45

6.4.

L. O'Glynh

Chelsea.

27th JUNE 05.

THIS BLESSED PLOT

ALSO BY HUGO YOUNG

The Crossman Affair

One of Us

THIS
BLESSED PLOT

Britain and Europe from Churchill to Blair

HUGO YOUNG

MACMILLAN

First published 1998 by Macmillan

an imprint of Macmillan Publishers Ltd
25 Eccleston Place, London SW1W 9NF
and Basingstoke

Associated companies throughout the world

ISBN 0 333 57992 5

Copyright © Hugo Young 1998

The right of Hugo Young to be identified as the
author of this work has been asserted by him in accordance
with the Copyright, Designs and Patents Act 1988.

1 3 5 7 9 8 6 4 2

A CIP catalogue record for this book is available from
the British Library.

Typeset by SetSystems Ltd, Saffron Walden, Essex
Printed and bound in Great Britain by
Mackays of Chatham plc, Chatham, Kent

To L, of course

Contents

Acknowledgements

I WOULD LIKE to thank, first of all, my sources for this history, beyond the published works cited in the Bibliography. In the nature of things, many of them were quite old when I spoke to them, and a number have since died. Those whom I can only posthumously acknowledge, but from whom I captured moments of their fugitive wisdom early in my inquiry, include: Lord Amery (formerly Julian Amery), George Ball, Lord Gladwyn (formerly Gladwyn Jebb), Emile van Lennep, Emile Noël, Sir Frank Roberts, John Robinson, Maurice Schumann, Lord Sherfield (formerly Roger Makins), Dirk Spierenburg and Lord Thorneycroft (formerly Peter Thorneycroft).

Of living participants, whom I saw for the purposes of constructing the story, and who are mostly cited in the text, I would like to thank particularly: Lord Armstrong of Ilminster (formerly Robert Armstrong), Jean-René Bernard, Georges Berthoin, Jean-Pierre Brunet, Sir Michael Butler, William Cash, Lord Chalfont, Maurice Couve de Murville, Lord Croham (formerly Douglas Allen), Sir Roy Denman, Lord Hailsham, Sir David Hannay, Sir Edward Heath, Lord Hunt of Tanworth (formerly John Hunt), Sir Curtis Keeble, Sir Donald Maitland, Sir Michael Palliser, Lord Rodgers of Quarry Bank (formerly William Rodgers), Lord Roll of Ipsden (formerly Eric Roll), Sir Crispin Tickell, Ernst van der Beugel and Edmund Wellenstein.

There are a number of other public people with whom I have talked, in some cases often, about the themes and history the book addresses. They include: Antonio Armellini, Paddy Ashdown, Tony Benn, Lord Biffen (formerly John Biffen), Tony Blair, Sir Leon Brittan, Gordon Brown, Charles Clarke, Kenneth Clarke, Lord Cockfield, Robin Cook, Tam Dalyell, Jacques Delors, Andrew Duff, Lord Garel-Jones (formerly Tristan Garel-Jones), Lord Gilmour of Craigmillar (formerly Ian Gilmour), Lord Hattersley (formerly Roy Hattersley), Lord Healey (formerly Denis Healey), Sir Nicholas Henderson, Michael Heseltine, Lord Howe of Aberavon (formerly Geoffrey Howe), Lord Hurd (formerly Douglas Hurd), Lord Jenkins of Hillhead (formerly Roy Jenkins), Sir John Kerr, Neil Kinnock, Helmut Kohl, Norman Lamont, Ruud Lubbers, John Major, Peter Mandelson, Geoffrey Martin, Denis McShane, Sir Christopher Meyer, Lord Owen (formerly David Owen), Chris Patten, Michael Portillo, Sir Charles Powell, Giles Radice, Lord Renwick of

Clifton (formerly Robin Renwick), Sir Malcolm Rifkind, Lord Ryder of Wensum (formerly Richard Ryder), Robert Schaetzel, Richard Shepherd, Lord Shore of Stepney (formerly Peter Shore), Lady Thatcher (formerly Margaret Thatcher), Sir Roger Tomkys, Lord Tugendhat, William Walde-grave, Karel Van Miert, Lode Willems and Robert Worcester. I am more grateful to them than perhaps they, or I, knew at the time.

Among professional friends and colleagues in the same category are John Newhouse, Anthony Sampson and William Wallace.

I have some particular personal debts: to Anthony Teasdale, who instructed me a great deal in contemporary Euro-politics; to Phillip White-head, with whom I made a series of films for Channel Four TV, *The Last Europeans*, that provided substantial momentum for the book I had already begun; to Sir Christopher Audland, also a first-hand source, who read and helpfully commented on the early chapters; and especially to John Pinder, one of the great scholars of contemporary Euro-British history, who read the entire text, saved me from numerous errors of fact and nuance, and is at fault for none that remain.

As my agents, I am fortunate to have Graham Greene and Ed Victor, both of whom kept pushing this project on its way. At Macmillan's, I want to thank Ian Chapman, for his encouraging personal enthusiasm for the book as it emerged; Tanya Stobbs, for overseeing its transmission into print; and Josine Meijer, for her inventive picture research. A little beyond Macmillan's, Peter James again applied his unsurpassed punctilio as an editor, and Sarah Ereira compiled with her usual creativity what is an essential reader-service in this kind of book, the index.

Behind all these people, however, there is the most indispensable source of material for any history: other texts and papers. For their assistance and sometimes their tolerance with my delayed returns, I thank the staff of the London Library, the Chatham House Library and the Research Department at the *Guardian*. Still more vital is the Public Record Office at Kew: a luxuriant secret outpost of the public sector, where there is so much to discover, and the staff are very helpful. Of the many books listed in the bibliography, I feel a particular weight of gratitude to two, constantly consulted: Michael Charlton's irreplaceable work, *The Price of Victory*, and *The Penguin Companion to European Union*, by Timothy Bainbridge with Anthony Teasdale.

Closer to home, Dominic Young again helped generously to teach me how to use my systems, his tolerance for my computer-dumbness putting to shame the impatience I used to show when trying to teach him Latin. Most of all, though, my debt is to Lucy Waring Young, whose affectionate

---

enthusiasm, sustained over several years, has been my strongest influence. It was strange to discover the ways in which a maker of things seen is in the same line of creative business as a documentary writer, and can teach him a lot about how to tell a story. I owe her, in the largest sense, everything.

That said, this is my book. Nobody else is responsible for any part of it. It was finished, by chance, on the day in May when the terms and membership of the European single currency were formally agreed by the European Council, led by Tony Blair, in Brussels. There will be developments beyond that, to incorporate in another edition. There will also certainly be errors to correct and gaps to fill: and many readers, I am sure, could help improve the record. If they feel inclined, they could write to me, c/o Ed Victor Ltd, 6 Bayley St, Bedford Square, London WC1B 3HB.

HUGO YOUNG

Hampstead
3 May 1998

List of Illustrations

SECTION ONE

Winston Churchill (*Churchill Archives*)
Ernest Bevin (*Camera Press*)
Sir Henry Tizard (*Popperfoto*)
Edward Heath (*Camera Press*)
Robert Schuman and Jean Monnet (*European Commission*)
The Messina Six (*European Commission*)
Russell Bretherton
Sir Anthony Eden and R. A. Butler (*Hulton Getty*)
Harold Macmillan (*Hulton Getty*)
President Gaulle and Macmillan (*Hulton Getty*)
Macmillan and R. A. Butler (*Topham*)
De Gaulle (*Topham*)

SECTION TWO

Hugh Gaitskell (*Topham*)
Douglas Jay (*Hulton Getty*)
John Robinson (*Hulton Getty*)
Sir Roger Makins (*Camera Press*)
Sir Gladwyn Jebb (*Topham*)
Sir Con O'Neill (*Tom Blau/Camera Press*)
Sir Michael Palliser (*Hulton Getty*)
Sir Michael Butler (*Camera Press*)
Sir John Kerr (*Popperfoto*)
Harold Wilson, George Brown and Michael Palliser (*Popperfoto*)
Harold Wilson and Chancellor Kurt Kiesinger (*Hulton Getty*)
Christopher Soames (*Hulton Getty*)
Edward Heath (*Camera Press*)
Edward Heath and President Georges Pompidou (*Popperfoto*)
Enoch Powell (*Camera Press*)

This royal throne of kings, this scepter'd isle,
This earth of majesty, this seat of Mars,
This other Eden, demi-paradise,
This fortress built by Nature for herself
Against infection and the hand of war,
This happy breed of men, this little world,
This precious stone set in the silver sea,
Which serves it in the office of a wall,
Or as a moat defensive to a house,
Against the envy of less happier lands,
This blessed plot, this earth, this realm, this England.

William Shakespeare, *Richard II*, Act 2, scene 1

A day will come when you, France; you, Italy; you, England; you, Germany; all you nations of the continent, without losing your distinct qualities and glorious individuality, will merge into a higher unity and found the European brotherhood.

Victor Hugo, 1849

Introduction: The Plot

THIS IS THE STORY of fifty years in which Britain struggled to reconcile the past she could not forget with the future she could not avoid. It is the history of an attitude to history itself. It is a record not of triumph, but rather of bewilderment concerning a question which lay in wait, throughout the period, to trouble successive leaders of the nation, and which latterly tested some of them to destruction. Could Britain, the question ran, truly accept that her modern destiny was to be a European country?

At the beginning of the half-century, with a world war barely over, Winston Churchill first placed on record the outline of a new, united Europe. At the end of it, an agreement was signed, under the collaborative eye of Prime Minister Blair, who was at the time the chairman of what we mean by 'Europe', to create a single currency for the European Union. There was an uneasy continuity between these two moments of creative apotheosis. Both Mr Churchill and Mr Blair, at their different times and from their own vantage-points, were spectators rather than actors in a continental drama from which Britain, the island nation, chose to exclude herself.

Plots of several kinds run through the saga.

The first is certainly blessed. The mythology of the scepter'd isle, the demi-paradise, bit deep into the consciousness of many who addressed the question, beginning with Churchill himself. The sacredness of England, whether or not corrupted into Britain, became a quality setting it, in some minds, for ever apart from Europe. Tampering with this blessed plot was seen for decades as a kind of sacrilege which, even if the sophisticates among the political class could accept it, the people would never tolerate.

The island people were not only different but, mercifully, separate, housed behind their moat. They were also inestimably superior, as was shown by history both ancient and modern: by the resonance of the Empire on which the sun never set, but equally by the immediate circumstances out of which the new Europe was born, the war itself. In that war, there had been only one unambiguous victor among European peoples, and she was not to be found on the mainland. The defence of historic uniqueness, against contamination from across the silver sea, was one powerful explanation for the course the British took during these fifty years.

But the plot was also tortuous. Little in the story was very straight. The nation's thinking about itself lurched between different destinies. Hanging on to the past, in the form of the post-imperial Commonwealth, seemed for a time to be the answer. Remaining constant to the Anglo-American relationship, the most powerful bond in the English-speaking world, was apparently another necessity, which would be fatally compromised by the lure of something called the European Community. The idea that these amounted to alternative choices, the one necessarily imperilling the other, afflicted the decision of all leaders from Churchill to Margaret Thatcher, if not beyond.

Such convolutions, however, were also personal as much as collective. Every individual story, as well as the national story, had its complexities. On no question of this period did more people in British public life change their minds than on Europe. There were conversions from one side to the other, and sometimes back again, each position often being held with a passion summoned from the realm of faith more than reason, where there are secret uncertainties that only the loudest voice can mask. Many, who first opposed British entry, later decided they had been wrong. Many others, who helped take Britain in, became virulent critics of their own handiwork. This made for a serpentine plot on several levels.

On top of that, though, the story was also, in many eyes, devious: not just a plot but a conspiracy. The making of Britain into a European country was accomplished, according to a sceptical reading of events, only by deception. The *de jure* transformation brought about by the British signature on the Treaty of Rome was not, we learned, a true conversion. The full-hearted consent of the people was never obtained, for the simple reason that the true nature of the contract was never put to them. This was subterfuge most foul.

Such were the plots which history has to disentangle. Beside them stand two less complicated truths, that help make sense of the historian's task.

The first is that Britain's resolution of her destiny, while it grew out of many strands quite different from those that influenced the continental states, was dominated by one – above all others. For the makers of the original 'Europe', beginning to fulfil Victor Hugo's dream, their creation was a triumph. Out of defeat they produced a new kind of victory. For Britain, by contrast, the entry into Europe was a defeat: a fate she had resisted, a necessity reluctantly accepted, the last resort of a once great power, never for one moment a climactic or triumphant engagement with the construction of Europe. This has been integral in the national psyche, perhaps only half articulated, since 1973. The sense of the Community as a place of British failure – proof of Britain's failed independence, site of her failed domination – is deep in the undertow of the tides and whirlpools this book attempts to chart.

The second narrative truth here implied is more contentious. Hindsight may be an unrespectable tool, but there are times when its application is inescapable. High political misjudgement is the thread running through this history. This is not an opinion, but a surely incontestable fact. It is proved by the outcome, Britain's presence inside the European apparatus. Since this is what did finally come to pass, one is entitled to cast a jaundiced eye on the record of those who resisted its happening, believed it would not happen, asserted it did not need to happen, pretended to themselves and the country that alternative destinies would happen instead. These turned out to be misperceptions of the truth. The people who made the error had their reasons, but subsequent events show that, for too long, their attachment to Britain's cultural and historic differences got the better of their political judgement. Ultimately, Britain did choose the fate her leaders long resisted or failed fully to embrace – but only after a period in which much opportunity was, by sheer lapse of time, wasted.

One does not need to carry either of the labels pejoratively invented in this time – Euro-phile or Euro-phobe – to accept the force of that. If objectivity can, for once, be brought to a question long drenched in opinionated emotion, it might be commonly agreed. As an exercise in leadership, the extended episode of Britain in and out of the European Community reveals a mismatch between political judgement and eventual, irresistible fact.

This book is an account and study of leadership, up to and just over the threshold into the present era when its quality seems likely, at last, to be less conflicted. It is a history of the great question, and of why a nation found it so difficult to answer: and of how the blessed plot became, instead, the graveyard, where the reputations of a large political class lie buried.

1

WINSTON CHURCHILL

Rule Britannia

IN MAY 1945, when the second German war ended, British self-esteem was higher than it had been in living memory. The little island nation had played a decisive part in liberating the continent from the abominations of Hitler. Britain was Europe's rescuer, the only power in the land mass and archipelago that could be so described. The United States and the Soviet Union may have had greater armies, and taken most of the military pain. But Britain was unique, indisputably the chief among European equals. Directly from that fact – that exquisite sense of national selfhood, and the experience of vindication going with it – stemmed all the large decisions of British foreign policy for the next fifteen years. These were the formative years, of crucial choices and chances. The influence of this history did not stop in 1960, but reached decades further forward. It was the defining experience, at different levels of consciousness, of every British leader for half a century.

Bestriding the fifty-year story is the man who set it on course. Three months after winning the war, Winston Churchill lost the election and surrendered his post as Prime Minister. But the people who flung him from office were unable to remove him from their minds. He was the leader round whom the entire nation from left to right had gathered, and his political defeat in no way diminished the hold he exerted over the British imagination. This effect, too, reached far beyond his own time. When Margaret Thatcher placed herself in direct descent from 'Winston', as she often called him, she knew what she was doing. He was the hero from whom the British weakness for nostalgia gained its richest nourishment. The belief that Britain, under Churchill, had won the war in 1945 retained its grip, twitching the nerve-ends and coursing through the bloodstream of Euro-sceptics in the 1990s.

Anyone wishing to explore the puzzle of Britain's relations with continental Europe in the twentieth century's second part must begin with Churchill, and not just because he came first. In the history, Churchill's record plays as important a part as the aura that came after him. The last begetter of British greatness, he was also the prime exponent of British ambiguity. In him the two strains mingling in Britain's post-war presentation of herself – illusion and uncertainty – had their most potent source. He epitomized the characteristic consistently displayed by almost every politician, irrespective of party, who came after him: an absence of steady vision on the greatest question concerning the future of Britain in the last fifty years. But he also spoke, none louder, for the reasons why such unsteadiness did not matter: why the issue of Europe could always be the plaything of fickle British politicians, because there always existed other possibilities for Britain, growing out of imperial history and military triumph.

Churchill was called the father of 'Europe', and he said much to justify that label. But he was also the father of misunderstandings about Britain's part in this Europe. He encouraged Europe to misunderstand Britain, and Britain to misunderstand herself.

Nobody stood closer to history than Churchill. He had studied it, written it, made it. But Harold Macmillan once said that his real greatness lay in 'his extraordinary power always to look forward, never back'.[1] This prophetic quality was his chief claim to public trust. The people believed what he said and promised. He was the last British leader whose reputation for sagacity was incontestable. Such a man might have been expected to rise above some of the comfortable illusions that gripped the British in the aftermath of war. Instead, he was the first in a long line of leaders who shared them. Indeed, his very presence, as Leader of the Opposition, did an enormous amount to endorse the general sense that Britain, after the war, did not have too much to worry about.

This was, after all, a united as well as a triumphant nation. War had been a unifying experience. National unity, wrote Sir William Beveridge in 1943, was the great moral achievement of the Second World War. It rested not on temporary deals or party coalitions but on 'the mutual understanding between Government and people', and expressed 'the determination of the British democracy to look beyond victory to the uses of victory'.[2] Common sacrifices had produced a common sense of the future, in which even the class system, among other divisive British traditions, seemed to have liquefied. When a Labour government was elected in July to replace Churchill's wartime coalition, the peaceful transfer of power to a party of the left, summarily despatching the hero, registered a country apparently at ease with its capacity for renovation.

This country also appeared to be strong. It possessed not only the army but many elements of the economy of a great power, on course for post-war recovery. Despite heavy German bombing of many significant centres, Britain's industrial capacity was higher in 1945 than it had been in 1939. Although exports had fallen during the war, they recovered swiftly under a determined government and a stoically purposeful workforce, in which almost nobody was unemployed. In 1947, British exports were five times those of France, as large, in fact, as those of France, Germany, Italy, Belgium, the Netherlands, Luxembourg, Norway and Denmark combined.

The most devastated war powers – Germany, France, Italy, the Netherlands – ran huge and persistent deficits, whereas Britain was a creditor with the whole of Europe. Whereas Britain was in every respect a giant, Germany was a devastated country, her industrial power dismantled, her housing stock decimated. Germany's national income in 1946 was less than one-third of what it had been in 1938, and France's only one-half, with the franc an all but valueless international currency. In Italy, the national output in 1945 was at the level it had been in 1911, down by nearly half since 1938. Britain, by contrast, was galvanized by war to new levels of output, based on a sense of national endeavour that victory did not dissipate.

On the contrary, victory confirmed a good many things that the country wanted to know about itself. The expression of it – of the assurance it supplied to an idea of nation that long preceded it – reached beyond economists, generals and politicians. If you look at what British writers were saying about England before and after the war, you read for the most part a seamless paean to the virtues of the nation's strength and identity. It occurred to hardly anyone, whether in 1935 or 1945, to doubt the value of being British (for which 'English' was then a synonym the Scots and the Welsh tamely put up with). In both decades, plenty of argument raged around the British national interest in rearmament or disarmament, central planning or market economics. The value and purpose of Britain's contribution to the world was the natural sub-text of a lot of these debates. But the greatness of its scale, like the history behind it, was not a matter over which many of the British yet agonized; and the war confirmed them in their complacency. Almost all writers, from left to right, believed in the qualities of their country. It never occurred to them to do otherwise. The notion that Britain/England might reconsider her role in the world, relinquishing her status as a global power or doubting her contribution to the welfare of mankind, did not arise. Nor was this confined to little Englanders, or celebrators of narrowly English cultural virtues in the mould of J. B. Priestley. It was a 'European', Herbert Read, a high-flown prophet of the continental avant-garde, who in the mid-1930s caught a note that the defeat of Germany did nothing to diminish. Introducing his anthology, *The English Vision*, the dangerous anarchist sounded like a man with indestructible pride in the special qualities of his country. 'What I wish to emphasise most is the universal validity of this our vision,' Read wrote. 'Alone of national ideals, the English ideal transcends nationality.'[3]

This unquestioning sense of nation persisted through and after the war. There was a striking contrast with the national attitude after the First World War, with its powerful aura of hope betrayed. 'I feel a doom over the country, and a shadow of despair over the hearts of men, which leaves me no rest,' wrote D. H. Lawrence at that time.[4] The 1940s satires of Evelyn Waugh derided the English middle classes. But they stopped well short of apocalypse in their prediction for the future of England. Nobody in any walk of life imagined that this was a country whose future might have been rendered more rather than less problematic by military victory.

George Orwell's odyssey through the England of the war maps the typical experience. Orwell was an honest, unposturing man, whom the right wing disliked because he was a socialist and the left wing disliked because he told the truth.[5] His writings trace the evolution of a nation's feeling about itself.

Back from Spain, after fighting for the republicans in the civil war, Orwell rediscovers a country offering wonderful reassurance in the places of his childhood – but he also senses the imminence of some kind of explosion. The year is 1938, in 'the huge peaceful wilderness of outer London', with 'the barges on the miry river, the familiar streets, the posters telling of cricket matches and Royal weddings, the men in bowler hats, the pigeons in Trafalgar Square, the red buses, the blue policemen – all sleeping the deep, deep sleep of England, from which I sometimes fear that we shall never wake till we are jerked out of it by the roar of bombs'.[6]

When the bombs fall, however, Orwell's ambivalence vanishes. Mockery is overcome by patriotism, and the man of the people emerges to castigate the intelligentsia whose love of country he does not always trust. He still calls England 'the most class-ridden country under the sun', but is adamant about his belief in the virtues of simple national pride. 'We must add to our heritage or lose it, we must grow greater or grow less, we must go forward or backward,' he writes at the height of the Blitz. 'I believe in England, and I believe that we shall go forward.'[7]

When it is all over, this belief is shaken only slightly, if at all. Orwell expresses the sober, but ultimately sure, conviction that Britain could claim a role in the world sufficient unto itself. His conviction fell on receptive ears. The war was a period when the people especially revelled in their past. Huge commercial success, for example, attended G. M. Trevelyan's triumphalist *English Social History*, published in 1944. Orwell's version of how Britain could expect to perform after 1945 was no less gratifying than Trevelyan's account of the past.

He caught a glimpse of the problem that might beckon. If global conflict continued, he said, there might be room for only two or three great powers, and he conceded that 'in the long run Britain will not be one of them'. She was just too small. But she had great things to give the world, one of them 'the highly original quality of the English ... their habit of not killing one another'. There was now a decent chance of this imposing itself on others, as Britain/England defined a new kind of domination. 'If the English took the trouble to make their own democracy work, they would become the political leaders of western Europe,' he concluded, 'and probably of some other parts of the world as well. They would provide the much-needed alternative to Russian authoritarianism on the one hand and American materialism on the other.'[8]

Leadership, of course, was the point. Although a mere essayist, Orwell was quite influential at the time – far more so than any such writer in the 1990s – and his description was consistent with Britain's objective position vis-à-vis the mainland countries. If there was to be a leader, she was it. Her democracy, meanwhile, had in Orwell's terms worked. A few months after he set down these sentiments, the ordinary English did, as he advocated, 'get their hands on power' through the agency of a people's government led by Clement Attlee. They had demonstrated the proof of what the war was about, the capacity of men to choose and defend the peaceful transfer of democratic power.

Churchill's part in that, his humble acceptance of an almost incomprehensible result, served to increase his prophetic stature. Although he was rejected by the voters, who decided that the fruits of victory would be better distributed by the people's party, his was still the voice that resounded loudest through the opening discussion about the future of Europe, after Europe had been saved.

*

WINSTON CHURCHILL had no objection, emotional or political, to the idea of the unification of Europe. Compared with the defenders of sovereignty who took control of his party in the 1990s, he was untroubled by its impact on the sovereign nation. His attitude was pragmatic, and it had an instructive history.

As early as 1930, he came out straight. Writing in an American magazine, he argued the case for creating a United States of Europe. He understood better than many contemporaries the failure of the Treaty of Versailles, after the 1914–18 war, to produce a secure settlement of the historic enmity of France and Germany. 'The conception of a United States of Europe is right,' he wrote. 'Every step taken to that end which appeases the obsolete hatreds and vanished oppressions, which makes easier the traffic and reciprocal services of Europe, which encourages nations to lay aside their precautionary panoply, is good in itself.'[9] So he believed in a USE for political reasons. But he also saw 'Europe' in economic terms. He noted the underlying dynamism of the American economy, especially its respect for 'science and organisation', and pondered how the Old World might emulate the New. He proposed, as the model for his United States of Europe, the single market and unified governing principle of the United States of America.

This was not the utterance of a serving statesman, nor even of a representative party politician. Churchill at the time was parading round the political wilderness, earning what he could by his pen. His piece was sufficient to the moment and its market. Besides, as anyone quickly learns who ventures beyond the bare facts of political history, judgements on matters that don't require an immediate answer are always open to shifts of nuance, if not outright reversal. Politicians do not expect to be held to all their visions. The discussion of foreign affairs is a paradise for musing soothsayers whose ideas at any given time seldom have to pass exacting tests of consistency. They can drift from one interesting proposition to its opposite in the reassuring knowledge that disproof by events is unlikely. On the future of Britain in the world – more exactly, the future of the world as it revolved around Britain – there was room in the middle decades of the century for incessant adjustment of the point of view.

Above all other questions, in fact, Europe has been the prime example of such uncertainty among modern British politicians. The habit of constant revision, with violent contradictions sometimes emanating from a single mind, is an unvarying feature of the history. The sole consistent pattern to be found, from the moment debate began in earnest, is the inconsistency – casual or tormented, selfless or self-indulgent – that almost every protagonist has brought to it. Fittingly, it is Churchill, Britain's last geo-strategist of world significance, who established the pattern.

Nonetheless, what he wrote in 1930 has to be taken seriously. It indicated a willingness to think irregular thoughts. A man of large horizons was casting about to meet a crisis he believed the nation-state might not be able to avert. And when war happened, he continued to think adventurously about the future of the continent whose freedoms he was fighting to preserve.

Wartime diaries and papers, his own and those of others, reveal the constructive restlessness of a mind not content with the shape of things as they had been. It was moved by the horrors of the fighting to explore possibilities which, at the time, seemed to the colleagues who heard them inexplicably bold. For example, in December 1940, only six months after becoming Prime Minister, Churchill discussed with some intimates a version of the future that bore resemblance to the model of European unity that in fact came to evolve by the end of the 1980s. He saw a Europe of five single powers – England, France, Italy, Spain and what he called Prussia – along with four confederations covering the rest of the continent: 'These nine powers would meet in a Council of Europe which would have a supreme judiciary and a Supreme Economic Council to settle currency questions etc.'[10] The Council, moreover, would take the power to deal with any breach of the peace. This foreshadowed the court, council and commission of the European Community.

Two years later, he was still musing about a Council of Europe, which would also interest itself in a common continental market. In a minute to Anthony Eden, the Foreign Secretary, he identified 'Russian barbarism' as the future enemy and a united Europe as the necessary bulwark against it. 'Hard as it is to say now, I trust that the European family may act unitedly as one, under a Council of Europe in which the barriers between nations will be greatly minimised and unrestricted travel will be possible.' He also hoped to see 'the economy of Europe studied as a whole'.

He continued to amplify this line of thinking. At the beginning of

1943, in a paper dictated from his bed on an Orient Express wagon-lit in the middle of Turkey, where he had gone to consult about the dangers of Soviet influence when the war was over, Churchill reiterated the need for a Council of Europe. He called these 'Morning Thoughts', to mark the informality of their composition. But the paper had a perennial influence, if only on debate inside a sceptical Foreign Office.[11] An 'instrument of European government' was at the heart of it, to be distinguished from the project of world government so ineffectually expressed by the pre-war League of Nations. He followed this, in March, with one of his grander wartime broadcasts, publicly explaining the need to start thinking now about 'the largest common measure of the integrated life of Europe that is possible, without destroying the individual characteristics and traditions of its many ancient and historic races'.[12] A little later, in May the same year, a mixture of these half-formed thoughts appeared in a conversation Churchill had with a group of Americans at lunch in the Washington embassy. The European 'instrument', consisting of twelve states and confederations, had now evolved in his mind into one of three regional bodies covering the globe, which would be answerable to a World Council.[13]

So Churchill was fertile in his wartime thinking. The constraints of national politics did not inhibit his creative reach. Frontiers did not trouble him, as he cast forward from the terrible time through which he was living. Indeed, within a month of taking office he had put his name to the most ambitious plan for the voluntary subsuming and remaking of two great nations that had ever been conceived, when, in response to the fall of France, he took up the embryonic proposal for an Anglo-French Union. The way to sustain France, it was felt by leaders from both sides of the Channel, was to sublimate these two nations into an 'indissoluble union'. They would 'no longer be two nations, but one Franco-British Union', and every citizen of each would immediately become a citizen of the other. There would be a single cabinet and a single parliament.

This project never came to pass. Dreamed up by senior British officials working together with some of the leading Frenchmen in temporary exile in London, it briefly attracted the interest of the French Government. But the Government fell before the extravagant idea, some of whose progenitors would later become very important in the grander post-war European project, could be put to the test. Churchill's interest in it cannot be read as indicating any more than the extremes to which he was prepared to go to sustain the war effort and defeat Hitler. It was plainly not intended to form a template for the Europe he might be expected to favour when hostilities were over. Nonetheless, it showed a supple approach to nationhood. It suggested that a national interest, in Churchill's conception, might in certain circumstances transcend the boundaries of national sovereignty as usually understood. It is one of the early bases – there were more important ones to come – of the claim by later 'Europeans' in British debates that Churchill was one of them.

Even at this stage, however, such a claim was seriously flawed. And the fault in this version of Churchillism is relevant to the argument that came after him. It doesn't amount to anything so crude as the notion that Churchill was in reality a serious anti-European: the greatest Conservative icon made available, on further inspection, for retrospective recruitment by the Euro-sceptic camp. This, at times, was how 'Winston' was later claimed. But the claim was empty. On the contrary, he remained always a European of highly romantic disposition. His idea of Europe was benign and passionate, informed by the prescience of the historian as well as of the public man. The flaw lay in his description of what Europe was, where its limits lay. Although in the east these had generous scope, encompassing his Danubian and Balkan confederations, to the west they stopped at the English Channel. In short, Britain did not belong inside the Churchillian concept of 'Europe'.

At times this appeared to be a product of mere muddle and oversight. In the grand sweep of mid-war speculation about how the tectonic plates of the global system might ultimately be redesigned, confusion about Britain's exact place in it was perhaps a trivial detail. When Churchill propounded his first big scheme in December 1940, he assigned England both to the great new Council of Europe, with its new supreme judiciary and economic union, yet also to some place beyond it. Britain would belong, and yet not belong. For 'the English-speaking world', he wrote, 'would be apart from this', while at the same time being in some unspecified way 'closely connected'.

Most of Churchill's blueprints, however, placed Britain/England outside the European construct. Even his 1930 account, untouched by the triumphalism of victory in the war, put the country above and beyond the continent. 'We have our own dream and our own task,' he wrote. 'We are *with* Europe but not *of* it. We are linked but not comprised.'[14] Thirteen years later, in his notion of three Regional Councils responsible to a World Council, he instinctively distanced Britain from the role of equal partner in any European enterprise. Britain would be a kind of godmother or broker, her relationship to Europe very similar to that of the US. America was more like Britain's equal partner than Europe could ever be. Together the two Anglo-Saxon peoples, Churchill opined, would share the common problem of maintaining 'large numbers of men indefinitely on guard', to keep the continental peace.

For the visionary had other dreams, and the historian other romantic attachments. These coexisted with his ideas about Europe and, though he seldom discussed the contradiction, in practice overshadowed them.

The war-winner could in no way surrender his belief that the British purpose must be to sustain the status of a great power, as near as possible equal in political weight with the US and the Soviet Union: a belief in which Churchill was unexceptional in either the public world where national prestige could never be compromised or the private circles in which he moved. Hardly anywhere, on the left or the right, in the journalistic or literary or political milieus, was the concept of Britain's solitary greatness, uniquely positioned at the hub of several global groupings, subjected to serious reassessment. At the same time, the strategist could never forget the concept of the English-speaking world. He had written a four-volume history of it. Empire, and then Commonwealth, formed bonds that were a part of many British families' inheritance and every British leader's responsibility. They had helped to win the war. Here were truly indissoluble unions, and they were in conflict with any simple idea of European Britain.

Churchill's failure to resolve this conflict, or come anywhere near doing so, was not surprising. Most of his successors – in differing measures and with varying commitment, some addressing the same conflict, others discovering new fields of difference – failed in the same way.

The contradiction, however, did not inhibit Churchill from making the unity of post-war Europe the great cause of his years as Leader of the Opposition. He proposed himself as the intellectual prophet of the European idea, investing in it a large portion of such emotional reserves as were left over from political defeat. In doing so, moreover, he was not a lonely eccentric, but was speaking to a country already to some extent acquainted with the grand notions for which he appeared to be speaking: the idea that there might be a worthwhile entity larger than the nation-state, and a way of organizing Europe that might better guarantee the avoidance of war.

Federalism, a word which by 1995 epitomized all that was alien in the project of 'Europe', possessed a different aura fifty years earlier. It had a certain purchase on parts of the British consciousness. So did the concept of union, as applied to Europe.

Federalism had blossomed before the war. By June 1940, when the flame of Anglo-French Union briefly lit the scene, the British federalist movement, called Federal Union, had more than 10,000 members in over 200 branches. The failure of the League of Nations and the shock of Munich had spurred more support, sometimes from names that were widely known, for a federation of free peoples, a union of sovereign states, or whatever similar arrangement might lower the possibility of conflict. Adherents came from the usual cadre of pious dreamers. 'The whole scheme of Federal Union has made a staggeringly effective appeal to the British mind,' the Archbishop of York enthused in 1939.[15] The abandonment of sovereignty made a natural appeal to the parsonical tendency, hoping to avoid war at a stroke. But serious men of affairs also put themselves behind the cause. William Beveridge was a federalist, and so was Harold Laski. The *Manchester Guardian* and the *New Statesman* came out for the federal idea, as did a former editor of *The Times*, Wickham Steed. Lord Lothian, former Cabinet minister and later ambassador to Washington, was a federalist of long standing. Richard Law MP, son of Bonar Law, the Conservative Prime Minister, wrote a pamphlet on the subject. There was also heavy academic support. The historian Arnold Toynbee, the constitutional jurist Ivor Jennings and the two most illustrious economists of the day, Lionel Robbins and Friedrich von Hayek, all did serious work on the practicalities of a federal constitution and its implications for defence, economic policy, tax, justice and the rest of state activity.

So federalism at this time was not the obsession of some irrelevant cranks' corner of British public life. Important people had begun to see it as perhaps the only solid guarantor of peaceful coexistence between peoples. There was a sizeable British literature on the subject, with roots in the thinking of John Locke, and extended by such varied political thinkers as Lord Acton, James Bryce and Ernest Barker. A famous continental federalist, Altiero Spinelli, prime author of a 1944 manifesto for federalism, and a man of deep conceptual influence on the post-war idea of Europe, when reflecting on his own intellectual formation, attributed much to 'the clean, precise thinking of these English federalists'.[16]

This was part of the context into which Churchill projected himself in 1945. By then, admittedly, the federal idea had suffered some degradation. Strong at the beginning of the war, it lost support when the fact of battle, especially of victorious battle, exalted the loyalties attaching to the nation-state. Federal Union closed down many branches. The European dimension, moreover, was overtaken in many minds by the necessity for something much wider. Among British federalists, disputes broke out between those still mainly interested in a federation of Western Europe and those who thought that a world potentially at ransom to nuclear super-powers required nothing less than a complete World Federation. Crankdom beckoned. The limited project of a federal Europe, itself requiring enough massive adjustments in the thinking of several ancient nations, tended to become engulfed by the case for world government, which had the early effect of returning such credibility as federation had to parsonical irrelevance.

Churchill was never seduced by world government. But he had ideas for Europe that, while eschewing federalism, made the case for a European Union. He set about promoting them in irresistible style. Three great meetings, of which the highlight in each case was a Churchillian oration, have become benchmarks of his career as a hero of the European peace.

The first was in Zurich on 19 September 1946. One must remember the mantle of inextinguishable gallantry in which he was arrayed by his collaborators in the war. Nobody regarded him as less than the greatest man in Europe, even though his own people had rejected him. He came to the University of Zurich, in a country at the confluence of the peoples and languages that had almost destroyed the continent, to deliver a judgement which, he said, would 'astonish' his audience. What he called the United States of Europe, an idea then only vestigially dreamed of, was a project on which 'we must begin now'. And at the heart of it – this was the astonishing bit – there had to be a partnership between France and Germany. 'In this way only can France recover the moral and cultural leadership of Europe,' he insisted. 'There can be no revival of Europe without a spiritually great Germany,' he added. 'We must re-create the European family in a regional structure called, as it may be, the United States of Europe.'

The Zurich speech made a very great impact. It is less commonly remembered now than the speech Churchill gave earlier that year in Fulton, Missouri, when he publicized the phrase and fashioned the thinking about the Iron Curtain which the Soviet Union had brought down between the free and unfree worlds. But Zurich was a beacon. It inspired many continental politicians, then struggling to remake their ruined countries. It roused enthusiasts for a united Europe to ecstatic excitement. They really seemed to think it meant that Churchill, for Britain, was making a choice. Leo Amery MP, Churchill's Tory comrade, who along with his son Julian was one of the few politicians who saw no conflict between strong attachment to the British Empire and a commitment to European Union, marked his leader's card. 'The French are startled, as they were bound to be, but the idea will sink in all the same,' he wrote. 'As for the Germans, your speech may have been just in time to save them from going Bolshevist. You have done few bigger things, even in the great years behind us.'[17]

The Zurich speech, however, was once again 'European' only in a sense that placed Britain outside Europe. It was the speech of a grandiloquent map-maker who wanted to dissolve the emotional frontiers between warring continental countries, but was rooted in a system that cast Britain as facilitator, even mere spectator, of the process. It does not seem to have entered Churchill's mind that the destiny he envisaged for Europe, as the only way to prevent a repetition of the war, was something his own country should embrace. Far from plotting a clear course forward, Churchill's spumes of oratory proposed a feel-good world in which just about every country was involved. Britain and the Commonwealth and 'mighty America', he said at Zurich, 'and I trust Soviet Russia, for then all would be well', must be 'friends and sponsors of the new Europe, and must champion its right to live and shine'.

Britain, in other words, was separate from Europe. Her sense of national independence, enhanced by her unique empire, absorbed by all creeds and classes and spoken for by virtually every analyst, could not be fractured. Churchill urged Europe to become united, and set about creating a movement with this as its purpose. But to be achieved by what means, exactly? His only practical proposal involved a quite limited form of unity. He reiterated what he had said in private, and sometimes in public, during the war: that the first step should be the formation of a Council of Europe, which would not be some grandiose agent of European governance, still less a federalist super-state, but a forum for association between sovereign governments. The extravagances that he sometimes gave voice to – 'supreme judiciary ... supreme economic council' – were by now abandoned.

As a blueprint, Zurich was therefore quite a modest affair. It dripped with symbolism, and in its time and place, less than eighteen months after the slaughter had ended, was a bold response to popular alarms. Its particular genius, perhaps, lay in launching the idea of Franco-German partnership, allied to the concept, for these other countries, of a United

States of Europe. It was attacked in *The Times*, by a young leader-writer who later became a famous European, Con O'Neill,[18] on the ground that it was anti-Russian, when the world needed unity more than it needed some divisive new European institution. It was a grand idea, and gave birth in Britain to a United Europe Movement to which Churchill offered himself as chairman, and some excited old-style federalists immediately pledged their support. But it was never intended to be federalist.

For Churchill certainly wasn't a federalist, and nor was his chief lieutenant in these matters, Duncan Sandys, his son-in-law. Sandys, having lost his parliamentary seat in the Attlee landslide, became the main functionary of United Europe, a potent behind-the-scenes figure in the evolution of the Great European that Churchill gave such a large impression of being. Sandys's talents were not for the arts of persuasion. He was more the scheming manager. His energy helped shape the vaporous effusions of his father-in-law in a direction that was at once strongly European and quite unspecific as to what this might really mean. 'Duncan was an organizer and intriguer with a great capacity to manipulate people,' Lord Hailsham told me in 1993. 'I was at Eton with him, and he was a manipulator of great skill even as a schoolboy. I expect he manipulated Churchill.'[19]

Sandys locked United Europe into a non-federalist platform, but above all was anxious to ensure that Churchill got fully and publicly committed. This is what places Sandys among the most significant of the early British Europeans. At this stage, the movement stood for a loose and cautious association of governments, and the old man used his next great opportunity to rally support for the missionary undertaking. 'Let Europe Arise' was the title of his address to the Primrose League on 18 April 1947. The Albert Hall in London heard another Zurichean summons to European destiny. But, again, the inconveniences were glossed over. United Europe was the expansive theme, but Churchill's tone also reflected a message Sandys sent him the day before, warning that Conservative back-bench MPs felt out of touch with his European ideas, and urging him to do more to secure their support for 'our movement'. So the speech insisted on giving a higher place in the scheme of things to people who did not speak French, German or any other of the alien mainland tongues. 'We shall allow no wedge', the great voice intoned, 'to be driven between Great Britain and the United States of America, or be led into any course which would mar the growing unity in thought and action, in ideals and purpose, of the English-speaking nations, spread so widely about the globe, but joined together by history and by destiny.'

This was no more than an oratorical hors d'oeuvre. The movement expanded, and made links with similar groupings, more copious and still more passionately committed, across the Channel. With Duncan Sandys active in the back room, the idea was conceived for a great international congress to give continent-wide impetus to a European Union. The first Congress of Europe met in The Hague on 7 May 1948, with Churchill as the keynote speaker.

It was an extraordinary assembly. The big names gathered from all over West Europe. From France came Léon Blum, Paul Reynaud and Jean Monnet, from Italy Alcide De Gasperi, from Belgium Paul-Henri Spaak and Paul van Zeeland. From all over came many others who make prominent appearances later in this story. Altogether there were eight former prime ministers and twenty-eight former foreign ministers. No fewer than 140 British participants turned up, out of some 800 delegates all told, including Harold Macmillan and twenty-three of his party colleagues. Adrian Boult, the orchestral conductor, and John Masefield, the Poet Laureate, were among those whose presence showed that this was a movement appealing to instincts much deeper than the merely political. Among younger attenders, later to be leaders of their own political generation, were François Mitterrand and Christopher Soames. Soames, whom Churchill designated his personal assistant at The Hague, was another of his sons-in-law, thus a second lifelong 'European' in the family.

The assembly, however, was shot through with ambivalence. Its main promoters were federalists, of whom there were many more in high places in Europe than there ever were in Britain. Though Churchill was not a federalist, his presence at The Hague again blurred the truth about where he stood. His eminence persuaded continentals they had to have him, and his rhetoric gave small indication that he did not in his heart belong on their side. The occasion was the high point of Churchill's ambiguity, arrived at not by any calculating deviousness, but as the natural emanation of a man immersed in certainty that history entitled Britain to ordain the best of all worlds for herself.

The United Europe movement, Churchill told the Congress, was not of parties but of peoples. His speech was rich in the highest-flown rhetoric, and this style was more than decorative. It was meant to rouse and dramatize. Read half a century later, it still summons up the horror of war, and recalls the idly forgotten fact that fear of war and thirst for peace, above all else, were the sources for the extraordinary idea that national frontiers might be lowered. For many of those present at the Hague assembly, their project was a matter of life or death. Churchill appeared to speak to and for them. 'We shall only save ourselves from the perils which draw near', he said, 'by forgetting the hatreds of the past, by letting national rancours and revenges die, by progressively effacing frontiers and barriers which aggravate and congeal our divisions, and by rejoicing together in that glorious treasure of literature, of romance, of ethics, of thought and toleration belonging to us all, which is the inheritance of Europe.'

Political unity, he went on, must 'inevitably' accompany economic and military collaboration, a process, as he explained, that did not necessarily damage a nation. What he said about that might have had a special resonance down the years. It touched on the issue that raised the most enduring anxieties among the British, and was an occasion where Churchill got closer than he often did to a practical description of what he meant. 'It is said with truth that this involves some sacrifice or merger of national sovereignty,' he began. But then he added that 'it is also possible and not less agreeable to regard it as the gradual assumption, by all nations concerned, of that larger sovereignty which can also protect their diverse and distinctive customs and characteristics, and their national traditions'.

These words could have served as a text for the proponents of British entry into the European Community in the 1960s and 1970s. The 'pooling' of sovereignty, with its implication that all participants drew greater sustenance from a pond bigger than their own, became a favourite way of describing what happened inside the Community. But the national sovereignties Churchill contemplated curtailing again did not include Britain's. That appears to have been an idea beyond the reach of his imagination. As a result, his speech at The Hague, which was regarded at the time as an historic address, could in due course be more exactly seen as a source-book for the confusion he created, simultaneously giving succour to the federalists while intending to do no such thing.

What happened as a result of the Hague Congress was also, in the end, ambivalent. Churchill made a concrete proposal, building on his frequent allusions to a future Council of Europe. He now suggested that it was time for a new institution 'in one form or another', which he specified as a quasi-parliamentary annexe to the Council, some kind of European Assembly, to enable the voice of United Europe 'to make itself continuously heard'. Three months later, France formally proposed that the Assembly should be created, and within a year the statute of the Council was agreed and the inaugural meeting of the Assembly arranged, at Strasbourg. The first institution of 'Europe' was in place, divided between a Council of Ministers and a Consultative Assembly.

In its beginnings, moreover, the Council fulfilled both the federalist and the Churchillian ideals. They were apparently conjoined within it. Paul-Henri Spaak, the Belgian federalist, was its first president, and Churchill its first hero. On the evening it opened, 10 August 1949, Churchill addressed a rally of 20,000 people crammed into the Place Kléber. Every corner was filled with people from the city closest to the heart of Franco-German Europe, to hear the great man address them, which he did in better French than usual. Then, as the Assembly debates began, he threw himself into its proceedings with a verve that impressed a fellow delegate. 'This extraordinary man', Harold Macmillan wrote in a letter home, 'seemed to come down almost too rapidly to the level of normal political agitation.' His early interventions were calculated 'to reveal him as a parliamentarian, rather than as a great international figure. He certainly took more trouble to listen to the debates than I have ever known him to do in the House of Commons. He walked about, chatted to each representative, went into the smoking room, and generally took a lot of trouble to win the sympathetic affection of his new parliamentary colleagues.'[20]

He also made another speech. Again it had a grand, uplifting effect. He saw the Council of Europe as 'a European unit' in the United Nations, which had lately been formed. He regretted the absence of the countries of Eastern Europe, now suffering under the tyrannies of communism, and asked that empty chairs be left for their representatives to fill in good time. He also inquired, dramatically, 'Where are the Germans?', and demanded that the Government of West Germany should be invited into the Council, alongside France, Belgium, Italy, Holland and the rest, without delay. He had never lost the sense he expressed at Zurich three years before, that, if European harmony was to endure, Germany must be in the concert.

At the same time, Churchill never intended the Council to break the nation-state. Having apparently scorned the narrow view of sovereignty just a year before, he was now unwilling to investigate the ways in which it might be modified, even for countries other than Britain. What interested him was the development of mood and feeling. 'I hope we shall not put our trust in formulae or in machinery,' he told the

Assembly. It was by 'the growth and gathering of the united sentiment of Europeanism, vocal here and listened to all over the world, that we shall succeed in taking, not executive decision, but ... a leading and active part in the revival of the greatest of continents which has fallen into the worst of misery'.

The Europeans didn't see the limits this implied. They allowed themselves to be deceived. And Churchill allowed himself to sound terribly confused. Many years later, Macmillan wrote in his memoirs that Churchill had 'had no clear or well-defined plan'. He wasn't interested in details. He merely wanted to 'give an impetus towards movements already at work'.[21] But that wasn't quite how European leaders, desperate to be led out of the ante-chamber of another war, saw the matter. They exulted in Churchill's compelling rhetoric, without thinking very hard about the realities that underlay it. And the price of their deception was going to be quite great, both for them and for Britain.

*

THERE WAS, besides, another kind of deception. This wasn't so much in Churchill's rhetoric as in the British mind, and it concerned the state of Britain herself. The Churchillian view, against which there was very little argument, took for granted Britain's capacity for independent decision-making in any area her leaders chose. This rested on imperial sentiment and national pride and the other outgrowths of the victory that saved Europe. But it also made assumptions about Britain's enduring economic strength that did not entirely stand up to examination. Anglo-Saxon triumphalism blinded even as it exulted. The figures of comparative growth and production immediately after the war told the truth but not the whole truth. They said what was true in 1945, and even in 1948, but they ignored the trends that told what might well be true by, say, 1955.

Behind the superficial encouragement of selected statistics was another kind of reality. While Britain was by some measures strong, by others she was weak. The struggle against Germany had been immensely costly. During the war, a quarter of the national wealth, £7,000 million, was lost: twice as much as in the First World War and more, proportionately, than in any other combatant country. The exports of this trading nation had not just declined but plummeted: in 1944 they were only 31 per cent of their level in 1938. The gold and dollar reserves were seriously run down, and in November 1945 it was necessary, with great difficulty, to arrange an American loan of £3.75 billion. In a famous memorandum, the man who negotiated it, John Maynard Keynes, warned the Attlee Government of the scale of the crisis which was being masked by public euphoria. 'The financial problems of the war', he wrote in August 1945, 'have been surmounted so easily and silently that the average man sees no reason to suppose that the financial problems of the peace will be any more difficult.' But Britain, he judged, was facing 'a financial Dunkirk'.[22]

This ominous phrase remained in the private realm, for the eyes of ministers alone. In any case, the US cavalry arrived in the shape of the loan. In 1945, Keynes's meaning, reinforced by his warning that 'a greater degree of austerity would be necessary than we have experienced at any time during the war', did not seriously impress itself on the politicians of any party. They agreed the loan, but did not draw the conclusion, or even register the question, that Britain might no longer be able to afford her imperial role, stretched round the globe, while building a welfare state at home.

Other truths were also disguised. Although the speed of the post-war economic recovery was impressive, especially on the exports side, it was less impressive than that of other countries. The important figures were comparative. In isolation they might look reasonably encouraging, but in fact the competitive decline that was to continue for the next half-century started now. Growth among the defeated or ravaged powers was consistently faster than it was in Britain. An assortment of reasons contributed to this. With no unemployment and hardly any immigration, Britain had no surplus labour to cope with expansion: the continentals had a surfeit. Britain had huge overseas obligations, not least the cost of policing the defeated countries: Germany and Italy had no such costs. Britain under a Labour government was preoccupied with wealth redistribution, and operated a top tax rate of over 90 per cent: on the continent there was far greater concern to create the incentives that would remake ruined economies.

Victory, in other words, produced decidedly less dynamic energy than did defeat. As a result, between 1947 and 1951, while British industrial production rose by a gratifying 30 per cent, France and Italy achieved 50 per cent, and Germany 300 per cent. By the end of 1950, German production, after the devastation of the infrastructure, not to mention the controls imposed by the occupying powers, was back at pre-war levels. It is true that in that year the British economy, measured by gross national product per head of the population, remained the second strongest in the world, with only the US ahead of it. But Germany and even France were closing steadily.

This was knowable at the time. The trends and statistics were no secret. But it wasn't commonly apprehended, least of all in the quarters where it might have been most expected that the details would be closely studied, and the lessons honestly drawn. In government circles where, Keynes excepted, victory in the war had done more to fortify the conceptions of the past than provoke new ones for the future, the evidence was received, as it were, blindfold. Anyone who saw behind it to the truth tended to be ostracized.

One man who did was Sir Henry Tizard, chief scientific adviser at the Ministry of Defence. In 1949, he composed a telling minute, contesting the wisdom of the age. 'We persist in regarding ourselves as a Great Power,' Tizard wrote, 'capable of everything and only temporarily handicapped by economic difficulties. We are not a Great Power and never will be again. We are a great nation, but if we continue to behave like a Great Power we shall soon cease to be a great nation.'

This fine and prescient distinction gave an answer to Orwell's question. It did not go down well. Whitehall received Tizard's warning 'with the kind of horror one would expect if one made a disrespectful remark about the King'.[23]

So an imposing consensus presented itself. On the question of Britain's place in the world, most pillars of the society took a similar attitude. The spirit of the times said that Britain's destiny had been determined by her military victory, and nourished the illusion that war had increased the country's inherent strength, not sapped it. This strength was imperial and global, another source, almost everyone believed, of advantage rather than burden. 'Our empire illustrated co-operation without domination for the whole of the world – co-operation between countries without the domination of one over the other,' the Dean of St Paul's preached on Empire Day, 1945. 'It was probably the greatest creation of British political genius.'[24] The Dean spoke in the past tense, no doubt, because the Empire was in process of being converted into the Commonwealth. But this remained the British Commonwealth, run by one nation, to which others still owed fealty. As the historian of Empire has written of the British at the end of the 1940s, 'They believed in their hearts that things British were necessarily things best. They believed that they, above all their Allies, had won the war. They saw themselves still, like their grandfathers, as a senior and superior race.'[25]

This was the *Zeitgeist* with which British political leadership after the war had its ambivalent relationship. Churchill spoke for part of it. He continued to assure the Americans that 'only the English-speaking peoples count; that together they can rule the world'.[26] Although out of office, he carried the weight of ages with him. This massive iconic figure, absolved from bothering with details or structures, set the tone that many on the continent desired to hear. His oracular pronouncements were as ambivalent as those of the goddess-seer at Delphi, but with less cunning intent. They were as devoid of clarity about European institutions as they were of rigour about Britain's economic prospects. They had enormous force. But they addressed less than half the picture.

On the one hand, there was Churchill's world. Proud nation. Inventive people. Stubborn, stoical, self-confident people. Future stretching indefinitely ahead. Second great power of the Western world watching with sympathy, seldom with alarm, the efforts of its neighbours across the Channel to remake themselves. Europe a place to which the British felt ineffable superiority. Little Attlee, no less than Churchill, was fated to personify this national pride, which it had become impossible for most Englishmen to question.

On the other hand, there was the world as seen by Henry Tizard. To this world, Churchill was absolutely blind. So, as we shall discover, were most of the people who, unlike Churchill, had to deal with it as responsible ministers. The consensus in favour of being a great power was impossible to challenge. On the left as well as the right, it was a given of national politics. After all, 'greatness' expresses the commonest of all ideas that, in one form or another, democratic politicians promise their electors. 'If we continue to behave like a Great Power, we shall soon cease to be a great nation.' Such a possibility of loss was unimaginable to British leaders in the post-war world – as it has been to most of their successors.

2

ERNEST BEVIN

Great Brit

WHILE ONE MAN controlled the emotional tone of post-war Britain's self-regard, somebody else was in charge of what actually happened. Ernest Bevin was the only man in the Attlee Cabinet who faintly resembled Winston Churchill. They had in common a capacity for domination. Each deserved the overworked description of a force of nature. Each addressed events from a basis of conviction that carried almost all before it – against colleagues, against enemies, sometimes against their closest allies. But Bevin had the advantage. He held cabinet office for a continuous period of nearly eleven years, as Minister of Labour during the war and Foreign Secretary immediately after it, whereas Churchill was cut out of power after five. He was also present at the making of the post-war world. Churchill could write and speak about it, and enjoyed the uniquely lustred admiration of audiences everywhere. Bevin made decisions.

With the United States and the Soviet Union, Britain still belonged to what were called, awesomely, the Big Three. At this, the topmost table of global leadership, Ernest Bevin was the British representative. Over the future of Europe, in particular, this gave him great influence. Europe was the cockpit in which the new struggle for mastery was joined. In the years between 1945 and 1950, the key alliances of Western power were shaped, and the debate about what 'Europe' meant reached its first conclusion. It is with decisions Bevin made and defended in those years that a British attitude which has endured for fifty years was first defined.

In particular, he embodied the paradox that was to repeat itself in different guises for decades ahead. He speaks with almost the same eloquence as Churchill for the elusive nature of the European idea. But his position, like Churchill's, declined to address an inherent contradiction. On the one hand, he conveys a sense of European unity mattering intensely to him. On the other, he seems to regard the concept of 'Europe' as forever hostile to the British interest.

Bevin was an improbable figure to have become the arbiter of these matters. Before 1945, there had never been a Foreign Secretary who remotely resembled him. Having left school at eleven, he was uninstructed in the niceties of the French Revolution, the Franco-Prussian War or any of the other half-remembered intellectual baggage his predecessors brought to the office, and in particular to their consideration of European politics. But he is commonly judged a great Foreign Secretary, and, in respect of the scale of the decisions he made, the verdict is not disputable.

Attlee gave him the job because he was the largest man among the colleagues who took over power. The original plan had been to send Bevin to the Treasury and Hugh Dalton, an Old Etonian and bonhomous intellectual, socially a more much congruent choice, to the Foreign Office. But over a lunch-time the Prime Minister reversed himself. 'I thought a heavy tank was what was required, rather than a light sniper,' he subsequently explained.[1]

Born in 1881, Bevin had risen from the humblest origins, through service as a trade unionist organizing draymen and carters in the West Country, to become the most powerful trade union leader in the country before he was forty-five. By the middle of the 1920s, he had created his own union, the Transport and General Workers, which, when the Second World War began, was the largest trade union in the world. He was a union man through and through, personified the 'industrial' side of the Labour movement, for most of his life had a wary relationship with the 'political' side, and distrusted all politicians who might be categorized as intellectuals. He was always interested in politics, and the power to which politics gave access. But, in the beginning, he was not easily bonded to the Labour Party. He greeted the first Labour administration in history, Ramsay MacDonald's Government of 1924, with a national dock strike a month after it came to office. 'Governments may come and governments may go,' he wrote with bluff self-regard, echoes of which were later transposed to the international scene, 'but the workers' fight for betterment of conditions must go on all the time.'

For most of his life, Bevin was not a politician at all. Only after Churchill brought him into the wartime coalition as Minister of Labour did he become a Member of Parliament. In the 1930s, after the disaster of the National Government, he devoted much time to rebuilding the Labour Party as the political wing of the trade union movement. The singleness of his purpose, backed by the size of his union, made him the crucial influence in pre-war party conferences. He was the very prototype of union baron that was later feared, derided and ultimately legislated out of political existence. But orthodox parliamentary politics was not the natural arena of a man who nevertheless became, after Churchill, the British politician most celebrated in the chancelleries of Europe and the world. He was in no way *soigné*. His considerable bulk burst out from ill-fitting suits. He had little patience with the niceties of debate, and was given to malapropisms that sent the educated Foreign Office smoothies around him into transports of patronising admiration. For many of them, he was the first man of toil with whom they had ever had contact as an equal, let alone as their master. When he entered the world stage, it could never have been as a diplomatic technician. Roy Jenkins observed of Bevin as Foreign Secretary: 'There was no other position in the Foreign Office, unless it was that of a rather truculent lift-man on the verge of retirement, which it would have been possible to imagine his filling.'[2]

He had, however, given thought to foreign affairs in earlier stages of his life. As an important union leader, he was caught up in the crises of the inter-war years. In 1927, he persuaded the Trades Union Congress to pass a resolution in favour of the same 'United States of Europe' that Churchill advocated three years later. He, too, likened it to the USA and urged its merits 'at least on an economic basis, even if we cannot on a totally political basis'. Such a great free trade area, it was argued later, might even have precluded the war, by sustaining the Weimar Republic and forestalling Hitler. And federation of a kind spoke to the left's ever seductive dream of world government. When war broke out, the Labour leader himself subscribed to it. 'In the common interest,' Clement Attlee wrote in December 1939, 'there must be recognition of an international authority superior to the individual states and endowed not only with rights over them, but with power to make them effective, operating not only in the political but in the economic sphere. Europe must federate or perish.'[3] It was a classic statement of the British federal idea as espoused by many leading figures at different times: pious, trenchant – and of only passing seriousness.

A species of it survived when Bevin became Foreign Secretary. Labour feeling replicated what ebbed and surged in other intellectual quarters, after as well as before the war. Coinciding with the Americans' nuclear bombing of Japan, the union baron's arrival in Whitehall was accompanied by a grand resurgence of the case for inventing not merely regional but worldwide organizations for peace. Stafford Cripps, the new Chancellor of the Exchequer, made the case for world federation. Attlee wanted 'the rule of law to be established throughout the world'. Bevin himself, in the first speech on foreign affairs that secured him the universal approval of his own side, overflowed with lyricism for a power beyond that of the nation-state. He was ready, he told the Commons on 23 November 1945, to merge the power of the British Parliament 'into the greater power of a directly elected world assembly'. There would be 'a world law with a world judiciary to interpret it, with a world police to enforce it'. The assembly would be 'the world sovereign elected authority which would hold in its care the destinies of the peoples of the world'.

There was a more down-to-earth way of putting this, and a few days later Bevin found it, in what became the most famous single remark he made on international affairs. 'Someone once asked me when I became Foreign Secretary', he told delegates to the preparatory commission then meeting in London to create the United Nations, 'what my policy really was. I said I have only one: it is to go down to Victoria Station here, take a ticket and go where the hell I like without anybody pulling me up with a passport.'[4]

His conduct of British diplomacy, however, was based on more exigent realities. Whatever Bevin's emotional preferences might have been, he could not escape the world of frontiers and control, of great forces that were fully capable of unleashing another war, which would be far worse than the war the Germans had just lost. It is hard to exaggerate the domination that fear of war had over the minds of all statesmen at this time. The bombing of Hiroshima in 1945 exposed the horrendous potential of the nuclear age. The outbreak of the Korean War in 1951 fulfilled the worst anticipations of a world living on the edge of permanent hostilities. Between those two events, Bevin was preoccupied with the creation of a new order to stabilize not just Europe but the international arena, which was now dominated by the two greatest powers, the United States and the Soviet Union. Vacuous oratory aside, Britain, the third occupant of a seat at the top table, took the idea of 'Europe' into account only as a residual consideration, out of much larger forebodings.

When Bevin entered the Foreign Office, it was committed to a strategy that might have been expected to be congenial to the Labour Party. This was the end-of-war, merging into post-war, policy of collaboration with the Soviet Union. Such was the orthodoxy of the moment, shared equally by the Americans, who themselves lost no time in packing up and starting to go home from Europe. The notion of a kind of global peace best guaranteed by equalities of allegiance between the victorious powers was what the Foreign Office was devoting itself to advance. Gladwyn Jebb, one of its architects, summarized its essence: 'All our own papers were then based on the assumption that there should in no circumstances be any Anglo-US line-up against the USSR or indeed against Communism, until such time at any rate as the Soviets should have made it abundantly clear that they did not intend to co-operate with the West.'[5]

With the advent of the Labour Government, Jebb recalled, 'a fresh and determined effort was made to secure this vital co-operation'. It was a stance, however, with which Labour as a party was happier than the new Foreign Secretary. It spoke to Labour's socialist internationalism, but was soon exposed as a denial of any tenable reality. By March 1946, Churchill, who had also been bewitched by its possibilities, repudiated it with his Iron Curtain speech. Not much later, Bevin too began to move towards the conclusion that collaboration was no longer a possibility. He reached this opinion sooner than most of the civil servants with whom he now found himself consorting. His life's education – 'plucked from the 'edgerows of experience', as he once told King George VI – prepared him better than them for hard-headed scepticism. 'Ernie was one of the very few British ministers who'd read Karl Marx and who knew about Communism,' one of his senior officials later recalled.[6] He stood out from the mandarins whose enchantment with their own fine formulae and optimistic constructs sometimes failed to engage with the facts that a democratic politician could not overlook.

From this basis, Bevin fashioned a position that both enhanced the integrity of Western Europe and diminished the possibility of Britain allying herself, in any institutional manner, with the continental urge for a closer form of union. Russia's behaviour in the post-war years, culminating in the occupation of Czechoslovakia in 1948, removed the last illusions that she could be a partner in peace. The need for an American alliance became paramount. This, the return of American military power to Europe, finally expressed in the creation of the North Atlantic Treaty Organization, became Bevin's overarching objective. Without Bevin, to whom Attlee sub-contracted Labour foreign policy as an almost independent fiefdom, it is doubtful whether either Washington or the Labour Party would have seen Nato through to its consummation by treaty in April 1949.

Bevin was equally essential to the process of implanting the American economic programme, which preceded Nato as a vital prop to the uncertain European peace. His biographer Alan Bullock reckons this 'his most decisive personal contribution' as Foreign Secretary.[7] On 5 June 1947, General George Marshall, the US Secretary of State, with little warning to anyone, proposed an American aid programme for European recovery, which eventually became the fuel for the remaking of France, Germany and Britain in particular. The first Bevin heard of the Marshall Plan was when he was lying in bed listening to the radio. But his instincts were impeccable. He went into the Foreign Office next day and got to work to assemble a response. Unencumbered by mandarin caution, he thought the Secretary of State had made 'one of the greatest speeches in world history'. Marshall laid down a challenge to Europe. It had to decide what it needed. 'The initiative, I think, must come from Europe,' Marshall said. Bevin seized on this with a kind of visceral recognition. Whereas the Foreign Office was initially cool, and the State Department was unsure what its leader meant, Bevin determined to take him at his word and help him fulfil it. 'It was like a lifeline to sinking men,' he later told the National Press Club in Washington.

So Nato and the Marshall Plan were at the heart of Bevin's achievement. He was, in his way, as central to their architecture as were the Americans. They implemented a world view that was global, strategic and conscious of imminent apocalypse. In this sense, Bevin was Britain's first peacetime Atlanticist, the man who saw less ambiguously than anyone that Washington should be taken up on its offer to guide and protect the evolution of post-war Europe. He carried the bulk of his party with him on a painful journey, beginning with the discovery that Moscow was as great an enemy of British socialism as it was of Western capitalism. He maintained the stance of a great power despite his awareness that Britain's economic strength had been sapped by the war. 'If only I had 50 million tons of coal to export, what a difference it would make to my foreign policy,' he was fond of saying. But this didn't induce him to behave like the leader of a fundamentally weakened country. He saw the immediate problem but, in common with almost everybody else, got nowhere near understanding, if he ever heard, the prophetic quality of Tizard's warning that Britain stood in danger of ceasing to be a great nation.

These strands – the Atlantic priority, the British self-image – came together in Bevin's attitude to the idea of 'Europe'. In effect, he carried out, against the background of Churchill's periodic forays into the uplifting language of European pseudo-federalism, a policy that betrayed the same ambiguity. That is to say, it was confused if not duplicitous. The impression of certainty concealed a refusal to recognize hard choices. The promises of solidarity with the ravaged nations of the continent were qualified by Bevin's total hostility to any real 'Europe' that presumed to include Britain.

At the core of this was an analysis that Churchill famously made, and Bevin did not dissent from. Represented as the essence of wisdom, it could equally well be described as a biblical text for the justification of strategic indecision. Always remember, Churchill would pronounce, that the British interest lies in remaining at the intersection of three circles, representing the United States, the Commonwealth and Europe. Never, he said, permit Britain to escape from any of them. It was a diplomatic philosophy, reverently repeated and hardly ever challenged, that now made an enduring impact on the shape of the European circle in particular.

Bevin's personal attitude began with disdain for the sheer weakness of all continental countries, which was probably shared by most of the British. They were entities in which Britain could repose neither hope nor reliance. Bevin spoke of them with despair, echoing the image sometimes to be found in the Foreign Office documents of the period, which refer to the danger of Britain 'chaining itself to a corpse'. It was one of the things that made him so committed to reawakening Americans' belief that Europe was one of their own most vital national interests.

His definitive speech on the subject, one of what he called his 'tours de reason', was made to the House of Commons on 22 January 1948. It was as spacious as it was ambiguous, and in both respects deserved to be called Churchillian.

On the one hand, this was the moment when Bevin announced that any complicit alliance with the Soviet Union had finally been rendered impossible by Soviet tactics in Central Europe. To mark a new turn in history, he proposed what he called a Western Union. The Russians, he remarked, had prevented Eastern Europe from joining any collective enjoyment of the fruits of the Marshall Plan, and were doing their best through the activities of communist parties in the West to impede the economic recovery of Europe. This meant that the free nations of Western Europe must draw together. 'I believe the time is ripe for consolidation,' Bevin said. Moreover, it must involve as many nations as possible in 'the spirit and the machinery of co-operation', not excluding Britain. 'Britain', the Foreign Secretary said, 'cannot stand outside

Europe and regard her problems as quite separate from those of her European neighbours.'

This speech had a deep formative influence. It led directly to the Treaty of Brussels, which united Britain to the continent in a defence pact with France and the Benelux countries – Belgium, the Netherlands, Luxembourg – which in turn led on to the making of Nato. On the other hand, the speech gustily emulated Churchill's own rhetoric of imprecision, and was made by a man whose vision was quite sceptical of European, as distinct from Western, Union. It did not define what Western Union was – deliberately, says Bullock – because Bevin didn't know where his call to unite 'trade, social, cultural and all other contacts' among all available nations would lead. He saw a vast world beyond Europe, in which somehow all Britain's interests could be reconciled under one umbrella. There would be the 'closest possible collaboration with the Commonwealth and with overseas territories, not only with British but French, Dutch, Belgian and Portuguese', and between these and Europe there was no necessary conflict. But the role of Britain, especially in the defence of Western Europe, was left vague. In an earlier Cabinet paper, Bevin appeared to be groping for a distinctive European part in the scheme of things. We should, he suggested, 'show clearly that we are not subservient to the United States or the Soviet Union'. But at the same time, he said his aim was to achieve 'what I called a spiritual union of the West'.[8] There was, in short, a lot of unexamined woolliness about Bevin's world view. He acted on the presumption that Britain was, and would remain, a world power, while at the same time occasionally being prepared to recognize that economic weakness might undermine such a claim. He wanted the West to unite, but was quite unsure how this might best be brought about or who the candidates for union might be. He saw Britain, correctly, as the prime mover among the European powers, yet at every relevant moment, as we shall see, he directed a foreign policy that weakened the 'European' option.

In all these positions, he was supported by the Foreign Office. There was a community of attitude between the unlettered union leader, a man who had the greatest difficulty in writing down, in his almost illegible hand, the thoughts to which he usually gave rather meandering verbal expression, and the officials who called him, without knowing conde-scension, Uncle Ernie. Instinct, allied to reasoning that turned out to be less than prophetic, led minister and mandarins in the same direction.

Instinct, surprisingly, was as decisive in the processes of the officials as it was in the gut of the typical politician. Until 1949, they had no such thing as a planning staff to assist their policy-making. The notion that rational foresight, meditated carefully and subjected to collective debate, might assist the making of foreign policy was one that took some time to gain acceptance in the British Foreign Office. Lord Halifax said before the Second World War: 'I distrust anyone who foresees consequences and advocates remedies to avert them.'[9] Halifax, admittedly, was a politician. But the condition was departmental. When one senior official recommended to another, in June 1944, the case for a two-year foreign policy statement updated every six months, the recipient, Sir Alexander Cadogan, the permanent secretary, replied: 'That way lies Bedlam.'[10] When Christopher Mayhew, on becoming a junior minister at the Foreign Office in 1946, asked for a document outlining foreign policy, he was told 'not merely that no such document existed' but 'that it was really rather doubtful whether we had a foreign policy in the proper sense at all'.[11]

There followed from this lordly amateurism not only a bias against the making of hard choices, but a reluctance sometimes to obey the logic of an analysis that was at least half discerned. To try to maintain a central position in all three of the intersecting circles defined by Churchill was a sensible, indeed elementary, objective. But to ignore some of the facts that might soon make this an illusory proposition was less defensible. Yet that was the regular tendency of the Foreign Office in the post-war half-decade and beyond.

At least some officials understood well enough that the British claim to great-power ranking was already compromised by the facts of economic life. Their words may not have had the vivid finality of Henry Tizard's, but they knew the score even before the war was over. A paper written in March 1945 spoke of Britain's enormous external debts, and cautioned against making 'commitments which our economic strength will not bear' and 'another series of humiliations' comparable with the events of the 1930s to which these would give rise. If Britain did not make clear that it would overcome its difficulties, 'other countries will say the lion is in his dotage and try to divide up his skin'. The man who wrote this, Sir Orme Sargent, deputy under-secretary, did have the prudence to note that Britain was 'the weakest and geographically the smallest' of the great powers. She was like 'Lepidus in the triumvirate with Mark Antony and Augustus'. But no sense of restraint followed from these observations. On the contrary, said Sargent before the Cold War with the Soviet Union declared itself, it was 'essential to increase our strength', by taking on more responsibilities. Sargent's clarity of analysis was matched only by the utter perversity of the conclusion he drew. Leadership of the Dominions, and of France and Western Europe, would be 'the only way to compel our two big partners to treat us as an equal'.[12] The Foreign Office saw Britain as a global player for the foreseeable future.

In 1945, the apparent contradiction between economy and politics was mitigated by a large amount of hope. At that time, the formal position of the Foreign Office was that economic strain was a temporary phenomenon. 'This country possesses all the skill and resources required to recover a dominating place in the economic world,' it wrote. By 1947, however, such optimism should have been banished from its councils. The dollar drain was incessant, Palestine and India were in turmoil, the cost of the vast German garrison, by which Britain paid to protect the rebuilding of her defeated enemy, was crippling. 'We shall be on the rocks in two years unless we can redress our balance of payments,' Hugh Dalton minuted Attlee in December 1945.[13] Yet the Foreign Office view of Britain's place in the world went defiantly, perhaps routinely, unrevised. The official view did allow that 'we do not seem to have any economic resources available for political purposes' – which limited what Britain could do for European economic recovery. But the case for an independent British foreign policy was 'still valid'.[14] And the necessity for choice between competing interests in the three circles was almost nowhere recognized as a problem meriting serious thought.

In the European circle, moreover, challenges now presented themselves whose outcome was preordained. While Churchill, however deceptively, was emitting a stream of pan-European rhetoric and starting to organize a European Movement, the Foreign Office was closing down each practical opportunity to make of 'Europe' something more than a collection of rival governments. In this ruthless exercise there was nothing to choose between the adamancy of the minister and the limpid certainty of his officials, who included some of the most influential policy-makers in the history of the British civil service.

The three exemplary moments in the process need not detain us for long. They are mere preliminaries to the decisive event that occurred in 1950, when Britain, under Bevin's ailing but determined hand, excluded herself from what became known as the Schuman Plan. But the justifications for what happened in each case are resonant. They sound the authentic note of their time. They can also be heard echoing through much that happened from first to last, right down to the 1990s.

The Treaty of Brussels, following Bevin's big speech on Western

Union, might have been a great leap forward. Its early devisers were infected with federalist possibilities: a parliament, a mechanism for economic co-operation, as well as a mutual defence agreement between Britain, France and Benelux. The idea of supra-nationalism was appearing between the draft lines, a development which Attlee himself at one stage did not reject, averring that in Western Union 'we are prepared, with other powers, to pool some degree of authority'.[15]

In the event, the outcome was more modest. Economic co-operation was mentioned, and a Permanent Consultative Council was created. But nobody could pretend this was a parliament, and that was as the British wanted it. Britain's destructive role was later regretted by one of the officials who performed it as Bevin's agent. Other officials invariably defended their part in British negativism towards Europe, on the many occasions they were approached by historians in later years. But Gladwyn Jebb, Poo-Bah of post-war construction and intellectual butler to the ministers who shaped many of its institutions, did concede that he had made a tactical mistake. The Foreign Office, he recalled in the 1980s, had been right in 1948 to rule out Britain entering a supra-national organization 'because it wouldn't have gone through Parliament'.[16] All the same, the FO could have been cleverer. It could have gone to the Europeans, who were more federalist inclined, and told them to be patient. Britain would come round, Jebb reckoned he should have told them. This embryonic European parliament might come to something: that is what the British might have said from their position of influence as Europe's strongest nation. 'Even though it won't have many supra-national powers, it could have more as time goes on,' is the way Jebb could have allayed continental fears. But the British declined to offer that kind of hope. 'I blame myself for not having done that,' Jebb said.

This was of a piece with the second development, which started before the drafting of the Brussels Treaty and cast a long shadow beyond it. In 1947, talks began on the formation of a customs union in Western Europe, essentially an American idea. Lowering barriers and equalizing tariffs was a way of freeing up European trade. Freer trade within Europe would be the necessary prelude to the strengthening of both the European and American economies. But this initiative the British vowed from an early stage to obstruct and, if possible, prevent.

It summoned up another great spectre that alarmed British leaders about the idea of 'Europe'. First the Brussels Treaty – heaven forfend! – looked as though it might set up a body bearing the same name as the Westminster Parliament and perhaps challenging its power. Then a

European customs union, if completed, would compromise, perhaps ultimately destroy, the British Commonwealth – and the sterling area, which mainly consisted of the Commonwealth countries' monetary resources kept in London.

The case for a customs union, making Europe into a single market without barriers, was the classic free trader's argument, arising from the crippled circumstances in which war had left the world. The US had a vast trade surplus, but the European economies were so decimated that there was a danger of world trade drying catastrophically. This consideration was the moving spirit of self-interest behind General Marshall and his generous Plan. European free trade was pressed as a precondition of the Plan. But the terms on which it began to happen were, in the end, the minimalist British terms.

This was the last time Britain succeeded in stopping a European development she did not desire – and even then the success was only temporary. It is not too much to say that the customs union that didn't happen in 1948 became the Common Market that did happen, without Britain, in 1958.

Bevin himself wanted a customs union to happen, for political reasons – and yet, for different political reasons, did not want it in the form desired by other countries. We see the embryo of a dilemma that was to continue for fifty years. The politics of *economy* pushed Bevin one way. As late as November 1947, he was minuting the economic policy sub-committee of the Cabinet on the desirability of Western Europe attaining a measure of economic union 'if it was to maintain its independence'.[17] But the politics of *politics* pushed him in the opposite direction. Any union, in Bevin's view, had to be between sovereign governments, with no power ceded to a supra-national body.

Between these prongs of Morton's Fork, the Foreign Office decided early where it was likely to finish up. Whereas later, when economic and monetary union became a pressing issue in the 1990s, Britain faced a terrible choice between losing sovereignty through EMU and losing world influence by staying out of EMU, in the late 1940s the decision was seen as obvious, at least by the officials in charge of it. The most powerful of these, Sir Roger Makins, assistant under-secretary at the Foreign Office, wrote in August 1947 that any customs union implied 'social and political' association. For Britain, this could happen only at the expense of links with the Commonwealth, the weakening of which would lead in turn to 'the disintegration of the sterling area and spell the end of Britain as a world power'. The anti-European position, in

other words, was then the opposite of what it became. It was credibly
consistent with Britain's global aspirations. In fact, officials thought, it
was the only way to sustain them. Supported by the Whitehall economic
departments, the Foreign Office therefore set about undermining the
proposed union. There was a 'general decision to go slow on the whole
matter', Makins wrote. Reflecting on this later, he exhibited nothing
resembling the conversion experience of his contemporary-in-influence,
Gladwyn Jebb. 'We were fighting a rearguard action,' he said in the early
1980s. The Americans 'pushed us far too hard', were 'not sympathetic to
our colonial obligations' and 'never understood the sterling area'.[18]
Makins played a vital part in resisting what he termed the 'blackmail' of
Washington, which implied that the Marshall Plan might not be
launched if the customs union succumbed to British resistance.

The Cabinet decision against the union was prepared with care, with
Bevin in the lead. The British had the power to dictate the outcome, and
at this stage in history were able more or less to satisfy both sides of
their contradictory position. The Marshall Plan did get launched, and
the body that oversaw it did not exercise the supra-national powers
which the Americans at first envisaged and most other European
countries would have been content to surrender. The Organization
for European Economic Co-operation (OEEC) was a truly inter-
governmental body. The Americans, and the French, wanted this to have
its own secretariat, capable of taking initiatives, with the ultimate objective, as Marshall himself described it, of 'closer integration of Western
Europe'. Not only did the British reject that, they vetoed the man the
integrationists named to run it, Paul-Henri Spaak, the dynamic Belgian
leader, whom they saw as far too strong. 'We had absolutely nothing
against Spaak, who we regarded as being an absolutely first-rate fellow,'
Makins later recalled. 'We resisted because we felt that there should not
be an individual of that kind standing between the governments.'[19]

These were palmy days for British influence. Having evicted Spaak,
London secured control for its own man, the third in this trio of civil
servants who mattered so much more than any of their successors in
later decades. Alongside Jebb and Makins, Oliver Franks exercised an
influence on the Labour Government seldom matched by any official at
any other time. With Franks as chairman of the executive of OEEC,
Britain had established what Makins called 'a matter of principle': that
European integration, although espoused in numerous vague orations by
Ernest Bevin, should remove not one particle of power from individual
governments. And Franks, like Makins, later offered an unrepentant

explanation for the British attitude. Britain was always interested in co-operation, he told Michael Charlton, but objected to the *institutions* of co-operation.

He thought that being in at the beginning of a new European institution wouldn't necessarily be enough to guarantee the national interest. 'If', Franks said on the radio in 1982, 'you are part of, and subject to, an institution which in some degree has a life of its own, initiative, spontaneity, ability to formulate policy, then you are no longer as free as you were before. And this is the point. Even though you can help mould the institution, the facts about the institution remain even when you've had your influence. The problem has been that we have been very reluctant to submit ourselves, if you like, to the rulings of an institution.'[20] There could hardly be a more unbending statement of hostility to the notion at any time of entering the European Community.

So the British got their way. But it was not a painless victory. Nor was there universal agreement that the right course had been taken. The tide of Europeanism, which Churchill among others was accelerating in 1948, did not stop at Foreign Office command. The Hague Congress, great climax of quasi-federalist effusion, took place in May. But, before we come to that, the accuracy of rival prophecies about the future of Britain, a question that crops up time and again, needs to be touched on.

The Foreign Office position, defended in particular by Makins and Franks, rested on a prediction about the future state of British power, most notably economic power. The sterling area, they thought, was Britain's lifeline, and the Commonwealth a source of both raw materials and industrial markets that had no discernible end. 'People did not foresee then that the sterling area would one day break up, that the countries of the Commonwealth wouldn't all want to hold their reserves in sterling,' Franks said later. It actually began to happen in less than a decade. But 'none of this was foreseen at the time'.[21]

That wasn't quite true. Henry Tizard wasn't alone in his more sceptical apprehensions. Bridging the Foreign Office and the Treasury was a man called Edmund Hall-Patch, Bevin's economic adviser. Hall-Patch regarded the choice identified by Makins and Franks as a false one. In August 1947, he minuted Bevin that this claim of an either/or choice between Europe and the Commonwealth had 'successfully blocked for two years our efforts to look at these proposals objectively'.[22] We should be more imaginative, he suggested. The integration of the United States had its lessons. 'If some such integration does not take place, Europe will gradually decline in the face of pressure from the United States on the one hand and the Soviet Union on the other.'

Hall-Patch was an atypical mandarin. In early life, he had earned his living as a busker on the streets of Paris, and had served abroad, Oliver Franks remarked, in such out-of-the-way places as Bangkok. Talking later, Franks conceded that Hall-Patch was a prescient man. 'He was seeing ahead with very considerable accuracy.' But his views at the time did not carry weight. They weren't congruent with 'the structure of thinking in government departments', which was the thinking Makins, Franks and Jebb, to name its three most influential designers, did nothing whatever to question. Therefore Hall-Patch wasn't heard.

Nor, however, were mildly integrationist views consistent with majority desires in the Labour Party. The party was the other great engine of Bevin's foreign policy, alongside the Foreign Office. The Labour Party has much to say in this whole story. It was a vital player at all the critical junctures of Britain's engagement with the continent. But the Labour thinking as it bore upon Bevin had a special relevance to the moment at which he, who is almost classifiable as the leading Euro-sceptic of his day, came under most baleful pressure from the supposed 'European', Winston Churchill: the Hague Congress and its aftermath.

Bevin, as we have seen, had not been hostile to federalist tendencies in his younger days. Like Attlee, he put his name to motions and resolutions that carried the stamp of desperate men desiring almost any expedient that might avoid a European war. After the war, a federalist tendency subsisted among Labour politicians, as it did among Conservatives. Indeed, on the very brink of the Hague meeting, 5 May 1948, when a Labour motion was debated suggesting that MPs from all European countries should assemble to work out a federal constitution, Attlee, the Prime Minister himself, was not averse. Maybe this reflects the vaporous manner in which the idea was then contemplated. Perhaps Attlee did not intend to be taken as making any very meaningful commitment. Nonetheless, the *Hansard* record shows him saying: 'Ultimately I believe we must come to federation of Europe. I have often spoken against the continuance of some sort of sovereignty.' The question was how to work towards 'some sort of federation' by dealing with 'practical matters'.

As aspirational rhetoric, this wasn't something Bevin especially disagreed with. On the other hand, the faction in the party which most warmly espoused the cause was one that, for other reasons, he most heartily abominated. Federation, in those days, was the ambition of the left. In May 1947, the Keep Left group of MPs published a manifesto urging a federation of Europe as far as the Soviet frontier, starting with the 'less spectacular' collaboration of France and Britain, and leading, as they hoped, to the eventual raising of the Iron Curtain.[23] A minor feature of this was the evidence it offered that shameless personal inconsistency, a feature of Labour politics no less than Conservative, began early. Composed by Ian Mikardo, the pro-federal tract was signed by fourteen MPs, among them two later scions of the anti-European cause, Richard Crossman and Michael Foot. Its major political effect, however, was to rouse Bevin's fury. For the purpose of the left was blatantly anti-American. At the very moment when Bevin had determined there was no longer any alternative to enlisting the US in the defence of Europe, this not insignificant faction in his party, containing around 100 MPs, was canvassing for a 'Third Force' to stand between the US and the USSR and supposedly heal the breach between them.

Federalism's Labour friends, in short, constituted one reason for Bevin to view with chilly disapproval Churchill's venture at The Hague. But they were not the main cause of it. Other party pressures exerted themselves on Bevin which he was, for the most part, content to experience. The party man coexisted with the international statesman. Europe, after all, was hardly a socialist paradise. Here was a Labour government, at the head of what appeared to be the most powerful country, surrounded by enfeebled nations run by anti-socialists. Adenauer in Germany, Robert Schuman in France, De Gasperi in Italy headed Catholic parties running would-be capitalist economic policies. Labour politicians were instructed in the language of unambiguous party politics not to attend the Hague Congress. 'The National Executive Committee', wrote the general secretary, Morgan Phillips, 'is unconditionally opposed to any action which might appear to associate the prestige of the governing majority party in Great Britain, however indirectly, with an organisation calculated to serve the interests of the British Conservative Party.'[24]

All the same, twenty-six Labour MPs did attend at The Hague. This did not please Bevin any more than did the resolution passed there, which was to lead to the Council of Europe, and the creation of its Assembly in Strasbourg. Bevin by now detested the European Movement as much as he disliked the Keep Left group. On returning from The Hague, Churchill had even had the impertinence, as Harold Macmillan recalls in his diaries, to lead a march from Parliament to 10 Downing Street to insist on the Assembly being created. There had been 'trouble from this so-called European movement, not always in the open', Bevin later complained in a Commons debate, 'and it had been extremely difficult to carry on negotiations with this kind of semi-sabotage going on behind the scenes.' (To which Churchill replied: 'You are the arch-saboteur).'[25]

Like it or not, however, the Government was driven along the road towards creating the Assembly. In the second most quoted line he ever uttered, Bevin had bestowed upon it an image straight from the 'edgerows of experience. 'If you open that Pandora's Box,' he once said, 'you never know what Trojan 'orses will jump out.' But in November one thing led to another and the tame little Consultative Council, which was all that remained of the 'parliament' the Brussels Treaty was once intended to provide, met in Paris in order to consider a proposal for a proper parliamentary European Assembly.

Britain could not avoid attending. In fact she sent a high-level delegation, led by Hugh Dalton, the Old Etonian intellectual who thought he should have had Bevin's job, and staffed among others by the ubiquitous Gladwyn Jebb. It worked hard to prevaricate. Instead of an assembly, it suggested a non-parliamentary consultative body with limited terms of reference, to be controlled by the governments. An impasse beckoned, assisted not least by another strand in Labour anti-Europeanism which Dalton personified. Dalton was almost uncontrollably anti-German. He regarded Churchill's efforts to bring the recent enemy into the concert of nations as a betrayal. 'We'll gouge out their eyes! We'll stamp on their bellies! We'll tear out their livers!' he once sang to a friend on the way to a function where Germans were to be present.[26] Although Bevin took a more statesmanlike view, he agreed with Dalton's opinion that, if the Council had to happen, it should be minimalist in conception.

For the most part, it was. 'We'll give them this talking shop,' Bevin eventually conceded.[27] During the negotiations, he wriggled and writhed. He wanted delegations appointed by governments not parliaments, and voting done in blocs, controllable by governments, rather than individually. In the end, a compromise was again achieved, as a result of which the Council of Europe had no power and rather little influence, a condition for which the British Labour Government was responsible.

As well as Churchill, with his grand inaugural speech, many large figures attended the first meeting of the Strasbourg Assembly. The Conservative delegation included Harold Macmillan, Duncan Sandys, David Eccles and Robert Boothby. None was a federalist, but all were by their own lights passionate 'Europeans'. They wanted the idea of Europe to succeed, and thought Britain should consider herself a leader among partners. The Labour team was also talented. Led by Dalton, it included James Callaghan, Fred Lee, Aidan Crawley and the young international secretary of the party, Denis Healey. But the Labour prejudice, following Bevin's, was different – or at least more explicit and, as some might say, more honest. 'We could not approve any policy that took us further away from the Commonwealth,' Dalton wrote at the time.[28]

The Strasbourg federalists didn't give up hope. Although the Council's statute had been written, ideas were still in the melting-pot. That was the spirit of the time. Enthusiasm and uncertainty abounded. Not everything seemed to be fixed. No sooner had they gathered than the continentals were pressing forward, pushing at the first meeting for 'a political authority of a supra-national character' to be created without delay. The Assembly passed a resolution to this effect, enjoining the Council to develop such an authority 'with limited functions but real powers', words coined by the Labour MP Kim Mackay, and every British Conservative voted for it. Paul-Henri Spaak personified the atmosphere of optimistic rejoicing. 'I came to Strasbourg', he said, 'convinced of the need for a United States of Europe. I am leaving with the certitude that union is possible.'[29]

But this underrated the opposition. Led by the Labour Government, the Council's committee of ministers simply killed off the Assembly's initiatives. They refused to surrender the veto which Bevin and the Foreign Office had made sure they kept, ignored the demand for a political authority and even tried to prevent the Assembly discussing any matter that fell within the functions of any other international body such as OEEC or the United Nations. Of Strasbourg's grand aspirations, only a Commission and Court of Human Rights, enforcing a European Convention, were eventually permitted to have an existence that endured.

By early 1950, therefore, the scene appeared to be set, and it accorded more closely with the priorities of establishment Britain – the Britain of Ernest Bevin, the Foreign Office, the Treasury, the whole of Whitehall, almost the whole of the governing Labour Party – than it did with the rhetorical clouds put out with such captivating power by Winston Churchill. These clouds, moreover, proved on inspection to be little more than hot air. They enveloped what was actually a consensus, shared by an entire political class, indeed by most of the arbiters of an entire culture. This consensus agreed, all in all, that the island nation belonged not to the continent but to the world, and could better maintain its global importance by spurning every inducement to reconsider the continent. It saw such lures, whether from the United States or from Europe, as a trick. And it was able until this date to impose its own terms on these allies, who were either too distant or too feeble to count. It was the captain of its fate, or so it thought, and the dominant force among the countries it had to deal with: the leader, in a word, of a Europe congenial to it.

This, however, was the last time such a sweet picture could be conjured up. The claim to leadership, hitherto unchallengeable, raised a question that could not be answered for ever by reference to intersecting circles, or any other image that obscured the necessity for choice. The luxury of calm disdain for 'Europe' was a pose with a limited life. The first great moment of truth was about to present itself.

*

ON 9 MAY 1950, at six o'clock in the evening, the French Foreign Minister, Robert Schuman, held a press conference that he hoped would change the world. This hope was less than well illuminated by some of the circumstances of the occasion. Schuman's modest presence and hesitant voice did not convey a sense of history in the making. Moreover, there were 200 journalists present but no movie cameras. To make sure something was recorded for posterity, Schuman was obliged to re-enact the scene some months later. Nonetheless, 9 May 1950 was the day that established Europe as being more serious about 'Europe' than the British could believe.[30]

To Ernest Bevin, it was a day mingling fury with regret. These emotions, moreover, were suffused by illness. Bevin was by now a sick man. He had returned to work only the day before Schuman's press conference, after a month in the London Clinic following an operation to ease his respiratory system. He sometimes said himself that he was 'only half alive'. He retained control of foreign policy, and the power of his pre-fixed positions concerning the future of Europe remained the dominant influence over what now happened. It is worth remembering, though, that this was now a man who by his own confession had difficulty staying awake and, according to his subordinate, Kenneth Younger, chaired meetings at which 'he could barely read out the agenda, let alone take charge'.[31]

The reason for Bevin's professional fury was obvious. The announcement Schuman made had been cooked up without his knowledge, and partly as an act of deception against him. But Bevin got over that. What he couldn't overlook was the regrettable possibility that Britain had lost control of events. In the five years since the end of the war, she had been able to forestall questions that embarrassed her or ensure they were answered in her favour. The Schuman Plan was something else again.

It proposed the boldest fusing of the resources and interests of two great nations that modern Europe had ever seen. Coal and steel, the base materials of industrial economies, would cease to be controlled and sold by the respective governments of France and Germany, and would be subject to shared decisions. These decisions would be made not by national governments acting as sovereign powers, but by a new organization – a high authority – which they would agree to create, and to which they would, over these particular resources, surrender sovereignty. French and German citizens would run the Authority. But their role would transcend nation. They would be the functionaries of a new and formal community.

There was no model for a coal and steel community in European or any other history. And the creative mind that lay behind it, which was entirely French, was inspired in part by economic necessity. The French were alarmed by Germany's post-war industrial recovery. Steel, in particular, had always been cheaper there than in France, and the pattern continued. Victor and vanquished were already exchanging the economic as well as psychological advantages that 1945 might have been expected to bring them. Though German production levels were controlled by the occupying powers, France knew the Americans would always sympathize with German demands for more. Indeed, it was because the Americans and British, who controlled the Ruhr, were on the verge of raising the ceiling for German production that the French were forced to act fast. For France, there were immediate attractions to a scheme over which she would share control. For Germany, collaboration as an equal partner with France, five years after the war, offered an irresistible opportunity.

But economics was not the largest consideration. The most relevant propensity of coal and steel was their use in the tools of war. Above and beyond the likely economic consequences of German domination – dumping, protectionism, cartels and the stifling of free trade – were the political attractions of a new way of peace. Removing these elements of the war machine from national control would reduce the risk of a mainland war recurring. This would be the earnest of a new political intention: Franco-German reconciliation, the prize that would change future history.

The three men who made the Schuman Plan – the patron, the architect and the grateful supplicant – were men of mettle. They knew what they wanted. This did not discount or exclude Britain. But neither did it contemplate submission to Britain's superiority. With Bevin and with Britain, each had a complex relationship. These were Europeans it was not given to a Briton thoroughly, intuitively, easily to understand.

Robert Schuman, the patron, uniquely personified what the Franco-German problem was about. His home territory was Lorraine, borderland between Germany and France, for ever in pawn to the warring continent. In childhood, Schuman, though French by descent, was categorized German, spoke French with a Rhineland accent, and was conscripted into German uniform in the First World War. He became a Frenchman only at thirty-two. But as a Lorraine politician he understood about coal and steel. They were produced there, fuelling the wars that were fought there. This was a place where the Légion d'Honneur and the Iron Cross could sometimes sit on the same mantelpiece. Georges Berthoin, a young Schuman aide and later the influential EEC ambassador in London, told me he saw such juxtapositions. There are still memorials to both French and German soldiers in the same squares of the same towns of Alsace-Lorraine.

According to Berthoin, it was partly as a way of freeing his home territory from 'historical schizophrenia' that Schuman saw his famous Plan. He was an improbable vehicle for such a grand scheme. The inaudible voice issued from a thin, ascetic figure, who had characteristics seldom found among politicians of the time, let alone forty years later. He lived in monastic chastity, a bachelor and scholar, expert in philosophy and theology, his bookshelves bearing copiously annotated editions of Hegel and André Gide. But he was also a public man of iron, who clung with determination to the carousel of the Fourth Republic. In an earlier turn of the wheel, before he took charge of the Foreign Ministry at the Quai d'Orsay, he had been Prime Minister. As a serious Catholic, he knew how to forgive, but did not indulge in the disgrace of forgetting. Above all, he never forgot the causes of the war. 'As regards the Coal and Steel Community,' said Georges Berthoin, 'Schuman was a man absolutely aware he was fulfilling a historic mission.'[32]

He was not, however, the Plan's inventor. Jean Monnet, the architect, was the chief creative mind. And since Monnet was the godfather, if not father, of this 'Europe' that has caused the British so much trouble, he should detain us a little longer.

History sometimes reallocates the credit for great events, as time goes on. But, for the idea and fact of 'Europe', Monnet has never lost the credit or the blame. Among all who came to favour the idea, sometimes years late, he enjoys an admiration verging on sanctity, just as for its enemies he is the devil incarnate. In Britain, as much as anywhere, Monnet was duly infamous. I once heard Kenneth Baker, a senior Cabinet minister in the 1990s, refer from a public platform to 'Jean' Monnet, as if he thought he was talking about a woman.[33] Perhaps this was a calculated insult from a politician keen to stress his anti-European credentials in the debate then raging in the Conservative Party. But from the 1950s to the 1970s there was no member of the British establishment whose hand Monnet had not in all probability shaken.

He was an internationalist in a rare sense, contact man supreme, originally a brandy salesman born in Cognac, banker, tireless factotum to the diplomatic gentry. Arranging a loan for Poland in 1927, for example, he made the lifelong acquaintance of John Foster Dulles, the US Secretary of State two decades later. He had a formative period in London, where he learned about British ways. But America was his first base. Years before 'Europe' was thought of, Dean Acheson, John McCloy, Henry Stimson, Averell Harriman and other East Coast paladins were Monnet's friends. He gave early meaning to the label 'international civil servant', being on the payroll of the British Government in the First World War and the American in the Second, as well as, for a while, deputy secretary-general of the League of Nations.

Monnet wasn't elected. He was never more than an official at any time, and often not even that, flitting through the underworld of unpublicized influence in the capitals of the West. Elbow-gripper, shoulder-tapper, a wanderer with a fat address-book, he was also a man of action, determined to harness a vision, which anyone might have, to the means of advancing it in the real world, which the average visionary tended to neglect. Contemplating why it was that Monnet was thought both by admirers and detractors to be so extraordinarily effective, François Duchêne suggests in his biography, a marvellous work of scholarship and insight: 'His secret, if he had one, came from a combination of creative and critical faculties. He appealed to the romantic in people through the idealism of his goals, and to the expert in them through the realism of his means.' Making 'Europe' was Monnet's richest dream. What drove him was the experienced fact of war. He thought the reason the First World War lasted longer than necessary was that the allies had fought 'side by side and not as a single organised force'. He is that rare specimen, a public man with one driving idea, able over half a century to see this idea, the weakening of the nation-state, begin to come to pass. The Schuman Plan was the largest stride he took towards it.

It connected seamlessly with his past. He had been the fertile brain behind the plan for Anglo-French Union in the dark days of 1940. He it was who mainly persuaded both Churchill and General de Gaulle of its merits. But after the war he wanted to go much further than Churchill. He was a committed federalist, and could see that the ambitions of the European Movement, for all the exalted vapourings of the Hague Conference (which he did not attend), led no further than the Council of Europe, which was carefully limited to collaboration between states. What Monnet wanted was not mere co-operation, but the creation within Europe of a common interest, formally constructed and legally ratified.

In its final form, the Coal and Steel Community did not conform exactly to the Monnet blueprint. There were significant dilutions. He was, however, its undisputed originator, and has identified the moment when it took specific shape. In the middle of March 1950, he repaired to the Swiss Alps, as was his habit, for a walking tour to clear his head. We may picture this stocky figure, accompanied only by a guide, as his memoirs describe, for two weeks striding across the mountains from one overnight lodge to another, physically on holiday but emotionally and intellectually preoccupied with what he saw as an essential idea. Five years after the last war, how best could the next one be prevented? Actually, he wrote, 'we are at war already'. The Cold War, now burgeoning, was 'the first phase of real war', and the danger for Europe still lay in Germany – not because Germany was in a position to start war again, but because she was in danger of becoming the stake in a struggle to the death between Washington and Moscow. The Berlin blockade was less than two years in the past. What Germany needed was some dramatic readmission to the Western system.

This was what Monnet sold to Schuman, and what he had no difficulty, of course, in inducing the West German leader, Konrad Adenauer, the third founder of this 'Europe', gladly to accept. West Germany was less than a year past its rebirth as an independent country. The new Federal Republic still lived under the shadow of defeat and moral ostracism, and was still divided into four zones of foreign occupation, the symbol of its mistrusted and inferior status. Chancellor

Adenauer, fiercely rejecting neutralism, was always likely to be receptive to Monnet's design, once it was put to him. When Schuman's message came, he says in his memoirs, 'I agreed to his proposal with all my heart.' To Monnet he said, 'I regard the implementation of the French proposal as my most important task. If I succeed, I believe that my life will not have been wasted.'

Before these men put anything on the table, they represented, it has to be said, a problem for the British. There were certain anterior difficulties. If this was to be a project that enlisted Britain's support, as it was certainly intended to be, it had to overcome preliminary obstacles and prejudices. Even a great tide of history, if that is what was about to be launched, might be set back or somewhat diverted by quotidian flesh and blood.

Robert Schuman, for one thing, was Germanic not only by territorial origin but by cultural sympathy. He understood English but did not speak it well, knew little English history, had consorted no more than he had to with British leaders. 'He did not understand Britain,' Georges Berthoin recalled. Forcibly thrown together, Schuman and Bevin actually got on quite well. They shared a somewhat austere attitude to the extravagances of life, and prided themselves on their connection with ordinary people. But between the Cartesian intellectual and the uneducated West Country yokel the mutual cultural understanding that might have overcome their political differences did not exist.

In the case of Adenauer, there was no natural lack of empathy with Britain, but there had been an unfortunate event. After the First World War, when he was a rising leader in the Rhineland, the British had helped him to recover part of a pension that had been removed from him. So he was originally never anti-British. But he had a bad experience in 1945 when he was ousted from his post as Lord Mayor of Cologne on the orders of a British brigadier, and expelled into the countryside. This was an action grimly symbolic of the persistent British failure after the war to build a constructive relationship with Germany. Had a German alliance been foreseen as a crucial ingredient of foreign policy in any of the post-war decades, the entire history of Britain and the European idea might have followed a different course. But, in any case, there was something deeper with Adenauer which, as with Schuman, voided him of pro-British predilections. He simply thought other countries understood Germany's problems better. As one of his advisers testified: 'He did not see in Britain the same partner, with the same kind of antennae for European thinking, as he did in France with people like Monnet and de Gaulle, or in America with people like John Foster Dulles, John McCloy and Dean Acheson.'³⁴

Schuman and Adenauer composed a Germanic alliance, culturally speaking. Adding his part to it was the Italian Prime Minister, Alcide De Gasperi who – further to the endless fluidity of continental politics – had been a young politician in Vienna during the last days of the Austro-Hungarian Empire. De Gasperi was another German-speaker. Berthoin watched the *arrières-pensées* comfortably shared between them. But more significant was the religious affiliation of all three. They were more than routine Roman Catholics. Church was important to their project: a church the British never warmed to.

For the British, the Catholic nature of 'Europe' was a generous source of prejudice against it, adding to the others. Britain in 1950 was still an emphatically Protestant country, in which Catholicism was something foreign and therefore suspect. As a child at a Catholic prep school at the time, I was taught to see myself as a member of God's elect, whose earthly fate was to be excluded from the mainstream by the ignorant, anti-Catholic majority. My heavenly destiny, however, would be to look down upon these heathens paying for their errors in hell. In the senior reaches of public life, where there were almost no Catholics, this attitude was reversed. The Protestants were the chosen ones. Anti-Catholic prejudice was instinctive, and Ernest Bevin was one who exhibited it. Gladwyn Jebb records a scene on a journey with Mr and Mrs Bevin to a trade union conference in Southport: 'The train was rather full and people often went by in the corridor, including from time to time a Catholic priest in a soutane. Whenever this happened Mr and Mrs Bevin became uneasy and Mr Bevin muttered "black crows". I understood that he believed that Catholic priests brought bad luck, and nothing that I could say had any effect.'³⁵

These feelings were not limited to superstition. They acquired a strong political formulation among people who saw in the Schuman Plan the beginnings of a Vatican conspiracy or, even more luridly, an attempt to recreate the Holy Roman Empire. And such speculations were not confined to fusty old imperialists and Little Englanders. Kenneth Younger, Bevin's astute and educated junior, was one of the few politicians or officials sympathetic to the Schuman Plan. But his suspicions on this account were evidently important to him. Schuman, he noted in his diary in May 1950, was 'a bachelor and a very devout Catholic who is said to be very much under the influence of the priests'. The Plan, Younger felt obliged to admit to himself, 'may be just a step in the consolidation of the Catholic "black international", which I have always thought to be a big driving force behind the Council of Europe'.[36]

The post-war continental Church, moreover, was known to be anti-socialist. Denis Healey, as international secretary of the Labour Party, found alarming proof of this in Holland. 'The Dutch Social Democratic Party had completely reconstructed itself after the war and turned itself into a Labour Party with no Marxist dogma at all,' Healey remembered. 'Yet, in the first election after the war in Holland, the Dutch Catholic hierarchy excommunicated people who voted Labour.'[37]

Such was the background beyond politics to the case of Schuman and the British. There was a mountain of suspicion to overcome. But this was as nothing to the foreground, where Britain, instead of playing her accustomed role as orchestrator of weaker nations, found herself artfully outmanoeuvred. The sequence of events that now unfolded might have been calculated to enrage Britain and her Foreign Secretary. Were they so calculated? It is hard to be sure. What cannot be disputed is that the British Government, placing the worst interpretation on events, adopted a position calculated, with malice aforethought, to frustrate what the continentals wanted and, come what may, to exclude Britain from it. At this watershed, Britain decided that there would be no confluence.

The deception was clumsy, and perhaps unnecessary. Schuman was due anyway to meet Bevin and Dean Acheson, the American Secretary of State, in London in early May, to talk about Nato and other large matters. A serious argument beckoned. France wanted to curtail the effects of Germany's menacing industrial recovery, without incurring the hostility of the Americans, who wanted to encourage it. Schuman needed something to propose. There was thus a timely vacuum into which Monnet, with characteristic deftness, launched the idea of a coal and steel community.

The largest steel and coal producer in Europe, however, was not admitted to the secret before it was announced. Nor were many other people. It required what Monnet joyously called a 'conspiracy'. Having accepted the idea, Schuman took it over as his own, without informing the foreign policy officials at the Quai d'Orsay. But what was worse than Britain's exclusion from the cabal was the incorporation within it of the Americans. Dean Acheson appeared to be a co-conspirator. This Bevin could not forgive.

Acheson was passing through Paris, prior to the London meeting of the Big Three, and Schuman went personally to the American embassy to tell him of the Plan before it was announced. It came as a great surprise. 'I have just had a most startling statement made to me,' Acheson told an associate after the meeting.[38] And his first reaction was to sniff the beginnings of a giant European cartel that would damage the American steel industry. So Acheson was not, in the first instance, entranced by Schuman's Plan. He knew it would enrage the British, who saw him as one of the few men in Washington sharing some of their scepticism about the integration of Europe. But it didn't take long for him to be converted to the political and security benefits that might flow from the Monnet–Schuman concept. Almost overnight, he switched his allegiance. The scene was set for sulphuric encounters in London.

The first of these was with Bevin. Acheson arrived on the morning the Cabinets in both Paris and Bonn were reaching the conclusion Monnet and Schuman had conspired to produce. He was sworn to secrecy, a pledge it seemed possible for him to sustain during lunch that day with Bevin, but the duplicity of which became apparent earlier than he might have hoped, when the French ambassador, René Massigli, turned up unannounced in the Foreign Secretary's ante-room with an 'important message' to deliver. 'My embarrassment grew as the company speculated about this mystery,' Acheson later recalled.[39] When he returned to the Foreign Office that afternoon, after Bevin had found out what was going on, he knew what to expect. 'I kept a four o'clock appointment ... with dragging feet,' he wrote. 'Bevin asked me to see him alone. He was in a towering rage, and at once charged that I had known of Schuman's plan and had kept it from him. This, of course, was true and I said so.'[40]

Acheson later regretted what happened. He said Schuman had committed a 'stupid' mistake by appearing to conspire against Bevin, and so had he by going along with it. But, if this was a mistake, it was not, on the part of Monnet or Schuman, accidental. It was based on an appreciation of the obstructive power of British diplomacy if given forewarning of initiatives it did not like.

Monnet was pretty open about this. He said later that he always knew the British would reject the Plan, and he was determined that this attitude, coming from the major European power, should not be allowed to frustrate the Franco-German idea. Schuman was less candid, and also less certain that Britain could not be persuaded to go along. When the Big Three had their meeting, on 11 May, he insisted there was no question of the French seeking to create a *fait accompli*. The minutes make him sound like a bad newspaper editor, insincerely apologizing to fend off a libel action. Schuman, they record, offered 'personal regrets for any embarrassment that might have been caused'. The French, he said, were merely putting up a proposal.

But they had certainly wanted to break the diplomatic rules that normally obtained between allies. Both for Germans and for Europeans, Schuman explained to Bevin and Acheson, the French desired 'to produce a psychological shock'. And this purpose they achieved, to which could be added the equal shock to the Americans, who were not accustomed to being taken so violently by surprise by anything the French Government chose to do.

By this time, two days after the thunderbolt, Ernest Bevin, though still dozy from the effects of sedative drugs, had recovered some of his sang-froid. The disarray in Britain's immediate response to the Plan had, in any case, been worsened by other little accidents. On top of Bevin's own serious disability, Attlee and Cripps were on holiday in France when the shock arrived. But now they were back at the Cabinet table, where Bevin showed that his indignation had passed, and the Foreign Office was back in pragmatic business.

There followed, according to the minutes, a discussion that foretold in outline the hundreds, indeed thousands, of similar discussions that would take place at the same table, covering the very ground and raising the same anxieties that preoccupied other British governments over the next forty-five years. On and on these debates would go, through the governments of Eden and Macmillan, and that of Harold Wilson, here present on this day as a youthful President of the Board of Trade. Past Wilson in the 1960s, into the years of Edward Heath, then in turn through the time of James Callaghan, Margaret Thatcher and John Major, the same musings and fears would incessantly recur.

There is a temptation, reaching for the cliché, to describe this similarity between 11 May 1950 and a hundred other later dates as uncanny. But of course it is not. For, whether in 1950 or in 1995, the problems that bothered the British about European integration, so long as it was considered a contingent possibility open to infinite debate, were unlikely to differ very much. There was nothing strange about them. They have always been the essence of the matter.

Part of the British response to Schuman's proposition was peculiar to its time. Was this a French plot, someone asked (Cabinet minutes rarely say who), to save money on defence by creating a European Third Force that would do business with the Russians? This was a question which in due course ceased to have any significance. Mostly, the debate exuded suspicion on grounds that became exceedingly familiar through subsequent decades. The scheme threatened disaster for the British steel industry, the ministers felt. It would produce a protectionist cartel which Britain might feel obliged to join. Yet inside a cartel of private steel-makers the public ownership of British coal and steel, one of Labour's proudest achievements, might be compromised, and the iron and steel industry might be 'seriously reduced in size'.

So the proposed community, as they thought, was in every way an economic threat, and an intrusion on the sovereign decision of a Labour government to nationalize basic industries. But it compromised political sovereignty in other senses too. Once Britain entered the scheme, 'it could not easily retrace its steps if it disliked the effects'. (The same would be said forty years later about the continental ambition to create a single European currency. The fearful irreversibility of 'Europe' has always been an aspect the British were most aware of.) Moreover, if there was to be a coal and steel community of the kind Schuman described, the ministers concluded that 'political federation might be an essential pre-requisite'.

The Cabinet vowed to find out more. Jean Monnet, they knew, was the designated contact man. He would be approached with a view to answering the question that has continued to puzzle so many successors to this, the first generation of the British political class to be faced with a hard choice in Europe which they might not be able to bury. Their quandary was simple, but of epic proportion. They needed to determine, the men round the table are drily reported as agreeing, if the continental proposal 'represented an economic scheme which had been put forward at this juncture for political reasons, or whether the project was primarily political in character'.

Similarly prophetic in their tone were the first responses of the Foreign Office and the Treasury, each prepared with swift professionalism for the Cabinet committee. Both their May 1950 submissions reveal the first stirrings of awareness of the dilemma that became so familiar. They could see pros and cons to a coal and steel community. But they also contemplated the hitherto unthinkable possibility that something serious was about to happen on the continent which might curtail Britain's own freedom of choice.

The Foreign Office, through Sir Ivone Kirkpatrick, a peppery little Ulsterman, noted that it had been the declared policy of the Government 'to incorporate Germany into the Western comity of nations', a policy against which France had always raised more serious objections than any other nation. Here, therefore, was a device which might overcome an insoluble post-war problem. Kirkpatrick produced a substantial list of other ways in which the Schuman Plan would also be a triumph of diplomatic progress.

On the other hand he indicated that there were the difficulties. These benefits were highly desirable – as long as Britain didn't actually have to join. All the British needed was 'consultative association', he suggested. Anything fuller was 'likely to involve us in Europe beyond the point of no return', an implicitly undesirable condition. So Kirkpatrick was ready with his thoughts about damage-limitation, should the continentals decide to go ahead. Britain, he said, should not 'take the lead' in criticizing the Plan, because it was already proving quite popular. He advised a stress on the positive benefits of the Atlantic community, rather than on 'our reluctance to become excessively involved in Europe'. The Foreign Office began to prepare the defences. But the Treasury's paper was even more wary. In the short term, it said, the British coal and steel industries could hold their own whether outside or inside the Franco-German Plan. But the long term might be disastrous either way. If Britain stayed out, the integrated continental steel producers could 'attack our export and probably even our domestic markets'. Yet, if Britain went in, the High Authority might well see the economic logic in concentrating all steel production outside Britain, in Schuman's own territory near the Ruhr. Likewise with coal, the British market-share, already sliding in Europe, would diminish further. There was also the danger that the Authority would insist on equalizing wages and conditions, a 'social chapter'-in-embryo of the kind that divided European opinion in the 1990s.

This was a dismal picture, apparently inviting Britain to do all she could to crush the Plan by any means available. According to these officials, it had no real advantage of any kind. Moreover, the Treasury peered with the same incredulity as the Foreign Office at the implications for national independence. It thought a 'political federation' the likely consequence of a community for coal and steel, remarking that 'no national government could give up sovereignty over such essential elements in its economic structure without prejudice to its power of action in almost every other field' – another apprehension that was to echo down the years with respect to other commodities, including the very stuff of ultimate economic union, money itself.

These, then, were the first reactions: deeply suspicious, presumptively hostile, initial bemusement already crystallizing into a purposeful discussion of how the Schuman Plan might be frustrated. That should not be done openly. The aim should be to find out more without showing too much interest. 'A close interest in the technical aspect might give the impression that we were prepared to commit ourselves further than we actually wished,' murmured the committee of officials set up to handle the Plan.

Such was the climate when the arch-begetter, following Schuman's own visit, arrived to explain himself to the British. This encounter was not as sulphurous as Bevin's with Acheson. But it exhaled the noxious fumes of a disagreement reaching close to the bowels of two nations – or at least of the two political classes that represented them.

Jean Monnet had reason to be pleased with the first wave of responses to his brainchild. For this most committed of integrationists, they were encouraging. German enthusiasm was not very surprising, for the Plan was a way back towards international respectability. But the reception in France had been almost as keen. Collaboration with the Germans apparently did not horrify the nation. 'Considering recent history and the personal experiences of practically every living Frenchman,' the man at the British embassy reported, 'this is, to say the least, remarkable.' What France wanted, however, was British participation. The same embassy man found a wave of feeling in Paris that 'unless Britain comes in, the scheme cannot succeed'. His counterpart in the Bonn embassy stressed the judgement of the German Government, too, that without Britain all such schemes of European co-operation 'were bound to fail'. But this was not Monnet's opinion. Nor was it a consideration that moved the British Government – except perhaps to optimism.

When Monnet reached London, his first meeting gave unexpected reason for hope. Stafford Cripps, the Chancellor of the Exchequer, told him that in his opinion negotiations should begin at once. Cripps evidently wasn't bothered by the precondition that a high authority, Schuman's unique creation, should be accepted from the start. He wanted to go ahead with talks, mainly because he didn't think Britain 'would ever be able to come in later on a scheme which had been worked out by France, Germany and Benelux'. This opinion of Cripps is worth dwelling on. He was, of course, a former federalist – but then so were many others, and in any case the post-war Cripps was a different man from the pre-war anti-warrior who had spoken out in favour of world government. His reaction to Monnet now is interesting not as some cryptic integrationist gesture to satisfy the Chancellor's personal agenda. That wasn't the point. What the Cripps–Monnet conversation did mark, however, was both the first and the last moment of conditional enthusiasm for the Schuman Plan to be voiced by a senior British minister. Cripps may not have wanted to join, but he did want to talk. And it was talking – the sucking-in effect of formal negotiation – that the entire British political establishment now turned itself, in effect, to resisting.

Most appalled by Cripps's amiable reception of Monnet were the officials who witnessed it. Edwin Plowden and Monnet had known and respected each other during the war. Plowden now had the further connection of being the nearest thing to Monnet's equivalent in London: the industrialist-turned-planner whom the Labour Government had recruited to be Stafford Cripps's senior adviser on economic regeneration. (Monnet's formal job in Paris was as head of the commissariat for Le Plan, France's post-war blueprint for economic recovery.) As a young businessman, Plowden had slipped easily into Whitehall life during the war and remained there, to be burdened with every kind of establishment task and clothed with every honour, for thirty years beyond it. He wasn't clever, in the formal Whitehall way. 'He only got a poor third,' a subordinate noted of his university career. But he became a formidable in-fighter. 'He was very good at arguing with ministers,' his private secretary of the period, Douglas Allen, later head of the Treasury, told me. 'They had to listen to him because they'd made such a fuss about appointing him.'[41]

Allied with Plowden at this critical moment was the more bruising figure of Roger Makins from the Foreign Office, already established as a rabid Euro-sceptic. He took the official note of Cripps's meeting with Monnet, a record dripping with mandarin horror. So anxious and yet confident was Plowden that he felt quite free to intervene dismissively in the ministerial conversation he was witnessing. He did not hesitate to explain to Monnet, according to Makins, that 'these were just the Chancellor's personal views which he had not discussed with colleagues'. And on leaving the meeting, Makins immediately went away and minuted his Foreign Office boss on the urgent need for a Bevin corrective: 'This plunge of the Chancellor took Edwin completely by surprise. Edwin agreed that the S. of S. must be told, the question is when and how. R.M.'

It didn't take long. Bevin saw the Makins note that day, and Attlee saw it soon after. But these politicians were not the significant players during Monnet's visit. That distinction undoubtedly went to Plowden and Makins, who now met the Frenchman on their own, at breakfast next day in the Hyde Park Hotel, for one of the more crucial engagements of the early days of Britain's reluctant flirtation. The story of Britain and Europe is, among other things, a story of many meals. Seldom does a moment of history fail to be accompanied by some kind of banquet. This was an early meal that became famous in the annals of the courtship.

Unlike the French opinion sampled by the British embassy in Paris, Monnet did not regard British involvement in the Schuman Plan as essential to its success, and neither in the end did Schuman. Monnet, indeed, subsequently made this opinion crystal-clear with his claim to have understood all along that Britain would always wait to see how any European institution worked, and apply to join only when satisfied that it did. Certainly the set-up at the time, beginning with the shock announcement by Schuman and continuing with a meeting that the British officials found wholly lacking in reassurance, did not seem designed to increase the chances of collaboration. In fact it could have been programmed to repel.

For Monnet had few answers to their questions. The British record of the meeting exudes grim pleasure in the long list of issues the French had evidently failed to think about: how coal and steel would be priced, how sold abroad, where produced at home, how governed by wage equalization and so on and so forth. From their note, Makins and Plowden sound weary and disdainful – but also shocked. For on one point Monnet was unalterably plain. The treaty would have to be agreed and signed as a matter of principle, before all these pettifogging minutiae were decided. And the principle in question was the independence of the High Authority. It would, said Monnet, mean 'the surrender of national sovereignty over a wide strategic and economic field': a point the potential signatories would have to concede before negotiations began.

This was a severe requirement for the representatives of a country already reluctant to comprehend the smallest revision of sovereignty in any particular. 'It was, so to speak, sprung on us,' Makins later told me. 'Well, Jean, what's all this about?' he remembered asking, in a formula he grew used to delivering to any historian who turned up on his doorstep. 'Oh, I've got it all here,' Monnet replied. Whereupon 'he fished a piece of paper out of his pocket, and gave it to us to read. We said, "But it says here that the objective is to set up a European federal structure. You know the British Government is not in favour of that." And he just said, "Yes".'[42]

Interestingly, the official British record of the meeting makes no reference to the Schuman Plan portending a federal Europe. That apocalyptic interpretation came a little later. Even though the High Authority, within the bounds of coal and steel, was indeed a body that might have federalizing tendencies, and the Community itself had been announced as 'the realization of the first concrete foundations of a European federation', that was not yet anywhere in evidence. The High Authority involved merely ceding sovereignty to a supra-national body for a limited purpose. The achievement of wholesale federation was an enormous inference to draw, entirely dependent on what the members eventually did to bring it about, far down the road.

All the same, the 'federal' spectre has been prominent in all subsequent recollection of what happened in May 1950. It is because federalism seemed imminent that the British said they were suspicious of the Schuman Plan, hoped it would not work and did their best, behind a fair amount of diplomatic camouflage, to prevent it working. This is how Makins, in particular, has always recalled it.

Early in this inquiry I called on Makins at his Kensington flat. By then he was ninety, long ago ennobled as Lord Sherfield, imposingly tall, still with a vigorous manner and booming voice, and entirely unrepentant about his role in the history whose direction he did much to determine. His fine collection of pre-Raphaelite paintings, though acquired with the help of a wealthy American wife, somehow testified to that distant era when a civil servant might be grand enough to own such things. The mind was still confident that he had had no option but to advise against what he often referred to at the time as the 'institutional adventures' proposed by Monnet and Schuman.

Throughout his time in the Foreign Office, Makins was the epitome of the post-war Atlanticist. He devoted the serious part of his professional life to nurturing the American connection, protecting Britain's special relationship with Washington, and therefore – a logical consequence, as he saw it – seeing 'Europe' as an idea to be regarded with gravest scepticism. He had consistently taken the view that even if 'Europe' worked, which he doubted, Britain's future would always lie elsewhere. This judgement, of course, he had to revise, and he found a brisk way of doing it which deflected the blame to forces beyond his control. It was all due to the unpredictable failure of British industry in the 1960s, he told me with a gesture that swept away the intervening years, during which time he had had to change his mind – about the economy, if not about his advice on the chances of 'Europe'.

But another judgement was harder to explain. The British *idée fixe*, that the Schuman Plan would lead to a European federation, did not materialize. That analysis turned out to be premature, if not something of a hallucination. The Coal and Steel Community came into being, but it did not in reality diminish the economic powers of governments over vital resources. In later decades, certain species of federalistic power did develop. The European Economic Community took away individual governments' sovereignty over external trade, and the Single European Act their sole control over external trade. There was a momentum. But it did not attain a recognizable federation. The full grandeur of the Coal and Steel Community's aspiration proved to be rather empty.

This was the first large judgement falsified by later events. But at the time it dominated all that flowed from Monnet's visit to explain the Plan to London.

Stafford Cripps, after his own talk with Monnet, paid little attention to Plowden's anxieties. Next day he pressed the Economic Policy Committee of the Cabinet to set in hand a detailed study of the Schuman Plan with a view to ensuring 'a practical scheme. . . . not inconsistent with our essential interests'. But these essential interests imposed great caution. Care would have to be taken, the committee concluded, 'to prevent this plan from becoming involved with proposals for federalism in Europe'.

The work began.[43] Makins and Plowden were in charge of it. Their premise was not to rule out the possibility of a high authority being set up, nor British participation in some form. 'If the proposals are successful, the United Kingdom should be associated with them,' their committee agreed at an early meeting. The diplomacy of inclusiveness, however sceptical its purpose, gathered pace. In a couple of days, Makins was ready with his preliminary advice to Bevin, which again was conciliatory. Her Majesty's Government should encourage the French and Germans to start talks immediately, 'and should express a strong desire to take part in them from the start'.

But this desire was in fact so conditional as to be unreal. It was a fine example of diplo-speak. Monnet had ruled out any discussion about the precondition – the supra-national High Authority. The Makins advice therefore covered all the bases. On the one hand, we should take part from the start (paragraph 3). On the other, there was 'no justification' for taking part (paragraph 10), unless ministers were prepared 'to abrogate certain sovereign rights'. This impenetrable contradiction was resolved, however, by the informal footnote Makins attached to brief

Bevin for a meeting with Schuman. Here he was unambiguous about the follies of the French and the Germans: 'We shall have to do what we can to get them out of the mess into which they have landed themselves.'

When his comrade, Plowden, appeared to induce Monnet to soften his position, Makins was equally caustic. The files include the record of a telephone conversation between Plowden and Monnet in which the latter concedes that once negotiations opened 'each of the points put forward in the communiqué as bases for negotiation would itself have to be the subject of negotiation'. Did this foretell a willingness to talk about the High Authority, after all? 'I think this is rather a pity,' Makins comments. 'It would have been better to leave M. Monnet alone.'

An elaborate minuet now begins between London and Paris, ostensibly about the terms and conditions on which the Schuman Plan should be advanced. In fact it seems more like an exercise in preparing allocation of the blame for failure. Did France really want Britain to get involved? Was Britain in any circumstances ready to negotiate? Were any imaginable talks, from the British point of view, a step beyond the point of no return? Whatever – the stately dance accelerated through the last week in May.

On 25 May, a message from London to Paris crossed with one going the other way. Bevin formally told Schuman that the French and Germans should start talking. This should be a bilateral not an international conference, though Britain 'would like to participate' in order to get 'a clearer picture'. Meanwhile, though, France formally told London that the British Government 'must commit themselves to acceptance of the principles of the scheme before discussing it in detail'.

This seemed to be an impasse. But the diplomats scurried to open it. Schuman's top official, Alexandre Parodi, saw an opportunity for some soothing casuistry. Surely, he told the British ambassador, expressing a wish to participate 'meant acceptance by His Majesty's Government of the principle involved'? Accepting the invitation to talk 'would in no way bind us to accept the eventual treaty', the ambassador reported Parodi as saying. To which seduction, the ambassador, Sir Oliver Harvey, whose papers show that he was keener than most officials that Britain should get involved, faithfully came back with his master's voice. The British 'could not engage themselves at this point to accept the principle of pooling'.

In parallel there was further casuistry on the subject of what *kind* of British attendance might theoretically be appropriate. In one and the same telegram to Harvey, Bevin instructed him to deny the rumour that

Britain planned to attend as an observer, and urged him to make the case for all interested governments to 'sit in on' the Franco-German talks when they started. He told Harvey to be 'realistic', which apparently did not encompass a warm reception for another Schuman suggestion about how, with a little diplomatic finesse, Britain could participate without commitment. Another Schuman aide proposed that by accepting the 'principles' of the Plan a government did not commit itself to accepting the decisions of the High Authority. That could only be done in the eventual treaty: 'and if in the course of negotiations any Government did not like the terms of the treaty, then it would always be open to that Government to decline to become party to it'.

So there was evidence that the French desired to be helpful. They wanted to make things seem easier, find language that reflected this, lure the British in. And this tendency wasn't confined to officials. On 30 May, Schuman himself sent for the British ambassador to discuss further linguistic refinements. It had occurred to him, he said, that there was some confusion between the words 'engagement' and 'commitment' in the French and English languages. This, he thought, had perhaps made London think that the precondition was more binding than it was intended to be. All London had to agree was the final desired objective, but the negotiations always had the chance of failing, in which case the British would have lost nothing. They might engage to negotiate without committing to the outcome. Speaking for himself, Schuman sincerely hoped Britain would take part in the coal and steel pool. Couldn't Britain at least say it would *like* to belong?

Now it was Britain's turn to be Delphic. Harvey said the British had 'a completely open mind', but it was a question of 'honesty' and 'not encouraging false hopes'. Upon that basis, next day, London nonetheless agreed to amend the British position with its own new language. Britain could not enter a 'precise commitment', but would participate 'in a constructive spirit', hoping to produce a scheme the Government wanted to be a part of.

On the face of it, this went a fair distance to meet what Schuman said he wanted – but not, it turned out, far enough. Studying the British documents that chart the course of this critical week, one has a strong sense of minds that were never destined to meet. Each apparent gesture of good intention is followed soon enough by an agonized restatement of position that somehow effaces it. The British expression of desire to participate and the French attempt to make this seem possible turn out each to be misleading, within and perhaps beyond the normal canons of diplomatic manoeuvring. For now Schuman, having first sought words with which to square the circle, turns round and claims to have misunderstood the British line all along. While fully seeing that they couldn't commit all their coal and all their steel into the common pool before an agreement was reached, what he *hadn't* understood, he claimed, was the demand that the High Authority itself must be negotiable. This he could not stomach. He could delay no longer. The British would have to decide, yes or no, within twenty-four hours. Or, as Monnet later wrote, 'we had to make an end of it'.

Even then, there was one more attempt by Schuman apparently to make things easier for the British. Issuing his ultimatum to Harvey, he proposed a face-saving new formula. A new text was produced in which the participants were saying not that they had 'decided' to establish the pool and set up the Authority, but that they 'had the immediate aim' of doing so. Harvey reported that Schuman believed this 'would meet us since it did not involve any commitment'.

Whether or not this was sincerely meant, it did not impress itself on London. There the question had advanced from the primitive perception in which Makins had framed it, as a matter of bringing the French to their senses, or 'helping them out of the mess'. It now merited the Foreign Office's most solemn judgement. The rest of inner Europe beyond France and Germany were assembling behind the Schuman Plan. The Dutch were interested, and the Italians keenly pressuring London to stop quibbling over detail. The Italian Foreign Minister, Count Sforza, used a phrase redolent of what was often to divide the continent from its off-shore neighbours in future years. It was, he said, 'the music and not the words that counted'.

At the Foreign Office, the duty of advising the Cabinet passed from Makins to the topmost official, Sir William Strang, the permanent under-secretary. His opinion came like an organ-blast. 'We are called upon to take a decision of foreign policy of a fundamental character which will have far-reaching consequences,' he began. It could not be based on tactical considerations alone. Nor, it seemed, should the Quai d'Orsay's seductive wordplay be taken for more than that. 'The decision which the French are now summoning us to take is, in fact, the decision whether or not we are to bind ourselves irrevocably to the European community,' Strang wrote. This was something 'I cannot bring myself to recommend.' What was at risk from saying no was mere 'temporary embarrassment', a condition that could not compare with the virtue of 'a cool appraisement of the national interest in all its aspects'.

The Treasury made the same assessment, recoiling with horror from
the French suggestion. 'It has been our settled policy hitherto', wrote its
chief, Sir Edward Bridges, 'that in view of our world position and
interests, we should not commit ourselves irrevocably to Europe either
in the political or the economic sphere unless we could measure the
extent and effects of the commitment.' Britain wanted, in other words,
to know exactly where she was going. By not going into Schuman,
moreover, the British were risking nothing. It wouldn't stop them
'participating in European discussions in some manner later on', the
Bridges committee said. Even the direct consequences for the coal and
steel industries were now seen with less alarm than in the Treasury paper
just a couple of weeks before, which anticipated dire effects whether
Britain was in or out. Now, apparently, 'there need be no cause for
alarm if at this stage the French decided to proceed without us'.

Thus was the Cabinet advised. And thus did it agree. But the
circumstances in which it took the advice were, in the eye of history,
bathetic. They rather muted the trumpets from Whitehall.

By 2 June, when Schuman's ultimatum expired, the principal British
ministers were absent from the scene. Bevin was again in hospital, his
duties assumed by Kenneth Younger. Both Attlee and Cripps were back
on holiday in France, from which they felt no need to return. Herbert
Morrison, in charge on the evening the message from Paris arrived, had
to be rooted out of London's theatreland to respond to it – which he
did with a phrase that became famous for epitomizing the hearts-of-oak
mentality so important to British disdain for what 'Europe' is supposed
to mean.

It fell to Plowden to track him down, at the Ivy restaurant. 'We
retired to a sort of passage at the back of the restaurant where spare
tables and chairs are stored,' Plowden recalled. Whereupon Morrison
apparently stated: 'It's no good. We can't do it. The Durham miners will
never wear it.'[44]

Next day, he presided over what was left of the Cabinet, which had
heard the message of the Strang and Bridges papers. Bevin was consulted
in hospital, and delivered the predictable blast. No one present dissented,
which shows that too much shouldn't be made of the depleted attendance. A full turn-out would have decided no differently. Far from
promising to watch benignly from the sidelines as Schuman and Adenauer went ahead, the Cabinet took a harder position, ruling that there
should be a further attempt 'to dissuade the French from going forward
... without our participation'. Plowden and Makins were speaking for

an official British mind that gathered almost the whole governing class under its sway.

The very act of talking was what the British Government balked at. It wasn't simply the precondition about the High Authority, which Schuman had in any case found ways of softening, but the terror felt in Whitehall that misleading signals might be given out. 'Nothing would be more likely to exacerbate Anglo-French relations than for us to join in the discussions with mental reservations and withdraw from partici- pation at a later stage' was the pious thought with which the Cabinet excused itself.

*

THIS WAS NOT a marginal call. At the level where it counted, Britain decided that to negotiate as a signed-up partner in the Schuman Plan would be an absolute error. Makins and Strang and Bridges and Attlee and Bevin all thought that. But it was not an unthinkable thing to do. There were other voices that made sense of the idea. What told against it were not axioms about Britain's world role, but mere opinions about the nature of reality.

One voice, or at any rate opinion, was in the Government. Kenneth Younger was a relatively young man to be thrust, thanks to Bevin's incapacity, into the role of proxy Foreign Secretary. On the night the ultimatum arrived he set down privately on paper the pros and cons of Schuman's formula, and placed much weight on the dangers of rejecting it.

He listed the consequences of the Plan not succeeding: French humiliation, American displeasure, British culpability for the failure of this extraordinary act of Franco-German reconciliation. He also counted the costs of the Plan being successfully put in place without Britain belonging to it. The coal and steel industries would face fearsome competition. But there would be something worse. The case for procras- tinating, which was the fall-back position in the unlikely event that the Plan succeeded, would be seen to have a heavy cost. 'While we might be able to join in the Plan before it reached finality,' Younger wrote, 'we should, by failing to participate at the start, greatly reduce our chance of getting a scheme worked out on lines proposed by ourselves.'

Standing in for Bevin at the Cabinet, Younger did not make these points. He kept his prescience to himself. But later he wrote that the Schuman proposals were 'handled in a curiously offhand way' in

London, and 'largely by officials'. Quite soon he decided that this combination of hauteur and neglect had produced the biggest foreign policy failure since the war.

Parliament held a big debate before the end of June, and here pro-Plan voices did make an explicit counterpoint to the heavy official drumbeats. Anthony Eden, the shadow Foreign Secretary, said the Plan 'must not be allowed to fail'. It was in Britain's interest it should succeed and in her capacity, by talking, to see it did so. This wasn't, he said, an assault on sovereignty but 'a fusion of sovereignty or, if you will, its merger or extension'. Eden's driving passion was for peace in Europe. He saw the Plan as a way of thwarting both German and, ultimately, Soviet propensities to disturb it. He insisted that any project must be Atlanticist as well as European, keeping the Americans in Europe – which was a universal British obsession. But on the politics of British independence he sounded only slightly ambivalent. 'The acceptance of European federation was no part of the political declaration just signed,' he noted. The Dutch had agreed it on the explicit condition that they might not, in the end, accept the High Authority. They insisted this be negotiated. 'Would we be prepared to enter discussions as a result of which a high authority would be set up whose decisions would be binding upon the nations who were parties to the agreement?' Eden asked. 'My answer to that question would be yes, provided [Hon. Members: 'Ahhh,' *Hansard* reports] that we were satisfied with the conditions and safeguards.'[45]

Winston Churchill's line was more stratospheric. He couldn't imagine any significant strategic discussion anywhere taking place without Britain. But younger Tories addressed the particulars. David Eccles, later a Cabinet minister, deplored the 'smug self-satisfaction' he saw around him, and thought the British refusal to talk would be 'utterly incomprehensible' to the millions all over Europe who feared another war. He ridiculed inter-governmental agencies where the members were 'nothing more than delegates of national policies', and urged that under the Schuman Plan 'we must arrange matters so that they speak and act not as Frenchmen and Germans but as Europeans'.

Julian Amery, bearer of a family loyalty to colonies and Commonwealth, said, 'I look at this question primarily as an imperialist.' Imperial interests, far from debarring engagement, 'dictate our participation in the talks'. The young Quintin Hogg came in on the same side. He thought the Commonwealth would survive only if Britain joined Europe. Adopting 'constructive attitudes' or 'friendly poses', he said, was not an

alternative to 'adopting the principle of pooling resources or the institution of a High Authority'. A certain supra-nationalism was desirable,
irrespective of the short-term shock it might cause a proud people.
Hogg's memory, when I talked to him forty years later, was that 'all the
people whose reputation has endured, the brains of the younger generation, were on one side'. In which *galère* he included not only himself
and Eccles, but Peter Thorneycroft and another young man who was
later to make the deepest mark, Edward Heath. Given future events, it is
fitting that the Schuman Plan debate was the occasion for Heath's
maiden parliamentary speech. Late of the Heavy Anti-Aircraft Regiment,
Lieutenant-Colonel Heath had just been visiting Germany, where he had
seen an economy already recovering, and an interest in the Schuman
Plan 'governed entirely by political considerations'. The Plan, he wrote
at the time, was 'a great chance, perhaps the greatest in twenty years' for
Britain to influence the shape of things. It was being thrown away. In
the House, he said that the supra-national aspect was not a 'principle'
but an 'objective', and should not be feared. But his particular foreboding
related to the economy. 'By standing aside from any discussions,' Heath
predicted, 'we may be taking a very great risk with our economy – a very
great risk indeed.'

These speeches had no influence. A few days later, the Cabinet
committee deliberated as though Eccles, Hogg and Heath had not
spoken. There was 'general opposition on both sides of the House',
ministers comforted themselves in recording, both to a supra-national
body wielding powers over British coal and steel and to participation in
'any federal system limited to Europe'. Such reassuring 'unanimity'
meant that the issue could be closed.

Did this decision cost Britain the leadership of Europe? It is often
said so,[46] but there may be something politically incorrect about the
question. The Coal and Steel Community, which evolved into the
Common Market and the European Union, was not primarily about
'leadership'. It was an exercise in collaboration by which countries sank
some of the aspirations that keep the competitive quest for leadership
going. Who is going to be top dog in Europe was, after all, the question
that started most of the wars. Nostalgia for that missed moment when
leadership could have been seized, which is the way many British
'Europeans' have tended to think of it, perhaps exposes a congenital
inability to see what 'Europe' is all about, one reason why the British
mind and the European mind had such difficulty in meeting.

It is also possible to argue that, if Britain had jumped the other way,

'Europe' might not have happened. Britain had many reasons to hope
the Schuman Plan would fail. Bevin's desire to oversee Franco-German
reconciliation, and strengthen the Western Union against the Soviet
Union, didn't extend to seeing Britain's own heavy industries, which
were bigger than the continentals', compromised by some kind of
multilateral control, nor to presiding over the violation of national
sovereignty. Sovereignty mattered most of all to a nation that had
triumphantly exercised it in war, and still saw it reaching wherever the
map was painted red. If Britain had entered the talks in order to destroy
Monnet's vision, she might have done so – at least for the moment.
Britain, in other words, might indeed have enjoyed old-fashioned 'leadership', but over a 'Europe' she had prevented from coming to pass.

Neither of these hypothetical talk-outs for what happened strikes me
as convincing. The Europe of the Coal and Steel Community was going
to happen. The strength of feeling behind something of the kind was
enormous, and if Britain had entered only to destroy, she would have
hastened her exclusion not only from the European but from the
American intersecting circle of influence and interest. Nor did Europe,
in truth, occupy such a Utopian level of unreality as to exclude the
concept of leadership from its vocabulary. In both the Community and
the Union, there has been a spirit of collaboration and even of national
self-sacrifice. But both economy and geography impose the possibilities
of leadership, just as history shows that the struggle for ascendancy can
never be entirely extinguished. Power does not permit the existence of a
vacuum. Some dog is top, as Germany has found to her advantage. The
verdict of one of the men most influential in cultivating the atmosphere
of British non-participation, the mood and reading that infected just
about the entire senior political class, is the right one. 'The decision',
Oliver Franks wrote, 'cost us the leadership of Europe which we had
enjoyed from the end of the war until May 1950.'

In the end, three aspects of the decision and its making are washed
up on the shore for critical scrutiny, after the tide of history has moved
on.

The first is a double-whammy of misjudgement. Britain hoped the
Plan would not succeed, and did not think it would do so. The hoping
was shot through with ambiguity: not even Roger Makins could actually
have desired that a scheme for Franco-German reconciliation would
come to nothing. Disclosing one side of his schizoid calculations, Franks
said that bringing France and Germany together 'as Schuman described
it to me "in an embrace so close that neither could draw back far enough

to hit the other" was worth everything for the peace of Europe'. Nobody in London wanted to be charged with responsibility for making it fail, as most of the participants thought it would unless Britain went along. But the Public Record Office files are littered with sceptical judgements about the ability of France and Germany to make the necessary compromises over the future of their coal and steel industries. Well into 1951, British ambassadors round Europe are filing accounts of the widespread fear of German domination of coal as well as steel, and emphasizing the improbability of a deal being done. They plainly underestimated the political will to make progress, but they also could not believe what they were being invited to think about. Con O'Neill, a young diplomat in Bonn at the time, said years later: 'I'm ashamed to say that I did not realise its enormous importance.' He also said: 'The idea that there should be a body with real authority over the decisions of national governments was something we felt was grotesque and absurd.'

Second, the collective judgement in London seems to have been extraordinarily pessimistic about the possibilities of an advantageous negotiation. This, perhaps, is the best evidence that at bottom there was a mysteriously visceral hostility great enough to transcend any amount of cool calculation. It began with the belief that the French did not want Britain as a full member of the Plan: true, perhaps, of Monnet, at least until the supra-national institutions had become a 'fact', but not so obviously true of Schuman, whose conduct gives plenty of evidence to the contrary. Springing the Plan as a big surprise wasn't the best way of securing agreement, and was openly designed to forestall a British veto. The existence of something called a high authority was never going to be wished away. But the scope of this body, its relationship to governments, the measure of its supra-nationalism, and its federalist implications: all this was open for discussion. The other member states all found ways of accommodating the French coup and shaping the Authority into a body they could live with, which violated their sovereignty only in a specific and limited way. Britain was in a stronger position than any of them to exercise this kind of negotiating muscle, for Great Britain was the most desired of all allies. The Dutch, the Belgians and Luxembourg faced the need to join but also the discomfort of being caught between overbearing continental neighbours. On 15 May, the British ambassador in Bonn reported a talk with the German Vice-Chancellor as follows: 'During the whole conversation, Bluecher returned again and again to one theme, the necessity for British participation. Without Britain, schemes for West European co-operation were bound to fail.'

The third striking feature of Britain's blindness to this desire is how little credit it did the British governing system, in which it may be ministers who decide but officials are supposed to bring their matchless wisdom to bear, in a spirit of detachment, on the evidence their political masters consider. What happened in 1950, under the ailing ministeriat of Clement Attlee, was rather like what happened in the 1980s under the overmighty hand of Margaret Thatcher. That, too, was a period when the civil service, with detachment drained out of it, did a poor job for the country. The condition then was a bit different: of weak officials finding it easier to succumb to the unsupported certainties of the governing ideology rather than challenge them. In the 1950s, nobody would have dared call Makins, Bridges and the rest weak. They were at least equal partners in defining the orthodoxy as regards Europe. Only at the lower levels and in occasional outposts were there people who challenged the advice ministers were getting, and these were seldom heard. In the balance of intellectual power, Whitehall was in this era more than a match for a cadre of Westminster leaders who were in many cases exhausted, and in some, like Bevin's, getting ready to die. One incontrovertible message of hindsight, to put it no higher, surely is that the official advice on this occasion was laughably erroneous.

It was, however, Bevin's to take or to refuse. The officials knew what he wanted, and he knew how they thought. It was he, with their smooth assistance in the drafting, who defined the line epitomized at the end of the Commons debate by Stafford Cripps, who said on the Government's behalf: 'It seems to us that, even if desirable, such a scheme could hardly prove to be workable ... unless it were preceded by complete political federation.'[47]

Nine months later Bevin was out of office, and a month after that he was dead. The European Coal and Steel Community came into being on 18 April 1951, with Jean Monnet at its head, and it survives to this day.

3

RUSSELL BRETHERTON

The Sacrificial Agent

EUROPE WAS MORE THAN coal and steel. One community did not finish the job. In the 1950s, the idea, for those who believed in it, was a force with irresistible momentum. Its logic, the logic of alliance against war, reached into all corners. When next this logic presented itself at the door of the British Government, the response did not differ very much, save in one respect. But this difference told a story. The man positioned to stand against the European Idea – the capital letters that Foreign Office papers now accorded the Idea suggest it was beginning to engender mockery – was no longer a titan but a cipher. Not only was Bevin long dead, but Bevinishness, the loud, certain, confident, unignorable voice that ruled the roost on Britain's behalf, had gone as well. The Conservatives, by 1955, could produce nothing to match it. In place of a world figure, the public official they sent to deal with 'Europe' was a figure no one in the world had heard of.

Russell Bretherton was flesh and blood. He did what he was told, though as it happens he didn't like it. He was an obscure middle-ranking official, and that was the point. His presence at the scene of combat was designed not to intimidate but to insult. This already said something about Britain's altering place in the world, even though few of the citizens saw it that way. Mulish domination was subtly making way for something more like disdain, but a disdain edged with the beginnings of alarm, and Bretherton was its symbol. By showing that Europe mattered so little to Britain, perhaps Europe would be persuaded that 'Europe' ought not to matter so much to itself.

This was the meaning of Bretherton. He was the nominee, void of power or status or the faintest resemblance to the roaring British lion, whom the politicians sent to register their continuing absence from the integration of Europe. But, before his moment came, several matters had occurred.

The decision to reject participation in the Schuman Plan caused barely a tremor in the British body politic. It was thinly reported, and criticized by only one organ of opinion, the *Economist*. It played no part in the election campaign leading up to the defeat of the Labour Government in October 1951. Nor was interest in it revived by the reappearance in power of the party that had supposedly favoured Britain's involvement, and of the leader whose magnetism and grandiloquence had persuaded many European leaders that he was one of them. Winston Churchill's return to office, in plenty of time to reverse Labour's rejection of Schuman, produced no such outcome. The moment, if it ever was a real moment and not the indulgence of mere oppositionism, had passed. Once back at the helm, Churchill gave little thought to 'Europe', his ancient gaze being trained around the globe, where the Korean War had begun, and where there were American presidents to parley with and a Soviet menace to be confronted. Besides, Churchill was no longer energetic. At seventy-four, he was old and half exhausted.

The voice that spoke for Conservatism in the Schuman Plan debate, though plainly oppositionist, was also steeped in irony. Although Anthony Eden, at that moment, came on with passionate contempt for Labour's isolationism from Europe, his personal disposition was, in practical terms, similar. It was part of his complexity. Eden was a sensitive, erratic, romantic, anxious internationalist. These qualities were ominously appropriate for the first Conservative leader who had the opportunity to align Britain with the integration of Europe and failed to take it.

His parliamentary attitude in June 1950 was more than posturing. He did seem to want Britain to join the Schuman negotiations. The proposed self-exclusion aroused his apocalyptic sensitivities. Strolling in his garden, he told a friend at the time: 'I think this is so serious, our refusal to go into this and see what it's all about, and show willing – I think it could be the beginning of World War Three.'[1] Despite its evasiveness – 'aaaah' said the House – over the High Authority, his Commons speech gave the continentals every reason to anticipate a change in the British position once Eden became Foreign Secretary. The Churchill syndrome of false expectation extended well beyond the voice of the master.

Eden, however, had never been a Churchill in this matter. Like the Foreign Office, he had looked on the old man's grand, post-war forays with some disdain. He refused to go to the Hague conference, and was absent from Strasbourg. 'There was an element of distaste in Eden for this whole *emotional* approach,' one of his staff recalled. He was therefore outside the Tory mainstream, which in opposition was dominated by the Churchillians, who made their presence felt at all these assemblies in the persons of Sandys and Soames and Amery, as well as the rival whom Eden most apprehended, Harold Macmillan. For Eden, Europe, let alone 'Europe', would never engage the deepest feelings of the British people. 'What you've got to remember', he told his private secretary, Evelyn Shuckburgh, 'is that if you looked at the post-bag of any English village and examined the letters coming in from abroad, ninety per cent would come from way beyond Europe.'

During Eden's tenure as Foreign Secretary, from October 1951 to April 1955, such personal attitudes – prejudices, biases, atavistic passions, the instincts reason had to start from – made their way into the arrangement of his professional priorities. But these, in turn, were naturally influenced by facts of power and geography that nobody in that job could ignore. What happened to British foreign policy in the early 1950s was fruit of the reality that Britain did not have the option to overlook: the historic inheritance that continued, *pro tem*, to assign her the responsibilities if not the entire arsenal of a great power. There were 15,000 British troops fighting in the Korean War. The imperial sun had not entirely ceased to set. In these years, Eden, the spokesman for a country whose foreign policy was still rooted in a reddened map, was a decisive arbitrator in Indo-China, in Persia, in Cyprus, in Egypt, in India.

He was the obverse of a Little Englander. Unlike later Euro-sceptics, he was a man of European culture, spoke French and a little German, would never have dreamed of carrying a supply of corn-flakes on the Channel ferry. He simply did not think that 'Europe', on the model of Schuman and Monnet, would ever work. All his knowledge of history told him that nationalisms were for ever. They could not be abandoned. They were, at best, the raw material with which foreign secretaries did their work. Above all, British nationalism, generously present around the world, could never be buried in some alien construct. Somewhere between his apparent enthusiasm for the coal and steel idea and his resumption of power in the Foreign Office, his real opinion forced itself upon him. In a famous speech at Columbia University, in January 1952, he told the Americans what it was. There had been suggestions, he said, that Britain should join 'a federation on the continent of Europe'. This was something 'we know in our bones we cannot do'. It violated 'the unalterable marrow' of the British nation.

Later in life, when he was often named as one of the culprits for Britain's late entry into Europe, Eden detested the accusation. It was entirely wrong, he said, and his friends came to his defence, saying that 'he just had a totally different concept of what a united Europe should be about'.[2] It's interesting, all the same, to see how little space 'Europe' gets in Eden's memoirs. He evidently did not reckon the subject merited a place at the centre of the history he was concerned with.

He did, however, have one important part in its evolution. This was a backdrop to what was about to happen of more epic moment. It is, in its way, the perfect little microcosm of the troubled Anglo-Euro relationship as it failed to develop in these early, formative days. Foreshadowing the Common Market Britain didn't join was the Defence Community which she had, first, apparently advocated, then second, helped destroy by refusing to join, then third, thanks to Eden himself, retrieved from oblivion by a device that seemed blithely to ignore most of the objections she had raised against it in the second stage.

Churchill, it must be recalled, had included the idea of a European army among his pan-Europe effusions. He saw it as the apotheosis of what he was talking about, Germans included. As midwife at the birth of the Strasbourg Assembly, in August 1950 he caused an early post-natal sensation by declaring that such an army would be a message 'from the House of Europe to the whole world'. Warrior nations would now put their armies under unified command to defend the cause of peace against all aggressors. And Britain, it seemed, was not excluded. 'We should all play a worthy and honourable part,' Churchill said.

No sooner was the Coal and Steel Community on the way to being an accomplished fact than this Churchillian vision arrived on the agenda of practical Europeans. The rhetoric of the old man, by now in office, was put sharply to the question, and the main agents of this interrogation were his old and closest allies, the Americans. For believing and committed Europeans, too, it was a natural development. For the ending of war, one community was plainly only a start. America, however, had special reasons and, one would have thought, also had in Britain an ally whose special agonies in all these European speculations would have made her susceptible to American influence.

There was surely a benign kind of syllogism at work. First, British policy under both Bevin and Eden was driven by the desire to maintain special links with the US, keep America in Europe and strengthen the transatlantic alliance against Moscow. Second, US policy, under Presidents Truman and Eisenhower, plus Secretaries Acheson and John Foster Dulles, was to encourage the integration of Europe under the political leadership of Britain, Washington's special ally and nuclear friend. Given these two premises, logic dictated that Britain would incline positively towards the negotiation of a proper 'European' role as a way, not least, of sustaining her American influence. Instead of which, the opposite occurred. Throughout the Foreign Office files of the period, if one argument runs deeper than any other against these Community entanglements it is the dually destructive consequence that was seen to flow from them. First, by getting into 'Europe', Britain would lose her unique position in Washington, and second, by assisting at such integration, Britain would be an accomplice at what she least desired and the Americans then most wanted, some disengagement of US troops from Europe – 'letting them off the hook', as Roger Makins called it.

In Washington there was a further consideration. Superficially, again, it met a Churchillian point. Having assumed the global burden, America pressed Europe to take on a more substantial part of its own defence, something that could not be contemplated without raising the issue of the country at Europe's geographic heart. The Berlin blockade and the communist coup in Czechoslovakia, both in 1948, greatly reinforced America's will to rearm Germany. With French troops heavily engaged in Indo-China, and the British defence budget under acute strain, Germany, as Churchill had said, could not be left out of the picture. Yet how could France, in particular, tolerate German rearmament in any form? Only by means of the same principles that had guided Schuman and his Plan. Following the Schuman Plan, therefore, came the Pleven Plan, a scheme put together, again in Paris, and with strong American support, for a European army in European uniform under European command, to be assembled for an indefinite period as proof of solidarity and a bulwark against enemies both within and without.

Ultimately, the Pleven Plan did not succeed. The Benelux countries and, naturally, Germany were quick to ratify it, but it failed because the French Assembly declined to do the same. The idea of one branch of the French political class was vetoed, several governments later, by another. The prior accessory to failure, however, was Britain, whose conduct was a lugubrious foretaste of future episodes, and whose leader drew from his closest ally a verdict that sounded a tocsin. Britain, wrote President Eisenhower in his diary, in December 1951 just after his own first election, 'was living in the past'. As for Churchill, he refused 'to think in terms of today'. 'My regretful opinion', Ike concluded, 'is that he no longer absorbs new ideas.'

The new idea of the European Defence Community proved unabsorbable, notwithstanding the fact that Churchill was virtually its first begetter. And that was the prime sense in which it can be seen as establishing the British style. It contradicted promise. The new military protector of 'the House of Europe' quickly acquired another label. 'European Army! European Army! It won't be an army, it'll be a sludgy amalgam,' the old man muttered to himself in Paris in 1952. 'What soldiers want to sing are their own marching songs.'[3]

There were other harbingers of future politics. One was the abysmal confusion the EDC provoked inside the Tory Cabinet, and the reputation for evasion and duplicity that thereby received another lift among the continentals. The mixture of incompetence and bad faith was exquisitely prophetic. One minister, David Maxwell Fyfe, went solemnly to Strasbourg to let the Assembly know that Britain supported the EDC, and promised 'our determination that no genuine method shall fail through lack of thorough examination'. Construing his own words much later, he insisted that his message had been that Britain 'agreed to the principle of joining the European Army'. Mere hours later on the very same day, 28 November 1951, Anthony Eden told a press conference in Rome that 'no British military formations would be made available'. Maxwell Fyfe, a strong European, was furious. In his memoirs, he wrote that 'this, more than any other single act, destroyed Britain's good name on the continent'. But Eden was unrepentant. And it was Eden's position that held firm, to decisive effect. Britain's refusal to place sufficient soldiers in the sludgy amalgam under European command was, effectively, what drove French parliamentarians to kill the EDC.[4]

That wasn't the end of British perversity, however. At this stage, Britain was still just about as capable of rescuing a version of 'Europe' as destroying it, and Eden now did so. When the Pleven Plan collapsed, no one was more horrified than he. For little though he was convinced by its military quality, and hard though he fought to keep the British out, he knew better than anyone what Washington thought, and was appalled to hear that, as a result, Dulles might be on the brink of conducting what he was calling, in a famous phrase, 'an agonizing reappraisal' of American foreign policy.

So Eden now acted with speed and brilliance – and, as it seemed, bewildering volatility. Spurred by the threat from Washington, he built a framework for German rearmament within a few weeks. This involved cajoling the French and, in major substance, reversing the stubbornness with which Britain had assisted at the abortion of the EDC. The Western European Union, the invention that did this, had the crucial quality of retaining national rights. It was inter-governmental. British troops would not be sent to battle under a French or German general. But the numbers that were offered for assignment on the continent would have amply satisfied the French, had they been offered to the EDC. Germany was readmitted to the company of fighting nations. More important for Eden, Britain agreed to keep an army on permanent standby in Europe, the price he was prepared to pay, having previously rejected it, for guarantees of a continuing American presence as well. From 1955 to 2025, the British military presence would not be removed except by agreement with the WEU allies.

The WEU was Eden's contribution to 'Europe' and, like Nato, a notable despatch of some portion of the King's own sovereignty into the hands of other powers beyond the sea. Serious federalists were not best pleased: the collapse of the EDC was seen by the more missionary continentals as the prelude, quite possibly, to the end of the entire Community venture. But WEU, as a second-best necessity, was a deal that satisfied almost everyone. It was done – further strand of consistency both before and after – with little serious debate in government and none, until after the relevant hour, in Parliament. Even when Eden came for approval of his final plan, the full Cabinet did not assemble to consider it. This was surprising, given the seventy-year military commitment the deal involved. Yet it was not so surprising, when considered in a pedigree line which shows that every positive development that has eventually succeeded in positioning Britain inside a European venture has been characterized, by its proponents, as doing nothing terribly significant.

The rule of thumb is roughly as follows. On those occasions when an agreement finally becomes expeditious, or impossible to avoid, let the world be informed of its banality, its minimal implications for the constitution, the utter impossibility of its changing reality in ways that anyone would notice. When, on the other hand, a proposition beckons which the politicians, for any or all of a host of reasons, do not like, or fear to try and sell, let it be stigmatized as an insupportable assault on the British way of life.

And let Mr Russell Bretherton or his heirs be sent to deliver the message.

*

MESSINA, A SMALL town on the north-east point of Sicily, is an improbable site for the birth-place of a great idea. In a country of immortal cultural repositories, it is notably lacking in grandeur. Discriminating visitors have always tended to stay at Taormina, down the coast. But the reason Messina occupies an indelible place among the benchmarks of modern history is unusually apt. It is famous as the fount of the European Economic Community – once the Common Market, later the European Community, now the European Union – owing to a pressing circumstance of strictly national politics. Ministers of the Coal and Steel Community were due to meet in Italy at the beginning of June 1955. But Gaetano Martino, the Italian Foreign Minister, had a problem. His power-base was Sicily, and an election was imminent there. He was not prepared to hold the conference in Rome. His colleagues, the foreign ministers of France, Germany, Belgium, the Netherlands and Luxembourg, were obliged, a little frostily, to accommodate him.

They thereby registered from the start a truth that would never subsequently be erased. The EEC, the culminating creation of the 'European Idea', was born in the way it would continue: as a dream of supra-national union modified, for every leader who has ever taken part in it, by the mundane accidents and irresistible demands of survival as a national politician. Martino, incidentally, won his election.

Messina, for the British, was the next European challenge: further proof, bewildering and enraging by turns, that after the failure of the Defence Community to happen in the way the continental integrationists wanted it, there was still life in the Big Idea. At the time Messina precisely took place, that first weekend in June, it meant virtually nothing. Not being a member of the Coal and Steel Community, Britain was not present at the meeting, and nor were British correspondents. Had the word Messina entered the columns of British newspapers, the resonance it drew would have been far from the world of high diplomacy. For the meeting coincided with the Old Bailey trial of the brothers Messina, charged with pimping and racketeering. It was the biggest tabloid story of the time. For most of the British, mention of Messina inspired only thoughts of prostitution and extortion by oily Italians running a corner of London gang-land. Indeed, exchange 'Messina' for

'Brussels', in the modern era, and you have a fair evocation of what the most extreme of British phobes and sceptics continue to think about the entire project that Messina began.

Less than two months before Messina, Anthony Eden succeeded Churchill as Prime Minister. Less than a week before, he was confirmed in office at a general election. The British had other things on their mind than the evolution of 'Europe'. But once again they were drawn, ineluctably, in. They were outside 'Europe', but were still a great European power. They could not be avoided. They had acquired associate status – country member, no voting rights – with the Coal and Steel Community. It was second nature in Europe once again to invite them to negotiate the new project, but this time without preconditions. After Messina, there began another minuet resembling what occurred in May 1950, which had similarities to, but also a difference from, the earlier experience.

The difference was simple. What took about a week in 1950 took six months in 1955. The similarities are more jarring. The passage of years had not rendered any clearer Britain's view of herself and her destiny. The pattern turns out to be very much the same. Confronted with an invitation to talk, the political class shudders and prevaricates, half-heartedly inches forward and then passionately withdraws. The same language of disbelief courses through the Foreign Office files in 1955 as five years before. A new generation of officials gives different ministers the same advice they want to hear. Ministers accept, still less questioningly, the old assumptions on which this advice is based. The one significant evolution is towards a hardening of both advice and response. Whereas Schuman, though widely predicted to fail, was regarded with pragmatic affability in London once it had come to pass, Messina was designated, almost from the start and certainly by the end, for destruction with extreme prejudice. The shift is a measure of Britain's sharpening vanity – but also of her fear-filled diminishment.

The change of cast occurred not only in London. New figures were taking centre stage in Europe. First on the agenda at Messina, curiously, was the fate of Jean Monnet, who had announced his resignation as head of the Coal and Steel Community with a view to resuming his role as manipulative activist on behalf of 'Europe', following the collapse of the EDC. At this beginning of what became the Common Market, its visionary begetter returned to the shadows where he had always been more at home and perhaps more influential. But Monnet had his proxies, none more important than the Belgian Foreign Minister, Paul-Henri

Spaak, a name to remember. Spaak stepped forward as the new, presumptive father of 'Europe', a role for which he had, among other things, the usual British credentials. He had spent most of the war in London, passionately desired British involvement in Europe, believed in Winston Churchill.

Spaak was one of the two facilitators of what happened at Messina. He wasn't, in fact, the original begetter of the idea of a customs union, which is what 'Messina' became and which he began by opposing. That credit did not even belong to Jean Monnet, who was also at first sceptical of its possibilities, and had to be persuaded. The true fount and origin was a man seldom heard of since, named J. W. Beyen, the Dutch Foreign Minister. It was Beyen who persuaded Spaak, who then incontestably became the politician chiefly responsible for what happened afterwards.

After disposing of the Monnet problem, the foreign ministers got down to serious, ambitious work. They had before them a proposal jointly fashioned by the small members – Belgium, the Netherlands, Luxembourg, collectively known as Benelux – which, to begin with, disturbed and rather horrified the larger ones. This, in the words of the preamble to the document they all eventually agreed to discuss, committed them to the belief 'that it is necessary to work for the establishment of a united Europe by the development of common institutions, the gradual fusion of national economies, the creation of a common market and the gradual harmonisation of . . . social policies'.

This might, the proposal stated, be approached in different ways. It was for discussion. Possibly the right way – this was at first Spaak's own preference – was through the creation of several new communities to deal with different functions. After coal and steel, we give you land transport, air transport, conventional energy, nuclear energy, whatever. An alternative or perhaps parallel way – favoured and prepared by Beyen – would be through a customs union yoking these six national markets into one. Two days were spent by the Sicilian seaside discussing each of these ideas, and not deciding between them. In the end, the discussion would go on, the Messina Six decided, across the whole field. There would be joint studies made by experts, some of them about 'functional' possibilities – improved canals, better railways and roads, exchange of gas and electric power, pooling atomic know-how – some of them about a 'common market', which would involve a common customs barrier with the outside world as well as common tariffs within, and the possible harmonization of social laws and monetary policy.

This, if meant seriously, was a bold agenda. Spaak's memoirs describe the end of the Messina conference as an apotheosis almost resembling the dramatic exhaustion described by Gibbon on completing *The Decline and Fall of the Roman Empire*. 'Each morning,' he writes, 'we prepared the day's agenda in the hotel gardens, surrounded by flowers ... On the last day of the conference we had to work through the night, drafting the final communiqué. The sun was rising over Mount Etna as we returned to our rooms, tired but happy. Far-reaching decisions had been taken.'[5] To others, however, the very spaciousness of the communiqué suggested that nothing had been decided and nothing, therefore, was likely to happen. *Il Tempo* described the communiqué as 'another unnecessary document'. The British ambassador in Rome reported his Dutch colleague as saying that the meeting was never intended to achieve anything, 'but all the foreign ministers enjoyed their holiday in Taormina'.[6] The Luxembourg representative, Joseph Bech, said on his return that the most significant thing about Messina was its omission of any smell of a high authority, Schuman-style, to ruffle the sovereignties of the French, or the British. Messina, he wrote, 'had not made the mistake that had bedevilled European politics during the last few years of trying to steal a march on time'. Monnet himself deemed it a 'timid step towards the making of Europe', all too likely to end in mere co-operation between nations.

There was, however, plenty to play for. The studies would now begin, and Spaak, the most dynamic man at Messina, would be their chairman. An amazingly short deadline, 1 October, four months hence, had been set for their completion. Even Monnet, a sceptic about other people's efforts in this field, opined that 'they could hardly end just in smoke'.

From the beginning of the process, Britain, as if by automatic right, was given special treatment accorded no other non-member of the ECSC, nor to any collective grouping of nations who might think they had a right to be kept informed. Spaak showed the Benelux draft to the British before he ever got to Messina, and before he showed it to the Germans, the French or the Italians. His first priority, he told the British ambassador to Belgium, was not to be seen doing anything behind Britain's back. For this favour, Spaak was most grudgingly rewarded.

The Foreign Office, despite experience with the Schuman Plan, at first approached the document he had considerately handed them as if it were a novel exercise in mystification. It was 'woolly', 'a hotch-potch', 'intangible', but clearly to be resisted. Two weeks before Messina, the relevant desk officer minuted that Britain should 'continue to deprecate, if asked, any further measures of economic integration at this stage'. The day before the meeting began, judgement came from higher up the hierarchy. 'There can of course be no question', wrote John Coulson, the senior line official, 'of our entering any organisation of a supra-national character.' But, in any case, it was far from clear that anything would emerge. Messina would be designed mainly to give 'an impression of activity'. If there was any question of her attending post-Messina meetings, Britain should 'think very carefully before accepting'.[7]

These, in fact, became the two preliminary issues to test the judgement of London. On neither was the official performance very acute.

Most officials thought nothing at all would happen. Coulson, taking the temperature at a meeting of the OEEC, found nobody that mattered who was interested in hastening the pace of supra-nationalism. Gladwyn Jebb, now the ambassador in Paris, cut through the subtleties of French ambivalence with a fine flourish. The Foreign Minister, Antoine Pinay, he judged to be anxious to keep European unity alive without making commitments. Pinay was 'thinking of organisations which had the power of decision (and were therefore supra-national) but whose decisions would be reached unanimously (and were therefore inter-governmental)'. 'This sort of double-talk does seem to keep the Europeans quiet,' the ambassador noted scornfully, before offering the opinion that no spectacular developments out of Messina were likely, and that progress in coming months 'will be purely verbal'.[8]

The collective Whitehall view, in short, was that what Spaak and the others had launched at Messina was almost certainly going to be a mess. The practical question on this occasion, unlike with Schuman, was not whether Britain should be present at the working out of this mess, but in what guise and on what assumptions her presence should be offered. Although the formal invitation had yet to arrive, it was made known through several embassies, immediately after Messina, that London's presence would be unanimously welcome.

Here, however, the ambivalences in London began. Something called the Mutual Aid Committee first expressed them. This, a Whitehall power-centre controlled by the Treasury not the Foreign Office, was charged with matters of European integration, as if to emphasize the exclusively economic, indeed eleemosynary, tests by which the project might be thought to have measurable relevance to Britain. Mutual Aid has the antique feel of post-war recovery, as far away as possible from the futuristic adventure of European integration. The MAC agreed that it would be 'politically embarrassing' to refuse to attend, and that it would be as well to send 'something rather more than a mere observer'. On the other hand, watch it. The British should make clear they were not taking part 'as a seventh member of the group', and did not necessarily accept the Messina objectives of a merger between economies and a harmonization of social policies. Now, also, the politicians came into the picture. This part of Messina was Schuman all over again. Preoccupied with the election, no Cabinet minister features in any of the relevant files for May 1955 as having an opinion about Messina, or even being sent a paper advising him what to think. Early attitudes are all struck between officials. No need to trouble the great men with so trivial a distraction. But, as June begins, the silence starts to be broken.

The first to speak was R. A. Butler, Chancellor of the Exchequer. Chairing an OEEC dinner a few days after Messina, he was loftiness personified. This was a time, as he reminded a later inquirer, when Britain was 'the normal chairman of Europe'.[9] From this elevated seat he remarked that he had heard of 'some archaeological excavations' at an old Sicilian town, in which Britain had not taken part. This did not go down well. It sounded as though Britain regarded the venture as digging up a past that would better remain buried. Either that, or he was offering a superior classical reference, the kind of Delphic little joke with which he often loved to tease. Butler, as we shall see, never was a 'European'. In June 1955, his tone did not misrepresent British establishment opinion.

The decision on whether to get involved in the post-Messina process was, initially, Butler's call. Not only was the MAC, the superintending committee, run from his department, but the new Foreign Secretary, Harold Macmillan, was abroad.

Butler was extraordinarily disengaged. 'Very weak and uninteresting', he scribbled in the margin of the first Treasury paper he saw, setting out the Messina communiqué.[10] Additionally, he suffered a visit from Beyen, Spaak's co-visionary from Holland, who arrived in London to press the case for British involvement. Beyen was a silky operator, exotically sophisticated by Dutch standards. He put himself about, stressing his Anglophile tendencies and waxing about our two 'sea-faring countries' which would never want to exclude 'the other world'. In private, he began to sharpen up Messina, conceding that the British were against supra-nationalism, but filling out the possible shape of the new 'Community' he wanted them to get involved in talking about. Butler couldn't stand Beyen. 'He was a very pushing man ... always telling you what to do,' he later said.[11] Despite it all, Butler recalled that he had manfully 'overcome my personal repugnance to him'. But the visit did not send him rushing to Brussels, where the post-Messina studies were supposed to start in early July. His department by now had got closer to a considered assessment.[12] Mutual Aid notwithstanding, the Treasury view was that Messina was 'inspired as much by political as economic motives', and was a way of 'binding Germany into western Europe'. But the economic plans were highly suspect. A common market was an unacceptable objective 'for ourselves', though if others wanted one 'among themselves', we could not object. As for taking part in talks, we didn't like being asked the question just yet. We would have preferred 'a pause for thought'. We didn't like Beyen's ideas, but 'this may be an argument for joining the discussions'. By joining the Six at the table, we might 'guide their thoughts towards suggestions for forms of co-operation in which we might be willing to join'. We should do so, however, only as observers, and should open proceedings with a statement making clear we fundamentally objected to the supra-national basis of the enterprise.

It was some time before Macmillan, the Foreign Secretary and real opposite number of Spaak and Beyen, could get involved in this. He was away in San Francisco celebrating the tenth anniversary of the United Nations, and these were days when news travelled slowly. He read of Beyen's visit only in the press. The fax did not exist, telephone and telegraph appear to have been sparingly used. Even within Europe itself, many of the messages cited here took days to arrive. But Macmillan did send a message, after reading his newspaper, that he wanted the Messina decision postponed until he got back. When he did so, however, it was with no immediate countermand to Butler. 'Europe' apparently featured no higher in his mind than in anyone else's. Since taking over from Eden, he had made one foreign policy speech, in which Messina was not mentioned. His department had reached the same view as the Treasury, that an 'observer' only should be sent to Brussels.

But Macmillan's antennae did begin to twitch. A Cabinet meeting to decide the matter was due on 30 June. Europe was still not at the top of the agenda. This was a Britain much more preoccupied with imperial and domestic problems. The Kenyan Mau Mau guerrillas competed for quality political time with incessant dock strikes, and, challenged by traffic congestion in Park Lane, the Cabinet solemnly decided to consider the novel remedy of something called a 'dual carriageway'. But it also decided about Messina, and meanwhile Macmillan had slightly changed the Foreign Office mind.

Instead of an 'observer', he told his top mandarins the day before the Cabinet, Britain should send a proper participant. He positively enthused about a new 'relaunch' of Europe, and if this was to be a version in which the British could join, they had to be there to shape it.[13] Supra-nationalism was to be avoided, and perhaps it could be. To the Cabinet he said, 'We might be able to exercise greater influence in the forthcoming discussions if we were to enter them on the same footing as the other countries and not in the capacity as an observer.'[14]

The Cabinet didn't have much of a discussion, if the minutes are to be believed – which is not always the case, though this time it is quite believable that the Park Lane dual carriageway might have seemed more absorbing. Insofar as the minutes reveal anything, it is the reek of anxiety and doubt. But the ministers agree that Britain should go to Brussels. And Butler and Macmillan are sent away to settle the details, which they do after a telling little interchange.

Butler was the first to compose a draft. It accepted Beyen's invitation, but proposed to make something clear. 'There are, as you are no doubt aware,' Butler wrote, 'special reasons which preclude this country from joining a European common market.' A categoric assertion, it seemed, that 'Europe' should understand there would always be a distance between them and us. 'Preclude' sounds adamantine. A sense of the axiomatic breathes from the Butler formula, and Macmillan noticed it. He made a subtle adjustment, of which the carbon copy in the Public Record Office bears the mark. A handwritten amendment deletes 'preclude'. Instead of 'special reasons which preclude', there are 'special difficulties for this country in any proposal for "a European common market".'

The Macmillan version, softening the sense of absolute negative inevitability, was the one that was sent to Europe. It might have been received in a spirit of some optimism. After all, it had seemingly found the language of negotiation. 'Difficulties' could always be ironed out, if the goodwill was there, which the further promise, to examine all problems 'without prior commitment and on their merits', suggested would be so. There was a lot of room for creative diplomacy in the fashioning of what this common market might eventually add up to.

Britain, moreover, would send no mere observer – though the designation arrived at was still perhaps a little opaque. She would, the

Foreign Secretary announced, 'appoint a representative to take part in these discussions'.

*

A POLITICIAN pressed hard to be that representative. He was Anthony Nutting, Minister of State at the Foreign Office, Eden's protégé and admirer, and one of very few out-and-out 'Europeans' anywhere near relevant office in the Government. Bevin had his Younger, Eden his Nutting, and each was treated with identical scorn by his master. 'I begged Anthony to let me go as an observer, just to sit there, just to show some presence,' Nutting said many years later. 'But he turned against *any* participation once he got into office.'[15]

To send a minister would at least have ensured a certain equality of representation. 'Europe', for the most part, ensured that the game now beginning in Brussels was played by its First Eleven. Paul-Henri Spaak, the dominating presence, was a foreign minister, and so was the chief German representative, Dr Walter Hallstein. The French team was made up of senior *énarques* from the Quai d'Orsay. But that degree of distinction, favouring 'Europe' with its brightest stars, was precisely not what Whitehall wanted. At two days' notice, a name had to be selected, and the one that presented itself was Russell Bretherton.

Bureaucratically, Bretherton had the right credentials, which were professional yet insignificant. He was an economist connected not to the Treasury or the Foreign Office but, well down-table, to the Board of Trade. He was already much involved with European trade issues, having been his department's representative on OEEC for the past year. Before that, he had been at the conference that set up the Marshall Plan in 1947, and then again on the economic side of the discussions that led to the formation of Nato. He had now attained the princely rank of under-secretary, but his experience was entirely relevant to the task of keeping an eye on what Spaak and his burgeoning committees might get up to, insofar as it affected trade. Trade was what Bretherton was about, and trade was the level of discourse at which London had decided to pitch its contributions to a process which, for the most part, it would have deeply preferred not to be having.

Quite soon, however, it became apparent to Bretherton that trade was an inadequate description of the issues on which he, the senior and effectively solitary British representative at the table, would be required to intervene.

He was, in fact, a man whose character spilled beyond the confines of his arid curriculum vitae. There was more to him than the grey template of a trade economist. For one thing, he wasn't just a career civil servant, but had spent time teaching economics at Oxford, where he was a fellow of Wadham for seventeen years, before he got into the Board of Trade. For another, one of his students there was Harold Wilson, a statistician-economist who went into politics – a happening that later produced a career-intersection unusual even in the tight little world of the British political class. In 1947, when Wilson became President of the Board of Trade, at thirty-one barely out of college, who should he find toiling on the lower corridors but the tutor, ten years older than himself, who taught him much of what he knew about economics.

Bretherton had admirers before and after his work on the Spaak committee. He made a personal mark, even in obscurity. A short, spare man, easily missed in a crowd, he was very clever. 'He didn't put you at your ease,' Roy Denman, a young BoT entrant in Bretherton's time, told me. 'He worked on the basis of intellect. His meetings used to be called audiences, because when Mr Bretherton spoke, nobody dissented.'[16]

His political boss at the time of Messina was also fulsome. Peter Thorneycroft, President of the Board 1951–7, told Michael Charlton that Bretherton 'was one of the most brilliant officials I've ever had the privilege of working with'. That was in 1982. When I went to see Thorneycroft in 1993, not long before he died, the glow of memory was more refulgent still. I didn't entirely trust Thorneycroft's recollection. Depicting himself as one of the Eden Cabinet's only real Europeans, he cast Bretherton as an indispensable aide. Thorneycroft's memory of himself was a shade romanticized. Although it is perfectly true he opposed imperial preference – the trade system that gave all Common-wealth countries big advantages – and faced down the Conservative Party conference to press the point, it is less clear what risks he took to push a sceptical Cabinet towards Europe in 1955. Nevertheless, remem-bering Bretherton, he thought the world of him, especially over Europe. His words are part of the record. 'You need a minister, like me, who has a view. But he needs some prophet, some man of real enthusiasm who in moments of weakness will help him struggle on. Bretherton was superb, a marvellous man. A real believer in the European cause.'

Bretherton's own beliefs are not yet relevant. Later they become so. The last reason he was sent to Brussels was because of any known enthusiasm for what the Messina powers were trying to put together. If anything, the opposite. But the matter did become an issue, when history

casually demonized the British representative as the man who walked
Britain out of the Common Market.

Arriving in Brussels, his first reaction was one of amazement at being
treated on the same level as the German Foreign Minister. 'Never before
or since have I been called Your Excellency,' he remembered a long time
later.[17] He did not, however, so far lose his sense of balance that he
could not almost immediately see what was going on: or, as much to the
point, see how it diverged from what London thought was likely to
happen.

The Whitehall position was, in the broad, to wait and see. But even
before their man was installed in Brussels, a series of studies had been
set in train to examine the implications. Although these tracked the
Brussels agenda, examining case by case the different functional integra-
tions – electricity, canals, air transport and so on – these were, with one
exception, never taken as seriously as the studies of the Common Market
itself. The exception, naturally, was atomic energy, a field in which
Britain had all to give and almost nothing to gain in any new community, being the only atomic power between Washington and Moscow.
But it was the idea of a common market, with its consequences for
industry, for agriculture, for the Commonwealth, for almost every aspect
of the gross domestic product, which attracted the highest level of British
concern. That is what engaged the Whitehall combatants, and gave rise
to the bedrock objection which became the tactical, if not quite the
strategic, base of Britain's attitude. The strategic case concerned sovereignty, supra-nationalism and high politics. The tactical argument to
support it, which contained substance as well as stratagem, was that any
new institution was essentially unnecessary. It could only duplicate
OEEC, the multi-national, inter-governmental body Britain already
chaired. This was the position that Britain was endlessly to repeat.

It was accompanied, at this early moment, by another, which was
more covert but of seminal importance. Whitehall continued to believe
that the Messina process was not, ultimately, serious. It would not lead
anywhere. The conflicts of national interest were too great. The proposed
Customs Union would find the parties violently disagreeing about tariff
levels. Protectionist France, in particular, would find it no easier to
surrender high tariff barriers than to liquidate any part of her sovereignty. Even the trading aspects of the plan would founder. As for the
political entity people like Johan Beyen spoke of, it would not get off
the ground.

Bretherton's first report from Brussels was painfully disabusive. He did not tell his superiors what they wanted to hear. The first meeting of the Spaak committee, he wrote, had shown 'firm determination to implement the Messina proposals'. The project was indeed 'predominantly political'. On his first trip back to London for face-to-face talking, he told colleagues that his brief, which was to 'steer Spaak Britain's way', was unlikely to be achieved. So much for the 'purely verbal' progress predicted by Gladwyn Jebb. The Customs Union was already almost agreed in principle. An atomic energy committee had been set up over his objections. Bretherton was already, it seemed, more observer than achiever. 'I still see his face in front of me,' said one of his European interlocutors, remembering the scene. 'He usually had a rather cynical and amused smile on his face, and he looked at us like naughty children, not really mischievous, but enjoying themselves by playing a game which had no relevance and no future.'[18]

It sounds as though Bretherton was playing the part he had been instructed to play, more than halfway outside the enterprise. But this was to some extent a masquerade. In less than a month he became well aware that Messina had more relevance and more future than anyone in London dared imagine.

He was also acutely sensitive to what was soon happening to his own position. It should be remembered that he was on his own, unhooked from ministerial or Whitehall control. In 1955, communications were far too slow to permit him to be briefed on his response to every turn in the discussion. The diplomatic bag took four days to reach Brussels. Bretherton saw himself getting drawn in. 'Influence' and 'steering' were, he began to realize, chimerical delusions. 'If we take an active part in trying to guide the final propositions', he wrote to a colleague on 4 August, 'it will be difficult to avoid later on the presumption that we are, in some sense, committed to the result.' How could Britain insist on such-and-such a point, get it accepted into the conclusions, and then renege on the whole deal? 'On the other hand, if we sit back and say nothing, it's pretty certain that many more things will get into the report which would be unpleasant from the UK point of view whether we in the end took part in the Common Market or not.'[19]

Between 1955 and 1995, the British dilemma, in a sense, never changed. Although it is true that the 1990s opt-out from economic and monetary union, EMU, preserved Britain's right to take part in all the preliminaries without obligation, the 'sucking-in' effect of involvement in any talks on any subject was what the latter-day enemies of 'Europe' regarded as the lesson of history, which they were determined not to see repeated. In exactly the same way, the ins and the outs constituted an axis of tension: choosing to be 'out', in the 1990s as in the 1950s, by no means disposed of any problem caused by the 'ins'.

Bretherton had to pass the ball back to London. He did not have plenipotentiary powers. And the thinness of London's commitment to the process did not take long to show itself. Before the end of August, the Mutual Aid Committee instructed him '*not* to imply, in saying that certain features of the proposals would make it very difficult for the UK to join, that we would join if our points were met'.[20] In plainer language, even if Bretherton won every point Whitehall wanted, Britain wouldn't necessarily accept the bargain.

Actually, and surprisingly, one school of thought had by now developed in London which considered that the case for joining what Brussels might give birth to was strong. Treasury economists had been studying the consequences of some kind of European customs union for several years, and concluded that the benefits it brought Britain would exceed any loss of preference in Commonwealth markets. They repeated this work now, and reached the same conclusion. Although other Treasury divisions had a different gloss, the majority judgement was that, in economic terms, Britain would be better advised to join than to stay out of a common market if it was put together. Looking at trade, taxation, commercial policy, labour and capital movement, the economists concluded that, although short-term calculation favoured abstention, in the long term its disadvantages would become clear.

Economics, however, wasn't the name of the real game, and the Treasury at this stage was not a place of decisive influence over major questions of external policy. What mattered was the high political judgement. And here, as autumn beckons, one begins to sense from the documents the gulf widening between the Whitehall panjandrums and the functionary they had sent to handle the case in Brussels.

Bretherton, on the spot, was beginning to be aware of how much there might be to gain. In his August letter, he had already written: 'We have, in fact, the power to guide the conclusions of this conference in almost any direction we like, but beyond a certain point we cannot exercise that power without ourselves becoming, in some measure, responsible for the results.' Within his brief he was doing his best. At one point, Spaak openly thanked him for his co-operative attitude. A Frenchman noted that his manner had become collaborative: 'You really could not make a distinction between Britain and the rest.' And speaking at a distance, much later, Bretherton revealed himself, at least by now, to be the man Peter Thorneycroft fondly imagined him to have been all along. The process, he said, changed him. 'Did you yourself begin to change your mind while this conference was going on?' Michael Charlton asked him. 'Oh yes,' he insouciantly replied.[21] In particular, he recollected, France was determined that British entry was a precondition of her own, and was prepared to pay a British price for that. Again in recollection: 'If we had been able to say that we agreed in principle, we could have got whatever kind of Common Market we wanted. I have no doubt of that at all.'

This, then, was Bretherton's position. He thought the Common Market was on the way to happening. He believed Britain could shape it. He put this advice on paper more than once. But, he said, 'I don't think anybody took any notice.'

He was right about that. The big guns were turning in the opposite direction.[22] The Treasury man who headed the MAC, William Strath, said mid-September would be 'a convenient moment to disengage'. Edward Bridges, still the head of the Treasury, now told Butler it had been 'a great pity' anyone had been sent to work with Spaak. He was firmly convinced Britain should have no part in this 'mysticism', which 'appeals to European Catholic federalists and occasionally, I fear, to our Foreign Secretary'. But the Foreign Office, in truth, was just as sceptical. Whereas the Treasury at least thought the Common Market might happen, the FO still believed there was almost no chance. It criticized the 'highly doubtful assumptions' of Treasury papers. What both departments agreed on was that the failure of the project should be encouraged to happen. Burke Trend, a rising star in mandarin Whitehall who later became Cabinet secretary, was the drafter of the final advice to ministers. They should be told, he wrote, that it would 'on balance be to the real and ultimate interest of the UK that the Common Market should collapse, with the result that there would be no need for the UK to face the embarrassing choice of joining it or abstaining from joining it'.

Trend also discussed tactics. Outright withdrawal would be 'a quite considerable gamble'. The Six *might* go ahead without us, and they *might* pull it off. Equally, they might fail, in which case we might be accused of sabotage, the implications of which 'are not pleasant'. But playing for time had its risks too, because the British were likely to find it harder to withdraw the longer they stayed in the talks. Nor was the idea of steering the Six towards OEEC very persuasive either. It would either be seen as another form of sabotage, or perhaps lead to the Six eclipsing OEEC and destroying it from within.

We see, all in all, what a damnable nuisance the idea of 'Europe' had now become, what a no-win situation it was beginning to present to the power that had grown accustomed over many years to securing what it could call victory, in all three of the intersecting world circles that uniquely defined Britain's range and role. The best advice that Trend could think of was to try and find some 'bribe', as he put it, which would lure the Six towards a free trade area rather than a customs union. Special tariff benefits, and a bit of British generosity on the nuclear front, he wrote, might be enough to do the trick.

Even if every policy carried risks, and no tactic could conceal them, however, there was never any doubt what the final Whitehall advice would be. On 27 October, the MAC, mindful of its audience and banishing the counter-views which at least one body of economists had submitted, loaded its assessment on the entirely negative side. There were, it said, four 'decisive considerations' against British membership. One, it would weaken Britain's relationship with Commonwealth and colonies. Two, Britain was a world power, and the Common Market would run against world free trade. Three, membership would lead to further integration, and perhaps federation, which the public would not accept. Four, British industry would no longer be protected against European competition.

There remained the end-game. It had to be accomplished with as much finesse as possible. In the various accounts of what happened next, we witness the usual distortions of memory and desires for self-vindication, of countries and politicians and officials who do not want to be blamed for the terminal event that now occurred. At this distance of time, the details may be of rather modest relevance – by comparison with the outcome. But Russell Bretherton, inevitably, is at the centre of them.

The extreme and most remembered version is also, naturally, the most alluring: the one that seems to reflect a due momentousness. Spaak, it is not disputed, had called a meeting for 7 November which was designed to bring matters to a head. This was a piece of blatantly aggressive chairmanship. In place of the sub-committees working on different aspects of the putative 'Europe', he proposed that all the work should now be subsumed into a single report, produced under his hand, coming to firm conclusions that would implement the Messina communiqué. Suddenly confronted with this coup, Bretherton is supposed to have summoned up a burst of Disraelian grandeur, expressed with Macaulayesque symmetry. Before rising from the table, he is alleged to have declared: 'Gentlemen, you are trying to negotiate something you will never be able to negotiate. But if negotiated, it will not be ratified. And if ratified, it will not work.'[23] To anyone who might doubt the probability of a trade economist, however clever, coming up with this impromptu formulation, the further word comes, from some sources, that Bretherton's text was drafted in Anthony Eden's own hand.

There is no documentary evidence that anything so exciting occurred. Marginal support might seem to emanate from the reaction of Spaak to Bretherton's intervention. 'Spaak just blew up at that point,' Bretherton himself said.[24] But such a response might as easily have been provoked, at this sensitive moment, by the rather more mundane expressions which there is some evidence the British representative did use. 'I had what amounted to almost a written instruction,' he remembered. It is in the PRO file. 'Following for Bretherton,' says a ciphered message sent, with rare speed, by bag to Brussels on 5 November. Therein he is given the words he must read out, which, for the first time, is what he does. They pour cold water, above all, on the duplication which this idea of a common market will entail. 'The main point I wish to make', the draft says for him, 'is that, to an important extent, the studies undertaken by these committees relate in varying degrees to matters within the competence of existing and broader institutions, and in particular to OEEC.'[25]

This was certainly enough to enrage Spaak. Bretherton's memory of what the Belgian said is unlikely to be precise, but the sense of it is surely faithful. 'Spaak just said, "Well, I am astonished and very hurt at this. You are just sticking to your guns. England has not moved at all, and I am not going to move either."'

Further evidence that Bretherton did not, in fact, make the spectacular exit legend attributes to him is supplied by the fact that his bosses in London never gave this meeting, either before or after it, quite the decisive importance which in retrospect it came to deserve. They told Bretherton to say what he said, but saw it as a form of prevarication, a delaying mechanism until they had worked out exactly when and how to achieve the same result, namely Britain's formal withdrawal from the Spaak committee. Later in November, Whitehall is still seething with disagreement about exactly what should be done. Ambassadors bombard London with questions. What exactly is going on, they ask? Our man at the ECSC complains at being 'left in the dark as to what HMG's policy really is'. Our man in Bonn says that, from what he has heard, we are taking the economic issue too narrowly. His superior at the FO messages back that yes, some Treasury economists favoured Britain joining, but it was for the Foreign Office 'to supply the spectacles of political reality as to how much of "Messina" will come to pass and, if it does, how it will fit in with our interests'.[26]

Plainly nothing had been decided exactly on 7 November. No doubt it is this that produced the lengthy argument, which zealots have conducted over decades, as to whether Britain withdrew from the Spaak committee, or was thrown out of it. Bretherton always insisted he did not withdraw. And that is technically quite true. He did not leave the room, and Britain did not there and then announce that she would take no further part. It does not even seem as though Spaak, for all his hair-trigger bombast, was on that very date laying down terms and conditions that banned Britain from taking further part.

On the other hand, that was Bretherton's last meeting. He never did return. The moment had presented itself, to both Spaak and the man who was chiefly in charge of the end-game in London, R. A. Butler, when Britain's pretence to any further allegiance to the project had to stop. Spaak's final report could be completed only by people who were committed to its recommendations. London, collective London, had decided it could not comply. At the edge of this Anglo-Europe consensus, London's part of the decision was the more definitive. Such was Spaak's keenness for Britain to come in – and his certainty, like Monnet's, that if the Six got their project together Britain would want to join it – that he would have been perfectly prepared for Bretherton to remain as a presence until the final proposition was agreed, which it was in early 1956. But then Bretherton would have had to be well and truly an 'observer', occupying the limbo between compliance and dissent, free to bark but not to bite, semi-acquiescent spectator at an event which Britain had decided to refrain from trying to control.

Against that alternative, absence was no doubt a more convincing option. But it committed Britain to the objective Whitehall had always put at the head of its wish-list, while desiring not to be seen to do so: assisting the Common Market, in Burke Trend's clinical judgement, 'to collapse'.

Mountains of words have issued forth about this sequence of events since it unfolded forty years ago. To a subsequent inquirer, curious to map the pathology of the political class most influential in shaping it, and to ask about the weight of countervailing wisdom at the time, two contributions cut the sharpest across any tendency to lie down tolerantly in front of the immutable facts of history.

The first is R. A. Butler's. Butler's relationship to 'Europe' was influenced by a considerable accumulation of interests and memories, some perhaps more admirable than others. For one thing, as a farmer who represented farming interests in Parliament, he was always likely to be wary of a project that might upset his personal and constituency arrangements. For another, he was among those Conservative politicians who were usually more sensitive to what the party might not like than to what it ought to be persuaded, against its instincts, to accept. Although a reformer, he seldom went about the business of social change by means of explicit challenge to the past. He did not, in that sense, have a brave political imagination.

Infusing this muted, oblique, crabwise character was a complicated past, especially as it had been touched by Europe. He was not at ease with all parts of his record. As an under-secretary at the Foreign Office, he had been closely associated with Neville Chamberlain, the Prime Minister who famously went to Bad Godesberg as an emissary seeking appeasement with Hitler. Butler was embarrassed by this connection with a man whose name for ever summoned up the image of two appurtenances: the famous 'piece of paper' he brought back ensuring peace in our time, and the furled umbrella that was his trademark. Later, Butler was always in a hurry to explain that he had had nothing to do with the formulation of Chamberlain's policy. It had just been his bad luck, so he said, to be the spokesman for it in the Commons, since the Foreign Secretary was in the Lords. But, as he knew, this didn't entirely wash. He had been in the appeasement camp, something he went to such lengths to obliterate as would intrigue any psychiatrist specializing in the behaviour of public men. The extent of it was revealed suddenly, when he himself visited Bad Godesberg many years later, as Chancellor. His memory was triggered. Out walking beside the Rhine with his private secretary, Robert Armstrong, he flourished the silver-headed cane that he invariably favoured, and, recalling his time with Chamberlain, said: 'Since then, I have never carried an umbrella.'[27]

So Butler lacked natural affinity with the Europe question, other than as the guilt-ridden veteran of a past that made it harder than usual for him to think straight. What should one make, nonetheless, of his apologia many years later?

When he was an old man, he looked back at the past with a candour that might disarm criticism, if it did not also carry an aura almost of complacency about it: shoulder-shrugging before whatever fate might bring. There was, he told Michael Charlton, 'a definite lack of foresight

on the part of myself, and a much bigger lack of foresight on the part of
the Treasury, and a very big lack of foresight on the part of the Foreign
Office'.[28] But it was really all down to the advice the politicians were
getting, especially about whether Messina would come to something.
'That is how the bad start, the late start for Europe, really started.' The
withdrawal of Bretherton, Butler thought, had come about more than
anything 'through boredom'. 'Anthony Eden was bored by this. Frankly
he was even more bored than I was.' It was certainly 'a mistake', Butler
said. But there was a consolation. 'I wasn't blamed at the time at all.
And I have not been blamed very much in history.'

It may be a bit of a rarity to come across so open a confession of
error. And perhaps the faintly comical world-weariness, the air of
plangent and inexplicable non-sequitur, comes straight from the style-
book of a notorious *flaneur*. But, conveying as he does London's
fundamental lack of serious or constructive interest, Butler rather under-
mines any defence there might be for the manifest error of judgement
that occurred in the second half of 1955. If 'history' has any part in
allocating 'blame', the exoneration of the Chancellor of the Exchequer,
or the other ministers who would have said very much the same as he
did, cannot be guaranteed in perpetuity.

Their lack of awareness, even, one might say, of intelligence, becomes
the more painful when set beside the evidence of what some other minds
were saying. This was long before 'Europe' had become a fractious
political subject, on which all factual assessments became hopelessly
contaminated by attitude-striking. Measured, cold-eyed calculation could
still be made without prejudice.

In February 1956, the Federation of British Industries, forerunner of
today's CBI, sent its international affairs man for a round of talks in
Brussels and The Hague. His name was Peter Tennant, and he had been
recently recruited from the Foreign Office. After a distinguished wartime
career serving MI6 from the British embassy in Stockholm, Tennant
moved, via Paris, to be Deputy Commandant in the British Sector of
Berlin. Perhaps his provenance imposes the need to give some small
recognition, after all, to the prophetic capacity of at least part of the
public service. Tennant, now private industry's top adviser, returned
from Europe with a very different verdict from the sonorous vacuities of
the Foreign Office.

The Messina process, he judged, was far from being 'purely idealistic,
impractical Europeanism'. He found the urgency surrounding it greater
than at the start of either OEEC or the ECSC. Nor were the participants

doctrinaire about supra-nationalism of the Monnet variety. The UK attitude, which Tennant characterized as lurching between belligerence and indifference, he found extremely puzzling.

He saw the political dilemma. Protectionism, sheltering behind imperial preference, was a hard nut to crack. But Tennant criticized the thinking about the emerging Common Market, which 'seems to have resulted in the advantages and disadvantages appearing to cancel out and thereby producing inactivity'. Inactivity, he went on, might be justified 'if one were not dealing with a reality'. Messina might produce a mess, and probably would do unless it had the benefit of British advice and experience. But the mess 'would for us be just as serious as a successful outcome from which we were excluded'. Imperial trade might presently account for almost 50 per cent of Britain's market, but this would inevitably shrink under pressure of more competition. Britain couldn't afford 'to be excluded from 20 per cent of our trade by the formation of a common market between six European countries, which might be joined by others and which, as a unit, would inevitably represent increased competition and bargaining power against us in third markets'.

What Tennant saw was an opportunity sliding away. Instead of identifying ourselves with Europe 'on our own terms', we were 'leaving events to proceed outside our control'. Unless this policy was somehow reversed, the result would cause far more disruption to the economy than any inconveniences that had to be dealt with now. 'We will be faced some 10 or 15 years hence with a decision to join the club on its terms and at a high entrance fee.'[29]

Russell Bretherton appears to have known that as well. Such was his own account of his judgement when he was released from the inhibitions of professional neutrality. But it also fits in with what he plainly thought at the time. Late in my inquiry, I came across a letter he wrote to Frank Lee, his permanent secretary at the Board of Trade. Dated 17 November 1955, on his return from Brussels, this already reflects on the crisis to come. 'I only wish that I felt happier about the line we are taking,' Bretherton said. 'I think that we underestimate the amount of steam, both political and economic, which is still behind the Messina ideas, and also the dangers for the UK in a purely negative attitude on our part.' The message about Bretherton's differences with his masters emerges at a later moment too. The last time we come across him in the official documents of this period, he has returned to his role as a Board of Trade civil servant. Eden is preparing for a visit to President Eisenhower, in the course of which he knows he will need to explain Britain's negative attitude to the integration that Washington had always been keen to foster. Peter Thorneycroft is asked to produce a paper, and Bretherton, who drafts it for him, dutifully assembles a measured case explaining why the Customs Union would be against the British interest. It is a professional piece of work, reflecting the stance to which the Government was now committed.

His official superiors, however, scrutinizing it before it was sent up to Thorneycroft, didn't like it. The draft, wrote Sir Edgar Cohen, second secretary at the BoT, was 'too reasonable'. What was required, to make the British position unmistakably clear to the Americans, was 'to sound a note of hysteria'.[30] Wiping out Bretherton's cool words, Cohen rewrote Eden's brief, in the kind of language that did proper justice to the mentality these esteemed masters of the universe were beginning to depend on.

4

HAROLD MACMILLAN

Agonizing for Britain

THE TREATY OF ROME, providing for a common market and an ever closer union of the peoples whose leaders invented it, was signed on 25 March 1957.[1] British hysteria, whether applied directly to the Messina Six or mediated via Washington, did not succeed in impeding the creation of a customs union, together with the apparatus of court, commission and council that was needed to make it work.

Hysteria of a different kind was adjacent to the scene. Here the word didn't describe a Foreign Office aspiration, a tactical ploy to fend off the future. It was the right word for the feeling that was engendered, behind the usual front of British sang-froid, by the diplomatic disaster, military humiliation and psychic catastrophe known forever after under a generic name: Suez.

'Suez' and 'Europe', concepts that billow beyond the words that represent them, are the two motifs twined round Britain's definition of herself in the second half of the century. That the Suez disaster and the Rome Treaty occurred almost simultaneously – November 1956, March 1957 – was an accidental fact. But their repercussions one upon the other were, from the British standpoint, intimate. They shaped the British political realm as it has subsequently existed. Together they raised the question of national identity as a predicament that has perhaps been experienced more acutely in Britain than in any other European nation. Suez, the terminal calamity of Empire, infused the British mind at the moment when the European dilemma, which has tormented it ever since, was already beginning to assume massive importance.

Britain's self-exclusion from the Treaty presented itself, to the small coterie of people who were even aware that it was happening, as a deliberative act. The official papers abound with rational arguments. In fact, it had much more to do with inchoate feelings about where Britain belonged in the world: visceral sentiments of grandeur that Suez, eventually, made untenable. But such awareness of the limits of instinct took time to dawn. Meanwhile, the stirrings of something new in the official mind were beginning very slightly to make themselves felt.

In one respect, the Foreign Office attitude to the Common Market – that it would never happen – was perfectly intelligible. It revolved around France, and France did not come smoothly to the party. The French attitude to nation and sovereignty resembled Britain's, with a preference for putting country before continent, and a measure of protection for traditional markets before the internal free trade the Market aspired to. French ratification was at times in doubt, and in any case had to be carried through by a government other than the one which had negotiated and signed the Treaty. It was at all times a risky venture, upon whose failure British diplomats rested their faith. But it happened. France surmounted her doubts and difficulties. She negotiated terms for her colonies, the equivalent of the British Commonwealth – for which Mother Britain found it inconceivable that a negotiation should even be attempted. Deploying their considerable negotiating panache, the French political class came round to falsifying the predictions and smashing the hopes of almost all their British counterparts.

Almost all, but not quite. In London there were the beginnings of dissent from the ideology that gripped upper Whitehall. The presence of these murmurings now needs to be registered. In the Whitehall of the middle 1950s, they did not get a hearing, but they did exist. The dominant culture belonged to Sir Roger Makins, but not everybody in it had drawn the same lessons from the war as he had done. These new men knew well enough that Atlanticism, the American relationship, the god before which Makins and his generation worshipped, was at the heart of the British national interest. The war and the victory had proved it. But theirs was a different kind of war, far from the armchair generalship that had imparted to older men a single-minded obsession with the Pax Americana. For them, the shot and shell of the front line were what they could never forget. Their war gave them a different perspective. And since they were the men of the future, many of whom rose high in the Foreign Office by the time the prejudices of their elders proved to have been misdirected, they are a cadre of some interest.

Consider Donald Maitland, born in 1922, whose diplomatic career crested as ambassador to the European Communities, 1975–9. In 1955, Maitland wasn't involved with Europe. What was quaintly known in the Office as an orientalist, he had learned Arabic and served, in his early career, in Baghdad and Lebanon. He spent his war not in Europe but in Asia and the Middle East. But the experience left him sceptical of the British orthodoxies. 'I came back from the war absolutely persuaded that the imperial idea – the idea of us ruling other countries – was finished,' he told me in the 1990s. 'We had to decolonize, and if we were going to do that we had to have another kind of foreign policy.'[2] The only basis for this, he thought as a young man, was Europe. He didn't pretend to know how it might happen, but he regarded as elementary the need for structures and treaties that were likely to stop Europe ever going to war again.

To anyone who thought like that, Messina was obviously a missed opportunity. But the official policy said otherwise. As the files voluminously show, from the moment Bretherton got to Brussels, the discussion in London centred not on how he might constructively use his seat but how he might gracefully vacate it. Quite a lot of Maitland's generation believed as he did. To me he named, among others, Oliver Wright (b. 1921), Brooks Richards (b. 1918), James Murray (b. 1919), Anthony Montague Browne (b. 1923), a varied group of distinguished career diplomats. There were others of similar age. But they never officially discussed Europe. Strong convictions produced no debate, a silence that reflected the lack of excitement, or even argument, in the wider world. 'We all worked terribly long hours,' Maitland remembered. 'There was no opportunity to talk except in the canteen or the gents.'

Some of them, occasionally, had opportunities which they took to extremes. The first posting of Christopher Audland (b. 1926) was to the UK high commissioner's office near Bonn, where the capital of the new-born German Federal Republic had just been established. There, at the age of twenty-three, he was the British negotiator of one of the Bonn Conventions, which were to lead to the full independence of West Germany. In this work, he took part in meetings with Konrad Adenauer once a week. Not surprisingly, he became immersed in Germany, and saw at close quarters the need for German integration into the European system. His next posting was to Strasbourg and the Council of Europe, where he decided that the Monnet approach to European unity, via a community, was much preferable to the inter-governmental approach favoured by Britain. 'In this I was thought very eccentric,' Audland later said. 'I was seen as having gone native.' But such Europeanism permeated all the advice he gave to his superiors when he returned to the Foreign Office to spend much of a decade involved in the great question, and then set the seal on his commitment by becoming a full-blooded

Eurocrat, working for the Commission in Brussels from 1973 until retirement. Thus Audland can be seen from the early 1950s as part of a new generation, unheard but significantly aberrant, which presaged a Foreign Office that sooner or later would be ready to revise its Euro-scepticism.

Among this youthful crowd was a figure who could be called, in retrospect, its leader. Personally, he collected more Euro-credentials than anyone else. Professionally, his career turned out to track with metro-nomic regularity Britain's European policy throughout the thirty-five years it took him to rise to the senior post in the Foreign Office.

Michael Palliser (b. 1922) spent his war in Europe, in the Coldstream Guards. He was part of a tank brigade, and what he remembered when I talked to him forty years later was not so much the war itself as the scenes it left behind, the towns that even tanks could not traverse for rubble. 'Simply taking a train journey from Berlin through the Ruhr and up to the Hook of Holland, you saw a place that was absolutely flattened,' Palliser said. It made a powerful impression on him. 'I came out feeling that this was something one simply can't allow to happen again. It hit you like a kick in the stomach.' In his chosen profession of diplomacy, that kind of youthful memory can have a potent afterlife. 'If you go into the international field,' Palliser said, 'the gut feeling perhaps continues in a way it does less in other jobs. Your view of the world can be formed by instinct as much as reason.'[3]

Like Audland, Palliser chose to live at first hand through Germany's post-war experience, remaining in the army for eighteen months, watching 'the deliquescence of a society'. He found himself poised between despair for what Germany had done and great personal sympathy for individual Germans. 'Here were people who were basic human beings, who had been appallingly knocked about. At nightfall, all you could see were piles of rubble, but then at daybreak people climbed out of the cellars and went to work.' In the Foreign Office, Palliser's first job was as secretary of the allied powers' committee that settled output levels for the German steel industry. Not long after, at the birth of the Schuman Plan, he spent three years dealing with Germany in all her aspects.

It was a formation that never left him. He could still recall in 1993 his disgust at watching the senior Foreign Office mandarins disposing of questions raised by Herbert Morrison, who succeeded Bevin as Foreign Secretary, concerning coal and steel policy and its relationship to the Schuman Plan. Makins was the lordly agent of the Labour politician's correction. His scornful minute, repelling all temptations to make common cause with 'Europe', was circulated 'in the print', a category of despatch that made sure the entire foreign service would see it. 'I remember being immensely discouraged by that,' said Palliser, 'and thinking, for God's sake, these people are living in the wrong world.' But, being near the bottom of the pecking-order, he could do nothing about it.

Palliser qualifies to be called the archetypal British 'man of Europe'. Although in the early days he was professionally frustrated, he secured some compensation by marrying, in 1948, the daughter of none other than Paul-Henri Spaak. The young diplomat was received into the European purple, at some cost to the political reputation of the Belgian Foreign Minister. For Palliser was a Catholic and Spaak was not, and Spaak had to tell his anti-Catholic socialist party to go to hell when Michael and Marie were married at the Papal Nunciature in Brussels. But that was only the beginning of Palliser's declaration for Europe. His later career was lived there. He was in Paris when the Rome Treaty was signed, in Downing Street when Britain made her second attempt to accede to it, in Paris again when the third and last attempt was made, in Brussels as ambassador when Britain finally limped into the Community, and in London as permanent under-secretary when the last undone piece of business relating to British membership was on the verge of being completed.

But in the middle 1950s, he was a man before his time. So were they all. They were no match for the great men of the Foreign Office, who had not only the rights bestowed on superior status but the belief that their wisdom was as incontestable as their position. If Makins was the high priest of Atlanticism, our man at the Paris embassy when the Treaty of Rome was signed was a Poo-Bah of still more eclectic range.

Sir Gladwyn Jebb (b. 1900) is, in his way, as emblematic of his time and class as was his subordinate, Michael Palliser. Jebb it was who, writing to London from Paris, reassured his department on numerous occasions that what had happened at Messina would come to nothing. He exposed occasional crevices of doubt about the advisability of London taking *quite* such an openly hostile attitude to all matters European, but he did not challenge the essential orthodoxy. Yet – and here is where he is typical of his time as well – this didn't remain his position. Quite the reverse. Jebb was the most eminent official whose trajectory on the Europe question follows the tortuous path taken by almost all the politicians whose lives it touched: from scepticism to enthusiasm – and sometimes back again. Jebb himself eschewed the last of these manoeuvres. He, who had called the Hague conference of the European Movement an 'ill-considered and emotional hullabaloo' and pursued an official career which had seldom challenged that premise, changed his mind for ever. On retiring from the Foreign Office in 1960 after thirty years' service, he began an opposite line of service that lasted another thirty years. Lord Gladwyn, as he was soon entitled, became a missionary European. The filling-out of Europe, with Britain at the heart of it, became his later life's work. When I saw him in 1993, he was still struggling through the consequences of a stroke to preach the cause in the House of Lords in speeches which the shorthand writers were hard put to decipher into an accurate note. But I couldn't help being more struck by the fact that, in his middle nineties, Gladwyn Jebb was far more interested in the likely results of the Treaty of Maastricht than in details of the history of Messina.

To listen to such prophetic concern was an impressive experience. But in the days when he counted for a great deal Jebb was no more prescient than any of his colleagues. He was a clever, arrogant man, a bully, whose flamboyance, Donald Maitland recalled, spread itself through the Foreign Office wherever he was posted. 'He was good with ministers. With their similar background, he could take on Eden on equal terms. And he got on very well with Bevin.'

He was, in a word, an official who counted more than any official could expect to in the 1990s. He belonged to a lost breed. And lest there be doubt about that, it is necessary to refer only to his memoirs, where the recitation of the author's achievements conjures up a forgotten world of British greatness, epitomized by none more spaciously than himself. 'The European Advisory Commission was, in varying forms, first advocated by me,' he writes. 'The famous "Four Power Plan" (which ended up with the United Nations) was originated by myself. It was I who first prepared a draft for an "Atlantic Treaty", which blossomed out eventually into Nato. The German Occupation Zones (which, for good or evil, largely shaped the whole post-war development of Europe) were at any rate prepared in the committee of which I was chairman. And, above all perhaps, suggestions for some kind of Western European Union (which ended up in the Brussels Treaty Organisation and in the WEU) were, so far as I know, first formulated in that dark back room [the room Jebb occupied at the Foreign Office, 1935–7, 1942–4].'⁴ Gladwyn was not troubled by modesty. The list speaks for a breathtaking intellectual aggrandizement. But it is not complete. The memoirist says something else that reveals a certain inflation of memory. 'If there has been any idea to which I have been exceptionally faithful over the years,' he writes, 'it has been "Europe" ... This is something I feel I really do know something about.'

What he knew in the middle 1950s, however, proved to be false. It reflected rather than challenged the mind of middle England. Jebb was a Euro-sceptic in every sense except the one most necessary, namely the capacity to apply a doubting mind to the orthodoxy that had taken Bretherton away from Spaak's table, or an anxious one to the economic prognosis which supported that political gesture.

For this was also an economic question. In the Foreign Office, the economic issue tended to be swept aside as if it barely needed addressing. Could Britain survive unscathed the creation of an economic zone across the Channel of which she wasn't part? Was the British economy, rooted in trading patterns far beyond Europe, strong enough to be indifferent to what happened there? These were always pressing questions, but had invariably been spared rigorous examination. In the run-up both to the Schuman Plan and to Messina, official analyses were sufficiently agnostic to give succour to the many people whose strong preference was for persuading themselves that the politics of 'Europe' required Britain, whatever the economic facts, to keep out.

By the middle 1950s, however, such a stance was beginning to be taken with somewhat less confidence. Some economists in the Treasury saw reasons for worry. Self-excluded from Messina, Britain embarked, as we shall see, on a defensive strategy which revealed a certain anxiety. The truth was becoming available, for those who could count.

The illusion of Britain's economic strength received plenty of reinforcement, not all of it mendacious. Both 1953 and 1954 were years of success. In 1953, there was a surplus on the balance of payments, which reflected an increase in output and exports. Stability was seemingly being followed by expansion. This remained, moreover, the enterprise of a great power that believed in its historic role. In 1955, befitting her history and status, Britain still spent 9 per cent of her gross national product on defence, financing massive troop encampments in the Middle and Far East. The military budget dominated both the shipbuilding and engineering industries. The island people continued to give a passable performance as a warrior nation of which the entire world had to take note.

Other trends, however, were more ominous, and they are not all the evidence of hindsight. Between 1954 and 1959, unit labour costs in manufacturing industry rose by 25 per cent in Britain, twice as fast as in other industrial countries. In 1958, the relentless trend line of German growth produced the cross-over between the economies of the war winners and losers: that was the year the German economy grew bigger than the British, and German exports first exceeded British exports. It was the climax of a period, 1950–8, in which the annual percentage growth rates for manufactured exports were as follows: West Germany 15.0, Netherlands 9.8, Italy 8.9, Britain 1.8.[5] Annual average growth rates overall, 1950–60, were: West Germany 7.8 per cent, Italy 5.8, France 4.6, Britain 2.7. Of course, the continentals had started from a lower base. But this was the seed-bed of the pattern of which the economist Peter Oppenheimer was obliged to write in 1970: 'It was estimated that all the other countries of north-western Europe [except Ireland] had surpassed Britain in output per head by the time the Conservatives left office' in 1964.[6]

There was, retrospect shows, a dire match between economic trends, on the one hand, and the political judgements that ignored them. The very year of Messina, 1955, was actually the moment when the balance of payments, the crucial residue of these trends, began to falter. The balance returned to deficit, the sterling reserves took a downward turn and there was no quick recovery from either development. The complacency of the Chancellor, R. A. Butler, based on the 1953–4 performance, began to be overtaken by a sense of depression, especially at the state of manufacturing industry.

This depression, however, was as yet far from terminal. It wasn't deep enough to prompt a serious re-examination of what government might do to give manufacturing a higher priority, and address the competitiveness problem. This was a nation whose thinking was hard to shake. In official circles, the conventional wisdom had never cared much about manufacturing anyway. Compared with the continentals, the Conservative governments of the 1950s were mistrustful of anything like an industrial policy, and pursued trading and commercial priorities which grew out of geo-strategic attitudes rather than any committed idea of the interests of Great Britain Ltd. International finance and the role of sterling continued to be the determinants of most British official thinking. Relationships with the Commonwealth retained a much tighter grip on the Tory, and for that matter the Labour, mind than the awkward realities of a trading bloc of expanding economies across the Channel. The politicians persuaded themselves, in the teeth of the trends, that they could survive and perhaps defeat the economic power of 'Europe' anyway. They were able to pretend that the world had not changed for ever, still believing, for example, that the main reason for

German and French success was the wartime destruction those countries had suffered. Therefore, they assumed, it would not last.

When I talked to Roger Makins in the 1990s, and asked him to explain why, in his rejection of 'Europe' in the mid-1950s, he had been so spectacularly wrong, his answer acknowledged the error but deflected the blame. After Messina, he had been transferred from the Foreign Office to the Treasury, where he was permanent secretary from 1956 to 1959. What he said to me conveyed the amateurish puzzlement that was often a convenient bolt-hole, an ironic escape, for the tigerish certainties of the post-war mandarinate. 'What I didn't foresee,' Makins told me, 'and what many people didn't foresee, was the total failure of British industry in the 1960s and 1970s. It was not to be foreseen. I agree that, if I'd read the statistics, I should have known we were bound to go downwards. But as permanent head of the Treasury, you weren't allowed to deal with anything under ten million pounds. As for reading obscure statistics, that was for somebody else.'[7]

But not all mandarins were so flippant. If one is looking for a beginning to the slow, stuttering reversal of Whitehall opinion about the proper relationship Britain had to have with the European Common Market, it can perhaps be located at a critical moment of decision in the career of Roger Makins's successor at the Treasury, Sir Frank Lee. If the worm was turning, the manoeuvre could never be accomplished by Michael Palliser and the other committed young Europeans at the Foreign Office, but it might be assisted by a fearless mind of suitable seniority. Frank Lee became that mind.

Lee had shown counter-cultural tendencies on occasions in his past. Seldom has a British civil servant combined intellectual independence, career success and collegial admiration to the extent that he did. He was a small, ugly man with a large spirit and a rasping voice. His Whitehall experience was wide beyond the dreams of any modern successor. He began in the Colonial Office, went to the Treasury, thence to Supply, more than once to Washington. He was a compleat mandarin of the meritocratic breed, becoming top man at Food, then top man at Trade, and finally the topmost of men, permanent secretary at the Treasury. But he remained, throughout, a leader in tight control of all that happened. One of his successors, Douglas Allen (Lord Croham), told me that, however high Lee rose, he would never delegate the main task of an official. 'He drafted everything himself. He was a brilliant draftsman, and an excellent chairman. He was one of my heroes.'[8]

Roy Denman is another witness to the impression Lee made. 'His appearance', writes Denman, 'suggested a more than usually dilapidated, second-hand suit which had spent the night in a hedgerow. His voice was like the creaking of a rusty gate. But he spoke with force and fire and with an intellectual clarity few could match. To hear him laying down the law to a minister was an experience not easily forgotten.'[9]

Along the line, Lee had challenged some sacred cows. When at Trade, he was the force behind Peter Thorneycroft's desertion of imperial preference. Given the Tory Party's imperial preferences, this was as defiant an attitude for Lee as it was a risky one for his minister. But still more significant was the choice he made in November 1955 to decouple from the Whitehall wisdom that decreed Bretherton's withdrawal from the Messina process. When the official paper went forward to the politicians, the name of the permanent secretary at the Board of Trade was among those appended to it, but he had in fact dissented, as the files record.[10] Being in a minority of one, he chose not to press his case. While acknowledging that ministers were taking a political decision, he told his colleagues that in his opinion the economic argument for entering the Messina project with a view to joining the Common Market was persuasive.

It was to be some years before Lee saw this opinion bear fruit. But he had made plain that it existed. For the first time, it was heard at a high level. It could be a catalyst, when the time came. It was lying in wait, as it were, for the moment when ministers themselves, and a larger handful of politicians, and a growing segment of the business community, and even a few flexible intellects near the top of the Foreign Office became ready to embrace the recognition that the world had changed.

In fact, it already had. By the time Britain's decision to exclude herself was set in metal in the Treaty of Rome signed by the Messina Six, Suez had knocked aside the main assumptions on which this withholding was based. That wasn't fully perceived in November 1956 when the fiasco occurred. Suez was too profound an event for its implications to be immediately understood, still less gathered into clear enough shape to prompt a change of policy towards Europe. But it was the death-blow for Britain's fading belief in her imperial reach, and should have told the governing class to re-examine their ideas about British independence.

Actually, the link between Suez and Europe emerged as a creative possibility before the disaster occurred. There were those who hoped for a synergy. The war-planning process brought France and Britain close.

Both countries saw their interests at stake when the Egyptian President, Colonel Nasser, seized the Suez Canal. Their leaders were deeply embroiled together in the middle months of 1956. The French Prime Minister of the time, Guy Mollet, a socialist and Anglophile, saw an opportunity, in preparing the conspiracy by which the Canal would be retaken with Israel's assistance, for the more durable involvement of Britain in the European system. He was still interested in readmitting Britain to the Messina process, advanced though that then was. 'There was a real spirit of confidence between the British and French leaders,' said one who witnessed it.[11]

The man who told me this was Mollet's secretary, Emile Noël, later the first secretary-general of the European Commission. Of the many old men I talked to during this inquiry, none had a more energetic memory than Noël. The mental habits of the old, their reliability on points of history, and their interest in reviewing their versions of it, could be a capacious sub-plot of any work that relies at all on oral reminiscence. Old men with an important past, I have learned, cover the gamut of truth between self-vindication and self-knowledge, vagueness and precision. But Noël, even at seventy-three, had the best-stocked recollection of detail of anyone I met. The formal histories seldom, if ever, contradicted it. Noël seemed to have an exact memory of every European Council meeting he ever attended. On the events of 1956, he confirms what was only to be expected. In the four months of meetings that led up to Suez, Selwyn Lloyd, the British Foreign Secretary, Harold Macmillan, by now the Chancellor, and Anthony Eden, Prime Minister, met their French equivalents Pineau, Bourges-Manoury and Mollet many times. 'In the margins of those meetings,' Noël recalled, 'Guy Mollet tried to convince his counterparts to make a move into the European Community, and said that France would make it easier for them. But there was no answer.'[12]

Nor could there have been. The leap of imagination required for such a move had been considered and definitively rejected, as we have seen, a year before. It never occurred to any of the British leaders that the enterprise they were now plotting might reopen the matter. And when it ended in disaster, after a single week's abortive engagement with Nasser, it had driven the French and British perspectives on Europe far apart.

To France, Suez greatly reinforced the case for concluding a treaty of European union. Negotiations were far advanced, but still incomplete. Before Suez, there was a substantial chance that French politics, moved by many similar considerations to the British, would not permit the Economic Community, as it was coming to be called, to be created. After the event, opinion swung round, and saw Europe more as a boost than a threat to French influence. 'The Suez fiasco had generated a new wave of "Europeanism",' writes one analyst, 'and had visibly strengthened the feeling in France that only through European unity could France regain a position of power and independence in the world.'[13] And without, if necessary, the British. It was, after all, the British who called a halt to the Suez operation, under pressure from their American friends. To any Frenchman still inclined to hesitate before sinking the nation's destiny into a construct among neighbours, Suez could only erode his scepticism. So France, after Suez, moved decisively to push her version of a union to the front of the agenda. She got her colonial empire included, and insisted on provisions for agricultural support that did not sell the birthright of French farmers.

Suez thus helped bring the European treaty to a constructive climax. But on Britain the immediate effect was very different. A lesson reveals itself, concerning the durability of British prejudices. For it was indisputably true that the American connection had shown how little it could be worth. The operation ended because Washington declined to help sustain it. What brought Britain to her knees wasn't military but economic weakness. In the run-up to hostilities, the sterling reserves fell by £20 million in September and £30 million in October. After two days of battle round Port Said, Macmillan felt obliged to warn his colleagues that maybe another £100 million had left the British vaults in the first week in November. He begged them to surrender. As the flight from sterling accelerated, national ruin loomed, and the Americans refused all requests for a bail-out. Eisenhower and his advisers decided to let Britain swing impotently in the wind. Yet, despite this lack of comradeship in the country's hour of need, the British leadership reacted to Suez first and above all by seeking to remake the Washington relationship. The Europeans had hoped for a different outcome. From Paris, Gladwyn Jebb, unconsciously prefiguring later alarms about the magnetic attraction of the Pacific Rim to the American mind, wrote: 'Some Frenchmen are comforting themselves with the thought that American policy favouring the Asiatic races will drive the United Kingdom further in the direction of Europe.'[14] But America, not Europe, was still Britain's uncontested priority. Preserving the sterling area, where Commonwealth countries kept their funds, continued to eclipse any thought of European solidarity. Keith Kyle has put it aptly: 'The sterling area gave some lingering substance to the notion that Britain was still a World Power. It was to uphold that notion that Britain was at Suez. One aspect of fading greatness was sacrificed to save another.'[15]

In some fields of policy, this greatness was soon seen to have been compromised fatally. In defence matters, for example, the imperial lion sacrificed her pretensions with extraordinary speed. Less than a year after Suez, the Government set in train a huge military shift by ending conscription, and reducing the British presence east of Suez, which was the border-line of Empire, and even to some extent in Europe. It was a seminal moment, which did further European damage by apparently reneging on the pledges France understood to have been given about Britain's commitment to the Western European Union. Simultaneously, Suez was a watershed for British colonialism. Although decolonization had begun with India in the previous decade, India is where it had stopped. It was no coincidence that it should resume in 1957, after a decade when the Conservative Party's strong colonial prejudices had continued to be just about sustainable. After Suez, resistance to independent nationhood for Nigeria, Tanganyika, Cyprus, Uganda and the rest evaporated. The fight, perhaps the romance, had gone out of the nation. It had been taught no end of a lesson.

What took longer to follow was the quest for an alternative, a new matrix within which to fit Britain's strategic objectives. The Empire was fraying at the edges and softening at the centre. The writing was on the wall for those prepared to read it, and to study with detachment the financial data that underpinned its meaning. A number of important people were beginning to examine it, finally moved by some apprehension at what they could see of both the political and economic future. But they needed a leader who was prepared to grasp the nettle of the past: someone who came from the past and understood it, and gave the reassuring impression of being steeped in its wonderful, heroic qualities, but who seriously suspected its time had come.

*

SUEZ WAS THE END, of course, of Eden. The pressures, of duplicity and failure alike, were too much for his health, which at the best of times was not robust. His successor as Prime Minister had no more honourable a record in the crisis than he did. Of all the ministers around Eden, Harold Macmillan played the most ignominious role, being among the first into the breach and the first to leave it. As Chancellor, he was the man who felt most directly the cold American withdrawal of financial support. But his response, which was to tell the Foreign Secretary, Selwyn Lloyd, that 'in view of the financial and economic pressures, we must stop', was singularly shameless. 'Considering the role he had played so far, his talk of "all or nothing", of "selling Britain's last securities", of "dying in the last ditch",' Keith Kyle writes, 'this was a sensational loss of nerve.'[16] But it was one for which the Conservatives did not punish him.

As was the practice of those days, Macmillan 'emerged' as their chosen leader. Had there been a leadership election, it is possible he wouldn't have done so. The favourite candidate, in the sense of the man most widely expected to win, was Butler, who deputized when Eden fell ill and was seen, especially by the press, as his senior heir apparent. But, when soundings were taken across the party, Macmillan was clearly preferred.

The choice had its European aspect. By contrast with the 1990s, Conservatism in the 1950s did not make 'Europe' the test of a politician's standing. In keeping with the absence of public debate throughout the Messina process, not even the faintest question about their continental attitudes affected the party's assessment of what kind of a Conservative Macmillan, on the one hand, or Butler, on the other, might be. Butler, however, was blackballed by significant numbers of Tory MPs and peers because of his record as a pre-war appeaser: which was one sort of European credential. And, by preferring Macmillan, the party was choosing the man who had already distinguished himself from his rival by desiring at least to send Bretherton to the Spaak committee. Unlike Butler, Macmillan declined to associate himself with statements of incredulity at the notion of Britain being an active partner in the development of 'Europe'.

Insofar as Europe did intrude on this leader's background, it seemed not to be an idea he resisted. Personal attitudes and instinctive attachments always matter in politics, and Macmillan had given plenty of thought to Europe, most of it comradely.

It began a long time before. When Harold Macmillan referred, as he often did, to 'the war' the allusion was usually not to Hitler's conflict but to the First World War, in which he had fought and had seen many friends, the flower of England, die. Throughout Macmillan's life, memories of the Somme appeared regularly in his discourse, and deeply penetrated his attitude to foreign relations. He was an internationalist, as beguiled as Eden by the fascination of foreign affairs, though he spent

Winston Churchill, Strasbourg, 1949: Europe, your Europe.

Ernest Bevin, Foreign Secretary 1945–51: the first Euro-sceptic.

Sir Henry Tizard, Chief Scientific Adviser, Ministry of Defence: the first realist.

Edward Heath MP: smoothly against the grain.

Robert Schuman and Jean Monnet, 1951: beginning with coal and steel.

The Messina Six; from the left, foreign ministers
Johan Beyen (Holland), Gaetano Martino (Italy), Joseph Bech (Luxembourg),
Antoine Pinay (France), Walter Hallstein (Federal Republic of Germany)
and Paul-Henri Spaak (Belgium).

Russell Bretherton, under-secretary, Board of Trade, 1955: the sacrificial agent.

Sir Anthony Eden and R.A. Butler, 1955: these excavations do not concern us.

Harold Macmillan, prime minister, Conservative Party Conference, 1962:
let us face the future – and the past.

President de Gaulle and Macmillan, 1961: old men don't forget.

Macmillan and R. A. Butler: a definite lack of foresight.

De Gaulle, 14 January 1963: what could be more obvious than '*Non*'?

much less time involved with them professionally. One reason Eden removed him from the Foreign Office after barely six months, in 1955, was his dislike of Macmillan's creative independence in the field Eden regarded as his personal domain. Nor was Eden the only Prime Minister who preferred an unthreatening subordinate in the job. Macmillan himself, when the time came, retained there Selwyn Lloyd, an incorrigible second-rater, and then appointed Alec Douglas-Home, shrewd and fearless but, as a disfranchised peer, a man who knew his place.

By pedigree, Macmillan was a Churchillian. Before the Second World War, he echoed the great man's vision of a single continent, with the off-shore island apparently included, brought together for the survival of the species. 'If western civilisation is to survive,' he wrote in 1939, 'we must look forward to an organisation, economic, cultural and perhaps even political, comprising all the countries of Western Europe.' When the war was over, and a version of this dream, minus the island, was being preached from the rostrums and grandstands of continental capitals, Macmillan was again of the company. In the Tory divide over the Council of Europe, he was unambiguously with Churchill, unlike Eden and Butler who were always disdainful.[17] He favoured the European Army, declaring to the Strasbourg Assembly that 'Britain's frontier is not on the Channel; it is not even on the Rhine; it is at least on the Elbe.' As the European Movement developed in the first few years, he consistently supported it.

Unlike Churchill, moreover, Macmillan carried this position into office. At the time of the Schuman Plan, his feelings had contrasted with the routine oppositionism of the party line. His critique of the Attlee Government's refusal to join it rested on a desire, within limits, for it to succeed. When the Tories took over, and Macmillan became Minister of Housing and Local Government, he infuriated more senior colleagues by circulating a disrespectful attack on the conventional wisdom that favoured Britain's aloofness. His line was a mixture of contradictions, of the kind that were still richly present in political argument in the 1990s. He wanted 'to attach Germany permanently to Western Europe'. Yet he also feared 'a German-dominated Continental Community' that might one day side with the Russians. But his driving belief was that Britain should get intimately involved. In March 1952, he wrote privately to Churchill after a Cabinet meeting that had poured cold water on the idea of European unity, flaying the 'continued opposition of the Foreign Office, in big and small things alike', to the whole European movement, and reminding the old man of the inconsistency between what he had said for years after the war and what he was now saying in government. The Foreign Office had produced 'a quite dreadful paper' on Europe, Macmillan wrote. According to his biographer, Alistair Horne, he now came closer to resigning than on any other occasion in his career.[18]

So this was a European. That designation wasn't as definitive in the mid-1950s as it became forty years later. Like every Conservative of the period, Macmillan was also a man of Empire. For the country that found it hard to contemplate the thought of no longer being a big player in the world, Empire was a timeless seduction. As the Foreign Office discarded Europe, Macmillan easily ruminated on alternative visions. A club-land diarist, Jock Colville, wrote of him in May 1952: 'Harold Macmillan said to me at the Turf yesterday that he thought development of the Empire into an economic unit as powerful as the U.S.A. and the U.S.S.R. was the only possibility...'[19] But his sense of both history and geography kept him nagging away at the prime option, which he saw Churchill and Eden neglecting at the country's peril.

Europe, however, wasn't by any means a fixed objective. Macmillan's disagreements with Eden went only so far. The moment of truth, Messina, occurred on his watch as Foreign Secretary, and he didn't grasp its importance. That short span, from April to December 1955, enclosed the whole evolution of British decision-making on Messina and the Spaak committee, and the 'European' at the Foreign Office presided over it with notable indifference. When, for example, the foreign ministers of the Six met to review progress, at Nordwijk in September 1955, Macmillan was invited, but said he was otherwise engaged. 'If they ask me, tell them I'm busy with Cyprus' is how he instructed his staff to deal with the matter.[20] He also swallowed Gladwyn Jebb's prediction that the Spaak operation would get nowhere. 'The French will never go into the "common market" – the German industrialists and economists equally dislike it,' he wrote in his diary, when visiting Jebb in Paris in December. And although it was Macmillan who got Bretherton to Spaak's table, he appears not to have lifted a finger to keep him there.

He was, therefore, a European only of his time and place, which is to say a tormented and indecisive one. He had a more open mind than Butler, but the idea that Britain might join or lead the continental venture as defined by the heirs and allies of Jean Monnet was still beyond the reach of Macmillan's imagination. When Eden moved him, against his will, from the Foreign Office to the Treasury – 'from geography to arithmetic', he mordantly reflected – he became the prime orchestrator of Britain's attempt to outflank if not wreck the great idea, because that rather suddenly became an essential British interest.

For, contrary to so many expert prophecies, the European Idea did move, within months, from fancy to reality. Although not signed until March 1957, the embryonic Treaty of Rome became a hypothesis to reckon with much sooner than that. Driven by Spaak, and led by France and Germany, the continentals were not giving up. Within three months of Bretherton leaving the table, they reached outline agreement on the principles of a common market, thus confronting Britain with a prospect that galvanized the political class out of the vacillating torpor in which their negative prognosis had allowed them to indulge. They now had to act, and Macmillan, sitting in the Treasury, was their agent. He devised a plan, saw it through the corridors of British power, and all the time exhibited a kind of helpless ambivalence, a lurching between the cool and the warm, that revealed him at this stage to be less a disciple of Jean Monnet than a seamless successor to the post-war Winston Churchill.

Plan G, as it was known, was plucked from an alphabetic list of Treasury options, and consisted of a proposal for a European Free Trade Area: all the trade and none of the politics. Although the Six were far advanced, their project had not reached its final shape before Plan G emerged, and it was the British ambition to supplant their fierce and narrow concept with a softer, broader one. The Six would be at the core of the EFTA, but the membership would be wider and there would be no common customs barrier: this would not, in other words, aspire to be a single unit, trading globally, with all the apparatus for negotiation and adjudication that converted it into a semi-political body, but would exist essentially for free trading within its own frontiers. The members would continue to have their separate tariffs against the outside world, thus disturbing none of Britain's historic buying-and-selling links with the Commonwealth. Moreover, EFTA wouldn't include agriculture at all. All the old preferential deals for food would stay. This would be a purely industrial arrangement. It was an entirely different concept from the one the continentals had already expended massive political resources on trying to achieve.

Macmillan saw this as 'European', but also as British, which was only appropriate for the people who regarded themselves as the senior European nation. His troubled mind expressed itself over many months. In February 1956, a hitherto unimaginable spectre was beginning to take shape there. 'I do not like the prospect of a world divided into the

Russian sphere, the American sphere and a united Europe of which we are not a member,' Macmillan wrote to his permanent secretary, Sir Edward Bridges.[21] The evolution of Plan G was propelled alongside the final, painful phases of negotiating the Rome Treaty: an irritant to the continentals, a delusion to the British. In January 1957, Foreign Secretary Lloyd produced a wrecking blueprint for a so-called "Grand Design", to unify all existing institutions in and out of the Six into a "General Assembly for Europe". It did nothing but open people's eyes to Britain's increasingly desperate antagonism to the Six. But in April 1957, by now Prime Minister, Macmillan was even more panicky. 'What I chiefly fear, and what we must at all costs avoid,' he wrote, 'is the Common Market coming into being and the Free Trade Area never following.' This would lead to German domination and 'put us in a very bad position'.[22] By July, with the Treaty signed, the matter had become one of open contest between the ins and the outs. 'We must not be bullied by the activities of the Six,' Macmillan told a colleague. 'We could, if we were driven to it, fight their movement . . . We must take the lead, either in widening their project, or, if they will not co-operate with us, in opposing it.'[23]

Macmillan understood, in short, that 'Europe' was an abiding and central interest to Britain, for which the idea of 'Empire' was not a serious alternative. He might flirt with that around the club fireplace, but he was beginning to concede its unreality. And yet, at the same time, addressing a 'Europe' that was now becoming real was a task which exposed all kinds of hideous difficulties.

On 1 January 1958, 'Europe' finally happened. The European Economic Community of the Six came into being, and the balance of power as between the makers and the supplicants dramatically shifted. Their differences became more prominent than the interest in compromise between them. Britain, a free-trading nation with a low-tariff tradition sustained by its worldwide Commonwealth, faced a Europe largely shaped by France, a protectionist nation, jealous of Britain, determined to protect the agriculture Britain wanted to leave out. After the *fait accompli*, the drive was accelerated for a Free Trade Association, a Europe of the Seventeen, as it was conceived, but it was doomed by a series of inherent conflicts of national interest. That would probably have been so even if General de Gaulle had not been summoned to power in France following the fall of the Fourth Republic in May 1958. As it was, late that year, de Gaulle brought negotiations to an abrupt and final close.

This, de Gaulle's first crucial intervention, recalls, incidentally, how copious are the accidents of history, how decisive the comings and goings of personalities who might have shaped the story differently. The General spent the formative years, when 'Europe' was being put together, distanced in his village of Colombey-les-Deux Eglises, from where he opposed the sacrifices of national sovereignty it entailed. Had he come to power mere months before he did, he might have been able to prevent French accession to the Treaty of Rome. But when he did attain the presidency, he was clear and ruthless in advancing the French interest in a project it was too late to change. Similar fortuitous chances, with large results for the Europe project, can be readily picked out in the careers of both Edward Heath and Margaret Thatcher: in the whole later history of British Conservatism, in fact. Like so much else, the shaping of post-war Europe came about through a delicate interlacing of the strands of geo-politics, on the one hand, and half-chance arrivals and departures on the other.

Macmillan's first reaction to de Gaulle's return was to make a radical proposal. The two men went back a long way. During the war, Macmillan had spent time along with de Gaulle in Algiers, where he was sometimes known as "Viceroy of the Mediterranean", and had been embroiled with the Free French forces that de Gaulle was orchestrating from exile in London. Macmillan, indeed, had been responsible on more than one occasion for saving de Gaulle's political life, when it was threatened with termination by Roosevelt and Churchill. So these two leaders, now thrown together at the peak of their careers, were steeped in the history of the century and, if international affairs had anything to do with sentiment, the one was owed a debt of gratitude by the other. Macmillan thought he saw his chance to put Anglo-French relations back on a proper course when he visited Paris soon after the General was installed there. De Gaulle's memoirs recount an embarrassing scene. Macmillan, he writes, suddenly 'declared to me with great feeling: "The Common Market is the Continental System all over again. Britain cannot accept it. I beg you to give it up. Otherwise we shall be embarking on a war which will doubtless be economic at first but which runs the risk of gradually spreading into other fields!" '[24]

This became a familiar British plaint, amounting almost to a threat. The greater union of Europe, designed to avoid war, contained within it, so they claimed, the seeds of war itself. An almost identical analysis was being proposed forty years later by British opponents of the greater European Union, who saw in the single currency the likely source not of unity but of quite possibly bloody division. It was an unsubtle way of attacking an enterprise which, for all kinds of other reasons, Britain did not desire to see to go ahead. De Gaulle in 1958, like Helmut Kohl in 1997, rejected the destructive invitation.

And, quite soon, Macmillan had no alternative but to withdraw his suggestion. An EFTA of Seven came into being: Austria, Denmark, Norway, Portugal, Sweden and Switzerland, alongside the prime economy among them, Britain. It was a trading organization, supposedly defending these countries against the might of the Six. But there was no 'permanent and comprehensive settlement' of the kind Britain had been seeking. Though the Germans had been receptive, de Gaulle had stopped it. The merger of interests having failed, Macmillan was obliged to embrace the reality which, in June 1958, he was still hoping to suffocate, and of which he said, at a small meeting of colleagues not long afterwards, that 'there were three elements who wanted supra-nationalism and who were playing no small part on the Commission ... the Jews, the Planners and the old cosmopolitan élite'.[25]

In December 1959, he put the awful truth into words, in a message to his Foreign Secretary. 'For the first time since the Napoleonic era,' he wrote, 'the major continental powers are united in a positive economic grouping, with considerable political aspects, which, though not specifically directed against the United Kingdom, may have the effect of excluding us both from European markets and from consultation in European policy.' The Common Market, it had to be admitted, was here to stay 'at least for the foreseeable future'. Trying to disrupt it would upset the Americans, play into the hands of the Russians and 'unite against us all the Europeans who have felt humiliated during the past decade by the weakness of Europe'.

The question had at last apparently defined itself. It was, Macmillan wrote, 'how to live with the Common Market economically, and turn its political effects into channels harmless to us'.

*

THE START WAS TENTATIVE. Actual membership was still not easily imaginable. But economic realism began to exert a mighty power. It was economics that effected the beginning of conversion. The argument economics made coexisted with political attitudes that were still almost completely hostile to its logic: that were, indeed, more often by-passed than addressed. The political vision, the dream, the ideal, the grand shining project, of European union were but spectral notions, discernible only by a privileged few Englishmen, and they always have been. From the start, a divide set into the British mind between economic necessity and political resistance which continued as a live and present force, in different degrees at different times, for the rest of the century.

The change of perceptions in this great matter began with the people whose concern with politics was smallest: officials, not politicians. Two months after de Gaulle closed down the prospect of an EFTA–EEC union, a despatch to London from the embassy in Bonn made the kind of points from which no sentient politician, and certainly not Harold Macmillan, could avert his gaze.

James Marjoribanks, minister (economics) at the embassy, wrote as follows. Unless the Free Trade Area, covering a population of 90 million, was able to reach a practical understanding with the Economic Community, an industrialized and rapidly growing bloc of 160 million, Britain faced 'disaster'. Our exports would fall, our economic power diminish. 'Our position would be changed from the biggest market, and the second largest exporter of manufactured goods to Europe, to a member of what would be very much a second eleven scattered round the fringe of an increasingly powerful and rapidly growing United States of Europe.' We were, added Marjoribanks, living under a misapprehension if we believed the Six were prepared to make a lot of concessions to let us into their industrial market while permitting our agriculture, and our Commonwealth food, freedom from their rules. 'I think it is vitally important for us all to rid ourselves of the feeling that the Six cannot do without us . . . The consequences for them of the United Kingdom being excluded are far less than the consequences for the United Kingdom of being shut out of Europe.'

This was an early voice. Like others, it hastened to reassure the audience that nothing so impractical as British *membership* of the Common Market was being proposed. But it was part of a gathering chorus of reassessment that began to be heard that year and next. In Paris, the false prophet Jebb, for one, announced his conversion from disdain to optimism. 'I believe that we rather tend to exaggerate the horror of our one day actually joining the Common Market,' he wrote to Macmillan in May 1960. 'For instance, if we ever did, we should be no more committed to the prospect of an actual federation than the government of General de Gaulle, that celebrated nationalist.'[26]

More influential than these comments from the outposts was a voice from the heart of government, the Treasury. We rediscover the rasping tones of Sir Frank Lee. By 1960, the discreet opponent of Bretherton's removal from the negotiations had become a positive exponent of the case for the closest possible association of the Seven with the Six: so close, in fact, that it was hardly distinguishable from membership itself.

Lee was interested in economic realities, and during the summer of 1960 did his best to acquaint a reluctant Cabinet with them. On 23 May, he described, to a special sub-committee Macmillan had established, what was now going on. Officials were working, in effect, on a scheme under which EFTA (for which, in the circumstances, one could read 'Britain') would accept most of the conditions the Six insisted on. They were looking at a common external tariff with modestly special treatment for the Commonwealth: at concessions to the European model for agriculture and horticulture: at harmonized social charges: at majority decisions on trade, rather than a national veto.

A few days later, the forceful official delivered the paper he had masterminded, of which his report to the sub-committee was merely a taste. This made an emphatic case that membership of the Seven was not enough: 'It cannot be compatible with either our political or our economic interests to let the situation drift on indefinitely on the basis of a divided Europe, with the United Kingdom linked to the weaker group.' A wider grouping, said Lee, was inescapable, and an Atlantic Free Trade Area – that distracting jade so often summoned up by critics of European integration – was 'not a practicable objective'. Nor was the Commonwealth a realistic alternative. The Commonwealth, Lee noted, depended essentially on the economic well-being of Britain and the strength of sterling. If Britain was shut out of growing European markets, the Commonwealth 'is not likely to flourish'.[27]

The paper despatched any number of illusions. Since the Common Market was already a success, if we wanted a deal we must be 'prepared to go much further than we have hitherto contemplated'. We must 'put out of our minds' the idea that we could 'secure our objective on the cheap'. Industrial free trade, without a price that recognized the political and economic strength of continental farmers, was simply out of the question. Realism demanded 'difficult and unpalatable decisions', including the contemplation of some surrender of sovereignty.

Lee conjured up a word for what all this meant. It came fresh out of the lexicon of a Whitehall that was sensitive to the implications of what the Treasury was proposing. The idea of *membership*, of course, still had to be eschewed. So crude a proposition would have fallen victim to the fit of vapours it would instantly have induced among the politicians. But, equally, Lee wished to make it plain that the time was past for a status so unreal as mere association. The concept he therefore coined may not have had much ring to it, but it perfectly caught the mood of tentative boldness, of fantastically daring half-heartedness, that now seemed to be called for. Britain and the Seven, he suggested, should seek 'near-identification' with the Common Market.

Macmillan received this proposition with considerable pain. It was not what he wanted to hear. On the other hand, he wasn't very clear what he did want to hear. The record of the Prime Minister's response, in discussion of the Lee memorandum on 27 May, suggests a man at war with himself. Could there not be some other solution, he is saying? 'Was it necessary for the United Kingdom to give up all hope, even as a long term objective, of an industrial free trade area?' he asked. Trying to secure a large single market is all very well, but consider what Britain would have to give up: control over tariffs, the cohesion of the Commonwealth, her own kind of agricultural support, some of her sovereignty and all the rest of it.

Something else, however, emerges from these ministerial deliberations. By the end of the discussion, which the minutes record with unusual fullness, it is articulated by Macmillan himself. Near-identification was fraught with problems. It would require big changes. So big, in fact, that perhaps it might make more sense 'to go into Europe fully', which might bring scarcely larger problems but carried more possibilities. The two policies, the Prime Minister concluded, were 'so similar that one might lead to the other, and if we were prepared to accept near-identification it might be preferable to contemplate full membership'. The time had possibly come to end 'our traditional policy of remaining aloof from Europe'. Further study was therefore set in train, under Frank Lee's direction.

In the evolution of Macmillan's attitude, one catches the anguished reluctance of the nation he led. Part of him, as we have seen, knew that a sundering from Europe would be fatal. As a student of history, he was as sensitive to the continental interests of his country as to its global reach, and he knew the latter was in retreat. Four months before, he had gone to Cape Town and given the most famous speech he ever made, on the winds of change that were blowing through once imperial Africa. He had always resisted both the low politics and the inflated grandeur – the farmers and the fantasists – that treated opposition to a European venture as axiomatic. And yet even now, with the writing etched ever more insistently on the wall, he was slow to move. The duty of leadership came upon him uncomfortably. It wasn't, yet, the political risks that deterred him, but something deeper. Although the Tory Party would have to be faced in due course, that wasn't the immediate problem What still gripped Macmillan were the tectonic plates of history, no slight matter to shift.

History, however, bore down on him at this moment in another way as well. For a man of private moods, who felt the power of public events moving in his bones, May 1960 had been a bad month. On the 16th, a great-power summit meeting in Paris, which he had done much to promote, ended in futile and dangerous disarray, when Nikita Khrushchev took the downing of an American U2 spy plane over the Soviet Union as the pretext to abandon all progress towards international *détente*. 'It is impossible to describe this day,' Macmillan wrote in his diary, 'I am too tired.' In his memoirs, he called the day 'one of the most agonising as well as exhausting which I have ever been through except, perhaps, in battle'. The fiasco produced in him a 'disappointment amounting almost to despair – so much attempted, so little achieved'. Reflecting in old age, he termed it 'the most tragic moment in my life'.

This trauma occurred a week before the EEC–EFTA debate in Cabinet committee started to get serious. Nothing so coarse as a direct connection between the collapse of the Paris summit and the mounting of an application to join the Common Market can be inferred. But the bleakness it engendered affected the mood. Thrown into the already crumbling certainties about Britain's role in the world, it made its contribution, not least to Macmillan's deepening gloom. His diary entries continued to sweep around the forces of history with a broad, puzzled brush. 'Shall we be caught between a hostile (or at least less and less friendly) America,' he wrote in July, 'and a boastful, powerful "Empire of Charlemagne" – now under French but later bound to come under German control? Is this the real reason for "joining" the Common Market (if we are acceptable) and for abandoning a) the Seven, b) British agriculture, c) the Commonwealth? It's a grim choice.'

Very, very slowly, however, the choice was beginning to disclose itself. Lee's next paper was more pressing.[28] He had proposed to Macmillan that it should be produced in the form of answers to questions: Will the Six develop into a powerful unit? How would Britain's influence from outside compare with her influence from inside? To what extent would entry put Commonwealth preference at risk? And so forth. There were twenty-three such questions, framed by Macmillan under Lee's advice and answered by a team of officials under Lee's control. The answers were getting less ambiguous, though they still clung respectfully to old household gods, opining, for example, that if the Commonwealth connection were weakened 'our standing in the world would suffer'. But the analysis of an entry-scenario now emphasized the advantages slightly more than the problems, in language whose sense of the positive sometimes looks quite startling four decades later. To concede, as it did, that membership of a successful EEC 'might change our concept of what were vital UK interests' revealed a largeness of spirit and intellect that had been entirely banished by the 1980s. Talking about 'our participation in majority voting in the Council of Ministers' as a guarantee rather than a destroyer of British influence was not something widely heard thirty years later. The full Cabinet, which was having its first discussion of the subject, received the Lee questionnaire with the usual agonizings, but also with a certain open-minded equanimity. Ministers' conclusions talked about the unripeness of time but also the need for choice, about fear of federalism but also about confidence in 'a loose confederal arrangement', about loss but also gain. Momentum for change was discernible. The plates were beginning to rumble.

We should note again how this had come about. It was without benefit of the usual ministerial initiative. Although Macmillan blessed it, this was an officials' operation. What happened on 13 July 1960 was a Cabinet decision that launched the process that concluded with Britain's application to join the Common Market, yet no ministerial paper preceded it. According to Roy Denman, for many years a senior official dealing with international trade problems, never before had a major new direction in foreign policy been opened on the basis merely of an official submission. And yet that was profoundly symbolic. It was consistent with the history. Both the Schuman Plan and Messina had been approached under much the same rubric of political detachment. It reflected a state of mind. In 1960, as in 1950, there was a sense in which the politicians were so paralysed by the awesome nature of necessary decisions that they preferred to delegate rather than lead. None was prepared to commit himself full-bloodedly to a single course of action. It was left to others to map the ground. And the officials, who had obliged in one direction in the earlier phase, now saw their duty as the opposite.

Proceeding crabwise, however, Macmillan himself did now get a little more political. He didn't commit himself to applying for entry, but began to prepare the ground for what such an epic decision would entail. He knew he would get nowhere unless he had the right people in place, and a Cabinet reshuffle on 27 July put them there. Nowhere, at the time, was it noticed that this was a 'European' reshuffle, although Edward Heath was appointed Lord Privy Seal, inside the Foreign Office, with responsibilities for what was thereby admitted publicly to be the major issue of relations with the Common Market. Christopher Soames and Duncan Sandys, two champions with a pedigree going back to Churchill's long march round Zurich, Strasbourg and the other shrines, were put in charge of the likely enemy camps of Agriculture and Commonwealth Relations.

Not that this was the signal for anything precipitate. What happened over the next few months was a continuation of the old mud-wrestling, as Macmillan's Cabinet grappled with its own anxieties, on the one hand, and with the continentals, above all France, on the other. Much time and argument had to pass before the leader finally forced himself to accept the unpleasant conclusion his country had spent a decade resisting.

What the British still wanted was a trading arrangement. Macmillan's own contributions between July 1960 and July 1961 are dominated by a kind of elegiac longing for the unattainable. 'If it were impossible to obtain true intimacy in the Councils of the Six without serious disruption of our relations, both economic and political, with the Commonwealth then we are better off outside . . .', he wrote in a minute on the Lee questionnaire. In August 1960, he met the German Chancellor, Adenauer, from whom he drew some apparent comfort that such painless involvement might be available. Adenauer suggested a process that examined the strictly economic difficulties, with a view to economic association, to be followed by unspecified moves towards an 'acceptable political relationship with the Six'. So the economics, in this phase, were the focus of attention. The Commonwealth bulked very large. There are reams of papers from the Treasury and the Board of Trade exploring different outcomes for tropical foodstuffs and temperate foodstuffs, woodpulp and aluminium, Rhodesian tobacco and New Zealand butter. Through the autumn, it is the Commonwealth that starts being squared, or not, as the case may be. With enough derogations and special concessions, the match might be made. London persists in the belief that 'the economic advantages of full membership of the European Economic Community' could be obtained by an association 'with no manifest political content'. The Germans, along with the Benelux countries and the Italians, were sufficiently eager for Britain's involvement to give some grounds for belief, to those with misty eyes, that she might indeed be able to have it both ways.

This was, however, a fantasy, and the people who made that clearest were the French. The old mistrust expressed itself in a new and obvious realism. Britain could not be permitted special treatment for her Commonwealth preferences, nor could she expect to sustain the cheap food policy that went with them. Through the winter of 1960–1, Ted Heath, under Macmillan's direction, pursued the fantasy down many avenues. France was the clearest of the Six in rejecting it, during numerous talks that took place at many different levels from de Gaulle downwards. The leading French official on the case, Olivier Wormser, told Heath that there could be no *modus vivendi* between 'the two regional economic systems – the Commonwealth and the EEC'. There were, of course, other French demons at work, springing out of a Gaullist view of destiny and history and the like. But hard practicalities, rooted in measurable money and countable votes, were France's fixed preoccupation. As late as May 1961, nevertheless, Macmillan was still telling the Commons that there was no question of entering the EEC without giving both the farmers and the Commonwealth what they wanted.

An interesting aspect of the 1961 deliberations is the increasing dominance they gave to these two issues, food and Empire. Time and again, as the pace of ministerial meetings increases, we hear Macmillan reciting his anxieties about Commonwealth reactions to any change in the relationship. The farmers, for their part, had R. A. Butler, now Home Secretary, on their side. The old sceptic had not changed his mind. At a Cabinet meeting in April he was talking as he had always talked, about the 'insuperable difficulties' of joining the Common Market, and the 'very grave political difficulties' of antagonizing British agriculture. This was Butler's song. Years later, as a rather late entrant to the ranks of politicians who felt obliged to concede that they had once got 'Europe' wrong, he tried to explain himself. He had taken his line, he said, because he had always had an agricultural seat. He knew the British farmer. But, he confessed, 'I now think I ought to have been more far-sighted.' He had an excuse, he ventured, in the fact that there had been no pressure to think differently. 'So it was not, so to speak, my fault. But I think that, being a prominent citizen and having a brain, I ought to have looked further ahead.'[29]

What plays rather slight part in the discussion is the matter of national sovereignty. It is present, and yet not present. It underlies, inevitably, the feelings that have made the British so resistant to throwing in their lot with countries that come from the same continent but from what has often seemed a different world. Yet the appearance of this consideration, which had been decisive at the time of the Schuman Plan and resumed a venomous place in the argument forty years later, is in 1961 no more than episodic. A strange combination of forces seems to be at work. On the one hand, sovereignty is just a far less urgent pressure than the baying of farmers and the affronted roars of Robert Menzies (Australia), John Diefenbaker (Canada) and other guardians of the white imperial inheritance. Diminished national sovereignty did not press itself as a real and present danger, at a time when in any case neither the institutions nor the ambitions of the Common Market were fully formed, and de Gaulle was busy frustrating their development. On the other hand, its power to get the project off on the wrong foot was great. It lurked, as something that might better not be mentioned. Looked at in a certain way, it might be too hot to handle.

Macmillan was not ignorant of the size of it. In November 1960, he caused Heath to seek the opinion of the Cabinet's leading lawyer, Viscount Kilmuir, the Lord Chancellor. For this was essentially a legal matter. Kilmuir, a veteran of Strasbourg, a post-war Macmillanite and Churchillite, was a European. But he did not pull his punches. His reply to Heath laid out each of the major constitutional aspects of 'Europe' that have since been treated, by the Euro-sceptic faction, as catastrophic encroachments of which the British knew nothing at the time.

Kilmuir was clinically clear.[30] To sign the Treaty of Rome would be to legislate for a loss of national sovereignty in three respects. First, Parliament would surrender some of its functions to a Council of Ministers which could, by majority vote, make regulations that became the law of the land. Second, the Crown's treaty-making power would in part be transferred to an international organization. Third, British courts would sacrifice some of their independence by becoming subordinate in some respects to the European Court of Justice. These were, he said, serious matters. 'It will not be easy to persuade Parliament or the public to accept them.' There would be objections. But, Kilmuir urged, they should be 'brought out into the open now', because otherwise 'those who are opposed to the whole idea of joining the Community will certainly seize on them with more damaging effect later on'. A prophetic warning, as to which, after many years of relatively acquiescent silence, there grew up some of the most bitter arguments in the whole of this history.

The subject, however, featured little in the April Cabinet meeting. The voices were heard, but their doubts were mainly about other matters. Macmillan placed the matter in the Cold War context, indulging his usual gloom about Britain being squeezed between larger powers and groups. He had begun the year by circulating to his colleagues some apocalyptic ruminations about the state of the world, which concluded, among other things, that the rise of Soviet blackmail and Asian neutralism might well indicate that 'the long predominance of European culture, civilisation, wealth and power may be drawing to a close'.[31] It was against this take that he looked on the Common Market. The Cabinet went round the old, old cycle of pros and cons, except that this time the bias was different, the balance of least-worst options weighted grudgingly towards the positive more than the negative. The future of British influence was more copiously cited, alongside the forecast that, when Adenauer and de Gaulle were gone, Britain's task might be to save Europe from itself. Grandiosity died hard.

It was as if the Cabinet, preparing to face the economic necessity of membership, needed to pump up its belief that it would be negotiating from strength not weakness. At another meeting, on 4 July, it talked about the prize of a large expanding market for Britain's goods, and about the danger of industrial decline if she stayed outside any longer. But there was political consolation for national pride. It was expressed in a sentence that showed how slender was the appreciation of what had been happening during the British absence. 'It tended to be overlooked', ministers agreed, 'that if we entered we might be the most powerful member, and be able to exercise a strong and sometimes a decisive influence upon [the Community's] policies.' Macmillan himself put this in the vernacular, with words which showed that British thinking had made no decisive break with its post-war pedigree. Challenged one night on the dance-floor about the rumours that Britain wanted to join the Common Market, he replied, holding his partner tight, 'Well, my dear, don't worry, we shall embrace them *destructively*.'[32]

This unrealism was part of a pattern, induced by the visceral uncertainties that attended Macmillan's entire approach to Europe. There was much whistling in the wind. France's repeated insistence, for example, that neither the Commonwealth nor agriculture would attract any more than the most minor concessions if Britain did apply was simply, it would seem, buried in the sands of disbelief. The British were angling, in effect, to change the Rome Treaty, and M. Wormser told them it was impossible. Reginald Maudling, the most Euro-sceptic

Cabinet minister, drew from this the conclusion that it was 'pointless talking about any negotiations with them', and criticized a strategy that depended on 'trying to entice an unwilling France to the conference table by successive concessions on our side'. But Maudling was the only minister in the inner group, as a decision neared, to oppose making an application for entry. Macmillan and Heath were determined to press on – but in the most defensive spirit. The Cabinet decision to make the application, taken at meetings in the last week of July, was as niggardly as it could be: not a decision to join, but a decision to establish whether satisfactory terms for joining could be negotiated – after which Britain might or might not decide to accept them.

When, after a good lunch, Macmillan went to the House on 31 July to announce this, he was, he says in his diary, nervous. This was not a man about to announce a glorious new departure for the British nation. The leader could hardly fail to be affected by the moroseness of the Cabinet debates, which seemed to revert, as the moment approached, to the old, neurotic negativism. He had to strike a 'delicate balance', he noted to himself, between giving the impression that Britain had decided to accept membership whatever the terms and 'suggesting to members of the Community that we had no real will to join'. He was sensitive, also, to the fact that none of this was mentioned in the 1959 election manifesto. Above all, he was caught by a quite insidious contradiction.

It is obvious that his own motive for engineering the Conservative Government's change of heart was political. His grand disquisitions on the state of the world meant something. He saw European civilization under threat, and Britain's place within it in danger of being marginalized. He had received telling signals from the new American President, John F. Kennedy, of Washington's undeviating commitment to European integration, and diminishing sympathy in that quarter for British hesitation. Americans never did have much time for the imperial so-called Commonwealth. The economic danger posed by a strong Six mattered a lot, but Macmillan placed this first and foremost in a geo-political context. Safeguarding British power was what, in Macmillan's mind, it was all about: a large, resonant purpose.

But he did not have the nerve to present it in that way. His opening statement was fuller of negatives than positives, of doubt than exhilaration. He emphasized all 'the most delicate and difficult matters' that had to be negotiated, and the many consultations, even permissions, that would be sought thereafter. After the opening announcement, eight months passed before Macmillan made another speech of any significance on the subject. Nowhere did he allow his public discourse to reflect what seemed to be his private feelings, for, if he had, he would have conceded that his geo-political apprehensions about Britain's future in the world might need to be met by something more profound than a commercial deal – which is how it suited him, for the most part, to represent the Common Market negotiations. No sooner had he led the Cabinet to take the plunge than he did almost everything to pretend, to the world outside, that the water was tepid and its depths were shallow.

Thus the political formula was established which has laid its hand on the British approach to Europe ever since this first effort was undertaken. It could sit aptly as an epitaph. It dictated the way every subsequent leader presented every move towards Europe. It speaks loud and clear from the record of Harold Wilson, of Margaret Thatcher, of John Major, and even to some extent of Edward Heath. It was, in essence, a lie. It said, on the one hand, that this move, whatever it was, was absolutely essential for the British national interest. But at the same time, it asserted, nothing whatever would change in the British way of life and government.

In Macmillan's version of his case, for example, the sovereignty issue barely featured. He gave no prominence to the contents of Kilmuir's letter to Heath. His entire tone was weary, pessimistic and above all, on this central point, silently evasive. The implications for Parliament were not mentioned, nor were those for the legal system. He told the Commons on 2 August that 'this problem of sovereignty . . . is, in the end, perhaps a matter of degree', and he addressed only the grandest, most extreme hypothesis: that the EEC might develop into some kind of federation. Naturally, he resisted that, and spoke for 'a confederation, a commonwealth if Hon. Members would like to call it that', as the 'only practical concept'. There is no reason to doubt that he meant it. It was just that he preferred not to think through, and certainly not to pronounce upon, the fact that this was, in two senses, primarily a political venture. It had a political object, to make Britain part of 'Europe'. And it had a huge political result: to reduce the independence of both Parliament and the courts.

This minimalism, it was often said, was a negotiating tactic. The most authoritative history of the time endorses the claim by ministers that, if they became missionaries for Common Market membership, the continentals would harden their terms.[33] In fact, their pinched, apologetic stance had the opposite effect. In the absence of a lead, British public opinion drifted from wary approval to a level of scepticism that was quite unhelpful. Support for the policy peaked in December 1961 at 53 per cent, but by May 1962 Gallup showed it had fallen to 47 per cent (with 32 per cent undecided), dropping to 36 per cent a month later. There were many causes for the failure of the negotiation, but it was certainly not helped by the inflexibility imposed upon the British position by a public opinion which nobody had prepared, still less won over, for a visionary leap into the Common Market.

Besides, the ambivalence was not a tactic. It registered the state of the heart of Harold Macmillan.

*

THE NEGOTIATIONS were always going to be difficult. Here was a project, in existence for less than four years, still forming itself, not ready for the easy accession of a country that had variously spurned and tried to spoil it. It hadn't yet shaped the modalities of its system of agricultural support, a vital matter for its largest members. It was in the middle of discussions about the kind of political union it might now embrace, on top of the economic community. It was, moreover, already coming to be disproportionately influenced by France, the member state with most to lose from British entry, and therefore always likely to be the most sceptical. This was itself a turnaround, poignant proof of the penalties of delay. Was it not France that had, at the time of Messina, most desired Britain to join in, and had even at times made Britain's entry a condition of her own? Now the balance was entirely different. France had got the Treaty of Rome written to suit her more than any other member, and in so doing, Miriam Camps wrote, 'had exploited to the full the advantages of negotiating from weakness, an art the British seem not to have mastered'.[34] Now under de Gaulle, who paraded French nationalism on a continental plane, she negotiated from strength.

The state of supplicancy was central to this British weakness. For all the hauteur that seemed to be implied by Macmillan's posture – that she was negotiating not for membership, but to discover whether satisfactory terms might be available should she graciously decide to accept them – Britain was essentially the beggar. And that wasn't the only problem. The British leader was also faced with several competing audiences. The Commonwealth, the farmers, the Tory Party, the public at large all required reassurance and even (if he were bold) visionary encourage- ment. The European Community, on the other hand, needed to be told that Britain would be a serious European but also to be alarmed by the possibility that she might not become one. Strategically, Macmillan had to show he was serious, to negotiate in credible good faith, and to rally maximum support for this truly historic enterprise. But his perception of tactics required of him an absence of zeal, a dignified coolness, and the assertion that 'Europe' might never be more than one among the several spheres of British interest.

A man of subtlety as well as history, Macmillan did his best to straddle these competing requirements. He undoubtedly wanted the negotiation to lead to British entry; its failure brought an end, in effect, to his political career. He was very well aware, none better, of the strategic reverberations of what he was attempting. But, looking overall at his performance, one can't help concluding that, in this war for the British soul, caution triumphed over boldness, tactics over strategy. Macmillan knew that accession could be achieved only by the sacrifice of Tory shibboleths, yet this perception was one he shrank from fully addressing.

Once the decision to negotiate had been taken, the British put their best feet forward, in the form of a team whose personal calibre nobody on either side ever doubted. They were the cream of the talent available in Whitehall, under the leadership of a politician, Edward Heath, who was close to Macmillan and whose zeal for the cause of European union had been apparent from the moment of his maiden speech in the Commons urging British participation in the Schuman Plan. Between autumn 1961 and January 1963, a detailed negotiation unfolded. Under Heath's direction, the intricacies of farm support, of Commonwealth imports of every kind from New Zealand butter and Indian tea to aluminium and woodpulp and lead and zinc, of the arrangements that needed to be made for other EFTA countries, of tariff quotas and non-tariff barriers and preferential entry and 'comparable outlets' for this or that commodity, were carried, in some cases, towards points of laborious agreement. Mercifully, the nooks and crannies of all this need not be investigated here. A shrewd and lengthy account of the negotiations was published, with a speed that did not compromise its thoroughness, within a year of the breakdown. Miriam Camps's excellent book has since been supplemented by any number of monographs and papers, as well as biographical studies, drawing on the cornucopia of official documents that began to be released in the early 1990s.

There were oddities and difficulties about the way the British went about this great historic venture. Below Heath, the leadership of the official team was handed to Sir Pierson Dixon, who succeeded in insisting that he would accept the task only if he was allowed to retain his other job as British ambassador in Paris. Heath complied, and the British delegation felt broken-backed as a result. Even though Macmillan wrote in his diary that Dixon 'has the most subtle mind in Whitehall', the choice seemed to confirm the half-heartedness which the confusing mode of the British application already implied. Moreover, it was arguable that the negotiation was allowed to get quite excessively bogged down in detail – a natural consequence, perhaps, of the intense reluctance of the British mind to look at the matter on the grand scale rather than as another complicated trade deal.

But the larger story is so well known that it has acquired the status of folklore. Virtually all accounts agree on the shape of it: the negotiation began in good faith, it was carried on toughly but fairly by Heath's team, they enlisted the support of the Five, they even got pretty far down the road with the French: after laborious if over-extended discussions a complete deal was close to being on the cards, it required only a couple more long sessions – until the whole endeavour was wrecked, on 14 January 1963, by the iron whim of General de Gaulle, President of France, killing off any further talks by exercising his veto on the very principle of British membership of the Common Market.

This familiar account is not false. De Gaulle did stop the whole process in its tracks, against the wishes of all five of the partner states. It was a brutal display of the deformities for which he was best known: unapologetic grandeur, the pursuit of the French interest, the association of the French interest completely with himself. But the story begs some questions. It exonerates Macmillan from any blame for this outcome, and at the time that was probably the only conclusion a reasonable observer could reach. Given what happened later, however, it is less easy to sustain. Whereas, in his own time, Macmillan seemed to be the statesmanlike victim of a malign and unreasonable opponent, subsequent events suggest that his own analysis was fundamentally at fault.

Hindsight, it may be replied, is a fine thing. But, on this question, the judgement of hindsight should at least be exposed, even if the verdict allows a plea in mitigation. And hindsight homes in on a simple fact. The only future for Britain, it soon turned out, was the one Macmillan sought to bring about. His problem was that he did not try hard enough to achieve it. Even as he plunged towards the future, he was besotted and ensnared by the past.

De Gaulle was certainly a bloody-minded antagonist, and there is no better vantage-point from which to watch the unfolding of his bloodiness than the post closest to it, the British embassy in Paris. After the veto, Pierson Dixon, from his double-duty perspective as ambassador and negotiator, wrote a blow-by-blow account that focused with bitter bemusement on the puzzle of the General.[35] Dixon's subtleties of interpretation prove to be well suited to the deviousness, the apparent contradictions, the indecipherable layers of meaning that lay behind a style that was well epitomized by another British diplomat, Sir Evelyn Shuckburgh. De Gaulle, Shuckburgh once wrote, 'does not exactly "conceal" his intentions; he mystifies his adversaries so that they do not quite believe what they suspect to be his motives'.

The mystery, here, was whether the General really did, or really did not, desire Britain to be admitted to 'Europe'. The ambiguity began at the beginning. When Macmillan visited him in January 1961, to sound the waters, de Gaulle was both positive and negative. Dixon reports him saying that he wanted Anglo-French relations to be 'very close', that he had no desire to 'upset' the United Kingdom, and that he certainly didn't envisage the Common Market always being limited to its present Six members, but also that the UK's 'island position and Commonwealth naturally made her look outwards across the oceans', and that he 'wondered how long it would be possible for the United Kingdom to pursue both a European and an American policy simultaneously'.

This set the style for two years of fencing. It had to be remembered, of course, that de Gaulle was involved in a great deal else besides the European Community, principally Algeria, from which he was in the midst of attempting to extricate France for ever. But when told in late July of Britain's intention to apply, he expressed, says Dixon, 'no pleasure at the news, in contrast to the other Heads of Government who received similar messages'. 'He looked distinctly vexed as he read the Prime Minister's letter.' And when, in November, he came at his own sugges-tion to Macmillan's country house, Birch Grove, he began by being no happier. As Macmillan pleaded the case, based, in this version, on the political need to unite Europe in face of the Soviet menace, his interlocu-tor agreed – but also said 'he had difficulty in seeing how the United Kingdom would fit into this beginning of Europe'. He was bothered by all the historical baggage. 'He admitted that the British were Europeans in our own special way and said that he and the French wanted the British in Europe. But the French did not want the British to bring their great escort in with them. India and African countries had no part in Europe.' Opaqueness, however, ruled. It was, indeed, part of the dis-course of both these men, though it was the British who were constantly the more mystified. For example, the General also said that 'Europe had everything to gain from letting serious-minded people like the British in. British entry was certainly in the common interest; it would hold Europe together and it would add enormously to its influence in the world.'

That was perhaps the high point of Britain's reading of de Gaulle. Never again did his loftiness appear to be directed in Britain's favour. Actually, his driving motives were always pretty familiar. He did not like the Common Market. When Britain applied, he was in the middle of trying to impose on it a form of political union which would in fact have deconstructed it, supplanting its community institutions with mere inter-governmentalism. But, if the Community survived, he wanted France to dominate it, and feared the British would threaten this. A metaphor gained wide currency, both in secret papers and in newspaper cartoons: 'There cannot be two cocks on the dung-hill.' For most of 1962, de Gaulle was making ever clearer who would rule the farm-yard.

On 16 May, the Paris embassy gave it as their considered opinion, in a despatch to the Foreign Secretary, that the General wanted the negotiations to fail. This was signed by Dixon himself, though drafted by a young man, Michael Butler, another of the Euro-diplomats from the Palliser cohort who subsequently trod every step up the ladder in support of a policy they passionately believed in. (In 1997, Sir Michael, whose last FO job was as British ambassador to the European Communities, 1979–85, showed the durability of the truly dedicated believer by becoming personal adviser on Europe to the new Foreign Secretary, Robin Cook.) A few days later, de Gaulle gave direct support to Butler's judgement in a conversation with Dixon. 'He said it was too early for us to enter the Common Market, and spoke a great deal about the difficulties for the Commonwealth.' While denying that he was formally opposed to British entry, he said he thought it would be difficult 'at the present time'.

Successive summit meetings confirmed this. At the Château de Champs, in early June, the two old lions once again surveyed the world. Both were far more interested in politics than economics, and they spent none of their time talking about levies on pig-meat. Great sweeping discourses about the shape of alliances, and the role of the Russians and Americans, were exchanged between them. Macmillan felt that 'after Europe had been created there must be discussions about the political and defence aspects and an attempt made to create a European world position'. The nuclear question was raised again, a subject of the greatest sensitivity to de Gaulle, and one on which subsequent papers and studies teem with argument as to whether or not Macmillan offered nuclear collaboration, whether he was in a position to do so, whether de Gaulle would have been open to seduction by such an offer which, according to some, was never actually made anyway. 'We were all rather baffled by the Champs meeting,' writes Dixon. But the thread of it did not lead anywhere new. The picture one collects is of Macmillan pleading for recognition of 'an important and decisive moment in history', and de Gaulle toying with Britain's historic unsuitability to meet it. 'It would have been possible', as Dixon wearily summarizes, 'to produce evidence in support of almost any interpretation of General de Gaulle's attitude.'

Even then, the British did not regard the situation as doomed. They still believed that the issue in the real world was the negotiations, not the principle: in other words, that de Gaulle wanted the negotiations to fail, but did not want France to take responsibility for the collapse of the enterprise. On this point, Dixon is self-flagellating. Having correctly divined the General's attitude, the embassy had underestimated his capacity to see it through. 'I and my staff were too categorical about General de Gaulle's unwillingness to take the blame for a breakdown,' Dixon reflects. Even by the time of the final summit, at Rambouillet in December, the message has not fully penetrated. The General 'was as negative as he could be', and was, in addition, 'furious' at having been, in Dixon's loyal opinion, out-argued by Macmillan both in private and then more publicly in front of his ministers. Confronted by Macmillan, for once, with the direct charge that he was raising objections in principle to Britain's application, de Gaulle still felt forced to deny it and to say that 'France desired Britain's entry.' Despite the assessment Michael Butler had sent in May, some elements in the Paris embassy were still, amazingly, prepared to take a morsel of succour from such ritualistic statements.

It was perhaps only after the General had applied his political veto, on 14 January 1963, that Dixon got the measure of what he was dealing with. Why had the General done it? 'It is when one attempts to answer a question like this that one finds oneself in a Kafka world,' Dixon writes. 'Hypotheses form and dissolve. There are morasses and mirages everywhere.' The farm-yard returns, as an analytical safe haven. 'There was never room for more than the Gaullist cock of the European roost.' The bewildered envoy concludes on a note that reflected the almost universal opinion of the time. The history of de Gaulle's conversations with Macmillan 'demonstrates, I am afraid, that he is not open to rational discussion'.

From France's viewpoint, de Gaulle's stance, at least to some people, looked different. It arguably had rationality about it. But, even if it didn't, the question of Macmillan's response to the menacing titan across the Channel can't be treated with such sympathy as it has received from many biographers and historians. Could his preparations have been different? Was his strategy flawed? Did he misjudge the weaknesses and strengths of his position? Was the failure of this historic venture absolutely inevitable? It had such immense consequences that the questions are worth posing.

The main case made against Macmillan concerns timing, and the way timing interacted with a decision to contest, for many months, every refined last detail of any deal, especially over agriculture and the Commonwealth. The negotiations dragged on past the summer of 1962. Just when the Europeans were expecting Heath to return with a comprehensive *démarche* in the autumn, they found the British preoccupied with a Commonwealth conference. There followed some unhelpful developments. In November, elections for the French National Assembly produced a Gaullist majority. From a position of perilous weakness, about to lose a referendum on the revision of the constitution, de Gaulle squeaked home on the referendum and swept aside all internal opposition at the polls. He could dig himself in deeper against the British. Moreover, the continuing impasse in Brussels led to an unfortunate coincidence. When Macmillan went to Rambouillet, he was obliged to confirm to de Gaulle, which he did with some airiness, that he was about to attend a summit meeting with President Kennedy at which he hoped to negotiate the supply of a new generation of intercontinental missiles to carry British nuclear warheads: confirmation, if the General required it, of Britain's indissoluble bondage to Washington.

The Rambouillet discussions, which took place in the shadow of the Cuban missile crisis, naturally dwelt on the state of the world on a wider plane than Europe. De Gaulle admired the way Kennedy had handled the crisis, but that didn't weaken his perception that Britain must, in a sense, make a choice between Europe and the Atlantic if she wanted to be taken seriously as an EEC applicant. Macmillan, arguing the opposite, was at one point reduced to tears by the General's unwillingness to share his own sentiments about the common interests of the great powers, among whom he counted France. De Gaulle recounted the occasion, with lordly derision, at a Cabinet meeting a few days later. 'This poor man,' he said, 'to whom I had nothing to give, seemed so sad, so beaten that I wanted to put my hand on his shoulder and say to him, as in the Edith Piaf song, "*Ne pleurez pas, milord.*"'³⁶

Had everything moved faster, which was within British power to achieve in alliance with the Five, de Gaulle might have had smaller opportunity to deploy what was plainly his settled prejudice. Even he had to pay some attention to his political base, and it would have been more vulnerable. Arguably, Macmillan should have been sensitive to the weakness behind Gaullist bluster in the early stages, the better to pre-empt the General's later strengthening.

This matter has been endlessly discussed, in the copious outpourings of scholarship that have long been part of the Britain-in-Europe indus-try.³⁷ It even has its own term of art: the 'summer' argument, meaning that Britain should have worked harder to close the deal before the autumn. Edward Heath, the chief negotiator, has always resisted this. 'I've never thought that,' he told me in 1994. 'I'm sure there were some people in the Foreign Office who were fed up with a negotiation going on and on. But I don't think it affected the French. You see, they all expected it at that time to be successful. They didn't know what de Gaulle was going to do. I don't think the summer argument has ever held water. It's just people who want to find some other excuse, and somebody to blame.'³⁸

In any case, it is at best a subsidiary point. The altogether larger question concerns the nature of the approach: a conditional and tentative venture, creeping in a state of high suspicion towards this moment of historic destiny, declining to make a commitment until the Europeans had shown what ground they were prepared to surrender, and reserving even then the option of a British veto. This was formulated, remember, against a background of enthusiasm on the continent. The Five were well disposed towards British entry into their half-formed project. Even France, at the beginning and in all formal statements, said the same. Yet the British were not prepared to do more than negotiate and hesitate. They were not, actually, applying. They made it clear that they wanted the Treaty of Rome, which they had declined to participate in drafting, unpicked in certain parts, and weren't willing necessarily to accept the *acquis communautaire* – the patrimony of principles, policies and laws already agreed by the Community – that were the basis of the great project.

They had some reason for concern about the details of what membership would require. Plainly the differences between the British

way of subsidizing farmers, and the Common Agricultural Policy the
EEC had just with agonizing difficulty agreed, posed a great problem.
How temperate foodstuffs like butter, on the export of which New
Zealand wholly depended, could go on being admitted tariff-free to the
British market was an issue that obviously foreshadowed long nights of
haggling. But the chosen method magnified the difficulties. It opened
the door to every vested interest to start lobbying intensively. It invited
the Commonwealth countries to make as many objections as they could:
a context which New Zealand handled reasonably, but in which the old
white bastions, like Robert Menzies of Australia and John Diefenbaker
of Canada, deployed massive hostile pressures. It also intensified such
opposition as there was in Europe. The Europeans did not want all their
acquis dismantled, by negotiators who in any case promised nothing in
return. They were driven into highly defensive mode. The momentum
that might have been established by a new status quo, namely the
unalterable new fact of a British decision to which other members had
to accommodate, was lost. This was the most grandly half-hearted
gesture on which any leader ever rested the fate of himself, his government and his country.

The reason lay partly in his political judgement of what was possible,
but also in his vision of what was historically desirable. In the first of
these, Macmillan lacked courage, in the second he failed to rise above
Britain's national disease: aversion to realism.

Macmillan's view of history continued to bestow a specious aura
of reality on the British Commonwealth. Although the very notion of
possibly joining the EEC implied a distancing from the old impedimenta
of Empire, the lure remained strong. This wasn't merely a feeling to
which the Conservative Party was still vulnerable but one that Macmillan
plainly experienced himself. When he said in the first Commons debate
on the application, in August 1961, that the Commonwealth 'has real life
and unity . . . [and] is something precious and unique', he was speaking
of an entity which, although it would now be invited to coexist with the
Common Market, remained in his view central to Britain's own future
interests as a world power. The protection of Commonwealth trade and
the maintaining of Commonwealth links were an essential part of the
negotiations, and became a point of maximal pressure, whether from
distant leaders or local Tories, against their succeeding. For more than a
year, the parading of the timeless Commonwealth connection, and all
the emotional baggage that went with it, was allowed free rein. Fired up
by the Beaverbrook press, something called Empire loyalism made its

way into popular consciousness, ranging white British stock against the sinister continental losers of the last war. Never did Macmillan find the words entirely to repudiate this sentiment, or to scotch with the necessary brutality the notion that the Commonwealth offered any kind of matrix for the economic future of Britain.

Even on the evidence available at the time, the potency of the Commonwealth myth was a rebuke to politicians who allowed themselves to be seduced by it. Suez, surely, had put an end to the political dream into which the Commonwealth fitted, that of Britain as world power. The enlargement of the Commonwealth that followed Suez – with independence for Ghana and Malaya in 1957, for Nigeria in 1960, with a steady stream of African and Asian countries following in the next few years – brought the opposite of greater power: far less coherence. Trading patterns had long since begun to work against the British connection, because that suited the old Commonwealth countries. Well before the 1960s, Canada was becoming more dependent on the United States, and Australia was starting to recognize her Asian destiny. They were plainly not good bets as the basis for British trade. The Commonwealth's own interests, member by member, diverged sufficiently from the British, and from each other, to drain most of the meaning out of any such thing as a Commonwealth bloc.

The bonds of history and culture, however, were stronger than the facts of economic life. They were white bonds, heavily connected to the old rather than the new Commonwealth, and they gripped hard on the British mind. In the 1961 debate, Member after Member rose from the Tory benches to laud the Commonwealth connection, yearning for the vanished, English-speaking world. 'We have since the war devised every sort and kind of scheme for economic co-operation in Europe,' moaned Lord Hinchingbrooke, 'but we have practically nothing comparable in the Commonwealth.'

In retrospect, the blinding emptiness of this suggests that Macmillan's willingness to submit to any part of the Commonwealth argument was more culpable than it seemed at the time. At the time, indeed, hardly anyone looked upon it that way. But here is a moment at which hindsight may be instructively, and not unfairly, consulted. Insofar as the Commonwealth was seen, in any scenario, as an alternative basis for Britain's economic future, this vision was pitifully false. The trade figures indicated it then, the subsequent history proved it afterwards. One may accord a deal of sympathy to the errors of politicians at any given time, but less so when the source of the error is a reluctance, through

sentiment or pain or misbegotten pressure or sheer intellectual feebleness, to acknowledge the harshness of facts that palpably will not change:
facts, moreover, that were well documented by Whitehall departments
which had shed their own illusions before 1961.

The Commonwealth argument was not, admittedly, the only pressure bearing down on Macmillan. Perhaps it wasn't the strongest. The
case of the domestic farmers, who were then so influential in the Tory
Party, was more insistent, and was represented in the Cabinet by the
tocsin-voice of R. A. Butler. But, together, these questions impressed
themselves as a mighty force on Macmillan's mind, contributing to the
dank uncertainty that surrounded the entire enterprise. Although he had
come to the conclusion that Britain *ought* to belong to the European
Economic Community, Macmillan was not prepared, until very late in
the day, to elevate this cause to a rank meriting his full-blooded
leadership of party and public opinion.

A year passed before he began to sell it at all. Only on 13 September
1962 did the Cabinet decide that public opinion was getting dangerously
sceptical and needed correction. Until then, it took the view that any
degree of enthusiasm shown by British leaders might work against their
negotiating position. If Britain got too keen, tactics might harden against
her. But, on the contrary, the failure to prepare and educate opinion at
home produced a scepticism which made it ever harder to risk the kind
of concessions that might have accelerated the negotiation. In the depths
of the impasse, in autumn 1962, heroic failures tended to be politically
more attractive than calculated concessions. As a way of appeasing
opinion, this dismal pattern was often repeated after Britain had got in,
reaching its apogee during the sterile years when John Major (1990–7)
was presiding over the near-disintegration of Anglo-European relations.
Now, in 1961–3, it played its part in dragging out the negotiations,
justifying a counter-scepticism on the part of the Five as well as the
Sixth.

Behind this was Macmillan's pessimistic reading of the Tory Party.
He felt its breath down his neck even when, with a majority of 100 in
the Commons, he had less to fear than any modern Conservative leader
except, twenty-five years later, Margaret Thatcher.

From the beginning, the measure of party scepticism was unimpressive. At its first test, after the August 1961 debate, the Government won
a vote by 313 votes to 5, with twenty abstentions and only one Tory,
Anthony Fell, deeming the leader 'a national disaster'. At that year's
party conference, 40 votes out of 4,000 were cast against the platform.[39]

In March and July 1962, back-bench motions insisting that there should be no deal without special terms for the Commonwealth showed the core figure of Tory Euro-dissenters in the Commons to be between thirty and forty. But they hung heavy over the proceedings. 'One cannot think that when the chips go down people like this will count for much,' Macmillan's press secretary, Harold Evans, noted in his diary. But Macmillan could never lose sight of them. He seemed to fear the vocal minority more than he relied on the majority that was deferential to his wishes. And it was only quite near the end of the road, in autumn 1962, that he began to come out fighting.

When he did so, it was to try and meet head-on the banked-up arguments the sceptics had been assembling, and he was, at last, quite forthright. His language, in a propaganda pamphlet he finally decided to produce, found some urgency. By negotiating for entry, the Government had taken what was 'perhaps the most fateful and forward-looking policy decision in our peace-time history . . .' 'The economic opportunities . . . greatly outweigh the risks involved.' 'A Britain detached from Europe would mean inflicting permanent injury on our common cause.' 'In the past, as a great maritime power, we might give way to insular feelings of superiority over foreign breeds,' but now 'we have to consider the state of the world as it is today and will be tomorrow, and not in outdated terms of a vanished past'.[40]

To modern readers, what Macmillan had to say about sovereignty, at this late stage, is particularly interesting. Up to now, he had not been very explicit. There had been little demand for it: sovereignty was much lower among public anxieties than it became by the 1990s. Others, however, had addressed it. The facts were on the record. Lord Home, the Foreign Secretary, told the Lords in August 1961: 'Let me admit at once that the Treaty of Rome would involve considerable derogation of sovereignty.' Nor would this be confined to the economic area. The consequences would be 'different in kind from any contract into which we have entered before'.

Now, Macmillan himself remained a little more cryptic. He openly acknowledged that political unity was the central aim of the Six, and said, 'we would naturally accept that ultimate goal'. The case for being inside, to influence this process, made its hallowed appearance: the case that Macmillan, in 1957, when offered the chance of belated entry to the Messina process, hardly looked at. 'As a member of the Community,' he wrote, 'Britain would have a strong voice in deciding the nature and the timing of political unity.' By remaining outside, she risked decisions being made 'which we could do nothing to influence'. Besides, under the Rome Treaty, 'in renouncing some of our own sovereignty, we would receive in return a share of the sovereignty renounced by other members'. This he called 'pooling', the term of art already formulated that would be much heard in later years. The obligations that flowed from it wouldn't alter the position of the Crown, he declared, 'nor rob our Parliament of its essential powers, nor deprive our Law Courts of their authority in our domestic life'.[41]

Thus the plainer depictions of Lord Chancellor Kilmuir were watered down for public consumption, and a repetition of Lord Home's crystal clarity was not attempted. But at least Macmillan's pamphlet addressed the anxieties of a public opinion that was doing nothing to help Heath and his colleagues in Brussels, as they struggled to keep the negotiation alive.

A prolific sub-division of the academic discipline that goes by the name of European Studies is devoted to the question of why General de Gaulle brought the negotiation to an end. Was the veto premeditated? Was it precipitated by British errors? Was it always on the cards? Who deceived whom? How these questions are answered seems almost a matter of personal taste. Since the General never gave an *ex cathedra* explanation, there is freedom to speculate.

In my inquiry, I heard many versions, all uttered with conviction. Michael Butler still says it was clear for weeks if not months what would happen. 'The veto certainly shouldn't have come as a shock,' he said, looking back in 1993. 'De Gaulle was absolutely consistent and really very predictable.'[42] Sir Edward Heath doesn't think so. 'The talks weren't always doomed to break down, and there's a lot of evidence to support that,' he said in 1995. Two days before the veto, he was in Paris having a delightful lunch with the French Foreign Minister, Maurice Couve de Murville, exchanging views about the differences between French and British literature and doing some last-minute political business. As Heath remembered, 'Couve said, absolutely clearly, "Nothing can now stop these negotiations from being a success." '[43] As for Couve himself, a serpentine figure even in his near-dotage, he told me in 1994 that there had never, in fact, been a veto. Couve admitted that he had thought de Gaulle's press conference speech unnecessarily irritating to his allies, and advised him to tone it down. 'I think the end of the negotiation should have been announced in a softer way,' he said. 'The press conference is the basis for what is universally called de Gaulle's veto. Which is the wrong way to describe it. Everyone agreed that Britain wasn't ready, though only France said that she should wait. The right way to describe what happened is that the negotiations did not succeed.'[44]

To me, the persuasive evidence derives from the pattern of de Gaulle's behaviour over many years. The odds were long against him ever welcoming Britain into the EEC, if he could find a way of keeping her out that was congruent with his political power at the given moment. Unwilling to take a risk with British opinion, Macmillan gave him the opening he needed. Certainly by the time of the Rambouillet summit, it was clear beyond doubt that the General's intentions were unalterable, and Heath, for one, deluded himself in supposing otherwise. The long delay, culminating with the trip to Bermuda to negotiate Polaris missiles out of President Kennedy for the next generation of British nuclear defence, gave de Gaulle both the opportunity and the ammunition he needed. Even Heath, in general a defender of all that happened, says Macmillan made a mistake there. Being filmed with Kennedy, insouciantly inspecting the troops on parade in Bermuda, was a way of showing the priority de Gaulle most detested. 'He was terrified we might be left without any nuclear weapon,' Heath told me. 'It would leave him in a very weak position with Parliament, and was going to do him enormous damage with the party. So that was what was on his mind. The other aspects just didn't make an impact on him.'

This is, to some extent, an academic discussion. What happened, happened. De Gaulle, without doubt, treated Macmillan monstrously, whichever way you look at it. Either he was going through an elaborate charade, holding summit meetings which he knew would lead nowhere, dragging out an enormous expenditure of effort in Brussels which he always intended to fail. Or, almost quixotically, he decided at the last moment to intervene against the wishes not only of his old antagonist but of all his continental partners – save Chancellor Adenauer, who was giving Macmillan a hard time for almost as long.

What wasn't academic was the consequence. Britain had embarked on a venture that did not succeed. Despite its tentative, conditional nature, the quest to join the Common Market was Britain's only shot. She was not prepared for it to fail, and had no contingency plan ready when it did so. For Macmillan, therefore, the event was catastrophic. He did his best to keep a stiff upper lip, falling into pettiness only once or twice with gestures he regretted, like withdrawing permission for Princess Margaret to visit Paris. In public, he remained dignified and didactic, resuming his global stance. 'A great opportunity has been missed,' he said, in a broadcast to the nation. 'It is no good trying to disguise or minimize that fact ... France and her government are looking backwards. They seem to think that one nation can dominate Europe and, equally wrong, that Europe can or ought to stand alone. Europe cannot stand alone. She must co-operate with the rest of the Free World, with the Commonwealth, with the United States in an equal and honourable partnership.'

But the private man was in a state of greater turbulence. 'I do not remember going through a worse time since Suez,' he wrote to Lady Waverley. In his diary he said, 'French duplicity has defeated us all,' and that Couve had 'behaved with a rudeness which was unbelievable'. But so what? 'All our policies at home and abroad are in ruins.' 'I had terrible difficulties with Macmillan afterwards,' Ted Heath told me. 'He wouldn't do anything, wouldn't concentrate on anything. This was the end of the world.'

In less than a year, he was gone. Other political problems beset his government, including a concatenation of events that would, in a later time, have been categorized as serial sleaze. Scandals of sex and espionage overwhelmed him. But the failure of his European venture removed from him his *raison d'être* in high politics. In October, pleading prostate cancer, he left the leadership of party and country. This proved to be a wrong diagnosis, but he didn't wait for the best specialist who might have told him he had a decent chance of living another quarter-century, which is what he did, dying only in 1986. Instead, Harold Macmillan became the first in a long line of Conservative politicians whose careers were broken on the wheel of Europe.

After the veto, his private office tried to prepare him for the next stage. The Public Record Office files contain an exchange between officials, who note that a good deal of speech-writing would be necessary in the next few weeks, and offer a selection of quotations for possible use. 'I began composing a little anthology,' writes G. H. Andrew to A. W. France. For example, from Laurence Sterne: 'Strange! Quoth I, debating the matter with myself, that one and twenty miles sailing, for 'tis absolutely no further from Dover to Calais, should give a man these rights.' Or Napoleon's: 'Du sublime au ridicule il n'y a qu'un pas.' Or from Thomas Moore: 'How shall we rank there on glory's page / Thou more than soldier and just less than sage.' Or how about *The Merchant of Venice*? 'What? Would'st thou have a serpent sting thee twice?'[45]

Several other amusing little piquancies suggested themselves to well-stocked mandarin minds. But on reflection, Herbert Andrew confessed, none of them would do. Imagining them in the mouth of Macmillan, he realized they wouldn't sound right. 'It is surprising', he concludes, 'how easy it is to strike a false note, and I have ended up with an anthology of false notes. It may at any rate remind you of a few things to avoid.'

5

HUGH GAITSKELL

Progressively Backwards

HAROLD MACMILLAN was not alone in his embroilment with the past. As the leader of the nation, he reflected a national condition. The British could hardly be said to be thirsting for a new kind of world which threatened to dislocate the allegiances they understood. In fact, by the standards of his time, Macmillan, tentative though he was, and neurotically respectful of the forces around him, was the boldest man alive. He was surrounded by people even more cautious than he was. Though he acted, and, by action, challenged the cycle of conservative contentment, he belonged to a kind of national consensus that regarded such action as almost impossibly risky – and perhaps, as his enemies said, quite unnecessary.

Just as important in this *histoire* as Macmillan's attempt at action was the certain belief, in several quarters, that his chosen line of action was an error. There was a lot of opposition, all of it from one direction. Usually, the political leader finds himself picking a way between one lot of people who say he is going too far and another saying that he isn't going far enough. But this did not describe Macmillan's position when applying for a British place in the Common Market. He had no opponents, as it were, to the left of him. There was no body of opinion, in fact not a single public voice that I have traced, which said that the British approach should be more vigorous: that the conditional basis of the application was too defensive, or a bolder plunge was demanded by Britain's parlous situation. Such criticisms were often heard later. But, at the time, there were no Tory federalists to speak of, and no force in Parliament demanding more urgency rather than more caution. What Macmillan faced was a small army of opponents, in all parties, who found different reasons for saying that the whole idea of British membership of the European Economic Community was a mistake.

This opposition mattered. It played its part in creating the climate in which the consideration, such as it was, of Britain's historic destiny took place. De Gaulle was the agent of failure, but the ground had been prepared at home. Opposition entailed a kind of full-throated roar in favour of the status quo, offered regardless of the fact that those who exhaled it were sometimes also critics of the status quo in other ways: alarmed by lagging competitiveness, hostile to imperial illusions, generally craving for modernity. But the critics were, for the most part, blind to this contradiction. Addressing a choice between past and future, they were conflicted. The tone they set was to resonate for decades.

The opposition was not devoid of reason. A large amount of abstruse ratiocination can be found in the archives concerning the pros and cons of entry as it would affect economic output, the balance of trade, the cost of food, the outlook for invisibles, the future of the Atlantic alliance and so on. The economic case was far from open-and-shut. Treasury and Foreign Office reworked the ground that previous officials had pored over in 1951 and 1955. Publicly also, there is no doubting the earnestness of the debates Macmillan's decision unleashed. In their combination of honest conviction and courteous disagreement, the 1962 debates were without doubt the best of the series that erupted, in the landmark years, with steadily more violent climaxes: 1967, 1971, 1975, 1984, 1992, 1993, 1997.

But overshadowing reason was the mighty power of sentiment: sentiment about the past, on which was based an incorrigible complacency about the present and the future. These attitudes grew one upon the other. They were righteously, unchallengeably, intertwined. Reading, in the 1990s, the arguments against Macmillan which held him half in thrall, one is struck by its marriage of the soft with the hard. There was some hard disagreement, as there was bound to be: contention about the facts, argument about the economic prospects in or out of the Common Market. Going into Europe, whichever way you looked at it, was a life-changing decision for a nation. But the overall timbre of the case made against Macmillan was irredeemably soft- rather than hard-headed.

It did not acknowledge the need for a truly sceptical, realistic look at the future economic prospects for Britain outside Europe, and it rested heavily, instead, on the ultimate recourse of many soft-headed British politicians of that time: the Commonwealth. Concern about the Commonwealth was marked by a double self-indulgence: an unrealistic assessment of what the Commonwealth could do for the British economy, coupled with a fanciful concern for what Britain owed the

Commonwealth. This attitude met with no shred of gratitude from those whose interests the mother country thought she was defending alongside her own.

So the nature of the debate reflected the frightening scale of the decision. Just as history rendered decisiveness impossible, so it produced a debate that was less than open-eyed. The shadow of the past reached forward to darken the British mind, making it reluctant to look too directly into a future whose discomforts were better left unexamined.

The main opposition player in this argument was Hugh Gaitskell, the leader of the Labour Party. For him, one must immediately acknowledge, it did not begin as an argument about national destiny. In its earliest manifestation, the Europe decision did not touch Gaitskell's ample store of passion. It took time to attain a status that would place it near the top of his political concerns. The subject was 'a bore and a nuisance and it has always been so', he once told a friend, and he expressed versions of this sentiment often. It was his preferred posture, about something that caused him much trouble. But even in those days, before Europe had destroyed a single British politician, calling it a bore and a nuisance scarcely met the case. This was an attitude that a good many Labour politicians found themselves falling into in later years. Combined with the sense that Europe 'didn't really matter', it supplied useful cover for a politician who could not make up his mind what he thought about it: a common frailty, later brought to a unique pitch of sophistication by Gaitskell's ally, Denis Healey.

Gaitskell would have liked to remain indifferent to Europe. When it unavoidably presented itself, he was still surviving the after-burn of two great arguments that had already wracked his party, and he could have done without another. At the 1959 party conference, he had fought, but failed, to secure the rewriting of Clause Four of the party constitution, the commitment to public ownership: an article of faith that survived another thirty-six years before Tony Blair succeeded in extinguishing it. In 1960, the party was further torn apart by an attempt to commit it to unilateral nuclear disarmament. This was enough for Gaitskell, as it would have been for any leader. Compared with these great questions of principle, Europe could be presented as speculative, almost otiose, which is how the leader originally preferred to see it.

The political context mattered in another way, which also had the effect of lowering Europe from the heights of grand principle. Parliament was halfway through its term, and a general election couldn't be far away. For Gaitskell, as for Macmillan, political survival infiltrated its way into the matter. That is often forgotten, in the endless dissections of what might have been. High politics cannot exist without considerations of the low. It was the Labour Party's opinion that the main reason Macmillan had embarked on the venture was because he needed a grand gesture of this kind to distract attention from the sense of party failure and national decline that surrounded his government. R. H. S. Crossman, the propagandist and senior leftist MP, told an American audience at the time that applying to get into the Common Market was 'an attempt by a most adroit and ingenious politician to extricate himself from his domestic difficulties and manoeuvre himself into a situation where, having successfully negotiated terms of entry, he could appeal to the country posing as the greatest statesman since Disraeli'.[1] Crossman might have added that the imminence of the election was intended as a bludgeon to keep Conservative MPs in line behind a policy which some of them fiercely disagreed with.

So the politics of party bulked large for Gaitskell – necessarily so. He had been leader since December 1955, and had already failed in the first shot at his appointed task, the winning of an election in 1959. Nothing could matter much more than winning next time. His party was divided over nationalization, divided over nuclear weapons and, as any student of the history could not fail to know, divided over Europe. The divisions of the 1950s lived on: federalists against Bevinites, Europeanists against globalists, left against right – although the cast of characters had sometimes changed sides. It is not hard to see why part of Gaitskell's response to the reappearance of Europe at the heart of British politics was to wish that it would go away.

Nor can one be surprised that this condition gave birth to a certain vacillation in the Leader of the Opposition. If the issue was a bore, and didn't really matter, and if it had to be considered primarily as a matter of manoeuvring towards a species of party unity, then it was to be expected that the Gaitskell record should show, at one level, and over quite a short period, the lurching inconsistency of line that has characterized so many politicians.

He gave many different impressions at different times. During 1960, when the issue first seriously began to surface, he was taken, according to his official biographer, to be a cautious supporter of entry.[2] After Macmillan's application, he maintained an elaborate public agnosticism, which he insisted should be the position of the party as well. It all depended, he said, on the terms the Government could secure. The question was 'tricky and complicated', he wrote to his daughter at

Oxford, and it would be 'absurd' to decide the Labour line too soon. As a party manager, he was determined, above all, to take no line at all until he had to, but on the issues of principle he was, in the beginning, dismissive of the common phobias. These, the political objections, he rejected for fully two years. In the summer of 1961, he strongly criticized a paper from Transport House, the party headquarters, which, he thought, much exaggerated the political drawbacks of British entry. In October, he expressed revulsion from the alliance between Little Eng-lander rightists and pro-Soviet leftists who made up most of the numbers in the hard anti-Market position. He thought they by no means spoke for mainstream public opinion. In early 1962, he wrote: 'provided the terms are satisfactory, I doubt if the country is going to be very anti'. In May, in a broadcast to the nation, he sounded about as far as Macmillan was from believing this would be the end of Britain as we know it. He said: 'You hear people speaking as though if we go into the Common Market ... this is the end as far as an independent Britain is concerned. That we're finished, we are going to be sucked up in a tunnel of giant capitalist, Catholic conspiracy, our lives dominated by Adenauer and de Gaulle, unable to conduct any independent foreign policy at all. Now frankly, this is rubbish, on the basis of the Treaty of Rome.'

He also said, in a memorandum around that time, that many of the fears, whether about competition from cheap labour or about a federal European super-state, were groundless. 'French or German votes could not decide British foreign policy.' But the Market existed. 'If we stay out of it,' he wrote, in terms that might have been taken from Macmillan's own lexicon, 'we run the risk of becoming nothing more than a little island off Europe. We shall be dwarfed politically by the Six.'

Thus, in half of himself, as he addressed the issue Macmillan had laid on the table, Gaitskell was drawn beyond agnosticism to a position echoing that of his chief political friends. For Europe divided the parties within themselves more emphatically than it separated Labour from the Tories, and in that divide Gaitskell's allies, on the right of the party, were for the most part pro-European. The 'Frognal Set', labelled after the location of the Gaitskell home in Hampstead where his friends often met, contained, among others, the most committed pro-European poli-ticians, in either party, among the post-war generation, chief among them Roy Jenkins but also, if waxing and waning, Anthony Crosland, Patrick Gordon Walker and John Harris. They had been central to his positioning on both unilateralism and Clause Four. They wanted him to be a European, and he gave them grounds to think he was.

But then he said other things as well. Some of this was on the economic side, where he argued – it was one of his more consistent lines – that the benefits to Britain couldn't be assessed at better than fifty–fifty. He ridiculed the flighty prophets departing from what he saw as his own impeccable economic rationalism. But he was hostile to other sorts of irrationalism as well. In April 1962, Roy Jenkins brought Jean Monnet, the founding father, to speak to a dining club they both belonged to and administer a dose of faith. He hoped Monnet would dispel Gaitskell's doubts. But Gaitskell, at his most sceptical, pressed Monnet with an hour's relentless questioning, at the end of which the little Frenchman was pleading for mercy. 'Well, one must have faith' was his despairing curtain line. 'I don't believe in faith,' Gaitskell replied, 'I believe in reason, and there is little reason in anything you have been saying tonight.' Jenkins wrote in his memoirs: 'I have never seen less of a meeting of minds.'³

This, then, was a fickle and troubled leader. No more than many other people did he know exactly where he stood on Europe. Though pushed by his friends, he listened almost as attentively to his enemies, the left of the party, Harold Wilson to the fore. While explicitly rejecting their main argument, that the EEC was a capitalist cartel that would be the death of socialism, he shared their generally sceptical, suspicious, very *British* attitude. And it was his enemies rather than his friends he finished up by pleasing.

*

FOUR DECADES ON, now that we have been pounded for many years by the orthodoxy of Euro-scepticism, the seminal moment of the creed holds one particular fascination.

When the political opposition to British entry into the Common Market was first compelled, by Macmillan's overture, to express itself, what case did it make for another way of being an off-shore island? Confronted with a proposition to do one thing, what did it have to say about an alternative? Gaitskell did not like being challenged thus. 'Nothing annoyed him so much as the question, "But what is the alternative?"', his daughter Julia told his biographer. Too bad. It is a question that every generation of Euro-sceptics has found different ways of imperfectly addressing.

In August 1961, after the opening decision, Gaitskell did not lead for the opposition. He was committed to waiting-and-seeing, and, by comparison with the right wing of the Conservative Party, was a model of disinterested investigation. However, a fiery inquisition did immediately begin. It is of special interest to modern readers, not least because it was of very little interest to people at the time. It did not answer the question about an alternative, but that very void is itself illuminating: it shone down the decades, issuing as vacantly from the mouth of William Cash, a Tory Euro-sceptic MP of the 1990s, as it did from that of Sir Derek Walker-Smith, his more winning predecessor of the 1960s. To them, essentially, the emptiness did not need filling. They thought that what mattered above all else was not what the future held for Britain if she did not belong to the Community, but the manifold horrors, the treacheries on history, the depletions of national sovereignty that were the certain, intolerable consequences of belonging.

In his presentation, Macmillan made little of the sovereignty question, as we have seen, and, throughout his engagement with the issue, was seldom pressed to address it. It remained in the margins of his discourse, being considered far less important than the price of food or the future of the Commonwealth. Macmillan invariably got away with a few well-wafted allusions to sovereignty being 'perhaps a matter of degree', and the Treaty of Rome not involving 'any kind of federalist solution'.[4] Hardly anyone contradicted him. Gaitskell began by similarly down-playing the alarms. These moved a few people to distraction, but in 1961–3 they were not the main source of anxiety: and in any case de Gaulle was surely a safeguard against them.

It is worth recalling, however, that quite a lot was said. The constitutional consequences of entry into the Common Market were not concealed. At the same time as Macmillan was making his statement, a parallel debate took place in the House of Lords, in which the Lord Chancellor, Lord Kilmuir, described what would happen. Both the courts and Parliament would be living in a new environment. The UK courts would have to defer, in the final analysis, to the European Court on matters in the Treaty, and British citizens would be obliged to pay European penalties, if imposed. 'I am quite prepared to face that,' said Kilmuir. 'There is this limitation to the interpretation and the carrying out of the Treaty.' Sovereignty would be lost in a different, more contractual way from previous such poolings, through Nato or the OEEC or the United Nations, and this would be 'an unprecedented step'.

This account, it has to be conceded, was less graphic than it might have been. Earlier in the preparations, in a private letter to Ted Heath, Kilmuir had remarked: 'I find the constitutional objections serious.' That didn't mean he found them 'conclusive'. But signing up for membership meant, in practice, transferring to the Council of Ministers Parliament's 'substantive powers of legislating over the whole of a very important field'. His words, already alluded to in the last chapter, bear repeating. 'I am sure it would be a great mistake', he went on, 'to under-estimate the force of the objections ... But these objections ought to be brought out into the open now because, if we attempt to gloss over them at this stage, those who are opposed to the whole idea of joining the Community will certainly seize on them with more damaging effect later on.'[5]

This proved to be a prophetic statement. As late as the 1997 election, the Referendum Party exhumed Kilmuir's letter from the files, displaying it as evidence of the establishment conspiracy of secrecy which Sir James Goldsmith and other RP zealots believed to have been at the core of Britain's entry into the EEC. And it is true that perceptions of what membership meant for sovereignty were more luridly understood in 1997 than thirty-five years earlier. But that was not, I think, primarily owing to the calculated neglect of the politicians of the day. Kilmuir did tell the House of Lords the essence of the matter, albeit without excitement. The Bow Group, under the direction of a young Tory politician by the name of Geoffrey Howe, produced a legal study in July 1962 which foreshadows with great exactitude the effect the Treaty of Rome has had on British law.[6] In August 1962, Kilmuir's successor, Lord Dilhorne, again went over the ground in a Lords debate, explaining in laborious detail how both judges and politicians would fall under the sway of the European system.

So there was no secret about any of this, for those who wished to know. To the extent that the British could ever justly claim to have been taken by surprise, the culprits were not the ministers who wished to start the entry process in 1962 so much as the nation itself, at the time. The trends and facts and probabilities were, for the most part, exposed. But they were seen through a haze of uncertainty. They achieved no real focus. They simply did not concern the political class in the way they came to do a few decades later.

Whether this reflected people's excessive confidence in British power, their lack of serious interest in the detail, or merely the embryonic evolutionary stage the Common Market had attained, is a question to be answered differently in different cases. In the most important case, that of Macmillan, the power relationship was dominant. Although sensitive to the fuss some people might make about sovereignty, he plainly did not believe it was a real issue. He could not imagine this move except as a way of reinventing British greatness. Time after time, in the documents and in his speeches, he rests his case on the Community as a theatre in which British power will be enhanced, not diminished: a place where Britain will lead, not one where there was intended to be no leader. Macmillan, steeped in great-power thinking, never did really understand this essential aspect of the Monnet–Schuman creation.

Not that the matter was left entirely undiscussed. For one school of Conservatives, the issue of Britain's survival as a sovereign nation was the inextinguishable heart of the matter. Derek Walker-Smith MP was one of them. A capable planning lawyer, Walker-Smith was at one time a man on the rise. He got as far as being Minister of Health, but in 1960 he was sacked, with only a baronetcy to console him. It was no doubt accidental that he should be the very first back-bencher who was called to speak in the debate on the Macmillan announcement, and at the time it didn't signify much. Although he made a brilliant speech, he wasn't talking about the issue that concerned most MPs. As a harbinger of history, however, no one could have been better chosen. He put into words the problem which, in due time, would tear the Conservative Party apart. The central argument he made, while having little impact on the politics of the moment, said what none put better in the years to come.

Unlike many of his successors, who later made Euro-phobia into an instrument for the wrecking of their party, Walker-Smith was a gentleman. His stance towards the Community was exquisitely polite. 'I would associate myself with no derogatory observations that might be made at this or any other time about the Community or the six nations that compose it,' he told the House with palpable sincerity. 'I salute, and all should seek to share, the sense of Christian purpose which animates their aims and aspirations.'

But he was unforgiving on the matter of sovereignty, dissecting with care the ways in which the Treaty took power from the nations, whether on trade relations or labour laws, or through its explicitly political aspirations. The question, he said, was not whether sovereignty was being sacrificed for good purpose, but whether it needed to be sacrificed at all. Could trading not be as favourably governed by inter-national as by supra-national agreements? Did we really need to join up, in order to achieve economic growth? 'I find something humiliating', he said, 'in the proposition that the only way to bring economic realism to a great industrial people is to join the Common Market.' For its component nations were different from Britain. Sovereignty came late to most of them, the detritus of the Holy Roman Empire. 'Their evolution has been continental and collective, ours has been insular and imperial.' They looked to share their practices with each other, 'but not with us'. To forget all this, 'as a sort of postscript to an economic arrangement', was deeply wrong, Walker-Smith thought. 'There are considerations here which go beyond the considerations of the counting house.'

He went on: 'If we adhere to the Economic Community now and the Six proceed, as they are entitled to proceed, to the next stage of political union, what then is the position? If we do not want to go along with them on the political side, could we stay in on the economic side, or could we get out at that stage if we wanted to? Or is the real position this, that if the decision is taken now, we forfeit the power of political decision? ... If we tried to come out of the Community in those circumstances, would not the Six be justified in saying to us, "But you knew all along of our enthusiasm for the next political step. If you did not share it, why did you join us in the first place?" '[7]

This was quite a prescient accounting. Long after Britain joined, these questions began to reappear in the minds of Walker-Smith's successors, gaining an almost violent urgency from the fact that, by the 1990s, they had become impossible to answer by a simple assertion of British independence. What should Britain do?, Walker-Smith asked himself rhetorically. The answer was simple. Tell the Six Britain wishes them well, she desires to co-operate, but she seeks no more than to associate with them, never to belong: exactly what Mr Cash and his friends, with a kind of hopeless longing, wanted to do thirty years later.

This was not, however, the line that Gaitskell took in the beginning, though he later drew potently on the emotional charge it generated. 'I have never been much impressed with the argument about loss of sovereignty,' he told the Commons in June 1962. His first concern, as he often said, was with the economic reckoning. And his parallel compulsion was with the matter of honour: with kith and kin, with our island's global story, with our historic obligations: in short, with the Commonwealth. It was here that he made common cause with politicians he otherwise despised, on the right of the Conservative Party, and with instincts he was not prepared to question, in the heart of the British people.

By both birth and formation, Gaitskell had some of these instincts within him. He was infused with the imperial connection that found its way into the lives of so many of the British professional classes. His father Arthur joined the Indian Civil Service, and spent all his professional life in Burma, though Hugh was born in Kensington. His elder brother, Arthur Jr, the founder of a peasant co-operative in the Sudan, spoke for the same dutiful attachment to public service on the global scale, and Hugh absorbed the family tradition. He was always, for example, especially involved with India, and had many close Indian friends, one of whom, K. B. Lall, India's ambassador in Brussels, is credited with turning him, finally, against the Common Market. He was also strongly pro-American. But just as, with a future generation of British leaders, the nuances of their speeches are examined for clues to where they really stand as between Europe and America, in Gaitskell's time the dichotomy was with the Commonwealth, and in his own utterance it was the Commonwealth connection that invariably came through strongest. The need to 'carry the Commonwealth' became one of the earliest tests he determined to apply to the European venture.

The Commonwealth, moreover, had become the acme of political correctness in the wider Labour Party. The anti-imperialists had made their mark by granting India independence in 1947, and watched the evolution from Empire into Commonwealth with unqualified approval. When Macmillan talked about the Commonwealth problem, he was referring invariably to the 'old', therefore white, Commonwealth, whereas for Labour it was a multi-racial entity – 'one of the great progressive manifestations of the history of mankind', said Maurice Edelman MP[8] – in which the tropical produce of Ghana mattered as much as New Zealand butter, and the flourishing of Asian rather than Canadian manufactures would be the crucial test case for the Community's good faith.

It is hard, as the century closes, to re-create the sway which these considerations held over the British political class in the 1950s and 1960s. Any 'weakening of Commonwealth links' was spoken of as if it constituted the death-knell for Britain's honour as well as her self-interest. 'We shall be sacrificing so much that I am proud of and value in this country,' said a Tory MP, R. H. Turton, in arguing that negotiations should not even begin. 'The future of the world will depend a great deal', he thought, 'on how far by this multi-racial partnership we can bring the continents together.' The instant alarm expressed by every Commonwealth government at the prospect of changing trade patterns impressed him and many of his colleagues direly. Not a few Labour MPs were similarly struck. In the August 1961 debate, the most emotional speech came from Lynn Ungoed-Thomas, a senior Labour man, who bemoaned a proposal 'which is alien to the mind of this country [and] is ruinous to our Commonwealth connection'. He went on: 'Right from its earliest days – the days of Wellesley, of Cornwallis, of Warren Hastings – there has been as a continuous thread amongst the best of our people the conception of the Empire as being a trust to develop into a Commonwealth of all our peoples, including the coloured peoples.' 'If there has to be a choice,' said Harold Wilson, 'we are not entitled to sell our friends and kinsmen down the river for a problematical and marginal advantage in selling washing machines in Düsseldorf.'

The betrayal of the past wasn't the only argument the emotionalists made. They had to do better than talk in terms of Armistice Day parades. Recognizing the need for something more concrete, they constructed some elaborate economic fantasies. The Commonwealth, they persuaded themselves, could be made into a viable economic partner, a growing force, if only London set its mind to the task. For there was certainly an economic downside to entry, in the form of higher food prices. Once Britain was in an arrangement that provided for open frontiers and nil tariffs between members, while abandoning the preferential arrangements to anyone outside the frontiers, New Zealand butter, cheap though it was, wouldn't stand a chance against the French. The charge developed that Britain had shamefully neglected Commonwealth trade for many years. It should now be boosted by all manner of devices. Viscount Hinchingbrooke proposed a Commonwealth Payments Union and a Commonwealth Bank, to help finance British exports. All Britain needed, belatedly, was a positive policy for Commonwealth trade rather than for European trade. 'We shall have tremendous opportunities if Britain will really get down to it,' Turton vigorously enthused. The debates of 1961 and 1962 contained much wild thrashing about in search of economic nostrums, to avert the unthinkable political outcome.

The trading arguments, however, were not very convincing. They defied patterns that were already visible. For example, Commonwealth exports to Western Europe were already rising, while those to Britain were declining. The share Europe took of British exports was rising, admittedly from a low base, while that of exports to the Commonwealth was falling. This was from a high base (40 per cent), but the pace and quality of expansion in the advanced industrial societies across the Channel far exceeded what was likely to be available across the oceans, in countries that were in any case interested in diversifying their trade away from Mother Britain. There could never be a customs union with

Canada or Australia, Ghana or Malaya, for the simple reason that none of these places would have an interest in doing British exports a special favour against their own developing industries.

Besides, the Commonwealth was already showing its hand. Some members, like Canada, looked to the United States, some, like India and Ghana, to the Soviet Union. Others would soon be looking to the Common Market, with or without Britain, because of the quantity and quality of what it offered. The contempt of one Conservative MP, Peter Smithers, for the prevalent economic illusions was as withering as that of Walker-Smith, from the other side, for the political. How could a nation of 50 million provide the finance and know-how for a Commonwealth of 600 million? he asked. 'If we value the Commonwealth, can we really hope to hold it together all by our little selves? ... My belief is that the antithesis put before the House and the country of a choice between Europe and the Commonwealth – ayes to the right, noes to the left – is entirely false.' On the contrary, Smithers insisted, if we fail in Europe, the Commonwealth itself would probably have no future.

Thus even the pro-Europe faction was careful to protect the Commonwealth. An open federalist such as Jo Grimond, the Liberal leader, felt compelled to say that the Commonwealth has 'a great future', to which Britain must contribute. Roy Jenkins conceded that the Commonwealth was 'greatly valuable', before insisting that it couldn't be a substitute for Europe. Nobody could afford to say, because few allowed themselves to understand, that the Commonwealth was destined for the margins of world economic power, and therefore of the British economic interest, before another decade passed.

Hugh Gaitskell himself was in this pickle, but was reluctant to face it. Though he was born of Commonwealth stock, and was to conclude by appealing to its meaning with all the force at his command, in between he sang an uncertain song. He said different things about the Commonwealth at different times, just as he said many different things about Europe. As a leader, though he went out in a gale of rhetoric, he was more the weathervane than the wind of change. He was true, in short, to the British tradition of not being certain what to think.

He always maintained, like everyone else, that the historic links had to be sustained. Meeting the needs of the Commonwealth members must be a basic test, he said, of the conditions Macmillan was able to obtain. But he wasn't always intoxicated by the possibilities. 'Are you sure that in ten or twenty years' time the Commonwealth will be there?' he ruminated in front of a group of Commonwealth MPs, in July 1962.

The ties, he noted, were getting weaker anyway. India seemed to be drifting away, the African countries were drawing closer to each other, the old white countries might be looking more to the USA. Maybe Britain would soon become 'just a little island off Europe', he again speculated, which couldn't depend on the Commonwealth, since this wasn't a military alliance, nor a customs union, nor even 'entirely a community of democracies'. He openly feared Britain being 'excluded from a tough, strong European state', and he told the Commonwealth MPs not to traduce Macmillan for investigating the alternatives. 'It is not fair to denounce the Government as though [negotiation] was a plain act of treachery,' he said.

So Gaitskell was not an all-out nostalgia-merchant. His rational mind could make the Commonwealth sound like a bad bet. He understood its weaknesses. On the other hand, he allocated it a veto over Macmillan's negotiations, telling numerous Commonwealth leaders, as his position hardened, that if their summit, scheduled for September 1962, was not satisfied, 'then the Labour Party would come out in strong opposition to our entry'.[9] He almost goaded them to reject the deal. Commonwealth governments 'should know the power they have to influence British opinion . . . is very great indeed', he said. He told the Australian Labour leader to 'regard it as your job to see that [Robert Menzies, the Prime Minister] does not sacrifice Australian interests'.

In reaching his final position, Gaitskell was naturally touched by his inner uncertainties, which were themselves influenced by the state of his party. In fact, he privately reflected on how well it would suit him if the agreement Macmillan was able to reach was so bad that the Commonwealth, the farmers and the Tory Party all vehemently rejected it. He did not *desire*, he said, to be obstructive, and he sometimes appeared not to be so. A party political broadcast he gave in May was judged to be a model of fairness, *The Times* remarking on 'his obvious devotion to truth and principle'. He was not, apparently, being oppositionist. The pro-Market forces in the Labour Party, a group of about fifty MPs for whom Roy Jenkins continued to be the most prominent spokesman, acclaimed his words as 'a great advance' – which reflected how they were more generally regarded, as a nuanced statement that came down, in spite of the recent, repellent meeting with Jean Monnet, in favour of British entry.

This ground which Gaitskell uncertainly occupied, however, was shifting beneath him. For few members of the Labour Party did Europe pose a clear issue of principle, and not all his colleagues on the right were reliably among them. The left, by now, were solidly opposed. But, when some of the key figures who had assisted him in his prior battles against the left, over nationalization and disarmament – Patrick Gordon Walker, Michael Stewart, Denis Healey, James Callaghan – began to move towards the anti camp, Gaitskell could not but take notice. Swinging erratically between his view of the Common Market, on some days, as a bore, on others as a test for Macmillan's negotiating skills, and on yet others as a matter of the highest principle, Gaitskell did not seem to have a secure anchorage. He could be mightily influenced by the last person who spoke to him. On a summer visit to Brussels, for example, he was destabilized when Paul-Henri Spaak made the unsurprising observation that the Community was destined to progress towards more political as well as economic unity. There was a terrible row. This continental line, which Gaitskell had heard many times before, now had a big effect on him. The man who had once called Europe a bore addressed the question with growing earnestness, but was also evincing more acrid scepticism.

This reached an interim climax when the Commonwealth prime ministers met together in early September, in London, where the Leader of the Opposition could be conveniently present in the corridors. Many had come with their own opposition leaders in tow, looking over their shoulders. Hostility abounded. For the terms negotiated thus far by no means satisfied all the Commonwealth demands. Though Foreign Office officials were able to paper over the disagreements, and achieve a public presentation of unity that later spin-doctors would have marvelled at, the white Commonwealth especially was seething, which provoked Gaitskell into mounting his highest horse of indignation. The personal bitterness between him and Macmillan reached a new pitch of venom. Referring to Australia, Gaitskell confided that the proposed terms were 'another example of Macmillan's smashing our relations with these people for personal political advantage'. Macmillan snarled in his diary: 'A very tense atmosphere everywhere. Gaitskell going about smiling ... as if he had just kissed hands.'

The Labour Party conference now beckoned, and there was no doubt that Europe would be the vibrant issue. Gaitskell anticipated it with another broadcast, ripping into the emptiness of the promises Europe was prepared to make to New Zealand, Canada, India and the rest. He insisted he wasn't negative about Europe, but said the political case for entry derived largely from what the Commonwealth could bring to it. As a way of avoiding a choice, he searched for ways of yoking the two together. Bridge-building between First World and Third, between black, brown and white races, between the tight little crypto-federation of Western Europe and the world beyond the seas where the map was coloured red: these were now Gaitskell's criteria for blessing the enterprise. Although intelligible as an ideal, they were a distraction from the main question with which the country was confronted.

Gaitskell wanted to have it both ways, which is, arguably, what every leader seeks for his country. But, if that is the object, there has to be congruence in his approach to the competing interests. In particular, the short-term positioning required to satisfy one set of pressures has to avoid, as far as possible, foreclosing longer-term interests that point the other way. This rule the Labour leader now proceeded to ignore.

All along, as his private conversations show, he explained himself as a man who, at the right time and on the right terms, positively wanted Britain to go into the Common Market. He insisted that he was pro-Europe, pro-EEC, pro-British membership. He was aware that if he attacked Macmillan's terms too strongly he might be mistaken for someone who wanted to keep out altogether. There were plenty of people like that, and Gaitskell affected not to be one of them. He probably wasn't. 'The problem really has been how to maintain our position against going in on the present terms and yet reply effectively to the Government's obvious intention to take us in on any terms,' he told a correspondent later in October. To Alistair Hetherington, editor of the *Manchester Guardian*, whose diaries record more than a hundred private conversations with the Labour leader,[10] he claimed that Labour, on getting into power, would reopen negotiations with the Six immediately.

And yet, in defiance of all these cautions, outright opposition is what he finally produced, in language which nobody could mistake for a temporary, transitional, negotiating position. For that reason, Hugh Gaitskell deserves recognition as the first of the 'Euro-sceptics', in the rather special sense which that term gathered round itself. The label wasn't current in the early 1960s, and it later became a misnomer, because it conferred a spurious aura of detachment on a school of thought that was, in fact, passionately opposed, at any given time, to the project known as 'Europe'. The anti-Europeans of the Thatcher years were the first to lay claim to its undoubted seductiveness. But Gaitskell came before them, as the representative of a state of mind for which 'sceptical' was a misleading description. Just as William Cash purloined the epithet for a school of thought whose intellectual manners belied it, the scholarly Gaitskell chose to invest this same subject with a reviling, unsceptical passion that no one had ever heard from him before. It is probably fair to say that he was not, in the depth of his being, opposed root and branch to British Europeanism. He was by no means Europhobic. But it also has to be said that his political rhetoric in the autumn of 1962 conveyed entirely the opposite impression. It gave coherence to an attitude of out-and-out hostility.

For help in the preparation of his conference speech, he turned to one faction among his friends and not the other. The Jenkinsite segment of the right could already see what was coming. Peter Shore, the party's international secretary, a lifelong zealot in the anti-EEC cause, produced a draft party statement on Europe that Gaitskell forced him to revise. The leader thought it went too far. But it was Shore rather than George Brown, Gaitskell's deputy leader, who was privy to the process by which Gaitskell determined his final position. When Brown went to Gaitskell's room in the conference hotel the night before the speech, he was persistently refused sight of the text. Gaitskell kept it covered up on the table. Brown, who would have to wind up the debate, asked, 'You're not going to switch the line, are you?', and the leader embraced him, saying, 'You know me better than that. I'd never do a thing like that.' And that is doubtless what Gaitskell sincerely thought. It is certainly what Brown said about him later: that he did not really intend to do what he did. To the end, in short, he was determined to have it both ways: to blow Macmillan's project out of the water, while insisting that he was not in principle opposed to it.

The speech he delivered to a large audience at the Brighton ice rink on 3 October 1962 was, to some who heard it, the greatest he ever made. By modern standards it was of Gladstonian dimensions, lasting 105 minutes, and it began in a calm, evaluative tone of voice. The leader rejected some of the oldest shibboleths of his party: that entry into the EEC would be the end of socialist planning, or that the Community might somehow be wished out of existence by Britain's remaining outside. But this didn't last long. Although he continued to insist that his only objection was to the terms Macmillan would settle for, the entire message of the speech seemed to be that a version of triumphant British isolationism should stretch forward into the indefinite future.

For one thing, Gaitskell abandoned his earlier line, that the economic arguments were evenly balanced. Now he loaded them all one way, deriding the notion that Britain could expect any benefit from expanding her European markets while losing in Canada, Australia and the rest. He

dismissed the view that a large domestic market of 250 million consumers offered an enticing prospect. 'Would we necessarily, inevitably,
be economically stronger if we go in and weaker if we stay out?' he
asked. 'My answer to this is . . . NO. Is it true to say that by going in we
should become all that more prosperous . . .? Again my answer to that
must be NO.' But economics was no longer what most interested this
proudly rational man. What moved him was a series of arguments that
could have been used at any time and in any circumstances, almost
irrespective of the infamous 'terms', to exclude British membership
indefinitely.

For membership, Gaitskell said, would change everything. Britain,
he had discovered, would no longer be Britain. 'It does mean', he said,
'the end of Britain as an independent European state.' He would make
no apology for repeating this, he said, his voice rising. 'It means the end
of a thousand years of history.' For the EEC, he insisted, was all about
European federation. 'How can one seriously suppose that if the mother
country, the centre of the Commonwealth, is a province of Europe,
which is what federation means, it could continue to exist as the mother
country of a series of independent nations? It is sheer nonsense.'

Moreover, Europe itself harboured a series of menacing absurdities.
These had now, apparently, become clear to him. Whereas the old
dominions once stood beside Britain against continental enemies at
Gallipoli and Vimy Ridge, he thought he had discovered in the Treaty of
Rome evidence that the EEC itself, including the Germans and Italians
and French, now had pretensions to becoming a military alliance. This
was bad enough – but, in another field, there was much worse. The
Common Agricultural Policy was 'one of the most devastating pieces of
protectionism ever invented': so bad that mere negotiation away of its
rougher edges could not meet the case.

All in all, Macmillan's project now merited the most strident
language Gaitskell could produce. Europe's proposed treatment of the
Commonwealth and the Government's assurances on that account were,
he said, 'astonishing' and 'odious'. As for the assumption that only top
people understood the issue, it seemed to imply that popular opinion
should be excluded from the reckoning. Here was something no sentient
politician could contemplate. It provoked Gaitskell to a peroration of
purest demagoguery – 'what an odious piece of hypocritical, supercilious,
arrogant rubbish is this!' – qualified only by a dying fall in favour of
British entry. If the EEC would review this catalogue of its defects, maybe
Britain could one day join.

'I still hope profoundly', this teetering Janus declared, 'that there may be such a change of heart in Europe as will make this possible.'

Before conference Gaitskell never had such a reception from the party as he had for this speech. Hardly anyone ever had. Throughout its length, 'nobody coughed or stirred', wrote the *Evening Standard*. For this one and only occasion, according to Peter Shore, Gaitskell 'won not only the minds but the hearts' of the conference. Backed by only half the right, the left, uniquely, supported him, which produced his wife Dora's famous *mot*: 'All the wrong people are cheering.' The leading dissident of the right, Douglas Jay, the only member of the Frognal Set who backed Gaitskell as strongly on Europe as they all did on Clause Four and nuclear disarmament, was still foaming with admiration two decades later. 'It was unique among all the political speeches I ever heard,' Jay wrote in his autobiography. 'It can only be described as an intellectual massacre.'[11]

Intellectual, however, is hardly the word to apply to Gaitskell's speech. It wasn't devoid of factual content, and it asked some hard questions about where the EEC thought it was going. Parts of it could be counted sincerely sceptical, especially about the meaning of union. 'Not all political unions are necessarily good in themselves,' he fairly noted. 'It all depends, does it not? ... It is not a matter of just any union, it is a matter of what are the effects of union. Is it an aggressive one? Is it damaging to others? ... Does it erect barriers as well as pull them down?' These were questions, he said, that had to be asked and answered, before deciding.

All the same, the speech wasn't intellectual so much as intensely, manipulatively emotional. For more than an hour, it plucked the mystic chords of memory. Gaitskell seemed so anxious to propitiate the past that he felt obliged to deny any real urgency about the future. He poured out all the most compelling reasons for Britain to believe that this was not a turning-point, nor the time to address the strategic question which underlay Macmillan's application to join the Common Market.

The speech was also, one must say, more than an instant success. One of Gaitskell's longer-term ambitions was clearly met, in that the party was commonly judged to be, for practical purposes, united. There was no great outcry against what he said, even though this offended an important group of Labour politicians: another way in which the Gaitskell period first exhibited trends that later made themselves felt consistently. Not only did this leader prove himself to be a sceptic in the vulgar as well as better sense, he also established that anti-Europe speeches usually got the loudest cheers and elicited the softest rebellions against them. This was to happen time and again, in Conservative as well as Labour epochs. There were salient exceptions, when anti-Europeanism had drastic effects on political leaders. Both the birth of a new party, the Social Democrats in 1981, and the deposing of an old leader, Margaret Thatcher in 1990, could be partly accounted acts of punishment against excessive displays of Euro-hostility. But a continuing thread of the pro-Europe cause has been its restraint in both victory and defeat. There are reasons for this, not the least of them being that this is the side that eventually won the argument, occupied power, saw its ascendancy take root, could therefore afford to be magnanimous: a complex, significant story. It remains a telling fact, however, that for most of this history it is the anti-Europe cause that has had the greatest resonance: made the most noise, named the most enemies, touched the most doubting nerves.

The post-Brighton politics of Labour saw the beginning of this pattern. Though many of Gaitskell's friends were disappointed, they were almost all forgiving. They did not stir up trouble, nor did they very vigorously fight back. Friendships did not collapse, and Gaitskell went out of his way to offer reassurance. 'He was still faithful to the old rule of the primacy of personal relations,' Roy Jenkins writes in his autobiography. Although there were meetings of hurt and puzzled pro-Europeans, who gathered to talk about ways of stemming the tide, the party was actually more united now than at any other time in the Gaitskell years, because the left, for the first and only time, were on his side. His enemies were his friends, and few of his friends became, even transiently, his enemies.

As an exercise in leadership, however, Gaitskell's European performance does not stand up well to retrospective consideration. It was full of passionate doubt, but almost totally devoid of prophetic insight. It spoke with overwhelming eloquence for the importance of the past. The hard questions about the future it did not really address. It set a standard which others, over the years, were to follow, whereby the alternative to 'Europe' was never very coherently put together in the speeches of people who found this construct a hideous spectre which they couldn't accept.

At this stage in the argument, the economic picture was certainly confused. By far the most convincing doubt concerned the price of food. Entry into the Common Market, just as the Six were finalizing their Common Agricultural Policy, would mean a switch in the method for subsidizing farmers, and, after the elapse of a transitional period, the end of the system whereby Britain bought her food from wherever it was most cheaply available. By taxes and outright bans, the CAP would stop all that, and force British consumers to buy continental, often at higher prices than free trade would have allowed. There was no doubt about this, though the Government, naturally, slid over the detailed implications. Since 30 per cent of UK imports consisted of food, and the average family spent about 30 per cent of its income on food,[12] it was certain that such a change of regime would have important effects on British labour costs and on the balance of payments. This was an important downside to the project. For some protagonists, notably Douglas Jay, it remained the most reasoned reason for lifelong hostility to Britain belonging.[13] It also played a large part, as it had to, in the Treasury's unenthusiastic analyses, all the way from the 1950s to the 1970s, of the economic consequences for Britain of going into Europe.

There was, however, an upside to the project: or rather, a danger which loomed so large that, if she didn't enter the project, Britain would face disaster. She had to trade to live. The market of the future was growing next door, across the Channel, and the figures were already telling, there for all to see. In the old Commonwealth countries, let alone the new, imports had been moving slowly for years. They wanted to create their own industries, and were in any case inherently smaller scale than the US and Western Europe, to which world exports had more than doubled in the past few years. The trend was relentless, and the absolute figures, not just the rate of growth, were already showing it. In the first four months of 1962, as negotiations proceeded, 31.6 per cent of British exports went to the Commonwealth, 38.6 to Western Europe. This was before the full rigour of internal tariff-lowering had taken place in Europe. When the internal tariffs were gone, British exporters to Germany, France and the rest were certain to be badly hit in the market where, the evidence now incontrovertibly showed, expansion was going to be relentless.

That was the economic argument made by many MPs, in the two major Commons debates of 1961 and 1962. Gaitskell never frontally disposed of it, relying instead on plausible, but over-convenient, contentions out of the economist's locker: that Europe's expansion was not, in fact, due to the existence of the EEC as such, or that there could be no guarantee of Britain specially prospering under continental rules, or that regional blocs were a poor substitute, in the long run, for proper global trade bodies. The thread running through Gaitskell's economic agnosticism, as through the hostile doubts of others, was an exercise in self-persuasion. Probably the majority of British politicians at this time, whatever their long-term attitude to Europe, wanted to persuade themselves the economy was not in bad shape: the prospects were reasonable: industry was surviving, or better: and there was no overwhelming need, therefore, to plunge into the political pain – it always was a pain – of aligning our institutions with the EEC's, while spitting on the Commonwealth. That is what Gaitskell insisted. It seemed to be his way of avoiding what he called 'humiliation'.

It also pre-empted the pressure for a Great Alternative. If the problem wasn't terminal, why accept an argument that said: if not the EEC, what? So this, too, Gaitskell didn't speak of, though others did and produced a revealing glimpse of a debate.

To the extent that there was an economic problem, some argued, it should be met not by joining the EEC as a full member but by seeking mere 'association' with it. Some of the Tories were keen on that, and the Government's response wasn't always logical. When this dilute expedient was put to Macmillan – to become 'country members, so to speak', the club-man drawled – he said it had been considered but rejected, on the ground that it had no advantages. To become merely a free-trading associate, he said, would 'raise all the same problems for British agriculture and Commonwealth trade', without giving Britain a position of influence within the Community to address them.[14] In other words, all the duties without the say. Edward Heath put it rather differently. Britain seeking a free-trade relationship, he said, 'is one of the things that raises the deepest suspicions of everyone in Europe'. She had been trying to secure one, without success, ever since the Community got going. All that had happened was that in 1958 de Gaulle vetoed a British attempt to get a free-trade area for all of wider Europe, and Britain had to make do with a separate body, of the 'out' countries, called the European Free Trade Association, the weaker brethren, some of whom would now seek entry to the EEC on Britain's coat-tails. The problem, Heath implied, was the opposite of what Macmillan said: the belief, among EEC members, 'that we want all the advantages of the developments in Europe without undertaking any of the obligations of the other members of the Community'.[15]

Whichever was the real reason – and both men, as usual, said different things at different times – it is plain that the free-trade alternative did not enter the agenda, even of the main opponents of the

Macmillan deal. Gaitskell did not push it. He did not seem to believe, at this stage, that Britain's economic situation demanded any drastic rearrangement of external relationships.

It has to be remembered, of course, that he was operating in the hottest political environment. He was concerned as much with the next election, coming soon, as with strategic national judgement, so one can't take as conclusive the omissions in his public thinking. Perhaps it is fair to decide that his opinion was not yet ripe. Charitably, you might say he wasn't ready. In any case, speaking as a domestic politician, he had plenty to say about the mess the Tories were making of the economy. He just didn't seem to think the future of Britain was yet, necessarily, wrapped up with the future of Europe.

Charity, however, doesn't deal with all questions. Gaitskell's major premise was spectacularly wrong. He hung more of his argument on the Commonwealth than many in his party, but as a lynchpin of either the economic advance or the political influence of the off-shore island, the Commonwealth was unreal. Many people did see this, however decorously they chose to make it clear. There was nothing perverse or mysterious about their judgement. They were simply readier to apply a cool head to factual evidence, undistorted by wishes or nostalgia. They were right, and Gaitskell was found to have brought the Brighton conference to its feet on a series of emotional appeals which events did not take very long to falsify.

This must necessarily colour the assessment of what Gaitskell would have done later in the piece, when, perhaps, he had become Prime Minister. There developed a lively academic industry in Gaitskell studies, some of which was devoted to the question of what he really thought about the Common Market. He said more than once, in his meandering odyssey, that he was sure there would be another application if this one didn't come off. It was, he insisted, all down to the terms, and these, he sometimes speculated, would one day change, perhaps when de Gaulle was no longer the commanding presence on the scene. One of the more consistent themes Gaitskell voiced concerned Britain's vital role in diverting the EEC from the dire but, to many, plausible fate of what he thought might become an inward-looking, tight little regional federation. As late as 21 September, just days before he raised the roof in Brighton, he spent a party political broadcast ruminating about the desirability of a wider Europe, and saying what a force for good in the world it might be. He was not, in any crude or adamant sense, anti-European, and no trace of xenophobia disfigured him. On the contrary, the position he arrived at was driven by a concern for more global internationalism. The Commonwealth kept eating at him. He wanted 'a bridge between the Commonwealth and Europe', which could not be constructed 'if we destroy the Commonwealth by our entry'.

At the back of this was a claim he made with great emphasis to President Kennedy, that he did not object in principle to British entry. In December 1962, he wrote a long memorandum to his fellow progressive, explaining why he had taken the negative line he did. 'I myself and my leading colleagues', he said, 'all happened to believe and still believe that the arguments of principle were fairly evenly balanced for and against, and that the balance would be tipped in favour of entry only if our conditions were fulfilled.'

It is in the belying of that statement, however, that Gaitskell made his mark. Although he certainly believed it to be true – which means, in the major sense, that it *was* true – his political performance gave the opposite impression. Its impact was quite different. The small print and the qualifying clauses were effaced by the brute power of his categoric rejection. Far from being finely balanced, the argument from principle came from his mouth in an overwhelmingly one-sided way. Whatever he may have desired, he became a propagandist against the European project at home, as well as doing much to fortify the scepticism of anyone abroad who was already disposed to doubt whether Britain seriously wished to become a European country.

This stance had some important effects. It was a sort of bellwether for the future, marking the path for later leaders, setting a standard that others emulated. In two ways, in particular, we can see Hugh Gaitskell as the forerunner of many politicians who mistook the truth about what 'Europe' fundamentally required of Britain.

The first is elementary and, of the two, is much the more excusable. Europe was a divisive issue for Gaitskell the party leader, as it was to be for every Labour leader until Tony Blair. Party management heavily influenced his thinking. 'The terms' were for Gaitskell what they became for Harold Wilson: the pretext which allowed him to avoid taking a clear policy position that half his party might have opposed. 'If I had urged unconditional entry (thus going further than the Government),' he told Kennedy, 'there would have been bitter opposition from a minority which was basically hostile to our entry. If I had urged opposition whatever the terms, this would also have been bitterly opposed ... In either case, there would have been a major split in the party, which, following the great dispute on defence, would have been fatal to our prospects.'

The trouble was, though, that Gaitskell's chosen way of dealing with this did not present him as a man sitting on the fence. His decisive oration showed no positive sympathies whatever towards Europe. It was the pro- not the anti-Europeans he decided he could take for granted, a choice whose influence reached well beyond the Labour Party. It helped to spur anti-Europe feeling in the country. At the end of 1961, after the application, public opinion, while still heavily laden with 'don't knows', surged in support of the idea of joining Europe. Labour support increased along with that of loyalist Tories, and was at one stage said to encompass more than half of Labour voters.[16] As the Labour leadership became more sceptical, public support, though still far from negligible, somewhat waned. To the extent that Gaitskell wanted to keep open the European option, his impact on public opinion, with the extremity of his utterance, was poorly judged. He immediately became the chief rallying-point for Euro-scepticism.

And yet, in some ways, he did not intend to be so: and this is the second sense in which he was a trail-blazer for successors. There was a discrepancy between the outcome he desired and the method by which he chose to reach it. He wanted to keep the issue open, but played his part in helping to close it. Gaitskell's most obvious heir in this mode of politics probably never gave him a thought, but her identity proclaims itself. Gaitskell wanted, at some time, to see Britain join Europe, but he preached relentlessly against it. Likewise, Margaret Thatcher spent a decade taking Britain ever deeper into Europe, yet simultaneously did her best to rouse public opinion against everything that 'Europe' represented.[17]

Along with serial inconsistency, this discrepancy between deeds and words is the political style that infuses, time and again, the history of Britain-in-Europe. Fatally aberrant, often counter-productive, these are practices the political nation has regularly adopted as its only way of coping with the project that dominates its existence.

What Gaitskell 'really' thought became, by a fateful intertwining, an academic question. The veto, of course, swept aside any immediate interest in the ongoing reality of British entry. But, only four days afterwards, Gaitskell himself was dead. At the age of fifty-six, unfulfilled as a statesman of major rank, he died from a viral infection that got at his lungs and eventually his whole immune system.

An epitaph, however, had already, in a sense, been declared on his attitude to Europe, which, because of the timing of his death, became the position for which he was most sharply remembered. In early December 1962, not long after the Brighton conference, the former US Secretary of State, Dean Acheson, made a speech which contained a phrase that has never been forgotten. 'Great Britain', Acheson told the graduating class at the West Point military academy, 'has lost an empire and has not yet found a role.' It was a speech about larger strategic matters, but also went on to ridicule British pretences about 'a "commonwealth" which has no political structure, or unity, or strength'. The British self-image, whether as economic master of the sterling area or broker between Washington and Moscow, imagined, Acheson said, a role that 'is about played out'.[18]

The speech caused an amazing eruption of outrage in Britain. Everybody who was anybody had their say. Ambassadors on both sides of the Atlantic had to devote their full time, for some weeks, to smoothing out the trouble. Macmillan wrote an open letter to the people, rebuking Acheson for 'an error which [had] been made by quite a lot of people in the course of the last four hundred years, including Philip of Spain, Louis XIV, Napoleon, the Kaiser, and Hitler'.

There could be only one explanation for the depth of this outrage, namely that Acheson had touched a recognizable nerve. In a single pithy phrase, he summed up what the British, in their heart of hearts, knew to be the truth: the truth which Gaitskell's had been the most resonant voice to deny. I could find no evidence that the Brighton speech actually prompted Acheson to say what he said. But indisputably it was the most authoritative recitation of the fantasy which Acheson despaired of, and which Macmillan, to do him justice, was attempting to challenge and, as he hoped, extinguish from Britain's view of the world.

'You know, the Common Market breakdown was a bigger shock for us than you chaps realised,' R. A. Butler affably told the Labour politician Anthony Wedgwood Benn a month after the veto.[19] The misapprehension, however, was rooted in a reason that extended far beyond itself. Since Labour wanted the breakdown to occur, the party and its leaders took some time to address the scale of what it really meant.

6

JOHN ROBINSON

A Conspiracy of Like-Minded Men

A MONTH AFTER de Gaulle's destructive intervention, a memorandum arrived at the Foreign Office from the British delegation in Brussels. Entitled 'The Next Steps', it showed that some British officials could produce a more hard-headed response to the collapse of Macmillan's policy than by merely toying with elegiac quotations to season the speeches of their disappointed ministers. It was addressed to the head of the Office's European Economic Organizations Department, and reported on the post-veto mood of the Community with a sinewy sense of diplomatic purpose.

The despatch began by considering the Italians. The Italians, said the writer, were furious at what had happened. 'I am told that the Italians have said to the Dutch in Rome that their anger at de Gaulle's behaviour will last longer than the anger in Holland.' All except the Luxembourgers, he said, were disgusted with the French. They had wanted the nego- tiations to continue and, if possible, succeed.

On the other hand, London should be wary. Whitehall ought not to suppose that this sense of solidarity would last long. 'While there are many individuals (most Dutchmen ... the German Economics and Finance Ministries) who will not forget or forgive,' the memorandum advised, 'the anger at the French is bound to wear off.' Officials had their jobs to do, and would 'sooner or later want to fall back into the former rhythm'. Their anger, in any case, was not primarily sympathetic but self-pitying. It was 'based more on the damage done to Community co-operation ... than on the resulting exclusion of Britain from the Community'. Britain's exclusion, however regrettable, would soon be accepted as a fact. Therefore, the author suggested, the British should be aware of a certain urgency. Their objectives might not yet be finally decided, he noted, but whatever they were, 'it would be easier to realise them this month than next, and progressively more difficult as we advance into the spring and summer'.

There were other complications. The Five were by no means agreed among themselves. The Germans and the Belgians, though tempted by vengeance against the French, thought it impossible to hold up the work of the Community for long. Only the Dutch, the author judged, 'are seriously considering punitive action in this field'. While the Germans were interested in stopping the passage of any regulations that might create still more obstacles against Britain joining one day, they saw 'juridical difficulties' in an attempt by the Five to engage in subversive consultations. 'The French would, it must be assumed, not take part. In their absence it would be difficult for the Five to pretend to the French that they were not consulting us multilaterally. And there would be two substantial difficulties: first, Luxembourg would keep the French fully informed, and might be even more active on France's behalf; secondly, as time went on, it would only be realistic to suppose that one or other of the Five would have interests not altogether divorced from those of France, the united front of the Five and Britain would be broken, and our own position might be very difficult.'

Of one thing, however, the author was certain. The idea of mere 'association' with the Community, which had always been the ambition of Conservative politicians who wanted to have it both ways, was unacceptable. Many schemes to this end were already floating round Brussels, many ways of getting Britain at least half engaged in the European enterprise, with some of the benefits and fewer of the costs and much of the great advantage, as the Five saw it, of a British presence in counterpoise to the French. But those who favoured this 'do not seem to have thought out the practical difficulties in any detail'. 'I have firmly stated our objections to any form of Association,' the writer reported, 'especially the fact that it would not provide for "political" relations with the Community.'[1]

This was a grand announcement, especially coming from a relatively junior man on what remained of the UK delegation to the Brussels negotiations. The texture of the despatch – cold-eyed analysis, anonymous sourcing, conspiratorial realism – had a personal flavour. Its tone, confident, assertive and effortlessly Machiavellian, is to be found littered through the public records extending down many years of the British engagement with 'Europe'. Its author, in the British way with civil servants, was and is almost unknown outside the circle of government. Yet in Whitehall and Brussels his name acquired the aura of a legend, which is duly celebrated in the secret, official history of the negotiations that finally secured British entry into the Community in 1972.

'To get into the Community,' the Foreign Office's official historian wrote, 'this country had to follow an extremely strait and narrow path, maintaining the true objective, overcoming disappointments, above all resisting the temptations of plausible but inadequate alternatives. The man who did most for many years by rigorous argument and strong determination to hold us to this strait and narrow path is Mr John Robinson.'[2]

In 1963, John Robinson was thirty-eight, and in the middle of a Foreign Office career which had not by then taken on the aberrant aspects it later acquired. His formation was conventional: private education at Westminster School, followed by Oxford, where he read Greats at Christ Church – though a hint of perversity is supplied by the absence of either of these details from his entry in *Who's Who*. Between school and university, he did service in the Air Force, as a non-commissioned officer, just getting in on the war. In 1949, he sat the Foreign Office exam, and was one of eight applicants, out of 400, selected for entry: those were the days when the brightest and the best still saw public service as a career-option of unrivalled fascination. In his first six years, Robinson did a tour in Delhi, another in Helsinki, as well as time in the FO bureaucracy at home. It was an ordinary beginning.

In 1956, he was sent to Paris, to Gladwyn Jebb's embassy, and this was the beginning of something else. This something else, the unique attribute Robinson was allowed to acquire, was summarized by the official historian: 'For some fifteen years he has worked in Paris, Brussels and London, uninterruptedly on Community affairs, and has become an unrivalled authority upon them.' In a department famous for despatching Japanese linguists to Bogotá, and Arabists to Iceland lest they get too familiar with the natives of the Middle East, Robinson was allowed to become a real European expert.

When Edward Heath was assembling the team to do Macmillan's work, Robinson was, through previous experience in Paris, a natural candidate. When that work collapsed in ruins, furthermore, it was Robinson who stayed behind in Brussels for the next four years, reading the runes, working the chancelleries, laying the basis for what he could not help becoming: the keeper of the memory of every telling detail, and every significant character, in the lengthy saga that was played out between the preparation for Britain's first application in 1961 and the consummation of her last in 1972.

So this made Robinson rare enough. He was maintained in place, allowed to absorb a history, perforce became the continuity man during the lean years between the first and final acts. His performance at the climax drew an official verdict that verged on the ecstatic. 'In the negotiations, he knew everyone, understood everything, foresaw everything, did everything,' the history records. Yet even that, apparently, didn't quite say enough for Robinson, all things considered. The author wanted to be more precise. 'His most important service, I think, came in the years *between* the first and last negotiations.'

Robinson was not a conventional Foreign Office type. Though formed normally, he sometimes behaved abnormally. Urbanity, for example, was not his style. 'He was a wild man,' one ineradicably urbane contemporary told me. Another remembered that he did not always play by the diplomatic rules. There were better ways, he thought, to serve his country. When Heath was negotiating on Macmillan's behalf in 1962, Robinson's main task was to act as an intelligence agent in the rival camps. He moved behind enemy lines, gaining unrivalled knowledge of their intentions. 'At our meetings to work out the next week's negotiating problems,' a member of the team told me, 'Robinson would produce a complete dossier on the thinking of the French and the others. We thought he bugged their offices.'

'In brilliance, in knowledge of Europe, in his readiness to confront the grandest in the land, John was unique,' said Roy Denman, a Whitehall partner-in-belligerence.[3] But these very qualities made him, as it was said, 'difficult'. Robinson himself, when I met him in retirement in the mid-1990s, talked self-effacingly about the mundane life he had led in Whitehall, doing the job he had to do for 'my shop' – otherwise known as the Foreign Office. His conversation revealed little of the brilliance, still less of the burning commitment to European integration (this was the time of deep controversy over the Treaty of Maastricht, for which he did not seem to be an enthusiast), that his reputation led one to anticipate. But another of his contemporaries, David Hannay, himself no paragon of modesty, called Robinson 'unbelievably able'. 'He was a brilliant civil servant, he drafted beautifully, he was a superb, ruthless negotiator.'[4]

Yet what singles Robinson out for a place in both the history and the bureaucratic anthropology of these years is something else again. Not only is it unusual for a Foreign Office official to retain the same professional interest for more than a decade, it is rarer still for members of that department, especially junior ones, to become associated with –

indeed, to form the militant vanguard of – a distinctive policy position. The Foreign Office has been marked often enough by an attitude, a state of mind, an institutional bias that became in due course the object of wrath and castigation by those, whether contemporary politicians or retributive historians, who disagreed with it. But such intellectual phases have usually been driven from the top. The appeasement of pre-war Germany, the adulation of post-war America, the seductions of Arabism, the lure of power as against the case for an international morality: all are deformities plausibly laid at the door of the institution which has seen party politicians of every stripe take their transitory place under its grand imperial ceilings. And the collective orthodoxy of the Foreign Office throughout the 1950s was, of course, decisive in shaping, rather than challenging, the responses of politicians who, at bottom, wanted most of all to see their own anti-Europe prejudices reinforced.

In 1961, when Macmillan redefined Britain as a country whose interest lay in seeking to join the European Economic Community, the Office responded smartly enough. It did its duty without objection, for those who run it have always been realistic about the locus of power. It had begun, indeed, to do more than that. Among Whitehall departments, it showed the most enthusiasm for Macmillan's idea. It was beginning to share his anxiety about the condition of a Britain that was in danger of ostracism from the table of the great powers. Alongside the Treasury's pessimism about the economic case for British entry into the Common Market – otherwise put, the Treasury's blind optimism about the stand-alone potential of the British economy – sat the Foreign Office's burgeoning pessimism about the political consequences of Britain's exclusion from influence in Europe, something which the whole of British history had been devoted to retaining.

Even so, when the veto occurred, it could not be said that the Foreign Office was well prepared for the future to which Macmillan and the Government were committed. The European culture-graft had by no means fully taken. There were numerous officials, especially in the higher ranks, whose background left a stamp they found hard to obliterate, even in the rather rare cases when they tried. Trained in Anglo-Americanism, pickled in the heritage of Commonwealth, they were slow to remake themselves as Europeans. Many of the senior people never really did so. Throughout Whitehall, Europe was a generational, as well as an attitudinal, issue. Burke Trend, who was soon to be the Cabinet secretary, continued to show the hand he had exhibited as the author of the crucial pre-Messina exercise in Whitehall scepticism.[5] An inveterate

Commonwealth man, Trend once confided to a friend that his career would ideally have culminated not in the Cabinet Office but as high commissioner to Canada.

On the other hand, not only the Macmillan initiative but the passage of time left a significant residue of committed talent, of which John Robinson was but one element. The young men who had despaired of their superiors' hidebound disdain for the Schuman Plan and the Messina project were rising up the hierarchy. The emblematic figure of Michael Palliser, Spaak's son-in-law, having watched post-Suez politics from the Paris embassy, was made head of the Planning Staff in 1964, a plum position of influence. Donald Maitland, though still mainly an Arabist, was personally selected to be in charge of the vital task of press relations for the Heath delegation. Oliver Wright had moved into 10 Downing Street, as the foreign affairs private secretary.

And other contemporaries, later to play a significant part in the acting out of Britain's struggle to become – or avoid becoming – a European country, now begin to make their appearance. For the first time the name of Michael Butler, probing and enraging Gaullist circles from his position as first secretary in Paris, emerges in the PRO files, the beginning, as he rather grandly put it in a retirement memoir/polemic, of 'my long *servitudes et grandeurs européennes*'.[6] Butler, who rose through every important European policy job to become the UK ambassador to the Community during the sulphuric years of Prime Minister Thatcher, 1979–85, was, along with Palliser, the archetypal Foreign Office European, sharing with Robinson a trait that made both of them especially mistrusted in the rest of Whitehall. Neither was prepared to leave the accountancy side of the enterprise to the Treasury's exclusive judgement. Butler, like Robinson, could not be accused of being economically illiterate. Each man added this dimension to the otherwise threadbare credentials of most British diplomats to talk about the intricacies which are at the heart of all European negotiation. Whether calculating the odds on cereal deficiency payments or mastering the finer points of the hard écu, cocktail urbanity would never be enough.

Emerging here, in short, was a new, younger breed of Foreign Office orthodoxy, to replace the old scepticism. An elite regiment was taking shape. Europe wasn't yet the path of choice for every ambitious diplomat, but it promised to be much more interesting than the Commonwealth, and offered a prospect of influence greater than anything else available in a second-order power engaged with the global rigidities of the Cold War. By 1963, a corps of diplomats was present in and around the

Foreign Office who saw the future for both themselves and their country inside Europe. The interests of their country and their careers coincided. It was an appealing symbiosis. The fact that France had, for the moment, obstructed it was less a deterrent than a challenge to their ambition.

As a torch-bearer for this challenge, its most obdurate and devious exponent, nobody, as the historian implied, had a longer record than John Robinson. But one man, in the core years of the period, was more senior and therefore more important still than Robinson, and that man, as it happens, was the historian himself.

Sir Con O'Neill, the author of the secret history, was writing about the period when he was Robinson's immediate superior. O'Neill led the enterprise on which Robinson served, the final negotiations for entry, 1971–2. In the project of Europe, they were comrades: as exotic, by Foreign Office standards, as each other: a most potent combination of talents.

O'Neill's peculiarity lay not in his manner, which was diplomatic if somewhat professorial. Nor did he acquire enemies through an overbearing policy commitment that he was determined, by any devious means, to force past other Whitehall departments: the way Robinson is remembered. O'Neill, a man of great reclaim in Foreign Office mythology, was singular for twice quitting the department on matters of principle, or at least rebellion, beginning with a protest against the pre-war appeasement of Hitler. His role as official historian of his own work was the culmination of another sudden departure and return. Refused the ambassadorship to Bonn in the mid-1960s, he left the Office in a huff. But ministers summoned him back, having decided he was the indispensable figure to lead the official side of the negotiations. In that task, he regarded nobody as less dispensable than John Robinson, to whom he paid an extraordinary epitomizing tribute from one bureaucrat to another. 'I sought his advice many hundreds of times,' O'Neill the historian writes, 'and can scarcely remember an occasion when I failed to follow it.'

They became a professional pair, O'Neill the senior, Robinson his earth-scorching ally: Robinson the man of fire, O'Neill the restraining force. 'If Con hadn't been there,' said Michael Palliser, 'John might have wrecked everything by his single-minded determination to win, and not minding how he did it.'[7]

On the matter of Europe, O'Neill went back a long way: most distantly to his disgust for appeasement, but more recently to a misjudged response to the Schuman Plan. We have heard his name before.

After the war, employed as a leader-writer on *The Times*, he directed the paper's European policy with a sceptical bias against Churchill's grand effusions. 'A premature attempt by governments to force union on Europe, before it is wanted, can only make divisions deeper,' is a sample of his early post-war thinking about the earliest efforts that were being advanced, especially, by the Americans.[8] Back in the Foreign Office, he was posted to Germany in 1948, where he decided that the Schuman Plan could be ignored. 'I am ashamed to say that I did not realise its enormous importance,' he later told Michael Charlton.[9] The misjudgement, which was just about universally shared, did not damage his career. He served, with angular distinction, more an intellectual than a social man, in Peking and Helsinki, before returning to his prime focus of interest.

In 1963, O'Neill became head of the United Kingdom delegation to the European Communities (the plural signifying that there were still separate communities: for the Market, for Coal and Steel and for Euratom). Here he reacquainted himself with Robinson, whom he had previously met when they were both involved in the early phase of Macmillan's conversion, Robinson as an under-strapper, O'Neill in a more senior position. Robinson, in particular, was committed to this cause. His contemporary, Christopher Audland, remembers their time together, after Macmillan had begun to feel his way round the issue, sitting in the same Foreign Office room, sifting the replies from Whitehall to the Prime Minister's questionnaire, shaping the responses in the right direction. They were not bloodless officials, but men who had decided what they thought and were now determined to help bring it about.

It is Audland's opinion that Robinson's contribution was the biggest of all, even though his rank was never high. 'He was the most influential official from 1961 to 1973,' he told me in 1994. 'He knew what he wanted. He was very clear strategically, but also tactically.' O'Neill, however, was the senior of the two, and therefore possibly the more important. Let us say that each, in his way, made a significant contribution to British history. In the middle years of the 1960s, followed by the early years of the 1970s, these two men had as much as anyone to do with keeping alive the conception that Britain belonged in the Common Market, and then bringing the embryonic idea to birth.

Something broader was also signified in their appointment to Brussels. It marked the establishing-in-place of the elite regiment. The Foreign Office was not yet run by Europeans, but the positions of influence on the Europe question were given to people who believed in its importance. They were a minority in the Office, but had majority control of the policy they cared about. The sceptics preferred to go, or were sent, elsewhere. Not that they were seen as sceptics. Such a term would imply the existence of an argument in which there had been winners and losers, an environment, such as developed in politics twenty years later, where sides had to be chosen and opinions were taken down in evidence. But in the early 1960s the new orthodoxy had not seized general hold. For many in the Office, and more in Whitehall as a whole, Europe was still a side-show. If anything, 'Europeans' were seen by their elders as a little off-centre: people who, because they happened to be captured by this unpromising cause which de Gaulle now appeared to have nullified, could be allowed to roam around their chosen play-ground.

The regiment, however, was disciplined. It knew where it wanted to get to, even though O'Neill and Palliser and Robinson and Butler were each men of different stamp, their intellects and emotions about Europe differently arranged. Whereas Palliser had a credal, not to mention family, affiliation, Robinson always claimed to be no more than a mechanic. He despised 'belief'. When I saw him thirty years later, he represented himself as a man who had merely done his best for 'my shop'. His allusions to his work, which were reluctantly given, emphasized its technical aspects: his reading of de Gaulle's intentions, his secret connections with the Dutch (always his best sources), the optimal ordering of papers to be circulated, or not, around Whitehall, the need to match the self-interested brutalities of the Quai d'Orsay. In the many interviews and conversations I had before writing this book, nobody's language was freer than Robinson's of the prophetic abstractions that so often accompany the European discourse. He was a practical man, from the beginning. 'I wrote a paper after the veto,' he said, 'pointing out how many telephones, how many refrigerators, how many washing-machines there were per 100,000 inhabitants of France. Things we'd been absolutely convinced we were superior in. But we were not superior. Nobody troubled to look them up, but I'd looked them up. My figures were accepted.'[10]

But not by everyone. At least, not by everyone immediately. For the elite regiment was taking shape before its generals, the politicians of the new Labour Government, had reached the same level of strategic certainty.

The story of the 1960s, after Macmillan and after Gaitskell, reveals a contrast of mentalities. On the one hand, officialdom, the diplomatic side of Whitehall, was beginning to nurture, at its policy-making core, a conviction that there was no alternative to British membership of the Common Market: a view accompanied by no less adamant professional vows that the French must be defeated in their refusal to permit this to come about. On the other hand, the politicians of the moment remained less sure. In politics, to begin with, nothing was changed by the veto. If anything, it stimulated a rebirth of the old hostility, and it certainly rekindled the old and chronic disagreements. Among the relevant politicians, with a handful of exceptions there was no matching clarity of purpose, no parallel willingness to shake off the incubus of past glories and future fantasies. De Gaulle's conduct, apart from rendering early entry impossible, had, for many politicians, only assisted in confirming their native dislike of Europe, and their suspicion of its schemes and stratagems.

This did not last very long. The influence of the committed soon began to bear down on the uncertain heads of those who would ideally have preferred not to be obliged to make a choice. The logic of the washing-machine was communicated from Robinson into the reluctant, but finally unresisting, mind of a new Prime Minister. Ultimately, the political class was cornered.

Two groups of public servants, who admittedly displayed different levels of angst, now made a serious effort to succumb to reality: the younger vanguard at the Foreign Office, and the inheritors, both young and old, of the mantle of British socialism. We are now entering the middle period of the saga of political ineptitude: of prolonged and agonized uncertainty, followed by the most grudging submission to trends that had been visible for a long time before.

*

LABOUR WON THE ELECTION, in October 1964, without any serious debate about Europe having taken place. The application for entry was Macmillan's last throw, and the veto was his last straw, as Rab Butler smirkingly indicated to Anthony Wedgwood Benn. So the issue was latent, a large failure added to the other disintegrations which his successor, Sir Alec Douglas-Home, was obliged, after thirteen years of Tory rule, to try and defend. But it was not made much of. The Labour manifesto clung to the old world, in which choices could be blurred. 'Though we shall seek to achieve closer links with our European

partners,' it said, 'the Labour Party is convinced that the first responsibility for a British Government is still the Commonwealth.' The party
stood by the five conditions it had defined as central in 1962: 'binding'
Commonwealth safeguards, freedom to pursue an independent foreign
policy, pledges kept to partners in EFTA (the residual second division of
non-EEC members), the right to plan the British economy, guarantees
for British agriculture.

Labour also had a new leader, with strongly anti-European credentials. Harold Wilson came from the left of the party, which had for many
years, after its early anti-American flirtations with European federalism,[11]
folded an anti-EEC position into its collection of socialist concerns.
Gaitskell, in declaring against the 1961 application, chose to betray his
friends before his country; for Wilson there was no such complication.
He had led the conference in rising to Gaitskell's glorious philippic. But,
to be elected leader, he did not need to state a position on European
integration: in the 1960s, as in the 1950s when Macmillan beat Butler
for the Tory leadership, the issue was low to the point of obscurity in
the assessment of the relevant electorate. More pleasing to the Labour
MPs of the day was Wilson's way with words, his brilliant capacity to
have it both ways, the scornful elegance he brought to bear on the
frailties of the other side. Although the veto, by keeping Britain out, had
saved her from the fate that Wilson as well as Gaitskell affected most to
fear, the new leader-presumptive did not hesitate to ridicule Macmillan's
failure. 'Naked in the conference room is one thing,' he told the
Commons on 31 January 1963. 'Naked and shivering in the cold outside,
while others decide our fate, is an intolerable humiliation.'

In the beginning, the new Government could believe its fate was in
no one's hands but its own. It, apparently, was the master now. That
was the state of mind in which it entered power. It seemed to recognize
that the Commonwealth, however keenly defended by Labour romantics,
did not close the argument about the British economy which, all Labour
spokesmen vowed, would be placed on the road to recovery only by the
application of socialist remedies. The economy, they knew, was what
mattered, and they did not doubt that the Tory record of low growth
and persistent balance of payments crises could be reversed. Shortly after
de Gaulle's veto, Richard Crossman, Wilson's leading propagandist, told
American readers that Britain's attempt to enter Europe had derived
from a pessimism spreading through Whitehall, industry and the City
which was 'completely foreign to the mood of the Labour Party'. 'Surely
it is a good thing', he added, 'that one of Britain's two great parties is

still passionately convinced that this country has a future – outside the Common Market.'[12]

This was what the party, with only a few exceptions, thought. Even the core of Labour pro-Marketeers grouped around Roy Jenkins, the *salon* of Gaitskell's *refusés*, found themselves for the moment put still further out of face by the General. Anthony Crosland, though not so committed a European as Jenkins, was a bellwether figure, the party's most celebrated ideologist. In the revised (1964) edition of his essential text, *The Future of Socialism*, there is no reference to the EEC.[13]

Other matters dominated the early months of the 1964 Government. A National Plan, designed to end the stop–go cycle that had been the curse of the post-war economy, was wheeled enthusiastically into place. Planning in one country was seen not only as the apotheosis of a modernized socialism but a repudiation of the European alternative: most of Wilson's main speech against the Macmillan application, delivered in the Commons in June 1962 when he was the shadow Foreign Secretary, had attacked the Treaty of Rome and the culture of its signatories on the specific ground that they were profoundly anti-socialist. 'The plain fact is that the whole conception of the Treaty of Rome is anti-planning, at any rate national planning,' Wilson then said. The only planning allowed in Europe was 'for the one purpose of enhancing free competition', he railed. To the enactment of this paean of belief in state economic planning the Wilson Cabinet turned most of its energies between 1964 and 1966. The European option was relegated to a negligible parenthesis.

This condition was replicated in Brussels, where the British option seemed equally void of relevance. One of Con O'Neill's jobs, as the new head of delegation, was to submit an annual report on the EEC's goings-on. At the end of 1964 he was obliged to record that British relations 'appeared to drift even further away from the foreground of Community thinking'. He added: 'The fact that our most positive contacts with the Community throughout 1964 concerned the subject of patents typifies the trivial level to which our working relations with the Community are now confined.' The Community itself, meanwhile, was developing fast. The rage against the French soon dissipated, and the regiment did not hesitate to warn its masters about what could be discerned. O'Neill quietly set down the ominous words. 'The inexorable process of adding little by little to the corpus of intra-Community decisions, doctrine and commitments has brought further divergence,' he noted.[14]

For a time, as it happened, this analysis was overtaken by events. In the middle of 1965, the Community experienced a heavy crisis that brought divergence within rather than without. The Treaty of Rome, one must always remember, was a beginning and not an end: since its signing, every year had been devoted to the practical evolution of its meaning in terms of real agreements, serious surrenders of national sovereignties, collective study and action on the common policies it envisaged. Through 1964, these had progressed so well – it was O'Neill's point – that the prospect arose of a full customs union, covering both agricultural and industrial products, being completed by mid-1967, more than two years ahead of the target date laid down in the Treaty. But in June 1965 there was another crisis of the French. The Council of Ministers failed to agree on arrangements for the future financing of the Common Agricultural Policy, the lynchpin of French design and interest. Not only did France, having failed to get her way, temporarily withdraw her ministers from meetings of the Council, bringing its policy-making to a halt, but General de Gaulle used the moment to launch a wide attack both on the powers of the Commission and on the very existence of majority voting in the Council, due, according to the Treaty, to start in 1966. Never an admirer of the Monnet–Schuman concept, the General came to power too late to stop it happening, but was regularly searching for ways to undermine its artefacts of supra-nationalism. An impasse developed. For the rest of 1965, nothing of substance occurred. For that period, the congruence between Britain's official lack of interest and the EEC's manifest inertia rendered O'Neill's gloom a little academic.

The inner momentum carrying the island towards the continent, however, had not entirely stopped. Although Wilson was comfortable with his anti-Europe railleries, and believed in his stand-alone National Plan, it is clear enough that he never repudiated Macmillan's ambition. Nor, at bottom, had Gaitskell done so. Gaitskell's summons to what sounded like a millennial battle for an independent Britain in fact concealed, as he disarmingly stated, the intention to resume the attempt to enter the EEC at some future date. Even in his ferocious defence of a thousand years of history, he kept open the door for a five-year change of mind. Deep down, and aware of the economic realities, he had to be ambivalent. Yet any ambivalence Gaitskell could muster was but a prelude to the efforts of Harold Wilson, a man whose entire political nature, what some might call his genius, was defined by his mastery of ambiguity.

Very soon, in the documents, the nuances are beginning to change. This starts, naturally, with the officials. Already in April 1965, Michael

Palliser, from the Foreign Office's Planning Department, gives an early glimmering of revisionism. Noting the abruptness with which some junior minister has recently invoked Labour's five restrictive conditions for contemplating accession to the Community, Palliser circulates an advisory rebuttal, cast in words of painful respect, suggesting that the reiteration of these conditions is no longer helpful. 'It is not for me to comment on the political importance within this country of laying emphasis on the five points,' Palliser disingenuously states. But the Government was now conducting 'a genuine reappraisal' of Britain's role in Europe, and 'any continuing insistence on the five conditions will seriously hamper HMG's efforts in this direction'. It would 'keep ... suspicion alive', and 'disturb our friends'.[15] Although it is true to say that, for much of 1965, the tone of the Foreign Office files reveals a state of extreme pessimism about Britain's prospects of *ever* getting into the Community, the regiment is plainly preparing to play a long game.

In the early days of 1966, it takes another stride forward. O'Neill, who has agreed to make a public speech in the Netherlands, submits the text of it for approval by the Office, with a mordant covering note that says, 'I think the general effect is fair and loyal enough to present British policy – or rather lack of policy.' He uses the opportunity to stress as much of the positive as he can, remarking how much attention the British were paying to the Common Market's French-inspired crisis, which 'proves how far my country has gone towards thinking of the fate and fortunes of the rest of Western Europe as inseparable from its own'. He has no doubt, this unelected officer says, that British public opinion is 'more and more coming to see our future as involving closer and closer connections with the rest of Western Europe'. He mentions the problem of sovereignty only, soothingly, to dismiss it: 'Experience in many fields has taught us that every international relationship affects our sovereignty and that exaggerated national independence is ineffective.... The problem lies more in the practice than in the principles.' As for O'Neill's conclusion, which the Office does not restrain him from uttering, it is extravagantly prophetic. 'I venture to express the purely personal view', he told the Dutch, 'that, should we ever succeed in joining the Community, we may well be found to be the champions rather than the opponents of its "supra-national" aspects.'

To balance this enthusiasm, he counsels against excessive zeal, urging that the wish to join the Community was 'not the same thing as the wish to undergo conversion to a new religion'. Although some regarded the Treaty of Rome 'as Holy Writ, whose every comma breathes divine inspiration ... I hope the Community will not insist on baptism by total immersion'.[16] But O'Neill's underlying message, approved by London, speaks for a Britain whose eagerness is qualified only by stoic resignation to facts of life that are probably temporary.

And so it proves, at a higher level as well. Some time in January, the wheels begin to turn a little faster, not just among officials but among a secret group of ministers. On 26 January, a minute records the formation of a committee of top officials to recommence the work of examining the overall economic impact on Britain, especially of the Common Agricultural Policy. Chaired by Sir Eric Roll, a key member of the Macmillan negotiating team and now permanent secretary at the Department of Economic Affairs, it includes unusually senior people from the Treasury, Foreign Office, Board of Trade and so on, and will operate under special conditions. Its brief has been approved by Prime Minister Wilson and his Foreign Secretary, Michael Stewart, but no other minister is meant to know that the committee even exists. Collective responsibility will be delayed. The rubric is explicit. 'Officials would neither report to ministers that they were working on questions connected with our future relations with Europe, nor inform them how the work was progressing.' Only after the work was completed would the Prime Minister decide whether to inform his colleagues.[17]

Nothing of this tendency, so far, was public. At the March 1966 election, which he called to improve on Labour's modest 1964 majority, Wilson continues to present himself as a leader who holds the continentals in utmost suspicion. Scepticism is his tone, though he affects a grudgingly open mind. If the conditions are right, Britain will consider it, he says, parading himself as a hard-nosed negotiator. 'My own experience of negotiations goes back twenty years,' he told an election audience at Bristol. 'It started with the most difficult of the lot, the Russians.' His best-remembered line, reeking of John Bullish defiance, was a riposte to the recent welcome which his main opponent, Edward Heath, had given to the ending of the Common Market's crisis, and to new murmurings of fraternity from the French. 'One encouraging gesture from the French Government,' Wilson spat, 'and the Conservative leader rolls on his back like a spaniel ... Some of my best friends are spaniels, but I would not put them in charge of negotiations into the Common Market.'

Already, however, Wilson was setting course for an attempt at entry. Never did a cure-all economic nostrum have a shorter life than his National Plan. As the Roll committee started work, word was seeping out to supportive ministers like George Brown, the most senior and voluble pro-European in the Cabinet. It began even before the election. On 20 January, Brown goes to lunch with the newspaper tycoon, Cecil King, chairman of the *Daily Mirror*, who records in his diary Brown excitedly bringing the lunch forward a week 'to tell me that Wilson is deciding to enter the Common Market!'[18] The King diary, coming out of a newspaper that was close to Labour and strongly pro-Europe, tracks the private world of Wilson and Brown, the tycoon's regular lunch companions, through 1966. Wilson's own conversion seems to have been sealed much earlier than he let on. Less than three weeks after the election, on 19 April, after seeing Wilson for an hour, King recounts: 'About Europe, he said he thought we should be in in two or three years.'

It was not only the logic of the elite regiment that effected this change in the prevailing bias of the Government. Events themselves were exposing the thinness of the alternative analysis. Consider, for example, the Commonwealth. Wilson, like Gaitskell, was by temperament a Commonwealth man. Although the evidence of a long-term downward trend away from Commonwealth trade could not be refuted, this special British relationship with a multi-racial Third World was something with great appeal to the Labour soul, of which Wilson always considered himself the prime custodian. But the middle 1960s saw a rending of both the economic and political ties with the Commonwealth. In November 1965, Rhodesia declared for unilateral independence, which laid on Wilson's back the burden of trying to undo this intolerable exercise in white supremacy. The task preoccupied him, humiliatingly, for years, and he never succeeded. His failure, therefore, also provoked great bitterness against Britain from much of the rest of the Commonwealth, especially in Africa but also, before long, in white Canada and Australia. Sentiments of affection, which in 1964 were proposed as a central feature of Labour's world view and the viable basis for an alternative to Europe, began to vanish on both sides.

Simultaneously, the defence aspect of British globalism was being exposed as a costly charade. The country's role as a kind of deputy world policeman, alongside the US, could not be sustained. Here the soul of Labour had long been pressing the party's leaders to cut defence spending, but the leaders, for the first couple of years, resisted these emotional directives. In the case both of the currency and of the military, Wilson was bent on proving to the people and the world, and perhaps to himself, that Labour government was not to be associated with retrenching the symbols of national greatness. Such an ambition could not last long. Retreat from the world forced itself on the managers of the nation's finances, and in July 1967 the process culminated in a defence white paper announcing the end of Britain's presence East of Suez by the mid-1970s. The Commonwealth was shocked. The Australians were 'appalled and dismayed', the leader of Singapore, Lee Kuan Yew, was 'fighting mad' and threatened commercial revenge.[19] The American President, Lyndon Johnson, declared an epitaph, writing to Wilson of his disappointment 'upon learning this profoundly discouraging news ... tantamount to British withdrawal from world affairs'.

But the consequence was, surely, obvious. With the political and the military engines of neo-imperialism all but turned off, a reassessment of Britain's role could produce only one conclusion. Whether or not she entered the Common Market, it was in her local region, grappling with her age-old neighbours, under the umbrella of Nato but also in some kind of new political and economic alignment, that her future was bound to lie.

The final awareness of this was borne in on Wilson only months after he had vowed never to be a spaniel. The Government experienced the first of several economic crises. In July 1966, a run on the pound was followed by a heavy deflationary package that put paid to the extravagant growth targets on which most of Labour's promises were based. The Crossman pronunciamento – 'this pessimistic conclusion ... completely foreign to the Labour Party' – was shattered. As if to underline one inner meaning of this, in the Cabinet reshuffle that followed, George Brown became Foreign Secretary. To the enemies of 'Europe', this was a fatal signal. It could just as easily have happened that Brown should resign. At the time, he was making one of his frequent threats to do so. Had this been allowed to happen, reflected one of the enemies – deploying a level of hyperbole with which students of Britain's European argument would become more and more familiar – 'the application to join the Market would probably never have been made'.[20]

Crystallizing his plans, Wilson had to take account of these enemies. Not long ago, after all, he had belonged in their camp. But it is entirely improbable that Brown's presence, as a passionate European in charge of the department that would be responsible for implementing the policy, alone prompted the switch that they detested. Long after the event, anti-EEC politicians continued to ponder explanations for the volte-face that Wilson, their reliable friend, appeared to have performed. Douglas Jay,

President of the Board of Trade at the time, could barely credit it. Did not the political and economic case against entry remain exactly as it was when Wilson made his derisive election speech in Bristol? 'An intelligent man', wrote Jay, 'does not, on rational grounds, alter his entire view on a fundamental issue affecting the whole future of his country in six or seven months, when the facts have not changed.' Jay put the conversion, which he regarded as a kind of treason, down to Wilson's susceptibility to pressure, especially from the press, along with the arrival of George Brown to articulate it. The figure of Cecil King, 'a pro-Market extremist' and a friend and former employer of Brown, looms large in the Jay demonology. And, in the Wilson years, King was indeed a sinister presence who tainted them, not long after this, by seeking, until removed by fellow directors alarmed for his sanity, to deploy his newspapers in support of an anti-democratic coup against the elected Government and the installation of a ministry of unelected talents, including himself.

More reliable witnesses to the Wilson odyssey in this matter are to be found among colleagues who, while being almost as sceptical of Europe as was Jay, retained a certain dispassion in their observation of the leader's tactics. Both Richard Crossman and Barbara Castle, in their diaries for 1966, reveal mounting suspicion of what he was up to. Never did he openly explain what he intended. That was the Wilson way, surrounded as he was by Cabinet colleagues who split about evenly in their enthusiasms, with eight of them firmly against any new application for entry.[21] Although Wilson was going round among his non-political friends like King vowing to be 'one politician, and a Prime Minister at that, [who] is honest with the public', neither the public nor his colleagues were yet judged ready for the revelation. Mrs Castle, however, knew what he was doing, and summarizes a technique that describes his entire approach to managing power in the fractious Labour environment of those years. 'I remain convinced he is anxious to get in,' she wrote, 'and he has succeeded in guiding us into a discussion of the details, which is more effective than anything else in making principles look less important.'[22]

The regiment, meanwhile, was pushing Wilson forward. O'Neill, in particular, was active, after close consultation with Eric Roll. In August, he wrote a paper, 'How to get into the Common Market', in which his realistic analysis of French intentions concluded with a list of concessions Britain should make to gratify them.[23] He noted that the Ministry of Agriculture was against any softening of the terms, and the Treasury was increasingly alarmed by the short-term ('and not only short-term') disadvantages for the balance of payments. The economic advisers, O'Neill noticed, thought the economy would be unfit to enter the competitive world of a tariff-free Europe for another five years. But he himself saw the matter quite differently. He thought time was ever more of the essence. 'Though the consequences of early entry into the Community may seem economically bleak,' he wrote, 'the long-term economic consequences of continuing on our present relatively indepen- dent course look much bleaker; and as time passes, the difficulty and the price of entering the Community will both grow greater.'

O'Neill, in this crucial phase of Wilson's strategic evolution, had become an almost open proselyte. Wilson called an all-day Chequers meeting, on 22 October, at which the Cabinet, after being kept in the dark about Downing Street's machinations, would have its first full European discussion. The Prime Minister was about to spring upon them his own surprise. But among the mass of preparatory papers ministers received was a report from the head of the UK delegation in Brussels which opened with a lapidary statement designed to lift their minds to matters more elevated than mere accountancy: to a vision of high politics, in fact, of the kind that civil servants seldom feel it is their place to articulate.

'For the last 20 years,' O'Neill wrote, 'this country has been adrift. On the whole, it has been a period of decline in our international standing and power. This has helped to produce a national mood of frustration and uncertainty. We do not know where we are going and have begun to lose confidence in ourselves. Perhaps a point has now been reached when the acceptance of a new goal and a new commitment could give the country as a whole a focus around which to crystallise its hopes and energies. Entry into Europe might provide the stimulus and the target we require.'[24]

No politician could have said this in public, and few of the relevant ministers were prepared explicitly to contemplate it in private either. It was, after all, a painful condemnation of what their profession was supposed not to allow to happen. The idea that the country might not know where it was going, after two years of the blessings of Labour, was uncomfortable to contemplate – and some of the Chequers discussion, on the part of the less reverent participants, was devoted to demolishing the premise. Crossman's diary entry for 22 October reveals a strand of Cabinet opinion resisting the insinuation that lay behind the O'Neill note, its search for a new way of being Great Britain. The diarist spoke up for Little England. 'I regard Little England as the pre-condition for any successful socialist planning whether inside or outside the Common Market,' he stated. Along with this should go devaluation of the pound, which the Treasury said was the necessary concomitant of entry, but which Wilson would not hear of. When Crossman declared that 'they shouldn't go into Europe in order to remain great', some other ministers, he says, gave him 'a great deal of support'. Among them was a colleague who was in the middle of one of the many reversions and reconsiderations that have marked his own career. 'Tony Wedgwood Benn', Crossman writes, 'made an extremely good speech asking what was European about us and what was American and whether the Anglo-American relationship isn't worth a great deal more than entry into Europe.'

O'Neill's rendition, however, got close to epitomizing what was present, if only half articulated, in the mind of the Prime Minister. Wilson came to Chequers with a plan up his sleeve which he saw as the necessary prelude to another attempt at entry. He was meticulous, as always, in his dissembling. With a large minority of his friends dead against an application, he needed to couch his strategy as merely indicating a desire to probe the possibilities. But here and now, writes Douglas Jay, 'the fatal slide began'. 'There must be no leaks,' Wilson instructed. 'It would be fatal to have any suggestion which would commit us either for or against entry.'[25] But what he desired not to leak was a decision that had much significance as a gesture towards the truth of O'Neill's analysis. He and George Brown, he said, would embark on a tour of the EEC capitals to sound out the current state of opinion there.

The Probe, as it came to be officially called, was the beginning of a recognition on Wilson's part – never explicitly stated, but surely alive in his subconscious – that Britain did indeed need a new focus for 'its hopes and energies': that, what with Rhodesia and the economic crisis and the sense of drift that was everywhere a subject of media discussion, the Government itself would benefit from a revivalist project: that 'Europe', however regrettably, was becoming the only place to look.

The Wilson–Brown tour of Europe, from January to March 1967, was in many ways the acme of Wilsonian politics. It applied to Europe several of the defining traits of this remarkable leader. It put on show his fascination with tactics, his professional vanity, his impressionable mind, the grandeur of his self-confidence, his refusal to acknowledge the realities of international power. It was at times comical, at others almost calamitous. But, seen from this distance in history, it did, for all its travails and its ultimate nullity, deposit in the realm of inarguable fact the public commitment of a Labour Cabinet to British entry into the Common Market.

The tour, announced in the Commons on 10 November, began in Rome on 15 January. Already Wilson had enraged his Cabinet critics by stepping up the language of intent. 'We mean business,' he told the Commons and several other audiences – it became his pugnacious little catchphrase. The usage, according to Jay, 'went beyond the spirit of the ministers' agreement at Chequers'. Having Brown alongside, moreover, was no consolation to those who hoped this would indeed be no more than a probe. Wilson explained the two-man aspect of the act as being a matter of reassurance: he was the sceptic, Brown the zealot, and they would balance each other out.

Brown's presence, in fact, contributed more to the farcical than the substantive nature of what occurred. Although Wilson, in his own book,[26] records his colleague as giving capable and thorough accounts of the agricultural side of the problem in all six capitals, Brown, as a well-known European, was of small interest to the continental interrogators. His behaviour, in any case, was often an embarrassment. He was frequently drunk, as was his habit at home as well. As a man to work for, his aggression and unpredictability placed the heaviest strain on officials' respect for what they could see as the sound, intuitive, if not exactly Bevin-like, instincts of the unlettered working-class politician. 'When the buzzer went in the private office, one didn't know who would be sitting behind the desk,' Donald Maitland, who had a charitable recollection of working for Brown, told me. 'We were like subalterns leading troops over the top. Either the machine-gunner would open up, or he would be charming. He was completely volatile.' In Europe, he was given to a buccaneering familiarity with people whom, as a sound European, he always thought he could deal with. 'This little Brown,' de Gaulle allegedly once said. 'I rather like him – in spite of the fact that he calls me Charlie.'[27]

The man who mattered, plainly, was Wilson, whose intentions nobody in Europe could divine. And Wilson, from his earlier position of scepticism, now began to find the words that seemed to incorporate Europe into his grander political scheme. From being the enemy of planning, the EEC was now, apparently, the ally of another of his deeper-felt propositions: the need for Britain to become the molten creative centre of the 'white heat of the technological revolution', a phrase he had earlier used to distinguish his own modernizing, futuristic Labour Party from the anachronistic Tories. It now became his bond with

Europe. Much concerned with the danger of what he called the 'industrial helotry' of Europe vis-à-vis the USA, he presented Britain as
Europe's best agent of escape from this fate. What he wanted to see, he
said just after announcing the Probe, was 'a new technological community'. It was his way of persuading Labour that the European option
had a proper link with the party's modern credo. It was also a way of
amplifying one of France's well-known obsessions: of postulating, in
effect, a shared objective. *Le Défi américain* was not only the title of a
famous recent polemic[28] but a summarizing statement of French, and
especially Gaullist, alarm at the penetration of American industry and
technology into their country. Wilson waxed eloquent about the opportunity, together, to reverse the terms of trade.

At each stop, he returned to the technological community, which
had suddenly become, as he saw it, Britain's major selling-point. He
stuck to a hard line on the terms and conditions – the Commonwealth,
EFTA, agriculture, the sterling balances – but did his best to advance
positive messages in favour of a 'strong and independent European
computer industry' and much else on the cutting edge.

More striking than this, however, is the development of his public
discourse. Before the end of January, Wilson was giving the open
impression of a fully evolved European. 'We mean business' was left far
behind by a grand statement not only against industrial helotry but in
favour of the notion that the off-shore island was itself the creation
of the continent, its people indistinguishable from those with whom he,
as the British Prime Minister, was now conversing. Delivered in Strasbourg, the key speech summons up unmistakable echoes of another
speech delivered in the same place fifteen years before, with the same
gaseous promise of a Britain and a Europe that had much more in
common with each other than the actions of either speaker, in reality,
were ever prepared to underwrite.

Wilson's Strasbourg speech in 1963 resembled Churchill's in 1949.
Its appeal to history could not have been more different from those he
had previously uttered, in his guise as a worshipful defender of the
Commonwealth. Our kith and kin, previously the emotive bond with
Commonwealth interest, had, with brilliant facility, changed their location. Two thousand ago, Wilson said, the British people were already
created out of continental stock. And 2,000 years, the statistician typically noted, was only 'the last one-ten-thousandth' of the period for
which man was estimated to have been on earth, 'less than half a second
of man's hour of history'. A thousand years ago, he went on, the very

name 'England' reflected the origins of European invaders and settlers (presumably the Angles), and modern English law began with the super-imposition of Norman-French laws and forms. The nineteenth-century nation-state, Wilson also emphasized, had given way to concepts of unity and international co-operation. In short, Britain's very history, far from severing her from the continental vision, would apparently be betrayed were she to spurn this natural culmination, the logic of a perfect union.

Douglas Jay does not precisely record his reaction to this effusion, but it must have ignited his worst fears about a former friend for whom his memoirs, by this stage, can only summon up the words 'Wilson oracular, not to say incoherent'.[29]

The tour concluded. The French phase of it, which was obviously the most sensitive, was ruffled by nothing more disturbing than an outburst of boorishness by George Brown, directed at the wife of the British ambassador, Sir Patrick Reilly, whom he profanely chastised for the shortcomings of her staff.[30] But Wilson's approach to de Gaulle did not meet with universal admiration. Crispin Tickell, a coming member of the regiment, recalled being unimpressed by his presentation. Accompanying Wilson, he drew an embarrassed contrast between the Prime Minister's clutter of files and de Gaulle's capacity to hold in his memory everything he wanted to say. This was, Tickell thought, part of a wider pattern. 'I have noticed', he told me, 'that in Anglo-French dealings the French nearly always think their positions through more carefully than we do. We are quicker on our feet, because of ministers' training in the House of Commons. We are more inventive and creative. But in set-piece discussions we tend to be less well prepared, less directed.'[31]

Be that as it may, the encounter appeared to register some meeting of minds. Wilson, at any rate, thought so. When the General opined that he 'had the impression of an England which now really wished to moor itself alongside the continent and was prepared, in principle, to pledge itself to rules in the formulation of which it had played no part', Wilson replied that he felt this reference to 'mooring alongside' was 'important, even historic'.[32]

He soon persuaded the Cabinet that much had been achieved. His own momentum was now unstoppable. The colleagues were summoned, in mid-April, to be told there should be no delay in renewing the application for entry. He found them surprisingly compliant, 'a real turn-up for the book', he telegraphed to Brown, who was in Washington. The fence-sitters had moved over. Only Jay and Healey remained utterly opposed. Everyone else agreed 'we should "have a bash" and, if excluded, not whine but create a Dunkirk-type robust British dynamic'.[33] When, a few days later, Wilson presented a draft statement on the British application and requested unanimous Cabinet support, not one voice was heard to say no.

This now became a public fact – the announcement of the second try was made to the Commons on 2 May – and what is notable is how much had changed in public thinking about Europe during the six years since Macmillan first attempted to interest the British in a change of direction. Though the veto was a setback, it did not put an end to the European debate in Britain: rather, the opposite. After initial anger, the mood settled more closely into one of anxious alarm at what Britain might be missing. For example, Jim Callaghan, the Chancellor of the Exchequer, who was formerly hostile, announced his conversion in terms that probably spoke for many: 'My experience over the last two-and-a-half years has led me to the conclusion ... that nations are not free at the moment to take their own decisions.' International factors, said Callaghan, had an effect 'which is much more than I had assumed when I took office ... The argument about sovereignty is rapidly becoming outdated.' The arguments raged back and forth, but the weight of them, in the media and industry and the City and pretty well every interested forum outside politics itself, was leaning ever more consistently on the side of regarding British entry as a probable necessity – if not yet an inevitability.

A welcome sign of this was the increasing honesty of official statements, beginning with Wilson's announcement. In it, he did not pretend there were no uncomfortable aspects. Whereas Macmillan was terrified of specifying openly any of the inconvenient particulars, Wilson did not balk at the consequences of the EEC's now finalized agriculture policy which, he said frankly, would mean food prices rising by 10 to 14 per cent, and the cost of living by 2.5 to 3.5 per cent.[34] To this would be added negative effects on the balance of payments. These had always been the main fears of Jay and his allies, worked out in elaborate and scholarly papers which argued, in effect, that the food-price effect was so enormous, and its inflationary impact on wages so certain, that *nothing* could justify Britain contemplating membership of the Common Market. Wilson rebutted them with the contention, which became the core case for entry and membership for many years after, that, along with finding a place for Britain in the larger political world (a strong Europe, he said, would be able to exert more influence in world affairs 'than at any time

in our generation'), membership would be worth all this economic pain
because it would lead to a higher rate of industrial growth and an
increase in exports.

With one of Wilson's audiences, this found overwhelming favour:
the Commons approved the decision by 488 votes to 62. With another,
its reception was sceptical to the point of insult: inside a week, de Gaulle,
while noting 'with sympathy' Britain's apparent movement towards
Europe, held a press conference in which he spoke of the danger of
'destructive upheavals' as a result of British entry into the Common
Market, the 'complete overthrow of its equilibrium' that would result,
the weakness of sterling and its unsustainable pretensions as a reserve
currency.

Wilson was unperturbed by these mixed responses. It was time,
instead, for his 'cheeky chappie' side, his stubborn defiance in adversity,
not to mention his superior view of the forces of history, to take the
field.

Although de Gaulle's verdict, while claiming not to be a veto, was as
negative as any sentient observer could imagine, Britain's reaction, voiced
by Wilson and not significantly disputed in the country, was to deny its
meaning. The leader, committed to an exercise in national assertiveness,
was insouciant. In June he visited the General for a tête-à-tête, to exercise
what he regularly insisted was his professional gift for diplomacy. When
Crossman urged that the Probe be conducted not by Wilson and Brown
but by professional diplomats, Wilson had replied, 'I am a professional.
I *am* professional, Dick.' 'Harold's illusions of grandeur in foreign policy
scare me stiff,' the diarist recorded a little later.[35] The illusionist now
assumed a patronizing attitude towards de Gaulle, telling him, as he
reported to the Commons, 'why we do not intend to take no for an
answer'. Privately, he informed George Brown of the impression he had
gained in Paris: 'I found myself watching this lonely old man play an
almost regal "mine host" at Trianon, slightly saddened by the obvious
sense of failure and, to use his own word, impotence that I believe he
now feels ... Against this background I feel paradoxically encouraged.
He does not want us in and he will use all the delaying tactics he can ...
but if we keep firmly beating at the door ... I am not sure that he any
longer has the strength to keep us out.'[36]

Wilson actually told a French journalist that he believed de Gaulle
would soon support British entry: a pathetic misreading, as Denis Healey,
to do him justice, had always foreseen. He also stepped up his threats of
the consequences that would follow any refusal by de Gaulle to acknow-

ledge how seriously the British meant business. One of his junior, but personally intimate, ministers, Lord Chalfont, briefed journalists with a list of the retaliatory measures the Prime Minister was contemplating if the old man did not comply. They reeked of extravagant unreality: abandoning all Anglo-French projects, perhaps withdrawing the entire British Army of the Rhine, maybe refusing to renew the Nato Treaty. When journalists bridled at the improbability of this, the minister said he had come straight from Wilson and dared them not to print it. The little man had mounted his highest horse.[37]

But de Gaulle's impotence, far from inducing him to lower his resistance, soon led him to declare it absolute once again. Britain's own dire condition gave him the pretext, if he needed one. The words he spoke in May, casting doubt on the state of sterling, came ignominiously true in November, when Wilson and his Chancellor, Callaghan, having resisted devaluation for three years, had it forced upon them. From that, it was but a small step to another lecture from Paris, and on 27 November de Gaulle delivered it. It was the usual gnomic performance, critical of Britain's insistence on trying to enter, yet also sardonic in its account of her earlier refusals and delays. The Common Market, the General said, was incompatible with everything that mattered: Britain's relationship with the USA, the way she fed herself, the state of sterling, her enormous external debts. He was not without a certain condescending goodwill towards his wartime ally. He wished 'to see her one day make her choice and accomplish the enormous effort that would transform her'. But there was 'a vast and deep mutation to be effected'.

*

THE SECOND TRY assembled, for the first time, a critical mass of support among the political class for the proposition that Britain should become a European country. The Government was committed, the Opposition agreed, the moving powers in business were desperate, and the people did not dissent. Public opinion, though rattled by the ups and downs and still heavily laced with respondents who said they didn't know what to think, was broadly supportive. There was a national crisis in November 1967, but its cause was devaluation, the great Satan that Wilson had determined to repel which now had its debauching grip upon the currency. The Cabinet did not leave Nato, but it did lose the pound. If anything, Europe now seemed more urgently necessary as a way out of the British crisis. Far from inducing Dunkirkism, the

General's second veto intensified the island's desire to make common cause with the continent. Next day Wilson told the Commons he had no intention of withdrawing the British application. De Gaulle, he said, was in error on sixteen points of fact, which he then recited. 'The great debate will continue, not only in Britain but throughout Europe.'

There was, however, another reaction, which showed that the debate would not continue entirely on Wilson's terms. Coexisting with the anxious passion of the ruling establishment was an opposite sentiment. The conversion was not complete, and the anti-Market ministers by no means gave up. The leader's volte-face, had it produced a result, would have led, as he well knew, to a grand internal struggle: something he thought he could face with confidence but which others were delighted not to contemplate. Now, mercifully, the blurring did not have to continue. 'There was an overwhelming sigh of relief from a clear section of the Cabinet that de Gaulle had saved the Labour Party from having to go ahead with Europe,' one of its members recalled.[38]

This was not the feeling of the Foreign Office, where some new dispositions were being made. The best places were not yet all reserved for the regimental cadres, their allocation showing, rather, the purposeful eccentricity George Brown brought to his role as the maker of top appointments. An obsession with class drove even this passionate pro-European to assign Europe a lower place than some other matters. He promoted into the top job, as permanent under-secretary, Sir Denis Greenhill, not one of the obvious candidates, whose main credential in Brown's eyes was that he was the son of a railwayman. It didn't seem to matter than Greenhill was also soaked in Atlanticism and the Commonwealth, a man whose juices did not rise to Europe. More bizarre was the case of Con O'Neill, who should have been the obvious official ally of any Europeanist minister. O'Neill was due to move from Brussels and become ambassador in Bonn, a post he coveted; but Brown stopped it on the ground that, as an Old Etonian, O'Neill might be unappealing to the leader of the German Social Democrats, Willy Brandt. Annoyed at being passed over, O'Neill promptly resigned from the Office, for the second time.

But O'Neill was not finished, and his allies were moving ahead. The take-over of pro-Europeans in many of the nerve-centres of government was well under way. Michael Palliser, installed in 1966 as the Prime Minister's private secretary, felt he had to warn Wilson before taking the job that he was a passionate European and might therefore be a bad choice. 'We shan't have any problems over Europe,' Wilson assured him, and they never did.[39] Michael Butler, though no longer in line command, having left Paris in March 1965 for a senior post on the Joint Intelligence Committee, remained, as such, an influential watcher. Donald Maitland was Brown's private secretary. Crispin Tickell was head of Chancery in Paris. Increasing numbers of the Palliser generation, coming up behind Greenhill, were in position to fortify, shall we say, those ministers who wanted to pursue rather than challenge Harold Wilson's stated purposes.

Not to be excluded from their number was John Robinson. After four years diligently pursuing the British interest in Brussels, the hench-man and then, more formally, the deputy to O'Neill, he returned to London at the end of 1966. 'I expect you've had enough of the subject, after all these years,' noted a sympathetic young *naïf*, writing from headquarters to Robinson as he was about to leave Brussels.[40] But Robinson was only just beginning the core phase of his career on the European project.

His reporting from Brussels in the lean years was merely a prep-aration for his activities in Whitehall in the fat ones, lasting from the late 1960s through the early 1970s. He returned not to deal with Bolivia, but as a leading operator in the European Economic Organizations Depart-ment, a wanly neutral designation which he immediately set about lobbying to change. The names, he always thought, were revealing. 'It used to be called Mutual Aid, for God's sake,' he expostulated to me. 'That's the way it was looked at in the fifties, a sub-branch of economics which the Foreign Office could let the Treasury and the Board of Trade get on with.' In May 1968, Robinson became head of an office that soon declared itself with unvarnished candour to be the European Integration Department.

He took it over when integration was hardly topmost in the mind of many political leaders. This was an unpropitious time for governmental projects in either Europe or Britain. May was the month of *les événements* in Paris, the pivotal moment, in both time and place, of the social rebellion that marked the multiple liberations of the 1960s. At the height of the Vietnam War, recrudescent Marxism met the Age of Disrespect in an attempted undermining of the established order in many parts of the developed world, France and Britain prominently among them. In France, de Gaulle was struggling to control events inside his own country, let alone remake the shape of Europe. In Britain, devaluation, far from releasing the suppressed energies of the economy, had unleashed a wave of national self-mortification. 'I'm Backing Britain' was the cause to which people were being urged to attach themselves as a patriotic gesture, in lieu of any imperative market reason for doing so. A mood almost of apocalypse prevailed. It had been anticipated a few months earlier by Quintin Hogg MP, who told the Commons: 'Can anyone doubt ... that we are a people that has lost its way? Can anyone deny that the British people is in the act of destroying itself: and will surely do so if we go on as at present?'

Such was the atmosphere of moral decline, the distracting pessimism, with which those who favoured the integrationist project had to grapple. Yet, unpromising though it looked, the period had positive consequences. It turned out, indeed, to be pivotal in another way as well, the beginning of the end for Britain's most formidable antagonist. It set the scene for de Gaulle's final thrust against the British ambition to join the European Economic Community – and for the decisive victory the elite regiment of the Foreign Office finally gained against him.

The central player in this episode, which displayed the regimental influence with rare and brazen clarity, was not, in fact, one of them. This was more than an ironic detail. Brown's eye for unorthodox appointments produced some brilliant, as well as some absurd, results, and one of them was the decision to send as ambassador to Paris not a regular diplomat but a Conservative politician, Christopher Soames. It was one of many signs of the intention, felt by Wilson as strongly as Brown, somehow to 'get through' to de Gaulle, better to read his mind, to cosy up to France, to try and replace an arid defensiveness with intimations of something warmer.

On his frequent, lurching journeys to Paris, Brown found the embassy a terrible place. 'When I used to visit there,' he wrote, 'I seemed to arrive just as they were trying to get the dust-sheets off the furniture; sometimes they didn't even bother to do that.'[41] Soames could be relied on to change all that, being a gregarious man, large of both body and soul. But perhaps his best credential was that he was married to Winston Churchill's daughter Mary, a British connection that even de Gaulle would hesitate to patronize. He was a European of long, consistent stripe, with good French which he disguised in suitably Churchillian *gaucherie*, and an acquaintance with the continental political class that stretched back to the Hague assembly and the other post-war manifestations over which Churchill had presided.

Soames took up his job in Paris in September 1968 naturally intending an audience with de Gaulle to be one of his earliest priorities. The General did not readily make himself available, but on 4 February 1969, a Tuesday, he received the ambassador and his wife at lunch at the

Elysée Palace. For Soames it was a big moment, much manoeuvred for, long anticipated. For de Gaulle it was – who can be sure what it was? Nobody, in the incessant scrutinies that followed, was certain what the General had intended by the occasion: whether, indeed, he intended anything more to be heard than the vaporous ruminations of an autocrat at the lunch-table. Was this a calculated move in the highest of high politics? Or one of those conversations, of which high politicians are sometimes more victim than perpetrator, that acquire, by a series of accidents, a mythic importance far exceeding anything they intended?

At any rate, a conversation took place, the substance of which has resolved itself, over the years, into a residue that is not seriously disputed. It was more a monologue, in which the General described the kind of Europe he would like to see developing. This would be a very different 'Europe' from the EEC, a looser yet broader construct, with more members and wider tasks, yet liberated from some of the supra-national pretensions and invasions of national sovereignty that so offended Gaullist France. Such a Europe, de Gaulle speculated, would be led by the powers that possessed serious armies: France, Great Britain, West Germany and Italy. When Soames commented that the arrangement took little account of the existence of Nato, de Gaulle portrayed it as something necessary in anticipation of the day the Americans departed, and Europe had to look after itself. He did not, he said, conceive the idea as anti-American. But he did propose a radical alteration in the concept of what 'Europe' meant, and who should be allowed to consti- tute it. Ireland, Norway and Denmark would obviously belong, but most important was Britain, now offered not only membership of the group but a seminal role in discussions leading up to its possible formation. For what the General seemed to be proposing was a series of secret bilateral negotiations between Britain and France, to be followed, if they succeeded, by a British launch of the grand plan, which France would then be heard to endorse, and others invited to join.[42]

There are nuances in this scheme, if it was anything so definitive as to merit that word, which could still be disputable. Its substance was, at one level, not surprising, being of a piece with what the General was always known to believe. He had often hinted at his restlessness with the status quo. In January 1967, during the Probe, he dangled in front of Wilson mysterious talk about the need for 'something entirely new' in Europe, and he repeated the thought when administering his immediate near-veto in May. He never liked a Europe that did not look after its own defence, under the leadership, naturally, of France. And he was

always irked by having come to power too late to abort the Treaty of
Rome. More than many of his contemporaries, he was also gripped by
the case for a Europe that was a player in the mighty hypotheses of the
Cold War, a bulwark against the Soviet Union, a pillar of order in a
possibly collapsing world. One British observer, close to Soames, read
the initiative as a 'consequence of the events of May '68', and added that
the occupation of Czechoslovakia by the Russians had also 'inclined him
to open the doors of Europe to Britain'.[43]

Whatever his reasons, his proposition startled Soames, who rushed
back to the embassy to begin to dissect its meaning, with the help of his
diplomatic colleagues. This had to start with getting down on paper
what the old man had actually said: not a simple task. Though Soames
had many qualities fitting him for the ambassadorial role, retaining
details of a conversation was not a skill that sat effortlessly alongside his
expansive manners and somewhat unrefined intellect. 'He was a tremendous life-force, and he had a broad sweep of understanding of big
problems,' said one of his admirers, David Hannay, the senior man on
Soames's staff in his later incarnation as a Brussels commissioner. 'He
could absorb masses of detail, though never in writing. It always had to
be oral. He was one of the only grown-up men I've ever known whose
lips moved when he was reading.'[44]

Even on the oral side, untrained as a professional diplomat, he had
limitations. In the hearing of Crispin Tickell, who was among the
embassy staff keenly waiting to hear what de Gaulle had said, Soames
likened the process of recollection he now attempted to 'trying to tickle
bits of garlic out from behind his teeth'.

The mouth and mind, however, were cleaned out to general satisfaction. So sensitive was the conversation that Soames sent a copy of his
version of it to de Gaulle's office the next day, for verification. There
were hazards in this procedure. The General, speaking as usual without
notes, had made no record of his own, and his officials were uncertain
exactly what had passed. But, three days after the lunch, word came back
from the Quai d'Orsay that the Foreign Minister, Michel Debré,
accepted, except for a few phrases, the Soames account.

In Paris, therefore, both the British and the French, while recognizing
that something big may have been floated into the diplomatic air,
conducted themselves with reasonably measured calm. Later, many of
them had their say about what should have happened next. The British,
however excited they felt, could have asked for further and better
particulars: could have launched an orderly inquiry before giving a

response: might then have insisted, if these inquiries got anywhere, that the Gaullist vision should be communicated to the Five, the EFTA countries, and in due course to the Americans, and altogether located in the regular channels that one might expect of an enterprise which, if it were to succeed, demanded fullest consultation with the many allies whose perspectives would be radically altered by it. Soames himself, reflecting later, thought as much. He told Cecil King in April, when the dust had faintly begun to settle on the most incandescent bilateral row between France and Britain since the war, that such a procedure, concerning an offer he personally took seriously, would have been proper. De Gaulle might not have agreed to it. But in that case the talks would not have started, and Britain, thought Soames, would have been 'out in the clear'.[45]

As it was, London's response was quite different. The Soames communiqué arrived in the Integration Department and caused immediate consternation. Here, in the spiritual home of the regiment, the enemy was seen to be striking at their central preoccupation. To John Robinson, as head of the department, and Patrick Hancock, his superintending under-secretary, it was perfectly obvious what de Gaulle had held out to Soames: the wreckage of 'Europe', and the discrediting of all Britain's ambitions to become part of it.

Hancock and Robinson immediately engaged the Foreign Secretary. George Brown, by this time, was no longer in office, his erratic emotions having driven him, finally, to resign. Instead, the Office was now run by the schoolmasterly, punctilious, sometimes rather moralistic Michael Stewart, an obliging pair of hands who had been drafted into the job once before, in 1965, when the chosen incumbent couldn't secure a parliamentary seat, and now returned after Brown had been caught drunk in charge of British diplomacy once too often. Stewart, though a faithful Wilsonian, was at this stage less interested than Brown in Europe. Vietnam and the Biafran secession from Nigeria were the questions that most engaged his capacity for passionate fluency in debate. But plainly the Soames–de Gaulle conversation was a matter of unavoidable priority.

The thesis constructed by Robinson, with Hancock alongside, was that de Gaulle's proposition constituted nothing but a devilish trap. Whichever way you looked at it, it presented Britain with ruinous options. What de Gaulle sought, Robinson insisted, was not to help Britain into Europe but to destroy her chances of ever building the alliances necessary to get there. She faced two possibilities, both of them congenial to de Gaulle's objective and destructive of her own. On the one hand, if Britain accepted the plan for secret talks to reshape and rescue Europe, she would be helping the General towards the kind of looser Europe he wanted and, in the process, would be revealed before the Five as conspiring against their project. To her friends she would be hardly better than a traitor. On the other hand, if Britain refused the bait, de Gaulle would increase his leverage with the Five. He would be able to say that he had offered Britain a role, had made the overture, but that the British weren't interested in talking.

Thus spoke the representatives of the regiment, and thus were they mostly heard. The conclusion that this was a Gaullist ploy, rather than the ruminations of an old man on the future of the world, was rapidly reached in official London, and subsequent events did not incline the main official participants to revise it. 'The analysis we made was right,' Palliser told me, years later. 'If we'd played it the General's way we might well have found ourselves being accused of breaking up the EEC, and if we didn't play it his way he would exploit that against us.' But, Palliser added, 'the handling of it was undoubtedly wrong'.[46]

The handling, however, had the effect the Palliser elite desired. It kept British loyalty to the EEC on track, in the eyes of people who would eventually matter more to Britain than de Gaulle did. But, before that could be established, time, chance and a show of remarkable Robinson-ian ruthlessness had to work their way through the process.

The chance that intervened was a date, long scheduled in the diary, for Wilson to visit Bonn for a routine meeting with the West German Chancellor, Kurt Kiesinger. He was due in Germany even as the Soames telegram was being evaluated in London. Thus, de Gaulle's infinite cunning was now overlaid by a dilemma he could not have imagined being brought into play so soon. Should Wilson explain to Kiesinger anything of what had passed in Paris, thus risking the fury of the French at their secret overture being unilaterally disclosed? Or should he remain silent, play dumb about what de Gaulle seemed to be up to, and thus behave with unforgettable discourtesy to the power that was his strongest and most necessary ally in the quest for EEC membership?

Wilson's own first instinct was to say nothing. What de Gaulle had said privately could be explained away, if necessary, as simply repeating what he had said publicly about the need for 'something entirely new'. Britain owed no obligations to the Germans, at this stage. Palliser, his private secretary, was advising him otherwise, but, to Wilson, there seemed no great merit in '[presenting] ourselves as a rather priggish little Lord Fauntleroy who had resisted the General's anti-EEC blandishments'.

Britain should take her time, and if necessary get into further talks with him, an entirely proper thing to do as long as she kept the Five informed. So, at any rate, Wilson presents his attitude in the memoirs he wrote in 1971, after his Government fell.

The Foreign Office, however, determined on a different strategy. Robinson told me: 'It's the only occasion I can quote to you from my career where officials – I won't say dictated – but suggested policy, and it was accepted.' Michael Stewart took the line the officials pressed upon him. On the plane to Bonn, he advised Wilson to tell Kiesinger the gist of what had passed. There was a big argument among the politicians and the travelling diplomats about how this should be done. In discussions at the Bonn embassy late into the evening, Wilson writes, 'I continued to express my distaste for the proposal.' Robinson recalled him 'swirling the brandy and saying he was going to go to Paris to talk to de Gaulle and poke Kiesinger in the eye'. For Wilson, as Palliser told me, valued – 'over-valued' – his relations with the General. 'He was squirming at the suggestion of offending him.' However, goaded by telegrams from London, pressed by Robinson and others on the spot, he eventually agreed to mention 'in a few simple sentences', without lurid overtones, what de Gaulle had said.

When he did so, Kiesinger was at first baffled. Wilson put it as a casual thing: ambassador called in, the General suggests refashioning EEC, British a bit puzzled, and so on. Kiesinger thought the interpreter must have made a mistake, muddling up the EEC with the Organization for Economic Co-operation and Development, the successor body to the OEEC. Surely it was the OECD de Gaulle wanted reorganized, the Chancellor inquired. No, said Wilson, it was the EEC. Robinson remembered Kiesinger urgently sending an aide out of the room to call Paris and find out what was going on.

The fall-out from this relatively modest disclosure might have been containable. But something else, rather less defensible, had occurred. This was Robinson's finest, or alternatively his basest, hour. To prepare Wilson's mind for the Kiesinger meeting, and help ensure this went the way they wanted, the FO team wrote a memo. Wilson had asked that this be 'brief and anodyne', suitable to his modest purpose. When he got it next morning, he found it was 'the full works'. 'I made it clear that I was furious,' Wilson writes. He had to take trouble to avoid speaking directly from it.

His caution, however, was otiose. For the contents of the full works were already on the wire, despatched openly round all relevant British embassies, allegedly to keep them in the picture about developments of which, thus far, they were entirely ignorant. Both the contents of the Soames telegram, and the full conspiratorial take on it, were written up by Robinson's team, with effects that did not take long to materialize.

The French, whom Soames informed of the circulation, were soon enraged. Their first tactic, now they were forced into semi-public mode, was to challenge the version they had originally agreed, saying they particularly rejected the item that most offended the Five: the concept of a leadership group, a *directoire*, consisting of themselves, the Germans, the Italians and the British. Equally, they sniffed out what they said were deliberate British distortions, making the General's words sound more anti-American and anti-European than they were. The very act of requesting confirmation of the Soames version in the first place was now seen to have been a British trap. For, if the French said they had agreed the Soames version, that lent colour to the Wilson position. Yet by contesting it they put themselves under pressure to supply an alternative account, a demand that inevitably stuck in their throat.

There then began a battle of the leaks. Until the middle of February, two weeks after the Elysée lunch, all this was happening in secrecy. Nobody outside government knew that Soames had met the General. But inquiries were beginning to be made. Soon enough, a sketchy French version of the Soames Affair appeared in the Paris newspaper *Le Figaro*, which was the pretext for the Foreign Office's final act of vengeance, its conclusive gesture ensuring that de Gaulle's seductive manoeuvre was destroyed. Thus liberated from all normal protocols – 'We've got the bastards at last,' one FO man, who sounds very like Robinson, John Dickie quotes exulting – the Office's chief spokesman summoned selected correspondents, to 'correct' the French account. He read to them, verbatim and *en clair*, large chunks of Soames's original despatch, giving rise to an international furore that put paid to anything serious de Gaulle might have had in mind. 'De Gaulle's Secret Offer: Scrap Six', the headline read. Exposed to the public eye, it was an offer nobody could fail to refuse.

Was this a case of serious mishandling, as Palliser came to judge? Certainly it produced a great coolness between London and Paris. Soames was summoned and rebuked by the Quai d'Orsay for his Government's numerous malefactions. Diplomats, especially those committed to the enterprise in question, never like to fall out with such venomous feeling as temporarily engulfed the two capitals. As for de Gaulle, his biographer writes that 'it would have been quite impossible to describe the General's furious reaction', though he also asks: 'Could he expect the country of Pitt and Churchill to overlook the snubs of 1963 and 1967 and not resort to one of those acts of revenge that only very old families and very old diplomatic services are capable of exacting?'[47]

In Britain, those who certainly thought the episode an error were the group of ministers still committed against British entry. To them, the crack-up of the Community was a heaven-sent chance for Britain to do what they had always wanted: to have it both ways: not to be excluded from modest European enterprises, but not to be required to join anything so ambitious as the Treaty of Rome. They were aware that 'Europe' could do Britain damage if she did not belong, and were no longer entirely blind to the economic consequences of a common, becoming a single, market across the Channel. The de Gaulle proposition, for a Community that interested itself in foreign policy co-ordination but renounced its pooling of economic ambitions, left them with hyperbolic frustration at the ruin of what might have been.

Thus Crossman, the sceptic, delivered a punishing verdict on 'the infantilism of Harold and Michael Stewart, priggish children who showed moral disapproval of the de Gaulle overture'. Douglas Jay, the phobic, called this overture 'a new and wonderfully far-sighted offer to Britain, whose rejection by a muddled Government was as catastrophic a blunder as Chamberlain's rejection of Roosevelt's offer in 1938'. A group of Foreign Office officials, Jay went on, 'did an incalculable disservice to this country. Seen dispassionately in retrospect, the wrecking of this offer without even further discussion was a more calamitous error, because it may well prove irrevocable, than Munich or Suez.'[48]

Seen by those public officials, however, their tactics were in pursuit of a government policy that had now been extensively debated and, for the first time, agreed with all relevant majorities in the British body politic. Anything else was a side-show. The officials, seized of this policy, saw it as their job to protect ministers against being fatally distracted from it. That, at least, is the high-ground argument they can make. It was the special credit O'Neill gave Robinson, in his retrospective official history: the man deserved remembering above all for 'resisting the temptations of plausible but inadequate alternatives'.[49] By wrecking de Gaulle's destructive proposition, they were saving Harold Wilson from himself.

In the event, they were justified. The event was the passing of de Gaulle. Robinson thought he could see it coming. That is what he

reckoned he was playing for. 'In February 1969, it seemed a possibility
that de Gaulle would disappear,' he told me. 'It was worth keeping the
rails open for that.' Had the General remained in place, the damage
done by the Soames Affair would have lasted a long time. It is unlikely
that he would have spoken to Soames again; Wilson himself would have
had to go on his knees for an audience. As it was, the General remained
in power for less than three more months, deposed by his own hand
when he called a referendum on reform of the French constitution.
Quixotically, he defined it as a vote of confidence in himself. When he
lost, he resigned – and the regiment saw the vindication of its judgement.

*

LONDON DID NOT immediately respond to de Gaulle's retirement. There
was no instant leaping into the arms of the Common Market. Gaullism
remained in power in France, with the election of Georges Pompidou to
succeed the General. Although Pompidou was a very different character,
unencumbered by an historic obsession with Anglo-Saxons, and in
principle more amenable to British entry, the brute fact of French
interest remained. Indeed, it was in this period, not the earlier one, that
a final obstacle was wheeled into place to impede the development of
British enthusiasm for entry even though the basic decision, the great
existential lunge of the political class, appeared to have been made. The
French saw an opportunity to secure what de Gaulle had failed to get in
1965 and to use the eagerness of the Five for British entry as the lever.
They insisted that the Six must conclude an agreement among themselves
on the agricultural system and its financing, which was always by far the
largest part of the Community budget. When this was hammered out in
December 1969, it fixed in place a system that put the Community,
rather than its nation-state members, in charge of its own resources, and
allocated disproportionate quantities of these to the support of farmers,
the most potent political lobby in France. This ensured that the food-
price consequences of membership would become even more gloomily
debated in Britain. It became a commonplace among both officials and
ministers, watching in the wings from Whitehall, that the financial
structure had been designed with the positive intention of raising the
price of Britain's entry-ticket, without possibility of concession.

Wilson, however, did press on. He already had a minister for Europe,
George Thomson, whose activities were beefed up before the end of the
year. There were more tours of the capitals. 'There is no need to be

obsessed by safeguards and the negative aspects of our application, though the Government has these fully in mind,' the Prime Minister minuted the Cabinet. 'There are plenty of positive points to put across about the opportunities that membership of the Community would offer for our influence abroad and economic well-being at home.'[50]

The Cabinet, of course, did not unanimously agree. And Wilson, getting ready for an election, took care not to cut off all escape-routes. The white paper he published in February 1970, on the cost of entering the Common Market, could not be accused of disguising unpalatable truths. The damage-assessment much increased the 1967 figures: food prices up by 18–26 per cent, the cost of living by 5 per cent, huge multiples to contemplate. The balance of payments burden could, the paper said, be anything between £100 million and £1,100 million. Although George Thomson told the Commons that this was about as useful as saying that a football game between his home-town teams might end 'somewhere between eight–nothing Dundee and three–nothing Dundee United', the propaganda effect was capable of being alarming. The Labour manifesto retained the old caution – for entry, provided the terms are acceptable – adding the defiant rider that 'if satisfactory terms cannot be secured . . . Britain will be able to stand on her own feet outside the Community'.

The large signals, however, pointed only one way. Speaking of the application, Stewart, the Foreign Secretary, told the Commons in February: 'It stands, we press it, we desire that negotiations should be opened, we are anxious that they should succeed.' If Labour won, Stewart was going to be replaced by Roy Jenkins. This had been agreed with Wilson: the placing at the Foreign Office of the man who, in the absence of George Brown, was the party's first European. The practical arrangements were all in place, moreover. Along with most of Britain, Wilson thought he would win the 11 June election, and he scheduled the renewal of his Euro-venture accordingly. The speech of application was drafted in the middle of the campaign, to be formally delivered in Luxembourg, by the newly mandated Foreign Secretary, on 30 June.[51] Everything was prepared for a seamless transition between one government and the next.

Except that the prophets were mistaken. Labour did not win the election, but lost it to a thirty-seat Conservative majority. And the seamlessness Wilson had prepared for turned out not to extend to the handover from one party to another, despite the fact that these parties fought the election on the same positive, if wary, platforms of support for entry. Having reached the brink of a commitment, and moved far enough to make Europe a seemingly common cause, Labour was about to prove that there was more life in the pattern of perpetual revisionism. Another story for another chapter.

Continuity, however, did not cease in the other part of government, John Robinson's shop. He remained in charge of Britain's European policy for another three years, stoking the fire, repelling all boarders from more sceptical departments, conducting himself as ruthlessly with Whitehall as he had always done against the French. Hardly anyone I came across in this inquiry wanted to qualify very much Con O'Neill's encomium for the man who 'knew everyone, understood everything, foresaw everything, did everything', though they usually remarked also on the enmities he created.

In the summer of 1993, I went to visit Robinson at home. It was more than a decade since his retirement from the Foreign Office, and he lived outside Cordes, at the heart of *la France profonde*, a choice of location that seemed to substantiate the label always put around his neck as a Euro-fanatic. In fact, he said, this was something of an accident. After Europe, his postings had been abroad, and he needed a house to retire to, in a country where he could take his dog without the expensive rigmarole of six months' quarantine. Plainly his tongue was in his cheek when he tried to persuade me of this. Actually his search had always been for a place in the sun, and his chief focus of study, before choosing Cordes, was the rainfall map. Neither his friends nor his colleagues ever doubted how strongly he was driven, well before Macmillan's decision, by the belief that Britain must get into the EEC. Married to a Swiss-French woman, with an Alpine plot to which he repaired every spring to plant his potatoes, he was a true continentalist, with a special under-standing, so one of his colleagues said, of the French administrative mind. But such are the defences a Whitehall official may need to erect, even in retirement, against the fatal charge that he was committed to a cause.

If Robinson had a single reason to live in France, I guessed, it was to escape the reach of an establishment to which he never belonged. He personified the FO line on Europe, but the institution was indeed 'my shop', and his approach to the work made him enemies along the way. Although he did much for Britain-in-Europe, Europe did little for him. This may have been more his own fault than anyone else's, but he takes his place in the line of public people whose careers have been blighted, sometimes ended, by the Europe question.

For one thing, it induced in him a conspiratorial attitude to life. Decades of trying to outwit the continentals, while suppressing the influence of other Whitehall departments, left their mark. Sitting in the sun in his garden, which he padded about in the guise of a gnarled French peasant – he was known locally as 'le fonctionnaire' – I got my first glimpse of it through the anxiety he expressed about the imminent availability of PRO files covering the Heath–Macmillan negotiations. He feared the exposure of his Dutch sources, possibly forgetting that he had seldom, if ever, committed their names to paper. Not surprisingly, he mentioned with some relish the fact that he had not long before destroyed all the files he kept on the Soames affair. I was further startled to be told, when he settled down to talk, that our interview could not be taped. It took half an hour to persuade him that, after my recording of many previous interviews in and out of Whitehall, such rule-book punctilio in the middle of the French countryside seemed a little excessive. Even then, there was much elaborate covering of the microphone at moments he still deemed sensitive thirty years on.

His former colleagues were not surprised to hear this. To them, he had never been able to shake the habit. 'Conspiracy was valuable when we were negotiating to get in,' said one. 'But, the day we joined, you couldn't afford to be conspiratorial any more. John couldn't adapt. You had to have open relationships with other ministries, and he wasn't prepared to do that. He intrigued, and kept secrets, and didn't tell people what he was up to. That might have worked in the French system, but it didn't work in the British.'

Nor did it work for Robinson's subsequent career, which he conducted with an unusual disrespect for the rules. After so many years engaged in the intriguing delights of multilateral diplomacy, the impositions of embassy life were as boring as they were bureaucratic. The Office finally inflicted its norm upon him, removing him from what he knew better than anyone, and Robinson did not react well.

His first post-Europe job was as ambassador to Algeria, selected presumably in recognition of his knowledge of the French. Although he survived his allotted three years, he didn't enjoy the work and didn't mind who knew it. Not long after getting there, he told friends in the Foreign and Commonwealth Office that he doubted the merit of maintaining a British embassy in Algiers at all. Certainly, he thought, two-thirds of its officials could be redeployed without any damage to its effectiveness. He was rare, possibly unique, in the annals of the foreign service as an ambassador who objected to an FCO inspectorate report because the staff cuts it recommended for his embassy were not deep enough. In assessing his host country he was no less rigorous. His valedictory despatch, circulated round the service, opened with a sentence that challenged the normal diplomatic niceties. 'Algeria is a country built on the organising principle of theft,' he mordantly wrote – a verdict which in the 1990s, when innocent Algerians were being murdered by the hundred, looked like an understatement.

His later appointments were no more satisfactory. Palliser, by now head of the diplomatic service, found Robinson a slot in Washington, as number two to Peter Jay, a prime minister's son-in-law, who was controversially sent there as ambassador in 1977. It was thought that the brilliant parvenu would be assisted, as well as quietly overseen, by the unorthodox veteran. Within an institutional framework, Jay thought, two intelligent men could work out any difficulties. But, again, the posting came to grief, Robinson's complaint being much the same as it had been in Algiers. There wasn't enough to do. He had been given a 'non-job', he told Palliser and Jay after a few months. He also brought his pro-Europe prejudices with him, which offended Jay, an instinctively anti-EEC man, like his father Douglas. By the end, the ambassador and his deputy were communicating only by letter, and Robinson, exiled to New York, would make business visits to Washington only after being assured that Jay was out of town.

The Office did not give up. A job fell vacant that at least involved serious work, the ambassadorship to Israel. Robinson went there in 1980, and before long was letting slip his opinion that the Israeli case against the Arabs was a weak one. Again, he didn't mind who knew what he thought, but this time the consequence was terminal. After a year, the ambassador was withdrawn, in the tacit knowledge that otherwise Israel would have demanded his expulsion. So he was obliged to retire, four years early, from the shop and office to which he had given exceptional service.

In recent Foreign Office legend, that is what Robinson is remembered for: the man who decided Algeria didn't matter, and exposed himself in Israel to the charge of being an Arabist of matchless indiscretion. When he died, in January 1998, a singularly crass obituary in *The Times* found little else to write about him, almost entirely neglecting the discreet but potent work at the centre of his career.

Having left the Office and disappeared to France, he returned deeper into the obscurity which he had always favoured when pursuing his métier as a European schemer. When I saw him, in his little rural fastness, he minimized what this European part had really been about. 'What was it based on?' he asked sardonically. 'Turning up at meetings and remembering what happened five years ago. Also knowing all the people, who hadn't changed on the other side. They always stayed put. At the Quai, it was the same old faces, again and again. I think there was a decision on our side to have at least one historical memory that went back over the months and years.'

Whatever the intention, the effect was something more: the creation of a single-issue diplomat, whose issue happened to set the path and dominate the argument of British politics and foreign policy for the next thirty years.

7

EDWARD HEATH

The Triumph of the Will

MANY FEATURES COMMON TO politics in every era and every dispensation are to be found in the history of Britain's reluctant binding to Europe. There is vacillation and concealment. There is progress followed by regress, and all the time an argument about the real meaning of each of these forms of motion. There is, near the top of the list, the question of national pride and what it means, allied to the question of the popular will and how it can be handled: and there is the claim always to be satisfying these potent values, while at the same time regularly redefining them. Also present is genuine uncertainty. The leaders often did not really know what would be the consequences of their action, or inaction.

Another thing that marks this history is the accident of timing, especially as it touched the life of Charles de Gaulle. Had de Gaulle been summoned to power a few months earlier than May 1958, it is possible that the Treaty of Rome would have been unilaterally aborted, and the Common Market as we know it never have come into being. A diverting speculation. The other end of de Gaulle's political career produced a more concrete fact – but again the consequences were fortuitous. A conjunction occurred that produced results which would otherwise, in all probability, not have happened in the same way, if at all. De Gaulle, having put his position on the line and been defeated, was succeeded as president by Georges Pompidou. A year later, Britain elected a new government, led by Edward Heath.

These men were not almighty movers of events. Each was carried by deep tides and other more fractured forces to the confluence they reached. Impersonal pressures – economic demand, political push, perceived strategic necessity – brought their two countries to a point where Britain's desire to be admitted to the European Economic Community, and France's readiness to contemplate her reception positively, were creating a coercive influence. Even without the men, the measure might have passed. Pompidou depended on anti-Gaullist allies and rivals, notably Valéry Giscard d'Estaing, who were more volubly pro-British than he was. He may not have been indispensable to the project. It is more debatable whether Harold Wilson, had he won the 1970 election, would have made the necessary connection with Pompidou, but the pressures might eventually have been strong enough to overcome even their mutually repellent personalities.

The chosen men, nevertheless, did matter greatly. In particular, Heath did. His presence rather than anybody else's at the helm of British policy from June 1970 until the moment of British entry, in January 1973, was singularly appropriate. He might not have been there. He could easily have lost the election, and before that he might well not have won the party leadership, in 1965. Had he failed to get that, the Tory leader and Prime Minister would have been Reginald Maudling, who was a sceptic about British entry and had been the enthusiastic point-man in Britain's doomed attempt to confine her part in the enterprise to a free trade area. As it was, Heath was chosen, without any special interest one way or the other in his European credentials, and thereby brought to the leadership, and then the job of Prime Minister, a collection of baggage which gave a clearer prominence to the European quest than any other Conservative politician at that time was prepared to offer.

Ted Heath, therefore, cannot help being the nodal figure in this story. The most qualified 'European' in Tory politics assumed the leadership of Britain at the time when the question of entry into Europe was ready for its final resolution. He was made a European, not least, by his formation, but he was made a European leader by his character. What he brought to the table, compared with every predecessor, was not merely a 'European' policy but exceptional single-mindedness in pursuing it. Not for Heath the anguish of Macmillan or the dissembling of Harold Wilson. For him the door to the future had been opened, to reveal a vision of blinding clarity, where every prospect led in one direction. That was how Heath thought of 'Europe'. Directing Britain towards it was a task he accomplished with an élan that put previous history to shame: a shame deriving not so much from the decisions as the indecision. Heath's performance in this matter was a text-book exercise in most of the arts of government, which produced a rare phenomenon, the complete attainment of a political objective.

So his place in the story is unchallengeable. He is, as he never let anyone forget, the father of European Britain, and for that is perceived worldwide as a statesman: the only post-war British Prime Minister in that category, distinguishable as such from Margaret Thatcher who, while more resonant and certainly more notorious than Heath, left no legacy that history will call, strictly, statesmanlike. Yet to say that of Heath is not to say everything. Such eminence brings with it responsibilities. The test he invites can't be satisfied merely by acknowledging that he took Britain into Europe, large task though that was.

At one level, he shaped an epoch. At another, his part was more enigmatic. What exactly Heath thought he was doing when he took Britain in is a different matter from the fact, the impressive fact, of doing it. What Britain-in-Europe was *for*, in his mind, is a question to which the answer is elusive. Closely related to it is the question of what the British people were told it was about and, still more puzzling, what this leader, having accomplished the brute fact of entry, did and didn't do to move the British towards starting to becoming truly European people. Heath brought an end to the unfortunate record of two decades. But he was by no means free of the foibles that rendered British policy, in some ways, as unsatisfactory after the event as before it.

*

HEATH'S CREDENTIALS began at the beginning. To be born, as he was, facing Europe, in Broadstairs, on the coast of Kent, within sight of the coast of France, is perhaps of no more than symbolic interest. One cannot pretend that the boy grew into a young man while staring with conscious forethought at his destiny. But at least Europe was not an alien place in his family. His mother, in service as a maid, had often travelled with her employers to the continent.[1] Although he came from humble stock, his father a carpenter, the family's cultural horizons were never confined to the English-speaking peoples.

As soon as he was old enough, the boy began crossing the Channel himself. When he was fourteen, he went to Paris on a school trip and fell immediately in love with the idea of travel. No particle of anxiety appears to have touched him as he wandered the streets of the foreign capital struggling with a foreign language. His memoir of the time recalls the 'heavenly anguish' of selecting which restaurant to enter, and the 'lucidity and clarity' of the French literature which, while he never became a very convincing exponent of spoken French, Heath always claimed to admire.[2] During summer vacations from university, he practically lived on the continent, especially in Germany, to which music drew him as much as politics. It was often forgotten, in later life, that Heath was an organ scholar at Oxford. He was steeped in European creativity, a condition that went well beyond the dilettante liking for a bit of Beethoven, which marked the cultural frontier of most English politicians.

These early excursions, however, had more to them than concert-halls and pavement cafés. When he got to Oxford in 1935, Heath soon involved himself in politics, through the Conservative Association, and displayed a seriousness about events on the continent that led to encounters which did decisively shape his European destiny. He had adventures that set him apart among Conservatives. In the summer of 1938, he went to Spain to see fascism in action, calling on the outposts of the anti-Franco government, being shot up and bombed as he travelled around the environs of Barcelona.[3] The young undergraduate spent days in intense political conversation with student-soldiers, assuring himself they were not primarily Marxists but genuine seekers after democratic freedom. He was not, however, lecturing them from the safe ground of British complacency. By his own account, he was obviously a serious fellow, drawn to the sea and soil of the Mediterranean, but engaged more by deep alarm at the tyrannies engulfing Europe.

Germany was where, in this formative time, he had the most astounding experiences. He became a wide-eyed tourist of the Third Reich. In Munich, in summer 1937, he made for the cellar where Hitler had first gathered the cronies who took him to power, and watched the changing of the guard at the Nazi memorial, 'steel-helmeted and goose-stepping with extraordinary precision', as he wrote. The German Embassy in London had given him an invitation to attend the Nuremberg rally. At the indoor conference preceding it, he witnessed Göring, Goebbels and Himmler at close quarters. As Hitler marched down the aisle, Heath was aware of him 'almost brushing my shoulder'. At the outdoor rally, he had a seat close to Hitler's box, and heard the leader's oration with traumatic horror. 'This man', he concluded, 'was obviously capable of carrying the German people with him into any folly, however mad.' Later, he went to a party where Himmler was the host – 'I remember him for his soft, wet, flabby handshake' – and Goebbels made himself known, 'his pinched face white and sweating – the personification of evil'.[4]

In the prelude to war, Heath had no doubt where he stood, against the appeasement policy of Prime Minister Neville Chamberlain. He took that side at Oxford, and helped fight a by-election in the cause. Even as war was on the verge of breaking out, he was to be found on another tour of future killing-fields, this time as far east as Warsaw. It was as if he could never satisfy his curiosity, just could not bear to keep away. It is an irony, therefore, that, when he volunteered for action, he should have spent most of the war years on the island, not the mainland. Only in the final year of combat did his unit move on from anti-aircraft duty, protecting Britain, into France and the Low Countries, participating, most memorably for him, in the liberation of Antwerp. The immediate aftermath, however, retained him on the continent, and deepened the meaning he took from what had happened. He went back to Nuremberg, this time for the war crimes trials, a spectator at the judgment on Göring, Hess, Ribbentrop and the rest, for their murderous depravities. 'As I left the court,' he later wrote, 'I knew that those evil things had been beaten back and their perpetrators brought to justice. But at what a cost. Europe had once more destroyed itself. This must never be allowed to happen again ... Reconciliation and reconstruction must be our tasks.'

So this was a very European man. His collection of first-hand European experiences was as large and memorable as any young English-man anywhere could boast of. Nobody from the traditional seed and shire of British Conservatism could get near it.

In his memoir, Heath claims to have had no foresight about what the war and its threat to European civilization would mean for his professional life. 'I did not realise that it would be my preoccupation for the next thirty years.'[5] But, indisputably, the experience entered into his blood and bone, as it did for those diplomats of his own generation, like Michael Palliser, whose lives were definitively shaped by the conflict they took part in. They were a particular kind of club, qualified in a different way from other kinds of public men. It probably mattered quite a lot to the direction of later events that in early September 1939, as Ted Heath was making it back to Britain from Poland by the skin of his teeth before war was declared, Harold Wilson was motoring to Dundee to deliver an academic paper on exports and the trade cycle, and that later, while Heath was training to run an anti-aircraft battery, Wilson became a potato controller at the Ministry of Food.[6]

Heath's opening bids in Parliament reflected this experience. Europe, especially Germany, was his prime, dominating interest. Germany both-ered him, even as she absorbed him. In 1948, while wholly accepting Churchill's view that Germany must be readmitted into some version of 'Europe', he had no illusions about the Germans. He said his knowledge of their pre-war mentality led him to believe that many of them still looked back on the Hitler years with favour. They should be encouraged to recover, but not allowed to fight: an 'interestingly doubled-edged view', as his biographer notes.[7] By 1950, when he made his maiden speech, this clarified into a heartfelt certainty that the European project of the period, the Schuman Plan, should involve Britain as well as the continentals.

The maiden speech adds to the incremental symmetry which was to conclude with Prime Minister Heath leading Britain into the European Economic Community – the 'Monnet–Schuman system', as it continued to be regarded by *aficionados*. Characteristically, Heath was able to deliver the speech just after returning from a tour of Germany, on whose condition he reported to the Commons at first hand. Having talked to both Christian and Social Democrats, he said, he was convinced that they wanted reconciliation and that the Schuman Plan for a coal and steel community was the way to begin the task. The 'binding in' of Germany – the notion of a European Germany not a German Europe – was not a concept then explicitly articulated by anybody. It awaited another generation of German politicians to be put quite so candidly. But this was the thought that underlay Heath's speech, and the statement he made that Britain must be part of the enterprise. He scorned the Labour Government's argument that Schuman was a capitalist ramp. He feared the consequences for the British economy – 'a very great risk indeed' – of self-exclusion from a community that would galvanize our continental competitors. And he said this with quite searing conviction, which distinguished him from his leaders, Churchill and Anthony Eden. They, too, attacked the Government, but for crudely oppositionist reasons. They said we should be there, but they didn't mean it and didn't take their own chance to do something about it when they reached government next year. For Edward Heath, it was an article of faith: and it was rendered the more prominent in his credo, the more vital in his personal history, by the fact that it turned out to be not only his maiden speech but the one speech of any significance he made as a back-bencher in Parliament, before soon being hoisted into the Whips' office and thence, after nine years of managerial silence, to a front-bench position where he spoke from the despatch box.

It is appropriate that this speech should stand in such solitary isolation. It was a personal announcement, which rang down the decades, taking the position from which Heath never deviated, using arguments that swept aside what he would always regard as marginal irritations –

such matters as the effect of 'Europe' on national sovereignty, or the precise nature of the terms of entry. Coming from his heart as well as his head, it was the first piece of the political platform that launched him and his country, twenty years later, into the Common Market.

The second, of course, was that he had been there before. He had sat at the table, sweated through days and nights in the smoke-filled chamber, haggled with counterparts over pigmeat and cashew nuts and the sterling balances, watched his mind go numb absorbing the tenth new scheme for dealing with New Zealand butter. From his experience as Macmillan's negotiator, he was a master of the European scene, knew the shape of every committee-room and the frailties of the players in them, many of whom had not changed in the space of the decade.

Heath's sheer range of acquaintance was enormous, and on many of its members he had made the best possible impression. His opening statement at the 1961 negotiation revealed to them a more direct approach than Macmillan's. The application, he told them, was not tactical and wasn't based on narrow grounds. He swept aside the conceit, much cultivated by his party-fearing colleagues in the Cabinet, that this wasn't an application at all, but simply an inquiry to see if decent terms might be available. 'We recognize it as a great decision,' he had said on the first day, 'a turning-point in our history, and we take it in all seriousness.' It was what Macmillan meant, but not what he dared to say. This spirit Heath maintained until beyond the end. His speech after the veto culminated in a statement, partly penned in his own hand, which said that Britain would be back. The veto should not jeopardize European unity, he said. 'We are part of Europe by geography, tradition, history, culture and civilization. We shall continue to work with our friends in Europe for the true unity and strength of this continent.' It was one of very few occasions on which Ted Heath, earnest to a fault and one of the least inspiring speakers of modern times, brought tears to the eyes of some of those present to hear him.[8]

There has been argument about Heath's tactical appreciation of the dealing he was involved in. Did he drag out the negotiations too long? Miss a crucial opening in the summer of 1962, like some First World War general failing to anticipate a breakthrough in the Maginot Line? This is fertile ground for speculation in Euro-academia, whose output on the point approached industrial-scale with the opening of the relevant British files in the Public Record Office.[9] But the episode made no dent on Heath's reputation, supreme among all Conservative and most

Labour politicians of his era, as the man best equipped to take advantage of an opening across the Channel, should this appear.

Before it did, a third element of his relevant curriculum vitae began to disclose itself. He made himself into something of a Euro-intellectual, again an unfashionable development in a Tory politician. His conviction was clear from 1950, his experience established by 1963. Then, in 1967, he gave shape to his view of the future with a series of lectures at Harvard University.[10]

These caused little stir at the time. It was a period when the whole EEC project was becalmed. The world view Heath set forth, however, was strikingly Euro-centred, undeflected by Wilson's charge that his enthusiasm for Brussels and all its works could be likened to that of a submissive spaniel. It prepared the ground for a break not only with Macmillan's priorities – the Atlantic relationship, the Commonwealth – but with the ongoing sensitivities of the Conservative Party.

Heath summarized the state of things in Europe. Since the project was under the influence of French obstructionism, he said, British policy faced a paradox. 'On the one hand, if the Community gathers speed and begins once again to progress towards economic and political union, it will inevitably make fresh arrangements and develop fresh institutions to which Britain will then be asked to adhere without having had any say in their formation.' The once and future dilemma, what Russell Bretherton had noted a dozen years before: how to combine influence with exile. But now there was a new development. 'On the other hand,' Heath went on, 'a stagnant Community has proved increasingly unattractive to British opinion.'

To ward off such corrosive damage, he recommended a missionary approach. Public support would be recovered only if people knew what Europe was about. 'This can only be done by setting out the prospects honestly and showing that when we talk about the unity of Europe we mean not a vague concept, but the habit of working together to reach accepted goals.' Heath, in other words, was framing a political future for the Community, and the flesh he put on it was fattest in the realm of defence. He harked back to a European defence community, and in the process declared himself, by the standards of post-war convention, a less convinced Atlanticist than any other British leader. He talked up the sacrilegious idea of nuclear pooling between France and Britain, and openly canvassed for 'an eventual European defence system'.

This was the working out, in opposition, of new and distinct priorities which, while little noticed by the Conservative Party, became disturbing to the Americans. Heath was never anti-American, in the way the Labour left had spent a lifetime being. Yet here was the emergence of a philosophy, a harbinger of his years in power, which foretold a drastic change not only from Macmillan's intimacies with John F. Kennedy but from Wilson's cringing submission to Lyndon Johnson. In this, Heath was to remain consistent. Henry Kissinger, in his memoirs, recalled a Prime Minister who 'dealt with us with an unsentimentality totally at variance with the "special relationship"'. Unlike other European leaders, who 'strove to improve their relations with us . . . Heath went in the opposite direction'.[11] It was a conscious choice, based on the perception that the old concentric circles were no longer quite as equi-cyclical as they were when Churchill talked about them. Europe, in Heath's assessment, had to become the largest: a position that actually gave him much in common, paradoxically, with de Gaulle. From time to time, Heath made speeches that could be called Gaullist, talking about the need to 'redress the balance' against the dollar, and speaking with disapproval of 'an allegiance foreign to Europe'.[12] The Godkin Lectures at Harvard were where they took coherent shape.

Also while in opposition, he began to lose all patience with the third of these circles, the Commonwealth. It became as much of a curse for him as it was for Wilson, and he lacked any of the family background, the emotional bonding, that might have sustained the myth of kin against the glaring fact of irrelevance and even, on the matter of Rhodesia, enmity. From the moment Heath became Tory leader on 1965, white Rhodesia, declaring independence in the same year, gained virulent support from a faction in the Tory Party, which delighted to goad him. It would be wrong to call Heath a lifelong anti-Common-wealth man. During the 1962 negotiations, he worked hard to defend Commonwealth interests, and travelled across many red parts of the map to get agreement for the results. He was proud to say that, before the veto, 'these were worked out in great detail almost to the point of completion'.[13] But by 1970 such feeling as he had for the Common-wealth, black or white, had drained away.

It had become, along with almost everything else, a residual in the great equation he desired to make between Britain and Europe.

*

EVEN SO, Heath was cautious. While his personal commitment was deepening, so was the country's scepticism. The idea of Europe was seldom to be so popular as in the first flush of the early 1960s, when Macmillan's anxieties contrasted with the bright-eyed zeal that developed, especially in the business world, for an exciting idea which looked like the way of the future. The veto, followed by the EEC's inability to decide where it was going, topped off by Wilson's candour about the effect on food prices, took the shine off the vision. In April 1970, two months before the general election, a Gallup poll found only 19 per cent of voters favouring British entry, with more than half of them rejecting the idea of even getting into talks. Popular feeling for the whole idea was at rock bottom. Heath's manifesto was calibrated accordingly. Whereas in the first election which he fought as party leader, the 1966, the Tories promised to 'seize the first favourable opportunity of becoming a member of the Community', the pledge now was much more guarded. At the 1970 election, the Conservatives promised only to negotiate – 'no more, no less'.

The negotiating modalities, however, were already in place. Such was the seamlessness. Whoever won the election, the ground was prepared. All Heath had to do was pick up the briefs and files that had been in the making for three years. This bears a moment's contemplation, given what later happened in the Labour Party. The official historian records a depth of continuity that was greater than has often been understood. The Heath negotiation, he writes, was based 'in all essentials' on the statement made by George Brown on 4 July 1967, prior to Wilson's abortive venture. It wasn't a case merely of picking up the baton that de Gaulle's second veto had forced out of Britain's hand in November, but of being the beneficiary of unremitting work that had gone on ever since. Brown stated a position that never changed, and, right up to and through the election, the fine-tuning and detailed timetabling of a process scheduled to start on 30 June was going on. The historian lists the quantity of work that was by then out of the way: 'The decision to apply for membership; its endorsement by Parliament; the necessarily deliberate response by the Community, involving, among much else, an opinion by the Commission; the preparation of negotiating positions by the Community and by ourselves.' To Heath, he says, this was 'of enormous value'.[14]

Likewise, the team that would handle it was already in place. The biggest thing Heath wanted to do was done by people Labour had picked. The caravan was rolling, and by now it was full of believers. The Whitehall hesitations of a decade before had not entirely vanished, but the political commitment to succeed, through the men selected to do the work, was now pretty well absolute.

At their head was Con O'Neill, restored to the Foreign Office after his brief tiff with George Brown, and put back in place there thanks, in part, to the ministrations of John Robinson. Within days of de Gaulle's departure, the signal that serious business might begin, Robinson proposed O'Neill's return, and went round to his flat to make sure that, if drafted, he would serve.[15] Other members of the Euro-sodality were placed alongside. Robinson himself was the most prominent, O'Neill's trusted ally, the continuity man who knew where every French body was buried. Raymond Bell came from the Treasury, as he had in 1961. Freddy Kearns from the Ministry of Agriculture and Roy Denman from the Board of Trade were already steeped in Europe, through regularly negotiating with the Commission as part of their daily work. The members of the regiment and their allies were in place, before the election was held to decide which party they would be serving.

So was the structure within which they operated. It had been decided that the negotiation should be handled not, as last time, from the Foreign Office, an arrangement that tended to sharpen differences in Whitehall, but from the Cabinet Office, where it could be better subjected to central control. There needed to be smoother co-ordination, and a more reliable facility for riding over and dissolving the residual antagonism in Whitehall.

For antagonism there still was. Part of it was departmental: the bull-headed determination of the Ministry of Agriculture, for example, to defend the interest of British farmers against negotiating concessions. But the problem was more than sectional. While Whitehall officials were trained in nothing if not detection of the way the wind was blowing, active enthusiasm for the Common Market was still not universal.

One man who noted this was John Hunt, whom Heath appointed to run the Cabinet Office operation in the final stages of the negotiation. Not long after, Hunt was to become secretary of the Cabinet. To be aggressively keen on Europe at this time, Hunt thought, remained proof of slight eccentricity. With a pedigree by Treasury out of Commonwealth Relations, he had come to his own supportive opinions a little late, but, as Whitehall co-ordinator of the team, was struck by its members' maverick quality. 'Most were not naturally people who were going to go to the top of the mainstream civil service,' he later reflected. 'I think some of them had been shoved into this job because it was one that nobody else was keen to do, and they happened to believe in it.'[16]

This set them apart from their superiors. Burke Trend, the Cabinet secretary, as we have seen, was classically sceptic, vowing to defend Atlantic and Commonwealth links at all costs. 'He was profoundly against Europe,' Hunt told me. It led to much awkwardness with Heath, his direct master. But Trend wasn't alone. There was considerable twitching from the old order. When Wilson insisted on trying to negotiate, Denis Greenhill, Brown's appointee as head of the Foreign Office, came into Robinson's office, which overlooked Downing Street, and, staring across the road, declared with utmost gloom: 'I think it's a question of flogging a dead horse' – a statement of dissidence which Robinson found very shocking.

The Treasury, also, remained officially against British entry. That is to say, its judgement of the economic consequences was negative, and it submitted a paper to that effect. The permanent secretary, Sir Douglas Allen, was roused to unusually vigorous displays of disdain when the economic arguments for entry were set in front of him. Not for him the balanced agonizing of the 1950s. Now that the Common Agriculture Policy, with its massive disbursements for farmer-heavy countries like France, was set in place, the advantages, he thought, were far outweighed by the costs. Whatever the political gains, there would be losses both to the balance of payments and to the economy generally. The Treasury paper, however, was dismissed. When Heath came to publish a white paper, it simply buried the Treasury arguments. 'We were prepared to put the pros and cons,' Allen, by now Lord Croham, told me, 'but to argue that this would be beneficial to the economy, on the terms offered, was something we could not accept. Although the white paper said that, the official Treasury dissented.'[17]

By now, however, these views were a side-show. The momentum that had built up since 1967 overrode such fiddling particulars. On 30 June, a different minister showed up in Luxembourg: the Tory, Anthony Barber, rather than the Labour man who had supervised all this work, George Thomson. A different man again, Geoffrey Rippon, led the actual negotiations, owing to Barber's sudden elevation to the Treasury, on the untimely death of the ablest man in the Government, Iain Macleod. Rippon's presence probably made some difference. A more roguish and laid-back politician than Barber, though not a Heath familiar, he was a capable lawyer and a keen European, formerly chairman of the Tory delegation to the Council of Europe. He had a swift mind and a broad brush, and an unlawyerly impatience with detail. Curious traits for a negotiator, perhaps: but attractive to his official team, who were happy to look after the mountains of small print while Geoffrey took care of the big picture, along with the claret and cigars, marks of his personal style, which delighted them almost as much as finding he was the first man most of them had known who kept a telephone in his car.

The negotiations began without delay, and they were, despite all the preparations, a process of extended complexity. They were sometimes nasty, and occasionally brutish, and they were indisputably long, lasting from July 1970 until January 1972. But they were also engulfed by a paradox. On the one hand, they had to take place. There was no way round the need to nail down every kind of transitional particular about the way Britain – along with Denmark, Ireland and Norway, who were also negotiating for entry, on the greater British coat-tails – would be allowed to make her way into the burgeoning network of Community governance. And yet there was a charade-like aura about them. In deep reality, they were, according to a well-qualified participant, 'peripheral, accidental and secondary'. For a large anterior fact dominated everything that happened, namely the imperative that Britain should join the continent. 'What mattered was to get into the Community, and thereby restore our position at the centre of European affairs which, since 1958, we had lost.'[18]

This lapidary opinion was no throwaway line. It didn't come from a commentator, or a careless politician, or a *post facto* surveyor of events, but from someone as close to the official British mind as it was possible to be: someone, indeed, who arguably *was* the British mind: at any rate, an interpreter of it second only to Edward Heath in his capacity to put judgement into action.

The author was Con O'Neill himself, the chief official negotiator, from whose work we have already heard in the last chapter. For nearly thirty years, this secret text, the Foreign Office's own history of the negotiation, more than 300 pages long, has lain in the vaults unread. Quite early in my own inquiry, someone kindly slipped me a copy of what is a *tour de force* of diplomatic writing, the ultimate insider's account, which O'Neill completed, extraordinarily, within six months of the negotiation ending. In its combination of narrative drive and penetrating analysis, together with the unique authority of its standpoint, there can be few state papers that surpass it. One cannot say it should have been published earlier, for the enlightenment of the British people about events that have bothered them ever since. It contains too many candid indiscretions concerning the stance and character of Britain's interlocutors, particularly the French, many of them still alive. But as a source-book for the intricacies of the process – a case-study of how a certain kind of multilateral diplomacy is conducted between sophisticated operators in Europe – it is without rival.

It is, of course, only a British account. And it is vastly longer than a secondary author such as this one could accommodate. But I rely on it for the next few pages. Fragments seem worth exposing, for the light they cast on what happened in Brussels in the prelude to Heath's defining triumph. As to both tactics and method, they have a lot to say. As to the errors made, and the imperfections of the outcome, O'Neill is also not entirely silent: another reason, no doubt, for having withheld an eminently publishable tome from publication for as long as possible.

One gets from it, to begin with, a sense of the scale of what entry now meant, by comparison with 1961. There had been an immense accumulation of Community rules and precedents, even though half the decade had been spent, thanks to de Gaulle, in a condition of stasis. O'Neill puts with startling candour the fundamental fact that lay behind the negotiation, the existential reality about 'Europe'. 'None of its policies were essential to us,' he writes. 'Many of them were objectionable.' But they had to be accepted, for the larger purpose. They had grown up in our absence. If the British had been there, he says, 'we would never . . . have allowed a situation to develop which made it so difficult, for instance, to ensure fair arrangements for New Zealand dairy products or developing Commonwealth sugar, or to create a situation of equity in respect of our contribution to the Budget.'[19] These, along with fish, proved to be the most contested items in the deal. But, as a result of the British not being there from the start, the fresh enactments they had to address amounted to some 13,000 typewritten pages. By 1970, as a German official of the Commission wrote, 'an almost inconceivable flood of European law . . . had to be accepted by the candidates'.[20]

A great deal of this was absolutely non-negotiable. That stance was laid down from the beginning, and within three months the British accepted it. They started off by reserving the right both to try and change Community policy and to postpone some difficult matters for settlement until after membership had been agreed. 'By October 1970 we had shelved these possibilities,' O'Neill writes.[21] Even the countries most anxious for British entry, like Italy and the Netherlands, were determined to play a hard game. Their conversational flexibility proved to be 'little more than politeness and a desire to please'. The Community's principle, he adds, was 'swallow the lot', and, musing about why this should be – why they wouldn't accept 'some compromises, some fresh starts, some changes of existing rules' – he lights upon a truth that would apply throughout the Community's history, right down to the present day, with the close of the century in sight. It was an articulation of the famous saw, *Les absents ont toujours tort*, describing the predicament of every outsider trying to get in, not as a result of malice or political enmity but of simple inexorable fact. 'Almost every conceivable Community policy or rule or enactment', O'Neill concluded, 'is the resultant of a conflict of interests between members, and has embedded in it features representing a compromise between the interests.' Open it up, and the whole laborious compromise will fall apart. Make exceptions, just because the British argument is strong and the matter of no great importance, and you create a precedent. So the rule became: 'Swallow the lot, and swallow it now.'[22]

This, in turn, defined the limit of what negotiation could be about. It was, essentially, about mitigation not change, about transitional arrangements not the remaking of rules to fit a new situation. There were nuances to this. Actually, in the thickets of the argument about the access of Caribbean sugar producers to their traditional British market, or of New Zealand's butter to the country on which her economy substantially depended, the Community agreed to adjust its rules. But usually, only for a while: five years was the norm for the transition. Beyond that, there could seldom be any special privileges against free trading within the EEC, especially in agriculture, or against the imposition of tariffs on outsiders. For who were the beggars now, the *demandeurs*, in Euro-parlance? There had almost been a category-shift since 1961, when the British still felt strong enough, rightly or wrongly, to make their approach from a position of strength, inquiring if satisfactory terms might be available prior to them deciding, from their great height, whether to dignify Europe with their presence. Ten years later, it was a case of taking what they could get.

The physical arrangements for this work are not without interest. There were often more than a hundred people in the room, with delegations from each of the Six, as well as the Commission and the president pro tem of the Council – French for the first period, German for the second, Italian for the third – who was the only one allowed to talk for the Europeans. 'A series of short and stilted dialogues' ensued between the president and the British delegation. But this wasn't where the real business was done. Everything that mattered took place in the corridors, and the long interludes between quite short formal meetings. Even the all-night sessions were not as arduous as they have always been represented in European folklore, with British ministers tottering back to London after defending the national interest into the small hours. 'The general image was conveyed', O'Neill writes of his work in 1971–2, 'of the British Delegation locked for 15 or 20 hours at a stretch in debate with the Community Delegation, as statement or proposal, reply, rebuttal or rejoinder, compromise or counter-compromise were volleyed across the table. This was not the case.'

In fact O'Neill could not recall a single continuous session between European ministers and Geoffrey Rippon that lasted as long as an hour. By far the greater time was taken up – 'twenty or thirty times as much' – by the Community partners haggling with each other, rather than in meetings with the British. On the British side, many more weeks were spent in London, preparing for the next session and sorting out White-hall turf-wars, than in Brussels, though by the end of the piece more than 140 officials from seventeen departments had made the cross-Channel journey: testament to the immersion Europe already required of any applicant member, and a harbinger of what was to come – the infusion of European matters into the life of the bureaucracy more deeply than into any other class or category in the whole of British society.

Whitehall was the battlefield where John Robinson, in particular, came into his own. Guarding the negotiators' flank against enfilading fire from colleagues in the home civil service was his special task, carried out with the secrecy and conspiratorial dissembling of which he was the FO's acknowledged master. It was also Robinson who laid down a fundamental rule of British negotiating procedure. When there was a breakdown, he wrote, it would be crucial to pin the blame on the other side. In a formulation Machiavelli would have rated, he identified 'the all-important point that, if the Community cannot make joint proposals to us which lie within the range of what we would regard as reasonably negotiable, we want the Community to fail to agree on joint proposals to us. We want the crisis on each subject to be within the Six rather than between the Six and ourselves.' O'Neill thought so well of this strategy that he cites it specially in his history.[23]

From the start, the British had a date in mind. Their objective was to gain entry on 1 January 1973, which was what in fact occurred. Robinson drew up a critical path that proved to be extraordinarily prescient, marking down, two years ahead, often to within days of the event, what ought to happen when and where.[24]

Keeping the Community, and especially the French, to the wheel was therefore the first strategic priority, closely followed by a decision to bid low rather than high when putting forward proposals. Not too low, but, more important, not too high, on account of the publicity. For this was a negotiation, as everyone understood, conducted in public – which had its virtues and its vices. A merit of the Community, O'Neill drily notes, 'is that they find it almost impossible to maintain any security for their transactions'.[25] As a result, the British usually saw the texts of what the other side were going to say before they said it. The state of prior knowledge was 'virtually complete'. On the other hand, such habitual transparency in the Community culture carried penalties. A proposal pitched too high could have calamitous effects, for it had to be assumed that in Brussels there were no secrets. To fail to secure a British demand, even in those days of relatively calm journalism, was to court political disaster. 'Nothing', says O'Neill, 'could have created a more damaging impression, in the press and in Parliament, than for us to have demanded a particular solution, and then be seen to be beaten back . . . into having to accept something much more modest.'[26]

There were exceptions to this tactic. On the biggest imponderables – sugar, dairy products and the contribution to the budget – Rippon and O'Neill put forward 'maximum demands', in order to keep the producer lobbies in the Caribbean and New Zealand happy, and to establish a rigorous base-line for what they knew would be the hardest deal of all, over finance. Here, O'Neill records, both press and Parliament were obliging, and understood very well that the bids were certain not to succeed. On other matters, the team saw low bidding as a form of toughness. It was their own way of playing hard ball. From the armoury of recognized negotiating tactics, such an approach contrasted with the more usual continental flamboyance. 'We stuck to it as long as we could,' O'Neill writes, 'and refused to become engaged in a descending order of compromise.'[27]

The O'Neill history gives lengthy and meticulous accounts of the handling of each subject on the table. The chapters often run to dozens of absorbing pages, capable, even thirty years later, of arousing the interest, perhaps the outrage, of the industries that were made or broken in the process. We learn that while the Foreign Office received most letters on the question of sugar – Tate & Lyle, and the sugar industry generally, having a long record of successful pressure on Tory governments – New Zealand butter and cheese was the likeliest deal-breaker, being the subject on which the parliamentary muscle of British kith and kin was most easily mobilized. If Britain, dealing on their behalf, accepted a settlement which the New Zealanders rejected, Parliament's approval could not be relied on. 'We were in a dilemma,' says O'Neill. 'The New Zealanders had us over a political barrel. They did indeed, to some extent, hold a veto over our entry into the Community.' The New Zealand Prime Minister, the historian judged, 'went on asking for more until, in almost every respect, he got it.' He was 'more successful in the negotiations than anyone else'.[28]

The most unexpected problem was the fate of the sterling balances, debts held in London, mostly to Commonwealth countries which had traditionally kept large quantities of their reserves there. 'No subject ... was more elusive and mysterious,' O'Neill writes. 'In no case was it harder to grasp clearly and firmly what were the issues at stake and what we would be asked by the Community to do.' The French were the ones who most cared, linking the question to the weakness of the British economy, a consideration that remained, for them, one which they took very seriously. But the British couldn't get to the bottom of French concern. 'It was never quite clear whether the reserve role of sterling was more objectionable to the French as something which gave us an unusual privilege and advantage, or as something which would represent an unacceptable liability and risk.'[29]

The French, indeed, were permanently captious. Though others occasionally raised their own special difficulties, the negotiation was essentially with the French, on whose style O'Neill had every reason, by the end, to regard himself as a world authority. As one professional to another, he wasn't entirely unimpressed by the French. It was they, he complained, who for months kept all parties in 'unnecessary and agonising suspense'. But he admitted that in one way this paid off. By stonewalling, he concedes, France kept control of the sequence of events. This resulted in a linkage being made – an entirely adventitious nego-tiator's linkage – between a successful deal on New Zealand's dairy products and a settlement on the Community budget. This worked out much to Britain's disadvantage. To keep New Zealand happy, the British were forced to worsen their budget terms.

This was by way of being a secular French triumph. On the other hand, O'Neill decided, they often seemed to be playing games. 'The French take an unusual satisfaction in the conduct of negotiations for its own sake,' he writes. 'They like the tensions it can engender, and the careful orchestration of innumerable themes. For the French, negotiation is an art form, or even a sport.' At the end of one all-night session, he was greeted by his French counterpart who said: 'Congratulations! *Vous avez très bien négocié.*' 'It was as though we had just finished a particularly exciting, hard-fought and enjoyable game of tennis,' the author comments.[30]

As to who had won this game, O'Neill acknowledged only one British disaster. His history concludes with two chapters of evaluation. One of them asks: Did We Make Mistakes? The other: Did We Get a Good Bargain? For the most part, he answers no and yes, respectively – but with a single large exception.

On New Zealand, he thought, the Antipodeans got more than they deserved. Political pressure probably required it, but the price was too high. 'I still feel it is something of a blemish on the outcome that we ourselves had to pay so much on New Zealand's behalf.' New Zealand herself would have settled for less, had the British ignored the cunning threats of her Prime Minister. Getting what she got, because it involved concessions on the British budgetary contribution, cost the British Exchequer, O'Neill reckoned, £100 million in 1972 money over five years (or £750 million in 1998 terms).[31]

On the financial deal itself, there is also a modicum of self-criticism. Having started with an absurd demand, that Britain should pay only 3 per cent of the EEC budget in the first year, 1973, O'Neill and his negotiators had to settle for 8.64 per cent, rising to 18.92 per cent in 1977. Bidding too toughly here had a bad effect. The minuscule opening shot produced, says O'Neill, 'an exceedingly hostile reaction from virtually all quarters of the Community'. 'A better atmosphere might have led to a better settlement.'[32] On the other hand, he decides that, ultimately, the final deal could not have been very different from what in fact was achieved.

On fish, however, he enters only a modest defence. This is the great exception. It was a complex, disastrous story. The Community concluded its own Common Fisheries Policy within hours of the enlargement process commencing, which looked like an amazing piece of chicanery. Having hung fire for years, the issue of access to coastal waters was resolved between the Six to the extreme disadvantage of the four candidate members, who would bring to the Community far longer coast-lines and double the fish-catch. Of all the matters on the agenda, fish was therefore the least prepared by the British. Since it was also the one question on which the Labour Party wasn't hopelessly compromised by its own activities in government from 1967 to 1970, Harold Wilson and his colleagues leaped with special relish to attack the Government, driving home the scandalous nature of the deprivation facing in-shore

British fishermen at the hands of predatory Frenchmen who, at one stage, seemed likely to be able to fish 'right up to the beach'.

There were, and are, inherent conflicts of interest in the seas of Europe which were always certain to cause trouble. They could never have been resolved to everyone's satisfaction. But here, at least, O'Neill does admit to error. He and his team, he says, wholly miscalculated the support which the plight of plucky trawler-men could engender, vastly disproportionate to their numbers or their economic importance. The CFP opened the way for foreigners to enter what had always been regarded as British waters, and O'Neill could understand the consequences without finding a way of dealing with them. Sea fisheries, he noted, were the only significant economic activity of developed countries that are a form not of harvesting or processing but of hunting. So he diagnosed the feelings they arouse to be both deep and ancient. 'As a fisherman myself,' he wrote, 'I understand these feelings. If I ever find someone else engaged in fishing a pool which by law, convention or comity I have a better right to be fishing at that moment than he, I experience feelings of sheer rage.'[33] The thirty pages he devotes to the fish issue are the most brilliant in his history, recounting the apparent modesty of the issue at the beginning and the life-and-death struggle it became by the end. But they tell a sorry story.

O'Neill asks himself, in conclusion, whether, taking one thing with another and considering them all in the balance, Britain got terms that were 'reasonable, advantageous and not too onerous'. And he has no doubt about it. He answers with an 'unhesitating affirmative'.[34] Yet he does not claim all, or even the essence, of the credit. As he noted from the outset, his own negotiations were, for all their length, peripheral and secondary. What mattered was the politics, and the over arching agreement secured between two politicians.

We return to the role of Prime Minister Heath, and his fellow protagonist in the quest for a solidarity between national interests, Georges Pompidou. If these terms were satisfactory, it was because the leaders desired the negotiation to succeed. And, in particular, Pompidou desired it, as he showed by engineering – or allowing to be engineered, it matters little – a summit meeting between himself and Heath which was decisive in securing British entry. It is rare to be able to say as much about any moment of diplomacy. Usually, every moment belongs to a skein of events made up of complex interconnections, all or perhaps none of which seem to be absolutely crucial. But, in the British negotiation with Europe, one truth which nobody contests is that the

Pompidou–Heath summit on 19–20 May 1971 was the moment that decided everything.

Pompidou, though he had been de Gaulle's Prime Minister, was not in fact a Gaullist *croyant et pratiquant*. He was not another Couve. When I talked to M. Couve de Murville in Paris in 1994, he told me dismissively that Pompidou's interest in getting Britain into the Common Market was a matter of domestic politics. 'He wanted to show he wasn't like de Gaulle,' said Couve.[35] A banker and a countryman, proud of his peasant origins, Pompidou, it is true, had never been very interested in foreign affairs. Insofar as he had an interest, he was more inclined to be anti-German than anti-British, and lacked most of the Gaullist rage against the imagined conspiracies of Anglo-Saxons. As President he soon made foreign policy his private domain. Not least of his reasons for this was a determination to contest the dominance of the unreconstructed Gaullists, the heirs and allies of Couve, at the Quai d'Orsay.

The reasons why he favoured British entry, if he could secure conditions that continued to favour France, were the usual mixture of the political and the personal. It is ever thus: but here, perhaps, the personal, involving Heath, were indispensable.

In terms of politics, Pompidou thought, the time had probably come. His closest aide in 1970, Jean-René Bernard, told me in 1994: 'It was the right moment for a real choice. There were no special reasons to refuse, if the negotiation was good. If we refused, we would have had a severe crisis inside the Common Market. And we would have been on very bad terms with the British for fifty years.'[36]

There was a tide in the affairs of continent and archipelago, carrying them together. A Dutchman, Emile van Lennep, secretary-general of the OECD, saw a lot of Pompidou at the time. The French understood, he thought, that the Common Market would become weak and undirected if it did not grow. They didn't like it, because it would reduce their control, but they had to accept it. 'I found out very early that there was not to be another veto,' van Lennep recalled. 'Britain would succeed. Not because Britain had changed, but because the application couldn't be resisted any more. British membership became a political necessity not just for the British but for the others as well.'[37]

All the same, a question remained: who would do the deed? At the time these thoughts were percolating through the Elysée, the British Prime Minister, his application on the table, was Harold Wilson. Had Wilson won the 1970 election, the ineluctable forces of history might have had to bide their time. Roy Denman, one of the negotiators, says in his book (published in 1996) that, if Wilson had turned up in Paris for a summit meeting, he 'would have been shown the door and Britain to this day would have remained outside the Community'.[38] Michael Palliser, Wilson's private secretary at the time, recalled his own modified pessimism. 'I'm absolutely convinced he wouldn't have been able to persuade the French to let us in,' Palliser told me. Much is also made, in Foreign Office lore, of an unforgettable blunder the Prime Minister made in 1967, when he arrived very late for a dinner at the French ambassador's London residence. Pompidou, visiting as Prime Minister, was supposed to be his host. Not only was he unimpressed by Wilson's excuse, that he had had to attend a Commons debate on Vietnam, but the French saw a certain symbolism in Wilson's dishevelled appearance. 'You could almost feel the self-satisfaction when we met them next day,' Palliser remembered. 'They looked at this Government which had just had to devalue, which was in an economic mess, and there they were with the strong franc. It was a real reversal of roles, after years of us looking down on them.'[39]

More seriously, Wilson failed to pass the old Gaullist test, which still applied even though de Gaulle had gone. Did Britain really mean it? Was she prepared to make an unconditional commitment to Europe as it was? The French were not convinced in 1970 that Wilson could be relied on not to think first about the Atlantic and the Commonwealth.

Heath, on the other hand, was seen quite differently. He came with credentials, vouched for from within the vast freemasonry of his acquaintance. He told me about it himself. It all began on a beach in Spain, in 1960, where he had gone to diet. Whiling away the time, he noticed a Frenchman, sitting two tables away with his American wife and their son. One day, the Frenchman came over to him and said: 'If you don't eat any more, you'll never be able to deal with de Gaulle.' Thereafter, the two men lay on the beach for many mornings, drinking sherry and eating prawns. It was the beginning of quite a momentous friendship.[40]

It is typical of Heath's guardedness, as a source for almost any information about his life, that having told me this story he declined to tell me the name of his friend. Until he wrote his own memoirs, he was extraordinarily coy: possessive of anything to do with Europe, in particular: the jealous guardian, it seemed to me, not only of a certain point of view but of sacred details of the story that everyone else showed a bottomless capacity, whether malign or otherwise, to get wrong.

It wasn't hard to complete the picture, however, since coyness had failed to conceal the name from several of Heath's colleagues who got their memoirs in first. The man on the beach was Michel Jobert, who happened later to become Pompidou's private secretary. They kept in touch. Naturally, Heath sent his Harvard lectures to Jobert, who translated them for Pompidou, who pronounced himself delighted with their message, especially Heath's idea for Anglo-French nuclear sharing. 'This shows that Heath is European,' Pompidou told Jobert. 'Pompidou knows you are serious,' Jobert told Heath. 'That contributed very largely to the result,' Heath told me in 1994.

Although this sounds like an exaggeration, its truthful aspect should not be underestimated. It was important to Pompidou, if he was to change the French position, to be certain he was dealing with someone whose attitudes and commitment he could trust. Around the axis of the Heath–Pompidou relationship, the negotiations for British entry rotated towards a successful conclusion.

The climax came in Paris, in the middle of May 1971. Industrious though O'Neill and his interlocutors had been, progress until that point had been sticky. There was known to be a political will, in London and, at least in the person of the President, in Paris. Yet the negotiators lacked the power to make, on either side, the concessions to express it. Pompidou and Heath settled all that, in twelve hours of deeply private talks, with interpreters only, of which we know more about the essence than we do about the detail.

There had been a big build-up, the usual elusive feints and weaves, neither lot of diplomats wanting to be the first to propose the summit lest this show some sign of weakness. The French officials, indeed, who were Gaullist to a man, did not want to propose it at all. The divisions between the President and the Quai persisted, to such an extent that Pompidou stipulated to London, when the idea was in the air, that the French Foreign Minister, by now Maurice Schumann, should be told nothing about it. Con O'Neill's history describes the lengths to which the British were compelled (by Jobert, acting for Pompidou) to go to ensure that the Quai d'Orsay was 'completely excluded', and the French ambassador in London, Baron Geoffroy de Courcel – 'aloof, frigid and critical', says O'Neill – kept wholly in the dark.[41]

In some ways, however, Heath's role vis-à-vis his own officials was not dissimilar. The Foreign Office, as the history showed, had as deep a suspicion of the French as the Quai did of any breach with Gaullist orthodoxy. Preparing for the summit, Heath was on guard against the diplomats. 'PM cross with FO for, he thinks, anti-French mutterings,' Douglas Hurd, his political secretary, wrote in his diary.[42] He also applied his own caustic interrogation of the Treasury's sceptical submissions. For several days, a length of time appropriate to the magnitude of the moment, Heath sat on the Downing Street lawn, wading through departmental briefs, challenging officials on the sterling balances, New Zealand butter, Caribbean sugar and the rest. Even though there was a shared intention that nobody should be a loser, he was getting ready for man-to-man combat.

In the event, it was not a hard contest. An army of advisers journeyed to Paris. 'The knights in full cry, especially on sterling,' Hurd noted, of Britain's mandarin negotiators, after the first day. But their role was mainly confined to gossiping in the corridors, as 'the great men strolled and talked, and talked and strolled again', watched only at a distance by auxiliaries who became increasingly puzzled as to what was going on. Even when it was over, there was some uncertainty. 'We ran into an unusual and potentially awkward situation,' O'Neill writes. The precise nature of agreement on the main issues 'was not made known'.[43]

Such are the perils of staffless diplomacy. That the meeting was a success, however, was eventually not in doubt. The two men, both highly proficient at engaging with the detail, devoted many more of their hours to the big picture. They disposed of the sterling problem – 'a totally unexpected settlement', O'Neill recorded – in short order. Their aides worried about the delays, but the principals were in fact progressing towards the definitive deal. There were great meals, as there have been from beginning to end of this history. Ambassador Soames gave a grand lunch to which the President, unusually, came: a real tribute, in Heath's opinion. Then Pompidou laid on his own splendiferous banquet. Such was the paucity of outcome thus far, however, that Hurd, fretting, began to think it was all going wrong. After the first day, he writes, 'we were dismayed to find how little had been decided'. Heath, as he remembered it, took mischievous pleasure in failing to reassure his political secretary and the rest of his staff about what was happening. 'All the press thought the thing was a flop and we were covering it up,' Heath told me, smirking at the recollection, even twenty years later.[44]

The press conference to announce that it was far from a flop took place at 9 p.m. on the second evening. With style and courage, Pompidou arranged for it to take place in the Salon des Fêtes at the Elysée Palace, the room where de Gaulle had announced the veto in 1963.

The negotiations, of course, were not over. There remained seven months of detailed work ahead, before they were completely finished. But the President gave the signal. 'It would be unreasonable now to believe that an agreement is not possible,' he said. 'The spirit of our talks over the past few days enables me to think that the negotiations will be successful.' As for Britain and France, recent history could be regarded as undone. The ghost of de Gaulle was, apparently, laid to rest.

'There were many people', Pompidou told the press, 'who believed that Great Britain was not European and did not wish to become European, and that Britain wanted to enter the Community only to destroy it. Many people also thought France was prepared to use all kinds of means and pretexts to propose a new veto to the entry of Great Britain into the Community. Well, ladies and gentlemen, you see tonight before you two men who are convinced to the contrary.'

So: the political class had at last succeeded. The men of topmost power were finally of one mind. There is a guileless excitement about Heath's first literary effort to say what it meant to him. 'It was one of the greatest moments of my life,' he simply said.[45] Though there was more to do, he had done what mattered: come out, by his lights, triumphant, from what O'Neill calls 'by far the most significant meeting that took place in the whole course of the negotiations'.[46]

It was, however, only the beginning of his struggle: a point he never entirely got the measure of. After the captains and the kings, there was another constituency to take account of.

*

THE DEAL DONE in Paris, and eventually ratified in Brussels, was a big deal. But it was not about the biggest matters. It didn't address any of the great issues – future policies of the Community, its relations with the rest of the world, the reform of its institutions and how they should work. Nor did it have anything to say about the larger future of Britain. The deep, existential *meaning*, for Britain, of getting into 'Europe' was not considered. The way Britain would have to change had no place in the work of the technocrats. The future of the nation-state wasn't on the agenda. If the (unindexed) O'Neill history gives any attention to the question of sovereignty, I overlooked it.

At one level, this was to be expected. It wasn't the negotiators' business to open up these profounder matters. The great issue was taken as read: Britain was ready to make the national adjustments involved, as long as the technical terms were right. Indeed, there was a school of thought in London so passionate for entry that it thought the debate should be terminated there and then. A Tory MP, Sir Anthony Meyer, told the Commons in January 1971: 'Frankly, I do not think it depends on the terms at all. I believe it would be in the interests of this country to join the EEC whatever the terms.'[47] In the Lords, six months later, Lord Crowther said: 'You do not haggle over the subscription when you are invited to climb aboard a lifeboat. You scramble aboard while there is still a seat for you.'[48]

Heath, however, knew better. He had done for some time. Before the election, he coined a phrase that never died – one of the few he ever contrived – which was to become a text much pored over, twisted and turned, in the coming years. Speaking of the proposed enlargement of the Community by four more countries, he offered the opinion that this would not be appropriate 'except with the full-hearted consent of the parliaments and peoples of the new member countries'.[49]

This speech was actually meant to be a warning to the Six. It was saying: Don't press us too hard, we have to get this thing past our own democratic tests. It was a negotiator's speech, delivered when he didn't know whether he or Wilson would be sitting at the table. But it became a rod periodically lying heavy on Prime Minister Heath's back. Hurd wrote that it 'fell victim to Wilson's talent for distortion', in the sense that Wilson found it convenient to construe its meaning as the promise of a referendum – whereas neither leader, in those distant early 1970s, made any such commitment. The idea of a referendum was briefly discussed by Heath's team, only to be rejected as unBritish. Wilson, in office, thought the same. In the language of that time, it was apparent that what Heath meant by consent was the consent of Parliament, as filtered through a perhaps more than usually thorough awareness of public opinion.

The phrase, nonetheless, set a benchmark. It became, for ever afterwards, the test which the Heath Government, and its successors, could be said at convenient moments to have passed only by fraud. Full-hearted consent? When did the British people ever agree to be ruled by the bungling tyrants of Brussels? And so on.

But there is a subtler gloss to be made. It tells us something about the state of the argument at the time. In saying what it was that people had to consent to, Heath was very specific: it was the nature of the settlement. This, he said, must not be 'unequal and unfair', and the test that counted was 'primarily the effect upon the standard of living of the individual citizen'. He made little mention of those spacious questions about the future of Britain as an independent country. Although that was the question on which the people were later said not to have given

their opinion, full-hearted or otherwise, it wasn't the question Heath
meant. Heath was talking cost of living, not cost of nationhood.

Nor, to be clear, did that differ from the state of the national
discussion as hitherto conducted. Returning with his deal, Heath faced a
brand of scepticism that had changed little since the first negotiation.
Compared with the furies emerging in the 1990s, the critics of EEC entry
in his own party then remained severe but gentlemanly, and not very
numerous. They were mostly concerned with the old issues, like the
damage that would be done to the Commonwealth. Some contested the
economic case, but none of them desired to bring down the Government.
Although now, as before, some voices took the sovereignty point, they
did not, with one exception, seize the public mind. Sovereignty wasn't
what the main discussion was about in the Labour Party either: or at any
rate, if it was, it was indirect, the old complaint that membership of the
EEC was the kiss of death for the future of socialism in an independent
country. Of the rich grammar of sovereignty, and the seductive investigations it prompted into the meaning of nation, little was heard in the
early 1970s.

The exception, however, mattered. He was a bit of a prophet: not a
successful prophet, because he roundly lost his cause, but a foreteller of
the concerns that were eventually, much later, to grip the British psyche.
He was the one thing that did register a change. Through him, for the
first time, a demon began to stir that had not been fully wakened before,
except briefly by Hugh Gaitskell. The pitch he made shifted the argument
from fuddy-duddy concerns about the redness of the map to anxieties
closer to home. Instead of worrying about other people's countries, the
British were invited, by a harsh, haranguing, driven voice, to think about
their own.

Enoch Powell, bringing overt and eloquent nationalism into the
European argument, had the beginnings of a visceral effect. Along with
the rod of 'full-hearted consent', Powell was a cross Ted Heath had to
bear. He is worth a little inspection, for he was in many ways the
godfather of the successor tribe, to whom nation was not merely
something but everything. He had historic relevance in another way as
well, as a perfect example of the oracular disfigurement that marks
generations of British politicians talking and thinking about Europe: the
louder the voice, the surer the chance that it is contradicting itself.

Mr Powell, former classics professor, compelling orator, One Nation
Tory, MP for Wolverhampton South-West since 1950, was, it is true,
always a kind of English nationalist. He could utter, without flinching,

endless romantic paeans to those 'who felt no country but this to be
their own'.[50] But, when Europe first came to the forefront of British
politics, Powell evidently saw no contradiction between preserving such
essential nationhood and entry into the Common Market. In fact, he
had a special connection with the project. By an enjoyable irony, the one
year Powell ever spent in anybody's Cabinet, as Macmillan's Minister
of Health, happened to be the year, 1962–3, when entering Europe was
the Cabinet's all-devouring purpose, something to which he raised no
objection.

When the party was driven from power, and Heath became its
leader, Powell's enthusiasm for Europe did not diminish. The One
Nation group of MPs published a pamphlet, *One Europe*, that was little
short of a federalist tract. Powell was not the only future sceptic to be
associated with it. It was edited by his friend, Nicholas Ridley, then a
passionate supporter of British membership of a united Europe and a
federalist[51] who was later, when a minister under Margaret Thatcher, to
be another exponent of the Principle of Voluble Contradiction. Powell,
it was reported[52] and never denied, wrote 25 per cent of *One Europe*, a
paper that advocated 'the full economic, military and political union of
Europe'. Addressing the problem of sovereignty, the paper noted that
already, through Nato, the IMF, the GATT and other international
affiliations, 'we have lost much sovereignty', and that each move towards
European unification 'requires that extra political step'.[53] Rather few
British politicians have been associated with anything so extremely
federalist as this effusion. In keeping with it, after the 1966 election,
when his election address supported British membership, Powell, as
shadow spokesman on Defence, objected to a Labour plan for withdrawing some troops from Germany on the very grounds that it would
imperil the larger objective. 'All our professions of anxiety to enter the
Common Market would be discounted,' he said. As late as April 1967 he
attended a conference at Cambridge University, where he hob-nobbed
with the likes of George Ball, Kennedy's hyper-keen European at the
State Department, and Pierre Uri, a draftsman of the Treaty of Rome.
The idea of the conference was specifically to promote European unification, and Powell was an uncritical participant.[54]

Not long after this, however, he underwent a conversion experience.
As often happened on the right – it was especially noticeable among the
intimate minions of Margaret Thatcher – this took radical form. From
apparently supporting political union, Powell moved in four years to the
opposite extremity. Instead of acknowledging political union, he utterly

rejected it. It was the very essence, he said, of the horror of the EEC. As the leading voice of English nationalism, he became Heath's most implacable opponent. The people, he told the 1971 party conference, would not tolerate British 'sovereignty being abolished or transformed'. Fusing a rhetoric of anti-black immigration with a bitter discourse against all things 'European', he took the independence of old England, which he might reluctantly extend to 'Britain', further out than any politician since Oswald Mosley.

For Powell, in effect, wanted no alliances of any kind. He was an anti-imperialist from way back, and a scornful critic of the Commonwealth. Equally, he built a long record as a critic of the Atlantic alliance, ridiculing America's global pretensions and overtly hostile to her management of the Cold War. The distancing from Europe was therefore added to a portfolio of isolationism, which left the Soviet Union as the only international entity for which Powell offered his occasional support. 'We do not need to be tied up with anybody,' he said in 1969, when making his formal break with the earlier pro-Europe position. 'We earn what we earn by our work and our brains ... We are not a drowning man clutching at a rope and screaming for someone to throw him a lifebelt.' Britain Alone seemed to be the Powellite message from the moment Heath began.

This genius of international statesmanship nonetheless had his followers, indeed his worshippers. They were not upset by his lurching transformations. Nor did they explore with much rigour the way he justified them.

His talk-out was, for a man of fastidious intellect, confusing. The confusion might even be said to shade into a kind of unconscious dishonesty, if such is possible to credit to so self-regarding a mind. What Powell said, when interviewed on the question in 1994, was that in the 1960s he never really understood what the EEC was all about. He claimed to have judged the matter of the 1961 application entirely in economic terms. 'I said to myself,' he recalled, ' "That's going for free trade. I'm in favour of free trade." '[55] This was an odd statement, given that the EEC was not about free trade but precisely about a customs union that protected trade against the outside world. But it was even odder, given the plain recognition in One Europe that some kind of political unification was the inescapable meaning of a signature to the Treaty of Rome. Indeed, it is quite incredible to imagine Powell, a particular student of constitutional matters throughout his political career, being unaware that the entire nature of the EEC – visible in all its founding documents, spelled out in the countless speeches of its founders, recognized in numerous Whitehall studies prepared before, during and after the Messina conversations fifteen years earlier – tended towards the ever closer union of political Europe.

By saying that he had thought it was all about economics, however, Powell proved himself a kind of intellectual leader. He was an apologist for amnesia, a condition in which he had a host of successor-disciples. A similar case was made by many latter-day Euro-sceptics reluctant to recall their earlier Euro-enthusiasm, including some whose customary attention to detail rendered it especially hard to believe their pleas of surprise at the turn events had taken. What Enoch Powell said about the Treaty of Rome, Margaret Thatcher closely mirrored when she came to defend, in her new guise as a ferocious anti-European, her signature on the Single European Act in 1986. Nobody, she said, had told her what it really meant.[56]

Since these explanations are hard to credit, one must search for other clues. I suspect they are intrinsic to the psychological, as much as the political, aspects of the 'Europe' question in recent British history. In the Thatcher case rather more than the Powell, the record suggests a leader in an advanced stage of denial. The past, in some sense, simply did not occur. So engulfing is their present rage at what is happening that these people simply can't accept they were ever in a different condition, other than as a result of gross deception. Aware of their apparent inconsistency, they writhe in a serpentine struggle to deny the possibility that this same, sentient, political person could have taken one position – often acting under many heads to advance it – only to adopt another that implies they were once profoundly wrong.

Powell was the path-finder for this tendency. And in 1971, when Heath had to get the product of his negotiation through Parliament, he was the siren voice that summoned forty Conservative MPs to oppose what the Government was doing. This much affected, though it did not determine, the course of events.

At this stage, we may deal briskly with what happened in Parliament. Plainly, the governing party would be split, and its majority of thirty was not sufficient to accommodate the dissenters without help from some-where else. Since the Labour Party was also split, everything rested on the Government business managers selecting the most judicious tactic to maximize the chance that Labour pro-Europeans would endorse the historic moment that now appeared. They were highly motivated, but they needed the proper encouragement. They did not, of course, include the leadership. In a collective renunciation, of near-Powellite proportions, Wilson and the majority of his colleagues made plain soon after the election that the process they had begun could no longer rely on their support. Later, they found, as they were bound to do, that the terms secured by O'Neill and Heath were bad enough to justify the party doing everything it could to ensure that entry did not happen. But there were powerful resisters of this instruction – Roy Jenkins, Shirley Williams, Harold Lever, others – who were to mark the history deeply.

Heath's contribution to securing their votes was, at first, astonishingly unhelpful. Although he had been Chief Whip for many years, and party management was supposed to be his forte, he persisted in the stubborn pretences of party discipline until the eleventh hour, before conceding to his Chief Whip, Francis Pym, that a free vote on the Tory side was the surest way of liberating the principled rebels on the other side. On 28 October 1971, this duly occurred, with sixty-nine Labour MPs, led by Roy Jenkins, the deputy leader, walking through the Government lobby, and helping to provide Heath with a majority of 112 in favour of the principle of entry on the terms he had secured.

Not everything was such plain sailing. During the passage of the European Communities Bill, most of the Labour rebels did not feel able to oblige. There were some narrow scrapes, though on every occasion enough backstairs intelligence was collected by Labour pro-Europeans to ensure that the Bill stayed on course. The Government majorities fell to single figures several times. But there were 104 votes, and not one of them was lost. The Bill passed unamended into law. And, on 1 January 1973, Britain entered the Common Market.

What, however, did people think they were doing when this happened? What did Heath think? How much was known, or unknown, or perhaps concealed from view?

In making the great leap, how conscious were the British, either at the top or among the masses, of precisely what it meant? These questions, in retrospect, have acquired more than academic importance. They will continue to reverberate through the story. They have become, for some people, the essence of the matter. And since these people have been among those most potently driving the debate – the apparently unresolved struggle inside the national mind – a quarter-century later, the aspersions they cast deserve to be studied: are, indeed, a central part of the biography of Edward Heath.

For Heath, two epiphanies marked the triumph of his life. First, there was the conclusion of his meeting with Pompidou, the great moment, as he later wrote, that he could never forget. Second came the night when he got his majority of 112, which he celebrated, while everyone else was going to parties, by returning to Downing Street, sitting quietly at the clavichord he had installed in his flat and playing the first of J. S. Bach's forty-eight preludes and fugues. An awkward, remote, emotionally secluded leader experienced a cathartic victory. But what, in truth, was it all about?

At one level, not only was the purpose clear but it received the fullest possible attention from the organs of British democracy. Entering the European Community, the purpose of three successive governments since 1961, plainly and substantially changed the nation's direction, and everybody in the country was made aware of it. How could its meaning be missed, after a decade of vexed probing, several hundred hours of debate in both Houses of Parliament, a public discussion that surged, with only occasional ebbings, through the media, and an inexorably growing awareness that this was the question, for better or for worse, that preceded all others bearing on the future of Britain?

Nor did these deliberations suffer from a want of official guidance on the facts. From 1967, dossiers and statements poured off the government presses, explaining how both Labour and Conservative Cabinets regarded the available evidence on the gamut of economic and political consequences that would flow from the success of their policy. Especially substantial was Heath's own white paper, published in July 1971, which gave a long account of what had been negotiated. It was not a piece of special pleading. Heath admitted, for example, that food prices would certainly rise, though by rather less than Wilson had put forward eighteen months earlier. He conceded, at least by implication, that the British share of the EEC budget might become a serious burden unless – a likely story! – the Common Agriculture Policy was drastically reformed. Somewhere or other, it is possible to locate official texts and formulations covering every aspect of what Britain was about to do.

On the other hand, there were ways and ways of presenting them to the public, and the most open way was not always selected. That was especially true of the deepest, most inchoate question: what membership of 'Europe' truly meant for national sovereignty. This was the issue which, if it proved to have been falsely handled, lay in wait to invalidate at its innermost core the nation's 'full-hearted consent'. And, long afterwards, this became the argument. When Euro-scepticism secured its tightest grip on the throat of government, in the later years of John Major, the sense moved powerfully through the Conservative Party that British entry was originally approved on false, even fraudulent, pretences.

The Heath white paper, whatever its other merits, handled this matter with some opaqueness. Phrases were dreamed up that could mean all things to all men and women. 'There is no question of any erosion of essential national sovereignty,' the paper said. 'What is proposed is a sharing and an enlargement of individual national sovereignties in the general interest.'[57]

This was open, as intended, to many constructions. It conceded that entry into Europe would certainly do something to the popular concept of an independent nation. The curtailment of such separateness, and its replacement by selective immersions in a larger pool of multi-national power, presided over by a supra-national body, was the essence of the European idea. But by inserting 'essential' into the account of what would not be lost, the authors left it open to readers to make their own assessment of what aspects of sovereignty were included. Was the supremacy of European law a breach of 'essential' sovereignty? What about the special power of the Commission, as the sole permitted initiator of European policy? Where, on this scale, did one place the advent of majority voting, on issues which might thereby pass out of British control?

So 'essential' glided into the vocabulary of reassurance. It offered the Government deniability. For who could ever say the promise had been broken? The accompanying phrase – 'a sharing and an enlargement' – was even more impenetrable. How individual national sovereignty could be shared, while at the same time being enlarged, without compromising its individuality, was a question to baffle any casuist.

It was not entirely indefensible, if you assumed, as Heath did, that sovereignty wasn't a theoretical concept but a many-headed instrument – sometimes solitary, sometimes pooled, exercised separately or together according to the needs of the moment – to be judged by its pragmatic usefulness. Heath developed many metaphors to try and get this point across, including, in later life, the image of the miser. 'Sovereignty isn't something you put down in the cellar in your gold reserve, and go down with a candle once a week to see if it is still there,' was one I heard him proffer to a meeting in 1994.[58] The problem was, however, that the white paper phrases, however explicable, and even defensible, were a hostage to anyone who later desired to mount a case for saying there had been a crucial element of dissimulation in what the world was told.

If nothing else, they lowered the guard of a nation supposedly on watch for any fundamental change that entry into Europe was about to impose upon it.

This tendency continued in the House of Commons debates of 1971–2. Ministers did not lie, but they avoided telling the full truth. They refrained from stating categorically that the law of the European Community would have supremacy over British law. This was a conscious, much deliberated choice. The Bill did not contain, as it might have done, a clause stating in terms the general rule that Community law was to be supreme. There were, it could be argued (and was, especially by Geoffrey Howe), technical justifications for this. It could be defended as an economy of drafting, leaving it open to the courts, in due course, to make the necessary assertion that such supremacy was a fact.[59] But the more potent reason for leaving this inexplicit in 1972 was political. Spelled out in a clause that had to be openly debated and passed, Community supremacy would have had explosive possibilities. The Government lawyers knew perfectly well what the legal consequences were. 'Does he think we were all complete idiots?' one of them riposted, when a professor suggested many years later that the degree of subordination of British law to European law had come as a surprise.[60] Of course they knew. But the draftsmen had been instructed to tread carefully, knowing, in this man's recollection, that full and open admission of what was being done to parliamentary sovereignty would be 'so astounding' as to put the whole Bill in danger.

Nor did ministers state that the European Communities Act would be, in practice, irrevocable. They preferred to repeat the correct but essentially academic formula that what Parliament had passed it could always repeal. Somehow their capacity for dramatic excitement eluded them when it came to giving due emphasis to the startling proposition that Parliament was surrendering some of its independence to the clauses and powers of a written constitution, namely the Treaty of Rome.

They put it, in short, more gently, quietly, obscurely. Heath himself seldom talked about sovereignty being surrendered. He was not prepared to concede, in cold fact, that although there might be a gain in power there would be a loss of independence. Winding up the historic debate in October 1971, the word he chose was as soporific as could be: 'In joining we are making a commitment which *involves* our sovereignty, but we are also gaining an opportunity.' Geoffrey Rippon, his lieutenant, occasionally had more accurate formulations dragged out of him, but Heath himself declined to yield an inch of ground, even to those who thought the very point of the Common Market was to reduce national independence, and thereby enlarge the collective power of Germany, France, Britain and whoever else belonged.

This disguising was part of an intensely political process. Only by sweetening the truth about national sovereignty, apparently, could popular support be kept in line. There was another confusion as well, perhaps less calculated but also having its place in an intellectual contest that has never really ended. To what extent could the whole venture be called 'political' in its very nature? This too was much muddied, much obscured.

At the time, the vanguard of the Government's case was invariably economic, and the arguments gaining most purchase on the public mind concerned the impact of entry on jobs, on prices, on industry, on the likely fate of a once-great economic entity now seen to be lagging behind the continent. Whenever 'the political' was mentioned, it tended to be projected forward into a vague and indecipherable future.

Sir Alec Douglas-Home, the Foreign Secretary, was always reassuring. There would be no 'political' aspect of the Community without Britain's agreement, he insisted. All development would depend upon consensus. 'Decisions on the political evolution of the Community', he said in the October 1971 debate, 'are not for now, even for tomorrow, but for the future. Any decision made on political advance must have the unanimous support of all the members of the partnership.' Whether Europe would develop any kind of political identity was also addressed by Prime Minister Heath. In the same debate, he presented the issue as a blank sheet of paper. 'What we shall have', he ventured, 'is an opportunity, which we do not possess and will not possess unless we join, of working out schemes for the future of the major part of Europe.'

As stated, this was true enough. But, as an answer to the preoccupations that later came to obsess people, it did not meet the point. It contained its own form of deception. In later years, the intrinsic nature of the European project was always referred to as political – which, indeed, was the truth. Historians and participants alike agreed that, *au fond*, politics was what the Community was about and politics was what British entry was about. Heath himself, in elder-statesman mode, invariably used the most emphatic language to drive from the field the numerous antagonists who pretended not to have known that. 'From the first, the Community was political,' he stated in the first Franco-British lecture, in 1992. 'It is still political. It will always be political.'[61] His derision for those who imagined otherwise could not have been more eloquently conveyed.

At the time, however, Heath did not put things so clearly. To have done so might have frightened the horses. In any case, this wasn't what most bothered people who talked about the political ramifications of entry. What they meant wasn't the future aspiration of a political Europe, so much as the likely emasculation of a politically independent Britain. Both, eventually, mattered. But in the early 1970s, it was the latter rather than the former that was capable of being addressed with more certain clarity than Heath was ever willing to supply.

This charge of near-duplicity, when levelled during the ferocious Sceptic Years, drew a response of equal indignation. Heath himself, when I interviewed him in 1995, put it down to the ignorance of a new generation. They were simply unaware of history, and did not know how much he had said at the time about the political nature of the enterprise, and how much, in any case, the sovereignty of nations was already diluted by such bodies at Nato. Pressed to show that the people had been fully informed, he referred me to the phrase in the Treaty aspiring to 'an ever-closer union among the peoples of Europe'. 'That embraces everything,' Heath said, with conclusive satisfaction,[62] before embarking on a little lecture designed to show that, because Britain had been responsible for creating federal states in Canada and Australia, there was something contradictory about the British fear of a federal United States of Europe.

That isn't the only defence, or the best one. A better effort can be made by Geoffrey Howe, the chief political draftsman of the European Communities Bill, and a man with his own claim to a central role in the history. As a lawyer, Howe is and was a punctilious respecter of words, and has a large repertoire of evidence that the legal issue, in particular, was well addressed in 1972, as it had been ten years earlier, often by himself. And this is true enough. Legal supremacy, which was the prime *casus belli* of Conservative Euro-sceptics in the middle 1990s, became a settled question many years before Britain joined the Community. As early as 1963, the European Court of Justice pronounced that the Treaty of Rome had, among other things, created a new legal order in international law 'for whose benefit the States have limited their sovereign rights'.[63] Subsequent cases had clarified the point that Community law applied by direct effect in each member state. The Court, along with the Commission, the Council of Ministers and even the European

Parliament, possessed superior powers that were identified as long ago as 1962, by Macmillan's Lord Chancellor Lord Dilhorne, who laid them on the line. 'These organs', he said, 'have in the spheres in which they operate ... certain supra-national powers which override those of the national constitutional bodies, and which are also incapable of challenge in the national courts of the member States.'[64] No more limpid statement of lost independence is to be found from beginning to end of this history.

Howe himself, to clinch the proof he needed that everything was open and above board, gave a lecture in October 1972 which spelled out, as he would say, the circumstances in which United Kingdom laws would be rendered invalid by Community law. It was a long, detailed, pretty scrupulous performance. In later years, he would often point to it. It did contain words that could be said, in a roundabout way, to acknowledge the subordination of UK laws. And because the subject clearly bothered him, he kept returning to it with further academic lectures designed to prove that sovereignty had been dealt with properly and/or that it was not a problem.[65]

But it was also Howe's opinion, in retrospect, that he could have been clearer. In the Commons, his words read like calculated waffling. Where there was a conflict, he said in 1972, the courts would just have to do their best to reconcile the 'inescapable and enduring sovereignty of Parliament' with the need to give effect to Treaty obligations. They would somehow interpret statute accordingly, and if there was a problem, he concluded limply, 'that would be a matter for consideration by the Government and Parliament of the day'.[66] Nobody challenged him to fill the lacunae this formula obviously left. But surveying his performance twenty-five years later, Howe wrote to an old colleague: 'I ... remain at least plausibly exposed to the charge that less of [our] thinking than was appropriate was explicitly exposed to the House of Commons at the time the Bill was being passed.'[67]

Whatever was said, in any case, was directed to an academic audience, and not designed for the enlightenment of the mass electorate. The political emphasis was not on what would change but almost entirely on what would not change. Nobody talked about the new legal ascendancy in the way Lord Denning later did. The Treaty, he said in a famous case in 1974, was 'like an incoming tide. It flows into the estuaries and up the rivers. It cannot be held back.'[68] Instead, political leaders placed their heaviest emphasis on the inviolate continuity of the common law and the unfettered independence of English courts and judges.

In short: examining the record, scanning those hours of democratic argument, one cannot but be struck by the thinness of their attention to what became the preoccupations of the 1990s. Anyone outraged by what 'Europe' seemed to have become could easily find themselves scandalized by the absence of official statements saying that this is what would happen. From there, it is not too large a stride to the construing of a conspiracy of silence.

The case, however, is not conclusive. It neglects the historical context. For the 1970s were not the 1990s. In two respects, the violence with which Heath was later attacked depends on seriously aberrant hindsight.

First, the sovereignty question was much less on people's minds in the 1970s than twenty years later. This is not an accidental, still less a manipulated, fact, but one that says something about the condition of the country. Sovereignty did, of course, have its day in the court of Parliament. It was the devouring obsession of Enoch Powell. Another eloquent prophet of the end of British independence was Anthony Wedgwood Benn, as he was still known.[69] A scattering of MPs took up the point. It throbbed through the visceral concerns of dissenters on the Tory side. But it was not dominant. Questions of economics seemed to be far more important: would the Common Market *really* be good for British industry, could our manufacturers compete against the Germans, what about the balance of payments, and so on? Even the future of the Commonwealth, in 1972, attracted more parliamentary anxiety than the future independence of Parliament. The price of food was of more concern than the coming irrelevance of debate.

Why was this? One must recall another part of the context. Hovering around the Common Market debate in those formative days was the wider question of international security. The Cold War was at its height, and Britain still thought of herself as a major player in its evolution. Macmillan had sought British entry into Europe as a way of staking a position from which she could continue to matter globally, as he showed in numerous gloomy prognostics about the fate that might grip a small country caught in the sights of the Russian bear. Prime Minister Heath's speeches were less copiously internationalist in the same sense, but his Foreign Secretary, Douglas-Home, often showed that Macmillanism was not dead. A pamphlet Home wrote in July 1971 was introduced as one that 'raises the level of the debate from groceries to survival'. Pressing the case for entry, Home said it would be 'a step of the utmost political significance', by which he meant that it would be a way of shoring up Britain's security interests in a more collective Europe.[70]

Alongside the micro-economic questions, therefore, it was the prospective realignment of Britain internationally that moved the debate, more than her reduction domestically: the shifting of a nation that retained a certain political self-confidence, rather than its fearful submission to the tyrannies of Brussels, and all the other impositions which, in the dialectic of the 1990s, allegedly reduced a once great nation to a satrap of scheming continentals.

In a word, the Britain of 1972 was not a nation dominated by fear. She did not doubt her future as a country that mattered. She was in economic trouble, but this had not yet drained her of self-belief. In particular, 'Europe' still seemed less like the threat it became, in some people's eyes, in the 1990s than the zone of promise it had been in 1960.

This is explicable by the second factor called to the defence of Heath. His critics tended to imagine he always had secret plans to achieve in and with Europe an integrated, or 'federalist', future which the people, had they been told about it, would never have supported. Again, the truth is messier. On the one hand, there was no such worked-out scheme. On the other, insofar as political leaders had thought about the future, they had done so very publicly.

In the early 1970s, the shape of the European Economic Community was in many respects uncertain. For a start, it was still known by that name, the *economic* community, designating economics as its prime sphere of action. Its political character was quite immature. The European Parliament was still described, in the official English version, as a mere Assembly, and was not developing into anything much more than a talk-shop. The Luxembourg Compromise operated. This had been introduced in 1966 to surmount the impasse de Gaulle inflicted on the Community by refusing to accept majority voting. The Compromise conferred an informal right of veto by any member state that considered a 'very important' national interest was being imperilled: an important reassurance to the anxious British.

Such a level of uncertainty fortified several of the more thoughtful contributors to the Commons debates, including former or even present sceptics who decided there was no grievous threat to independent British nationhood. Sir Harry Legge-Bourke, for example, said he had originally been against the European venture. In 1951 he thought the Schuman Plan amounted to supra-national government, but now he thought differently. 'The more one studies the way in which Europe is working out,' he said in October 1971, 'the less likely it is that there will be close-knit federation.' He saw the 'old, traditional differences' between the nations alive and well, and did not believe that the final shape of Europe was anywhere near ready for definition.[71] Angus Maude, another Conservative MP, refused to support Heath, but based his case entirely on economic grounds. He thought the political argument of little importance. 'There is no political unity in the Six,' he said, 'and the likelihood is that there will not be any for a generation.' Nor did he believe 'that there is any serious risk of a major or total loss of sovereignty'.[72]

This perception, often deployed by Heath's defenders, has its problems. It does not sit comfortably with the parallel assertion they have made to squash all subsequent objectors: namely, that such people have no right to speak, since it was clear from the start what the country was signing up for. The Treaty of Rome says everything: the British signed it: end of story. So went the triumphalist case. The contempt inherent in it has been the greatest flaw in the prosecution of the pro-Europe cause in British politics for twenty years.

Nonetheless, the practice of reading into the era of the early 1970s the assumptions of the middle 1990s produced a false indictment. Heath's own speeches reflected uncertainty more than a grand, fixed plan. He was inviting the nation to engage with forces of history that had yet to show what they could do. 'Working out schemes for the future of the major part of Europe' was an activity he sincerely looked forward to, in the national interest. Presenting his case to Parliament, he enthused at the prospect of a summit meeting that had been called by France and Germany for some time in 1972, which he foresaw as some kind of Congress of Vienna, settling monetary and trading matters, and 'future political development'. When this summit came about, in October 1972, Britain, though not yet formally a member of the EEC, was present, and contributed to an outcome Heath never forgot. The communiqué that resulted from it, half of it written personally by President Pompidou, was, he stated on numerous occasions for years afterwards, 'the finest international communiqué ever written'.[73]

An element of this communiqué, moreover, challenges the other part of the charge-sheet: that the plan for the Community was secret. Far from it. Even before Heath became Prime Minister, Europe had pledged itself to something called economic and monetary union. At a meeting in The Hague in 1972, promoted by Pompidou and supported by the West German Chancellor, Willy Brandt, the Six pledged themselves to achieve EMU by 1980.

Although EMU didn't happen, its presence on the agenda makes another point. It was there, believed in by some, doubted by others, but

‗arousing terminal hostility hardly anywhere. It may not have seemed real; and, very soon, turbulence in the exchange markets, together with the quadrupling of the price of oil, put paid to it for the duration. The 'snake', an arrangement by which European currencies – including sterling – locked into narrow bands of fluctuation against each other, was torn apart. But before that, as a concept, EMU aroused little outrage on constitutional grounds. At this first mooting, its role in history is surely to be the proof not of a secret federalism at large among the makers of Europe but of the indifference with which such possibilities were once regarded.

The critique to be made of Heath is real, but it is different from the one which is usually mobilized. As the nearest thing to Britain's father of Europe, he had significant shortcomings.

Though possessed of a great idea, he was congenitally unable to convey its resonance to the nation he wanted to believe it. Whether you liked it or not, his idea was the most discrete and particular Big Idea that any British leader had seized on since the war. Yet he could never make it sing. As already noted, he was an entirely uninspiring orator. For a people as reluctantly European as the British, this was an unfortunate conjunction. It meant that, in this formative period, when there was much cynicism to be lifted from the nation's soul, the voice at the top had the levitation of a lead balloon.

This wasn't merely a matter of rhetorical technique. In retrospect, what Heath seems to have lacked, rather surprisingly, was a coherent vision of what Europe, and British membership of Europe, ought actually to mean. If the message did not get across as it deserved to, perhaps this was because the content, as much as the form, was deficient.

Getting into Europe was plainly a Heath objective to which he applied every ounce of energy and resource. Nobody could fault his commitment. But there were officials who saw this as a purpose without a clear enough objective. Was getting in for its own sake, to Heath, enough? Michael Butler was a key panjandrum of the Europeanized Whitehall machine, who spent six years as Britain's permanent representative to the Communities. In Heath's time, Butler was head of the European Integration Department at the Foreign Office. As such, he talked to the Prime Minister often, and found him, he once told me, 'extraordinarily Gaullist'. That is to say, Heath saw the EEC not so much as a community of theoretical equals, rather as a theatre for his own domination. There were decisions in the early 1970s, for example about the location of an embryonic central bank, which Heath approached from the start with a veto mentality, Butler told me. Even though everyone else had agreed the bank should be in Luxembourg, Heath simply thought his own preference, which happened to be for Brussels, was the only solution. Though he was exultant at being at Europe's top table, Heath's temperament, wasn't really, in the concessive sense, properly *communautaire* at all. 'I always wonder to what extent Ted really understood what it was all about,' Butler said in 1993.

So did someone closer to him, Robert Armstrong, his private secretary, fellow music-lover and a zealous European. Armstrong saw Heath's Europeanism as rooted in the war. He shared with the continentals, thought Armstrong, the overriding belief that war must not happen again, and that the EEC was the way to avoid it. Britain should belong as part of this anti-war alliance, and also to subject her own industries to a reviving jolt from European competition. But Heath's larger purpose Armstrong found a little mystifying. He told me: 'It always seemed to me that, for him, getting in was an end in itself. I did not have the impression that he had at that time a coherent vision about what to do with it when we were in, how it would evolve and therefore how we would try and make it develop.'[74]

It was of much historic importance, all the same, that Heath remained in office for merely a single year after British membership began, in January 1973. It was probably a great misfortune. If Butler and Armstrong are right, one can't be sure how much Britain would have added any momentum towards a coherent, active 'Europe', had the Conservatives won the election in February 1974. The middle 1970s were a time of stasis in Europe, for reasons that transcended any one country's power to overcome them. But history would certainly have been different, if Heath had won: as different, perhaps, as if Wilson had won in 1970. There can be no doubt that Heath, the most committed European to lead the country between 1945 and 1997, would have tried to impose a personal stamp of Euro-enthusiasm. As it was, his year in office as an EEC head of government was not just pathetically brief, but was overwhelmed by domestic crises to which he was obliged, unavailingly, to give his entire attention.

Thereafter, he did not remain silent. And there was a long thereafter. In it, bitterness and rectitude vied to be the controlling presence in his output. In 1996, reviewing a new book, called *A History of Modern Europe*, he was not impressed. 'The sole reference to me describes me as "a yachtsman",' he complained.[75] An obtuse verdict, he felt, and sadly misinformed. But nautical metaphors are nonetheless in order. For the quarter-century after he was deposed from power, he wandered the world like some Flying Dutchman, destined never to disembark into the haven of a 'European' Britain which he should have been instrumental in creating. Alternatively, he was the Old Man of the Sea, symbol of a burden nobody else succeeded in discharging.

He remained, however, vigorous. He carried Europe with him wherever he went, castigating the fainthearts at home and abroad. I witnessed him at the age of eighty-one, in a seminar in Munich, rise from semi-slumber at the dinner table to deliver a word-perfect diatribe against doubts that had just been expressed by the Prime Minister of Bavaria about the wisdom of starting the European single currency in 1999. In his own mind, he was a major historical figure, justified in requesting, as he did, that the several parties his friends organized for his eightieth birthday in 1996 should be sure to include on the guest-list both the Queen Mother and the Prince of Wales, as well as every famous conductor old enough to be his contemporary. His contribution to Britain's destiny, he plainly felt, deserved nothing less.

And he was, in his way, not mistaken. Whatever shortcomings there were in his approach to the great adventure, he was the man who saw it through. He finally carried Britain over the threshold that the islanders for so long did not want to cross.

8

ROY JENKINS

The Fissile Effect

THE EUROPE QUESTION, ever since it presented itself, has been shot through with beguiling paradoxes for the British political system. It is not like other issues. For thirty years, it has not obeyed the rules.

It has, for example, ranged majorities against minorities, with aberrant consequences. Ever since Britain entered the Common Market, there has been a large parliamentary majority in favour of the enterprise – yet, throughout the period, this majority has at times had difficulty expressing itself. Dissenting minorities, for different reasons in different seasons, have had potent influence. There was a natural majority – 112 Heath got – for entering, in 1971, and a natural majority for remaining, throughout the years of Margaret Thatcher and John Major. But you might never believe it, looking at the history, whether in 1974, when Labour returned to power, or 1994, when the Conservative Party showed signs of incipient break-up after ratifying the Treaty of Maastricht. Europe tore politics apart, while enjoying steady majority support. The system, as organized, couldn't handle the issue in a way that reflected the majority consensus of the politicians the people sent to Westminster to represent them.

There are different ways of looking at this. It could be an example of politics at its most refreshing: men and women of conscience, liberating themselves from party disciplines, voting with their brains, holding out against the mighty power of government machines: a cross-party alliance of righteous free-thinkers, using all available procedures to impede the onward march of conventional, erroneous wisdom.

Alternatively, it could be something else: political failure on a heroic scale, the frustration of national purpose by unrepresentative ultras, a history of self-indulgent escaping from reality, through which the majority was regularly held hostage in the name of anti-Europe attitudes that were seldom formulated into a coherent alternative policy.

Whichever of these views has most appeal, one truth is incontestable. The closer Britain moved towards entry, the more ineluctably 'Europe' became a question that split the Labour and Conservative parties. Entry was meant to settle Britain's national destiny, but in politics it settled nothing. It was immediately an agent of fracture, not of healing, a propensity it has never shaken off.

The first victim was the father himself, Edward Heath. Losing office in February 1974, Heath could not blame the result on his Europe policy. It had nothing to do with the hideous mess he had made of a counter-inflation strategy that culminated with a battle against the coal-miners, in which the electorate failed to support him. But there was an overhang of Europe, in the insidious persona of Enoch Powell. Powell, who in 1968 had been sacked from the shadow Cabinet for a speech that fomented racial hatreds, had many complaints against Heath. 'One cannot but entertain fears for the mental and emotional stability of a head of government to whom such language can appear rational,' was his comment on one of Heath's defences of a statutory incomes policy.[1] But Europe did most to fire this devouring contempt. By 1974, Heath's 'surrender' of the sovereign powers of the Westminster Parliament had determined Powell to come out in support of the Labour Party which, so Harold Wilson said, opposed it. By force of oratory, as well as his mesmerizing disregard for party, Powell came close to dominating the last days of the campaign, and had some effect on the outcome.[2] Arguably, he swung enough seats, in a very close battle, to render Heath incapable of forming the new government. But whether he did or not, his conduct was a signal. It showed that, for some people, the Europe question transcended every other. Powell in 1974 was the harbinger of a faction for whom he remained an immortal hero in 1994. He was proof that Europe could divide a party and its leadership: the loudest voice to date in a long line of Conservative politicians – some before him, many after – whose careers Europe dominated and whose ambitions it, effectively, ended.

So the Tories were the first to be affected in government by the responsiveness of this great question to minority opinion. But Labour, in its turn, was also shattered. In the end, Labour was formally broken, along a line whose deepest cut was made by the Europe issue. The minority here had the opposite purpose from the Powellites. It enlisted itself, across party, in service of the broad majority which narrow party disciplines usually had the effect of frustrating. It had a determining effect on the 1971 vote, and on other occasions later. But it, too, was a symptom of the breakdown of a system. A system that was supposed to clarify political choices, through the deep, long rooting in of class- and interest-based parties, produced an outcome that was thoroughly confusing for the voters. The competing zealotries had almost nothing to do with divisions between the left and right which they were used to and could understand. For any voter who cared about Europe one way or the other, party was no longer a concept to be relied on.

Another paradox, therefore, shimmers to the surface. The people needed guidance, but they couldn't get it from the usual agencies. The parties wanted popular support, and the issue demanded the full-hearted consent Heath spoke of. But the average voter, deprived of clear party lines, was spectator to what seemed an increasingly private conflict, in which politicians showed many unsettling traits.

There was the divide within parties, the quartering rather than halving of the familiar political landscape between the two main protagonists. There was also the divide within politicians themselves: the near-impossibility of finding senior leaders who now thought the same as they thought ten, five or even two years before or who, if they did, hadn't reversed themselves, in some cases more than once, in the intervening period.

This was bound to be bewildering, especially at such a time. For it occurred in a context when the public was supposed to matter especially. Popular assent was required – yet the 'Europe' issue was already showing one of the traits it never shook off, an ambiguous relationship with public opinion. On the one hand, the combatants always claimed to be speaking for the public, often a public whose 'real' attitude was supposedly antagonistic to the whole European enterprise. On the other hand, the behaviour of politicians became increasingly like that of members of a private club. For twenty years their antagonisms, and the sacrifices some of them were prepared to make for their position, seemed like those of people detached from the wider world, engaged in a struggle to the death, over ideas that engaged the great mass of ordinary people with far less ferocity.

Never was such turbulence more in evidence than in the two years after Heath. They were the hinge moment, when anything might have happened. Entry was effected, but its permanence wasn't guaranteed. In the sceptic English dog, there was another bark yet. In fact there would be many, over the years. The people most responsible for silencing this, the first and decisive one, were, as they had to be, Labour politicians.

A Conservative leader took Britain in. But hardly less impact all round was made by the Labour politician who insisted that Britain must remain: the guarantor of Heath's majority, and architect, as it turned out, of Labour's crack-up.

*

WHEN HEATH LOST, and Labour took over the country, it also took over its own past. It could not avoid an encounter with the history for which it was responsible. In the recent phase, this had a distinct and ominous shape. When in opposition, up to and including 1963, Labour had opposed British entry. When in government, 1967–70, it had favoured and rather desperately sought British entry. When it was back in opposition, 1970–4, oppositionism asserted itself once again. Opposition, in short, gave control to the instincts of the party, government gave it to the perceived necessities of the country, and between these positions there was an absence of much grey area. The two attitudes were black and white. Moving from one to the other, in the early spring of 1974, barely a year after British membership had become an objectively existing fact, Harold Wilson faced a transition that would challenge even his famous mastery of manoeuvre.

Over all this period, one man mirrored and enhanced the dilemma through his own emphatic whiteness, or perhaps blackness. More than anyone, Roy Jenkins ensured that greyness, ultimately, was not an option. In government, he was Wilson's prop, little though he was welcomed as such: he stood for the position that Prime Minister Wilson found it inescapable to advance. Once George Brown disappeared into drunken oblivion, he was the leader of the Labour Europeans. But in opposition Jenkins was Wilson's curse, making it impossible for the leader to glide painlessly back into the arms of the sceptic party. With a group of allies, he stood inflexibly against the party line, an abomination for which he was not being readily excused even twenty years later. Interviewed in 1995, Barbara Castle, his Cabinet colleague of the period, asserted that she could still never forgive Jenkinsites for their 'party treachery' in 'putting Europe first', and recalled with relish how she had 'described the pro-Market fanatics as sanctimonious, middle-class hypocrites, and I meant it'.[3]

Jenkins always was a 'European'. Admittedly, he did not join Heath in supporting the Schuman Plan. For a young Labour MP to have jousted with Foreign Secretary Bevin would have been *lèse-majesté* demanding more confidence than Jenkins had at the age of thirty. He says that he 'meekly' accepted the party line.[4] But a few years later he went as a Labour delegate to the intermittent meetings of the Council of Europe in Strasbourg, a posting whose term was deliberately limited by the party to avoid its tenants going native. On Jenkins this precaution did not have the intended effect. In a total of seven weeks, spread over the two years, exposure to continental politics and politicians, he writes, 'sowed the seeds of my subsequently persistent conviction'.

By 1961, he was a fully fledged and active proponent of British entry. He had opposed EFTA, the second-division periphery Macmillan tried to organize into a rival grouping, and, when the time came, got himself made deputy chairman of the Common Market Campaign, already a cross-party affair, and then became chairman of the Labour Committee for Europe. From this period onwards, his commitment was steady, 'and at most times dominant in my life'. 'By the standards of the pioneers,' he adds a little sheepishly, 'I was a latter-day convert, although one well before the bulk of, say, the Foreign Office, City or Conservative Party opinion. When eventually enlightened I remained so, and with some fervour.'

He was not alone. Actually, the Labour Committee for Europe, as well as coming to the aid of a Conservative initiative, was in these early days cross-factional within the party. A number of MPs on the left continued to carry the banner of a united Europe once borne aloft by the likes of Michael Foot and Richard Crossman.[5] Names such as Eric Heffer, Sid Bidwell, Stan Newens and Marcus Lipton are to be found on the Europeanist roster. But the core of the cohort came from the liberal internationalist tradition more numerously represented on the right. William Rodgers made his maiden speech as a Labour MP in June 1962, supporting the Macmillan Government's policy for entry. Roy Hattersley was another, unbreakably consistent since 1958. Tam Dalyell, Douglas Houghton, Joel Barnett and a few others with a long parliamentary life ahead of them resisted their friend Hugh Gaitskell's determination to see the imminence of entry as the betrayal of a thousand years of history. Not all the right were with Jenkins. As well as Douglas Jay, Gaitskell's particular ally and intimate, some surprising younger men were still also hesitating. David Marquand, one of the most creative and influential thinkers behind social democratic revisionism in the 1980s, recorded his attitude to the Common Market as 'very sceptical, indeed hostile' when it first appeared as a British issue for decision.[6] But Europeanism was already a cult in the Labour Party, and Jenkins something like its high priest.

There was another aspect that helped give him that suitably awesome status. Although born modestly in Wales, he was a social as well as a political internationalist. He travelled much, conversed and wrote easily on a global stage, gathered a wide acquaintance, especially European and North American. He was as much at home in Tuscany, possibly more so, as in his constituency of Stechford in the bleak West Midlands. It would never have occurred to him, as it did to Douglas Jay, to carry a supply of British cornflakes on journeys he was required to make across the Channel. By 1970, he had had frequent personal dealings with just about every continental politician of note. Jean Monnet, Willy Brandt, Valéry Giscard d'Estaing, Helmut Schmidt, not to mention Kennedys, Achesons, Rockefellers, Bundys and a hundred others from points west and east of the British Isles, are grist to his memoirs, as they have been to his life.

This cosmopolitan figure was rooted in different terrain from other chieftains of his party, Wilson not least. The continent made Wilson uneasy. Europeans, 'especially from France and southern Europe', according to one of his close advisers, were to him alien. He disliked their food, 'genuinely preferring meat and two veg with HP sauce', and went on holiday to the Scilly Isles, 'which enabled him to go overseas and yet remain in Britain'.[7] Wilson was a miserly, north-country non-conformist, who delighted, as Jenkins never did, in keeping every particle of his background on display. James Callaghan, while perhaps a little more internationalist by instinct, also came from the part of the Labour Party that was, socially if not politically, cabined and confined. Jenkins, in this company, was a faintly exotic beast, which did little for his fraternal popularity. Among the baggage that went with it was a different relationship with 'party'. This shouldn't be exaggerated. He understood well enough that his party base was the source of all political power, and paid close attention to Stechford's requirements. But part of his 'European' stigma, among those who regarded it as such, lay in the distancing from traditional good old Labourism which it apparently signalled. There were faint traces, in the Jenkins of 1970–4, of the superior disenchantment – Barbara Castle's 'treachery' – that was to be exhibited, also somewhat *de haut en bas*, by Tony Blair after 1994. The link, as we shall see, was one of which Blair became extremely conscious.[8]

When Labour went into opposition in 1970, it did two things simultaneously. Its MPs elected Jenkins as Wilson's deputy leader. And the party as a whole, not discouraged by most of its leadership, moved into its familiar opposition mode of rejecting British entry into Europe as Heath was promoting it. This contradiction helped stave off the moment when opposition became absolute. But it exposed the split mind that eventually produced a split party.

Labour, under Wilson's guidance, eased rather than hurtled into rejectionism. Awareness percolated through even its extremer fringes that the U-turn should not be too abrupt. The party conference, which in 1967 voted by 2:1 to support entry, in autumn 1970 rejected, albeit narrowly, an 'anti' resolution. For the next three years, in fact, Wilson successfully prevented the conference from passing any motion of wholesale opposition in principle to membership. The old leftist opponents, supplemented after the election, especially by leading trade unionists, were held at bay.

The spirit, however, was with them. It called forth a countervailing force, which had the deputy leader at its head and was now free to exhibit a full emotional commitment. As prelude to its own scheme formally to oppose Heath's deal, the party's National Executive Committee summoned a special conference in July 1971, where feelings would be ventilated but no vote taken. On this occasion, the party's divisions became absolutely apparent, and, for the first time, the pro-Marketeers proved themselves the ultras in the argument. That was the flip side of the pattern, as between government and opposition. When Labour was in power, nosing towards entry, the leading antis had to keep their mouths shut. When Labour was out of power, preparing to reverse its position, no such restraint afflicted the other side.

Jenkins himself, being deputy leader, was not allowed to speak at the 1971 event. But his supporters reached full flood. John Mackintosh, MP for East Lothian, delivered a coruscating attack on the fainthearts who feared for national sovereignty and worried about economic growth. This speech was remembered in the annals for ever after. Re-read, it sharpens a large truth about the history: that, of all those who contributed to it, none has been more eloquent, more completely and defiantly committed to Britain's European destiny than the Labour pro-Europeans of the Heath period. They put Heath's own faltering locutions in the shade. Unencumbered by the need to negotiate, or to box the compass of a party navigating through fierce contrarian storms, they took the fullest responsible advantage of their lack of responsibility.

It was inevitable, when the question was put, that they would answer it in complete awareness of what they were doing. Europe needed them, Britain needed them, and they lived down to Mrs Castle's derisive expectation that they were the kind of people who would put these considerations before the overriding need, on the widest grounds of socialist politics and economics, to get the Heath Government out. On 28 October 1971, sixty-nine members of the parliamentary Labour Party voted with the Government to pave the way in principle for entry, and twenty others abstained from opposing it.

Without this support, the motion would have fallen. Almost certainly, Heath's effort would have been unsustainable in the British Parliament, and Britain would not have entered – then or, possibly, ever. The terrifying evidence of national decline might have impelled some future government to make yet another approach to Europe, but no one can have much idea what would have become of it. Jenkins and his people were thus determinant at one defining moment – and this wasn't the last.

By the protocols of parliamentary behaviour, their vote was a heinous crime. Once again, Barbara Castle can be our witness. 'I used to respect you a great deal, but I will never do so again as long as I live,' she hissed at Jenkins in the Commons members' dining-room, in the middle of the party imbroglio when he was making his intentions clear.[9] He didn't have the nerve to carry on in the same vein. When, after the paving motion was won by 112, the Bill itself came for passage, the rising, responsible men in the Jenkins group avoided voting with the Government. The majorities, clause by clause, came tumbling down, and were often crucially dependent on the saving interventions of a handful of Labour people – Tam Dalyell, Austen Albu, Michael Barnes, Freda Corbet – too old or unambitious to be intimidated, to keep the Bill intact. When Harold Lever, dutifully obeying Wilson, voted against the second reading of the Bill, he retired to the gentlemen's lavatory to be physically sick. Others, such as Bill Rodgers, felt demoralized, having voted tamely for the party after riding the high of their October principles. Jenkins, looking back, was penitent. He and his friends had been 'cowering behind the shields of these men older or younger than us who were braver'.[10] When he was challenged to run again for deputy leader, his ambition to keep the job made him blur his voting intentions as the Bill was in transit, and, even though this was enough to keep him in the post, he bitterly regretted it. 'It was weak and equivocating . . . a major tactical error,' he judged later.[11]

Nonetheless, the Bill went through, and Jenkins was the key accessory before, if not during, the fact. The October vote was a watershed moment. It established the presence of a hard-core Europeanism in the Labour Party, which others would ignore at their peril. It singled out a section of the party that was not prepared to be seduced by the ambiguity of others, separating them by style as much as content. In their way, these people were being unpolitical, if party and politics are to be treated as coterminous notions. They thereby ranged themselves against three types of ambiguity, the three threads of behaviour that evinced a quite different way of handling the 'Europe' question – even, one might say, a quite different political psychology.

The first was best personified by Anthony Wedgwood Benn, whose conduct about this time coincided with the prophetic elision of his name to fit the proletarianism which was to be Labour's signature theme in the coming years. At some moment, precisely unspecified, he had become Tony Benn. He had also become an anti-European.

Tracing Benn's personal European odyssey ought to be a relatively simple task, since his diaries constitute one of the most extended tours of a leading politician's mind ever made available.[12] The task is complicated not by lack of candour on the diarist's part, so much as by the mercurial approach, the ever imminent sense of messianic revelation, he brought to this subject in common with most others. His history plots a course from suspicion, through flirtation, into consummation, followed shortly by passionate rejection.

Benn was against the Macmillan application, proclaiming that he knew it would fail. And quite soon he was expressing admiration for the agent of its failure, General de Gaulle. 'I am really a Gaullist,' he says on 20 July 1964, 'and in favour of positive neutralism.' Gaullism litters his diary talk at this time, driven on by the dilemma he faced concerning the Americans. As a junior minister, Postmaster-General, in Wilson's first Government, Benn retained a leftist's deep dislike of America's military intentions, musing on 14 January 1965: 'The choice lies between Britain as an island and a US protectorate, or Britain as a full member of the Six, followed by a wider European federation. I was always against the Common Market but the reality of our isolation is being borne in on me all the time. This country is so decrepit and hidebound that only activities in the wider sphere can help us to escape from the myths that surround our politics.' Later that year, he solves the problem by offering covert support to colleagues working against British membership and in favour of 'an all-European group which I wholly support and have done for many years'.

Before the 1966 general election, he was still an anti, voting vainly against the manifesto phrase 'Britain should be ready to enter Europe'. But he was seducible. Later that year, seeing the way the wind appeared to be blowing, he prepared to yield before it. 'I came to the conclusion that Britain would be in the Common Market by 1970,' he writes with some prescience, after the October Cabinet meeting that approved the Wilson–Brown Probe. When the time came to decide, he spoke up clearly in Cabinet. 'I said we had to cut Queen Victoria's umbilical cord,' he reports on 30 April 1967. This 'created a favourable impression with the pro-Europeans, who thought me anti-European'. A week later, speaking as the Minister for Technology, he uttered a strong appeal for technological co-operation in Europe. This, he said, 'requires an inte-grated commercial market'. Bilateral dealings might have some value, 'with professors crossing the Channel both ways to read learned papers to each other'. But they would never be enough. 'If that is all we can achieve in Europe, then we shall be condemned . . . as a continent to the status of industrial helotry with all that that means in terms of world influence. And history may well say that we deserve it.'[13]

Benn thereby observed the pattern. In government, he favoured Labour's positive intention. In October 1971, equally, he conformed to type. What he once called the 'managerial phase' of his politics ended with the loss of power in 1970, and was succeeded by an ever leftward progression which included ever stronger anathemas against the Com-mon Market. These began with a becoming linguistic modesty. 'I make no apology, in the course of having thought about this issue, for having changed the emphasis of my view at different stages,' he said in the great 1971 debate. Since the world was changing fast, what virtue was there in an unbending consistency? Besides, he confessed, he had had his doubts, even when supporting the application in 1967. It was, I suppose, his plea for recognition as a man who had never wholly changed his mind. But it hardly conceals the fact that Benn's reversion to his original hostility described a perfect parabola of contradiction.

This was one kind of ambiguity. It didn't guarantee Benn a wholly adoring reception back into the arms of those whose drive towards the last ditch never deviated: Barbara Castle, Michael Foot, Peter Shore, several others on the left; Fred Peart and a few others on the right. But together they composed one version of how Labourism, socialism, nationalism, internationalism, call it what you will, should answer the Europe question.

What united this school was the belief, above all, that Europe mattered deeply. That much they shared with Jenkins. The two sides reached opposite conclusions, but neither doubted that the issue touched the soul of the party and the future of the country. The contrast between them was in their attitude to it. The contrast between Jenkins and a second type of ambiguity was more subtle, and possibly more startling – certainly harder to comprehend – not least because it separated him from some of his natural political allies.

Denis Healey had a longer history in the matter than any of his colleagues. He was the international secretary of the Labour Party from November 1945 until he became an MP in 1952. For a young man who had seen war at first hand, this was an extraordinary time to occupy such a post: extraordinary, in particular, for the range of connection it gave him in European politics. Here he was, close to the heart of affairs, in the only socialist party then running a government in Europe, whose place as the dominant power there was taken for granted. Not only was Healey the intimate servant of Foreign Secretary Bevin, he fraternized incessantly with European socialist leaders. His catalogue of memories goes on and on. He was in at the beginning of the re-formation of the German Social Democrats. Ancient and modern socialists, from Norway and Belgium and France and Austria, received him gratefully in the post-war years. He knew the Italians, and in 1949 took a personal hand in selecting a suitable socialist leader for the Greeks. Further afield, he became best friends with Teddy Kollek, later Mayor of Jerusalem, close friends with Jayaprakash Narayan, and received Roy Welensky, the leader of the Rhodesian Labour Party.[14] He was, it can be seen, an impeccably international man. And so he remained. A feature of the superb autobiographies which both Healey and Jenkins composed in retirement is the reminder they provide of what expansive horizons some British politicians' lives encompassed in the first three post-war decades, something nowhere to be found in the 1990s, the first seven years of which were spent under the leadership of a Prime Minister who, before he became Foreign Secretary, had never visited the United States.

It follows from this history that Healey had a long engagement specifically with the question of European union. He was much involved in securing European socialist support for the Marshall Plan. In 1948, he wrote a pamphlet, *Feet on the Ground*, arguing against any idea of European federation, then much in vogue. Federation, he insisted, worked only in empty continents, like America or Australia. If European federation were imposed on countries that had separate national existence, it 'would require forcible sanctions against secession', for which 'the prolonged and bloody American Civil War is not an encouraging precedent'. He was and is a believer in the divisive relevance of the 'olive line', north and south of which, he contends, Europeans have different attitudes to authority, corruption and work.[15] The Mediterranean might be a good place to enjoy the food and pictures, but the littoral people were unreliable. However, Healey is at least willing to apologize for one thing he wrote in 1948, that Europe should concentrate on producing 'cheap cheeses for mass consumption instead of luxury cheeses like camembert and gorgonzola'. 'I still blush to remember,' he writes.

His anti-federalist position, reflecting that of most of the Cabinet he served, moved on to a higher plane. In 1950, he drafted another pamphlet, *European Unity*, which appeared under the party imprint at the very moment when the Schuman Plan was sprung on Bevin, and contradicted the emollient tone of the Government white paper. In retrospect, Healey was enough of a realist to regret the adamancy of Labour's hostility to Schuman, and more particularly the Conservative exercise in boat-missing at Messina. 'It was a terrible error,' he told me in 1995.[16] All the same, he was closely involved with Gaitskell's evolution into an anti-European who could not contemplate the end of a thousand years of history. He had reached the same conclusion.

He maintained this position in government, when he was Secretary of State for Defence, 1964–70. But here the shadings and complications begin. On the one hand, in this role, Healey negotiated the definitive post-war realignment of the British posture towards the world, by organizing and pushing for military withdrawal from East of Suez. He applied his powerful mind and rounded international expertise to the necessary task of locating Britain's mission within range of her economic capability – which is to say, broadly speaking, within Europe, the field of Nato. On the other hand, he continued simultaneously to oppose British entry into the Community, or at least any effort to secure such entry in the 1960s.

Healey was one of the last hold-outs against Wilson's 1967 venture, which was an object of his most hectoring scorn in Cabinet on the ground, he grandly stated, that de Gaulle would never take it seriously. When, in 1971, Labour swung into opposition to Heath, he therefore found it easier than almost anyone to argue with great brutality against the terms Heath got. He led for Labour at the beginning of the great debate, and took apart the speculative economic promises on which Heath's case was based. He didn't believe the growth forecasts, twisted the British budgetary contribution into its most dismal magnitude, and defined the project as being all about teaching the unions a lesson in a competitive jungle of Euro-capitalism that no decent Labour politician could stomach.[17]

This was preceded by his own version of the vacillation that has afflicted the majority of politicians in this story. For Healey, too, had his little flutter. In May of that year, he became one of the bigger catches of the Jenkinsites, as they rounded up signatories for an advertisement announcing support for what Heath was doing. This appeared days before Heath's climactic meeting with Pompidou, as if to emphasize the breadth of serious national backing the Prime Minister had, and Healey allowed himself to join a company of 100 Labour MPs to say so. He followed this up with other gestures, speaking for Europe in the shadow Cabinet and, on 26 May, publishing an article in the *Daily Mirror* under the headline 'Why I Changed My Mind'. It seemed to be the defiant assertion that a reasonable man could ultimately be persuaded of the whereabouts of the light. A reckless conclusion. At first it looked sound enough. 'I've changed my mind too,' he wrote. 'I know it's unfashionable. Some of my friends say it is politically inconvenient too. But the world has changed a lot in the last nine years and so has the Common Market ... failure in Brussels will be a great chance lost for everyone concerned.' But he was soon disclaiming responsibility for the headline, and pointing to the sceptic tone between the lines. 'If our economy is strong when we go in we should reap a splendid harvest,' he had written. But also: 'If it is weak, the shock could be fatal.' Having changed his mind within a month, he changed it back again within another. 'By July Healey was stridently back into the other camp,' Jenkins notes.[18]

The distinctive feature of Healey's position as against Jenkins's, however, was something different. The two men had been rivals, while also in a sense political brothers, ever since their years at Balliol College, Oxford. At that time, admittedly, Healey was a communist while Jenkins was already a social democrat, but their rise in parallel through the Labour Party was that of two immensely able progressive politicians, the cream of their generation. It was perhaps inevitable that they should have watched each other closely, and diverged in matters of style if not, in all seriousness, of content. Jenkins, though more distant from the soul of the Labour Party, was much the abler cultivator of party support, the more attentive to the arrangement of its factions at any given time. Healey, ostensibly the more emphatic in his opinions and certainly the more aggressive in conveying them to lesser mortals, was also more inclined to judge, flaunting his intellectual scepticism, that no issue was worth defining as a matter of incontrovertible principle.

So it was with Europe. Professional indifference became Healey's way of dealing with the passions that raged around him left and right. He thought Europe and the zealotries it induced were a distraction from what he regarded as the 'real issues'. He was joined in this posture by a man of similar intellect, but whose bias shaded in the opposite direction, Anthony Crosland. Crosland, a better friend of Jenkins and basically a supporter of British entry, also opined with some disdain that the Jenkinsites were making far too much of it. It wasn't one of the major questions of domestic politics, he thought.

This was the line that he and Healey persisted in through all the arguments in the Labour Party for the decade following the 1967 application. In one way, it may have had the merit of reflecting the attitude of the British people. It spoke for their agnosticism, trying to find a way of fending off the wild obsessions over Europe which have been an enduring difference between the political class and the voters who put them where they are. Is that enough, however, to justify the persistent refusal of senior politicians to give a lead to people who, unlike them, are not paid to have opinions, and who expect to be instructed on complicated matters?

Healey, evidently, thought so. When I interviewed him in 1995, as feelings over the Treaty of Maastricht swirled even more violently round the British political system than they had over the Treaty of Rome, he remained unapologetic. I accosted him with his shiftiness in the face of a hard decision, yes or no, on the idea of British entry, on which the people themselves, not long after, were required to give their own verdict. Were they not entitled to the clear opinion of one of the cleverest men in British politics? Healey replied with the consummate pride of the distanced intellectual, an approach almost as far removed from Jenkinsism as it would be possible to invent, short of outright Bennery: 'I made it clear that people should use their brains, as I was using mine, and take a final decision in the light of the situation as it developed.'[19]

So here were two strands of Labourism in the early 1970s. One, which finished by merging with the do-or-die opponents, reached that position having previously assisted the leadership's strategy for taking Britain in. The other, though opposed to the leadership plan, was even more opposed to those who most fiercely pushed it, and defined the issue as one not worth the attention focused on it. This was uncertain ground on which a leader might hope to base a firm stand of his own. In any case, such firmness wasn't Harold Wilson's natural mode of leadership even on simple questions. Inevitably, a third type of ambiguity assembled itself. It could have only one objective: to make sure these elusive strands continued to belong, alongside the uncompromising veins of Jenkinsism and Castlery, in the body of a single party.

More than anyone, Wilson bore the brunt of Labour's change of persona between government and opposition. One might say that he was himself, cynically, the essence of the shift, and did not try to resist it. After all, hardly anyone doubts that if Wilson had won the 1970 election he would at some stage have resumed his effort to get in. But that won't suffice as a verdict on his conduct when Heath took Europe back to the top of the agenda. Ambiguity was forced upon the Leader of the Opposition. Perhaps it even became more like duplicity. This can be called, nonetheless, one of Wilson's finer hours, in which he did for the Labour Party what at the time was his prime duty – to hold it mostly together.

It couldn't be done on Jenkins's terms. No amount of aggressive leadership would have altered the fact that, with the party out of power, a commitment to back Heath would have split the shadow Cabinet and been resisted by the party conference. But Jenkins's desired result, all the same, could be secured. That was what Wilson wanted. The one thing with which his conduct is consistent is a desire throughout that no organ of the party should commit itself to taking Britain out. Deep down, Wilson was, however reluctantly, a Marketeer. He never said as much. He may well have thought that he could get better terms than Heath: indeed, that if Heath fell he could immediately take over the negotiations and emerge triumphant. But he always stopped short of getting into bed with Barbara Castle.

Besides, he had another problem. The Europe issue did not stand alone, divorced from everything else that was happening in the party. The Labour Party of that time, from the mid-1960s to the mid-1970s, that is the entire Wilson period, was suffused by a permanent state of disloyalty at the top. It wasn't that overt plotting against Wilson went on all the time. There were whole years when his position was secure. It was just that faction and the rivalry between factions were a kind of given of Labour society. Manoeuvring around, if not against, the person of the leader was a condition of existence in the Cabinet, a necessary conse-quence of its division into left and right, a faculty without which any

Labour politician of consequence could hardly be taken seriously. Regular contestation between these groups was positively expected, was allowed for in all Wilson's decisions about who held what job, and was met on a daily, indeed hourly, basis by his own pre-emptive manoeuvres.

This wasn't, in other words, a government of straight and simple men. Europe, like everything else, played its part in larger battles, among them the question of the leadership. Throughout, Jenkins's ambition was the prime feeder of Wilson's paranoid anxieties. Jenkins, moreover, made little secret of it. His autobiography is honest about his desire to lead the party, and how his conduct fitted at any given moment into this life-plan. Actually, by that account, he had given up some of his hope a little earlier. His real chance, he felt, had been in the summer of 1968, when Wilson was presiding over a fractured government and deeply unpopular both inside and outside it. Looking back, Jenkins saw, after that moment, 'a career punctuated by increasingly wide misses of the premiership'.[20] When the Europe question exploded three years later, he might already have been out of the hunt. But that wasn't the way it seemed at the time to Wilson's friends – or his enemies. For some of these, 'Europe' was the instrument through which the treacherous little man might be disposed of. If they could trap him into supporting 'Europe', thereby sacrificing his traditional power-base on the left, the right thought they would have him by the vitals. Bill Rodgers is recorded as saying at the time: 'If Wilson loses his support on the left, he won't have any at all. And we'll cut his bloody throat.'[21]

So 'Europe' was not an academic argument between members of a respectful fraternity. Behind the issue was an ever present sub-text. Wilson was no keener to lose his head than to let the Jenkins ultras split the party.

The evolution of his tactics has been chronicled by several hands. In February 1971, he still thought trouble might be staved off. Jenkins went to warn him privately that, if the Government struck a deal with the Community, he and his faction would be determined to support it. The only way to minimize the coming upheaval, Jenkins suggested, was to have a free vote. But Wilson at that stage was saying he could do better. 'I am more optimistic than that,' he told Jenkins. 'I hope that we may be able to get the party officially to vote in favour.' The free vote would be a last, worst resort.

The year, however, saw a steady decline from this high expectancy. On 26 April, Wilson began to show tentatively anti-European colours, making a speech that canvassed the appalling possibility of an invasion

Hugh Gaitskell,
Labour Party
Conference, 1962:
cry God for England
and a thousand
years of history.

Douglas Jay,
President of the
Board of Trade, 1964:
never go abroad
without the
cornflakes.

Labour changes course: Harold Wilson, prime minister, and George Brown, with Michael Palliser, private secretary, lurking between, Paris, 1967.

Dumbfounded by de Gaulle: Wilson and Chancellor Kurt Kiesinger, Bonn, February 1969.

The ambassador and the president: where the Soames Affair began.

Edward Heath,
prime minister
1970–74: there
is no alternative.

Heath and President
Georges Pompidou:
entente cordiale,
at last.

Two faces of 1972.
Enoch Powell (above):
ferocious sceptic.
Sir Geoffrey Howe:
cryptic zealot.

Into the continental embrace, 1972: prime minister Heath signs the
Treaty of Rome, flanked by Geoffrey Rippon, chief negotiator (right), Sir Alec
Douglas-Home, foreign secretary (left) and (far left) the documentation
of 'Europe' thus far.

of 'Italian black-leg labour' if Britain went in. It was the beginning of a precautionary populism, in which mood he was soon spurred to further lengths by the intervention of a man he feared more intensely, though perhaps less consistently, than Roy Jenkins: the former Chancellor and ever lurking shark, James Callaghan. In May, Callaghan delivered a burst of anti-Europeanism that would have sat comfortably in the mouth of a Tory Euro-sceptic of the 1990s. France's approach to the EEC, he said, would mean 'a complete rupture of our identity'. We were about to exchange our old friends in the Commonwealth and the United States for 'an aroma of continental claustrophobia'. Callaghan was especially concerned about the future of the English language. 'The language of Chaucer, Shakespeare and Milton' – late arrivals, one imagines, over Callaghan's known cultural horizon – was, he chided, threatened by the French demand for linguistic hegemony in the EEC. If French was to be the dominant language of the Community, then he had something to tell the Froggies in a demotic they might understand: 'Non, merci beaucoup.'[22]

For the rest of 1971 and through 1972, Callaghan vocally opposed British entry, and Wilson began to travel the same road. Callaghan invented a formula that Wilson seized on, to cover the charge of inconsistency with earlier policy: that entry was unacceptable on the terms Heath had negotiated. At the end of June 1971, Callaghan was telling Jack Jones, leader of the Transport Workers Union, that they should unite round three supreme objectives: to beat Heath, keep the party united and 'stop us going into the Common Market'.[23] At the special conference in July, Wilson, who had allied with Jenkins to resist its being called, made a speech of such negativity as to cast him finally and definitively, in the current terms of the argument, as anti-European. 'It was like watching someone being sold down the river into slavery, drifting away, depressed and unprotesting,' Jenkins said.[24]

Wilson's real depression at the time, however, had another source. Though few people believed he was really as hostile to entry as he felt it prudent to indicate in his conference speech, this did not secure him remission from the harsh verdict of the pro-Europeans. Quite the opposite. They felt he should be more honest. On 9 June, he had allowed Jenkins to give him a little lecture about straightness. While conceding that the leader had a hard problem to deal with, the deputy told him, insufferably: 'What is most damaging to your reputation and position in the country is that you are believed, perhaps wrongly, to be devious, tricky, opportunistic.' By sticking to the Europe position he had taken in government, said Jenkins, Wilson would not only do some good to the cause and the country but might make people see him as a man of principle.[25] Not only that – here came the twist of the knife – but he would be rewarded by a guarantee that the Jenkinsites would not endeavour to replace him, with or without the intriguing Callaghan.

The leader, writes Jenkins, received all this 'with perfect good temper'. Such tolerance seems all the more heroic, since the homily was delivered in response to Wilson's complaint about his difficulties, toying with an agonizing choice, which he compared self-pityingly with the simplicities confronting a man like Jenkins whose choice was already made. Later, he put the point more graphically. Exasperated by his posturing colleagues, he told them one day: 'I've been wading in shit for three months to allow others to indulge their conscience.'[26] When Jenkins, shortly after the July conference, delivered a scintillating pro-Market philippic to the parliamentary party, Wilson was beside himself, ranting to Tony Benn, a visitor to his home in Lord North Street: 'I may just give up the Party leadership, they can stuff it as far as I am concerned.'[27] 'He was full of boasts,' writes Benn, 'but underneath was desperately insecure and unhappy.' He was beginning once again to see Jenkins's people as an anti-party fifth-column, just like the Gaitskellites in an earlier phase, gathering in private rooms and flats to plot against him. 'A party within a party is not less so because it meets outside the House in more agreeable surroundings,' he told the parliamentary Labour Party, with vintage sarcasm, the very night he was telling Benn he might quit.

Come October, of course, he was still there. He always was, until a moment, years later, when he stunned the world by resigning with clear blue skies apparently all round him. Now, squeezed between right and left, Europe and anti-Europe, he told the world that what he wanted was a united party, a phrase which at this particular moment meant that the pro-Europeans should not be penalized. It was apparent, as Jenkins had warned, that significant numbers would refuse to be dragooned into opposing the vote-in-principle for entry, and the leader felt obliged to make the best of it. In exchange for the freedom to do that, they would sacrifice their freedom to support the passage of the Bill, and Harold Lever would take his conscience to the lavatory. Wilson, for his part, would sustain the line that all he objected to were the terms, the infamous and terrible terms by which Heath had failed to secure a decent deal in the cause of a great leap forward which the Labour Party continued to imply that it did not, in principle, oppose.

There was, however, one more condition, another shard in the mosaic of Wilsonian ambiguity. He found an additional way to confuse the matter, in order to simplify his life. It had first emerged some time earlier, out of the teeming mind of Tony Benn. In his new raiment as man of the people, Benn had proposed that Europe was so large a question that it should be put to a referendum: not a wholly new idea, but one which he laid on the table at the perfect moment. What the party could not agree, let the people settle! It was an irresistible lure to a leader pressed by short-term considerations of party unity.

At first, Wilson opposed the referendum. 'I understand you are suggesting a plebiscite on the Common Market,' he said acidly to Benn on 5 November 1970. 'You can't do that.' When Benn put it to the party's National Executive around that time, he couldn't find a seconder. But he persisted, writing a long letter to the electors of Bristol, the seat of his constituency, presumptuously challenging a more famous message delivered to the same electors, in which Edmund Burke, on becoming the MP for that parish in 1774, laid out the doctrine of representative government: 'Your representative owes you, not his industry only, but his judgement; and he betrays you, instead of serving you, if he sacrifices it to your opinion.'[28] 'If people are not to participate in this decision, no one will ever take participation seriously again,' Benn riposted. A less romantic voice, impressed by the needs of party rather than the voguish concept of participation, was that of Callaghan. He was among the earliest to dabble with the referendum, calling it 'a rubber life-raft into which the whole party may one day have to climb'.

The whole party, however, declined to do so. Although Wilson changed his mind under pressure from the left, Jenkins and his friends saw the referendum as the beginning of the end. It became, for them, a *casus belli* requiring an extreme response.

Though achieving a measure of unity in the short term, its ultimate role was the opposite. In the end, it marked a stage on the road to a great sundering.

Wilson never liked it. In deflecting Benn, he only repeated what he had said when asked the question during the election. All three party leaders had rejected a referendum, none more vehemently than the Prime Minister. 'The answer to that is No,' he said. 'I have given my answer many times ... I shall not change my attitude on that.'[29] Nor did he want to do so. A referendum, while superficially attractive in certain circumstances, has the large disadvantage, to a party leader, of surrendering control. Only a more threatening source of such prospective impotence could induce him to revise his opinion.

The process of emasculation now unfolded. Adamantly negative in November 1970, Wilson, under slow torture, was obliged to switch sides in March 1972. The regular 1971 party conference, in October, came close to deciding against entry in principle. Those were still the days when massive union bloc votes, wielded by grotesquely power-proud barons, affected to determine party policy, and only the jousting of the Transport baron, Jack Jones, against the Engineering baron, Hugh Scanlon, ensured that the line was held. By another typical perversity, the conference at that point rejected the seductive middle option, a referendum, by a larger margin. But this wasn't the end of the matter. As the European Communities Bill began passage through Parliament, the Heath Government was in trouble on many other fronts. To the Labour Party, Europe or no, it presented an irresistible target. Any issue on which it could be defeated roused the blood of every Labour politician not prepared to regard entry into the Common Market as a sacred purpose. The referendum became such an issue.

Its transforming into party policy was engineered by its latter-day inventor, Tony Benn, a master not only of rhetoric but of manoeuvre. On 15 March, the shadow Cabinet, despite the rage for unhorsing the Government, had considered and rejected support for a referendum that would have thoroughly embarrassed Heath. On 22 March, Benn got a gently lisping little motion carried by the National Executive asking the shadow Cabinet if it would be good enough to look at the referendum again. This was passed 13–11, with Wilson, Callaghan and Jenkins absent. A Tory back-bench amendment to the Bill, promoted by Enoch Powell among others, was due to test Commons opinion very shortly. So, a week after the NEC, the shadow Cabinet did what it was asked and, this time, reversed itself, voting 8–6 to support Powell's parliamentary ploy.

The ploy, as it happens, got nowhere. When it came to a vote, there were enough Labour abstentions to kill the amendment. Inside the party, however, this proved to be a truly historic moment: a second occasion when Jenkins was determinant. He, Lever, George Thomson and others lower down regarded the referendum not merely as defective in itself and a betrayal of parliamentary democracy, but, perhaps more important, as a device designed, should they support it, to nullify what they had achieved by voting against the party line and sending the Bill exultantly on its way the previous October. To them, it was as much a matter of what would happen to their faction as what would happen to their cause. Watching Wilson's switch, particularly his willingness to call the second shadow Cabinet meeting, Jenkins concluded that 'he must have fixed upon a strategy of forcing us into submission or resignation'.[30]

If so, the strategy succeeded. Not long after the shadow Cabinet vote, Jenkins resigned as deputy leader, taking Lever and Thomson with him. Alongside and below, the advice to him split on lines that are of interest. They began partly to foretell the shape of future allegiance. Roy Hattersley, though a totally committed European, was emphatically against resignation. David Owen, then a Labour European of similar stamp, advised against but, says Jenkins, supported it 'almost enthusiastically' when it happened. Bill Rodgers, while not wanting to put the pressure on, was thoroughly pleased. Lever, back from playing the tables at Deauville, said simply, 'Thank God.'

What Wilson said was nothing much. He made a token attempt to change his deputy's mind, but was otherwise calmly acquiescent, especially when Jenkins assured him that he would not be making a challenge for the leadership, at least in the coming autumn.

The Jenkinsites, after all, were isolated. Even as they gained approval in the press, they soon became unpopular in the party. Most of the younger ones opted not to leave their front-bench jobs, and Wilson, fortified by the referendum commitment, was able to see off what he regarded as the threat that mattered most, the left's demand for exit. 'Harold said that to be committed to come out would be impossible for him, and that he would have to resign,' Benn's diary records on 3 May 1972. An exit resolution loomed at the party conference. In fact, it was defeated, by the narrowest margin – 2,958,000 so-called votes in favour, 3,076,000 against – and Wilson, on the basis of a colourful promise of what could be gained by root-and-branch renegotiation, achieved the impression of unity which was, to him, what counted most.

Looking back, many have criticized Wilson's handling of events. Bill Rodgers once went so far as to say of the October 1971 vote: 'He could have held the party together by voting for entry.' So widespread was moral repugnance against Wilson's deviation, Rodgers thought, that the damage it did was far worse than any split provoked by the opposite course. Many more than sixty-nine MPs, he judged, would have voted for Europe if the leader had led them in that direction.[31] On the same retrospective occasion, Jenkins himself reflected that a lot of trouble might have been avoided if Wilson had chosen to act, in a sense, even more ambiguously than he did: keeping the temperature down, not imposing the whip, allowing free rein to party disagreements, not taking a black-and-white position himself.

Outright support, the Rodgers line, was, I think, impossible. The presence of anti-Europeanism, both numerically and emotionally, was dominant in the Labour Party of this period. It was supplemented by the usual ferocious anti-Tory feeling that justified, for many Labour politicians, adversarial combat on any and every issue. Overt backing for Heath's initiative would not have been tolerated.

On the other hand, only an illusionist could seriously suppose that the opposite approach would produce a settled unification. A time of functional tranquillity might now eventuate; but it was the calm before the crack-up.

*

WHEN WILSON walked into Downing Street in early March 1974, for his second tour as Prime Minister, Britain had been a member of the European Economic Community for fourteen months. It would have been easy for an outside observer, especially a European, to conclude that she did not intend to stay there much longer. The early gestures of the ministers that mattered seemed to signal hostility, verging on contempt.

Jenkins did not matter. Though at one point slated to return to the Treasury, he was obliged to settle for a more remote reprise, at the Home Office, which he had last run in 1967. Here he was parked well away from Europe, which was placed, instead, in the beady care of Callaghan, the new Foreign Secretary. The Labour election manifesto had pledged the party to a 'fundamental re-negotiation of the terms of entry', a promise decked out with some spacious presumptions. The manifesto said, for example, that pending a successful renegotiation Britain would feel free to ignore Community rules which didn't suit her. There was more of this kind of posing arrogance. Callaghan set about engaging in the Euro-world with a notable brutality of purpose.

Ambassadors were summoned to London for induction into the new coolness. Having spent a year trying to demonstrate that Britain was now keen on 'Europe', they were told to reverse course. 'I want you to understand that all this European enthusiasm is not what we're in business for,' the Foreign Secretary instructed one of them. 'I need to know whether you can do the job.'[32] Michael Butler, under-secretary in charge of the European Community, who prepared the Foreign Office briefing papers in response to the manifesto pledge, was called to a man-to-man meeting. Callaghan thanked him for the papers, but added an admonition. 'They tell me you really care about Europe. Is that right?' he asked the official. Butler, though worried about hanging on to his job, nevertheless said yes, that was so, he did care a lot about Europe. 'Very well,' the Foreign Secretary replied. 'But just remember. I really care about the Labour Party.'[33]

He carried his offensiveness abroad. Visiting Brussels for the first time, he wasted no charm on François-Xavier Ortoli, the president of the European Commission. 'He was extremely rude, and treated Ortoli like a second-rate official,' said a witness. The negative effect of the aggressive formal statement he made to a meeting of the Council was mitigated only by a sudden distraction: the death of President Pompidou was announced in the middle of it. But in his hostility Callaghan spoke for a new regime infused by suspicion of Brussels and most of its works. Other visiting ministers varied in their handling of the problem. Though Peter Shore, the Trade Secretary, was the most fundamental of critics of British membership, he behaved, from officials' point of view, impeccably. Tony Benn, the Energy Secretary, intrigued more deviously against Community initiatives. He was now an out-and-out enemy of Brussels, declining to conform to pattern. Reappearance in government made no difference to Mr Benn. 'I felt as if I was going as a slave to Rome,' he wrote on 18 June. 'My visit confirmed in a practical way all my suspicions that this would be the decapitation of British democracy without any countervailing advantage, and the British people, quite rightly, wouldn't accept it. There is no real benefit for Britain.'

In the topmost reach of government, however, the old normality prevailed. Staying in was Wilson's objective, through dense veils of hostile obfuscation. While Callaghan seldom relented in his aggression, even allowing it to be put about that, like it or not, a British exit might be inevitable, that doesn't seem to have been his end-game, and it certainly wasn't Wilson's. Renegotiation, a term that promised everything but might mean rather little in the end, was to be the salve for Labour's gaping wounds.

It could not begin in earnest until there had been another election. In March, Wilson was a minority Prime Minister unable to put forward proposals that the Community would have to take seriously. Every week, the talk was not of governing but of the next election, to acquire a proper majority. When the election happened, in October, the majority it produced was only three, enough to rule if not enough to dominate, and the inescapable basis on which anti-Marketeers could increase their influence over the renegotiation process.

Interestingly, they had not been able to insist on a categoric commitment to a referendum. In October, as in February, the pledge the party made was only to 'consult the people through the ballot box' after new terms had been negotiated. Even now, Wilson and his friends recognized the importance of the Europe faction enough to use these ambiguous words, as Jenkins writes, 'rather than to flaunt the red cloth of "the referendum" in my face'.[34] But this was indeed no more than face-saving. A referendum, rather than yet another general election, was clearly the instrument of choice. The balance of forces favoured the anti-Market side. They were, after all, in a majority in the conference and related organs. They had a strong grip on the Cabinet and the parliamentary party. They stood for an attitude, an emotion, a defiant rejection of the capitalist imperatives that the Market then seemed to embody, which Wilson had done little to argue down.

He did, however, hold the initiative, and something that could be called a renegotiation began. It was not without substantive potential. Certain matters had been postponed by Heath, most obviously the size of the British budget contribution. After so short a period of membership, the presence of serious financial inequity, sufficient to trigger the correcting mechanism the Heath deal contemplated but did not define, was hard to establish. But its likely occurrence was widely agreed. Brussels's own forecasts showed that the inequity – Britain contributing more than she would get, and more than her national income indicated as her due – would get worse in future years. Likewise, the Common Agricultural Policy, the source of most of this imbalance, was penalizing New Zealand, for which Wilson had a special soft spot, and the Caribbean. All the old issues, in other words, were deemed fit for grievance-mongering by the British. And all were in some manner at least addressed in the process which the British obliged the continentals, saddened but resigned, to reopen.

It was an extended process. Wilson briefed himself diligently on each of the seventeen aspects of the Heath deal Labour said were unacceptable. Over the winter of 1974–5, Callaghan flew to and from Brussels incessantly. The existing apparatus of Cabinet committees was fortified by another two, one for Euro-strategy, one for tactics. Regional policy, industrial policy, energy policy, overseas aid policy, the policy for Value Added Tax: these were just the beginning of the struggle. The entire structure of O'Neill's negotiation, if the static generated by ministers was to be believed, was up for detailed discussion. At the heart of it was the money, a matter on which Wilson regarded it as important to be able to show he had got something back.

Three aspects of the renegotiation, however, are more telling in retrospect than the barren matter of the sums. The sums, in fact, added up to very little. Despite the length of the process, which reached its climax at a summit in Dublin, Britain gained nothing that could be counted. The German Finance Ministry dreamed up a new formula for calculating a British rebate, to apply once Britain's gross national product per head was lower than 85 per cent of the Community average. In the event, it was valueless. According to Michael Butler, the British official closest to the renegotiation and one of the few Foreign Office men who does not look back on it with scoffing cynicism, it 'never produced any financial results'.[35] Since it was the only item in the list that was strictly quantifiable, rather than susceptible to linguistic blurring, this could have been damaging to Wilson's strategy. But its emptiness became apparent only after the moment of political crisis had passed.

And politics was the issue. This is the first aspect worthy of attention. 'It soon became clear to me', said Michael Palliser, at that time the ambassador in Brussels and a key player in the renegotiation diplomacy, 'that the whole object of the exercise was to keep Britain in, and get something that could be presented to the British as politically adequate.'[36] What was actually obtained mattered much less than the impression that, whatever it was, it was quite enough. This was part of the reason for the elaborate, long-drawn-out nature of the dealing.

Quite early in the piece, Wilson was daring to let it be known that he wanted a success, and that when the ensuing referendum took place he would be in a position to support a Yes campaign. For Jenkins especially, this was an important moment. It signalled that Wilson had, in effect, changed sides. Instead of sucking up to the left with anti-Market nuances, he was putting himself in a position where he had to make common cause with the Jenkins faction, little though he cared for them. 'By December I was not in serious doubt that Wilson would recommend a "yes' vote and that Callaghan as Foreign Secretary would do the same,' Jenkins writes. 'I did not therefore feel that there was any need for me to contemplate a second resignation.'[37] Subsequently, Wilson had so hard a time from the left – 'He was almost beside himself . . . The venom poured out of him,' wrote Barbara Castle, after an especially heated confrontation with his old allies[38] – that he once again waved around resignation threats. The renegotiation, thin though its eventual outcome was, in effect obliged him to come out for the first time as an open pro-European.

The second piece of hindsight to which this gives rise concerns the forbearance of the Europeans. Never was their desire for British participation so sharply manifested as during the elaborate dance that Wilson now conducted with his party, a period of uncertainty which occupied another fifteen months after the mere fourteen that Britain had so far belonged.

Wilson's peer-group of European leaders put up, first of all, with his theatrically extreme demands, some of which appeared to be challenging the very clauses of the Treaty of Rome. They went along with the implication that British membership thus far had somehow lacked political legitimacy. They put themselves to much trouble, going through the motions of meeting and deliberating and haggling, with a view to producing what might be represented as a fresh basis of British membership. With some boldness, they even brought their own skills to bear on the British political process direct, through the intervention of the new German Chancellor, Wilson's fellow leftist, Helmut Schmidt.

When Schmidt became Chancellor, in place of Willy Brandt, he was commonly construed to be an Atlanticist rather than a European. This was how Callaghan saw himself, and the false dichotomy, so popular in British politics, was planted on the Germans as though they were as much in thrall to it. Callaghan looked forward to dealing with an American German. But Schmidt, while certainly a friend of Nato, was not a critic of European integration. More than that, he was willing to argue for Europe in the temple of British anti-Europeanism, the Labour Party conference. In November 1974, he came to the platform at Central Hall, Westminster to speak, in effect, in Wilson's cause, and brought the rapt assembly of sceptics to their feet. I was present myself, as a journalist. It was hard to know which to admire most, his command of irony in a second language, or the way he elevated the Europe discourse to a level which the British were so seldom capable of addressing: its geo-political, even its moral, dimension as a force for good in a dangerous world.

Schmidt's presence that weekend was key in another way too. It encouraged Wilson to align his public mind with his private intention. There was a session between the two of them at Chequers, at which the German promised his British counterpart enough help with the renegotiation to satisfy Wilson that it would succeed. In return for German backing, he induced the Prime Minister to prepare to come out into the open, and to visit Paris to inform the new French President, Valéry Giscard d'Estaing, as well that he was about to do so.

Interviewed twenty years later, Schmidt took a sardonic view of this whole encounter. The renegotiation, he said, was face-saving, a cosmetic operation for the British Government. 'If, from British hindsight, it worked as a cosmetic operation, then the rest of the members were successful,' he reflected drily.[39] But at the time, his presence looked entirely different. It had a galvanizing effect. One official who was present at the Chequers session regarded it, indeed, as the final conversion of Harold Wilson to a course of conduct that concluded by keeping Britain in the Community.

'After Schmidt had gone,' the official told me, 'Wilson retired to his room. He spent about three hours there. He made one telephone call, to Jim Callaghan. By the time he came out, he knew exactly what he wanted to do and where he wanted to go. He clearly understood that if he tried to pull us out of the Community, he would split his party and Roy would take out however many people. He would get the Cabinet to agree to have a referendum, to agree that it was government policy to stay in, but that Benn and Shore and Castle would be free, exceptionally, to argue that we should come out. I think he had thought all that out as a tactical operation when Schmidt left. After that, it was just a question of making sure it happened.'

'I don't think it was a matter of principle for Wilson,' added the official, a man who saw many British ministers at close quarters throughout his life. 'But I thought his performance was staggering.'

He now had to carry it into the Cabinet room. With the renegotiation formally concluded in March, he needed to count the heads before the inevitable division, which he was prepared to legitimize for this one occasion, became public. It took two days, and the spilling of a great deal of acrimony. Presenting himself as an open-minded doubter to the end, Wilson, like Callaghan, spoke for a positive recommendation only on the second day. His attitude, in fact, remained Healeyesque. 'The decision is a purely marginal one,' he told Barbara Castle a little later. 'I have always said so. I have never been a fanatic for Europe. I believe the judgement is a finely balanced one.'[40] But there came a point, and it was now, when he could not avoid staking himself to a position that did not admit of such convenient cerebration. You were either for it or against it, and as Prime Minister, having promoted the entire process that culminated with this choice, you would find it harder than most to pretend that there was somewhere in between.

Some of the Cabinet were enraged. The diarists, especially Barbara Castle, excel themselves in their depiction of Wilson's alternation between fury and self-pity, as his dream of a well-mannered disagreement – 'a dignified parting of the ways', Ben Pimlott writes[41] – gave way to violent exchanges of abuse. Driven into alliance with his scheming rival, Jenkins, he boiled over with indignation at Jenkins's growing contacts with pro-European Tories getting ready for a Yes campaign in the referendum. 'Most unusually for him, Wilson was out to make himself unpleasant,' Jenkins writes.[42] To his oldest friends he seemed to be self-flagellating, as he contemplated the break with them. 'Harold was talking of resigning or of calling the whole thing off,' Michael Foot recalled. 'He kept saying the humiliation was so awful, the attacks of the press were so awful . . . He was in a state of emotional fury about it.'[43]

Such was the condition of the Prime Minister, as he edged the apparatus of politics in the direction he knew it had to go. His near-derangement, which was not construed by anyone as a tactical invention, did not, however, divert the course of events. The Cabinet majority of 16–7 for a positive recommendation of the new terms included five members previously on the other side, who were now won over by a combination of wheedling and enforcement, mainly by Callaghan.[44] Without them, the vote would have been 12–11 against staying in the EEC. For all his inner, and sometimes outer, turbulence, Wilson managed to guide the machine of government against the opinions of all his closest political friends, not to mention most of his personal coterie of advisers who were committed anti-Marketeers.

He also did so against the bulk of opinion throughout the Labour Party. However open Wilson is to the charge of slipperiness, and of complete, studied, sedulous failure to lead popular opinion in the direction he presumably wanted it to go, his managerial talents – deployed, it would seem, only semi-consciously, with him half-resisting himself all the time – produced an extraordinary reversal of political normality. When the Cabinet decision was put to Parliament, it received a large majority, entirely thanks to the Tories. But, of Labour MPs, 145 were against, only 137 in favour, with 33 abstentions. Counting all ministers, fewer than half voted for the Government line. Later in April, at a special party conference, there was a massive majority, 3.7 million to 1.98 million, for coming out of the Common Market altogether. Wilson had to remind them that coming out was not yet the issue: this was what the referendum of the people, not the party, would decide.

All the same, true to the position he had taken throughout this latest phase, Wilson made a speech that nowhere contained a statement saying he was personally in favour of staying in Europe. Already, thus, he was hedging against a No verdict. One may look with awe on his tactics in the Cabinet, but there is surely a limit. Even while he was judging an issue so important that it had to be sent to the people, he was reducing to the minimum his own responsibility, guarding against the worst, omitting to rise with even a single enthusiastic phrase to the occasion.

But there is something else worth noting about this phase of Wilsonry, which has particular piquancy in the 1990s. It is the third large insight to be legitimately enriched by hindsight.

As early as April 1974, scarcely a month into power, and still baring his teeth at anyone who looked like a pro-European, Callaghan was already beginning to learn something about the EEC that he liked the sound of. There began to emerge a collective opinion that the Community should find ways of taking a more active interest in foreign policy: what was known, in the language, as political co-operation. This was not entirely what he had looked for. As a noted Atlanticist, he watched with some distress the fiasco of the so-called 'Year of Europe' which his friend, Henry Kissinger, the US Secretary of State, had invented as a way of diminishing transatlantic rivalries. The resignation of President Nixon, running from impeachment, was one of several events that compromised the Year of Europe. But it did become apparent to Callaghan, pushed by the Foreign Office, that some kind of consultative approach to foreign policy by the Nine – Nine, instead of Six, was now the number, Denmark, Ireland and Britain, but not Norway, having seen their applications through – might be a way of increasing Britain's weight in the world.[45]

At the time, this awareness played its part in Callaghan's adjustment – conversion would be far too strong – from an adversarial to a mildly co-operative role in the renegotiation. Seen from afar, its casual treatment in 1975 recalls the lack of neuralgic sensitivity which then attached to anything that resembled political collaboration. Such ideas were then part of an ongoing, exploratory dialogue, towards a possible end which nobody could clearly foresee but which nobody fundamentally opposed. It is one example of how the context has changed, but also a cautionary item to insert into the 1990s argument about the alleged deceptions being perpetrated twenty years before. The observable historic fact is that, while political collaboration – a version of political unity – was in the air, it wasn't concealed. Rather, it was almost completely ignored in the debates that went on about the future of the nation.

There is parallel evidence of this in the still more neuralgic field of the currency. Economic and monetary union, EMU, was, as we have seen, on the Community agenda at the time Heath signed the Treaty. Serious leaders of serious governments made a commitment to introduce it in 1980. When Wilson displaced Heath, this objective was still nominally in place, though the oil shock meant that most bets were off. Nevertheless, it appeared on the agenda of a summit Wilson attended in Paris in December 1974, and he signed up to the declaration which said that, on EMU, the will of heads of government 'has not weakened, and that their objective has not changed'. 'The time has come', it went on, 'for the Nine to agree as soon as possible on an overall concept of European Union.'

Wilson, it is true, signed this in a spirit of confident agnosticism. He thought it wouldn't happen for some time. Other governments, he told the Commons, now had a different attitude towards 'the practicability of achieving EMU by 1980'.[46] He said the objective had been 'tacitly abandoned'. And plainly he did not want it. In their grapplings with him, the anti-Europe keepers of the diaries show him caustically promising that EMU is out of the window.

But fury at the prospect, all the same, was muted, by comparison with what came later. It didn't touch the British at that time on a spot where Europe really hurt. Although that can be attributed to its remoteness from reality, it dilutes the case of the conspiracy-theorists, whose retrospective vision depends so heavily on the notion that Europe was, all the time, cooking up plans that neither they nor their leaders knew anything about.

Few people, in truth, knew exactly where they were going. And now it was time for the British people as a whole to make what they could of the prospect.

*

IN THIS GREAT ARGUMENT, the people had thus far been only occasional contributors. Their voice had not been heard. Or perhaps they didn't have a voice. This was as real a possibility. The people hadn't spoken, in part, because they hadn't been asked. But also they didn't always have much to say. Now they were invited to take part in a referendum which, though termed merely consultative, would be decisive. It was the first national referendum in the history of the United

Kingdom: an alien deviation from the trusted path of party and parliamentary government.

'The people' were always hitherto a tool in the debate, their feelings handled warily by pro-Europeans, deciphered with confident presumption by the other side. But, insofar as they had been able to give a political opinion, this was inevitably buried in the mix of a hundred issues that were at stake in parliamentary elections. Their real responses, when put to it, were a bit of a mystery. Nobody had reason to be certain *what* they felt about this single question.

From public opinion polls, which were taken regularly from the late 1950s when Europe first became an issue, it was possible to deduce three characteristics of the public attitude to Britain's entry and membership. It was changeable, ignorant and half-hearted.

At the beginning, it tended to be favourable by a wide margin.[47] A Gallup poll in March 1959 showed that those in favour of opening negotiations to join outnumbered the antis by four to one, an order of magnitude that broadly held good until the beginning of the Macmillan event. This was a period of some excitement at the prospect of what beckoned, though there were palpable class differences: Europe has always been an idea more favoured by middle-class voters than the rest. Between June 1961, when Macmillan was preparing to decide, and January 1963, when de Gaulle administered his veto, there were fluctuations. Possibly the most significant figures, thrown up at different times in 1962 by Gallup and National Opinion Polls (NOP), were those showing the 'don't knows' as quite often larger than either the pros or the antis.

After the veto, it didn't take long for a majority to say it wanted negotiations to resume: 46 per cent against 25 per cent, according to Gallup in June 1963. The later 1960s, however, were not a good time for the European idea in Britain. In fact, an enduring shift began in the year Wilson decided to make his first overture, 1967. Disapproval of the initiative stood at 26 per cent in February, 41 per cent in May (when Wilson announced it), 45 per cent in November when the General said no again. Ignorance and indifference were still conspicuously prevailing conditions, measuring well above 20 per cent at all times. Of one feature there could be no doubt throughout the period: the high proportion of the people who found themselves unable to share the fascination of the politicians with this subject.

Not surprisingly, therefore, Europe never achieved then, and hardly ever has done since, what opinion pollsters call salience. It did not stand out, among the range of matters that troubled the typical British mind. It was seldom a preoccupation, by comparison with prices and jobs and schools and health and the other quotidian realities. The popularity of the Community has had its ups and downs, and has never been so high as it was in the late 1950s when Britain did not belong. But even at the depths of its unpopularity it did not really set the electorate's pulses racing. There were always things that mattered more. In October 1974, only 10 per cent of voters logged it as an important question. Through the 1980s, this was consistently down to low single figures: between 1986 and 1988, the monthly average was 2 per cent.[48]

Now, however, the voters were obliged to take it seriously, because they were being asked to vote. The question could not be avoided. 'Do you think that the United Kingdom should stay in the European Community (The Common Market)?' And at the moment the question was put, they were readier to give the answer the Government wanted than they had been for a long time. For all the shenanigans in the Cabinet, the coolness of the national leadership and the limited popularity of all things European, as the inevitability of the campaign came finally into view the polls showed Yes votes outnumbering No votes by two to one, a lead they never lost.

The referendum was happening, it should be remembered, at a time of considerable national anxiety. In thirty years, the atmosphere had completely changed. When Ernest Bevin and Clement Attlee decided to have nothing to do with the Schuman Plan, they did so as leaders of a country still deeply conscious that it had won the war, and still imbued with a grim self-confidence to match: still blind, also, to the comparative industrial weakness that loomed not far down the track. 'Europe' remained a speculative venture, all right for other countries, quite unlikely to come to anything, and, in any case, a project that could never dent the immortal verities that sustained the independent British state. Had there been a referendum in 1951, asking whether Britain should enter the Coal and Steel Community, it would have produced an overwhelming majority in favour of roast beef and Old England, along with the near-universal opinion that our Spitfire pilots surely had not died in vain.

In 1975, it was all quite different. The national psyche had been battered by many intervening events, not least those of recent memory. For one thing, the country saw itself as being in desperate economic straits. Crises of several kinds seemed capable of destabilizing it, beginning with the aftermath of the event that had pushed Heath out in the first place. In the winter of 1974, the British underwent the economic damage and national trauma of a three-day week brought about by a dispute between the Government and the miners. Alongside this disruption was a world oil crisis, further weakening people's expectations of normality. This was a time of great churning, even a certain panic. Inflation had lately reached 25 per cent, and Britain was simultaneously experiencing widespread, sustained unemployment for the first time since the 1930s. So unpredictable were world events that responsible pundits and politicians began to fear for a shortage of raw materials and basic foodstuffs: a phenomenon, incidentally, which neatly finessed any argument there might be about the cost of the Common Agricultural Policy. In this context, the Common Market had become a reassuring fixed point in the status quo. The people looked ready to be persuaded that anything which put jobs at risk, and might add yet another element to the turbulence, was an adventure not worth undertaking. Christopher Soames, by now the senior British Commissioner in Brussels, was widely quoted as saying: 'This is no time for Britain to be considering leaving a Christmas club, let alone the Common Market.'

Nor was it just a matter of the economy. Political developments also hung like an albatross round the national mind. There was the horror of Irish terrorism on the British mainland: the bombings now reached out of Belfast and Derry to London, Guildford, Birmingham. In Scotland and Wales, votes for national independence peaked in the October election, another disturbance. Scottish nationalism, which took 30 per cent of the vote, was to become a familiar feature on the British scene over the next decades, but at this time the English had difficulty putting it into perspective. They thought it could be the beginning of a break-up, against which, ironically, Europe might provide some kind of unchanging bastion. These things played their part in the formation of a consensus, in the middle of 1975, which was always going to be hard to persuade to take a plunge into what amounted to the unknown. Already, perhaps oddly, Europe was normality. *Quieta non movere*, let sleeping dogs lie, an axiom of British political management ever since Robert Walpole, was likely to work to the advantage, in such a climate, of the most revolutionary change in constitutional status visited on the country since that venerable eighteenth-century leader first introduced the title of prime minister into the English language.

The consensus, certainly, was wide and strong. Roy Jenkins, fittingly, was placed at its head. As a senior minister, he carried the authority of

the state. As an enthusiast for Europe, he divested Wilson of responsibility for a cause the leader did not himself care for. The arrangement
was, relatively, congenial to all parties.

It was also supported by most organized segments of British society.
Business, of course, was universally in favour of a Yes vote. A survey of
company chairmen, carried out by the Confederation of British Industry,
showed no fewer than 415, out of 419, saying that Britain should stay in
the Community. Donations poured into BIE, Britain In Europe, the
umbrella group set up to conduct the Yes campaign. The press was
equally united. Though some newspapers opposed the holding of a
referendum, and all treated the conduct of it as more or less of a bore,
none campaigned for a No vote. The *Daily Express*, once the last bastion
of Empire loyalism and, in 1962, a dedicated enemy of what Macmillan
was trying to do, had by now come round to the view that there was no
alternative to the Common Market. There was no lack of coverage of the
No campaign,[49] but nor was there ever a sense that this was an argument
that evenly split the leaders of opinion in any sphere. Even in church, it
was impossible to get away from the uplifting case for Britain's place in
Europe. Every Anglican bishop supported it, prayers were said in half
the Anglican churches, any lingering whiff of Europe as a project
designed for the furtherance of rule by the Vatican was thereby helpfully
dispelled.

What happened was that all the acceptable faces of British public life
lined up on one side. While Jenkins led the cross-party campaign, Heath
was just as active and Jo Grimond, the leader of the Liberals, had equal
standing. Whitehall set up its own task forces and liaison committees
with the unfamiliar role of supporting one side in a quasi-electoral
argument. The old begetter of the deal, Con O'Neill, was recruited as the
chief administrator of BIE, though he found the chaos of electioneering,
the sheer disorder of politics as against diplomacy, hard to handle, and
he was quietly sidelined. A fraternity of the middle-minded carried all
before it, towards the continent many of them knew rather well. The
historian E. P. Thompson thought of them as people who defined 'white
bourgeois nationalism as "internationalism"', and he satirized their
cultural habits. 'The Eurostomach', he wrote, 'is the logical extension of
the existing eating habits of Oxford and north London. Particular
arrangements convenient to West European capitalism blur into a haze
of remembered vacations, beaches, bougainvillaea, business jaunts and
vintage wines.'[50]

The No campaign, by contrast, enlisted a different breed. What united them wasn't just their attitude but their effect: their oddity, by and large, their position outside the mainstream of governing politics, their resistance to the edicts of centrism in both its behavioural and intellectual mode. Enoch Powell, Tony Benn, even Peter Shore, certainly Dr Ian Paisley, the leader of the Ulster Democratic Unionists: these were not smooth, concessive or readily pleasing politicians. They were edgy, passionate, admirable for their very refusal to conform: not qualities often rewarded by the mass of a cautious and conservative nation. A Harris poll taken at the beginning of the campaign tested public reactions, on a personal level, to twenty-two leading political figures who were involved in it. Each of the fourteen pro-Market names drew a positive reaction. Six of the eight antis scored negative, Powell and Benn, their most important voices, among the most extremely. Paisley, the worst, racked up 62 per cent who did not like him.[51]

They were supported by groups and hangers-on who were usually still more outlandish. The National Front made its presence felt at too many meetings. Missing from the mix was any ballast from an institution the public could respect and understand, such as a political party. For although the Labour Party in conference had voted to pull out of Europe, and the majority of its MPs agreed, it was forbidden to have any presence in the No campaign. Wilson and the leadership insisted on silence from the party, obliging the licensed dissenters to make no official connection with it.

There were attempts, by both sides, to submit a conclusive economic case. For economics was what the campaign ranged most consistently around, and in particular the question of prices. Prices were the key: that was felt by Robert Worcester, the head of MORI, pollster for the Yes campaign.[52] He found that for 58 per cent of people the cost of living was the prime concern, and for 37 per cent food prices specifically. Unemployment, by comparison, worried only 15 per cent. Yet although these were the prime subjects of debate, and had the attraction of apparently being quantifiable, they existed, in the end, more in the realm of fear and speculation than in that of hard evidence. The No campaign, for the most part, said that prices would rise, and that the iniquitous CAP would be a blight on the British housewife. Probably the height of its effectiveness was reached with a scare story launched by Tony Benn, to the effect that 500,000 jobs had already been lost to Europe. This contradiction of the assurances that Heath had given three years earlier secured a lot of publicity. For its part, the Yes campaign could do little more than go on making the same point. It found a hundred different ways of saying, though none of proving, that the general economic prosperity eventuating from Britain's deepening membership of the EEC was a prospect it would be insane to give up.

In the late 1990s, however, the interest of the 1975 referendum campaign lies in something different. What was really said about the issue that came to matter most? In what state of mind, as regards the future of the British nation, did the people make their choice? Were there things they did not know, whose absence from the debate somehow invalidated the verdict? Was there, in particular, a conspiracy of conceal-ment about what Europe meant for national sovereignty?

As Euro-scepticism reached a crescendo, driven with special vituper-ation by politicians who had been part of the Yes campaign twenty years before, these questions acquired new potency.[53] The answers are more complex than they were sometimes made to seem.

The sovereignty issue was raised with passion and prominence by the anti-Marketeers. This camp divided into two: those like Barbara Castle and Douglas Jay, whose main concern was food prices, unemploy-ment and related economic matters: and those like Enoch Powell and Tony Benn, who, while also plunging into the economics, preached great warnings about the end of Parliament and the abolition of Britain's independence. The official No campaign's propaganda document ran through the fundamental dangers. The Common Market, it said, 'sets out by stages to merge Britain with France, Germany and Italy and other countries into a single nation ... As the system tightens – and it will – our right, by our votes, to change policies and laws in Britain will steadily dwindle. . . . Those who want Britain in the Common Market are defeatists; they see no independent future for our country.' This was distributed at government expense to every household in the country.

Along with it went verbal paeans to the greatness of the nation that was and is. 'What the advocates of membership are saying, insistently and insidiously,' Peter Shore declaimed as the campaign was ending, 'is that we are finished as a country; that the long and famous story of the British nation and people has ended; that we are now so weak and powerless that we must accept terms and conditions, penalties and limitations, almost as though we had suffered defeat in war.' This was the kind of line heard much from Michael Foot as well. 'The British parliamentary system has been made farcical and unworkable by the superimposition of the EEC apparatus,' Foot said. 'It is as if we had set fire to the place as Hitler did with the Reichstag.' On the whole, it was the more floridly effective parliamentarians who voiced the most eloquent concern for the shell that Parliament, they said, was about to become. But they were often not very specific. There certainly were losses of specific bits of sovereignty – legal supremacy especially – involved in membership of the Community. But these critics, by and large, preferred the grand sweep of their own unhorizoned rhetoric, prophesying the end of life as we know it: a tactic that may not have assisted in diminishing their faintly crackpot aura.

The Yes campaign dealt with the matter differently. I traced no major document or speech that said in plain terms that national sovereignty would be lost, still less one that categorically promoted the European Community for its single most striking characteristic: that it was an institution positively designed to curb the full independence of the nation-state. Seldom, if ever, did the leading speakers address specifically the implications of the European Court of Justice. There was plainly much wariness about exactly how much to say, and in what context. The official Yes campaign document described the legal question, for example, as follows (italics in the original): 'English Common Law is not affected. For a few commercial and industrial purposes there is need for Community Law. But our criminal law, trial by jury, presumption of innocence remain unaltered. So do our civil rights. Scotland, after 250 years of much closer union with England, still keeps its own legal system.'

While not untrue, this could be said somewhat to understate the matter. It certainly conformed, as did the entire Yes campaign, to the old familiar rule, the golden thread of deceptive reassurance that runs through the history of Britain's relationship with the European Union up to the present day: our entry was essential, our membership is vital, our assistance in the consolidation is imperative – but nothing you really care about will change.

On the other hand, it cannot be contended that the Yes campaign was silent on sovereignty. The words are there, the allusions are made. They just sought to change the way people thought about the concept. 'So much of the argument about sovereignty is a false one,' the document said. Sovereignty wasn't a 'dry legal theory', but had to be tested in the wider context of British interest in the world. 'The best way is to work with our friends and neighbours,' it said. If Britain now said No, 'the Community would go on taking decisions which affect us vitally – but we should have no say in them. *We would be clinging to the shadow of British sovereignty while its substance flies out of the window.*' The Community, it went on, recognized that every nation was different.

There was a balance to be struck between national and communal desires. '*All decisions of any importance must be agreed by every member.*'

While again it can be said that all these statements are defensible, they begged some questions. What did *any importance* mean, in the last one? The Treaty of Rome provided for majority voting, for example about agriculture. The agreement of every member wasn't always necessary. That was part of the point about the Community, but one the Yes campaign did not dare address. It did not deal, in all its subtle intricacy, with the straitening of the sovereign nation, or the climate of collaboration that would begin to produce majorities which it became impossible or imprudent to resist. The pro-Europeans did not try to foretell, in other words, the extent to which *political* union would begin, as a matter of political reality, to emerge. Their statement did say in terms, disposing of another 1990s canard, that while some people 'want us to be half-linked to Europe, as part of a free trade area', this wasn't possible because 'the European Community doesn't want it'. But the extent to which the project was political at all became masked: another well-chewed bone of contention with 1990s sceptics, who blame Messrs Heath, Jenkins and the rest for having failed here, above all, to tell the truth.

To this charge, Heath and Jenkins have their answer. They sometimes sound incredulous. When I interviewed Jenkins in 1995, he said the campaign had been almost all about politics. 'We're accused of having presented the case as just a useful trading arrangement and not facing up to the broader political issues,' he said. This was the reverse of the truth. He remembered a celebratory dinner, after the referendum, at which he and Heath had sat on a sofa together and shared experiences on this very point. 'We both agreed', he told me, 'that we had had some great meetings, very well attended, two thousand, three thousand people. In all of them, it was when one talked about the political issues that one got those moments when there is a sort of silence, a positive silence that meant one was gripping the attention of the audience.'[54]

Heath himself remembered the same kind of thing. When, in early 1997, he was goaded into contesting the claim that he had always disguised the political implications of going into Europe, he replied by producing chapter and verse from long-forgotten statements. Had he not said, to *The Times* on 7 April 1975, 'Britain – as a member of the Community – now belongs to the greatest political grouping in the world'? And what about this from the *Guardian* a month later: 'For the first time in their history, the ancient nation-states of Europe are coming together to learn the lessons of history and to avoid a repetition of its mistakes ... We have a unique and crucial role to play in building a Europe others have only dreamed of: free from tyranny and bloodshed, living in peace and prosperity, and meeting its responsibilities in the wider world'? To anyone who said he had not talked about the politics, he simply said, as he once said to me: 'They're just ignorant.'

This is not quite good enough, however. The arguments about Europe, like many political disputes, often come face to face, only to pass each other at the moment when they should lock horns. While it is true that membership was always a political act, and also true that it was discussed as Heath, Jenkins and many others remember it – as the avoidance of war, the closer union of friendly peoples, and so on – those weren't the hard issues. They were about Europe as a political entity, but not about Britain as a country constitutionally altered. They were politics in one sense, but not the other. As to that other sense of politics, the combatants today are apt to fall back on the suggestion that everyone knew that national sovereignty couldn't last anyway. Pressed on the suggestion that he had evaded the issue in 1975, Jenkins said: 'I don't think one ever dodged it. But certainly I would never have pretended – because I always believed it was absolute nonsense to say that you will preserve every bit of your sovereignty.'[55]

So the pro-Europeans' defence, in retrospect, is not satisfactory. Its frailties, however, are to a substantial extent made good by two aspects of the 1970s often lost on the fevered minds of the 1990s.

The first, already touched on, is the genuine and almost universal uncertainty about where the Community was going. The British referendum took place at a time, after the oil shock, when Europe was inert. Nothing much was happening. Jacques Delors, the next urgent driver towards more integration, was almost a decade away from taking the presidency of the Commission. For a minister to say, as many did, that nothing big could be decided without Britain's agreement was no more than the truth at the time: and, since nothing big of any kind was on the horizon, it was not a statement that immediately aroused speculative curiosity. The enemies of the project did their best to chill the people's blood, but their scenarios were drawn from their version of the literal meaning of the Treaty – its meanings and possibilities, on which they turned out to be quite largely correct – not from actual future pro-grammes that anyone knew were in the works. Even EMU, though affirmed as an objective, was, as Wilson spotted, no longer very real.

The second point is still more telling: a natural trap for modern sceptics to fall into, but a trap all the same. The truth, incredible though it may seem twenty years later, is that the public were not interested. The potential loss of sovereignty did not bother them. Not all the rhetorical feats of Bennery could make them take it seriously. If the voters said Yes to Europe, it was because they did not care about the arguments pressed hardest on them to make them say No.

This is not merely a deduction. It can be measured. In the MORI opinion poll already cited, which showed 58 per cent of people concerned about the cost of living, the number registering alarm about sovereignty or national independence was no more than 9 per cent. Nor was this an aberration. Polling by NOP, which asked the same question at regular intervals between June 1961 and July 1971, found that, in a list of the aspects of Europe which people most disapproved of, having 'no say in our own affairs' scored remarkably consistently: at 3 per cent rising to 4 per cent.[56] If not enough was said by the Yes campaign about these matters which later became so sensitive, it may partly be because the campaigners knew that prices rather than independence, money rather than nation, was where the voters needed reassurance.

There was a congruity between these points. The absence of a future integration plan and the absence of public concern about integration no doubt reinforced each other. That doesn't mean 'Europe' did not develop, as sceptics were to claim, in ways unimagined by the voters of 1975. But it does raise a question about the percipience of those, especially the professional politicians, who claim to have been comprehensively hoodwinked when the Community, with Britain a compliant and fully voting member throughout, developed in the way it did. Misjudgement, maybe: conspiracy, surely not.

At any rate, the vote was won. The margin stayed the same, 2:1, as the polls had said it was in mid-March, though further polling implied that the campaign had not been entirely wasted, since perhaps 14 per cent of people changed their mind one way or the other. What settled it, by common agreement, was fear rather than exultation: the fear of the unknown, as represented by a world outside Europe which the No campaigners were unable convincingly to describe: not, alas, the enthusiasm of the British people for dealing in their newly discovered destiny. Just as there was a great contrast with the atmosphere that made membership of 'Europe' unthinkable in 1951, so there was another with the mood prevailing in 1961–3, when the EEC debate revolved round such confident questions as whether Britain would 'realise her full potential' in the EEC or as leader of a multi-racial Commonwealth. Now sullen apprehension was more the ticket. Survival, rather than potential, was what dominated the national mind. One woman's story spoke for many. The day after the referendum, a Cabinet minister told a civil servant outside the Cabinet room: 'I went to my constituency and an old lady said to me, "I don't like this Community, but I voted to stay in for my grandchildren." '[57]

What, however, did the outcome mean? It was supposed to be conclusive. The people had spoken. Robert Armstrong, later to be Cabinet secretary, said in my presence a few days later that, as a strong European, he was delighted to think that the issue had finally been put to bed. He spoke for the entire establishment of the political class and their auxiliaries, who had first opposed the referendum but then, after winning it, thought it would exorcize doubt at every level, from the Euro-stomach to the European peace.

It wasn't merely the winners who took this view. Tony Benn himself was man enough to embrace the outcome of the enterprise he had got under way. The populist did not unsay what the people said. 'I have just been in receipt of a very big message from the British people,' he came to his doorstep to declare on the morning after. 'I read it loud and clear. By an overwhelming majority the British people have voted to stay in and I'm sure everybody would want to accept that. That had been the principle of all of us who advocated the referendum.'[58] It sounded as though the participants might now go back to their party benches, and normal hostilities resume.

For careful observers, though, there were more interesting signals to consider, which raised some doubt about that. The meaning of party, and its connection with the Europe enterprise, might perhaps have been fatally compromised.

For one thing, it was obvious who had been most exhilarated by the campaign. 'It is a perverse but indisputable fact', writes Roy Jenkins in his memoirs, 'that the event I most enjoyed during 1974–6, my second and last period in a British government, was the one which I had striven most officiously, even to the point of a resignation which may have cost me the prime ministership, to prevent taking place.'[59] At the head of a cross-party organization, a truly national leader for the first time, Jenkins had made a temporary escape from the body that both succoured and, increasingly, alienated him, the Labour Party. It was the beginning of what might become a habit. Europe had supplied the excuse for this separation. It could yet become the pretext, the inescapable reason, for something more enduring.

The real leaders of the Labour Party, meanwhile, had conducted themselves with an equal and opposite lack of interest. While Jenkins was rising above party to preach Europe, Wilson and Callaghan rose above Europe to maintain, as they saw it, party. Their lack of zeal in the campaign was singular to behold. They refused to be seen under the cross-party umbrella, and did not speak at BIE occasions, for which stance Callaghan offered a significant rationale. There were, he said, three sides to the argument – the pro-Marketeers, the anti-Marketeers and 'the truth', which he represented. The BIE, though campaigning for the outcome the two men were banking on, was stained by prejudice, and therefore beyond the pale. They appeared occasionally under the banner of the Trade Union Alliance, but never under that of the Labour Campaign, a sub-group within BIE. Wilson made eight speeches, often at ill-arranged meetings, and Callaghan five: far fewer than they would do in an election campaign. Wilson's most memorable line used a cricket metaphor, uncomfortably mixed with sailing, to express the wholly defensive nature of the case he was presenting. Britain could not maintain world influence, he said, 'by taking our bat home and sinking into an off-shore mentality'. All in all, both men took care to remain eloquently distanced from the action.

Wilson carried his coolness even to the moment of victory. On the steps of 10 Downing Street, he gave a prepared speech which noted the size of the majority – bigger than any government ever got at a general election – and said it mapped the way forward to 'join wholeheartedly' with the rest of Europe in working together. The result, he added, meant that fourteen years of argument were over. But he refused to say he personally welcomed the result. Advised to do so by Bernard Donoughue, the only pro-Europe man in his entourage, he pointedly declined.[60]

And somebody else was absent from the popular consultation, Wilson's opposite number in the Conservative Party, Margaret Thatcher, who had been elected leader in Heath's place a few months before. She made her excuses, and let others carry the torch. She counselled a Yes vote, but said she thought Heath should take the thunder. Like Wilson, she had nothing to do with Britain In Europe.

Both main party leaders, therefore, were disclaiming some portion of responsibility for the watershed. They chose not to be fully engaged. It was a telling sign. The parties, through these leaders, distanced themselves from Europe in a way they would never contemplate over any other issue. It was as if, great though it was, they did not see it as a party question. They shrank from it personally, but they also recoiled from the political implications of an issue which party could not accommodate. It was unavoidably fissiparous – and the agent who might prise apart the fault-line was still at large.

*

THE REFERENDUM did not determine much. It settled the argument in British politics for a while. Not for some time was there any more talk, even from the serious anti-Europeans, about getting out of the Community. The decisive vote seemed to be the end of that debate. At the same time, it was the start of almost nothing. It failed to ignite a new collective effort in the chambers of government to take positive advantage of the Europe connection. In terms of British policy, as opposed to Labour politics, it was almost as if the referendum had never happened.

In less than a year, Wilson resigned the premiership, Callaghan replaced him, and Jenkins signified his intention to depart from British politics, accepting a four-year term as president of the European Commission.

Callaghan was not the man, any more than Wilson, to see in his post-referendum situation an historic opportunity. Presented with this result, this apparent settlement of a dispute that had rendered full-hearted membership, *croyant et pratiquant*, of the Community impossible, he allowed little of his natural scepticism to be reconsidered. The voice of the people had no effect upon him, perhaps because he didn't believe that, even with such a clear discrepancy between one side and the other, it was in any meaningful sense 'pro-European'. He construed the voice as identical with his own: cautious, suspicious, defensive and – most complacent of Callaghanesque postures – famously pragmatic. As a factual description, this was probably correct. What it left out of account was how a political leader, if he had any ambition to change the world, might steer Britain into making sense of what had now been definitively confirmed as the main part of her political destiny.

Callaghan's attitude, however, was congruent with his weak political position. By the time he became Prime Minister, his party had lost its majority and the anti-Europeans in his cabinet and party had not surrendered their opinions. Although the exit option had gone, the line of least collaboration remained stubbornly attractive. Any more positive engagement with the Community, besides offending many of the antis, would have been a distraction from other problems that were crowding in. In the autumn of 1976, after all, the economy appeared to be in such parlous imbalance that the Government became a supplicant at the court of the International Monetary Fund, whose officers temporarily seized control. Neither the leader nor his circumstance were conducive to truly constructive reconciliation between the island and the mainland.

For Jenkins, the prospect was very different. He may have been finally frustrated in his desire to be Prime Minister: he secured only 56 votes out of 314 in the contest to fill the Wilson vacancy. But he was, at last, a European leader. Taking up the presidency in January 1977, he made his break with British and Labour Party politics, to which, interestingly, he had already indicated to Callaghan he would probably not return. This wasn't made public at the time. But he told Callaghan that he 'did not want a future in British politics in their existing shape'. He could only envisage returning to 'a reshuffled pack', in which Labour's anti-European prejudices had somehow been finessed. 'Callaghan', Jenkins writes, 'looked surprised and pensive rather than hostile.'[61]

In his new task, he was at first frustrated. Impasse and lack of optimism still prevailed, the continuing fall-out from the oil-based recession. But eventually he became the prime instigator of the modern Community's most far-reaching project to date, a forerunner, in its way, of the system that was to come to full flower in the 1990s, leading, indeed, to many of the developments which ensured that 'Europe' would remain for the duration a festering source of division in British politics. In effect, Jenkins invented the European Monetary System, within which was sited the Exchange Rate Mechanism, out of which was begat the economic and monetary union that became scheduled to start for real on 1 January 1999. The dream so sanguinely defined by Pompidou and his colleagues in October 1972, having sunk almost into oblivion under the weight of quadrupled oil prices, now acquired definition once again.

Jenkins did not, of course, bring the EMS about. Though still in once sense a political leader – the first in his post, incidentally, to be admitted as an equal partner to world summit meetings of the Group of Seven – he was now formally an official. He could propose but not dispose. He did propose an outline for the EMS, dreamed up, as he records, on a picnic outing to the Forêt de Soignes – shades of Jean Monnet, devising the shape of the Coal and Steel Community as he strode across Alpine fields.[62] The case for a new currency regime, it seemed to him, was overwhelmingly made by a comparison between the 1960s and 1970s. In the 1960s, with fixed exchange rates, European economies had done well, at least keeping pace with America and Japan. In the middle 1970s, with rates unpegged and oscillating sometimes wildly, the performance had been dismal. For a few fleeting weeks, Britain had belonged to what was called the currency snake, the 1972 agreement allowing Community currencies only narrow fluctuations against the dollar, and so against each other. By 1976, it had been abandoned under the pressure of events, by all members except Germany and the Benelux countries. Now a 'zone of monetary stability', possibly leading to full monetary union, became Jenkins's crusade, as much, it would seem from his own account of it, because it might be a device to relaunch the flagging European idea as for its substantive virtues.

After breaking it to the world in a speech at Florence, he did much private politicking to enlist the support of the political leaders who mattered, Helmut Schmidt and Giscard d'Estaing. Though both were wary, and both otherwise preoccupied, it appealed to some of their pre-existing instincts. Giscard had to be ready to face down Gaullist resistance in his own coalition. Schmidt was initially reluctant, but then suddenly changed his mind, an occasion on which Jenkins lavishes a self-conscious cliché. Schmidt's enthusiastic account of the benefits of an EMS was the turning-point. 'I shall never forget how my heart leaped during that exposition,' the stylist apologetically writes.[63] The usage is a measure of his commitment to the project – which did not, however, find much favour with Callaghan.

It was, first of all, sprung on Callaghan unawares, at a summit in Copenhagen in March 1978. Although Callaghan had in fact heard Schmidt expounding a version of it before, he had not been listening, because he was simultaneously trying to get Schmidt to listen to his own initiative for closer links with the dollar. On that occasion, Jenkins writes, they 'had passed like two friendly ships in the night, close but not seeing or at least not listening to each other'.[64] But, in any case, Callaghan was by no means a solitary British sceptic. He was advised by the senior Treasury official on hand at Copenhagen, Kenneth Couzens, to reject it: and though he did not do this *tout court*, showing Jenkins an unaccustomed measure of polite interest, there was never much doubt that the Cabinet would find reasons to resist any active British involvement.

In fact, the Prime Minister himself seems to have become, if anything, a little more interested in the EMS than his Cabinet colleagues. 'World statesmen', wrote Edmund Dell, a Cabinet sceptic, later, 'have often proclaimed the benefits of stability in currency markets': they were attracted by 'an excuse to interfere' in the erratic and irrational performance of the markets, where the recent era of floating rates had a poor record.[65] When the Government produced a green paper, designed as a basis for rejecting the Jenkins–Schmidt–Giscard initiative, the Prime Minister insisted that it at least contain a commitment to the *principle* of stable exchange rates. Indeed, Callaghan's flirtation with the idea grew stronger in his memory as time passed. He apparently regretted accepting what was in 1978 the conventional Treasury and Whitehall, as well as political, advice. Some years later, when Giscard came to deliver the annual Ditchley Lecture, at Ditchley Park outside Oxford, he alluded to Britain's failure to join the operative element of the EMS, the Exchange Rate Mechanism. The meeting was chaired by Sir John Hunt, the former Cabinet secretary, by now Lord Hunt of Tanworth, who thanked the former French President for his brilliant presentation, remarking, on the side, that he himself had always believed Britain should have joined in the first place. Lord Callaghan was sitting in the front row, and said in a voice that echoed round the room: 'Pity you didn't say so at the time.'[66]

The European Monetary System came into operation in March 1979. In May, Britain elected a new government, which did not immediately manifest any greater desire than its predecessor to plunge whole-heartedly into the European enterprise. And even as it was in the throes of being elected, Jenkins was given what turned out to be his opportunity to make good what he had Delphically foreshadowed to Callaghan before he went to Brussels: that when he returned, he would be reluctant to re-enter the tribalism of British party politics as then arranged. The fissile effect of the European experience was about to reach its explosive moment.

It would be a simplistic error to say that the founding of the Social Democratic Party was due wholly, or even mainly, to the disagreement about how Britain's European relationship should essentially be conducted. It answered a more pervasive call, in and out of the Labour Party, for a new grouping on the centre-left. It sprang from histories, arguments and rivalries going back a long way, reaching deep into the very fundaments of Labourism and socialism, Marxism and Methodism, all the competing strands that had brought the party to a pitch where they had ceased, in practical effect, to coexist together as a governing force. Europe was only one of the questions at stake. There was nationalization, there was defence, there was the constitution of the party, there was so-called elitism versus so-called populism, there was a host of dissatisfactions that drove a collection of professional politicians, supported by many unprofessional but active citizens, to depart an old allegiance and fashion a new one. However, Europe was, of all these questions, perhaps the most specific catalyst.

It played this role in several ways. First, there was Jenkins himself. The prophetic send-off, which Callaghan could scarcely believe, was amplified during his time in Brussels, where he became both fully European and ever less fully a British politician of the kind his life thus far had shaped him into. At the end, the EMS mattered far more to him that what the Labour Party thought about the EMS. Though he was incessantly busy, ranging round the continent and maintaining dialogue with every European figure that mattered,[67] he attained a distance from the British scene that gave him the opportunity to deepen his perception that it was in serious trouble.

He put this into words in late 1979, when the absent statesman was given an hour's free time to address the nation on BBC television. Jenkins's Dimbleby Lecture, as it was called, became a text marked down as an early pointer towards political reform, in which he proposed to play a major part. It was a philippic against excessive partisanship, a diatribe against the sterile party system, a paean for the virtues of coalition government. It sought to map out a new political creed, towards which such coalitionism might lead the country: less penal taxation but better public services, more respect for market forces but less unregulated worship of them, more state benignity but less state omnipotence, objectives, he called them, which 'could be assisted by a strengthening of the radical centre'.

The lecture rose above Europe, barely mentioned it. But it came out of Europe, and affirmed respect for modes of politics, such as coalitions, that were and are European. This was before the Labour Party lurched towards the extremity favoured by Tony Benn, but Jenkins spoke in the full knowledge that Europe would be a war zone for the now unconstrained Opposition. His own history, culminating in his departure from the deputy leadership, had singled Europe out as the issue above all others that moved his wing of the party to do unusual things. Though most of them felt as strongly about nuclear disarmament, this wasn't something they'd had to fight for so hard, since here the Wilson leadership felt the same. By many devices – calculated resignation, organized defiance of the whips, even the building of something close to a party within a party – Labour pro-Europeans had shown for many years the special potency of the attitude Jenkins stood for.

This points to the second European stream in the confluence of the SDP. It was a matter of organization as much as ideology. The referendum campaign blurred the Labour divisions but laid bare the way they might later be pursued. Many significant people acquired the habit of structured disagreement, discovering the pleasures, not to mention the culminating triumph, of working outside normal party lines. The list of pro-Europe activists in 1975 can helpfully be read alongside the roster of founding members of the SDP. William Rodgers and Shirley Williams were high in the councils, and other names leap off the page. Among Labour MPs later to go over were George Thomson, Dickson Mabon, Tom Bradley, David Marquand, Ian Wrigglesworth, John Roper, all of whom were heavily engaged as Jenkins lieutenants. Dick Taverne, who had gone so far as to resign his seat at Lincoln to fight a mid-term by-election in March 1973, to make his point against Labour's anti-Europe position, was another prominent cross-over.

There were exceptions. Roy Hattersley, a prime and undeviating Labour Europeanist, was also a categoric and unflinching Labour loyalist. He never contemplated surrendering either Europe or Labour, and by the middle 1990s, while mutating into a Grand Old Man of Labour orthodoxy in face of the New Labour model of Tony Blair, was happy to declare himself a European federalist.

David Owen was another case again. Like Hattersley, he spoke and voted for Europe in October 1971, having been a combative pro-Europe MP from the moment he got into the House in 1966. 'My political career has been dominated by the question of British membership of the European Community,' he starkly wrote in his autobiography.[68] He resigned from a junior post, with Jenkins, in 1972, and then again in 1980, from the shadow Cabinet, when Michael Foot became leader of the party. Though rather slower than Rodgers or Shirley Williams to welcome Jenkins's path-defining Dimbleby Lecture, he signed up with the two of them to make the Gang of Three that was preparing to leave the Labour Party, and then the Four that made the SDP.

But for Owen, it seems, Europe never had quite the prominence, as a mould-breaking issue, that it did for Jenkins. He was by this time more concerned with the defence question, and the attempted reconstituting of Labour Party power away from its MPs to the unions and the rank and file. In 1977, Callaghan had made him Foreign Secretary at the age of thirty-seven. He thus spent two years dealing with Jenkins, in a sense, as his political superior: the youthful politician surpassing the now unelected bureaucrat. During this time, moreover, the politician had acquired a certain dyspepsia with Europe, priding himself on the diffi-culties he was able to cause the Brussels bureaucrats, and rooting out the 'federalists' he thought were dominating the upper reaches of his department.[69] These people, he said, were the 'biggest source of friction' he had to contend with. When he had left office, he once marked the card, for my benefit, of an entire generation of Foreign Office grandees, divining several of the top men as lacking prime loyalty to the British nation. 'I have never been at any stage a federalist,' he writes, preferring to guard more jealously the independent muscularity – 'the sinews of nationhood' – that also might be said to describe, exactly but fatally, his own political style.

For Jenkins, however, Europe was the source of his ultimate liberation. It drew him out of one party into another: and with him much, in the end, of the tradition he stood for. This awaited reabsorption, more than a decade later, into something also exalting itself, in terms, as the radical centre: the old party becoming New.

9

MARGARET THATCHER

Deutschland Über Alles

FOR THE FIRST SIX YEARS of British membership of the European Community, Britain was led by men who were otherwise engaged. Ted Heath, preoccupied with domestic survival, did not begin to make an impression. Harold Wilson and Jim Callaghan, though compelled to give the matter some attention, were always trying to fend it off. Their successor was the first in the line to see Europe as a subject not for apologetic reticence but for triumphal prominence. For eleven of the first seventeen years, the tone was set and the policy made by someone who, at important moments, gave Europe the loudest place on her agenda.

This had a transforming effect. As the inheritor of unfinished business, Margaret Thatcher was well cast to conclude the deal neither Heath nor Wilson could close. But the loudness eventually brought with it confusion and calamity. As British steward of the Europe connection for twice as long as anyone before or since, she imposed on it a contradiction that had an influence no other leader came near to matching.

This was the Thatcher hallmark. In her time she took Britain further into Europe than anyone except Heath. Institutions and markets and laws became far more deeply imbued with the Europe effect. In one shining case, with the British leader's creative and voluble support, the project underwent a step-change from unanimous to majority rule. This was big, adventurous stuff, in a period of rich expansion for the Community idea. Mrs Thatcher, at every stage, was part of it. Yet simultaneously all her political energy was directed against what she herself was doing. Even as she took Britain further in, she stoked the fire of those who opposed this every step of the way.

One way of describing her performance was put to me by Robert Armstrong, now Lord Armstrong of Ilminster, her Cabinet secretary for much of this time. As a pro-European, Armstrong was impressed. 'She was more skilful than anyone I've ever met', he said, 'in combining rhetoric which was faithful to her principles with policies that were totally pragmatic.'[1] But another reading also has to be considered: that the rhetoric so far drowned out the pragmatism as fatally to complicate the most elementary task of the politician – securing popular support for the policies her Government is actually pursuing. As time went on, she allowed her very personal obsessions to confuse, even corrupt, her role as a national leader.

Seldom in the recent record of democracy, and never in this story of Britain-in-Europe, has a lengthy course of events been attributable so particularly to a single character. For all her eleven years, Prime Minister Thatcher was in disagreement, on Europe, with most of her significant ministers. In this central phase of Britain's accommodation to the reality it had finally chosen, the country had a leader who was more potent than any since the war, but was formed by influences which could have been selected, unless she overcame them, to bring her into collision with the European idea.

To begin with, she was Britain's first post-war Prime Minister. That is to say, she did not know the war at first hand, whether as a potato controller or a soldier. Born in 1925, she was still at school when it began and at Oxford when it ended. She could not, like the Macmillans and Heaths and, for that matter, Pallisers, call to mind images of a continent reduced to rubble, which left such men with the inextinguishable belief that European nations must devote their future lives to ever closer union. The echoing afterlife of remembered battle was not available. So she did not participate in the experience that defined the convictions and fired the practice of the main contemporaries who gathered with her, decades later, round the table at the European summit.

Her war, instead, was spent in the small middle-England town of Grantham, thinking about the Germans. Her father, Alfred Roberts, the shaper of her mind and life, was intensely suspicious of foreigners. Whereas the Heath family's gaze drew on experience across the Channel, the Roberts family were navel-watchers, supremely proud of Englishness. 'I would sooner be a bootblack in England', Alfred told the Grantham Rotary Club, of which he was president, in 1937, 'than a leading citizen in a good many of the other leading countries of the world today.' He seems to have detested, in particular, France, which he called 'corrupt from top to bottom'.

It was Germany, inevitably, that dominated table-talk in the Roberts household. 'I knew just what I thought of Hitler,' Margaret Thatcher recalls in her autobiography.[2] It is hard to decipher, as one reads this work, how much of it is a genuine recollection of the time, and how much the pasted-on hindsight of a retired politician. Whether, for example, the thirteen-year-old girl was as conscious as she states of the iniquity of Hitler's invasion of Sudetenland is difficult to judge: as is the representation of herself as someone who always knew that the pacifism in Britain in the 1930s was not exclusively, as she insists, a disease of the right. However, her retrospective conclusion about the Germans is eloquent. That even 'a cultured, developed, Christian country like Germany had fallen under Hitler's sway' showed that civilization, in the hands of weak people, could never be taken for granted. As the bombers droned over Grantham, the nature of the enemy, and the contrast they made with the British, impressed itself on a youthful mind. 'I have to admit', she writes forty years later, 'that I had the patriotic conviction that, given great leadership of the sort I heard from Winston Churchill in the radio broadcasts to which we listened, there was almost nothing that the British people could not do.'[3]

Europe, as this child's mind reached adulthood, acquired no prominent, still less a visionary, place in its hierarchy of interests. There is no record of what she thought of the Schuman Plan. By the time of the Macmillan application, she has reached Parliament, and is, as a dutiful Conservative MP, in favour of it. Indeed, she remembers thinking, after the event, that we had missed the boat at Messina: 'There was a general sense, which I shared, that in the past we had underrated the potential advantage to Britain of access to the Common Market.'[4] All the alternatives, she also thought, were inadequate: neither EFTA nor the Commonwealth nor the USA could meet Britain's trading needs.

With hindsight, however, she is a wistful Gaullist. It is the earliest of many regrets, misjudgements, errors and reversals that litter the Thatcher career on this subject. Writing in 1995, she confesses she did not know at the time what the Treaty of Rome was all about. She was in favour, she says, of a common market, 'and neither shared nor took very seriously the idealistic rhetoric with which "Europe" was already being dressed in some quarters'. Again in retrospect, she looks on de Gaulle's veto as an opportunity that should, in ways she does not describe, have been somehow seized. He had said, in his veto statement, that the breakdown of negotiations need not prevent 'an accord of association designed to safeguard exchanges', or 'close relations between England

and France'. This, the elder stateswoman reflects, would have been better than British membership on the terms eventually negotiated. She concludes: 'We may have missed the best European bus that ever came along.'[5]

Such a perception had not been borne in on her by 1971. When Heath made his second try, she was a Cabinet minister and 'wholeheartedly in favour of British entry'.

De Gaulle's departure had 'transformed the prospects'. Though a mere onlooker at the detailed negotiations, she had the opportunity to contemplate the meaning of Community membership for the grand principles of sovereignty, both national and parliamentary. Enoch Powell and others, after all, brought them to everyone's attention and Powell was one of her heroes. But she looked on his arguments as 'theoretical points used as rhetorical devices'. She did not, at that time, dispute what Geoffrey Howe, piloting the European Communities Bill through the Commons, said about the potential conflict of laws, namely that in any dispute 'the courts would . . . try to interpret statute in accordance with our international obligations'. For it could not be disputed. Only much later did she come to regard the white paper's talk about there being no loss of 'essential' national sovereignty as 'an extraordinary example of artful confusion to conceal fundamental issues'. In 1971, it evidently made perfect sense.[6]

By 1975, the year of the referendum and of her ascent to the leadership, it still made sense. She wasn't, at that stage, too keen on the referendum device, and made her maiden speech as party leader attacking it. Again we find a belated confession of error. At the time, she argued that a referendum, whose implications for parliamentary sovereignty would always be 'profound', was conceivable only 'in cases of constitutional change'. The Europe connection, in 1975, evidently did not measure up to this requirement. Twenty years on, now positioned somewhere between the sceptic and the phobic concerning British membership of the European Union, Baroness Thatcher found herself to have been mistaken in supposing that the Treaty of Rome did not entail a constitutional change. It was 'at least part of the way' towards a written constitution, she now considered.[7] By this time, the middle 1990s, a referendum on the next development, a single currency, had become, in her raucous opinion, essential.

As party leader, she had from the beginning a world view shaped much more by the Cold War than by the European Idea, and it was in this respect that she was able to muster most enthusiasm for the meaning of the Nine. 'I did genuinely believe that it would be foolish to leave the Community,' she writes. But she always saw the bond between West European countries as a strengthening of freedom against the menace of the Soviet bloc, and from time to time urged them, while not diminishing from Nato, to strengthen their attitude to collective security. Speaking in Brussels in 1978, she said: 'Who is there in the EEC deliberations to speak up for defence? I feel no assurance that all these connected matters are being looked at together.' In December of that year, it should also be noted, she was even derisive of the Callaghan Government's refusal to get involved in the foundation of the Exchange Rate Mechanism (ERM) of the European Monetary System. 'This is a sad day for Europe,' she said in the Commons, under a Labour government 'content to have Britain openly classified among the poorest and least influential members' of the Community. She seemed to want in. But the defence dimension concerned her most. For all the economic collectivism of Brussels, which became a source of maximum suspicion, strategic collectivity was an attitude to be encouraged.

Member though Britain was, however, the Community, even before she had to grapple with it, represented much that Mrs Thatcher did not like. She may have brushed aside as meaningless its absurd aspirations, but there was no getting away from its history and composition. For someone as instinctively suspicious of Roman Catholicism, for example, the spectre of *Europe Vatican*, once to be found among the nightmares of socialists like Ernest Bevin and Denis Healey, was not entirely absent. Catholic social teaching, if not the threat of papal conspiracy, was a menace to the project of a leader bent on liberal market economics. Worse than that was the very style of politics that Europe lived by. It had been exalted by Heath, frantically trying to pull election victory out of the fire in October 1974, when he suddenly proposed a so-called Government of National Unity, a non-party administration of all the talents, to tackle the British crisis. Mrs Thatcher silently seethed against the very idea. That was one reason why she took little part in the referendum: the Yes campaign was a plain affront to the supremacy of party, and the war between parties, which was the only political style she understood. Europe, in its larger way, constituted a lifelong exercise in the haggling and dealing, the compromise and consensus, that the lady most despised.

To the objective problems Europe presented to any Prime Minister, therefore, was added, in Mrs Thatcher's case, a more personal challenge. Christopher Soames, whom she put in her first Cabinet, had a good phrase for her, and the truth of it endured at least through her office-holding, Europe-engaging life. 'She is an agnostic who continues to go to church,' he once told me. 'She won't become an atheist, but on the other hand she certainly won't become a true believer.' Europe contended with most of her natural instincts, none of which she desired to overcome. Thatcher *contra Europam* was the stance that she adopted. Although it produced some significant positive results, her long tenure was more notable for its encapsulation of the vices, the English diseases, to be found at one time or another throughout this history.

Somewhere, they can all be seen in the Thatcher years. There is straightforward inconstancy: once routinely favouring Europe, she became its passionate enemy. There is more than a touch of dissimulation: though apparently the upholder of the sovereign nation, she acted to increase the collective powers of the Community. There is the preaching of illusion: as Prime Minister she fully understood the interlocking of Britain with Europe, but when she left she flirted with the dream of Britain Alone. There is contradiction: leading Britain further in, she tried to talk Britain further out. And there is incompetence: she lost four senior ministers to the Europe question, a record of instability that culminated in her own eviction.

One does not need to be a critic of the Thatcher approach to pick out the shape of this saga. The country she took over was in a poor way. What Sir Henry Tizard had said all those years ago – 'We are not a Great Power, and never will be again. We are a great nation, but if we continue to behave like a Great Power we shall soon cease to be a great nation' – received, at the very moment of her arrival in power, an eerie modern gloss from the British ambassador in Paris. Sir Nicholas Henderson, whose confidential valedictory despatch in June 1979 contrived to be published in full, offered a less elegant, but no less telling, update. 'Our decline in relation to our European partners', Henderson wrote, 'has been so marked that today we are not only no longer a world power, but we are not in the first rank even as a European one.'[8]

The three parts of Mrs Thatcher's response to this condition were phases first of triumph, then of confusion, and finally of collapse.

*

NOT ALL THE EUROPEAN business she inherited was unfinished. The thing had not been a total failure for Britain. Since the moment of entry, there had already been some gratifying successes. Food prices were one example. Predicted, even by Heath, to rise by 16 per cent, in the first two years they actually fell – by just over 1 per cent.[9] Britain paid that much less inside the Nine than she would have done outside, because world food prices happened to rise above the level at which they had been fixed in the Community. In some later years of the 1970s, Britain did have to pay more. But here was a case that showed how little was predictable in the finances of the Common Market.

More viscerally pleasing was what had happened to the status of the English language. This was a triumph to satisfy even the most sceptical Thatcherite. In the Heath negotiations, language had been a problem. Con O'Neill even offered the opinion that France's fears for the primacy of French 'had lain for years behind earlier French determination to exclude us from the Community ... It was seldom referred to in public; but it loomed and swelled in the background.'[10]

Heath, to placate Pompidou, had said that the old linguistic ascendancy would be sustained, and he instructed British officials, when they arrived in Brussels, to continue the practice under which all negotiation was conducted in French. It was a moral obligation he felt it incumbent on him to fulfil. The Danes and the Irish, however, had given no such undertaking, and made clear from the start that they wanted to speak English. Even though the Dane in question spoke excellent French, he was under instruction from Copenhagen to use his even better English. Once that happened, the Englishman, Michael Palliser, decided it was a practical impossibility for him not to do likewise. At that point, however, other national representatives were under their own instructions to take defensive action against both English and French. An elaborate minuet began in the Committee of Permanent Representatives, or Coreper, in which the Italian, another good French speaker, started speaking Italian, and the Dutchman Dutch. Michael Palliser, the Englishman in question, recalled: 'We had the effect, more through the Danes and the Irish, of turning the committee into a Tower of Babel.'[11] But the consequence was to erode the supremacy of French. Texts in other languages slid quietly into Euro-practice. By the time Mrs Thatcher came to power, French was no longer the exclusive first-draft usage. English was on the way to a place of equality, even, in practice, superiority.

Money, however, remained an unresolved problem. The Heath arrangement had left open the possibility that, if an 'unacceptable situation' arose concerning the British contribution to the Community budget, something would be done. That was what the Wilson renegotiation had mainly been about; but it had produced no more money. The formula depended on many elements, the net effect of which was to disadvantage a member state which (a) collected more tariffs and levies on goods imported from outside the EEC, and (b) had an efficient agriculture sector, with much lower manpower costs than other members, and was therefore rewarded with much lower subsidies from Brussels. This was a description of Britain. Labour had got the formula adjusted, to give more weight to national wealth: gross national product per head. By 1970, after all, Britain was already less rich, in those terms, than France, Denmark or the Netherlands. However, with North Sea oil on stream by the later 1970s, the Wilson formula produced nothing. Some richer countries continued to be net beneficiaries, while the new Thatcher Government was looking at a net contribution in 1980 of £1,000 million, rising fast.

The very calculation of this figure was, in its way, a heresy. Community idealism had always frowned on the concept of a fair national return, the infamous *juste retour*. This was not supposed to be the way true Europeans thought about their joint endeavour, an elevated view which did not, however, exclude certain more familiar considerations. The net beneficiaries didn't want the net balances even to be published. 'The Danes, in particular,' writes Michael Butler, one of the Foreign Office's champion number-crunchers at the time, 'were passionate in their opposition, lest giving publicity to their net gains lead to their erosion.'[12] So great was the commitment to the pooling of resources, after their collection according to the neutral formula laid down, that some continentals had serious difficulty understanding why the British had a problem. Butler and David Hancock, the Treasury man in charge, were reduced to drawing elementary graphics in order to explain how British taxpayers' money was being routed into the pockets of German farmers. 'There was a real intellectual problem,' Hancock told me. 'Some of them couldn't see what the fuss was about.'[13]

The new Prime Minister, immediately briefed, had no such difficulty. The sensibility of 'Europe' was soon swept aside, and the *juste retour* enshrined in the demotic: 'our money', sometimes corrupted into 'my money', became the watchword, and the demand for its return the focal point of all Mrs Thatcher's early forays into European diplomacy. It was, for her, an almost perfect issue. The problem suited her angular mind and her instinct for aggression. It was very black-and-white. The outcome, instead of being lost in swathes of Euro-babble, would be starkly measurable. There would be a winner and a loser, and only the winner would have justice on her side.

The battle over the budget contribution, however, set the scene for contests which lasted much longer, against two categories of enemy that became a demonic presence in Mrs Thatcher's world throughout her decade in power.

In the first category were the other European leaders. She met them early, and did not like what she found. Her first foreign visitor to Downing Street was Helmut Schmidt, the German Chancellor, with whom, in one way, she got on quite well. Though Schmidt, as leader of the Social Democrats, was theoretically a socialist, she sometimes joked with him that, being seriously interested in market economics, he was well to the right of half her Cabinet. Their relationship testified to her ability to rise above, or perhaps descend below, mere ideology to make instantaneous judgements about whether X or Y was someone with whom, almost chemically, she could do business. I even found the same myself: despite producing a good deal of critical journalism, I was somehow never banished to the darkness, and was even credited as a person with 'convictions'. So it was, at a much superior level, with politicians. Just as there were progressives she could tolerate, there were conservatives she disliked, and high in this category was Schmidt's European partner, Valéry Giscard d'Estaing, the French President, whom the British leader thought cold and patronizing. 'Olympian, but not patrician', she acutely called him.

Over the budget question, they were both her enemies. When the matter came for what was supposed to be settlement, at a summit in Dublin six months after she got in, she inaugurated the new, Thatcher, era of European diplomacy. It was to be characterized, on her part, by hideously plain speaking, and a triumphant lack of sensitivity to other people's problems.

The Europeans behaved badly at Dublin. In response to her unsubtle demands for a fair deal, they were rude and derisive, and determined not to meet her anywhere near halfway. Roy Jenkins, a witness, writes that Schmidt feigned sleep during one of her harangues. At another point, Giscard had his motorcade drawn up at the door, engines revving, to signal that he would delay no longer. 'I will not allow such a contemptible spectacle to occur again,' he said as he departed. On the other hand, the lady's own performance had broken all the rules. She marked out the last ditch she would defend with total intransigence for as long as it took. The smootheries of conventional diplomacy, the spirit of give-and-take on which the whole European edifice depended, were plainly values she could never be relied on to observe.

No deal was done at Dublin, and, as the argument rumbled on, the other object of Mrs Thatcher's undying suspicion began to emerge clearly into view: the Foreign Office, and – a rather larger compass – all who stood in unquestioning emulation of the Foreign Office attitude to international life.

Quite a lot had happened to the Foreign Office since the days of Roger Makins and Gladwyn Jebb, and even since those when John Robinson was holding the European fort. Europeanism, non-existent in the 1950s, remained an eccentric allegiance as late as the middle 1960s. Since Britain was still outside, Community affairs hadn't yet become the obvious career-path of choice for all young diplomats in search of stimulus and influence. Older men had to see their careers out, and older men were Commonwealth or American men, not, by and large, Europeanistas. Equally, however, the middle generation was moving towards the higher reaches, and this group was different, being constituted by many of the people who had once despaired of the Euro-scepticism above them.

In the topmost place, when she got in, Mrs Thatcher found ensconced none other than Michael Palliser. Palliser, a two-time veteran of the Paris embassy, hand-holder to both Wilson and George Brown during their European ventures, first UK mission chief to the European Communities after the joining, continued to regard the closer union of Europe as the core British interest the Foreign Office should be defending. He had lived and breathed it throughout his professional life, and was now at the head of the institution that could do most to advance it.

He was not alone. The Office Mrs Thatcher inherited was, according to David Owen, who bequeathed it, a hotbed of Euro-federalism. In his memoirs, Owen writes about this aspect of his time as Foreign Secretary with some venom. A number of officials, he says, 'had become zealots for the European Community and all its works'. Instead of behaving like diplomats, they had taken up 'a campaigning role'. Too many were reluctant to do anything that would put them at loggerheads with the rest of the Community, still less to 'spill a little blood on the diplomatic carpets of Europe', which was Owen's own ambition from time to time. Nor did they easily submit to political control. Owen notes scornfully that the politicians they mainly associated with – Heath, Jenkins, Grimond – 'were federalists, and when I joined the Foreign Office they too easily assumed . . . that I would be too'.[14]

With uncharacteristic tact, Owen withholds the names of the officials he has in mind. And he probably exaggerates the semi-conspiratorial influence he attributes to them. There were certainly diplomats who didn't accord with his description. But it is not hard to know the people he was talking about. One of them, I easily surmise, is Palliser, a man Owen says he 'liked and respected', but whom he then compares, under the thinnest disguise, with the patriotic high-flyers of the Quai d'Orsay who 'talk European and think France', who 'fight at every level for France', unlike the British, who mostly lacked the tenacity to do likewise. Another name surely marked by Owen's federalist stigma is that of Michael Butler, a cunning, thick-skinned negotiator, whose passion for 'Europe' nonetheless implies a view of the British interest that would be uncongenial to a nationalist politician, whether one at heart a European, like David Owen, or an anti-European, like Margaret Thatcher. Other figures who could easily have attracted Owen's suspicion were John Fretwell, later ambassador in Paris, Michael Jenkins, a Europeanist many times over, who finished his career as ambassador to the Netherlands, and Christopher Mallaby, soon to go to Bonn.

It is not a crime to be a federalist, and, besides, the term has a variety of meanings. Few of these distinguished public servants would accept the label without careful qualification. The two I asked, Palliser and Butler, denied the charge as made, each producing a set of definitional nuances that rendered it meaningless. Nevertheless, officials are not elected politicians, and are wont to have less sensitivity than ministers to problems of popular consent. Their institutional bias is to get things done, to wrap up the business, to achieve consensus between the high negotiating parties without excessive regard for the possibly cussed reaction of the mob: indeed, perhaps seeing their public duty as being to help their minister forget such considerations, which might otherwise divert him from the national interest. Making 'Europe' work, which inevitably meant reducing to their lowest the imperatives of narrow nationalism, was the institutional bias of the Foreign Office when it came under Mrs Thatcher's command.

She had some difficulty commanding it. When, a little later, she found an ambassador in Paris by the name of Reg Hibbert, who urged her to keep up the heat on the French in some negotiation, she was amazed, and inquired how he had ever been appointed.[15] In fact Hibbert, a noted contrarian, whose previous ambassadorship was in Outer Mongolia, was put there by Owen. For the rest, she found people who far from satisfied her requirement that they be One of Us. 'I think she tended to feel that the Foreign Office was so committed that it wasn't on our side at all,' Lord Hunt of Tanworth said.[16] Along with its ministers, it was horrified by what had happened in Dublin, and these ministers, Lord Carrington and Sir Ian Gilmour, wet Europeanists both, were left the task of picking up the pieces.

Another lesson in diplo-Thatcherism had to be taught them first, however. The Dublin offer was for a refund of no more than £350 million, one-third of the British deficit: quite unacceptable. The Thatcher demand was for 'broad balance' in the sums, which, interpreted literally, would have required the whole imbalance to be wiped out. The Foreign Office set its sights on two-thirds, and, through a series of complex formulae and adjustments batted to and fro with Schmidt's and Giscard's people, got close to a net figure which was near that. But it offered no permanent promises for the future. The discrepancies produced by the system would remain as irritants every time the budget came up. It took another FO negotiation, using FO methods, which included a modest amount of stick as well as carrot, to reach the two-thirds reduction for two years, with the promise, in certain circumstances, of a third.

What was seen as a triumph by Carrington and Gilmour was regarded differently elsewhere. This was the lesson. No negotiation could be permitted smoothly to succeed if it was conducted by a minister other than the Prime Minister. Farcical and phoney scenes had to be gone through before a deal was recognized as done. The ministers, arriving at Chequers uncertain what to expect from the compromise they had agreed over the midnight oil in Brussels, were met by the leader's almost uncontrollable wrath. As she appeared at the door, Gilmour recalled, she was 'like a firework whose fuse had already been lit; we could almost hear the sizzling'.[17] She accused them of giving in, and settling for a worse deal than she had already rejected. Officials were summoned to settle the point one way or the other. The Treasury official, Rachel Lomax, then a relatively junior economist who happened to be on duty when the telephone rang, briefed herself in the car to Chequers, and proved, perhaps woman to woman, to be the only person capable of persuading the Prime Minister, calmly but insistently, that the figures added up to Britain's advantage. 'It was beautifully done,' writes Gilmour. 'What a pity, I thought, that Mrs Lomax is not in charge of the economy.'

After many hours of rancid discussion, followed by a full Cabinet meeting, the new arrangement was accepted, though in the leader's case still through gritted teeth. As an early indicator of the Europe problem and the Thatcher way of meeting it, the episode had aspects which are of some enduring interest.

At this stage, for example, the issue remains one of cost, not sovereignty. The lady's ferocity is addressed to the unfairness of the balance-sheet, not the existence of the enterprise. Though exulting in her freedom to break the diplomatic rules and cause maximum annoyance, she is playing the Community game, albeit with a ruthlessness hitherto visible only behind the better manners of the French.

Moreover, she was addressing a real, undeniable problem. The budget imbalance was the product of a financial scheme quite deliberately set in place, under French direction, before the Heath negotiation began, to ensure that within the existing *acquis*, the European patrimony, another item was stacked against the British. It wasn't the first time such a ploy had been worked. Both the Common Agricultural Policy and, even more particularly, the Common Fisheries Policy, were concluded under pressure of the applications for membership from a country, Britain, that stood to be disadvantaged by them. The loophole in the budget rules – the allowance for a possibly 'unacceptable situation' that needed to be changed – was one of which the British were absolutely entitled to take advantage, if they could negotiate an outcome. The seven-year transitional phase Heath and Pompidou originally negotiated was, in any case, coming to an end as Mrs Thatcher took over.

But, in the negotiating task, normal manners had got nowhere. Though both Roy Jenkins and Ian Gilmour claim in their memoirs that the Thatcher style gained nothing extra, several officials I interviewed – Palliser, Butler, Hancock, David Hannay, most of the suspect *galère* – more or less disagreed. Some with reluctance, others like Hannay with bullish enthusiasm, thought her method, which was not always their method, had paid off. The budget question had to be settled, and her abrasion contributed to what amounted to a three-year deal. The spectacle of Helmut Schmidt kicking the furniture and unleashing a volley of German oaths after Mrs Thatcher had left the room, during an intervening summit in Luxembourg, was one that Michael Butler appears to have found thoroughly amusing.[18]

The story, moreover, had a satisfactory outcome. We leap forward four years from the Chequers fiasco: past the Falklands War, past the 1983 election landslide, into the middle Thatcher years when she was operating in all her amplitude. In that time, the 1980 formula had produced mixed results, again contingent on the impossibility of predicting EEC budgetary flows, which were themselves mainly influenced by the vagaries of agricultural production. For example, in 1981, amazingly, the British contribution netted out at merely *2 per cent* of the 1980 forecast.[19] In 1982, by contrast, the agreed deal was higher than predicted. But, in any case, these year-by-year haggles could not last. Though there had been the three-year comfort period, it guaranteed nothing for the future. The potential for continuing inequity, with Britain the substantial loser, remained. Any Prime Minister, whatever their position on the spectrum, would have been obliged to fight hard against it.

The 1984 contest ranged Mrs Thatcher against a new cast of main characters, who were to have more influence than their predecessors on her life. By now she was plainly at least an equal, rather than the tyro needing to go to extreme lengths to establish her position against Schmidt and Giscard. This was the mature Thatcher, who was dealing, however, with two new men who, in different ways, personified the Europe that disturbed and finally unhinged her.

Schmidt was succeeded in 1982 by Helmut Kohl who, as a Christian Democrat, nominally a conservative, might have been expected to be more like a kindred spirit to the British leader. But the law of perverse outcomes, an ordinance frequently at work in the radiations of the Thatcher personality, continued to operate. Kohl, a pawky Rhinelander, was a very German politician. He was not by instinct or formation an internationalist, like Schmidt. Nor was he, as a Christian Democrat, fully versed in the liberal economics now raging through the decimated heartlands of industrial Britain. Schmidt made no secret of his disagreements with Mrs Thatcher, and his near-contempt for her view of the EEC as an arena where the only thing that mattered was to be seen as 'winning': in conversation with me in 1985, he likened her, in this respect, to Harold Wilson.[20] But Schmidt she could understand, whereas Kohl she spent eight years regarding as a pain: verbose and difficult, and, more to the point, a leader whose views of the European project conferred on it steadily larger grandeur, even as hers were moving in the opposite direction towards, if possible, the complete unfettering of the nation-states.

They could not, for a start, speak the same language, a misfortune that partly lay behind her nickname for him: the gasbag. Often though they met, they never seemed to get any closer. For this she was most to blame, according to one of her devoted admirers, Charles Powell, her foreign affairs private secretary for six years. Powell, whose own Euroscepticism marched in line with hers, described to me how courteous Kohl invariably was, bringing her little gifts he had personally chosen, escorting her round his home town, trying to convince her that he was

'not German but European', as he once confided to the private secretary.
'I think Chancellor Kohl deserves great credit for working very hard on
the relationship,' Powell said. 'To be honest, he worked harder at it than
she did.'[21] But he did not succeed. Mrs Thatcher was both careless and
atavistically alarmed. Once, visiting the Rhineland-Palatinate in Kohl's
company, she responded to the welcoming ceremony by saying how
much pleasure it gave her to be in France.[22] Throughout, as Powell
reflected elsewhere, she was in thrall to childhood memories. 'For a small
girl growing up in Grantham,' he said, 'the Germans were about as evil
as anything you could think of.'[23] This opinion, though displaced by the
rise of Soviet communism, was never entirely abandoned.

As regards Britain's budget problem in 1984, however, Kohl was not
the prime object of Mrs Thatcher's attention. The moment of decision
coincided with France's term as president of the Council, which elevated
to critical prominence the other new butt of the Thatcherite approach to
Europe, François Mitterrand.

Giscard's successor as French president, a socialist, was, in historic
terms, hardly new at all. He was elected president, after many years'
trying, in 1981. Like Kohl, he came out of the deep past, formed and
tempered by the defining event that had been the origin of this 'Europe'
in which all leaders were now engaged. More passionately than Schmidt
and Giscard, Kohl and Mitterrand articulated an emotional commitment
to the European idea fashioned in the experience of war, which Kohl
(born 1930) had spent as a young spectator in the killing fields along
the Rhine, and Mitterrand (born 1916) as a shadowy operator in the
Resistance who still managed to keep his connections with the Vichy
Government.

These men were almost different species from Margaret Thatcher.
But the German and the Frenchman had swapped places in her esteem.
She admired Mitterrand almost as much as she disliked Kohl. Despite
being a socialist, Mitterrand had intellectual quality. 'He is a philosopher,
which she would like to be but isn't,' Powell once told me. Beside an
extraordinary political career, in which he was the left's presidential
candidate against de Gaulle as long ago as 1965, and then against Giscard
in 1974, ran a capacity for grandiose reflection which, oddly, Mrs
Thatcher did not always resist. A scornful enemy of Euro-guff – the
sweeping visions and journeys-without-maps which were alien to British
temperaments far beyond her own – she nevertheless appreciated a class
intellect when she saw one. Mitterrand's broad literary culture – he

could recite from memory the last lines of 'Ulysses', for example[24] – was something she could admire without ever approaching it herself.

Mitterrand, for his part, was fascinated by the lady, at least at the beginning. She was not without charm, and he not without a susceptibility to it. He once famously advised his Minister for Europe, Roland Dumas, to be aware of her dangerous qualities. 'Cette femme Thatcher!' he reputedly said. 'Elle a les yeux de Caligule, mais elle a la bouche de Marilyn Monroe.' Claude Cheysson, the Foreign Minister, observed the two together often. 'I've always been amazed by their mutual fascination,' he said. 'Each looked at the other, wondering how someone so strange could exist, trying to grasp who he or she was.'[25]

In 1984, they had each reached an important moment. For its first few years, the Mitterrand Government all but ignored Europe. The French Socialist Party was pursuing socialist economic policies that put it at odds with Germany. By March 1983, with the leftist faction in command, there had been two devaluations of the franc inside the European Monetary System, from which France was threatened with exclusion if she attempted a third. Only at this moment did Mitterrand change course, reinstating a more conventional economic policy and, at the same time, determining to get much more involved in the evolution of Europe. Indeed, he intended 'relaunching' Europe, along with himself. A senior French diplomat observed sardonically: 'Monsieur Mitterrand's term as president of the European Council has become his road to Damascus.'[26]

His involvement in this presidency was arguably greater than that of any national leader occupying the same six-month position in the history of the EEC. He began by touring all the capitals of the Nine, while Foreign Minister Dumas engaged in regular shuttle diplomacy between Paris, Bonn and London. Just as Pompidou's 1971 *démarche* over British entry had to be kept secret from the officials of the Quai d'Orsay, these efforts by Mitterrand were conducted against the opposition of the Quai and also his own left wing. Nonetheless, in this short period he met six times each with Kohl and Thatcher for bilateral talks. 'Europe', he had warned at the start of his term, 'is beginning to look like an abandoned building site.'[27] He was entirely committed to resuming construction, the principle edifices being agricultural reform, the accession of Spain and Portugal, the liberalization of the internal market and an increase in Community funds. Looming as an obstruction to all this dynamism, though, was the net British contribution to the budget.

This had already gone through many phases. The 1980 formula did not preclude an annual haggle over its particulars. Now, however, there appeared a possible parting of the ways. For, although Mitterrand wanted the question settled, he wasn't prepared to make all the concessions. It was in 1984 that talk of a Europe of two speeds – the ins and the outs, the core and the periphery, other incessantly deconstructed metaphors of what he now called *la géométrie variable* – began seriously to be heard, though it had been canvassed a decade earlier, in the Tindemans Report, as a way round the impediments placed by a previous British (Labour) government. With a summit due in June, at Fontainebleau, both Kohl and Mitterrand made clear their determination to move forward on a unity agenda, towards the completion of the internal market and more majority voting. Kohl said that the 'decisive conditions had been created'. Dumas, on Mitterrand's behalf, said that, if a budget agreement was not reached, France would call a meeting without the British to discuss political reform.

Thus, a repeat beckoned, on a smaller scale, of 1955, with another display of self-excluding British stubbornness which could never be relied on to impress the continentals. This has been the pattern of the relationship for half a century, hardly less visible in the 1990s than at moments in every other decade. The tactic of leaving an 'empty chair', and obstructing all Community business by refusing to attend, may have been exclusively a French device. But the British deployed an opposite and equal effect. They alone were able to exasperate other members almost enough to have an empty chair forced upon them.

On her way to Fontainebleau, Mrs Thatcher told the British officials travelling with her that she thought the meeting was doomed. Just before, she had let it be known how unimpressed she was by the threat of a two-speed Europe, and what it really meant. 'Let me tell you what I mean,' she told a newspaper, with characteristic subtlety. 'Those who pay most are the top group and those who pay less are not.'[28] In the car, she said: 'We're never going to settle this thing.' Her belief was that Mitterrand would refuse to move, even though it had been Kohl who got in the way of a previous near-deal in March. After all, any concession to the British, however justified in equity and logic, would be paid for by larger contributions from the others, which meant, in major effect, Germany.

By the time they reached Fontainebleau, the matter was down to a single issue. The structure of the arithmetic on which the British abatement should be calculated – the VAT factor, the tariffs and levies factor, the scalings down and leverings up, the link with an increase in the Community's total resources, and all the other haggled computations that are the stuff of Euro-negotiators' lives while remaining for ever outside the comprehension of every normal European citizen – was just about agreed. What it came down to was a percentage figure and a time-span. What per cent of the contribution that Britain was due to make under the regular rules would be deducted on account of Britain's special position? And would this last indefinitely?

Mrs Thatcher was determined to get 66 per cent, worth around £1,000 million of public spending: the cost, say, of the entire family doctor service in Britain. The occasion was laid on with a grandeur that fitted the spacious ambitions Mitterrand had set himself, but it got off to a start of precisely the unbusinesslike kind the lady most detested. First the French, aided by the European Commission, sought to set a time-limit on any deal, and to hustle it through in two hours before dinner. Then the President spent much of the meal briefing the colleagues about his recent visit to Moscow, which was followed by Kohl's interminable account of a journey to Hungary he had recently returned from. These were pitiful distractions from serious business. The British briefed scornfully against the Germans. Mrs Thatcher, retreating to confer with her officials, fumed against the general lack of gratitude. 'How on earth can Britain be treated in this way?' Robin Renwick remembered her saying. 'After all, we saved all their skins in the war.'[29]

When they got down to business next day, it was after all-night negotiations between officials. But the business, at European Council summits, is unusually dependent on the performance of the principals. Officials are seldom admitted to the room. Prime Minister and Foreign Secretary have to do the work themselves, and quite often the Prime Minister is alone with the peer-group. This was an aspect of the task at which Mrs Thatcher was uncommonly good. Not only was she briefed in great detail, a British style growing out of Question Time in Parliament, and also out of the British cultural obsession with the precise rather than the aspirational aspects of negotiation. She could take and remember the briefing to formidable effect, and was always armed with little lists, known to the officials who supplied them either as 'stiletto points' or, alternatively, 'handbag points', with which she would prick or batter her adversaries.

When the end-game started, most of the others, according to Michael Butler, who was in the thick of it, were talking a maximum of 55 per cent, while the leader's instruction to the British was to talk about

70.[30] 'It was quite *impossible* to go below that,' one of them was told, 'there could be no whisper of a thought of it *in any circumstances whatever.*' Many hours intervened. Talking along these lines continued. The Germans, 'a rugger scrum . . . round the massive figure of Chancellor Kohl', writes Butler, eventually said that 60 per cent was their limit, while Mitterrand, desiring to be the orchestrator of a settlement, said he might be pushed to 65.

Gathering her officials together, Mrs Thatcher found them of one mind. These were not, it should be noted, a collective from yester-year, the old gang, as she had perceived it, of typical Foreign Office gentlemen always prone to regard the other side as having a decent, or even the better, case. Butler and Renwick were hard-headed, highly combative men, aggressive and devious to a fault. Together with David Williamson, an old Community hand whom Butler describes as a born negotiator, they reached the conclusion, as did Geoffrey Howe, the Foreign Secretary, that they had got everything they could. And she agreed. 'It's time to settle,' she immediately said – but with one more shot to call, a percentage point which, if gained, would be worth at least £150 million to Britain over the next ten years. Approaching Mitterrand once more, she duly got it. It would be very helpful, she said, if she could hit the two-thirds mark, 66 not 65 per cent, to last for as long as the Community's take from VAT collected was pegged at the new ceiling of 1.4 per cent. The EC's desperate need for this new ceiling, up from 1 per cent, to pay its escalating farm subsidies, gave the British their negotiating leverage. And the Council, led by the President, surrendered, as the price for moving on to other things – such minor matters as the liberalization of the internal market, the abolition of customs controls, the radical reform of the institutions.

Mrs Thatcher, in her hour of victory, appeared to go along with these signs of the relaunch Mitterrand had set himself to getting started. She talked quite happily in terms of forward momentum. Reporting back to Parliament, she said: 'The way is now clear for the completion of the Common Market in goods and services.' Speaking to the Franco-British Council, she sounded almost ecstatic about the possibilities for collaboration across the board, listing as European objectives 'greater unity of the Community market, greater unity of Community actions in world affairs, greater unity of purpose and action in tackling unemployment and the other problems of our time'.[31] What a litany! No line was drawn, or so it seemed, beyond which 'Europe' might not have a beneficent role. Language which no Conservative politician, even of a pro-Europe persuasion, would comfortably be using in a decade's time now cascaded from the Thatcher lips. The deepest-dyed symbols of an entente were, at this stage, capable of being congenial to her. Visiting Paris in November 1984, for example, she took the first diplomatic steps towards Anglo-French agreement to build a tunnel under the Channel.

Such was the personal effect of a famous victory. She had been very effective, laying waste all critics of her confrontational methods. Emile Noël, the legendary French civil servant who was secretary-general of the Commission from the EEC's inception until 1987, told me that she 'obtained much more than was reasonable', an achievement for which the British taxpayer ought to be grateful.[32] 'The British got more than they really needed – in the opinion of a poor official!' The cost to the other members, Noël thought, had been outrageously high.

But, from now on, things got more complicated.

*

THE THATCHER TECHNIQUE was brilliantly successful in a certain task. It got the money back. She could measure the victory, and gloat over the consequences. But it had its costs, and these weren't a matter of mere caprice or jealousy on the other side. The confrontational method, even when deployed only once, cashed in a lot of chips, in a game where every player has only a limited number and can't acquire more by simply shouting.

Winning on the budget, especially in the way she chose, which was probably the only way she knew how, meant *inevitably* paying a price in other spheres. Her bad manners were certain to worsen the manners of everyone else she would need to help her at some other time. They raised the temperature and burned in the memory. They were the weapons of a leader who took a narrow view of her objective, forgetting that every other leader round the table was as much or little a sovereign leader as she was, with pride to salvage and voters to please, and just as deeply held a view of how Europe should develop. This was, after all, meant to be a team, an alliance, a jousting but ultimately fraternal partnership. For a body created to prevent war, battle was exquisitely inappropriate as the driving metaphor one of its members brought to the table. The Community way, which grew out of the coalition politics every continental politician absorbed at kindergarten, involved give-and-take, log-rolling, back-scratching, all rooted in a concept of 'victory' that couldn't be defined by anything as simple as the short-term interest of one country.

The mismatch between the Thatcher mind and the European mind took time to reach a climax. She went on thinking she could fashion Europe to her advantage, and in some measure she did. But in the second phase, the transitional sequence, there began to emerge the unsettling sense that she didn't know what she was doing.

As she told Parliament after Fontainebleau, the way was now open for great developments. The period of stasis, though she never used such a regretful expression, could be ended, with the Common Market being stripped of its protectionism and made truly common or, better put, free. She now had a project for Europe, the single market, to which, banishing most traces of scepticism, she was able to apply her talent for messianic zeal. It was the high point of her vision – the only time, indeed, when such a word could be aptly applied to her continental attitudes – yet within it can be seen the start of her undoing.

The single market was not a Thatcher idea, but a collective aspiration. As everybody knew, it made no sense, in a so-called Common Market, to have succeeded in lowering customs barriers but to leave in place many other blockages to open business dealings. So-called 'non-tariff' barriers, brought on especially by the 1970s recession, were ranged throughout the system: all the panoply of different national standards on safety, health, the environment: of half-closed frontiers across which labour and capital and services could not freely move: of discrimination against foreign products or tendering for public procurement: all the fences and ditches and slopes and biases that precluded the creation of that distinctively 1990s cliché, the level playing-field. The market could not be free or single until these had been removed. The Commission had long desired to do this, and the lists of what needed to be done had languished in its drawers for years. But now a critical mass assembled for action. To Mitterrand's desire for a relaunch, and Mrs Thatcher's perception of a single market beckoning, was added a third element, the arrival in the Commission presidency of a politician who wished to make something significant out of it, Jacques Delors.

Delors, at this stage, was a man the British much admired. There were, as ever, complications about the succession to his crucial post, which in theory was meant to go to a German. It was the Germans' turn. But they had recently done rather well in the international market for big jobs, and, in any case, also said they did not have a suitable candidate for the new vacancy. They ceded their place to France. Britain much preferred Delors to the Frenchman who was first put up, the Foreign Minister Claude Cheysson. Cheysson was regarded as uninterested in liberalizing the market, and besides, according to Robin Renwick, he had been 'absolutely hopeless' during the budget negotiations.[33] Delors, by contrast, was the Finance Minister who master-minded Mitterrand's reversion from socialism. He was a financial disciplinarian. 'He began imposing our policies,' Howe noted with admiration, 'a finance minister after our own hearts.'[34] Though talking left, he acted right. On Europe, however, he was an unknown quantity, as Howe, speaking ten years later, rather plaintively remembered: 'One never knows, you see, when people arrive in that job.'

It did not take Delors long to hit on his own project for the relaunch of Europe, though he came to it from an unThatcherite position. He favoured the single market because it made political sense: it was congruent with the right-wing ascendancies then to be found in many of the member countries. It also made economic sense, with a period of strong growth – always the condition in which the Community thrived – on the horizon.[35] But, for Delors, it had little to do with any deregulatory passion shared with the British. He was a tough, *dirigiste* French socialist, out of the Catholic social tradition. He was also an acquiescent, though not recklessly proactive, federalist. He became, in the European context, the enemy Mrs Thatcher often seemed to need for the successful prosecution of the politics of battle. The names of many defeated enemies were gouged on her tally-stick: Galtieri of Argentina, Scargill of the miners, Heath of Old Conservatism. Here was a European candidate who might soon be fit to join them.

This wasn't the tenor, however, of the first phase of Delors. There were difficulties, of a personal kind that Mrs Thatcher, as many rivals found, had an uncontrollable instinct to inflame. She was very patronizing, as if the president were no more than a bureaucratic flunky. At one early press conference which they were supposed to be conducting jointly, she left no space for him to speak, and, as her long harangues drew to a close, addressed him thus: 'Would you very kindly confirm that what I said was absolutely strictly accurate and that you are looking forward to this, and rising to the challenge it represents, and that you will hope to solve it during your coming two years of presidency of the Commission?' To Delors' monosyllabic grunt, she responded: 'I had no idea you were such a strong silent man.'[36] It was a snubbing Delors did not forget.

But in the beginning they shared an objective. And to advance it they brought in a man they both admired, though not at the same time. The Delors Commission, which started work in January 1985, produced a general post among commissioners and, most spectacularly, the rise to prominence of one of the odder protagonists in this story, a man named Arthur Cockfield.

Cockfield was an operator in the interstices between business and government, of long pedigree but almost zero visibility. Qualified as a barrister, he had joined the Inland Revenue as a tax inspector as long ago as 1938, rising high in that organization before starting a new career at the head of Boots Pure Drug Co., which he ran for much of the 1960s. He had his first public job under the Heath Government, as head of the Price Commission, a nerve-centre of the corporatism of the day. But hardly had Mrs Thatcher, the anti-corporatist, supplanted Heath as Tory leader than Cockfield was handed a peerage and a seat beside her as a kind of ideas-man, an apolitical wheeze-merchant, her loyal, unambitious, creative antidote to the scheming, soft-headed paternalists she was obliged to keep in the Cabinet. In 1982, Cockfield reached the Cabinet himself, as Secretary of State for Trade, a post in which his eccentricity proved as notable as his business sense. Reluctant to travel without his wife, but having a wife who resisted travelling anywhere by air, he once conducted a trade negotiation with Nigeria standing offshore, like an antique son of Empire, aboard an ocean liner.

To liberalize Europe's internal market, both Delors and Mrs Thatcher regarded Cockfield as the best-qualified agent. He set about the task with a purposefulness that soon proved more pleasing to the former than the latter, effecting as swift a transfer from the Thatcher project to the Delors as he had from the Heath to the Thatcher. Cockfield was that sort of man, anchored in the internal logic of whatever task he had been set, rather than riding the captious tides of what a real politician might call political reality. The technician became, in his way, an ideologue. What Howe, in his memoirs, called Cockfield's 'tenacious commitment' grew, as Mrs Thatcher saw it, into something more menacing. He seemed to move from deregulating the market, an authentic Thatcher goal, to reregulating it in the Delorsian name of harmonization. So zealous was he to strike down every barrier, even to the point of harmonizing national tax systems, that he became, she writes, 'the prisoner as well as the master of his subject'. 'Unfortunately,' she goes on, 'he tended to disregard the larger questions of politics – constitu-

tional sovereignty, national sentiment and the promptings of liberty . . .
It was not too long before my old friend and I were at odds.'[37]

It was a Frenchman who paid Cockfield the ultimate compliment,
by comparing him with Delors. Delors, he said, was the more intuitive
and flexible. But 'Cockfield is a cool Cartesian, whose logic is so deadly
that he can push systematically to extremes. You need that kind of mind
to work through the consequences of abolishing frontiers.'[38] Such a
laudatory epitaph from Paris was a kind of death-warrant in London.

Cockfield produced a white paper identifying 297 imperfections in
the single European market, with timetabled proposals for eliminating
them by 1992. At this stage, when they were still mere proposals, they
accorded with what Mrs Thatcher thought she wanted. She was still, by
her lights, in a 'European' phase – which is jolting to look back on from
the phobic years of her retirement. In the middle of 1985, she put
together and circulated a paper she calls 'ostentatiously *communautaire*',
which indeed it was. Not only did it talk about completing the internal
market, with decision-making changes to match, but it made the case
for a stronger European foreign policy, under the rubric of political co-
operation. The Falklands War, in which not every EC member had come
up to scratch, was still for her a living memory, and she thought 'how
valuable it would be if all Community members were prepared to
commit themselves to supporting a single member in difficulties'.[39]
'Europe: The Future', the document in question, might even be described
as a tentative approach towards that entirely unBritish concept, a phrase
never uttered by a British statesman in half a century, 'The Construction
of Europe'. Mrs Thatcher didn't go that far. But there was a whiff of
collaborative promise. This was a period in which the French newspaper
Le Matin could write of 'the spectacular evolution of the British position
. . . which will confuse those critics normally sceptical about Britain's
European enthusiasm'.[40]

There was, however, a limit. Britishness necessarily intervened, only
to be balked. How was the Cockfield–Delors programme actually to be
imposed? Mrs Thatcher and her Foreign Secretary favoured the informal
approach.

Plainly there would be no end to protection, no effective creation of
singleness, if any one country was able to block something it didn't like.
There would have to be, as all concerned seem to have recognized from
the start, an extension of qualified majority voting: a mechanism which
allocated voting weight to each country roughly according to its size,

and permitted a majority of such weighted votes to secure a decision binding on all members. It was known as QMV: one of the alphabetic short-hands which, along with ERM and IGC, came to occupy a special place of neuralgic infamy in Britain's later consideration of what 'Europe' meant, or might mean. But the method by which QMV would be installed, across a far wider range of Community business than it had ever touched before, was a question.

The Thatcher–Howe proposal was for a kind of constitutional convention – 'a concept more familiar to Anglo-Saxon than to continental minds', Howe concedes.[41] There would be a gentlemen's agreement, written but without legal force, to treat all the single-market agenda as though the unanimity rule had been set aside. For the British, accustomed to such half-worlds, this would be quite enough for QMV, and would have the merit of forestalling the need for an IGC, or inter-governmental conference, whose legalistic outcomes would in turn be capable of invoking the activity of another suspect abbreviation, the ECJ, or European Court of Justice. An IGC was the normal, indeed the only, way of securing amendments to the Treaty of Rome. The trick would be to pretend that QMV did not require such amendments. Above all, Britain wanted to avoid an IGC, which ministers felt might open the way for uncontrollable constitutional ventures, themselves likely to be federalistic, certain to be legalistic and, all in all, guaranteed to operate against the British interest. Even Howe, the European, felt this, though the Baroness, in her memoirs, charges him with giving in about it.

They were both, however, defeated. It was the first serious calamity of the Thatcher era, a pay-back, some said, for her discomfiting budget triumph. The Thatcher rule of negotiating conduct said that 'compromise' was an unmentionable word. This was formally laid down by No. 10, a curse on all normal diplomatic behaviour. In their briefs to the Prime Minister, throughout her time, officials were never allowed to use the term, commonplace though it was: they had to invent all kinds of circumlocution, if they were to do their job of giving tactical guidance on upcoming meetings. But in Milan, in June 1985, the tables were turned. No-compromise became the weapon of the other side. The European Council, the summit of leaders, did something it had never done before, taking a vote, which required only a simple majority, over the British leader's writhing, fuming body, to call an IGC.

The British went to Milan seriously believing this could not happen. They thought they had fixed enough support for their idea of a gentlemen's agreement. But meanwhile, there had been other developments propelling things in a different direction: the formal, dramatic, declaratory, treaty-bound direction most members usually preferred. At the very same time the budget deal was done at Fontainebleau, a committee was set up to investigate ways of making another leap forward in Europeanism. Chaired by an Irish politician, James Dooge, it was told to suggest improvements in European co-operation: which, by the time the caravan moved on to Milan, it had duly done.

Some of the Dooge proposals were congenial to the European Thatcher. They met her two largest demands: for a smoother internal market and closer political co-operation. But they were also, as she could see even then, ominous. They were an expression of momentum, of process, of the endless quest for ever closer intimacy under the Brussels umbrella. They talked about the 'achievement of a European social area', about 'institutional reform' and about the promotion of 'common cultural values': menacing portents of a new and pervasive unity, to be topped off by the rebranding of the Community as the 'European Union'. When the captains and the kings arrived in Milan, this was waiting on the table for their approval and, more particularly, for the summoning of an IGC which would certainly be the only way to enact its ambitious propositions.

At the beginning, it looked as though this might be avoided. Under the hand of Bettino Craxi, the Italian Prime Minister, the Thatcher approach seemed to gain ground. Craxi was 'sweetly reasonable' when the two of them talked, luring the lady into a state of security. 'I came away thinking how easy it had been to get my points across,' she writes.[42] Besides, she had taken trouble to get the Germans on side, entertaining Kohl for an entire, painful Saturday at Chequers. The first stage of Milan saw unanimous approval both for Cockfield's white paper and for the British proposal on informal improvements to decision-making.

But that didn't settle the matter. Both the Italians and the Germans turned out to be treacherous jades. The British idea wasn't seen as an alternative, but as a prelude to the real game. Discussion grew more rancorous, as Mrs Thatcher struggled to resist formal Treaty changes and the erosion of the Luxembourg Compromise – the Gaullist device of twenty years before, that had protected the veto rights of individual states. 'Margaret,' writes Howe, 'with more excuse for tetchiness than usual, contrived to get us emotionally aligned with [the Greek Prime Minister] Papandreou at his worst.'[43]

Then Craxi sprang his little trick. Without warning, he pressed for a vote on whether to hold an IGC, and easily secured his simple majority, a success Howe explains as 'a reaction above all to the sharp tone of British leadership'.

A decade later, Michael Butler, one of the posse of hard-faced Foreign Office men by Mrs Thatcher's side, was still ashamed of his lack of foresight. 'I was horrified at my own failure to see that this was what they would do to us if we went on being intransigent,' he told me in 1993. The British became nothing more than spectators at the Italians' 'enormous satisfaction' when they pulled off their coup.[44] For her part, the leader was furious at being bulldozed by a chairman she regarded as disgracefully partisan.

Her anger, however, did not yet drive her to folly. There now unfolded an example of something that became a Thatcher pattern through many of her European, and not only European, ventures. 'I saw it happen a thousand times,' said Butler, 'her reason overcoming her prejudices.' Instead of roaring out to denounce Craxi to the press, she listened almost immediately – it only took the lunch-break – to officials who pointed out the folly of declaring that she would have nothing to do with the IGC, which was her first instinct. The same prudence attended her report back to Parliament. Neither in hot blood nor in cold did she make anything so unwise as a pledge to reject any Treaty change. On the contrary, she sent her officials off to negotiate the kind of changes that would expedite internal-market decisions.

By this means Mrs Thatcher, instead of being the chief obstacle to further European union, became one of its chief architects. The Single European Act, which six months later became the concrete product of the Milan summit, was a fusion between the visions of Margaret Thatcher and Jacques Delors for the future of Europe. But for Thatcherites, and for the whole British argument against Europe, it has been alternatively a problem and an embarrassment ever since. So it merits some careful attention.

As the IGC proceeded, a sprawling agenda was laid before it, just as Mrs Thatcher feared. It was due to end in Luxembourg six months on, a tight schedule which assisted in limiting the scope and doing so quite largely in accordance with British desires. The British were the minimalists, and, since any changes needed unanimous support, the minimalists were strongly placed. They weren't alone. Other members, sometimes less voluble in their rhetoric, were as cautious in their surrenders of power, for example, to the European Assembly, now about to be called, at last, a Parliament. Small accretions were allowed to this body. Equally, the strengthening of co-operation on foreign policy was easily agreed.

There was more trouble over EMU, the dreaded economic and monetary union first cited as an aspiration in 1972 and never expunged from the gospel. Most continentals wanted to upgrade it to a Treaty objective, but the British would rather it weren't mentioned at all. They thought the Monetary System was progressing well enough on an informal basis. Here they lost a point. The Single European Act contains the first formal Treaty reference to EMU, albeit in a cautious mode that was to have much significance later. Any evolution of the Monetary System was listed as requiring unanimous approval: a condition which came controversially into its own, further down the line, in the Treaty of Maastricht 1992. The taxation ideas, apotheosis of Cockfield's harmonizing lunacy, as it was seen, were also kicked into the long grass with a heavy British boot.

These were satisfactory curtailments of what the Euro-visionaries, the Delors Commission among them, had hoped for. But the Single Act needed its positive side as well. This was the whole point of a strategy, the imperative British strategy, to liberalize the internal market in all the ways the British thought, for practical as well as ideological reasons, they could profit from. The new Treaty, if Treaty it had to be, needed to provide a thoroughgoing extension of majority rule for the immense range of decisions that touched on market matters. This was, in British parlance, a 'federal' proposition. It consciously diminished the power of nations, in these specific but large areas, to frustrate the collective will. Yet this did not debar it, in the slightest, from the approval of the British. Indeed, such a way of imposing a genuinely free market was allocated its own, faintly triumphalist, campaigning slogan: 'Thatcherism on a European scale'.

The British demanded, and got, one big exception to the regime of unimpeded movement. The island nation wanted to keep its right to control immigration. But, for the rest, the British placed their country not merely in compliance with, but rather in the vanguard of, the most practical advance towards the abolition of national frontiers and national powers that the Community had undertaken in the whole period of British membership. It had another wrinkle to it, moreover. There was a change in the power under which individual countries could secure exemptions. Under the Luxembourg Compromise, a nation could simply demand and exercise this power. After the Single European Act, a nation that needed an exemption from single-market rules by reason of *exigences importantes*, as they called them, put itself in the hands of the European Court if any other nation launched a challenge. The Court, along with the Commission – these supra-political embodiments of 'Europe' – were handed the power to determine what the Single Act, in hard cases, meant.

The Single Act was, in part, a triumph for Delors and Cockfield, though it didn't satisfy the president, who expressed himself dolefully about how little had been achieved. Most of Cockfield's 300 items had been put forward before by the Commission, but had always been rejected by the nation-states. The skill and drive of the two Commissioners now saw the Act past innumerable pitfalls. But it was also a triumph for Mrs Thatcher, in that, by common consent, the final agreement on most substantive issues satisfied the British more than anyone else.[45]

It certainly satisfied Mrs Thatcher. When she got back home, she called the result 'clear and decisive'. This reflected the general atmosphere in the Conservative Party at the time. Hardly anyone criticized the Act as a piece of crypto-federalism which wasn't all that crypto. The Prime Minister's enthusiastic report to Parliament was accepted in similar spirit.

Passage of the necessary measure was just as untroubled. When the European Communities (Amendment) Bill came to the Commons in April 1986, six days were required to see it through all its stages. After a mere three sessions in committee, a guillotine motion to cut off debate was proposed by the Government, through the mouth of the leader of the House, John Biffen. Biffen, who had been a Powellite on the subject of Europe many years before the term Euro-sceptic was invented, spoke to the motion with wry but determined awareness of what was now required, and it was carried by 270 votes to 153.

In the light of what happened later, the debate on the Bill deserves passing scrutiny. The Single Act, after all, was a major constitutional measure. Just as remarkable as the size of the majority for the guillotine was the indifference attending the matter in the minds of many MPs. On that occasion, with the Labour Party still supposedly in anti-European mode, there were 200 absentees from the vote. When it came to the third reading, the final moment of passage, there was an even more paltry tally of 149 supporters to 43 opponents. During the debates themselves there were contributions which, at the end of the 1990s, seem a little startling. Some of the usual suspects with whose names a later generation became all too familiar – Teddy Taylor, Tony Marlow, Nicholas Budgen – are to be found dominating the brief discussions that did take place, grinding on for some hours about the powers of the

European Court of Justice, and attacking, with Enoch Powell, the change of nomenclature by which the Assembly was to become a full-blown Parliament. But none of them joined their grand old hero in voting against the guillotine. Riotous rebellions on the Government back-benches, such as accompanied endorsement of the Treaty of Maastricht seven years later, were nowhere to be seen.

A fair number of latter-day sceptics supported the argument made with most notable passion by one George Gardiner, the MP for Reigate and a devoted Thatcher disciple, who in 1997 was so disgusted with the remnants of official Conservative Party enthusiasm for Europe that he fought the election in the interest of the Referendum Party instead. A decade earlier, Gardiner is to be found uttering a paean of desire for the 'economies of scale' of a united Europe to take on the Americans in high-tech industries, and making the case for qualified majority voting as the only way to defeat national protectionism.[46]

As we shall see, Gardiner was not alone in his painful lurching from one passion to another.[47] After a few years, many Conservatives were singing a different song about the Single Act. They came to regard it, not as a lynchpin of the liberalized market, but as an instrument through which the ever closer union of Europe made its way forward. They saw it, increasingly, as a moment of serious defeat, possibly of treachery against the nation: a treachery, even, for which they themselves might be somewhat responsible, and might therefore have a duty to make condign repentance by reneging on their own handiwork – however embarrassing such a manoeuvre is for any politician. Among these apostates was Baroness Thatcher herself. The architect of the Act became seriously disillusioned by its operation.

This raises quite a list of questions for the by-standing, voting citizen, who has no choice in high politics but to leave such important matters to the leaders of the day. What is he or she, who played no part in either the writing or the passing, to make of it? Was there some element of betrayal here, and if so, who betrayed whom? Did the continentals circumvent the revised Treaty of Rome, to accomplish more than they ever let on at the time? Or was it more a case of the British leader first misunderstanding what she was doing, and then, along with her allies in the party, searching for scapegoats to cover up what was either a change of perception or a change of heart?

There is no disputing that the Single Act worked both better and worse than its different founders intended. Delors and Thatcher saw it in different ways, and got different things from it. The more obvious parts of this outcome are the worst, the places where rather little happened, which Mrs Thatcher, presumably, should have had most cause to regret. For long after 1992, there continued to be many imperfections in the freedom of internal trade and movement. Some state-owned airlines, Air France conspicuous among them, were still being grotesquely over-compensated for their commercial failures, and the free markets in such sensitive services as banking and insurance were opened with agonizing reluctance. The cultural differences between the free-trading tradition, mostly but not entirely represented by Britain, and a continent with a long history of both social protection and privileged state enterprise, could not be wiped out by a single measure. The Act was the beginning not the end of a negotiation that would never cease.

This was one part the British didn't like. Nor were they invariably impressed by the ways in which the famous singleness – the harmoniza-tion, the union – did come about. They were soon confronted by the habit of the entire Euro-apparatus, mainly the Commission and the Court, of construing in a spirit of integration, when in doubt, the words with which the Act presented them. Incorporated in it, for example, was an article designed to achieve common standards of health and safety at work, a measure included in those that were manoeuvrable, like other level-playing-field items, by QMV. But what was 'health and safety', and where did you draw the line between it and general social policy, which required unanimous agreement? When attempts were made to broaden the definition, the British rightly felt cheated.

On the other hand, are we seriously to suppose that Mrs Thatcher had not examined the words she put her name to? This was the implication of the charge, familiar in the pathology of Euro-scepticism, that 'Europe' had somehow pulled a fast one. But, as to the words, there is copious evidence that she was aware, as her fascination with texts of all kinds would lead anyone to expect, of everything. I pressed a number of her officials about this. David Williamson, who at the time was her senior Europe adviser, said: 'I was present in 10 Downing Street on one occasion when Mrs Thatcher came down the stairs and said to me, "I have read every word of the Single European Act."'[48] For Michael Butler, any other behaviour would have been an offence against nature. 'I never remember an occasion in the six years when I worked for her', he told me, 'when she negotiated something without knowing what she was talking about.'[49] Geoffrey Howe says in his memoirs that she sat with the other leaders 'for no less than twenty-seven hours in two working days' talking through the draft of the Act, which was in any case quite largely a British text.[50]

So the notion that the Act, which she hailed as a triumph in December 1985, got past her on the basis of some kind of fraud will not do. But that doesn't mean she fully understood it. There is no necessary contradiction between British Tories, led by her ever more vocally in her retirement, saying that the Act did more than they intended, and this having come about, more than anything, through the peculiar combination of their innocence and hubris. Perhaps Mrs Thatcher wanted the Act to mean what she said it meant, and was simply not prepared to recognize that it might mean something else as well.

What it said in Article 1, for example, was: 'The European Communities and European Political Co-operation shall have as their objective to contribute together to making concrete progress towards European unity.' This came after a preamble that talked about furthering 'the European idea', protecting Europe's 'common interests', and 'investing this union with the necessary means of action'. Such federalist verbiage Mrs Thatcher, while signing up to it, was inclined to dismiss as claptrap that could safely be ignored. Asked about it in the Commons, she both chided and exonerated her continental counterparts: 'I am constantly saying that I wish that they would talk less about European and political union. The terms are not understood in this country. In so far as they are understood over there, they mean a good deal less than some people over here think they mean.'

But they didn't. They expressed an aspiration which it suited Mrs Thatcher, like almost all British politicians, to ignore by pretending it didn't really exist. This was a practised condition. In 1983, the British leader put her signature to the Stuttgart Declaration, which spelled out a pledge, supported by twenty pages of detail, to the cause of much more European union. It was the first big statement, promising institutional reforms of an intensely unifying kind in every field, that modern 'Europe' had ever attempted. The British, while signing, despised it. Looking back, Geoffrey Howe says the attention they had given it was 'less than we should have done'.[51] The Thatcher memoir says: 'The document had no legal force. So I went along with it.'[52] But the truth is they preferred not to address the language of their partners with the seriousness it deserved.

They thought of it as Euro-guff, or Euro-twaddle, a bizarre, cultish worshipping at the altar of Jean Monnet, which would mercifully never get anywhere near full transsubstantiation into the body of revealed and meaningful law. There had been similar words in the texts from the beginning. The Treaty of Rome, for example, placed high among its purposes 'to lay the foundation of an ever closer union among the peoples of Europe'. But few of the British, even among the political leadership, properly absorbed this. They never really penetrated the words, and, if they did happen to be vouchsafed a moment of enlightenment, it was to see them as a challenge, rather than a credo that had much to do with the island race. From that long history of recoiling from what Europe meant, the pretence followed almost naturally that the aspirations of the Single Act could best be treated in the same way.

Alongside this misperception was a mismatch in the British attitude to negotiation. In Europe, negotiation never ends. Membership is a process not an event, Howe once said. There is a sense in which nothing is ever finally settled. An agreement favourable to one country is merely the beginning of the next deal, and often vulnerable to being reopened under a different heading. Little is quite cut and dried, and, since cut-and-dried-ness was the part of her style in which Mrs Thatcher took most pride, there were always likely to be incandescent difficulties between her and the people she resolutely declined to see as partners.

Nevertheless, the Single Act was a fact. It surrendered sovereignty, accelerated momentum. That, at the time, was what the British leader thought she wanted, and urged the people to applaud. Though it wasn't what Jacques Delors envisaged, it seemed to signal Britain's open-eyed engagement with the dominant culture of the Community. Everyone in the Thatcher Cabinet backed it, and so did almost everyone in the Thatcher Party – storing up trouble for the day when it became an inconvenient memory.

For their eyes weren't open, and they couldn't really face the consequences of what they had done.

*

ONE OF THE MOST compelling, if unsung, visionaries of 'Europe' was Emile Noël, the first, and until 1987 only, secretary-general of the European Commission. For forty-five years Noël devoted himself to the cause, thirty of them as the wily, dedicated, self-effacing but all-knowing official at the heart of the Community's central machine.

Noël was, of course, a Frenchman. No other breed would have been considered for the top job in a bureaucracy fashioned on French lines to serve French purposes. But he rose far above nationality to become the complete European, wise in the objects of the enterprise, steeped in its history, dedicated to its oneness, observant of the foibles of the many political leaders who came and went. A measure of his importance, and the affection in which he was held by true Euro-cultists, was an all-day meeting held in London after he died in August 1996, to hear tributes from all manner of former Commissioners, ambassadors, directors-general and the like. Here he was placed, to general acclaim, in a bracket with Monnet, Schuman, Adenauer and Spaak as one of the great Europeans.

When I met Noël in 1993, he was in his retirement job, running the European University Institute in Florence. A small, quiet, unimposing figure, he still exuded the tireless absorption of the bureaucrat in the project on which he had spent his life. He loved talking about Europe, to whose history he brought a formidable memory, capable of instant recall of the proceedings of every summit he had ever attended. But this vast accumulation, together with the length of time, rivalling the monarch's, which he had in one job, supplied him, as well, with a conspectus of the ages.

Emile Noël watched the Thatcher phenomenon in Europe with interest and some admiration. He thought she got too much money at Fontainebleau, but saw this was to her credit. 'She was a real stateswoman, very efficient, very clear, knowing every significant point,' he judged. 'I cannot agree with the content of her position, but she was a very effective Prime Minister for a certain length of time.'[53]

Exactly when this time ended, Noël thought, was a matter for debate. He argued with himself as between 1984 and 1988. After the budget deal was done, he said, 'the Thatcher method became less and less efficient, year after year'. But the Single Act was a sort of victory. And in 1988, the battering-ram technique produced a refinement of the budget deal, locking the British rebate into a wider reform of agricultural spending. At that same meeting, on the other hand, occurred a more dismal Thatcherite watershed, showing how far she was from controlling the agenda any longer. Britain wasn't satisfied with the agriculture reform and threatened to veto it, a gesture that provoked a decisive move by the other eleven members. Noël said: 'This was the first time they were prepared, and even preferred, to go ahead without the British if the decision was opposed. It was the first time it was so clear.'

Whatever moment one might try to select as definitive, a trend established itself in the middle 1980s with which Mrs Thatcher could not easily cope. Settling the British budget problem was a doubled-edged event. It brought her back 'my money', but opened the way for new developments. Victory was the necessary prelude to something more unpleasant. Until it happened, the continental integrators were in balk. That is why Mitterrand needed to make concessions at Fontainebleau. After it happened, a sequence of events was liberated, all of them discomfiting because all spoke for the kind of momentum the British leader would prefer to think did not exist. At each colloquium of the leaders, in what became a decade of Community dynamism to follow the decade of stasis, something new was always edging forward. The agenda was always multiple, overlapping, relentlessly evolving. Just as the Single Act grew out of the budget deal, something more ominous began to take shape even as the Single Act was being finalized. The allusions to economic and monetary union, murmured during the build-up to the Act, turned out no longer to be mere aspiration but to describe the next great project.

From 1985, in fact, money began to be the core issue. If there was to be a single market, why then should there not be single money as well? This, to Margaret Thatcher's obvious bafflement, was something several of her peer-group, the leaders of Europe, apparently believed in, at least as a long-term goal. From now until the end of her prime ministership, aspects of the single currency – its preliminaries, its legitimacy, the prior binding of national exchange rates, the settlement of this goal as the new holy grail of 'Europe' – dominated an expanding acreage of the politics and economics of what used to be known, in distant halcyon days, as the Common Market. The prospect drew out the Thatcher scepticism, followed shortly by the Thatcher aggression. It came to dominate her political life, seizing her mind, devouring the unity of her Cabinet, to the point of being her nemesis.

For in parallel with this new momentum came another development. She began to show both an intensity and exclusivity of commitment on the Europe question that had hitherto been kept at bay. Early disagreements with Foreign Office ministers about how to handle the budget row had been superseded, on the whole, by a unified determination. She won the argument among her ministers, the prelude to winning the battle in Europe. Geoffrey Howe, Foreign Secretary from 1983, stood shoulder to shoulder, tolerant of her disdain, a solid ally in struggle. But for the colleagues, as for the Europeans, the new phase marked a change of atmosphere. There began to be a new argument, and new dissent. The politics of the personal began ever more insistently to intrude upon the politics of the nation. How currencies were managed, and how the Europe relationship was factored into them, were questions that called forth remarkable events in the annals of a prime minister and her government.

One strand concerned the currency itself. The European Monetary System (EMS) encompassed an exchange rate mechanism (ERM) locking the member currencies within bands of stability from which they could not, without agreement, shift. While embracing the innocuous aspects of the EMS – the 'zone of monetary stability' it proclaimed, and the European Curency Unit (écu) it controlled – Britain had kept out of the ERM ever since the Callaghan Government, saying only that sterling would join 'when the time was right', or alternatively 'ripe'.

So the ERM, in 1985, wasn't a new venture, wasn't part of some grand new European initiative. For Britain to join it, on the other hand, would be a European signal, as well as a decision to base economic, and especially anti-inflationary, strategy on the exchange rate, rather than on monetary indicators (M3, M0) whose chronic unreliability were at last depriving them of their mystic power over the minds of all true Thatcherites. In 1985, the leading minds in this category, Geoffrey Howe and Nigel Lawson, who was Chancellor of the Exchequer, made a big push to get into the ERM. Their reasons were economic, not European. But they didn't allow the European dimension to compromise their economic judgement. 'Europe' had not reached neuralgic status in the Tory Party, and besides, Howe, if not Lawson, was a lifelong devotee of all things continental.

The argument, at the economic level, had gone on for some time. Lawson was flirting with it as early as 1981, as a junior minister. Running the Treasury since 1983, he had grown more enamoured of the case, until it became for him the driving strategic objective. He was convinced that linking sterling to the Deutschmark, which was in effect what ERM membership meant, was the route to economic stability. It would protect business from exchange-rate gyrations and foster an anti-inflation climate. But he was unable to instil this opinion into those immediately around him. For most of two years, the senior Treasury officials and the top people at the Bank of England were, according to Howe, respectively 'sceptical' and 'cautious'.[54] The leader herself was still more heavily barricaded against conversion. Even after Lawson had managed to swing the Treasury and Bank, by early 1985, she still resisted. She didn't like the entrapment of fixed rates, the loss of political discretion and economic freedom. And she had an adviser off-stage, Alan Walters, who opposed ERM membership, in Lawson's phrase, as 'the work of the devil'. Walters, an aggressive professor of free-market persuasion and an intellectual base more American than European, was a Thatcher guru, an early presence in Downing Street fending off the wetter Cabinet ministers, who continued to exert much personal influence on his patron even after leaving London.

Lawson, however, did not surrender. As 1985 wore on, the lady herself seemed to be teetering. Howe records a moment when he caught her 'speaking of "when" not "if" we joined the Mechanism'. Joining was now almost conventional wisdom among mainstream Tory opinion. A meeting to fix it was set for 13 November.

This meeting wasn't strictly a "European' moment. The clash of mind-sets still related more to economic than to political ideas: to the currently inner meaning of economic Thatcherism, not yet the existential crisis about the future of an independent Britain. It was, nevertheless, significant in the evolution of Mrs Thatcher into a leader whom Europe would eventually undo. It marked the most strident moment yet recorded of her assuming a personal command that swept aside collective opinion, not by argument but by crude personal assertion, in a field adjacent to the Europe question.

Lawson presented the case he had long prepared the ground for, having circulated all present with reams of papers and tables laying out the economic advantages ERM members were gaining over Britain, and exposing the much lowered risks, in present circumstances, of deciding to belong. His listeners made an interesting collection. The Treasury and the Bank, both represented by their chiefs, were now solidly behind him. So were Howe, Deputy Prime Minister William Whitelaw, the Trade Secretary, Leon Brittan, and the party chairman Norman Tebbit, a man who later kept his elderly name alive by becoming a rabid Euro-sceptic. The chief whip, John Wakeham, offered the clear opinion that entry would induce no important back-bench rebellion. Only John Biffen, the sceptic from way back, opposed what Lawson wanted to do. Insofar as the collective was being consulted, it voted overwhelmingly to support the Chancellor.

But this was beginning not to be, in the old sense, a collective government. Having heard the opinions of her colleagues, the leader said sharply that she disagreed. Over her shoulder, it was apparent to Lawson, loomed the absent figure of Walters, and on her desk, plain for all to see, was a Walters communication. He had lately written an academic treatise denouncing the ERM root and branch.[55] Having delivered a crisp philippic against the entire idea of the European Monetary System, Mrs Thatcher responded to those who continued to make their pitch by saying: 'If you join the EMS, you will have to do so without me.'[56] In other words, the principle of time's ultimate ripeness was overturned. Government policy, which had hitherto accepted that one day Britain would join the ERM, was reversed by fiat of a Prime Minister who regarded her word alone as sufficient to kill it, apparently, for ever.

For Howe, it was all very bewildering. 'This was the first time that any of us had contemplated her exercising a veto of this kind,' he snuffles in his memoirs. Getting such high-handedness reversed, he muses, might require him and his friends 'to go almost off the constitutional map'.[57] A mysteriously menacing phrase. What could it mean? Impeachment? Or perhaps a rare, Howe-like mumble of total disagreement? Lawson felt much more explicitly outraged. It was 'the saddest event of my time as Chancellor', he writes, 'and the greatest missed opportunity'. He felt particularly vexed that it came about under the influence of a man, Walters, who had no place to speak at all, and he railed at the spectacle of the leader reversing Government policy without ever formally renouncing it: a recipe for confusion – but one, as we can now see more clearly, that was to become increasingly characteristic of Mrs Thatcher's dealings with the European Community.

The episode gave rise, in any case, to another bizarrerie. The passions let loose in this territory were beginning to produce many irregularities for constitutionalists to ponder. A Prime Minister personally reversing a policy was not an act without precedent, though this would normally – in the case of Harold Wilson, say, or Ted Heath – imply the presence of an unspoken Cabinet majority on the same side. By contrast, a Chancellor pursuing an exchange rate policy so secret that it is never disclosed to the Prime Minister, and a Prime Minister apparently so blind that she doesn't see what is happening until she reads about it in the newspapers, pushes forward the frontiers of the para-normal. Yet this is what began to happen little more than a year after Lawson was spurned in his desire to enter the ERM. Almost as a private frolic of his own, he began to have sterling shadow the Deutschmark, aiming to keep its value down to DM3.00. Selling sterling, the Bank doubled its foreign currency reserves within a year. Whether this really was secret from the Prime Minister, or something from which she preferred to avert her gaze, is a question to which the definitive answer is lost in the haze of muteness that sometimes surrounds actual financial operations. Eddie George, deputy governor of the Bank, later said: 'At no point did Nigel Lawson tell us there was to be a policy of shadowing the Deutschmark.' On the other hand there plainly was a shadowing, described by one Treasury official to Philip Stephens thus: 'It was exclusively a Lawson operation . . . [But] you will not find any papers in the Treasury setting out the policy of shadowing the Deutschmark.'[58]

These utterances from an arcane world are not satisfactorily clarified in the memoirs of any of the principals. What was indisputable, and required no great crystallizing, was the argument that underlay the matter. Argument, in fact, is too decorous a word. The contest of wills about exchange rate fixing, conducted with increasing rancour between the Prime Minister and her Chancellor, was a harbinger of what Europe at large, beyond the currency question, could do to the personal relations – the very solidarity – of her Government. The Prime Minister was ceasing to be all-powerful, even though in March 1988 she abruptly forced Lawson to end his intervention against the pound. Senior ministers, who had grown up as her protégés, were ceasing to respect her exclusive wisdom on matters either economic or European. A fissure was opening up, under the influence of acrid personal politics, and of developments in Europe itself which now became the dominating preoccupation of Mrs Thatcher's life.

This was the second strand of what it is hardly too much to call her slow disintegration. There were tides she could not control, and it became a matter for mounting rage that this should be so. Such was the nature of 'Europe', once that elusive entity was experiencing economic growth, and a certain political confidence, and was under the hand of a man who knew where he wanted to take it.

For the middle 1980s were also the palmiest days of Jacques Delors. Whereas for Mrs Thatcher the Single Act was, desirably, the apogee of Europe's trajectory, for the Commission president it was but a way-station on the path to a still more integrated future. Behind this vision, Delors gathered the great majority of continental leaders, including all the biggest ones. In 1988, it exposed itself, in ways that the British leader could neither endorse nor obliterate.

Delors was nominated, first of all, as master of the future of economic and monetary union, EMU. This followed his reappointment, *nem. con.*, to another term in the presidency. 'We were saddled with M. Delors,' the Baroness writes, and in the end she even seconded his name, finding to her annoyance that her favoured horse, the Dutch Prime Minister, Ruud Lubbers, refused to run.[59] A note of defeat is beginning to infuse her estimation of events. As foreshadowed in the Single Act – its stated 'objective of progressive realization of economic and monetary union' – progress was simultaneously set in train towards EMU. A committee was required and Delors was put in charge of it. 'I was having to recognize that the chance of stopping the committee being set up at all was ebbing away,' is the doleful Thatcher memory.

She secured some crumbs of comfort. The slant of the Delors committee was directed away from a possible European central bank: 'I restated my unbending hostility.' She even renewed an argument she had proffered earlier, that the terminology of the Single Act, buried in its ambiguous entrails, contemplated only economic and monetary 'co-operation' rather than union. The membership of the committee itself she also believed she had influenced to her advantage. It was to be composed of central bankers rather than officials: reliably flinty realists and sceptics, as she thought, about anything so delicate as tampering with currencies. The head of the Bundesbank, Karl-Otto Pöhl, almost resigned over the presence of Delors as the chairman, deeming him not to be a qualified 'expert'.[60] The governor of the Bank of England, Robin Leigh-Pemberton, was the British member, to whom, along with Pöhl, the Prime Minister looked 'to put a spoke in the wheel of this particular vehicle of European integration'.

Delors' agenda, however, was much wider. Elated by his nomination for a second term, he immediately repaired to Strasbourg, the home of the European Parliament, to set out an overview of where the Community might be going. There could hardly have been a more frontal challenge to the British leader's opinion, not merely of Europe but of the liberal *Zeitgeist* she was bent on infusing into the new age. Matching Delors' belief in a Single Act was his determination that Europe should be something more than a paradise for unchained capitalism. He believed in a 'social' dimension: took it, indeed, as a good socialist, to be a cardinal priority for his presidency. Addressing the parliamentarians, he sketched out the implications of both a social and 'political' Europe. Law-making, he said, was bound in some part to shift from the nations to the federalistic centre. 'In ten years,' he specified, '80 per cent of the laws affecting the economy and social policy would be passed at a European and not a national level.' He went on: 'We are not going to manage to take all the decisions needed between now and 1995 unless we see the beginnings of a European government.'[61]

Delors, a subtle as well as strategic man, saw this speech as a warning. It was not a mission statement so much as a provocation to national parliaments, inviting them to consider the political realities likely to flow from the momentum unleashed by the Single Act.

That wasn't how Mrs Thatcher read it. To her it seems to have come as a straightforward power-grab by a megalomaniac. She went on the radio to denounce Delors, saying that he had gone 'over the top'. He was frightening people with his visions. 'He would never say such extreme things to me,' she said. They were entirely 'airy-fairy'.[62] And they soon became even more intolerable. On 7 September, the French imperial socialist – no longer the man Howe once approved as 'after our own hearts' – was received with acclamation in a south coast resort by the British Trades Union Congress. Addressing the brothers and sisters, he assured them that the single market would have a social dimension and protect workers' rights. In return, they serenaded him with a rendition of 'Frère Jacques'. He shed an uninvented tear. The occasion marked an important moment in the conversion of the British left to 'Europe', not yet for its internationalist, still less its federalist, potential, but as the only available hammer that might dislodge Margaret Thatcher from her unsettling ascendancy.

By this summer, however, Mrs Thatcher, in a larger way, had had enough. Everywhere she looked, it seems, she saw developments that proved 'Europe' was getting out of hand. It was the final dawning of a light she had hitherto been finding many ways to resist: the light that gleamed from the formal pledge, written thirty years before, to an ever closer union, the illumination which showed there were many significant people who meant this seriously.

She writes about it in her memoirs with the fury of one belatedly discovering a truth that had been withheld. The European Commission, she found out, was being very active. It wasn't like the British civil service, the tool of elected ministers: hadn't, indeed, been set up like that in the first place. One of the uniquenesses of the Community from the start was the exclusive power it gave the Commission, the supra-national *apparat*, to initiate proposals, ideas, advances. These had to be approved by ministers before they could become part of Community law or practice. But the Commission never was as self-effacing as Whitehall, and was now, according to the raging adversary of Delors, excelling itself.

Assembling a charge-sheet, her officials listed what it was doing in 1988. She was appalled. It was 'pushing forward its "competence" into new areas', she writes.[63] These included culture, education, health, social security. 'It used a whole range of techniques.' It set up advisory committees 'whose membership was neither appointed by, nor answerable to, member states and which tended therefore to reach *communautaire* decisions'. 'It carefully built up a library of declaratory language, largely drawn from the sort of vacuous nonsense which found its way into Council conclusions, in order to justify subsequent proposals.' 'It used a special budgetary procedure, known as *"actions ponctuelles"*, which enabled it to finance new projects without a legal base for doing so.'

Most seriously of all, she goes on, 'it consistently misemployed treaty articles requiring only a qualified majority to issue directives which it could not pass under articles which required unanimity'. These were part of a tendency so pervasive and pernicious that it entirely overshadowed the merits of particular cases. The Baroness chronicles her difficulty in arguing against populist environmental and health regulations, for example, that came under this heading. Cunning Commissioners kept 'presenting themselves as the true friends of the British worker, pensioner and environmentalist'. And if ever they were challenged in court, the ECJ lined up with the Commission, 'twisting the words and intentions of the Council', always favouring 'dynamic and expansive' interpretations of the Treaty over restrictive ones.

Such was the catalogue of disgust. The more she considered it, 'the greater my frustration and the deeper my anger became ... I had by now heard about as much of the European "ideal" as I could take.'[64]

She therefore decided to say so, in whatever undiplomatic words she could get away with. A speaking engagement was already scheduled for early September in Bruges, at the College of Europe, a good platform from which to deliver the new vision of what Europe should be about.

The lecture she prepared was a clear break with the implicit consensus for which every British leader, herself included, had spoken since 1973.

It partly depicted Europe as a threat to what she had done for Britain. 'We have not successfully rolled back the frontiers of the state in Britain only to see them reimposed at a European level, with a European super-state exercising a new dominance from Brussels': this became the Bruges speech's single most famous line. But its deeper message was that Europe itself must redirect its priorities in the world. What mattered in Europe was not the Community, but the wider Europe to the east. 'We shall always look on Warsaw, Prague and Budapest as great European cities,' she said. In their enmity with the Soviet Union, these were the places where the lamp of decentralized liberalism really shone. As prisoners of Moscow, they valued nation-statehood more highly than the

West, where too many Community members wanted to move in the opposite direction. 'Willing and active co-operation between independent sovereign states' was the way to build a successful European Community, a 'family of nations' the image insistently preferable to anything that smacked of a single endeavour.

There was more in this vein. It was a long, vibrant, intentionally challenging speech, with a peroration that exalted above all else the Atlantic community – 'our noblest inheritance and our greatest strength'. By the time she wrote her memoirs, the author had enhanced the range of her European vision to stretch from the Urals to what she rather fancifully termed 'the New Europe across the Atlantic'.[65] Anything to lower the presumption of what was now no longer even the European *Economic* Community, but, menacingly, the European Community *tout court!* But just as interesting as the content of Bruges were its preliminaries and its aftermath. They throw light on her two *bêtes noires* respectively.

Before the speech, there were fierce exchanges between the Foreign Office and Downing Street. I have glimpsed some of the secret official papers, and they expose not only the mutual contempt now existing between the two power-centres, but also something of the tactics inside the Foreign Office as the mandarins considered how to deflect the lady. From scanning them, one learns quite a lot about the state of things in the mature years of her prime ministership.

The draft was prepared in Downing Street, by Charles Powell, her closest official. He sent it across to the FCO asking for comments and suggestions, and noting that 'it has been seen by the Prime Minister, who is quite attracted to it'. The draft was undeniably strident. Powell included, among other choice readings of his mistress's voice, a passage that talked about Britain alone having saved Europe from being united 'under Prussian domination', and some triumphalist paragraphs on the success of the British Empire by comparison with the imperial failures of France, Spain, Portugal and Holland. Similar tactlessness abounded, along with some threatening allusions to the growth of qualified majority voting and the intolerable loss of national independence.

This had a pained reception across the road. Foreign Secretary Howe was appalled. His private secretary, Stephen Wall (who ten years later was head of the UK delegation to the European Union), minuted the head of the European Department, John Kerr (who ten years later was permanent under-secretary, the top official in the Foreign Office), listing a series of *bêtises*. There were 'some plain and fundamental errors in the draft', Wall began. It also tended 'to view the world as though we had not adhered to any of the [European] treaties'.

The Foreign Secretary, he went on, 'does not like the suggestion that we were more successful colonialists than other European countries. Is it not anyway a fact that we lost our North American colonies before Spain lost her South American colonies?'

Nor was Powell's appropriation of freedom as an exclusively British concern acceptable. It 'implies that we alone fought against tyranny and for freedom, which is presumably what the French revolutionaries thought they were doing'. As for the proposition, declared by Powell–Thatcher, that we should 'forget a United States of Europe – it will not come', this elicited another tart history lesson. 'The Secretary of State agrees that a stronger Europe does not mean the creation of a new European super-state, but it does, has and will require the sacrifice of political independence and the rights of national parliaments. That is inherent in the treaties.'

After receiving and absorbing this minute, Kerr set about rewriting the draft. Circulating it to colleagues, he said that Powell's original 'seemed off-beam' and in some parts 'needlessly provocative'. He was also struck by an omission. In all the fervour of the lecture, it seemed to him 'eccentric to pass over in complete silence one of the principal themes of the UK's EC policy in recent years' – the need for evolutionary change in the Community. He therefore included a new passage on that, and sent the whole to other Euro-concerned departments – Treasury, Department of Trade and Industry, Ministry of Agriculture – though with a pre-emptive ban on letting Downing Street know who had seen it. 'I think it would be good tactics *not* to reveal this to No. 10 at this stage,' Kerr instructed. Let these departments make known their approval of the FCO version – but it will be best if 'such advice appears *sua sponte*'.

In his covering note to Powell, by contrast, Kerr was all emollience. The authors of *Yes Minister* couldn't have made it up. It was too beautifully tendentious even for them. 'The Foreign Secretary believes that the scope and structure of your draft are generally well judged,' the under-secretary purred. But to avoid 'rejoinders or rebuttals', it might be prudent to consider some reformulations such as are herein proposed.

A week later, Powell sent back another draft, 'substantially rewritten', which Kerr regarded, so he circulated colleagues, as 'buying 80 per cent of the suggestions sent out by the FCO'. In a further redraft, he tried bidding for another 10 per cent, saying that 'the remaining 10 per cent don't really matter (and concern areas where No. 10 are probably incorrigible)'. All in all, he could reflect on a Whitehall job well done. 'It looks as if our damage-limitation exercise is heading for success.' The Bruges speech might not take any tricks in Europe, but it would cause no trouble. Howe, by now travelling in Africa, didn't need to be disturbed.

As to the battle of the drafts, this was only partly correct. After the final exchange, some of the sentences got souped up again before delivery. But, as a prophecy, Kerr's conclusion was more seriously in error. There had been some pre-emptive damage-limitation, both by the softening that remained and by warning Brussels of what was coming – thus enabling Delors, for example, to cancel his plan to attend. But the speech, of course, made its mark with the enemies in Europe, and thus fulfilled the Prime Minister's intentions rather than the Foreign Office's. In her chapter on this passage of her premiership, subtly entitled 'The Babel Express', she can hardly contain her delight at the anger she had caused. 'Not even I would have predicted the furore the Bruges speech unleashed,' she writes. The reaction was one of 'stunned outrage'.[66]

Writing privately to a British official in Brussels, Powell defended the speech as a warning. This is also recorded in the secret file just cited. Perhaps Mrs Thatcher was trading warning for warning with Delors. The speech was directed against future losses of national sovereignty occurring 'by stealth rather than by design', Powell explained to William Nichol, who had a senior post at the Council secretariat. The outcry, he added, had come from 'those who did not like the implications of their small steps being exposed to public scrutiny'. In any case, the speech had been an exceptional political triumph. It attracted, he noted, 'more support and favourable comment than any since the Prime Minister has been in Downing Street'.

Recounting his own memory of the Bruges speech, parts of which he calls 'sheer fantasy', Howe sees it as the moment when his leader finally ceased to allow her head to rule her heart. Her rhetoric, certainly her private posturing, had often smelt like this, but her policies had invariably been pragmatic, not least under the helpful hand of her Foreign Secretary. 'No. No. Yes.' described the usual parabola of the Thatcher mind in addressing European suggestions, according to a later Foreign Secretary, Douglas Hurd. Now, it seems, she had moved beyond reason. 'She began readopting arguments which she and I had had no difficulty in rebutting in debates over the Single European Act only a couple of years before,' Howe writes.[67] The rupture between them was, he seems to have found, traumatic. 'It was, I imagined, a little like being married to a clergyman who had suddenly proclaimed his disbelief in God.'

Europe, however, moved on. So, for a time, did the power and influence of Howe and Lawson. This was the other oddity of the later Thatcher epoch. Though the Bruges speech set out a new agenda, and achieved maximum effect in the public arenas of politics, it stopped nothing happening. Nor did it have an instructive impact on any of her senior ministers other than to stiffen their resolve to defeat the philosophy it proclaimed. Apparently the height of presidentialism, it exercised little authority and attracted no respect among the colleagues who were, presumably, supposed to make it work.

There were, admittedly, differences between the two lieutenants. Howe was much the more 'European' in the old sense. He believed in the sweep of history, with himself somewhere near the centre, that must carry Britain, willy-nilly, closer to Europe; and he had no difficulty, in this context, imagining the congruences required by economic and monetary union. They did not frighten or repel him. Lawson, by contrast, more of an economic intellectual, was fiercely and publicly opposed to a single currency. He distinguished between the ERM and EMU, declining, unlike most of those who backed the ERM, to regard the one as mere prelude to the other. The ERM he saw as 'an agreement between independent sovereign states ... economic and monetary union, by contrast, is incompatible with independent sovereign states'.[68] For Lawson, 'Europe' could never be a cause strong enough to override his mistrust of a continental central bank and – Churchillian dream, or nightmare – a United States of Europe.

For the moment, however, the ERM was the issue: the diabolical invention that Mrs Thatcher had thus far successfully warded away from Britain, but the item on the European agenda that no single leader was able to snuff out. On this point, Howe and Lawson were together, indifferent to the ordinance of Bruges, and willing, as it turned out, to face down the leader whose declaration in September 1988 was supposed to shock Britain, as well as Europe, into a new way of thinking.

The momentum was continuing, inexorably. Lurking in the wings, unstoppable, was Delors' committee on EMU itself. The central bankers were working away, and the British representative, Robin Leigh-Pemberton, kept the ministers informed. At this stage they were anxiously agreed that Delors, while certain to propose a general signing up to ERM, should be restrained from plotting a definitive path to EMU;

and the governor, a Thatcher appointee, agreed on tactics to achieve this. But others, unfortunately, did not. The head of the Bundesbank, Karl-Otto Pöhl, having first resisted the very presence of Delors anywhere near the sacred ground of currency-management, edged feebly – 'a broken reed', writes Lawson – towards acquiescing in an EMU scheme. When the committee arrived at a three-stage programme for monetary union, Leigh-Pemberton, too, signed up, protesting to Lawson that he did not want to be in a minority of one. That was not a posture likely to recommend itself to the Prime Minister. After writing to her to explain himself, he never received a reply. I was told that, after the Delors Report was published, she refused ever again to talk to Leigh-Pemberton, crucial though his position was, about anything to do with Europe.

Thus far, Lawson, though favouring the ERM, was with her. But this couldn't last. These matters were not the stuff of a debating society. While EMU might unite the colleagues, EMU itself, here and now, was only peripherally the issue. The question posed by the Delors committee, which came for final settlement at a summit in Madrid at the end of June 1989, was whether or not Britain, though well understood to be more minimalist in her vision than other members, would sign the pledge – Stage One, as it was called – to enter the ERM. The way things had evolved, in this new Europe which had discovered a certain dyna-mism, meant that a negative answer to the question would imply a negative approach, in effect, to Britain's continuing presence as a big player in the entire 'Europe' project. Through the Thatcher eyes this might be seen as perverse, absurd, enraging. But it was a fact, of somewhat epic proportion. And it gave rise to events, where politics and personality entwine around each other, of similarly awesome moment.

Howe and Lawson were quite determined that the answer at Madrid should be yes, and went to considerable lengths to break down the lady's opposite opinion. At Howe's suggestion, the Dutch Prime Minister, Ruud Lubbers, one of the few Europeans she approved of, was invited to Chequers for a day's discussion. Though he was a potential ally in resisting Delors' proposal that Stage One should *inevitably* lead to Stage Three, the full EMU, the British leader destroyed her opportunity by lecturing Lubbers both on EMU and on his alleged feebleness over the modernization of Nato. When the Dutch Finance Minister suggested that her opposition to EMU would be much more influential if it came from within the ERM, she rounded on him with fury. The whole occasion, Lawson writes, was 'ghastly and embarrassing'.[69]

As their own preparation for Madrid, the two then composed a memorandum, with the aid of Treasury and Foreign Office officials who were now, it seemed, behind them to a man. It was a seductive memorandum, cleverly contrived, beginning with the strategic suggestion that the British priority, which was to derail EMU, would indeed be better achieved by first joining the ERM, or at least stating the firm intention to do so. To that extent, it played winningly to its audience of one. But it went on to say other things that were less ingratiating. The Howe influence was visible in his usual mantra about the risks of isolation in Europe, and both ministers, after much consideration, raised the ante further by proposing not merely a declaration for the ERM in principle but a deadline by which entry would be accomplished: at first shot, within a year, but then, in a spirit of pragmatism, the end of 1992.

The argument was a mirror-image of what had often come before, and what, indeed, would also continue to come afterwards. It was the case – the incessant, unexhausted, unembarrassed case – for the merits of being inside a European venture, helping it to happen: ranged against the case for being outside, watching it succeed or fail, and half hoping, let's face it, for the latter outcome. The Delors Report, the ministers said, was going to be accepted, whatever the British said. It was certain to have some kind of life and future. An attempted veto would not stop anything happening: would, indeed, make the project more likely to advance, and the emergence of a two-tier Europe more likely to occur.

This was a foretaste of a future argument – to name one moment out of many – to be held in 1997, when EMU had become a near-reality. Much the same parade of agonized sophistries, as between inning and outing, would unfold in the early months of the Blair Government. Then, at least, there was a difference of methodology. For one thing, the Howe–Lawson memorandum's curtain line was not yet applicable after six months of Mr Blair. 'Could we discuss this with you?' the Chancellor and the Foreign Secretary plaintively requested. Such was the state of the Thatcher collective.

Their hesitancy proved to be well judged. To begin with, the answer seemed to be no. Instead of meeting her senior ministers to get ready for Madrid, Mrs Thatcher assembled her senior Downing Street staff, who now included, as a returned adviser in full fig, the same Alan Walters who had set her against the ERM in 1985, as well as a chief policy man of similar kidney, Brian Griffiths. Powell, the Foreign Office sheep long since attired in Thatcherite clothing, was also there, along with her influential press secretary, Bernard Ingham. But the leader was the only elected politician. This was the kitchen cabinet which had now replaced the formal Cabinet as the forum of influence, and together it agreed that the Howe–Lawson memorandum was unacceptable. The ministers were altogether too soft. The conditions they wanted to propose to Europe – the universal end of exchange controls, fully free movement of capital – were insufficient. The prior requirements must now reach into realms that some might call unreal, including the complete deregulation of all national banking systems. There should be no acceptance in principle of the ERM, but instead the Europeans would be told at Madrid that the only worthwhile priority was another push to complete a long list of single market measures which had been either evaded or forgotten.[70]

Howe and Lawson could not stand for that. Rare though it was for two ministers, alone, to engage in what amounted to bilateral warfare with the Prime Minister, they now raised their firepower, insisting that she should meet them together, and not, as she would have preferred, singly. According to Lawson, it was 'the only instance in eight years as Cabinet colleagues when we combined to promote a particular course of action'. At a meeting on 20 June, she heard them out, and even promised to 'reflect further' on what they said. When, following a riposte from Downing Street, they sent a second joint minute and requested a second meeting, she tried to fend them off with separate telephone calls. But this underestimated their purpose. They were determined to push her to the limit. On the very eve of the Madrid summit, she felt she had no alternative but to receive them in Downing Street, where she heard, apparently to her astonishment, a solemn declaration from Howe, followed in like manner by Lawson, that if she remained totally unwilling to move forward on the ERM neither of them would feel able to remain members of the Government.

This was a new nadir for the Thatcher engagement with 'Europe'. In her book, it was an 'ambush' mounted by a 'cabal', a strange way to depict the posture of her two most important colleagues but not unjustifiable. This was what she had driven them to, by trying to gather to herself the exclusive, transcendent control of a national policy which she had reduced to a personal obsession. In the televised version of her book, when she gave her account of 'this nasty little meeting', the memory of it contorted her visage, even four years after the event, into one of loathing. The recollection of failure, as well as enmity, was etched on her mouth and in her eyes.[71]

For failure is what it was. Next day, she and Howe flew to Madrid.

They were on the same plane but did not speak. Howe's memoirs conjure up a state of things so bad that communications between them were passed back and forth, in written notes, through separately curtained enclosures on the aircraft. That evening, the Thatcher party, which included Powell and Ingham, declined to attend the British ambassador's dinner-party, leaving Howe and his entourage feeling 'strangely relaxed' at the table.

When the summit began, it was to hear, very soon, a speech from the Prime Minister whose content, Howe said, had not been vouchsafed to him. He had no idea what she would say. But, when she spoke, he was agreeably surprised, as much by the content as by the manner. She was 'calm, quiet and measured',[72] he writes. And she made the necessary, if unexpected, statement: 'I can reaffirm today the United Kingdom's intention to join the ERM.' It was as if there had been no other possibility. She stipulated some conditions, and declined to specify a date. She also reminded those present to remember that adoption of the single currency, EMU itself, would not be acceptable to the House of Commons. But the essential concession was made. Finance ministers could now get ahead with the preparation of a full ERM, and Britain would take her place within the process.

There were other developments. A proposed social charter, another Delors initiative, reached the table, only to be flicked at least halfway off it by the British. All in all, Madrid was seen to be a British victory: within that, moreover, a victory which both sides in the British argument could live with. Howe and Lawson had got just about what they thought they needed, and Mrs Thatcher, making much of the conditions she had imposed and the continuing imprecision of timing, had not lost face. She really could persuade herself it was her victory, over none more saliently than the enemy cabal within.

Once again, as with the Single Act, the House of Commons and the media greeted with unsullied acclaim the return of a Prime Minister who had authorized an advance in 'Europe'. They somehow persuaded themselves it was another victory for the nation over the tribe of Jacques Delors. The leader herself, in her own memoirs, has grown a little less self-deceived on this point. 'Only someone with a peculiarly naïve view of the world', she writes, could have expected the Madrid conditions for the ERM to modify the pace towards its happening – though that is rather what she was trumpeting at the time. In another respect, however, her recollection of triumph is undimmed. It is the triumph over Howe and Lawson. At the first Cabinet meeting, she gloatingly remembers, she did not, as was her habit, sit at the table while the members trooped in. 'This time . . . I stood in the doorway – waiting.' She was eager to watch the expressions, see as early as possible what anyone might be planning to do, after her great success. 'But there were no resignations.' The nasty little meeting a week earlier had been, to her satisfaction, turned against the men whose conspiracy produced it.

It wasn't long, moreover, before this was driven home. In the cool of the following month, the leader did not behave like someone whose victory reinforced her position, so much as one with the memory of insult, and the fear of its repetition, ringing through her mind. Quite suddenly, the Cabinet was reshuffled, and Geoffrey Howe, the great, grey, slowly flowing, never ceasing artery of Thatcherite, and for that matter Heathite and Macmillanite, Conservatism, was choked off from the heart of power. He was compelled to leave the Foreign Office, and offered, after a fair amount of jockeying and confusion, a job that didn't matter much, as Leader of the House of Commons.

'Something had happened to Geoffrey,' Mrs Thatcher darkly writes, implying perhaps that he had gone slightly off his trolley. In fact, it was simpler than that. He had ceased to be ready to agree with her, come what may, about 'Europe'. She also thought he was enjoying himself too much, jetting about the world at government expense with dubious regard to the national interest, and enjoying the grace-and-favour official residences where he could entertain her enemies. 'I was determined to move him aside for a younger man,' she explains, with parodic unawareness of the resonance of the dissembling cliché.

She would have reason to regret this ruthless sentiment. In due time, Howe made her pay for it with condign severity, and in retrospect she expresses some doubt about whether she did the right thing. But only because of the misfortune that was heaped upon it soon after. Nothing to do with what happened a year later. Unlike Howe's departure, Nigel Lawson's was not precipitated by her. Often though they had argued, and furtively though he had operated, she evidently did not want him to go. But Lawson went, a few months later, exasperated beyond endurance by the undermining interventions of her special adviser, Alan Walters. 'Perhaps if I had known that Nigel was about to resign I would have kept Geoffrey at the Foreign Office for at least a little longer,' the Baroness writes.

By October, both were gone, and she was left, as she thought, with more malleable successors, readier to pursue her vision of 'Europe'. This, however, was now menaced from a different quarter – by another tendency which the Iron Lady could not control.

*

IN THE COMPLEX of prejudices, whether rational or, just as often, visceral, that Mrs Thatcher brought to 'Europe', none was more potent than her attitude to Germany. Both positive and negative surges of sentiment concerning the European Community were warmly affected by it.

On the positive side, Germany was close to the heart of the matter. As we have seen, European security interested her more than economic integration. Well before she became Prime Minister, she earned the Iron sobriquet by declaring her non-negotiable hostility to the Soviet Union, and her determination to see that Britain made stronger contributions to the defence of freedom in Central Europe. Germany, the divided epicentre of this region, couldn't avoid being the focus of her interest. In 1978, she made a speech, entitled 'Principles of Foreign Policy', that spoke of the need to advance democracy throughout the world so as to reduce the risk of war. In this sense, she powerfully desired the Community to assume a political role. 'I did not regard the EEC as merely an economic entity,' she writes. 'It had a wider strategic purpose.'[73] The Community, because it bordered on the communist world, was the showcase and the magnet that might draw people away from communism.

To that extent favouring, if anything, a stronger political presence for the Community, Margaret Thatcher upheld the idea of 'Europe'. Indeed, she took it further than most of her contemporaries. She thought the EC should be the defender of freedom, alongside Nato but also in some sense additional to it, a view not shared by many continental leaders, who were wary of such a dimension. These doubters included German leaders themselves, of all parties – Kohl every bit as much as Helmut Schmidt, or Schmidt's predecessor, the architect of *Ostpolitik*, which the Iron Lady much disapproved of, Willy Brandt. It was, in a sense, a tribute to her fearlessness in face of what conventional opinion might term a contradiction that she was prepared to be, in one sense, a stronger integrationist, but, in another, the opposite.

The defence of German freedom, as part of Europe's freedom, was therefore a high purpose that excited Mrs Thatcher's interest in 'Europe'. Her doubts about the Germans, on the other hand, spoke differently.

What Hitler's war fired in an adolescent breast in Grantham did not disappear. The images fixed by Hitlerism extended into a picture of Germany as an expansionary power, out to dominate by peaceful means the Europe it had almost destroyed by war. Whoever was leader of Germany at any given moment, these feelings were seldom far away. Laced into them were threads of envy at the speed and depth of Germany's post-war recovery, which she thought was somehow unfair. That was the opinion of Charles Powell, who once instructed Helmut Kohl's closest adviser, Horst Teltschik, in the significance of his boss's 'wellspring of instinctive anti-Germanism'.[74]

For a full decade after 1979, the instinct ebbed and flowed with variable importance. No German was exempt from its consequences. Kohl, with whom she cohabited, as it were, for eight years, was never graced with forgiveness for his nationality. He it was who bore the brunt of an opinion she summarizes with remarkable candour in her memoirs. Dismissing those who think the German problem 'too delicate for well-brought-up politicians to discuss', she offers an emphatic view of her own. 'I do not believe in collective guilt,' she says. 'But I do believe in national character.' Since the unification of Germany under Bismarck, she opines, 'Germany has veered unpredictably between aggression and self-doubt.' 'The true origin of German *angst*', she rather more mysteriously writes, 'is the agony of self-knowledge.'[75]

Though these were awkwardly deforming opinions for one close ally to hold about another, they had no catastrophic consequences until 1989. In that year, however, the fall of the Berlin Wall and collapse of the Soviet Union put both the positive and negative segments of the broader Thatcherite view of Europe under grave strain. The positive side began to lose its rationale, while the negative side threatened to billow to bursting-point. With the end of the Cold War, what, any longer, could be relied on as the security argument for a more cohesive European Union? And with the death of communism, what, any longer, could keep the separate sectors of Germany, the Federal Republic and the Democratic Republic, apart – their only acceptable condition, in the eyes of anyone who was alarmed by what they saw as Germany's grandiose ambitions?

For Mrs Thatcher, this was a terribly destabilizing conjuncture. Nothing could have left her more conflicted. The Iron Lady rejoiced to see Moscow ruined, but was appalled to imagine Berlin reborn as the home of a new Reich. Not that many people expected this to happen. Weeks before the fall of the Wall, with Mikhail Gorbachev dismantling

Soviet tyranny, a *Financial Times* columnist was thought very daring when he wrote: 'The future period during which German unity could be regarded as feasible has suddenly shrunk from a matter of decades to perhaps only 10 or 15 years.'[76] The prophecy of Professor D. Cameron Watt, a celebrated international scholar at the London School of Economics, seemed nearer the mark: 'There will still be two Germanys 50 years from now.'[77] This was certainly what Mrs Thatcher wanted, as she did not hesitate to inform Kohl, Gorbachev, the American President George Bush and – the only Westerner who agreed with her – François Mitterrand.

Attempting to stop German reunification was one of the more bizarre initiatives in the Thatcher foreign policy record. But that is what she did. It took less than a month for her to fail, with Chancellor Kohl having the nerve to set out his own ten-point plan for a German future which included the goal of federation between the two Germanys, to be followed by 'the reattainment of German state unity'. Germany was deciding her own future, with the support, incidentally, of British voters, whom opinion polls in October 1989 registered as 70 per cent in favour. This did not console their leader. In the first half of 1990, she exposed her doubts to all who would listen, telling the House of Commons, the Polish Prime Minister and the Board of Deputies of British Jews, among others, that boundary changes in Central Europe were governed by the Helsinki Final Act and should not be attempted without 'massive consultation'. Her attitude towards the old enemy was more intransigent, and ruinously outspoken. In July, at the fortieth-anniversary celebration of the Konigswinter Conference, the Anglo-German get-together that had done much to improve relations between the two national establishments, she told a former German ambassador it would be 'at least another forty years before the British could trust the Germans again'.[78]

So this was a settled opinion. And it had recently received intellectual endorsement of a kind which, in her opinion, clinched the point. Earlier in the year, she had registered the special place of Germany in her concerns by organizing, extraordinarily, a day-long conference at Chequers. What other nation ever got such treatment? None. Not even the Soviet Union – with whose leader, Gorbachev, she was in any case now rather more cosily in sympathy than she was with Kohl. The Chequers seminar on Germany became part of Thatcherite Britain's downward slide, away from European fraternity, into the grip of the leader's private world.

It assembled half a dozen academics, American and British, to speak to an agenda prepared by Charles Powell.[79] The agenda set out the persistent Thatcher concerns. 'What does history tell us about the character and behaviour of the German-speaking people of Europe? Are there enduring national characteristics? Have the Germans changed in the last 40 years (or 80 or 150 years)? Is it better psychologically to "stand up to Germany"? Or to pursue a friendly approach?'[80] Scores of similar questions, homing in on the German national character and what could best be done about it, were listed for the academics to think about.

During their day's discussion, they did not wholly satisfy Mrs Thatcher's requirements. Though they were a mixed bunch, among whom were three of her known political supporters, the more she talked, the more anxious they seem to have been to disabuse her of some of her assumptions. One of them, George Urban, later set down his own account of what happened. Urban has the historians unanimously challenging some of the Granthamite generalizations the leader found it hard to let go of. To the suggestion, for example, that the German people had not changed, Urban himself, along with the two other sympathizers, Hugh Trevor-Roper and Norman Stone, responded by saying that Germany herself had changed a great deal. Germany had remade liberal democracy, reinforced her institutions, shown every sign of being a constructive and pacific European power. Likewise – another Thatcher *idée fixe* – German minorities scattered round Eastern and Central Europe would not, these scholars thought, become a fifth-column working to destabilize the continent. All in all, they declined to subscribe to the nightmares summoned up by Mrs Thatcher and her faithful scribe, Powell. Before arriving, they had not known who else would be present and had not got together, yet, according to Urban, several of them remarked, as they departed, on the similarity of their assessments.[81]

What happened next, however, was indicative of the lady's intellectual methods, as well as her incorrigible attitudes. Powell's fidelity as a scribe proved more closely pinned to prior prejudice than to the truth. His minute of the meeting became famous, because it was leaked some months later to a newspaper. According to this account, the seminar had reached conclusions which gratifyingly confirmed most of what the leader suspected. It had picked out the essence of the German national character: '*angst*, aggressiveness, assertiveness, bullying, egotism, inferiority complex, sentimentality', according to Powell. It had found reason to fear for the future in the Germans' 'capacity for excess, to overdo things, to kick over the traces ... to over-estimate their own strengths and weaknesses'. It had agreed there were still questions to be asked about 'how a cultured and cultivated nation had allowed itself to be brain-washed into barbarism', and whether 'the way in which the Germans currently used their elbows and threw their weight about in the European Community suggested that a lot had still not changed'.[82]

Such was the collective wisdom it pleased Mrs Thatcher to come away with. It is interesting that in her memoirs she makes no attempt to soften the verdict, or correct the impression the public – and the Germans – got of the Chequers seminar. Could the Germans be *trusted*? That was the question, according to Urban, to which she kept returning, while reciting many reasons to give a negative answer. Although the participants were quite prepared to consider that there was a complex of issues that might be summarized as 'the German question', they did not go along with the simplistic version from which the Prime Minister could not be shifted. Another of those present, Timothy Garton Ash, told me Powell's account was 'extremely tendentious'. No one has contended otherwise, save Powell himself, who responded with a combination of bullying and vanity that aptly reflected the tenor of the times in Downing Street as the Thatcher era drew to a close. 'I've been taking minutes for a long time but nobody has yet accused me of fabrication or inaccuracy,' he bellowed to the participants who challenged what they read.[83]

The fact is that angst was more prevalent among the British leadership than the German. They worried about the Germans more than the Germans worried about themselves, fiercely conscious though Kohl was of the need to placate European anxieties over the message of history. He himself did worry. That was the reason for his large, undeviating commitment to the unity of Europe, and the axiom he had placed at the base of his political life: Thomas Mann's famous affirmation – 'not a German Europe but a European Germany'. But his worries did not exceed those of Mrs Thatcher and her friends, who thought nothing of saying and believing about Germany things which, if a German had ventured similar generalities about the British, would have precipitated a nervous breakdown in the tabloid press.

Even Mrs Thatcher was obliged to recognize some constraints of political decency. When Nicholas Ridley, the Trade and Industry Secretary, attacked Germans in an open interview, she accepted his resignation. In the summer of 1990, it seemed some manner of taboo still operated. By stating to a magazine editor that European integration was 'a German racket designed to take over the whole of Europe', Ridley somehow put himself beyond the pale. German behaviour, said the minister, was 'absolutely intolerable', and Kohl would 'soon be trying to take over everything'. The Germans were a menace 'because of their habits'. Six columns of this stuff provided sufficient circumstantial static, the editor thought, to justify him running a cartoon depicting the Chancellor as the reincarnation of Adolf Hitler: which in turn affronted public opinion so much that Ridley had to be asked to leave the Government.[84]

But Mrs Thatcher was sorry to lose him. Not only did he know about the Germans, he understood the frailties of the ERM. On this point, he was 'almost my only ally in the Cabinet', she writes.[85] There is an eloquent beauty about this combination of truths and accidents. They are a kind of epitaph anticipating the lady's fall. A minister who agreed with her, on both the questions that now most gripped her mind, was obliged to depart. She could not save him. He joined the line of ministers, all likewise once her close allies, who, one way or another, had also left because of the Europe question: a question that by now was raised to a new pitch of explosive sensitivity by her handling of it: a question which she thrust to the forefront of British politics, even as her treatment of it ensured no other colleague who mattered agreed with what she wanted to do. Could there be a more ominous foretelling of Armageddon?

New ministers, meanwhile, were in place. But they did not prove more malleable than Howe and Lawson. One of them, Douglas Hurd, could never have been expected to. As Foreign Secretary he had entered the place for which his life hitherto was preparing him, which meant, by definition, that he was unlikely to agree with his leader about the Germans. Over Europe, he was not a federalist. In fact, as the 1990s proceeded and the issues became yet more divisive, Hurd was to show himself less steeped than Geoffrey Howe in the juices of European integration. But he was a Foreign Office man to his roots: trained there as an embryonic mandarin, embraced there as Heath's private secretary when the 1971 negotiation took place, already with form as a junior minister there in the Thatcher years, altogether an entirely unsuitable appointment for a Prime Minister whose stance towards the place was studiously adversarial. It is a commentary on the condition of the Government that Hurd selected himself. By late 1989, no other candidate for the post was remotely as credible.

Alongside Hurd, from the same date, was a new Chancellor of the Exchequer who, on the face of things, might have been more persuadable to the Thatcher viewpoint in his particular field of operations, the ERM.

John Major was, to all appearances, a Thatcherite, personally nurtured by the leader through a career that saw him rise from his first junior ministerial post into the Cabinet in less than four years. Major had no form, one way or the other. He seemed a willing follower of the orthodoxy of the leader, without diversionary ideas of his own. It was the only position for an ambitious young Tory, without previous convictions, to adopt. That, along with a general industrious competence, was the way he had got on. Compared with Lawson's formidable, aggressive intellect, Major's was untutored and, on matters of economic theory, apparently timid.

The Thatcher orthodoxy on the ERM, however, was contested. And Howe, bearer of the old wisdom, remained, unlike Lawson, in the Government. Even from a backwater as Leader of the House, he could still make speeches, and he lost little time in emphasizing in public, for example, how imperative it was that Britain 'stuck in good faith' to the ERM terms agreed at Madrid. This wounded the leader. She later called it an act of 'calculated malice'. But the fact was that orthodoxies could not necessarily be shifted by a reshuffle. Inside the Treasury which Major took over, the ERM lobby was fully formed. His officials were by now entirely in favour of entry as the route to a more solid basis for the war against inflation. Though Mrs Thatcher exerted episodic influence from No. 10, thereby inflicting some confusion in the early days of Major, he soon became a Chancellor with an agenda that decisively preferred the economic orthodoxy of the Treasury to the political imperatives of Downing Street. With Hurd as his reliable ally – they met regularly together for breakfasts that appeared on nobody's public schedule – he soon began to reinforce rather than challenge the Madrid commitment. In this period, Hurd, when asked privately about daily speculation then occurring on ERM matters, was quite happy to reply that his young colleague Mr Major, far junior to himself on the time-line of Tory hierarchy, was the most powerful man in the Government: even, he would mischievously imply, more powerful than the Prime Minister herself.

For both Hurd and Major knew they were in a strong position. Having already lost both a Chancellor and a Foreign Secretary, even a leader as well accustomed as Mrs Thatcher to riding out storms of her own creation could hardly afford to lose another from either post. The two of them began a process of persuasion, and ultimately enforcement, which casts a strange light on her eternal reputation for getting her own way. By the time she reaches this part of her memoirs, faced with the forces ranged against her, she is almost bleating with self-pity, as well as implied self-exoneration. 'There are limits', she writes, 'to the ability of even the most determined democratic leader to stand out against what the Cabinet, the parliamentary party, the industrial lobby and the press demand.' Wrong though she thought it was, this majority, alas, might finally be capable of imposing itself upon her. With only Ridley for an ally, she goes on, she was not strong enough 'to state that on grounds of principle we would not have sterling enter the ERM now or in the future'.[86]

It took time for Major and Hurd to get there. There were a number of intervening moments.[87] Apart from the objective need for technical preparations, and a reasonable alignment of economies, the argument itself continued. The leader did not end her struggle, and her colleagues were not so adamantly convinced of their rightness as to fight her in open court. Major, for example, was happy to engage in the distracting quest for an alternative to the goal of EMU, a search that had been legitimized at Madrid. An old Lawson idea for 'competing currencies', whereby all twelve national denominations would be legal tender in every EC state, was explored, as was a complex scheme promoted by Major himself for a so-called 'hard' écu – the European Currency Unit, the basket of national currencies in which much Community business was done. This was conceived as a possible but highly contingent route towards full EMU, more experimental and less frightening than the big bang the Delors committee proposed. Major espoused it strongly, as an appealing way to persuade the leader towards an ERM that would not, if the écu scheme triumphed, necessarily be the prelude to full EMU. It involved him in many hours of linguistic negotiation, to ensure the right nuances of conditionality. The 'would–could–should' problem became famous in the conversations of the higher Treasury at the time. 'The écu would be more widely used,' Major said when he announced the plan in June. 'It *would* become a common currency for Europe. In the very long term, if peoples and governments so choose, it *could* develop into a single currency. But that is a decision we *should not* take now, for we cannot yet foresee what the size and circumstances of the new Europe will be.'

These ideas, however, received little support in Europe. 'Competing currencies' was simply dropped, and the main value of the hard écu was political: the luring of Mrs Thatcher, along with Ridley while he still mattered, towards the moment when entry into the ERM, as long as it could be portrayed as much less than an automatic staging-post to EMU, was deemed to be inevitable. Even as such, the hard écu did not attract unanimous agreement. The game kept being given away by other players. The Prime Minister might say, as she did, to the Commons: 'Those who wish to use the écu in place of their own national currency may. I do not believe we shall.' But the governor of the Bank could not help but describe the hard écu as a step on the way to full monetary union. Nor could the entire Thatcher philosophy of Europe avoid being seen as a minority position, standing against an attitude for which the new Foreign Secretary spoke as firmly as the old – his counsel against Britain being 'prickly, defensive or negative', his fear lest 'we isolate ourselves by shutting ourselves off, raising the drawbridge of argument, acting as if we were a beleaguered island'.[88]

When the fateful moment of entry arrived, on 5 October 1990, the circumstances were related intimately to the past, the present and the future of the island's relations with the mainland, and the Conservative Government's custodianship thereof.

It happened then because it had not happened before. The force of events, almost unanimously supported by the political class of all persuasions at the time, drove sterling in. Yet entry took place when the relevant exchange rate index stood at DM2.95 to the pound, a rate that was already higher than it need have been and, within two years, was to prove unsustainable. In the matter of timing, the decision was calamitous. It thus takes its place in a category that has become familiar in this history: of climactic moments long postponed, then urgently desired, then achieved at a conjunction of time and place producing less, sometimes much less, advantage than might have been previously attainable. The sequence began in the 1950s, and would be equally visible in the later 1990s. It was now operative at the start of the decade. Once again, what appeared to be the logic of the present cast heavy doubt upon the judgement of the past.

In the case of entry into the ERM, indeed, this absence of an earlier decision perhaps had an especially corrosive effect. It contributed to the building of a conventional wisdom that turned out to be as potent as it was unfortunate. Though seemingly a success for the European wing of the Cabinet, it eventually helped to strengthen anti-Europe feeling, especially in the Tory Party. Although Thatcherite opposition to the ERM rested as much on an ideology of floating exchange rates as on hostility to 'Europe', the counter-attack, welling up in most corners of business and the press, and much of the parliamentary party, was in part born of resistance to the entire direction of the leader's European policy.

Out of her excessive hostility grew the misdirected zeal of the other side, which allowed itself to be deceived into ignoring the downside of entry into the ERM at the chosen moment: a moment that came about not through any perfect economic logic, but more because it happened to be the moment when the leader's resistance at last collapsed.

In the longer term, this had a still weightier effect, redoubling the scale of the defeat that awaited those who thought that, by entry, they had won. The mistimed entry, when followed two years later by humiliating exit, discredited the very concept of a fixed exchange rate in the period when EMU, from being a speculative dream, had become an imminent reality. When a serious British debate about EMU should have begun, it was impeded not least by sick memories of the ERM experience. For years after October 1990, all British politicians found it hard to speak of the ERM without being drowned in hoots of derision. In Conservative circles, the infamous alphabetic sequence was literally unmentionable. In the Blair Government, it was considered so explosive that the then Chancellor of the Exchequer, while announcing that Britain would enter EMU if and when the time was ripe, felt obliged to deny that he had any intention of joining the ERM beforehand, as the prevailing Treaty stipulated.[89]

The ERM, in short, became the Great Satan. It was placed beyond the edge of rational discussion. Such was the consequence of the October climax in 1990, for which the supporters of 'Europe', it can be seen in retrospect, were as much to blame as the enemies. Indeed, since it was only later that a good many of these supporters became enemies, perhaps one should say that the 1990 friends of the ERM were almost entirely to blame for the disastrous connotations which thereafter hung around it.

Politically there was a more immediate result. Joining the ERM was the penultimate episode in the self-destruction of Margaret Thatcher. Never before had she been driven to an action she was so reluctant to endorse. Even the 1985 Anglo-Irish Agreement, which she signed with gritted pen, had, by comparison, its merits. After the ERM moment, it was very soon apparent that she could not forgive herself. Her response was in keeping with the general tendency to over-compensate for defeat, which was by now infecting all sides of the 'Europe' argument in Britain. This mighty Prime Minister, once the lord of so much she surveyed, had lost the decision. But she was determined not to let the consequences slip away from her. The decision must in some way be countermanded. She therefore set out to make clear what this baleful defeat for her did not mean.

It was the beginning of the end. And the scene of its unfolding opened, fittingly, in Rome, home of the originating Treaty that was responsible for luring the island towards this benighted continent in the first place. At a summit called there by the Italians, EMU was eased relentlessly on to the agenda. There emerged a plan to fix a date by which the second stage of the Delors committee's proposal should be set in place. Thus, a mere three weeks after Britain dragged herself into the ERM – Stage One – the continentals were already plotting something else: a rather vague, but nonetheless insistent, pushing forward.

In fact the summit turned out less threatening than it might have been. It agreed to delay the Stage Two deadline by a year, from January 1993 to 1994. The communiqué made no explicit commitment to a single currency in the future. But the Thatcher boiling-point was lower than before. The very looseness of the communiqué, shaped in part to suit the lady, attracted her scorn for its 'grand and vague words'. She made a vigorous assault on 'non-urgent and distant things' that were far from 'the nitty-gritty of negotiation'. 'People who get on a train like that deserve to be taken for a ride,' she said at a press conference when the summit closed. The vehicle was on its way to 'cloud-cuckoo land'. When M. Delors predicted that a single currency would be created before 2000, she retorted that the British Parliament would never agree to it, and would stop it in its tracks. 'We shall block things which are not in British interests, of course we shall,' she promised, goaded onwards by the reckless aggression of much of the tabloid press. It was to this moment that the *Sun* pinned the famous ranting headline – 'UP YOURS DELORS'.

Returning home, she had not cooled off. True, as quite often happened in the Thatcher decade, the relevant Whitehall officials effected a certain hosing down. In her report to the Commons, Mrs Thatcher read out a text that gave off a different level of heat. By comparison with Rome, she sounded almost emollient, even alluding with approval to Major's hard-écu plan and acknowledging the possibility – the remote and undesirable but nonetheless real possibility – of it eliding into a single currency if the people and governments chose that route. But this was merely the text. When she came to the questions that followed it, and there was no text to hold her down, the politics of the intensely personal resumed their sway.

The European Commission, she said, was trying to 'extinguish democracy'. She would never stand by while a federal Europe was created 'by the back door'. This is what a single currency would amount to. Having suggested earlier that the écu could develop into a single currency, she now insisted that it would not, in the real world, be widely used. Therefore it could not develop. Therefore, by implication, there could never be a single currency.

As for M. Delors, he had many federalizing schemes. For all of these she had a simple answer. It became, in its monosyllabic brutality, the rubric of one of her most famous parliamentary moments, leaping with rage, ringing round the chamber, startling even those who in eleven years had much experience of the Thatcher vocabulary on Europe. 'No . . . no . . . no,' she bawled, her eye seemingly directed to the fields and seas, the hills and the landing-grounds, where the island people would never surrender.[90]

*

LOOKING BACK FROM 1998, one finds it hard to credit the circumstances of Margaret Thatcher's undoing.

Here was a Prime Minister who had won three general elections, and still bestrode politics. The people had elected her, kept on electing her, and her party in the country continued to greet the super-star wherever she went. She was not a fading force, nor had she suffered the kind of parliamentary defeats that begin to unpick the position of a leader in place for more than a decade, as she had been. All these were points of astonishment when her assassination occurred, but the aspect of it that grew most arresting as time passed was different. In 1998, it was utterly jarring to recall that the prime cause – at least the indispensable pretext – of Mrs Thatcher's removal was that Conservative Members of Parliament were unable any longer to trust her hostile conduct of British relations with Europe.

There were other influences. She seemed to some of them to be losing her touch in a more general way. The most worrying proof of it was her inability to draw the deadly electoral sting of the new local property impost, the so-called poll tax, which she had been determined to put in place. This tax roused even the stoical British to riot in the streets, an event whose rarity made it very potent. The poll tax also hit Tory MPs where it hurt them, often being a gauge, measurable between one locality and another, of their prospects of holding on to their seats at the next election. Anxiety about survival, their Government's and their own, was the *sine qua non* of the uprising in the parliamentary party that drove Mrs Thatcher from office.

Europe, however, fired anxiety to its decisive pitch. It was her performance at and after Rome that determined the manoeuvres of the decisive players against her. It supplied them with the material for attack, and enriched the atmosphere of alarm into which they deployed it. The leader was suspected, even by some of her supporters, of becoming wayward, excessively emotional, often, in the bar-room demotic of the Commons, a little crazy. One Cabinet minister told me around this time that she was 'absolutely barking' – which, coming from an opponent of ultra-Thatcherism, was discountable, but, because it reflected what was being loosely put about by a wider range of politicians and editors, suggested her position might be crumbling. Even though her climactic roar in the Commons, the triple negative, was answered with deep-throated pulsations of approval behind her, the Tory Party in the autumn of 1990 was inwardly conflicted. It still warmed to the defiant chauvinism that was her standard mode of speech. But it could also respond to the inducements of those most worried by the stance which she was, incorrigibly, taking.

The pro-Europe segment of Conservatism secured the strongest purchase on these contradictory feelings. Mrs Thatcher was challenged by people whose sharpest identity was 'European'. She was voted out of office by a party which, at this time, came to be repelled by the extremity of her anti-Europeanism. Written in 1998, that is a statement it is hard to come to grips with. By 1998, there was almost no limit to the Euro-scepticism that would find favour in the Tory Party. But in 1990 it was Mrs Thatcher's almost demented fervour over Europe that convinced enough Tory MPs of her wider ineligibility to be the leader who could guarantee them a fourth election victory.

The first signal came a year before. After Lawson and Howe left the great offices, turbulence in the party did not abate. The Tories hadn't recovered from their last electoral disaster, the European elections in summer 1989, when the leader's ferocity was given full expression in party propaganda – to unimpressive effect. The campaign was conducted on the basis that Europe was the enemy, and its Parliament a near-absurdity. This did not strike a chord with the British people. Urged to be fearful of 'a Diet of Brussels' and suchlike puerilities, less than 28 per cent of those who turned out voted Conservative, the lowest share of the vote ever recorded by the party in a nationwide election.

The leader, therefore, was challenged in December 1989. The challenge did not succeed. But the man who made it, an otherwise obscure baronet, Sir Anthony Meyer MP, was best known for his European dimension. Though generally unsympathetic to all that Thatcherism stood for, he responded to a specific stimulus. 'I made no secret of the fact that it was her manifest distaste for everything that emanates from Europe that finally decided me to launch my challenge,' Meyer writes in his own memoir.[91] He persuaded sixty MPs not to vote for the lady. It was a harbinger. Although she paid little attention, it rendered thinkable what had previously been viewed with incredulity.

The same definition, the European, applied with much greater sharpness to the man more seriously lurking in the Conservative politics of the later 1980s, the politician who, shortly after the débâcle in Rome, was obliged to conclude that his time had come.

Michael Heseltine stood for nothing if he did not stand for Europe. The continental connection infused, with Heath-like intensity, every part of the politics that interested him. There were differences with Heath. For Heseltine, the drive had less to do with worshipping alongside the post-war cult of Jean Monnet than with a view of economics, especially the economics of size, and the over arching necessity of Britain submerging herself in the only entity that would give her a chance of survival in global competition – except that survival was not a concept Heseltine ever discussed. His obsession was with 'winning'. The pitch he always made for Britain-in-Europe was that this was the only road to 'victory', the mythic objective beloved of many politicians: an expression which comes from the same root as the Thatcher concept of 'battle'. Heseltine, who wrote a substantial book on the subject, called it *The Challenge of Europe: can Britain win?* – a question to which there was a positive answer, but only on one condition.

In 1990, Heseltine had been absent from governing politics for nearly five years. He had walked out of the Cabinet in 1986, ostensibly on a Europe question – the obscure but fiery matter of whether Britain should build military helicopters under licence from American or European suppliers. Surrounded by static of the most explosive kind, emanating from the Thatcher personality and the Thatcher style of governing and Heseltine's lordly impatience with his inability to get his way, that was the core issue in what became known as the Westland affair. Every week and every month thereafter, Heseltine devoted himself to avenging not just the personal defeat he had suffered – always the most powerful impulse, demanding the ultimate retribution – but also the political misjudgement he thought this defeat entailed. He was passionately committed on Europe. He wrote his book, which was a serious, thorough, constructive compilation, and a polemic in favour of closer integration.⁹² He also spread the word. I saw him a number of times during his wilderness years, and never failed to receive a lecture about the leader's European follies: how she had got the Germans hopelessly wrong, had put a succession of anti-Europeans in charge of Britain's trading policy, did not know or care about the needs of British business. 'Germany and France will go ahead with some sort of monetary union,' he told me in March 1990, 'and Britain will simply slide slowly out of the picture, mainly owing to one woman's prejudice.' He was appalled to think there was nothing more to it than that.

But Heseltine had to be careful. Though it was common knowledge that he thirsted to depose the woman, prudence said he should never indicate, by a half-sentence of public disloyalty, that this was the case. The quantity of his menace depended on the quality of his silence. Maintaining his air of mystery, Heseltine loomed ever larger as the raw lineaments of Mrs Thatcher were finally demystified. It required the intervention of another force, creating another climacteric of the European argument, to bring him into the open.

The most avid listener to the triple negative had been a minister who was supposed, under collective responsibility, to endorse it. Geoffrey Howe was still a member of the Cabinet. But after hearing it, and reflecting on the excitement it induced on the benches behind, he decided he had had enough. A relationship which, he mordantly calculated, had stretched through at least 700 meetings of Cabinets and shadow Cabinets, was brought summarily to an end by his resignation. Or rather, its positive aspect was concluded. Their twenty-year professional connection had one more element to disclose, a final disgorging of emotion laid out for the witness of the world.

They exchanged letters of departure with mutual incomprehension. He wrote: 'We must be at the centre of the European partnership, playing the sort of leading and constructive role which commands respect. . . . I now find myself unable to share your view of the right approach to this question.' She wrote: 'Your letter refers to differences between us on Europe. I do not believe that these are nearly as great as you suggest.' They were ships passing in the day, never mind the night. She also wrote, material for greater retrospective puzzlement, 'We want Britain . . . to be part of the further political, economic and monetary development of the European Community.'

But these were merely the formalities. There remained the opportunity for speech, and Howe determined to make the most of his: the resignation speech, customarily heard in silence by the Commons, in which he would explain himself with the most devastating effect he could summon from a rhetorical style never previously noted for its power. It is another measure of the 'Europe' question, its capacity to grip the hearts as well as the heads of many different kinds of British politician, that, at this terminal occasion, it propelled Geoffrey Howe to heights of oratory more disdainful and more lethal than he had ever reached before.

It was the occasion, as much as the words, that mattered. The words were damaging enough. They spoke of Europe and they spoke of style, intimating that Cabinet government, over Europe, had all but come to an end. They described as 'futile' the task of 'trying to stretch the meaning of words beyond what was credible and trying to pretend that there was a common policy'. They offered self-laceration, from a man who had 'wrestled for perhaps too long' with his conflict of loyalties. But what made the moment decisive was its timing. Enough MPs knew, in their inward minds, that Howe was not speaking out of pique so much as desperation. They recognized, even if silently, the picture that he drew. They looked to their own seats and their own future if that picture was permitted to prevail. And they were aware of both the man and the moment that might supply an immediate opportunity for relief. If the annual leadership election, provided for in party rules though never activated before 1989, had not beckoned, nothing might have happened. As it was, after Howe spoke, the calendar set the tumbrils rolling.

For Heseltine, it was now or never. Howe's speech drew him from cover. The urge for a contest reached even those who never wanted Heseltine to win it. They could not deny the divisive nature of Mrs Thatcher, in substance as well as style. One of her most obsequious flatterers, Paul Johnson, was driven to write in the *Daily Mail* of 'the real weakness of Mrs Thatcher's leadership – her inability to unite the party over Europe, or even to convince it that she is doing her best to keep it together'. And so enough of the party thought, proving the truth of the perception by splitting almost down the middle when it came to the vote. There were 152 votes for Heseltine, 204 for Mrs Thatcher – a majority four short of what the arcane rules required for a first-round victory. The lady was now for burning.

There was something dramatically satisfying about these final days. The locations were somehow appropriate. After spitting on the Treaty in Rome, the leader was on her way to Versailles when she first heard that she was to be consigned to the guillotine. She did not immediately offer her head. Having heard, while in Paris for a European meeting, that the vote had left her short, she fulfilled her Versailles engagement with aplomb. Her old adversaries were considerate. François Mitterrand, the host, delayed proceedings for an hour until she arrived. Helmut Kohl, she records in her memoirs, came straight to the point, advising her not to bottle up her feelings. She had plenty to say against Kohl but at least, she writes, he was 'never devious'. 'He had been determined to devote this evening to me as a way of demonstrating his complete support.'[93]

Kohl, however, did not have a vote. And it must be doubted whether, if he had had one, he would have cast it in favour of survival. As it was, the leader did not survive, falling by her own hand two days later, when she was persuaded by a stream of colleagues that a second round of voting would not supply the victory, or at any rate the mandate, she needed to carry on.

So passed the longest-lived leader of Britain's European connection. Though Heseltine plunged the dagger, after Howe had drawn the first blood, he did not succeed. He could spark the party into a negative act, but not a positive one on his own behalf. Instead of him, it elected as replacement the most obscure of the candidates, with the most opaque record on all matters, Europe among them.

As to what this meant, hindsight is again a good and faithful servant. Only at a distance is it possible to reckon out the truth, and get a measure of the ambiguity in the Conservative Party at that time.

Ostensibly, the deposing of Margaret Thatcher was the conclusive triumph of Tory Europeanism. Here was the largest Conservative, now ranging the party openly against the objectives of the Treaty of Rome – 'an ever closer union among the peoples of Europe'. She might cavil at that description, saying that a union of peoples should be distinguished from – would be violated by – a union of governments or states. No matter: addressing Europe's evolution as attained by 1990, she was anti-'European'. And she lost. She terminally antagonized two major figures, both of them paradigm 'Europeans', who routed her from the field. What Helmut Schmidt called her defining characteristic, her love of war, was not enough to win the last battle. This was decided not just by Heseltine and Howe but by the party at large, in Parliament and, to sufficient extent, outside as well. When she left, the nation and much of the party exhaled a long sigh of relief. They were relieved at the new possibilities: of collective decision-making, of reasoned discussion, of government that started from the belief that Europeans were not enemies but colleagues with whom business could be done. The first continental act performed by the new man, John Major, was a declaration that he wanted Britain to be 'at the very heart of Europe'.[94] It seemed to settle the tenor of a more stable time.

Such was the apparent truth. But it was wholly deceiving. Actually, these events were the prelude to something like the opposite. After a brief period of tranquillity, the expulsion of Mrs Thatcher led to more turbulence than ever before. It settled nothing. 'Europe' was the pretext for the great defenestration, but settling the Europe question was not what the party was in any state to do. By her departure, Mrs Thatcher gave way to the 'Europeans' – yet also exposed how little they had prepared the ground for their own victory.

A question was answered: for how long could the country stand a leader whose Europe policy, founded on aggression, became totally divisive? But another question was asked: how could the party that first took Britain into Europe still be vulnerable to the prejudices which the bloody victors thought they had expelled?

10

WILLIAM CASH

Europe Made Me

EURO-SCEPTICISM, though it did not enter the language until the 1980s, penetrated the bloodstream of the Conservative Party in the early 1950s. From the moment 'Europe' began to be invented, there were Conservatives who thought Britain should have nothing to do with it. There were Labour people too. The names have changed, the numbers surged and fell, but the institutions have always harboured this strain of feeling. It is a persistent, rooted thing, which some Tories and some progressives alike cannot regard as inconsistent with their party allegiance, even when party leaderships have been long committed to Europe. Indeed, especially on the Tory side, they see their tenacity as a noble duty, for which they will one day be rewarded by seeing their party redirected towards the course of national righteousness.

This phenomenon is not in the least surprising. What is at stake has always been fundamental. It hasn't always been presented that way. Enthusiasts for entry, as we have seen in the cases of Edward Heath and Geoffrey Howe, felt it prudent to mask the radical nature of the transaction they were proposing. But 'Europe' involved an organic shift in the nature of the nation-state. This hit some people in their guts. They could never get over it. It broke with a history they revered, notably the Commonwealth connection. It seemed to imply a threat to the heart and soul of Britishness. For some politicians, driven by a sense of existential crisis, opposing it became the central purpose of their life.

Some of the early opponents of entry proved to be less driven. Peter Walker, later a Cabinet minister under both Heath and Mrs Thatcher, is an example. As a youthful tyro, Walker acquired notoriety for tramping round the Commonwealth to oppose the Common Market. Getting into Parliament in 1961, he immediately set about attacking the Macmillan negotiations then in train. His reasons were mainly to do with a judgement about trade, laced with his preference for the multi-racialism of the Commonwealth. He came at Europe from the left of the party. 'It was proposing external tariffs against the rest of the world,' he later wrote. 'And it was totally white, while I believed that Asia and Africa were the emergent powers.'[1] Walker seriously believed that Commonwealth trade could build the future of British prosperity. But not for long. By the end of the 1960s, with Heath on the brink of office, Walker had seen the error of his ways. 'I became more and more convinced of the wisdom of my conversion,' he writes, 'when I became a minister, attended EEC Councils of Ministers and began to see the value of co-ordinated European action.'

This element of self-interested rationality – the lack, in the end, of gut feeling – helps account for Walker's rare status as a committed sceptic who then enthusiastically went over to the other side. There were more startling versions. In June 1971, Nicholas Winterton secured the Tory nomination for the Macclesfield by-election as an anti-Marketeer, and won it in September as a pro-Marketeer.[2] The conversion experience litters this story, but mostly, as time goes on, the other way. Economics was never enough to breed undying hostility. For that, it was necessary for the viscera to be fully engaged.

In history, the core of scepticism has been about the visceral question. In the 1972 debates, the few incorrigible Tories who opposed Heath were moved by thoughts of nation more than economics. Their parliamentary resistance was mannerly, tenacious and almost entirely uninfluential. Insofar as they mattered, it was to achieve the ironic effect of pushing alarmed ministers to dissemble about what they were doing. They had no effect on the decision. But they kept the flag flying, and a sceptic core intact, and some of them still mattered a quarter-century later.

John Biffen, for example, was proud to have voted more often against the European Communities Act 1972 than any other Tory. He even beat his hero, Enoch Powell, on the count. In the style of that era, he maintained a stance of perfect parliamentary civility, which carried on through a career that crested as a member of the Thatcher Cabinet. Biffen's lightness of touch, combined with the remarkable bipartisan regard in which he was always held, made him a kind of licensed sceptic even when belonging to a government which officially embraced the European project. But on this subject, he was granite. He believed in nation as the only entity capable of commanding popular authority. For many years he carried in his wallet a dog-eared sheet on which he had inscribed a quotation to remind him where he stood. It came from de Gaulle's memoirs. 'Now what are the realities of Europe?' the General asked. 'What are the pillars on which it can be built? The truth is that those pillars are the states of Europe ... states each of which, indeed, has its own genius, history and language, its own sorrows, glories and ambitions; but states that are the only entities with the right to give orders and the powers to be obeyed.'[3]

Biffen didn't make many speeches on the subject. Compared with later sceptics, he was as short on didactic ranting as he was on bile. He thought enlargement might be the answer, but underestimated the capacity of the Community to absorb new nations without sacrificing its momentum towards integration. In 1977, he wrote that the accession of Greece, Portugal and Spain, then being discussed, would make the Common Agricultural Policy a dead letter, and monetary union 'well nigh impossible'. He added: 'I am certain the Treaty [of Rome] cannot prescribe the political forms to govern a Europe of Twelve.'[4] None of this having come to pass fifteen years later, the arguments continued and Biffen was part of them. The Twelve had become Fifteen and Brussels was not broken. But it might be. A new generation of Tory MPs arrived in the Commons, equipped with Biffen's firm purpose and their own brand of streetwise ferocity. In 1992, as a back-bench elder statesman, Biffen rejoiced to see himself as teacher and strategist, the old brain behind the young. He once told me that he was now the Fagin of Euro-scepticism.

This school had other ancients who went back to the beginning. One of them was a Scotsman, Teddy Taylor, also present at the creation which he adamantly opposed. Unlike Biffen, Taylor bore all the signs of becoming a single-issue politician, as well as an unlucky one. Having fought the Heath application, he was installed in the Thatcher shadow Cabinet but then lost his seat at the 1979 election. Re-elected, for a seat in the south of England, he was never invited on to the front bench again, largely because he was an anti-European. This stance he took with unshakeable earnestness, though again, like Biffen, he was short on acrimony and capable of self-mockery. 'You see I am terribly obsessed about the European Community,' he told an interviewer, looking back on his life, in 1996. 'This is probably a problem. I am the biggest Euro-bore there ever was.'[5] Though he participated keenly in every anti-European rebellion of the 1990s, unlike most of his friends he didn't need the sting of betrayal to get him going. He knew in 1972 what Europe meant for national independence. He thought entry would be a disaster, and left the Government on account of it. But Heath, he said, also knew what it meant and did not conceal it. Unlike all the modern ultras, Taylor never pleaded deception by the former leader as the reason for an uprising. 'He didn't hide the consequences,' Taylor reflected. 'The tragedy is that few listened.'[6]

So here were two exemplars of a steady trend. There always were Tory politicians who detested British membership of the European Community from start to finish, top to bottom. They were part of the scenery, to whom nobody objected because fundamentally they didn't matter. They were admitted, sustained, even promoted, in polite society. But for many years they also seemed irrelevant, a fringe group of tolerated cranks. What they stood for had, after all, been defeated. Minorities deserved to have their voice, but this one was faced by some inconvenient developments.

The first was the 1975 referendum, in which all the Tory sceptics of the time naturally played a part. The result of the referendum appeared to close the gut argument. Belatedly, the anti-EEC position had been displayed and tested before the people, of whom two-thirds turned out not to be impressed. There remained plenty of negotiating to be done, to defend the British position, but the fundamentalist line was finished: a reading emphatically reinforced by the second development, the election of Margaret Thatcher. Everything about Mrs Thatcher's prime ministership seemed to render the sceptic cause, politically, void of rebel fire. On the one hand, she absorbed it into her own strategies towards Europe, especially over the budget. On the other, by taking Britain into more intimate congress with the Community, she seemed to be confessing that there was no longer any future in root-and-branch hostility. As proof of this, nothing could have been more eloquent than Biffen's own piloting of the Single European Act through a guillotined House of Commons.

When the lady herself was overthrown, this reading seemed to be confirmed. It was surely implausible to suppose that the forces of reason, of power, of acquiescence, of establishment conformity – everything that 'Europe' conventionally represented – could now be displaced. If that were to happen, it would argue for the presence in the Tory soul of a force quite different from the ineffectual fragment of gentlemanly politicians who disclosed themselves twenty years before. This force, if it existed, would have to be outside the realm of the hitherto known: a voracious beast not yet sighted: a spirit still capable of being moved uncontrollably by the visceral impulses most people thought had been put to sleep.

*

WILLIAM CASH was not present in 1972. But he was there in 1990, and still there in 1998. As the personification of the Tory Euro-sceptic spirit in this new, unfettered guise, he became the single most notorious operator, at a time when these people finally came to matter. In his person he does as much as anyone to show how and why, after Mrs Thatcher was deposed, the beast that had failed to defend her was let loose, avenging the years of impotence, on what was now supposed to be a European country.

Cash was born in May 1940 – on the day, as it happens, that Churchill became Prime Minister – child of a father killed in Normandy four years later. Whether this was already a defining moment is hard to say. It cannot have given the Germans a high place in the youthful Cash's hierarchy of esteem: and Germany bulked large in the nightmare visions he later had of Europe. Another feature worth pondering is his Catholicism. Educated by the Jesuits, at Stonyhurst, he might, simplistically, have been expected to gravitate towards the pro-Europe camp. After all, wasn't the Community a Catholic conspiracy, orchestrated from the Vatican, mistrusted on that account by Ernest Bevin and Denis Healey, not to mention, in fragmentary moments, Margaret Thatcher, a notorious incomprehender of Catholicism? It is a feature of modern scepticism, however, that the religious stereotype has been copiously reversed. Maybe this attests to the dwindling power of the Vatican, maybe to the fact that other spectres came to dominate the fear-filled minds of those who dislike everything epitomized by 'Brussels'. Among the more tireless critics of British policy, and even membership, in the 1990s were well-known Roman Catholics such as the editor of the *Daily Telegraph*, Charles Moore, the former editor of *The Times*, William Rees-Mogg, the incontinent columnist Paul Johnson. The Catholic fraternity included converts, both to their new Church and/or to a view of Europe opposite to the one they had held before: suggestive indicator, perhaps, of a cast of mind that entertains flexibility of doctrine, while needing it to coexist with blazing doctrinal certainty at any given moment.

Cash was a Catholic from the start, but not an anti-European. As it happens, I knew him in our youth, when we played cricket together on the fields round Sheffield. He remained a fanatic for the English game, captaining parliamentary teams into later middle age. But more formative was his induction into English history, which he read at Oxford. The appurtenances of history began close to home, with his descent, as he seldom missed an opportunity to recall, from John Bright, the Victorian social reformer. When totally immersed in the anti-Europe cause, he sometimes raised his eyes from the latest statutory excrescence to remind one that he was not, like most of his factional colleagues, a right-winger. In his early days, he was saluted by Shelter, the housing charity, and also recognized as a campaigner for the relief of Third World debt. But the defence of the nation, as a nation, became his cause, and revelling in its history was his pastime. His country home in Staffordshire, he was proud to think, once belonged to the British ambassador to Hanover in the late 1690s.

Cash started professional life as a lawyer: useful avocation for what was to come. Installed first in a family firm of solicitors, he took up the recondite work of a parliamentary agent, assisting businesses and local authorities with the promotion of private bills. At a young age he was a legal adviser to the Confederation of British Industry. Later he got deeply involved with large-scale measures such as paving the way for submarine pipelines and repatriating the Canadian constitution. It was activity that kept him in the purlieus of Westminster, and made him familiar with statutory exegesis: a talent which, in later years, his contemporaries, obliged to watch him deploy his indefatigable capacity for deconstructing European legislation, had as much reason to regret as to admire.

It took Cash some time to reach the heart of Westminster. As a young man, he worked away at the party grass-roots, spent holidays helping older MPs keep their seats. His power-base, if it could be called such, was the Primrose League, an antediluvian Tory sub-group, originally the magnet for the party's recruitment of women, which, according to one reliable history, had 'passed its peak in most areas by 1906'.[7] At least fourteen parliamentary seats declined to make Cash their Tory nominee, before he closed in on Stafford and won a by-election in 1984. He was no worse a candidate for politics than a hundred other Tories. He was pleasant, serious and committed to the public good, if prone to deeper-delving obsessions than his contemporaries. But he came with neither the connections nor the charisma for stardom. Arriving in the House, he seemed destined for an ordinary career of public service that would never make him famous.

Almost immediately, however, he plunged into the Europe question.

Somebody recognized the textual appetites of the budding legislator, and
put him on the Select Committee on European Legislation, which has
the task of trying to scrutinize the outpourings from Brussels. The job
put Cash's Europeanism on the line.

For he regarded himself as a European; and he certainly wasn't a
cradle sceptic of Biffenish mien. In the 1975 referendum, he voted Yes,
and was then involved in founding something called the Westminster-
for-Europe Group. More than that, he prided himself on his Euro-
awareness from a legal point of view. Long before Britain signed the
Treaty of Rome, he urged his law partners to remember that this would
be a superior law, when it came into force. The European Court of
Justice would hand down superior judgments. He thought the partners
should know this, and prepare for it. Always a fearless letter-writer to
the powers-that-be, the young Cash widened the audience for his
message. 'I wrote to the President of the Law Society and the Prime
Minister to get people to realize that they had to have course studies for
the solicitors' exams in European law as an absolute fundamental,' he
told me.[8]

While anxious to open other people's eyes, however, it turned out
that he had not fully opened his own. Neither the statutory nor the
political momentum towards integration, which the Treaty expressed,
had apparently crossed his consciousness. He did not believe in momentum, nor in the desire of some Europeans to achieve it. His arrival on
the select committee seems, for all his vaunted attention to the subject,
to have produced a terrible awakening. 'It was then that I realised what
was really going on,' he writes. 'The European Community was in danger
of rapidly becoming a political federation.'[9] A visit to Brussels with the
committee exposed the fuller dimensions of the nightmare. 'I was
disturbed by the number of officials I met from the European Commission whose federalism was beyond doubt.'

Shattering though it was, this *aperçu* did not at first divert Cash from
supporting the Government's own Europeanism. No sooner did he
arrive in Parliament than the Single European Act reached the agenda
for debate and decision. At this stage in the evolution of the 'Europe'
question, he played a role that confirmed the innocence of his legal
understanding, while simultaneously enraging those with a longer sceptic
pedigree than he had. It was where, however, he first established a
reputation, the *sine qua non* of 1990s Euro-scepticism, for interminable
fascination with the small print behind which one should always assume
the likely presence of ministerial subterfuge. He was making his mark as

a Euro-bore, even as he rebuked others for mistrusting the Single
European Act more than he did.

On second reading, he warmly supported the Act. Though he
thought the Community's 'mechanisms' needed careful watching, and
cautioned that 'we must be sure we know what we are doing', he pointed
to the global competitiveness the single market would bring, and added
a reassurance: 'We tend to exaggerate the dangers of majority voting.'[10]
On the committee stage, which was dominated by the sceptics, he again
affirmed the obvious truth, that majority voting could work to Britain's
advantage. He twitted Enoch Powell with the reminder that, in 1972, the
sage had prefaced his attacks on British entry with the words: 'I come
to speak to you as a European, among Europeans.' Not having been
present himself in 1972, Cash felt free to patronize those who had
missed the point about what the Treaty of Rome really meant. They had
been 'a little disingenuous ... and did not consider the treaty in its full
context ... They should not be so surprised to find that these things are
happening now,' he solemnly chided.[11] Given his own seeming lacunae
of understanding, his listeners could have been excused if they regarded
this as faintly insufferable. Whereas Teddy Taylor, Enoch Powell and
others voted steadily against the Bill, Cash reliably supported it, even
speaking in favour of the guillotine, albeit on condition that time be
allowed for some substantive speeches by all those, himself included,
who hadn't been allowed to say enough.

On third reading, he did open up some anxieties. The generalized
alarm about the looming, spreading, all-consuming monster of Brussels
was beginning to express itself. Familiar buzz-words vaporized across the
sky. 'It is essential', he said, 'to maintain the democracy of this House
and its sovereignty and to ensure that we do know that the legislation
done in our name is known to have been done on behalf of the people
of this country.'[12] Indeed, he had tabled an amendment asserting, with
the kind of grandeur that teeters between the definitive and the meaningless, that 'nothing in this Act shall derogate from the sovereignty of the
United Kingdom Parliament'.

But the amendment was ignored, and Cash's vote was unaffected.
Essentially, he was a Thatcherite. What Mrs Thatcher believed, he
believed as well: that the preambles and codicils about closer union did
not mean what they said, and that Britain, in any case, could, under the
lady's vigilant leadership, prevent further outrages occurring.

He had, however, now been ineradicably infected with the pleasures and the pains of notoriety as an anti-Brussels, if not wholly anti-Europe, politician. The pleasures, on the whole, were ascendant. The by-line of William Cash began to appear with some regularity, especially in *The Times*. These pieces, in turn, would be alluded to as reinforcements of his speeches in the Commons. He began to travel the continent in search of kindred spirits, journeys from which he would return with extensive lists of names to be dropped and many hours of intimate discussion attested to. A German banker here, a French Gaullist there, seminars in Madrid, weekend conferences in Schloss this or that, all were fluid matter for Bill's torrential, single-issue conversation, the proof that he was not alone in the scepticism he felt about the European project.

An obscure, even mildly comical, politician was on the way to becoming an international celebrity, whose voice counted for something in a government to which he would never belong.

*

THOUGH MRS THATCHER WENT, Cash did not. Nor did any of the others who thought like he did. In the leadership contest, they were defeated by the forces of reason, of fear, of, among other things, 'Europe': the defenestration was opposed by every sentient Euro-sceptic. But then they colluded in the nomination of her successor. John Major, the chosen leader, was supposedly their man. He could not have been elected without them. They had a veto on the alternative possibilities. While the lady's departure seemed to signal the triumph of the Europeans, less remarked was that Major's installation was contingent on the anti-Europeans. This was a party already in subterranean conflict with itself, even as it rallied round a new, more collegiate, more consensual leader. The mainstream establishment had won. But the potential of Euro-scepticism, lurking just below the skin of the staid and stolid centre of the party, was greater than anyone understood in November 1990.

It came in several clusters, which had different roots.

The old guard was still represented. Many veterans of 1972 were dead or departed, and Biffen's impersonation of Fagin awaited the 1992 election, when the new young boys would come aboard. But there remained the hardest of hard-liners, including Teddy Taylor, and a farmer named Richard Body who had pushed the cause for twenty years. Body's opposition embraced any forensic attitude that lay to hand, not excluding a paranoia that qualified him, from way back, to keep

company with the younger Euro-phobes. It was Body who in 1975 first
sought an audience for the claim that the CIA station chief in London
was the hidden hand behind the Yes campaign in the referendum.[13]

A second group, almost as strongly pedigreed, came to full flower
during the Thatcher years. Nicholas Budgen, Powell's successor in
Wolverhampton from 1974, was a thinking, practising sceptic who joined
Taylor and Co. opposing the Single European Act. So did names of past
and future obscurity such as Ivan Lawrence and Bill Walker. Edward du
Cann, former party chairman and never much of a supporter of what
Heath did in the beginning, was of the company.

But the case of the Single Act presented problems which foreshadowed divisions in scepticism that continued, in various forms, to dog it
as a source of belief and unified allegiance. Down the years it attracted
free traders, on the one hand, protectionists on the other: currency fixers
as well as currency floaters: the right and, occasionally, the left: Little
Englanders, yet alongside them globalists who regarded Europe as too
small a span to work with. On the Single Act itself, an exemplary figure
is that of George Gardiner MP. This was a politician so loyal to Mrs
Thatcher that he spent the years from 1990 to 1997 conspiring against
her successor, and so full of loathing for European union that he finally
bolted the party. But in 1986 he was more emphatic than Bill Cash about
the need to pass the Act, making, as we have seen, a speech in praise of
the economies of scale as the only way by which Europe could challenge
America's technological supremacy. Gardiner's attack on national protectionism, and his defence of majority voting to make the market function
better, could not have been improved on by Ted Heath himself.[14]

This highlights a third strand of the sceptic phenomenon: numerically, and politically, the most arresting. Bill Cash and George Gardiner
were not the only converts. This was a church full to overflowing with
apostates of one kind or another, and it was the brutal eviction of
Margaret Thatcher that tended to persuade many of them to clarify their
new position. Many who had served in her Government, but were not
inclined to break with her even after they had left it, came forward with
an anti-Europeanism freshly minted. Her departure removed their heroine, in some cases their very reason for supporting Conservatism.
Exposing anti-Europe feelings at least as strong as hers was one way of
securing revenge for what the other side had done. Not all the scepticism
that soon began to swirl round her successor can be attributed to such
personal sourness. But what is indisputable is that the parting of Mrs

Thatcher from her job accelerated the parting of many politicians from their support for the official party line on Europe.

The conversions came in many times and shapes. There is a variety of motive and explanation, of fame and obscurity, to be sampled.

The sceptics of the 1990s included some exceptional enthusiasts of the 1970s. An example was John Wilkinson. As Conservative MP for Ruislip Northwood, he joined every group, however disloyal, that strove to make life insupportable for the Major Government on Europe: the most obdurate Old Etonian to be found on that side of the argument. Yet who is this, during the pathfinding debate of October 1971, leaping from his place to harry and hector anyone who dared challenge Heath's great scheme? The same Mr Wilkinson, then MP for Bradford West.

In 1965, a Labour MP named Woodrow Wyatt wrote to *The Times* announcing himself as a European more *pur et dur* than the grand master, Heath himself. This was during the wilderness phase, after the failure of the Macmillan negotiation and before Harold Wilson had begun to think about taking up the cause. Wyatt pleaded for a gesture that would cut through the agonizing, saying: 'We should make the historic and brave decision to sign the Treaty of Rome as it stands.'[15] He held to the pro-Europe line through and beyond the referendum. But, having shifted parties, in conformity with a powerful adoration of Mrs Thatcher, he also reversed his attitude. His experience resembled that of Cash. The enterprise turned out to be not as he imagined. What he had once regarded as 'unattainable pious hopes' now offended him by their apparent substance. The European Court of Justice, a basic lynchpin of the Community idea, now had no acceptable place. 'The court,' Wyatt wrote, 'steeped in continental law, expresses its judgements in terms frequently offensive to our understanding of law.' 'We are as alien to the major players on the mainland as they are to us,' he went on.[16] By the end of 1996, Wyatt was advocating Britain's immediate exit from the European Union.

A similar odyssey was traversed by another convert peer, the historian and scholar Max Beloff. In 1969, Beloff published a book on British foreign policy arguing that Britain's destiny was to assume the leadership of Europe 'which she rejected almost a quarter-century ago'. The logic of the argument that the European nation-state is 'for many purposes obsolescent' was, he wrote, 'unanswerable'. It followed that Britain should 'come out as an advocate of a European federal system'.[17] Yet in 1994 he was telling the Lords that Britain was 'becoming simply a unit in a federal system', and on that account might justifiably be expelled from the Commonwealth of independent nations. It was Gait-skell's old point. Why should the other countries, Beloff argued, 'be prepared to regard as an equal a country which has no more constitu-tional status than that of, let us say, an American state or a Canadian province?'[18] In 1996, another Beloff book directly contradicted the thesis of thirty years before, contending that the basic differences of outlook between island and mainland, combined with the deception by which successive statesmen had sought to bury them, cast fundamental doubt on the future of the European Union.[19]

There were more vulgar and spectacular shifts. In 1975, Alistair McAlpine, wealthy scion of a construction business, served as an active treasurer of the European League for Economic Co-operation (ELEC), the all-party body that fathered the Yes campaign. By 1997, after several years as chief fund-raiser for Mrs Thatcher's election campaigns, he had moved to the Referendum Party, founded by Sir James Goldsmith as the chief gathering-place for anti-Europeans. For McAlpine, who scorned Major more loftily *de haut en bas* than his own formation, either social or educational, in any way justified, was the extreme case of a convert fired by Thatcherite revenge. He simply adored the lady. Goldsmith himself, though, also did service in 1975, chairing the food sub-com-mittee of the Yes campaign – where, according to one admiring col-league, he was 'extremely creative in finding arguments to justify the CAP'[20] – before turning into the most florid, profligate opponent of 'Europe' in the history of Britain's membership.

Some of the Euro-patterning was, by contrast, subtle. Jonathan Aitken is a case in point. Great-nephew of old Lord Beaverbrook who spoke for Empire in the 1950s and 1960s, Aitken voted Yes in the referendum, but No, as an MP, to the Single Act. The Single Act, he thought, was the beginning of the end for Parliament, where he and Teddy Taylor had spent many a fruitless night dividing the House against Brussels directives that would otherwise have gone through on the nod. On the Treaty of Maastricht, by contrast, he was heterodox in his scepticism. As we shall see, the Treaty became fount and focus of the most violent hostility to Europe that ever managed to assert itself. But to Aitken it was acceptable. By then he was a minister, but told me that, had he been a back-bencher, he would still have supported Maastricht, on the ground that it gave Britain all necessary protections.

So Conservative Euro-scepticism, beginning to erupt even as it saw its heroine depart, had rich and various origins. It was a confederacy of zealots and lurchers, with the latter amply outnumbering, and often outreaching, the former. One might venture some conclusions from their history. Some were moved by disappointment born of failed ambition. They resented their exclusion from office sufficiently to allow an embryonic scepticism, hitherto suppressed, to prepare them for full rebellion. Others were pushed, by personal loyalty to Mrs Thatcher, over an edge they had already spent some time looking across. They hadn't all cast an anti-Europe vote, insofar as one was available, in the leadership election. Biffen, for instance, voted for Douglas Hurd, and Richard Shepherd, whose position sprang from an almost Cromwellian romance with the historic sovereignty of Parliament, supported Heseltine. But, for them both, Euro-scepticism served what they had long known. Others again, Cash-like, thought they now knew what they didn't know before.

Considered as a group, they were cantankerous, mostly humourless, and acquired a single-mindedness sufficient to elude, in a way the British system cannot readily tolerate, party discipline. The lurchers, however late, became zealots.

The two categories shared in common one overriding consideration. They were determined, above all else, not to let themselves or the country be deceived. Deception, they felt, was close to the heart of the story so far. The old believers were never misled. That was the source of their particular pride. They had always known what Europe meant and, knowing it, rejected it. The converts, by contrast, had something to answer for. All these protestations, whether by William Cash or Woodrow Wyatt or Max Beloff or, supremely, Margaret Thatcher, that they never really knew what Europe stood for, cast doubt on their political judgement, and secretly they knew it. They needed to make up for it. An element of the post-Thatcher zealotry, among Thatcherites including the lady herself, was a kind of guilt at the errors of the past: at their complicity in the momentum towards European integration which they imagined was not really happening. For more than a decade, after all, Mrs Thatcher had been running the country while the incremental growth of European common rules and action – community, in another word – was developing under her very eyes, and sometimes under her active hand. For a visceral anti-European, this was a shameful record to have to contemplate.

All conversion events have their ambiguity. There is a gain, for those who experience it, in terms of truth. Here and now, the converts, as they imagined, could at last see Europe plain. This was offset, however, by a certain weakening of credibility. Were such erratic insights really to be trusted? No matter. If the occasion arose again when the European juggernaut could be stopped, it would be met by a resistance that poured repentance for all those errors of the past into one mighty last stand.

*

ALTHOUGH THESE PEOPLE counted for little in November 1990, from April 1992 they counted for everything.

John Major won the general election, but with a majority of only twenty-one. The result consigned him into the hands of politicians who, though they had mostly chosen him to be their leader, spent the next five years tearing his leadership to pieces. The beast was let loose. And an occasion appeared that brought into the open the pent-up rage which the years of surrender to Europe now, in feral eyes, required.

There was nothing sudden or unexpected about this moment. It arose, as ever with Europe, out of the continuities. The Delors committee on economic and monetary union had reported. Mrs Thatcher had uttered her shrieking triple negative against it. But the momentum to implement it, and much else besides, had not been impeded. An inter-governmental conference, necessary to change the Treaty of Rome, was scheduled. It would take, inevitably, a large stride towards a greater Europe, unless it was stopped. And it could not be stopped. Convened for its decisive session in December 1991, in a Dutch town which until then had impinged on the mind of hardly anyone in Europe, the IGC produced the Treaty of Maastricht: a name to live in infamy in the annals of British Euro-scepticism.

The Maastricht Treaty was a watershed. It was, formally, a Treaty on European Union. 'The Union' became an entity in international law, and those who lived within its borders became 'citizens of the Union'. The British, already optional possessors of burgundy-coloured, malleable Euro-passports, replacing the straight-backed navy blue of home, would now be holders of European citizenship whether they liked it or not. Words like the 'coherence', 'solidarity' and 'borders' of 'the territory of the Union' were enshrined in treaty language. The word 'Economic' was dropped from the old designation, European Economic Community: a deeply sinister development. And that was only the beginning. In institutional terms, the Treaty had much to offer, much to threaten. It increased the power of the European Parliament, installing it as a co-decision-maker, in some circumstances, with the Council of Ministers. It extended the reach of a common social policy. It struck out in the direction of 'the eventual framing of a common defence policy'. It provided for more collaboration on foreign policy, and proposed 'a single institutional framework' within which matters of justice and home affairs would also, in due course, be encouraged to fall. Most specifically, it provided for the creation of a European central bank, the non-accountable, non-democratic power-centre that would invigilate 'the irreversible character of the Community's movement to the third stage of Economic and Monetary Union'.

From some of these particulars, Britain secured exemption.[21] She removed herself from the protocol redefining the social chapter that appeared in the Treaty of Rome. She asserted, and it was agreed, that, unlike every other member state except Denmark, she would not automatically take her currency into the monetary union once economic conditions made it eligible for membership. These were serious exemptions, tenaciously negotiated. But they did not prevent the Treaty, if ratified, from existing. They did not alter the character of the Treaty of Maastricht as it was regarded by its architects, particularly President Delors and Chancellor Kohl.

'In Maastricht,' said Helmut Kohl, 'we laid the foundation-stone for the completion of the European Union. The European Union Treaty introduces a new and decisive stage in the process of European union which within a few years will lead to the creation of what the founding fathers of modern Europe dreamed of after the last war: the United States of Europe.'[22]

For British sceptics, that was exactly the problem. Kohl put in a verbal nutshell what they knew 'Europe' now to mean. For some, Maastricht was the confirmation of what they reckoned they had always known but been unable to instil into the convictions of the brethren. For others, it was the final eye-opener. It put indisputable words round the proposition they had hitherto found ways of obscuring: that the Single Act was indeed but a step along the path to something greater. Kohl and the sceptics, in effect, had a meeting of minds. They agreed about the object, while utterly disagreeing about its desirability. Together they left John Major and the Government floundering somewhere in between. The Kohl analysis, endorsed with horror by more British politicians than had ever shown their faces before, gave rise to the climactic battle of the Thatcher–Major era: the bitterest struggle, indeed, of the entire period of British membership of the Community.

Maastricht provoked, first of all, a flowering of the sceptic intellect.

There was a great outpouring of books and tracts. William Cash, now consumed by his life's work, was first into the lists. Characteristically, he got in there ahead of time, with his dense volume *Against a Federal Europe*, which appeared while Maastricht was still in negotiation.

The book revealed the fruits of many journeys to and from the continent, into and beyond the minds of a great variety of Europeans. It was anxious to establish that the author wasn't anti-Europe, only anti-'Europe'. No xenophobe he. And this wasn't a false claim. Nobody who disliked foreigners could have spent as many hours as Cash parading through the ante-chambers of European chancelleries, offering their occupants the burden of his limitless knowledge. On the other hand, Germany kept recurring as an object of suspicion. The more journeys Cash made, the more confident his generalizations became. 'The problem of German national identity has been intractable,' he wrote, 'largely because there is simply no credible political model in German history for the Germans to follow.' 'For long Germany had a political inferiority complex,' he further ventured. 'Germany's failure to achieve political greatness further encourages the view that she has a great future before her,' he cunningly opined. 'As Nietzsche wrote', 'as Fichte addressed the German Nation', as Adenauer implied, as Genscher hinted: the texts came thick and fast, all tending to suggest that Germany was an arrogant menace to the peace, epitomized in the observation that 'her previous bids for power have been made in the name of "Europe."'[23]

Engulfed within the German menace was, in Cash's confident belief, the coming end of British sovereignty. The draft texts of what became Maastricht were already available, and foretold the ascendancy of central banks, the sacrifice of national autonomy to common policies of numerous kinds. This gave rise to ominous reflections. 'One of the most baffling phenomena in the debate about Europe is that Britain seems to be the only country worried about national sovereignty,' the author wrote. He demystified the matter by asserting that no other country was sufficiently interested in parliamentary democracy.

But above all what Cash saw – what nobody, actually, could deny – was the irrevocability of the scheme that was on the verge of enactment. Once created, the new currency was intended to be for ever. The structure supporting it would become a permanent government. There was to be no opening for exit or, quite possibly, refinement. Moreover, the existence of British opt-outs from the social chapter and the single currency would be of modest consequence. They would not stop the Treaty happening. And the Treaty, once written into law, would affect every European Union member, whether or not they signed up to every piece of it. It would be the new norm, the base-line, the objectively existing fact against which every country would be obliged to measure its real independence. What was signed in 1991, and ratified in 1992, would become one more item in the integration of Europe, another stage on this long and stealthy journey, obliging Britain to travel on – or risk exclusion from the engine of the train she had joined twenty years before.

The fact that Maastricht would be irreversible was an electric prod. It finally galvanized British Euro-scepticism to assemble the accoutrements – ferocity, stubbornness, venom, suicidal will – appropriate to a last stand. For Maastricht needed the support of every member state. Britain, along with the others, had power of veto. And if the leadership wouldn't use this veto, which Major hadn't, perhaps Parliament could be made to use it instead, by rejecting the necessary legislation and thereby bringing the entire Community venture to a juddering halt.

Investigations into doubt therefore ranged much wider round the Conservative Party. This was the period of maximum growth, in an output where scepticism elided readily into phobia. By the time the Maastricht Treaty came to dominate politics, no fewer than twenty-seven separate organizations existed in Britain with the sole purpose of contesting this or that aspect of European unification.[24] In the wake of the Treaty, pamphlets flooded from the presses attributing its acceptance by the Government variously to national self-hatred, castles of lies, the road to serfdom or a hundred different varieties of incomprehension as to the consequences of economic and monetary union.

Conservative MPs, not usually counted among the book-writing classes, followed Cash into the literary field, driven by the common perception that what was now at stake was the survival of Britain. In *A Treaty Too Far*, Michael Spicer expressed the bewilderment of a European who had perhaps misled himself.[25] Like many Tories, Spicer's main interest was in free trade. His book rehearsed the patchy history of the implementation of the Single Act, and while he refrained from the callow criticism that the Act had produced far too many Brussels directives – how otherwise could the market be made free and fair than by imposing Europe-wide regulations? – he found that Britain was the only member state genuinely acting out its belief in free markets. The case for 'working from within' was, for Spicer, finished. The evidence proved that Britain's influence was feeble. She was constantly being outflanked by the scheming continentals.

The thinking, though often phobic, didn't always reek of phobia. Phobia is a sort of madness. Like Spicer, a good many adherents to the sceptic cause were now developing a reasoned critique. The Commons debates, over the period, had at times the air of an extended seminar in the higher constitutionalism. Fertilizing the guilt about the past was a scholarly demand for exactness about the future.

'The most extraordinary thing about the United Kingdom is that traditionally expenditure and taxation were decided by the House of Commons,' said Sir Trevor Skeet. 'In future these matters will not be decided here for many of them may be transferred to Europe.' 'Are we prepared to put our signature to a treaty which will erode the power and influence of Members of this House to such an extent that they are incapable of delivering the natural and legitimate aspirations of their constituents?' asked Christopher Gill. 'What have we joined? We have joined a centralized unitary state, and at some stage we shall have to ask the people, "Do you want to go this way, or do you not?"' said Sir Teddy Taylor. James Cran said: 'I am concerned only about the kind of Europe that we will have. I wish to see an evolutionary Europe. Institutions are much better if they are allowed to develop slowly. I take exception to the fact that the people who are deciding matters at inter-governmental conferences want to force the issue of unification far faster than I would wish.' On 20 May 1992, when the Maastricht Bill came for its second reading, these words were as quizzical as they were emphatic. Scepticism seemed a well-merited designation. From the real meaning of subsidiarity to the presumed logic of a common foreign policy, the aspirations of the Treaty were subjected to worried scrutiny.

It was not, however, an academic exercise. It might have been that. In fact, almost everyone expected it would be. These solemn utterances, after all, came a very few weeks after the Government had won its fourth election victory. Governments at that time in the cycle usually get their way. And, at the beginning, Major did get his way. The second reading of the great measure, the European Communities (Amendment) Bill, was won by 336 votes to 92, with Labour officially abstaining and only twenty-two Tories declaring themselves incorrigible sceptics by voting against. That was on 21 May. The next stage, committee, was scheduled for 4 June. The Government planned to whip Maastricht through with all deliberate speed, on the tide of victory, leaving an autumn uncluttered for other legislation. The collective beast of scepticism, sublimely convinced though it was of its own rectitude, did not believe it could roar its destructive way through the whipped acquiescence of conventional political lore and practice.

But then something happened that opened the cage. Ironically, a European country paved the way for attack by Britain's anti-Europeans. On 2 June, even as the Whips were finalizing their plans for disciplined passage, a referendum in Denmark produced a negative result. By 50.7 to 49.3 per cent of the vote, the Danish people refused to endorse the Treaty. If Denmark said No, then the Treaty would become a nullity everywhere else as well. Short of by-passing Denmark – in effect, expelling the Danes from the EC – there was no way the architects of Maastricht could hope to get their creation into place. It was a moment to test the entire apparatus of the Euro-debate, not least in Britain, where the argument was much more sulphuric than anywhere else. The moment revealed the rather different temper of the Cabinet from that of its die-hard opponents in the ranks.

The Government temporized. It promised statements, immediately choosing not to drive home its election victory and carry on regardless but, rather, to fall into the arms of the Euro-sceptics and see what they would accept. The House, ministers conceded, needed to be told what the Danish vote meant. The committee stage should be postponed, pending clarification.

The sceptics, on the other hand, were jubilant. They saw their moment. There is nothing like the possibility of victory to shift dithering souls from one camp to another. The twenty-two dissenters of 21 May grew to sixty-nine, who signed a motion against Maastricht on 3 June. They immediately diagnosed a gap wide open for the total renegotiation of the Treaty, a 'fresh start with the future development of the EEC'. They were tremendously excited. Having shown them a chink of hesitation, Major, with his small majority, was about to surrender himself into their hands. 'It seems irrefutable', said Kenneth Baker, 'that last week tore a gaping hole in the Maastricht Treaty ... The Danes have given us an opportunity to think again about the next step forward.' Baker, as Home Secretary, had belonged to the Cabinet that negotiated and approved Maastricht. During the election, he was particularly robust in its defence. But Baker had now lost his job. Not for the first time, this experience of loss helped ease the machinery of a flexible mind. The conversions were coming as if by mass baptism. The parliamentary veto now beckoned, Major having so signally failed to do his duty and force the whole of Europe to march in step with the island race.

I had several conversations with Bill Cash around this time. He was a man the Government now took quite seriously. Douglas Hurd, emollient diplomat, had tried to buy him off with a job. These blandishments seemed to produce in him equal amounts of pleasure and contempt. In 1991 there was apparently a parliamentary private secretaryship on offer, which might be traded up in due course for a minister of stateship. But Bill would have none of it. He was also asked by Hurd to contribute draft material to the 1992 manifesto, another gesture that suggested his European opinions were beginning to get a grip, which was far more important to him than office. As the Maastricht negotiation was coming to a head, he seems to have had ready access to the top people. 'I saw John Major the day before he went to Maastricht,' Cash told me. 'He asked to see me. I said, "You must use the veto and you must stop what effectively would be a German Europe, because I think that's the direction in which all this is going." '[26] Having neglected to take this advice, Major had to face the full weight of the sceptics' punishment. There is a sense in which they were now controlling, if not quite running, the Government. Certainly it was true that Major could hardly make a move, at home or abroad, without first considering the response it would receive from the likes of William Cash.

The parliamentary history of the European Communities (Amendment) Bill, once its timing had succumbed to the vagaries of the Danish voter, was a drama containing some elements unprecedented in this century. Having put off the committee stage until the autumn, the Government gave scepticism free rein to establish itself at the centre of political debate. At last it moved in from cranks' corner, becoming the main dynamic element to which all other forces had to adjust. It was boosted by a cognate government disaster, the forced removal of sterling from the European Exchange Rate Mechanism in the middle of September.[27] No Euro-sceptic could have written a more perfect script to legitimize the contention that 'Europe' was bad for Britain, and the entire project of currency alignment a malign federalist fantasy. The righteousness of scepticism discovered no more potent image than that of the Chancellor of the Exchequer, Norman Lamont, scuttling white-faced from the pavement outside the Treasury after announcing, on 16 September 1992, that British membership of the ERM was over. It set the stage for a process which, while it ended in the passage of the Bill, destroyed the fabled unity of the Conservative Party, perhaps for decades.

The Bill was driven through every imaginable legislative contortion. Each vote had the capability of being lost. The business managers kept being forced to buy off trouble with the promise of future votes, or underpin the critical moments of passage by threatening votes of confidence. They began with a so-called 'paving' debate, promised after the Danish fiasco, which itself was nearly lost. It was carried by 319–313 only after the Prime Minister had been obliged to assure the sceptics – curious testimony to the sovereignty of the British Parliament – that completion of the Bill's passage would be delayed until after the Danes had held a second referendum. So the dance went on. Tactical manoeuvres by the Labour Party ensured, as they often had in history, that the natural Commons majority for Europe which, now thanks to Labour, still existed, might not necessarily express itself. At the last throw, in July 1993, weeks after the formal stages of passage were complete, on another special vote that the Government had been obliged to concede in order to worm out of a byzantine trap set six months earlier, they were actually defeated. At this high moment, twenty-two Conservatives voted for destruction, only to be overturned by a confidence motion the following day.[28]

This performance, lasting from June 1992 until July 1993, provided many field days for Euro-sceptic ultras. Cash was prominent among them. The period was, in a sense, his apotheosis. It was not quite true, as he told me later, that he 'organized the whole thing'. There were several contenders for the title. Factions on the right are no less vulnerable than factions on the left to the old political truism that the more passionately an ideology is preached, the more vicious are the jealousies, and sometimes the disagreements, between those who preach it. The Euro-sceps and the Euro-phobes who flourished under the Major Government had their sub-sections. Cash's relentlessness, and the fame that clung to the tall ungainly figure in the stridently chalk-striped suit, did not enjoy universal approval even among his allies in the division lobbies: perhaps, on occasion, especially among them. Nonetheless, it is a fact that he personally crafted 240 amendments to the three-clause Bill, and that he was proud to have voted forty-seven times, more than any other MP, against the Government when three-line whips were in place. He was the most frequent as well as the most creative exploiter of the parliamentary facilities to hammer home, regardless of what anybody thought, the Tory opposition to the newest, most menacing artefact of European union.

As such, he was part of something wider as well. He belonged within a segment, almost a movement, that was changing the terms on which Tory politics were done. In the political generation that was growing up behind him, Europe was producing a new breed of politician, harsher and more disrespectful than any Tories that had gone before. This is what Europe, among other things, did. Ambitious young MPs would tread modestly during their first few months in the Commons. Cash had done that himself. And nobody could accuse him, in these middle years, of modesty over Europe. But, just as Cash was rougher than Biffen, there were younger men a lot rougher than Cash. Within weeks of arriving in the House, they were strutting about as the saviours of party and country from the European menace.

Running into a group of them in the autumn of 1992, I was given a dose of their aggression. In ascending order of passion, they were against the ERM, against Maastricht and against the party leader. Their deconstruction of the texts produced cries of mirthful triumph, as they discovered yet another sub-clause proving the Treaty's menace to sovereignty, or its irrelevance to Europe, or – a favourite insight – the inherent likelihood of it leading to a new European war. But their real passion was for deconstructing John Major. Six months after he had won them their seats, they wanted him out. The longer the Maastricht crisis could be made to last, they felt, the more satisfactorily it would eat away his authority. Though admitting they would have voted for him had they been MPs in 1990, they now thought him a traitor to the right, who had acquired a European conviction in outrageous defiance of those who put him where he was. They were the first significant cohort of Thatcher's children, as they called themselves, to get into Parliament. There had been a time-lag before this happened, producing a Thatcherized party only after the heroine had gone. But these people had won their rightist spurs at university. They were 'combat-trained', as one of them, Alan Duncan MP, coolly put it to me. They could bide their time before they really took over the party, meanwhile marking the cards of Major's successors with ideological severity. They wanted Major to fail, not least over Europe. And they thought he would.

In the days when Biffen, and then Cash, entered the Commons, such treacherous conversation would have been unthinkable. Issuing from the mouths of tyro parliamentarians, it would have crossed all frontiers of political propriety. But it would also have seemed, in the watches of the night, seriously deluded: a speculation outside the realms of political reality. In the old days, party leaders were far beyond the reach of such underlings. It wouldn't have occurred to a single member of the intake of 1970 or 1979 that they were in a position to conspire against Mr Heath or Mrs Thatcher.

The combination of Europe and John Major, plainly, was different. The potency of the one and the weakness of the other changed the rules of political conduct.

*

THE TREATY OF MAASTRICHT was, however, ratified. There were no backsliders. All twelve member states of the European Union pushed it through. Denmark was smuggled back on board, after securing still wider exemptions than Britain and running a second referendum that produced a majority of 56.8 per cent. France, where a referendum was very nearly lost in 1992, resumed her customary role at the heart of European activities. Germany, perversely, was the last to ratify, after Maastricht had been taken to the Constitutional Court. Britain's final act of passage, in July 1993, was eased by the politics of personal survival. Neither William Cash nor anyone else, save a single abstaining eccentric, was prepared to withhold support from a confidence motion. They were, after all, professional politicians. Their own frailty stared them in the face. No Conservative, whatever his state of combat-readiness, wanted to fight a general election which the party was certain to lose by a landslide. So the governing establishment won. It is a moment to survey the wreckage.

By 1994, Euro-scepticism was a, perhaps the, factor the Conservative leadership had to reckon with. It had become a term of art, as well as a famous force. This was a period, also, when its different designations began to matter: just as there were factions within the faith, there were labels registering different levels of refinement. 'Scepticism', an attractive state of mind implying a quest for objective truth, scarcely seemed to do justice to some of the raging furies that sheltered behind the name. To some observers, therefore, 'phobia', with its staring-eyed connotations, now became a truer designation for certain members of the camp. So the sceps became the phobes, at any rate among Euro-philes who wanted to make a propaganda point. But the philes, in turn, resented such labelling on their own account: philia could sound even more dangerous than phobia. A contest thus established itself for ownership of the most sententious vacuity: 'Euro-realism'. We are the Euro-realists now, every faction claimed. As a convenience, and a courtesy they hardly deserve, I will continue to refer to Cash and his rivals as Euro-sceptics.

By now they had a considerable grip on the parliamentary party.

Around the Major Government's mid-term, some academic research investigated the attitudes behind this.[29] These were pretty extreme. No fewer than 56 per cent of Tory MPs wanted an Act of Parliament passed which would 'establish explicitly the ultimate supremacy of Parliament over EU legislation'. Behind such an apparently righteous clarification lay a radical idea. It meant, quite simply, tearing up the Treaty of Rome. But how many of the respondents understood this, even as elected legislators, may be doubted. Some of the other answers were contradictory, revealing an alarming incomprehension about the most basic elements of Community life. For example, 55 per cent of these MPs thought the European Court of Justice 'a threat to liberty in Britain', but 67 per cent said they wanted the ECJ to have greater powers – to enforce the single market, which already represented much of its active jurisdiction. This seemed very muddled thinking. But there was no mistaking the sway of the sceptics. The sense of the majority was clear enough. They wanted to turn back the tide of integration, with a reduction in qualified majority voting and an attack on the powers of the European Commission. In the ideal world of the average Tory MP, both the Commission and the European Parliament would be put back in boxes that could never be opened except with the approval of national legislatures.

There was no let-up, either, in parliamentary activity. Maastricht's passage merely fuelled the sceptics' capacity for outrage. Buried in the Treaty was a pledge, agreed to by Britain, to increase the annual contribution of member states to the EU budget. This had to get through Parliament as a separate matter. By the time it came up, by-election defeats had whittled the Tory majority down to fourteen, so Major moved once again to make the matter one of confidence – a vote no Tory MP could dodge with impunity. Eight MPs, however, dodged it. Their own opinion that the vote, as framed by the Government, was a constitutional outrage met the response that their abstentions were a disciplinary disgrace for which the only appropriate punishment was withdrawal of the whip. Joined by one other, the 'Whipless Nine' were born: including Taylor and Budgen and Gill and Shepherd and Wilkinson and Body, of the names already mentioned: supplemented by politicians who strained to breaking-point the decorous intellectualism implied in the bearing of a sceptic. Teresa Gorman, MP for Billericay, and Tony Marlow, MP for Northampton North, brought to the Europe argument the complacent, guttural boorishness of the authentic British nationalist. Marlow, indeed, was regarded by some party managers as possessing attitudes so far to the right on these matters that he did not properly belong in the Conservative Party.

Bill Cash refrained from joining this company. He thought Community finance was the wrong issue on which to break with the party, he told me. But not far distant from this stance were the ever present strands of personal rivalry. Politics may usually be thought of as a trade conducted by means of collective action, as party solidarity, but in the taxonomy of Euro-scepticism there were almost as many categories as there were Tory politicians espousing that general allegiance: each of them with a slightly different history, his own studious analysis, a mildly divergent set of obsessions, a discrete tactical appreciation, a more or less grandiose vision of his own contribution. Cash, in a sense, was just such a solitary. He did his own thing, to which he brought the necessary degree of passionate certainty, together with enviable indifference to the effect he sometimes had on others. But he remained within the encampment, to play his part in the irresistible growth of Euro-scepticism that was making its inexorable way, as Biffen once put it, 'like weeds through concrete'.[30]

What, however, was this designed to achieve? What world did it stand for? What was the mind-set that drove it forward?

The sceptic mind, belying its label, was prone to anxieties that were the opposite of cool. Paranoid fear became one part of its stock-in-trade. An image Cash seized on, and often toyed with, was one that Geoffrey Howe had once used when explaining how sovereignty should be seen as fragmented rather than solid. Consider a bundle of sticks, said Howe. That, he recalled, was how he once heard a Cambridge professor talking about the freehold ownership of property: something which could be likened to the possession of a bundle of sticks, each of them deployable as a different form of ownership – lease, partnership, licence and so on. So it was with sovereignty. Like property rights, 'sovereignty may be seen as divisible, and exploitable, in the interests of the nation whose sovereignty it is, and in a thousand different ways and circumstances'.[31]

This might be thought a somewhat recondite metaphor, not best calculated to clear the mind of the ordinary citizen puzzling over political abstractions. It struck Cash as tremendously significant. 'It is difficult not to notice', he wrote, 'that the "bundle of sticks" is reminiscent of the Roman *fasces*, the bundle of rods with a protruding axe-head, carried before Roman consuls as a sign of the state authority of Rome, and adopted by Mussolini as a symbol of the movement he led to power in 1922, whence the word "fascist."'[32]

Cash stops short of calling the EU and its supporters fascists, though clearly the parallel with the *fasces* made a big impression on him. He came back to it – 'sticks wrapped in a silken cord' – when I interviewed him in 1998. To him, the unaccountable authoritarianism of Brussels and all who support it is, at the least, fascistic. The fear of fascism also overhangs the sceptic vision of what could most easily go wrong in Europe if there is any more integration: a disorder not so much of Brussels as within nation-states that can no longer express their independence, especially over economic policy. 'I think we're heading for the possibility of a new fascism on the back of unemployment,' Cash said. This is a more respectable fear than the spectre of European Commissioners parading with their *fasces*. But the word became easily thrown around, tossed lightly into the demagogic pot, sometimes by voices, such as that of the plutocratic James Goldsmith, which themselves seemed to have a closer affinity with fascist tendencies than any Cockfield or Jenkins or Delors.

Reaching further into the murky depths, the Conservative historian Andrew Roberts published a futuristic novel, *The Aachen Memorandum*, built round the heroes of a body called the English Resistance Movement.[33] Their sacred task is to resist the new Nazi Reich which the European Union has re-created. This totalitarian monster features German functionaries embarking on the extinction of old English virtues. They assassinate Baroness Thatcher, punish women who shave their armpits, rename Waterloo Station after Maastricht, force letter-writers to use the postcode. The Movement takes vengeance against them, retrieving the Union Jack from the ignominy depicted on the cover of the book, where it is shown being burned away to reveal yellow stars – ambiguously Jewish or European – beneath. This version of patriotism locates Europe with communism, Jewish finance and black immigration as the enemy of the British, more particularly the English, people.

Roberts's idiom was satire, but his meaning was plain. As an extreme English reactionary, he certainly wasn't satirizing himself. He was exalting the past, over which no shade broods more lushly than the hero of this school of Englishness, Enoch Powell. 'Backward travels our gaze,' Powell once epically intoned, 'and there at last we find them, or seem to find them, in many a village church, beneath the tall tracery of a perpendicular east window and the coffered ceiling of the chantry chapel. From brass and stone, from line and effigy, their eyes look out at us, and we gaze into them, as if we would win some answer from their inscrutable silence. "Tell us what it is that binds us together; show us the clue that leads us through a thousand years; whisper to us the secret of this charmed life of England, that we in our time may know how to hold it fast." '34

A blunter version of this romantic quest came readily to the minds of a certain class of Tory politician. The Roberts satire was not a joke. During the 1980s Europe induced a more fully developed paranoia concerning the future of the British essence than it had done thirty years before, sometimes coming out *en clair* and directed at the dark forces that now ensured the supremacy of European thinking in the secret cabals of the power elite. Alan Clark, then Minister for Trade, on encountering a Foreign Office official who seeks to enlighten him on some aspect of European Community policy towards Chile ('All crap about Human Rights'), notes in his diary: 'This man is exactly the kind of mole who is working away, eighteen hours a day, to extinguish the British national identity.'35

So the supposed defence of Englishness was one impulse of political Euro-scepticism. However honestly the fears were felt about the homogenization of a nation under rule from a distant capital, they did not produce a debate that was either generous or enlightened. Vicious language and poisonous thought abounded in the Tory Party. 'It is a party where one Conservative hostile to the European Community can accuse another in favour of it of being "a Pétainist" adapting himself to the new European order, as one such person did to me only two nights ago,' Lord Thomas of Swynnerton reported to the House of Lords. 'This mood derives not from national pride or even a memory of past greatness but from a new mood of provincial nationalism which is extremely destructive.'36

Woven into this feeling – those viscera talking again – was the pain of an inner intellectual conflict. Should sceptics want 'Europe' to work or not? In particular, was the legal order, which the Treaty of Rome created, something that should impose itself on the constantly wayward continentals, who were always wanting to blur its effect, for example, on the enforcement of the single market? Or must it at all costs be stopped from imposing itself on the sovereignty of the British Parliament – even, in the more extreme version, the supremacy of the British courts? It couldn't do both things, couldn't bring French protectionism into line without extending its reach into the regulation of the British fishing industry. British sceptics forced themselves into painful contortions to have it both ways.

Plainly there had to be a European Court of Justice. Its role was fundamental to the functioning of the Community from the start. It also had to apply its jurisdiction equally between the members. That was the whole point of the enterprise. This did not impede the onset of ever more insistent appeals for British exceptionalism. Aware that the ECJ could not be abolished, some sceptics began to work up arguments for special opt-outs. One of them introduced a Bill, for example, 'to provide by Order in Council for the disapplication within the United Kingdom of judgments, rules and doctrines propounded by the European Court'.[37] Introducing it, Iain Duncan Smith sought to undermine the strictly legal basis of the ECJ. It was, he said, 'a political court'. It had 'huge licence to make legislation that national governments must obey.' Parliament, therefore, must reclaim its sovereignty, review the judgements 'and, where necessary, seek to change them politically'. It must, in other words, amend the British Act of 1972, from which all this had sprung.

The measure got nowhere. But it was a *cri de coeur* against what have unquestionably been the integrationist tendencies of the Court. The ECJ paid attention to the preambles and codicils, as well as the formal texts, of the treaties. It developed into a constitutional court, gradually establishing, as one scholar put it, 'an overarching legal order which is greater than the continuing consensus which originally created it'.[38] The effect has been 'the creation of a European federal legal system to which the legal orders of the member states of the Community are subordinated'. Although implicit in the Union enterprise, and discernible as happening many years before Britain became a member, this can rightly be called a political evolution. It discomfited and enraged a growing segment of the Tory Party, including members of the Government. The Home Secretary of the period, Michael Howard, while part of an administration that often invoked ECJ jurisdiction, became spokesman for radical proposals to escape what the British didn't like about it. 'Some countries', Howard said in 1996, 'may wish to withdraw from elements of the treaties.' 'This may indeed mean', he went on, 'that some states would be able to repatriate powers which are currently exercised in Brussels.'[39] Repatriation, a vogue word for the old Tory right when Enoch Powell was inflaming the populace with his responses to immigration, was reborn as their magic solution to the problem of a court they couldn't escape but had come to detest.

The apostate Lord Beloff put it more graphically. Laws made in Brussels and adjudicated by the ECJ were 'a challenge to Britain's sense of identity'. Most of the British, he went on, 'have an idea, however vague, of the benefits they derive from the common law and of its

superiority to continental codes'. The continentals were natural law-
breakers, 'prepared to vote for anything at Brussels in the confident
knowledge that they will only enforce what suits them'.[40] So spoke the
Oxford scholar, striking a chord that rang sweetly, though without avail,
through the noisy forums where sceptics assured each other of the
terrible fate that had befallen Britain.

Their inner conflict went further. United by the infamies of Brussels,
they were still a mass of disagreements within and between themselves.
Majority voting posed such a quandary. A Euro-sceptic who wanted to
minimize the role of Brussels on the matter of funds for the Common
Agricultural Policy could only favour any system that reduced the power
of small countries to block reform. Extension of the dreaded QMV
could, in some fields, enhance the power of large member states like
their own. But, as a totem looming over national sovereignty, it had to
be regarded, at some higher level of principle, as a menace. In short, the
Euro-scepticism of a fully paid-up EU member could not readily accommodate the contradiction such a stance entailed. For a people that was
inside the Union, the quest for solutions, to satisfy the ever more
passionate anxieties of a class of politician that could not abide what was
happening, was destined to be frustrating.

At the peak of these frustrations was the climactic problem. What
could the sceptic mind offer as an alternative to British membership of
the European Union? This intellectual instrument, a mélange of logic
and rage, became well practised in arguing the case against the EU.
William Cash had his own litany, much recited. The EU was bureaucratic
and centralized. It would not take seriously the Maastricht promise of
more 'subsidiarity' – power to the members. It was moving outside
political control. It wasn't doing enough to make the single market real.
It was spreading its tentacles, largely through the Court, into areas it
should never touch. It had ambitions, sometimes open, sometimes secret,
for wholesale political union. It was the heart of an emerging super-state.
It was run by majority rule, which might leave Britain on the thin end
of an argument. Even where unanimity was required, the EU had its
own momentum. It couldn't be stopped without a massive, perhaps
destructive, effort. All these features rendered it an unlovely, sometimes
highly dangerous, menace to the British way of life and government.
Above all, perhaps, it was not British. As the years passed, a critique
developed which asserted that the differences between island and mainland were written into history: were unalterable: were, sadly, part
of the ineluctable order of things. There is, wrote Michael Spicer, 'a

fundamental difference in the philosophy which lies behind the British constitution and those of her continental partners'.[41] The one, he added, wasn't necessarily 'better' than the other. Just different, as it always had been – something everybody ought to have realized long ago.

So what should be the response to this? One approach, the Government's, was to develop the concept of 'variable geometry': different members moving at different speeds, with different opt-outs and the like. The images acquired their own surrounding theology. Variable geometry, implying some kind of structural measurement, did not stand up to rigorous examination. 'Multi-speed', on the other hand, got close to implying a multi-divisional Europe, which was obviously dangerous ground. Nor did 'concentric circles' do the trick for everyone.

The harder sceptic was not in favour of any of this. Cash was especially emphatic in his denunciations. 'A two-tier or two-speed Europe *is a most unattractive idea* [italics in the original],' he wrote in the manifesto advice Hurd asked him to prepare for 1992. 'We would be marginalised, lose authority and involvement, and would not catch up.' The concentric circles were even worse, implying France and Germany at the centre, and Britain on the fringe, of an organization to which she would nevertheless have to subordinate large swathes of her legal independence. 'This is a lego-political power-play,' Cash obscurely sniffed.[42] He was especially horrified by a suggestion that once came out of Helmut Kohl's office, proposing 'observer status' for any member state unwilling to join a full United States of Europe.[43] This smacked of relegation, perhaps along with the Baltic states and other fringe supplicants, into some kind of 'Association of European States'. Cash smelt a federalist rat of peculiar pungency. 'How *communautaire* is it for Britain to face the threat of being forced out if she does not comply unquestioningly with proposals to which we have never agreed?' he asked.

So Cash, at this stage, seemed to favour staying in the EU at its very centre. The proper solution would have been to veto Maastricht outright, making it impossible for the EU to proceed as the majority of its members wished. But short of that, it seems, the Cash position saw variable geometry as a trick. Yet this surely contradicted another strand of sceptic thinking: the proposition that Britain should renegotiate her terms of membership. In the 1990s, the idea of a merely trading partnership began to acquire friends in the Tory Party. It seemed the perfect way to secure the economic benefits of EU membership without making the political sacrifices, as Tories saw them, presently required. Michael Spicer was representative of this opinion. He had ambitions to see the whole EU revert to 'an association of freely trading and co-operating independent states', but, failing that, he thought Britain should go it alone. Those European countries outside the EU, he believed, had done better economically than EU members. Mimicking their position had no dangers, he thought. Trade would continue as before, since this would be in the EU's interest. The 'fresh start' a lot of Tories signed up for saw 'a place for Britain in a loose European commonwealth'. She would have her own currency and her own market liberalism, thereby rejecting, among other things, 'the specious fear of isolation'.[44]

Seductive though this sounded, it took incomplete account of the evidence. True enough, Sweden, Finland and Austria, outside the Community in 1990, had a higher per-capita income than either Germany or Britain. Each, however, was seeking to get in, and later did so. Rich though they were, they judged exclusion from the EU, despite the burdens of membership, to be imprudent for their countries. This seemed to turn part of Spicer's case against him. He did not explain, moreover, how the sweetheart deal he envisaged for Britain – all the benefits, none of the burdens – would be consummated with a Union that might not look kindly on a partner who lived by different rules of market conduct, and was seeking to retreat from full membership precisely in order to secure advantage on the notorious unlevelled playing-field.

Among honest sceptics, in short, there was a lot of thrashing about. They knew there was a problem. They didn't hesitate to join the more phobic elements by seizing every opportunity to intensify anti-Europe feeling. Without a blush they could expostulate against Beethoven's 'Ode to Joy', chosen as the theme tune for Euro 96. How could German music be allowed to infiltrate the European Football Championship England was hosting? They couldn't modify feelings that were intestinal in origin. In fact, these became steadily more powerful. Yet the logic of the alternative caused them problems every time they confronted it – mainly because of their reluctance to embrace the true logic of their guts, if not always their minds, which was for Britain to leave the European Union.

It took some time for such a dramatic option, full exit, to begin to emerge, even as a rhetorical possibility. Even the less rarefied sceptics were aware it might not be popular. Quite apart from their own intellectual problem, there was the political question, which exposed another of their awkward contradictions. Much of their case rested on the contention that the EU was deeply unpopular: that the people were being led by a smooth, deceiving political class: that another referendum on Europe would turn the tables. Yet they also weren't sure enough of that to make an open case for a new arrangement which faced the people with the awesome possibility of actually disengaging from 'Europe'.

The first time this happened, it caused a bigger row in the Eurosceptic camp than in the world outside. The first serious politician to try it on was Norman Lamont, the former Chancellor of the Exchequer, a prime negotiator of the Maastricht Treaty, on whom, however, the experience seems to have left an indelible loathing of the Union. It was the Cash and Thatcher case all over again: the self-hatred, among other things, of the politician who had once voted for 'Europe' but now had his eyes opened. At Maastricht, Lamont suddenly discovered what he was dealing with. He had been a minister for twelve years, many of them spent negotiating in European councils, but evidently hadn't understood what was really going on. 'For the first time in my life,' he told me, 'I really came face to face with people who in private would say to me "There will be a United States of Europe and I want to see it." '45

Lamont began to ventilate the case for exit at the Conservative Party conference in 1994. 'I do not suggest that Britain should today unilaterally withdraw from Europe,' he said. 'But the issue may well return to the agenda.'46 Britain was 'on a collision course' with her partners. She was frustrating their plans, and they were understandably annoyed. She couldn't simply veto new political developments. Far preferable would be to negotiate 'outer tier community membership . . . which involved only the free trade parts of the Treaty of Rome'. This wouldn't be a 'two-speed Europe'. It would simply recognize that Europe was moving in 'two completely different directions'.

This was a somewhat fumbling approach to exit. It still pretended to have things both ways, wanting all the trade benefits and none of the political consequences. But it opened up the real argument. It began to face anyone prepared to listen both with the extremity of one Conservative opinion and with the adjustment that serious scepticism, applied to the real world of running Britain, would involve.

*

IT DID NOT, however, please William Cash. Only part of this displeasure arose from the challenge Lamont's thesis presented to the notion, espoused by Cash and many others, that to favour two speeds, outer circles and all that stuff was to cave in to the Eurocracy. Lamont's 'exit' headlines irritated not Cash the thinker but Cash the impresario. His school of scepticism had taken a new turn, and recruited a tigerish force with the capacity to propel the cause far beyond the picayune world of Parliament. In Parliament, after all, it had failed. Maastricht was law. A national movement was now required, and Cash, with some important assistance, placed himself at the head of it.

The same day Lamont made his speech, a new body, named the European Foundation, held a rally in a Bournemouth hotel, where the room was packed with the sweating bodies of Conservative Party activists in town for the conference. It wasn't the first such meeting, but it was the most exultant, and it introduced fully frontal into the political arena the most imposing grotesque to enter the modern Euro-debate, Sir James Goldsmith. Cash, the Foundation's founder and only chairman, led up to the Bournemouth stage Jimmy Goldsmith, its biggest patron, a man of gigantic wealth who had the quixotic idea of using some of it to promote the anti-EU cause in Britain.

Goldsmith was, in a special sense, a European, having a mother who was French and a life-style that bridged the Channel as well as the Atlantic. A formidable private accumulator, he had hankerings to be a public man somewhere in the regions of politics. In the 1970s, he tried to force his way in by starting a glossy British news magazine, which failed. From time to time, he would be heard from on trade matters, where he had become an articulate protectionist, railing against the damage done by global corporations, not dissimilar from his own, to the life of Third World countries in particular. Then, earlier in 1994, he entered politics proper, by founding, with others, a political movement in France that went by the name of L'Autre Europe. Europe, he thought, was, while protectionist within its borders, another iniquitous agent of the evils of globalization. It was also bureaucratic, and distant from democracy: the creation and feeding-ground of what he called, in conversations I had with him, 'the political caste . . . the elite that begins to think it owns what it runs, which can be a nation-state or a local community, the Mafia or Europe'.[47] This was the breed that Goldsmith most detested, and from which he saw his own entry into politics as offering some kind of rescue.

It will be seen immediately that he was far from the model of a Conservative Euro-sceptic. Apart from his grand manner and bottomless pocket, his ideas about trade were anathema to most Tories. But this they put on one side. Under the banner of his new party, Goldsmith got elected as a French Member of the European Parliament in summer 1994, prepared to take his scorn for the entire EU project to Strasbourg

– though in the event, as was true of many MEPs elected on party lists in France and elsewhere, his attendance in the Parliament was seldom recorded. In his other home, England, he set about creating a movement which, under guise of neutrally pressing for a referendum on British membership, mobilized phobo-sceptic opinion wherever it came from.

Another way Goldsmith was different was that, in his way, he was an intellectual. Having made his pile, he went into retreat to improve his mind, journeying privately round the globe to conduct ground-level investigation of the case for protection. He published books – *The Trap, The Response* – that spelled out with statistical support the dire state of the world resulting from the mismanagement of everything from education to nuclear power.[48] The books reached far beyond the question of Europe. But their alignment was sensitive to the author's different European constituencies.

The French edition of the first, *Le Piège*, argued for a strong Europe, which could 'protect its economy against America and Japan as well as developing countries'. Brussels, said Jimmy (he was James only in Britain), must have 'central powers' to control diplomacy and defence, the latter 'consisting of exclusively European forces'. How this sat with his general loathing for 'Brussels' was never fully explained. He even argued, in the French version, for a European central bank, to prevent 'competitive devaluations'. But none of these prescriptions appeared in *The Trap*. There he called the European Parliament 'either a waste of time or downright destructive', words that don't appear in the French text.[49] To the French he was as pro-Europe as, to the British, he was anti, offering the indignant excuse, when pressed about these apparent contradictions, that they were differences brought about by 'the evolution of my ideas' (*Le Piège* appeared in Paris a year before, in 1993) or mistranslation. To the innocent observer, it may have seemed only that he had taken to characteristic extremes a trait of the profession he most despised. He had become, with tycoonish contempt for subtlety, a politician.

It was as a politician that he agreed to meet me. He said he was used to complicated contracts, but had seen nothing like the Maastricht Treaty. 'I've spent three years studying the Treaty and the protocols, the way it works, how the institutions work,' he told me. 'I've done practically nothing else. Twelve hours a day.'[50]

By this time, rivalling Cash as the world's greatest living expert on Maastricht, he had moved on from the European Foundation to full-blown campaigning activity as leader of his own party, the Referendum

Party, which was getting ready to run a candidate in every seat in the 1997 election. The only exceptions would be places where the sitting MPs, through conviction or terror, were persuaded to come out for a referendum on their own account. Otherwise, £20 million of the Goldsmith fortune would be available for the great assault, the best-breeched single-issue campaign in the history of British democracy. 'I've had tens upon tens of Tory MPs coming here to plead with me not to run against them,' the grinning autocrat told me in his Belgravia drawing-room. There had been some attempt to negotiate at a higher level as well, with Prime Minister Major engaging in more than one conversation, in which the vague promise of a referendum was dangled in front of Goldsmith in the hope that he might withdraw.[51] This showed as much naïvety about his pliability as about his calculated interest in what he might actually achieve. He assured me that even if he secured only a single vote, his own, the Party would have been worthwhile. 'I do what I must do,' he said. To an important extent, the whole campaign was a self-indulgent ego-trip, not susceptible to conventional inducements from the governing class.

'I vomit on the Government,' Goldsmith said to me more than once, sitting in his private booth in Wilton's Restaurant, readying himself for action. Such was the unsettling force under whose generous sway quite a number of Tory Euro-sceptics, in both the Commons and the Lords, were happy to place themselves in the post-Maastricht period.

But, all in all, Goldsmith was an embarrassment rather than a credit to the cause. For one thing, his £20 million got it nowhere. When the election took place, the Referendum Party, fighting nearly 550 seats, got an average of 3.1 per cent of the vote. This was better than any minor party had ever done before; it was also consistently better – as it should have been – than the other anti-Europe entity, the shoestring UK Independence Party. Goldsmith had some influence. Arguably his mere presence deepened the split in the Tory Party, by increasing the number of Tory candidates who felt obliged to trumpet their sceptic tendencies as a way of trying to see him off. But the number of seats his party's presence swung was minuscule, if indeed they existed at all. The most learned scrutiny concluded, after poring over a complicated matrix of hypotheses, that there might have been four Tory seats lost because of the Referendum Party's intervention, offset by three that were probably held for the same reason. 'Insofar as the objective of Sir James Goldsmith's campaign was to inflict losses on the Conservatives,' the scholars write, 'it must largely be deemed to have been a failure.'[52]

More problematic still was what he left behind for the politicians, not least William Cash. When Goldsmith got his party going in 1996, as a rival to the Conservatives, the Foundation had hurriedly to regroup. Cash, about to fight the election in the Tory interest, couldn't go on getting money from a political opponent. He was always coy about how much Goldsmith gave, and more emphatically reticent about the donor who stepped in briskly to replace him: Baroness Thatcher. 'Who is the lunatic who advises her on these things?' asked one back-bench Tory, faced with his former leader funding an operation diametrically opposed to the official party line.[53] She was certainly warm to Bill.

He continued, inexhaustibly, to perform, unimpressed by the status of his opponents. Germany still bulked large in his forebodings. When Chancellor Kohl dared to suggest that Europe, without a political union of the EU, might slide into war, Cash and a colleague composed an entire pamphlet in rebuttal.[54] 'We have no desire to return to the nation-state of old,' Kohl said. 'It cannot solve the great problems of the twenty-first century. Nationalism has brought great suffering to our continent.'[55] Cash, echoing a lot of sceptics, rejected this inconvenient recollection of why the European Community had been started in the first place. He could see why Kohl was bothered. 'Germany has in the past found it difficult to reconcile nation-statehood and democracy,' he sneered. But for other countries, like Britain, it was different. She had no problem with democracy, nor the slightest need to fear a war – unless it came about through the forced unification of Europe under German domination.

Nor was Cash's zeal diminished when his faction had lost their power over government. The old language continued, even though delivered into the political void represented by the benches opposite: the massed ranks of Labour politicians with a majority of 179, who could afford to relocate him where he began – as a bit of a joke. This didn't deter him in the slightest. By now he could call on some of the appurtenances of a budding elder statesman in the cause, remarking to the tyros that he was in his fourteenth consecutive year as a member of the Select Committee on European Legislation, of which commodity, he warned them, there was 'masses in the pipeline' that would be 'a fraud . . . on the people of this country'. When the next post-Maastricht event, the Treaty of Amsterdam, was debated in December 1997, his fulminations were divided between 'the ideology of the European Coal and Steel Community, which stinks', and all the measures on which the new Government was embarked, which 'are inviting the chaos, the disorder and the implosion of the European Community'.[56]

This was an article of faith. Having failed to stop the momentum of the Union, sceptics were resigned to sitting back and waiting for the end. They had made the most of their period of potency, avenging the past, including, in many cases, their own past. But it hadn't been enough. Faced by a new government which aspired without ambiguity to be pro-European, they got most of their kicks by looking back: towards the ministers whose own weakness had made them, for five years, strong – and whose influence they wanted finally to extirpate from the modern Conservative Party.

11

JOHN MAJOR

At the Heart of Darkness

IT IS THE FATE of modern British governments, however sceptic they are in theory, to be in practice 'European'. The facts of life are European. Europe shapes the everyday reality with which all public people have to grapple. What Lord Denning said of law – 'the Treaty is like an incoming tide. It flows into the estuaries and up the rivers. It cannot be held back' – could be said as graphically of governance. The existence of the European Union is a condition infusing the bloodstream of every British official and politician. But it reaches deepest into the life of ministers especially. Where others protest and complain, ministers act. Others lament, but ministers carry on. They are not only the governing class of Britain, they belong to the governing class of Europe: knowing each other, haggling together, cutting deals, a kind of masonic fraternity, assisting daily in the onward passage of a project they regard, however much they may sometimes dislike it, as a given. No member of the Union can operate in its own national interest without a leader who understands the meaning of this axiom.

One person who understood it, for most of her time, was Margaret Thatcher. She fought the Union, but lived under it and did much to advance its integration. When the Conservative Party came to choose her successor, it never occurred to anyone to seek a leader who rejected it. No such candidate existed. In fact, there was barely an MP – certainly not Bill Cash – who subscribed to any other idea than continuing acceptance of this norm of British life. We are all Europeans now, they could still credibly declare in 1990.

There was a range of options when the choice arose, within which, admittedly, the European credential of the available leaders was an element to be considered. Two of the candidates were prominently European. Douglas Hurd had worked with Ted Heath, and was tarred as a Foreign Office alumnus from the beginning of his career. He was thus assumed to be, among other things, a Europe man, which, by and large, he was – though he usually spoke with a more guarded sense of distance than, for example, Geoffrey Howe. Michael Heseltine was more fiercely of the faith, having written a book-length panegyric to Britain's coming 'victory' on the continent, and having placed the issue in the vanguard of his argument against Mrs Thatcher. If the party had chosen either of them, it would have announced that it was opting with enthusiasm for Europe simply by the fact of rejecting the third candidate, who seemed perfectly to exemplify what it thought it needed: nothing more nor less than constructive agnosticism. Both parts of that label mattered equally. There had to be a lack of zeal, which was a matter of character. But there should also be an intention to build rather than destroy, which was a matter of politics.

John Major was made leader for other reasons than his ideas about Europe, but his general political character, which is what got him the job, imparted itself to that question as well as all others. Where Mrs Thatcher was strident, he was emollient. Where she burned with conviction, he could see all sides of the argument. Where she tore the party apart, he was elected to keep it together. Where she became the enemy of 'Europe', he pronounced himself its friend, and was chosen for the very reason that, by style as much as content, he would enable hostilities to cease. Though approved by the allies of the departed leader, he was picked as someone who would not give full voice to their prejudices.

He was, in other words, a simple party man. He actually liked the Conservative Party. Long before he became its leader, it was by far the most important influence in his life. Keeping it one and whole was to be the defining task of his leadership. When he had retired from the front line, after Cash and his friends had brought this task close to the most ruinous failure, Major said to me, musing socially, by way of explanation of all he had done: 'I love my party. That was the point. She never loved the party. That was the difference.'[1]

Major's origins supplied no formative twist to his ideas about Europe. He neither fought the Germans, nor heard the Luftwaffe overhead, nor lived with the oppressive knowledge that his father had been killed in action. In his roots, there was nothing to indicate that he could aspire to be a public man, let alone dream of the heroic course his life might take.

He was born in 1943, in a forgettable patch of suburbia on the southern edge of London. For many years the only exoticism in his life was supplied by his father, a circus artiste, later the owner-operator of a business manufacturing garden gnomes. The family was chronically short of money, and its youngest child short of sufficient ambition to keep him at school past the age of sixteen. In adolescent years, therefore, he was constructing no intellectual hinterland, historical or otherwise. When his contemporaries were preparing to go to Oxford or, as mostly happened for his generation of Conservatives, Cambridge, he was looking for clerical work, or helping his father and brother with the gnomes. Ambitious young Tory swells of the period began to strike attitudes round the Macmillan application and the de Gaulle veto. For someone coming of age in the early 1960s, it was the issue of the moment, which might mark the definitive end of a politics still trapped in the penumbra of the Second World War. University Conservatism billowed with earnest argument about the Common Market, and its superiority, for a modern-minded person, over the Commonwealth. On the streets of Brixton, where the young Major lived, such matters were barely heard of.

The boy did, however, discover politics. After school, his further education was supplied by the Young Conservatives. With their help, he ceased to be a rather lonely social reject. His frontiers stretched out from Brixton to the alluring seaside resorts where the Conservative Party held its annual conference. The party, he later said, brought him alive. Quite soon, he became a political junkie, hooked on street politics, tramping the far corners of the local borough in search of a seat on the council, advancing a career that reached an interim apotheosis as chairman of the Lambeth housing committee. It was the prelude to fulfilling the ambition he formed quite early in his startling shift from drop-out to mainline politician: to enter the House of Commons.

This was an intensely local beginning. Major reached Parliament, in May 1979, without having been obliged to express, possibly even to hold, an opinion on any international question. He was apparently present as a Yes voter in the 1975 referendum on Europe, but at the time of the debates on entry, in 1972, he wasn't heard from. His tireless official biographer could find nobody with a recollection of him having taken a position.[2] Whereas for many future Conservative politicians, the Heath event, the successful entry, was a defining moment, which shaped their very commitment to modern Conservatism, the future leader was not engaged.

He may even have been something of a closet sceptic. While persistent deviation from the party line would have been out of character, he did give one indication of less than reverential loyalty to the European

Idea. Six months after getting into Parliament, he signed a letter to *The Times* which addressed itself to the Community budget negotiations Mrs Thatcher was then furiously embarked on. This called for fundamental reform of the Common Agricultural Policy, as the necessary basis for 'new and permanent financial arrangements'. Such thoughts were commonplace; all Tories agreed that we should get 'our money' back. But the letter concluded on a note of sulphuric menace that was not often heard at the time. 'Unless we can jointly work out the radical changes needed and put them speedily into effect,' it said, 'the case for Britain staying inside [the EEC] becomes increasingly difficult to sustain.'[3] Appearing in November 1979, this was a lonely sentiment to be heard from anyone outside the ultra-phobic bunker. Since one of Major's co-signatories was Tony Marlow MP, a lifelong and unregenerate anti-European, it is fair to assume that the climactic recommendation was seriously intended.

For Major, however, it represented only a brief squirt of rebellion against conventional wisdom. He had put his name to something no other ambitious mainstream Tory would have dreamed of uttering. But then he disappeared into the silence of junior office, first as a whip and then in the necessarily parochial enclave of social security administration. These were the days of the final European budget negotiation – the 'new and permanent arrangement' – and then of the Single Act, neither of which required a junior member of the Government to take any other position than the acquiescence that was now, on all subjects, Major's natural demeanour. He was making his reputation as an efficient minister and amenable Thatcherite, on whose relatively inexperienced head the lady's eyes were coming to be trained with serious admiration. She was ever watchful for allies who might become protégés, younger politicians to earn admission to the rank of One of Us. Many, after early promotion, failed to satisfy her expectations. A Cabinet in which the most senior posts continued to be held by men she successfully made into her enemies was in need of loyalist replenishment, and Major fitted the description. He duly received preferment, on an unusually fast track from the back-benches. As Chief Secretary to the Treasury, which he became in 1987, he conducted himself with punctilio and charm, winning more friends than enemies among the spending ministers whose ambitions it was his job to curb. When larger posts fell vacant, owing to the furies let loose around the work of, first, Geoffrey Howe, and then Nigel Lawson, the same capable, deferential replacement was standing quietly by, eager to accept the extravagant patronage of his leader.

The first of these promotions took him wholly by surprise, and required him, among other things, to make his first serious excursion into the 'Europe' question. Until then, he had still managed to remain outside it, even as a Cabinet minister. The Thatcher–Howe and Thatcher–Lawson imbroglios largely passed him by, though he was in Lawson's ministry. Faction, at that point, had not established itself as the organizing mechanism of the Conservative debate on Europe. But, suddenly, Major became Foreign Secretary, a task for which his background in no way prepared him. He was the minister for Europe, without a record of experience to draw on even from ministerial visits to the plethora of European Councils, since his particular jobs had seldom required them.

He was an *ingénu* and he knew it. When he got the news, he told Douglas Hurd how impossible he thought the job would be. 'He was rocked right back on his heels,' Hurd told me. 'He was very unhappy.' Elsewhere Hurd has recorded the reason for this. Major had said to him: 'There's a world full of 150 countries, always exploding into bits and pieces, there are boxes full of stuff about places I have never heard of. And I am expected to take decisions about that!'[4] It is true enough that, in the later twentieth century, it is no longer the ambition or aptitude of every rising Tory to follow in the footsteps of Curzon, redrawing the map of the world. But, even in his own time and place, the Foreign Secretary Mrs Thatcher chose to appoint in July 1989 was uniquely under-qualified for the work.

As it happened, Europe was not the place that felt the consequences of this disability. Major occupied the post for barely ninety days, July to October, for part of which the continent was on holiday. Other matters – Cambodia, Hong Kong, a Commonwealth conference – pressed unavoidably in. It was also as Foreign Secretary that Major made the first trip of his life to the United States. The global rather than the regional was what arrived on his desk in this short span.

He was not, however, silent on the Europe question. And since the politics of the matter had been given a new dimension by Mrs Thatcher's speech at Bruges in September 1988, it was beginning to become impossible for any ministerial utterance to be taken at face value. In this period of endless textual deconstruction, the Bruges speech set a benchmark, with its assault on the socialism emanating from Brussels and its aggressive defence of the nation-state. The nightmare of the super-state, in particular, was born. Any speech that failed to amplify it was capable of being seen as subversive.

Yet the Bruges philosophy was not one with which the new Foreign Secretary was instinctively imbued. Though expressed by the Prime Minister, it remained more a defiant challenge than an agreed definition. Least of all was it well regarded in the department which this unformed man, this unlettered internationalist, had been put in charge of. If there was a teacher and a student in their bureaucratic relationship, the leader and the led, departmental orthodoxy inevitably began by having the upper hand. Naturally, therefore, what Major said about Europe reflected the wisdom Mrs Thatcher had not yet succeeded in rendering unconventional. Delivering the annual British *tour d'horizon* at the UN General Assembly, a year after Bruges, he spoke of the need for a 'stronger, more united Western Europe', and asserted that 'our active membership of the Community is a fixed point in our future'. In normal times, these would have been trite banalities. In 1989, they were seen by the Thatcher circle as signs of the new man's susceptibility to the Foreign Office, an impression not diminished when they were repeated in the Foreign Secretary's speech that year to the Conservative Party conference.[5]

Yet to have said anything else would have been, for the ministerial Major, an offence against his nature. Even at this early stage in his prominence, he behaved like a man whose task was not to amplify the more abrasive messages of his leader, but the reverse. He wasn't an anti-Thatcherite. Though Mrs Thatcher was his patron, and the definer of his core ideas about economic policy, he wasn't burdened with her extreme convictions, and positively disapproved of the disunity these brought with them. Over Europe, he was already seeking to dissolve differences and heal wounds.

Such was to be his mission as leader too: a period that could later be regarded as a six-year exercise, painfully unsuccessful, in trying to persuade the Conservative Party there was a middle way between the anti-Europe passions of its most vocal minority of politicians and the pro-Europe necessities that came with the task of government.

Undefiled by awkward prejudices of his own, Major naturally clothed himself in the orthodoxy that was the pragmatic wisdom of the moment. As Foreign Secretary, this led him to the extraordinary insight that British membership of the Community had its merits. In his next post, however, it required something a little more daring: a posture and a choice, in fact, that turned out to touch his life for many years ahead.

It was at the Treasury, not the Foreign Office, that the 'Europe' question drove into the heart of Major's political life. Once again, he arrived at a new department in the wake of the personal turbulence

which Mrs Thatcher made inseparable from her governing style. Nigel
Lawson had resigned, and not the least of his grounds for doing so was
the persistent intervention in his work of Alan Walters, the leader's
personal economic trainer, who was particularly exercised over the
matter of the European Exchange Rate Mechanism (ERM). Walters
assisted Mrs Thatcher in preventing Lawson from doing what he wanted.
The ERM, as we have seen, was then the fiercest *casus belli* in the
Thatcher Government.[6] While it largely passed Major by when he was at
the Foreign Office, at the Treasury it became the issue that defined him
as what he was: an absorber of establishment wisdom, and a tenacious
functionary in the task of seeing it to enactment.

He first addressed it as a sceptic: or rather, a more suitable designation for Major, as a man without opinions. 'I am an agnostic,' he told a
Foreign Office official.[7] In his early days at the Treasury, he remained in
the same condition, but was surrounded by some objectively existing
facts he was never likely to resist. The Government was already committed in principle to entry to the ERM, when the time was ripe. That was
the consequence of the blood spilled at the summit in Madrid in June:
the victory over the leader that had cost Howe his job as Foreign
Secretary. More than that, by autumn the entire senior collective at the
Treasury were of the opinion that the time had come to convert the
commitment into fact.

Seldom, indeed, in the entire history of Britain's membership of the
European Community has there been such unanimity, concerning the
next integrationist development, as that to be found in the debates about
entry to the ERM in 1989 and 1990. This did not, it is true, indicate a
sudden upsurge of Euro-idealism. The proximate cause was the decline
in the value of the currency throughout 1989: the pound, worth DM3.28
at the beginning, dropped to DM2.72 by the end, a fall of 17 per cent.
This gravely damaged the prospects of a fall in the inflation rate, and
became a self-accelerating vortex that threatened to consume defenders
of the exchange rate, chief among them the new Chancellor of the
Exchequer. The need for a reliable counterweight, an anchor, became
apparent.

All the same, it is remarkable that the ERM, which existed as a
studied preliminary to a European single currency, was almost universally seen as the right way to construct the anchor. Officials, politicians
and other observers had been through a variety of intellectual odysseys
before reaching this position. Lawson himself, for example, while an
unwavering believer in the ERM and fixed rates, was powerfully opposed,

in all circumstances, to entry into a single currency. At the Bank of England, Eddie George, the future governor, was less sure about the ERM than Robin Leigh-Pemberton, the present governor, whose signature on the Delors committee's recommendation of a critical path leading to EMU had infuriated Mrs Thatcher.[8] But, as the currency slid and inflation rose, the Chancellor soon decided that the ERM offered him his best hope, and he had almost everyone who mattered on his side, from the Treasury to the Bank to the Foreign Office, from the old guard like Howe and Lawson to his new, most intimate colleague, Foreign Secretary Hurd, from the CBI to the Labour Party, from the *Financial Times* to the *Guardian, The Times* and the *Daily Telegraph.*

His conversion was due to economics, but not entirely devoid of a sense about European politics. As befitted a politician who was nothing if not sensitive to the locus of power, he knew that entry into the ERM club would also align Britain more favourably in discussions about the future of Europe. Such discussions – how relentless was the European dynamo! – were already scheduled. The leaders had agreed in December 1989 to call an inter-governmental conference – the Maastricht of two years ahead – to agree the changes to the Treaty of Rome that were necessary for a single currency. Major didn't need to be Howe-like in his Euro-philia to want to influence this, if necessary by joining the ERM. It was the normal instinct of any minister not barricaded behind an over-mastering scepticism about the European project – which meant almost all ministers except the leader herself, who was, even at this late stage, wholeheartedly supported only by one Cabinet minister on the verge of departure, Nicholas Ridley, and another too junior to matter, Michael Howard.

However, once Major was himself persuaded of the case, she had to be carried to the point of decision. It was not a simple task. He did not, to begin with, show his hand. After all, for a new, young Chancellor to presume to push the Prime Minister off the course she still preferred was a large ambition, even though Hurd was his ally. Hurd and Major met frequently for breakfast, picking a way forward, in the knowledge of realities that favoured their ambition. The first of these was that any reneging on the Madrid commitment would have a disastrous effect on the Government's credibility in the City, the second that they were both uncommonly secure in their positions. Neither, in effect, could be sacked. They were therefore well placed to impose upon Mrs Thatcher, a point she appears to have taken with some bitterness. As her discussions with Major proceeded in the spring of 1990, she could see where he was headed. 'I was extremely disturbed to find that the Chancellor had swallowed so quickly the slogans of the European lobby,' she writes in her memoirs. 'It was already clear that he was thinking in terms of compromises which would not be acceptable to me, and that intellectually he was drifting with the tide.'[9]

He dabbled with alternatives to the culminating concept of full economic and monetary union. These had been half formulated in Lawson's time: the notion, for example, of 'competing currencies', whereby the market rather than a European central bank would determine how far sterling was replaced in daily transactions by the Deutschmark and the franc. The contribution of Major himself was to encourage development of another idea, partly fathered by the old Eurocrat Michael Butler, for a 'hard écu': a possible stepping-stone to a single currency, but not inevitably destined to produce one. Each of these schemes, besides any virtue it had in itself, was designed to render more palatable to the leader the case for entry into the ERM. Each, however, was without significant support elsewhere in Europe. They were of little more than academic interest: steps along the way, down a path Mrs Thatcher would eventually find it impossible to impede.

When she conceded, on 13 June, it was to Major personally. 'I had too few allies to resist and win the day,' she laments. By that time, even her personal staff, from which Walters had retired, were pushing in the same direction. The logic and the pressure, orchestrated by the Chancellor, set Britain on the threshold, after a decade's resistance, of absorption into the European monetary project. His instincts, moreover, were already pointing him beyond that. He was at least toying with the politics of EMU itself. He saw the possibility, as he minuted the Prime Minister in April, of a 'two-tier Europe', from which Britain would be excluded if she did not take EMU seriously. He plainly thought this would be very bad news. The leader's recollection of his message is witheringly scornful. Major, she thought, had 'a tendency to be defeated by platitudes', and should not have cared about the two tiers 'if the other tier is going in the wrong direction'.[10] But, on the immediate question, she had had to bow to him. All that remained, as regards the ERM, was to settle the date of entry, which was finally agreed between them to be 8 October – as long as it was accompanied, at her insistence, by a 1 per cent cut in interest rate.

For anyone watching Major's evolution as a European, this saga offers a number of illuminating lessons, the first of which concerns his susceptibility to the fashion of the moment. There was nothing wicked about this preference, nothing that was even aberrant: after the ERM decision was debated in the Commons, only eleven Conservative MPs, led by John Biffen, refused to support it. When the overwhelming weight of expert opinion, both political and economic, lies on one side of an urgent argument, the stubbornness required to resist it can derive only from the kind of systemic prejudice that had no part in Major's make-up. Even that cussed quality, as Mrs Thatcher herself proved, was not enough. The fact remains, however, that the decision came to be almost as widely criticized after the event as it was supported before. Not *quite* so widely. In the controversies that rattled round the Tory Party's European debate for years ahead, there were always defenders of the therapy which ERM disciplines had worked on the economy. But it did become commonly agreed that the pound, which after falling so far in 1989 appreciated steadily in 1990, was put into the mechanism at a rate, DM2.95, which was higher than could be sustained, even within a 6 per cent band of flexibility either way, and much higher than any figure reflecting the real competitive relationship between the German and British economies.

Major knew most of this at the time. 'It was the only occasion I ever witnessed him having a fundamental row with Margaret Thatcher,' one of his closest political friends told me. He had wanted a lower rate, she an even higher one. Later, Major himself, in my hearing, specifically denied the existence of such a disagreement. But the final figure was certainly a compromise, which also had to reflect, of course, what the existing members of the ERM would accept.

Whatever the array of forces on this point, the material consequence was a lowering cloud over Major's career. What he had joined together as Chancellor, he was obliged to put asunder as Prime Minister two years later. His conduct generated a feeling, moreover, that he was a politician for whom conviction tended to follow action, rather than vice versa. Not many people thought, looking back, that he had ever really believed in the ERM from a position of principle. He took it up as an anti-inflationary weapon, but, for him, it did not fit into the kind of grand European scheme of thinking which persuaded some of his contemporaries, who had had a different education, of the need always to take one side in the great European debate – for fear of being stigmatized as a member of the unwashed and unenlightened. It was as a trimmer, not an ideologue, that Major led the making of a decision that became the first item in the charge-sheet his former friends eventually raised against him.

But, secondly, another signal was there for those who wanted to see it. Major was not a visceral anti-European. He had, at this stage, no particle of the faith that might persuade him to worship at the same altar as William Cash. His form, on the subject of Europe, was shallower than that of Hurd and Heseltine, and much less rooted in the past, but it was also fresher. It had been proved, as it were, in battle. He had shown that his gut feelings didn't carry him into the same blazing empyrean, afire with anti-continentalism, where Margaret Thatcher defiantly took up residence in her final months.

He was therefore never really qualified for the task which his supporters, retrospectively, reviled him for failing to fulfil. Hurd, his friend and rival, always knew this. Major never was a rightist, in this or, for the most part, any other matter. He slipped into the mainstream of the moment, always moderately rather than with Thatcher-like zeal. 'We used to have lunch occasionally, when I was Home Secretary and he was Chief Secretary,' Hurd said some years later. 'He talked perfectly clearly about his views. I've never understood (a) why she thought he was a protégé, or (b) why the right wing in 1990 thought "Here's our guy." '11 They all just wanted to believe it, Hurd thought.

Major, moreover, was happy to allow them. Also dating from his time as Chief Secretary, a journalist recalled an evening at a party conference when he had 'bumped into one of the most pro-European Tory MPs' and later 'had a drink with a fiercely Euro-sceptic right-winger'. Both had been impressed by the little-known Mr Major. 'Why? Because he had given both of them the impression that he agreed 100 per cent with their views.'12

Such was the figure in whose hands was now placed the task of sustaining party and government into another election, while pursuing the work that was axiomatic to Britain's place in the world: the recovery of some influence in Europe.

*

As Prime Minister, Major wanted, above all, to restore normality. The period of one-woman rule, an unsuccessful experiment in quasi-presidential government, should come to an end. Not least was this so over the question that had brought the lady down. The very night of his election as leader, he kept a date in the inconvenient town of Altrincham to make a party speech, in which he said, among other things, that he thought Britain should stop shouting from the terraces and start playing on the field of Europe.

This was a mood he was fully permitted to engender: the change of leader was, for a time, cathartic. It would not be long before the historical rhythm which the great Arnold Toynbee divined in his survey of the ages, whereby every action is eventually followed by a hostile counter-action growing out of it, would reassert itself, to memorable effect, in the annals of the Conservative Party. The underlings at Major's back would soon make sure of that. More than 130 Tory back-benchers had joined what they defiantly named the Bruges Group, to keep faith with the famous text. But they had also chosen Major, and they wanted him to succeed. For a while, therefore, the governors governed. Their perspective, rather than that of their tormentors, was reaffirmed. Events could be seen from their point of view, rather than that of a rank and file that was not yet driving events. The sides coalesced, to resemble a fully functioning political party.

There came a time when this would not be easy to remember – but it did happen, in Major's first few months.

He started with the advantage of not being repelled by foreigners. He was intensely English, and, in his somewhat self-conscious attempts to fill out an otherwise vacant personality, Englishness was pushed to the fore. One of his few extra-mural passions was cricket, and the author he most regularly said he read was Anthony Trollope. When I saw him, later in his time, in his flat in Downing Street, he proudly displayed his cricketing memorabilia; and the collected works of Trollope, he said, lay alongside *Sense and Sensibility*, which he was re-reading, by his bed. One of the lines that clung to him was pilfered from George Orwell, to convey an image of Englishness he exalted, reaching back from the 1990s, as he recited it in a speech, to another England of 'long shadows on county grounds, warm beer, invincible green suburbs, dog-lovers, and old maids bicycling to Holy Communion through the mist'. This reeked of nostalgia. Warm beer came to seem a refreshment that was especially congruent with the Major personality. But he was not the kind of Tory who needed to define his love of one country by the ferocity of his dislike for others.

In particular, he had no hang-up about the Germans. He knew they were the key to a more diplomatically constructive future for Britain in Europe, and was critical of his predecessor for her neglect of this. He once gave me a learned little lecture on exactly why her attitude –

reflecting, it must be said, what successive British leaders had done ever since the war – contrived to perpetuate Britain's most unfortunate missed opportunity.[13] It had been, he said, 'an historic error of very great proportions'.

His opening gesture as Prime Minister was to set about correcting the error, by seeking the special friendship of Chancellor Helmut Kohl. Kohl was by now in his prime as a statesman: after German reunification, indisputably the dominant European figure. From the beginning, the two men warmed to each other in gratitude: the one for his release from the didactic tyrannies of Mrs Thatcher, the other for the sympathetic understanding he received from the more experienced politician.

It was natural that Major should choose Bonn as the place where he would make his first speech as Prime Minister outside Britain, and almost as predictable that it would aim to establish a tone that was different from what had gone before. This much it did. But it also became something of a *cause célèbre* in Major's evolution, and as such repays a little study.

His main purpose was indeed to change the climate. After lauding what the Conservative Party and Kohl's Christian Democrats shared between them – 'the great Conservative values: stability, opportunity, community, identity' – he talked about his vision of a free-market Europe, and an enlarged Europe open to the new democracies in the East. He made clear that, so far as monetary union was concerned, 'we think it best to reserve judgement . . . we cannot accept its imposition', and he offered a finely inconclusive assessment of the proper place of nation, in the scheme of things, as against Community. 'Europe', he said, 'is made up of nation-states: their vitality and diversity are sources of strength. The important thing is to strike the right balance between closer co-operation and a proper respect for national institutions and traditions.'

But the most remembered passage was the one that really did appear to foretell a change of aspiration: 'My aims for Britain in the Community can be simply stated. I want us to be where we belong. At the very heart of Europe. Working with our partners in building the future.'[14] So important were these words to Major that some of them appeared on the draft in his own hand: 'At the *very* heart,' he wrote.[15]

It is in the aftermath, as much as the fact, of this speech that its interest lies. It sounded like a manifesto for at least the long-term purpose of shifting Britain closer to the centre of the Community: not towards agreeing a federalist agenda, but surely breaking with the insistent separatism that had hitherto spoken from most of the sub-texts. Yet it turned out that this was not quite meant to be so. While, at the time it was given, the speech caused rather little turbulence, and passed the test of substantive, if not tonal, consistency with what had gone before – the *Daily Mail* rejoiced to conclude that 'the carping has stopped' – this verdict eventually changed. When the Euro-sceptic atmosphere reheated in the Tory Party, the speech became subject to revisionist assessment.

A minor sign of this is to be found in the flexible verdict of Charles Powell, Mrs Thatcher's influential, and brazenly loyal, foreign affairs adviser, who stayed on with Major for his first few months. At the time of the Bonn speech, Powell pronounced it satisfactorily Thatcherite. There was nothing in it, he said, that could not have been said by his former mistress.[16] Later, Powell had a different recollection. He told Major's biographer that he had said the speech 'went much too far in the Europhile direction of Heath'.[17]

Such, apparently, was the suppleness of judgement exacted by the changing circumstances in which it had to be delivered. But Major himself also came to rewrite his purposes. He had never intended, he later insisted, to say what his words apparently said. What he meant was not that Britain should be at the heart of Europe, but at the heart only of the European debate. 'I emphatically did not mean ever Britain slavishly following on at the behest of whatever the fashionable European majority opinion of the day happened to be,' he said in 1995. 'What I meant is that we should engage in the argument ... and argue the British case from the heart of Europe.'[18]

This was a retrospective apologia. One thing that certainly did not happen under Major was the location of Britain at the heart of Europe, and some explanation was now required for those who had briefly been led to expect otherwise. But the regime did change in other ways.

One of them was via the ascendancy allowed to Hurd, and with it the rehabilitation of Jacques Delors, the Commission president, as a man with whom it was not only necessary but valuable to do business. Hurd was a serious admirer of Delors, a case of one quality mandarin recognizing another of the breed. Although Hurd spent his entire time as Foreign Secretary insisting he wasn't a federalist, and cautioning against the centralist tendencies of Brussels, he always saw Delors as an ally, rather than the demonic enemy of Thatcherite imaginings. We need Delors 'to keep us straight', he said to me on one occasion. He regarded the Commission as mostly a guardian of practicality, and Delors himself, in particular, as someone who understood the need to decentralize: a proponent of 'subsidiarity', the ugly abstraction that entered the vocabulary of Euro-speak in the 1990s. Delors had often told him he wished some of the other Commissioners – for example, an Italian transport Commissioner trying to lay down the law about British roads – 'would not be so silly'.

Hurd himself pushed in this direction, urging Brussels to keep out of 'the nooks and crannies' of national life. But his main contribution was as a tutor in foreign affairs whom Major was happy to learn from: a key influence, therefore, on the calmer, more moderate, more bureaucratic context in which, the leader hoped, 'Europe' affairs would once again be conducted.

For he couldn't escape the heat indefinitely. The Maastricht summit beckoned. There was no getting away from it. Some kind of deal had to be arranged that would satisfy both Major and the party: satisfy Major *because* it satisfied the party. The relationship was symbiotic. The party chose Major, and wanted him to succeed – but on its terms. Major accepted the brief, and wanted to deliver – but on terms which he, as a national leader, could pragmatically live with. Running up to Maastricht, which was fixed immutably for early December 1991, the Prime Minister began to show the tortuous subtlety for which, devoid of any excessive zeal, he was to become well known.

There are other ways of describing that faculty. The time came when it would have to be called weakness, or empty deviousness, or bare-faced contradiction. But, before and during Maastricht, Major was subtle, prescient and pretty effective. The regime outfaced its opponents, abroad and at home.

The opponents abroad wanted Maastricht to be something big. After the Single Act, it would be only the second substantial revision of the Treaty of Rome since the great document was written in 1957. Not one but two inter-governmental conferences, one on economic and monetary union, the other on closer political union, were labouring towards conclusions. For federalists, therefore, it was a moment of opportunity and truth, and they did not want to waste it.

At their head, it turned out, was the Dutch Government, who would be in the chair at Maastricht. The Dutch weren't always enemies of the British view of 'Europe', but in their present configuration they were, in British terms, 'federalist', and first used their presidency to favour proposals massively enhancing the power of Brussels. The political union IGC was all about this argument, and especially the extent to which foreign and security policy could and should be drawn under the Community umbrella. The Gulf War was only just over when the argument got going, and the terrible bloodshed in Bosnia continued throughout, a rebuke to the inability of 'Europe' to act together on its eastern doorstep. The Dutch, ditching more cautious proposals that were on the table, produced a draft treaty that put both foreign policy and interior-ministry affairs under the hand of the Commission and the Court of Justice. This was federalism writ heavy. Besides risking confusion about the role of Nato, and the Americans, in the future defence of Europe, it would constitute a serious step towards political union, if not, yet, exactly a European government. To explain and justify it, its defenders offered the image of the Community as a tree, springing from deep roots into well-spread branches which grew, however, from a single trunk.

Not only Britain but France rejected this. A creative Frenchman propounded the rival model of Europe as a Greek temple, whose façade consisted of three pillars. Although these all propped up the Council of Ministers – the national government leaders – only one consisted of powers that were truly integrated: the existing Community, based on the Treaty of Rome, and covering mainly matters of markets and trade. The other two would consist of foreign-and-security policy, and justice/home affairs/immigration and so on. These, while expressing a European dimension, would admit of less intervention by the Commission, the Parliament, the Court, the artefacts of 'Europe'.

Naturally, this model appealed much more to the British, and they appropriated it as their own. In the intensive discussions that revolved around the shape of future political union, moreover, they played a more constructive role than had been true in the recent past.[19]

The British, of course, never wanted a treaty at all: that was still their fundamental position. As a journalist, I was reminded of this, at moments when the Maastricht process was striking them as especially arduous, by just about every minister involved. The Treaty was the tool, they thought, of politicians who took seriously that very unBritish term 'the construction of Europe', and was therefore, at some level, deeply undesirable. To that extent, a certain seamless continuity prevailed from Thatcher to Major, indeed from Major, interrupted only by Heath, all the way back to Ernest Bevin and Winston Churchill.

But Major and his people played a decent hand. This required a great deal of diplomatic energy, coupled with a modicum of reassembled goodwill, which would not have been available under the previous dispensation. For there were plenty of other points of contest, notably about the role of the European Parliament, which the Germans especially, as their price for economic union, wanted to see enhanced in a matching upgrade for political union. Delors himself, though an integrationist on foreign policy – and a constant lamenter of the weakness of the political side of Maastricht – joined with the British in resisting the extension of Commission 'competences' into such fields as energy, tourism and disaster relief. In all these preliminaries, the Major style did roughly what seemed to be required by the people who had been so horrified by Mrs Thatcher's declarations of war. It got to grips with the reality of continental negotiation. There was a lot of fine-tuned preparation, for an agreement to which the British, for once, were as committed as the Europeans – as long as they secured some important positions.

For the Thatcherites had not gone away. They were the opponents at home, who had equally to be propitiated by the party manager. He did the work with aplomb, and a certain amount of political courage.

The Cabinet was kept involved with a thoroughness to which few of its members were accustomed. It contained, as we shall see, its quota of naturally severe Euro-sceptics, who were biding their time. But the leader comfortably boxed them in. It was a member of this group who exulted to me about how attentive Major was being in keeping them informed. 'There has never been a European summit on which so many ministers were able to have their say,' this man said. Parliament was given the opportunity to speak as well, before Maastricht began. Major, rather riskily, laid his position on the line. He would accept no taint of federalism in the Treaty, he said. He would insist on his 'pillars', would reject any compulsion, such as the other countries were contemplating, to join up to economic and monetary union.

The temperature was beginning to rise. Led by Mrs Thatcher, some sceptics could already see the Maastricht trap, as a now-or-never last chance to exercise a British veto over integration which would, if it was enacted, be irreversible. Opt-outs and special British exceptions were in the air, but they wouldn't stop the caravan moving forward. At the head of her friends, Mrs Thatcher demanded at least the gesture of a promise to hold a referendum on EMU, should Britain ever decide to join, and called Major arrogant when he refused either to rule out for ever British membership of the single currency or to promise a national consultation if the time came.

An issue thus was born, Yes or No to a referendum, which was to invade Tory politics for the duration, the litmus-test of his honour, his nationalism, his respect for party – his whatever – that Major kept facing for the next five years. This, also, was when William Cash came to thump the table.

But only six Tory MPs, including Biffen and excluding Cash, voted against the pre-Maastricht declaration of support. Sent on his way with a parliamentary majority of 101, Major arrived at the place, whose unheard-of name would one day be engraved dolefully on his heart, with his Cabinet and his party behind him, and with skills that had now been honed in the European arena for a year. He might not be a visionary, but the little lessons in dealing with people, acquired in Lambeth street politics, developed in the corridors of the Commons, enhanced at the Treasury, were what he thought would see him through.

He was, indeed, a student of people, the lowest and the highest. It was his special trick. Douglas Hurd noted it as one of Major's early consolations when he was plunged into foreign affairs. 'He is a collector of people,' Hurd told me, after retiring from the Foreign Office. 'In a way, going into foreign affairs was like enlarging his collection.' At the negotiating table, watchfulness, along with an intense application to detail, was his principal weapon. 'He's a student of body language,' Hurd went on. 'He watches, more carefully than anyone I've ever known, how people conduct themselves when they're with him. He used to say to me, because I was often with him at diplomatic discussions, "But you didn't watch what his hands were doing. You didn't see what he was doing with his hair at that point." Which I hadn't.'[20]

When I once put this to Major, he cringed, but did not deny it. His own body visibly stiffened. Plainly I had stumbled on the protective device of an outsider from way back. 'Yes,' he said, his cover blown. 'I look at the body language at least as much as I listen to the words. I have always done it, as far back as I can ever remember.'[21]

At Maastricht, these were necessary, though not sufficient, skills. Since national leaders are decisive figures at European summits, often negotiating only with a foreign minister beside them, their personal faculties matter keenly. But Major's tenacity was as important as his sensitivity. When it came down to the wire, there were two issues that mattered more than any others to the British.

One was EMU, not a new problem. It had been obvious for more than a year that EMU would be at the heart of Maastricht, its central purpose. It had been equally obvious that Britain, for one, would be unwilling to collude as a signed-up member in a scheme that required the solemn disclaimer of monetary sovereignty for an indefinite, perhaps permanent, period ahead. If the Maastricht version of EMU contained such a sense of both the automatic and the perpetual, and if it was to be accomplished within the legal order of the Community rather than as a separate enterprise outside the Treaty of Rome, Britain, and perhaps others, would have to retain the option not to belong.

How was this to be arranged? The months before Maastricht were occupied with numerous arguments about the shape of EMU, the role and status of a new European central bank, the number of currencies necessary to make a viable quorum, the relationship between coercion, veto and arbitrary exclusion as these might affect different countries. Of particular controversy was whether Britain should be treated uniquely. Britain didn't want to be. Norman Lamont, the Chancellor, at the last meeting of finance ministers before Maastricht itself, argued for a generalized opt-out, on which any country could draw, something that might conceivably prove attractive to the Germans, always the most delicately poised, as regards EMU, of the continental powers. But Lamont did not gain his point. Only Denmark, in any case, was as interested as Britain in retaining freedom of monetary manoeuvre. The Lamont proposition was defeated 11–1.

In Maastricht, the final EMU opt-out was secured only with difficulty. The precise text of the protocol, giving Britain her special privilege, had to be agreed, and the others insisted on going through it. This was the day Lamont later said that his eyes were opened to the hideous federalist impulses of his fellow finance ministers. It was also a moment concerning which some ugly little retrospective squabbles broke out, prompted by the now Euro-phobic former Chancellor, as to who precisely deserved the credit for the British opt-out. There had been stories of dramatic walks-outs from Maastricht committees, and the Chancellor banging vainly on the door of a room where Major and the Dutch leader, Ruud Lubbers, stitched up the final deal. 'I just produced a piece of paper at the last meeting deleting everything and saying it didn't apply to Britain,' Lamont later claimed. And of the opt-out: 'I did that.' At which Major said he was 'very surprised ... [and] so will everyone else be who was actually there at the Maastricht negotiations'.[22]

The second British point was less well prepared for. Bruges 88 lived in the collective Tory memory, and its statement of revulsion against the reappearance of socialism via the ordinances of Brussels was shared throughout the Major Government. Since Maastricht was destined to include an expression of the 'social dimension' of Europe, this had to be eluded as firmly as EMU. It brought back some of the arguments from the very origins of 'Europe', which the Labour Party had first opposed, among other reasons, as a capitalist plot. In a certain context, 'Europe' was an exercise in free-market protectionism: in another, it could be seen as a form of Christian socialism. It all depended where you looked from. In fact the British, taken as a whole, were never consistent about where to place the EEC on this left–right spectrum. The critics in either party could always find convenient reasons to put it at the opposite end from their own. But in 1991, without doubt, Maastricht's prospective social chapter seemed wholly ominous to the reigning British orthodoxy.

It was not, however, easy to dispose of. And the way this happened, while successful in the outcome, was a harbinger of the Tory struggle which, in due course, insinuated its way up from the back-benches into the Cabinet itself.

The issue was not the fact but the content of a social chapter, and on this the continentals at first seemed ready to negotiate. Some of the partners – French, Italian, Belgian – saw it as a text that should seriously enhance the rights of workers to be consulted about decisions in the enterprises where they worked. Major's position was that this would impose huge costs on industry, and sacrifice jobs. But since there had been no agreement in principle before Maastricht, one way or the other, a poker-game ensued. As things stood, Britain could wreck the Treaty by rejecting the chapter, and for most of the two-day summit the Europeans judged that Major wouldn't dare to carry his resistance that far. They thought he must be bluffing.

But Major had some uncompromising forces at his back, whom he seemed almost to beg to apply their pressure. The Employment Secretary, Michael Howard, had stated his own unyielding hostility to any version of social chapterism. Although he wasn't at Maastricht, Major instructed that he be kept informed and given, in effect, a veto on what might be proposed. So Howard, when asked by telephone, seized his chance, threatening that he might resign if Britain signed up.[23]

This early version of a regular Major tactic – 'the more you pressure me, the more readily I will agree with you' – had the desired effect. When Lubbers, who as the summit chairman needed to save the Treaty, sought to seduce him with a much watered-down social chapter, Major said no as clearly as he knew how: words to the effect, according to his biographer, of 'It's no good asking me. I can't do it. And I won't do it.' For the last six hours of Maastricht, in fact, Major sat solemnly, almost pleasurably, declining to accept the logic of being one against eleven, sticking to his solitary negative on several issues, periodically reminding his colleagues that it was they, not he, who wanted the Treaty anyway. Finally impressed that the British meant what they had been saying, Lubbers produced his own alternative – a social chapter that was technically outside the Treaty, which meant that Britain's dissent, her formal refusal to sign up, could be permitted without jeopardizing everything else.

And so a Treaty of Maastricht was agreed. The process had a number of aspects, some of which are so startling that they deserve a special place in any reflection on Britain's relations with this mysterious collection of countries and cultures across the Channel.

The least surprising concerned Major himself. He conducted a canny, patient negotiation. He wasn't the main architect of Maastricht, a title which undoubtedly belongs to Ruud Lubbers, Dutch grand-master of the politics and game-playing required to keep a complex coalition of political interests moving forward. The only mistake Lubbers made, he told me afterwards, was in not appreciating the adamancy of Major's position on the social chapter. As the author of the chapter, he thought he had contrived the proper degree of unoppressive subsidiarity within it, sufficient for Britain to sign up. As he reflected on what had gone wrong, Lubbers took an almost academic interest in his own chairmanly performance. 'If I had known that John Major needed in all circumstances an opt-out, I would have played it differently,' he said.[24]

But he admired Major's trajectory as a negotiator. 'There are two models of negotiation,' the scholarly deal-maker explained. 'The model of using arguments, trying to convince people, doing that in a good sequence, with good timing. And then you have the other model, negotiating emotionally. However strange this may sound, most political leaders do it emotionally. Margaret Thatcher. Helmut Kohl. Also Mitterrand, a bit less. They shout at you that such-and-such is absolute nonsense. But John Major never. A gentleman, well briefed, rational, well informed.'

It was not surprising, either, that Major should make the most of what had been achieved. His spokesman went too far in saying that the result amounted to 'Game, set and match' to the British. Even had this been true, it was a foolish piece of triumphalism that was pinned, owing to the anonymity behind which British official spokesmen then sheltered, to the Prime Minister. Even though he didn't say it himself, he offended both Lubbers and François Mitterrand. 'Mitterrand was very irritated,' Lubbers told me. 'It was as if he said to Mitterrand, "I managed

A united vision: Harold Wilson goes European, with Helmut Schmidt,
the German Chancellor, Labour Party conference, 1974.

All about the price of bread: Barbara Castle (left), shopping for a No in the
referendum, June 1975.

Margaret Thatcher and friends: the Dublin summit of the European Council, 1979.

The President and his patrimony: Jacques Delors, European Commission, 1985–95.

Margaret Thatcher: disdaining Europe and, with Helmut Kohl (below, right), failing to understand the Germans.

The phobic faces of the 1990s: Sir James Goldsmith (above),
and William Cash.

John Major, prime minister, 1990–97: my hesitation is final.

Bastards and others: John Redwood (to the right of the blazer), and his campaign team for the challenge to Major, June 1995.

Roy Jenkins: from Wilson to Blair, and goad to god-father.

The militant tendency:
Conservatives for
Europe, Kenneth
Clarke (above) and
Michael Heseltine.

Tony Blair, Paris, March 1998: *Je suis un homme d'Europe.*

Maastricht, not you, or Kohl, or anyone else."' It also incurred Lubbers's disapproval for its crassness as a piece of domestic political management. 'After all, he was apparently saying that all the elements of Maastricht where I *don't* have an opt-out are excellent! Because I managed it! If you're going to say that, you should at least go hell-for-leather for parliamentary approval, instead of leaving time for a controversy to start.'

That, as we have seen, is not what happened. However, given that there had to be a treaty, this one was as good as Britain could have expected. Besides, there was an excuse for Government exuberance in the ecstatic reception the conquering hero received on his return from the Netherlands.

Given the odium subsequently heaped on Maastricht, and its luminous place in the catalogue of infamy that became the bible of Conservative Euro-scepticism, it is worth recalling what these people were saying at the time. This is another testament to the waywardness of judgement that has been characteristic of many a sceptic mind: its capacity for sharp reversals of opinion not only about the matter of principle, but about the correct interpretation of matters of fact: its sheer want of scepticism, in the proper sense, at moments of excitement.

For the anti-Brussels camp also, like Major himself, thought he had had a triumph. 'He went. He stood firm. And he prevailed,' said the *Daily Mail*. 'When the test came, Mr Major was ready for it. The moment found the man of consensual instinct with more than a touch of steel.'[25] Paul Johnson wrote: 'John Major's Houdini-like escape from the toils of the Eurocrats at Maastricht is a personal victory which may well go into folklore.'[26] 'In almost every sense, it was a copybook triumph for Mr Major, the stuff of Foreign Office dreams,' reported the *Daily Telegraph*'s man in Brussels, Boris Johnson.[27] The *Telegraph* itself editorialized as follows: 'Mr Major deserves the heartfelt gratitude of his party for averting a disaster which might have made election victory unattainable.'[28] *The Times* leader described the whole event as an 'emphatic success'.[29]

What unifies these voices most remarkably is not that they approved of Maastricht and Major in 1991, but that each one of them, in less than a year, came to write about Major in the most scathing terms, and cite the Treaty of Maastricht as the main evidence against him. A variety of explanations might be ventured. Since all supported the Conservatives, and an election was coming, they were doubtless eager to fortify the leader of their party at what might otherwise have been the wrong sort of turning-point. In addition, the very fact of doing down the continentals, by securing the opt-outs while remaining somewhere near the centre of European activities, could only be a source of pleasure to papers and writers much concerned about the future of British national sovereignty. Once again, we seemed to be having it, rather comfortably, both ways. In any case, the level of these people's expectations for Britain in Europe was different from what it became. For one thing, they still wanted Britain to be in there, making the most of the EU and pushing the British interest. The *Daily Mail* verdict, for example, was predicated on the need for what it called an effective defence 'of our country's interests in shaping an ever closer European union'. The paper speculated optimistically on a new currency that would one day 'be worth having'. A few years later, no reader of the *Mail* would believe it could ever have taken such positions.

Nothing, however, had changed about Maastricht in the intervening time. The Treaty was the Treaty was the Treaty, for better or for worse. Only later, it seemed, did these unsceptical sceptics fully understand what it was about: or at any rate decide to bewilder people with second thoughts which they seldom, if ever, acknowledged as such.

Another thing that happened, though, was that Major became committed to the Treaty. He saw himself as its maker. From the British point of view, he owned it. Seeing it ratified was, for him, a matter of honour as much as politics. However loud the roars and devious the manoeuvres of the Cashites, there could never be a question of withdrawing the European Communities (Amendment) Bill from the parliamentary process. He would use every disciplinary device, and all his political capital as leader, to prevent Britain being responsible, by her non-ratification, for the failure of Maastricht to become a fully functioning treaty of the Union.

This was the high point of Major the European, the governing man, declining to be fettered by the party politicians around him. But it marked the last real ascendancy of the senior colleagues – a dwindling collection, as it turned out – who backed him in his earnest desire, ineptly expressed, to be at the heart of Europe.

*

ON 9 APRIL, Major did what he had been chosen to do, in the general election which almost nobody expected him to win. To common amazement, he acted out the scenario that was only a wishful dream for most Conservative MPs. There were a good many reasons for this, which had less to do with him or his party than with the Labour Party and its leader. But the election took place in the shadow of Maastricht. The campaign unfolded, therefore, within the outer edge of the phase when the Treaty was still being written about as an unqualified triumph, burnishing Major's name as a man of competence. To that extent, Europe played its role in helping him to win the 1992 election.

If anybody saw this at the time, however, it was only for an instant. No election, won by a clear majority, has been followed by a sharper reversal of the mandate which it might normally be thought to have created. Never in modern British democracy was so much confidence, given by so many people, so swiftly removed from the Cabinet on whom it was conferred. If Major's version of Europe helped him win, it was also responsible for withdrawing the palm at record speed.

For the disagreements in the party had not been resolved, merely forgotten as a pre-electoral act of convenience. They were, in fact, incapable of resolution. They related to a question, the very nature of an independent Britain, which was, in the eyes of quite a number of Tory politicians, uncompromisable. These ultras did not exist merely at the lower levels, where Cash sported and Teddy Taylor played. They had their representatives all the way up the Government, reaching into the Cabinet itself. Such sceptics had been silent until now. Sometimes, as with Michael Howard and the social chapter, the leader was careful to humour them. Their presence at all levels constrained his negotiating stance – though in directions with which he himself was, for the most part, content. At no stage could Major have been called a thunderous Euro-phile. But now he was about to discover a different order of disagreement among high colleagues, a new brand of hostility to himself within the privy group, which he was driven to match at similar levels of revulsion. Such, within a few months, was the dire influence of 'Europe' on the Conservatives' fourth, apparently triumphant, term of office, now about to be destabilized by men whom the Prime Minister defined in a word seldom heard as an officially listed category of colleague: 'the bastards'.

Events, rather than people, started this descent. There was the Danish referendum on Maastricht in June 1992. What the British voters gave – newly mandated tranquillity – the Danes were allowed to take away. This transformed the realm of the possible, galvanizing anti-Maastricht feeling, reopening the Tory divide that had been more or less disguised since the removal of Mrs Thatcher. It soon exposed the fact that this was not a strong government, but a brittle one, with pieces flaking away as readily as in the Thatcher years. But there was a difference with the Thatcher experience. Whereas, under her, dissidence over Europe produced six sackings or resignations from the Cabinet, under Major the dissidents, in every case except one, remained inside, free to argue and corrode, challenge and dissent, from within the portals of power. A style first welcomed as the soul of consultative collegiality, after years of Thatcherish autocracy, became a vehicle for entrenching treachery on the one hand and weakness on the other. It was the defining element in the decline and fall of John Major's Government.

This first surfaced, appropriately, in the person of a Major ally. Norman Lamont had been, after Mrs Thatcher, his most important friend. In some respects, he was all that Major wasn't. After schooling at Loretto, a famous private establishment in Scotland, he moved on to Cambridge. In 1964, the year Lamont, as president of the Cambridge Union, was reaching the pinnacle of a conventional political apprenticeship, Major was a clerk in a dead-end job at the London Electricity Board. What they shared from that period on, however, was a dedication to Conservative politics, and an inexhaustible desire to succeed. The crooked path of political ambition had carried them, by 1990, to a point where one, Lamont, was subordinate to the other in their Treasury posts, and became, by inevitable and self-interested osmosis, his closest ally in the contest to get the top job. Lamont managed Major's campaign, and Major rewarded him with the chancellorship. Thus were they bound together in what became a crisis far exceeding the Danish referendum in potency as the unraveller of the mandate.

For Lamont was by now presiding, *ex officio*, over Britain's membership of the European Exchange Rate Mechanism, the ERM. This was Major's baby, his claim, in a sense, to be a man of power: certainly the policy initiative that had carried him through the fire against Mrs Thatcher, in defence of which he had emerged triumphant on the other side. But, Chancellor Lamont was now in charge, the man who had to worry every day about the exchange rate and the interest rate that supported it.

By the summer of 1992, it was clear that the story of the ERM was not an entirely happy one. Sterling's membership had served one purpose, as a suppresser of inflation, pretty well. But as the second year of the experience progressed, the economy was caught in a familiar, alarming bind. A startling aspect of the election victory was that it had been achieved against a background of rising unemployment and economic recession. With house prices falling and business bankruptcies almost as rampant as they had been in the early Thatcher years, however, restiveness on the Conservative back-benches wasn't stifled by the recentness of MPs' return to Westminster. It was infiltrated by their other discontents, mainly Europe and the imprisonment which Europe, via the ERM, was enforcing on what they liked to think of as the sovereign domestic economy.

Along with the fresh-discovered, supra-national evils of Maastricht, in other words, came a more ominous count against the continental enterprise. For the ERM required sterling to be held within fixed bands against the Deutschmark, and during 1992 this was proving difficult to achieve. The markets' faith in the maintenance of the rate, given the parlous state of the economy, was beginning to drain away, demanding, if the Government were truly serious, a rise in interest rates. Yet such a rise was exactly what the depressed national economy did not require. The viciousness of the circle could hardly be more apparent, and nor could the vulnerability of the British situation to external developments, such as a rise in Germany's own interest rates for Germany's own domestic reasons.

Much of the summer was spent in semi-public arguments about how this dangerous impasse might be addressed. There was a case for raising interest rates. There was a case for 'realigning' sterling in the ERM, a euphemism for devaluing. There was even a case for leaving the ERM altogether. There were reckless shouts from some Tories in favour of lowering interest rates, and to hell with the ERM. And over all these arguments hung an air of impending crisis, which the Government chose to resolve by a statement of adamant support for the currency as it was, inside the ERM, within the present bands. Lamont made the statement.[30] It was a ringing defence of the principle of fixed exchange rates, and a challenge to anybody who dared to say that Britain's present economic difficulties had anything to do with ERM membership. Floating or devaluing, said the Chancellor, would lead not to lower interest rates but, in all probability, higher, because of the influence exerted, in or out of the ERM, by interest rates in Europe.

The political significance of this speech, in the evolving pathology of Euro-scepticism, became apparent only later. For Lamont subsequently laid claim to being a deep sceptic at heart, so his utterance, which I witnessed him giving with severe and unchallengeable assertiveness, becomes one more display-piece in the well-stocked museum of inconstancy on the subject of Europe. At the time, however, it stated an official policy which no minister seems to have contested.[31]

It was also the prelude to disaster. Having pledged themselves to the ERM and the rates it required, Major and Lamont were driven to tactics and performances they would later have preferred to forget. The management of Britain's exit from the mechanism – the sundering of what Chancellor Major had joined together – was one of the most embarrassing, as well as politically calamitous, episodes in the post-war history of British economic policy, a period not short of contenders for the title. Major always defended entry, seeing it, he once told me, as a lynchpin in the assault on inflation which he regarded as his central political task, and whose success he was incorrigibly proud of. 'Between 1990 and 1996 we moved from an inflation-prone country to a disinflationary country,' he said. 'I am happy to let history make a judgement about whether the short-term pain was right for the long-term gain.' But on the coming-out, he thought, history could already speak. 'It was a disaster, a political disaster. There is no doubt about that. It was an embarrassment for the United Kingdom.'[32]

Such clinical blitheness did not prevail when events were unfolding. They featured, mainly, the blundering of Lamont, a man of whom it was often rumoured that he would no longer have been Chancellor at all, but for the surprising defeat of an abler politician, Chris Patten, in his seat at Bath. In the event, this was perhaps a mercy for Patten. From the moment the Cabinet decided to remain in the ERM, mere ministers lost control to the overwhelming power of the financial markets. On 26 August, Lamont stood on the Treasury steps to announce that 'we will do whatever is necessary' to maintain sterling's parity. The world was to have 'no scintilla of doubt' about this. On 4 September, he travelled to Bath for a meeting of EC finance ministers which he was chairing. Dismal scenes ensued, in which the Chancellor took it on himself to lecture the Bundesbank on the need to cut interest rates, and advanced an extensive critique, to anyone who would listen, of German policies. He seemed to be following, punily, in the Thatcher line, emulating her performance in Dublin in 1979 which almost caused Helmut Schmidt to walk out. Now Lamont performed a little foot-stamping of his own that had the same effect on Helmut Schlesinger, the chief German central banker. It was 'the most ill-tempered meeting I had ever attended', another banker recalled to Philip Stephens. The opening, that might have existed, for a negotiated realignment of sterling's value was lost in the rage that Lamont, on Britain's behalf, felt at the suggestion of the pound being treated in the same way as the peseta and the lira.

Major, too, was firm. Maintaining the pound's value had become for him, as for many of his predecessors, a totem. Their wretched history in this matter did not caution him. Rather, the reverse. 'All my adult life,' he told Scottish industrialists on 10 September, 'I have seen British governments driven off their virtuous pursuit of low inflation by market problems or political pressures. I was under no illusions when I took sterling into the ERM. I said at the time that membership was no soft option. The soft option, the devaluer's option, the inflationary option, would be a betrayal of our future.' He recalled the Harold Wilson devaluation in 1967, doubtless imagining there was no possibility of his being forced down the same track. He spoke with contempt of those who would, as Keynes said, 'debauch the currency'.

The speculators were active, however, against currencies both in and out of the ERM. Early on 16 September, the game was almost up. The pound continued to slide, and, to begin with, the Major–Lamont response was to raise interest rates from 10 to 12 per cent. When this had no market impact, they announced another rise, to 15 per cent, for next day, in a last, near-hysterical punt to defend their sterling policy. They got all the leading Cabinet ministers lined up in support of this, 'to put their hands in the blood', as Kenneth Clarke described it. These ministers had not been directly included in policy-making up to this point, and not made aware, at the time when it was still relevant, of the options that might have been available. But the more emphatic pro-Europeans – Clarke, Hurd and Heseltine – were especially implicated, and especially willing to test the 'European' option to the limit, though more than $10 billion had already been spent by the Bank, to no effective purpose other than the enrichment of speculators.

This could not last. As night fell, Lamont made another appearance outside the Treasury, to announce that his economic strategy had been destroyed. 'Massive speculative flows', he said, were continuing to disrupt the exchange markets. So the judgement now had to be reversed. The 15 per cent interest rate already announced would be revoked, and sterling's membership of the ERM would be suspended. Most of the words in his July speech, he might have added, had now to be eaten.

Though the overt events of this disaster were bad enough, it had other layers and reverberations which, had they been known at the time, would have heightened the sense of a government out of control of events: something governments are never meant to be. Some of these were merely comical, if revealing. The absence of command reached into the most elementary areas. It happened, for example, that Downing Street was under repair at the time, and Major was occupying emergency quarters in Admiralty House, where, though this was 1992, there was no proper telephone switchboard and no direct line to market information. The high command of British economic management, including the governor of the Bank and the First Lord of the Treasury, were huddling over a crisis they were unable to measure from moment to moment. Even a radio could not be found when it was wanted.

More enduring was the memory of some of the ministers who were kept out of the information loop for more purposeful reasons. Although Douglas Hurd was Foreign Secretary, and therefore running a Europe policy of which the ERM was a central element, he recalled later how shocking these events had been. The day was immediately known as Black Wednesday, a correct label for what was a national humiliation, though one which was in due course reversed – White Wednesday – as a political statement by anti-'Europe' elements wishing to emphasize the therapy of liberation from the ERM. Hurd thought he should have known about the possibility of Black Wednesday some weeks before it happened. So did Kenneth Clarke, the Home Secretary, who discovered most of what he knew about Lamont's Treasury operations from reading the newspapers. He told a group of journalists some years later: 'I reflected on that day that I'd never been in a government that didn't have an economic policy. I waited with interest to see what it would be by the end of the day.'[33] None of this was a happy augury for the four years in which Britain was liable still to be governed by the Major Administration.

But the most testing impact of these days and weeks was felt, naturally, by Major himself. To him, the outcome was a failure he took very personally. It bothered him deeply. There is good evidence that he considered, on a day-to-day basis, the case for his resigning. Hurd was one person who listened to him agonizing. 'Quite clearly, he and the Government would have to start again from the bottom up,' Hurd recalled. 'He was not sure he was the right person to do that.'[34] Major's official biographer has amplified this account, reporting that on 23 September the Prime Minister got as far as drafting, in his own hand, the script of a resignation statement he would broadcast to the nation, prior to making way, as he hoped, for his preferred successor, Clarke. He showed the text of this to one of his private secretaries, Stephen Wall, who refused to contemplate the possibility. 'Wall and Major talked for two hours,' writes Anthony Seldon. 'Major subsequently regarded this conversation as crucial to his decision to carry on.'[35] According to Hurd, he was still thinking about quitting a fortnight after Black Wednesday.

London wasn't short of people who thought he should do so. It was from this period that can be dated the unprecedented accumulation of enemies gathering round Major's person. There had been nothing like it since the depths of Harold Wilson's unpopularity – and Wilson, reviled though he often was, lived in a time when a minimum of good manners still applied to the media's performance. It wasn't permissible, nor even contemplated, even in Wilson's worst days, for a newspaper to imply that he was mentally deranged. Nor did editors vilify him to his face. Throughout the Thatcher decade, indeed, they had lost the habit of sceptical detachment of any kind, when addressing the leader. For Major, after the ERM débâcle, different rules applied. And it was apparent that Europe, including some sharp revisionism concerning the Europe of Maastricht, was the driest tinder on the fire.

A heavy rumour circulated that, at some point on 16 September, Major was so completely laid low by the destruction of his policy, and the colossal outflow of reserves, that he had some kind of nervous breakdown. So great was the pressure on him that a brief retreat from reality might have been understandable, though also, of course, discreditable. I made intermittent efforts over the years to get the episode confirmed, but the quality of the denials was impressive: enough, at any rate, to render any perpetuation of the rumours thoroughly dishonest.

But this did not deter all newspapers closer to the moment. *The Times* published a lengthy examination of the Prime Minister's mental health, by two reporters whose lack of medical qualifications, let alone their distance from the scene, did not deter them from asking whether Major 'can take the strain' and concluding that quite possibly he could not. They adduced a variety of gossipy circumstantial evidence, from 'dramatic weight loss' to the fact that he 'has given up alcohol' and was 'having his hair tinted at Trumpers'. He was 'lonely', 'unhappy', and might well be suffering from conditions that are triggered by extreme stress, of which 'heart disease and mental ill health are possibilities'.[36] On this miserable basis, it wasn't hard to construct the picture of a disintegrating Prime Minister.

While not all papers were so extravagant in their speculations, many began to cause Major problems. They drove a reasonably balanced man into a species of neuroticism. There is no sight quite so characteristic as that of the British press hammering a man when he is down, a practice that gains in venom when the same organs have been largely responsible for raising him up in the first place. So it was with Major, who heard multiple voices around this time telling him he should quit, and became an obsessive accumulator of resentments concerning material he couldn't stop himself reading. A kind of fusion was beginning to appear between strands of polemical opinion that were to remain ever present in the future demeanour of most of the Tory press: a ferocious line in Euro-scepticism, bound together with a deepening contempt for the unleaderlike leader who was failing to show the same exuberance for the cause as they did.

Major didn't often call up newspaper editors on the telephone. But over the ERM he later admitted to doing so. To small effect. Self-serving though it is, the account given by the *Sun* editor, Kelvin MacKenzie, of one such conversation is worth putting down. When the Prime Minister called, shortly after the débâcle, MacKenzie alleges he said to him: 'I've got a large bucket of shit on my desk, and tomorrow morning I'm going to pour it all over your head.'[37]

But another fusion materialized, forming a critical mass with potentially still greater explosive qualities. There were people in the Government whose visceral feelings about Europe resembled those of the editors: had probably existed, indeed, for rather longer. A consequence of the ERM humiliation was the reassembling of these feelings by ministers who had tended to suppress them, but who saw September 1992 as a watershed that ought to carry the Conservative Party back towards its latter-day preference for floating currencies, as well as a proper hostility for further European integration. What united most of these men was their intense, sometimes tearful, loyalty to Margaret Thatcher in the hour of her deposing: an emotion so spacious that it could entirely overlook, when the ERM exit occurred, that it had been Mrs Thatcher who authorized entry in the first place. Attitudes to the ERM became the touchstone of a neo-Thatcherite revival, crystallizing the presence of enemies within as well as behind and below the Government. These enemies were a mixture, as ever, of erratic converts, their ambitions thwarted, and discreet zealots, with ambition awaiting satisfaction.

In the former category, Norman Lamont was the leading member. He struggled on as Chancellor for eight months after the cataclysm, his life increasingly marked by a lack of either public or personal discipline. The man who, in July, said ERM membership was the irreplaceable centrepiece of his economic strategy reported, in September, that he had been 'singing in the bath' when exit was accomplished. Explaining himself afterwards, Lamont always said he had been agnostic-to-sceptical about the ERM in the first place, but, having inherited the policy when Major gave him the Treasury, had gone along with it uncomplaining. A pliant politician had blown with the wind.

It took the loss of office to sharpen Lamont's decision as to where his agnosticism ended. Before this trauma, he gave little hint of the depth his Euro-phobia would soon reach. What he said was certainly not enough to spare him the merciless hounding of the Tory press which, on that point, might have been willing to protect him had they known what he really thought. When Major sacked him, in May 1993 – the only political enemy to suffer that fate in six years – Lamont trampled derisively on the leader's grave, delivering the effective curtain line that his Government gave 'the impression of being in office but not in power'.[38]

Having left government, it must be said, Lamont became one of the more serious scrutineers of the EU. He developed a critique acknowledging, as we have seen, the need to consider the truth that momentum could draw Britain in one of two directions: towards greater federalism or, alternatively, towards a looser relationship that amounted to a form of exit.[39] But he entered a category already created by another departed minister, Kenneth Baker, a Home Secretary who did not survive past the 1992 election, and then discovered, having been a key supportive figure in the Maastricht negotiation, that he was a Euro-sceptic after all. There was something tainted about these reconsiderations. The attraction that might be claimed for an open mind was nullified by the sense that loss of office, rather than any irresistible novelty of evidence, had something to do with stimulating the conversion.

The same charge could not be made against the sceptics who remained in high office, and were, if anything, cosseted and promoted by the Prime Minister. Their self-defined though usually unadmitted mission, at the heart of government, was to achieve an ever greater distance from the heart of Europe. They weren't in the topmost jobs, but they were both a threat and, as Major saw it, an indispensable necessity to the leader. That was the context in which he gave them their famous name, while talking on an inadvertently open microphone to a television reporter in July 1993. Beset by the fiery divisions attending the final parliamentary vote on Maastricht, Major bemoaned the size of his majority and the incipient split that he was striving to prevent. People, he noted, were always telling him to do 'all these clever, decisive things', to reassert his control on the Europe question among others. But the party was still 'harking back to a golden age that never was'. In this fantasy-land, he speculated, 'You have three right-wing members of the Cabinet who actually resign.' But what happens then? They simply join the ranks of the dispossessed, causing all sorts of trouble. 'We don't want another three more of the bastards out there,' he concluded.[40]

He could as easily have said four not three, though he apparently thought of Michael Howard, whom he had made Home Secretary, as excluded from the coven. Howard, along with the two of them then present – Peter Lilley, the Social Security Secretary, and Michael Portillo, Chief Secretary to the Treasury – had pressed for Maastricht to be abandoned after the Danish referendum: the voices of Cashism above the salt. They had pressed the case further, after the ERM fiasco, when it looked likely that a referendum in France might kill the Treaty anyway: a prospect which Major himself, Lamont told me, saw as an escape-route from his troubles. According to Lamont, Major hoped the Danes would vote Yes but then the French No: which, if true, is a neat measure of his passing disillusionment. When the French failed to oblige, and Maastricht became a commitment the Cabinet could not avoid, the bastards were the ones expressing an inability to see why the British should exert so much effort to rescue a Treaty they had never wanted in the first place.

Lilley was the senior among them, who had been in the Cabinet the longest. Born in 1943, he was a right-wing economist of quite serious pedigree, an investment adviser before getting into politics, who wanted not just to halt but to reverse the process of European integration. In private, he advanced the concept of a 'nuclear Switzerland' as a model the British should aim for, believing it to be wholly absurd to suppose that a country with 56 million people couldn't survive as an independent economy making trade agreements with its neighbours. Lilley was quite an absolutist. For instance, the political nature of the European Court of Justice, in his view, didn't even need to be debated. It existed as an ominous, repellent fact. He was also an optimist, believing with some certainty that 'Europe' would wither away, once the old men, Kohl and Mitterrand, had faded from the scene, and the rest of Europe came to see that genuine reform, of such matters as agricultural and regional policies, would be achieved only at the expense of national interest – and would therefore never be attempted. This prospect, with its potential for the long-term destruction of the EU project, Lilley found agreeably exciting.

He was a studious figure, notably lacking in charisma. In polls that were taken to find out which ministers were best recognized by the public, there were years when Peter Lilley barely troubled the scorers, though he had been minister for a decade. His one occasion of prominence, when he paraded a different personality, was the party conference. Here the shy, high-voiced nonentity tried hard, not without success, to sound like a ranting demagogue, with a strident line of invective against the continentals, in their guise, for example, as welfare scroungers. At the 1993 conference, Lilley seemed to revel in his new bastard ranking, treating the faithful to a speech of xenophobic ridicule which also, in its sub-text, tweaked the Prime Minister's nose.

A rather different place in the *salon des salauds* was occupied by Michael Portillo, who began the Major period as Chief Secretary and finished it as Secretary for Defence. Portillo, potentially a larger politician than Lilley, was driven by opinions that extended beyond law and economics. What bothered him was the future of Britain and Britishness in their grandest meaning.

How much this was due to Portillo being the son of a Spanish immigrant was a question to evoke any amount of amateur psychology in reply. Whatever the reason, this was a very *British* right-winger who, in conversations I had with him over a three-year period, often lamented the absence of more national pride in his countrymen. He seemed to regard British irony, including self-irony, as a disease not an attribute, comparing it unfavourably with the Germans and, especially, the French, who expressed old-fashioned attitudes to the superior merits of their own goods and services.

He wasn't always a sceptic on the Europe question, however. It didn't present itself to him as an issue until late in the 1980s. He had voted for the Single European Act, he once told me, without any reservation. He simply didn't know anything about its deeper meaning, he confessed. But then came Maastricht and the single currency, to which, while keeping silent in public, he was fiercely opposed. He admired the meticulous way Major had handled the politics of Maastricht, culminating with its appearance as a manifesto commitment. But by 1994 he had reached the conclusion that it had become impossible to keep the Tory Party together while keeping the EU together, in its present shape, at the same time. Besides believing that the single currency simply would not work, unless it was supported by an equivalent political structure, he adopted a hard attitude towards the need, at all costs, to preserve national power unfettered. It was the veto, not the size of Britain's weighted vote in Community councils, that concerned him. The British interest, he thought, almost never lay in getting things done, almost always in stopping things we didn't like. There had never been an occasion, he contended, when Britain had been frustrated in her objectives by other countries mobilizing a majority vote against her. He was utterly convinced that only the veto, the undying symbol of a negative attitude to Europe, could defend the British way of life.

The strength of his opinions about this led Portillo to circulate the news of where he stood, but without ever being disloyal. He was not the most deft performer on the tightrope, though he knew that the sentiments of the back-benches were collecting themselves into a reliable safety-net for anyone of his persuasion. He, too, couldn't resist the lure of the party conference, raising the roof, as Defence Secretary in 1995, with some spectacularly tawdry jibes at the inferiority, even the cowardice, of the European partners. These followed a reckless charge that many European students were 'cheats' who got their degrees by paying for them. On each occasion he had to withdraw or rephrase what he had said. But his mistakes, he seemed to think, were merely tactical. On the substance he was moved by juices for which he would never apologize. For another conceit was that he held his convictions about Europe more strongly than anyone on the other side held theirs: and this, in his belief, guaranteed that in the fullness of time there could be only one outcome to the story which had begun with the historic error made twenty years before, when Britain misled herself into believing that 'Europe' was her inevitable destiny.

Here, therefore, were two alien presences alongside Major, not yet formidable for their political weight, but known to hold opinions about the Europe policy that echoed those of the volubly sceptic cave on the benches behind. Despite their obvious hostility, Major chose to do nothing about them. Indeed, in May 1993, he added to their number, bringing into the Cabinet John Redwood, who was made Secretary for Wales.

As a candidate for bastardy, Redwood was in some ways the most eligible of the three. Certainly in the eyes of Major's friends, he became the most ridiculed and reviled. Again with a pedigree in the City, he was also a former Fellow of All Souls, the Oxford college distinguished as a scholarly enclave but seldom as a supplier of durable performers in the practical world of high politics. Redwood was a Thatcherite by specific definition, having headed the policy unit at 10 Downing St in the middle 1980s. He climbed, as an elected politician, under his patron's welcoming eye. When she was removed, he was among the most despondent of her followers but, because he was cleverer than many high Euro-sceptics, he became accepted as one of their necessary representatives in government in the post-Thatcher world.

But Redwood was a disturbing figure, a kind of *idiot savant* as some saw him. He was obviously very bright but, equally obviously, rather unreliable. There was something other-worldly about him, a quality that might be attributed to his academic origins but was supplemented by an appearance which the press could not resist turning into a joke, depicting him as a Vulcan from outer space. Redwood knew he had this effect on people, and trained himself in attempts at populism: for example, while Welsh Secretary, modifying his reputation as a rigorous Thatcherite enemy of public spending by mobilizing a campaign in defence of local cottage hospitals. But on 'Europe', he was the most ultra of ultras, a powerful disbeliever in integration, and an expert casuist in defence of the common sceptic proposition that being against the European Union was the only way, in truth, to show that you were a real European.

Major did not like these people. As dissenters from the Maastricht process through the first half of 1993, they remained within the bounds of formal propriety while being, in their hearts and deeper stratagems, unreliable colleagues, as he indicated by his private crudity about them. By the end of Maastricht's passage, he was utterly exasperated. Yet this was an emotion he did not feel able to take much further than a muttered aside to an accidental television microphone. The bastards, allied with the friends of William Cash, had another effect as well. By the autumn of 1993, Major was beginning to understand how he might need to make common cause with them. This was the moment when that famous capacity to convince each faction in the argument that he was really on their side can be seen slipping one way rather than the other.

From now on, Major's survival instincts started the process of converting him from a genuine sceptic – quizzical, calculating, negotiating – into something more like what 'sceptic' had become as a term of art, which is to say an enemy of 'Europe' and a disbeliever in its driving purposes. How much this was due to canniness under pressure, and how much to what passed for his genuine convictions, became a subject of some controversy. He was indignant that anyone should suppose he ever acted out of anything but his real beliefs. The fact is, however, that he now made his first utterance to rank with the Thatcher speech in Bruges. He declared for a kind of British scepticism that puzzled and dismayed the continentals as severely as that famous eruption had in 1988. After a five-year interval, the world was put on notice that British Conservatism, in this as in most other respects, had not actually changed.

Significantly, Major chose not to place this statement in the Europhobic press, or to make a speech before a select audience, but to write a piece in a magazine, the *Economist*, with an international audience.

He sounded extraordinarily hostile to what 'Europe' was now doing, and positively jubilant at Britain's reluctance to go along with it. 'We take some convincing on any proposal from Brussels,' he proudly wrote. 'We counted the financial cost of our membership. Others counted their financial gain. We subjected each proposal to the scrutiny of Parliament. They relaxed in the sure knowledge that their public opinion uncritically endorsed the European idea. Hang the detail. Never mind the concession of power to Brussels.'

The future, he said, recapitulating the Bruges address, must be built around the nation-state. Insofar as the vision of Monnet and other founders had proposed a weakening of nation, the time for any more of that was over. 'The new mood in Europe demands a new approach . . . It is for the nations to build Europe, not for Europe to attempt to supersede nations.' As for the main project now on the table, EMU, this would, in Major's opinion, simply not happen. 'I hope my fellow heads of government', he wrote, 'will resist the temptation to recite the mantra of full economic and monetary union as if nothing had changed. If they do recite it, it will have all the quaintness of a rain dance and about the same potency.'[41]

As a piece of prophecy, this joined quite a long line of British misjudgements. But, as a piece of politics, it showed that Major the man of government had decided, once Maastricht was safely written into law, to allow himself to be gradually superseded by a character with ambitions that turned out to be more futile: Major, the man of party, susceptible to the most insistent voices that could be heard at any given time.

*

HE WAS NOT a failure, as a European governing politician. He entered the freemasonry with aplomb. Ruud Lubbers and Helmut Kohl were not the only leaders to notice and relish the change of style he brought, after the wholesale depredations of Mrs Thatcher. He could carry on, as a regional diplomat, even when under the most extreme pressure as a domestic leader.

The hideous débâcle of the ERM, for example, occurred in the half-year when Britain took the presidency of the European Council, and Major was therefore chairing all meetings among the leaders. He continued to do this punctiliously, and to some effect. A summit held in Birmingham shortly after the ERM exit was very testing. He had called it, partly to make up for such destabilizing events as that one. The Danish and French referendums also seemed to call for some reaffirmation of the Euro-order, an acknowledgement of discontents. Major hoped Birmingham would see an increase in subsidiarity, handing powers down to the national level, and a reduction in the reach of the Commission. Jacques Delors wasn't pleased, and Anglo-German relations were still suffering from what the British regarded as the Bundesbank's betrayal of Kohl's apparent promises to help keep the pound in the ERM.

But the regular summit at the end of the presidency, held in Edinburgh in December 1992, was regarded as a little masterpiece of Major-ry. He was the consummate chairman, of an unusually heavy agenda. There was the Danish position to be agreed: how many more opt-outs could Denmark be permitted as the price for getting a second referendum launched and carried? This was essential if Maastricht could survive. There was the perennially delicate issue of the Community budget, over which Major used the chair to secure a lower increase than many other members, especially the small ones, hoped for. Enlargement, subsidiarity, changes to the European Parliament: all these required the preparation, the mastery of detail and the nerveless elbow-gripping of the quiet fixer Major liked to see himself as being. Now, too, his study of body-language was attaining senior-wrangler excellence. His swotting up of European history evidently enabled him to make some uproarious little jokes featuring the medieval St Hubert of Maastricht in the punchline.[42] Now he had made it quite apparent that he was determined to see Britain ratify rather than destroy Maastricht, despite his difficult parliamentary situation, pretty well everyone in the masonry was his friend and admirer once again.

In particular there was Kohl, his original friend, who held for him and his entourage a special fascination. Kohl was terribly helpful at Edinburgh, taking instruction from Major on the quiddities of the British parliamentary system as the reason why, contrary to the demands of Delors and others, Britain could not guarantee to pass Maastricht by a

given date. Later, Kohl, an exacting judge of the mastery he thought all
leaders needed to show over their parties, was to become very scornful
of the British leader. There was a severe withdrawal of affection. But in
1992 the reappearing spectre of Margaret Thatcher, now situated in the
eccentric but unavoidable legislative assembly called the House of Lords,
united them in watchful understanding. The Majorites could never think
of Kohl without a certain toffish mirth, especially at his physical presence,
eloquent even before it began to move. They relished the memory of
him in Major's Edinburgh hotel suite, almost crushing the low-slung
furniture, 'this great bull on a little velvet chair', slapping down any
colleague who dared raise an objection, the antithesis of any posture
Major could hope to bring to his own situation. British condescension
for the foreigner could extend even into the most pro-European circles
of government. 'I would guess there must be about 20 stones' worth of
Jerry there,' a jocularity perhaps permissible in private conversation, was
a phrase committed shamelessly to print by none other than the minister
for Europe at the time, Tristan Garel-Jones.[43]

Garel-Jones was an under-strapper, but men like him, the pro-
Europe figures, were essential to the Major prime ministership. They
were the counterpoise to the sceptics, the other force the leader had to
reckon with: the ones who, in their way, he necessarily relied on, and
whose line, as a governing man, he supported while never wanting to be
so clear about this as to rouse the fury of the other side. That, essentially,
was the story of John Major's term of office for the last three years:
holding a balance in which, as part of the task, he deemed it critical
never to disclose for certain where he finally stood, or what might be
regarded as his bottom line: a task rendered manageable, however, by
the palpable fact that he didn't really know what these positions were
himself. He was prepared to settle for almost anything, as long as it
satisfied the cardinal necessity of sustaining, in formal terms, the unsun-
dered union – though not, of course, the unity – of the Conservative
Party.

To finesse their difficulty, the men of government came up with a
verbal formula, of which Douglas Hurd seems to have been the main
author. He developed the conceit that Europe was 'moving our way'.
Those who called on him heard these words often. So did the Cabinet.
They were a way of arguing that, if you took the long view, the problem
between, say, Portillo and a pro-Europe man like Michael Heseltine
might be said not really to exist. For Britain's objectives were coming
about anyway. 'The climate is changing,' Hurd told me on several

occasions between 1992 and 1996. The Commission, repeatedly, was said to have got the message about subsidiarity. So had Delors and Mitterrand personally. There was now a new stream of higher wisdom percolating through the Community from its source-bed in London. Ideas that had once been regarded as 'heresies, eccentricities of British thought' were now beginning to prevail, a development that made it 'not sensible to back off into noisy and destructive isolation'.[44]

Major himself also believed this. He was convinced the Germans would soon be as keen decentralizers as the British, spurred on by the demands of the *Länder* for their regional rights to be recognized against Brussels' impositions. France, he thought, was moving in the same direction. More than once, I saw him gleaming with certainty that the priorities of the big three EU countries would conspire in favour of the British view, on this subject at least, and that future enlargement would bring about the wholesale review of EU spending he always wanted.

Nor was this posture always nervous and defensive. Though Major cultivated a Hamlet-like demeanour in the matter, Heseltine continued capable of bursting on the scene with the dismissive fierceness of a Falstaff. Preparations for the 1994 European elections began in an atmosphere of anxiety, reflecting the divisions in the party and the tormented dithering of its leader. Ministers came and went, suggesting to the manifesto committee the compromises they thought essential in any form of words the party wrote. When Heseltine's day arrived, he made a statement of unmitigated Europeanism, explaining to the assembled functionaries that the present climate of scepticism was nonsensical, and that he personally would play no part in the election campaign unless the party line returned to the heart of Europe. He challenged them to account for their feeble-minded collapse into the arms of the anti-Europeans. Hurd, who was chairing the committee, thanked him for his robust statement, but the bald declaration left everyone stunned. The intervention was barely comprehensible. 'It was so utterly unfamiliar to hear anything like this from a minister,' one witness told me next day. And the party, incidentally, fell some way short of the eruptor's demand, when the time came.

Hurd and Heseltine were large figures. Though Major had defeated them in the leadership contest, they were, in a sense, larger than he was. He won not because he had the most friends but because he had the fewest enemies: on account not of his forensic brilliance but of his emollient competence. Hurd and Heseltine, Foreign Secretary and President of the Board of Trade, stood for something, not only as leftist

Conservatives but as politicians whose experience in government gave
them considerable standing outside. They personified the governing
world, the politico-business establishment, the whole inheritance of
which Europe was deeply a part. Together with Kenneth Clarke, they
formed the bastion that protected Major against the sceptics' onslaught,
while also preventing him from sliding, as he sometimes seemed about
to, wholly into the sceptic embrace. They were his haven of escape from
the bastards, without ever becoming, however, a force strong enough to
erase the strong neo-Thatcherite colouring that Major soon felt obliged
to give his Europe policy.

As Chancellor from May 1993, succeeding Lamont, Clarke was in as
prominent a position as his colleagues. He was a robust, often aggressive
character, more than a match for the sceptic snipers behind him, meeting
fire with fire and eschewing the sibilant formulations of some other
Europeanists. Heseltine, for example, usually took the line that public
rows should be avoided. However emphatic he was in private, he
declined to retaliate against the steady stream of anti-Europe speeches –
coded from the front bench, ever more scathing from the rear – on the
ground, as he would say, that 'I won't stir it up unless I'm forced to.'
Clarke was temperamentally less willing to leave the field to the enemy.
As the Major years wore on, he became defiantly assertive in his
positioning, so much so that by the end of them he had been promoted
to the top demonic rank in the sceptic calendar.

For the notion of Europe 'going our way' was constantly under
challenge. These governing figures of high Tory politics could never rely
on events to bear them out. Eminent though they were, they had to live
with both the neuralgia of the party and the capacity of the leader, in his
tortuous uncertainty, to make a difficult situation worse.

One episode put all these features on display with an especially lurid
clarity. For Major it was his worst crisis since the ERM exit, and for
Hurd 'the worst episode', he said, in nearly six years as Major's Foreign
Secretary.[45] For the governing class, its outcome put them closer than
ever to being overpowered by the bastard rabble beneath.

Its origins lay in a Europe policy that Britain not only supported but
had promoted: enlargement from a Union of twelve members to one of
sixteen, with the addition, if their people agreed, of Austria, Finland,
Norway and Sweden (though the people of Norway, once again, voted
No). Enlargement, for any member state that rejected the integrationist
model of the existing EU, was a natural objective, but it had inevitable
consequences for the balance of power. In particular, for the zones of

EU action that were subject to qualified majority voting (QMV), additional members would raise a question about the size of the majority needed to act, and of the numbers needed to qualify it. Under rules that had existed for quite a time, votes were weighted according to each country's size, and twenty-three such votes were enough to create a 'blocking minority' – the collective veto, which Michael Portillo was not alone in believing to be the vital fall-back weapon in defence of the British national interest. If the EU was enlarged, should twenty-three votes still be sufficient to block? If so, a smaller proportion of the whole would be able to frustrate the wishes of the majority. Twenty-three votes could already be assembled merely by two large countries and one small one, but, under enlargement, small countries could get together to defeat what all the larger powers, notably France, Germany and Britain, might want. Plainly this was a serious issue, which would require fundamental attention, as to the size–vote ratio as well as the scale of the blocking minority, when enlargement actually occurred. But meanwhile, without changing the votes-per-country to reflect population size more accurately, the majority of members wanted to raise the twenty-three to twenty-seven – well short of the figure that would have accurately reflected the change in numbers that was about to happen, but still a dilution of existing veto power.

At that modest level, the change did not need to present itself as a massive question. It might have been treated as almost technical in nature. To the bulk of people outside the political class, and a good many within it, it was, if not unintelligible, extremely obscure. Before it attained incandescence, quiet compromise, pending more permanent arrangements, might have been available. Differently handled, the bulk of sceptic Tory MPs would, in the judgement of several of them after the event, have settled for twenty-seven, this being so much smaller than it might have been. But here Major's famous talents as a manager completely deserted him. For most of March 1994, he became the author of a political exercise that ended in near-disaster, especially for himself.

Hurd could see what was coming, but Major declined to go along with him. Isolated in the foreign ministers' council, Britain nonetheless decided to appeal to the grandstand of domestic public opinion by declaring that this was a great test of national sovereignty. She would settle for twenty-three or nothing, even if this meant her being solely responsible for delaying the next stage of enlargement, on which Major had hitherto played a constructive role, encouraging the momentum for entry in the applicant states, especially during his presidency. 'We aren't going to do what the Labour Party do, which is to say "yes" to everything that comes out of Europe without any critical examination,' he shouted to the Commons. 'We will not be moved by phoney threats to delay enlargement.' The Labour leader, John Smith, who challenged him, was dubbed, in the relentless, faintly whingeing locutions of sub-cockney, known as 'Estuary English', that Major retained, 'Monsieur Oui, the poodle of Brussels'.[46] In its invocation of the dog, this recalled Harold Wilson on Ted Heath: in its deployment of a bit of French, the sarcastic knowingness of Jim Callaghan playing to the gallery before the 1975 referendum: a wretched, but telling, ancestry.

The Cabinet, offered the opportunity to tie Hurd's hands when he went into the negotiation, duly did so. With two exceptions, all the voices favoured sticking at twenty-three. Neither of the contrary opinions, it should be noted, came from Heseltine or Clarke: a measure of how fast the issue became one of national pride, and how sensitive even these pro-Europeans were to the desirability of being seen on the pro-British side of the argument, in the event of the leader's position becoming untenable.[47] For the vultures were circling. Major's future was the stuff of daily speculation. The post-ERM frailty reappeared, and with it the sense that he very likely could not last. Discussion was openly taking place as to why Heseltine, having recovered from a recent small heart attack, could now be considered to have overtaken Clarke as the party's likely favourite.

When the foreign ministers met, at Ioannina, Hurd had a very hard time. The absolutist position was untenable, and he had been left a small amount of leeway, something about 'preserving the substance' of the existing position. This he proceeded to exploit, with help from the Germans, who in effect supplanted the Greeks as the deal-makers, and from his friend Jacques Delors. Only by keeping the French out of the room at a critical moment was he able to construct a communiqué which had a chance of satisfying his colleagues without imperilling the next stage of enlargement. Even by Europe's standards, the compromise was convoluted, stating that if the potential blocking minority mustered between twenty-three and twenty-six votes, then, though that didn't meet the agreed figure of twenty-seven, the relevant Council would do 'all in its power', within a 'reasonable time', to reach a consensual solution. The deal had stretched everyone's diplomatic powers, and risked enraging those who were excluded from the final fix. 'I could never do this again,' Hurd mordantly reflected to me soon after returning.

His reception, however, was far from grateful. The Ioannina compromise made Major very nervous. In the political arena, it would be seen only as a climb-down, however much sense it made as an act of government: the more sense, indeed, given the real world of actual European decision-making, where these computations of voting power would hardly ever come into play. This was a supremely totemic controversy. Symbol, power, ambition, politics: all mattered more than the substance of the issue. Such was the state to which Britain's 'Europe' problem had once again degenerated.

The Cabinet sceptics, naturally, opposed Ioannina. Howard made the main statement of dissatisfaction, which the other side found 'long and able', Hurd told me. Portillo, Lilley and Redwood chimed in. Clarke, however, did not. Having spoken before for twenty-three, he was prepared to settle for Hurd's 23–26 deal. His governing persona reasserted itself. Not only Hurd but Major needed to be guarded against the fury of a party that now seemed gripped more widely than ever by the sense that its leader, irrespective of the line he took, was forfeiting its confidence. Quite a number of middle-of-the-road MPs were unable to understand how he had ever got into the Ioannina crisis in the first place, and others were more brutal. Tony Marlow had been his collaborator on the occasion of Major's first known Europe intervention, writing a letter to the papers favouring possible exit from the EEC. To him, Major must have been a particularly sad disappointment. Now Marlow stood up and told him to depart, with a directness no backbencher had summoned up since Anthony Fell said the same thing on the same issue to Harold Macmillan – 'make way for somebody else who can provide the party and the country with direction and leadership'.[48]

I saw Major to interview him around this time. He much resented the common belief that he was being pushed around by forces he couldn't control. Too many people, he thought, were in the grip of a fallacy. 'The fallacy', he said, 'is that I am wholly reactive, and only concerned with one side of my party or the other. It might perhaps occur to people that I feel pretty strongly myself about what is the right thing to do . . . I happen to be doing what I believe to be right.'[49]

In his own eyes, his role was still more creditable than that, both abroad and at home. His calculations about Europe, he said, had to take into account the line-up on the other side, especially the fact that the other powers all had natural friends – 'an entailment of allies', as he rather curiously put it. 'Partly because we are an island, partly because of history, we don't have an entailment.' The skills he brought to this national condition, he thought, were just as valuable on the domestic front. Indeed, they were probably irreplaceable. Gazing round the empty Cabinet table at which we were sitting, the embattled Prime Minister checked off the ghosts in the chairs, enumerating the reasons why each of them, were they to take his place, would split the party. 'If there hadn't been a consolidator sitting in this chair since 1990,' he said, 'I think it would all have broken up.'

The process of consolidation, nevertheless, tended now to move all in one direction. What might be called Major's genuine feelings did play some part in this. He had begun thoroughly to dislike what he called the continental way of doing things: the refusal to be precise, the preference for grand generalities, the slack briefing, the reluctance to conduct a meeting in the cut-and-dried way the British favoured. But more, surely, had to do with a political predicament in which he knew where his most potent enemies were to be found.

His speeches and stances became more desperately appealing to them. One strand tried to reassure them, and perhaps himself, of the unreality of their nightmares, especially about the single currency. 'My scepticism is about the economic impact of it,' he told a German magazine in April. 'You would need proper convergence of the econ-omies across Europe. They would all need to be operating at the same sort of efficiency. I know of no one who believes that is remotely likely. It is simply not going to happen.'[50]

During the European election campaign, which culminated in June, he delighted Euro-sceptics by putting fresh words to his vision of Europe. We should now see the Union, he said, as 'multi-track, multi-speed, multi-layered'.[51] This was a new British formula, first alluded to by Hurd, to permit the continentals to make swifter progress towards integration, while ensuring Britain's legitimized separateness. But the speech did not appear to have been well worked out. A few months later, close to the anniversary of his groundbreaking effusion in the *Economist*, Major contradicted himself. 'I see real danger', he said at Leiden in Holland, 'in talk of a hard core, inner and outer circles, a two-tier Europe. I recoil from ideas of a Union in which some would be more equal than others.' This was puzzling in the detail: having favoured a multi-speed Europe in May, how could anyone but a hair-splitting casuist recoil from a two-speed version in September? But there was no mistaking the consistency of tone. Major was now speaking for nation more than Community. 'The Maastricht Treaty strained the limits of acceptability to Europe's electors,' he said. 'Europe's peoples in general retain their favour and confidence in the nation-state. I believe that the nation-state will remain the basic political unit for Europe.'[52]

These declarations of independence were not confined to the verbal. The 1994 John Major was happy to cast a solitary vote against the agreed successor to Delors as president of the Commission, Jean-Luc Dehaene, the Belgian Prime Minister, who had been approved by every other member. Reasons were invented for stigmatizing him as a federalist, a designation that could just as easily be applied to the fall-back candidate who eventually got unanimous support, the Luxembourger Jacques Santer. This was pettiness by Britain – but pettiness with a domestic purpose: the invention of a defect, said to apply uniquely to the porky Belgian, for no better reason than the pleasure of being able to demonstrate, to a press and a party thirsting for continental blood, that nothing could cut more sharply than a bit of British steel.

*

THIS WAS NOT ENOUGH, however, to staunch the flow of bile around and out of the Tory Party. To accomplish that, the leader judged he owed them, in the last analysis, the opportunity to dispose of him.

Major was, by comparison with other prime ministers, a quite frequent contemplator of resignation. It hardly needs to be said that he had a lot of iron in his make-up, the material without which he could never have made his unassisted journey from Brixton to Downing Street. But there was also a certain self-effacement, a looming excess of modesty: a vulnerability, therefore, to depression when things were going badly, and a capacity at least to wonder whether, in all circumstances, he continued to be the right man for the job. There is no record of any such apprehensions having crossed the mind of Edward Heath or Jim Callaghan, though Wilson planned his exit, for reasons of exhaustion as much as anything, more than a year ahead. When Mrs Thatcher talked about quitting, which she did quite frequently, it was, on all occasions save one, a threat designed to pull people into line behind some policy they seemed in danger of not supporting.[53] She threatened, as it were, from strength. Major thought about it from weakness, at different moments of the Maastricht ratification process, and then, folded into that, when he had to get out of the ERM.

In June 1995, however, he produced a different effect. Surrounded by enemies, he exercised his right to surprise, by jauntily walking on to the Downing Street lawn and announcing that he had resigned as leader of the Conservative Party. There would now have to be a leadership election, in which he would stand as a candidate. Under party rules, every autumn brought the possibility of such an election, and every autumn since 1992 there had been discussion of some enemy or other making use of this opening to challenge him. By the summer of 1995, two years from the end of the present Parliament, and with three years of accumulated fire banked up against the leader, the talk of an autumn challenge was more unquenchable than ever. The Government was being chronically destabilized. So Major threw down the gauntlet to his party. 'It is time to put up or shut up,' he said.

This was a challenge, essentially, to the Euro-sceptics. Although he had been appeasing them with almost every gesture he could find, the appetites of the people who thought like William Cash and Michael Portillo were, as is usually the case with the appeased, insatiable. To their ideological hostility was added the dismay of a wide variety of Tory politicians who, if the opinion polls were indicative of any durable truth, faced the imminent end of their careers. For the first time in many of their lives, the Labour Party was a credible alternative government, now twenty-five points ahead.

Thus challenged, the sceptics duly rose. Lamont, skulking, was the first bet to lead them. But Lamont was not the most undamaged of goods. Redwood also lurked, unable to decide. Portillo hovered, waiting to see what Redwood might do, and thinking he might come into the contest if the first round was inconclusive. Portillo, by this stage, was extraordinarily alienated. The pervasive European issue of the moment was the prospect of another inter-governmental conference, the follow-up to Maastricht, which would take the EU into further realms of integration, with more QMV, more streamlined institutions, perhaps a more powerful Strasbourg Parliament. On this, Portillo favoured the most radical of British nationalist strategies. Complete rejectionism – the antithesis of the way Major and Hurd did business – was the right line both for Britain and for the electoral prospects of the Tory Party. The straddling of the sides should end. Portillo was even prepared to talk, in my hearing, about the desirability of a formal splitting of the party.

But Redwood it was who ran, and scepticism paraded in full regalia behind him. At his first appearance, the nine MPs from whom the whip had been withdrawn were his prominent henchmen: a bad start. His alternative programme proved more eccentric than substantial, though it promised a clear and absolute No to Britain joining the single currency. The sceptic press came out in force. 'Redwood vs. Deadwood' is what the *Sun* called the contest. Elsewhere, it was Major's lack of leaderly qualities, his shortage of officer-class command, as much as his want of Euro-phobia, that gathered the voices against him. But, to him, the presentation of himself as a man who could appeal to the sceptics as much as anyone else was a crucial objective. When Clarke, for example, emerged with typical brutishness to say that an ultra right-winger like Redwood could not win an election for the Conservative Party 'in a thousand years', Major's people were horrified.[54] They feared this might make their man sound insufficiently right-wing. And when Hurd let it be known that he would resign as Foreign Secretary immediately the election was over, the word went out that his replacement might well be a sceptic.

With the help of these signals, and the slightness of the opposing candidate, the parliamentary party was persuaded to reinstate the leader. More than a third of them didn't vote for him: he won by 218 to 89 votes, with twenty abstentions. Immediately announced as a decisive victory, it did become, as far as Major's ongoing position was concerned, conclusive. But, as regards the issue, the result was no more than cosmetic. It settled, after a fashion, nothing. For the pro-Europe people, Major was, of course, the only option – though there were some, possibly even some who secretly went as far as casting a tactical vote for Redwood, who thought Heseltine, coming in after a non-result, might be their saviour. But the anti-EU faction simply resumed the struggle for Major's mind, and the enforcement upon it of their visceral prejudices.

The degeneration of the Conservative Government, therefore, entered its terminal phase. A ruse designed to solidify it actually produced no change in its condition. And this happened at a time when the great question continued to obtrude, quite unrelentingly, on the consciousness of politics.

On the one hand, EMU beckoned – with decisions required, of both an economic and political character, by 1997. Choosing between 'never' and 'some time, maybe' was not the most uplifting of arguments to be having, but it was around that bleak axis that the entire end-game of the Major period would now revolve. At the same time, the IGC, equally undeflectable, had to reach its conclusions either shortly before or shortly after the British general election. What Europeans saw, as they made their own preparations for another group of epic developments, was a government in London that was not so much indecisive as, quite probably, incapable of taking a decision. It was no longer a question of seeing which side the British would come down on, but of addressing the palpable, if rather pathetic, reality that their internal condition debarred their leader from being taken seriously, whatever he said.

Government did go on. The seat at the table continued to be occupied. Hurd duly departed, to be replaced by Malcolm Rifkind, the Defence Secretary, whose past performance did not appear to qualify him as the promised sceptic. If Rifkind had a definable origin, it was on the left of the party, as a supporter, for example, of Scottish devolution, and a rising minister who was not entirely trusted by Mrs Thatcher. Amid a cluster of vaguely centrist positions was thought to go a more Hurdish than Portilloite attitude to Europe. That perhaps was the case. In my own first conversation with him, however, soon after he became Foreign Secretary, he greeted these suggestions cautiously. When I noted that he was a pro-European, he instantly denied that he had ever been a strong one 'if by that you mean someone who wanted more integration'. He challenged me, with a gleam of triumph, to find a single press release throughout his career that might indicate otherwise – although I knew that in a previous role, as Minister of State in the Foreign Office, and the British representative on the Dooge committee in 1985,[55] he had had to be restrained by none other than Geoffrey Howe, then his boss, against being too European. Rifkind hoped to show he had never changed his mind, but he seemed like a piece of fluff blown on the sceptic wind now breezing irresistibly through the party.

Nothing could happen without reference to this torrid zephyr. It generated, simultaneously, the oxygen on which most of the Tory Party existed, its life-support system, yet also the poison that seeped through it, corrupting all coherence.

Adventitiously, too, scepticism was given another twist, and Major an uncontrollable blow, by a threat to the nation's health that had nothing directly to do with either Europe or political leadership, but soon carried both issues to a yet deeper nadir of aggravation. In March 1996, the Government was forced to disclose that a cattle disease, BSE, might be linked with brain disease in humans, a new strain of Creutz-feldt-Jacob, or CJD. Though BSE had been present in the nation's beef herd for some years – a consequence, it was often argued, of the deregulatory, anti-inspection prejudices of high Thatcherism – the human link had not been authoritatively made. Now a Government scientific committee said it might exist, and ministers felt they had no choice but publicly to endorse the finding.[56]

The statement produced an immediate national panic but, almost as importantly, a series of repercussive degradations – if that were possible

– in relations with the European partners. For Britain exported beef and its products to Europe, and the European Union, as the controlling agency of both trade and public health rules, imposed an immediate British beef ban not only in Europe but worldwide. Farming was put on the rack. A great British industry, which was a traditional bulwark of the Conservative Party, found itself a prisoner of Brussels.

Evaluating the Major years after they were over, some Downing Street insiders called the BSE crisis the most difficult single issue of the premiership.[57] Heseltine told a group of journalists at the time that it was 'the worst political problem I have ever had to confront': a large statement for one whose ministerial career went back twenty-five years. The successor Government, after an early trawl through its Whitehall inheritance, said the BSE problem, which was still quite unresolved, constituted much the most chaotic mess it had to deal with.

For Major himself, however, it was the intermingling with Europe that caused him most grief. Part of this was his own, rather typical, British fault. A decision had been taken, when the CJD link was first adumbrated, not to advise, still less consult, the European Commission beforehand. Justified on the grounds of preserving secrecy, this showed some contempt for the body which, after all, would have decisive influence on the regulatory consequences, and represented millions of European nationals whose health was potentially under threat from British negligence. It was a studied choice, contributing to a long-drawn-out absence of mutual co-operation, which in turn did much to transmute the scepticism of many of the island Tory politicians into downright phobia for the continent and all who made decisions there.

The crisis swiftly escalated. At its first emanation, a summit in Turin to launch the plenary stage of the post-Maastricht IGC, the Europeans were actually quite helpful, promising Major financial help for the destruction of older cattle on a vast scale. But he took an abrasive line, attacking the beef ban as an exercise in 'collective hysteria', and already preparing the ground for what became the most surreal, yet strangely persistent, feature of the British position: that 'Europe', rather than Britain, was responsible for the BSE catastrophe. As the ban continued, Britain got ready to retaliate. A number of options were prepared, including a counter-ban against European meat products and, more dramatically, the leaving of an empty chair at all EU discussions. This, the de Gaulle tactic of the mid-1960s, could not have had the same paralysing effect as it did then. The only victim would have been Britain, unable to exercise her veto. A substitute ploy was therefore invented: to obstruct all decision-making that required unanimity. After the veterinary committee in Brussels had persisted in its dissatisfaction with Britain's safety measures, Major rose to his full parliamentary height to announce a policy of 'non-cooperation' with Europe,[58] as a result of which British ministers succeeded in blocking as many as seventy measures, including several, for example against EU fraud, which they themselves had been promoting. With very little to show for this, after a month's obstruction, serious thought was given in London to refusing to attend the next EU summit, in Florence, at the end of June.

The overall effect of the grand gesture of non-cooperation was merely to increase the number and deepen the resonance of the Prime Minister's critics, wherever they were. It was the worst breakdown since Britain joined the Community in 1973. For the Europeans, it marked the beginning of the end of their respect for him. Though the bastard faction in the Cabinet, led by Howard, were pressing for the empty chair, Major did, of course, go to Florence. He thought he could get some kind of beef deal, which, in the event, he did. The ban would begin to be lifted, in line with a cattle-slaughter programme that EU vets would invigilate and approve: a conjunction, as it turned out, which took a very long time to come about. But the damage done to the British leader's relations with his continental peer-group was considerable, going on terminal. Before Florence, the Commission president Jacques Santer spoke of an imminent 'moment of truth' for Britain, a menacing phrase which nonetheless reflected the genuine opinions of most of the member states. They could not but see Major, occupying what they ridiculed as the 'half-empty chair', as increasingly petulant, and obviously not in control.

Pressing on him more strongly, however, were the people who supposedly belonged to the same political enterprise as he did at home. Stamping his foot in rage at what he regarded as the unscientific politicking of the continentals was an attitude which, far from gladdening the Tory Party, only rendered its divisions more combustible. The beef row somehow excited the famous viscera to more turbulent agitation than ever. Was this because the substance at issue was the Roast Beef of Old England, the complete culinary symbol of British eating? Major himself, hinting as much to a Spanish audience, called beef 'part of the psyche of our nation', to be reckoned alongside forests for the Germans.[59] Might poisoned lamb, or contaminated chicken, have touched a less sensitive national nerve? Or was the problem that this aggressive interference from Brussels, even on a matter requiring urgent attention, exposed to apparent ridicule Major's much pleaded case for subsidiarity, and Douglas Hurd's insistence that things were 'moving our way'? Whatever the reason, BSE unleashed the media dogs, barking at Major with renewed ferocity. Around this time, one measured comment, not untypical of the general tone, said that here was 'a weak man trying to look strong', who presided from his half-empty chair over 'a half-dead Government'.[60] Having excited the mob by going to war, Major had inflamed it yet further by retreating into peace and calling this, emptily, a victory.

Sceptic appetites had been whetted by an earlier gesture, concerning the matter that vibrated with still more potency than BSE. For the manoeuvrings over the single currency never ceased. Though Major was an open sceptic on this matter, he never wanted to declare against EMU in perpetuity. The governing man in him regarded that as hopelessly imprudent, though the political man kept inventing formulae to put off the evil day when he might have to confront the other side of the party, whether at Cash's level or Portillo's, with the choice.

This political man had thought of a device that might assist him towards a haven of tranquillity, where the forces around him temporarily ceased to battle. For a year or two, he was toying with the case for promising a referendum. This, he privately suggested, could be pledged to happen before any decision was taken to put sterling in the single currency. It became the touchstone of most Euro-sceptic politics from now on. Anyone opposed to a referendum announced himself, by implication, as an anti-populist and probably an anti-democrat. So said the body of Euro-sceptics. They were goaded by the overbearing Jimmy Goldsmith, who made an all-embracing Europe referendum the core purpose of his new party. But they worked out to their own satisfaction that, in a referendum on EMU *tout court*, they couldn't fail to win the argument to which many of them had devoted the prime of their political lives.

The referendum, therefore, became the question, as the factions in the party looked fit finally to split apart. But the referendum did not enjoy universal approval, even among Euro-sceptics. Portillo opposed it on democratic grounds: also, perhaps, because he could see more clearly than some of his colleagues that it was a duplicitous expedient which, if it endorsed the wrong decision, would close the argument, and pre-empt parliamentary sovereignty, for the indefinite future. The more important opponent, however, was Kenneth Clarke. He it was, as Chancellor and man of unshiftable conviction, whom Major knew he had to carry in all these matters.

But Clarke was manoeuvrable, if not directly carriable. The referendum argument rumbled through the Cabinet before and after the BSE bombshell burst; its outcome became part of beef's collateral damage. It appeared, in late winter, that some sign of official sympathy for a referendum would be the most promising way to sweeten the atmosphere in the party that was now boiling with hatreds. One day in the Commons, Major duly dropped the hint. There would be study of the subject, he said. That was as good as saying that there would be a referendum pledge very soon. Clarke was not amused. He detested the way he had been bounced, and so did Heseltine.

Heseltine was to murmur, some time later, that the Tories' commitment to a referendum on EMU was one of the great disasters of the final months. Once made, it would extract, he thought, a matching commitment from Labour – which it duly did. And, once that happened, any government's EMU options would sharply close – which they did. To both Heseltine and Clarke, placing the single currency in hock to the popular will would immensely complicate the task of remaining anywhere near the centre of Europe. Nonetheless, the commitment was made, in a protocol stating with rare public formality that if a newly elected Conservative government were to contemplate entry into EMU, it would hold a referendum first. This was issued not from the Government but, eloquently, from Conservative Central Office. There was no signature, but those silently taking the pledge were Major, Clarke and Heseltine, with the sceptics alongside, and Rifkind piping up for the usual pretence that this was all part of an ordered continuity. 'The Government made quite clear some considerable time ago,' he said at a press conference, 'that we are not going to rule out the possibility of joining a single currency in the next Parliament.'[61]

From the anti-sceptic point of view, there was only one merit to this document. Its promise was restricted to the life of a single parliament, and was solemnly, if privately, sworn to be the last concession Major intended to make to the Cabinet's bastard strain. There would be no further yielding, Clarke was given to understand, on the policy that the Government would 'wait and see' if sterling should one day belong to the single currency. The famous bottom line – or was it the infamous line in the sand? – was now definitively drawn. O fond illusion!

The pressure for another pledge did not let up. The real goal of Euro-scepticism, about which the Tory press, quite unimpressed by the referendum decision, kept hammering on, was to secure sworn testimony from Major that he would not enter EMU. Between the referendum pledge and the election campaign, exactly one year passed. There was no week when this question failed to intrude upon the life, and dominate the manoeuvres, of the grimly tormented figure in 10 Downing Street.

In the middle of this period, I had a conversation with him, in which the subject of Europe could never be far away.[62] He presented himself as a man of competing convictions, yet also one who denied the need to make certain kinds of choice. He seemed puzzled by what confronted him.

Like all post-war prime ministers before him, he rejected any suggestion that 'Europe' represented some kind of an alternative to the Atlantic relationship. America's defence role in Nato was central to European security, and 'we are the second nation of Nato'. In his experience, there had never been a serious difference between Britain and the Americans on the big issues, a fact which pointed the way towards one of Britain's most necessary interests. 'Every time the Europeans have tried to do something without the Americans on defence,' he said, 'they have made a bog of it.' All this suggested to him that the British problem could never be resolved by making a strategic choice, loaded one way rather than the other. 'Unlike any other European nation, we are genuinely split as to where our interests lie,' he said. The country, he thought, was 'pretty evenly split' about which way to go. 'So I ask myself,' he said, 'why do we have to choose one or the other? Why should we make an artificial choice when our interests are almost equally divided between two great blocs – the Americas and Europe? My answer is that we would be mad to make such a choice.'

It followed that we would be equally mad to contemplate leaving the European Union, as some sceptics were now implying. 'It is nonsense, copper-plated nonsense,' he said, 'that we would leave the European Union and form some Atlantic alliance.'

At the same time, however, the Europeans were 'going too far, too fast'. They were moving in the wrong direction. They should be thinking about enlarging to the east, letting in the poor countries like Poland and Hungary, rather than deepening relations among the rich Western nations. 'I profoundly believe that is the wrong choice after a century, for half of which these countries have been to all intents and purpose enslaved.' It was all very well for Helmut Kohl, who also wanted enlargement, to be pushing for more integration. He had the luxury of being in charge, 'driving the motor'. Equally, Major could see why Spain and Portugal wanted a strong European Union: 'not all that many years ago, they were run by men in epaulets and dark glasses'. But for Britain, he said, it was otherwise. 'It is a different prospect for a nation traditionally used to doing things in its own way, suddenly finding that it may not be able to do so.'

In particular, he added, the single currency would make for a situation that was very different. It would remove power and responsibility from elected politicians. 'I wouldn't like to be the Chancellor of the Exchequer', the Prime Minister mused, 'who went to the despatch box and said: "Well, I no longer have any control over interest rates. I am sorry they've gone up by three per cent but it's nothing to do with me, Guv!"'

What seemed most to frustrate him about the present situation was his own confusing locus, blown about between the people of Britain and the European ruling class. The people, on the one hand, he regarded as not being fundamentally chauvinistic. 'They are not anti-European at all,' he said. What bothered them, he thought, was that 'we often seem powerless to prevent things happening'. On the other hand, it was the perception of public opinion, and its effect on him as leader, that weakened the message he was constantly trying to get across to the Europeans. The press, falsely representing the people, was responsible for this. He was unable (as he did not say) to discover a way of asserting his command over the deluge of polemic and propaganda it evacuated over him. The 'nature of the debate here' was unhelpful: that was the way he put it. 'The problem I face in Europe', he concluded forlornly, 'is that the Europeans are never certain whether the position I take is because I believe it or is a reflection of political necessity.'

Whichever of these two influences was the greater, one more, fateful stride had to be attempted, into the arms of the anti-Europeans. Though the referendum pledge was supposed to be the last such move, Major was uncomfortable with the vague, procrastinating, palpably evasive, intentionally contorted words he was being required to say about the single currency. Much of the last part of 1996 was spent, on the one side, trying to make sense of them, and on the other trying to take them apart. It was another period of textual deconstruction, sufficiently reductivist and passionate to recall the medieval school-men. Every word spoken on the subject of 'Europe' by Major, by Clarke, by Rifkind, by a club of bastards that was growing in number, was scrutinized for its inner meaning with respect to possible shifts on the single currency, probable rejection elsewhere in the party, and proof that the leader either was, or was not, about to convert fully to scepticism, perhaps either before or after sacking his Chancellor of the Exchequer. The quotation about a notional Chancellor, cited two paragraphs above, which appeared in a piece of mine published in February 1997, was just one example of an utterance seized on by the media, held up to the light and rotated through all planes of inspection, before being pronounced incontrovertible proof that Major had changed his mind again.

It seemed he half had. Certainly he imposed one more sceptic concession on Clarke, who regarded it as impossible to resist, on account of the proximity of the election. Again, looking back, one can hardly see in this the cause for civil war. What the Cabinet agreed was that it should now be said the single currency was 'very unlikely' to start, as intended, in January 1999. Further, 'if it did proceed with unreliable convergence [of the economies of member states] we would not of course be part of it'.[63] This was a neat way of avoiding the sceptics' stipulated demand, that the Tories should fight the election pledged against entering EMU in the first wave of currencies to join it. By postulating delay, the Cabinet could be said to neutralize the question. But this wasn't the way the adjustment was interpreted – or intended to be. It was a sop to the Euro-sceps, falling short of sufficient provocation to Clarke to resign.

This was the posture in which the election was fought – or rather, in which the leader tried to fight it. 'Wait-and-see with extreme scepticism' might be a way of encapsulating it. But the message, already baffling enough to voters less schooled in medievalism than Conservative politicians, was overlaid by the more strident complication that more than half the party's candidates rejected it. As Major, with the support of some of his Cabinet, stuck doggedly to his final final position, many Tory election addresses were being crafted with words of total commitment against a single currency in any circumstances. Financed by a phobic businessman named Paul Sykes, and under the gun from Jimmy Goldsmith, a great cohort of would-be Members of Parliament sought to arrive there on the basis of a position that swept aside the agonized syntax – his last attempt to present himself as all things to all Tories – of the party leader.

For the man whose chief credential, when he became party leader, was supposed to be his mastery of the arts of political management, ironic is hardly the word to describe his fate. Over the seven years, the Conservative Party, under his decent and well-meaning hand, had all but disintegrated. And it duly lost the election, in which the Labour Party secured a majority unimaginable by any post-war government, ending 179 seats ahead of all its rivals put together.

What was the role in this cataclysm of 'Europe'? Directly, a rather small one. The Tories could not make it a great question, since that would only draw attention to the party's divisions, a condition which voters, waking from slumber to pay their quinquennial attention to the political scene, are known particularly to dislike. Apart from one rather passionate statement, in which he pleaded – pleading was by now the only mode he knew – for his party not to 'bind my hands', Major didn't talk about Europe much. Labour, for its part, took up a circumspect position, desiring above all to give no hostages to sceptic fortune. So the most divisive issue in British politics was not presented in full vigour to the electorate, at this classically healing moment in the democratic calendar.

On the other hand, Europe was proxy and proof for other things, to do with leadership style and party credibility, with competence and with plausible purpose. On all those counts, it did more than any other issue to wreck the Tory Government and obliterate any possibility of it being re-elected. And the outcome of Major's handling of it summoned up some troubling ghosts.

He was the sixth Conservative Prime Minister since Churchill to have grappled with the Europe question. In a way, he was discernibly of the lineage. In his particular time and place, fifty years on, he represented in his person some of the same hesitations and anxieties that had afflicted all his predecessors save one. In Churchill's case, the divided national psyche was barely visible, beneath the imperial certainties and the grand continent-building for which he spoke. But the separateness of the island and the unthinkability of it itself being part of the continental project were a part of almost all Tory instincts. Under Eden, who disdained to go to Messina, this continued, only marginally abated. Under Macmillan, followed by the afterthought of Douglas-Home, the balance changed but the divide remained. In their hearts, very many Conservatives were only half ready for the enterprise which de Gaulle saved them from having to choose. They backed Macmillan's attempt to edge Britain towards a different kind of future, but few hoisted into their minds a true understanding of what it would mean. They thought they could probably go on having it all ways, without the need to make a new statement of dependency, still less allegiance, as the founding fact of existence in the European Community.

Heath, of course, was the aberrant case. He was unreserved in his belief, if not wholly clear or candid in his vision. Had Heathite Conservatism survived more than a year after entry, winning rather than losing elections, no one can know how different Britain's European settlement would have been, or whether the Euro-scepticism that destroyed Major would have had half the purchase it subsequently gained on the Tory Party. But Heath lost, and his cause, while rooting itself in the practical business of British life, captured the minds and hearts of Conservatives only imperfectly. A decade of Mrs Thatcher, exciting the Tory divide even as she conducted policies that were supposed to carry the nation, gave Major a legacy whose true nature was unresolved. It matched, all too aptly some would say, his own uncertainties. If the Conservative Party in 1990 needed the firm stamp of a European, ready to embrace the destiny towards which Britain had limped for fifty years, Major was certainly not the man to deliver it.

In some ways, even, the past spoke more loudly through him than the future. Churchill, after all, had at least welcomed every sign of European unification. He was the benign, and not inactive, spectator at a process he regarded as essential. Integration, at that early moment, was something even the Labour Government could acquiesce in.

By Major's time, the prevailing attitude was different. His true forebear, perhaps, was Eden. By Eden's time, while the agreement to European unity was still extant, the belief that it would work was fraying. When the next stage of it, the Common Market, was being conceived, the main British attitude was that it didn't stand a chance. R. A. Butler spoke, consummately *de haut en bas*, about the comical 'archaeological excavations' going on at Messina. This was the beginning of a line of analysis, often repeated, which consisted of the British persuading themselves that the Europeans were engaged on an impossible endeavour. Apart from producing a series of false prophecies, this did not make for fraternal warmth. It wasn't seen as the thinking of a friend. In international affairs, predictions of failure do their bit to ensure their own fulfilment.

The last days of Major eerily replayed them. First, he decided it was time to tell the European Union to rethink its place in the world. Rifkind, the Foreign Secretary, was sent on a tour of the capitals to explain to a succession of political and business elites that they were leading Europe in the wrong direction. The Union should become less integrated, more of a partnership of nations. Rifkind began his tour, calculating on special resonance, in Zurich, where Churchill had launched his own vision of a United States of Europe in 1946. Did he imagine he could lay claim to the smallest scintilla of Churchill's authority, or the tiniest fragment of his audience, for the view Britain was now, in her wisdom, prepared to vouchsafe to her continental neighbours? His lectures continued, round half a dozen capitals, chipping away at EU institutions, warning against 'jumping blindly' towards more integration, pressing the virtues of British parliamentary democracy.

Coming from a strong government, credibly committed to the European enterprise, this might have been a little hard to take. A German foreign minister, touring Britain with a series of Euro-philiac lectures, was a spectacle as hard to imagine the Germans proposing as the British permitting. But the Rifkind exercise was launched by a government no European had listened to for a long time, which was on the verge of collapse, and whose every word on Europe, as they saw it, was dictated not by a serious judgement about how the Union might develop but by sceptic stranglers with their hands round the party's neck. Rifkind's final journey was one of the most humiliating, as well as ridiculous, acts of British foreign policy in the fifty years of which he was so proud to speak.

It wasn't the only echo of the past, however. Still more damaging was a replication of the prophecy made with such confidence in 1955 that the Common Market wouldn't come to birth. Nor, Major and his Government were almost certain, would the current project of economic and monetary union. In 1993, someone had produced for Major the uncharacteristically vivid phrase he was proud of, in which he said that EMU had 'the quaintness of a rain-dance, and about the same potency'. This was still the analysis, which lay, among other things, behind the pre-election compromise, making the wish father to the thought that EMU would not happen at the appointed moment in January 1999. Even Clarke and Heseltine thought that much. Major and most of the others thought more. They believed, both before the election and for some time after it, that EMU was essentially nonsense. Even the Europeans, when they stared it in the face, would surely see this, and retreat before political and economic realities so fraught with danger.

So saying, the British made themselves pretty much detested, certainly ignored, by the leaders whom Major had once imagined he would join at the heart of Europe. These leaders had pursued difficult policies, sometimes strongly against the pattern of their nations' economic history, in the belief that they could make EMU happen. They were now about to do so. What could be said for Major was that, in his error, he himself had exhibited a certain historical consistency. Most of his predecessors would have recognized his problem – though vacillation, the chronic disease, took none of them as close as him to the heart of darkness.

12

TONY BLAIR

Leading from the Edge

John Major was removed from office in the twenty-fifth year of Britain's membership of what was now the European Union. The anniversary, when it finally arrived on 1 January 1998, went unremarked. There were no newspaper supplements, no television retrospectives. In a media world that feeds avidly on the convenient predictability of such moments, the silence was remarkable. But it was also eloquent. It spoke for the dismal state of relations Major left behind. By far the greater portion of the belonging had been spent under the hand of ministries, culminating in Major's, that never – not too strong a word – found a single thing to exalt about membership of 'Europe'. Destiny had dragged Britain there, but the British discourse seldom moved beyond the narrow modes of complaint, lecture and demand. Sympathetic recognition of the quarter-century would therefore have been, as a mirror of history, somewhat unreal. Celebration was out of the question.

Whether this would have been any different if another group had been in power for all or some of the time is, of course, an academic matter. For nearly twenty years, Conservative politicians and politics shaped the relationship alone. But the speculation isn't worthless, and the most likely conclusion to be drawn from it is salutary. Although the Tories were in power, they weren't opposed, for much of the time, by a coherently organized party able to see Europe more clearly than they did. They were at the head, one might say, of an entire political system, the very structure of British politics in the 1980s, which allotted the 'Europe' question an auxiliary, and almost always negative, place. The Liberal Party had long been a minority voice for closer union with Europe, but it was almost never heard. The Liberals' small importance only emphasized the extreme apprehension, sharpened by erratic aggression, with which both the big battalions habitually treated the subject.

The Labour Party's history in the matter promised terribly little. Go back to the last time they were in the frame of government. It was the culmination of extensive deviousness. Harold Wilson, as shown above,[1] played a critical role in keeping Britain in Europe, by organizing the 1975 referendum. The Labour leadership was then, to that extent, European. But this was after a series of shifts that spoke for a collective scepticism, a riven and unresolved party mind, which would have been hard for any party leader, even from the seat of government, to fashion into the kind of positive Europeanism that Margaret Thatcher, despite the many integrationist steps she took, spent a decade teaching the people to vilify. Wilson and his successor, James Callaghan, let's not forget, opposed the Heath Government's negotiated entry, having spent the three previous years themselves seeking to take Britain in. And they played the smallest part they could in the referendum campaign.

It can be said that these leaders were prudently hedging their bets. On their own account, they would probably contend that my version of what happened gives too little weight to Wilson's problems of party management at all stages. Maybe so. Like John Major, Wilson was prepared to abandon any consistency, let alone vision, as regards Europe for the sake of keeping his party in what could be construed as one piece: and this purpose, though ultimately unsuccessful, wasn't indefensible. But in the case of the last Labour leaders in government, before the two-decade ice age of powerlessness, it also expressed their personal ambivalence. Neither Wilson nor Callaghan were, in any but the most reluctant and instrumental sense, 'Europeans'. They did nothing whatever to teach the party or the country to embrace the continental connection. It is hard to imagine how their immediate successors, if miraculously given the opportunity, would have produced a very different atmospheric context from the one Mrs Thatcher set about creating on her first encounter with European leaders, and never ceased to poison thereafter.

On the other hand, something did happen to the Labour Party in this time, which might not have happened if it had been in government. Under the curse of what seemed to be the interminable status of opposition, it evolved. This occurred not because it saw the light but because it tired of the darkness, the experience by which most political change is propelled. Labour didn't suddenly become seized of the higher Euro-wisdom, perhaps after re-reading the sacred texts of Jean Monnet

or Roy Jenkins. No great access of supra-national idealism could be
detected, percolating round the corridors and smoke-filled rooms of
Blackpool and Brighton, as the party struggled through its annual conferences during the barren years. What happened was a reaction to the
much larger political reality that dominated its existence: the hegemonic
rule of Mrs Thatcher. Challenge and response, action and reaction:
eventually, the classic pattern began to surface through the tundra.

Largely, though not entirely, because Mrs Thatcher was anti-Europe,
Labour became pro-Europe. Because Thatcherism dominated the power-
structure of Britain, socialism, as it was still called, sought and found
another outlet. Over time, strands in the progressive left that had parted
fused together once again. Europe, which had contributed mightily to
their division, became a kind of therapy, even, in some ways, a unifying
balm.

The middle 1990s were the first occasion, in all this history of British
membership, when Europe not only brought parties together, but, in
due course, ceased to be a destructive agent at the heart of government.

*

AFTER 1979 and the Thatcher victory, Labour reverted with great speed
to the anti-Europe stance that had been its instinct to adopt at almost all
times when the party wasn't burdened with office. Even in government,
it had never been the party of Europe. Ernest Bevin, under Attlee, was
the Foreign Secretary who sanguinely watched the Schuman Plan pass
him by: the first leader of the left who rejected 'Europe': the man who
stood at the earliest gateway and was certain Britain's future lay in
turning her back on it. In opposition, as we have seen, Labour's heart
persisted in this prejudice for the next twenty-five years. Now in
opposition again, the party reassumed the line, almost as if it had had
nothing to do with the unfortunate accident that put a Labour government in charge of Britain-in-Europe for five of the country's first six
years of the relationship.

Labour had already shown something of its hand. At the last
conference before the 1979 election, party instructed government in an
impossibilist agenda, supporting a resolution which asserted a series of
unilateral priorities. Britain, the conference said, should pass a law
enacting Westminster's power to override any EEC regulation: should
abolish the CAP, insist on the right of nation-states 'to pursue their own
economic, industrial and regional policies', and reject any increase in the

powers of the European Parliament (then still a mere Assembly). This, let's say again, was the party still in charge of national policy, still the Government. For the bulk of the party, plainly, the 1975 referendum meant little. It was only natural therefore that, when office was removed, it should make the next leap, after demanding impossible reforms from within, to the straightforward position that Britain should leave the Common Market. A motion to that effect was duly passed in October 1980, exchanging the scorned religion of Europe for something more pantheistic. The next Labour Government, it said, should 'disengage Britain from the EEC institutions and in place of our EEC membership work for peaceful and equitable relations between Britain and all nations in Europe and the rest of the world'.

This was carried by 5 million to 2 million, a result greeted with exultation by Tony Benn, the one-time pro-Europe man and inventor of the referendum whose result, at the time, he had humbly accepted. 'That is sensational, a fantastic victory,' he wrote in his diary on the day of the 1980 vote.[2]

Anti-Europeanism hadn't always been the position of the Labour left. It was the left's flirtation with European federalism, back in the post-war period, that particularly enraged Ernest Bevin. The left, at that time, saw nascent 'Europe' as the desirable counterpoise to the American super-power, an attitude Bevin abominated. But time, naturally, changed everything, and long before 1980 the 'Europe' question divided the Labour Party on left–right lines which placed the left, almost entirely, on the anti-Europe side. In the afterburn of the 1979 defeat, Europe became part of the radical leftist catalogue that captured the party: a reversion somehow rendered more satisfying by the fact that one of those old federalists, Michael Foot, who had long ago forgotten he ever embraced such heresy, was elected to be the Labour leader.

In parallel with this, as we have already seen, was a compatible development. Roy Jenkins, having left London to become president of the European Commission, gave every indication that he would make good his private vow at that time never to return to the Labour Party. Six months after the 1979 election, he delivered the Dimbleby Lecture, canvassing a new, coalitionist party of the centre. Not long after that, when he began to attract allies to this cause, they came from among people moved first and foremost by the anti-Europe stance that Labour was already taking.

The fissile effect of Europe on the Labour Party was thus matched by its coagulant influence on everyone, high and low, involved in the construction of something else. It wouldn't be true to say Europe was the biggest single motivating element in the formation of the Social Democratic Party, the SDP, under Jenkins's leadership. Nuclear defence, and the Bennite onslaughts in the name of party democracy, were still more jarring pretexts for some of those involved. But Europe was first in time. The most authoritative history of the SDP records the moment. After the first Labour *démarche* to unpick the primacy of the referendum verdict, Shirley Williams met David Owen and William Rodgers in her flat. The date was 6 June 1980. They were all, in different degrees, strong Europeans, as well as former ministers, high in the Labour hierarchy. They agreed to issue their first joint statement of dissent from a party position, and agreed it must focus on Europe, though on condition that this 'would be only the first thing they did together'.[3]

Europe, therefore, had become a defining reason for some senior people to leave the Labour Party. By the same token, it was by now an issue on which the party insisted that an unyieldingly negative position should be adhered to by all who stood in the Labour name. The departure of the SDP MPs cut the ground from under the already waning support for Europe. There were a few resilient members of the right and centre, whose personal record on Europe would have made any surrender of their position laughable even by the relaxed standards of consistency on this issue that British politics has long observed. But only they could afford to make clear their dissent from the line Foot keenly favoured, and with which he led his party to the most spectacular electoral defeat in its post-war history. For the most part, there was at least token solidarity for a simple repudiation. 'British withdrawal from the Community is the right policy for Britain,' said Labour's 1983 election manifesto. This would be 'completed well within the lifetime of the Parliament'. In one easy swoop, a Repeal Bill would abolish the present powers of the Community in Britain, and then repeal the 1972 Act once negotiations on withdrawal were complete.[4]

What role this startling commitment played in the near-terminal withdrawal of the British people's support from Labour at this election cannot be precisely assessed. In a document that was described by one of its more sardonic dissenters as 'the longest suicide note in history', degrees of culpability as between the promise of unilateral nuclear disarmament, the pledge to renationalize swathes of industry and the commitment to get out of the EEC are hard to distinguish. Suffice to say that, on Europe, the opinion polls at the end of the campaign were putting the Tories 23 per cent ahead, one of their largest measured advantages on a policy issue.[5] When Foot was ushered off the scene, soon after the electoral disaster, his Europe policy was one of the first that began to disappear after him.

One of its apparently more ardent supporters became the promoter of, once again, a Labour reversal of position. But on this occasion it was a reversal in favour of a more positive line, conducted, not grudgingly under the pressure of being in government, but with all deliberate urgency, after the party had finished an election with 188 seats fewer than the Tories and come close to being relegated to third place in the popular vote by an alliance of the Liberals and the SDP.

Neil Kinnock, a man of the left, had always been, in conventional terms, an anti-European. His attitude was gathered almost blindly into the familiar leftist cluster. But when Kinnock became party leader in the autumn of 1983 he soon understood that a shift was compellingly desirable – if for no better reason than that elections for the European Parliament were due in June 1984, and supplied an early focus for the revisionism that the recent catastrophe indicated was necessary across the board. But there was more to it than that, Kinnock subsequently indicated. He represented himself as never having been an anti-European in the manner of late-period Tony Benn. Changing the line on this subject, one of his associates confirmed, was nothing like so difficult for him as the personal renunciations of conscience involved in abandoning unilateral nuclear disarmament or supporting the sale of council houses, two requirements of political realism he accepted through gritted teeth. He was already, he himself once told me, dissatisfied with the straight pledge to get out of the Common Market: and he also wished, as he looked back on it, that when he began to change the party line he had done so more emphatically. As it was, he indicated at the start of his leadership only a conditional resumption of a hypothetically pro-Europe position. The EEC had to prove itself 'a source of tangible value to the British people', he wrote. 'We could only realistically accept enduring membership if, at the very least, we suffer no significant material loss or disadvantage.'[6]

This was a cautious advance, conducted against the grain of a still highly militant left. Kinnock wrote those words while a miners' strike, which he felt obliged against his better judgement to support, was testing the very life of the Thatcher Government. He had to be careful with this other inflammatory issue. But, in any case, the new stance conformed to the barren realities of all but a small fragment of British Europeanism. It was defiantly minimalist: pragmatic, rather than in any way visionary. It

posed the test of economic advantage, which was the way most Labour
people ever since Wilson preferred to look at the matter. Insofar as it
touched on more philosophical issues, Kinnock's statement represented
Europe as a concept to be considered within the approved canons of
nationalism, rather than by acknowledging any positive virtue in sinking
some of Britain's economic identity into a larger whole: again, a familiar
stance for all British party leaders, with the partial exception of Heath.

The change was, however, significant. And it became decisive. It was
cabined and qualified by all manner of oppositionism, and by a persistent
reluctance to admit that Labour was now a European party. In 1986, the
party opposed the Single European Act, putting up one of its most
stalwart pro-Europeans, George Robertson MP, to say that this measure
was 'wholly irrelevant', and 'a diversion from the real task before us'.[7]
Under Kinnock's successor, the better-credentialled European John
Smith, Labour's incessant parliamentary manoeuvres, against a government without a majority, almost succeeded in destroying the Treaty of
Maastricht. The tradition of putting party before issue, and victory
before anything discernible as a principle, was carried over seamlessly
from the Wilson era. But the course was set for a different sort of Labour
approach to Europe. The recognition was established that, without this,
the party might find it much harder to exploit the growing frailties of
the Thatcher, and then the Major, Government.

For the first time, one is beginning to see, Europe became, in the
late 1980s, an arena whose role in British politics was changing. While it
continued to tear successive Cabinets apart, there appeared the novel
prospect that, to other politicians, it might offer some advantage.
Perhaps, they dimly saw, there was actual political gain to be made by
adopting a stance that was positive rather than negative.

Labour lost the 1987 election, even though it abandoned its Year
Zero extremism on Europe and several other matters. But Kinnock was
becoming a European politician, at least in Europe. He was an assiduous
attender at meetings of continental socialist parties, and became friends
with leaders such as Willy Brandt, in Germany, Michel Rocard, in
France, and the Italian nemesis of Mrs Thatcher, Bettino Craxi. In 1985,
he was invited to Spain by the Prime Minister, Felipe González, to speak
in the local referendum campaign to authorize accession to Nato.[8] These
were socialists with actual experience of real power, the proof that
progressive politics need not consign its leaders into the oblivion which
Thatcherism had thus far dealt to the British Labour Party.

The European Community, moreover, was itself an embodiment of that kind of politics. What post-war Labour saw, not incorrectly, as a threat to the freedom of the great British nation-state to organize its coal and steel industries under public ownership had become, by the lights of the Thatcherite world, a repository of socialism. 'We have not successfully rolled back the frontiers of the state in Britain', the lady said at Bruges, 'only to see them reimposed at a European level.' As well as marking the moment of her new belligerence, this signified the very reason why, in the same month of September 1988, the British Trades Union Congress received the president of the European Commission, Jacques Delors, as if he were a prophet. Delors, whom the brothers serenaded as Frère Jacques, to the tune of the only French song most of them knew, came from Brussels to explain that there was another world, beyond either the free market or the command economy, which 'Europe' existed to promote. His words became a mantra, his very presence a beacon, for the beleaguered rabble that the island's Labour movement, after a third election defeat, was in danger of becoming.

This was, once again, more a facing of reality than a deep conversion experience. Europe, for Kinnock's evolving Labour Party, did not represent a dream of union but the Utopia where power might lie. The debates which began to revolve around it in the party concentrated, as usual, more on the economic than the political dimensions. Could the Community become a power-house of economic growth, or were the anti-inflationary biases of the Bundesbank a threat to British industry? The discussion that ensued had a rationality, notwithstanding the strength of the sceptic left, that barely allowed itself to be touched by the primeval demons simultaneously at large among Conservatives. National sovereignty was an issue that no longer stirred the left. Kinnock himself, after all, was Welsh. John Smith, his successor, was Scottish. Many of their strongest lieutenants were also Celts. Such politicians, coming from a tradition steeped in forced submission to the English, were always less likely to be disturbed in their viscera by the occasional importunities of what might be decided in Brussels.

A collection of influences was therefore developing that now united rather than divided all the important forces opposed to the Conservative hegemony. This wasn't enough to save them from yet another election defeat, in 1992. But both the old party, Labour, and the new party, known as Liberal Democrats and still significantly peopled by those who had left the old in acrimony, now made common cause on the principle of the Europe connection.

There were still hold-outs on the further left. Tony Benn continued to preach, a voice of undiminished eloquence: in support of a case, however, of much diminished political strength among his fellow leftists. Benn's allies were on the Government benches. He spoke with enthusiasm of young William Cash, though he would never join Cash on a platform, and wrote with horror of his nationalist opinions.[9] Among the centre left, hardened by its decades of impotence, a moderate degree of Europeanism now seemed the touchstone not only of distinctiveness from the other side, but of Labour's fitness, at last, to be taken seriously by the people.

*

IN THIS EVOLUTION, some Labour politicians played a more heroic role than others. The old found it considerably easier than the young. Only the most ancient allegiance to 'Europe' was enough to fortify resistance to the party line in the early 1980s. Indeed, it was only through having lived and fought the struggles of the 1960s and 1970s, or so it seemed, that a Labour politician of the Year Zero period was capable of attaching any real importance to the continental question, as something he or she needed to think about. I have been unable to trace any Labour MPs, making their first entry into Parliament in 1983, who proclaimed themselves opposed to the party's pledge on immediate exit from the Community.

Certainly, the aspirant Member for Sedgefield, in the county of Durham, didn't. And the absence of such a statement from Tony Blair's first successful personal manifesto is indicative of a number of truths.

One is that Europe, at this stage, had entirely lost its inspirational place in social democratic, or indeed any other, British politics. Seen from 1983, the idealism that once swirled round this issue, the oxygen that pumped the very heart of Roy Jenkins, John Mackintosh and their friends in the Wilson era, was untransmutable into a contemporary force. It did not reach the youthful progressive mind. This was partly because the Community, now that Britain belonged, had become a banal, merely functional extension of the business of governing, and as such incapable of inspiring anyone. But it also reflected the decade since entry, in which Europe was downplayed by Wilson and Callaghan, prior to resuming its place as nothing more than a commodity in the marketplace of Labour faction: an issue whose main sensitivity for an ambitious politician, therefore, was that it should not be seen to damage him.

Europe, in other words, was something on which hardly any sensible young Labour person would dare to challenge the orthodoxy. It simply wasn't big enough, as a question on which to break with the party so early in a political life. It wasn't even a subject where one tended to have terribly prominent opinions either way, certainly not in a favourable direction.

This illuminates something else behind the Blair abstention from dissent, which is immediately worth noting given what happened later. In that era it was possible, often essential, to sublimate personal conviction, on almost any subject, to the quest for preferment in the party. The true state of a tyro Labour mind was very often impossible to discern. Opinions didn't seem to be the point, as the prudent tyro was the first to see. Routine promises of fealty were the way to get ahead: which, in Blair's case, at least placed him, on Europe, as securely in the line of his ancestors as John Major was in his. He was true to the past in one definitive respect. Like every other Labour leader before him, when Blair assumed the succession in July 1994 he had to account for the fact that he had apparently changed his mind on Europe.

Whether this really was a change raises quite profound questions about the nature of conviction. Certainly Blair *said* he was against British membership of the Community. But at that time virtually any opinion a Labour person had could be regarded as an opinion of convenience. Blair's real opinions in 1985 were often as obscure as, ten years later, they were clear. Dissimulation and agnosticism were among the intellectual diseases from which he began to release the party when he became leader. But in his personal case, on the 'Europe' question, the cure was quite a long time coming.

Born in 1953, Blair matured when the Second World War was a distant memory. The formative events of 'Europe' had made no impact on him. He was two when Messina happened, ten when de Gaulle said no, fifteen when Wilson tried again, twenty when Britain got in. Besides, he was not, in the conventional sense of most progressive youth, political. The son of a barrister who was also a law lecturer, he imbibed such politics as he did from, as it were, the wrong side of the fence: Leo Blair was chairman of the Durham Conservative Association. Subsequently, Tony Blair would recollect that it was the disabling stroke his father suffered at the age of forty that started him, the son, on the road to politics. He rather consciously took over some part of his father's frustrated ambition for a public life, albeit with a different party base. Occurring when he was only ten, the illness and its consequences for the family also seem to have supplied the first stirrings of ideas such as service, and community, and fairness, and the need to do something about them.[10] However, Blair did not become a university politico. Going up to Oxford in 1972, he might have become involved in all manner of political causes. His years there coincided with the degeneration of the Heath Government under the weight of some massive industrial struggles, and the return to power of a Labour leadership roiled in much disputation. For any young man drawn to politics, there was a great deal to argue about. But Blair appears not to have been interested, finding the greater part of his moral development, and his concern about public questions, in the religious rather than the political sphere.

One of his earliest recorded political acts, as it happens, was European. He voted Yes in the referendum in 1975, the year he also joined the Labour Party. This didn't signify a crusading interest in Europe, which could hardly, in any case, have been a sufficient reason at that time to persuade any person, young or old, to sign up with the party. It was simply a natural marriage of positions for any burgeoning progressive who did not side with the hard left. It was a normality Blair observed, without making any fuss about it or needing to strike any kind of posture, but it can surely be said to have defined him as by instinct a pro-Europe man: a regular, unzealous absorber of Europe into the routine attitudes of someone who was now beginning to think he might like to be a politician.

By the time this became a possibility for him, however, the definition of what was routine had changed. His first intervention in national politics was as Labour's candidate at a by-election in the Tory stronghold of Beaconsfield, in May 1982. With Michael Foot at the helm, the official party line already proposed exit from the EEC, and the youthful candidate did not openly dissent. According to his biographer, indeed, he 'made Europe one of his main themes'.[11] He wasn't quite categoric in his adoption of the exact party position, which stated, in *Labour's Programme 1982*: 'We do not believe a further attempt to change the nature of the Community would be worthwhile. . . . Britain must therefore withdraw.' Blair voiced a faintly less extreme position, with a timid parenthesis in a letter to the local paper, which supported 'the Labour Party's present leadership' on all important matters, including, he wrote, 'withdrawal from the EEC (certainly unless the most fundamental changes are effected)'.[12] He was anxious, he also made clear, not to be labelled 'a Benn-backer'; but he took up something close to the Benn position. His way of putting this was interesting. He said he had come to these positions, which included nuclear unilateralism, 'as a Labour Party man, not as a "Bennite" or any other "ite" '. It was the same, evidently, with Europe. 'Come out if we must, but not as an article of socialist faith,' was how he described it to the *Guardian*.[13] And all his specific observations were critical. 'Above all, the EEC takes away Britain's freedom to follow the economic policies we need,' his official election leaflet said.

How much he agreed with all this is a moot, and perhaps an academic, point. When he became more prominent, it was normal to assert without qualification that he never had done.[14] But in the general election a year later, when he fought the safe seat of Sedgefield, was he also, therefore, expressing false sentiments? His election address said: 'We'll negotiate withdrawal from the EEC, which has drained our natural resources and destroyed jobs.' These words subsequently gave him trouble with the Tories, who used them to undermine his image as a sincere and, above all, consistent party leader. A talk-out has been constructed, to the effect that they were written in a hurry, after he got the Sedgefield nomination very late, and that they merely summarized party policy: what his leaflet called 'Labour's Sensible Answers'. His 'Personal Message', on the other side of the leaflet, contained no mention of Europe – evidence, so it is contended, that he didn't really mean it.[15]

All that this demonstrates, perhaps, is the problem of conviction, in that era of Labour politics. There is not much reason to doubt that, in his heart, Blair had little problem with British membership of the EEC – but had still less problem with adapting his public words to get into Parliament, and thus position himself to help rescue the party from the attitudes that were making it unelectable. When Tories attacked his seeming shift, they were misunderstanding the nature of the Labour debate on Europe – as if to say that every piece of positioning on the matter was like their own, drawn from the bone and soul and gut. Very few of Blair's generation in the Labour Party felt anything like that about Europe, or any other issue save the need to get rid of the Tories and install the progressive left in government.

It has to be said, nonetheless, that these sinuous duplicities, however well intentioned, became, justifiably, an embarrassment. They were yet further examples of the confusion that has been the mode in which the British political class chose, times without number, to present its views on Europe to the people. In his early days, Blair treated Europe as a subject about which it was dangerous to tell the truth: risky, even, at his early stage of initiation into the class, to decide and stake out a position

on what the truth really was. While plainly untouched by Cashite
nationalism, he was reluctant in the beginning, whatever he actually
believed, to address the fact that being pro-European might require a
commitment to look Euro-scepticism square in the face and stare it
down.

The youthful Blair was the exponent of a national habit with a long
pedigree. Whether he could shake the habit was to become one way of
defining the challenge Europe presented to his quality as a political
leader.

In the contest that put him in that place, after John Smith died in
May 1994, the 'Europe' question played no part. The Kinnock evolution
was carried on by Smith and, apart from unregenerate Bennites, attitudes
to the European Union had long since ceased to be a litmus test of
whether a Labour politician was sufficiently red or blue. The years after
Bruges, and then Maastricht, imparted to the Labour Party not only a
warm acquiescence in what 'Europe' might do to revive social democratic
politics, but a considerable satisfaction in their own beautifully moder-
ated unity compared with the turmoil on the other side. They could sit
quiet and smug, as the bloody oppositionism that reached into the
Cabinet itself performed, more than adequately, the task of giving the
Prime Minister a hard time. Not the least damage, indeed, that the state
of the Tory Party did to the 'Europe' issue for most of the 1990s was to
absolve the Labour Party from seriously engaging with it.

I had many conversations with Blair in the five years of the 1992
Parliament.[16] Whatever his judicious hesitations in the past, he was by
now plainly a proper European. Once installed in the Commons, he had
been totally supportive of the Kinnock–Smith shift, and now personified
the sense in which every mainline Labour politician of his vintage could
be presumed automatically to be, with greater or lesser zeal, pro-EU.

With him, this opinion was more than automatic. Quite regularly,
he would describe himself as 'passionately' European, and he was never
less than realistic about continental developments. As early as May 1993,
barely six months after the ERM débâcle, he was expressing his disappointment that the entire press, which had pushed so hard for British
membership, now directed the same unanimity in the opposite direction.
He could already see that EMU and the single currency were likely to
continue being pushed forward by most other EU members, and he
meditated on the certainty that the case for some kind of British
attachment to the ERM would be revived. What was most striking at
this time, however, was the way he located the 'Europe' question within

the wider Labour predicament: that, along with Kinnock's other shifts on the importance of markets or nuclear defence, the conversion on Europe had been a matter of expediency not conviction. The party was still addressing all these matters, Blair thought, as if nothing fundamentally needed to change. 'Conversion', as such, was almost being avoided: certainly relegated to a second-best option, pending the moment when the timeless Labour values and positions, in faintly new cosmetics, could be reaffirmed. That might be necessary for party management, he thought, but was quite insufficient as a way of making Labour credible in the wider world.

This attitude prefigured Blair's strategy when he became leader. From the moment he began his leadership campaign, up to and through the moment when he won the 1997 general election, he took it as axiomatic that Labour must change 'from within', and be seen to do so. This didn't touch on the party's Europe position anything like so sensitively as on many other questions: in the context of the time, the party was already seen, and saw itself, as 'European'. But it meant, for example, that Labour shouldn't fear to concede that there were occasions on which the British interest was served by adopting lines that ran with the grain of Europe rather than against.

This, when Blair began to put it into words as leader, had a startling effect on the climate. His position, he said, was that 'the drift towards isolation in Europe must stop and be replaced by a policy of constructive engagement'. He wasn't uncritical of the EU or the Commission, but he wanted to establish an atmosphere in which criticisms were not assumed to denote anti-Europeanism. Britain should be 'at the centre of Europe', 'should set about building the alliances within Europe that enable our influence to grow'. This, he thought, was about more than fulfilling our national interest. To hesitate before our European destiny, he rather more boldly said, was 'to deny our historical role in the world'. The role was to be 'a major global player', and would be forfeit unless we accepted Europe as our base.[17]

This was a measured beginning, a cautious introduction to what Blair called 'the patriotic case', in which he quoted Palmerston and Kissinger but neglected to name with approval a single continental politician, living or dead. It provoked, nonetheless, a sensation in the Conservative Party. In the course of his speech, Blair proposed that qualified majority voting, the dreaded QMV, might be extended to social, environmental, industrial and regional policy decisions taken in the EU Council. It was a modest suggestion, carefully and conditionally couched, but to many Tories it seemed like a staggering gaffe. The 'four vetoes' and the pathetic innocence with which Blair had 'thrown them away' became the mantra of many a Conservative seeking succour from the Government's own crises. I met a number of ministers around this time who were almost literally foaming with disbelief that the young man could have said such a thing, their reaction lurching between the jubilation of party politicians who were certain they had got him, and the dismay of national chauvinists who saw Britain on the brink of being sold down the river to Brussels.

But Blair made one or two other speeches reiterating the position, and trying to broaden the impression of a leader thinking in a quite different spirit from the reigning sceptic orthodoxy. Their defensiveness reflected the spirit of politics at the time. They were hot for European reform, especially of the institutions and the agriculture policy, and they stressed the need for popularizing what Europe might mean for people's everyday lives. 'If we do not now make persuasion the condition of moving forward,' he said in Bonn, 'then the initiative will pass to those hostile to the whole project of Europe.'[18] He wanted to make very clear, to the Europeans, that they could expect, if Labour won, something better than the impotent posturing of Major: while also making it clear enough to the British that the national birthright would be safe in his hands. He was convinced, he always told me, that the country wasn't anti-European in the Tory way, and that the task was carefully to convince it that it was losing out as a result of Major's imprisonment by his party.

Here was another aspect of Europe, for Blair the student of political authority. It was blinding evidence of the single thing he most despised about the other side, to which he was determined never to succumb – control of the leader by the party, rather than the party by the leader. The same perception drove him with equal rigour to minimize the opportunities for forces to arise that might be beyond the leader's power to resist.

His opposition leadership, therefore, was marked by tactical manoeuvres, not all of them very creditable. Under his predecessor, as already noted, Labour had risked wrecking the Maastricht Treaty for the sake of possibly bringing down the Major Government. The jockeying went on through Blair's three years. He used to be opposed, for example, to another Europe referendum. When the question arose over Maastricht, he rejected the idea emphatically, saying in 1992: 'The right place for the debate to take place is in Parliament, where people can express different views.' He also said, in 1993: 'Our mandate is derived from our ability as Members of Parliament to represent our constituents.'[19] But in 1994, in his very first joust at Prime Minister's Question Time, he chose to try and goad Major into pledging a referendum on further European integration, knowing it to be a live issue between him and Kenneth Clarke. Not long after that, he made a commitment on the point himself. In the event of 'a major and fundamental constitutional change', said the Leader of the Opposition, 'there is clearly a case for ensuring that the decision can be very clearly taken by the British people'.[20]

Referendum politics continued to dominate, as EMU became the most crucial question on the table. In my talks with him in the earlier 1990s, Blair never expressed any hostility to EMU, or the single currency, in principle. He explicitly said he favoured it, if it could be made to work. By mid-decade he was being more sceptical, in the proper sense. His anxiety always was a practical one: whether, as the undoubted route to greater stability and lower transaction costs and (probably) lower interest rates, it could be sustained within the vast economic discrepancies between the different regions of the EU. This greatly bothered him, and he gave voice to the sceptic sentiment often enough in private, it seemed, to awaken the mistaken excitement, once again, of the Tory Party. Themselves mired, throughout 1996, in Major's strife-torn hesitations about exactly what words, to strike what policy, the party should be using about EMU, some Tory managers became convinced Blair was about to commit Labour against entry in the life of the next Parliament – the very line they were pleading with Major to adopt.

I asked Blair at the time about this rumour, and he was bewildered. Such a position was never on the cards. On the other hand, after Major promised an EMU referendum, Labour promised the same thing a few months later. It feared any challenge to its populist credentials. The leader took a lot of trouble to explain that this was merely the logical consequence of the fact that EMU itself was now impossible for any country to decide on before May 1997, the last date for a British election. This meant there couldn't be a manifesto commitment on entry, which in turn meant that a later referendum was the only way to secure the people's consent. It might look like a surrender to the anti-Europeanism which the Tories had long cultivated in the country, but it wasn't.

'My strategy is *not*, underline three times, to run as a Euro-sceptic,' Blair told me. It was, instead, to wait and see, just like the Conservatives. Or rather, since each party had improved on that tepid usage, Labour's plan was to 'protect and advance' – a formula fresh from the same words factory as its resounding Tory competitor, 'prepare and decide', a phrase much trumpeted by the ever resonant Michael Heseltine. Labour would presumably *protect* the issue by the referendum promise, then in due course *advance* the argument for a Yes: which was perhaps less bleak than the insinuation from the other side, that Britain would *prepare* for a single currency other people were inventing, and then *decide* not to buy it.

This, then, was the basis on which Blair moved into the election campaign which nobody except he and Major thought he might conceivably lose. In it, Europe played a smaller role than many Tory managers wanted it to, and Blair was therefore not put to a question that might compel him, in his caution, to appear more sceptical than he felt. If Major had done what the managers urged, and forced Clarke to swallow an outright pledge against EMU entry in the coming Parliament, he would have hoped to throw down a gauntlet to his Labour rival – yet there was no reason to believe the rival would have picked it up. Watchful EMU-readiness, moderate Euro-enthusiasm, a worldly-wise absence of zeal on either side of the question: these were the vibrations Blair sought to convey, which he knew were quite enough to distinguish him from the Conservatives, and reassure the electorate that it would be safer with him than with them.

This was what he won with. And immediately he had won, the caution of it was swept up into the more spacious rhetoric growing out of the greatest British election victory of modern times. 'Europe', along with other matters, became infused, as an issue, with the self-confidence, the freshened certainties, even the didactic exuberance that naturally comes over a party which has had such an uplifting experience at the hands of democracy.

For the first time in all this history, Britain had a 'European' government with a long life ahead of it. If there were resisters in the governing party, they were irrelevant, all importance drained by the massive numbers of MPs who would do anything the leader asked of them. It is not too much to call this a revolutionary moment. It was – could be – the moment when passion dulled and struggle ceased: when vituperation and bullying and gut-driven piety and the sanctimony of exclusive patriotism, all the coinage of permanent threat which had been the currency of political trade in this matter almost since the beginning, finally lost their power of command. This was the opportunity the leader had made for himself. As a therapy for the nation, it would be disturbing, after so many years in a different psychological condition. How, one had to wonder, would he use it?

He had already foreseen the early days in power, and dwelt upon how they would be handled. The European calendar laid down a post-Maastricht summit, concluding another long-drawn-out inter-governmental conference, to be held at Amsterdam within weeks of the election. He had thought about how different he would make the British tone, how altered would be the atmosphere in the Commons, as compared with the triumphalist bull-pit favoured by both Mrs Thatcher and John Major, when he reported back from the summit. He would use the language of collaboration not confrontation. He would claim positive results not negative triumphs. It would be the signal that, as well as what happened to Britain, what happened in Europe would matter too: the theatre where Labour's victory was displayed could be, in a sense, all-encompassing.

And so it proved, after a fashion, to be. In Opposition, Blair put an old Euro-sceptic, Robin Cook, in charge of foreign affairs. Cook had campaigned for a No vote in the 1975 referendum. But the Cook who became Foreign Secretary had long since changed his own mind, and become a European: quizzical, practical, Scottish, but European. The Conservatives, who had built Amsterdam into an occasion when the very lifeblood of the British nation would be in danger of dripping from the table, sincerely believed that Blair would be incapable of preventing it. How could anyone lacking the matchless experience of their own, battle-hardened, superlatively successful Mr Major hope to take on the likes of Helmut Kohl? But this turned out to be a false apprehension. Extravagantly so. It was true that the European leaders welcomed their counter-parts from the new British Cabinet. The change of atmosphere was instant and, to them, stunning. Accustomed to British delegations that were not only hostile, but incapable of guaranteeing the passage of any agreements they did manage to complete, the continentals were now dealing with a country that aspired to make Europe work, and a leader, aided by a Foreign Secretary, whose skills as a bargainer immediately made themselves felt in the Treaty of Amsterdam. 'You can't imagine how wonderful it is to feel you are actually being listened to,' a British official, steeped in the pessimism of the Major years, told a journalist.[21]

But nobody could say that Amsterdam made large integrationist strides. It left institutional reform in abeyance, and only with difficulty managed to keep EMU on track. It was, in the end, a minimalist

conference which witnessed, among other things, the ironic spectacle of
the British prime minister seeking to extend majority voting which, in
some of the most important cases, was resisted, for their own domestic
political reasons, by the Germans. What emerged, in fact, was a possible
confluence, further simplifying the British task, between the greater
readiness of London to enlist for a positive European project and the
status of that project in the minds of many Europeans. Maastricht, many
thought, had already brought to an end the full Monnet vision of ever
closer integration, concluding with a United States of Europe. The
pillared structure, dividing up the areas that would remain with governments from those that were covered by the EU Commission, Court and
Parliament, was, from the viewpoint of fully centralizing super-statists,
an eyesore; and Amsterdam did little to improve the landscape.

Just as Blair, in other words, was taking the heat out of 'Europe' by
the fact of his victory, Europe, with the fiery exception of EMU, looked
as though it was cooling down to an atmosphere dominated by compromise, and endless, boring, relatively uninflammatory pragmatism. At
Amsterdam, the British confirmed their border controls, backed more
collaboration on crime control, did more than they ever had under the
Tories to try and rescue the lost cause of the domestic fishing industry.
It was unglamorous, mostly uncontentious, stuff. Within six weeks of
the election, Europe was rendered into a part of quotidian banality.

Blair's area of contest, in fact, was different. But he did choose one.
It was the sign that a big victory did bring with it a certain arrogance.
Having won Britain as new Labour, he soon set about persuading Europe
that new Labour's remedies were the route to salvation for social
democrats everywhere. Within a month of gaining power, he had been
to Noordwijk in the Netherlands and Malmö in Sweden, and delivered
what amounted to lectures on the liberal economy and labour market
flexibility, the notorious Anglo-Saxon economic model the continentals
were supposed to learn from. In effect, he was asking them to abandon
the social Europe of Jacques Delors, or at least minimize its place in the
big picture. *Le grand tableau* was the catchphrase, virtuously self-
conscious in its chosen language, with which Blair invariably reminded
himself and his colleagues that the broad brush made the images that
mattered. Always remember *le grand tableau.*

In Blair's Euro-version of the big picture, the man with the most
enviable mandate in the Union began to redraw the ideological map
which most of his peer-group had grown up with. Government's job, he
said, was to enable people to make the most of themselves, 'in an

economy based on knowledge, skills and creativity'. 'This is the third way,' he told the European Socialists Congress, 'not old left or new right, [but] a new centre and centre-left agenda.' It was the route, among other things to 'a people's Europe'.[22] If nothing else, Blair wasted no time in conveying to his audience his mastery of the essential modern art of the soundbite.

This kind of lecture might be said to have something of the Rifkinds about it. It was, after all, telling the Europeans what to do – though it refrained from explaining how to run 'Europe' as such, and did come from the mouth of a new leader whose sympathies in that respect could not be doubted. There was still the faint whiff of hubris. After Malmö, the Dutch Foreign Minister, Hans van Mierlo, was heard to remark sardonically that some things never changed – another British leader telling the Europeans where they were going wrong.

All the same, as most continentals recognized, Britain had changed. The leader *saw* himself as European, and didn't fear to say so. For one thing, he felt quite at home in their countries, holidaying naturally in Tuscany and speaking French with facility. When he delivered a speech in French to the National Assembly in Paris, in March 1998, there was wild excitement on both sides of the Channel: as much a tribute to the stubborn mono-linguism of his predecessors as to his own rare brilliance.

His political relations with the French were not perfect. Lionel Jospin, elected Prime Minister at just about the same time as Blair, personified the socialism that had never died in France, and whose success at the polls was a rude counter to the Blair thesis that the 'third way' was the only way progressives could win. Jospin was also of a slightly different era, not quite part of the 'young continent' Blair wanted to position alongside the 'young Britain' which he had fashioned as the defining, if somewhat vacuous, image of his time and place. Though not as old as Helmut Kohl, whom the Blair people, come 1998, were beginning to paint as yesterday's man, Jospin was an awkward ingredient in the 'modernized' Europe for which the British leader seldom stopped preaching. As a leader who prided himself on having no enemies, Blair took time to find himself congenially alongside the French socialists.

In his European role, however, he enjoyed the blessing of old men. He was a source of relief to Kohl, in whose presence I sat for some hours in October 1997, listening to him expatiate not only on the future of Europe but on the role it was now open for Britain to play there.[23] Blair, one of the Chancellor's staff said, had told Kohl, when they met for their first intimate talk, that he looked forward to 'a relationship of equals'.

But Kohl had forgiven such startling presumption. Britain now had a leader, he was pleased to say, who saw the point about Europe. With Mrs Thatcher, any dialogue on the point had been 'hopeless'. With Major, who at least understood the problem, it had been almost as bad, because he had put so many anti-Europe people in his Cabinet. With Blair, Kohl believed, there was a good chance of fulfilling the maxim to which he had always held, that Europe could ultimately succeed 'only if Britain joins in'.

Another old man could also feel a sense of vindication. Blair's arrival in Downing Street completed, in a sense, the odyssey Roy Jenkins had begun. The party Jenkins left had become the party he would not now have needed to leave. The 'Europe' question, on which he mainly left it, was being addressed with more effortless aplomb by Blair than by any Prime Minister of his lifetime. There was something singularly fitting in the fact that Jenkins was now permitted to become a man of influence once again, the private godfather, some called him, to a leader who had still been in short trousers when Jenkins first began trying to persuade Labour leaders – Gaitskell, then Wilson – to adopt the cause to which he gave the largest part of his political energy. Blair was Jenkins's natural heir. He seemed to be launching a decade in which Britain would move, for the first time, full-hearted into Europe.

Yet the past could not be shed quite as easily as that. It lingered heavy in the air. There was a limit to Blair's Europeanism. No longer fearful of the 'Europe' that compromised old definitions of the nation-state, Britain still hesitated to follow the continental agenda. The traditional posture – fifty years of history, in a sense – remained palpably present in the consciousness of politics, an emanation the new Prime Minister did not desire instantly to ignore. While in favour of 'Europe' in general, the Government was ambivalent concerning the project that most countries of the Union cared most about, economic and monetary union, EMU: the project, indeed, on which the very future of 'Europe' was now most heavily staked.

Tony Blair, as we have seen, never wholeheartedly believed in an EMU which included, from the start, the pound sterling. He placed himself in the classic line of those British politicians who, while not part of the Whitehall conspiracy to wreck Messina, were sceptical about the success of the weird integrationist scheme, and argued that we must wait and see if the Common Market worked, which it probably wouldn't. The same line of reasoning would apply to the single currency. The propaganda of the deed, after all, has always played the most persuasive role in Britain's eventual embrace of 'Europe'. In the autumn of 1997, when Blair made the British decision not to join the monetary union that was scheduled to start on 1 January 1999, he submitted to a tendency that was hallowed not only in the politics but, one might say, in the culture and psychology of his country.

The occasion was a moment of mismanagement as well as disagreement, frailties which showed that Europe could still be a neuralgic issue, even behind a Commons majority of 179. While Labour, through Blair's own voice, had long ago declared there to be 'no overriding constitutional barrier' to EMU,[24] the question of the promised referendum had not been settled. Where, exactly, should it be fitted into the critical path of the Government's progress towards a second term? In October 1997, the leader took the line of least resistance. The pledge which neither he nor Major was prepared to offer before the election, that they would exclude entry into EMU in the lifetime of the coming Parliament, was now, bizarrely, made good.

Much confusion attached to it. It became the most damaging item in the process – an incessant deformity in the Government's methods – by which ministerial spin-doctors, the new masseurs of information, sought ascendancy over each other on their masters' behalf. The chain of half-promises and quarter-denials through which the decision eked into the public realm supplied an early lesson in public disbelief for what any unelected Labour spokesman had to say. But on 27 October the Chancellor, Gordon Brown, told the Commons that more time was needed. Britain and Europe were at different stages in the economic cycle. Brown was known to be less sceptical than Blair about the workable merits of EMU as a technical construct, but he had not fought hard against the prevarication he was now announcing. As well as the convergence of economies, the better preparation of opinion was required. This was what the Government would now embark on, but the task could not hope to be completed, on either the economics or the politics, until another election had taken place.

Six months after the 1997 election, this was a bathetic apotheosis for Tony Blair, on the issue where he hoped to make a serious difference. As such, it was unfortunate, but revealing. Maybe it would, in the end, be a temporary position. But, for the moment, it showed him straddled between the intensity of pressures from the past and the extremity of his ambition for the future.

The past was not represented by members of the previous government, since they were now irrelevant. Nothing the Conservative Party had to say could make any impression on the public. But their scepticism still had its proxy messengers, which Blair took much more seriously. The loudest voices in the print media remained Euro-sceptic, and were virulently opposed to the single currency.

It was perhaps a reflection of Blair's belief in the transience of political power that he regarded these voices as a threat which even his luxuriant Commons majority could not be sure of repelling. And no anti-EMU voice was more influential, he thought, than the one which most of both old and new Labour united in abominating, that of the Australian-American tycoon, Rupert Murdoch, speaking through his four national newspapers and, less important, his monopoly satellite TV station. Blair gave inordinate attention to cultivating Murdoch before the election. Now, by sidelining EMU from immediate decision, he was pre-empting a Murdoch onslaught which, he feared, might undercut his prospects of a second term.

That wasn't the only reason for delay. There were genuine disjunctions between island and mainland economies, though it wasn't clear, if this was to be the test, when and what manner of convergence was to be expected. The media priority, however, was there. Blair took the view, he had often said, that once the economic argument was convincing, public opinion could be won in favour of EMU. But he was anxious, I think, about the process. He foresaw an all-or-nothing battle, which the referendum would constitute. Ranged against him would still be the product of two decades' worth of accumulated scapegoating of Brussels and all its works: the ferocity of printed xenophobia, which a reasoned case found hard to match: the baying voices of publicists and politicians ready to die in the last ditch, in defence of a Britain that was as sentimental as it was vestigial, but which nonetheless, if challenged at the wrong moment, might rise and smite its leader. He wanted to be certain he would win.

Until this test was faced, however, Blair's claims for his future European life were bound to be ambiguous. He stated his purpose. He wished to be a leader of Europe; and he had both the domestic base and the political charisma to make this a credible possibility. But hard on his self-exclusion from EMU came the involuntary, though entirely predictable, exclusion of Britain from the committee that would shape and run the single currency from the moment it became a near-reality. Blair and Brown mishandled that, provoking a further excitation of sceptic rage by insisting Britain should belong, even when every argument undermined the case, as the French Finance Minister said with notable relish, for the marriage-chamber to be occupied by anyone except the wedding party.

It was an irony, but not an empty one, that the first half-year after Blair pulled back from EMU was occupied by Britain's turn in the presidency of the European Union. The Prime Minister conducted this with much efficiency. The Foreign Office lived up to the reputation it had enjoyed since John Robinson's day, as the most professional, best-resourced diplomatic service in the Community. Much was quietly done, for example, towards the enlargement of the Union – though not as much, inevitably, as the trumpets had predicted. In the slow progress of Europe – now accelerating, now retarded, here sometimes gliding, there more often stumbling – Britain was now able to play a part no longer poisoned by sectarian aggravation.

But the climactic act Blair performed as President produced a moment of uncomfortable symbolism. He was an umpire not a player, on 3 May 1998, when eleven members of the Union took the field and pledged to complete their economic and monetary union. He chaired the meeting, but did not sign the pledge.

He left his country, for the moment, in limbo, back from darkness and willing to be saved, but not yet ready to name the day or the hour when the old world would end.

*

THE WAY IN WHICH the new world would ultimately develop was a matter of far-ranging doubt. The single currency, the euro, was about to be minted in the tabulations of bankers and accountants. In eleven countries there would soon no longer be national coins of the realm. But the future of the European Union – its shape and its numbers, its power and its relevance – were debated seriously. One could easily forget, in the often crude cacophony of the British argument, that the EU had genuine problems, about which responsible intellectuals could take sober, critical positions.

On the large scale, what was the EU any longer for? Born out of one war, it had prospered during another. The Monnet people conceived it, and secured the political argument for it, as a compact to prevent Germany and France from ever destroying the peace of Europe again. That was the provenance, and the point had now been made. One of the beauties of Six, then Nine, then Twelve, then Fifteen groups of national politicians spending their waking hours in wearisome dialogue with each other was that the experience left no possibility of war. Moreover, anachronism was surely redoubled by the ending of the Cold War and the redrawing of the internal continental frontiers. Neither hot nor cold war any longer made 'Europe', as hitherto understood, an axiomatic necessity. The deeper unification of what used to be Western Europe was arguably a project that took too little account of greater Europe: was perhaps, indeed, inimical to the countries struggling to rebuild their economies and democracies after the communist catastrophe. What did Brussels have to offer Warsaw and Budapest, let alone Latvia and Bulgaria?

Timothy Garton Ash was an intellectual whose credentials as a European were quite satisfactory: one of those, for example, who had been summoned to Chequers to instruct Mrs Thatcher in the iniquities of Germany and been dismayed to experience the depth of her anti-German sentiments.[25] But in 1998 Garton Ash was a sceptic about the need for, or wisdom of, the pursuit of unity. Post-war integration, he noted, was the product of external influences, first the Soviet Union and second the United States: Moscow driving Western Europe together for its security, Washington encouraging this process as a precondition of the Marshall Aid that rescued Europe's economies. Together with the cutting-off of Eastern Europe, these pressures created 'a historical con-stellation that was particularly favourable to a particular model of West European integration'. But the end of the Cold War had ended the need for it.[26] Now, it could be argued, the EU was a threat to the liberal order rather than a guarantee of this paradigm being broadened and deepened around the continent. If integration succeeded, Garton Ash seemed to say, it would be a threat to the greater Europe and possibly the world. If, more likely, it failed, the formidable achievements that were to the credit of those who had built the European Community could well be destroyed.

At a still loftier level, the Anglo-American scholar Tony Judt was pessimistic about the continuing value of any attempt at unity. 'I am enthusiastically European,' he wrote in early 1996. 'No one could seriously wish to return to the embattled, mutually antagonistic circle of suspicious and introverted nations that was the European continent in the quite recent past.' But, he went on to argue, 'A truly united Europe is sufficiently unlikely for it to be unwise and self-defeating to insist upon it. Unlike Jean Monnet, the founder of the European Community, I don't believe that it is prudent, or possible, to "exorcise history", at any rate beyond moderate limits.' Judt therefore urged the 'partial reinstatement ... of nation-states', and contended that it might be 'the better part of wisdom' to stop promising the former communist states of Eastern Europe that they could expect to become members of a fully integrated continental system.[27]

The fumbling performance of the EU, in trying to construct a policy that inserted 'Europe' into the Yugoslav tragedy of the 1990s, fuelled the pessimism of this and other observers. It had shown, Judt wrote, 'the compulsion to avoid engagement, and the absence of any agreed strategic interest beyond maintaining the status quo'. 'The myth of "Europe"', he went on, 'has become little more than the politically correct way to paper over difficulties, as though the mere invocation of the promise of a united Europe could substitute for solving problems and crises in the present.' Events in the Balkans had shown that this Europe was 'fundamentally hollow, selfishly obsessed with fiscal rectitude and commercial advantage'.[28]

The possibly overreaching ambition of EMU wove itself into this thesis. Monetary union is a high-risk project, based on a very optimistic assessment of how the economies of eleven countries, and the politics of those economies, can be made to coexist and fructify. It imposes huge demands for economic reform on societies that are not necessarily prepared to abandon the social protections which more market-driven, liberalized economic rules will imperil. The usual flexibilities, whether of wages or jobs, that need to exist within a zone that has a single interest rate will take years to develop. The central controller of monetary policy will be not a group of elected politicians, but the European Central Bank, whose susceptibility to political influence is one of the most imponderable elements of the future 'Europe', but whose likely propensity to favour deflation is well attested and is, indeed, enshrined in its formal rubrics. Who will be to blame for rising unemployment? Garton Ash's answer exposes one of the many problems EMU will encounter. 'As elections approach, national politicians will find the temptation to "blame it on EMU" almost irresistible,' he writes. 'If responsible politicians resist the temptation, irresponsible ones will gain votes.'[29]

The case that has driven EMU has not been, essentially, economic. It is a political venture, as its critics have inexhaustibly pointed out. But the economic test is the one it has to begin by passing. Its prime – indispensable – justification will be if it produces more reliable economic growth, behind lower interest rates and the illumination of transparent prices. One of the extraordinary features of the euro, in anticipation, was the depth of the uncertainty, on every side of the argument, whether, and if so when, this decisive economic improvement would begin to happen. Similarly absent was any agreed prediction about the role of the euro vis-à-vis the US dollar. But, irrespective of the politics, the euro's creators were placing themselves behind a massive bet that the economic effects would be positive. And on top of that there certainly will be the politics: the asymmetry between regions, the contest between nations with different interests at any given time, the relationship between belongers and non-belongers, the impact of these great issues on the future of the EU as a sustainable, developing enterprise.

At more mundane levels, forty years on from the operative beginning of the Treaty of Rome, there were many problems too. Enriching the accountability of 'Europe' to the people was a task in which several generations of leaders in every member country had failed. The bureaucracy of Brussels, though numerically smaller than some individual Whitehall departments, continued to defeat the political intention that its power should be reduced – or at least was perceived as doing so. After Maastricht, there was meant to be more 'subsidiarity', used as a synonym for national decision-making. It was taking time to come about. Even Helmut Kohl, bestriding Europe as the prophet of closer integration, attacked Brussels as a place out of which came 'a lot of nonsense'. 'It is full of people who never face an election,' he said at the occasion described above. 'When you go on the hustings, you have to answer questions.' A question he was having to answer, in a country now ready to overcome its reluctance and endorse his case for abolishing the Deutschmark, was how 'Europe' could be said to belong to the people.

On behalf of the British debate, it could be said that these and other questions had at least been raised. The ferocity of the Conservative argument drove an intense public discussion of what 'Europe' meant, what it might or might not do to the British nation, what role Parliament could any longer play. The British parliamentary culture encouraged the adversarial approach, and when the Government was in daily danger of being defeated, maximum coverage in the press and on television was assured. This was true, as in no other country, from the beginning to the end of the Major years. Major's first EU summit as Prime Minister, in Rome in December 1990, was a big moment on the road to EMU, and the occasion for extensive debate on all British TV channels about what it meant. Its outcome got blanket treatment. By contrast, on the final night the main 8 p.m. television news in France had no report from Rome, though on the midnight bulletin the communiqué did scrape in as the tenth item.[30] For many years, the question of Europe held little importance for the domestic politics of the continental member states, a condition that had its merits but also carried its penalties. It showed that Europe had become an everyday reality of life, hardly worth reporting: a norm which all parties accepted. But it also deprived both people and politicians of the obligation to examine serious questions. Jacques Delors, the great high priest, was one of those who most deplored this. 'You have to keep the British in the EC for their democratic tradition if nothing else,' he once said. 'They have the best journalistic debate, the best parliamentary committees, the best quizzing of prime ministers after a summit.'[31]

Insofar as this was true, it came about not as an observance of text-book democracy but as a consequence of passion. Sheer intensity of feeling, boorish and blinkered though its exponents sometimes were, produced an air of combat that invigorated the democratic challenge to executive action which other countries dozily nodded through. Yet it is hard to take Euro-sceptic passion, after all these years of deploying everything it's got, as a persuasive matrix for the Blair Government's approach to the new world.

It remained, for one thing, incorrigibly petty, beneath its grand themes of national survival. Its antagonisms knew no limit. When Beethoven's 'Ode to Joy' was chosen as the theme tune for TV coverage of Euro 96, the soccer competition for the European Championship, Tory MPs attacked the BBC's suspect patriotism, the party chairman said fans would be upset because this was the EU anthem, and the Education Secretary, Gillian Shephard, called for a 'rousing' work by an English composer to be played instead.

British Euro-scepticism was seemingly unembarrassable. It formally complained about a children's TV programme because this 'contained positive statements about EU membership and nothing to indicate there were other viewpoints', a charge to which, in the climate of the times, the BBC director-general, John Birt, felt obliged to assent.[32] A hideous episode in serial paedophilia, occurring in Belgium, was seized on by the *Daily Mail* as something much more than a sex crime. How appropriate, wrote one of the paper's star performers, that the Belgian capital should also be the capital of the EU. Her tortured reasoning produced a linkage typical of the sceptic mind. Thanks to the paedophiles, she asserted, 'the Europhile fantasy that Belgium was a successful precursor of a European super-state, happily uniting all ethnic, religious, language and histori-cal divisions, now lies in tatters'. The Belgian political class, 'and by extension the EU political class', would now (somehow) realize that 'cosy deals, cosy corruptions which exclude the people can no longer be tolerated'.[33]

Not all anti-EU material reached such a depth of xenophobia, but the instinct often lurked. Fear and loathing, far beyond the realm of Bismarckian exegesis, was present in many of the attitudes to Germany. The Mafia-corruption of Italians, and animal torture by the Spanish, were national stereotypes regularly deployed as part of a mentality deeply preoccupied not just with the defence but with the inherent superiority of Britishness.

Britishness, however, is complicated. This was another problem with the Euro-sceptic synthesis. It proposed a rather simple narrative for our island story, as dubious in its descriptive accuracy as it was confused in analysing Britain's contemporary options. It depended on a claim to the purity of Anglo-Saxon lineage which the facts do not sustain. In this sense, Englishness, as an identity to be defended in the last ditch, was as unconvincing as Britishness. The English, like the British, were an ethnic mixture going back into the mists of time, wherein we find the Teutonic tribe of Saxons, and thus an early German connection. The inter-penetration between island and continent, beginning with the British monarchy, obscured exactly what specialness of national character was being threatened by the continental connection.

Besides, many points of reference that had uniquely defined the British were now in jeopardy, for reasons quite apart from the existence of the European Union. Linda Colley, in her book *Britons*, identified them. Protestantism, once the vital cement, no longer had much influ-ence on British culture. Recurrent wars with continental Europe, in which identity had been forged against the enemies without, were a thing of the past. The commercial supremacy of the eighteenth century, and the imperial hegemony of the nineteenth and twentieth, were gone. 'No more can Britons reassure themselves of their distinct and privileged identity,' writes Colley, 'by contrasting themselves with impoverished Europeans (real or imaginary), or by exercising authority over manifestly alien peoples. God has ceased to be British, and Providence no longer smiles.'[34]

This is not to say the British don't have different customs and manners from their closest European neighbours, the French. At every level, from politics and the structure of the state, to sport and culture and the arrangement of leisure and, indeed, the manifestations of chauvinism itself, these are distinctive countries. They each have traditions to protect, and national rules of conduct their people resolutely decline to modify. So does every other country in the EU. This very fact, however, throws doubt on some of the nightmares peddled by anti-EU propagandists in Britain. Six of these countries have been together in this Union for forty years. They have created a single market, subjected themselves to common laws, taken seats in a European Parliament, sunk some of their economic sovereignty in the institutions of Brussels. But who will say that any particle of the Frenchness of France has been sacrificed, or the Italianness of Italy, and so on? If such attenuations have occurred, they derive from the universal impact of American culture and commerce far more visibly than from the impositions of the Union.

Here, then, are two unpersuasive weaknesses in the spirit of anti-Europeanism at large in Britain. Its scepticism has a phobic edge, and its fear for the national identity is, on the available evidence, a hallucination.

It can be argued, however, that even these, though powerfully felt, are not the point. And they may not be. In some ways, Euro-sceptics, especially at the lower end of print journalism, make the worst of the case by constantly harping on about them. The serious case, surely, is not about the survival of cricket versus *boules*, or even about the relative propensity of French and British dock-workers to take direct action against the travelling public, but about national control over big decisions. The European Union renders collective a decision-making process, in some areas, that was once exclusively national: and sometimes without the protection of a veto.

But this is where the anti-EU case begins to wobble, attacking the status quo but unable to mark out a foothold on a different sort of future. Lack of realism has been its problem throughout the history, and this continues. At every stage, those of the British who did not want 'Europe' to develop have predicted it would not: and in every case, except over the European Defence Community in the mid-1950s, they were wrong. False prophecy about EMU, the total improbability of it actually happening, was uttered with mandarin certainty by a variety of Cabinet ministers, right up to 1 May 1997.

Similar unrealism affected the main thrust of the sceptic attack on the way the EU actually functions. The European Court of Justice was a frequent target. During the later Tory years, ministers developed a deep-felt line that the Court should be brought to book. The 'repatriation' of its powers became a familiar theme of the then Home Secretary, Michael Howard. The proposition was discussed as though this was a matter for Britain alone, omitting to address the elementary fact that any body like the European Community or Union needed some mechanism for resolving disputes, and the further fact that one of the main beneficiaries of this arrangement was Britain. Since, from the start, it was one of Britain's distinctive peculiarities to observe Community rules, and the practice of many other members to evade them, the ECJ was not obviously an institution that operated against the British interest. Yet sceptics were enraged by its integrationist tendencies, when interpreting the treaties. So they seemed to think nothing of unilaterally demanding its reform, and overlooking the need to persuade not merely some but all member states of what they had in mind.

A deeper speculative fantasy came to pervade them, as the years went by. This was the belief that the European Union somehow did not constitute 'Europe'. There was a decent impulse behind such a conceit. Some Euro-sceptics, unwilling to be cast as xenophobes, desired to parade their international, and especially their European, credentials. 'I have always been a supporter of moves to greater co-operation in Europe,' wrote William Cash.[35] He spoke for many, aware of the pitfalls of simple nationalism. Tuscan home-ownership and gastronomic tastes were proofs, so they said, of a veritable lack of insularity. More seriously, the collaboration of free nation-states was what they said they had always favoured. The post-Cold War world, as many added, created an opportunity to expand the true dimensions of the European House, which the existing definition circumscribed. At its worst, some said, the single currency could lead to disintegration, if not war. They, the true Europeans, were here to prevent that happening.

The possible narrowness of 'Europe' was a legitimate concern. But the notion that the EU did not constitute 'Europe' was wishful thinking. The Union existed, the product of several decades' history. This history could not be undone. It had created, for better or for worse, the main framework within which the great majority of European nations wished to pursue their own development. EMU itself, problematic though it was, was backed by an enormous collective political will to make it work. For all the EU's frailties, there were far more countries wishing to join it than depart. In fact, with the possible exception of Denmark, none even thought about quitting. For some reason, all were content with the prospect that their economic decision-making would now partly become collective, and confident enough to stake their future on what could be made, for the betterment of things, out of the extraordinary experiment set in train by the Treaty of Rome. The European Union was, quite simply, the largest fact objectively existing across the terrain of the continent and its archipelago.

The discomfort that this engendered was displayed in the Conservative Party's debate. It was a very awkward fact to have to confront. The discussion, both before and after the 1997 election, thrashed about, pitching between horror, as most Tories now felt it, at the prospect of further European integration, and inarticulate timidity, as their leaders showed, before the task of defining an escape-route from this fate.

There were attempts. William Waldegrave, for seven years a Cabinet minister, made an ambitious one. Though a pro-Europe man, Waldegrave always had a certain scrupulousness about what this meant. Long before, as Edward Heath's political secretary, he was so disgusted by the dissembling and evasion he saw in the Yes side's preparations for the referendum that he withdrew his services for the duration of the campaign. But he belonged to the party's European wing, and never qualified as a term-of-art sceptic. While in office, however, he was privately thinking about ways of escape from the continental clutch, and preparing to recognize, he once told me, that claims for British global influence might have to be abandoned. The need for this influence, paramount possession of an old imperial power, was the case most pro-EU politicians made. Only through Europe, they said, could Britain count or, in the Heseltine formulation, 'win'. Waldegrave decided that counting might not matter. He set supreme store by what he thought could still be called the sovereign independent nation – despite the network of international obligations and uncontrollable pressures that binds every modern country within it. His plan, published after he lost his parliamentary seat, was for 'a sort of European Canada'. This way, Britain, having left the EU, could remain prosperous, in the shadow of a more powerful state: free of central economic control, yet benefiting from the proximity of a vast market. 'No more sitting at the top table any more,' Waldegrave ventured. 'No more punching above our weight.' After a decade or two, he blithely admitted, 'we would have as little say over what happened in our end of the continent as do the Canadians in theirs: not *no* say, but not much say'.[36] But we would not be under Brussels's thumb.

This was a very unTory attitude, challenging the party's age-old assumption that Britain must, above all, count. As such, it was far too painful for many Tories to think about. It also overlooked the influence Brussels still would have. Continuing free trade with the EU required submission to EU rules, while surrendering influence over how those rules were made. Norway, the model more commonly put up for emulation, was the proof of it. Though Norway wasn't in the EU, it was subject to all the laws in the EC treaties, through membership of the European Economic Area, the basis for its trading relationship. The entire apparatus of EU rules on immigration, transport, manufacture and trade in goods and services applies in Norway. Norway's courts and companies live under law as interpreted by the European Court in Luxembourg. This is the precondition for Norway's trade with the EU, unmediated, however, by the presence of any Norwegian ministers at the political table.

Still, the Waldegrave version had the merit of intellectual honesty. It went further than some of the earlier logicians, like Norman Lamont, who favoured permanent exclusion from EMU, while being unwilling to describe what would happen next in respect of membership of the EU. Even the most serious and deep-dyed of Euro-sceptics quailed before this task. Michael Portillo, like Waldegrave and Lamont, was also out of the Commons, and therefore, it might be felt, free to explore what had previously been unthinkable. In April 1998, he gave a serious speech, dissecting the dangers of a common European foreign policy, and calling for some 'honesty' in Britain. Honesty, he thought, had been most conspicuously lacking. 'If we adopted an honest policy from now on,' the former minister said, 'we could hope markedly to improve the esteem in which our partners hold us, and so increase our influence.'[37]

We would, however, still be partners. Portillo did not propose a British exit. Yet he said that 'we in Britain have in mind a completely different destination from that cherished by our partners', and attacked the failure of successive politicians to make that clear. Our willingness to criticize, but then acquiesce in, Europe's project 'makes us look ridiculous ... robs us of influence,' he said. It was, further, 'a myth that we can influence the development of Europe by being an enthusiastic participant in its future development' – the scornful opinion Portillo had always had of the Major–Hurd belief in a Europe that was 'moving our way'. Britain needed the 'courage to move against the throng', and should not fear to instruct Europe in the overriding virtue of liberal markets and sovereign nation-states. But, even in Portillo's view, it seemed that Britain should still be there. Some might say he revealed a lack of personal courage, or perhaps an access of private realism, by not being ready categorically to say otherwise.

If official Conservatism represented one pole of the British argument, it stood in deep, but suggestive, confusion. Waldegrave and Portillo defined the long-term problem, but left it unresolved. At the same time, the party leader, William Hague, teetered between rejecting EMU for five years or for ten, concluding with the longer period. Those in the party who thought a certain fluid agnosticism would be more prudent were, for the moment, routed. But, silently, they mattered. A part of Hague's dilemma was that, hardened sceptic though he was, he was also ambitious, and knew somewhere in his head that the business wing of the party had to be retained: something unlikely to be made easier if the euro happened, and did not fail to work, and young Mr Hague were still found sitting on the shore beneath the white cliffs of Dover declining to learn the lesson King Canute had vainly tried to teach.

Pending the divulgence of this moment, most sceptics were limited to making prophecies of doom. They said that EMU would not work. They went through the motions of adding that they hoped they were wrong. For the failure of EMU would certainly be a catastrophe for every economy in Europe. But, as politicians, they had vested much in being right. Their intellectual position left room for no other outcome than the collapse of the project. They needed EMU to fail. 'Its end will come,' Lamont intoned. There was certain to be 'a massive political crisis'. 'The people will kill the euro,' said his last, lapidary piece of wisdom before the die was cast.[38]

The impression one had of Conservatism summoned up the image of another King, famously cavorting on the same outcrop of land. Here, surely, was an existential condition more like that of Lear, railing against unalterable Fate: aware of the tragedy of history that had brought Britain, at the hands not least of many of the Conservatives' own leaders, to a destiny which their inheritors now regretted – but could find no way to change.

As a model for a new government, this was not encouraging. Though politicians like Portillo and Waldegrave asked serious questions, their responses conformed with those of the rest of the sceptic school, and added up to a counsel of despair. The world they defended seemed, in the end, to be nostalgic and narrow: assailed by demons, racked by existential confusion. They were incapable of absorbing the possibility that 'Europe', by immensely strengthening the post-war local economies, might have been the making not the breaking of the nation-state in the modern world.[39] They could see no future good, of that or any other kind, in 'Europe'. All in all, by 1998, many had lost the faculty of rational detachment. Their opinions were strongly felt, but incoherent: sincere, but baffled: certain, yet unsure: speaking from the gut, but incapable of satisfactory engagement with the neurons in the head.

Behind their inchoate power, also, was a challengeable piety. 'The people', who Lamont thought would kill the euro, had played an important part in the sceptic demonology for many years. Indeed, mistrust of what the people would stand for ran through the history of both sides. It explained Macmillan's hesitations, as well as Heath's reluctance to explain the drama of the revolution he was proposing. Claims about what the people wanted had been the cat's-paw of every politician, assuring some, alarming others. Yet British public opinion about Europe was always hard to gauge reliably. It did not take 'Europe' for granted, as opinion did among the people of the original Six. It varied from age to age. If it revealed a consistent pattern, however, it was this one: that the people tended to go wherever they were led by the political class.

As a new political class settled in for a long innings, a significant question bonded the future to the past. It was the question that Tony Blair, if he wanted to lead from anywhere more fruitful than the edge of Europe, needed to address more urgently than any other. What was the real relationship between the voters, the politicians and Europe, and how could this be intensified, for the first time in twenty-five years, as a force for positive rather than negative developments?

The truth about opinion on Britain's Europe connection was that it ranged between fickle and indifferent. For example, there wasn't a single month, between September 1974 and November 1991, when it had higher saliency – mattered more – than prices or law-and-order or education, in the public mind.[40] As the Conservative blood-letting over Maastricht began to dominate the news, this changed a bit, though even then most of the bread-and-butter issues bothered people more. In the week when the political class, in the shape of the Major Government, came closest to collapsing in the wake of a Maastricht-based confidence motion in the Commons, unemployment, the NHS, law-and-order and the state of the economy were regarded as more important than the European issue.[41]

Against this background of relative indifference, the British could not be listed among the most consistently pro-Europe people. When asked specific questions, they have reflected the vagaries of the time. The European Commission maintains a 'Eurobarometer' of public opinion, inquiring into issues of the moment, which is published twice a year. Among the questions regularly asked is: Do you think the European

Community is a Good Thing, a Bad Thing, or Neither? In 1973, the year of entry, 31 per cent of the British said it was a Good Thing; in 1975, referendum year, 50 per cent; in 1981, the depth of the Thatcher winter, 21 per cent; in 1989, the penultimate Thatcher year, 52 per cent; in 1991, Major's first year, 57 per cent; in 1997, his last, 36 per cent.[42] So the picture changes, between pretty wide extremes. There doesn't always seem much rhyme or reason about it.

The same lack of steadiness emerges in answer to the opposite question, though perhaps, in this case, with an explanation that shows a growing awareness of practicalities. Asked, after ten years of membership of the Community, if Britain should withdraw, 42 per cent of people said yes. When the same question was asked after twenty years, the percentage for exit was down to 17.[43] Some might say, given the unrelenting barrage of hostility to Europe which the dominant political class delivered in this time, that it is surprising to find any serious percentage of the British still expressing positive opinions. But in 1991, even the unenthusiastic *Daily Mail* gave prominence to a poll it had commissioned, which found that 43 per cent favoured joining 'a federal Europe', with only 31 per cent against.[44]

As EMU approached, the percentages in favour, already unimpressive in several European countries, weakened. In Britain, announced as a non-candidate for entry, 61 per cent said in April 1998 that they would vote No in a referendum.[45] But the question could be differently asked, and get a different kind of answer. A MORI poll for the European Movement found that 57 per cent believed EMU membership 'could offer advantages, but Britain should only join when the economic conditions are right'. Seven out of ten people were also found to agree that Britain 'should support closer co-operation between the countries of Europe'.[46] Another trend also diminished the succour which sceptics could take from these surveys. It appeared that the pro-integrationists were generally younger and better educated than the antis. A MORI poll in June 1996 showed that pro-Europe feeling was ahead by 35 per cent in social class AB, the upper-income professionals, and by 30 per cent among voters aged between eighteen and thirty-four.[47]

The only safe conclusion to draw from the history of these surveys was that opinion was not settled. The propaganda of the deed was working. When asked, irrespective of their preferences, what they *expected* to happen, most people registered their belief that the European Union would become more important in their lives. This, they thought, was an inevitability. But the propaganda of the word, to explain and justify it, had hardly started. The question remained enmeshed in the damaging perception that it wasn't primarily the business of the people anyway: that Europe was owned, as it always had been, by the political class.

Such, indeed, had been its history. Escaping from this history, and rectifying the disastrous record of this class in this arena, was the best summation of the task Tony Blair had to undertake if he was to begin making good his desire to be a leader in Europe.

The British political class. These are the people this book has been about. And it is true enough that Europe has been their preoccupation, far more than the people's. Out of this grows the common depiction of 'Europe' as a conspiracy against the people, the most potently felt of the righteous arguments made against everything that has happened. The case is falser than its makers contend – yet also truer than those who resist it have ever been prepared to recognize.

The Euro-sceptics, who make this case, themselves belong to the political elite. They are of the class they criticize, and as vulnerable as their opponents to the charge that they speak from and about a private world. To a significant extent, their concerns are about that world rather than the wider world. They hate 'Brussels' not only because they don't like the decisions that are made there, but because the place supersedes *their* place, which is Westminster. The more honest of the sceptics are prepared to admit this. Portillo once conceded as much to me. The prospect of losing power makes occupancy of political position so much less attractive. There is a way of locating this argument on the high ground: by talking about the loss of national and parliamentary sover-eignty, and the damage this does democracy. But the low ground is more important than is often admitted: the place where MPs posture and speechify, where national ministers like to think they are making big decisions: the playground from which the decision to join the European Union removed some favourite toys.

That is one reason why the issue has become most loudly owned by the chattering classes – but not just by one faction among them. The elitist disease, spreading through the hot-house of Westminster, affects all sides. The sceptic chatterers fear, as much as anything, their own diminishment, in the grand political role they probably once imagined it would be their life to play.

As a case against 'Europe', this is badly flawed. Even granting that politicians are entitled to the sensation of power, one cannot say that 'Brussels' has uniquely prevented modern Members of Parliament from enjoying it. All national parliaments, like all national governments, now live under a range of inhibitions. The power of markets, like the influences of intermeshing alliances, have cut them down over a long period. No land is an island, least of all this particular scepter'd isle and blessed plot, which was always global in its range and now depends on the Europe connection to protect what remains of its worldwide reach. But the reduction of Westminster's power and glory belongs to a wider trend, which has not happened by accident. Decentralizing government is supposed to be the acme of modernity, agreed on all sides. While Conservatives didn't agree with the Labour hand-over of regional power to Scotland, they defend subsidiarity as a principle. Under the Blair Government, starting with Scotland, it is happening. 'Europe' is but one of the agents draining the decisive life out of Westminster. Theoretically, Westminster will still be sovereign over Scotland, and retains the power to revoke devolution. In practice, such sovereignty is a chimera. It will not be exercisable. Power has gone, as it has also gone to the European Union. So railing against Europe on that account makes a seductive, but hardly a sufficient, case.

What we have here is more like another illusion – passionately felt, but remote from the facts. Just as it is doubtful whether Euro-scepticism has any special connection with some embittered, unrepresented, forcibly silent majority, so it is misleading to portray the spokesmen for this cause as protecting Britain against an onslaught uniquely threatening to the British national character, or the British sovereign Parliament, or both. What these people more exactly represent is the sceptic elite's collective inability to tolerate the notion that the future of Britain now depends on securing the agreement of politicians who come from other countries.

The British failure to absorb this, however, isn't only, or even mainly, their fault. Another elite has been part of the performance. More clearly than the sceptics', its record measures the scale of the task Blair took on when he vowed to move his leadership from the edge to the centre of Europe.

One of the most instructive talks I had, while probing around this subject, was with the former Dutch Prime Minister Ruud Lubbers. He said something I never forgot. Here he was, a modern leader of one of the founding Six, which was a country usually to be found among the most keenly integrationist, renowned for its European instincts, living proof that the smaller countries feel little need to be defensive about their nationalism, and have electorates who don't give a second thought to membership of the European Union. Yet it was Lubbers's opinion that none of this was immutable. 'If I and others went on television for a few nights, to make a case against the integration of Europe,' he told me, 'I think the Dutch people could easily turn round.'[48]

One way to read that is as proof that 'Europe' is indeed an elitist project. In the beginning, like all original ideas in democratic politics, it certainly was. Lubbers was saying that this, in a way, continues. 'It is a very difficult idea,' he said. 'You have to keep nurturing it, supporting it.' In other words, it remains an experiment. What began as a structure to rule out war continued, he implied, to be vulnerable to the human propensity for conflict. Nationalism remained a force, perhaps the strongest force among people who were given any encouragement to express it. The duty of the elite was to exercise their skill and wisdom against this force, as well as creating the political context that underpinned the huge benefits Europe stood to gain, in the global context, from economic integration. While the EU had popular support – was part of the unquestioned order of things – this was still always contingent on leadership. If the elite gave up, the experiment would fail.

That certainly describes a project which can be defined, or stigmatized, as the work of the political class. Such were the people – Monnet, Schuman, Spaak, Beyen – who thought it up: and equally the people – Pompidou, Schmidt, Mitterrand, Delors, Kohl – who applied the further impulses that made it live. The European Community was a heroic endeavour, undertaken against great odds, which built a record of assisting peace and prosperity among European nations that has not been surpassed. The political elite of the continent, though open to criticism for many false steps that had to be corrected, created an entity that justified their claim to leadership.

The British pro-Europe elite has more to answer for. Leave aside its collective lateness to get the point. Forget the recurrent theme of individual hesitation and serial apostasy. Consider only the scale of what it did, beside the puny skills it brought to the task of proclaiming what this meant.

One signal weakness was misrepresentation. It was as if the makers did not dare to tell the truth. Though Edward Heath showed the tenacity to do what had to be done, he could not liberate himself from the nation-state mythology to which his country was in thrall. Beginning with him, the idea that one of the virtues of the EEC lay in its dilution of national sovereignty could seldom be openly described. During the 1975 referendum, Heath spoke, quite reasonably, not only of 'extending

Britain's influence in the world', but also of the 'controlling interest' which membership of the Community would confer on this one country.[49] A version of this triumphalist philosophy always remained in currency. While no British leader could seriously talk for much longer about 'control', the sense of 'winning' a constant series of zero-sum games against partners who were really opponents continued to be the narrative-line of the story governments told. I have found no trace of any Prime Minister, from Heath to Blair, returning from an EU summit to report that he had supported, or else opposed, a decision solely because such a course was best for the future of 'Europe'.

Starting from such an attitude, the political class failed to convey, perhaps even to experience, a sense of idealism about the project. It has been an ineffective missionary for the change it brought about in 1973. This was true almost from the start. David Watt, reporting on the referendum campaign, detected little positive enthusiasm on either side. He found both the pros and the antis were essentially negative, worrying about the price of food or the effect on jobs. 'Idealism of any kind does not enter into the equation,' Watt wrote, 'and there is neither zest nor vision in most of what is being said on platforms up and down the country.'[50] True in 1975, this became more apparent in the decades following, when the sceptical tone of successive prime ministers helped to dampen such ardour as existed among the lower ranks.

In place of zeal came its natural opposite, complacency. The most corrupted trait I kept encountering was the sense, so prevalent among the Euro-elite, that having won the decision, they had won the argument. Many exhibited the unmistakable opinion not only that the battle was over but that the other side, however loud it shouted, had simply lost and should now shut up. The noisier the contest became during the early 1990s, the heavier the silent gloating that accompanied it, from the class that knew it commanded every operational forum from the ante-chambers of Whitehall to the board-rooms of big business, from Brussels committee-rooms where a thousand lobbyists thronged, to the outposts of the Commission whence arrived the subsidies that were, for many people up and down the land, the way they got to know most about the European Union.

'Europe' was extraordinarily bad at preaching its message. So were the politicians, designated, *ex officio*, to be its intermediaries. They talked, for the most part, to each other. Dank seminars for the enlightenment of the converted took precedence over effective proselytizing of unbeliev-ers. Out of the back-streets of Westminster, from the offices of the

European Commission or the European Movement, came messages that
reflected chronic uncertainty about how to deal with the British condition. In sum they rendered the pro-Europe side as cultish a faction as
the sceptics: a private group, with the establishment behind it, baffled
into near-obscurity by the belligerence of those whose weapon of choice
was the Union Jack. So deep-seated was the British tradition of
aggression towards Brussels that it cowed into calculating reticence even
those whose entire purpose was to advance the opposite case.

In this climate, there were some severe derelictions. Consider one of
them. A consistent weakness of the EU, as perceived by sympathizers as
well as sceptics in the British Parliament, was the inadequate scrutiny of
its decisions by democratic assemblies. This became a constant complaint, and it was justified. Westminster, in keeping with its claims to be
a superior parliament to any other in the Community, made more effort
than many, but this was still inconsequential. Commons sub-committees
toiled over Brussels directives, but had meagre success in persuading
Parliament as a whole to take their reporting seriously and still less in
influencing the words that became Community law. This was a democratic affront, yet nobody did much about it. Nobody dared suggest that,
if Parliament meant what it said about dictatorship from Brussels, it
might itself sit a few more weeks of the year to ensure that the ministers
who act as legislators in the Council are properly accountable to it: an
example, perhaps, to less developed assemblies. That would not have
been convenient to the executive. It could have been proposed by serious
pro-Europeans, or, for that matter, by the Thatcher camp. But in those
years ministers of neither stripe felt moved to do this.

The losers from this negligence were the citizens of Britain and, dare
one say it, Europe. The underinvigilated network of national bureaucra-
cies, together with the Commission, continued on its way. But the
political losers in Britain were the Euro-elite. For a quarter-century, they
were prime accomplices in the failure of 'Europe' to infuse itself into the
democratic culture, preferring that it should be retained in the executive
zone of private deal-making and unaccountable, invisible decisions, for
fear of being exposed to the incessant hostilities of the other side.

As a result, the practical benefits of the Europe connection were, for
most of this period, minimized. There were many areas where these
existed – but often in the teeth of British politicians' resistance rather
than with their creative support. The huge inward investment by car
and electronics industries into Britain in the 1980s was a direct result
of the European Union. Britain became the main access point for Asian

businesses into the continental market. But the explanation for this was a matter of discomfort to the governing party. At the 1996 Conservative Party conference, the Scottish Secretary, Michael Forsyth, and the Welsh Secretary, William Hague, each recited his magnificent record in steering investment into his territory. But in neither case could they acknowledge, by even a word, the indispensability of Europe to this performance. The Union, though central to the lives of these ministers, was literally unmentionable, except perhaps as an expletive.

The omission went wider. European oversight was heavily responsible, for example, for cleaner water and beaches, and other bits of environmental progress. Yet most British ministers built a record of resisting rather than advancing it. It took its place in the expletive-driven world that passed for the British European debate, where the language of antagonism singularly failed to elicit a matching vocabulary of support. Likewise, over a far longer period, human rights in Britain were fortified by the European Convention on Human Rights, administered by a court and commission in Strasbourg. The Convention was actually a British creation of the post-war years, long predating the Treaty of Rome. But by the end of the Conservative years the very fact that it occasionally produced judgments overturning British practice was swept up into the tide of ministerial hostility to all things European, which the other wing of the political elite made only feeble efforts to challenge.

This was Blair's inheritance, as the first British Prime Minister elected on a ticket that said he was entirely comfortable to be a European. The aura of Euro-scepticism was still palpable, especially in the press. The sense of Britain being, among other things, a European country was not yet coursing strongly through the land. In many influential minds, the belief that the European Union would, for the indefinite future, be grappling with enormous problems still half effaced the belief that Britain must be centrally involved in addressing them. Escapism, combined with vilification, continued to lure a segment of the political class, pulling some of the intellectual and journalistic class behind them.

Blair started from a quite different position. He could look forward with some confidence to a decade of power, in which these national attitudes might be fundamentally altered. It would be a many-faceted task, turning round the accumulations of fifty years which successive leaders had always shrunk from addressing squarely. But, in the likely process, two broad elements were perhaps discernible.

The first was the work of persuasion. A government united in a

sense of Euro-realism would set about demystifying – better, disinflam-
ing – the question. The discourse would become sober, rather than
perpetually contentious. In place of a government that rejoiced in the
failures of 'Europe', and returned from every summit defiantly proclaiming that it had again been defeated by the mad continental integrationists, a new leadership began telling the country something it was actually
better pleased to hear. In due course, one might expect some explicit
statements that the EU brought advantages to Britain which did not
deserve the neurotic suspicion the people had long been taught to apply
to everything coming out of Brussels. This shift was unlikely to encompass visionary paeans of adulation for the great European Ideal – but
then, those had stopped being heard, anywhere in Europe, years ago.
The Blair approach would need, first, to carry him past the EMU
referendum which it was plainly his intention to conduct, if possible,
before the notes ands coins of euro-land came into circulation on 1
January 2002. But, even before that, the teaching process was gradually
beginning. It was already plausible to believe that, deprived at last of a
government it thought it could overturn, the Euro-sceptic minority was
being set back.

   Whether this would soon create a sense of European community in
Britain was another matter. Truly European consciousness is an elusive
faculty on the off-shore island, and dependent on a popular involvement
that certainly hasn't been available by means of politics, though travel
and culture and the general first-hand experience of non-political Europe
have surely changed the national outlook: changed it, perhaps, closer to
the attitude Ernest Bevin articulated, but did nothing to bring about,
when he claimed that the object of his foreign policy was a world in
which he could 'go down to Victoria Station here, take a ticket, and go
where the hell I like without anybody pulling me up with a passport'.[51]

   That was in 1945. Closing on 2000, the millennial leader spoke at
least for a frontier-free mentality, if not the abolition of passports. He
brought an end to defiance, as the leitmotif of Britain's self-image. A
master of public rhetoric, especially on the electronic media, Tony Blair
was unlikely to miss his opportunity to reposition the national mind,
and thereby permit a more angst-free contribution by Britain to the
great questions concerning the future of Europe: the enlargement of the
Union, its economic management, its political institutions: all in all, the
diversity it was prepared to tolerate within its integration, without
speeding its own dissolution.

   Secondly, however, there were facts. The European Union existed. It had survived for many decades. Its leaders were determined that this should continue. It would be the context, the given reality, round which their other problems would revolve. It would set the terms on which these problems would have to be addressed. There wasn't any other way, they thought, to protect and advance their nation-states. That, as it turned out, was the way for Britain too.

This was not a new truth. The history suggested strongly that no alternative had existed for fifty years. But there was now a Prime Minister who did not fight it, and, untroubled by the demons of the past, prepared to align the island with its natural hinterland beyond.

Notes

1. WINSTON CHURCHILL: RULE BRITANNIA

1 Michael Charlton, *The Price of Victory* (BBC Publications, 1983), 12.
2 William Beveridge, *Pillars of Society* (1943), cited in Kenneth O. Morgan, *The People's Peace: British History, 1945–1989* (Oxford University Press, 1990), 3.
3 Herbert Read, *The English Vision* (1933), cited in David Gervais, *Literary Englands* (Cambridge University Press, 1993), 134.
4 In *Return to Bestwood*, cited in Gervais, *op. cit.*, 99.
5 The phrase is stolen from Freeman Dyson, *Weapons and Hope* (Harper & Row, 1984), 129.
6 George Orwell, *Homage to Catalonia* (1938).
7 George Orwell, *The Lion and the Unicorn* (1941).
8 George Orwell, *The English People* (1944).
9 *Saturday Evening Post*, February 1930.
10 John Colville, *The Fringes of Power: Downing Street Diaries, 1939–1955* (Hodder & Stoughton, 1985), 13 December 1940.
11 'Morning Thoughts': Notes on post-war security by the Prime Minister, 1 February 1943, appears as Appendix V in Michael Howard, *Grand Strategy*, iv (London, 1972), 637–9.
12 BBC Home Service broadcast, 23 March 1943.
13 See W. F. Kimball (ed.), *Churchill and Roosevelt: the complete correspondence* (Princeton University Press, 1984), ii, 222.
14 *Saturday Evening Post*, February 1930.
15 *Federal Union News*, 23 December 1939, cited in John Pinder, 'British Federalists 1940–47: from movement to stasis', a paper given to a conference of historians, Brussels, May 1993.
16 Altiero Spinelli, *Come ho tentato di diventare saggio: Io, Ulisse* (Bologna, 1984), 308.
17 Martin Gilbert, *Never Despair* (Minerva, 1988), 267.
18 See below, pp. 224ff.
19 Interview, Lord Hailsham, 12 January 1993.
20 Harold Macmillan, *Tides of Fortune, 1945–1955* (Macmillan, 1969), 175.
21 *Ibid.*, 217.
22 CAB 129/1 CP (45) 112.

23 Margaret Gowing, *Independence and Deterrence: Britain and atomic energy, 1945–52,* vol. i (Macmillan, 1974), 230.

24 *The Times,* 25 May 1945.

25 James Morris, *Farewell to Trumpets* (Penguin, 1979), 473.

26 Eisenhower Library, Ann Whitman Files, State Department dinner 12 April 1954.

2. ERNEST BEVIN: GREAT BRIT

1 Quoted by Roy Jenkins, *Nine Men of Power* (1974), 75.

2 *Ibid.*

3 C. R. Attlee, *Labour's Peace Aims* (Labour Party, 1939), 13.

4 29 November 1945, quoted in Alan Bullock, *Ernest Bevin, Foreign Secretary* (Heinemann, 1983), 198.

5 FO 800/493, 5 May 1947, cited in Bullock, *ibid.*, 396.

6 Frank Roberts, in Michael Charlton, *The Price of Victory* (BBC Publications, 1983), 48.

7 Bullock, *op. cit.*, 857.

8 Cited in Charlton, *op. cit.*, 54.

9 Anthony Sampson, *Anatomy of Britain* (Hodder & Stoughton, 1962), 311.

10 FO 371/40741.

11 Anthony Adamthwaite, 'Britain and the World, 1945–49: the view from the Foreign Office', *International Affairs* (Spring, 1985).

12 Roger Bullen and M. E. Pelly (eds), *Documents on British Policy Overseas,* series ii, vol. i: *The Schuman Plan, the Council of Europe and Western Europe Integration, 1950–1952* (HMSO, 1986), No. 102.

13 Cited in Adamthwaite, *op. cit.*

14 FO 371/66546.

15 House of Commons, *Hansard,* 5 May 1948.

16 Charlton, *op. cit.*, 55.

17 FO 371/62732.

18 Charlton, *op cit.*, 59.

19 *Ibid.*, 74.

20 *Ibid.*, 72–3.

21 *Ibid.*, 70.

22 *Ibid.*, 71.

23 Richard Mayne and John Pinder, *Federal Union: the pioneers. A history of federal union* (Macmillan, 1990).

24 Walter Lippgens and Wilfried Loth (eds), *Documents on the History of European Integration,* vol. iii: *The Struggle for European Union by Political Parties and Pressure Groups in Western European Countries, 1945–1950* (de Gruyter, 1988), 698.

25 House of Commons, *Hansard*, 13 November 1950.

26 Ben Pimlott, *Hugh Dalton* (Jonathan Cape, 1985), 568. The friend who reported it was Nicholas Davenport.

27 To Christopher Mayhew, his junior minister: Charlton, *op. cit.*, 77.

28 *Daily Telegraph*, 9 September 1949.

29 Cited in Anthony Nutting, *Europe Will Not Wait* (Hollis & Carter, 1960), 25.

30 The initial circumstances of the Schuman Plan are especially illuminated in 1950 PRO documents: CE 2141, 2219, 2328, 2330, 2339, CAB 130/60, GEN 322/3; CAB 134/293.

31 Kenneth Younger, Diary, 14 May 1950, cited in Peter Hennessy, *Never Again: Britain, 1945–1951* (Jonathan Cape, 1992), 400.

32 Interview, Georges Berthoin, 1 July 1994.

33 Conservative Party conference, October 1993.

34 Karl-Gunther von Hase, spokesman, German Foreign Office, 1958–61, quoted in Charlton, *op. cit.*, 209.

35 Lord Gladwyn, *The Memoirs of Lord Gladwyn* (Weidenfeld & Nicolson, 1972), 176.

36 Younger, *op. cit.*, 14 May 1950.

37 Quoted in Charlton, *op. cit.*, 121.

38 *Ibid.*, 95.

39 Dean Acheson, *Present at the Creation* (Hamish Hamilton, 1969), 385.

40 Dean Acheson, *Sketches from Life of Men I Have Known* (Hamish Hamilton, 1961), 44.

41 Interview, Douglas Allen (Lord Croham), 27 May 1993.

42 Interview, Roger Makins (Lord Sherfield), 6 May 1993.

43 For the later passages of decision-making on the Schuman Plan, see 1950 PRO documents: CE 2342, 2376, 2468, 2470, 2526, 2568, 2569, 2615, 2659, 2772, 2773, CAB 129/40, CAB 134/293, CAB 128/17.

44 Bernard Donoughue and G. W. Jones, *Herbert Morrison: portrait of a politician* (Weidenfeld & Nicholson, 1973), 981.

45 House of Commons, *Hansard*, 26 June 1950.

46 Most eloquently by Edmund Dell in *The Schuman Plan and the British Abdication of Leadership In Europe* (Clarendon Press, 1995), a masterly history of the episode.

47 House of Commons, *Hansard*, 27 June 1950.

3. RUSSELL BRETHERTON: THE SACRIFICIAL AGENT

1 Anthony Nutting in Michael Charlton, *The Price of Victory* (BBC Publications, 1983), 169.

2 Robert Carr in *ibid.*, 157.

3 According to Roger Makins in *ibid.*, 151.
4 For detailed survey of the Fyfe–Eden conflict, see H. J. Yasamee, *Anthony Eden and Europe, November 1951* (Foreigh Office Historical Branch, Occasional Paper, 1987).
5 Paul-Henri Spaak, *The Continuing Battle* (Weidenfeld & Nicolson, 1971), 227.
6 FO 371/116040.
7 For Foreign Office reactions to Messina, see PRO documents FO 371/116038–40.
8 FO 371/116038.
9 Charlton, *op. cit.*, 194.
10 T 230/394, 18 June 1955, cited in Simon Burgess and Geoffrey Edwards, 'The Six Plus One: British policy-making and the question of European integration, 1955', *International Affairs* (Summer, 1988).
11 Charlton, *op. cit.*, 190.
12 For Whitehall debates over British response to Messina, see 1955 PRO documents: CAB 134/1026, CAB 129/76, CAB 128/29, T 230/394, FO 371/116042.
13 FO 371/116042.
14 CAB 128/29, 30 June 1955.
15 Charlton, *op. cit.*, 169.
16 Interview, Sir Roy Denman, 1 February 1994.
17 Charlton, *op. cit.*, 178.
18 Robert Rothschild, head of Spaak's Cabinet, in *ibid.*, 180.
19 CAB 134/1044, 1955.
20 CAB 134/1026, 1955.
21 Charlton, *op. cit.*, 184.
22 For Whitehall analysis and tactics re the Spaak committee, see 1955 PRO files: CAB 134/1044, CAB 134/889, T 232/433, T 234/181, FO 371/116045–8, FO 371/116054–5.
23 Sir Roy Denman (interview, 1 February 1994) gave me this account, which he had heard from a member of the French delegation, J.-F. Deniau.
24 Charlton, *op. cit.*, 188.
25 T 234/181, 1955.
26 Late November exchanges in FO 371/116056.
27 Interview, Lord Armstrong of Ilminster, 3 December 1993.
28 Charlton, *op. cit.*, 194.
29 BT 11/5402, 1955.
30 *Ibid.*

4. HAROLD MACMILLAN: AGONIZING FOR BRITAIN

1 There was a second treaty, signed on the same day, which set up the European Atomic Energy Authority, known as Euratom.
2 Interview, Sir Donald Maitland, 4 February 1993.
3 Interview, Sir Michael Palliser, 4 July 1993.
4 Lord Gladwyn, *The Memoirs of Lord Gladwyn* (Weidenfeld & Nicholson, 1972), 2.
5 Cited by Alan S. Milward, *The European Rescue of the Nation State* (Routledge, 1992), 128. Several statistics in this passage come from Milward's ground-breaking work.
6 Peter Oppenheimer, in Robert Skidelsky and Vernon Bogdanor (eds), *The Age of Affluence* (Macmillan, 1970), 146.
7 Interview, Roger Makins (Lord Sherfield), 6 May 1993.
8 Interview, Douglas Allen (Lord Croham), 27 May 1993.
9 Interview, Sir Roy Denman, 1 February 1994.
10 CAB 134/889 (1955).
11 Interview, Emile Noël, 28 October 1993.
12 *Ibid.*
13 Miriam Camps, *Britain and the European Community, 1955–63* (Oxford University Press, 1964), 77.
14 FO 371/124421, cited, along with several other documents in this passage, in James Ellison, *Harold Macmillan's Fear of 'Little Europe'* (Leicester University Press, 1995).
15 Keith Kyle, *Suez* (Weidenfeld & Nicolson, 1992), 556.
16 *Ibid.*, 464–5.
17 Roger Bullen and M. E. Pelly (eds), *Documents on British Policy Overseas*, series ii, vol. i: *The Schuman Plan, the Council of Europe and Western European Integration, 1950–1952* (HMSO, 1986), Nos 406, 424, 437.
18 Alistair Horne, *Macmillan, vol. i: 1891–1956* (Macmillan, 1988), 351.
19 John Colville, *The Fringes of Power: Downing Street diaries, 1939–1955.* (Hodder & Stoughton, 1985), 30 May 1952.
20 Sir Nicholas Henderson, speaking on *The Last Europeans*, Channel Four TV, 26 November 1996.
21 Cited in Ellison, *op. cit.*
22 PREM 11/2133, 18 April 1957.
23 PREM 11/2133, 15 July 1957, Macmillan to Thorneycroft.
24 Charles de Gaulle, *Memoirs of Hope* (Weidenfeld & Nicholson, 1971), 188.
25 PREM 11/2679, meeting at Chequers, 29 November 1959, cited in Milward, *op. cit.*, 432.
26 FO 371/150282.

27 CAB 130/173, CAB 134/1820, 1955.

28 CAB 129/102, 1955.

29 Michael Charlton, *The Price of Victory* (BBC Publications, 1983), 258.

30 FO 371/150369, 1955.

31 PREM 11/3325, 1961.

32 According to Georges Berthoin, chief representative of the ECSC in London at the time. (Interview 1 July 1994).

33 Camps, *op. cit.*, ch. 10.

34 *Ibid.*, 371.

35 FO 371/171449.

36 John Newhouse, *De Gaulle and the Anglo-Saxons* (André Deutsch, 1970), 211. Newhouse's brilliant book offers a very full account of the Rambouillet meeting, which appears to derive from close inspection of the official minute taken by the British.

37 See Camps, *op. cit.*; Charlton, *op. cit.*; Richard Lamb, *The Macmillan Years, 1957–1963* (John Murray, 1995); Alistair Horne, *Macmillan, vol. ii: 1957–1986* (Macmillan, 1989); and, interstitially, every political memoir and history of the Macmillan period. See also Nora Beloff, *The General Says No* (Penguin, 1963); Robert J. Lieber, *British Politics and European Unity* (Berkeley, 1970); J. W. Young, *Britain and European Unity, 1945–1992* (Macmillan, 1993); George Wilkes (ed.), *Britain's Failure to Enter the European Community, 1961–63* (Frank Cass, 1997). A monograph I found useful here: N. Piers Ludlow, 'A Mismanaged Application: Britain and EEC membership 1961–63' (paper presented to the European Liaison Committee of Historians, March 1996).

38 Interview, Sir Edward Heath, 8 February 1994.

39 Several figures in this passage are taken from a useful study: David Dutton, 'Anticipating Maastricht: the Conservative Party and Britain's first application to join the European Community', *Contemporary Record* (Winter 1993).

40 Rt Hon. Harold Macmillan MP, *Britain, the Commonwealth and Europe* (Conservative Political Centre, September 1962).

41 *Ibid.*, 6–7.

42 Interview, Sir Michael Butler, 30 January 1993.

43 Sir Edward Heath, speaking on *The Last Europeans*, 26 November 1995.

44 Interview, Maurice Couve de Murville, 30 June 1994.

45 FO 800/889, 1963.

5. HUGH GAITSKELL: PROGRESSIVELY BACKWARDS

1 R. H. S. Crossman, 'British Labour Looks at Europe', *Foreign Affairs* (July 1963).

2 Philip Williams, *Hugh Gaitskell* (Jonathan Cape, 1979), 702–49 contains many of the quotations that follow in this passage.

3 Roy Jenkins, *A Life at the Centre* (Macmillan, 1991), 145; Douglas Jay, *Change and Fortune* (Hutchinson, 1980), 282.

4 House of Commons, *Hansard*, 2 August 1961.

5 FO 371/150369.

6 Dennis Thompson, *The Rome Treaty and the Law* (*Crossbow* supplement, July–September 1962).

7 House of Commons, *Hansard*, 3 August 1961.

8 House of Commons, *Hansard*, 6 June 1962: which, along with the August 1961 debate, is the source of all the quotations in this passage.

9 Letter to Arthur Calwell, Australian Labour leader, August 1962, cited in Williams, *op. cit.*, 721.

10 The most easily available source for these is Philip Williams's biography, *op. cit.*, which uses them copiously.

11 Jay, *op. cit.*, 286.

12 Central Statistical Office, *Annual Abstract of Statistics 1965*.

13 See, notably, Jay's contribution to Brian Brivati and Harriet Jones (eds), *From Reconstruction to Integration: Britain and Europe since 1945* (Leicester University Press, 1993).

14 Harold Macmillan, House of Commons, *Hansard*, 2 August 1961.

15 Edward Heath, House of Commons, *Hansard*, 3 August 1961.

16 Kenneth Younger, 'Public Opinion and Foreign Policy', *International Affairs* (January 1964).

17 See Chapter 9.

18 See Douglas Brinkley, *Dean Acheson: the Cold War Years, 1953–71* (Yale University Press, 1992), 176–82, for the text of Acheson's speech and a helpful discussion of it.

19 Tony Benn, *Out of the Wilderness: diaries 1963–67* (Hutchinson, 1987), 20 February 1963.

6. JOHN ROBINSON: A CONSPIRACY OF LIKE-MINDED MEN

1 FO 371/171420, 8 February 1963, Robinson to Keeble.

2 Sir Con O'Neill, 'Report on the Negotiations for Entry into the European Community, June 1970–July 1972' (Foreign Office, unpublished, 1972).

3 Interview, Sir Roy Denman, 1 February 1994.

4 Interview, Sir David Hannay, 26 August 1994.

5 See above, p. 91.

6 Sir Michael Butler, *Europe: more than a continent* (William Heinemann, 1986), 4.

7 Interview, Sir Michael Palliser, 7 May 1993.

8 Leader, *The Times*, 15 May 1947.

9 Michael Charlton, *The Price of Victory* (BBC Publications, 1983), 105.

10 Interview, John Robinson, 20 August 1993.

11 See above, p. 41.

12 R.H.S. Crossman, 'British Labour Looks at Europe', *Foreign Affairs* (April 1963).

13 Noticed by Donald Sassoon, *One Hundred Years of Socialism* (I. B. Tauris, 1996), 237.

14 FO 371/182299.

15 FO 371/182377.

16 FO 371/188327.

17 FO 371/188328.

18 Cecil King, *The Cecil King Diary, 1965–70* (Jonathan Cape, 1972), 20 January 1966.

19 Reported by George Thomson, the minister sent to convey the news. See Philip Ziegler, *Wilson: the authorised life* (Weidenfeld & Nicolson, 1993), 331.

20 Douglas Jay, *Change and Fortune* (Hutchinson, 1980), 363.

21 Jay identifies these accurately: Denis Healey, Fred Peart, Herbert Bowden, Dick Marsh, William Ross, Barbara Castle, Anthony Greenwood and himself, with Jim Callaghan and Richard Crossman 'wobbling'.

22 Cited in Ziegler, *op. cit.*, 334.

23 FO 371/188346.

24 FO 371/188347.

25 Richard Crossman, *The Diaries of a Cabinet Minister*, ed. Janet Morgan, vol. ii (Hamish Hamilton and Jonathan Cape, 1976), 22 October 1966.

26 Harold Wilson, *The Labour Government, 1964–70: a personal record* (Weidenfeld & Nicolson, 1971), 327–44.

27 Lord Jenkins of Hillhead, speaking on *The Last Europeans*, Channel Four TV, 26 November 1995.

28 Jean-Jacques Servan-Schreiber, *Le Défi américain* (Paris: Denoel, 1967).

29 Jay, *op. cit.*, 363.

30 Ben Pimlott, *Harold Wilson* (HarperCollins, 1992), 439.

31 Interview, Sir Crispin Tickell, 19 January 1993.

32 Wilson, *op. cit.*, 341.

33 Ziegler, *op. cit.*, 335.

34 Cited in Elizabeth Barker, *Britain in a Divided Europe, 1945–70* (Weidenfeld & Nicolson, 1971).

35 Crossman, *Diaries*, vol. ii, 21 April 1967.

36 Ziegler, *op. cit.*, 335.

37 This episode, on 26 October 1967, became known as the Chalfont Affair,

and is well described by John Dickie, *Inside the Foreign Office* (Chapmans, 1992), 171–5.

38 George Thomson, 'The Labour Committee for Europe: a witness seminar', *Contemporary Record* (Autumn 1993), 393.

39 Sir Michael Palliser, cited in Ziegler, *op. cit.*, 332.

40 FO 371/188348.

41 George Brown, *In My Way* (Victor Gollancz, 1971), 131.

42 Apart from interviews with officials cited in the text, the published sources relied on here for the content of what de Gaulle said to Soames are: Jean Lacouture, *De Gaulle: the ruler, 1945–1970* (Harvill, 1991), 475–7, Dickie, *op. cit.*, 166–71, Wilson, *op. cit.*, 610–12.

43 Bernard Ledwidge, *De Gaulle* (Weidenfeld & Nicholson, 1982), 392–7. Ledwidge was the minister in the Paris embassy at the time.

44 Interview, Sir David Hannay, 24 August 1994.

45 King, *op. cit.*, 21 April 1969.

46 Interview, Sir Michael Palliser, 7 May 1993.

47 Lacouture, *op. cit.*, 477.

48 Jay, *op. cit.*, 433.

49 See above, p. 175.

50 Ziegler, *op. cit.*, 337.

51 George Thomson, 'The Labour Committee for Europe', 394.

7. EDWARD HEATH: THE TRIUMPH OF THE WILL

1 John Campbell, *Edward Heath* (Jonathan Cape, 1993), 5.

2 Edward Heath, *Travels* (Sidgwick & Jackson, 1977), 10.

3 *Ibid.*, 40.

4 *Ibid.*, 31.

5 *Ibid.*, 115.

6 Ben Pimlott, *Harold Wilson* (HarperCollins, 1992), 69–70.

7 Campbell, *op. cit.*, 65.

8 According to Sir Michael Butler, who was in the room (interview, 30 January 1993).

9 Much of it helpfully summarized, as well as added to, in George Wilkes (ed.), *Britain's Failure to Enter the European Community, 1961–63* (Frank Cass, 1997). See especially ch. 12.

10 Edward Heath, *Old World, New Horizons*, Godkin Lectures, delivered in March 1967 (Oxford University Press, 1970).

11 Henry Kissinger, *Years of Upheaval* (Weidenfeld & Nicolson, 1982), 141.

12 See House of Commons, *Hansard*, 16 November 1966.

13 Heath, *Old World*, 30.

14 Sir Con O'Neill, 'Report on the Negotiations for Entry into the European

Community' June 1970–July 1972' (Foreign Office, unpublished, 1972), ch. 34, para. 9.

15 Interview, John Robinson, 20 August 1993.

16 Interview, Lord Hunt of Tanworth, 13 January 1993.

17 Interview, Lord Croham, 27 May 1993.

18 O'Neill, *op. cit.*, ch. 36, para. 1.

19 *Ibid.*

20 *Ibid.*, ch. 4, para. 11.

21 *Ibid.*, para. 8.

22 *Ibid.*, para. 16.

23 *Ibid.*, ch. 7, para. 16.

24 See *ibid.*, annex 1, section B.

25 *Ibid.*, ch. 6, para. 4.

26 *Ibid.*, ch. 7, para. 10.

27 *Ibid.*, para. 11.

28 *Ibid.*, ch. 15, paras 15, 22.

29 *Ibid.*, ch. 14, paras 1, 4.

30 *Ibid.*, ch. 32, para. 16.

31 *Ibid.*, ch. 35, para. 3.

32 *Ibid.*, para. 20.

33 *Ibid.*, ch. 25, para. 2. This and the next two chapters discuss the fisheries question.

34 *Ibid.*, ch. 36, para. 4.

35 Interview, Maurice Couve de Murville, 30 June 1994.

36 Interview, Jean-René Bernard, 1 July 1994.

37 Interview, Emile van Lennep, 18 June 1993.

38 Roy Denman, *Missed Chances* (Cassell, 1996), 232.

39 Interview, Sir Michael Palliser, 9 July 1993.

40 Interview, Sir Edward Heath, 21 May 1994.

41 O'Neill, *op. cit.*, ch. 33, para. 15; ch. 32, para. 5.

42 Douglas Hurd, *An End to Promises* (Collins, 1979), 62.

43 O'Neill, *op. cit.*, ch. 7, para. 19.

44 Interview, Sir Edward Heath, 21 May 1994.

45 Heath, *Travels*, 5.

46 O'Neill, *op. cit.*, ch. 33, para. 17.

47 House of Commons, *Hansard*, 20 January 1971.

48 House of Lords, *Hansard*, 27 July 1971.

49 Speech to the British Chamber of Commerce, Paris, 6 May 1970.

50 Cited by Robert Shepherd, *Enoch Powell* (Hutchinson, 1996), 248. Several of the quotations that follow were first collected in Shepherd's valuable book.

51 See Nicholas Ridley MP, *Towards a Federal Europe* (European Forum, 1969), published text of a speech delivered at a European federalist conference.

52 Andrew Roth, *Enoch Powell* (Macdonald, 1970), 372.

53 *One Europe* (One Nation Group, 1965).

54 G. R. Urban, letter, *Sunday Telegraph*, 29 December 1991.

55 Shepherd, *op. cit.*, 248. The interview was conducted for a Channel Four TV programme, *What Has Become of Us*, screened November–December 1994.

56 See Chapter 9.

57 *The United Kingdom and the European Communities* (HMSO, July 1971), Cmnd 4715.

58 European Movement meeting, London, 7 May 1994.

59 Which they duly did, though only with categoric finality in 1989, in *R* v. *Secretary of State for Transport, ex parte Factortame Ltd*, 1990 ECR 1–2433.

60 Private information.

61 Franco-British Lecture, delivered at the Foreign Office, 15 October 1992.

62 Sir Edward Heath, interview for *The Last Europeans*, Channel Four TV, July 1995.

63 Case 26/62, *Van Gend en Loos* v. *Nederlandse Tariefcommissie* (1963) ECR 1.

64 House of Lords, *Hansard*, 2 August 1962.

65 Notably: 'Sovereignty and Interdependence: Britain's place in the world', the London School of Economics Alumni Lecture, 8 June 1990, published in *International Affairs* (October, 1990); and 'Euro-Justice: Yes or No?', a paper delivered at the Bar Conference, London, 30 September 1995, published in *European Law Review* (June 1996).

66 House of Commons, *Hansard*, 13 June 1972.

67 Private information.

68 *Bulmer* v. *Bollinger* [1974] 3 Weekly Law Reports 202.

69 See, notably, House of Commons, *Hansard*, 27 October 1971.

70 Sir Alec Douglas-Home, *Our European Destiny* (Conservative Group for Europe, July 1971).

71 House of Commons, *Hansard*, 21 October 1971.

72 House of Commons, *Hansard*, 27 October 1971.

73 I heard him say this in the Franco-British Lecture, *op. cit.*, and modified versions of it on several other occasions.

74 Interview, Lord Armstrong of Ilminster, 2 December 1993.

75 *Sunday Times*, 7 July 1996.

8. Roy Jenkins: The Fissile Effect

1 *The Times*, 30 November 1973.

2 The measurable Powell effect is helpfully discussed in Robert Shepherd, *Enoch Powell* (Hutchinson, 1996), 448–51.

3 Barbara Castle, interview for *The Last Europeans*, Channel Four TV, July 1995.

4 Roy Jenkins, *A Life at the Centre* (Macmillan, 1991), 104. Other references

in these paragraphs to Jenkins's early positions are drawn from the same source.

5 See above, pp. 41–3.

6 House of Commons, *Hansard*, 27 October 1971.

7 Bernard Donoughue, 'Renegotiation of EEC Terms: a witness account', in Brian Brivati and Harriet Jones (eds), *From Reconstruction to Integration: Britain and Europe since 1945* (Leicester University Press, 1993), 204.

8 See Chapter 12.

9 Jenkins, *op. cit.*, 323

10 'The Labour Committee for Europe: a witness seminar', 12 June 1990, *Contemporary Record* (Autumn 1993), 409.

11 *Ibid.*, 416.

12 There are six volumes, covering the years 1940–90.

13 House of Commons, *Hansard*, 8 May 1967.

14 These and many more are itemized in Denis Healey, *The Time of my Life* (Michael Joseph, 1989), 70–96.

15 *Ibid.*, 116.

16 Denis Healey, interview for *The Last Europeans*, June 1995.

17 House of Commons, *Hansard*, 21 October 1971.

18 Jenkins, *op. cit.*, 318.

19 Denis Healey, interview for *The Last Europeans*, June 1995.

20 Jenkins, *op. cit.*, 260.

21 Ben Pimlott, *Harold Wilson* (HarperCollins, 1992), 583.

22 Speech, Southampton, 25 May 1971.

23 Kenneth O. Morgan, *Callaghan: a life* (Oxford University Press, 1997), 395.

24 Jenkins, *op. cit.*, 320.

25 *Ibid*, 319.

26 Healey, *op. cit.*, 360.

27 Tony Benn, *Office without Power: diaries, 1968–72* (Hutchinson, 1988), 20 July 1971.

28 Edmund Burke, *Speeches at his Arrival in Bristol*, 3 November 1774.

29 Quoted in David Butler and Uwe Kitzinger, *The 1975 Referendum* (Macmillan, 2nd edn, 1996), 11, on which I have drawn for some other details in this chapter.

30 Jenkins, *op. cit.*, 343.

31 'Labour Committee for Europe', *op. cit.*, 397.

32 Private information.

33 Sir Michael Butler, speaking on *The Last Europeans*, 3 December 1995.

34 Jenkins, *op. cit.*, 389.

35 Sir Michael Butler, *Europe: more than a continent* (William Heinemann, 1986), 93.

36 Interview, Sir Michael Palliser, 3 September 1993.

37 Jenkins, *op. cit.*, 399.

38 Barbara Castle, *The Castle Diaries* 1964–70 (Weidenfeld & Nicolson, 1984), 19 March 1975.

39 Helmut Schmidt, speaking on *The Last Europeans*, 3 December 1995.

40 Castle, *op. cit.*, 26 April 1975.

41 Pimlott, *Harold Wilson*, 656.

42 Jenkins, *op. cit.*, 405.

43 Pimlott, *Harold Wilson*, 657.

44 Bernard Donoughue, *op. cit.*, 200. Donoughue, a key Wilson aide at the time, names the five as Merlyn Rees, John Morris, Fred Peart, Reg Prentice and Lord Shepherd.

45 Butler and Kitzinger, *op. cit.*, 32.

46 *Hansard*, 18 April 1975.

47 See F. Teer and J. D. Spence, *Political Opinion Polls* (Hutchinson, 1973), 108–19, from which several of these figures are taken. Also Butler and Kitzinger, *op. cit.*

48 According to MORI's monthly polls.

49 See Butler and Kitzinger, *op. cit.*, 228, 240.

50 *Sunday Times*, 27 April 1975.

51 Butler and Kitzinger, *op. cit.*, 256.

52 'The 1975 British Referendum on Europe: a witness seminar', 5 June 1995, *Contemporary British History* (Autumn 1996), 98.

53 This phenomenon is discussed at greater length in Chapter 10.

54 Lord Jenkins of Hillhead, interview for *The Last Europeans*, July 1995.

55 *Ibid.*

56 Teer and Spence, *op. cit.*, 118.

57 Recalled by Sir Patrick Nairne, 'The 1975 British Referendum', *op. cit.*.

58 Butler and Kitzinger, *op. cit.*, 273.

59 Jenkins, *op. cit.*, 399.

60 Donoughue, *op. cit.*, 205.

61 Jenkins, *op. cit.*, 442.

62 See above, p. 48.

63 Jenkins, *op. cit.*, 470.

64 *Ibid*, 477, which is part of a naturally positive history of the episode. For the fullest first-hand sceptical account, see Edmund Dell, 'Britain and the Origins of the European Monetary System', *Contemporary European History* (March, 1994), 1–60. Also see Healey, *op. cit.*, 438–40.

65 Dell, *op. cit.*, 4–5.

66 Valéry Giscard d'Estaing, the Ditchley Lecture, 1985.

67 His book, *European Diary, 1977–1981* (Collins, 1989), attests to this for nearly 700 pages.

68 David Owen, *Time to Declare* (Michael Joseph, 1991), 66.
69 *Ibid.*, 248.

9. Margaret Thatcher: Deutschland Über Alles

1 Interview, Lord Armstrong of Ilminster, 2 December 1993.
2 Margaret Thatcher, *The Path to Power* (HarperCollins, 1995), 26.
3 *Ibid.*, 31.
4 *Ibid.*, 126.
5 *Ibid.*, 127.
6 *Ibid.*, 207–11.
7 *Ibid.*, 330–3.
8 Sir Nicholas Henderson. The text is reproduced in Henderson, *Channels and Tunnels* (Weidenfeld & Nicolson, 1987), 143.
9 Simon Harris and Tim Josling, 'A Preliminary Look at the UK Food Industry and the CAP', paper delivered at Agra Europe Conference, 20 April 1977.
10 Sir Con O'Neill, 'Report on the Negotiations for Entry into the European Community, June 1970–July 1972' (Foreign Office, unpublished, 1972), ch. 33, para. 19.
11 Interview, Sir Michael Palliser, 3 September 1993.
12 Sir Michael Butler, *Europe: more than a continent* (William Heinemann, 1986), 93–4.
13 Interview, Sir David Hancock, 26 February 1993.
14 David Owen, *Time to Declare* (Michael Joseph, 1991), 245–8.
15 *Ibid.*, 281.
16 Interview, Lord Hunt of Tanworth, 13 January 1993.
17 Ian Gilmour, *Dancing with Dogma* (Simon & Schuster, 1992), 238–41, gives a full account of the scene. Another colourful version of the early Thatcher approach to Europe appears in Roy Jenkins, *A Life at the Centre* (Macmillan, 1991), 491–508.
18 Interview, Sir Michael Butler, 30 January 1993.
19 Nine million écus (the EEC unit of currency), against the forecast 700 million. See Butler, *op. cit.*, 100.
20 Interview, Helmut Schmidt, 6 February 1985.
21 Sir Charles Powell, interview for *The Last Europeans*, Channel Four TV, July 1995.
22 Witnessed by David Marsh: see his book, *Germany and Europe: the crisis of unity* (William Heinemann, 1994), 44.
23 *Ibid.*, 45.
24 Adam Gopnik, *New Yorker*, 3 June 1996.
25 Claude Cheysson, speaking on *The Last Europeans*, 11 December 1995.

26 Cited by Andrew Moravcsik, 'Negotiating the Single European Act: national interests and conventional statecraft in the European Community', *International Organisation* (Winter 1991).
27 Speech to the Netherlands Government, 7 February 1984.
28 *Daily Express*, 4 June 1984.
29 Sir Robin Renwick, interview for *The Last Europeans*, July 1995.
30 Butler, *op. cit.*, 108.
31 Speech in Avignon, 30 November 1984.
32 Interview, Emile Noël, 29 October 1993.
33 Sir Robin Renwick, interview for *The Last Europeans*, July 1995.
34 Lord Howe of Aberavon, speaking on *The Last Europeans*, 11 December 1995.
35 See Charles Grant, *Delors: inside the house that Jacques built* (Nicholas Brealey, 1994), 66.
36 *Ibid.*, 77.
37 Margaret Thatcher, *The Downing Street Years* (HarperCollins, 1993), 547.
38 Michel Petite, an intimate of both men, quoted in Grant, *op. cit.*, 68.
39 Thatcher, *The Downing Street Years*, 548.
40 Quoted in Geoffrey Howe, *Conflict of Loyalty* (Macmillan, 1994), 409.
41 *Ibid*, 407.
42 Thatcher, *The Downing Street Years*, 549.
43 Howe, *op. cit.*, 409.
44 Interview, Sir Michael Butler, 30 January 1993.
45 For a careful assessment, see Moravcsik, *op. cit.*
46 House of Commons, *Hansard*, 23 April 1986.
47 See Chapter 11.
48 David Williamson, speaking on *The Last Europeans*, 11 December 1995.
49 Sir Michael Butler, speaking on *The Last Europeans*, 11 December 1995.
50 Howe, *op. cit.*, 454.
51 *Ibid.*, 307.
52 Thatcher, *The Downing Street Years*, 314.
53 Interview, Emile Noël, 29 October 1993.
54 Howe, *op. cit.*, 448. Nigel Lawson, *The View from No. 11* (Bantam Press, 1992) supplies rivetingly detailed accounts of every significant meeting, including all Europe-connected ones, he attended from 1983 to 1989.
55 Alan Walters, *Britain's Economic Renaissance* (Oxford University Press, 1986).
56 Lawson, *op. cit.*, 499.
57 Howe, *op. cit.*, 450.
58 See Philip Stephens, *Politics and the Pound* (Macmillan, 1996), 77.
59 Thatcher, *The Downing Street Years*, 740.
60 Grant, *op. cit.*, 121.
61 Speech to the European Parliament, 6 July 1988.

62 *Jimmy Young Programme*, BBC Radio 2, 27 July 1988.

63 Thatcher, *The Downing Street Years*, 743.

64 *Ibid.*

65 *Ibid.*, 744.

66 *Ibid.*, 746.

67 Howe, *op. cit.*, 538.

68 Speech at Chatham House, 25 January 1989.

69 Lawson, *op. cit.*, 916.

70 The arguments surrounding this are more fully chronicled in my book, *One of Us* (Macmillan, 1989), 554 ff. Lawson, *op. cit.*, 898–936, Howe, *op. cit.*, 566–84, and Thatcher, *op. cit.*, 688–752 are indispensable sources for the phase.

71 Interview with David Frost, 24 November 1993.

72 Howe, *op. cit.*, 582.

73 Thatcher, *The Path to Power*, 347.

74 From Teltschik's own memoirs, cited by Alan Watson, 'Thatcher and Kohl – old rivalries explained', in Martyn Bond, Julie Smith and William Wallace (eds), *Eminent Europeans: personalities who shaped contemporary Europe* (Greycoat Press, 1996), 266.

75 Thatcher, *The Downing Street Years*, 791.

76 David Marsh, *Financial Times*, 30 September 1989.

77 Letter, *Daily Telegraph*, 6 September 1989.

78 Karl-Gunther von Hase, cited by Watson, *op. cit.*, 267.

79 The academics were Fritz Stern and Gordon Craig, both US-based, along with Timothy Garton Ash, Norman Stone. Hugh Trevor-Roper and George R. Urban.

80 The complete agenda is printed in George R. Urban, *Diplomacy and Disillusion at the Court of Margaret Thatcher* (I. B. Tauris, 1996), 147–9.

81 *Ibid.*, 128.

82 Printed in the *Independent on Sunday*, 15 July 1990.

83 Urban, *op. cit.*, 153.

84 *Spectator*, 12 July 1990.

85 Thatcher, *The Downing Street Years*, 722.

86 *Ibid.*, 723.

87 See Stephens, *op. cit.*, 140–67 for the best account of these.

88 Douglas Hurd, Scottish Conservative Conference, 11 May 1990.

89 House of Commons, *Hansard*, 27 October 1997

90 House of Commons, *Hansard*, 30 October 1990.

91 Anthony Meyer, *Stand Up and Be Counted* (William Heinemann, 1990), 162.

92 Michael Heseltine, *The Challenge of Europe: can Britain win?* (Weidenfeld & Nicolson, 1989).

93 Thatcher, *The Downing Street Years*, 842.
94 Speech, to the Konrad Adenauer Stiftung, Bonn, 11 March 1990.

10. WILLIAM CASH: EUROPE MADE ME

1 Peter Walker, *Staying Power; an autobiography* (Bloomsbury, 1991), 30.
2 Uwe Kitzinger, *Diplomacy and Persuasion* (Thames & Hudson, 1973), 177.
3 Charles de Gaulle, *Memoirs of Hope* (Weidenfeld & Nicholson, 1971), 194.
4 John Biffen, *Political Office or Political Power?: six speeches* (Centre for Policy Studies, 1977).
5 *Observer*, 18 August 1996.
6 Letter, *Daily Telegraph*, 21 January 1997.
7 Anthony Seldon and Stuart Ball (eds), *Conservative Century* (Oxford University Press, 1994), 273.
8 Interview, William Cash, 27 January 1998.
9 William Cash, *Against a Federal Europe* (Duckworth, 1991), 3.
10 House of Commons, *Hansard*, 23 April 1986.
11 House of Commons, *Hansard*, 27 June 1986.
12 House of Commons, *Hansard*, 10 July 1986.
13 Recounted by Body in 'The 1975 British Referendum on Europe: a witness seminar', 5 June 1995, *Contemporary British History* (Autumn 1996), 93.
14 House of Commons, *Hansard*, 23 April 1986.
15 *The Times*, 18 February 1965.
16 *The Times*, 7 May 1996.
17 Max Beloff, *The Future of British Foreign Policy* (London, 1969).
18 House of Lords, *Hansard*, 27 April 1994.
19 Lord Beloff, *Britain and European Union* (Macmillan, 1996).
20 'The 1975 British Referendum on Europe', *op. cit.*, 96.
21 For an account of the Maastricht negotiation, see Chapter 11.
22 Speech at the Bertelsman Forum, Petersburg Hotel, 3 April 1992.
23 Cash, *op. cit.*, 68–83.
24 Chris R. Tame, *The Euro-Sceptical Directory* (Bruges Group, 1997) lists both the bodies and the people considered to have contributed helpful work to the cause.
25 Michael Spicer, *A Treaty Too Far: a new policy for Europe* (Fourth Estate 1992).
26 Interview, William Cash, 27 January 1998.
27 See Chapter 11.
28 For the best account of the parliamentary trials of Maastricht, see David Baker, Andrew Gamble and Steve Ludlam, 'The Parliamentary Siege of Maastricht 1993: Conservative divisions and British ratification', *Parliamentary Affairs* (January 1994).

29 'Backbench Conservative Attitudes to European Integration', *Political Quarterly* (April–June 1995).

30 John Biffen, speaking on *The Last Europeans*, Channel Four TV, 11 December 1995.

31 Sir Geoffrey Howe, 'Sovereignty and Interdependence: Britain's place in the world', the London School of Economics Alumni Lecture, 8 June 1990, published in *International Affairs* (October, 1990).

32 Cash, *op. cit.*, 40.

33 Andrew Roberts, *The Aaachen Memorandum* (Orion, 1996).

34 Speech to the Royal Society of St George, 1964: cited in Kenneth Baker (ed.), *The Faber Book of Conservatism* (Faber, 1993), 205.

35 Alan Clark, *Diaries* (Weidenfeld & Nicolson, 1993), 14 April 1987.

36 House of Lords, *Hansard*, 8 March 1995.

37 House of Commons, *Hansard*, 23 April 1996.

38 Aidan O'Neill, *Decisions of the ECJ and their Constitutional Implications* (Butterworths, 1994), 17. O'Neill offers an admirable analysis and discussion of these questions.

39 Michael Howard, speech, 18 May 1996.

40 *The Times*, 4 July 1994.

41 Spicer, *op. cit.*, 193.

42 William Cash, *Democracy in the European Community: arguments against federalism* (Bow Group, 1991).

43 See Michael Mertes, *Frankfurter Allgemeine Zeitung*, 19 September 1989.

44 Spicer, *op. cit.*, 198–200.

45 Norman Lamont, interview for *The Last Europeans*, July 1995.

46 Speech to the Selsdon Group, 11 October 1994, reprinted in Norman Lamont, *Sovereign Britain* (Duckworth, 1995).

47 Interview, Sir James Goldsmith, *Guardian*, 12 October 1996.

48 *The Trap* (Macmillan, 1994); *The Response* (Macmillan, 1995).

49 Examined by Denis McShane, 'The Altered Ego', *Guardian*, 4 July 1996.

50 Interview, Sir James Goldsmith, *Guardian*, 12 October 1996.

51 See Alistair McAlpine, *The Times*, 7 October 1997, for a heavily Goldsmithite account of this transaction.

52 John Curtice and Michael Steed, Appendix 2, in David Butler and Dennis Kavanagh (eds), *The British General Election of 1997* (Macmillan, 1997), 308.

53 David Nicholson, MP for Taunton, who subsequently lost his seat. *Daily Telegraph*, 15 June 1996.

54 Bill Cash MP and Iain Duncan Smith MP, *A Response to Chancellor Kohl* (The European Foundation, 1996).

55 Helmut Kohl, speech to the University of Louvain, 2 February 1996.

56 House of Commons, *Hansard*, 3 December 1997.

11. John Major: At the Heart of Darkness

1 Conversation at the Guildhall, London, when Chancellor Kohl was made an Honorary Freeman of the City, 18 February 1998.

2 Anthony Seldon, *Major: a political life* (Weidenfeld & Nicolson, 1997), 46.

3 Recalled by William Rees-Mogg, *The Times*, 5 August 1996.

4 Seldon, *op. cit.*, 88.

5 *Ibid.*, 95.

6 See Chapter 9, pp. 340ff.

7 Seldon, *op. cit.*, 110.

8 See Philip Stephens, *Politics and the Pound* (Macmillan, 1996), 151–3.

9 Margaret Thatcher, *The Downing Street Years* (HarperCollins, 1993), 721.

10 *Ibid.*, 724.

11 Interview, Douglas Hurd, 28 October 1996.

12 Andrew Marr, *Independent*, 23 April 1997.

13 Interview, John Major, 1 November 1993.

14 Speech to the Konrad Adenauer Stiftung, 11 March 1991.

15 Interview, Sarah Hogg, 24 October 1996.

16 See Sarah Hogg and Jonathan Hill, *Too Close to Call* (Little, Brown, 1995), 78.

17 Seldon, *op. cit.*, 167.

18 *Daily Telegraph*, 22 November 1995.

19 The best account I came across of the preliminaries to Maastricht appears in Charles Grant, *Delors: inside the house that Jacques built* (Nicholas Brealey, 1994), 181–210.

20 Interview, Douglas Hurd, 28 October 1996.

21 Hugo Young, 'The Last Tory?', *New Yorker*, 3 February 1997.

22 Both Lamont and Major spoke on *The Poisoned Chalice*, BBC TV, 30 May 1996.

23 Seldon, *op. cit.*, 247.

24 Interview, Ruud Lubbers, 22 October 1996.

25 *Daily Mail*, 12 December 1991.

26 *Ibid.*

27 *Daily Telegraph*, 11 December 1991.

28 *Daily Telegraph*, 12 December 1991.

29 *The Times*, 12 December 1991.

30 Speech to the European Policy Forum, 10 July 1992.

31 The most accessible account of the ERM crisis appears in Stephens, *op. cit.*, 193–260.

32 Interview, John Major, 25 November 1996.

33 Private meeting, 2 July 1996.

34 *Panorama*, BBC TV, 9 June 1997.

35 Seldon, *op. cit.*, 321.

36 Graham Paterson and Andrew Pierce, 'Can Major Take the Strain?', *The Times*, 21 October 1992.

37 Andrew Neil, *Full Disclosure* (Macmillan, 1996), 9.

38 House of Commons, *Hansard*, 9 June 1993.

39 See his speeches, gathered in *Sovereign Britain* (Duckworth, 1995).

40 Off-the-record remarks to Michael Brunson, Independent Television News, 23 July 1993.

41 *Economist*, 25 September 1993.

42 Seldon, *op. cit.*, 350.

43 *Sunday Telegraph*, 17 December 1995.

44 Douglas Hurd, speech to the European Union of Women, London, 30 June 1992.

45 Seldon, *op. cit.*, 454.

46 House of Commons, *Hansard*, 22 March 1994.

47 The two were John Gummer, Environment Secretary, and Gillian Shephard, Minister for Agriculture.

48 House of Commons, *Hansard*, 29 March 1994.

49 *Guardian*, 25 March 1994.

50 Interview in *Der Spiegel*, 25 April 1994.

51 Speech at Ellesmere Port, 31 May 1994.

52 Speech at Leiden, 7 September 1994.

53 The exception was in January 1986, when she thought her resignation might be compelled by the Commons over the Westland affair. But Neil Kinnock, the Labour leader, missed his chance.

54 Seldon, *op. cit.*, 578.

55 See above, p. 331.

56 House of Commons, *Hansard*, 20 March 1996.

57 Seldon, *op. cit.*, 642.

58 House of Commons, *Hansard*, 21 May 1996.

59 *ABC* (newspaper), Madrid, 20 June 1996.

60 William Rees-Mogg, *The Times*, 23 May 1995.

61 Press conference, 3 April 1996.

62 Interview, John Major, 25 November 1996, preparatory to a *New Yorker* profile (*op. cit.*).

63 John Major, House of Commons, *Hansard*, 23 January 1997.

12. Tony Blair: Leading from the Edge

1 See Chapter 8.

2 Tony Benn, *The End of an Era: diaries, 1980–90* (Hutchinson, 1992), 1 October 1980.

3 Ivor Crewe and Anthony King, *SDP – The Birth, Life and Death of the Social Democratic Party* (Oxford University Press, 1995), 43.

4 A useful summary of the Labour history is to be found in Kevin Featherstone, *Socialist Parties and European Integration: a comparative history* (Manchester University Press, 1988).

5 David Butler and Dennis Kavanagh, *The British General Election of 1983* (Macmillan, 1984), 143.

6 'New Deal for Europe', in James Curran (ed.), *The Future of the Left* (Polity/New Socialist Press, 1984).

7 Cited in Featherstone, *op. cit.*, 66, from House of Commons, *Hansard*, 23 April 1986.

8 Giles Radice, *Offshore: Britain and the European Idea* (I. B. Tauris, 1992), 167.

9 Benn, *op. cit.*, 9 March 1989.

10 John Rentoul, *Tony Blair* (Little, Brown, 1995), 14.

11 *Ibid.*, 83.

12 *South Bucks Observer*, 16 April 1982.

13 *Guardian*, 10 May 1982, cited, as are some other quotes, by Rentoul, *op. cit.*.

14 For example, see Rentoul, *op. cit.*, 72.

15 *Ibid.*, 135.

16 Notably on 4 May 1993, 6 December 1993, 15 June 1994, 3 November 1994, 30 January 1995, 20 February 1995, 16 June 1995, 15 July 1996, 8 May 1996.

17 Speech at Chatham House, London, 5 April 1995.

18 Speech to the Friedrich-Ebert Stiftung, Bonn, 30 May 1995.

19 These quotes come, first, from BBC TV, 27 September 1992, and second, from House of Commons, *Hansard*, 1 February 1993, both cited by Rentoul, *op. cit.*, 438.

20 House of Commons, *Hansard*, 1 March 1995.

21 *Financial Times*, 17 June 1997.

22 Speech to the European Socialists Congress, Malmö, 6 June 1997.

23 Dinner at the Chancellor's Residence, Bonn, 29 October 1997.

24 As note 18.

25 See above, pp. 359–61.

26 Timothy Garton Ash, 'Europe's Endangered Liberal Order', *Foreign Affairs* March–April 1998.

27 Tony Judt, *A Grand Illusion?: an essay on Europe* (Penguin, 1996).

28 Tony Judt, *New York Review of Books*, 11 July 1996.

29 The most extensive and narratively revealing, if embittered, case against EMU was made by a former EU official, Bernard Connolly, in *The Rotten Heart of Europe: the dirty war for Europe's money* (Faber, 1995).

30 *Antenne 2*, 14 December 1990. William Cash, *Against a Federal Europe* (Duckworth, 1991), 58.

31 *Marche du Siècle*, French television, 26 February 1992.

32 *Daily Telegraph*, 7 August 1996.

33 Ann Leslie, 'What the Murder of These Girls Tells Us about Corruption at the Heart of Europe', *Daily Mail*, 21 October 1996.

34 Linda Colley, *Britons* (Yale University Press, 1992), 374.

35 Cash, *op. cit.*, 3.

36 William Waldegrave, 'Freedom v Empire', *Daily Telegraph*, 24 November 1997.

37 Michael Portillo, lecture to the Windsor Leadership Trust, 16 April 1998.

38 Norman Lamont, 'The People Will Kill the Euro,' *Daily Telegraph*, 30 March 1998.

39 The thesis brilliantly worked out in Alan S. Milward, *The European Rescue of the Nation State* (Routledge, 1992).

40 MORI series, inquiring into 'the most important issue' and 'other important issues', 1974–1991.

41 MORI, week of 22–26 July 1993, testing 'important issues': Unemployment 66 per cent, NHS 32 per cent, Economy 31 per cent, Law-and-Order 24 per cent, Europe 19 per cent.

42 European Commission, *Eurobarometer*, Nos 31 and 32, 1989; No. 36, 1991; No. 47, 1997.

43 *British Social Attitudes*, 12th report, 1995–6 edn (Dartmouth Publishing, 1996).

44 ICM poll, *Daily Mail*, 26 June 1991.

45 *Guardian*/ICM poll, *Guardian*, 8 April 1998.

46 MORI poll for the European Movement, published 16 February 1998.

47 Reported in the *Guardian*, 21 June 1996.

48 Interview, Ruud Lubbers, 22 October 1996.

49 *Financial Times*, 30 May 1975, in David Watt, *The Inquiring Eye* (Penguin, 1988), 62.

50 *Ibid.*

51 See above, page 29.

Bibliography

There is an immense literature bearing on the British relationship with Europe, and I make no pretence here to list it. Some of the academic papers and books I cite in the Notes contain several pages of references to other academic works, in several European languages. These are the works I have found helpful, or have in some way drawn on.

Noel Annan, *Our Age* (Fontana, 1990).

Timothy Bainbridge with Anthony Teasdale, *The Penguin Companion to European Union* (Penguin, 1996).

Kenneth Baker (ed.), *The Faber Book of Conservatism* (Faber, 1993).

George W. Ball, *The Past Has Another Pattern* (New York: W. W. Norton, 1982).

Elizabeth Barker, *Britain in a Divided Europe, 1945–70* (Weidenfeld & Nicolson, 1971).

Correlli Barnett, *The Audit of War* (Macmillan, 1986).

Lionel Bell, *The Throw that Failed* (Lionel Bell, 1995).

Lord Beloff, *Britain and European Union* (Macmillan, 1996).

Max Beloff, *The Future of British Foreign Policy* (London, 1969).

Nora Beloff, *The General Says No* (Penguin, 1963).

Tony Benn, *Out of the Wilderness: diaries, 1963–67* (Hutchinson, 1988).

Tony Benn, *Office without Power: diaries, 1968–72* (Hutchinson, 1988).

Tony Benn, *Against the Tide: diaries, 1973–76* (Hutchinson, 1989).

Tony Benn, *The End of an Era: diaries, 1980–90* (Hutchinson, 1992).

Martyn Bond, Julie Smith and William Wallace (eds), *Eminent Europeans: personalities who shaped contemporary Europe* (Greycoat Press, 1996).

Douglas Brinkley, *Dean Acheson: the Cold War years, 1953–71* (Yale University Press, 1992).

Leon Brittan, *Europe: the Europe we need* (Hamish Hamilton, 1994).

Brian Brivati and Harriet Jones (eds), *From Reconstruction to Integration: Britain and Europe since 1945* (Leicester University Press, 1993).

George Brown, *In my Way* (Victor Gollancz, 1971).

Tom Buchanan and Martin Conway (eds), *Political Catholicism in Europe, 1918–1965* (Oxford University Press, 1996).

Roger Bullen and M. E. Pelly (eds), *Documents on British Policy Overseas*, series ii, vol. i: *The Schuman Plan, the Council of Europe and Western European Integration, 1950–1952* (HMSO, 1986).

Alan Bullock, *Ernest Bevin*, 3 vols (Heinemann, 1960–83).

David Butler and Dennis Kavanagh (eds), *The British General Election of 1983* (Macmillan, 1984).

David Butler and Dennis Kavanagh (eds) *The British General Election of 1997* (Macmillan, 1997).

David Butler and Uwe Kitzinger, *The 1975 Referendum* (Macmillan, 2nd edn, 1996).

David Butler and Martin Westlake, *British Politics and European Elections, 1994* (Macmillan, St Martin's Press, 1995).

Sir Michael Butler, *Europe: more than a continent* (William Heinemann, 1986).

John Campbell, *Edward Heath* (Jonathan Cape, 1993).

Miriam Camps, *Britain and the European Community, 1955–63* (Oxford University Press, 1964).

William Cash, *Against a Federal Europe* (Duckworth, 1991).

Barbara Castle, *The Castle Diaries, 1964–70* (Weidenfeld & Nicolson, 1984).

Michael Charlton, *The Price of Victory* (BBC Publications, 1983).

Alan Clark, *Diaries* (Weidenfeld & Nicolson, 1993).

Lord Cockfield, *The European Union: creating the single market* (Wiley Chancery Law, 1994).

Linda Colley, *Britons* (Yale University Press, 1992).

John Colville, *The Fringes of Power: Downing Street Diaries, 1939–1955* (Hodder & Stoughton, 1985).

Bernard Connolly, *The Rotten Heart of Europe: the dirty war for Europe's money* (Faber, 1995).

Ivor Crewe and Anthony King, *SDP – The Birth, Life and Death of the Social Democratic Party* (Oxford University Press, 1995).

Richard Crossman, *The Diaries of a Cabinet Minister*, ed. Janet Morgan, vol. ii (Hamish Hamilton and Jonathan Cape, 1976).

James Curran (ed.), *The Future of the Left* (Polity/New Socialist Press, 1984).

Alex Danchev, *Oliver Franks, Founding Father* (Oxford University Press, 1993).

Edmund Dell, *The Schuman Plan and the British Abdication of Leadership in Europe* (Clarendon Press, 1995).

Roy Denman, *Missed Chances* (Cassell, 1996).

John Dickie, *Inside the Foreign Office* (Chapmans, 1992).

Bernard Donoughue and G. W. Jones, *Herbert Morrison: portrait of a politician* (Weidenfeld & Nicholson, 1973).

François Duchêne, *Jean Monnet: the first statesman of interdependence* (W. W. Norton, 1994).

James Ellison, *Harold Macmillan's Fear of 'Little Europe'* (Leicester University Press, 1995).

Kevin Featherstone, *Socialist Parties and European Integration: a comparative history* (Manchester University Press, 1988).

Charles de Gaulle, *Memoirs of Hope* (Weidenfeld & Nicholson, 1971).

Stephen George, *Britain and European Co-operation since 1945* (Basil Blackwell, 1992).

Martin Gilbert, *Never Despair* (Minerva, 1988).

Ian Gilmour, *Dancing with Dogma* (Simon & Schuster, 1992).

Lord Gladwyn, *The Memoirs of Lord Gladwyn* (Weidenfeld & Nicholson, 1972).

James Goldsmith, *The Response* (Macmillan, 1995).

James Goldsmith, *The Trap* (Macmillan, 1994).

Margaret Gowing, *Independence and Deterrence: Britain and atomic energy, 1945–52*, vol. i (Macmillan, 1974).

Charles Grant, *Delors: inside the house that Jacques built* (Nicholas Brealey, 1994).

John Gunther, *Inside Europe* (Harper & Brothers, 1936).

Denis Healey, *The Time of my Life* (Michael Joseph, 1989).

Edward Heath, *Old World, New Horizons* (Oxford University Press, 1970).

Edward Heath, *Travels* (Sidgwick & Jackson, 1977).

Nicholas Henderson, *Channels and Tunnels* (Weidenfeld & Nicolson, 1987).

Peter Hennessy, *Never Again: Britain, 1945–1951* (Jonathan Cape, 1992).

Michael Heseltine, *The Challenge of Europe: can Britain win?* (Weidenfeld & Nicolson, 1989).

Sarah Hogg and Jonathan Hill, *Too Close to Call* (Little, Brown, 1995).

Martin Holmes (ed.), *The Eurosceptical Reader* (Macmillan, 1996).

Alistair Horne, *Macmillan, vol. i: 1894–1956* (Macmillan, 1988).

Alistair Horne, *Macmillan, vol. ii: 1957–1986* (Macmillan, 1989).

Geoffrey Howe, *Conflict of Loyalty* (Macmillan, 1994).

Douglas Hurd, *An End to Promises* (Collins, 1979).

Douglas Jay, *Change and Fortune* (Hutchinson, 1980).

Roy Jenkins, *European Diary, 1977–1981* (Collins, 1989).

Roy Jenkins, *A Life at the Centre* (Macmillan, 1991).

Roy Jenkins, *Nine Men of Power* (Hamish Hamilton, 1974).

Christopher Johnson, *In with the Euro, Out with the Pound: the single currency for Britain* (Penguin, 1996).

Tony Judt, *A Grand Illusion?: an essay on Europe* (Penguin, 1996).

Paul Kennedy, *The Rise and Fall of the Great Powers* (Vintage Books, 1989).

Cecil King, *The Cecil King Diary, 1965–70* (Jonathan Cape, 1972).

Henry Kissinger, *Years of Upheaval* (Weidenfeld & Nicolson, 1982).

Uwe Kitzinger, *Diplomacy and Persuasion* (Thames & Hudson, 1973).

Uwe Kitzinger, *The Second Try: Labour and the EEC* (Pergamon Press, 1968).

Keith Kyle, *Suez* (Weidenfeld & Nicolson, 1992).

Jean Lacouture, *De Gaulle: the ruler, 1945–1970* (Harvill, 1991).

Richard Lamb, *The Macmillan Years, 1957–1963* (John Murray, 1995).

Norman Lamont, *Sovereign Britain* (Duckworth, 1995).

Nigel Lawson, *The View from No. 11* (Bantam Press, 1992).

Bernard Ledwidge, *De Gaulle* (Weidenfeld & Nicholson, 1982).

Robert J. Lieber, *British Politics and European Unity* (Berkeley, 1970).

Harold Macmillan, *Tides of Fortune, 1945–1955* (Macmillan, 1969).

Donald Maitland, *Diverse Times, Sundry Places* (Alpha Press, 1996).

David Marsh, *Germany and Europe: the crisis of unity* (William Heinemann, 1994).

Richard Mayne and John Pinder, *Federal Union: the pioneers. A history of federal union* (Macmillan, 1990).

Anthony Meyer, *Stand Up and Be Counted* (William Heinemann, 1990).

Alan S. Milward, *The European Rescue of the Nation State* (Routledge, 1992).

Jean Monnet, *Memoirs* (Collins, 1978).

Kenneth O. Morgan, *Callaghan: a life* (Oxford University Press, 1997).

Kenneth O. Morgan, *The People's Peace: British History, 1945–1989* (Oxford University Press, 1990).

James Morris, *Farewell to Trumpets* (Penguin, 1979).

John Newhouse, *Europe Adrift* (Pantheon Books, 1997).

Jim Northcott, *The Future of Britain and Europe* (PSI Publishing, 1995).

Anthony Nutting, *Europe Will Not Wait* (Hollis & Carter, 1960).

Aidan O'Neill, *Decisions of the ECJ and their Constitutional Implications* (Butterworths, 1994).

George Orwell, *The English People* (London, 1994).

George Orwell, *Homage to Catalonia* (London, 1938).

George Orwell, *The Lion and the Unicorn* (London, 1941).

David Owen, *Time to Declare* (Michael Joseph, 1991).

Peter Paterson, *Tired and Emotional: the Life of Lord George Brown* (Chatto & Windus, 1993).

Ben Pimlott, *Harold Wilson* (HarperCollins, 1992).

Ben Pimlott, *Hugh Dalton* (Jonathan Cape, 1985).

Giles Radice, *Offshore: Britain and the European idea* (I. B. Tauris, 1992).

John Rentoul, *Tony Blair* (Little, Brown, 1995).

Nicholas Ridley, *My Style of Government* (Hutchinson, 1991).

Andrew Roth, *Enoch Powell* (Macdonald, 1970).

Anthony Sampson, *Anatomy of Britain* (Hodder & Stoughton, 1962).

Donald Sassoon, *One Hundred Years of Socialism* (I. B. Tauris, 1996).

Anthony Seldon, *Major: a political life* (Weidenfeld & Nicolson, 1997).

Anthony Seldon and Stuart Ball (eds), *Conservative Century* (Oxford University Press, 1994).

Jean-Jacques Servan-Schreiber, *Le Défi Américain* (Paris: Denoel, 1967).

Robert Shepherd, *Enoch Powell* (Hutchinson, 1996).

Robert Skidelsky and Vernon Bogdanor (eds), *The Age of Affluence* (Macmillan, 1970).

Paul-Henri Spaak, *The Continuing Battle* (Weidenfeld & Nicolson, 1971).

Michael Spicer, *A Treaty Too Far: a new policy for Europe* (Fourth Estate, 1992).

Dirk Spierenburg and Raymond Poiderin, *The History of the High Authority of the European Coal and Steel Community* (Weidenfeld & Nicolson, 1994).

Philip Stephens, *Politics and the Pound* (Macmillan, 1996).

F. Teer and J. D. Spence, *Political Opinion Polls* (Hutchinson, 1973).

Margaret Thatcher, *The Downing Street Years* (HarperCollins, 1993).

Margaret Thatcher, *The Path to Power* (HarperCollins, 1995).

Hugh Thomas, *Ever Closer Union: Britain's destiny in Europe* (Hutchinson, 1991).

Christopher Tugendhat, *Making Sense of Europe* (Viking, 1986).

George Urban, *Diplomacy and Disillusion at the Court of Margaret Thatcher* (I. B. Tauris, 1996).

Peter Walker, *Staying Power: an autobiography* (Bloomsbury, 1991).

Alan Walters, *Britain's Economic Renaissance* (Oxford University Press, 1986).

David Watt, *The Inquiring Eye* (Penguin, 1988).

George Wilkes (ed.), *Britain's Failure to Enter the European Community 1961–63* (Frank Cass, 1997).

Philip Williams, *Hugh Gaitskell* (Cape, 1979).

Harold Wilson, *The Labour Government, 1964–70: a personal record* (Weidenfeld & Nicolson, 1971).

Hugo Young, *One of Us* (Macmillan, 1989).

J. W. Young, *Britain and European Unity, 1945–1992* (Macmillan, 1993).

Philip Ziegler, *Wilson: the authorised life* (Weidenfeld & Nicolson, 1993).

Index

DICTIONARY OF
BEHAVIORAL SCIENCE

DICTIONARY OF BEHAVIORAL SCIENCE

Compiled and Edited by

BENJAMIN B. WOLMAN

In Collaboration With

Gerhard Adler
Kurt A. Adler
George W. Albee
Anne Anastasi
Petr K. Anokhin
Silvano Arieti
Benjamin Balinsky
Nancy Bayley
Leopold Bellak
Lauretta Bender
Arnold Bernstein
Manfred Bleuler
Medard Boss
Francis J. Braceland
Jerome S. Bruner
Charlotte Buhler
Leonard Carmichael
George M. Carstairs
Raymond B. Cattell
Isidor Chein
Lee J. Cronbach
Florence L. Denmark
Gordon F. Derner
Morton Deutsch
John Dollard
John C. Eccles
David Elkind
Albert Ellis
John E. Exner
H. J. Eysenck

Charles B. Ferster
Anna Freud
Erich Fromm
G. Allen German
Eleanor J. Gibson
Gustave M. Gilbert
Edward Glover
Joy P. Guilford
Harry F. Harlow
Donald O. Hebb
Edna Heidbreder
Harry Helson
Mary Henle
Ernest R. Hilgard
Robert R. Holt
Lewis A. Hurst
Lothar B. Kalinowsky
Abram Kardiner
Otto Klineberg
David Krech
Wolfgang Kretschmer
Lawrence S. Kubie
Stanley Lesse
Konrad Lorenz
Juan J. Lopez-Ibor
Arthur R. Luria
Margaret S. Mahler
Jules H. Masserman
David C. McClelland
Margaret Mead

Neal E. Miller
Henryk Misiak
Jacob L. Moreno
O. Hobart Mowrer
Gardner Murphy
Lois B. Murphy
Theodore M. Newcomb
Joseph M. Notterman
Carl Pfaffmann
Jean Piaget
Karl H. Pribram
Harold M. Proshansky
John D. Rainer
Carl R. Rogers
Nathaniel Ross
William N. Schoenfeld
Robert R. Sears
Hanna Segal
Virginia S. Sexton
B. F. Skinner
M. Brewster Smith
Hans H. Strupp
John J. Sullivan
Leona E. Tyler
David Wechsler
Michael M. Wertheimer
E. D. Wittkower
Joseph Wolpe
Paul T. Young
Joseph Zubin

M

First published in the United States 1973
First published in the United Kingdom 1974

Reprint published in the United Kingdom 1975

Published by
THE MACMILLAN PRESS LTD
London and Basingstoke
Associated companies in New York
Dublin   Melbourne   Johannesburg and Madras

SBN 333 16787 2

Printed in the United States of America

PREFACE

There are hundreds of thousands of professionals and millions of college and university students who read psychological, psychiatric, and related literature and millions of interested laymen who are unable to avail themselves of useful information because of the barriers of technical terms. There are, indeed, a few dictionaries on the market covering partial areas, but at the present time, there is not even one comprehensive and authoritative dictionary that covers the entire field. The need for such a dictionary has been apparent and the authors of the present *Dictionary of Behavioral Science* intend to fill the gap.

Our Dictionary covers all areas of psychology such as experimental and developmental psychology, personality, learning, perception, motivation, and intelligence. It also includes all aspects of applied psychology, such as diagnosis and treatment of mental disorders, and social, industrial and educational psychology. The Dictionary covers the disciplines of psychiatry, biochemistry, psychopharmacology and clinical practice. The Dictionary includes terms related to neurology, neurosurgery, genetics, endocrinology, and presents the concepts and techniques of the orthodox and non-Freudian psychoanalysis. The motto of the Dictionary is *Concision and Precision.*

The planning of the Dictionary was done according to the specific disciplines, but it is printed in alphabetic order. Compiling and editing of this Dictionary resembled the writing and editing of close to 20,000 short papers. It certainly required the joint efforts of a large team of prominent psychologists, psychiatrists, and other scholars, and the help of a selected group of editorial assistants and secretarial staff. I am deeply indebted to all of them.

I must thank especially Drs. G. F. Derner, E. Glover, R. R. Holt, and H. Proshansky for their wise comments. Mr. Mike Hamilton gets the credit for initiating this project and Mr. Barry R. Nathan and Mrs. Alberta W. Gordon have earned my profound gratitude for their most cordial help.

B. B. Wolman

ACKNOWLEDGMENTS

I would like to express my profound gratitude to the following people who helped in many ways in the preparation of this DICTIONARY.

Editorial Assistants

Melvin Crosby
Patricia Edstrom
Cecille Freilich
Susan Knapp

Barbara Leavy
Ella Lenoff
Michael Moskowitz
Sally Moskowitz

Anne Mulvey
Irwin Schatz
Leonard Temme

Secretarial Staff

Robin Haber
Kathy Mankes

Naomi Mankes
Margaret Wiener

We are deeply indebted to the following Publishers who permitted us to adapt their copyrighted material.

(1) Appleton-Century Crofts

Adapted material from "Schedules of Reinforcement," C. B. Ferster and B. F. Skinner, copyright 1957 by Appleton-Century-Crofts, Inc. Reprinted by permission of Appleton-Century-Crofts, Educational Div., Meredith Corp.

(2) Harcourt Brace Jovanovich, Inc.

Adapted material from "Introduction to Psychology," Fifth Edition, Ernest R. Hilgard, *et al.*, copyright 1953, 1957, 1962, 1967, 1971, by Harcourt Brace Jovanovich, Inc. Reprinted with their permission.

Adapted material from "Personality and Motivation Structure and Measurement", Raymond B. Cattell, copyright 1957 by Harcourt Brace Jovanovich, Inc. Reprinted with their permission.

(3) Houghton Mifflin Co.

Adapted material from "Abilities: Their Structure, Growth and Action," Raymond B. Cattell, copyright 1971 by Houghton Mifflin Co. Reprinted with their permission.

(4) Penguin Books Ltd.

Adapted material from "The Scientific Basis of Personality," Raymond B. Cattell, copyright 1965 by Penguin Books Ltd. Reprinted with their permission.

(5) American Psychiatric Association

Adapted material from "Diagnostic and Statistical Manual of Mental Disorders (DSM-II)," copyright 1968 by American Psychiatric Association. Reprinted with their permission.

(6) American Psychological Association

Adapted material from "Ethical Standards of Psychologists," copyright 1963 by the American Psychological Association, Inc.

EXPLANATORY REMARKS

The guiding ideas of this Dictionary are usefulness, simplicity, and flexibility. We have tried to keep matters as simple as possible and to avoid whatever could hinder easy access and readability. There was no reason to mark the pages with phonics, phonetics, etc. We have assumed that people who read psychology in English do not need to be instructed in spelling.

We have avoided as much as possible superfluous indicators such as q.v., see, synonym, opposite, for we do not believe that someone looking for a specific fact, e.g., a definition of operant conditioning, must be bothered with a host of signs indicating related terms. If he looks for them, he will find them easily; if he does not seek them, there is no need to inform him that the terms he did not seek have been defined elsewhere in the Dictionary. Thus, the word "see" was used sparingly and only when it was absolutely necessary.

The logic of a dictionary required giving priority to nouns. For instance, "phlegmatic type" was defined under "type, phlegmatic." It was necessary, however, to cross reference many terms, and the "phlegmatic type" was listed as "see *type, phlegmatic.*" The same principle was applied to several key terms such as complex, conditioning, reinforcement, scale, syndrome, test and type. Abbreviations have been avoided for they are usually more handicap than help. Adjectives were defined only when necessary; e.g., "narcotic" was defined as a noun. When a term was spelled in more than one way, in most cases, both types of spelling followed one another, divided by a semicolon; e.g., aboulia; abulia.

No entries were signed; the name in front of an entry does not give the author of the entry, but rather indicates the author of the concept, idea, or technique.

The term "mental disorder" was used interchangeably with "behavior disorder."

Finally, the reader will find two appendices of special interest. These are the American Psychiatric Association's Classification of Mental Disorders and the American Psychological Association's statement of Ethical Standards of Psychologists. We believe that these appendices greatly enhance the Dictionary's usefulness and scope.

B.B.W.

DICTIONARY OF
BEHAVIORAL SCIENCE

A

A   See *angstrom.*

a%   A traditional Rorschach scoring calculation, representing the proportion of animal content responses in a protocol. Since it is easy to see animal forms in the inkblots, it is expected that they will represent from one-third to one-half of all the responses in most records. Unusually high numbers of animal responses are generally associated with constriction and/or stereotypy while unusually low numbers are associated with the records of the more seriously disturbed subjects.

A scale   See *scale A.*

AA   See *achievement age.*

AAT   See *test, auditory apperception.*

A/S ratio   (D. O. Hebb) Association-sensation ratio.

Abadie's sign   (J.M.C. Abadie) The absence of pain when pressure is put on the Achilles tendon.

abalienated; abalienation   Obsolete terms meaning mental illness or insanity.

abalienatus   Total destruction of the senses; loss of mental faculties. This term is no longer in use.

abasement   Degradation of oneself; excessive complying, surrendering, accepting punishment.

abasement need   See *need, abasement.*

abasia   The inability to walk due to lack of motor coordination, usually the result of a psychological disturbance rather than an organic cause. This condition often accompanies hysteria. Types of abasia: 1) Astasia-abasia involves the inability to stand or to walk as a result of mental conflict. 2) Ataxic abasia is awkward locomotion. 3) Choreic abasia—the inability to walk because of muscle spasms in the lower limbs. 4) Paralytic abasia—the inability to stand or walk due to organic paralysis. 5) Paroxysmal trepidant abasia—a form of astasia-abasia in which the legs become spastic when walking is attempted. 6) Trembling abasia—the inability to walk because of continuous trembling in the legs.

abative scoring standardization   (R. B. Cattell) The third possibility in standardization, after *normative* (across people) and *ipsative* (across the same response to different stimuli). Like the ipsative score, it is standardized within one person, but with regard to the same response to the same stimulus *made across a population of occasions.* (Hence, P-technique gives abative standardization.)

ABBA   Counterbalanced order of presentation of independent variables in a psychological experiment. The one independent variable, condition A is followed by the second independent variable condition B, this followed first by condition B then A.

abclution   (R. B. Cattell) One of the personality dimensions characterized by rejection of acculturation and refusal to conform to cultural patterns.

abderite   A stupid person.

abdominal reflex   See *reflex, abdominal.*

abducens nucleus   A mass of nerve cells located in the fourth ventricle from which the abducent nerve originates.

abducent nerve   See *nerve, abducent.*

aberrant energy expression   The abnormal and unorganized methods of releasing energy that are found as symptoms in the psychoses and neuroses.

aberration   1. A deviation from the normal or typical. 2. In an optical system, the passage of light by any pathway other than the most efficient; particularly, passage of light in such a way that rays emanating from the same point fail to converge on the same focus.

aberration, mental   Deviation from normal mental functioning.

abetalipoproteinemia   See *syndrome, Bassen-Kornzweig.*

abience   Avoidance. Abient behavior moves the organism away from exposure to a stimulus.

1

ability The power to perform an act, either physical or mental, whether innate or acquired by education and practice. *Ability,* as distinguished from aptitude, implies that an act can be performed now. *Aptitude* implies that the individual can develop by training the ability to perform a certain act. *Capability* is the maximum effectiveness a person can attain under optimal conditions of training.

ability grouping Dividing pupils into relatively homogeneous groups with regard to ability, either in a specific subject or in general ability.

ability test See *test, ability.*

abiotrophy An early loss of function or vitality of cells or tissues.

ablation Removal of all or part of an organ, often with the purpose of studying its function.

ablution 1. The act of washing the body. 2. A form of hydrotherapy given for insomnia that usually brings quiet, restful sleep. This treatment involves vigorously rubbing with water and then drying each part of the body.

ablutomania A preoccupation with thoughts about washing that frequently accompanies an obsessive-compulsive neurosis.

Abney's Law The principle that the luminance of a given monochromatic light is proportional to the luminosity, *V*, of the light and the radiance, *E*. In mathematical form the law is expressed as follows:

$$B = K\zeta \, V\lambda \, E\lambda \, d\lambda$$

where:

   B = luminance
   $V\lambda$ = relative luminosity at wave length
   $E\lambda$ = energy distribution of light according to a specified physical measure
   K = a constant allowing for differences in the magnitude of B and E.

abnormal 1. Diverging from the normal, not conforming with the general rule. The term usually connotes pathology or deviation from what is considered psychologically adjustive. 2. In a statistical distribution, descriptive of scores which are outside the normal or expected range of scores, departing from the mean interval of the distribution.

abnormal impulse to work See *ergasiomania.*

abnormal polychromate An individual who is able to distinguish most color except for one or two which he fails to perceive or confuses.

abnormal psychology See *psychology, abnormal.*

abnormality Deviation from the norm. The various definitions of abnormality depend on the kind of norm one has in mind: 1. (Statistics) Deviant from the mode, mean, or any other statistical norm. Also unusual, rare, coincidental, improbable. 2. (biology and medicine) Sickness, disease, defect, malformation, malfunction, invalidism and any other somatic or physiologic pathology. 3. (psychology) Disturbed, disorganized, maladjustive behavior; irrational, dis-

turbed, uncontrollable and disbalanced mental processes and/or disintegrated personality structure.

aboiement The uncontrollable and involuntary production of abnormal or unusual sounds. For example, some severely regressive schizophrenic patients make many animalistic noises.

abomination A term that has been used to convey loathing for food. Presently it is used only to express a general loathing and extreme disgust.

aboral The region of the body opposite to the mouth. The term is used in animal psychology.

abortive decision Rushed, premature, ineffectual decision.

aboulia; abulia Inability, usually pathological, to make decisions; loss of will power, inability to carry out decisions.

above and below (A. Adler) The unconscious belief that maleness is superior to femaleness; the conception of man as above and female as below. According to Adler, femininity is a position of inferiority; masculinity is to be strived for as a goal of superiority.

Abraham, Karl (1877-1925) One of the earliest disciples of S. Freud and the first German psychoanalyst. Developed a theory of etiology of mental disorders linked to Freud's psychosexual stages and wrote extensively about characterology and manic-depressive psychosis.

abreaction (psychoanalysis) Lessening the anxiety associated with an experience that originally involved the repression of emotions, by reliving the experience in feeling, thought or action. The freeing of psychic energy by converting repressed ideas or experiences into consciousness. In the early stages of psychoanalysis, abreaction was part of the cathartic method.

abreaction, motor (psychoanalysis) Living through an unconscious emotion or experience by muscular or motor expression.

abscissa 1. The horizontal line used as a base line in a two-dimensional graph of Cartesian coordinates. Used to plot measures of the independent variable—synonym: *X* axis, horizontal axis. 2. The distance of a point *P* along a line parallel to the *X* axis as measured from the *Y* axis (or vertical axis)—synonym: *x* value, *x* distance.

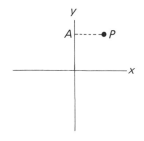

XX is the axis of abscissa.
AP is the abscissa of *P*.

absence The short period of time when there is a temporary loss of consciousness during attacks of hysteria and epileptic seizures. During this loss of consciousness there is either suspended or merely automatic activity. Also there is amnesia for the events that occur during such periods.

absentmindedness The tendency to be largely unaware of surrounding conditions due to absorption in one's own thoughts.

Absicht (from German ab-sehen). Absicht refers to an intention, aim, goal, or purpose. The usage arises when conceiving of humans as cognitively purposive or as controlled presently by anticipated future states or conditions. The term was important in ethics, for a traditional distinction is made between intention, action, and results. Ethical responsibility, particularly in the Graz school at the beginning of the 20th century, was viewed as residing in the intention. Intention has frequently been confused with intentionality, which as a primarily perceptual or cognitive term does not imply purposive behavior. The root notion is the Aristotelian conception of four types of causality: material, efficient, formal, and final. In human actions Absicht refers to a final causality.

absolute 1. Independent of comparison with other objects of judgments; not relative. 2. Not subject to change with time or circumstances.

absolute accommodation See accommodation, absolute.

absolute error See error, absolute.

absolute impression See impression, absolute.

absolute judgment See judgment, absolute.

absolute-judgment method See method, absolute-judgment.

absolute limen (RL) See threshold, absolute.

absolute luminosity See luminosity, absolute.

absolute measurement See measurement, absolute.

absolute pitch See pitch, absolute.

absolute refractory period See period, absolute refractory.

absolute scale See scale, absolute.

absolute sensitivity See sensitivity, absolute.

absolute threshold See threshold, absolute.

absolute value See value, absolute.

absolute zero See zero, absolute.

absorption 1. Focusing attention on one object, thereby excluding other objects. 2. Excluding reality because the focus of one's attention is on autistic thoughts.

abstinence syndrome See syndrome, abstinence.

abstract (noun) 1. A summary. 2. That which contains within itself all the essential qualities of a larger thing. (adjective) 1. Referring to a quality or aspect that is considered apart from other qualities or from the object itself. 2. That which is applicable in general rather than in concrete or particular situations. (verb) 1. To separate a part from the whole, to consider a single quality or aspect of an object apart from other aspects and from the object itself. 2. To briefly and uncritically summarize the content of a piece of writing.

abstract intelligence See intelligence, abstract.

abstract symbolism See symbolism, abstract.

abstract thinking See thinking, abstract.

abstracting-sensation (C. G. Jung) The isolation of a content or meaning, characterized by sensation, from other irrelevant elements.

abstracting-thinking (C. G. Jung) Bringing out a content or meaning that is distinguished from other elements by its logical and intellectual qualities.

abstraction 1. Separation and isolation of a particular aspect from a concrete whole; the development of a concept by drawing from a class of objects or events. 2. The concept arrived at by the isolation of a meaning or characteristic from the specific totality considered. 3. Inattention to surrounding situations due to an absorption with one's own thoughts.

absurdities test See test, absurdities.

absurdity Something self-contradictory or meaningless.

abulia See aboulia.

abulic An individual or act characterized by abulia, loss of will power.

abundancy motive Desire to experience enjoyment, to obtain gratification, to seek novelty, to discover and understand, to attempt to achieve and create. This motive includes the goals of satisfaction and stimulation. It may often involve the search for tension increase rather than tension reduction.

AC/A (psychophysics) The ratio of accommodative convergence to accommodation; it is a description of the near response of an individual which is constant for that individual.

academic 1. Relating to formal education, particularly involving the study of books. 2. Pertaining to the theoretical rather than practical issues. In psychology, referring to those experimental programs and schools of thought whose goals are theoretical as opposed to practical application.

acalculia A form of aphasia that involves the loss of ability to carry out even simple arithmetic operations.

acanthesthesia A variety of paresthesia in which the individual experiences the sensations of pin pricks.

acarophobia 1. A morbid fear of mites. 2. Extended to include a wide variety of small animals and objects.

acatalepsia Abnormal inability to understand or to reason; impairment of reasoning function.

acatalepsy An obsolete term that was used as synonymous with dementia.

acatamathesia 1. Inability to understand perceived objects or situations. 2. Impaired ability to comprehend the meaning of spoken language.

acataphasia The inability to arrange words in the correct phrasing and sentence structure of common speech. Also called syntactical aphasia.

acathexia Partial or complete inability to retain secretions and excretions of the organism.

acathexis (psychoanalysis) The absence of a cathexis. Particular ideas or thoughts that hold no feelings or emotions for an individual are said to be acathected.

acathisia The inability to sit down because the thought of such an act or the act itself produces intense anxiety in the individual.

acathisia paraesthetica Presently called paresthetic acathisia; another name for acathisia—the inability to sit down due to emotional factors.

acathisia psychasthenica Presently called psychasthenic acathisia; the inability to sit down because the thought of such an act or the act itself produces intense anxiety in the individual.

acathisia spastica Presently called spastic acathisia; the inability to sit down because the thought or act of sitting results in hysterical convulsive seizures.

acceleration 1. A quickening or speeding up. 2. An increase in the rate of change. Constant acceleration—an increase that is the same in each successive time unit. Positive acceleration—an increase that increases with each successive time unit. Negative acceleration—an increase that is less with each successive time unit.

acceleration, developmental Uneven growth; precocious growth of some or all functions.

acceptance 1. A positive attitude toward an idea or judgment. 2. A relationship or attitude that involves the recognition of an individual's worth without condoning or condemning the person's behavior or verbalizations and without implying emotional attachment.

acceptance in social relations (B. B. Wolman) Social relations are viewed in the two dimensions of "power" and "acceptance," power being measured in terms of the ability or inability to satisfy needs and acceptance in terms of willingness or unwillingness to do so. Individuals who are willing to satisfy the needs of others are perceived as friendly, those who act against the needs of others are perceived as hostile.

acceptor of action results (AAR) An apparatus of the functional system which corresponds to decision making. The apparatus of AAR consists of several functional structures. One of them concerns the ascending tonic influences of the hypothalamus and reticular formation. These influences sustain AAR as a rather heterogeneous apparatus in a long-lasting stable state until the program of action is formed and the result that was programmed is attained. Another mechanism of the AAR can be called the "Mechanism of collation." Due to the afferent synthesis the afferent features of a probable result are mobilized from memory, as predicted. By means of return afferentation at the acceptor of action results, a collation of features of the real result is combined with the features of what has been predicted by the AAR.

accessory Additional help, contributory, assisting. Used to refer to those parts of a sense organ that aid in the organ's more effective functioning.

accessory catalepsy See *catalepsy, accessory.*

accident Unusual, unpredictable event, usually harmful.

accident, cerebrovascular Apoplexy; stroke. A serious and sudden damage caused to the cerebrum by hemorrhage or thrombosis or embolism, associated with partial or complete paralysis, brain damage and psychotic state.

accident, intentional An accident occurring because of an unconscious motive.

accident prone person A person who acts out and discharges a forbidden and unconscious impulse through accidents.

accident proneness 1. Tendency to experience harm or damage. 2. Unconscious wish to be harmed.

accident, purposeful An accident that satisfied some need of the individual. Also called intentional accident. See *accident, intentional.*

accidental chaining See *chaining, accidental.*

accidental errors See *errors, accidental.*

accidental reinforcement See *reinforcement, accidental.*

accidental stimuli See *stimuli, accidental.*

accommodation 1. The adjustment and adaptation of an organ, a part of an organ, or an organism to existing situations. 2. The changes in the lens and ciliary muscle of the eye for focusing at different distances. 3. (J. Piaget) The modification of an existing schema by which a person perceives or thinks as a result of new experiences.

accommodation, absolute The adjustment or change in the shape of the lens in response to different distances as considered for each eye separately.

accommodation, binocular Simultaneous accommodation of both eyes.

accomplishment quotient Also called achievement quotient; the ratio of achievement age, the actual performance in school or on a standardized test and the performance level expected, indicated by the chronological age or estimated by the mental age.

acculturation 1. The processes by which children learn the characteristic behavior patterns of their social group. 2. The processes through which an individual learns the behavior patterns of a particular group, thus enabling the person to get along within that group. **3.** The acquisition of the cultural elements of one people by individuals of another group or culture.

accuracy 1. Pertaining to exactness, freedom from error. **2.** Relating to the degree of correspondence between that which is said or measured and a fact, thing or event. **3.** Ratio between number of test items correctly answered and the number of test items attempted.

accuracy compulsion (Rorschach) A tendency of the subject to be overly concerned with the form of the inkblots and dissatisfied with his own associations or responses.

accuracy score See *score, accuracy.*

accuracy test See *test, accuracy.*

ACE Test See *test, ACE.*

acedia Listlessness, carelessness, melancholia, and apathy. (This term is rarely used.)

acenesthesia Absence or lack of the feeling or perception of one's own body.

acerophobia Also acerbophobia; an intense fear of sourness.

acetylcholine A compound released at the endings of parasympathetic postganglionic and all preganglionic nerve endings. This base is believed to be responsible for the passage of impulses across synapses thus activating muscles. It also lowers blood pressure and increases peristalsis.

acetylcholine, metabolism of Acetylcholine, produced from acetylation of choline by the enzyme choline acetylase is present in the brain almost entirely in bound form. On nerve stimulation, it is released in its "free" form and is rapidly inactivated by the enzyme cholinesterase through hydrolysis to acetate and choline.

Ach, Narziss Kaspar (1871-1946) Member of Oswald Külpe's "Würzburg school" of imageless thought in Germany, later professor of psychology at Berlin, Königsberg, and Göttingen. His 1904 work on the determining tendency in thought (such as being ready to add or to multiply two digits before they are presented) was a landmark in the psychology of set.

achievement 1. Accomplishment, success in bringing about a desired end. **2.** That which is successfully attained. **3.** The degree or level of success in some specified area or in general. The level of proficiency attained in scholastic or academic work.

achievement age Achievement described in terms of age; the level of attainment that is considered normal for a particular age; the chronological age that is equivalent to a specific level of performance.

achievement battery A group of tests that measure the degree of attainment of skills and knowledge in several areas.

achievement drive See *drive, achievement.*

achievement motive (D. C. McClelland) Technically in psychology a concern to improve, to do things better than one has done them before; measured by counting the frequency with which people think spontaneously in terms of improvement in imaginative stories; related to certain action characteristics like taking moderate risks and preferring concrete feedback on quality of performance which in turn facilitate entrepreneurship and rapid economic growth. Not related to fame or school achievement, or to one's own opinion of how concerned he is to get ahead.

achievement need See *need, achievement.*

achievement quotient Less commonly called accomplishment quotient; the ratio of actual performance level to the expected level of performance.

achievement test See *test, achievement.*

Achilles jerk The reflex movement of the ankle when the Achilles tendon is tapped lightly.

achluophobia An intense fear of darkness.

achromatic 1. Lacking in chroma; that is, possessing no hue or saturation but only the dimension of brilliance. Such stimuli are considered "colorless colors," running from black through gray to white. **2.** Referring to a lens that has been corrected for chromatic aberration.

achromatic color response A type of Rorschach response in which the black, white, and/or grey features of the inkblots are specifically used to represent color, as for example, "a *black* bat." The scoring symbol 'C' is generally used to denote such responses.

achromatism Complete color blindness.

achromatopsia Inability to discriminate between all hues; all stimuli are perceived as achromatic-gray; total color blindness; also called achromatism.

acidosis, diabetic Occurs in diabetes mellitus and is due to a loss of base in the urine along with the accumulation of ketone acids in the tissues and blood. May result in coma.

acmaesthesia Also acmesthesia; perceiving sharp points by touch but lacking the sensation of pain usually associated with such perceptions.

acme 1. The highest point. **2.** The highest point of pleasure occurring during sexual intercourse. **3.** (medicine) The critical stage or crisis point of a disease.

acolasia An old term for unrestrained self-indulgence or lust.

aconuresis Also enuresis; the uncontrolled or involuntary passage of urine.

acoria 1. An insatiable desire for food because the individual never feels full after eating. **2.** A form of hunger as a result of the absence of feeling satiated after a meal.

acoumeter Also acumeter; an instrument used to determine auditory acuity or sensitivity of hearing.

Hearing loss is measured in terms of decibels at the various frequencies within the normal range of sensitivity. More commonly called audiometer.

acousma A simple auditory hallucination such as hissing or buzzing. A condition on the borderline between illusion and true hallucinosis.

acoustic spectrum The range of sound waves within the range of human hearing from about 16–20,000 hertz.

acoustico-mnestic aphasia See *aphasia, acoustico-mnestic.*

acousticophobia A morbid fear of sounds.

acoustics **1.** The science of sound, specifically the physics of sound. **2.** Those characteristics of a room that affect the distinctness with which sounds can be heard within that enclosure.

acquired **1.** Obtained. **2.** (psychology) Behavior or response that is gained primarily through practice, experience and learning. **3.** (biology) Development that is due to environmental influences.

acquired amentia See *amentia, acquired.*

acquired drive See *drive, acquired.*

aquired fear Fear resulting from conditioning.

acquisition **1.** That which is gained or added by the organism, such as ideas, information or new ways of responding. **2.** Increase in the response strength after the behavior has been rewarded.

acquisition cumulative curve See *curve, acquisition cumulative.*

acquisition curve See *acquisition cumulative curve.*

acquisitiveness A strong tendency or desire to possess, and sometimes to hoard certain objects.

acrai An Arabian term, no longer used in the United States, that is synonymous with nymphomania and satyriasis.

acrasia, acrasy Absence of self-control; intemperance.

acratia Impotence; inefficiency; loss of power.

acroaesthesia Also acroesthesia; exaggerated sensitivity in the extremities, especially to pain.

acroanesthesia Loss of feeling or sensitivity in the extremities.

acrocinesia Also acrocinesis; excessive motion or movement as sometimes observed in certain cases of hysteria.

acrocyanosis Blueness of the extremities as a result of a vasomotor disturbance. If this condition is chronic and progressive, there is hypertrophy of the soft tissues of the hands and feet. One of the symptoms which accompany severe schizophrenia.

acrocyanotic Pertaining to the condition characterized by bluish discoloration of the extremities.

acrohypothermic Relating to abnormal coldness of the extremities.

acromania An obsolete term that was used to refer to a chronic, incurable and violent form of behavior disorders.

acromegaly A condition involving the overgrowth of bones and connective tissue caused by hypersecretion of the anterior pituitary gland during adulthood. The characteristics are enlarged head, hands, feet and some internal organs.

acromicria Term used in constitutional medicine, especially by E. Kretschmer and N. Pende, for a condition characterized by the underdevelopment of the extremities and the skull as compared to visceral development. Acromicria congenital is an expression introduced by C. E. Benda for mongolism. See *Down syndrome.*

acroparesthesia **1.** A sense of numbness, sometimes recurring, in the extremities. **2.** A neurosis, chiefly seen in middle-age women, involving tingling or crawling sensations and coldness in the hands.

acrophobia An intense fear of being in high places.

act "Act" is a basic or primitive term in Act psychology, but in Association or Gestalt psychology is a derived term. The "act issue" is whether to conceive relations or acts as primitive terms of a theory of mind. If mental acts are basic, then relations between elements of experience are formed by mental acts. If relations are embedded in the nature of experience (Stumpf, Wm. James), then both mental acts and Laws of Association, which function to relate elements in experience, are not necessary.

If relations are formed by the integrative action of the nervous system (Koehler), then both mental acts and Laws of Association are not necessary. The act issue starts with two notions: that experience comes in mosaic-like elements and the unity of consciousness is a psychologically real phenomena which must be explained. For Aristotle the common sensibles related the elements of experience; for the British empiricists after Locke, Laws of Association performed that function; for Gestalt psychologists the integrative activity of the nervous system related elements of experience; but for act psychologists the unity of experience is achieved by means of cognitive functions of mind.

act–habit Repetitive activities on the part of a child that represent habituation and personality-rooted character traits. This term points out the importance of different cultural aspects of the environment in influencing the development of certain aspects of a child's personality.

act psychology Within the domain of mental phenomena act psychology can be distinguished on ontological grounds from other psychological constructions as follows: (1) what exists are contents and their relations (Wundt), (2) what exists are contents, relations, and mental acts or functions (Külpe), and (3) what exists are primarily mental acts within which contents have a secondary existence (Brentano).

Some forms of act psychology, following Aristotle's and Aquinas' philosophical realism, also assert the existence of objects external to the individual. For the Brentano school only real objects are capable of being presented in the sensorium. This position leads to controversies about the existence of objects like mermaids, golden mountains, etc. A realist position was defended by B. Russell, who made a distinction between knowledge by acquaintance and knowledge by description. A mermaid is known not by acquaintance but by description.

Closely related to the tradition of act psychology is J. P. Guilford's Structure-of-Intellect model. In this model knowledge is categorized by contents (figural, symbolic, semantic, behavioral) and form (units, classes, relations, systems, transformations, implications) and mental operations, or acts, into cognition, memory, divergent production, convergent production, and evaluation.

Act psychology can be distinguished from two other views: Association Psychology and Gestalt Psychology. Association Psychology relations arise as a result of the operation of laws of association; in Gestalt Psychology they arise as a result of an integrative activity of the nervous system; in Act Psychology they occur by a mental act.

act, pure stimulus; r (C. L. Hull) An act which, although it does not serve to move the organism closer to a goal, initiates the proprioceptive stimuli that tend to elicit the appropriate operant response.

ACTH See *adrenocorticotropic hormone.*

acting out (psychoanalysis) The reproduction of forgotten attitudes, memories or conflicts by action rather than words without conscious awareness or recognition on the part of the individual. Carrying into action behavior patterns that are appropriate to an older situation but are brought out by the symbolic similarity of the present situation. During psychoanalytic treatment the patient behaves toward the therapist in ways that are reproductions of past attitudes toward parental authority. This is called "acting out in the transference." Acting out can occur outside of the analytic situation but related to it. In these instances, the patient projects his feelings toward the therapist onto people in his everyday environment. Externalization of conflicts through acting out can, with some persons, occur without being related to treatment, as in character disorders. The term acting out, is often applied indiscriminantly to any aggressive or anti-social activity. Such behaviors have an unclear relationship to acting out and, therefore, the term lacks precision except within the context of an analytic situation.

actinic rays Short wave-length light rays, violet and ultra-violet, which produce chemical change.

action currents The changes in the electrical potential of nerves or muscles that occur during physiological activity.

action, deferred (psychoanalysis) When an experience becomes significant and meaningful not at the time the experience took place; that is, when the original experience is revived by some subsequent occurrence.

action interpretation (S. R. Slavson) The nonverbal reaction of a therapist to the statements or acts of a patient. A technique used almost exclusively in activity group psychotherapy.

action potential The entire sequence of changes in the electrical potential associated with impulses in nerves and muscles. Often used as synonymous for action current.

action, psychomotor A behavioral response or action that is the direct result of an idea or perception.

action psychotherapy See *psychotherapy.*

action research Scientific programs or studies designed to yield results that are practical rather than theoretical.

action, symbolic Unconscious and automatic actions that are considered accidental by the individual doing them. These acts may be simple or complex; but either type conceals a definite meaning. Symbolic actions may manifest themselves in such unconscious mannerisms as jingling coins or playing with a moustache.

action system 1. All the glands, nerves and muscles involved in the production of a particular response. 2. All the physiological and psychological structures participating in accomplishing a specific behavioral result.

activation A desynchronization of the electrical recordings made from the brain (EEG) when the organism becomes alert.

activation theory of the emotions The assumption that defines emotion as one end of a continuum of activation. The continuum ranges from sleep (no activity) to violent emotion (maximum activity).

active 1. Dynamic, functioning, working. 2. Possessing the qualities of movement or change. 3. Alert, showing spontaneity or initiative. 4. Causing action.

active analysis (psychoanalysis) A technique in which the analyst takes a more dominating role in the treatment process. The analyst would offer advice, give interpretations, and give suggestions for the direction of free association. Wilhelm Stekel and Sandor Ferenczi advocated various types of active psychoanalysis.

active fantasying A psychotherapeutic procedure involving the analysis of the patient's spontaneous imagery. Through the analysis of fantasied images, the analyst can uncover the unconscious roots of the patient's conflicts and help the patient bring them into conscious awareness.

active imagination See *imagination, active.*

active-passive 1. A polarity believed to be important in governing mental life and most commonly applied to opposing aims of instinctual drives. Activity is evident when a person seeks objects to gratify his needs. Passivity is manifested when a person wishes to have someone gratify his instinctual needs, with him being the receiver of gratification. 2. The child moves from passivity to activity as he learns to perform for himself functions previously performed for him by adults. 3. A specialized psychoanalytic usage referring to the structural concepts of id, ego, and superego, which are considered to be, at various times, either active or passive in relation to one another.

active therapy See *psychotherapy, active.*

activities, graded Occupations and handicrafts that have been classified according to their difficulty; that is, the amount of mental and physical effort needed to complete them. This system is used in occupational therapy to make possible a simultaneous increase in difficulty and in the patient's capacity to perform.

activity catharsis A catharsis in which the repressed feelings and thoughts are conveyed through action rather than verbally. This situation occurs often in activity group psychotherapy.

activity, group An activity in which several individuals participate. In occupational therapy, the main value of such a group is its socializing effect upon the members.

activity, group immobilizing (S. R. Slavson) A form of group psychotherapy in which activities are limited to one specific interest or task for the purpose of binding libidinal energy.

activity group therapy See *psychotherapy, activity group.*

activity, libido-binding (S. R. Slavson) Activities that tie an individual to a particular interest or occupation.

activity, socializing Referring to therapy groups, any activity that results in the interaction of an individual with other members of the group.

activity wheel A drum in which the subject, usually a rat, may run turning the drum. The measure of the activity is the number of revolutions of the drum.

actual neurosis See *neurosis, actual.*

acuity The accurateness or sharpness of perception.

acuity grating A square with alternate black and white lines printed very close together, used to measure visual acuity by determining the minimum separability that is needed so that the objects will be perceived as two distinct things.

acute 1. Sharp or pointed at the end. 2. Sensitive to fine discriminations in both perception and thinking. 3. Severe or sharp pains. 4. Of rapid onset and lasting a short time. 5. An angle of less than 90 degrees or containing one or more angles of less than 90 degrees. 6. (psychopathology) Acute disorder or disease with a sudden onset and usually short duration.

acute affective reflex See *reflex, acute affective.*

acute brain disorder A complex of symptoms resulting from temporary impairment of the functions of brain tissue such as the disordered behavior occasionally induced by drugs.

acute delirium A condition of mental confusion and excitement characterized by convulsions and sometimes death.

acute hallucinosis A condition in which the individual experiences hallucinations for not longer than a few weeks. Hallucinosis is typically toxic in origin, particularly associated with acute alcoholism.

acute mania See *mania, acute.*

acute preparation An animal that must be destroyed for humane reasons following an experiment involving unusual surgical techniques.

acute shock psychosis See *psychosis, acute shock.*

adaptation 1. (physiology) The change or adjustment of a sense organ to the incoming stimulation. Sensory adaptation—a) decreased sensitivity to stimuli due to prolonged stimulation, also called negative adaptation; b) continued effective sensory responsiveness under changing stimulation. 2. (biology) Structural or behavioral changes of an organism or part of an organism that fits it more perfectly for the environmental conditions under which it must live; changes that have survival value. 3. More generally, any beneficial modification that is necessary to meet environmental demands. Social adaptation—accepting and meeting societal and interpersonal demands. 4. Elimination of irrelevant behavior as learning progresses. 5. (A. Adler) A process of upward adjustment and compensation for man's innate deficiencies. 6. (E. Fromm) Modifications in drives, attitudes and emotions in adjusting to the environment. Although man can adjust himself to most circumstances, there are some limits to the malleability of human nature. 7. (H. Hartmann) A critical concept in Hartmann's theory of the ego. The newborn child has an innate perceptual and protective apparatus which, after the id-ego separation, becomes the conflict-free ego sphere. This apparatus performs the tasks of mastering the reality, called by Hartmann adaption.

adaptation, brightness A decrease in the brilliance of a stimulus which is caused by an increase in the general illumination of the surrounding visual field.

adaptation, color See *color adaptation.*

adaptation level (H. Helson) 1. A hypothesized momentary state of the organism at which stimuli are neutral or indifferent on any attribute. The stimuli above this point have specific characteristics and those below have complementary qualities. For example, in the transition from pleasant stimuli to unpleasant stimuli there is a stimulus or group of stimuli that is neutral. This transitional zone represents the stimuli to which the organism is adapted so far as the particular quality, magnitude or attribute is concerned. 2. Also known as AL, the adaptation level can be operationally defined as the value of that stimulus which elicits a neutral response when a subject judges a set of stimuli in terms of qualitative or numerical rating scales. 3. The theory of adaptation level attempts to evaluate the factors that influence this neutral zone in terms of focal, background and residual stimuli. The AL is seldom, if ever, at the center or at the arithmetic mean of the series. The phenomenon is called decentering. As a result of decentered AL the usual tendency is to overestimate small values of stimuli and to underestimate large values of stimuli although the contrary is sometimes found. These and other puzzles in classical psychophysics are easily explained if it is assumed that the prevailing AL is the effective norm in psychophysical judgments. Harry Helson and his co-workers have proposed quantitative theories embodying AL as a parameter to deal with difficulties in such classical formulations as the Weber-Fechner law and phenomena associated with changed states of adaptation in color vision. It is generally accepted that AL is a weighted geometric mean of focal, background (or contextual), and residual stimuli. While AL denotes the value of stimulus that elicits a neutral or indifferent response, to predict or fit the responses to each of the members of a class of stimuli being judged, it is necessary to know the proper type of S-R function or curve for the data in question.

The adaptation level theory has been utilized in studies of psychophysical judgment, sensory and perceptual processes, language and communication, and in aesthetic, social and personality studies, to mention a few of its numerous applications.

adaptation, photopic See *adaptation, brightness.*

adaptation syndrome See *syndrome, adaptation.*

adaptation time The duration of time from the onset of a stimulus to the moment when the consequent changes in the sense organ being stimulated cease.

adaptational psychodynamics See *psychodynamics, adaptational.*

adaptative Relating to that which aids in adjustment or improvement; appropriate.

adaptive act (H. A. Carr) Adaptation to the environment is of central importance. In the adaptive process motives act upon the organism; there is always a sensory situation and a response to the stimulus. Response is the activity that leads to a change in the entire situation in the direction of satisfaction of the motive. Once the motive is satisfied, the organism does not react to it any longer. The object by which the motive is satisfied is called an incentive. A motive represents a genuine need; the satisfaction of a motive is necessary for the survival and the well-being of the organism. When the adaptive act is completed the action of the motivating stimulus is terminated and the goal of the response accomplished.

adaptive behavior Any behavior that aids the organism in meeting the demands of its environment; adjustive or appropriate responses.

adaptometer Any instrument used to measure the degree of sensory adaptation, but specifically applied to a device that measures dark adaptation.

addiction **1.** Compulsive craving for something. **2.** Overdependence on the intake of certain substances such as alcohol and drugs, or performing certain acts such as smoking, etc. **3.** Inability to overcome a habit or behavioral pattern.

Addison's disease A progressive condition of anemia accompanied by digestive disturbances, weakness, and some pigmentation of the skin, which is caused by ineffective functioning of the adrenal cortex.

additional response Used in Rorschach testing to note instances in which the subject reports a percept during the inquiry phase of the test which he did not report during the free association period.

additional scores See *scores, additional.*

additive scale See *scale, additive.*

additive W A type of response to the Rorschach inkblot test that involves the report of details which the subject eventually combines to form a whole response. See *Rorschach inkblots.*

ademonia A term used in the past for severe mental anxiety or distress; sometimes used as synonymous with melancholy.

ademosyne A term that was used as synonymous with nostalgia.

adenoid type A hypertrophied pharyngeal tonsil or adenoid that is believed to be a sign of a serious constitutional problem. The extreme cases of this type are frequently associated with cretinism and deaf-mutism.

adephagia Also addephagia; a term used in the past indicating an abnormal and insatiable appetite; synonymous with bulimia.

adequate stimulus See *stimulus, adequate.*

adermonervia An obsolete term for anesthesia.

ADH Antidiuretic hormone. See *vasopressin.*

adhesion **1.** (physics) The molecular attraction between body surfaces that are in contact with one another. **2.** (medicine) The abnormal connection betwen organs or parts of organs due to inflammatory growth of new tissues. **3.** The connection or sticking together of substances, events, or ideas.

adiadochokinesis Also adiadokokinesis or adiadokokinesia; adiadokocinesis or adiadokocinesia. **1.** Inability to perform movements that involve rapid alteration. **2.** Continuous movement.

adience (adient behavior) Behavior that moves the organism toward a specific stimulus or exposes the organism to more of the stimulus through action that maintains the stimulus.

adiposogenital dystrophia Also called Froehlich's syndrome. Retarded development of the gonads and increased sugar tolerance, usually occurring in individuals during the pre- or post adolescent period. This condition is the result of an impairment of the pituitary gland or the hypothalamus.

adj schedule See *reinforcement, schedule of: adjusting.*

adjunctive psychotherapy See *therapy, adjunctive.*

adjusting (adj) schedule See *reinforcement, schedule of: adjusting.*

adjustment **1.** An harmonious relationship with the environment involving the ability to satisfy most of one's needs and meet most of the demands, both physical and social, that are put upon one. **2.** The variations and changes in behavior that are necessary to satisfy needs and meet demands so that one can establish a harmonious relationship with the environment.

adjustment inventory See *inventory, adjustment.*

adjustment mechanism A fairly permanent, habitual form of behavior that is adjustive.

adjustment method A psychophysical method in which the subject adjusts a stimulus object in relation to a constant or standard stimulus. The mean of the series of adjustments is taken to be the most representative score. A measure of variability, such as the standard deviation, is also calculated as indicative of the subject's variability.

adjustment of observations; measurements 1. Statistical correction of observed data to allow for atypical or disturbed conditions. 2. The use of the principle of least squares to obtain the best value to represent a series of measurements. See *least squares method.*

adjustment, optimum Survival under the best possible conditions which is the goal of psychotherapy.

adjustment path analysis (R. B. Cattell) A standard framework for analyzing a person's attempts at adjustment in terms of basic alternative paths which can be followed.

adjustment procedure (psychophysics) A means of arriving at the threshold of error by taking the average of the deviations when a subject adjusts a stimulus object until it appears equal to a criterion object.

adjustment process analysis (APA) chart An abstraction and reduction to a system of the sequences of response possible to the organism in its goal-seeking behavior. An attempt at comprehensive schematization of successive paths and choice-points (Dynamic Crossroads) in the adjustment of the organism, including possibilities for frustration, conflict, and personality learning.

Adler, Alfred (1870-1937) Viennese psychiatrist, an early associate of Sigmund Freud and one-time president of the Vienna Psychoanalytic Society. He broke with Freud in 1911, rejecting Freud's instinct (libido) theory and stressing instead an ego-psychology, and a social personality theory and social psychiatry, calling it "individual psychology". He saw man as aiming towards his own, self-created goals, rather than as the victim of his inherited drives; he viewed man's problem in his insecurity, which is apt to mislead him to emphasize his self-interest only, instead of uniting it with the interests of the community of men of which he ought to feel a part; he believed that neuroses and psychoses are generated by an insufficient development of social feelings towards others. His greatest influence has been in Child Guidance, and his theories sparked Child Guidance movements in Europe and the U. S. A. He lived in New York City from 1926, lecturing and practicing psychiatry, and was professor at the Long Island College of Medicine 1932-37. Among his many books are: *Theory and Practice of Individual Psychology, Social Interest, A Challenge to Mankind, Problems of Neuroses, What Life Should Mean to You, Understanding Human Nature, The Education of Children, The Problem Child* and many others. His theories and techniques are taught and practiced in many Adlerian Institutes and Adlerian Clinics in the U. S. A. and abroad, by societies bearing his name.

ad lib body-weight The weight approached or reached by a mature organism under continuous access to food.

ad lib feeding Providing continuous access to food.

adolescence 1. (biology) This approach considers early adolescence as beginning with the onset of the pubescent growth spurt until about a year after puberty. The pubescent growth spurt is marked by a spurt in physical growth, changes in body proportions and the maturation of primary and secondary sex characteristics. Puberty is the climax of pubescence and is characterized by signs of sexual maturity such as the menarche in girls and the presence of live spermatozoa in the male urine. Late adolescence is considered to last until physical growth is relatively complete at which time early adulthood begins. These biological changes vary according to individual, age-stage, and sex. 2. (chronology) Early adolescence is designated as the age period of 13 through 16 and late adolescence as 17 through 21. Sometimes the age periods established for girls and boys are different, 12 through 21 and 13 through 22 respectively. Either designation is misleading for neither biological nor psychological maturity proceeds at the same rate in all individuals. In addition, all aspects of biological or psychological maturity do not develop at the same rate in the same individual. 3. (sociology) Considered to be largely a creation of the Western world, social adolescence involves outgrowing the social status of a child but not yet being accorded the privileges of the adult. 4. (cross-cultural) Adolescence is viewed according to the way of life of the youth through the years and in different parts of the world. By such a comparison certain constants can be identified as characteristic of adolescence regardless of culture. 5. (theoretical) Adolescence may be defined according to a particular theory. For example, the phenomenologist places emphasis on the adolescent's perception of himself and his environment. In contrast, the psychoanalytic approach, based on Freudian theory, considers early life stages as highly significant and each stage as important for the subsequent stages. 6. (developmental) Adolescence is considered in relation to other developmental stages and in terms of the psychological dynamics involved. Looking at the role that adolescence plays in total development and in helping the individual establish identity is an example of such an approach.

adolescent crisis 1. The emotional changes that occur during adolescence. The adolescent ego is confronted with new challenges: achieving independence, casting off old emotional ties and developing new ones. Both physiological and psychological events, during this time, present problems for the adolescent to deal with before reaching maturity.

2. Radical shift of moods typical of adolescent period.

adrenal cortex The outermost portion of the adrenal glands where cortin is produced.

adrenal glands See *glands, adrenal.*

adrenal medulla The part of the adrenal gland which secretes the hormones adrenalin and noradrenaline.

adrenalin Also called epinephrine; a hormone secreted by the adrenal medulla. Its general effects are to mobilize the body's resources to cope with an emergency or stressful situation. Specifically, adrenalin stimulates the production of sugar from the liver, increases heart rate, facilitates muscle contraction and inhibits digestion.

adrenalism A condition resulting from impairment in the functioning of the adrenal glands. Also called suprarenalism.

adrenergic **1.** Pertaining to the type of chemical activity characteristic of adrenalin (epinephrine); adrenalin-like action. **2.** Characterizing the action of certain nerve fibers of the sympathetic nervous system that produce sympathin which is an adrenalin-like substance.

adrenergic-response state (R. B. Cattell) A personality dimension showing characteristics generally indicative of high levels of adrenalin secretion, such as high blood sugar, rapid pulse and high blood pressure.

adrenin Also adrenine; trade names for adrenalin (epinephrine).

adrenochrome An oxidized derivative of adrenaline which has psychotomimetic properties and is believed to be present in an excessive amount in schizophrenic people.

adrenocortical hormones See *hormones, adrenocortical.*

adrenocortical insufficiency See *Addison's disease.*

adrenocorticotropic hormone See *hormone, adrenocorticotropic.*

adult analysis **1.** (psychoanalysis) Refers to the psychoanalysis of adult patients. **2.** May refer to non-Freudian approaches to analysis used with adults.

adult-child interaction test See *test, adult-child interaction.*

adult maladjustment, simple A category including individuals who appear maladjusted although there is no evidence of psychosis or psychopathic personality. Their difficulties and lack of adaptive capacities are seen in relation to specific areas such as marriage or occupations.

adultomorph (L. S. Kubie) Refers to psychoanalysts who interpret infant's fantasies in adult terms.

advantage, law of See *law of advantage.*

adventitious deafness See *deafness, adventitious.*

adventurousness **1.** Characterized by risks and hazards, thereby being adventurous. **2.** Possessing courage.

advisor system A program established by the United States Service Unit in which groups of platoon leaders were trained in practical psychology. The purpose was to sustain the morale of the soldiers and prevent mental breakdowns. Training included being made aware of the importance of: (1) having an interest in and helping to solve the soldiers' problems; (2) explaining details to new members of the unit; and (3) the proper assignment of tasks. Platoon leaders were carefully selected, for emotional stability was an important factor. They were then trained to create good will within their unit without any loss of fighting efficiency. This program successfully reduced psychoneurotic reactions as well as absences without leave.

adynamia Loss of strength; weakness; debility. Also called asthenia.

aedoeomania An obsolete term for nymphomania.

aerial perspective See *perspective, aerial.*

aero-acrophobia Intense fear of being in places that are both open and high; such as in an airplane.

aëroasthenia See *aëroneurosis.*

aëroneurosis A type of psychoneurosis found in aviators. This condition is characterized by restlessness, anxiety and varying physical manifestations.

aerophagia Automatic swallowing or gulping of air, a common symptom of neuroses particularly of hysterical patients.

aerophobia A morbid fear of fresh air or drafts.

aerumna A term that is no longer used to refer to depression that accompanies a physical disease.

aeschromythesis The foul or obscene language of the maniacal or delirious person. This term is no longer used.

aesthesiometer Also esthesiometer; an instrument used to measure tactile sensitivity. It is a compass-like device that determines the threshold or minimum spatial separation on the skin at which two points are perceived as two separate points.

aesthete Also esthete; an individual who emphasizes the importance of the beautiful as part of experience; one who is very sensitive to beauty.

aesthetic type; esthetic type See *type, esthetic.*

aesthetics Also esthetics; the study of the constituents of beauty. If such study is experimental it is considered a branch of psychology. However, if such study is rational and a priori it is considered a branch of philosophy.

affect **1.** A class name given to feelings, emotions, or dispositions as a mode of mental functioning. **2.** The name given to specific emotions or feelings. **3.** (K. Pribram) A state generated when motivated action becomes unfeasible.

affect block The inability to love due to a fear of love and a fear of emotional ties. As a result of the blocking of affect, this condition involves the incapability for strong emotions and the avoidance of loving by using doubts and uncertainties.

affect, conversion of (S. Freud) Wish-impulses arise during the period of infantile sexuality. At a later time when these impulses are fulfilled, the resulting emotional state is pain rather than the previously felt pleasure. This change or conversion of affect is the essence of repression. These impulses are repressed; and, subsequently, they are symbolically represented in some physical manifestation. The physical symptom is held to be the way that an internal conflict is externally expressed.

affect, detached (S. Freud) An emotional component that has been separated from the idea with which it was originally associated because the idea was unbearable to the ego. Instead the affect becomes attached to other, more acceptable, ideas, which grow to be obsessions.

affect-energy When a stimulus is applied to a whole human organism excitement is produced. The energy resulting from this excitement is called affect-energy or affective energy.

affect, fading of (S. Freud) The dimming of the emotional, as well as ideational, components of impressions as they become more and more remote in the past. Freud conceives of these changes as being the work of the preconscious.

affect-fantasy See *affect-phantasy.*

affect, flattening of In pathological states, a general impoverishment of emotional reactivity which is characterized by incongruous or inappropriate affective behavior or a total lack of response to emotionally tinged stimuli.

affect, hunger (D. Levy) The human being's craving or desire for emotions. This term was originally described with regard to the emotional hunger for maternal love, protection and care that arises when a child is deprived of such parental affection. A more descriptive and precise term would be affection hunger.

affect, inappropriate The display of emotions which are incompatible with the demands of a particular situation.

affect, inversion of (psychoanalysis) A manifestation of ambivalence in the form of a sudden change in emotion from love to hate or vice versa.

affect, organ localization of An emotion may be felt in any body organ. An effect is usually localized in those organs that are reached directly by the autonomic nervous system, such as the stomach, heart and lungs.

affect-phantasy; affect fantasy (C. G. Jung) A fantasy, imagined event or object, that has a strong emotional component attached to it.

affect, somatic factor In addition to the subjective emotional state through which an affect expresses itself, there are physiological or somatic accompaniments of emotional states. A few examples of these physiological changes are nausea, palpitations and sweating.

affect-tonus A basic and normal state of affect; that is, the affect is at an even level due to continuous and stable stimulation. This situation is analogous to muscle tonus. Changes in this normal level represent emotional reactions.

affect, transformation of in dreams (psychoanalysis) The representation of an emotion in a dream by the opposite emotion. A feeling, usually a repressed one, is transformed into its exact opposite and incorporated into a dream. This is one of many processes by which true meaning is obscured in dreams.

affectability An individual's ability to express feelings or emotions.

affectation To assume or exhibit unnatural feelings; an artifical manner in behavior or speech meant to impress the listeners or the onlookers. This manner may be often seen in hysteria or in the manic phase of manic-depressive psychosis.

affectio hypochondriaca An obsolete term for hypochondriasis.

affection 1. A general term for feelings and emotions. 2. Caring or loving; tender attachment.

affection, masked (W. Stekel) The display of tender behavior by an individual who is actually feeling hostility and hatred. In addition to referring to an unconscious defense reaction, this term may also refer to a conscious deception.

affective Pertaining to affect or feeling.

affective arousal theory (D. C. McClelland) An attempt to account for the arousal of positive and negative affect in terms of the degree of discrepancy between adaptation level (or expectation) and what actually happens to the organism. If what happens coincides exactly with expectation, no affect is aroused; if it deviates slightly from expectation, positive affect is aroused; if it deviates markedly from expectation, negative affect is aroused. Used to explain how motives become directed toward increasingly sophisticated and complex goals. As cognitive expectations become more complex, moderate deviations from them needed to give positive affect—i.e., new goals—also become more complex. Used also to explain why aesthetic taste moves from simple to more complex forms with growing experience.

affective disorders More recently called affective psychoses. A group of psychoses that are characterized by derangements of emotional expression or mood. The exaggeration of emotional expression is accompanied by signs of intellectual disturbance. Also characteristic of an affective disorder is the rapidity with which symptoms change. In these conditions, all emotional distortions range between the two poles of manic elation and deep depression; the affective psychoses tend to occupy the extremes.

The transition from emotional excitement to depression can occur in various ways. The onset of either an extreme depression or elation does not seem to be related to a specific precipitating life experience and therefore, is distinguished from psychotic depressive reaction and depressive neurosis.

The Diagnostic and Statistical Manual of Mental Disorders of the American Psychiatric Association, 1968 (Second Edition, DSM-II) categorizes the major affective disorders (affective psychoses) as follows:

I. Involutional melancholia
II. Manic-depressive illnesses (manic-depressive psychoses)
   1. Manic-depressive illness, manic type (manic-depressive psychosis, manic type)
   2. Manic-depressive illness, depressed type (manic-depressive psychosis, depressed type)
   3. Manic-depressive illness, circular type (manic-depressive psychosis, circular type)
     a. manic-depressive illness, circular type, manic
     b. manic-depressive illness, circular type, depressed
III. Other major affective disorder (affective psychosis, other)
IV. Unspecified major affective disorder

affective energy See *affect-energy.*

affective epilepsy See *epilepsy, affective.*

affective eudemonia Escape from an unbearable reality by fleeing into mental illness. This term puts emphasis on secondary gains which are important in the following examples of affective eudemonia: faxen-psychosis, the Ganser syndrome and certain cases of hypochondriasis.

affective experience See *experience, affective.*

affective processes in ament (A. F. Tredgold) Emotions are weaker in both duration and intensity in a mentally deficient individual than they are in normal people. The acquisition of sentiments consisting of the association of an emotion and an abstract idea are even more markedly defective.

affective psychosis See *psychosis, affective.*

affective ratio See *ratio, affective.*

affective reaction type See *type, affective reaction.*

affective reintegration The reorganization of affects or emotions into harmony following their previous disintegration during the affective psychoses.

affective rhythm (psychobiology) An expression used to mean the routine that utilizes the individual's emotional mood.

affective state A condition involving the experience of emotions.

affective syndrome Another term for affective psychosis which is the category of disorders in which the main symptoms are inappropriate or exaggerated emotional reactions.

affective tone 1. The generalized mood or feeling of an experience. 2. (E. B. Titchener) The pleasantness or unpleasantness with regard to a specific stimulus. 3. The subjective correlate of acceptance-rejection behavior.

affective transformation 1. (psychoanalysis) The representation in consciousness of a repressed emotion usually by its opposite. 2. The law of affective transformation says that emotionally emphasized values continue to strive to increase their area of dominance. This process is often noticed in schizophrenia and may be observed in other behavior disorders as well.

affectivity 1. The tendency to react emotionally. 2. A generalized emotional experience, one that is not identifiable as a specific emotion or with a particular stimulus. 3. The amount of emotion or feeling evident at a specific time.

affectomotor Displaying both muscular activity and emotional excitement. This combination of symptoms is common to many behavior disorders, but affectomotor is usually used to refer specifically to the manic phase of manic-depressive psychosis.

affectomotoric Characterized by intense mental tension and muscular activity.

affecto-thymia (R. B. Cattell) The positive pole of the A personality factor, re-named from Cyclothymia vs. Schizothymia because, though it supports in factorial experiment, the dimension of Bleuler and Kretschmer; it may represent easy versus inhibited emotional response.

affectus animi An expression that was used in the past as a general term for any psychiatric disorder.

afferent Carrying toward; concerned with the transmission of neural impulses toward the central nervous system.

afferent apraxia See *apraxia, afferent.*

afferent interaction See *interaction, afferent.*

afferent motor aphasia See *aphasia, afferent motor.*

afferent paresis See *paresis, afferent.*

afferent stimulus interaction 1. (C. L. Hull) A postulate which holds that all afferent neural impulses active in the nervous system at any given time interact and in the process of interacting, modify one another. The behavioral effects of these impulses are more than the mere summation of the effects of each taken separately. 2. This principle is an attempt to provide a behaviorist explanation for patterns of stimuli and other configurational problems dealt with by the Gestalt psychologists. See *Gestalt psychology.*

afferent synthesis The initial stage in the formation of the functional system. It is indispensable for every functional system and precedes "decision making" for the system. As a rule, "decision making" occurs only after the stage of afferent synthesis comes to the end. The afferent synthesis comprises the four most main components: dominating motivation at a given moment, situational afferentation, stimulus afferentation, and continuous extraction of the former experience from memory. All these processes are processed on separate neurons at the very beginning, and only after this processing there takes place integration of many decision making neurons, the processing of four heterogeneous excitations on the neuron synaptic organization is realized in uninterrupted dynamic processes, facilitating mobilization of the indispensable interneuronal connections. Such dynamic processes include ascending activation of the reticular formation, hypothalamus facilitating effect, increase of discrimination, cortico-subcortical reverberation, centrifugal facilitation of excitability of the receptors, etc. All these dynamic processes facilitate the choice of the most adequate aim for the given motivation and a given situation. The existence and interrelations of all the dynamic processes mentioned on separate neurons have been experimentally demonstrated.

affiliation **1.** Connection or association. **2.** (H. A. Murray) An individual's need to draw near and enjoyably cooperate with another, to form friendships and remain loyal, to please and win affection of important others. Also called affiliative need.

affiliation need See *need, affiliation.*

affiliative behavior Behavior designed to establish friendly and satisfying interpersonal relationships.

affiliative motive See *motive, affiliative.*

affiliative need See *affiliation.*

affinal **1.** From the same origin. **2.** Related through marriage.

affinity **1.** Attraction and relationship. **2.** (biology) The relationship between certain groups due to their mutual resemblance which is indicative of a similar origin.

affusion **1.** To pour water upon the body. **2.** A form of hydrotherapy during which the patient stands or sits in a bathtub with a sheet around his body while water is poured on him. Then the patient is towel rubbed until a reaction is observed. The purpose is to reduce fever and calm nervous systems.

after care Treatment and rehabilitation services provided by the community for patients discharged from hospitals.

afterdischarge The continuing discharge of neural impulses after the stimulus has been removed.

aftereffect **1.** An aftersensation. **2.** A sensory experience that continues after the stimulating condition ends. **3.** (learning) The strengthening of the connection between a stimulus and a response because the consequence of the act are satisfying. See *afterimage.*

aftereffect, figural The distortion or displacement of visual objects that are placed in a region which had previously been occupied for some time by other visual objects, such as dots, lines, or figures.

afterexpulsion Secondary repression.

afterimage The persistence of sensory excitation in a given sensory system, following the removal of the adequate stimulus. The most readily observed afterimages occur in vision. There are both positive and negative visual afterimages. A positive afterimage occurs when the observer sees a patch of color similar in both brightness and hue to the original. In negative afterimage, every color appears as the complementary in hue to the original and is opposite in brightness. Also called aftersensation. See *Purkinje afterimage.*

afterimage, memory An afterimage consisting of the revival of an experience immediately after it has occurred.

afterimage, positive Experience of a visual stimulus after it has been removed. The brightness and hue of the afterimage are almost the same as the actual stimulus.

aftersensation The continuation of a sensory experience after the removal of its stimulus. In vision, a positive aftersensation is one in which the image is brighter than the surrounding field and a negative aftersensation is one in which the image is less bright than the surrounding field. Also called afterimage. See *Purkinje afterimage.*

agamma globulinemia Disease caused by sex-linked recessive gene resulting in absence of gamma globulin which is necessary for antibody formation. Not clinically detectable at birth and not damaging unless offending organisms or toxins are present. The body is unable to synthesize antibodies to fight the invasion and survival is made unlikely.

agastroneuria A condition of the stomach characterized by lowered nervous tone. Sometimes called neurasthenia of the stomach.

AGCT See *Army General Classification Test.*

age **1.** The period of time from birth to any given time in life; the time an organism has lived; chronological age. **2.** One of the stages or periods in life; as, middle age. **3.** A lifetime; the entire time of a being's existence. **4.** The time in life when a particular capacity or qualification arises; as, school age. **5.** A particular period in the history of man; as, stone age. **6.** (psychology) An individual's development, either mental or anatomical, etc., that is measured by the number of years expected for like development in an average child. Distinguished from chronological age and always with a qualifying expression; as, mental age, anatomical age. Called age equivalents.

age critique (French) Menopause or period of time during which menstruation ceases.

age equivalent The level of an individual's development, regarding any trait or characteristic, that is expressed as equal to the chronological age at which the particular level is normally or on the average attained. Therefore, the mental development characteristic of age eight is designated as mental age eight.

age-equivalent scale See *scale, age-equivalent.*

age-equivalent score See *score age.*

age-grade scaling See *scaling, age-grade.*

age norm   1. The average score attained by a large group of children on a standardized test; a representative performance of children at a given age level. 2. The chronological age at which a given score is usually achieved.

age ratio   The chronological age of a child at one testing divided by the child's chronological age at a later testing. This ratio is a crude measure of a test's predictive power. The test's predictive power depends on the age at which the test is given and the length of time between tests. The younger the age of the child, the poorer the predictive power of the test. The longer the interval between tests, the poorer the prediction from one test to the next. Therefore, prediction will probably be better from ages 5 to 6 (ratio 5/6) than from ages 3 to 4 (ratio 3/4).

age scale   See *scale, age*.

age score   See *score, age*.

agenesis; agenesia   Also called aplasia. The failure, either total or partial, of tissues to develop.

agenetic   Characterized by the absence or imperfect development of one or more parts of the body.

agent, catalytic   1. (chemistry) A substance that changes the velocity of a chemical reaction without being altered itself. 2. (psychology) The patient who initiates catharsis in other members of the psychotherapy group.

agent provocateur   Varying kinds of influence that act as precipitating or exciting causes of events, diseases or disorders.

ager naturae   (Latin) The field of nature; the uterus.

agerasia   An old age that shows youthful appearance, health and vigor.

ageusia   Also ageusis and ageustia. An impairment or deficiency in the sense of taste. The cause of such a disorder may be either physiological or emotional. There are three types of ageusia which are distinguished on the basis of the location of the defect causing the disturbance in the gustatory apparatus. If the cause is a cortical lesion, the disorder is called central ageusia. If the lesion is located in the nerve between its origin and distribution, the disorder is called conduction ageusia. However, if the defect is in the nerve endings, peripheral ageusia is the name given to it. This condition is common in psychiatric patients, particularly in the depressions. It has also been observed to occur in schizophrenia and hysteria.

agglutinations, image   See *image agglutinations*.

aggregate   1. A mass of distinct units; a group of objects, thoughts, persons, etc. that are brought together but remain separate entities. 2. (mathematics) A sum of a number of quantities.

aggregation theory   (W. C. Halstead) A theory of intelligence in neurological terms. It postulates that intelligence is a function of the coordinated effort of various sensory and motor areas located throughout the cerebral cortex.

aggression   1. Attack or hostile action that may take any form from physical assault at one extreme to gentle verbal criticism at the other extreme. This type of behavior may be directed at any thing or person, including the self. 2. (S. Freud) Aggression is one of the primary instincts. One's natural aggressiveness against the self may be directed against the outer world. Thanatos is, primarily, an instinct of death and all of us carry a certain amount of self-destructiveness within ourselves. It seems that people have to destroy things and other people in order not to destroy themselves. In order to protect oneself from the tendency toward self-destruction, one must find external channels for aggressiveness. 3. (A. Adler) In Adler's theory, aggressiveness is the most general human striving and is a necessity of life. Self-assertion is the underlying principle of aggression. The aggressive drive is the drive to overcome one's feeling of interiority. 4. (J. Dollard & N. E. Miller) According to the frustration-aggression theory interference with goal directed behavior is frustration, and frustration leads to either a substitute response or to aggression, which is also a kind of substitute. If aggression if blocked, it may be directed against a substitute or turned inward to become self-aggression. 5. (H. A. Murray) An individual's need to forcefully overcome opposition, to fight, to punish another, to injure or kill another and to revenge an injury.

aggression, animal experiments of   Several brain centers have been found to be important in the control of aggressive behavior. Afferent stimulation of the hypothalamus in a decortical cat produces quasi rage. Focal lesions of the hypothalamic ventromedial nucleus results in an exaggeration of aggressive tendencies. The medial hypothalamus appears to be inhibitory for this behavior while the lateral area is excitatory. Stimulation of the amygdala in intact animals also induces rage responses while ablation of this area produces docility in a variety of animals. In monkeys, amygdala lesions are followed by changes in position in the hierarchy of dominance-submission. The function of the amygdala seems to be the control of the excitability of lower central mechanisms for aggressive behavior.

aggression, antisocial   Unjustifiable aggression from a socially evaluative standpoint; e.g., instrumental, retaliatory, spontaneous.

aggression need   See *need, aggression*.

aggression, prosocial   Allegedly justified aggression, e.g., in children, tattling, belligerent rule-stating; in adults, punitive discipline of children and criminals, expressions of moral indignation and outrage, violence in a "good cause" (as in lynching, book or witch-burning, destruction of property/persons conceived to differ in values from one's own, revolution).

aggressive behavior   The acts of behavioral responses of an organism that display the quality of aggression.

aggressive instinct   See *Thanatos*.

aggressiveness   1. The tendency to display hostility by performing acts of aggression. 2. The tendency to overcome opposition of being self-assertive pushing forward one's own interests. **3.** Showing enterprising or energetic behavior. **4.** The tendency to be dominating in a social situation.

agitated depression   See *depression, agitated.*

agitation   **1.** Restlessness. **2.** Excitement. **3.** Set in motion. **4.** Hurrying.

agitolalia   Also agitophasia. Excessively rapid speech due to emotional excitement or stress. Speech is cluttered with sounds that are slurred, omitted, or distorted.

agitophasia   Also called agitolalia. The cluttered speech that results from extremely rapid speaking while under excitement and stress. Cluttering involves the omission, slurring or distortion of sounds.

agnosia   **1.** A complete or partial inability to recognize and attach meaning to the impressions of a sense organ. **2.** The loss of the memory of familiar objects. An individual with agnosia is unable to correctly perceive and identify familiar objects. This condition can involve any sensory system and is often the result of cortical damage. In visual agnosia, for example, the individual is able to perceive whatever is within his visual field but is unable to recognize what he is seeing.

agnosia, apperceptive visual   (H. Lissauer) A form of visual agnosia which is characterized by a disturbance of the visual synthesis of individual cues.

agnosia, associate visual   (H. Lissauer) A form of visual agnosia characterized by an inability to recognize the meaning of objects when perceiving their outline.

agnosia, left-right   See *apractagnosia.*

agnosia, speech   A disturbance of phonemic hearing resulting from damage to the posterosuperior portion of the left temporal lobe characterized by the lack of ability to distinguish sounds and words and repeat them, to produce words spontaneously, difficulty in naming objects and in writing and in general, an impairment of the analysis and synthesis of speech sounds.

agnosia, tactile   **1.** Agnosia due to lesions in the postcentral cortical areas which are characterized by difficulties in the tactile recognition of objects, especially the analysis and synthesis of tactile and kinesthetic stimuli. There are two forms: Wernicke's agnosia and asymbolia. **2.** See *agnosia, Wernicke's.* **3.** See *asymbolia.*

agnosia, visual   Agnosia due to lesions in the secondary visual cortex characterized by an inability to recognize objects or the meanings of objects. There are two forms: apperceptive visual agnosia and associate visual agnosia.

agnosia, Wernicke's   (S. Wernicke) A form of tactile agnosia in which the identification of objects through touch is impaired usually associated with lesions closer to the secondary areas of the cortical nucleus of the cutaneous-kinesthetic analyzer.

agoraphobia   An intense fear of open spaces.

agrammaphasia   Also called agrammatism. A type of aphasia in which the individual forms sentences without regard to grammatical rules.

agrammatism; agrammatologia, agrammata; agrammataphasia   A type of aphasia; the inability to communicate that involves the absence of grammatical rules in the formation of words into sentences. Such a loss of the ability to speak coherently may be the result of brain injury or it may accompany a severe mental disturbance such as schizophrenia.

agraphia   A type of aphasia; the inability to communicate, characterized by the loss of the power to write any or all of the following: individual letters, syllables, words or phrases. This impairment in the ability to write is usually due to a cerebral lesion but occasionally may be the result of emotional factors. Acquired agraphia is the name given to the condition that results from brain injury or disease which causes a loss of the individual's previous ability to write. Congenital agraphia refers to the situation in which the individual has unusual difficulty learning to write, difficulty that is not consistent with his other intellectual accomplishments.

agraphia, visual   Disturbances in writing due to lesions of the occipitoparietal areas characterized by inability to differentiate by writing letters, numerals, or words.

agreement coefficient   See *coefficient, agreement.*

agriothymia   A term used in the past to mean maniacal or insane ferociousness.

agriothymia ambitiosa   A morbid desire to conquer and/or destroy nations.

agriothymia hydrophobica   Also called hydrophobic agriothymia; an irresistible impulse to bite.

agriothymia religiosa   A morbid desire to destroy other religions and the people advocating them.

agromania   An extremely intense impulse to live in open country or in isolation.

agrypnia   A term to describe the inability to sleep, specifically a chronic condition of sleeplessness. Such a condition is also called insomnia. Sleeplessness that is associated with mental excitement is called agrypnia excitata. Agrypnia pertaesa is the inability to sleep due to a physical disorder. The sleeplessness brought on because of old age is referred to as agrypnia senilis.

agrypnocoma   Also called coma-vigil. A deep sleep from which the person can be easily awakened; sleepless coma. A condition involving variations of coma and wakefulness that can be observed particularly in patients with an organic brain disease.

agrypnotic   Relating to, producing or displaying insomnia.

agyiophobia   A morbid fear of streets; fear of crossing streets.

aha or ah-ah experience   Also called ah-hah experience. The name given to the moment of insight or the realization of a solution in a problem solving situation. The time when all the perceived parts of an experience fit into a meaningful pattern.

ahedonia Inability to experience pleasure.

ahistorical A theoretical approach to the study of behavior that emphasizes present conditions, both within and without the organism, as a means of understanding the present behavior of that organism. The use of any item from the past history of the organism is minimal when present behavior is the object of study.

ahypnia; ahypnosia Terms applied to extremely severe cases of insomnia; inability to sleep. See *agrypnia*.

aichmophobia A morbid fear of pointed objects.

aidoiomania Another term for erotomania; a morbid inclination to love.

aids The development of systems of cognitive ability to cope, through the discovery of some particular response formula which is successful and generates many associated performances.

ailment, functional A mild, temporary symptom resulting from disturbed physiological functioning such as the somatic expression of emotional conflicts.

ailurophobia Also called galeophobia and gatophobia. Morbid fear of cats.

aim-inhibition See *drive, aim-inhibited*.

aim of instinct The aim of an instinct is to return the organism to the relative state of balance that existed before the instinct was aroused. The term homeostatic equilibrium has been used by W. B. Cannon to refer to this state. The aim of an instinct is the disappearance of an unpleasurable state while the object of an instinct is the means through which the aim can be achieved. The psychoanalyst's constancy principle represents a view similar to Cannon's.

aim-transference The shift of objectives from one life situation to another in which the goal is more likely to be achieved. For example, if the goal is success, aim-transference may involve the switch from activities in sports to activities in music.

aiming test See *test, aiming*.

air-swallowing See *aerophagia*.

akataphasia See *acataphasia*.

akinesia algera (P.J. Moebius) A form of hysteria characterized by a general painfulness accompanying any type of movement. Moebius associated this symptom only with conditions of psychogenic origin.

akinesis; akinesia The absence or impairment of voluntary movement. Frequently observed in psychiatric patients, akinesis is usually of functional arigin.

akinesthesia The absence or impairment of the kinesthetic sense which includes the muscles, tendons and joints. This condition involves the inability to perceive movement of one's own body.

akinetic Relating to or characterized by lack of mobility.

akinetic apraxia See *apraxia, akinetic*.

akoasm; acoasm A simple, auditory hallucination of sounds such as crackling or buzzing. See *acousma*.

AL See *adaptation level*.

alalia Speechlessness; the complete absence of the ability to talk as a result of functional causes.

alarm reaction The release of metabolites in the affected tissues as a response to stress. See *adaptation syndrome*.

albedo The reflecting power of a surface or object described in terms of the ratio of the light reflected by the object to the light falling upon that surface. This ratio is completely independent of the degree of illumination. The ratio of reflectance is the same whether the illumination is weak or intense.

albedo perception A form of brightness constancy in which the discrimination or perception of surfaces is made only with regard to their albedo (ratio of reflectance), while disregarding the variations in degree of illumination.

Albee, George W. (1921-) American psychologist, concerned with manpower and the sociology of professions. His survey of the nation's needs and resources for professionals for intervention and prevention, and his long-time advocacy of the position that disturbed behavior does not reflect illness but a damaging and inhumane environment, has affected mental health planning. His research interests in psychopathology have focused on intellectual development of seriously disturbed adults. He served as President of the Division of Clinical Psychology (1966-67) and as President of the American Psychological Association (1969-70).

albinism A congenital deficiency in pigmentation of the skin, hair, and eyes. In extreme cases the skin is a milky color, the hair is very light, and the eyes have deep red pupils and pink or blue irises. This condition also involves color blindness.

alcheringa According to the mythology of the Arunta tribe of Australia, alcheringa is the "dream time" or period in which the subhuman ancestors of their race lived.

alcoholic A person addicted to alcoholic beverages.

alcoholic dementia See *dementia, alcoholic*.

alcoholic hallucinosis See *hallucinosis, alcoholic*.

alcoholic psychoses See *psychoses, alcoholic*.

alcoholic psychosis, paranoid type See *psychosis, alcoholic, paranoid type*.

Alcoholics Anonymous Also called A.A. An organization formed in 1935 by former alcoholics aiming at helping alcoholics in overcoming their addiction to alcohol.

alcoholism 1. Addiction to alcoholic beverages. **2.** Alcoholic poisoning.

alcoholomania An urge for drinking alcoholic beverages.

alcoholophilia A liking for alcoholic beverages.

aldosterone A steroid isolated from substances of the adrenal cortex and from human urine which causes sodium retention and potassium loss.

alector A term that was used to refer to any individual who was unable to sleep.

alertness Being quick to understand and to act; rapid perception; watchfulness.

Alexanderism An uncontrollable desire to conquer and/or destroy nations; also called agriothymia ambitiosa.

alexia Also called word blindness and visual aphasia. A form of aphasia in which there is an absence of the ability to grasp meaning from or to read the written or printed language. This condition is the result of organic brain damage and does not involve any impairment in vision or intelligence. The loss of a previous ability to read is called acquired alexia. If the condition involves an inability to learn to read that is not consistent with the individual's mental age and other intellectual achievements, it is referred to as congenital alexia.

alexia, visual Disturbances in reading due to lesions of the occipitoparietal areas and characterized by inability to recognize individual letters, numerals, or words.

algebraic value The numerical value that includes the plus or minus sign that preceeds the number.

algedonic Pertaining to that dimension of experience or emotion characterized by pleasantness-unpleasantness.

algesia; algesis Sensitivity to pain; the ability to feel pain; sometimes referring to a capacity to experience pain that is above the average.

algesimeter; algesiometer An instrument with a sharp, pricking stimulus used to measure sensitivity to pain by pressing the calibrated needle against the skin.

algesthesia; algesthesis 1. Sensitivity to pain. **2.** General hypersensitivity (hyperesthesia).

algolagnia (Schrenck-Notzing) Sadomasochism; experiencing perverse sexual arousal or sexual pleasure as a result of either receiving or inflicting pain. Active algolagnia- sadism; passive- masochism.

algolagnist An individual who achieves sexual excitement by either experiencing or inflicting pain.

algometer An instrument used to measure sensitivity to pain by employing the pressure of a blunt stimulus against the skin.

algophilia Masochism. Experiencing pleasure as a result of receiving pain.

algophobia An intense fear of pain.

algopsychalia A symptom expressed as pain in the mind that is distinguished, by the patient, from organically caused pain. This symptom is character-

istic of some hypochondriacal, depressed and schizophrenic patients. For example, the hypochondriac complains of severe head pains resulting from the pressure of unbearable anxiety.

alienatio mentis Literally, alienation of the mind; in general, it denotes insanity.

alienation 1. Estrangement; breaking down of a close relationship. **2.** (social psychology) Disruption of feeling of belonging to a larger group such as, for instance, the deepening of the generation gap or increasing of a gulf separating social groups from one another.

alienist A physician, usually a psychiatrist, who is considered by the courts to be an expert on mental disorders. Such an individual is accepted as an expert witness regarding the mental responsibility of persons involved in legal actions.

alimentary behavior, brain mechanism in The limbic and hypothalamic areas of the brain have been found to be important in the control of alimentary behavior. Stimulation of the lateral hypothalamus causes eating behavior while lesions in this area results in aphasia. The ventromedial hypothalamic areas are important in satiety. Stimulation of this area ends feeding while lesions result in hyperphagia. The hypothalamic areas which control drinking behavior are adjacent to those which control eating. While eating depends on adrenergic excitation, drinking is caused by chalinergic excitation. Empirical studies have used a variety of methods to control feeding and drinking behavior resulting in a multiple-factor theory of regulation of feeding and drinking which seems to be generally accepted. Experiments focusing on the EEG activity during alimentary behavior suggest that satiety may express an internal inhibition which, after consummation is achieved, plays a important role in bringing innate behavior to an end.

alimentary canal The body organs from the mouth to the anus, including the esophagus, stomach, and small and large intestine. This system is involved in the passage, digestion, and absorption of food, as well as the elimination of waste products.

alimentary orgasm (S. Rado) The period of satisfaction that occurs after hunger is satiated. In psychoanalysis, the gastro-intestinal tract is considered to be important with regard to emotional investment and action.

allachaesthesia; allesthesia Also spelled allachesthesia; allaesthesia. Experiencing a tactile sensation at a place other than the point actually stimulated.

allegoric interpretation See *interpretation, allegoric.*

allegorization (A. Neisser) The formation of new words or phrases; a process frequently observed in schizophrenic patients.

allele; allelomorph Alleles (allelomorphs) are alternative forms of a gene found in the corresponding loci on homologous chromosomes. Only two alleles can be present in any one individual, one derived from each parent that have segregated at meiosis. Multiple alleles is the term to designate the situation where more than two alleles exist for a given locus in the population. Each allele carries contrasting Mendelian characteristics and goes to different mature germ cells.

allelic; allelomorphic Referring to, pertaining to or having the characteristics of an allele or allelomorph. For example, blue eyes and brown eyes are allelomorphic characteristics.

allergic potential scale See *scale, allergic potential.*

allergy (C. von Pirquet) An acquired, altered reaction capacity of the tissues to specific substances that are harmless to most people. This involves an antigen-antibody mechanism that is characteristic of many disease processes and causes physical disturbances that may range from mild irritation to shock. The antigens (allergens) may be either proteins, lipids, haptens, or carbohydrates; however, the antibodies are not always demonstrable. There are four general classifications of allergic diseases: (a) Serum sickness, (b) Contact dermatitis, (c) Atopic diseases are those that depend upon an inherited reaction capacity, such as hay fever, asthma and drug sensitivities, (d) Anaphylaxis refers to those responses that are induced by previous sensitization.

allergy, cerebral Bizarre and unusual cerebral disturbances occurring as symptoms in allergic individuals.

allergy, extrinsic An allergic reaction resulting from an allergen that originates outside the body.

allergy, intrinsic An allergic reaction caused by an allergen that originates within the body.

alliaceous (Zwaardemaker) One of the classes of smell sensations, of which garlic is a typical example.

allied reflexes See *reflexes, allied.*

allocentric Referring to those senses that are oriented objectively such as seeing and hearing.

allocheiria; allochiria A condition involving the experiencing of a tactile sensation at a corresponding point on the side of the body opposite to the side that had actually been stimulated.

alloerotic Pertaining to sexual excitement that is directed to or induced by others; referring to the extension of libido outward, upon other individuals; opposite to the self-directed, autoerotic sexuality.

alloerotism; alloeroticism Directing sexual or erotic tendencies toward others and away from the self.

allolalia Unusual or abnormal speech.

allophasis An obsolete term meaning incoherent speech.

alloplastic (psychoanalysis) Referring to directing libido away from the self toward other persons and objects.

alloplasty (psychoanalysis) The process through which the adaptation of libido to the environment occurs; directing libido energies away from the self toward other individuals and objects.

allopsyche Another person's mind or psyche.

allopsychic Denoting mental or psychic processes in the world outside the individual himself.

allopsychosis Referring to psychological processes that are directed outside the self. For example, allopsychic delusions involve the projection of the individual's own impulses and feelings into others.

all-or-none response A reaction, involving individual neurons and muscle fibers, that is either of maximum strength or not at all. Such a response shows no gradation regardless of the intensity of the stimulus, as long as it is above threshold strength.

allotriogeusia; allotriogeustia 1. An abnormal appetite. 2. An unusual or perverted sense of taste.

allotriophagy An intense desire or need to eat unusual foodstuffs.

allotropic 1. Relating to or exhibiting allotropy. 2. (psychiatry) A personality that is concerned with others; how they feel, what they think.

allotropy 1. The occurrence of an element in two or more separate forms with different physical properties. 2. A strange or unusual form. 3. An attraction between unlike structures or cells. 4. The term Adolf Meyer used for allopsyche.

Allport, Gordon W. (1897-1967) American psychologist, personality theorist, and researcher. Received his Ph.D. in psychology (1922) from Harvard where he served as professor of psychology from 1930 until his death. Known principally for his innovative contribution to the psychology of personality. Allport's theory emphasizes unique individuality, human maturity, and conscious forces. Among his many works are *Personality: A Psychological Interpretation* (1937), *Becoming* (1955), *Pattern and Growth in Personality* (1961). In the area of social psychology he also contributed *The Psychology of Rumor* (with L. Postman, 1947), *The Individual and His Religion* (1950) and *The Nature of Prejudice* (1954).

Allport A—S Reaction Study (G. W. Allport and F. H. Allport) An example of a unidimensional approach to the measurement of personality. The Allport A—S Reaction Study is a test designed to measure the incidence in the personality of two traits, ascendance and submission. It is theorized that one trait would be prominent and the other subordinate. The method is to present verbally certain life situations and require the subject to select from the standardized choices the type of behavior most characteristic of his own adjustment to such situations. There are two forms available, one for men and another for women. The score is an algebraic summation of the number of situations in which the person felt that he would be dominant. Such a score is assumed to be representative of some general tendency on the part of the subject. An example of a typical situation is as follows:

a. At a reception or tea do you seek to meet the important person present?

Frequently
Occasionally
Never

b. Do you feel reluctant to meet him?

Yes, usually
Sometimes
No

Allport — Vernon — Lindzey Study of Values (G. W. Allport, P. E. Vernon, and G. Lindzey) Revision of Allport — Vernon Study of Values. A questionnaire designed to yield measures of six attitudes believed to be the most revealing aspects of personality. The scoring shows the individual's emphasis on social, theoretical, economic (interest in acquisition of material things), aesthetic, political (interest in interpersonal power relations), and religious values. This instrument is appropriate for use with late adolescent or college age subjects. Each individual is given a total of 180 points which is distributed among the six values; therefore, the scores for each value is the relative strength of that value within the person. The resulting scores are significantly related to various educational and occupational groupings, as well as to academic achievement. This technique requires responses to 15 four-alternative items and 30 two-alternative items. An example of a four-alternative item is the following:

1. Do you think that a good government should aim chiefly at:

a. more aid for the poor, sick and old
b. the development of manufacturing and trade
c. introducing more ethical principles into its policies and diplomacy
d. establishing a position of prestige and respect among nations.

The subject indicates his order of preference by writing 1, 2, 3, or 4 before each alternative. A two-alternative item is illustrated as follows:

2. The main objects of scientific research should be the discovery of pure truth rather than its practical applications.

(a) Yes   (b) No
Agreement with (a) and disagreement with (b) is shown by writing 3 under (a) and 0 under (b). A slight preference for (a) over (b) is indicated by writing 2 under (a) and 1 under (b). The opposite is done if the agreement or slight preference is for (b).

alogia 1. Senseless or stupid behavior. 2. Inability to speak because of defects in the central nervous system such as a brain lesion; expressive aphasia. 3. The type of mutism, due to lack of ideas, that may be observed in an idiot or imbecile.

alogous A term used in the past to mean irrational or unreasonable.

Alper's disease Severe mental retardation combined with seizure state, caused by destruction of cerebral neurons, while the myelinated structures remain unaffected. The disease is nonlipid and it is most often caused by cerebral anoxia. It is also called progressive infantile cerebral poliodystrophy.

Alpha, Beta, Gamma hypotheses (K. Dunlap) Three hypotheses concerning the relationship of frequency of repetition to the rate of learning. Alpha states that frequency of repetition promotes learning. Beta indicates that frequency of repetition has no effect on the rate of learning. Gamma proposes that frequency of repetition hinders learning. See *hypothesis.*

alpha error See *error, alpha.*

Alpha Examination; Alpha Test A group general intelligence test consisting of eight subtests given to military personnel during World War I. See *test, Army Alpha.*

alpha movement See *movement, alpha.*

alpha press See *press, alpha.*

alpha response A response, in a conditioning situation, that is not considered to be true learning but rather is believed to be the result of sensitization.

alpha rhythm Also called Berger rhythm, Berger wave, and alpha wave. The most common brain waves of the adult cortex. During rest the oscillations are regular and smooth, occurring at a rate of 8-12 per second with an amplitude of 5-15 microvolts.

Alpha Tests See *test, Army Alpha.*

alphabet content (H. Rorschach) The scoring system used when letters of the alphabet are given as responses to the inkblots.

alt schedule See *reinforcement, schedule of: alternate.*

alter To change, vary or modify. In psychology: An individual's concept of another person as distinct and separate from himself.

alter ego; alteregoism A very intimate friend that is considered by the individual as a second or other self. Alteregoism is a close feeling about another person in the same situation as oneself.

alternate form See *form, alternate.*

alternate responses test See *test, alternate responses.*

alternating personalities The appearance, independently, of more than one organization of the mental, social, and moral qualities of an individual as manifested in the person's relations with his social environment.

alternating vision The process of using first one eye and then the other eye for seeing. In most situations, one eye has dominance over the other and suppresses its incoming sensory information.

alternation of neurosis An older expression referring to the temporary or permanent cure of a behavioral disorder by the occurrence of an acute physical ailment.

alternation problem, double See *problem, double alternation.*

alternative (alt) schedule See *reinforcement, schedule of: alternative (alt).*

alternative hypothesis See *hypothesis, alternative.*

alternative reinforcement See *reinforcement, alternative.*

altitude A dimension of intelligence described as the level of difficulty of the problems that an individual can solve. Other dimensions are extent of intelligence, the variety of problems that can be solved, and speed of intelligence, the time required to solve certain problems.

altitude test See *test, altitude.*

altophobia Morbid fear of heights.

altrigenderism The natural, nonsexual and non-amorous activities that occur between individuals of opposite sexes. Heteroerotism refers to amorous, though not overtly sexual interests. Heterosexuality is the term used when the sexual element becomes involved; heterogenitality is the expression used when referring specifically to sexual intercourse.

altruism (A. Comte) Consideration, concern and affection for other people as opposed to self-love or egoism.

altruistic Relating to or characterized by altruism; that is, by constructive consideration and interest in others.

alucinatio A term that literally means wandering of mind, but is used to refer to an hallucination.

alusia An obsolete term for insanity. The literal meaning is to wander in mind.

alveolar Relating to an alveolus: 1) A cavity, pit, depression or cell. 2) A cell of air located in the lungs. 3) The bony socket of a tooth.

alysm The restlessness that is displayed by persons who are ill.

alysmus The mental anguish, anxiety and depression that accompanies an illness.

alysosis Also called otiumosis. Boredom; may be observed in simple schizophrenia.

Alzheimer's disease (A. Alzheimer) A rare presenile psychosis that is associated with cerebral sclerosis. There is a rapid deterioration of the brain causing progressive mental disorder accompanied by speech difficulties. The individual is hyperactive and restless, displaying both defective memory and disorientation. Although all the symptoms of senile psychosis may be manifested, this disease may occur at a comparatively early age, such as in the forties.

amacrine cells Also called inner horizontal cells or association cells. Amacrine cells are retinal cells that connect the bipolar or second order neurons. Although they appear to be without axons, the bodies of these cells are located in one of the lower rows of the inner nuclear layer. The importance of amacrine cells is believed to be their involvement in summation effects.

amathophobia A morbid fear of dust.

amaurosis The partial or total loss of sight, from any cause, without changes in the structure of the eye. The temporary blindness that may result from sudden acceleration is called amaurosis fugax. Amaurosis partialis fugax is the partial blindness that may accompany headaches or vertigo. The condition characterized by total blindness existing at birth is called congenital amaurosis. Introducing various poisons and toxic products into the body may result in a type of blindness known as toxic amaurosis. Another type of toxic amaurosis is uremic amaurosis. See *Tay-Sachs disease.*

amaurotic family idiocy See *Tay-Sachs disease.*

amaxophobia An intense or morbid fear of being in, or riding upon, any vehicle.

ambidextrality Referring to or characterized by the use of both sides of the body.

ambidextrous 1. Having no preferred side in performing motor functions. The ability to perform motor acts equally well with the right side of the body as with the left side. 2. Equal skill or ability with both the right and left hand.

ambiequal (Rorschach inkblots) A personality dimension described as a well-balanced amount of both introtensive and extrotensive tendencies. The person does not appear as either excessively dependent upon others or particularly egocentric.

ambiguity, intolerance of A psychological state manifested in a rigid individual and characterized by the tendency to overlook differences and to simplify the environment.

ambiguity tolerance The ability and willingness to handle situations in which there are conflicting or alternate outcomes or interpretations, without undue difficulty.

ambiguous 1. Unclear; vague; having several meanings. 2. Referring to statements, objects, or situations that have two meanings or give rise to two intepretations.

ambiguous figure Any one of a large group of figures which are subject to continuous change in perspective or interpretation when regarded steadily for a period of time. The Necker cube is the most common example.

ambitendency The co-existence of opposing actions, each existing independently of the other.

ambitent A Rorschach postulate, referring to those instances where the sum of human movement responses is essentially equal to the weighted sum of color responses. When the ratio (Erlebnistypus) manifests such features, the person is considered naturally prone to derive basic gratifications either from within himself or from interaction with his environment.

ambivalence 1. The co-existence of opposing emotions, attitudes or traits in the same individual. **2.** The rapid alternation of emotional attitudes towards another. **3.** Being able to attend to or view two or more aspects of an issue or to view a person in terms of more than one dimension or value. **4.** (K. Lewin) The state of being pushed towards or pulled between two opposite goals.

ambiversion (C. G. Jung) A personality type balancing between introversion and extroversion, these two traits being present in about equal amounts.

ambivert (C. G. Jung) An individual having ambiversions as the prominent personality trait.

amblyopia Poor vision having no known connection with any organic defect or problem in the refracting mechanism of the eye. It has been associated with color blindness, albinism, and tobacco, alcohol and other toxic states.

amblyoscope An instrument used to determine the point at which two separately presented visual stimuli fuse.

ambrosiac A class of odors of which musk is an example.

ambulatory automatism See *automatism, ambulatory.*

ambulatory psychotherapy See *psychotherapy, ambulatory.*

ambulatory schizophrenia See *schizophrenia, ambulatory.*

amelectic A state of indifference; apathy.

ameleia Indifference, morbid apathy.

amenomania 1. A mild form of mania the symptoms of which are gaiety, a fondness for clothes, etc. **2.** Morbidly elevated affective state. **3.** (B. Rush) A term applied to the manic phase of manic depressive psychosis. **4.** A delirium marked by joyousness.

amenorrhea An absence of menstruation resulting from emotional conflict situations where a suppression of menstruation in young women is a defense against sexuality and where heterosexual fantasies substitute for the unacceptable aspects of femininity.

amentia Obsolete term for mental deficiency.

American Psychiatric Association, classification of mental disorders See *classification of mental disorders.*

Ames demonstrations Situations devised by Adelbert Ames, Jr. allowing distortions of depth perception by the use of one cue at a time to eliminate conflicting cues.

ametropia Errors of refraction due to a defect in the refractive apparatus of the eye. Usually affecting the visual acuity and accomodation of the eye.

amimia Language disorder in which the person is unable to communicate with the help of gestures or signs.

amine Any compound formed by placing one or more of the hydrogens of ammonia by one or more organic radicals such as $R \cdot NH_2$, $R \cdot NH \cdot R'$ and $R \cdot N \cdot (R') R''$, where R, R', and R'', may or may not represent the same radical.

amino acid Organic compound resulting from the hydrolysis of protein and having the basic formula of $NH_2 - R - COOH$ where R = aliphatic radical. These compounds are used by the body of an organism to resynthesize its proteins.

aminoaciduria A disorder of amino acid metabolism causing elevated concentrations of one or more amino acids and the presence of excess amino acid in the urine.

aminoacidurias, no-threshold Disease in which enzymatic deficiencies are present but in which no increase in plasma concentration of the amino acids occur. See *homocystinuria.*

aminoacidurias, overflow A type of aminoacidurias in which amino acid appears in the urine as a result of increased plasma concentration of one or more amino acids, due to an enzymatic deficiency. See *phenylketonuria; maple syrup urine disease; histidinemia; tyrosinosis.*

aminoacidurias, renal A group of aminoacidurias which are the result of faulty mechanism of reabsorption of amino acids in the renal tubules. See *Hartnup disease; Joseph's syndrome; methionine malabsorption.*

amitosis Cell division with no splitting of the chromosomes.

amitryptiline An antidepressant drug of the tricyclic compound group used in the treatment of depressions.

amnemonic Relating to an impairment in or loss of memory.

amnesia 1. A deficiency in or lack of memory, either partial or total. **2.** An inability to recall past experiences.

amnesia, anterograde Loss of memory for those experiences and events following the physical or psychical trauma.

amnesia, autohypnotic (C. G. Jung) Descriptive term for repression.

amnesia, catathymic Memory loss delimited and confined to a certain recollection or experience.

amnesia, circumscribed Memory loss in which the beginning, or the termination of the memory loss is fairly easily defined.

amnesia, continuous See *amnesia, anterograde.*

amnesia, episodic Forgetting of particular important incidents only.

amnesia, epochal Loss of all memory of a certain past period or epoch of one's life usually precipitated by a sudden shock or trauma; the forgotten period varies from a few days to several years.

amnesia, infantile Loss of memory for the years from birth to about five years to age necessitated by the unacceptable nature of memories concerning the rise of the sexual life and the limits imposed upon the infant's power.

amnesia, post-hypnotic Loss of memory for what occurred during hypnosis.

amnesia, retrograde Loss of memory for those events and experiences preceding the cause of the amnesia.

amnestic aphasia See *aphasia, amnestic.*

amnestic apraxia See *apraxia, amnestic.*

amniocentesis Recovery of embryonic cells from the amniotic fluid for genetic prognosis assessment purposes.

amobarbital The generic name of a five-ethyl-five-isoamylbarbituric acid whose trade name is amytal.

amobarbital sodium The generic name of the sodium derivative of amobarbital which is a central nervous system depressant producing sedation or hypnosis depending on the dose given.

amphetamines A racemic drug, $C_6H_5CH_2CH(NH_2)CH_3$ used in medicine and psychiatry as a stimulant in depression and a diet pill in obesity.

amphierotism (S. Ferenczi) Condition in which the individual is able to conceive of himself as a male or a female both together.

amphigenesis Ability of a primarily homosexual individual to have normal sexual relations with a member of the opposite sex.

amphigenous inversion See *inversion, amphigenous.*

amphimixis 1. Contribution by both parents to the heredity of the offspring. 2. (S. Ferenczi) Refers to the union of anal and genital eroticism.

amplitude 1. Size or amount of the movement from point zero during any one cycle of a variable. 2. Size of a sound or light wave from point zero, related to the psychological dimensions of loudness and brilliance respectively.

ampulla That enlarged area of the semicircular canals where they connect with the vestibule of the inner ear, containing the hair cells serving as the end organs of the sense of equilibrium.

amputee, castration anxiety See *castration anxiety, amputee.*

amuck; amok A state of murderous frenzy. Amuck patients attack murderously whoever is in their way until they themselves collapse. Hypothetically related to psychomotor epilepsy. The term amuck is borrowed from Malayan amog.

amusia Impairment or loss of ability, most likely due to brain damage, to comprehend or reproduce musical tones.

amychophobia Morbid fear of being clawed or scratched, of lacerations.

amygdaloid nucleus; amygdala Almond-shaped mass of grey matter in the cerebrum located approximately under the anterior tip of the temporal lobe. Thought to be one of the interconnected emotional and motivational centers of the old brain.

amyostasia Muscle tremor.

amytal interview See *interview, amytal.*

amytal; sodium amytal Trade name for a barbiturate used widely as a sedative and hypnotic. Known popularly, and incorrectly, as "truth serum" since it effects lowering of inhibitions but does not allow confession against the individual's will.

anabolism Synthetic metabolism involving the restoration and building up of tissues.

anaclisis 1. Condition of emotional dependence on others. 2. (psychoanalysis) A condition in which another instinct conditions the satisfaction of the sex drive.

anaclitic depression See *depression, anaclitic.*

anaclitic object choice Choice of a loved object based on the unconscious wish to receive passive gratification.

anacusia; anacusis Complete and total deafness.

anaesthesia See *anesthesia.*

anaesthetic See *anesthetic.*

anaglyph Stereoscopic picture printed in two complimentary colors that are slightly offset which, when viewed through lenses of the same colors, gives the illusion of depth.

anaglyptoscope; anaglyphoscope Instrument used to demonstrate the importance of shadow and light in perception by reversing the lighting of an object.

anagogic 1. Referring to the spiritual interpretation of words and the Scriptures. 2. Allegoric Scripture interpretation looking for hidden meaning for future life. 3. Of or pertaining to ideals, to the significance, spiritual or ideal, of behavior or the content of the psyche. 4. (C. G. Jung) The ideal, moral or spiritual striving of the unconscious. 5. Dream interpretation which emphasizes the philosophical meaning of the dream.

anagogic interpretation See *interpretation, anagogic.*

anagogic symbolism See *symbolism, anagogic.*

anagogy, anagoge 1. Interpretation or application of needs that is spiritual in nature, as with the Scriptures. 2. Scripture interpretation, allegorical in nature, seeking obscured meanings concerning future life.

anal birth Dreams and fantasies whose anal erotic content is expressed in a symbolic wish to be reborn through the anus.

anal character See *character, anal.*

anal eroticism The experience of sexual arousal or excitement through the stimulation of the anus or by activities associated with the anus such as defecation.

anal-expulsive stage (K. Abraham) Subdivision of the anal stage in which erotic pleasure is experienced by the passing of the feces. There is little interest in or caring for the external object (parent) and the passing of the feces often has sadistic overtones.

anal personality See *character, anal.*

anal-retentive stage (K. Abraham) Subdivision of the anal stage in which the child experiences pleasure from holding on to his feces, which may become his love object. Considered to be the source of tenderness.

anal sadism See *sadism, anal.*

anal-sadistic love Object relationship characterized by a high degree of aggressive as well as love impulses, typically seen in the anal stage.

anal-sadistic stage See *anal stage.*

anal stage (S. Freud) The second stage of psychosexual development occurring in the second year of life during which the child derives sexual pleasure from the stimulation of the anal zone by the elimination and retention of feces. This stage is characterized by an ambivalence concerning masculine and feminine impulses manifested as active desires to manipulate and to master, and passive wishes to be dependent and taken care of.

analgesia, analgia Insensitivity to pain.

analgesia, congenital Insensitivity to pain which exists from birth.

analgesic, analgetic 1. Pertaining to analgesia. 2. A drug which relieves pain.

anality 1. The component of libido which is localized at the anal zone. 2. Instinctual conflict observed during the anal stage of development. 3. Anal eroticism reflecting a fixation of the anal stage.

analogies test See *test, analogies.*

analogy period (Rorschach) A type of directive inquiry recommended in the Klopfer approach to the Rorschach. In the formal inquiry all questioning concerning responses must be non-directive, and for this reason, some information provided by the subject may lack clarity. The analogy period permits the examiner to ask direct questions after the formal inquiry has been completed.

analysand One being psychoanalyzed.

analysis 1. Process of reducing or separating out the constituent parts of a complicated phenomenon. 2. Method of understanding a phenomenon in which the conditions under which it occurs are varied. 3. See *psychoanalysis.*

analysis, character See *character analysis.*

analysis, content (sociology) A method of transcribing qualitative material into quantitative form by counting. The process consists of determining how to break up the data, how to categorize the

units, and of forming an appropriate scoring guide which independent judges can use reliably.

analysis, direct (J. Rosen) A psychotherapeutic technique of treating psychotics based on modifed psychoanalytic theoretical formulations in which the therapist enters the patient's delusional system and literally interprets his primary process verbalizations. The psychotic symptoms are believed to reflect unconscious processes directly without the erection of defenses or resistances. The therapist utilizes the patients' delusional system, offers support and provides corrective experiences.

analysis, ego Interpretation of ego defenses in psychoanalytic treatment leading to an understanding of the reason for the defense against the impulse.

analysis, graphic (statistics) The use of graphs to discover significant relationships among variables.

analysis, group The investigation of social pathology in a group.

analysis, intent Measurement of social interaction by categorizing verbal statements in terms of their intent or purpose, such as seeking support or comfort.

analysis, item 1. The process of determining the difficulty, discriminability, internal consistency, and reliability of a test item. 2. The determination of item validity.

analysis, latent structure (P. F. Lazarsfeld) A technique for scaling answers to an attitude questionnaire based on the assumption that inconsistent replies can be explained in terms of a deeper, underlying class or classes of attitudes.

analysis, link See *link analysis.*

analysis of covariance (statistics) The method used to determine whether differences in variance of two or more related dependent variables exposed to two or more experimental conditions are significantly different from what would be expected by chance while controlling the intercorrelation of the various variables.

analysis of variance (statistics) A method used to determine whether the differences in the variance in the dependent variable under different experimental conditions could have occurred by chance only.

analysis, orthodox See *psychoanalysis.*

analysis, pattern 1. A technique for the search of clusters of items which belong together according to a particular criterion. 2. A technique for finding a group of items which are superior in predicting the criterion to each single item along.

analysis, propaganda An assessment of propaganda by the study of its techniques, agencies, materials and contents.

analysis, scalar See *scalar analysis.*

analysis, scatter An analysis of the amount or qualitative pattern of scatter for the purpose of finding significant relationships among the various subtest scores on a test.

analysis, self The attempt to understand one's own motivations, actions, and feelings without the aid of professional guidance. Freud originally suggested all psychoanalysts undergo self-analysis to avoid potential counter-transference problems but later changed this view in favor of a training analysis.

analysis, syndromal (D. Horn) A simplified type of factor analysis in which rated variables are intercorrelated and combined distributions are performed for highly intercorrelated groups of variables.

analysis, training Personal psychoanalysis of the future psychoanalyst for the purpose of training.

analysis, transactional See *psychoanalysis, transactional.*

analyst See *psychoanalyst.*

analytic group psychotherapy See *psychotherapy, analytic group.*

analytic process See *process, analytic.*

analytic psychotherapy See *psychotherapy, psychoanalytic.*

analytic therapy See *psychotherapy, analytical.*

analytical psychology See *psychology, analytical.*

analytical scale See *scale, analytical.*

analyzer (I. P. Pavlov) The first part of a reflex arc which begins in the natural peripheral end of the centripedal nerve and ends in the receptor cells of the central organ.

anamnesis **1.** Recollection or recalling. **2.** Events prior to the onset of a disorder in a personal, medical or family history which are remembered by the affected individual and sometimes considered pertinent to the disorder.

anancasm Stereotyped, repetitious behavior which produces anxiety if not performed.

anancastia; anankastia An obsessive, compulsive or phobic condition in which the individual feels he is being forced to act, think, or feel against his own will.

anandia See *aphonia.*

anandria The absence of male characteristics or of masculinity.

anaphase (biology) The third stage of mitosis in which the halves of the chromosomes migrate to opposite poles of the spindle.

anaphia Loss of the tactile sense, or some deficiency in it.

anaphrodisia The absence of sexual feeling.

anaphrodisiac That which causes or pertains to a lack of sexual or erotic feeling.

anaphylaxis Extreme susceptibility, particularly an allergic condition in which there is hypersensitivity to proteins taken into the body.

anarthria A partial or total inability to speak articulately.

anasarca hystericum **1.** A temporary swelling, usually of the abdominal area, in a hysterical person. **2.** Phantom tumor.

Anastasi, Anne (1908-) American psychologist. Chairman Psychology Department Fordham University. Principal research concerns test construction and evaluation, factor analysis, nature and origin of psychological traits, and role of cultural and experimental factors in the development of individual and group differences. Author of *Differential Psychology* (1958), *Psychological Testing* (1968), *Fields of Applied Psychology* (1964). President of the American Psychological Association, 1971-72.

anathymiasis **1.** (philosophy) Obsolete Greek term for soul. **2.** An obsolete term for hysterical flatus.

anatomical age A measure of skeletal development based on the rato of the ossification of wrist bones to the area of the "carpal quadrilateral."

anatomy response (An or At) (Rorschach) A scoring code for internal bodily details which can be seen only through the use of X-ray or by dissection.

anchorages **1.** Perceptual anchoring. **2.** The standards or reference points against which judgments are made.

androgen A sex hormone present in both sexes but in greater quantity in males which influences the structural and behavioral characteristics associated with maleness.

androgenic That which causes maleness or contributes to maleness.

androgyneity (anthropology) Belief that the individual has bipolar sexual potential until he is transformed into a particular sex by tribal ritual.

androgynoid A male with hermaphroditic features who often appears to be female.

androgynous, androgynal, androgynoid, androgynic The presence of both male and female characteristics in one individual.

androgyny Condition of being androgynous.

andromania Erotic craving for men in a female; nymphomania.

andromenecism See *hermaphroditism.*

androphobia Morbid fear of men.

androphomania Obsolete term for mental disorder characterized by homicidal tendencies.

anecdotal evidence Casual, unsystematic observations which is rarely sufficient evidence for generalizations but can be used to make hypotheses regarding further investigations.

anecdotal method (G. J. Romanes) A method of presenting data using popular accounts based on observation. This method was introduced in 1882 in the book, *Animal Intelligence* which presented data on animal behavior from scientific and popular accounts.

anechoic Echo free, especially in reference to a room or enclosed area.

anemia An abnormal reduction of the amount of oxygen transported by the blood due to a decrease in the number of erythrocytes per cubic millimeter, in the hemoglobin concentration and in the volume of red cells and characterized by pallor and weakness.

anemia, cerebral Impairment of the cerebral blood circulation which can be produced artificially by the injection of mescaline, adrenaline and other toxic elements. These injections can produce symptoms similar to those of catatonic schizophrenia.

anemia, sickle-cell A genetically determined metabolic defect, generally found in dark-skinned peoples, especially of African origin, which is characterized by the displacement of a part of the normal hemoglobin by a slightly different and ineffective variety, resulting in a lowered oxygen carrying capacity by the blood. An individual may carry the gene but exhibit no clinical signs of malfunction unless he moves to a high altitude whereupon the disease becomes manifest.

anemotropism A response of orientation of the body as a unit to jar currents.

anencephaly Absence of the cerebrum and cerebellum and of the flat skull bones.

aneneia Deaf-mutism.

anenthanasia Painful death.

anergasia (A. Meyer) Loss of functional activity due to structural brain disorder.

anergastic Pertaining to or the condition of anergasia.

anergia, anergy Absence of energy; weakness; passivity.

anerotic pulse Weak pressure wave preceding the main pulse beat.

anerotism Sexual negativism; avoidance of sexual relations.

anesthesia; anaesthesia Impairment or loss of sensitivity to internal and/or external stimulation from functional causes, drugs or neural damage.

anesthesia, hysterical A psychogenic disorder in which sensory feeling is absent in a part or parts of the body.

anethopathy (B. Karpman) Personality disorder characterized by a lack of moral inhibitions and unethical behavior and also including narcissistic sexual behavior and general egocentricity. Individuals afflicted with anethopathy do not respond to therapy.

aneuploid A chromosome number which is not an exact multiple of the haploid number.

Angell, James (1869-1949) American psychologist and educator. Graduated U. of Michigan (1890) and Harvard (1892). Studied at University of Berlin and at Halle. President of Yale University (1921-1937). Before switching to administration Angell won distinction for promoting the Functionalist viewpoint in contrast to Wundtian and Titchenerian structural psychology which he believed could not cope with the expanding problems of the then new psychology. Opposing the stand that the chief purpose of psychology is analysis of immediate experience into its elements and their qualities by introspection, functionalism employed introspection and objective methods in studying consciousness. The latter is regarded as a psychophysiological process having adaptive value in adjusting the organism to its environment. Author of *Psychology* (1904) and *Chapters from Modern Psychology* (1912).

anger An intense emotional reaction elicited by threat, interference, verbal attack, overt aggression or frustration and characterized by acute reactions of the autonomic nervous system and by overt or covert attack responses.

angiogram Procedure enabling the study of blood distribution in the brain by the injection of a dye with a different x-ray density from blood or brain tissue into blood vessels in or near the brain.

angstrom (Å) Unit of length measure especially of light wave length, 10^{-10} meter; $\frac{1}{100,000}$ micron = 0.001 mm. or 0.1 Å.

angular perspective See *perspective, angular*.

anhedonia Lack of reaction to pleasure producing stimuli; inability to experience pleasurable sensations.

anima (C. G. Jung) The archetype that is the feminine component of a male's personality, resulting from the accumulated racial experiences of men with women.

animal magnetism See *magnetism, animal*.

animal phobia See *phobia, animal*.

animal psychology See *psychology, comparative*.

animism 1. Ascribing life to inanimate nature. **2.** (J. Piaget) This phenomenon has been observed in children who ascribe friendly or hostile intention to inanimate objects.

animistic reasoning Illogical reasoning based on natural coincidences, such as, for instance, the belief that putting up storm windows will cause a heat wave.

animus (C. G. Jung) The archetype that is the masculine component of all women's personalities resulting from the accumulated racial experiences of women with men.

annoyer (E. L. Thorndike) Any factor that obstructs stamping in of a response thus preventing learning.

Anokhin, Petr K. (1898-) Soviet neurophysiologist, had been working for many years over the functional system theory which he formulated in 1935. This theory made possible creating a new approach towards study of behavioral acts, and to reveal detailed neurophysiological mechanisms of the conditioned reflex of the behavioral act and the psychic activity. The functional system theory permitted 1) formulation of a new theory in evolution of functions, 2) creation of a neurophysiological basis to study psychophysiological peculiarities of behavior and 3) the general theory of functional systems also helped in deciphering of cybernetic, medical, pedagogical and many other regularities where a researcher deals with biological systems. See *functional system; afferent synthesis; acceptor of action results; systemogenesis; biocybernetics; general systems theory.*

anomalies of sex chromosomes See *chromosomes, sex, anomalies of.*

anomaly See *abnormal.*

anomaly, autosomal Defect of number or form of a chromosome other than the sex chromosome.

anomia The difficulty of recalling names; a type of aphasia.

anopia Blindness.

anorexia nervosa (W. Gull) Severe loss of appetite.

anoxemia Oxygen deficiency in the circulatory system.

Anschauung (German) 1. Observation. 2. Vantage point. 3. Point of view.

antagonists 1. Drugs that neutralize the effect of each other. 2. Muscles that act in an opposite direction to one another, such as extensors and flexors. 3. Two colors that produce together an achromatic color.

antedating response See *response, antedating.*

anterior pituitary gland See *gland, anterior pituitary.*

anterior-posterior gradient See *gradient, anterior-posterior.*

anthropocentrism 1. The assumption that the man is the center of the universe. 2. Relating the laws of nature to the laws governing the human mind. The philosophical systems of Kant and Hegel are examples of such an approach.

anthropoid Resembling human beings; e.g., chimpanzees are anthropoid apes.

anthropology The science of the human race. Physical anthropology studies human organisms in their evolution and adjustment to the changing physical environment. Cultural anthropology studies the customs, manners, morals and social structure of prehistorical, primitive and contemporary men.

anthropometry Measurement of physical characteristics of the human body.

anthropomorph 1. Man. 2. Of the human species or having a human form.

anthropomorphic Having a human form or human characteristics.

anthropomorphism Attributing human characteristics or abilities to gods, animals, or objects.

anthroponomy (W. Hunter) The science of human behavior; psychology.

anthropos (C. G. Jung) The archetype of primal man.

anthrotype (biology and medicine) Biological type of human organisms; human phenotype.

anticathexis (S. Freud) The energy invested by the ego in keeping repressed material in the unconscious; cathexis used for the blocking of unconscious material.

anticipation method See *method, prompting.*

anticipatory error See *error, anticipatory.*

anticipatory response See *error, anticipatory.*

antidromic conduction See *conduction, antidromic.*

antigen A substance that stimulates and/or activates the production of antibodies.

Antigone complex See *complex, Antigone.*

antisocial behavior Behavior which violates explicit or implicit rules of property and personal rights or explicit or implicit rules meant to maintain group cohesiveness and interpersonal trust.

antisocial reaction (Psychopathic personality) A "character disorder" in which the individual displays immature behavior in the form of persistent, socially incapacitating tendency to seek immediate gratification. There is also a marked inability to discern the consequences of his behavior and to learn from his experiences.

anvil Incus.

anxiety 1. (S. Freud) The ego's reaction to external threats is called fear. When the ego is exposed to threats from within, that is, coming from the id or the superego, its reaction to such a threat is called anxiety.

The term anxiety has several connotations. Originally Freud believed that anxiety was the result of blocking of sexual impulses. The combination of unsatisfied libido and undischarged excitation was supposed to be the cause of anxiety neuroses, and the thwarted libido was believed to be transformed into a state of anxiety.

Three years after having presented the structural theory in 1923, Freud introduced a new theory of anxiety. The new theory did not discard the old one but reduced the scope of its meaning to particular cases. According to this new theory (1926) anxiety originates from the infant's inability to master the overflow of excitations. A neonate is usually exposed to more stimulation than he can possibly master. Excessive stimulation may become traumatic, and hence create the painful feeling of primary anxiety.

O. Rank (1929) assumed that the birth-trauma is the prototype of all anxiety states. Separation from mother is another severe anxiety-producing factor. Castration fears, guilt feelings, fear of abandonment, and rejection are the most frequently experienced anxiety-producing situations. The feeling of helplessness is one of the most frequent symptoms of neurotic disturbance; it is especially typical of traumatic neuroses. Also the inability to control one's own excitement (whether aggressive or sexual) may create a state of anxiety.

Freud's early theory of anxiety became incorporated in the new and more broadly conceived theory. Since the satisfaction of instinctual demands may create a dangerous situation the ego must control the instinctual impulses. A strong ego accomplishes this task easily, but a weak ego has to invest more energies in an anticathectic effort to ward off the unconscious impulses.

Anxiety is "a specific state of unpleasure accompanied by motor discharge along definite pathways," Freud wrote in 1926. Ultimately, the three types of anxiety-producing situations in childhood can be put together and reduced to one fundamental cause, namely, loss of the love object. Thus, being left alone, being in the dark, and finding a strange person in place of the mother are the main anxiety-producing situations which reflect the feeling of loss of the loved person. In other words, anxiety is a reaction to the absence of, or separation from, the love object. This feeling of loss is experienced in the birth-trauma, in weaning, and later on in castration fear. In all these situations, loss of support causes increased tension, and an economic disturbance demanding some discharge of energy.

The infant longs for the sight of the mother because he knows from experience that she gratifies all his needs without delay. The situation which the infant appraises as "danger" and against which he desires reassurance is therefore one of not being gratified, of an increase of tension arising from non-gratification of his needs—a situation against which he is powerless (Freud, 1926). A strong ego can cope with danger, but a weak ego reacts with anxiety. When the ego is threatened by external reality it develops reality-anxiety. When the superego attacks the ego, feelings of guilt and inferiority, called moral anxiety, ensue. When the id's pressures threaten to break through the ego controls, neurotic anxiety develops.

Reality-anxiety is a reaction of the ego to a danger from without. Anxiety-preparedness may develop in one of the two following manners: either an old danger-signaling experience called "anxiety development" is re-experienced, or a past danger having a paralyzing effect on the individual, is re-experienced. Neurotic anxiety manifests itself in three ways. The first is anxiety-neurosis, typically felt as an overall apprehension and a sense of oncoming doom. Anxiety neurosis is usually caused by the existence of undischarged excitation when blocking libido energy is transformed into an anxiety state. Neurotic anxiety is manifested also in hysteria and in other neuroses. Certain ideas attached to libido become repressed and distorted, as a result of which the energy, whether libidinal or destructive turns into a state of anxiety.

2. (H. S. Sullivan) Anxiety results whenever the biological needs of an individual cannot be satisfied in a socially acceptable way. The individual develops a feeling of insecurity and uneasiness. It is always connected with an increased muscle tension. Muscles ready for a socially unacceptable action become inhibited since their activity is likely to invite disapproval. Anxiety is a socially produced muscular tension which interferes with other tensions or normal mental functioning. The relief of this socially created tension brings the pleasant feeling of self-esteem and self-respect, the antithesis of anxiety.

3. (K. Horney) See *anxiety, basic*.

4. (B. F. Skinner) Anxiety is the result of conditioning. It is the response to a neutral stimulus which has been associated with an aversive stimulus. It is not an inner state but a group of emotional tendencies which are elicited by a specific situation.

anxiety attack, equivalent of See *anxiety equivalent*.

anxiety, basic (K. Horney) Each individual has two fundamental needs: safety and satisfaction. The gratification of the satisfaction needs without feelings of safety and acceptance produces basic anxiety, a basic feeling which leads to the development of a neurosis. Neurotics fear the world and view it as an unsafe and hostile place, and defend themselves against basic anxiety in four ways: by seeking affection of any form, by being submissive, by gaining power, or by emotional withdrawal.

anxiety, castration Anxiety experienced as a defense against castration anxiety, with regression to the anal area as the primary instinctual zone.

anxiety equivalent (psychoanalysis) Intense physiological response or bodily disturbance such as rapid heart beat or loss of breath which replaces conscious anxiety or fear.

anxiety fixation See *fixation, anxiety*.

anxiety hysteria See *hysteria, anxiety*.

anxiety, objective Anxiety for which there is an identifiable and intelligible cause or precipitant.

anxiety, real Anxiety caused by an actual external danger.

anxiety, socialized (A. Davis) The anticipated fear of punishment for a socially unacceptable behavior.

anxiety tolerance The ability to function despite anxiety.

anxiety, urethral Anxiety associated with urination.

apandria Having an aversion to males.

apareunia The inability to have sexual intercourse.

apastia Abstaining from eating food; a symptom of psychiatric disorder.

apathy 1. Absence or deficiency of emotion, excitement, or interest; indifference. 2. Lack of interest in things which others find interesting or stimulating.

apeirophobia Fear of boundlessness or infinity.

aperiodic reinforcement See *reinforcement, aperiodic*.

aperture, color See *color aperture.*

aphakia Loss of the crystalline lens of the eye due to injury or defect.

aphanisis (E. Jones) Extinction of sexuality.

aphasia Loss of or impaired ability to speak, write, or to understand the meaning of words, due to brain damage.

aphasia, acoustico-mnestic Aphasia resulting from lesions of central portions of the left temporal area or of deep portions of the temporal cortex characterized by difficulties in remembering word lists, comprehension and reproduction of long sentences, comprehension of words, and in the ability to name objects.

aphasia, afferent motor Aphasia resulting from lesions of inferior portions of the post-central area characterized by a disturbance of fine oral movements associated with a loss of precise kinesthetic feedback.

aphasia, amnestic Disruption of language usage, involving a memory loss for specific words.

aphasia, auditory Inability to comprehend the spoken word. A form of sensory aphasia.

aphasia, conduction A form of aphasia characterized by impairment of the ability to differentiate and repeat speech sounds accurately rather than difficulties in spontaneous articulation and associated with lesions in the post-central cortical areas.

aphasia, developmental Retardation in the child's learning of language which is often out of phase with mental age, and other developmental levels, and trends. Associated with general sensory, perceptual and intellectual inefficiency, perseveration, emotional inability, and often hyperactivity.

aphasia, efferent motor Aphasia resulting from lesions of the lower part of the left premotor area and characterized by difficulties in the transition from one sound to another, in the smooth articulation of the speech sequences both in repetition and spontaneous speech.

aphasia, expressive Language disorder characterized by the inability to speak or write appropriately and sometimes accompanied by the inability to perform related gestures.

aphasia, global Complete loss of all motor and sensory uses of oral and written speech.

aphasia, jargon Fluent but inappropriate use of words.

aphasia, motor Inability to speak words.

aphasia, nominal Inability to speak the intended or correct word.

aphasia, semantic Impairment or loss of the ability to comprehend the meaning of words.

aphasia, sensory Inability to comprehend the spoken or written word, with the damage in the dominant hemisphere.

aphasia, syntactic Impairment or loss of the ability to employ correct grammatical constructions.

aphasia, visual Impairment or loss of ability to comprehend the written word.

aphemia Obsolete term for the inability to speak due to a functional or an organic disorder.

aphephobia Morbid fear of being touched.

aphonia; aphony Speech loss caused by defects of the larynx or emotional disorder.

aphonia, hysterical Sudden loss of voice due to emotional problems.

aphoria (P. Janet) A state of general weakness and lack of energy which does not disappear with regular exercise or physical training and is considered to be a symptom of neurosis.

aphrasia The inability to understand or articulate correctly phrases or groups of connected words even though single words may be comprehended and spoken correctly.

aphrenia Loss or impairment of the functioning of the conscious mind.

aphrodisia Sexual excitement.

aphrodisiac That which stimulates sexual excitement or is associated with it.

aphtongia Type of motor aphasia characterized by the inability to control muscle spasms of the tongue.

apiphobia Abnormal fear of bees.

aplasia; aplasy See *agenesis.*

aplestia Extreme greed.

apocleisis 1. Lack of desire for food. 2. Aversion to food.

apopathetic behavior Behavior clearly influenced by the presence of others but not directed toward them.

apoplectic type See *type, apoplectic.*

apoplexy Sudden loss of motor control and consciousness due to a blocked blood vessel or cerebral hemorrhage.

a posteriori 1. Arriving at the cause of an event by inductive reasoning; i.e., deriving general principles from observation and generalization of specific, observed facts. 2. Of reasoning that starts from observed facts; designating what can be known only after actual occurrence of an event.

Apostle of the idiots Name given to Edouard Seguin (1812-1880) because of his extensive involvement with the care and welfare of the mentally retarded.

apparatus, lie detector See *lie detector.*

apparatus, mental (S. Freud) The three mechanisms of personality, the id, the ego and the superego, or the dynamics of the mind upon which the psychoanalytic model of personality structure is based.

apparatus, psychic See *apparatus, mental.*

apparent movement See *movement, apparent.*

apperception **1.** Clear perception and awareness of something which occurs in the last portion of attentive perception. **2.** Process of recognizing relationships between a particular object and the already existing knowledge of similar or related things in such a way that a particular object is more clearly understood. **3.** (J. F. Herbart) Theory that learning and understanding occurs through finding relationships between new facts and one's previously existing experience and knowledge.

apperceptive visual agnosia See *agnosia, apperceptive visual.*

appersonation; appersonification Delusion in which an individual takes on the characteristics and situation of another person, usually an important figure.

appetite **1.** A motivation, desire, or impulse which stems from internal physiological conditions, though external conditions may serve as influences. Appetites include hunger, thirst, sexual drive, need for air and for rest. **2.** The sensory and affective mental processes which are influenced by such physiological conditions mentioned above. **3.** (W. McDougall) The building up of instinct energy. **4.** (E. C. Tolman) A state of excitation leading to consummatory responses which bring physiological queiscence. There are six appetites, namely food, sex, excretion, specific contact, rest and sensory-motor.

appilledema Choking of the optic nerve at the optic foramen caused by abnormal intracranial or intranentricular tension which is usually due to a brain tumor.

applied psychology See *psychology, applied.*

apprehension **1.** Direct, immediate act or process of becoming aware of something, whether objects or facts. **2.** Anxiety stemming from fear of some future event.

apprehension, implicit Awareness of the sum of items comprising and affecting a total sense experience without discrimination of the particular items themselves.

approach-approach conflict See *conflict, approach-approach.*

approach-avoidance conflict See *conflict, approach-avoidance.*

approach gradient See *gradient, approach.*

approach learning See *learning, approach.*

approach type (Rorschach) Description or classification of a response according to how the individual approaches the inkblot which might be in terms of the whole or of details, according to shading or to color or through concern with some combination of aspects.

approximation conditioning See *conditioning, approximation.*

appurtenance (Gestalt) The mutual influence between parts of a field.

apractagnosia Agnosia resulting from lesions of the parieto-occipital areas of the cortex characterized by an inability to analyze the spatial relationships represented in pictures, disturbances of movement and action and of memory for spatial schemata.

apraxia Impairment or loss of ability to perform purposeful movement, caused by lesions in the motor area of the cortex but with no sensory impairment or paralysis.

apraxia, afferent Apraxia resulting from lesions of the post-central cortex characterized by disturbances of the voluntary control of complex movements associated with defective kinesthetic feedback from the motor acts.

apraxia, akinetic A condition involving the loss of ability to move spontaneously.

apraxia, amnestic Impairment or loss of the ability to remember or act upon a command.

apraxia, dynamic Apraxia resulting from lesions of the premotor cortex and characterized by the loss of the continuity of movement.

apraxia, efferent See *apraxia, dynamic.*

apraxia, ideational Impairment or loss of the ability to conceive a plan for a whole behavioral movement or sequence. Individual acts may be properly carried out but there is a dislocation of the correct overall sequence.

apraxia, motor Disorder in which uncomplicated movements become clumsy. Movement of individual fingers is often impaired or lost.

apraxia, sensory **1.** Inability to distinguish among objects or to identify objects by touching them. **2.** Disorder in which the individual is unsure of how to use familiar objects.

a priori **1.** Arriving at the effect of an event by deductive reasoning; i.e., arriving at the consequence of a specific event on the basis of definitions or general principles which are assumed to be true. **2.** Designating that which can be known through reason alone, without necessity of experience of an actual event. Usually with the connotation of assumption on inadequate grounds of proof.

aptitude Capacity or potential ability to perform an as yet unlearned task, skill, or act.

aptitude, mechanical The inborn ability to deal with and manipulate mechanical objects and machines.

aptitude, scholastic The likelihood of achieving a given degree of success in academic pursuits, based on data such as high school record, personal characteristics and achievement tests and estimated in quantitative terms.

aptitude test See *test, aptitude.*

AQ (Sometimes A.Q.) The ratio between the actual level of scholastic performance and the level which is expected. Actual performance is measured by achievement age or educational age; expected performance is measured either by chronological age or by mental age. The relation between school achievement and chronological age is phrased as acceleration or retardation. The relation between school achievement and mental age is phrased as overachievement or underachievement. These ratios tend to be unreliable.

aquaphobia Morbid fear of water and drowning.

aqueduct of Sylvius See *cerebral aqueduct.*

Aquinas, St. Thomas (1225-1274) Christian theologian in the Middle Ages who discussed social and political questions concerning property, economics, and the political community within a theological framework. He incorporated Aristotelianism with a Christian outlook and emphasized the importance of reason and nature in the universe.

arachnophobia Fear of spiders.

arbitrary origin See *origin, arbitrary.*

arbitrary response (Rorschach) A response which is not related to any of the particular characteristics of the inkblot upon which it is based.

archetype (C. G. Jung) The structural component of the collective unconscious which is inherited. It is a deep unconscious representation of an experience that has been common to a human race for countless generations. The archetypes form the core of autonomous partial systems, independent of the consciousness. If one becomes stirred up, the archetype takes "possession" of the individual and causes neurosis. The archetypes are called primordial images, dominants, imagos, mythological images and behavior patterns. The anima, animus and the shadow are the main archetypes.

area sampling See *sampling, area.*

Ares 1. The god of war in Greek mythology. 2. (B. B. Wolman) The destructive drive, introduced instead of S. Freud's *Thanatos,* the god of death. It reflects the fight for survival. When there is a threat to life, the general drive for life (lust for life) is channeled into Ares which is more primitive and more powerful than Eros.

aretic behavior Destructive, hostile, aggressive behavior.

aretic syndrome in childhood schizophrenia (B. B. Wolman) Childhood schizophrenia in which the child displays unusual aggressiveness and unprovoked cruelty. Corresponds to paranoid schizophrenia in adults.

argininosuccinic aciduria Metabolic disorder possibly transmitted by a recessive gene, with a deficiency in argininosuccinase causing an excess of argininosuccinic acid. Main clinical features are gradual mental retardation, thinness of hair, convulsions, and systolic murmur.

Argyll-Robertson pupil A pupil which contracts in the appropriate way in accomodation and convergence but which does not contract adequately in response to light. This is a symptom of neurological damage usually caused by syphilis.

Arieti, Silvano (1914-   ) American psychiatrist born in Italy. Author of *Interpretation of Schizophrenia* (1955), and *The Intrapychic Self* (1967). Editor-in-Chief of the *American Handbook of Psychiatry,* and editor of the *Journal of the American Academy of Psychoanalysis,* and of the *World Biennial of Psychiatry and Psychotherapy.* Pioneer work in the office treatment of schizophrenic patients. Research in the psychodynamics and thought disorders of schizophrenia; in the creative process; in cognition and volition in normality and mental illness.

Aristotle (384-322 B.C.) Greek philosopher. He believed that the universe is comprised of matter (hyle) and form (morphe). The soul is the form, the body is the matter. The soul functions on three levels, the vegetative, sensory and rational. Aristotle introduced the idea of association based on contiguity, similarity, and contrast.

Aristotle's illusion See *illusion, Aristotle's.*

arithmetical average See *mean.*

Army Alpha Test See *test, Army Alpha.*

Army Beta Test See *test, Army Beta.*

Army General Classification Test See *test, Army General Classification.*

arousal An increase in the complexity (amount of information, uncertainty) of neural organization manifest by desynchronization of electrical recordings made from the brain (activation).

arousal threshold See *threshold, arousal.*

arrhythmia An absence of rhythm of the heart due to functional or organic causes.

arsenic poisoning See *poisoning, arsenic.*

art therapy See *therapy, art.*

arteriosclerosis Proliferative and degenerative changes in arteries causing thickening of the walls, loss of elasticity, and sometimes calcium deposits, with a resulting decrease in the flow of blood.

arteriosclerosis, cerebral Arteriosclerosis affecting the vessels of the brain and usually occurring in old age. Symptoms vary, but usually include headache, dizziness, noises in the ears, irritability, loss of power of concentration, memory defect, vague dyesthesias and some hypertension.

arthritic diathesis See *diathesis, arthritic.*

arthritis, rheumatoid A chronic arthritis of organic or psychogenic etiology affecting multiple joints. Psychogenic causes consist of inhibited hostile, aggressive wishes which cannot be expressed.

Arthur Point Scale of Performance Tests See *scale, Arthur Point Of Performance Tests.*

artificial selection See *selection, artificial.*

artificialism (J. Piaget) The tendency of children to attribute the occurrence of natural phenomena such as rain or sunshine to artificial causes or to the intentions of a person.

as if (H. Vaihinger) According to Vaihinger's idealistic positivism, human life is guided by goals and ideals which are not necessarily true, but people act upon them "as if" they were true.

ascendance-submission A bi-polar continuum in which the ascendance extreme represents tendency to dominate and the submission extreme the tendency to be dominated in social relations. The Allport A–S Reaction Study is used to measure this dimension.

asemia Loss of ability to understand or to utilize communication symbols of any sort including words, signs, and gestures.

Ashby's Law of Requisite Variety A mathematical statement about information processing which describes the procedure of choosing correct alternatives and rejecting incorrect ones.

asonia Inability to distinguish among pitch differences.

aspiration level (K. Lewin and K. Dembo) The expected level of future performance. In Lewin's theory the level of aspiration is presented in realistic or unrealistic psychological fields and the degree of reality of a goal influences the individual's estimate of his achievements.

assertive responses Aggressive behavior which a person learns to use in anxiety-provoking situations where he feels intimidated and taken advantage of, as a means to reduce the anxiety which is incompatible with the assertive response.

assertive training A behavior therapy technique by which anxiety habits of response to interpersonal situations are overcome by encouraging the patient to express other spontaneously felt emotions in the actual situation. For example, he is encouraged to express his habitually inhibited anger when someone takes unfair advantage of him, e.g. pushing ahead of him in line. Apparently, because such expression potentiates the anger or other relevant emotion there is inhibition of anxiety, leading to weakening of the anxiety habit.

assets-liabilities technique A counseling technique which requires the client to list his personality assets and liabilities and to work on eliminating the liabilities.

assimilation 1. (physiology) The transformation of food into the substances used and stored in the body. 2. A learning process whereby new material is modified and made part of the existing knowledge. 3. (E. Hering) The production of retinal materials when the blue, red, or green cones are stimulated. 4. (J. F. Herbart) The understanding of new material in terms of what is already known. 5. (C. G. Jung) The lateration of an object or situation to fit the needs of the self. 6. The perception of a new situation in a way which makes it appear identical to a familiar situation. 7. (E. L. Thorndike) The animal's reaction to a new situation as if it was a familiar one because of their similarities. 8. (speech) The adjustment of letter sounds to appear like neighboring letter sounds in the mouth position and/or sound

itself. 9. The acceptance of a negative fact about oneself into one's experience.

assimilation law See *law of assimilation.*

associate visual agnosia See *agnosia, associate visual.*

association 1. A functional connection between psychological phenomena established through experience or learning whereby the occurrence of one tends to evoke the other. 2. A bond between ideas. 3. The second part of an associational sequence. 4. The strength of the postulated bond between associated members.

association by contiguity The law that upon the occurrence of two events close in time, the subsequent occurrence of one event will evoke the other.

association coefficient See *coefficient, association.*

association, constrained In an association test, a response which is specified in terms of its relationship to the stimulus.

association cortex See *cortex, association.*

association fiber A neuron which connects different centers in one hemisphere of the brain.

association, free See *free association.*

association, mediate An ideational association between two terms which is made by indirect linkage through intervening terms.

association method See *method, association.*

association, neutral 1. The process of joining independent neurons to produce a result. 2. Postulated neural pathways between various structures of the body.

association of ideas (history) The process of joining or connecting ideas to form new compound ideas.

association psychology See *associationism.*

association-reaction time The time between a given stimulus and a response in the form of an association to the stimulus, especially in a word association test.

association-sensation ratio (D. O. Hebb) The ratio of the association cortex to the sensation cortex which is considered an index of general learning ability: the larger the ratio the greater the learning potential. Also called A/S ratio.

association test See *test, association.*

association time 1. See *association-reaction time.* 2. The association-reaction time minus the simple reaction time, an obsolete method of measuring association-reaction time.

associationism The theory that the mind consists of irreducible simple elements which are combined by association to produce learning. Aristotle introduced this principle stating four laws of association: the laws of similarity, contiguity in time, difference, and contiguity in space. Rudiments of this theory which became prominant at the beginning of the seventeenth century and continued to develop through the nineteenth century were established by

J. Locke (1632-1704) and D. Hume (1711-1776) who emphasized the importance of sensory perceptions and associations. D. Hartley (1705-1757) clarified this theoretical position in his work stating the principles of contiguity and repetition as necessary for association to occur. J. Mill (1773-1836) elaborated the theory further emphasizing temporal contiguity. Later British associationists such as A. Bain and J. S. Mill introduced other laws such as similarity, difference, intensity, and inseparability. In the nineteenth century, this position was developed by E. L. Thorndike who stressed connections based on contiguity of stimulus and response and I. P. Pavlov who viewed associationism as identical with conditioning.

associative inhibition See *inhibition, associative.*

associative memory See *memory, associative.*

associative process Process in the organism that is a part of an original unlearned or previously learned process.

associative shifting (E. L. Thorndike) The principle that stimuli presented in a similar situation as stimuli which evoked specific responses can evoke the same responses.

associative strength The strength of an associative connection as evinced by the frequency with which the stimulus evokes the particular response.

associative thinking See *thinking, associative.*

assonance A similarity of vowel sounds as in teeth, beach.

assumed mean See *mean, assumed.*

astasia Motor incoordination and unsteadiness in maintaining a standing position.

astasia-abasia See *abasia.*

astereognosis See *agnosia, tactile.*

asthenia Physical weakness or lack of strength and vitality.

asthenia, mental Inability to concentrate on an idea or thought for any length of time; mental weakness or fatigueability.

asthenia, neurocirculatory   See *neurocirculatory asthenia.*

asthenic **1.** Depressed or inhibited feeling. **2.** Linear-framed, long-limbed slender body-type. **3.** (E. Kretschmer) Body type associated with schizothymic temperament.

asthenic habitus Body-type characterized by slender linear frame and long limbs.

asthenic reaction A psychoneurotic reaction characterized by chronic aches, pains, physical, and mental fatigue. It usually occurs in young adults and is believed to result from sustained emotional stress which the individual cannot cope with.

asthenic type See *type, asthenic.*

asthenophobia Morbid fear of weakness.

asthenopia Weakness of vision due to fatigue of the ocular muscles or the eye in general.

asthma Symptom complex resulting in an impairment of breathing, especially respiration, and wheezing, caused by an increase of responsiveness to various stimuli of the trachea, major bronchi, manifested by extreme narrowing of airways to various reasons. It is believed that there may be an inherited vulnerability and that emotional factors are also contributory.

asthma, bronchial See *asthma.*

astigmatism Defective vision due to an abnormal curvature of one or more refractive surfaces of the eye such as the cornea, or the lens, which prevents light rays which enter the eye from focusing at a point on the retina. Instead, the light rays spread out in various directions depending upon the type of curvature.

astrology A pseudoscience which concerns itself with the influence of the movements of stars and planets on human events.

asylum, insane An obsolete term for a mental institution.

asymbolia A form of tactile agnosia in which the visual evaluation of tactile cues is impaired usually associated with lesions in posterior cortical areas and involving zones of overlap of the cortical parts of the cutaneous-kinesthetic and visual analyzers.

asymmetrical distribution See *distribution, asymmetrical.*

asymptote   A straight line which a curve constantly approaches, but never reaches, or a theoretical limit which a curve approaches.

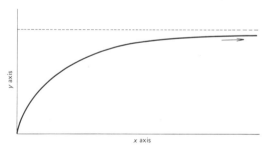

--------------------------------- asymptote

asymptotic curve See *curve, asymptotic.*

asyndesis Speech disorder characterized by the juxtaposition of elements without appropriate connections.

asynergia Faulty coordination of groups of muscles that are normally well coordinated.

asynergic speech Asynergia of the vocal apparatus usually due to cerebellar disease; speech becomes irregular, jerky, and explosive.

ataractic drugs Tranquilizers.

ataraxy Complacency; calm, unperturbed mood.

atavism Reappearance of ancestral characteristics after their absence in several generations.

ataxia Incoordination of voluntary muscular action.

ataxia, intrapsychic An emotional state observed in schizophrenics in which the individual appears to separate his own feelings from other mental phenomena.

ataxia, locomotor See *Tabes dorsalis.*

ataxia, mental Lack of correspondence between ideas and affects.

ataxiagraph A device for recording degree of ataxia.

ataxic abasia See *abasia.*

ataxic paraplegia Slow progressive degeneration of the posterior and lateral columns of the spinal chord causing weakness, spasticity, and incoordination of the legs.

ataxic speech See *asynergic speech.*

ataxic writing Uncoordinated writing due to brain damage or lack of skill.

ataximeter 1. A device for measuring involuntary sway of an individual standing erect with his eyes closed. 2. Any device for measuring involuntary movement.

ataxiophobia Morbid fear of disorder.

ataxophemia Incoherent speech.

ATDP See *scale, Attitude Toward Disabled Persons.*

ateliosis Dwarfism caused by pituitary disorders without physical malformation.

atephobia Morbid fear of being ruined.

athetosis Condition of slow recurrent apparently purposeless movement primarily of the toes and fingers which results from a brain lesion.

athletic type See *type, athletic.*

athymia (Hippocrates) Melancholy.

atmosphere effect 1. The production of a response which is due to habits of responding which are associated with particular words, portions or patterns of the stimulus. 2. Errors in thinking which result from an impression implicit in the statement of premises of the problem.

atom, social (J. L. Moreno) The psychological relations of an individual to the smallest social structure which is the patterns of relationship of the individual to other individuals toward whom he feels attraction or repulsion.

atomistic psychology See *psychology, atomistic.*

atonicity; atony; atonia 1. (physiological) Lack or reduction of normal tone or tension in the musculature. 2. (phonetics) Reduction of stress or tone.

atrophy, optic Degeneration of the optic nerve fibers which is classified either primary or secondary depending on the cause.

atropin Drug which relaxes smooth muscles and is used primarily to relax the pupil, the bladder, and the intestines.

atropine poisoning See *poisoning, atropine.*

attensity (F. B. Titchener) The characteristic of attracting attention of a sensation or sense datum.

attention 1. Selection and perception of a certain stimulus or of a range of stimuli comprising a part of a complex stimulus situation. 2. Adjustment of the sense organs and/or the central nervous system to allow for maximal stimulation. 3. (E. B. Titchener) State of sensory clearness and vividness; state of consciousness in which one mental content stands out clearly from the rest.

attention fluctuation Intermittent changes in the clarity of perception of an object under conditions of constant and unchanging stimulation.

attention-getting mechanism Behavior designed to gain attention, usually otherwise maladaptive.

attention reflex See *reflex, attention.*

attention-seeking Behavior that secures an orientation of others toward oneself.

attention-seeking, negative (R. R. Sears) Socially unacceptable forms of a.–s., usually considered as mixed with aggression; e.g., in children, temper tantrums, interrupting, disobedience; in adults, quarrelsome behavior, derogation of others, uncooperativeness, demanding aid, as in acute drunkenness, pretended suicide or proposed violence.

attention-seeking, positive (R. R. Sears) Socially acceptable forms of a.–s.; e.g., in children, asking help, talking, performing adult role behavior, asking questions, seeking reassurance, calling attention to successful performances; in adults, persistent talking, mild exhibitionism, pseudo-modesty, self-deprecation, gregariousness.

attention span 1. The amount of material or number of separate objects which can be noticed during one brief exposure. 2. The duration of time a person can concentrate on one event or thing.

attenuation 1. A reduction in the degree, amount, or worth of anything; to make slim. 2. (statistics) A reduction of a correlation coefficient due to unreliable measurements.

attitude A learned predisposition to react consistently in a given manner (either positively or negatively) to certain persons, objects or concepts. Attitudes have cognitive, affective and behavioral components.

attitude, masculine, in female neurotics See *masculine attitude in female neurotics.*

attitude scale See *scale, attitude.*

attitude, social 1. An attitude directed to interindividual or intergroup relations. 2. An opinion shared by many people.

Attitude Toward Disabled Persons Scale See *scale, Attitude Toward Disabled Persons.*

attonity Condition of stupor characterized by total or almost total immobility which sometimes occurs in catatonic schizophrenia and depression.

attribute 1. A characteristic or fundamental property that is predicted of a subject. 2. (structural psychology) The most fundamental characteristics of sensation; quality and sensation are the most universally accepted. 3. An independent dimension of sensation as indicated by discrimination tests.

Aubert diaphragm A device for controlling and measuring the amount of light passing through an aperture.

Aubert-Förster phenomenon The principle that it is easier to recognize small objects when near as compared to larger more distant objects even though the latter subtend the same visual angle as the former.

Aubert phenomenon An optical illusion in which a vertical line inclines to one side as the head is tilted to the opposite side when no other object is present in the visual field.

audile An individual for whom auditory rather than visual images are predominant or unusually distinct.

audio-frequency Sound waves which are within the range of human hearing, approximately 16-20,000 hertz.

audiogenic Caused or produced by sound.

audiogenic seizure See *seizure, audiogenic.*

audiogram A graphic record of an individual's auditory sensitivity across several frequencies in relation to established norms as measured by an audiometer.

audiogravic illusion See *illusion, audiogravic.*

audiogyral illusion See *illusion, audiogravic.*

audiometer An instrument for measuring the acuity and the range of an individual's hearing.

audiometric curve See *audiogram.*

audio-oscillator An electronic instrument capable of emitting pure tones of desired frequency and intensity.

audito-oculogyric reflex See *reflex, audito-oculogyric.*

auditory Pertaining to hearing.

auditory acuity Sensitivity of hearing measured in terms of intensity of sound waves; usually equivalent to auditory threshold.

auditory aphasia See *aphasia, auditory.*

auditory apperception test See *test, auditory apperception.*

auditory aura See *aura, auditory.*

auditory cortex See *cortex, auditory.*

auditory flicker See *flicker, auditory.*

auditory labyrinth The portion of the labyrinth of the ear having to do with hearing.

auditory or acoustic nerve See *nerve, auditory or acoustic.*

auditory ossicles The small bones in the middle ear which conduct sound from the eardrum to the cochlea.

auditory projection area The area in the posterior portion of the superior temporal convolution where the auditory nerve terminates and where auditory perception is mediated.

auditory spectrum See *acoustic spectrum.*

auditory threshold See *threshold, auditory.*

aulaphobia Fear of any contact with a wind instrument, especially a flute, which has been sometimes considered a phallic symbol.

aura 1. General term for a symptom which precedes the onset of physical or mental disorder and warns of its coming. 2. (parapsychology) Supposed emanations given off a person's body which are seen or picked up by others who are sensitive.

aura, auditory Form of epileptic seizure characterized by sudden occurrence of buzzing sounds sometimes but not always preceding the onset of a grand mal seizure.

aura cursoria Aimless running around usually occurring just before an epileptic seizure and associated with its onset.

aura, epileptic Psychic, motor or sensory disturbance which precedes an epileptic seizure, serving as a warning signal.

aura, visual Form of epileptic seizure characterized by the sudden vision of light flashes sometimes but not usually preceding the onset of a grand mal seizure.

aural Related to the ear.

auricle The ear flap or external part of the ear.

auroraphobia Fear of the northern lights.

autarchic fiction See *fiction, autarchic.*

authoritarian character See *authoritarian personality.*

authoritarian cultural lag (G. M. Gilbert) The persistence of authoritarian attitudes, identifications, and behavioral frames of reference long after a social revolution or upheaval has overthrown traditional authoritarian government. This is thought to make both individuals and their social institutions susceptible to authoritarianism in the guise of self-government and to lead to the establishment of dictatorship as a transitional form of social organization.

authoritarian group (K. Lewin) An experimental group in social psychology where all decisions are made by the leader.

authoritarian personality Referring to individuals who are characterized by a dependence upon clearly delineated hierarchies of authority.

authyphobatesis Obsolete term for spontaneous somnambulism.

autia (R. B. Cattell) The high-score of a personality dimension characterized by non-conforming, impractical, "Bohemian," dissociative behavior, with intensive subjective, autistic, inner intellectual life. Involves maladjustment to, and rejection by, social milieu. Appears as first-order questionnaire factor M+ and associated first-order objective test factor U.I. 34+.

autism 1. An extreme case of egocentrism, narcissism and inability to relate to other people. 2. Perceiving the outer world in terms of one's own personality, needs, thoughts and ideas, with little if any regard for the reality. 3. Tendency for withdrawal from real life and indulging in daydreaming and bizarre fantasies.

autism, early infantile 1. (A. Kanner) A cluster of severe symptoms occurring in infancy. The symptoms include withdrawal, language disturbance and often mutism, fear of change and insistence on sameness, inability to relate to people, repetitive rhythmical movements, apathy and emotional detachment. In some cases the early infantile autism develops into schizophrenia. 2. (M. S. Mahler) Early infantile autism is a type of early childhood schizophrenia, in which the instinctual forces of libido and aggression exist in an unneutralized form. The mother is not perceived by the infant as a separate entity but remains undistinguished from inanimate objects. 3. (B. Rimland) Early infantile autism is basically a cognitive dysfunction. It is the inability to relate new stimulus to previous experiences related to organic impairment, specifically reticular dysfunction. This dysfunction is probably caused by anoxia. 4. (B. B. Wolman) The early infantile autism is a name of a cluster of symptoms which 1) could be caused by organic causes or 2) by psychogenic factors. The latter is a syndrome typical of early childhood schizophrenia called vectoriasis praecocissima. The schizophrenic syndrome of autism is a regression of the infantile ego into the id.

autism, normal (M. S. Mahler) The first weeks of extrauterine life are regarded as the normal autistic phase. The instinctual responses to stimuli of a neonate and infant are on a reflex and thalamic level; his ego apparatuses are unintegrated and his defense mechanisms consist of overflow and discharge of somatic reactions. The libido position is predominantly visceral. In the autistic phase the young infant may be likened to a closed monadic system. Mahler conceptualized the state of the sensorium in terms of *normal autism*, for in the first weeks of life, the infant seems to be in a state of primitive negative hallucinatory disorientation, in which need satisfaction belongs to his own omnipotent autistic orbit.

autistic child A child who displays autistic symptoms such as repetitive rocking and head banging, apathy, fear of change, insistence on preservation of sameness, lack of interest in people, severe speech disorders with frequent mutism and extreme aloneness. Autistic symptoms start in early infancy and are linked either with organic causes or viewed as a syndrome schizophrenia in childhood. See *autism, early infantile.*

autistic schizophrenia See *schizophrenia, autistic.*

autistic syndrome in childhood schizophrenia 1. See *autism.* 2. (B. B. Wolman) Corresponds in childhood schizophrenia to simple deterioration and hebephrenia in adults.

autistic thinking See *thinking, autistic.*

autobiography 1. A biography written by the subject himself recounting memoirs of his life. 2. A document used for psychological, sociological and historicobiographical research which while having the disadvantages of bias due to the author's reasons for writing, his state of mind and age at the time of writing have the advantage of completeness and of being related to a particular area of interest.

autocentric Self-centered.

autochthonus 1. Found in the area or part of the body in which it originates. 2. Pertaining to ideas that seem to arise independently of an individual's own train of thought.

autochthonous gestalt A perceptual unity which arises due to factors that are innate to the perceiving organism rather than to the stimulus.

autochthonous variable See *variable, autochthonous.*

auto-echopraxia A form of stereotypy in which an individual continually repeats a previously experienced action.

auto-fellatio The self-gratifying act of placing one's penis in one's own mouth.

autofetishism Sexual feelings towards one's own material possession.

autoflagellation Whipping oneself.

autogenic, autogeny Self-generated or self-originated.

autogenic reinforcement See *reinforcement, autogenic.*

autognosis Self-knowledge.

auto-hypnosis Self-induced hypnosis.

autoimmune disease hypothesis (P.R.J. Burch) Statistically developed explanation for schizophrenia, manic-depressive psychosis, and involutional psychosis using genetic factors.

autoimmune response The manufacture of antibodies noxious to the organism's own tissues.

autokinesis Movement originated by stimuli arising within the organism.

autokinetic effect The illusory erratic and unpredictable movement of a luminous object, fixed in time and space, in an inarticulated surrounding such as darkness.

autokinetic phenomenon See *phenomenon, autokinetic.*

automata theory The mathematical study of the behavior of robots.

automated psychodiagnosis See *psychodiagnosis, automated.*

automatic action An act performed without self-awareness.

automatic writing 1. Writing while paying attention almost solely to the content rather than to the hand movements or resulting handwriting. 2. Writing of meaningful material unconsciously.

automatism, ambulatory Automatic activity which is rhythmic in form.

automatism, ambulatory comitial (D. H. Tuke) Automatic acts which are often observed in epileptics.

automatograph An instrument for recording automatic movements.

automaton 1. A mechanical figure designed to act in a self-motivated or human fashion; a robot. 2. A man who behaves in a machine-like way.

automaton conformity (E. Fromm) The posture adopted by a person in order to resolve his fears of freedom and the concomitant isolation by following society's prescription.

automorphic perception See *perception, automorphic.*

automysophobia Fear of being filthy or smelling bad.

autonomasia A type of amnesic aphasia characterized by inability to remember names or nouns.

autonomic affective apparatus See *apparatus, autonomic affective.*

autonomic balance A wholesome interaction between the divisions of the autonomic nervous system.

autonomic epilepsy See *epilepsy, autonomic.*

autonomic nervous system See *nervous system, autonomic.*

autonomy; autonomy drive (A. Angyal) The tendency to attempt to master or be effective in the environment, to impose one's wishes and designs on it.

autonomy, functional (G. W. Allport) The tendency for modes of behavior, once acquired, to become eventually independent of the drives or motives by which they were originally instigated.

autonomy need See *need, autonomy.*

autonomy, primary (H. Hartmann) In contradistinction to S. Freud, Hartmann postulated that the ego is endowed with an innate apparatus of a conflict-free sphere which includes the functions of motility, perception and thought. The fact that from its inception, the ego is equipped with such an apparatus was called by Hartmann primary autonomy.

autonomy, secondary (H. Hartmann) The acquired ability of the ego to resist regression. The stable patterns of the ego, its independence from the id-based impulses, the ability to retain developmental acquisitions are secondary autonomous.

autopathy A disease, handicap or disorder that has an afferent cause.

autophobia Morbid fear of oneself.

autophonia, autophony A condition characteristic of some middle-ear and auditory tube diseases in which the Eustachian tube remains open causing the voice to echo peculiarly.

autophonomania Obsolete term for a suicidal mental illness.

autoplastic Change, adaptation or alteration of the self.

auto-sadism (psychoanalysis) Sadistic tendencies defensively turned toward the self because of the anxiety and guilt associated with aggression directed towards others.

autoscope An instrument, device or technique used in the magnification of small, involuntary muscle movements.

autoscopy The seeing of one's self as a double, usually in the form of the face and bust which imitates the expressions and movements of the original. The copy is usually misty, hazy and partially transparent.

autosomal anomaly See *anomaly, autosomal.*

autosome Any chromosome other than the sex chromosomes. Man has 22 pairs and drosophila melanogaster 3 pairs.

autosuggestion Communication from oneself to oneself in the attempt to influence or improve health or behavior.

auxiliary ego 1. The person who consciously accepts another person's communications, needs, and purposes, in order to aid the other and increase his strength. 2. (J. L. Moreno) In psychodrama, a secondary actor who adopts and enacts supporting roles from the viewpoint of the other.

auxocyte A spermatocyte, oocyte or sporocyte during early growth.

availability principle The ease and readiness with which a response is elicited is dependent upon how ready for functioning that response is.

aventyl Common name for nortriptylene, an antidepressant drug.

average deviation See *deviation, average.*

average variation See *mean deviation.*

aversion therapy See *therapy, aversion.*

aversive conditioning See *conditioning, aversive.*

aversive stimulus See *stimulus, aversive.*

aviator's neurasthenia See *neurasthenia, aviator's.*

avoidance-avoidance conflict See *conflict, avoidance-avoidance.*

avoidance behavior See *behavior, avoidance.*

avoidance-avoidance conflict See *conflict,avoidance-avoidance.*

avoidance, free operant (M. Sidman) Procedure of aversive stimulation used in studying avoidance conditioning. The experimental animal is placed in a usual metal operant conditioning chamber containing an operandum appropriate to the organism. By means of programmed electronic equipment a series of intense but brief shocks are delivered to the subject through the floor of the chamber. The shocks are programmed by two recycling timers. When the subject does not respond to the interval between the shocks, the shock-shock interval or SS interval is specified by the first timer. If the animal responds, the shock can be postponed for the amount of time programmed on the second timer, the response-shock interval, or RS interval. Each shock starts the SS interval anew while each response terminates the SS interval and starts the RS interval. Thus by responding, the animal can reset the RS interval and postpone shock for as long as he responds.

There are no extroceptive stimuli indicating that a shock is impending. Since the duration of the shock is a fraction of a second, the animal does not terminate a shock, but postpones it every time it responds. Thus specification of the SS and RS intervals completely specify the free operant avoidance situation.

avoidance gradient See *gradient, avoidance.*

avoidance learning See *learning, avoidance.*

avoidance schedule, Sidman See *avoidance, free operant.*

awareness Being conscious of something; the state of perceiving and taking account of some event, occasion, experience or object.

axial gradient A graded difference that becomes progressively smaller between two aspects, states or conditions located along an axis of an organism.

axiology A branch of philosophy which deals with the study of values, such as those of religion, ethics and aesthetics.

axiom 1. A truth which is self-evident. 2. A proposition which is commonly accepted as true. 3. A proposition offered as true for the purposes of observing and studying the consequences which follow from it.

axis One of two or more straight lines meeting at a point called the origin. The horizontal axis is typically identified as the X axis, the vertical as the Y axis, and a third axis at right angles to the first two permits location of all points in three-dimensional space.

axis, vertical See *Y axis.*

axon The long and thin efferent part of the neuron. The nerve impulse, produced on the membrane of the axon, travels along the length of the axon.

axon reflex See *reflex, axon.*

B

B **1.** The total of an organism's body, excepting the nervous system. **2.** A symbol for luminance. **3.** A symbol for any number or variable. **4.** (C. L. Hull) The mean of the amount of responses in a response or alteration cycle.

babbling Meaningless vocal sounds uttered by infants prior to their ability to talk.

Babinski reflex (J. Babinski) The upward extension versus flexion of toes when the sole of the foot is gently stroked. This reflex is common in infancy but gradually gives way to flexion or contraction of the toes, called the plantar reflex. When this condition occurs beyond infancy it is a sign of neurological disorder—specifically lesion in, or depression of the pyramidal tract.

baby talk Early speech characterized by inaccurate pronounciation of various consonants. This form of speech is gradually outgrown unless it is reinforced by the child's environment or the result of some kind of more serious speech disorder.

bacilli, fear of See *bacillophobia*.

bacillophobia Morbid or pathological fear of bacilli or germs. The fear can extend to include all micro-organisms.

back disorders, psychogenic Backaches of emotional origin.

back wards Wards in mental hospitals which house severely disturbed patients.

backward association A verbal learning term referring to a connection between a particular item in a series and a preceeding item. See *association*.

backward conditioning See *conditioning, backward*.

bad-me See *personified self*.

bad object, good object (Melanie Klein) In the first year of life, at the paranoid-schizoid position, the infant introjects the breasts, and experiences a part of the introjected breasts as a good object and a part as a bad object, reflecting the death instinct. The bad objects are repressed.

Baillarger, Jules Gabriel Francois (1538-1616) A French physician considered to have been the first epidemiologist. He provided the first clear description of whooping cough and in a later paper apparently originated the term rheumatism.

Bain, Alexander (1818-1903) Scottish professor of philosophy at the University of Aberdeen. He wrote the first systematic textbook of psychology in English (its two volumes appeared in 1855 and 1859), published the first book on mind and body in 1872, and founded the first psychological journal, *Mind*, in 1876.

balance **1.** The state in which opposing forces are in an equal relationship. **2.** The state of upright posture characterized by the harmonious adjustment of the muscles against gravity. **3.** (K. Heider) A cognitive system which results when there is consistency in the relationship between either objects, persons, or an object and a person, and an individual's evaluation of them.

balance of minus judgements (experimental psychology) When the comparison stimulus is objectively equal to the standard stimulus, the amount of the difference between the percent of plus and minus judgements.

Baldwin, James Mark (1861-1934) American philosopher and theorist. Studied at Princeton and at Leipzig (under Wundt). Was professor of philosophy at the University of Toronto (1889-1893), of psychology at Princeton (1893-1903), of philosophy and psychology at Johns Hopkins (1903-1908). The next five years were spent in an advisory capacity at the National University of Mexico. For five years after that he was professor at L'École des Hautes Études Sociales in Paris. He founded laboratories at Toronto (1889); at Princeton (1903); championed work of Hall and Cattell by endorsing evolution, functional approach to psychology, and psychology of individual differences. Specialist in child and social psychology. Co-founder with Cattell of *Psychological Review* (1894) and *Psychological Index* and *Psychological Monographs* and *Psychological Bulletin* (1904). Also published a two-volume

Dictionary of Philosophy and Psychology (1901-1902). Wrote *Handbook of Psychology* (1889-1891), *Mental Development in the Child and the Race* (1895), *Social and Ethical Interpretations in Mental Development* (1897) and *History of Psychology* (1913).

ball and field test   See *test, ball and field.*

band chart   A chart which indicates, usually through the use of different colors, the number, amount or percentage of items, classes, or groups which make up a given total.

bandwagon effect   (social psychology) A social group phenomenon characterized by increasingly large numbers of people associating themselves with the dominant opinion.

Bar Diagram   See *Diagram, Bar.*

baragnosis   A loss of the perception of weight.

Barany Test   See *test, Barany.*

barbiturate   Any one of a class of drugs that act as central nervous system depressants.

baresthesis; baraesthesia   The sense of pressure.

barium poisoning   See *poisoning, barium.*

barognosis   The perception of weight; the ability to estimate weight.

barophobia   An extreme fear of gravity.

baroreceptors   Nerve structures (receptors) which are stimulated by changes of pressure within the organ in which they are located.

Barr body   The sex chromatin as seen in somatic cells of the female; named after the discoverer of sexual dimorphism in somatic cells, Dr. Murray Barr. It is best studied by the buccal smear or oral mucosa technique. The number of Barr bodies in a cell is one less than the number of X chromosomes.

barylalia   Thick, indistinct speech characteristically seen in patients with organic brain disease and common in the advanced stages of general paresis.

baryphonia; baryphony   A form of dysphasia characterized by a thick, heavy voice quality.

basal age   The lowest age level at which all items are passed in tests standardized in terms of mental age units.

basal ganglia   A group of structures of gray matter deep within the cerebrum which forms part of the neural system that aids in the control of motor responses.

basal metabolic rate   Represents the minimum energy expenditure required for the maintenance of vital functions.

basal metabolism   The amount of energy expended, measured in calories, per unit of time while at rest; measured after fourteen to eighteen hours of rest. The basal metabolic rate is the minimum energy expenditure necessary for the maintenance of vital functions.

base line   The abscissa, or horizontal axis, of a graph.

base rate problem   The occurrence of spontaneous remission in patients with or without treatment.

Basedow's disease   See *goiter, exophthalmic.*

basic anxiety   See *anxiety, basic.*

basic data relation matrix (BDRM)   A basically five dimensional (but possibly ten) score matrix containing all the particulars (coordinates) necessary to define a psychological event: a person, focal stimula, a response, an ambient stimulus (background condition), and an observer. Sometimes called "the data box" from which all correlational and analysis of variance procedures must begin. Its value is in pointing comprehensively to all possible relational analyses.

basic paranoid attitude   (Melanie Klein) The first stage of the oral phase in which the infant has no experience of the whole person, experiences no ambivalence, and has split his object into an ideal and persecutory one. The prevalent anxiety is of a persecutory nature—a fear that the persecutors may invade and destroy the self and the ideal object.

basic personality   (A. Kardiner) The constellation of personality traits which are present in all members of a given culture or society due to common child raising practices.

basilar membrane   The delicate membrane in the cochlea which supports the organ of Corti, the organ which converts movements of the basilar membrane into nervous impulses.

basophobia; basiphobia   An extreme fear of standing erect or walking.

Bassen-Kornzweig syndrome   See *syndrome, Bassen-Kornzweig.*

bath, brand   See *cold bath.*

bathophobia   A pathological fear of depths.

bathyesthesis; bathyesthesia   Deep sensitivity.

batrachophobia   An extreme fear of frogs.

battery of tests   See *tests, battery of.*

battle fatigue   State of physical and emotional exhaustion caused by stress situation in active combat or other hardships of war. It acts as a precipitating factor in causing a variety of behavior disorders. Battle fatigue was called shell shock in World War I.

Bayes' theorem   (statistics) An algebraic statement that the probability of an event's having been the consequence of another event is dependent upon the number of mutually exclusive events which may have given rise to that event.

Bayle's disease   An obsolete name for general paresis first described in 1822 by the French physician Antoine Bayle.

Bayley, Nancy (1899-   )   Developmental psychologist, at University of California (later also

National Institute of Mental Health). Studied psychological and physical growth of sixty healthy children from birth to 36 years. Made analyses of intelligence and of factors influencing IQ and rates of mental growth. Demonstrated low correlations between mental scores obtained before and after one year of age. Found sex differences in determiners of mental abilities, showing boys more permanently affected by early emotional aspects of parent-child interactions, proving that genetic factors play a greater role in girl's abilities. Devised a method of predicting children's adult height from x-rays of bone maturity.

Bayley scales of infant development See *scales, Bayley, of infant development.*

BDRM See *basic data relation matrix.*

Beard, George Miller (1840-1883) An American psychiatrist who introduced the term neurasthenia.

Beck system An approach to the Rorschach test developed by Samuel J. Beck following the basic guidelines set forth by Hermann Rorschach and Emil Oberholzer. It is generally considered one of the most conservative approaches to the test, empirically based and following the behavioristic traditions.

bedlam State of frenzy, tumult, wild excitement. Bedlam was the name of the Priory of St. Mary of Bethlehem, a mental hospital in London. Bedlam became the common name for any mental hospital and eventually came to its present meaning.

before-after design An experimental method or procedure in which all groups, control and experimental, receive pre- and post- tests.

behavior 1. The totality of intra- and extraorganismic actions and interactions of an organism with its physical and social environment. Psychology deals with three types of phenomena: 1) Observable behavior, such as nervous tics, stuttering, excessive perspiration, bed-wetting, compulsive acts, impotence, violence, suicidal attempts, etc. 2) Introspectively observable phenomena, i.e., behavior that is not easily observed from without, such as toothache, headache, worry, hunger, and fear. 3) Unconscious processes, i.e., those mental processes which are not accessible even to the experiencing individual himself. **2.** Any single activity, movement or response or group of activities, movements or responses of an organism; an activity, movement or response which alters the position of the organism or any part of the organism, in space. **3.** (behaviorism) The dependent variable in the science of behavior.

There is considerable disagreement in psychology as to what actually constitutes behavior, although there is a general agreement in that behavior is seen as the activity of an organism. The problem arises in the delimiting of those activities which are considered behaviors. For the behaviorists, an activity, to qualify as a behavior, must be directly observable and measurable. For other psychologists, activities that qualify as behaviors include ideas, thoughts, dreams, images as well as overt muscular and neuro-

physiological activities. There is also disagreement in distinguishing activities that are considered behaviors from those activities studied by physiology; i.e., the distinction between talking, perceiving, walking, on the one hand, and breathing, digestion, secreting bile on the other hand.

behavior, avoidance Behavior that postpones an aversive event thereby escaping from the conditioned aversive stimuli. The conditioned aversive stimulus is all the stimuli before the aversive stimulus presented minus the stimuli associated with the avoidance response. Thus avoidance behavior is a form of escape behavior.

behavior contrast (B. F. Skinner) The observation that in discrimination experiments the latencies of responses to stimuli that occasion reinforcement are longer than the latencies of responses to stimuli that do not occasion reinforcement, when such responses do occur.

behavior criterion A standard behavior with which other behaviors are compared.

behavior determinant (E. C. Tolman) Any variable which has a causal relation to a behavior.

behavior disorders A general term describing disorganized, disturbed, and deranged behavioral patterns. This term is used interchangeably with mental disorders, abnormal behavior, abnormal psychology, and psychopathology.

behavior dynamics 1. The study of causes and effects in behavior. **2.** Motivation.

behavior, extrinsic Behavior which does not have a specific response mechanism; such behavior can be performed in various ways using different kinds of mechanisms.

behavior field The sum total at any given time of all events, conditions, and stimuli that impinge upon and influence the behavior of the organism.

behavior genetics The field of study dealing with the genetic basis of mechanisms underlying specific behavior patterns.

behavior homology A generalization stating the principle of a continuity of behavior patterns from species to species, a specific class of behaviors in lower forms corresponding in function and pattern to that same class of behaviors in man.

behavior, intrinsic Behavior which is carried out through a specific mechanism or organ as, for example, eye-blinking.

behavior, maternal The behavior involving the care of the young.

behavior method An approach which is derived from behaviorism in that the methods and goals, but not some of the negations and philosophical postulates, are accepted. Behavior of organisms is systematically studied as an observable response to carefully defined stimuli. Introspection is not used and mental contents and processes are not dealt with. However, intervening variables that are not directly observable, such as hunger of the organism, are accepted as explanatory constructs if tied down to stimulus and response conditions and if defined in strictly operational terms.

behavior, molar 1. A large unified unit of behavior. **2.** A large unit of behavior which is not equal to the sum of its parts. **3.** (E. C. Tolman) Behavior which is modifiable by learning. The unit of purposive behavior. **4.** Behavior which is explained or defined in terms of psychological rather than physiological constructs.

behavior, molecular 1. Behavior described in terms of small units. **2.** Behavior described in terms of neuromuscular or glandular activities.

behavior object An object which usually elicits a socially standardized type of behavior, such as a chair or fork.

behavior observation (generic) The recording and measurement of behavior by use of a human observer; may be in naturalistic or controlled settings, with pre- or post-observational categorization with or without supplementary instrumentation. See *time-sampling; behavior unit observation.*

behavior, overt Behavior which is easily observable; behavior or response which is visibly accountable or tangible.

behavior pattern See *archetype.*

behavior rating 1. The observation and recording of the occurrence of specific behaviors or classes of behaviors. **2.** The assignment of a rank, score or mark to a specific observed behavior or class of behaviors.

behavior repertoire All behaviors which are possible for an organism.

behavior sampling The observation and recording of all the behaviors an organism engages in during prescribed segments of time so as to yield a representative sample of the totality of the organism's behavior.

behavior segment The smallest descriptive unit of a response to a stimulus.

behavior shaping Teaching of new and desired responses by using conditioning techniques of reinforcing any response that approximates the desired one until the correct behavior is learned.

behavior space 1. (E. C. Tolman) The space that contains objects perceived by the organism at any one time. The organism perceives the objects as being in a place at a distance and direction from the organism. **2.** (K. Lewin) The complex and total set of conditions and relations determining the behavior of the individual, at any given time. The set consists of memories from the past, present influences, contemplations of the future, the perceived objects and the relation between them, the perception of the self in the situation, and a system of values, attitudes and beliefs concerning objects and relationships in the set.

behavior, species specific 1. Behavioral patterns shown by most members of the same species when in similar or the same situation. **2.** Complex, stereotyped behavior appearing in most members of a species with no evidence of prior opportunity to learn it, thus assumed to be innate.

behavior, spontaneous Behavior that occurs ostensibly in the absence of any stimulus that could be shown to occasion, elicit or release the behavior.

behavior stream The continuous behavior output of an organism from which behavior theory abstracts such data terms as "response"; the term is paralleled by continuous energy input functions from which behavior theory abstracts such independent variable terms as "stimulus."

behavior therapy 1. The class of methods of changing unadaptive habits that is based on experimentally established paradigms. It is applicable to all unadaptive habits that have their origin in learning. The two major branches are classical conditioning, largely involving reciprocal inhibition and mainly applied to neuroses, and operant conditioning applied to unadaptive motor habits, notably those habits of schizophrenics that have been acquired by learning. **2.** (B. F. Skinner) Shaping of behavior through manipulation of reinforcement to obtain the desired behavior. The theory is that hypothetical emotional factors and mental states are useless data in the study of psychopathology. The overt behavior is critical which is determined by external forces. Psychopathology is believed to result from underlearning or from learning of inappropriate behaviors which are reshaped by externally given reinforcement. **3.** (J. Wolpe) Treatment of neurosis using learning theory techniques. Neurosis is believed to originate when a drive-motivated behavior is arbitrarily punished resulting in feelings of anxiety in similar situations. Therapy consists of reciprocal inhibition involving experimental extinction or counter-conditioning techniques. The patient is asked to perform the anxiety arousing behavior in fantasy or fact in a rewarding atmosphere resulting in the elimination of inhibitions associated with the behavior. Two major methods of behavior therapy are classical conditioning and instrumental conditioning. There are four forms of the latter method: reward training, avoidance learning, omission training, and punishment training.

behavior therapy, verbal conditioning The use of operant conditioning techniques in order to guide and increase the verbalized statements of the patient who can find out that his speech will not be disapproved of or punished.

behavior unit observation (BUO) Acts defined by pre-established categories are recorded as they occur, without reference to duration or time intervals; measure is either frequency of occurrences during a standard time period of observation, or frequency per unit of time when observations differ in duration.

behavior, verbal Behavior which employs words in any form-printed, written, oral, etc.

behavioral equation An equation, as follows, expressing the magnitude of a behavioral response act, a_{jh}, as a function of the subject's ability, A; temperament, T; and dynamic, D, trait endowments, of behavioral indices, b_j's, peculiar to the focal stimulus and response, j, and of modulating influences, s_h, peculiar to the ambient situation, h.

$$a_{ijh} = \Sigma b_{ja}A_i + \Sigma b_{jt}\, T_i + \Sigma b_{jd}s_{hd}D_i$$

(i being a particular individual). This is the simplest linear and additive form for factor analysis, but can be generalized.

behavioral genetics See *behavior genetics.*

behavioral information See *information, behavioral.*

behavioral oscillation $(_sO_R)$ See *oscillation, behavioral, or* $_sO_R$.

behavioral situation indices The values, which are factor loadings, usually written b or s in the behavioral specification equation, which show how much a given source trait is involved in that specific situation and response.

behaviorism A theoretical "school of psychology," created by John B. Watson, for which overt behavior was defined as the subject-matter of psychology; designed to broaden systematic psychological study to encompass the lower animals, children, and the mentally abnormal. An atomistic theory for which reflexes and the conditioned reflex were the basic units.

Behn-Rorschach Test See *test, Behn-Rorschach.*

Bekhterev, Vladimir Mikhailovich (1857-1927) A Russian neuroanatomist, neurophysiologist, psychologist, neuropathologist and psychiatrist. In 1878 he graduated from the Medico-Surgical academy and was assigned to the Chair of Psychiatry under I. P. Merzheyevskii. In 1884-1886 he worked abroad at the laboratories of Kronecker, Gudder, Westphal, Meinert, Wundt, and Flechsig. From 1893-1913 Bekhterev was the Head of the Chair of Psychiatry and Neuropathology of the Academy of Military Sciences in Petersburg. In that period he wrote *Transmitting Pathways of the Spinal Cord and the Brain, Bases of Theory on the Brain Functions* (7 volumes), *Objective Psychology* (3 volumes), *Psyche and Life, Suggestion and its Role in Social Life, General Bases of Diagnosis of the Nervous System Diseases.* He formulated the conception of "combined-motor reflexes" which was an application of the conditioned reflex theory to man. He discovered and described the following new nervous pathways and nervous centers bearing his name: a) a group of cells in the external region of Corpus Posterior; b) vestibular nucleus ("Bekhterev nucleus"); c) Formatio Reticularis; d) four bunches in Brachia Conjunctiva; e) stria medularis was determined to serve for unction of different cerebellum parts; f) external stria inside the brain cortex named after Bekhterev. During his last years, his activity concerned the foundation of the science of reflexology.

belief-value matrix (E. C. Tolman) The set of categorizations and classifications (judgments and values) which the individual brings to his interactions with the environment.

Bell Adjustment Inventory See *inventory, Bell Adjustment.*

Bell-Magendie Law See *law, Bell-Magendie.*

bell-shaped curve See *curve, bell-shaped.*

Bellak, Leopold (1916-   ) American psychiatrist, psychoanalyst, and psychologist. Attempted to bridge these three fields conceptually and experimentally. Created Children's Apperception Test (CAT), formulated multifactorial theory of schizophrenia, and was instrumental in creating Schizophrenia Research Center at National Institute of Mental Health. Organized the first 24-hour walk-in clinic (Trouble Shooting Clinic) and general hospital as community mental health center at Elmhurst General Hospital, New York City. Co-authored with L. Loeb, *The Schizophrenic Syndrome;* described his experimental studies in psychoanalysis in *Broad Scope of Psychoanalysis;* wrote *Emergency Psychotherapy and Brief Psychotherapy* (with L. Small), and *The TAT and CAT in Clinical Use,* and other works.

Bell's mania See *mania, Bell's.*

belonephobia An extreme fear of needles.

belongingness, principle of (E. L. Thorndike) A bond between two items is more readily formed if the properties of one item are closely related to the properties of the other item.

benadryl The trade name for diphenhydramine, an anti-histamine compound used orally, topically and parenterally for allergies and for hyperactive children with behavior disorders.

Bender, Lauretta (1897-   ) American child psychiatrist. Married to Paul Schilder (Austrian psychiatrist and psychoanalyst) until his death, 1941. Author of Visual Motor Gestalt Test (Bender Gestalt Test). Worked in New York City and State psychiatric hospitals for children from 1930. Special contributions made to childhood schizophrenia, brain damaged children, deprivation syndrome in children, learning disabilities, art of children, and physiological and drug-therapies.

beneceptor A receptor for stimuli which tend to promote the well-being of the organism.

Bennett Differential Aptitude Test See *test, Bennett Differential Aptitude.*

Bennett Test of Mechanical Comprehension See *test, Bennett, of Mechanical Comprehension.*

benzedrine A trade name for amphetamine.

benzodiazepine compounds Include librium and valium. It appears they act by a suppression of excitation in the reticular activating system; they promote muscular relaxation and block convulsive drug or electrically elicited activity. Sedative action seems to be between barbiturates and phenothiazines.

Berger rhythm See *alpha rhythm.*

Bergson, Henri (1859-1941) French philosopher, professor, whose writings contained much material relevant for psychology; opposed materialistic and positivistic philosophy and atomistic psychology; stressed the dynamic unity of mind and the ego as the unifying substratum of everchanging psychological states; favored intuitive rather than rationalistic approach to reality; received Nobel prize in 1927.

Beritashvili (Beritoff), Ivan (1885-   ) Soviet neurophysiologist. Worked under N.E. Vvedensky (1909-1914). In 1916-1919, Docent of Physiology at Odessa University. Since 1919, professor of the State University in Tbilisi; since 1935, Head of Sechenov Institute of Physiology. He established: 1) role of the spinal nervous elements such as intermediate, motor and gelatinous Rolando's substance in phasic coordinating motion of the extremities (1909-1914); 2) a rhythmic nature of the reciprocal inhibition of skeleton muscles (1912-1914); 3) a nervous mechanism of establishing of the jugular and labyrinth tonic reflexes (1914-1915); 4) formation of bilateral connections—progressive (direct) and return (feedback) under conditioning (1916-1922); 5) formation of conditioned reflexes under a reverse order of the combination, i.e., unconditioned first, then conditioned (1927); 6) appearance of the general inhibition together with inhibition of a definite complex of the brain neurons under each behavioral act (1927-1935); 7) individually acquired feeding or defensive behavior after a one-time perception of the food location or a damaging agent and its regulation by reproduction of an image of the food location or the enemy (1932—1935); 8) regularities of the image-driven psychoneural activity of neocortex (1935, 1947, 1969); 9) an automatized involuntary character of the conditioned reflex, based on structural development of the synaptic apparatuses (1961—1969); 10) a neuropsychic mechanism of orientation of animal and man in space (1959); 11) role of cortical and subcortical brain regions in the image-driven psychoneural activity (1961, 1969); 12) image-driven and emotional memory, its characteristic and origination (1968).

Berkeley growth study A study aimed at changes in intellectual ability with increasing age. Found that there is little stability in intelligence test scores obtained in testing in infancy and those 5 or 6 years later.

Bernard, Claude (1813-1878) French experimental physiologist, credited with coining of the term endocrinology.

Bernheim, Hippolyte-Marie (1840-1919) French psychiatrist who investigated hypnotism and suggestibility. Bernheim maintained that all people are suggestible. Bernheim was critical of Charcot's views and techniques.

Bernoulli trials (statistics) A series of trials in which there are two and only two possible outcomes

for each trial and the outcome of one trial in no way influences the outcome of any other trial.

Bernreuter Personal Adjustment Inventory See *Bernreuter Personality Inventory.*

Bernreuter Personality Inventory (R. G. Bernreuter) A questionnaire introduced in 1931 which measures six traits: neurotic tendency, self-sufficiency, introversion-extroversion, dominance-submission, confidence and sociability, the last two of which were added by J. C. Flanagan following factor analysis. This inventory is intended for use with children in grades 9 to 16 and with adults. The items are answered yes or no and each is scored in terms of its differentiating ability for a specific trait. Its value lies in initial diagnosis of persons at the extremes of the scale.

best answer test See *test, best answer.*

best reason test See *test, best answer.*

bestiality **1.** Any human behavior which is revolting and disgusting. **2.** Sexual intercourse with animals.

beta coefficient In multiple correlation, the amount that each variable must be multiplied in order to yield the highest correlation.

beta error See *error, beta.*

beta movement See *movement, beta.*

beta press See *press, beta.*

beta response An eyelid response which is delayed somewhat after the presentation of the conditioned stimulus.

beta rhythm; beta waves A pattern of brain waves observed on an electroencephalograph in which the waves are faster and of less amplitude than alpha rhythm.

beta test See *test, Army Beta.*

beta weight; β-weight (statistics) In a multiple correlation, the amount by which each variable is multiplied so that each variable or predictor will produce the highest possible multiple correlation with the dependent variable.

betz cells Large pyramid shaped cells located in layer V of the motor cortex.

Bezold-Brücke phenomenon With an increase in illumination, there is a shift in hue with colors tinged with red and green moving toward the yellow and blue side of the spectrum.

bias **1.** A tendency towards favoring a certain position or conclusion. **2.** A tendency to make errors in a certain direction. **3.** A factor in an experimental procedure which systematically introduces error or systematically distorts a set of data. **4.** An adjustable set point that regulates a servomechanism. Example: the adjustable setting on a thermostat.

bibliokleptomania A pathological tendency to steal books.

bibliotherapy Reading used as a therapeutic technique.

Bichat, Law of See *law of Bichat.*

Bidwell's Ghost See *Purkinje afterimage.*

bifactor method (statistics) A factor analytic procedure involving the extraction of a general factor and then the extraction of group factors, or factors of more limited scope.

bifactoral theory of conditioning See *conditioning, bifactoral theory of.*

bilateral 1. Having two sides. 2. Pertaining to both the right and left sides.

bilateral transfer The transference of a skill learned on one side of the body to the other side of the body.

bilirubin A chemical substance, the principal pigment of bile. Normally found in feces and, in cases of jaundice, in urine. See *bilirubin encephalopathy.*

bilirubin encephalopathy See *Kernicterus.*

bimodal (statistics) A descriptive term for a distribution which has two points at which the frequencies are significantly greater than at points on either side of those two points.

bimodal distribution See *distribution, bimodal.*

binary (number) system A system of numbers consisting of 1 and 0 used in electronic computers.

binaural A term pertaining to the functioning of the two ears together, as in normal hearing.

binaural beat See *binaural shift.*

binaural ratio The ratio of the sound intensities at the two ears.

binaural shift The periodic shift in localization or perceived intensity of the sound which occurs when two tones of slightly different frequency are perceived separately by each ear. The fluctuation rate corresponds to the frequency difference.

bind hypothesis, double See *hypothesis, double bind.*

Binet, Alfred (1857-1911) French psychologist. Director, laboratory of physiological psychology, Sorbonne, Paris; with Theodore Simon constructed first well-known individual scale of intelligence which determined mental age; builder of French psychology and objective scientific psychology, insisting on experimental basis for psychological data; experimented extensively and intensively on functions and phenomena, particularly on thinking; rejected associationism; founded and edited first French psychological journal, *L'Année Psychologique* (1895); author of *L'Étude Expérimentale de l'Intelligence*(1903).

Binet—Simon Scale See *test, Binet—Simon.*

Binet—Simon Test See *test, Binet—Simon.*

binocular accommodation See *accommodation, binocular.*

binocular flicker See *flicker, binocular.*

binocular parallax See *parallax, binocular.*

binocular perception See *perception, binocular.*

binocular vision Sight with both eyes fixated on the same object in space.

binomial expansion The result of raising to any power an algebraic expression containing two terms.

Binswanger, Otto (1852-1929) A German neurologist and psychiatrist.

biochemical research Research dealing with the effects of biochemical events on the behavior of organisms and of the reciprocal effect of behavior on biochemical events. Sensory and motor actions can be altered by the injection of chemical agents to particular areas of the brain. Behavior such as learning and memory has been found to affect biochemical systems at the molecular level.

biocybernetics A biological branch of application and elaboration of the cybernetic regularities. Mechanisms of self-organization in the living system with the "feed-back" as the decisive factor are the main issue of biocybernetics. A wide development of biocybernetics took place with the study of the neurocybernetic regularities, such as transmission of information, feed-back, reliability of neurocybernetic patterns, etc. The neurocybernetic approach to study of a neuron and of the brain enabled the building of a great number of models of a neuron and of the whole machine-electronic combinations, as for example, "perceptron" by McCulloch-Pitts. One must, however, notice that "neurocybernetics" is a somewhat artificial limitation of the biocybernetic regularities, since the brain becomes a biosystem if it continuously receives information from the external and internal stimuli through peripheral afferent pathways. At the same time, the brain performs its integrative functions through the activity of the peripheral motor and secretory apparatuses. The biocybernetic regularities are related to the deeper and more narrowly elaborated regularities of the functional system, which is the real working centro-peripheral organization. Biocybernetics also used distinguished properties of living organisms (fine sensibility, speed of movement, principles of organization, etc.) for a constructive improvement of technical and electronic machines.

bioelectrical potential The electric charge or potential shown by living tissues, such as neurons and the brain, at any given time.

biogenesis The origin and evolution of living things.

biogenetic law (E. Haeckel) Ontogenesis, that is the development of the individual, is an abbreviated replica of phylogenesis, that is the development of the species. Also called the law of recapitulation.

biographical method See *method, biographical.*

biological theories of personality See *personality, theory of: biological.*

Biographical Sketch of an Infant By C. Darwin, a diary of the early development of a child.

biometry   **1.** The application of statistical methods to the study of living organisms, their structures and functions. **2.** The calculation of the probable human life span.

bionomics   See *ecology*.

biopsychology   The field of psychology approached from a biological point of view, stressing the organism's adaptiveness to environmental demands and pressures through nervous system, endocrine gland, receptor functioning, etc.

biosocial theory   (G. Murphy) Biosocial theory posits the full continuous reciprocity of organism and environment. It emphasizes the fact that observation of personality is possible only when the organism is interacting with a social (or both physical and social) environment. Description of a personality as a self-contained unit (as often occurs in "personality research"), forgetting the situational-ecological context of all personal responses tends to be unrealistic. When considered in terms of the *time dimension,* the organism is continuously both giving and receiving social stimulation, and it is not the life history of the organism as such, but the history of its interactions with other personalities, that constitutes the best present direction for full-fledged personality study.

biosphere   **1.** The total area of the earth and the air surrounding it which contains and supports living organisms. **2.** The earth as an environment for living organisms.

biostatistics   The collection and analysis of data concerned with the lives of human beings, especially births and deaths.

biotype   **1.** (biology) A group of organisms which share a common hereditary background, although the individuals of the group may vary considerably. **2.** (E. Jaensch) One of two kinds of people characterized by an eidetic imagery thought to be physiologically based; the B type is associated with a tendency towards exophthalmic goiter; the T type is associated with a tendency towards tetany.

biotypology   The categorization of man into various types (biotypes) dependent upon psychological, physiological and anatomical considerations.

bipolar   **1.** Having two poles or branches at extreme ends. **2.** Referring to variables, tests or scales which are meaningful at extreme and opposite ends.

bipolar factor   See *factor, bipolar.*

bipolar neuron   See *neuron, bipolar.*

birth order   The relative order of age in the children of a family.

birth trauma   **1.** (psychoanalysis) The anxiety, thought to be the prototype of all later anxiety, experienced by the infant upon being born and being flooded with stimuli. **2.** A physical injury received at and during birth.

biserial correlation   See *correlation, biserial.*

bisexuality   **1.** The possession of the anatomical or psychological characteristics of both sexes. **2.** The condition of being equally attracted to members of both sexes.

bite   (operant conditioning) A deviation from a smooth curve on a cumulative record. It indicates a brief period of slow responding followed by a compensatory high rate which reestablishes the over-all rate.

bivariate correlation   See *correlation, simple.*

bivariate experiment   A form of design in which only two variables are measured at once, one of them commonly being manipulated and called the independent variable (sometimes called the univariate method). This may be called the classical, traditional experimental design in contrast with the multivariate experiment.

black box   A term for a formal model used in an attempt to develop hypothetical constructs to be used in explaining the behavior of organisms. Analogies are drawn between the organism and a black box, i.e., constructs are developed which will account for the output of the system given the input into the system.

blackout threshold   The point or level at which an organism loses consciousness, especially in conditions of oxygen deprivation.

Blacky pictures test   See *test, Blacky pictures.*

blank experiment; blank trial   See *experiment, blank.*

blanket group   A classification term referring to those items which do not fit in any of the prescribed categories.

blast-injection technique   A means of inducing convulsions in an animal by the prolonged exposure to air blasts or blasts of high frequency sound.

blastomere   A cell formed by the division of the fertilized ovum.

blastula   The stage of embryonic development formed by the cleavage of the ovum and characterized by a spherical mass of functionally identical cells with a central cavity.

blend response   A Rorschach response in which more than one feature of the blot, such as movement, color, form, or shading, contributes to the formulation of the percept. Generally considered to represent a complex affective-thought operation, each of the determinants is scored and given full weight in interpretation. See *additional scores* (for contrasting approach.)

blepherospasm   An involuntary spasm or blinking of the eyelids.

Bleuler, Eugen (1857-1939)   Swiss physician and psychiatrist. Introduced the word "schizophrenia" and the modern conception of this psychosis, stressed early in the 20th century the need of occupational, social and psychological treatment of schizophrenics and fought against the idea that schizophrenics cannot be successfully treated. The first academic clinician who recognized the significance of Freud's psychoanalysis and helped much in its development. Introduced many psychological and psychopathological conceptions: ambivalence, ambitendence, autism, autistic thinking, etc. Introduced ambulatory assistance to psychiatric patients. Pioneer in the fight against alcoholism and in developing treatment for alcoholics. Stressed the significance of mnemism in psychiatry.

Bleuler, Manfred (1903-   ) Swiss psychiatrist. Investigated the psychological sequelae of endocrine diseases and introduced the term "endocrine psycho-syndrome". Applied the Rorschach test for sociocultural research. Continued his father's (see Bleuler, Eugen) work on schizophrenia and discovered that the condition of schizophrenia begins to improve from the 5th year on, after the onset of psychosis. Found that children of schizophrenics are healthy and a few are psychopathic. Introduced the principle of active community ("tätige Gemeinschaft") in treatment of mental disorders.

blind diagnosis See *diagnosis, blind.*

blind-matching technique A validation procedure in which an observer, given one description of a person or event, is required to select another example of that person or event from an independent description of events.

blind spot An area of the retina insensitive to light due to the juncture of the optic nerve and the eyeball at that point.

blindness, hysterical Blindness occurring although the organ is functional and intact.

blinking reflex See *reflex, blinking.*

block design test See *test, block design.*

block sampling See *sampling, block.*

blood groups Five blood types, A, B, O, M and N which are due to the action of single genes. Groups A, B, and O which exhibit linkage are used as markers in experiments designed to map chromosomal pairs. M and N do not manifest linkage.

blood pressure The force exerted by the blood against the walls of the arteries. Systolic pressure is the maximum pressure; diastolic pressure is the minimum pressure. There are many physiological and psychological correlates with blood pressure change.

Blos, Peter (1904-   ) Clinical psychologist and child psychoanalyst. Main contribution in the field of psychoanalytic theory of adolescence. Subdivision of adolescence into five phases, metapsychologically defined and exemplified by clinical material. Similarities and differences established in the developmental lines of male and female adolescence. Adolescent changes in psychic structure are formulated as the Second Individuation Process of Adolescence, Late Adolescent Consolidation and Character Formation. The typical structural differentiations are cued by somatic, genetic and cultural influences. Adolescence is conceived as the terminal stage of childhood, rather than, exclusively, as a recapitulation of prelatency

psychosexual development. The oedipus complex reaches its definitive resolution with the closure of adolescence. The transformation of the negative oedipus complex leads to the formation of the adult ego ideal. Special clinical studies in Cryptorchism, Female Delinquency and Acting Out (family myth).

body build The individual's body structure taken from the point of view of the pattern of relationships among the members and features of the body-trunk length, girth, limb length, height.

body-build index (H. J. Eysenck) An index of constitutional types which groups individuals according to the value obtained from multiplying one hundred times their height divided by six times their transverse chest diameter: mesomorphs fall within one standard deviation of the mean; leptomorphs are those one standard deviation or more above the mean, and eurymorphs are those one standard deviation or more below the mean.

body image See *image, body.*

body-language The expression of thoughts, emotions, etc. through movement of the body.

body type See *type, body.*

body-weight (in control of level of deprivation) An accompanying effect of a food deprivation schedule is loss of body-weight which is used as a check on the schedule. Body-weight is usually measured prior to a session and is maintained by feeding the animal up to a prescribed weight following a session.

Bogardus Social Distance Scale See *scale, Bogardus Social Distance.*

Bogen cage A performance test requiring the solution of a maze problem in three dimensions.

bone-conduction test See *test, bone-conduction.*

Boolean algebra (G. Boole) An algebra of sets consisting of a system for forming and manipulating sets according to specific postulates.

borderline intelligence See *intelligence, borderline.*

borderline schizophrenia See *schizophrenia, latent.*

Boring, Edwin G. (1886-1968) Long-time head of Harvard's psychology department. Theoretical work on sensory processes, especially audition. Leading professional historian of experimental psychology, who gave particular attention to the competing influences of Zeitgeist and of persons on the development of science. First editor of *Contemporary Psychology.*

bound energy (psychoanalysis) Libido under the control of ego processes which is available for dealing with reality and not expended on fantasy and repression.

Bourneville's disease See *tuberous sclerosis.*

Braceland, Francis J. (1900-   ) American psychiatrist, clinician, educator, editor. Psychiatrist-in-chief, the Institute of Living, 1951-65, Senior Consultant, 1965—; Editor, *American Journal of Psychiatry,* 1965—; Chief, psychiatry, Mayo Clinic,

1946-51; Dean, Loyola U. Med. School, 1941-42. Editor and author of four volumes and over 200 psychiatric papers on various aspects of clinical psychiatry and psychiatric education. Chief, Psychiatry, U.S. Navy, WWII, Rear Admiral (Ret.) 1962; President, American Psychiatric Association, 1956-57; President, American Board of Psychiatry and Neurology, 1950-52; Vice President, World Psychiatric Association, 1961-66.

brachycephaly, brachycephalism Having a short or broad head with a cephalic index of 81.0 to 85.4.

brachydactyly Having abnormally short fingers or toes.

brachylineal See *brachymorphy.*

brachymorphy Having an abnormally short stature.

brachyskelic Having abnormally short legs.

brachytypical See *brachymorphy.*

bradycardia Slowness of the heart due to functional or organic causes.

bradyglossia Slowness of speech resulting from difficulties in the movement of the tongue.

bradykinesis, bradykinesia Slowness of movement due to functional or organic causes.

bradylalia Slowness of speech of psychological or organic causes.

bradylexia Slowness of reading of psychological or organic origin.

bradylogia Slowness of speech of psychological or organic causes usually resulting from slowness of thinking.

bradyorthia Slowness of speech resulting from organic damage of the speech mechanism.

bradyphasia Slowness of thought.

bradyphrenia Sluggish mentality of psychological or organic causes.

bradypragia Slow action usually referring to physical activity of the body.

bradypragic Referring to bradypragia.

bradyscope An instrument which presents visual pictures or objects at slow rate of speed.

bradytrophism Slow metabolism of nutrition or nutritive movement characteristic of certain diseases.

braidism An obsolete term for hypnotism.

Braille A system of writing and printing which enables the blind to read, utilizing different combinations of raised points for letters and signs.

brain The portion of the central nervous system, composed of nerve tissue, enclosed within the skull, including the cerebrum, midbrain, cerebellum, pons and medulla oblongata.

brain center 1. Any area which is the end-point of afferent neurons, or the starting-point of efferent neurons, or an intermediary between the two.

2. Any group of neurons in the brain which are hypothesized to perform a specific function.

brain damage, effect on IQ test performance Damage to the right hemisphere results in a lower after birth. Injury to different areas of the brain may result in focalized handicaps but may also result in general intellectual and/or motor impairment.

brain damage, effect on IQ test performance Damage to the right hemisphere results in a lower performance level and intact verbal performance while damage to the left hemisphere causes difficulties in the verbal sphere.

brain disorders Disorders that are caused by or associated with impairment of functioning of brain tissues and that generally manifest symptoms such as: impairment of orientation; memory impairment; impairment of intellectual functions including calculation, knowledge, learning, comprehension; impairment of judgment; shallowness and lability of affect.

brain field theory See *isomorphism.*

brain lesion, occipitoparietal 1. See *agnosia, visual.* 2. See *apractagnosia.* 3. See *alexia.* 4. See *agraphia.* 5. See *acalculia.* 6. See *aphasia, semantic.* 7. See *agraphia, visual.* 8. See *alexia, visual.*

brain lesion, of frontal lobes Lesions of the frontal lobes result in the impairment of abstract or complex gnostic and intellectual functions, loss of purposeful behavior, of complex forms of behavior, and perseveration. The size, location and extent of the damage to the frontal lobes determines the type of impairment which will occur.

brain lesion, of occipital lobe Lesions in the occipital area result in the inability to remember sequential elements of an act. The past is not forgotten.

brain lesion, of parietal lobe 1. See *apraxia, afferent.* 2. See *agnosia, tactile.* 3. See *aphasia, afferent motor.*

brain lesion, of premotor cortex 1. See *aphasia, efferent motor.* 2. See *apraxia, dynamic.*

brain localization The proposition that various behaviors and mental functions are associated with specific and localized areas of the brain.

brain potential The level of electrical activity or electric potential in the brain.

brain stem That portion of the brain which remains after the cerebrum and cerebellum are removed.

brain waves The spontaneous and rhythmic electrical discharges of the living brain, particularly of the cerebral cortex.

brat syndrome See *syndrome, brat.*

breakdown, nervous A popular term for a sudden neurotic or psychotic disturbance that incapacitates the individual, often to the point of requiring hospitalization.

breakthrough 1. Any significant advance, progress or development in research or theoretical knowledge. 2. (psychotherapy) A rather sudden movement towards a goal or manifestation of new and constructive work and attitudes after a period of resistance and little progress.

Bremerman's limit A law which designates the absolute limit to the amount of information processing at a particular time by the following statement: 1.5×10^{47} bits per second by one gram of matter.

Brentano, Franz Clemens (1838-1917) German philosopher and psychologist. Studied in Berlin under the Aristotelian scholar, Trendelenburg, and received his Ph.D. degree *in absentia* from Tübingen in 1862 for a thesis on Aristotle's different conceptions of Being. In 1864 he was ordained a priest in the Dominican Order. During the winter of 1866 he was habilitated at Würzburg, and was appointed extraordinarius professor in 1872. Brentano became embroiled in the ecclesiastical controversy over the dogma of the infallibility of the Pope and was allowed to resign from the Dominican Order. At the same time, in 1873, he resigned from Würzburg. In 1874 he was appointed professor at Vienna. He married in 1880 and as a result resigned his post at Vienna; however, he continued to teach as *Privatdozent*. In 1895 he left Vienna for travel and study in Italy. After the outbreak of World War I he went to Zürich where he later died.

Brentano revived an Aristotelian-type psychology. His ontological position is one that recognized mental acts, sensory phenomena, and objects in the external world. In the perception of an object there is simultaneously an awareness of the object and an awareness of the perceiving. There are three types of mental acts which are perceived: (1) Vorstellungen (presentations), (2) Urteile (judging), and (3) Gemütsbewegungen (emotions like love and hate). All thought has a direction and a reference or intention. The content or object of thought has a secondary existence within a mental act, which has primary existence.

Brentano had distinguished students to whom fell the opportunity of recreating European psychology and philosophy after the decline of Hegelianism, and to a lesser extent Kantianism. Among these were Freud, K. Stumpf, F. Hillebrand, K. Twardowski, A. V. Meinong, C. V. Ehrenfels, E. Husserl, A. Marty.

brevilineal A term used by Manouvrier to describe the constitution or body type characterized by a body with lines that are shorter and broader than the average figure.

brief-stimulus therapy (BST) A form of mild electro-shock therapy.

Briggs Law (L. V. Briggs) A statute of Massachusetts which required the psychiatric examination of people indicated for a capital offense and also those people indicated for a crime whose past history include more than one offense for any crime or a conviction on a felony charge. The report would be made available to the court, the probation officer, the district attorney and the defense attorney.

brightness 1. The intensity of all visual sense data. 2. The attribute of a film color allowing it to be placed in a series which ranges from dim to brighter

than white under similar viewing conditions. 3. An obsolete term for saturation. 4. A term for a high degree of intelligence understood in relation to those others in the life group of the individual.

brightness adaptation See *adaptation, brightness.*

brightness constancy See *constancy, brightness.*

brightness contrast See *contrast, brightness.*

brightness threshold See *threshold, brightness.*

bril A unit of brightness which has 100 bril equal to 1 millilambert. Smaller and lesser brightnesses are arrived at by the halving method.

bril scale See *scale, bril.*

Broca, Paul (1824-1880) French physician and surgeon. Authority on aphasia and pioneer in science of modern craniology. First to use clinical method successfully for demonstrating localization of functions in the cerebral cortex. Localized articulate speech in the brain (1861).

Broca's area The brain center, located in the inferior frontal gyrus in the left cerebral hemisphere of right-handed individuals, which is highly critical in speech functioning, primarily in articulated or spoken speech. Named after Dr. P. Broca who discovered it.

broken home A home with one parent absent due to divorce, separation, desertion, death, etc.

bromate poisoning See *poisoning, bromate.*

bromidrosiphobia A pathological fear of the offensive odors of the body.

bronchial asthma See *asthma.*

brontophobia The fear of thunder.

Brookland's experiment Demonstrated that adequate stimulation of mentally deficient children resulted in positive changes in social and emotional maturity, affective relationships, and social participation and in a significant increase in intelligence ratings.

Brosin, Henry W. (1904-) American psychiatrist and psychoanalyst. Worked on toxic-organic reactions including head injuries, malarial therapy, insulin therapy, artifically induced fever therapy; Rorschach method over a wide variety of disorders including the schizophrenias and psychosomatic disorders; psychoanalysis and psychotherapy in psychosomatic disorders and psychoses; since 1955 studied human communication systems including microanalysis of linguistic, kinesic (body motion) and visceral systems in different cultural settings (with G. Bateson, R. Birdwhistell, Charles Hockett, N. A. McQuoun, Frieda Fromm-Reichmann and William Condon).

Brown—Sequard syndrome A paralysis of one side of the body with sensory anesthesia on the opposite side which follows the sectioning of the lateral half of the spinal cord.

Bruner, Jerome S. (1915-) American psychologist. His work has evolved from an early interest in opinion formation and other social phenomena to concern with perception, thought, learning and language. In the mid-50's he focused on cognitive processes in children and with that, parallel work in the nature of the educational process. Since the late 60's, his subjects have grown younger and experimental apparatus more technical in order to study perception, attending, learning, memory, early language acquisition and problem solving in infants during the first two years of life.

Brunswik, Egon (1903-1955) Hungarian systematic psychologist and historian of psychology who, after founding the first psychological laboratory in Turkey, came permanently to the University of California at Berkeley in 1935. Founder of the school of probabilistic functionalism, he made significant contributions to the psychology of perception and to research methodology in psychology.

Brunswik ratio A measure of the perceptual constancy prevailing under different experiments, relating the subject's responses to the stimulus variable under various environmental conditions. In an experiment of the constancy of visual brightness the ratio is: $(R-S) / (A-S)$ with S the per cent of reflectance for the stimulus match, A the albedo, or percent of reflectance, for the object to be matched, and R the per cent of reflectance of the object the subject chooses as matching.

bruxism The grinding of the teeth during sleep.

Bryngelson-Glaspey test See *test, Bryngelson-Glaspey.*

BSR Basal Metabolic rate.

BST See *brief- stimulus therapy.*

buccal intercourse See *intercourse, buccal.*

Buerger's disease See *thromboangitis obliterans.*

buffoonery psychosis A type of catatonic excitement characterized by disconnected, caricatured grimaces and gestures, and either silence or illogicalities. Believed to be a contrived flight into mental illness in order to escape from reality since patients tend to remain well-oriented.

bug, cocaine A sensory disorder occurring in heavy users of cocaine and manifested as itching, biting, sticking and crawling sensations which are attributed by the user to the presence of insects.

bugger Colloquialism for homosexual or more specifically for a sodomite.

Bühler, Charlotte (1893-) Austrian, then American psychologist. Studied adolescents' problems using diaries. Developed methods for observing infants, experimenting with first social responses of infants. Demonstrated in further behavioral studies of infants, adaptivity and curiosity. Outlined childhood and adolescent development. Used biographies to outline life cycle phases and theory of human development through the life span. Wrote critical studies of psychoanalytic reality principle and of homeostasis theory. Developed the theory of four basic tendencies of life. Introduced values in psychotherapy. Was founding sponsor of Association for Humanistic Psychology and wrote (with Melanie Allen) a book introducing Humanistic Psychology.

Bühler, Karl (1879-1963) German physician and psychologist. After some work at Berlin went to Würzburg, as assistant to Oswald Külpe. Made the then final important contribution to the Würzburg School of imageless thought in 1907-1908. Was professor of psychology at Bonn (1909-1913) and then at Munich (1913). After military service during World War I he became professor at the University of Vienna. There, during the years before Nazi annexation of Austria, he gained international recognition for his contributions to the psychology of thought processes, of language, of perception, of Gestalt theory, of the mental development of the child. From 1939 to his death he resided in the U.S. in a kind of academic isolation.

bulb A term used for medulla oblongata.

bulimia Insatiable hunger related to both increased appetite as well as increased intake of food, often observed in psychotics. Also known as *hyperphagia.*

bulimy Bulimia.

Bunsen-Roscoe law The principle that visual threshold for light is a function of stimulus intensity multiplied by stimulus duration.

Buss-Durkee Inventory A scale which measures hostility developed in 1957 by A. H. Buss and A. Durkee. This inventory consists of a questionnaire made up of seventy-five true-false items which reflect two major factors in aggression: emotional hostility characterized by resentment, suspiciousness, and negativism and overt aggression characterized by verbal and indirect hosility and irritability.

C

C See *color response.*

C factor Factor of cleverness or quickness in thinking uncovered in some factor analyses of intelligence tests.

C group The control group.

C reaction A response to stimulation in the human embryo, in which the body bends into a C shape.

CA See *chronological age.*

cacergasia Mental deficiency.

cachexia, hypophysical (M. Simmonds) A state of pathology due to deterioration or traumatic destruction of the anterior lobe of the pituitary gland. The main symptoms are loss of weight, low metabolic rate, general weakness, states of disorientation and loss of memory.

cachexis, cachexia An advanced state of deterioration and weakness, most often caused by tuberculosis, syphilis, and carcinoma.

cachinnation Unrestrained laughter that appears to be inappropriate and/or without an evident cause. It is quite often manifest as a symptom of hebephrenic schizophrenia.

cacodaemonomania; cacodemonia; cacodemonomania A delusional state in which the individual believes himself to be possessed of or by a demon, an evil spirit, or a devil. It is sometimes observed as a symptom of hebephrenic schizophrenia.

cacogenic A term used to identify the most severely defective individual, physically and/or mentally.

cacogeusia The perception of bad taste; often reported by individuals with idiopathic epilepsy.

cacopathia A hippocratic term used to identify a severe emotional illness.

cacosomnia Insomnia; interrupted sleep; sleeplessness.

cadiva insania Epilepsy.

caduca passio Epilepsy; also called "The falling sickness."

caducus morbus Epilepsy.

Cain complex See *complex, Cain.*

cainophobia A fear of new, novel, or unfamiliar objects, surroundings, or people.

caintophobia See *cainophobia.*

California Achievements Tests See *tests, California Achievement.*

California first-year mental scale See *scale, California first year.*

California growth study Continuation of the Berkeley growth study.

California Infant Scale for Motor Development See *scale, California Infant, for Motor Development.*

California Personality Inventory (H. G. Gough) A set of seventeen scales introduced in 1957 for use with normal populations, ages 14 to adult in guidance. The scales assess the presence of traits such as responsibility, socialization and dominance.

California Test of Personality See *test, California, of Personality.*

California tests of mental maturity See *tests, California, of mental maturity.*

Calkins, Mary Whiton (1863-1930) American philosopher and psychologist. Completed work for doctorate at Harvard under James and Münsterberg, but denied degree because Harvard would not award degrees to women. Established the psychology laboratory at Wellesley, the first in a woman's college. Pioneer in dream psychology and one of the original contributors to the systematic psychology of the self. Elected the first woman president of the American Psychological Association. (1905)

callipedia The wish to bear a beautiful child.

callomania Delusions of beauty.

callosum or corpus callosum Commissural, myelinated nerve fibre that connects the two cerebral hemispheres.

calorimeter An instrument for the measurement of heat.

camisole A canvas shirt with extra long sleeves that is sometimes used to restrain violent mental patients.

campimeter A map of the visual field. See *perimeter.*

camptocormia A rare form of hysteria observed most often in soldiers. It is characterized by acute forward flexion of the spine. The patient has extreme difficulty in walking and often suffers tremors. Also known as bent back.

canalization 1. (neurology) Formation of neural connections which facilitate the flow of the neural current. 2. (G. Murphy) Establishing of preferences in patterns of behavior.

cancer, emotional factors in Emotional factors do not seem to cause malignant growths directly; however, reactions to these diseases are often pathological. Loss of an organ is sometimes responded to as loss of a loved object or as a punishment for a sinful act. Patients with leukemia contracted the disease subsequent to a mourning reaction which consisted of an identification with the lost object followed by a choice of another person as a vicarious object. These patients tended to have mothers for whom they were vicarious objects.

canchasmus Inappropriate giggling or laughter that is sometimes observed in patients suffering from hysteria, and frequently in hebephrenic schizophrenia.

canina appetentia See *bulimia.*

cannabis A narcotic and antispasmotic found in the flowering tops of the more potent Indian and the less potent American cannabis sativa plant which in large doses produced intoxication and mental exaltation. Also known as bang, bhang, gunjah, charas, churrus, hashish, and marihuana.

cannabis indica An intoxicant and narcotic that is obtained from Indian hemp.

cannibalism A psychotic impulse to eat human flesh.

Cannon, Walter B. (1871-1945) American physiological psychologist of motivation and emotion who held that emotion produces bodily changes that prepare the organism for fight or flight. In a pioneer experiment, he demonstrated (by measuring changes in the volume of balloons inflated inside human stomachs) that hunger pangs and stomach contractions are correlated.

capacitance The amount of electricity that a condenser or other electronic component can hold.

capacity An individual's maximum mental aptitude and/or physical capability.

capgras syndrome See *syndrome, capgras.*

captation An obsolete term used to identify the initial stage of hypnotism.

captivation A light, prehypnotic state.

carbon dioxide therapy (L. J. Meduna) The inhalation, through an anesthesia mask, of a mixture of 30 percent carbon dioxide and 70 percent oxygen. The usual procedure consists of a minimum of 20 treatments, 3 times a week.

carbon monoxide poisoning See *poisoning, carbon monoxide.*

carbon tetrachloride poisoning See *poisoning, carbon tetrachloride.*

cardiac psychoneurosis A psychoneurotic fear of coronary disease with no apparent physiological pathology.

cardiac psychosis The fearful and confused emotional state that often follows a coronary attack.

cardiazol The trade-mark for pentamethylene-tetrazol. See *metrazol.*

cardiograph An instrument which measures and graphically describes the amplitude and rate of the heart beat.

cardio-renal disease Disease of the heart and kidneys.

cardiotachometer An instrument that records the total number of heartbeats over extended periods of time.

cardiovascular Pertaining to the blood vessels and the heart.

cardiovascular neurosis See *neurosis, cardiovascular.*

carebaria Unpleasant sensations of heaviness and/or pressure in the head.

Carmichael, Leonard (1898-) American psychologist, physiologist and student of animal behavior. Extensive experimental research on the development of sensory processes and behavior in mammals before birth. With H. H. Jasper devised new apparatus and took the first human electroencephalograms in America. Student of visual fatigue and the electrophysiology of eye movements in reading and other visual tasks. During World War II, Director of office of over 400 workers who made an analytic punch card record of the special skills of all Americans with scientific and specialized skills needed in the war effort. Former President, Tufts University. Former Secretary (administrative head), Smithsonian Institution. Now Vice-President for Research and Exploration, National Geographic Society.

carnosinemia A rare aminoaciduria associated with mental retardation.

carotid sinus syndrome See *syndrome, carotid sinus.*

carphology Aimless picking at bedclothes or pajamas, etc. in patients with fever.

Carstairs, George M. (1916-) Scottish psychiatrist and anthropologist. Has carried out research in culture and personality in North India, research in social psychiatry in Britain, research in transcultural psychiatry in South India.

case history The complete medical, psychological, and social history of a patient. Psychological test data, personal documents, and transcripts of psychotherapy sessions are all part of a case history.

case study method An exploratory study of single cases which aims at discovering and forming hypothetical concepts. It deals with complex relationships and tries to discern the relevant variables out of a host of multivariate personality structures and relationships. Most of psychiatric discoveries starting with E. Kraepelin and S. Freud, have been made through detailed case studies of individual patients. Also the discoveries of W. Stern, V. Bekhterev, C. and K. Bühler, and J. Piaget are the result of careful observations conducted on individual cases.

casework, psychiatric The work with patients conducted by a psychiatric social worker. It may take place within the walls of a mental hospital or at the patient's home. It may be comprised of a few interviews or it may extend to a full fledged prolonged psychotherapy, conducted cojointly with a psychiatrist or a clinical psychologist or independently as the sole treatment.

castrate, castration The removal of the testes in the male or the ovaries in the female.

castration anxiety (S. Freud) A fear of genital injury or loss. It is an important part of the *Oedipus Complex* and a source of childhood anxiety. In adults it often manifests itself in the form of a displaced fear of harm to other bodily organs.

castration anxiety, amputee The amputation often represents symbolic castration. The phenomenon in lower-extremity amputees of the sensation during urination of the stump, rather that the phallus as the source of the stream, supports the psychoanalytic view of castration anxiety.

castration complex See *complex, castration.*

castrophrenia A delusion that occurs sometimes in schizophrenic patients, that their enemies are depriving them of and/or controlling their thoughts.

CAT See *test, Children Apperception.*

catabolism The process of breaking down complex organic substances into simpler forms. The reverse process of anabolism.

catabythismomania Impulse to commit suicide by drowning.

catabythismus Suicide by drowning.

cataclonia See *cataclonus.*

cataclonic Relating to cataclonus.

cataclonus Rhythmic convulsive movements of functional origin.

catagelophobia Fear of ridicule.

catalentia An obsolete term for epilepsy.

catalepsia cerea An obsolete term for catalepsy.

catalepsy 1. A trancelike state in which muscles are held rigid for a long period. 2. A conditon in which a person's limbs will remain in any position in which they are placed. Characteristic of catatonic schizophrenics and of some forms of hysteria. Synonymous with cerea flexibilitas, flexibilitas cerea, and waxy flexibility.

catalepsy, accessory The conditon called catalepsy involves the waxy flexibility of the muscular system that allows the limbs to be placed in any position, where they will remain indefinitely. Accessory catalepsy is a rarely used term that refers to the catalepsy associated with hysteria, mania, epilepsy, tetanus, and other disorders.

catalepsy, artificial Catalepsy occurring during hypnosis.

catalepsy, epidemic Catalepsy affecting many people as a result of imitation.

catalepsy, rigid See *catalepsy.*

cataleptiform Resembling catalepsy.

cataleptize Developing a cataleptic state.

cataleptoid Resembling catalepsy.

catalexia A reading disorder characterized by a tendency to reread words and phrases; a form of *dyslexia.*

catalysator; catalyzator 1. A catalyzer. 2. An external agent or stimulus that serves to loosen inhibitions.

catalytic agent 1. A chemical element or substance which increases the speed of a chemical reaction. 2. A member of a psychotherapeutic group who activates emotional discharges in other members.

catalyzing action of hypnosis The accelerating influence of hypnosis in psychoanalytically oriented psychotherapy such as hypnoanalysis.

catamite A rare term for a boy who submits to pederasty.

catamnesis 1. The history of a patient following the onset of an illness, mental disturbance, or behavior disorder. 2. The period following the initial examination, or following discharge from treatment.

cataphasia A disorder in the ability to use language, caused by brain lesions, and characterized by frequent and uncontrollable repetition of the same words or phrases without reference to their meaning.

cataphora Coma interrupted by intervals of partial consciousness.

cataplectic attack 1. A sudden loss of muscle tone, usually provoked by intense emotion. 2. Part of a syndrome called idiopathic narcolepsy characterized by a sudden urge to sleep and cataleptic attacks.

cataplexy 1. In some animals muscular rigidity caused by an overwhelming sudden emotion such as fear or shock. **2.** In humans, sudden loss of muscle tone provoked by intense emotion, often associated with narcolepsy. **3.** Hypnotic sleep.

cataptosis (C. Galen) An apoplectic or epileptic seizure.

catastrophe theory (S. Ferenczi) A theory which maintains that many neurotics view coitus as an activity which may be injurious to their genitals.

catastrophic behavior (K. Goldstein) Psychological adaptation to the organically determined disorders of language known as aphasia. This adaptation involved a tendency toward fanatical orderliness, disinterest and aversion as defensive measures to avoid "catastrophic embarrassment."

catastrophic reaction A breakdown resulting from an individual's inability to cope with his environment, which may in reality be threatening or dangerous. The individual feels anxious, helpless, and buffeted by his circumstances.

catathymia The existence in the unconscious of a complex which produces a pronounced effect in the consciousness.

catathymic amnesia Amnesia limited to circumscribed events or periods of a person's life.

catathymic crisis A violent nonrepeated act resulting from intolerable tension.

catatonia **1.** (K. L. Kahlbaum) First described in 1874 and thought to be a brain disease leading to disturbances in motility. **2.** In 1896 Kraepelin included it as one of three types of dementia praecox or schizophrenia. See *schizophrenia, catatonic.*

catatonia, depressive See *catatonic stupor.*

catatonia manic See *catatonic excitement.*

catatonia mitis A mild form of catatonia.

catatonia protracta A severe form of catatonia.

catatoniac An obsolete term for someone suffering from catatonia; synonymous with catatonic schizophrenic.

catatonic excitement Excessive motor activity and excitement sometimes seen in catatonic schizophrenia.

catatonic schizophrenia See *schizophrenia, catatonic.*

catatonic stupor The most prominent symptom of catatonic schizophrenia involving waxy flexibility, extreme negativism, sterotyped behavior and inaccessibility to external stimuli.

catatonoid attitude **1.** Behavior resembling catatonic behavior. **2.** Stereotyped behavior and emotional shallowness typical of latent schizophrenics.

catch trial (psychophysics) A trial in which no stimulus or stimulus difference is presented to the subject and a response is a "false alarm", responding to something that is not there. This is an attempt to control the subject's guessing or anticipating a stim-

ulus and for the nervous system producing its own stimuli.

catecholamine A group of chemical substances manufactured by the adrenal medulla and secreted during physiological stress.

categorical **1.** Pertaining to a classification or categorization based on qualitative rather than quantitative distinctions. **2.** Unqualified; absolute.

categorical imperative **1.** An unqualified demand or command. **2.** Kant's principle: "Act only on that maxim whereby you can at the same time will that it should become a universal law."

categorical judgment, law of See *law of categorical judgment.*

category **1.** A group having a set of common attributes or qualities. **2.** In statistics, a grouping based on qualitative rather than quantitative differences.

catelectrotonus Increased excitability of a nerve or muscle near the cathode, as an electric current is passing through the tissue.

catharsis **1.** The purging of emotions. **2.** (Aristotle) The purging or purification of emotions through artistic expression. **3.** (psychoanalysis) The expression and discharge of repressed emotions and ideas.

catharsis, community The purging of a community's feeling of guilt.

cathartic **1.** Relating to or using catharsis. **2.** A medicine used to produce evacuation of the bowels.

cathect; cathectize To charge an object or idea with affect or psychic energy.

cathectic Relating to investment of psychic energy.

cathectical method Instruction by the Socratic method of skillful questioning.

cathexis (psychoanalysis) The investment of an object or idea with psychic energy.

cathexis, fantasy The investment of psychic energy in wishes, or fantasies, or to their original source in the unconscious.

cathexis, hypervectorial (B. B. Wolman) The overinvestment of psychic energy in one's parents or parental substitutes characteristic of schizophrenics.

cathexis, interindividual (B. B. Wolman) The balance of emotional energy of libido or destrudo cathected (invested) in interraction between two or more individuals.

cathexis, intraindividual (B. B. Wolman) The balance of emotional energy of libido or destrudo cathected (invested) in various parts of one's personality and parts and organs of one's body.

cathexis, object The investment of cathexis in some object outside oneself.

cathexis, self The investment of psychic energy in oneself.

cathode The negative electrode of an electric circuit.

catochus 1. An obsolete term for catalepsy. 2. A phase of ecstasy or trance in which the person is conscious but cannot move or speak.

catoptrics Branch of optics dealing with the properties and phenomena of reflected light.

Cattell Infant Scale (P. Cattell) A scale of infant intelligence and development from 2 to 30 months, an attempt to extend the Stanford-Binet downward. From 22 months upward the test items include some items from the Stanford-Binet.

Cattell, Raymond B. (1905-) American psychologist. Applied factor-analytic developments and new behavioral test devices to the systematic taxonomy of unitary traits and states. Batteries of known validity provided for 30 indexed traits and 9 states, including anxiety, stress, arousal, etc., as distinct dimensions.
  Discovered most valid objective measures for motivation in men and animals, leading to the dynamic calculus of interest summation, conflict, resolution and integration. Applied this — as tri-vector description — to development of structured learning theory.
  Propounded psychometric and mathematical models — confactor rotation, ipsatization, the profile coefficient, taxonome, P — & dR — techniques, the personality sphere, fluid and crystallized intelligence, and formulae in social psychology for group syntality and leadership interactions.

caudal Pertaining to the tail or tail-end of an animal.

caudate nucleus Mass of grey matter forming part of the striate body in the subcortical region of the cerebral cortex; next to the thalamus.

caumesthesia The experience of heat even when the temperature is not high.

causal chain A series of events that are linked causally.

causal explanation in psychology 1. Explanation of behavior as the necessary result of antecedent factors. 2. S. Freud accepted a most rigorous determinism that says, "no causes without effects, no effects without cause." 3. K. Guthrie discarded the problem of causation and presented learning in a *post quod* (after which) rather than a *propter quod* (because of which) continuity. 4. C. G. Jung has accepted both Freud's determinism and Adler's purposivism. He held the Kantian position that both principles are methods of cognition rather than laws of nature. 5. K. Lewin viewed behavior and environment as simultaneous facts; the past only effects behavior to the extent that it remains in the present. 6. B. F. Skinner confined his system to description rather than explanation. According to Skinner, a "cause" becomes a "change in an independent variable" and an "effect" a "change in a dependent variable." 7. Some psychologists such as A. Adler, W. McDougall, K. Goldstein, and C. Tolman substituted the notion of causation in psychology by purposivistic theories.

causal nexus The causal interconnection between two events or successive phases of a one event.

causal texture (E. C. Tolman & E. Brunswik) The property of the environment of being made up of mutually dependent events. The degree of dependence is expressed in terms of probability and not in terms of causal certainty.

causalgia Burning pain not caused by heat, sometimes present in nerve injury, particularly injury of the sensory nerves of palms and soles.

causality An explanation of phenomena (effects) as the result of antecedent phenomena (causes). See *causal explanation in psychology*.

causation See *causality*.

causation, historical Explaining present behavior in terms of antecedent causes.

causation, principle of multiple The theory that many causes interact to produce an effect.

causation, systematic Explaining present behavior in terms of present causes.

cause and effect test See *test, cause and effect*.

CAVD test See *test, CAVD*.

CEEB College Entrance Examination Board.

ceiling 1. The maximum score attainable on a test. 2. In statistics, the maximum possible score possible on a test minus an allowance for chance error.

cell 1. The structural unit of living organisms. 2. In statistics a compartment formed by the intersection of a row and a column in a table.

cell-assembly or assembly (D. O. Hebb) A number of neurons acting temporarily as a system with self-maintained activity; hypothetically, its activity is a representative or ideational process, the unit of perception and thought. It is proposed that a primary assembly is organized as a result of a repeated stimulation such as the sight of a line of a certain slope or a particular hue, a touch at a particular point on the skin, a vowel sound, and so forth. Superordinate assemblies theoretically are organized by the activity of a number of primary assemblies. The assembly may be excited as the direct result of sensory stimulation, or by its associative connections with other assemblies.

cell, body Any cell other than a germ cell.

cell body The central part of the cell containing the nucleus.

cell division See *mitosis*.

cell, padded A room with padded walls and floors, used to confine acutely disturbed patients who are potentially destructive to themselves or others.

cell, Purkinje A large cell with many dendrites which is located in the middle layer of the cerebullar cortex.

cellular Pertaining to cells.

celom See *coelom*.

cenesthesia 1. The general feeling of the body. 2. The belief that certain bodily sensations are registered in the unconscious without the person being consciously aware of them.

cenesthesic Relating to cenesthesia.

cenesthopathic Relating to general feeling of physical illness.

cenesthopathy The general feeling of physical illness not related to any particular part of the body.

ccnophobia See *kenophobia*.

cenotrope; coenotrope An acquired pattern of behavior exhibited by all members of a particular biological group in a common environment and assumed to be the result of both heredity and environment.

censor, endopsychic (psychoanalysis) The agent within the preconscious responsible for the process of censorship.

censorship (psychoanalysis) The processes involved in the defensive activity directed against admitting to consciousness disturbing external stimuli or unacceptable impulse-derivatives from the unconscious.

censorship, dream (psychoanalysis) In dreams, the process which keeps unacceptable wishes or thoughts from breaking through.

center correlation See *correlation center*.

center, psychical An obsolete concept referring to the idea that mind and intelligence were localized in centers within the brain.

centile 1. Synonymous with percentile; a score representing the percentage of the distribution which falls below it. 2. One of 100 groups or divisions within a ranked distribution, each representing one percent of the distribution; or the rank order of any of those divisions.

centile rank The number of rank order of a centile; see *centile 2*.

central conflict (K. Horney). The conflict between the real self and the idealized self.

central constant (T. Burrow) Essentially homeostatic primary principle governing man's total action pattern; relates man as a species to his environment.

central fissure See *central sulcus*.

central force (C. G. Jung) Refers to the primal libido and means undifferentiated energy or life force.

central inhibition Inhibition of neural impulses by central nervous system processes.

central limit theorem (statistics) The principle that states that the sampling distribution of the means of random samples will be approximately normal in form regardless of the form of the distribution in the population if the sample size is large enough and if the population variance is finite. The more the population distribution differs from a normal distribution, the larger the sample size must be in order for this principle to be true.

central lobe See *Reil, island of*.

Central Motive State 1. (C. T. Morgan) Drive; motivating force, based on four phenomena: (1) persistence of motivation even when the initial condition does not exist any longer, (2) preparation of the organism for consummatory responses, (3) increased level of activity, (4) the consummatory responses. 2. Hypothetical processes in the central nervous system, not caused by present external stimulation.

central nervous system The brain and the spinal cord.

central processes Processes occurring in the central nervous system.

central scotoma See *scotoma, central*.

central sulcus Groove located in the middle of the lateral surface of the cerebral hemisphere, separating the frontal from the parietal lobe.

central tendency 1. (statistics) The general tendency for scaled ratings to gravitate toward the center of the scale. 2. (biology) The tendency of inherited biological traits to revert toward the norm.

central tendency measures Statistical measures which attempt to provide a single value representative of a distribution. The most commonly used measures are the mean, median, and mode.

central vision Vision which takes place in the region of the fovea; the area of clearest vision.

centralism; centralist psychology A position which maintains that behavior is a function of the central nervous system. The brain is viewed as the mediator and integrating center between the stimulus and the response.

centrifugal Moving from the center towards the periphery. Sometimes used to describe nerve impulses or fibers.

centrifugal nerve or neuron A sensory or afferent nerve or neuron.

centripetal Moving from the periphery towards the center. Sometimes used to describe nerve impulses or fibers.

centroid method (L. L. Thustone) A factor analytic method of extracting factors from a correlational matrix in which one axis passes through the center of gravity of the system and the others are orthogonal and thus uncorrelated. By rotating the axis to oblique positions, correlations among factors are revealed.

cephalad Toward the head.

cephalagia, cephalalgia Headache.

cephalagra Headache.

cephalic Pertaining to the head.

cephalic index See *index, cephalic*.

cephalization Concentration of important organs toward the head of the organism.

cephalocaudal Long axis of body, from head to tail.

cephalocaudal development The principle that development, especially the embryological, progresses from head to tail.

cephalogenesis In embryological development, the stage associated with the development of the primordia of the head. /

ceraunophobia See *keraunophobia.*

cerchnus Obsolete term for hoarseness.

cerea flexibilitas See *catalepsy.*

cerebellar cortex The gray, outer covering of the cerebellum.

cerebellar fit (H. Jackson) Tonic fit associated with tumors of the vermis and characterized by sudden loss of consciousness and falling, dilated and immobile pupils, and rigid extension of the body.

cerebellar gait Unsteady gait in which there is a disassociation of movement between the body and legs. The body either lags behind or is thrust forward, resulting in a "drunken" walk.

cerebellar peduncle See *peduncle, cerebellar.*

cerebellar speech See *asynergic speech.*

cerebellum Structure of the brain lying below the cerebrum and above the pons and medulla. Primarily concerned with the regulation of motor coordination.

cerebral anemia See *anemia, cerebral.*

cerebral anemia, acute Temporary reduced flow of blood to the brain caused by cardiac weakness, or intense fear or anxiety. Symptoms include dulled senses, noises in the ears and spots before the eyes. The skin becomes pale, cold and covered with perspiration.

cerebral anemia, chronic Chronic reduced flow of blood to the brain caused by such conditions as pernicious anemia, leukemia or repeated loss of blood. Symptoms include noises in the ears, headache, dizziness, poor memory and insomnia. There may be delusions and hallucinations.

cerebral anemia, local Temporary reduced flow of blood to a part of the brain due to a transient spasm or pressure from a tumor causing the closure of an artery. Symptoms reflect function of area involved.

cerebral aqueduct A slender elongated cavity in the midbrain connecting the third and fourth ventricles.

cerebral arteriosclerosis See *arteriosclerosis, cerebral.*

cerebral blindness An inability to see due to lesion or damage in the visual area of the cerebrum.

cerebral cortex Mantle of cells covering the cerebrum consisting mainly of cell bodies giving it a grey color. Phylogenetically, the more advanced part of the brain structure.

cerebral dominance 1. The principle that the cerebrum is the highest control center in the nervous system. 2. The fact that one brain hemisphere is dominant over the other in the control of body movement, especially handedness.

cerebral embolism See *embolism, cerebral.*

cerebral hemispheres The two symmetrical halves of the cerebrum which are separated by a deep fissure while connected by a broad band of fibers known as the corpus callosum.

cerebral integration The theory that the cerebrum is the integrating center of the organism, serving to integrate and unify all parts of the body and all behavior of the organism.

cerebral lipidoses See *lipidoses, cerebral.*

cerebral lipidosis, infantile See *Tay-Sachs disease.*

cerebral palsy 1. Paralysis due to brain lesion. 2. Infantile spastic diplegia.

cerebral peduncle See *peduncle, cerebral.*

cerebral syphilis See *syphilis, meningovascular.*

cerebration Cerebral physiological activity.

cerebrospinal Pertaining to the brain and the spinal cord.

cerebrospinal fluid Lymphlike fluid within the cerebral ventricles and between the arachnoid membrane and pia matter of the brain and spinal cord.

cerebrospinal system All the nerves in the body except those associated with the autonomic nervous system.

cerebrotonic type See *type, cerebrotonic.*

cerebrum 1. In vertebrates the largest portion of the brain occupying the entire upper part of the cranium and consisting of the right and left hemispheres. 2. The forebrain and the midbrain.

ceremonial A ritualized sequence of behaviors having symbolic and emotional significance beyond the act itself.

ceremonial, compulsive Ritualistic repetitive behavior characteristic of the obsessive−compulsive neurotic.

ceremonial, defensive An elaborate sequence of behavior devised unconsciously as a defense against anxiety and compulsively executed whenever anxiety threatens.

certification of psychologists A statement by an official body that a person has met the required standards and therefore may represent himself as a psychologist.

cervical Pertaining to constricted portion or neck.

CGS system The generally accepted system of scientific measurement using centimeters, grams and seconds.

Chaddock reflex 1. Extension of the big toe on stimulation of the external malleolus, seen in pyramidal tract lesions. 2. Flexion of the wrist and fanning of the fingers caused by irritation of the ulna in hemiplegia.

chaeraphrosyne An obsolete term for a state of cheerfulness.

chaeromania, chairomania See *cheromania.*

chain reflex of behavior A set sequence of behaviors in which the completion of one response is the cue (stimulus) for the next.

chain schedule See *reinforcement, schedule of: chained.*

chained reinforcement A schedule of reinforcement in which responding to a particular stimulus in one schedule is reinforced by a different stimulus usually under a new schedule, the new schedule being the one in which primary reinforcement takes place.

chained responses See *responses, chained.*

chained (chain) schedule See *reinforcement, schedule of: chained.*

chaining, accidental A process in which a response which frequently precedes a reinforced response shares in the effect of the reinforcement in such a way that the whole sequence becomes a stable part of the organism's behavior. A form of superstitious behavior.

chance **1.** The probability of an event occurring without any cause. **2.** An event is conceived of as being caused by any number of individually unknown factors which combine to give a stable quantititative value. **3.** The extent to which an event within a system is caused by factors not in that system.

chance difference A difference between two measures which cannot be attributed to a constant error or bias, nor to a true difference but is rather due to random influences.

chance error See *error, chance.*

chance halves correlation See *correlation, split half.*

chance variation Change in the inherited characteristics of an organism due to unknown causes.

change agent A term which grew out of the National Training Laboratory experiences with T-groups (T for training) and sensitivity training and which refers to the professional (usually a psychologist) who serves as a leader of the group. The leader conducts group sessions in such a way as to bring about changes in attitudes and behavior of the members of the group that can be brought back to their organizations and have an impact on them.

change of life Menopause.

changing, compulsive The compulsive need of an individual to continuously change either himself or his environment.

chaped disk See *papilledema.*

character **1.** A consistent and enduring aspect of an individual's personality. **2.** The integration of individual traits into a unified whole; personality.

character, anal A person with permanent and consistent patterns of overt and covert behavior reflecting issues that were important during the period of learning to control bowel movements. There is a fixation at the anal level due to the child's being unable to reconcile the wish for anal pleasure and the demands of society. The conflict might be resolved by the child's finding pleasure either in anal expulsion which results in such traits as extreme generosity, conceit, suspicion and ambition or in anal retention, resulting in such traits as obstinancy and defiance, parsimony and/or avarice, orderliness and compulsive behavior.

character analysis **1.** Treatment of a character disorder with psychoanalysis. **2.** (W. Reich) Psychoanalytic technique with primary emphasis on the interpretation of the patient's character expressed through his total behavior pattern, and character resistances as revealed in the analytic situation rather than on unconscious material. Unconscious material is interpreted only upon the successful interpretation of the patient's character resistances, an approach which enabled the psychoanalytic treatment of patients who had before been unamenable to psychoanalytic treatment.

character armor (W. Reich) An individual's pattern of defenses which are largely ego-syntonic and allow that individual to maintain a certain role in interpersonal relationships; a personality structure as a generalized defense against anxiety.

character, compliant (K. Horney) A person who is only submissive and self-effacing and who tends to move toward people.

character defense A defense against anxiety which is blended into the personality.

character disorders A group of disorders characterized by life-long patterns of deeply ingrained maladaptive behavior.

character, exploitative (E. Fromm) An individual who attempts to fulfill his wishes by exploiting others either by force or cunning.

character formation The processes leading to character formation; personality development.

character, genital (psychoanalysis) The adult stage of psychosexual development characterized by the fusion of pregenital impulses of the oral and anal nature and the primacy of genital eroticism in interpersonal relationships.

character, hysterical An individual having a character disorder characterized by excitability, emotional instability, overreaction, dramatization, self-centeredness, and overdependence on others.

character, membership **1.** (Gestalt) The quality of an element in a whole which is a function of its being a part of the totality. **2.** (Gestalt) The concept that the whole is influenced by a change in its elements and that the elements are affected by alterations of the whole.

character neurosis **1.** Neurotic symptoms which have become accepted by the ego and blended into the personality. **2.** (B. B. Wolman) The second level in neurotic deterioration according to the sociogenic classification of mental disorders. Character neurotics seem to have incorporated their neurotic symptoms in their personality structure; the character neuroses are divided into the hyperinstrumental type which corresponds to the sociopathic or psychopathic personality; the dysmutual type, the cyclothymic and passive-aggressive personality; and the hypervectorial type, tne schizoid and compulsive personality.

character, oral An individual with permanent and consistent patterns of functioning which reflect fixation on the oral stage as a result of abundant or more frequently, insufficient oral satisfaction. In the former case, the individual develops optimistic but overdependent attitudes; in the latter, depressive and aggressive tendencies may develop. In both cases, narcissistic supplies are demanded from without. The individuals are self-centered and characterized as selfish or "takers." They may be compulsive eaters, drinkers, smokers or talkers.

character, paranoid An individual characterized by hypersensitivity, rigidity, unwarranted suspicion, jealousy, envy, feelings of self-importance, and a tendency to blame others and ascribe or project evil motives to them.

character, receptive (E. Fromm) Personality type characterized by passivity in social relations, a strong need for support from others, and a dependence on things given to him.

character structure The integration of character traits into a unified character or personality.

character traits 1. Those aspects of an individual's behavior which are consistent, persistent and stable. 2. (G. W. Allport) Personality trait.

character, urethral (psychoanalysis) An individual with permanent and consistent patterns of overt and covert behavior reflecting issues that were most important during the period of learning to control urination. The urethral personality types have usually been punished for enuresis by being put to shame. The bed-wetter would like to hide his deed and to avoid shame; hence the "burning ambition" not to be shamed again and a feeling of envy toward anyone who has not been humiliated. He, however, usually lacks persistence.

characteristic, acquired 1. A change in the structure of an organism as a result of the influence of the environment or because of the organism's own activities. 2. A behavioral modification that is learned. See *Lamarck's theory.*

characterology A rarely used term for the branch of psychology dealing with character and personality.

Charcot, Jean Martin (1825-1893) French neurologist; professor of pathological anatomy, Paris (1860). Appointed to Salpêtriére (1862) where he established a neurological clinic which gained world-wide renown and attracted many students, among them Freud and Janet. Known for his study of hysteria and use of hypnotism.

Charpentier's bands Alternating black and white bands seen when a black disk with a white sector is slowly rotated. More rapid rotation causes pastel hues (Fechner's colors) to be seen.

Charpentier's law A law of visual perception which states that the product of the area of the image on the fovea and the intensity of light is constant for threshold stimuli.

chart A systematic arrangement of data in graphic form.

chasmus, hystericus Persistent yawning.

Checklist, Frostig Sensory-Motor and Movement Skills A list of various behaviors categorized within seven broad areas of sensory-motor and movement skills including coordination, agility, strength, flexibility, speed, balance and endurance, which was developed primarily as an aid for classroom teachers, school psychologists, and other professional school personnel in the observation and evaluation of selected aspects of the child's motor development. The instrument is not standardized and does not include developmental norms.

cheimophobia Fear of cold.

Chein, Isidor (1912-   ) American psychologist. Contributed to systematic philosophicopsychological theory through analyses of such concepts as attitude, behavior, consciousness and its negations, ego, freedom, heredity, intelligence, mind, morale, motivation, personality, power, prediction, psychological structures, self, typology. Also contributed to the development of the concepts, methodology, and substantive research in the field of *action research,* particularly in the areas of delinquency, drug abuse, intergroup relations, and psychological implications of minority-group membership.

cheiromancy See *chiromancy.*

chemical sense A sense which is affected only by chemical substances.

chemoreceptors Nerve structures which are stimulated by various chemical agents which are produced in or enter into the organism.

chemotaxis An involuntary movement of an organism involving change of position toward or away from chemical substances.

chemotherapy The employment of chemical substances to effect therapeutic ends, i.e. to cure pathology.

chemotropism An involuntary movement of an organism or cells involving change of orientation or growth toward or away from chemical substances.

cheromania An obsolete term for the manic phase of manic depressive psychosis.

cherophobia Fear of or aversion to gaiety or happiness.

chess-board illusion An optical illusion in which a circular black and white check pattern appears to have depth, and the checks seem progressively larger toward the circumference.

Cheyne-Stokes psychosis A psychosis characterized by anxiety, restlessness, and Cheyne-Stokes respiration.

Cheyne-Stokes respiration Breathing which shows a rapidly diminishing rate followed by a rapidly increasing rate found in premature babies and disorders such as cerebral arteriosclerosis, senility and heart disease.

Chi The Greek letter X sometimes used in statistical formulas.

chiaroscuro response Any Rorschach response which is determined by the distribution of light and shading in the inkblot. Most approaches to the Rorschach recommend subdividing chiaroscuro responses into three categories depending on whether the light-dark component suggest dimensionality, texture or shading. See *texture; shading; vista responses.*

chiasma The place where the optic nerves from each eye unite and then separate.

chiasms (R. B. Cattell) Choice points in dynamic adjustment, sometimes called 'dynamic crossroads,' where emotional expression is changed.

child-centered 1. Refers to a school or institution in which the primary goal is fulfillment of the child's present needs rather than preparation for adulthood. **2.** Refers to families where the child's needs are dominant.

child development The study of the child from the developmental point of view.

child guidance Methods used in the treatment of behavioral and educational problems in children usually in schools and clinics; generally prophylactic.

child guidance movement A movement to establish mental health facilities for children, whose inception was in 1909 with the founding of the Juvenile Psychopathic Institute in Chicago. This center offered performance and intelligence tests in addition to physical examinations while the early clinics were established to treat delinquents; they gradually broadened their treatment orientation to include other behavioral problems. In this milieu, the clinic team emerged consisting of the psychiatrist, clinical psychologist and the psychiatric social worker.

child-parent fixation (psychoanalysis) A child's emotional attachment of love, hate, or both toward one of his parents which is so firm as to interfere with his forming other relationships.

child, problem A child whose behavior deviates so widely from acceptable social norms that special methods are required for dealing with him.

child psychiatry The branch of psychiatry dealing with children.

child psychology The branch of psychology dealing with children.

childhood schizophrenia See *schizophrenia, childhood.*

Children's Apperception Test (CAT) See *test, Children's Apperception.*

chiromancy Palmistry.

chiromania An obsolete term and concept for the relationship between masturbation and psychiatric disturbance; a morbid impulse to masturbate.

Chi-Square (x^2) A formula which determines whether an obtained distribution differs significantly from the expected distribution to such an extent that it would be attributable to the operation of non-chance factors. The formula is:

$$x^2 = \Sigma \frac{(f_o - f_e)^2}{f_e}$$

Where x^2 refers to Chi-Square, f_o is the observed frequency, f_e is the expected frequency, and Σ means to take the sum of the values represented by the Chi-Square formula.

Chi-Square test of goodness of fit A comparison of an observed distribution with the expected or theoretical distribution of a given population to determine whether or not the two are in reasonable agreement.

chlorpromazine A tranquilizing drug. Its commercial name is thorazine.

choc An uncoordinated response elicited by a surprise sudden stimulus.

choc fortuit (A. Binet) An accidental mental shock usually of sexual nature.

choice point The point in a maze or other discrimination apparatus from which it is possible to proceed in more than one direction or make more than one response.

choice reaction A type of reaction experiment in which the subject must respond differently in different situations.

choice reaction time See *reaction time, choice.*

choleric type See *type, choleric.*

cholinergic Pertaining to the chemical activity characteristic of acetylcholine or to nerve fibers which release acetylcholine to activate effectors.

cholinesterase An enzyme found in blood and in various other tissues which breaks down acetylcholine. By preventing the buildup of acetylcholine at nerve endings it plays an important role in the transmission of nervous impulses.

cholinesterase, modification by behavior The alteration of the activity of cholinesterase by environmental stimulation.

chorda tympani A branch of the seventh or facial nerve carrying nerve impulses from the taste receptors.

chorea A neurological disorder characterized by irregular involuntary movements or spasms of the muscles of the extremities and the face.

chorea abasia See *abasia.*

chorea, epidemic See *choreomania.*

chorea, Huntington's (G. Huntington) Chronic progressive hereditary chorea characterized by loss of coordination, disturbance of speech and mental deterioration.

chorea rotatoria Chorea characterized by rotation or oscillation of the head, trunk, or limbs.

chorea saltatoria Chorea characterized by involuntary jumping.

chorea, Syndenham's The syndrome of chorea following an infection.

chorea, Syndenham's acute An actue toxic disorder of the central nervous system secondary to certain infections causing chorea; Saint Vitus' Dance.

choreiform Resembling chorea.

choreoathetosis Combination of chorea and athetosis. Irregular and involuntary movements of facial and limbic muscles (chorea).

choreoid Resembling chorea.

choreomania Dancing mania; epidemic of convulsive dancing which occurred in Europe in the fourteenth century, in the wake of the Black Death.

choroid 1. Membranous. 2. Choroid coat.

choroid coat Vascular layer of the eye that is continuous with the iris and lies between the sclera and the retina.

choroiditis Inflammation of the choroid coat.

chrematophobia Morbid fear of money.

chroma In the Munsell color system the dimension that corresponds most closely to saturation.

chroma-brightness or brilliance coefficient The ratio of hue to brightness (brilliance), which varies from a minumum in the yellow to a maximum in the violet.

chromaesthesia See *chromesthesia*.

chromatic 1. Pertaining to hue. 2. Pertaining to chroma. 3. Pertaining to the chromatic scale.

chromatic aberration Error in optical system resulting from unequal refraction of different parts of the spectrum causing indistinct images surrounded by a halo of colors.

chromatic color A color possessing hue and saturation.

chromatic contrast; color contrast Increased differences in hue between two colors presented simultaneously or in close succession.

chromatic dimming Decrease in saturation when light intensity is suddenly decreased after a period of fixation, due to successive contrast.

chromatic flicker See *flicker, chromatic*.

chromatic scale See *scale, chromatic*.

chromatic valence The power of a color stimulus to produce hue in a mixture.

chromaticity The quality of a color stimulus determined by its dominant wavelength and its purity.

chromaticness The psychological correlate of chro-

maticity determined by a color stimulus' hue and saturation.

chromatics 1. The science of color. 2. The chromatic scale.

chromatid A chromosome at prophase and metaphase can be seen to consist of two strands held together by the centromere. Each strand is a chromatid.

chromatin The easily stainable protoplasmic substance in the nuclei of cells.

chromatin negative Lacking sex chromatin or a Barr body. Normal males are chromatin negative.

chromatin positive Possessing sex chromatin or a Barr body, which represents a single X chromosome which is inactive in the metabolism of the cell. Normal females are chromatin positive.

chromatism See *photism*.

chromatophobia See *chromophobia*.

chromatopseudopsia Color blindness.

chromatopsia Seeing objects as abnormally colored under unusual conditions such as snow blindness.

chromatotropism An orienting response (tropism) toward certain hues or colors.

chromesthesia; chromaesthesia A form of synesthesia involving the seeing of colors upon hearing certain words, letters or sounds.

chromidrosis A rare condition in which perspiration is colored.

chromophobia 1. Fear of colors. 2. Excessive dislike of certain colors.

chromosomal aberration, chromosomal defect Nonfatal changes in the structure and number of chromosomes.

chromosome Chromosomes are the chromatin strands in the nuclei of somatic and sex cells along which the genes are arranged in linear order. They are composed of DNA on a framework of protein and are the carriers of genetic information. They are visible in a dividing cell as deeply staining rod-shaped or J-shaped structures.

chromosomes, sex, anomalies of Sex chromosomes in which there are different constitutions other than the normal XY in the male and the XX in the female. See *Klinefelter's Syndrome; Turner's Syndrome; Triplo-X Syndrome*.

chronaxia; chronoxic; chronaxy The excitability of tissues measured in units of time needed for the passage of electric current of voltage twice as intense as the threshold of voltage.

chronic constipation, psychogenic See *constipation, chronic, psychogenic*.

chronic diarrhea See *diarrhea, chronic*.

chronic electrode An electrode for according or stimulating central nervous system tissues implanted through a small hole made in the skull and fixed on the skull permanent.

chronic mania See *mania, chronic.*

chronological age The cumulative age of the individual from birth; calendar age.

chronological complex See *complex, chronological.*

chronological system See *complex, chronological.*

chronophobia Fear of time.

chronoscope An instrument used for the measurement of short intervals of time.

cibophobia Morbid fear of food.

cineplasty A restorative operation performed on a disabled hand which utilizes the remaining muscles in the amputated stump to attach them with ivory pegs through a yoke to an artificial hand.

cingulectomy A form of psychosurgery; surgical removal of the cingulate gyrus.

circadian rhythms Cyclic biological changes that occur within an organism.

circular conditioned response See *circular reflex.*

circular psychosis See *psychosis, manic-depressive.*

circular reaction A behavioral pattern in which the reaction to a stimulus evokes repetition.

circular reflex Special case of response chaining in which the response produces stimuli which themselves increase or prolong that reponse.

circumstantial (or indirect) validity Obtaining the validity of a test X against a criterion Y by evaluating the similarity of X's correlations with variables A, B, C, D, etc., to those of Y with the same variables.

cistron The smallest unit of genetic material that must remain intact to direct the synthesis of a specific polypeptide.

citrullinemia A rare aminoaciduria associated with mental retardation.

civesticism Dressing in inappropriate garments, e.g., an adult who dresses as if he were a little child.

clairaudience Hypothesized ability to hear without using one's ears or any known sensory mediation.

clairvoyance 1. A hypothetical ability to see without using the eyes or any sensory mediation. 2. Any sort of perception or knowledge of past, present, or future without known sensory mediation.

clang association Association of words based on their sound.

Claparède, Edouard (1873-1940) Swiss psychologist; functionalist. Established the *International Association of Applied Psychology* and organized its first international congress (1920); founded (with cousin, Théodore Flournoy) *Archives de Psychologie* (1901); studied psychological phenomena in terms of their usefulness in meeting individual's needs and interests; promoted animal psychology and child psychology; advocated improvement of teacher training; established the Rousseau Institute, famed for research in child psychology and development of progressive methods of teaching.

class interval See *interval, class.*

class, social A group of people who have similar level of income, or education, or vocation or inherited status. For instance a society can be divided (on the basis of economic criterion) into high, middle, and low income level classes; on the basis of inherited status in aristocratic class and commoners.

class theory A theory that describes objects or concepts on the basis of their belonging to a certain class.

classes, informational (J. P. Guilford) Conceptions underlying sets of items of information grouped by virtue of their common properties.

classical conditioning See *conditioning, Pavlovian.*

Classification of Mental Disorders Based on the Diagnostic and Statistical Manual of Mental Disorders of the American Psychiatric Association DSM-II, 1968. List of Mental Disorders with Their Code Numbers.

I. Mental Retardation
Mental retardation (310-315)
310 Borderline mental retardation
311 Mild mental retardation
312 Moderate mental retardation
313 Severe mental retardation
314 Profound mental retardation
315 Unspecified mental retardation
.0 Following infection or intoxication
.1 Following trauma or physical agent
.2 With disorders of metabolism, growth or nutrition
.3 Associated with gross brain disease (postnatal)
.4 Associated with diseases and conditions due to (unknown) prenatal influence
.5 With chromosomal abnormality
.6 Associated with prematurity
.7 Following major psychiatric disorder
.8 With psycho-social (environmental) deprivation
.9 With other (and unspecified) condition

II. Organic Brain Syndromes
(Disorders Caused by or Associated with Impairment of Brain Tissue Function) In the categories under IIA and IIB the associated physical condition should be specified when known.

II—A. Psychoses Associated with Organic Brain Syndromes (290-294)
290 Senile and pre-senile dementia
.0 Senile dementia
.1 Pre-senile dementia
291 Alcoholic psychosis
.0 Delirium tremens
.1 Korsakov's psychosis (alcoholic)
.2 Other alcoholic hallucinosis
.3 Alcohol paranoid state ((Alcoholic paranoia))

.4 Acute alcohol intoxication
.5 Alcoholic deterioration
.6 Pathological intoxication
.9 Other (and unspecified) alcoholic psychosis
292 Psychosis associated with intracranial infection
.0 Psychosis with general paralysis
.1 Psychosis with other syphilis of central nervous system
.2 Psychosis with epidemic encephalitis
.3 Psychosis with other and unspecified encephalitis
.9 Psychosis with other (and unspecified) intracranial infection
293 Psychosis associated with other cerebral condition
.0 Psychosis with cerebral arteriosclerosis
.1 Psychosis with other cerebrovascular disturbance
.2 Psychosis with epilepsy
.3 Psychosis with intracranial neoplasm
.4 Psychosis with degenerative disease of the central nervous system
.5 Psychosis with brain trauma
.9 Psychosis with other (and unspecified) cerebral condition
294 Psychosis associated with other physical condition
.0 Psychosis with endocrine disorder
.1 Psychosis with metabolic or nutritional disorder
.2 Psychosis with systemic infection
.3 Psychosis with drug or poison intoxication (other than alcohol)
.4 Psychosis with childbirth
.8 Psychosis with other and undiagnosed physical condition
(.9 Psychosis with unspecified physical condition)

II—B. Non-Psychotic Organic Brain Syndromes (309)

309 Non-psychotic organic brain syndromes ((Mental disorders not specified as psychotic associated with physical conditions))
.0 Non-psychotic OBS with intracranial infection
(.1 Non-psychotic OBS with drug, poison, or systemic intoxication)
.13 Non-psychotic OBS with alcohol (simple drunkenness)
.14 Non-psychotic OBS with other drug, poison, or systemic intoxication
.2 Non-psychotic OBS with brain trauma
.3 Non-psychotic OBS with circulatory disturbance
.4 Non-psychotic OBS with epilepsy
.5 Non-psychotic OBS with disturbance of metabolism, growth or nutrition
.6 Non-psychotic OBS with senile or pre-senile brain disease
.7 Non-psychotic OBS with intracranial neoplasm
.8 Non-psychotic OBS with degenerative disease of central nervous system
.9 Non-psychotic OBS with other (and unspecified) physical condition
(.91 Acute brain syndrome, not otherwise specified)
(.92 Chronic brain syndrome, not otherwise specified)

III. Psychoses not Attributed to Physical Conditions Listed Previously (295-298)

295. Schizophrenia
.0 Schizophrenia, simple type
.1 Schizophrenia, hebephrenic type
.2 Schizophrenia, catatonic type
.23 Schizophrenia, catatonic type, excited
.24 Schizophrenia, catatonic type, withdrawn
.3 Schizophrenia, paranoid type
.4 Acute schizophrenic episode
.5 Schizophrenia, latent type
.6 Schizophrenia, residual type
.7 Schizophrenia, schizo-affective type
.73 Schizophrenia, schizo-affective type, excited
.74 Schizophrenia, schizo-affective type, depressed
.8 Schizophrenia, childhood type
.90 Schizophrenia, chronic and undifferentiated type
.99 Schizophrenia, other (and unspecified) types
296 Major affective disorders ((Affective psychoses))
.0 Involutional melancholia
.1 Manic-depressive illness, manic type ((Manic-depressive psychosis, manic type))
.2 Manic-depressive illness, circular type ((Manic-depressive psychosis, circular type))
.33 Manic-depressive illness, circular type, manic
.34 Manic-depressive illness, circular type, depressed
.8 Other major affective disorder ((Affective psychoses, other))
(.9 Unspecified major affective disorder)
(Affective disorder not otherwise specified)
(Manic-depressive illness not otherwise

297 Paranoid states
.0 Paranoia
.1 Involutional paranoid state ((Involutional paraphrenia))
.9 Other paranoid state
298 Other psychoses
.0 Psychotic depressive reaction ((Reactive depressive psychosis))
(.1 Reactive excitation)
(.2 Reactive confusion)
(Acute or subacute confusional state)
(.3 Acute paranoid reaction)
(.9 Reactive psychosis, unspecified)
(299 Unspecified psychosis)
(Dementia, insanity or psychosis not otherwise specified)

IV. Neuroses (300)

300 Neuroses
.0 Anxiety neurosis
.1 Hysterical neurosis
.13 Hysterical neurosis, conversion type
.14 Hysterical neurosis, dissociative type
.2 Phobic neurosis
.3 Obsessive compulsive neurosis
.4 Depressive neurosis
.5 Neurasthenic neurosis ((Neurasthenia))
.6 Depersonalization neurosis ((Depersonalization syndrome))
.7 Hypochondriacal neurosis

.8 Other neurosis
(.9 Unspecified neurosis)

V. Personality Disorders and Certain Other Non-Psychotic Mental Disorders (301-304)

301 Personality disorders
.0 Paranoid personality
.1 Cyclothymic personality ((Affective personality))
.2 Schizoid personality
.3 Explosive personality
.4 Obsessive compulsive personality ((Anankastic personality))
.5 Hysterical personality
.6 Asthenic personality
.7 Antisocial personality
.81 Passive-aggressive personality
.82 Inadequate personality
.89 Other personality disorders of specified types
(.9 Unspecified personality disorder)
302 Sexual deviations
.0 Homosexuality
.1 Fetishism
.2 Pedophilia
.3 Transvestitism
.4 Exhibitionism
.5 Voyeurism
.6 Sadism
.7 Masochism
.8 Other sexual deviation
(.9 Unspecified sexual deviation)
303 Alcoholism
.0 Episodic excessive drinking
.1 Habitual excessive drinking
.2 Alcohol addiction
.9 Other (and unspecified) alcoholism
304 Drug dependence
.0 Drug dependence, opium, opium alkaloids and their derivatives
.1 Drug dependence, synthetic analgesics with morphine-like effects
.2 Drug dependence, barbiturates
.3 Drug dependence, other hypnotics and sedatives or "tranquilizers"
.4 Drug dependence, cocaine
.5 Drug dependence, cannabis sativa (hashish, marihuana)
.6 Drug dependence, other psycho-stimulants
.7 Drug dependence, hallucinogens
.8 Other drug dependence
(.9 Unspecified drug dependence)

VI. Psychophysiologic Disorders (305)

305 Psychophysiologic disorders ((Physical disorders of presumably psychogenic origin))
.0 Psychophysiologic skin disorder
.1 Psychophysiologic musculoskeletal disorder
.2 Psychophysiologic respiratory disorder
.3 Psychophysiologic cardiovascular disorder
.4 Psychophysiologic hemic and lymphatic disorder
.5 Psychophysiologic gastro-intestinal disorder
.6 Psychophysiologic genito-urinary disorder
.7 Psychophysiologic endocrine disorder
.8 Psychophysiologic disorder of organ of special sense
.9 Psychophysiologic disorder of other type

VII. Special Symptoms (306)

306 Special symptoms not elsewhere classified
.0 Speech disturbance
.1 Specific learning disturbance
.2 Tic
.3 Other psychomotor disorder
.4 Disorders of sleep
.5 Feeding disturbance
.6 Enuresis
.7 Encopresis
.8 Cephalalgia
.9 Other special symptoms

VIII. Transient Situational Disturbances (307)

307 Transient situational disturbances
.0 Adjustment reaction of infancy
.1 Adjustment reaction of childhood
.2 Adjustment reaction of adolescence
.3 Adjustment reaction of adult life
.4 Adjustment reaction of late life

IX. Behavior Disorders of Childhood and Adolescence (308)

308 Behavior disorders of childhood and adolescence ((Behavior disorders of childhood))
.0 Hyperkinetic reaction of childhood (or adolescence)
.1 Withdrawing reaction of childhood (or adolescence)
.2 Overanxious reaction of childhood (or adolescence)
.3 Runaway reaction of childhood (or adolescence)
.4 Unsocialized aggressive reaction of childhood (or adolescence)
.5 Group delinquent reaction of childhood (or adolescence)
.9 Other reaction of childhood (or adolescence)

X. Conditions Without Manifest Psychiatric Disorder and Non-Specific Conditions (316-318)

316 Social maladjustments without manifest psychiatric disorder
.0 Marital maladjustment
.1 Social maladjustment
.2 Occupational maladjustment
.3 Dyssocial behavior
.9 Other social maladjustment
317 Non-specific conditions
318 No mental disorder

XI. Non—Diagnostic Terms for Administrative Use (319)

319 Non-diagnostic terms for adminstrative use
.0 Diagnosis deferred
.1 Boarder
.2 Experiment only
.9 Other

claustrophilia A morbid desire to be confined in a small space.

claustrophobia A morbid fear of being confined in a small space.

clavus Severe headache.

cleft palate Congenital effect which results in a fissure of the palate. Its immediate cause is the failure of complete development, by eight to ten weeks, of one or more of the five embryonic processes of the fetus' face. Some children have hearing problems and often have speech problems, and there is, though infrequently, a mild degree of mental impairment and socioemotional deficits.

clerical test See *test, clerical.*

client (non-directive psychotherapy) A person who receives counseling or non-directive psychotherapy.

client-centered psychotherapy See *psychotherapy, client centered.*

climacophobia Morbid fear of stairs.

climacteric psychosis See *psychosis, involutional.*

climacterium 1. A critical period in life. 2. Menopause.

clinic An outpatient establishment for the diagnosis and treatment of illness. A mental health clinic deals with mental disorders. Most often mental hospitals operate clinics, but some clinics are operated by groups of psychiatrists, clinical psychologists, and psychiatric social workers.

clinical method A variety of research and diagnostic techniques such as interviews, life histories, testing, projective techniques, and case observation.

clinical psychology See *psychology, clinical.*

clinical psychology, legal status See *certification of psychologists.*

clinical practice Treatment of physical diseases and mental (behavioral) disorders.

clinician An individual qualified to practice treatment of physical diseases and mental behavior disorders.

clitoromania Nymphomania.

clock (operant conditioning) A stimulus, some dimension of which changes systematically with time.

clone A group of organisms of a common, non-sexual origin, such as, e.g. splitting in protozoa.

clonic Relating to clonus.

clonus Movement characterized by involuntary alternating rapid muscle contraction and relaxation.

closure (Gestalt psychology) The theory of electric circuit has been used by gestalt psychology in their study of brain mechanism. The brain activity follows the principle of equilibrium, and when there is a gap in the current, tensions on both sides of the gap and the electric current closes the gap. Hence the principle of closure which applies to the perception. When a figure is drawn with incomplete lines, the perceive completes it (closes) in his mind and perceives it as complete.

clouding of consciousness An impairment of perception and orientation associated with brain disorders.

cluster analysis (statistics) A technique for determining the presence of clusters by inspection of a matrix, or correlation table.

cluster correlation See *correlation, cluster.*

Clytemnestra complex See *complex, Clytemnestra.*

CNS Central nervous system.

coacting group (social psychology) A group of people cooperating with one another with little if any interaction with one another.

coaxing-hypnosis See *mother hypnosis.*

cocaine An anaesthetic which is also a mild stimulant.

cocaine bug See *bug, cocaine.*

cochlea A part of the inner ear which includes the hearing organ.

cochlear-palpebrol reflex Tightening or closing of eyelids in response to an auditory stimulus.

code capacity (information theory) The maximum of information that can be sent through a code channel.

code of ethics, ethical code for psychologists A set of standards for psychologists compiled from real problem situations which psychologists deemed to be of ethical importance. This code, developed by the American Psychological Association, differs from earlier codes which were based on existing codes of other professions in deriving its content from empirical situations relevant to psychologists.

code test See *test, code.*

codeine A depressant derived from morphine.

coding 1. (statistics) The process of transforming a set of scores into a more convenient set. 2. The transformation of messages into signals in an information theory.

coding key A list of the classes of data and their respective symbols assigned to each.

codon A triplet of three bases in a DNA or RNA which codes for a specific amino acid.

coefficient 1. (mathematics) A value by which other values are multiplied. 2. (statistics) A value stating the degree to which a characteristic occurs in specific instances.

coefficient, agreement Also called coefficient of agreement. 1. A measure to determine the degree of agreement between a specific item and the rest of the scale. The formula used is as follows:

$$CAg = \frac{a_1 + a_2 + a_3 \ldots + a_n}{N}$$

CAg is the coefficient of agreement, a_1 is the total number of responses for subject one that agree with his responses to the item in question, a_2 is the same calculation for the second subject and so on, and N is the total number of responses. 2. A measure to determine the amount of agreement among rankings or ratings. The formula that is used is as follows:

$$CA = 100 \left[\frac{\frac{1-\Sigma T-\Sigma B}{N}}{2(H-L)} \right]$$

CA is the coefficient of agreement, *T* is the top 50% of the rankings, *B* is the bottom 50% of the rankings, *H* − *L* is the range between the highest and the lowest rank, and *N* is the number of cases.

coefficient, alienation The measure of the degree of absence of a relationship or correlation between two variables. The coefficient is found by using the following formula:

$$k = \sqrt{1-r^2}$$

where *k* is the alienation coefficient and *r* is the product moment correlation for the two variables in question. See *product moment correlation coefficient.*

coefficient, association A measure of the correlation between dichotomous variables such as male-female.

coefficient, consistency See *coefficient of internal consistency.*

coefficient, contingency (*C*) A measure of the association of two different sets of data which determines the degree to which the variables are independent of each other and to what extent this can be attributed to chance. The mean square contingency coefficient, the most commonly used measure, is given by the formula; $C = \sqrt{\frac{X^2}{N+X^2}}$

Where *N* = the number of cases and X^2 is the symbol for Chi square.

coefficient, correlation See *correlation coefficient.*

coefficient, dispersion An index of variability; it is the ratio of any measure of dispersion over the mean and multiplied by 100. It allows for comparison between scores with unequal means.

coefficient, *j* (E. S. Primoff) An estimate of the predictive value of each of the subtests of a battery.

coefficient, multiple determination (*R²*) The degree to which the correlation of two variables in a multiple correlation can be accounted for by the influence of other variables.

coefficient, nondetermination The amount of variance in the dependent variable which is not accounted for by the independent variable.

coefficient of equivalence, Kuder-Richardson Any of several formulas which are variations on the chance-halves correlation, used for the estimation of correlation between comparable forms of a test on the basis of one administration. Also called K-R formulas.

coefficient of intelligence See *intelligence, coefficient of.*

coefficient of internal consistency See *internal consistency, coefficient of.*

coefficient, path choice (R. B. Cattell) Factor analytic technique which measures one person on one set of variables on different occasions.

coefficient, reliability Any measure of reliability which involves the use of correlation coefficients.

coefficient stability (r_{st}) The correlation between two applications of a test with a sufficiently large interval between them to reduce the differential effects of practice.

coefficient, variability See *coefficient, variation.*

coefficient, variation (statistics) A measure of relative variability in a frequency distribution given by the formula: $V=\frac{100\ \sigma}{M}$ where V stands for variability, σ is the standard deviation, *M* is the mean of the distribution.

coelom (celom) The embryonic body cavity formed in the lateral mesoderm during the tridermic stage of embryological development.

coenotype See *cenotype.*

cognition 1. A general term for any process which allows an organism to know and be aware. It includes perceiving, reasoning, conceiving, judging. 2. A postulated stimulus-stimulus association or perceptual organization thought to account for expectancies of an organism.

cognition, operation of (J. P. Guilford) Immediate discovery, awareness, rediscovery, or recognition of particular items of information; understanding or comprehension.

cognitive Of or related to thoughts and ideas.

cognitive-awareness level (G. A. Kelly) The extent to which a construct used in diagnosis and psychotherapy is useful, effective and noncontradictory.

cognitive consistency The notion that a person's cognitions (beliefs, perceived behaviors, etc.) will tend to be logically and psychologically consistent with one another. If inconsistencies are present, the individual attempts to reduce them by changing his cognitions, behavior, or both so that they are consistent with each other.

cognitive dissonance (L. Festinger) A motivational state which exists when an individual's cognitive elements (attitudes, perceived behaviors, etc.) are inconsistent with each other. The tension produced by this state may be reduced by adding consonant elements; changing one of the dissonant elements so that it is no longer inconsistent with the other, or by reducing the importance of the dissonant elements.

cognitive-dynamic investment strain (R. B. Cattell) A concept referring to the difficulty in having to remember and attend to a large number of minutiae, in order to achieve and maintain goal satisfaction.

cognitive map (E. C. Tolman) A perceptual representation of the maze which an organism develops based on environmental cues and the organism's expectancies, which teaches him the location of the goal.

cognitive reaction time See *reaction time, cognitive.*

cognitive schema 1. A perceptual pattern of past experience believed to be imprinted in the organism's structure to which past and future experience are referred for interpretation. **2.** (E. C. Tolman) Cognitive map.

cognitive sign principle The postulate that learning consists of the awareness of the relationship of stimuli to responses or goals rather than the learning of a series of responses.

cognitive structure (K. Lewin) The individual's organization of the world into a unified system of beliefs, concepts, attitudes, and expectations.

cognitive style The mode in which a person organizes and classifies his perceptions of the environment in order to impose order upon a confusing series of events.

cognitive theory of learning A theory of learning which postulates the existence of intervening central processes in learning which are cognitive in nature and which states that learning involves new ways of perceiving rather than of incorporating new responses into the behavior repertoire.

cognizance need See *need, cognizance.*

cohesion The attraction that a group holds for its members and which dictates the capacity of the group to resist dissolution. In order for a group to remain attractive to a member, the resultant force operating on that individual must be greater than zero.

cohesion, law of 1. The principle in learning that behaviors which are contiguous in time tend to unify into more complex, higher-order actions. **2.** The principle that parts of a gestalt tend to acquire coherence.

coitus interruptus Sexual intercourse voluntarily interrupted by the male.

cold spot Skin or membrane area sensitive to low temperature.

colitis Inflammation of the colon of organic or psychogenic origin.

colitis, mucous Chronic infection of the mucous membrane of the colon which is often seen in patients who have intense demanding personalities and suffer from constipation or diarrhea.

colitis, spastic Colitis associated with spasms of the colon of physical or psychogenic causes. The psychogenic conflict centers around intense oral aggressive and receptive needs.

colitis, ulcerative An inflammation of the colon characterized by ulceration of the mucosa.

collecting mania See *mania, collecting.*

collective behavior See *mind, collective.*

collective mind See *mind, collective.*

collective psychology See *psychology, social.*

collective unconscious See *unconscious, collective.*

colliculus A prominance in the nervous system, specifically one of the four prominances of the corpora quadrigemine in the brain stem.

colligation A combination of units in which the units remain separate from each other rather than losing their identity in the totality.

colligation coefficient (statistics) An approximation of the relationship between two dichotomous variables. It is a function of the square roots of the products of the frequencies in opposite cells in a four fold table.

colliquation A complete breakdown of cells and tissues.

color adaptation 1. The decrease of hue and saturation of a color when it is fixated upon for a prolonged period of time. **2.** Raising an individual's absolute threshold of sensitivity to hue.

color antagonism The mixture of colors which results in achromatic gray.

color aperture Color classified as film colors which are seen as spaces in neutral screens.

color blindness Total or partial inability to perceive colors. Total color blindness results in the perception of colors as shades of gray. The most common form of partial color blindness is the inability to differentiate reds and greens.

color, complementary A color, which when mixed with a particular other color produces gray.

color contrast See *contrast, color.*

color conversion (H. Helson) The changes in lightness and/or chromaticity in color due to any change in viewing conditions such as through simultaneous or successive contrast, changes in spectral energy of source of light, adaptation of the eyes, etc. Usually color conversion is restricted to changes occurring according to the principle of color conversion.

color deficiency See *color blindness.*

color, induced A change in the appearance of a color due to the introduction of another color into the immediate area.

color memory See *memory, color.*

color mixture The operation of combining two or more colors to produce an effect of fusion. The techniques used to accomplish this effect include rapid rotation of colors on a color mixer, simultaneous projection of colored lights on a screen and the mixture of pigments.

color naming A Rorschach answer in which the subject merely identifies areas of the inkblots as to their color. The symbol Cn is typically used to denote such an answer although the criteria for its use differs among various Rorschach systems. Klopfer and Rapaport both include Cn scoring whenever such a response occurs while Hertz and Piotrowski score Cn only when it is clear that the subject has given no thought to a meaningful interpretation of the blot. It is generally regarded as a constricted or disorganized type response.

color, primary **1.** In a loose sense, any of those colors which, in any system, are of special importance for color classification. **2.** One of those colors that cannot be broken down into other component colors: red, green, yellow, and blue. **3.** One of those pigments that can be mixed to yield, in reduced color saturation, all the hues: white, black, red, yellow, and blue.

color purity The extent to which a color is fully saturated.

color pyramid A graphic representation of the relationships of achromatic and chromatic colors to each other in the form of a double pyramid. The base of the pyramid is a triangle, square or circle, depending on which colors are considered to be primary. If the base is a triangle, the primaries are red, green, and blue. If it is a square, yellow is added as the fourth color. The assumption underlying the color base is that there is no basic color. The colors of intermediate hues are placed along the borders of the figures. The center of the geometric figures is gray. The radii extending from this point refer to degrees of saturation. The farther from the center a color is, the more saturated it becomes. The vertical axis of the pyramid represents the dimension of brightness with black at the bottom and white at the top. As one moves from the periphery to the center, the colors become less saturated but of equal brightness. Colors of different tints and shades are found on the sides of the figures from the poles to the periphery of the base.

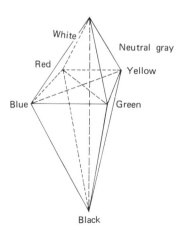

White / Neutral gray / Red / Yellow / Blue / Green / Black

color response (Rorschach) A class of Rorschach responses which includes use of the chromatic features of the blots. It is generally considered to represent affectivity and is weighted in relation to the use of form. Thus, form dominated color responses in

which the form component is secondary or nonexistent are considered as lability. Some approaches to the Rorschach, particularly Hertz, Klopfer, and Piotrowski also include special scorings and interpretations for color responses which appear to be "forced" by the subject, or where color is used in an arbitrary manner.

color shock An unusual, or startle reaction of Rorschach subjects to the chromatic features of the inkblots. It is manifest in delayed reaction times, sequence alteration, impairment of response quality, and general reduction in response frequency. Most Rorschach authorities have speculated that it is a valid index of neurotic features.

color sorting test See *test, Holmgren.*

color surface The plane surface obtained by cutting through a color pyramid at right angles to the vertical axis of brightness. The surface contains all the possible hues and saturations at that particular level of brightness.

color temperature The temperature of a black body or complete radiator at which it yields a color matching that of a given sample of radiant energy. It is measured on the absolute or Kelvin scale.

color triangle The plane figure forming the base of the color pyramid which shows the relationships between the colors, brightness and saturation.

color vision, theories of **1.** Theories which attempt to explain how light energy is transformed into visual sensations of different colors. There are three main theories: the Young–Helmholtz, the Hering, and the Ladd-Franklin theory. **2.** See *color vision, theory of: Young-Helmholtz theory.* **3.** See *color vision, theory of: Hering theory.* **4.** See *color vision, theory of: Ladd-Franklin theory.*

color vision, theory of: Hering theory (E. Hering) The perception of color is mediated by three processes in the retina, a black-white, a red-green, and a blue-yellow process. Each member of a pair is differentially stimulated by anabolic building up excitation which produces sensations of black, green and blue and catabolic tearing down stimulation which produces sensations of white, red, and yellow. Mixture of colors is due to the simultaneous stimulation of two halves of non-paired processes. Color blindness results from the absence of one or more of the chromatic processes.

color vision, theory of: Ladd-Franklin theory (Ladd-Franklin C.) An evolutionary theory stating that monochromism, total color blindness was the primitive form of perception followed by the evolution of yellow and blue receptors which were succeeded by the development of red and green receptors. The different forms of color blindness result from regressive loss of the use of specific receptors.

color vision, theory of: Young-Helmholtz theory (T. Young and H. von Helmholtz) The perception of color is explained by the presence of three types of cones in the retina, red, green and blue. While each cone responds to any wave length, the maximal response occurs to the wave lengths it is most sensitive to. Mixture of colors results from the simultaneous stimulation of two different cones. White results from the simultaneous stimulation of all three cones. Color blindness is due to the partial or total absence of cones.

color wheel An apparatus which mixes colors by rapid rotation of a variably colored disk to produce a fusion of the colors.

color zones Regions of the retina which respond differentially when stimulated by different colors. Normally, all of the colors can be perceived in the foveal region of the retina. In the middle zone, blues, yellows, and achromatic colors. In the periphery of the retina, all colors are seen as achromatic. The zones are not rigidly separated from each other.

colorimeter An instrument used to measure colors by comparing them to a known color mixture.

Columbia Mental Maturity Scale See *scale, Columbia Mental Maturity.*

column 1. (statistics) A vertical row of values in a statistical table. **2.** A bundle of neurons of similar structure and function which extends longitudinally for some distance. It is found in the central nervous system.

coma A state of unconsciousness during which most behaviors and reflexes are suspended.

coma, insulin Coma induced by a large dose of insulin either accidently or regulated for the purpose of shock therapy.

coma-vigil See *agrypnocoma.*

combat fatigue See *fatigue, combat.*

combat neurosis See *fatigue, combat.*

combination (mathematics) A set or group consisting of any number of object items in such a way that no two sets have exactly the same items although an item may occur in more than one set. The ordering of the items is unimportant.

combination, law of 1. The principle that two or more stimuli which are presented simultaneously or in close temporal proximity may combine to elicit a response. **2.** The principle that two responses which are made simultaneously or in close proximity will occur together upon presentation of the stimulus eliciting either response.

combination tone A third tone produced when two tones of similar timbre are sounded simultaneously. There are two kinds of combination tones: summation and difference tones.

comention (R. B. Cattell) A personality trait characterized by adherance to cultural prescriptions, obedience to authority and suppression of personal desires.

cometophobia Morbid fear of comets.

commensurable (mathematics) Referring to two or more variables which can be quantitatively assessed by the same unit of measurement.

commissural fibers See *fibers, commissural.*

common factor See *factor, group.*

common factor variance See *communality.*

common fate, law of (Gestalt) The principle that perceived elements which change or move in the same way tend to be apprehended as belonging together.

common trait A set of personality characteristics (dimension, trait) which has the same form or pattern of expression for all people and on which, therefore, all people can be given a meaningful numerical value.

communality That fraction of the total variance of a test which is due to factors common to all tests subjected to experiment.

communication 1. The transmission of energy change from one place to another as in the nervous system or transmission of sound waves. **2.** The transmission or reception of signals or messages by organisms. **3.** The transmitted message. **4.** (Communication theory) The process whereby one system influences another system through regulation of the transmitted signals. **5.** (K. Lewin) The influence of one personal region on another whereby a change in one results in a corresponding change in the other region. **6.** The message of a patient to his therapist in psychotherapy.

communication, consummatory (communication theory) Communication of the sender which expresses his feelings and ideas and which does not require an answer from the receiver.

communication, mass The dissemination of information through the mass media.

communication, mass media of The instruments of communication which disseminate information to large numbers of people at once such as newspapers, television and radio.

communication theory The branch of science which is concerned with communication whether it is physical, mechanical, psychological or social. Models for human communication are developed to parallel machine models.

communications unit (communication theory) A unit consisting of a sender, a channel and a receiver. The sender encodes messages to be transmitted via the channel to the receiver which decodes the signals. Parallels are made between machine systems and the human organism.

community 1. A group of organisms living in close proximity and having some type of social organization. **2.** A group of persons, not in close contact who share a common interest or purpose.

community catharsis See *catharsis, community.*

community-of-content theory The principle that different complex situations have certain stimuli in common which account for the consistency of responses from situation to situation.

comparable form See *form, comparable.*

comparative judgment See *judgment, comparative.*

comparative judgment, law of See *judgment, comparative, law of.*

comparative mava method A comparison of the estimates of the genetic and environmental variance components across a series of racio-cultural groups (made by the Multiple Abstract Variance Analysis Method) permitting inferences to be made about the environmental influences and genetic structures responsible for the observed variances. Thus, a correlation of variance on an environment feature with the environmental trait variance component permits an estimate of the regression of specific environmental characters upon the environmentally produced part of the trait as such.

comparative psychology See *psychology, comparative.*

comparison stimulus (Co) (psychophysics) Variable stimulus the subject adjusts until, for him, it and the standard stimulus are indistinguishable during a psychophysical experiment.

compensating error See *error, compensating.*

compensation The mechanism of covering up aspects of oneself which are unacceptable and substituting more desired traits in an exaggerated form.

compensation autonomic (E. J. Kempf) A reflexive action to counteract stimuli which produce a fear state in a person. For example, a feeling of social incompetency which causes fear, and reflexly initiates an action to counteract this feeling.

compensatory rate See *rate, compensatory.*

competence motive The individual's active attempt to contact and master his environment as an end in itself as apart from the practical benefits of this activity.

complacency, principle of (R. B. Raup) The tendency of organisms to maintain a physiological state of equilibruim and to return to this state when it is disturbed by external forces.

complementary color See *color, complementary.*

complementary probabilities See *probabilities, complementary.*

complete learning method; complete mastery method Method for measuring the rate of learning by the number of trials taken to learn items to a given criterion.

completion test See *test, completion.*

complex 1. A group of related or associated factors. 2. (psychoanalysis) A group of associated ideas and impulses having an emotional meaning which are partly or totally regressed because they are in conflict with the ego and/or the superego.

complex, Antigone (B. B. Wolman) An extreme case of non-sexual love and sacrifice of one's own life for the sake of a beloved person; borrowed from the Greek myth of Antigone, the daughter of Oedipus, who buried the dead body of her brother despite the threat of death penalty. Antigone was punished by death.

complex, Cain A complex characterized by rivalry, competition and destructive feelings toward a brother.

complex, castration (S. Freud) The castration complex is the result of childhood fears of punishment for forbidden sexual desires towards the parent of the opposite sex. In the male it is manifested in a fear of losing his genitals. In the female, it is manifested in the fantasy that the penis has been removed from her as a punishment.

complex, chronological (M. Paine) A systematized complex organized around the experiences of certain epochs of the life of an individual rather than the subject matter in the epoch.

complex, Clytemnestra The occurrence of the wife killing her husband.

complex, Diana Repressed desire of a female to be a male.

complex, Electra (psychoanalysis) Love a girl has for her father with accompanying hostility for her mother; attributed to jealousy of the mother for possession of the father, and to blaming the mother for not giving her a penis or for taking it away from her; feminine version of the Oedipus complex.

complex, Eshum Infrequently used term for castration complex.

complex, grandfather The desire to be the parent of one's own parents.

complex, Griselda Refers to the father's desire to keep the daughter to himself. The father's reluctance to part with his daughter is based on his own unresolved Oedipal conflict in which his yearning was for the mother.

complex indicator (C. G. Jung) In an association test, any behavior caused by a repressed complex such as blushing or responding slowly.

complex, inferiority 1. (A. Adler) An abnormal unconscious exaggeration of feelings of insignificance and insecurity resulting in defensive and compensatory behavioral manifestations. 2. (psychoanalysis) Repressed feelings of insignificance arising from the inability to reconcile Oedipal wishes with the reality of childhood inadequacy.

complex, Jocasta (R. de Saussure) An excessive and perverted love of a mother for her son.

complex, K A generalized cortical response evoked by an auditory stimulus occurring during sleep.

complex, Medea The death wishes of a mother toward her children as a means for revenge against her husband.

complex, mood (M. Prince) A systematized complex of dispositions, natural inclinations, desires, and modes of behavior which are suppressed or inhibited for one reason or another.

complex, Oedipus (S. Freud) Erotic involvement of a male child with his mother accompanied by hostile feelings toward the father. In females, called the Electra complex, it is involvement with the father and resentment toward the mother. Negative Oedipus complex is one erotic involvement with the parent of the same sex and resentment toward the opposite sex. The idea of Oedipus complex was borrowed by Freud from the Greek myth about Oedipus who killed his father and married his mother.

complex, Orestes (psychoanalysis) The repressed or unconscious desire of a son to kill his mother.

complex, Phaedra A sexual love of a mother for her son.

complex reaction See *reaction, complex.*

complex, subject (M. Prince) A systematic complex or complex of associated experiences organized around subjects or departments of human experience.

complex, systematized (M. Prince) Image systems of complexes or associated experiences which become organized and fairly distinctly differentiated in the course of the development of every one's personality. Many of these systems may be organized around a predominant emotion, tendency or feeling.

complication experiment See *prior entry law.*

component instinct See *instinct, component.*

compos mentis Of a sound mind; not mentally deficient.

composite image See *image, composite.*

composite norm See *norm, composite.*

composite score See *score, composite.*

compound A totality formed of independent parts.

compound eye See *eye, compound.*

compound reaction See *reaction, compound.*

comprehension test See *test, comprehension.*

comprehensive solution See *solution, comprehensive.*

compression 1. The use of one symbol to represent more than one thing at a time. 2. Condensation.

compromise formation (psychoanalysis) An action or behavior which represents both the work of repressed impulses and of the repressive defensive mechanism of the ego. It is allowed to occur because the repressed impulse becomes disguised in order to escape the censorship of the ego.

compulsion 1. The state in which the person feels forced to behave against his own conscious wishes and judgment. 2. The force which compels a person to action against his own will or forcing a person to act in this way.

compulsion neurosis See *neurosis, obsessive compulsive.*

compulsive behavior Irrational and irresistible impulse to perform some act repeatedly.

compulsive personality See *personality, compulsive.*

computer An instrument capable of solving problems by applying specific processes to given data and supplying the results of these operations.

computer synthesis scoring (R. B. Cattell) In a questionnaire containing several factor scales, the usual method scores each only on its own set of items. Computer synthesis allocates available contributions from all scales to any one scale. It increases velocity but vitiates estimates of correlations among the true factors.

Comte, Auguste (1798-1857) French sociologist who began the positivist movement. He rejected the validity of introspection; all science is social, he held, and deals not with the inferential or speculative but only with the directly observable.

conarium (R. Descartes) The point of union between the mind and the body in Cartesian philosophy.

conation The aspect of personality characterized by a conscious willing, strong and purposive action.

conc schedule See *reinforcement, schedule of: concurrent.*

concentration 1. Exclusive restricted attention to one object or area of study. 2. (I. P. Pavlov) The law of excitation and inhibition which describes the centralization of nerve processes within restricted cortical areas.

concept, congruence of images See *congruence-of-images concept.*

concept-formation tests See *tests, concept formation.*

concept-switching task A task which requires the subject to categorize objects according to one concept, then to find another concept according to which the objects can be classified.

concept validity See *construct validity.*

conceptual learning See *learning, conceptual.*

conceptual model See *model, conceptual.*

conceptual nervous system See *nervous system, conceptual.*

conceptual thinking and brain processes See *thinking, conceptual and brain processes.*

concommitant variations (J. S. Mill) A principle of inductive reasoning which states that when two phenomena vary together, they are either causally related as a cause and effect or have a cause in common.

concordance coefficient (*W*) (statistics) A statistical estimate of the degree to which judges agree with each other in ranking. The formula is:

$$(W) = \frac{12\Sigma(\Sigma R)^2}{nk^2(n^2-1)} - \frac{3^n+1}{n-1},$$

where ΣR stands for the sum of the k ranks assigned to each subject by the different judges, and n is the number of subjects.

concordant A term used in twin studies to indicate that both members of a twin pair exhibit the trait or disease in question. Concordance rates indicate the percentage of twin pairs in a study that are concordant. Higher concordance rates in monozygotic than dizygotic twin pairs give a preliminary indication of a genetic factor, which can be further explored by studying monozygotic twins reared apart. The twin studies of Franz J. Kallmann in schizophrenia, manic-depressive psychosis and other psychiatric conditions as well as tuberculosis and deafness exemplify this method and extend it by introducing further categories of blood relatives, resulting in a twin-family method.

concrete intelligence See *intelligence, concrete.*

concrete thinking See *thinking, concrete.*

concurrent operant See *operant, concurrent.*

concurrent (conc) schedule See *reinforcement, schedule of: concurrent.*

concurrent validity See *validity, concurrent.*

concussion Shock resulting from a blow or jarring of a part of the body. When blow is to the head, it may be accompanied by unconsciousness, and temporary paralysis.

condensation (psychoanalysis) The fusion of any group of unconscious elements into one more acceptable element in order to pass the censorship of the ego.

Condillac, Étienne Bonnot de (1715-1780) Influential French empiricist philosopher, who introduced Locke's philosophy to France. Against the doctrine of innate ideas, he developed the philosophy of sensationism: all mental life can be derived from sensory experience. Thus if a statue were endowed with a single sense, it would develop all the mental processes of man.

condition 1. The antecedent necessary for an event to occur. 2. The state of a person, situation, or object. 3. To establish a conditioned response. 4. To cause learning in an organism.

conditional factor A personality of ability factor found in variables presented under special conditions restricting the range of influences, e.g., without variance in motivation. Opposed to *naturalistic factors.*

conditional probability See *probability, conditional.*

conditional reflex See *reflex, conditioned.*

conditionalism (C. G. Jung) The view that an effect is explicable by its cause and that knowing the cause, one can predict the effect.

conditioned avoidance See *conditioning, avoidance.*

conditioned fear See *fear, conditioned.*

conditioned reactive inhibition See *inhibition, conditioned reactive.*

conditioned reflex See *reflex, conditioned.*

conditioned reinforcement See *reinforcement, conditioned.*

conditioned reinforcer See *reinforcer, conditioned.*

conditioned response See *reflex, conditioned.*

conditioned stimulus See *stimulus, conditioned.*

conditioned suppression See *suppression, conditioned.*

conditioning, approximation 1. Conditioning of a complex or rare response through successively rewarding first gross approximations and then closer approximations of the desired response until the desired response is attained and conditioned. 2. Shaping of behavior.

conditioning, aversive Form of counter conditioning through the use of punishment; occasionally used in the treatment of homosexuality, stuttering, or alcoholism.

conditioning, avoidance An extroceptive stimulus is presented to the experimental subject and after a period of time an unconditioned aversive stimulus is presented. The two stimuli usually overlap in time and terminate together. If the appropriate response is emitted before the onset of the aversive stimulus, it does not occur and the extroceptive stimulus is terminated. The presentation of the neutral extroceptive stimulus before the unconditioned aversive stimulus in a respondent, or Pavlovian conditioning procedure, the onset of the CS followed by the onset of the US. Thus the extroceptive stimulus becomes the CS and the aversive stimulus is the US.

At the same time that this classical conditioning occurs, operant conditioning occurs, since the operant response is reinforced by the termination of the conditioned aversive stimulus and possibly by the nonoccurence of the unconditioned aversive stimulus. In this procedure the conditioned extroceptive stimulus has several properties: (A) It elicits respondent behavior appropriate to the unconditioned aversive stimulus, (B) It is also a conditioned aversive stimulus removal of which is reinforcing. In this sense, avoidance conditioning becomes a special case of escape behavior, (C) It is a discriminative stimulus, it acquires stimulus control of responding.

However, another conditioned avoidance procedure has been developed, the free operant avoidance, in which there is no extroceptive unconditioned stimulus. The aversive stimulus, a very short, intense electric shock, is presented to the organism at regular intervals, say, every ten seconds. This is the shock-shock interval, S-S interval. Each response postpones the occurrence of the shock for a period of time, say twenty seconds. This is the response-shock interval, R-S.

Free operant avoidance behavior is maintained without a conditioned extroceptive stimulus. The stimuli controlling this behavior is still in dispute; thus, the nature of avoidance behavior itself is still unsettled.

conditioning, backward (Pavlovian conditioning) One of the common experimental temporal relationships, arranged between the unconditioned stimulus (US) and the conditioned stimulus (CS). Conditioning normally occurs when the onset of the CS is before the onset of the US. In backward conditioning the CS is presented after the onset of the US. If backward conditioning occurs at all, it is not very effective since it has never been conclusively demonstrated.

conditioning, bifactoral theory of The proposition that attitudes determine the probability of incidence of conditioning, and properties of the stimulus determine response magnitude.

conditioning, classical See *conditioning, Pavlovian.*

conditioning, cross 1. Conditioning to any situational stimulus which occurs at the same time as the unconditioned stimulus in the original conditioning procedure. 2. The conditioning of postural and tonic responses to commonly occurring stimuli.

conditioning, differential Establishment and maintenance of a conditioned response to one of two stimuli by reinforcing the response to the one and not reinforcing the response to the other.

conditioning, higher-order A type of Pavlovian conditioning in which the original conditioned stimulus is used as the unconditioned stimulus in a new conditioning procedure.

conditioning, instrumental Conditioning procedures in which the animal's behavior is instrumental in the obtaining of reward or the avoidance of or escape from punishment. The appropriate response must be performed prior to reinforcement in order to obtain it.

conditioning, operant (B. F. Skinner) A form of conditioning in which reinforcement is contingent upon the occurrence of the response. Instrumental and operant conditioning are distinguished primarily, methodologically. Operant conditioning involves the repeated emission of the same response, the operant, while for instrumental behaviors the reinforcement contingent response occurs only once per trial. Consequently the primary measure of operant conditioning tends to be the rate of responding.

Operant conditioning experiments usually involve a small number of subjects observed over a long period of time; thus providing a stable "baseline" or "steady state" with which to compare the experimental effects. With animal subjects the experimental apparatus is usually a sound proof, light resistant box. In its usual form the box contains only the operandum, that upon which the subject responds, sources for light and sound stimuli and a mechanism to deliver reinforcement, usually either food or water. Thus unwanted external influences are minimized and critical variables can be precisely controlled by the experimenter.

In operant conditioning the response conditioned is the operant which is any of a class of behaviors that are equally effective in achieving reinforcement. Thus an operant is defined by the situation in which it occurs. In the experimental situation the operandum defines the operant. When rats are used as subjects, the operandum in the experimental cham-

ber is a bar depressor which delivers reinforcement. In this situation the only behavior that is reinforced is the bar press. It makes no difference how the subject performs the operant, with its paw, nose, or tail; when the bar is pressed, the operant has been performed and the animal is eligible for reinforcement.

Since the dependent variable in operant conditioning is the response rate or the number of events in a given period of time, it becomes meaningful to talk about the amount of responding; twice as many responses mean twice as much behavior. A relationship which is less clear than some other measure is used, e.g. half the latency or half the amplitude. Thus response rate as a measure gives at least a simplicity, if not clarity, to the analysis and interpretation of data. Operant conditioning often leads to a behavior analysis in which explanation of behavior is reduced to description, and causation of behavior reduced to explication of functional relations. Thus the full description of an event is taken to include a description of its functional relationship with antecedent events. Attempts to account for behavior in terms of physiology or biology play little part in operant conditioning.

conditioning, Pavlovian (I. P. Pavlov) Often called classical conditioning, respondent conditioning, type 1, and type S conditioning. It is the procedure of presenting two stimuli in one of several temporal arrangements. One stimulus, the unconditioned stimulus, is sufficient to evoke an unconditioned response. By presenting the neutral stimulus followed by the unconditioned stimulus to the experimental subject for a number of times, the neutral stimulus evokes a response similar to the original unconditioned response, and the neutral stimulus becomes a conditioned stimulus capable of evoking a conditioned response. Furthermore, the conditioned response the neutral stimulus evokes through conditioning is a conditioned response, somewhat different and distinguishable from the unconditioned response.

Pavlov developed his theory of conditioning with a physiological orientation explaining the observed facts of conditioning by postulating events in the nervous system of the organism. His basic unit of analysis was the reflex-arc which he divided into three parts; analyzer, connection and effector. The analyzer begins at the peripheral sense receptor and carries the stimulation to the cortical receptor centers. Each analyzer has a special central territory in the cortex which represents a projection in the brain. The sensory stimulation is conducted along the analyzer pathway to its receptor center. The connection is between the receptor and effector. Modifications in the stimulus conditions lead to new connections which in turn lead to new behavioral patterns. Conditioning is the process of creating new connections. The effector is the motor response, or working part of the reflex. Pavlov eventually concluded that reflexes could be formed in the motor regions, therefore the motor region had receptor functions as well.

Three laws govern the excitatory or inhibitory passage of neural energy from one center to another, the process of forming connections: 1) Irradiation, the stimulation in a certain group of nervous cells irradiates over large parts of the cerebrum and the excitation started in a certain cortical point spreads in a wave to surrounding areas. 2) Concentration, the wave of irradiated excitation goes back to the starting point. 3) Induction, once an area is stimulated and irradiates, neighboring areas develop inhibition and force concentration of the stimulated area. This is positive induction. Once an area is inhibited, neighboring areas develop stimulation which force concentration of the inhibition. This is negative induction. Irradiation, concentration, and induction apply to inhibition as well as excitation.

Several types of classical conditioning experimental designs have commonly been distinguished. When the conditioned stimulus (CS) is presented to the subject a fraction of a second to a few seconds prior to the presentation of the unconditioned stimulus (US), the conditioned response (CR) occurs shortly after the CS. The delayed conditioned response occurs when the CS is presented continually for as much as a minute before the US is presented. When there is a pause between the termination of the CS and the presentation of the US it is called trace conditioning, so called because Pavlov concluded that there remained in the organism some trace of the CS after it is discontinued.

Other types of experiments include (a) higher order conditioning where one CS serves as the US for another, second, CS. (b) When conditioning has occurred and the CS will elicit the CR, generalization is said to occur when a wide range of stimuli will elicit the CR. (c) When the subject is trained to respond to one CS and not respond to other stimuli, discrimination is said to have occurred. Repetition of the CS without concomitant repetition of the US, leads invariably to a decline and the eventual extinction of the CR. Without the US reinforcement, extinction always occurs. Among the several types of internal inhibitions that Pavlov distinguished the first type was called extinction; repeated presentation of the CS without the US leads to the suspension of the CR. Another type of internal inhibition was retardation; in trace conditioning the CR does not occur upon the presentation of the CS but occurs after a pause shortly before the US is presented. Differentiated inhibition occurs in discrimination studies where one CS is followed by the US but another CS is not followed by the US. Eventually, only a CR to the former will be established while responses to the latter will be inhibited. Conditioned inhibition is when an indifferent stimulus is added to a well established CS, resulting in the nonoccurrence of the CR. Disinhibition occurs when an external stimulus acts upon the inhibited CS, removing the inhibition resulting in the occurrence of the CR.

conditioning, pseudo The elicitation of a response to a previously neutral stimulus when that stimulus is presented following a series of conditioned stimuli.

conduct Behavior.

conduction 1. The transmission of a neural impulse from one neuron to another. 2. The transmission of sound waves through the ear.

conduction, antidromic The passage of a neural im-

pulse from the axons to dendrites, in reversed direction.

conduction aphasia See *aphasia, conduction.*

conduction deafness See *deafness, conduction.*

conduction, neural The transmission of an impulse along nerve fibers and from neuron to neuron.

conduction unit 1. The unit whose function is the transmission of impulses from one part of the nervous system to another. 2. (E. L. Thorndike) The hypothesized system of neural connections underlying a particular action which occurs under specific conditions.

conductivity 1. The ability of a substance to transmit energy. 2. The ability of a neuron to transmit nerve impulses which is dependent on the size and metabolic state of the neuron.

cones Receptor cells in the retina which function to transform the energy of light rays into nervous impulses which produce daylight and color vision.

confabulated response (Rorschach) Originally defined by H. Rorschach as a response in which the subject interprets an area of the blot and then assigns the same interpretation to a larger area, or to the entire blot, with general disregard for the appropriateness of concept as related to the larger area. Most contemporary Rorschach systems incorporate this concept and use a scoring of DW or its variations. In the Rapaport approach to the Rorschach, the concept has been extended considerably to account for the broader category of "pathological" verbalizations.

confabulation 1. The falsification of memory due to partial amnesia. 2. (Rorschach) Arbitrary elaboration of responses to inkblots without objective support.

confactor rotation (formerly parallel proportional profiles) (R. B. Cattell) A method of sorting the rotation problem in psychological factor analysis which gives independence of the need for simple structure methods. It requires two experimental groups and seeks a functional proportionality of factor leadings on the same variables, thus treating factors as influences.

confession stage (C. G. Jung) The first stage of analytical psychotherapy in which the patient tells of all that is troubling him.

confidence interval The limits outside of which an event is not expected to occur by chance or the distance in sigma units between the fiducial limits.

confidence, level of See *limits, fiducial.*

confidence limits See *limits, fiducial.*

configural scoring See *scoring, configural.*

configuration See *gestalt.*

configuration principle Refers to the basic interpretive approach used in Rorschach testing, wherein the variety of scores, frequencies, percentages, and ratios are considered inter-dependent and interpretable only as related to each other. This principle generally *prohibits* the formulation of interpretive statements based on single scores or features such as the number of animal responses, or the number of color responses or a simple combination of score frequencies as is found in a psychogram.

confirmation (E. C. Tolman) The realization of an expectancy which has the value of a reward.

confirming reaction See *reaction, confirming.*

conflict Simultaneous instigation of two or more incompatible responses; *types* have been differentiated on the basis of whether the conflicting responses are approach or avoidance: I, approach-approach, II, approach-avoidance, III, avoidance-avoidance, IV, double approach-avoidance, conflict, internalized Type II.

The instigation is internal (e.g., aggressive or sexual feelings or drive vs. aggression or sex anxiety), thus leading to an approach-avoidance conflict with reference to manipulanda relevant to the drive.

conflict, actual (psychoanalysis) A present situation involving a struggle between conscious and unconscious desires, that is, opposite impulses. An actual conflict is believed to be the transformation of a root conflict which is the early source of the struggle. A root conflict remains unresolved in the unconscious, repressed since early infancy.

conflict, approach-approach Conflict which occurs when an individual is attracted by and wishes to move toward two positive, attractive goals which are completely or partially incompatible.

conflict, approach-avoidance Situation in which both positive and negative stimuli or both approach and avoidance stimuli are inherent in the same goal or in approximately the same place, whether psychologically, geographically or in the same life space. The organism cannot approach one and avoid the other simultaneously which presents conflict.

conflict, avoidance-avoidance Situation in which an organism faced with two negative goals or situations must move toward one of them in order to avoid the other. In such a situation, the avoidance gradient of the one being approached increases while that of the other decreases and vice versa, causing the organism to move back and forth if both situations are equally negative and resulting in great stress.

conflict-free ego sphere (H. Hartmann) The part of the ego which Hartmann called primary autonomy and which includes perception, motility and memory.

conflict index, C A statistic which gives an exact value for the total amount of energy which an organism (or other dynamic system) has bound up in internal conflict.

conflict, positive-positive See *conflict, approach-approach.*

confluence 1. The flowing together of elements which have been separate such as motives, responses or perceptual elements. 2. (A. Adler) The fusion of several motives into one.

confluent learning (R. B. Cattell) Personality learning in which responses are discovered giving simultaneous expression to tensions previously in conflict.

confusion scales See *scales, confusion.*

congenital Present at birth; not necessarily genetic.

congenital analgesia See *analgesia, congenital.*

congenital aphasia See *aphasia, developmental.*

congruence 1. Agreeable coexistence. 2. (C. Rogers) The integration of experiences into the self, executed on a conscious level.

congruence-of-images concept The idea that behavior in a family is partly an effort to develop and maintain shared and congruent images of the various family members; e.g., the image the father has of himself agrees with the daughter's image of the father.

congruent points Points on the two retinas which are involved in the perception of a point in an external stimulus.

congruity (Osgood, C. E. and Tannenbaum, P. H.) A cognitive state which exists when two objects which have the same evaluative meaning for an individual are positively related in a statement, or when objects which are negatively related have evaluative meaning of the same intensity but of opposite signs.

conj schedule See *reinforcement, schedule of: conjunctive.*

conjoint family therapy See *psychotherapy, family.*

conjugate movements Coordinated movements of the two eyes.

conjugate schedule See *reinforcement, schedule of: conjugate.*

conjunctiva The mucuous membrane of the inner eyelid and outer eyeball.

conjunctival reflex The closing of the eyelid when the cornea is stimulated.

conjunctive motivation See *motivation, conjunctive.*

conjunctive reinforcement See *reinforcement; schedule of: conjunctive (conj).*

conjunctive (conj) schedule See *reinforcement, schedule of: conjunctive (conj).*

conjunctivity (H. A. Murray) The coordination and organization of motives, and purposes with actions.

connection 1. A link between two phenomena. 2. The link between the receptors and effectors.

connectionism 1. The doctrine that the basis of all behavior and learning are connections of stimulus and response which are strengthened to produce stability. 2. (E. L. Thorndike) The theory that the functional bonds between stimulus and response are inherited or acquired neural connections.

connector 1. A nerve fiber which joins a receptor and effector. 2. A neuron which connects two neurons.

consanguinity Relationship by descent from a common ancestor. Raised consanguinity rates are found in the parentage of persons with recessive diseases.

conscience 1. The individual's set of moral values which was thought to be innate by theologians but is now believed to be learned. **2.** (psychoanalysis) See *superego*.

conscious or consciousness 1. Referring to the process of being aware or knowing. **2.** Characterizing a person who is aware. **3.** Pertaining to the ability to react to stimulation in the environment. **4.** Pertaining to that which is observable by introspection. **5.** (psychoanalysis) The upper part of the topographic structure where rational processes can take place.

consciousness, stream of See *stream of consciousness*.

consensual eye reflex See *reflex, consensual eye*.

consensual validation (H. S. Sullivan) Validating one's perception against the perception of other individuals, starts at the syntaxic mode or stage of development.

consentience (M. Jahoda) The agreement or acceptance of a certain attitude when corroborating evidence is introduced.

consistency The agreement of a test with itself. It requires three coefficients (Cattell's conceptualization): 1) The *reliability* (dependability) of a test-retest agreement (over time), 2) The *homogeneity* coefficient defining agreement of parts (over sections), and 3) the *transferability* coefficient expressing degree of agreement of validity over groups (over populations).

consistency coefficient See *coefficient of internal consistency*.

consistency index See *index, consistency*.

consistency, internal An index of the extent to which different parts of a test measure the same function. The degree of internal consistency can be estimated by noting the correlation of the two halves, or by correlating each score with the total score.

consolidation theory The theory that when learning ceases, the neurophysiological activities underlying learning continue to function. This hypothesis is used to explain phenomena such as retroactive inhibition.

conspect reliability coefficient (R. B. Cattell) The degree of agreement of two psychologists scoring the same recorded or observed responses.

constancy The stability of perceptions under varying external conditions.

constancy, brightness The fact that an object retains its normal or standard intensity independent of the surrounding stimuli.

constancy, color The fact that colors tend to remain the same despite changes in illumination or other conditions.

constancy hypothesis The principle that there is a rigid one to one correspondence between the proximal stimulus and the sensory response so that given a particular stimulus, the same response will occur independent of other conditions. This theory is presented as the antithesis of Gestalt theory which stresses relativism in stimulus-response relationships.

constancy of internal environment (W. B. Cannon) The postulated tendency for the internal state of the organism to remain relatively constant.

constancy of the IQ The tendency of the IQ measure to remain relatively constant from year to year when the individual's score is assessed with the same or similar test.

constancy principle (S. Freud) Organic nature tends to return to the initial non-organic phase.

constancy, size The stable perception of the size of objects under different viewing conditions.

constant 1. A mathematical value that remains unchanged under all conditions. **2.** An experimental condition that is not allowed to vary.

constant error See *error, constant*.

constant method See *method, constant stimulus*.

constant stimulus method See *method, constant stimulus*.

constellatory construct See *construct, constellatory*.

constipation, chronic, psychogenic Constipation of long duration due to psychological conflicts about giving and retaining.

constitution 1. The total hereditary and acquired characteristics which determine an individual. **2.** The nature of a thing.

constitution, epileptic psychopathic Complex of negative personality traits and progressive mental and intellectual deficiencies which are manifested by some epileptics and is thought to be related in some way to epilepsy.

constitution, hyperpituitary A constitutional type characterized by dysplastic features, massive body parts, and a restless, reasoning mentality. It is associated with pituitary hyperfunction at the end of the normal growth period.

constitution, hypoadrenal The constitutional type characterized by deficiency in adrenal activity.

constitution, hypopancreatic Condition resulting from progressive intolerance for carbohydrates. A transitory phase to diabetes.

constitution, hypoparathyroid The constitutional type characterized by inadequate secretion of the parathyroid glands.

constitution, hypopituitary (N. Pende) Constitutional type associated with inadequate secretion of the pituitary gland. Characteristically they exhibit immature secondary sexual features, asthenia, low blood pressure, polyuria, increased carbohydrate tolerance, slow pulse and apathy.

constitutional anomaly Anatomical and physiological disequilibrium between two or more systems of the body.

constitutional factors See *factors, constitutional.*

constitutional inadequacy See *inadequacy, constitutional.*

constitutional medicine See *medicine, constitutional.*

constitutional psychopath See *psychopath, constitutional.*

constitutional theory of personality 1. (E. Kretschmer) Personality theory based on the relation between body-type and mental disorder, especially schizophrenic and manic-depressive psychoses. Theory assumes a continuum between abnormal and normal personality types though typology is based primarily on investigation of psychotics. Four body types (see *asthenic, athletic, pyknic* and *dysplastic*) are related to two basic temperaments (see *schizothyme* and *cyclothyme*). These temperaments occur in normal and abnormal variations. Cyclothymic temperament and manic-depressive psychoses are associated with pyknic body-type while schizothymic temperament and schizophrenia are associated with asthenic and athletic body-types. 2. (W. H. Sheldon) Personality theory based on the relationship between body-type and temperament. Body type is classified in terms of three components: ectomorphy, endomorphy and mesomorphy. A person's somatotype is a combination of the three components, each of which is measured along a 7-point scale yielding many possible combinations or somatotypes. Personality is measured in terms of the intercorrelations of sixty traits related to introversion-extroversion and to temperament. The intercorrelation of these traits yields three clusters which constitute the primary components of temperament: cerebrotonia, viscerotonia and somatotonia. The three basic body types are correlated with the three temperamental components: ectomorphy with cerebrotonia, endomorphy with viscerotonia, and mesomorphy with somatotonia. Neither body type nor temperament is completely inherent; early nutritional variables and childhood experiences may influence physique and personality, respectively. Constitutional type provides a substructure of capacities and limitations.

constitutional type 1. A group of enduring physiological, anatomical and psychological qualities which are thought to be a basis for categorizing people. 2. The behavioral traits believed to occur in certain body types. 3. (Hippocrates) A group of characteristics which are believed to be associated with particular diseases. The habitus apoplecticus type was believed to occur in thickset, rounded people. The habitus phthisicus was thought to occur in slender, angular individuals. 4. (Galen) A constellation of traits based on the type of fluid which is basic in the body. The four types include the sanguine, melancholic, choleric and phlegmatic. 5. (E. Kretschmer) See *constitutional theory of personality.* 6. (W. H. Sheldon) See *constitutional theory of personality.*

constrained association See *association, constrained.*

constraint The compelling of someone to do or not to do something.

construct A formally proposed concept representing relationships between empirically verifiable events and based on observed facts. The term was suggested for use instead of concept by K. Pearson.

construct, constellatory (G. A. Kelly) A construct whose elements also belong to other constructs. The construct boy, for example, may also mean aggressive which is another construct.

construct, core (G. A. Kelly) A construct which partially determines how a person adjusts himself to the environment.

construct, empirical A construct determined as a result of experimentation.

construct, hypothetical Concepts introduced within the framework of a theory with the aim of explaining behavioral data. The logical constructs fill a gap in observation and experimentation, going beyond observable data. They are heuristic in theory formation for they bridge together empirical data and open new vistas for future research. Reinforcement, intelligence, adjustment, learning, superego, oedipus complex, equilibration, etc., are examples of logical constructs used in various fields of psychological theory.

construct, logical See *construct, hypothetical.*

construct, pre-emptive (G. A. Kelly) A construct which cannot be classified in any other way except as the given construct. Right and wrong exemplify such constructs.

construct, preverbal (G. A. Kelly) A construct having no word symbol which may or may not have developed before the person began to talk.

construct, regnant (G. A. Kelly) A construct consisting of elements whose function is to be a part of subordinate constructs.

construct validity (or concept validity) The extent to which a test or operation measures a defined concept or construct, as determined by a correlation coefficient. Since it is mostly factor concepts that can be given measurable form, the term as used in this book refers to a test or test battery's correlation with (loading on) a factor, where the factor is an operationally defined representation of a concept.

construction need See *need, construction.*

consultant psychologist See *psychologist, consultant.*

consulting psychologist See *psychologist, consulting.*

consummatory communication See *communication, consummatory.*

consummatory response See *response, consummatory.*

consummatory stimulus See *stimulus, consummatory.*

contagion The spread of behavior or feelings to

other people through suggestion, imitation or sympathy.

contagion, mass The rapid spread of behaviors among groups of unrelated people who are not necessarily in the same area.

contaminated response A Rorschach response in which an unrealistic mixture of content occurs within a single response. The merging of two or more entirely incompatible concepts makes for an obvious bizarreness indicative of serious disturbance in thought.

contamination 1. (experimental) A spurious relationship between two variables produced by the independent and dependent variables to influence each other. If an experimenter, for example, has knowledge about one variable, it may influence his findings on the other variable. 2. (Rorschach) The fusion of two responses which are objectively separate from each other.

contemporaneous-explanation principle (K. Lewin) The principle that only present events can influence present behavior.

content analysis See *analysis, content.*

content, dream, latent (psychoanalysis) The unconscious wishes and impulses whose meaning is hidden from the dreamer due to the transformation of this content into the manifest content by the dream work.

content, dream, manifest (psychoanalysis) The dream content as the dreamer perceives and remembers it.

content, informational (J. P. Guilford) A parameter of the structure of intellect; it is the substantive aspect of information, by which it is classified in broad categories—figural, symbolic, semantic and behavioral.

content, law of See *law of content.*

content psychology See *psychology, content.*

content response See *response, content.*

content scores One of the major components of Rorschach scoring or coding in which standard abbreviations are used to denote the class of content used in a response such as A for animal, H for human, Bl for blood, etc.

content validity See *validity, content.*

context, theory of meaning See *meaning, context theory of.*

contiguity The propinquity of objects or events in space or in time.

contiguity, law of 1. (Aristotle) The principle that learning is based on the occurrence of stimulus and response close in time or space. Then when one element occurs, the other follows. 2. (E. R. Guthrie) The principle that learning depends upon the proximity in time or space of stimulus and response alone. 3. (C. L. Hull) The hypothesis that learning is based on the proximity of stimulus and response in

time or space which is possible due to the gradual decay of the neural excitation underlying the variables. It is believed however that reward is a necessary adjunct to contiguity.

contiguous conditioning (E. R. Guthrie) The principle that learning is the result of an association of stimuli and response movements by contiguity. Conditioning occurs after only one trial. Forgetting and extinction result from the inhibition of old connections by new incompatible ones, not from the lack of reinforcement.

continence 1. Self-restraint or complete abstinence from sexual activity. 2. The retention of feces and urine.

contingency (statistics) The extent to which the values of one variable depend on the values of another variable.

contingency coefficient (*C*) (statistics) A measure of the relationship between two variables. The coefficient is a measure of the degree to which the variables are non-independent of each other more often than would be expected by chance. The formula is: $C = \sqrt{\dfrac{X^2}{n + X^2}}$ where n is the number of paired values in the two variables, and X^2 refers to Chi square.

contingency method (statistics) A method of measuring the degree to which two variables occur together: the function between actual cell frequencies and the expected cell frequencies in a two-way table.

contingency table A two-way table showing the frequencies of two variables which are entered in the vertical and horizontal rows of the table.

continuity The quality of uninterrupted movement from one element to another which may be temporal, spatial or logical.

continuity-non-continuity (in learning theory) (D. Krech) Terms for alternative assumptions concerning the effects of rewarded and punished responses during discrimination learning. Continuity assumes that the correct response is cumulatively strengthened or weakened with every rewarded or punished choice. Non-continuity assumes that typically the animal first responds on the basis of irrelevant discriminanda prior to making choices based on the correct cues and that only then do rewarded or punished choices affect the acquisition of the correct discrimination. See *hypothesis; discriminandum.*

continuity of germ plasm theory The theory that reproductive germ cells are derived from other reproductive germ cells, not from somatic cells so that any environmental influences on the body cells do not affect hereditary transmission.

continuity, social The transmission of cultural forms from generation to generation by institutions such as the family, school and church.

continuity theory of learning See *learning, continuity theory of.*

continuous avoidance See *avoidance, free operant.*

continuous epilepsy   See *epilepsy, continuous.*

continuous reinforcement (CRF) schedule   See *reinforcement, schedule of: continuous.*

continuous scale   See *scale, continuous.*

continuum   A curve, graph or variable which has no steps between any two points.

contour   The boundary of a figure.

contraception   The prevention of fertilization of the ovum by the sperm by artificial means.

contractility   A fundamental property of a living tissue of shrinking upon stimulation.

contracture   The failure of a muscle to return to its resting position after contraction.

contralateral   Referring to the opposite side of the body.

contrast   The intensification of the difference between two given stimuli produced by the contiguous presentation of these stimuli temporally or spatially.

contrast, brightness   The intensification of the perceived difference in brillance of two objects which results when two visual stimuli are presented either simultaneously or in close succession.

contrast, color   The effect which one color has on another when perceived simultaneously or successively. It involves enhancement of complementary colors by each other and the perception of the complement of a neutral surface when the stimulus color is fixated upon.

contrast, successive   See *contrast, color.*

contrasuggestibility   The tendency for an individual to take on an opposite attitude to that which was suggested to him.

contrectation   The touching of and fondling of another person, usually associated with genital excitation.

control experiment   See *experiment, control.*

control, experimental   The control and arrangement of all extraneous variables, i.e., all variables other than the independent variable, in order that any change in the dependent variable can be considered a function of the independent variable.

control group   See *group, control.*

control, social   The stipulation of rules of conduct by social institutions.

control, stimulus   See *stimulus control.*

controlled sampling   See *sampling, controlled.*

controlled variable   See *variable, controlled.*

conventions, social   The implicit rules and regulations of social conduct which are tacitly agreed upon by the members of the group.

convergence   1. The tendency to move toward one point. 2. The tendency of the eye to move inward toward the source of light so that the image will fall on corresponding parts of the foveas. 3. The inheritance of traits from both father and mother. 4. The principle that a trait is a product of both hereditary and environmental factors. 5. The meeting of two or more nerve impulses from different sensory pathways. 6. (M. Jahoda) The acceptance of an attitude or behavior contrary to one's own because it reflects other valid considerations.

convergence theory   The theory that psychological phenomena result from the interaction of hereditary or acquired specific traits with specific environmental conditions.

convergent production, operation of (J. P. Guilford) Generation of items of information from given items, where the needed information is fully determined by the given information; a search for logical imperatives.

conversion   1. A fundamental diametric change of belief or attitude as of religious beliefs. 2. (psychoanalysis) The transformation of psychological conflicts into physical symptoms. 3. (logic) A change of a proposition caused by interchanging the subject and the predicate which results in a distortion in logic. 4. (psychometrics) The translation of scores from one scale to another.

conversion hysteria   See *hysteria, conversion.*

conversion seizure   See *seizure, conversion.*

conviction   Belief without a doubt.

convolution   A fold on the surface of the cortex of the cerebrum.

convulsion   Involuntary generalized muscular contraction. May be tonic (without relaxation) or clonic (alternating contraction and relaxation).

convulsion, clonic   See *convulsion.*

convulsion, static   A special form of the motor aura of epilepsy which may include forward, backward or related movements.

convulsion, tonic   Persisting contraction of a muscle.

convulsive therapy   See *shock therapy.*

cooperative factor   A factor having the loading pattern on salient variables very similar to that of another independent factor with which its correlation may be negligible.

coordinate   1. (mathematics) A point or line of reference which is used to locate a point in space. 2. Equal in rank. 3. To arrange items according to a specific schema.

coordinated epilepsy   See *epilepsy, coordinated.*

coordination   1. The harmonious functioning of parts, especially of muscles in the performance of an action. 2. The similar relationship of two items of a class to a higher or inclusive class.

coping behavior   (A. Maslow) A behavioral pattern which facilitates adjustment to the environment for the purpose of attaining some goal.

coping style Means by which the person comes to terms with stresses and makes use of opportunities and also the unique organization suggested by the various means employed by the person in adaptive efforts.

coprolaba The uncontrolled use of obscene words.

coprophagia or coprophagy The eating of excrement.

coprophilia An extreme interest in, preoccupation with, or attraction to feces.

coprophobia Morbid fear of excrement.

core construct See *construct, core.*

corium The outer part of the dermis, the layer underlying the epidermis.

cornea The transparent outer part of the sclerotic layer of the eye.

corneal lens See *lens, corneal.*

corneal reflection The reflection of light from the surface of the cornea which is used as a technique for studying and photographing eye movements.

Cornell method (L. Guttman) A technique for determining whether an attitude is scalable by ascertaining whether the attitude in question is unidimensional.

Cornell Selective Index (A. Weider, B. Mittelmann, D. Wechsler and H. G. Wolff) A personality inventory introduced in 1944 designed to screen out psychologically unstable men from the armed forces. It consists of ninety-two questions some of which are starred for immediate attention of the tester.

Cornell Word Form Test See *test, Cornell Word Form.*

corollary 1. A principle which is deduced as a result of proving another proposition. **2.** A natural result.

corpora quadrigemina The four masses of nerve tissue at the posterior of the midbrain, one pair of which is the superior collinculi, the center for usual reflexes and the second pair of which is the inferior collinculi, the center of auditory reflexes.

corpus callosum See *callosum.*

corpus striatum See *striate body, or striatum.*

corpuscle 1. A small rounded particle. **2.** A specialized encapsulated sensory nerve organ. **3.** A cell which floats in the blood or lymph.

corpuscle, Krause's An encapsulated neuronal ending, found primarily in the conjunctiva of the eye, the skin of the nipples, and the genitals, and believed to be one type of receptor for cold. Also called Krause ending and Krause's end bulb.

corpuscle, Meissner An encapsulated end organ found primarily in the hairless surface of the soles of the feet and the palms of the hands which functions as a receptor for touch sensations.

correct rejection (signal detection theory) One of four possible outcomes in a single trial of a signal detection experiment. Noise is presented without a signal and the subject correctly detects the absence of a signal. The other outcomes are a hit, a false alarm and a miss.

correction 1. (statistics) The use of specific techniques to minimize chance errors. **2.** The use of lenses for the eye to improve impaired vision.

correctional psychology See *psychology, correctional.*

correlate (noun) **1.** A variable which is in some way related to another variable; a correlation exists. **2.** A principle that is logically related to another principle or conclusion. (verb) **1.** To put a variable, principle or conclusion in relation to something else. **2.** To calculate the coefficient of correlation.

correlation 1. Any relationship between two variables. **2.** (logic) Any relationship relating two variables such that a change in one of the variables results or is associated with, a change in the other. **3.** (statistics) A concomitant variation; the degree to which two variables vary together.

correlation, biserial (r_{bis}) A correlation in which one of the variables has only two parts or divisions and the other variable has many classes. For example the correlation of age into two classes, old and young.

correlation, bivariate See *correlation, simple.*

correlation center A neurological center where two or more afferent neurons unite to influence an efferent system.

correlation, chance halves See *correlation, split half.*

correlation, cluster A group of variables that are more correlated to each other than to any other group. Any correlation statistically derived from the cluster would be significantly positive.

correlation coefficient (r) (statistics) A numerical index that indicates the degree of relationship of two variables. The Pearson product moment correlation coefficient is the most widely used. The formula is:

$$r = \sqrt{\frac{\Sigma(\tilde{Y}-\bar{Y})^2}{\Sigma(Y_i-\bar{Y})^2}}$$

where $\tilde{Y}$ is the predicted value of Y, $\bar{Y}$ refers to the mean of the Y values, Yi is one of the variables under consideration and Σ means to mathematically sum the values represented by the expressions $(\tilde{Y}-\bar{Y})^2$ and $(Y_i-\bar{Y})^2$. The values of the correlation coefficient can range from -1.00 to $+1.00$ where positive values indicate that a low standing in one variable is associated with a low standing in the other. Negative values indicate an inverse relationship; high standing in one variable is associated with low standing in another.

correlation, curvilinear A correlation whose regression is not linear. It is represented by a curved, rather than a straight line.

correlation graph See *scatter diagram.*

correlation hierarchy A correlation table in which the values are arranged such that the magnitude of correlation either progressively increases or decreases from one corner to the other three. These correlations are seen to originate from common factors.

correlation, index of A measure of the relationship of two variables.

correlation, inverse A correlation between two variables in which increasing values of one variable are related to decreasing values of the other. Also called negative correlation.

correlation, linear A correlation in which the line of regression is in the form of a straight line indicating that for any change in one variable, a proportional change in the other will occur. The degree of correlation is measured by the coefficient of correlation.

correlation, matrix A table which includes the correlation coefficients of every variable with every other variable in a particular set. Each test's correlation with itself is usually included.

correlation, multiple (R) A coefficient showing the relationship between a number of independent variables and one dependent variable. The multiple correlation is most commonly used when a given relationship is due to multiple causation. The formula is:

$$R_{1.23} = \sqrt{\frac{r_{12}^2 - 2r_{12}r_{13}r_{23}r_{13}^2}{1 - r_{23}^2}}$$

where $R_{1.23}$ is the multiple correlation between the dependent variable 1, and variables 2 and 3, and r refers to the correlation between two variables which are specified by the subscripts.

correlation, negative See *correlation, inverse.*

correlation, partial The net correlation between two variables when the influence of other variables on their relationship has been eliminated. The formula is:

$$r_{12.3} = \frac{r_{12} - r_{13}r_{23}}{\sqrt{1 - r_{13}^2}\ \sqrt{1 - r_{23}^2}}$$

where r is the correlation between the variables specified in the subscripts.

correlation, Pearsonian See *correlation, product moment.*

correlation, point-biserial Product moment correlation of a dichotomous variable and a continuous variable.

correlation, polychoric A correlation between two variables which are both continuous and normally distributed. The correlations are plotted in a table containing more than four cells.

correlation, positive Correlation between variables in which great strength or quantity in one is associated with great strength or quantity in the other. The highest positive correlation is 1.

correlation, primary The relationship between two variables which cannot be ascribed to the influence of a third factor.

correlation, product moment The most common form of computing correlation, based on product-moments:

$$r = \Sigma xy / N_{\sigma x \sigma y}$$

which assumes rectilinear regression lines.

correlation, Q See *P technique.*

correlation ratio (η^2) An index of the degree to which a regression line is nonlinear. The formula most commonly used is:

$$\eta^2{}_{yx} = \frac{\Sigma\, n_j (M_{Yj} - M_Y)^2}{\underset{j}{\Sigma}\ \underset{i}{\Sigma}\ (Y_{ij} - M_Y)^2}$$

where $\eta^2{}_{yx}$ is the correlation ratio for the relation of Y to X, n_j is the number of sample observations in the treatment group j, M_{Yj} is the mean for the j observations in group Y, M_Y is the mean error of the total observations in the population Y, Y_{ij} is the value of the ith individual in the jth category in the Y population, and Σ means to mathematically sum all the values represented by the expressions $(M_{Yj} - M_Y)^2$ and $(Y_{ij} - M_Y)^2$.

correlation, secondary The correlation between two variables which is due to the existence of a third variable.

correlation, self Correlation between random halves of a test, two administrations of the same test or between a test and an equivalent form.

correlation, simple The magnitude of the relationship of two variables.

correlation, Spearman foot rule (R) (C. Spearman) A coefficient of correlation which is based on gains in rank from the first variable to the second. The formula is:

$$R = 1 - \frac{\sigma\ \text{x}\ \Sigma_g}{N^2 - 1}$$

where g is the gain by any individual from rank 1 to rank 2, Σ means to add all the values represented by the symbol g, and N refers to the number of cases involved in the ranking.

correlation, split half A method of estimating test reliability by determining the correlation between two comparable halves of a test and applying the Spearman-Brawn formula to compensate for attenuation causing by splitting the test.

correlation, spurious A correlation relationship which is caused by a factor or factors external to the variables involved.

correlation table A table showing the quantitative relationship between two variables. One variable is entered in the horizontal rows and the other in the vertical.

correlation, tetrachoric (r_t) A correlation of two variables that are both continuous and normally distributed, and expressed in terms of only two classes: male-female correlated with dullness-brightness would be an example.

correlation, total The most commonly used form of correlation in which each variable is represented by a series of individual events or scores. This is the correlation of two variables in their original form.

correlation, zero A correlation showing no relationship, or a correlation having a correlation coefficient of zero.

correspondence (statistics) A relationship of two variables such that every individual score of one variable is paired with a score of the other.

correspondence theory (philosophy of science) Also called correspondence rules. A formula translating data and concepts in one field of research in reductionism, when the data and concepts (theoretical reductionism) or the research methods (methodological reductionism) of one science have to be presented as derivations of corresponding data and concepts or research methods of another science.

corresponding points See *identical points*.

corterita, U. I. 22 (R. B. Cattell) The factor of cortical alertness and arousal in objective tests, such as reaction time, flicker fusion speed, etc.

cortex 1. The outer layer of an organ. 2. The cerebral cortex when used without qualification.

cortex, "association" Those parts of the brain which are not directly connected with sensory or motor functions. They are thought to be the areas in which sensations are associated or integrated with motor functions.

cortex, auditory The area of the cortex which registers auditory stimulation.

cortex, frontal The outer layer of the frontal lobes.

cortex, parietal, structure and function of The cutaneous-kinesthetic analyzer which provides the kinesthetic basis of motor activity. It is important for discrimination based upon deep pressure sensitivity. This area follows the principle of functional representation whereby the greater the functional significance of the organ, the greater its area of representation in this central area. In man, the inferior parietal cortex has cutaneous-kinesthetic zones which overlap with the visual analyzers.

cortex, sensory The part of the cerebral cortex which receives neural impulses from the sensory organs via afferent tracts; the sensory projection areas.

corti Refers to the structures of the inner ear such as the organ of Corti, the arches and the rods of Corti.

cortical center 1. Areas in the cortex which consist of the incoming sensory fibers. 2. Areas of the cortex which consist of efferent motor fibers.

cortical epilepsy See *epilepsy, Jacksonian*.

cortical gray The median gray color perceived by the dark-adapted eye under conditions of total darkness.

cortical satiation theory (W. Köhler and H.

Wallach) The representation of a stimulus in the brain involves electrical charges and currents which may, if prolonged due to neural defect or overexposure to the stimulus, so fatigue the cortical area that the flow of neural processes is impaired or stopped.

corticalization An increased control of processes by the cerebral cortex characteristic of organisms who are highly placed in the phylogenetic scale.

corticord substances Hormones secreted by the adrenal cortex which seem to regulate inflammatory reactions to infection.

corticosteroid toxicity See *toxicity, corticosteroid*.

corticotrophic hormone See *hormone, corticotrophic*.

cortin A substance made up of several hormones which is secreted by the adrenal cortex and is important in the regulation of the gonads and the control of salt intake.

cortisone One of the hormones produced in the adrenal cortex or synthetically which is used mainly in adrenal insufficiency.

co-twin control, method of An experimental method to ascertain the effects of environmental influence by keeping heredity constant in which one twin is subjected to an experimental manipulation while the other twin is not. The twins are subsequently compared to assess the differences due to learning or environmental effects.

counseling A form of therapeutic aid offered to individuals to help them understand and resolve their adjustment problems. A variety of diverse techniques are used including the giving of advice, mutual discussion, and administration and interpretation of tests.

counseling, directive A form of counseling in which the counselor controls and stipulates the condition of the interaction.

counseling, director Counseling in which the counselor directs the topics and actively suggests courses of action.

counseling interview See *interview counseling*.

counseling psychology See *psychology, counseling*.

counseling, vocational Counseling concerning employment and vocational adjustment.

counselor A professionally trained individual who practices counseling.

counter (operant conditioning) Stimulus, some dimension of which changes systematically with the number of responses emitted.

counteraction need See *need, counteraction*.

counterconditioning The formation of an alternative response to a stimulus through the establishment of another often incompatible response.

counterego (W. Stekel) The unconscious part of the psyche which is antagonistic to the ego.

countertransference (psychoanalysis) Unconscious feelings evoked in the psychoanalyst by the patient which may adversely affect the necessary objective attitude to the patient and interfere with the treatment.

courts, juvenile Courts of justice which deal with people below the legal age of adulthood. The philosophy of these courts is that the child requires rehabilitation, not punishment. Laws concerning juvenile offenses are vague allowing the judge the opportunity to provide the juvenile offender with the best alternative for obtaining help for his problems.

couvade The custom prevalent among primitive people of the father taking to bed when his child is born in order to recuperate from the pangs of childbirth.

covariance A tendency where a change in one variable is accompanied by a change in another. Covariance is given by the formula:

$$\frac{\Sigma XY}{N}$$

where X and Y are the deviations from the mean, of the two variables in the series, N is the number of cases, and Σ means to take the sum of the values represented by XY.

covariation chart (R. B. Cattell) A correlation chart having three dimensions, people (or organisms), tests (or behavioral preformances), and occasions (on which people and tests interact). The covariation chart shows exhaustively the possibilities of all behavior correlation.

cover memory See *memory, screen.*

covert response See *response, implicit.*

covert sensitization (J. Cautela) A method for overcoming unadaptive appetitive behavior, e.g. overeating or homosexuality, through the verbal evocation of unpleasant responses such as nauseation or disgust. The behavior to be extinguished and the aversive response are evoked simultaneously by verbal cues.

Coxsackie encephalitis See *encephalities, Coxsackie.*

CPI See *California Personality Inventory.*

cramp Painful contraction of a muscle or muscle group which is sustained for a period of time.

cranial capacity The cubic content of the cranium.

cranial division The upper region of the parasympathetic division of the autonomic nervous system.

cranial index See *index, cranial.*

cranial nerves See *nerves, cranial.*

cranial reflex See *reflex, cranial.*

craniography The graphing or photographing of the skull.

craniology (F. J. Gall) The belief that mental abilities are localized in different areas of the brain and that the presence of these faculties are determined by the contours of the skull.

craniometry The measurement of the skull.

craniosacral division The portion of the autonomic nervous system originating in the medulla and lower spinal cord which controls vegetative functions in the body.

cranium The skull, especially the part containing the brain.

creative resultants, principle of (W. Wundt) The principle that the totality of mental processes equals more than the mere summation of the individual elements.

cremnophobia Morbid fear of precipices.

Crespi effect A disproportionate increase in learning or the strength of a response in comparison with the reward given to this behavior.

cretinism Congenital hypothyroidism. Usually no physical signs at birth except for slow physical and mental development. The skin becomes gradually dry and coarse; vocal expression is hoarse; the genitalia remain infantile. Most cretins are of short physical stature and profoundly retarded.

crf schedule See *reinforcement, schedule of: continuous.*

cri du chat syndrome Severe mental defect caused by a portion missing from chromosome 5 and associated with oligophrenia, somatic hypotrophia, microcephaly and not uncommonly, congenital heart disease.

crime A major transgression of the law which is punishable.

criminal psychology See *psychology, criminal.*

criminal responsibility A term specified by law to delimit conditions under which the person is held responsible for his actions and can be punished for them.

criminology The scientific study of crime and criminals and of the social and psychological factors associated with them.

crisis theory See *theory, crisis.*

crisis therapy See *therapy, crisis.*

crispation Mild contraction of muscles, convulsive or spasmodic.

criterion analysis 1. A method of factor analysis using the criterion variable in the test matrix. 2. (H. J. Eysenck) A procedure of factor rotation using two homogeneous groups which are differentiated by the factor which accounts for the greatest amount of variance in the factor matrix.

criterion rotation A form of factor rotation in which the difference existing between a control and an experimental or criterion group is made to be the expression of a single factor.

criterion score See *score, criterion.*

criterion variable See *variable, criterion.*

critical flicker-fusion frequency The rate at which a flickering stimulus ceases to be perceived as such and is seen as a continuous fused stimulus.

critical incident technique See *technique, critical incident.*

critical period A point in development at which the individual is optimally ready to learn a particular response pattern. This concept is much like that of maturational readiness.

critical point 1. A point which has been designated as the dividing point which separates ranked scores into distinct groups with reference to some criterion. 2. (S. R. Slavson) Specific time or stage in therapy during which the individual realizes his problems clearly and decides upon a definite course of action to deal with them in a constructive way.

critical ratio (C. R.) The ratio of the difference between two statistics to the standard error of that difference. It is a measure of how probable it is that the obtained statistic is affected by chance. The most commonly used *CR* involves the difference between two means. The formula for uncorrelated means is $C.R. = \dfrac{M_1 - M_2}{\sqrt{\sigma^2_{M_1} + \sigma^2_{M_2}}}$ where M = mean, and σ = the standard error of the mean. The difference is not regarded as being significant unless the *CR* is at least 3.

critical score The score which divides a group of scores or values into distinct groups with reference to some criterion.

Cro-magnon man An upper Paleolithic man manifesting a high level of physical and mental development characteristic of modern man represented by skulls found in Western Europe.

Cronbach, Lee J. (1916-   ) American psychologist. Developed (with Meehl) theory of construct validation in psychology; developed (with Gleser) interpretation of tests as aid to decision making; formulated (with Snow) strategy for research on aptitude-treatment interaction; elaborated (with Gleser and others) theory of error and generalization in psychometrics; chaired first committee to develop standards for psychological tests; prepared major textbooks on psychological testing and educational psychology.

cross-adaptation The change in an individual's sensitivity to one stimulus as a function of his adaptation to another stimulus regardless of whether or not both stimuli are in the same modality.

cross-conditioning See *conditioning, cross.*

cross-correspondence (parapsychology) A message arising in automatic writing of one medium which can be understood only by another medium.

cross-cultural approach The study of the effects of social practices and environmental influences upon behavior through the investigation and comparison of several cultures.

cross-modal integration The ability to coordinate information acquired by more than one sense, for instance, tactile and visual, or auditory and visual. Reading is based on the ability to coordinate or integrate the visual sensation of a written or printed word with the sound of the same word spoken. Deficiency or failure of cross-modal integration is believed to be one of the causes of dyslexia (the disability to read).

cross-modality matching (S. S. Stevens) A psychophysical experiment in which the subjects are presented with several standard stimuli, for example, five weights, and the response is to adjust the value of a second continuum, such as loudness, so that the second continuum matches the psychological value of each of the standard stimuli.

cross-parental identification See *identification, cross-parental.*

cross-sectional method See *method, cross-sectional.*

cross-validation A method of determining the validity of a technique or research procedure by administering it to a second group to see if the results coincide with the findings obtained from the administration of this procedure to the original group with whom it has been found to be valid.

crossing over See *crossover.*

crossover Exchange of genetic material between members of a chromosome pair. The chiasmata seen at diplotene are the physical evidence of crossing over.

crucial experiment See *experiment, crucial.*

crude mode See *mode, crude.*

crude score See *score, crude.*

cry, epileptic Strange, abrasive sounds made by an epileptic just prior to the arresting of respiration in a grand mal; thought to be caused by the sudden release of air through the glottis which contracts as the tonic spasm begins.

cry, initial See *cry, epileptic.*

cryptogenic epilepsy See *epilepsy, cryptogenic.*

crystal gazing See *gazing, crystal.*

crystalline lens See *lens.*

crystallized general ability (R. B. Cattell) A general factor, largely in a type of abilities learned at school, representing the effect of past application of fluid intelligence, and amount and intensity of schooling, it appears in such tests as vocabulary and numerical ability measures.

crystallophobia Morbid fear of glass.

crystasthesia A form of perception which is not explainable in terms of known receptors such as clairvoyance or mental telepathy.

crytococcus meningitis See *meningitis, crytococcus.*

crytomnesia The appearance of ostensibly novel experiences, memories, or thoughts, which originate in forgotten or repressed experiences.

cue 1. A signal which elicits behavior based on previous experience. 2. A signal in the perceptual field which the organism uses to make a discrimination.

cue, incidental   See *stimulus, incidental.*

cue reduction   The phenomenon whereby one aspect of a stimulus can elicit a response which was previously evoked by the whole response.

cue reversal   The interchanging of a cue which signaled reward with the cue which signaled nonreward in an experimental situation.

Cullen, William (1710-1790)   Scottish physician who introduced a broad classification of diseases, inclusive of mental illnesses. He coined the term neurosis for diseases which had no local pathology nor caused fever. He divided all neuroses into comata (strokes), adynamias (diseases of the autonomic nerves), spasms (convulsions), and vesanias (mental deficiencies and insanities).

cultural adaptability   The ability of migratory groups to accept the culture of the country they migrated to. Also called acculturation.

cultural anthropology   A branch of anthropology which studies the manners, morals, and social relations of various societies, tribes, and ethnic groups.

cultural deprivation   Substandard living conditions and/or discrimination which prevent certain individuals from participation in the cultural achievements of their society. Cultural deprivation is often quoted among the causes of mental retardation.

cultural determinism   The belief that the culture determines personality structure.

cultural disorganization   A breakdown of traditional cultural bonds and of the importance of values due to transition within a society or the transition of an individual from one society to another.

cultural lag   Residues of cultural values from bygone days, not related to the present day culture.

cultural norm   A set of cultural values generally accepted in a given society.

cultural parallelism   (cultural anthropology) The appearance of similar cultures in two places or two epochs without any connections or influence between the two cultures.

cultural pressure   A dimension found by factoring variables defining modern nations and loading cultural productivity, e.g., Nobel prizes, urbanization, indices of frustration and sublimation, frequency of war, etc.

cultural relativism   The belief that mental health and mental disorder do not have a universal meaning but depend on cultural norms of each particular society. Accordingly people believed to be mentally disturbed could be believed to be normal in another society.

culture   1. The way a certain society lives. 2. The totality of manners, customs, values, of a given society, inclusive of its socioeconomic system, political structure, science, religion, education, art and entertainment. 3. The intellectual aspects of life, such as science, art and religion.

culture area   Geographical boundaries of a culture.

culture epoch theory   A theory that all societies pass through the same periods in their history. A. Comte's theory of the theological, metaphysical and positive stages, and Hegel's thesis, antithesis and synthesis theory are representative examples.

culture-free test   A psychological test that can be administered to individuals in any culture. Test results are not affected by cultural factors.

culture trait   1. Personality trait common to all people belonging to a certain culture. 2. A material or symbolic element of a given culture.

cumulative   1. Constituting that which has been successively put together or summed as each new quantity is added. 2. (statistics) Referring to a method of representing a distribution in which the sum of all elements is taken from the beginning to a certain point by adding each figure successively to the next until all the cases in the distribution have been represented.

cumulative curve   A graphic representation of the sums of the frequencies of a series of scores. Each point on the curve represents the summed total of the number of cases at and below that point (or at and above).

cumulative deficits phenomenon   (M. Deutsch) With persistent influence from a disadvantaged environment there is, over time, an increasingly larger negative effect on the behavior in question.

cumulative distribution   A type of frequency distribution where each plot represents the summed total of the number of cases falling at or below that point (or at or above that point).

cumulative frequency   A graphical or numerical accumulation of cases in which each new case is added to the preceding total.

cumulative frequency curve   See *cumulative curve.*

cumulative record   A continuous summative record to which new data are added to the preceding total.

cumulative scale   See *scale, Guttman.*

cumulative tests   See *tests, cumulative.*

cuneus   A wedge-shaped area on the middle surface of the occipital lobe of the cerebrum.

cunnilingus   Oral stimulation of the female genitals.

cunnus   The external genitals of the female.

Curtis completion form   Projective test used with children 11 and over in which sentences are completed. Scoring method is partially objective, yielding a cumulative point score.

curve, acquisition cumulative   The graphic representation of the rate of response in operant conditioning in which the slope of the cumulative curve reflects the response rate.

curve, asymptotic   A curve which constantly approaches a straight line but never reaches it.

curve, bell-shaped   The graph of a normal distribution.

curve, distribution Also called frequency curve, or probability curve, represents graphically the frequency of occurrence.

curve, fitting Finding the curve best representing particular empirical data.

curve, J (F. H. Allport) A graphic representation of the frequency with which individuals comply with a rule or standard lying within the range of their capacity. The curve approximates the shape of the capital letter J.

curve, Jordan (topology) A closed curve of any shape which does not intersect itself, usually used to define regions of life space.

curve, learning See *learning, curve.*

curve, logarithmic A curve in which each point along one coordinate is the logarithm of the value of the other coordinate. The equation is $y = \log x$. Also called logistic curve.

curve, mental growth A graphic representation of mental development as a function of chronological age in which mental age is plotted on the vertical axis and chronological age is on the horizontal axis.

curve, normal distribution (K. B. Gauss) A bell-shaped curve which is a graphic description of a theoretical function having as its domain all of the real numbers. It is continuous for all values of a variable x between $-\infty$ and $+\infty$; therefore the graph never touches the horizontal axis. The tails of the curve show decreasing probability densities as the values of x become extreme in any direction. The distribution is absolutely symmetric and unimodal. The mean, median and mode all have the same value of x. The height of the curve, denoted by y refers to the probability density for each value of x. The entire area cut off beneath the curve by any interval is a probability. The mathematical rule for a normal density function is

$$f(x) = \frac{1}{\sqrt{2\pi\sigma^2}} \, e - \frac{x - \mu}{2\sigma^2}$$

where π and e are mathematical constants, x is the value of the variable, μ is the mean and σ^2 is the variance.

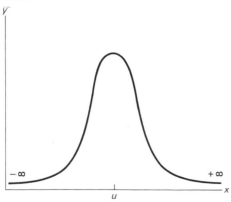

curve of rest A graphic description of the gradual change of the psychogalvanic skin response under conditions of no stimulation.

curve, percentile (statistics) An ogival-shaped cumulative frequency curve which indicates the cumulative frequencies as percentages of the total number of cases.

curve, performance Curve which measures and graphically illustrates performance of a particular behavior as a function of some other variable such as learning, incentive, or time. Such curves are often referred to as learning curves, though what is actually measured is performance.

curve, retention (H. E. Ebbinghaus) A graphic representation of the amount of learned material which is remembered over a period of time consisting of a measure of remembering on the vertical axis and a measure of the time elapsed since learning on the horizontal axis.

curve, S Referring to a curve that is shaped like an S.

curvilinear correlation See *correlation, curvilinear.*

curvilinear regression See *regression, curvilinear.*

curvilinear relationship A relationship between two variables which is graphically represented by a curved rather than a straight line.

custodial care Hospitalization without treatment. For a long time mental hospitals were (some still are) institutions that practiced custodial care.

cut-off whole A special classification for scoring Rorschach responses which involve the subject's use of two thirds or more of the blot and the deliberate exclusion of the remainder of the blot to make for a better response. This category, generally scored with the symbol W, was devised by Klopfer and has been adopted in most approaches to the Rorschach although strongly argued against in the Beck approach.

cutaneous sense See *sense, cutaneous.*

cybernetics (N. Wiener) A science of communication, information and of feedback and control mechanisms which uses servomechanisms.

cycle disorder Any behavior disorder with distinct reversal of moods. See *manic-depressive psychosis; dysmutualism.*

cycle, manic-depressive The change of mood from depression to elation and reverse, typical of manic-depressive patients.

cyclophoria A rotated deviation of the eye due to a muscular imbalance.

cycloplegia See *mydriasis.*

cyclothyme 1. One who exhibits alternating changes of mood from elation and hyperactivity, to depression and sadness. 2. (E. Kretschmer) Person who has a *cyclothymic* temperament, one of two basic temperaments.

cyclothymia Uneven pattern of mood changes from elation and hyperactivity to depression and sadness.

cyclothymic (E. Kretschmer) One of two basic temperament classification associated most frequently with the pyknic body-type and characterized by shifts in mood. The extreme cases of cyclothymics develop manic-depressive psychosis.

cyclothymic personality Also called affective personality with periods of depression, worry, low energy, pessimism and alternating periods of elation, ambition, enthusiasm and optimism.

cyclothymic type See *type, cyclothymic*.

cynonthropy A delusion that oneself is a dog.

cynorexia See *hyperphagia*.

cypridophobia An extreme fear of contracting venereal disease.

cystathioninuria A rare aminoaciduria associated with mental retardation.

cytogenetics Area of biology concerned with the study of heredity from the viewpoints of cytology and genetics.

cytology Area of biology dealing with the study of cells, their formation, structure and functions.

cytomegalic inclusion body disease A viral disease; when occurring in pregnant women may affect the fetus and cause congenital mental deficiency. Inclusion bodies can be discovered in urine and the cerebral fluid.

D

D **1.** Symbol for drive. **2.** (statistics) The symbol for the measure of the scattering of values around a mean or median which includes the middle four-fifths of the cases or the cases between the tenth and the ninetieth percentiles of a frequency distribution. **3.** (statistics) The difference between two scores of the same person. **4.** (statistics) The symbol for the measure of similarity between set of numbers given by the formula

$$D_{12}{}^2 = \sum_{j-1}^{k} (x_{j1} - x_{j2})^2$$

where $j=$ the number of k variables; the numbers 1 and 2 refer to the two sets of scores and x_{j1} and x_{j2} are the scores of the two sets on variable j. **5.** (H. Rorschach) A response to parts of an inkblot card in the Rorschach test, which are conspicuous in size. It is believed to indicate interest in the obvious, practical and concrete. **6.** (C. Hull) The symbol for the strength of the primary drive which motivates an animal to action after the acquisition of the specific habit involved in the action. It is computed by the formula:

$$D = \frac{D' \times D}{\overset{\circ}{D}}.$$

7. (K. Spence) The symbol for the logarithmic difference between the stimulus used to train an animal and the one used to test him.

d **1.** (statistics) Symbol for deviation. **2.** (statistics) The deviation of a class from the mean of a population. **3.** (statistics) The discrepancy between the rank a person receives on two tests. **4.** (Rorschach) A score for a response to small visual details of an inkblot card. **5.** Diopter. **6.** Drive. **7.** The number of just noticeable differences found between two stimulus groups.

d' **1.** (C. Hull) Symbol for $\overset{\circ}{D} - D$. **2.** (signal detection theory) An index of the subject's sensitivity in a signal detection sensory experiment. It is the difference between the mean of the distribution of the noise alone from the mean of the distribution of the noise and signal together divided by the standard deviation. The difference between the two distributions are given in terms of standard scores, like Z scores:

$$d' = \frac{M_{SN} - M_N}{\sigma_N}.$$

D' (C. L. Hull) The symbol of primary drive components not operative in the formation of a habit.

$\overset{\circ}{D}$ (C. L. Hull) The symbol of primary drive components not operative in the formation of a habit.

$\bar{D}$ (C. L. Hull) Symbol equal to the formula

$$100 \; \frac{D + D}{\overset{\cdot}{D} + Md.}$$

d reaction test See *test, d reaction.*

d reaction time See *time, d reaction.*

dacrygelosis An obsolete term which indicates alternate spells of crying and laughter.

dactylology 1. One-hand alphabet in which symbols are expressed with the fingers. **2.** Manual communication of the type generally used by deaf-mutes.

daemon; daimon 1. In ancient Greek mythology: a guiding spirit. **2.** In medieval terms: an evil spirit that enters a person's body and controls his mind and forces him to act in a bizarre and often antisocial manner.

daemonic; daimonic 1. An obsessive thought or feeling that dominates a person's behavior. **2.** (R. May) A powerful, uncontrollable drive; a blind push toward self-assertion mainly in rage and sex.

daemonic character (S. Freud) A self-destructive drive in masochistic individuals; an expression of the death instinct. The individuals with this self-destructive drive tend to repeat the same actions despite the damage caused to themselves, as if possessed by a daemon.

daemonophobia A morbid fear of being attacked by daemons.

dainties, craving for An uncontrollable desire for delicacies or some special food. See *opsomania.*

Daltonism Red-green color blindness after the English scientist John Dalton (1766-1844), himself color-blind, who gave the first description of this condition.

damping   The checking or restraining of the amplitude of a vibration either due to sudden or progressive external pressure or internal friction.

damping constant   The role of decrease of the amplitude presented by a mathematical formula

$$\frac{\sigma}{T}$$

where δ stands for the amplitude, and T stands for the period of time.

dance therapy   See *psychotherapy, dance.*

dancing madness   Frenzied dancing such as occurred in Germany during the 14th century. This type of convulsive dance seemed to spread among the masses like an epidemic. It accompanied the outbreak of the Bubonic plague or "Black Death." (1334-1351). See *choreomania* or *choromania; epidemic chorea.*

dancing mania   1. An abnormal impulse to dance. 2. A form of psycho-motor over-activity which may take place in conjunction with religious experiences. See *dinomania.*

dancing mouse   A breed of mouse with a characteristic walking pattern often used in psychological experimentation.

DAP   See *test, Draw-A-Person.*

dark adaptation   The process by which the eye becomes sensitive to visual stimuli illuminated by weak light. The process is dependent on the resynthesis of visual purple, rhodopsin, by the rod elements of the retina. See *scotopic adaptation.*

Darwin, Charles Robert (1802-1882)   Born in Shrewsbery, England and educated at the universities of Edinburgh and Cambridge. In "*The expression of emotions in man and animals*" and "*The descent of man and selection in relation to sex*" he made outstanding contributions to psychology by showing the possibility of not only the evolution of the organic structure but also of the mental functions. Darwin's theory of evolution has become a cornerstone in comparative psychology. Lloyd Morgan, Sechenov, Pavlov, Freud and the functionalists have been inspired by Darwin's theories.

darwinism   The theory of evolution proposed by Charles Darwin, that through the process of natural selection all organisms have evolved from earlier and primitive organisms. This results in a view of phylogenetic continuity from the primitive to the sophisticated species of organisms.

DAT   See *test, differential aptitude.*

data   Plural of datum. Group of factual items collected by observation or experimentation upon which inferences and conclusions are based.

data processing   A mathematical analysis and description of data.

datum   Singular of data. An item of information.

day blindness   An abnormality of the eye in which the central fovea of the retina does not accommodate to high intensities of light stimulation. In such cases, bright light is uncomfortable and vision is better in dim light.

day dream   See *dream, day.*

day-dreamer   One who indulges in waking reveries.

day hospital   See *hospital, day.*

day residues   Remembrances of experiences of the previous day which, in part, determine the manifest content of a dream.

daylight vision   See *photopic vision.*

daymare   An acute state of anxiety of distress induced by fantasies during the waking state.

Dd   (H. Rorschach) Response to small unusual details in an inkblot card which are perceptually well articulated and which reflect an interest in the fine aspects of situations.

dd   (H. Rorschach) Response to tiny unusual details in an inkblot card.

Dds   (H. Rorschach) A response to small unusual details having a small white space which is meaningful in determining the response.

DDT poisoning   See *poisoning, DDT.*

DdW   (H. Rorschach) A response to a whole inkblot card determined by a small unusual detail which suggests the given percept.

de   1. (H. Rorschach) Response to tiny unusual edge details in an inkblot card which is believed to indicate anxiety and evasion on the part of the subject. 2. See *threshold, difference.*

deaf mute   One who can neither hear nor speak.

deafness   Inability to hear sounds. Total deafness is an inability to detect all auditory stimuli. Selective deafness is the loss of sensitivity to a specific range of auditory stimuli. Adventitious deafness is due to injury to the ear, whereas congenital deafness is due to a defect in development. Cortical deafness is due to a malfunction in some area of the cerebral cortex; and nerve deafness results from a malfunction in the pathway from the inner ear to the auditory cortex.

deafness, conduction   Deafness due to impairment of the conduction structures, the outer ear, eardrum or the middle ear so that sound waves are obtained on their way to the inner ear.

deafness, hysterical   A form of deafness despite the apparent lack of physiological defect. Hysterical deafness is one of several psychoneurotic conversion reactions, in which the anxiety resulting from an unconscious conflict is converted to some debilitating organic symptom. The specific symptom that develops usually has some compensatory value for the individual.

de-anal   Transfer of instinctual impulses from the anal region to some other mode of expression.

de-anality   Referred to instinctual impulses when they find expression in ways unrelated to the anal region.

de-analize When instinctual impulses have been transferred from the anal region to some other mode of expression they are said to have been de-analized.

death Cessation of bodily and mental functions vital to the organism.

death feigning The immobility of some animals in the presence of a threat.

death instinct See *Thanatos*.

death phantasy Imagining oneself as being dead, and at the same time being aware of what is going on. Typical for manic-depressive patients who often imagine themselves lying in a coffin and watching the reaction of their families and relatives.

death rate The ratio of the number of individuals who died at a stated time and place to the total number of individuals at that time and place.

debilitas animi An archaic term for mental retardation.

debilitas erethisica An archaic term for pathological irritability.

debility A physical weakness and lack of vigor.

decadence The deterioration of an individual or society resulting from social rather than biological or physical factors.

deceit, studies of (H. Hartshorne and M.A. May) Studies of character reported in 1930 in which three areas of moral behavior were assessed: the subject's moral knowledge, his moral attitudes and opinions, and his actual moral behavior. Children, grades five to eight, were tested. Questionnaires and inventories examined moral knowledge and opinions and objective tests ascertained actual behavior. It is believed that these tests of honesty measure deceitfulness, dishonesty, and unfairness. The studies have been criticized because deceit does not seem to be a general measure but specific in particular situations.

decile Referring to a division which contains one tenth of the cases in a given distribution of ranked scores.

decontextualization (R. R. Sears) A defensive process in which external stimuli (e.g., persons, places, objects) associated with a previous anxiety-evoking experience are avoided or ignored.

defective, high-grade A classification of intellectual endowment ranging from IQ 50-69 referring to a person of subnormal intelligence who can adapt to concrete situations with a minimum of supervision.

defense, isolation (Rorschach) Isolated comments about the inkblots, rather than responses to them, thought to indicate an effort to avoid those aspects of the blots which may evoke feelings of conflict or anxiety.

defense mechanism The term "defense mechanism" was introduced by Freud in 1894. In 1936 Anna Freud described defense mechanisms in detail. Defense mechanisms are methods used by the ego in fighting off the instinctual outbursts of the id and

the attacks of the superego. A strong ego does not typically use defense mechanisms, but when it is unable to cope with id and superego pressures, it may resort to the use of these mechanisms. Therefore, all defense mechanisms, except sublimation, indicate an inner conflict and a state of anxiety.

defense, perceptual Selective perception of stimuli by which anxiety-provoking stimuli are kept from awareness. Experimentally it has been shown that taboo or offensive words, presented rapidly within a series of neutral words, are either not seen or misperceived, by the subject.

defensive strategies (G. M. Gilbert) In contrast to defense mechanisms, defensive strategies involve long-range and overt behavior patterns, especially social role assumptions and interpersonal relations, which serve the purpose of ego enhancement and defense. Examples are: manipulative or opportunistic affiliation, reactive or compensatory aggression.

deference need See *need, deference*.

deficiency, mental Subnormal intellectual development. Adaptation to the social environment and emotional adjustment as well as the development of learning ability are used in assessing mental-deficiency. IQ scores in intelligence tests more than two standard deviations below the mean are generally considered to be in the mentally deficient range but overall social or behavioral adjustment is the primary consideration in the determination of mental deficiency. IQ scores two to three standard deviations below the mean are in the range of mild mental deficiency; scores three to four standard deviations below the mean are in the moderate range; scores four to five standard deviations below the mean are in the severe range; and scores more than five standard deviations below the mean are in the profound range.

deflection strain The strain occasioned by the organism's acceptance of goals or paths-to-goals that are substitutes, in the sense of not being innately preferred; for example, escaping a fire by first moving towards it. Similar to the concept of sublimation, but broader in that it includes acceptance of substitute paths as well as substitute goals.

deletion A form of chromosomal aberration in which a portion of chromosome is lost, for example, of the short arm of chromosome 5 in the Cri du chat syndrome.

delinquency An infraction of the moral or legal code; if by an individual under 16 or 18 years of age, depending on state law, it is referred to as juvenile delinquency.

delinquency area A neighborhood in which the incidence of delinquency is disproportionally high.

delinquency, juvenile Relatively minor violation of legal or moral codes by a child or an adolescent which brings him to the attention of a court.

delinquent One who offends by negligence, neglect, or violation of a duty or responsibility, or by a minor infraction of a law.

deliramentum An archaic term for delirium.

deliratio senum An archaic term for senile psychosis.

deliration An archaic term for delirium.

délire A French term used sometimes to mean delirium, mania, or paranoia.

délire à quatre A shared, systematized set of delusions, often of persecution, originating first in one person but then spreading to three others.

délire d'emblée (E. Bleuler) A delusion that is complete and stabilized at its outset.

délire d'énormité (E. Bleuler) The delusion that the amount of urine to be passed will cause a flood. Consequently such patients may refrain from urinating for long periods of time.

délire de négation An archaic term for withdrawal symptoms.

délire de négation généralise An archaic term referring to a complete withdrawal from the world, in which the patient has come to believe that the world no longer exists.

délire du toucher A compulsion to touch things.

délire tremblant Delirium tremens.

delirium A non specific term for mental confusion. Often accompanied by delusions and hallucinations. It may be a result of organic brain damage, drugs, fevers, and shock.

delirium abstinence A delirious state caused by the discontinuation of the habitual use of one of several drugs or alcohol.

delirium, acute (E. Bleuler) A delirium thought to be caused by an infection or schizophrenic processes resulting in convulsions and often, death.

delirium, alcoholicum Delirium tremens.

delirium ebriosorum Delirium tremens.

delirium grandiosum Megalomania.

delirium metamorphosis An archaic term for the delusion that the individual's body has turned into a body of a beast.

delirium, oneiric An archaic term referring to a delirium accompanied by hallucinations of which the individual has no memory.

delirium sine materia An archaic term for a delirium with no apparent physiological cause.

delirium tremefaciens Delirium tremens.

delirium tremens An acute delirium precipitated usually by alcoholic poisoning but also occurring as a result of brain inflammation and senile psychosis. It is characterized by intense tremors, anxiety, hallucinations, and delusions.

delirium verborum A delirious state characterized by great verbiage.

delirium vesanicum A non-specific archaic term for a delirium that includes hallucinations, delusions, incoherence, illusions, etc.

delta movement See *movement, delta*.

delusion 1. A perception contrary to reality despite evidence and common sense. 2. An irrational and obstinate belief in an idea. 3. A system of irrational beliefs that the individual actively defends.

delusion, asthenic (P. Janet) Delusions accompanied by psychasthenic activity; the critical powers cease to function and all emotions, thoughts, and acts are expressed.

delusion, autopsychic (K. Wernicke) One of a classification of delusions suggested by K. Wernicke. When the individual's personality is the subject of the delusion, it is an autopsychic delusion. When the outside world is the subject of the delusion, it is an allopsychic delusion. When the individual's body is the subject of the delusion, it is a somatopsychic delusion.

delusion, catathymic (E. Bleuler) A delusion caused by the affective content of a complex in the unconscious.

delusion, expansive The same as delusion of grandeur.

delusion, explanatory (E. Bleuler) Refers to the evidence that an individual gives in offering proof of the truth of his delusions. The evidence itself is delusionary.

delusion, healthy (C. B. Farrar) The opinion that whether an idea is acceptable or is branded as a delusion depends on its source.

delusion of grandeur The exaggerated belief of the individual that he is a great man. He may believe himself to be God, Napoleon, a prince, or a general.

delusion of interpretation An interpretation of a delusion given by the individual himself.

delusion of observation The same as delusion of reference.

delusion of persecution An irrational belief that the individual is a victim of a conspiracy to kill him or to injure him or cause him to fail. It is most common in paranoid individuals where even seemingly innocuous events are taken as proof of the conspiracy.

delusion of reference The false belief of the individual that behaviors of others have malign and derogatory reference to the individual when in fact they have no reference to the individual at all.

delusion, psychasthenic See *delusion, asthenic*.

delusion, residual (C. Neisser) Refers to delusions that are formed in an acute state and maintained in a chronic state.

delusional system A system of false beliefs which is resistant to other points of view.

demand Any aspect of an organism's internal or external environment that results in a drive.

demand character (Gestalt) A stimulus arouses and

directs the appropriate behavior of an organism. The music demands to be listened to or the chocolate cake to be tasted.

dementia Non-specific but lasting deterioration of emotion or intellectual powers.

dementia agitata (R. Krafft-Ebing) An agitated state of individuals suffering from dementia praecox.

dementia, alcoholic The first state of deterioration in Korsakov's alcoholic psychosis.

dementia apoplectica The dementia due to cerebral hemorrhage or softening of brain tissues possibly due to cerebral arteriosclerosis.

dementia arteriosclerotic Dementia due to cerebral arteriosclerosis. The same as dementia apoplectica.

dementia atrophic Presenile psychosis.

dementia depressive (E. Kraepelin) See *schizophrenia, catatonic type.*

dementia, endogenous (E. Kraepelin) Dementias are endogenous if they: a) arise from internal causes, and, as far as can be seen, are not occasioned by external causes; b) result in more or less general enfeeblement. This distinction is now no longer maintained.

dementia, epileptic Deterioration in an epileptic individual, the cause of which apparently is variable from individual to individual.

dementia infantilis A degenerative disease of the neurons in the cerebral lobes occurring at about three years of age which leads to a rapid loss of speech and some impairment of motor functions.

dementia, paralytic See *paresis.*

dementia, paralytica Archaic term for paresis.

dementia paranoides (E. Kraepelin) Archaic term for schizophrenia, paranoid type.

dementia post-traumatic Impairment of intellectual functioning subsequent to a head injury.

dementia praecocissima (S. de Santis) Any of the schizophrenic symptoms appearing in children under five years of age.

dementia praecox Schizophrenia.

dementia praecox, agitated (E. Kraepelin) A subclass of schizophrenia or dementia praecox distinguished from other forms of schizophrenia by extreme agitation. This term was never widely accepted in the U.S.A.

dementia praesenilis Gradual loss of mental powers, intellectual or emotional, seen usually in elderly individuals; however, if observed in younger individuals called dementia praesenilis.

dementia, primary Simple schizophrenia.

dementia psychoasthenic (P. Janet) From an archaic nosology in which much behavior of schizophrenics is thought to be due to psychological exhaustion arising from uncontrolled thoughts, emotions, illusions, and delusions.

dementia sejunctiva Rare term for schizophrenia.

dementia semantica A verbal reaction void of feelings.

dementia, senile The impairment of intellectual functioning in elderly individuals. It occurs with senile brain disease.

dementia simplex Archaic term for simple schizophrenia.

dementia, traumatic Intellectual or emotional deterioration caused by injury.

dementive schizophrenia (B. B. Wolman) The final stage of deterioration in schizophrenia. The ego and superego no longer interfere with the action of the id, and personality structure breaks down.

demissio animi Archaic word for melancholia.

demi-vierge (M. Prevost) Refers to a woman that physically is a virgin but psychologically is not a virgin.

democratic group 1. Group based on democratic principles. 2. (K. Lewin) An experimental group in sociopsychological research, in which the group members are free to choose whomever they wish to work with, and the leader refrains from imposing his will upon the members of the groups.

demography The statistical study of human populations including birth and death rates, income, geographic distribution, mental measurements, etc.

demon See *daemon.*

demonia Morbid fear of demons.

demoniac Archaic term for a mentally disturbed person.

demonolatry Worship of a demon or devil.

demonology Study of folklore, mythology, and theology dealing with demons and evil spirits.

demonomania Obsession with demons.

demono-melancholia Same as demonomania.

demophobia Morbid fear of crowds.

demoralization, personal (R. Park) When an individual reorganizes some values and habits without a concomitant reorganization of his life.

demorphinization Termination of the use of morphine.

demyelination Loss of myelin.

denarcism When the individual is no longer attached to himself; when the psychic energy has been directed to objects external to the individual.

denatured alcohol poisoning See *poisoning, ethyl alcohol.*

dendrite The part of a nerve cell that receives an impulse from other nerves and carries the impulse toward the nerve body.

dendron Same as *dendrite.*

dendrophilia Love of trees.

dendropsychosis A strong interest in trees, not necessarily pathological.

denervation Prevention of the functioning of nerves in part of the body by removing or sectioning them.

denial Sometimes the weak ego rejects not the past but the present; the defense mechanism called denial is involved in such a rejection. When its actual current life becomes too painful to accept or too difficult to cope with, the infantile ego withdraws from reality, breaking away from the truth, and refusing to acknowledge the existence of painful facts. Memory and perceptions prevent an unlimited escape from reality; but in some pathological cases the hard-pressed ego gives up reality-testing and simply denies facts. Some persons go so far as to deny the loss of beloved ones by acting as if the latter were still around.

denotation Signifying or designating objects or concepts by some sign, gesture, symbol or word. Distinguished from connotation in which significant aspects are implied rather than denoted.

density 1. A quality characteristic of some types of stimuli; some psychologists maintain that an elementary characteristic of a tone is density, distinct from pitch, volume or timbre with its own absolute and differential thresholds. 2. In statistical theory the probability of instances of a range of events in a continuous probability distribution.

dental age Dental development measured by the number of permanent teeth a child has to the average number of permanent teeth for his age group.

dentate nucleus A complex of gray nerve cells, shaped like teeth, located in the cerebellum. There is some evidence that it is involved with the experience of emotion.

Denver system Classification of chromosomes in a descending order of magnitude, with number one the largest and twenty-two the smallest of the autosomal chromosomes.

de-oral Removal of oral impulses from the oral zones.

de-orality The expression of psychic energy normally expressed through the oral region being expressed through some other region.

dependence 1. A relationship between two phenomona in which the occurrence or maintenance of one phenomonon is a necessary condition for the occurrance or maintenance of the other. 2. A reliance on other individuals for the formation and maintenance of opinions and ideas.

dependence need See *need, dependence.*

dependence, oral (psychoanalysis) Wish to be taken care by the mother or a mother substitute.

dependency 1. An action system for which another person's nurturant, helping, caretaking and affectionate activities are the rewarding environmental events; supplicative behavior that elicits such responses from others. 2. (psychoanalysis) An emotional relationship, as above, established in the oral stage of infancy.

dependency motive Motivation based on a need to be cared for or to gain support through affiliation.

dependent 1. An individual whose social, economic or intellectual wellbeing is maintained by some other individual. 2. A factor contingent upon another factor.

dependent variable See *variable, dependent.*

depersonalization A feeling in an individual that he is no longer himself. His personality, his body, external events, the whole world may no longer appear real.

depolarization In the normal resting stage of a neuron an electrical equilibrium is established across the neural cell membrane such that the inside of the cell is negatively charged to usually about -70 to -80 millivolts. This is a result of a high concentration of negatively charged ions inside the cell and positively charged ions outside the cell. The membrane normally prevents the positive ions from entering the cell thereby maintaining the equilibrium. When the neuron is fired, the cell membrane permits the positive ions to enter the cell and the depolarization across the membrane takes place. This is the mechanism of neural transmission.

depraved appetite Archaic term for *pica*, a craving for unnatural foods.

depression Feelings of helplessness, hopelessness, inadequacy, and sadness. These may be symptomatic of several disorders; however, these feelings occur also in normal individuals.

depression, adolescent Mild depression often accompanied with hypochondria and anxiety, usually seen in young men and women.

depression, agitated A syndrome of abnormal behavior characterized by overactivity, restlessness and tension so that the patient can remain still for only short periods fo time. The agitated-depressed patient is extremely anxious and apprehensive, expecting impending doom. He tends to talk about his fears and despair, and often expresses self-hatred. He shows his depression and suffering as he paces back and forth, wringing his hands, moaning and crying. He is prone to acting out in a hostile manner against others as well as against himself.

depression, ambivalent (E. Minkowski) Depression in which ambivalence is an outstanding symptom.

depression, anaclitic (R. Spitz) Syndrome observable in infants having lost their primary care takers and/or object choices in which aggressive and sexual drives, due to the absence of the preferred and accustomed object, are turned inward.

depression, constitutional Depression thought to have been related to body type or physical constitution of the individual. However, there has been no proof of this.

depression, cyclical Another term for *manic-depres-*

sive, depressed type. A recurring mood disorder characterized by a severely depressed state and by mental and motor retardation; uneasiness, apprehension, perplexity, and agitation may also be present.

depression, involutional Another term for *involutional melancholia*; a mood disorder occurring in older age characterized by worry, anxiety, agitation and insomnia, often with guilt feelings.

depression, listless (J. MacCaudy) The individual responds to depressive ideas with effortless resignation.

depression, reactive A transient depression attributed to some experience; the individual usually has no history of repeated depressions.

depression, retarded A depression in which normal activities are impaired.

depression, stuporous A severe depression in which normal activities are omitted.

depressive anxiety The anxiety that may accompany a depression.

depressive neurosis An excessive depression due to an internal conflict or identifiable event.

depressive reaction A transient depression due to some event; the individual usually does not have a history of recurrent depressions.

depressor nerve An afferent nerve which depresses motor activity when stimulated, usually a nerve that lowers arterial blood pressure by vasodilation and lowering heart rate.

deprivation Dispossession or removal of a needed or desired object. Food and/or water deprivation is often used for a specified duration in animal experiments to create within the organism some definable level of drive; e.g. hungry 22 hours.

deprivation amentia (A. Tredgold) Obsolete term for mental deficiency due to the lack or insufficiency of some necessary factors. These factors may be physiological or social.

deprivation, sensory A level of stimulation that has been reduced or altered so that it no longer conforms to the individual's normal range or kind of stimulation. Two kinds of deprivations are absolute, reduction and reduced patterning. The former is an attempt to eliminate all stimulus inputs. The latter indicates a situation in which stimulus-input levels are maintained near normal but the patterns inherent in the input are modified or destroyed. Sensory isolation indicates a situation in which the social dimensions, interpersonal communication is limited or absent.

deprivation, sleep, effects of The chronic prevention of sleep causes psychotic behavior, a decrease in performance on psychological tests, and in EEG alpha activity. It was found that by the fourth day of wakefulness, the metabolism of carbohydrates increases providing the body with an emergency energy supply needed to master the stress of non-sleep. However, by the seventh day, these emergency provisions begin to fail, producing a decrease in arousal.

This decreased arousal has been suggested as the cause of the psychotic disturbance because of the partial or total blocking of sensory input associated with this level of arousal.

deprivation syndrome See *syndrome, deprivation*.

deprivation, thought A disturbance in which thoughts are interrupted either by the cessation of thoughts for various periods of time or a thought is obstructed and followed by another, unrelated thought.

depth In sensory psychology the perceived distance from the subject of visual or auditory stimuli.

depth interview An interview conducted in a permissive atmosphere with freedom for the individual to express himself without fear of disapproval, admonition, dispute, or advice, aimed at offering a comprehensive picture of the subject's feelings, beliefs, and motivations.

depth perception 1. Perception of distance between the stimulus and the subject. 2. Perception of three dimensionality or solidity of a stimulus.

depth psychology See *psychology, depth*.

derailment (E. Kraepelin) Archaic term used to indicate abnormal functioning or disorganization of psychological processes.

derailment of volition (E. Kraepelin) Archaic term for the disruption of volition.

Dercum, Francis Xavier (1856-1931) American neurologist.

Dercum's disease (adiposis dolorosa) Rare disease usually appearing about middle life characterized by obesity, sharp pain in the areas of abnormal fat deposits, and mental deterioration including loss of memory, decreased intelligence and emotional disturbance. Generalized epileptiform convulsions are not infrequent.

derealization The feeling that familiar surroundings or people are unreal or have become strange.

dereism Autistic thinking which ignores reality.

dereistic Unrealistic, fantastic.

derivative (psychoanalysis) Some activities by which the id may be expressed. They are usually disguised thereby permitting expression of unconscious wishes without anxiety.

derivative insight Insight arrived at without interpretation by the therapist.

derived emotion (W. McDougall) Emotions associated with a prospective outcome of an event, such as disappointment, hope, relief, etc.

derived need A need which has developed from a basic physiological need of the organism through association and generalization. The concept has fallen into disuse.

derived primary attention Habitual passive attention.

derived property (Gestalt psychology) The parts of a perceived object derived from the whole.

derived scale A scale of values obtained by some mathematical transformation of the original scores. This is usually done to facilitate analysis, standardize scores, or meet certain mathematical prerequisites which then permit further mathematical analysis.

derived score A score that is obtained by some mathematical manipulation of the raw data. It may summarize raw data, e.g. a mean data, or transform scores to a derived scale, e.g. z scores.

derma The sensitive layer of the skin below the epidermis.

dermal sensitivity, sense The cutaneous sensations associated with skin receptors.

dermatitis Inflammation of the skin of physical or psychological origin.

dermatography, dermatographa Skin writing; slight scratches or strokes on the skin causing welts.

dermatophobia Fear of the skin.

dermatosiophobia Fear of skin disease.

dermis The sensitive layer of skin, between the epidermis and the subcutaneous tissue.

dermography; dermographism Same as dermatography.

Derner, Gordon F. (1915-) American psychologist. Developed the first university based professional school in applied psychology at Adelphi University, Garden City, New York, a program which prepares students at the doctoral level and post-doctoral level for practice in consultation, psychodiagnostics, psychotherapy, psychoanalysis and clinical research; published first book in the United States on the psychology of the tubercular; published papers on diagnostic testing, psychotherapy, clinical supervision, clinical problems and professional problems; leader in establishing psychology as a legally recognized profession; early worker in group process; research and practice in control of smoking; active in cross-cultural and international psychology.

desanimania Archaic term for mental deficiency and/or without psychosis.

Descartes, René (1596-1650) Great early French Renaissance philosopher. Distinguished between mind (unextended substance) and body (extended substance), and held that the two interact. Only man possesses mind or soul; animals—and man's body— are strictly machines or automata. Invented analytical geometry and the graphic system now known as Cartesian coordinates.

descriptive average An estimated mean based on incomplete data.

descriptive principle A generalized description and catagorization of classes of events.

descriptive statistics See statistics, descriptive.

desensitization 1. Weakening of a response with repeated presentations of the stimulus. 2. See systematic desensitization.

deserpine A sedative; one of rauwolfia alcaloids.

desurgency (R. B. Cattell) Agitated, depressed behavior.

desexualization Removing sexual energy from an apparently sexual object; sexual detachment.

design, experimental Plan of an experiment structured to answer specific experimental questions. Design usually specifies: 1) Choice of subjects, species, age, sex, etc. 2) Apparatus used for stimulus presentation and response recording. 3) Experimental procedure. 4) Type of analysis of results.

design, factorial Experimental design incorporating one or more levels of two or more independent variables.

design, panel Study in which one sample of people is interviewed recurrently over a long period of time to investigate the processes of response change, usually in reference to the same variable.

designatory scale A numerical scale in which events or event classes are assigned numbers for identification purposes only; the number assigned is arbitrary and is not correlated in any way with any property of the event or class.

desoxyn Metamphetamine, a stimulant.

despeciation 1. Change in the characteristics of the species. 2.Formerly, the appearance in one individual of several extreme deviations in physical characteristics as a sign of biological inferiority.

Despert Fables (L. J. Despert) An English translation of the Düss Fables, a projective technique designed to determine emotional conflict areas in children. It consists of ten short fables, each of which presents a problem for the child to solve.

destination (communication theory) Recipient of message.

destiny, neurosis of Surrender to an allegedly predestined fate.

destruction method The surgical removal or destruction of a part of the nervous system so as to determine the functions of that part.

destructiveness Expression of aggressive impulses by destroying or defacing objects.

destrudo (B. B. Wolman) The emotional energy of Ares, a primitive, archaic, destructive energy which is normally fused with libido. When libido fails in a state of regression, the destructive energy takes over.

detached affect (psychoanalysis) An affect separated from its generating idea and attached to another idea because the original idea was too threatening, thus the original idea and its affect are maintained independently of each other.

detachment (K. Horney) A neurotic need for self-sufficiency and independence. The individual lacks both feelings for others and social involvement.

detail response (Rorschach) A response which involves the use of less than the entire blot. A variety of area descriptions have evolved in different approaches to the Rorschach. Most have sub-divided this category into large or frequently responded to areas, and small or infrequently responded to areas. Some approaches, such as Klopfer, have special score designations which differentiate frequently responded to areas into rare, tiny, edged, or internal categories.

detection theory See *signal detection theory*.

detentio Archaic term for immobility observed in catalepsy.

deterioration Progressive loss of a psychological function.

deterioration, alcoholic All psychotic, chronic brain syndromes caused by alcoholism, which are not included in Korsakov's psychosis.

deterioration, emotional Progressive lack of appropriate emotional behavior.

deterioration, epileptic Progressive intellectual and mental deterioration which occurs gradually in a small percentage of epileptics; the cause of this deterioration and its relation to epilepsy is not known.

deterioration index A measure by the Wechsler-Bellevue tests of the loss of mental functions with age. Four of the functions tested that show loss with age are called the "Don't hold functions"; these are: digit span, digit symbol, block design, and similarities. Four functions, called the "hold functions" do not show an appreciable decline with age; these are vocabulary, information, object assembly, and picture completion. The deterioration index:

$$= \frac{\text{Hold} - \text{Don't hold}}{\text{Hold}}.$$

deterioration, senile Progressive loss of mental functions associated with old age.

determinant An antecedent condition that in some way causes an event. Behavior determinants may be physiological, structural, environmental, and/or organismic.

determinant, Rorschach The characteristic of the stimulus pattern used to structure the individual's perception.

determinant score One of the major components in Rorschach scoring or coding which refers to the perceived feature or features of the blot, such as form, movement, color, or shading, that precipitate the response of the subject.

determinate reflex Response at the site of stimulation.

determination, coefficient of Proportional reduction in the variance of the dependent variable as a linear function of the independent variable. This coefficient represents the strength of a linear relationship between variables.

determining quality (S. Freud) The characteristics of the traumatic scene that determine the specific neurotic symptoms.

determining tendency (N. Ach) The presentation of the aim influences the reaction of the experimental subjects to the stimulus. The subjects' performance is determined not only by what they see but also by what they are requested to see.

determinism The doctrine that all phenomena, including behavior, are effects of preceding causes. Thus, with knowledge of the relevent antecedent conditions, the subsequent events can be predicted.

determinism, biological The view that constitutional and biological factors determine the psychological and behavioral characteristics of the individual.

determinism, biosocial The view that psychological and behavioral characteristics are the result of the interaction of biological and social influences upon the organism.

detour behavior Action that leads to a desired end when direct action is obstructed.

detour problem A design in problem solving tests in which the goal can only be reached by an indirect route.

detraction Lessening the amount of attention without shifting the point of focus.

detumescence Subsiding of swelling of the genital organs, after erection.

deuteranomaly In color vision, a condition in which an individual mixes unusually large amounts of green to red so as to match a yellow standard, indicating poor sensitivity to green color.

deutero-learning 1. Learning about the process of learning, learning the skills that make learning more efficient, learning about how to go about learning. 2. Learning to learn, learning set.

deuteronopia Green color blindness.

deuteropathy A secondary symptom.

deutero-phallic (E. Jones) Second stage of the phallic phase. When the child starts to suspect that not everybody has the same type genital organ but that there are two types of people, male and female.

deutoplasm Lifeless parts of the cytoplasm, especially food reserves such as the egg yolk.

Deutsch, Morton (1920-   ) American psychologist. Developed and experimentally tested a theory of cooperation and competition. Has shown that attitudes, perception, task orientation, and communication are profoundly influenced by type of social relationship. One of the first to study experimentally such topics as trust and suspicion, interpersonal bargaining, and conflict resolution. Has demonstrated that conflict becomes more destructive as factors making for a competitive relationship become more dominant.

development Refers to increasing complexity and/or organization of processes and/or structure.

development, genital-physical A conceptualization of sexual life based on psychosexual and emotional maturity rather than orgastic, anatomical and mechanical desires.

development, mental The progressive appearance, change and organization of mental processes and functions which occur from birth until death and which are due to maturation and/or learning.

development, prenatal The growth of structures and functions in the fetus while in the uterus. The growth occurring before birth.

developmental age An index of maturation determined by a psychometric method and expressed in years.

developmental aphasia See *aphasia, developmental.*

developmental levels Arbitrary division of the course of life into age ranges. These are: (a) infancy, from birth to 1 year, including the neonate, from birth to one month; (b) childhood, from 1 to 12 years, including early childhood from 1 to 6 years, mid-childhood, from 6 to 10 years, and late childhood, from 10 to 12 years; (c) adolescence, from 12 to 21 years, including early adolescence, from 12 to 14 years, mid-adolescence, from 14 to 16 years, late adolescence, from 16 to 21 years; (d) maturity, from 21 to 65; (e) old age, from 65 on.

developmental norm The level of development representative and characteristic of children at a specified age.

developmental psychology Concerned with the emotional, attitudinal, social and intellectual processes through which the individual goes during the life-span from conception to death. However, the principle orientation is toward the two decades from birth to about twenty years of age, i.e., the time when changes (both physical and mental) are rapid, and during which behavioral patterns are formed and become relatively stable. "Growth," "development," and "maturation" are often used synonymously to refer to change over time, primarily of immature organisms. See *growth; development; maturation.*

developmental quotient A psychometrically derived developmental age divided by the individual's chronological age.

developmental scale See *scale, developmental.*

developmental sequence In the course of the development of an organism there is a sequence of the appearance and development of structures in the organism. This sequence is, within limits, constant for all organisms of the same, or related species. It is usually assumed that this sequence is within limits, constant for all organisms of the same, or related species. It is usually assumed that this sequence is under genetic control.

developmental stage A period in the life of an individual during which specific traits or behaviors become characteristic. For example, during the Freudian oral stage, behaviors appropriate to that stage manifest themselves.

developmental tasks Achievements and skills obtained by the developing individual and regarded by a society or culture as appropriate and necessary to his level of development for the acceptable functioning of the individual in that society or culture.

developmental test of visual-motor integration See *test, developmental, of visual-motor integration.*

developmental units Units of an equal interval scale used to measure development. The IQ was intended to be an equal interval scale in which a change of one unit at age 10 and a change of one unit at age 11 were thought to be changes of equal amounts of development. Generally, however, these scales cannot demonstrate equal intervals.

developmental zero Hypothetical point at which life starts; generally agreed to be the moment of fertilization of the egg by the sperm.

deviate An individual who differs markedly from the social standard usually in terms of attitudes, moral standards and overt behavior.

deviation 1. A departure from the norm. 2. (statistics) The amount by which a score differs from some measure of the distribution of scores.

deviation, average The arithmetic mean of the absolute values of deviations of scores from some reference measure of the distribution of scores. The reference measure is usually a measure of central tendency. Absolute value means the numerical value alone regardless of sign, plus or minus; i.e., all minus signs are changed to plus signs before finding the arithmetic mean of the deviations.

deviation IQ A measure of intelligence with a test in which the scores are standardized with an average score of 100 and a standard deviation specific to the test used. One such test is the Stanford-Binet with a standard deviation of approximately 16. It is contended that the deviation IQ and the conventional IQ, the quotient between mental age and chronological age, have the same meaning.

deviation, median The midpoint of all of the deviations from a measure of central tendency.

deviation score See *score, deviation.*

devolution Retrograde development, degeneration or the undoing of evolution; involution.

dexterity Skill and ease in using the hands.

dexterity test See *test, dexterity.*

dextrad Toward the right side.

dextral Of the right side.

dextrality Favoring the use of the right hand over the left.

dextroamphetamine Form of amphetamine, commonly known as dexedrine; a stimulant.

dextrophobia Fear of objects on the right.

dextrosinistral An originally left-handed person trained to use the right hand.

diabetes A disease characterized by an excessive discharge of urine and by inordinate thirst.

diabetes insipidus Disease in which vast quantities of water are consumed and later eliminated as very diluted urine. Caused by damage to the region of the hypothalamus producing vasopressin.

diabetes mellitus An inherited disease characterized by a deficiency in insulin causing an excess of sugar in the blood (hyperglycemia).

diabetic acidosis See *acidosis, diabetic.*

diad 1. A social group of two individuals. 2. A unit of classification of social interactions. 3. Musical term for the simultaneous occurrence of two tones; a chord of two tones.

diagnosis 1. Identification of disease handicaps and disorders on the basis of observed symptoms. 2. Classification of individuals on the basis of observed characteristics and usually abnormalities.

diagnosis, blind A psychological evaluation based solely on test material without an interview or further clinical information about the patient.

diagnosis, differential Distinguishing between two similar diseases or disorders on the basis of their compared characteristics.

diagnosis, negative Identification of a disease or a disorder by elimination; identification of what the disturbance is not.

diagnosis, social Mostly used by psychiatric social workers to indicate environmental conditions of a client.

diagnostic interview See *interview, diagnostic.*

diagnostic test See *test, diagnostic.*

diagnostic word test See *test, diagnostic word.*

diagram, bar A visual representation of quantities consisting of a series of contiguous rectangles, of width proportional to the size of the class interval it represents, and in height proportional to the quantity in the various intervals.

dialectic A branch of logic that arrives at truth through deductive reasoning and counterposition of opposites.

Diana complex See *complex, Diana.*

diaphragm 1. A muscular partition especially the one that separates the thorax from the abdomen and is the chief muscle of respiration. 2. An aperture between a light source and a surface which controls the amount of light falling on the surface. 3. A contraceptive device.

diarrhea, chronic Diarrhea of long duration due to physical or psychogenic causes.

diarrhea, nervous Gastrointestinal malfunction characterized by frequent and fluid stools due to disturbances of the autonomic nervous system.

diary method Daily record of all events relevant to an object of investigation.

diaschisis Temporary cerebral shock; a sudden damage to a part of the brain causes shock to all connected parts. This results in a temporary cessation of function in the related parts.

diastole Period of the cardiac cycle during which the heart dilates and the ventricles fill with blood.

diastolic blood pressure The blood pressure obtained when the heart cavities are filled with blood.

diathermy The application of an oscillating electric current of high frequency for therapeutic purposes.

diathesis Inherited predisposition to a particular disease.

diathesis, arthritic A constitutional condition occurring in adults which includes the exudative and hypersecretory diathesis and arthritism, thought to occur in a megalosplanchnic hypervegetative constitution.

diathesis, explosive (A. Meyer) A subdivision of the traumatic neuroses manifesting intense irritability especially under the influence of alcohol which may lead to unmotivated acts of violence.

diathesis, exudative A constitutional condition occurring in children characterized by an irritable skin and chafing, eczema and high susceptibility to external irritants of the skin and mucuous membranes.

diathesis, neuropathic Neurasthenia.

diathesis, traumatophilic A predisposition to accidents.

diatonic scale See *scale, diatonic.*

diazepam See *valium.*

dichoglottic Of two separate areas of the tongue.

dichorhinic Of the simultaneous and usually independent stimulation of both nostrils.

dichotic Of separate and usually independent stimulation of both ears.

dichotonomously distributed data Data which are divided into two mutually exclusive categories on the basis of the presence or absence of a certain trait.

dichromatism Of a type of color blindness in which only two of the primary colors are seen.

dicrotic notch The notch in a pulse tracing of a peripheral artery.

didactic analysis See *psychoanalysis, didactic.*

didactic group psychotherapy See *psychotherapy, didactic group.*

diencephalon Part of the forebrain between the prosencephalon and mesencephalon, it includes the thalamus, epithalamus, and hypothalamus.

difference cannon (J. S. Mill) Any difference in otherwise identical effects are a result of differences in their antecedents.

difference threshold (limen) See *threshold, difference.*

difference tone A combination tone, sometimes heard when two tones of similar timbre are sounded together. Its frequency is often the difference between the two tones sounded.

differential aptitude test See *test, differential aptitude.*

differential conditioning See *conditioning, differential.*

differential diagnosis See *diagnosis, differential.*

differential extinction See *extinction, differential.*

differential growth See *growth, differential.*

differential inhibition See *inhibition, differential.*

differential R-technique (R. B. Cattell) The basic values are differences between scores on each of a set of variables measured at two occasions. These differences between scores are correlated and factor analyzed. One of the two main methods of determining dimensions of personality change-through-time (state factors). The other method is P-Technique.

differential reinforcement See *reinforcement, differential.*

differential reinforcement of inter response times See *reinforcement, schedule of: differential reinforcement of low rates of responding (drl); reinforcement, schedule of: differential reinforcement of high rates of responding (drh).*

differential response See *response, differential.*

differential scoring See *scoring, differential.*

differential sensibility See *sensibility, differential.*

differential threshold See *threshold, difference.*

differential tone See *difference, tone.*

differentiation 1. Process of becoming something different than it previously was. 2. (biology) Increase in complexity and organization of tissues during development. 3. (conditioning) Experimental procedure in which responses of a subject are changed from one type or class of responses to another class of desired responses by a process of selectively reinforcing successive approximations to the desired response. As the procedure continues for responses to be reinforced, they must approximate the desired response. 4. (mathematics) In calculus, the process of obtaining a differential coefficient. 5. An increase in the number of individual heterogenous aspects of an originally homogenous field.

differentiation of the life space (K. Lewin) A process of development increasing the regions of influence of an individual's life space, thus enlarging and diversifying the field of his activities and social interaction.

difficulty scale See *scale, difficulty.*

difficulty value See *value, difficulty.*

diffraction Bending of a portion of light as it passes the edge of an obstacle as when it passes through an aperture. This phenomenon is common to all wave forms.

diffraction grating An apparatus which produces the constituent wave length of an electromagnetic wave, often used to obtain monochromatic light from white light. It consists of a highly polished surface upon which are fine parallel slits. The wave length is of the same order of magnitude as the slit length.

diffusion 1. The spread of culture from one social group to another. 2. The scatter of light because of irregularities in the medium. 3. The spread of stimulation through cutaneous tissues.

diffusion circle An area of skin surface affected by pressure stimulation within the area.

digital computer A computer which can perform mathematical and logical operations with information, numbers, etc., represented in digital form.

dilantin Common name for diphenylhydantoin, an anticonvulsant drug used in the treatment of behavior disorders in children and adults and also migraine, neuromuscular disorders and a variety of cardiac abnormalities. It appears to act by decreasing the spread and amplification of the response to a stimulus, exerting a stabilizing effect.

Dilthey, William (1833-1911) German philosopher. Announced his cultural science psychology in the 1880's, but principal effects of its impact were not felt until early twentieth century. Emphasized critical study of man in society; regarded man as a unit, as an expression of human character, and led to a psychology of personality. Dilthey charged that laboratory psychology was inadequate to understand man; maintained that cultural science psychology *understands*, natural science psychology *explains*; believed that if human mind was to be understood by the psychologist, psychology had to be brought closer to history, art, literature and ethics; regarded psychology as fundamental to all cultural sciences; rejected natural science psychology; stressed understanding and holism.

dimorphic Characterized by two forms.

diphenylhydantoin See *dilantin.*

diploid The chromosome number of a gamete which contains both members of each chromosome pair. In man, the diploid number is 46, and in drosophila melanogaster it is 8.

diplopia Double vision; binocularly seeing two images when only one visual stimulus is presented usually as a result of trouble with motor coordination between the eyes or failure to focus properly.

dippoldism Flagellation of children.

dipsomania Mental disorder associated with alcoholism which occurs periodically following excessive drinking. It lasts several days, and is characterized by various patterns of responses depending upon the individual.

direct analysis See *analysis, direct.*

direct inquiry (H. Rorschach) Procedure used to supplement the regular inquiry, wherein the subject is provided information concerning the various determinants of responses and asked directly to specify which of those determinants were influential in his formulation of each response. The procedure, similar to Klopfer's Analogy Period, is designed to avoid the problems created by the non-directive questions of the regular inquiry.

direct measurement See *measurement, direct.*

direct psychoanalysis See *psychoanalysis, direct.*

direct reflex See *reflex, direct.*

direct scaling See *scaling, direct.*

direct therapy See *psychotherapy, direct.*

directed thinking Goal directed thought.

directions test See *test, directions.*

directive counseling See *counseling, directive.*

directive fiction See *fiction, directive.*

directive group therapy See *psychotherapy, directive group.*

directive (or determining) tendency See *determining tendency.*

directive therapy See *psychotherapy, directive.*

dirhinic stimulation Simultaneous stimulation of both nostrils by the same odor.

disability Loss or impairment of a bodily organ or a function.

disaesthesia Cutaneous and subcutaneous sensation of discomfort.

disappearing differences method (psychophysics) A modified method of limits in which an appreciable difference between two stimuli is gradually decreased until they appear identical.

discharge of affect (S. Freud) An active reaction to an emotional experience involving the whole range of voluntary and involuntary reflexes by which one's emotions are usually worked off.

discharge rate In institutional statistics, the ratio of the number of patients discharged in a given period of time over either the total number of patients in the original group or the number of patients admitted during the same time period.

discomfort-relief quotient (DRQ) Verbal expression of the ratio of feelings indicating satisfaction over feelings indicating dissatisfaction along some specified dimension, i.e., self or environment.

discontinuity theory of learning The hypothesis that for discrimination learning to occur the organism must attend to the cue of the stimulus upon which the discrimination is dependent. This view is related to insight learning but differs from it insofar as discontinuity theory accepts the possibility of gradual improvement in the task after the discrimination is established.

discontinuous variable A variable the values of which are not on a continuum but has discrete, sharp, and abrupt changes from one magnitude to the next magnitude.

discordant A term used in twin studies to indicate that one member of twin pair exhibits a trait or disease and the other does not. The discordance percentage in monozygotic twins in a systematic study provides a measure of the contribution of non-genetic factors operating from within or outside the organism.

discrepancy Disagreement between fact and theory or between two facts.

discrete distribution See *distribution, discrete.*

discrete measure Measures taken for a quantity that changes discontinuously or discretely.

discrete variable Same as *discontinuous variable.*

discriminal dispersion Frequency distribution of responses in a discrimination situation. The greatest number of responses is to the discriminative stimulus; the more different the stimulus is from the discriminative stimulus the fewer the responses made to it.

discriminal process The process of discrimination between stimuli.

discriminandum (a, pl.) (E. C. Tolman) A term referring to the relatively enduring sensory character of objects as modulated by the sense organ capacities of the given organism, and which permit that organism to make sensory differentiations. Thus discriminanda are differentiated from physical stimuli since discriminanda are defined by physical *and* behavioral-supporting attributes. See *physical stimulus.*

discriminated operant (B. F. Skinner) An operant occasioned by a stimulus as a consequence of previous training.

discriminating fineness (psychometrics) An index of the smallest difference in values of a variable detectable by a test.

discriminating power (psychometrics) A composite of several measures of the ability of a test to differentiate between testees on the relevant dimensions. It includes (a) probability of the test, the probability of correct discrimination among testees by the test (b) discriminating fineness, the smallest amounts of differences detectable by the test (c) discriminating range, the range of scores within which the test is a useful tool.

discriminating probability of the test (psychometrics) An index of the probability of correctly discriminating between testees or the relevant dimensions on the basis of the test. It is the proportion of correct to incorrect discriminations by the test.

discriminating range (psychometrics) The range of scores within which a test or index has reliable discriminating power and outside of which the scores may unduly be influenced by chance factors.

discrimination (R. Merton) Restrictive or hostile acts directed against some group.

discrimination, errorless (H. S. Terrace) Procedure used in operant conditioning to establish responding to the S^D and with an absence of responding to the S^Δ; Thus it is a procedure to establish without errors a discrimination between the S^D and S^Δ. Two ways of doing this are: 1) establishing normally with errors, a discrimination between the S^D and S^Δ, then superimposing new stimuli over the established discriminative stimuli, so each stimulus is a complex of the established discriminative stimulus and the new stimulus. Next, by slowly fading out the old discriminative stimuli, the new stimuli come to be the discriminative stimuli. Thus new S^D and S^Δ have been established with no responses or errors, to the S^Δ. 2) Presenting the S^Δ for periods of time, too short for the subject to respond, and at weak stimulus intensities and gradually increasing the duration and intensity of the S^Δ; the discrimination between the S^D and the S^Δ can be established without errors.

discrimination, index of (psychometrics) An index of the sensitivity of a test or test item to differences in testees on the relevant dimensions measured by the test.

discrimination reaction time See *reaction time, discrimination.*

discrimination, sensory The process or ability to recognize quantitative or qualitative differences between stimuli.

discriminative approach and avoidance responses A technique used by behavioral therapists to teach patients to discriminate between anxiety arousing and non-anxiety arousing situations.

discriminative learning A learning situation in which the subject learns that responses to one stimulus is reinforced while responses to other stimuli are either not reinforced or punished.

discriminative stimulus A stimulus that occasions the appropriate response as a consequence of conditioning.

discussion leader Individual who promotes free discussion and interchange of ideas in a meeting of usually small groups.

disease A lack of a state of ease; usually an abnormal condition of body or mind, synonymous with disorder, pathology, illness.

disease, Beard's (G. M. Beard) Archaic term for neurasthenia.

disease, Bell's (L. V. Bell) Archaic term for a form of manic type of manic-depressive psychosis.

disease, flight into It is generally recognized that gains and compensations as a result of disease or disorder can be motivating factors to become or remain ill.

disease, Friedmann's (M. Friedmann) Narcolepsy.

disease, Janet's (P. Janet) Psychasthenia.

disease, Little's (W. J. Little) Diplegia.

disease (or disorder), mental Psychopathy.

disequilibrium, mental (P. Dubois) Mental imbalance.

disgust A feeling, attitude or emotion of repulsion, aversion, withdrawal, loathing and possibly nausea.

disinhibition 1. (I. P. Pavlov) A temporary increase in the strength of the conditioned response upon introduction of an irrelevant stimulus. 2. The lessening of cortical control of impulsive or vegetative functions due to drugs or alcohol.

disintegration Disruption of the organization of a unified system; it may refer to disintegration of psychic and behavioral processes.

dismemberment, fear of A fear most often seen in involutional psychosis and in schizophrenia, that the individual is going to lose part of his body.

disorder, functional A pathological state of an organism with no organic basis.

disorder, impulse A category of psychopathic behavior characterized by symptoms or a character structure of impulsive action. The neuroses include kleptomania, pyromania, addiction, sexual perversions and catathymic crises caused by inner tension and unconscious conflict needs which cannot be controlled.

disorder, mental Any gross or disabling disruption of mental or behavioral processes of adjustment whether psychological, social, organic, or functional in origin, regardless of being relatively temporary or chronic. Also called behavior disorder.

disorder of volition See *parabulia.*

disorder, organic A pathological state of an organism resulting from physical or structural damage.

disorders, classification of mental See *classification of mental disorders.*

disorders, respiratory 1. Disturbances involving the respiratory apparatus. 2. See *asthma, bronchial.*

disorganized behavior Behavior, parts of which are not integrated and are often aimed at disparate ends, while the total behavior contradicts itself and leads nowhere.

disorientation Loss of the ability to comprehend spatial, temporal and social relations.

disparagement, mania for (P. Janet) Fear and jealousy of another's success and a desire for one's own triumph not really by success but by belittling the achievements of others.

disparagement syndrome See *syndrome, disparagement.*

disparate retinal points Areas of both retinas of one individual which in normal binocular stimulation give rise to the perception of different positions in space.

disparation The double visual image of an object when the fixation point is either in front of or behind the object.

dispareunia See *dyspareunia.*

disparity, retinal Differences between the projections on both retinas of one individual when looking at a visual stimulus. This occurs since both retinas are located at different views of the same stimulus complex. These differences in the retinal image are important cues for the perception of depth.

dispersion The extent to which scores vary among themselves or deviate from some reference point. Dispersion is measured by the average deviation, interquartile range, or most commonly, the standard deviation.

dispersion circle Usually a colored circular visual sensation when light rays from a point source are not focused on a single retinal point, but are dispersed over an area. This is achieved usually by a lens system.

dispersion coefficient See *coefficient, dispersion.*

displaced aggression An expression of hostility to an individual or object rather than to the source of the hostility.

displacement 1. A substitution of one response system for another when the former behavior is prevented in some way. 2. A distortion of eidetic image resulting in a rearrangement of recalled parts. 3. (Rorschach) Focusing attention on insignificant details of the stimulus complex so as to avoid more revealing responses. 4. (psychoanalysis) A defense mechanism; displacement is a shift of emotion, meaning, or fantasy from the person or object toward which it was originally directed, to another person or object. It involves a discharge of aroused emotions toward neutral or less dangerous objects.

displacement in dreams In the manifest dream a single element may stand for a whole conglomeration of unconscious, latent dream thoughts. In the waking state instinctual energies are bound and cathected in definite objects. In dreams these mental energy loads shift easily from one object to another. In some dreams significant issues are barely mentioned or represented by symbols while unimportant unconscious elements may be represented in a very clear manner. This phenomenon, displacement, occurs in dreamwork, transforming the psychical intensity, latent thoughts and wishes into sensory experience. The more obscure the dream is, the more displacement there is in the dream.

disposition 1. The arrangement of parts or elements of a system such that the action of the system is in part a consequence of its internal structure. 2. A hypothetical organization of psychological and physiological elements such that an individual's behavior in different situations will have similar characteristics. 3. A relatively stable and constant attitude. 4. (W. McDougall) All the innate tendencies and propensities of an individual.

disposition rigidity See *perseveration.*

disposition system See *complex, mood.*

dissected-sentence test See *test, disarranged sentence.*

disseminated sclerosis Multiple sclerosis.

dissimilation 1. Catabolism. 2. (C. G. Jung) Adjustment of the individual to external forces and consequent estrangement of the individual from himself.

dissimulation Feigning or concealing one's real emotions.

dissociation A process of preventing motivational systems, complex psychological processes and activities from entering consciousness because of intolerable anxiety. These processes function independently of the rest of the personality.

dissociative reactions Neurotic reactions to extreme stress, characterized by the repression of entire episodes in life as in amnesia, fugues, and multiple personalities.

dissonance (music) Any combination of tones sounded simultaneously, the effect of which is conventionally heard as being in unrest and tense, and needing at least one other simultaneous group of tones following it for resolution and completion. Dissonance is a matter of degree and contemporary music theory redefining it.

dissonance, cognitive See *cognitive dissonance.*

dissonance reduction (L. Festinger) The principle that when a tension producing dissonant situation occurs, an individual seeks new information or behaves in a way to reduce the dissonance.

distal 1. Far from some reference point. 2. (anatomy) Away from the center of the body or point of attachment to the body.

distal stimulus See *stimulus, distal.*

distal variable See *variable, distal.*

distance receptor Receptors capable of responding to stimuli that are separated from the body by some distance. Among these are visual, auditory, thermal, and olfactory receptors.

distance vision See *vision, distance.*

distoceptor A distance receptor.

distortion, parataxic (H. S. Sullivan) An aspect of interpersonal relations of perceiving and relating to a person as if he was a person with whom one has related to in the past, independent of his objective characteristics.

distortion, perceptual An absence of correspondence between the common perception of a stimulus and a perception by an individual.

distribution, asymmetrical A statistical distribution in which there is a lack of similarity between the two halves as divided by the mean or median.

distribution, bimodal A distribution that has two points at which the frequency is considerably greater than on either side of the points. The points need not be of the same frequency.

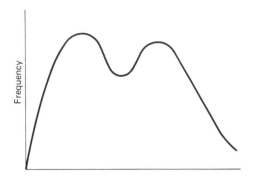

A bimodal distribution

distribution, binomial See *normal frequency distribution.*

distribution, cumulative frequency See *cumulative frequency distribution.*

distribution curve Curve of a frequency distribution; on the horizontal axis the items or values are plotted, and on the vertical axis the frequency of their occurrence is plotted.

distribution, discrete A frequency distribution consisting of distinct, separate steps.

distribution-free (statistics) Pertaining to nonparametric methods which make no assumptions about the form of distribution of scores in the sampling universe.

distribution, Poisson (statistics) A binomial distribution in which the probability of a given event is extremely small.

distribution, ranked A distribution of scores or values arranged in order of increasing of decreasing magnitude. A particular rank is indicated by a number specifying its position.

distribution, rectilinear A distribution of scores in which each category has approximately the same frequency of cases as opposed to a normal distribution which is characterized by the largest number of cases falling near to the mean.

distribution, self (Gestalt psychology) The involuntary change in dynamic relations of a sensory field which results in a higher organization of that field.

distribution, truncated (statistics) A distribution having no extreme points due to a failure to obtain extreme cases or an intentional removal of them. It may be unilateral or bilateral.

disuse principle The theory that the tendency to make a learned response to a stimulus decreases with disuse over time.

diuresis Increased production and secretion of urine.

divagation Rambling and incoherent speech.

divergence 1. Turning out of both eyes when the distance from the subject to the binocularly fixated point increases. 2. A permanent turning out of one eye respective to the other; wall-eyed.

divergent production, operation of (J.P. Guilford) Generation of items of information from given items, where the emphasis is upon a variety of output from the same source; a search for logical alternatives.

Dix, Dorothea Lynde (1802-1887) Left home at ten years of age and at fourteen began teaching school at Worchester. Because of tuberculosis she resigned her regular duties and began to give Sunday instruction to women prisoners. This was her first view of prison life, which led her to investigate conditions at poorhouses, insane asylums, and jails. She believed that the living conditions of the insane were due to an antiquated, ignorant, and callous system which needed reform. She was instrumental in the formation of more than thirty institutions for the insane and for having millions of dollars appropriated for improved care in public institutions. In England she was instrumental in having a royal commission investigate insane asylums in Scotland. In Rome she was a moving force in the foundation of a new hospital.

dizygote twins Twins which grew from two separate eggs; fraternal twins.

DL See *difference threshold.*

d-lysergic acid dietymide See *lysergic acid diethylamide.*

DNA (deoxyribonucleic acid) The nucleic acid of the chromosomes, in which genetic information is coded.

doctrine of interest See *interest, doctrine of.*

doctrine of temperament, Galen's (Galen) The belief that personality characteristics result from the different combinations of the four basic elements: earth, air, fire and water, in the physical composition of the person. Sanguine, choleric, phlegmatic and melancholy dispositions were thought to result from different amounts of these elements.

dolichocephaly Having a long, narrow head with a cephalic index of less than 75.

dolichomorph Tall thin bodily shape.

doll play, permissive Examiner is permissive of commonly forbidden thematic content (e.g., aggression), avoids interpretation, and limits interaction to reflection of child's performance.

doll play, projective (R.R. Sears) A procedure in which a child is presented with dolls and a doll house or other environmental materials, with encouragement to manipulate them either thematically (e.g., "show what the family does here") or organizationally (e.g., "make a scene").

Dollard, John (1900-) American psychologist. Made a pioneering behavioral study of the caste system in South. Best work done with Neal E. Miller, relating reinforcement learning theory to psychoanalysis and culture theory. Imitation is learned; neurosis is learned. Personality is learned and it varies according to the laws of learning and the specific social conditions under which it is acquired. See *reinforcement learning theory; neurosis; psychotherapy*.

domal sampling A form of area sampling in which a sample of houses are designated and a specific member of each household is interviewed.

domatophobia Fear of being in a house.

dominance 1. A drive or desire for ascendancy, being more important or prominant in a relationship. A tendency to control others. 2. When two or more responses are occasioned by a stimulus, one of them is more likely than the other. 3. Preferential use of one side of the body over the other; handedness.

dominance, genetic (genetics) The phenotype of one gene of an allele pair is expressed while the phenotype of the other recessive allele, does not appear in the characteristics of the organism.

dominance, hemisphere One hemisphere of the brain controls movement of the body more than the other hemisphere, resulting in handedness.

dominance, lateral 1. The tendency for dominance of one side of the brain over the other in most functions. 2. Preferential use of one hand or side of the body.

dominance need See *need, dominance*.

dominance, ocular The preferred use or greater use of one eye rather than the other which is one form of lateral dominance.

dominance-submission See *ascendance-submission*.

dominant wave length Wave length of a color which when mixed with the appropriate amount of white yields a color that matches a given color.

dominant (genetics) A gene is dominant if it is expressed when heterozygous.

dominant gene See *gene, dominant*.

dominator-modulator theory In color vision the hypothesis that there is a dominant receptor for brightness perception; color discriminations are a function of another receptor, the modulator, which modulates the response of the dominant receptor.

Donder's law See *law, Donder's*.

Doolittle method (statistics) An efficient and systematic method of finding the unknowns in a set of normal equations. This method is often used in solving multiple correlation problems.

Doppler effect If the distance between a sound or light source and an observer changes, the sound pitch or light color appears to change. Thus, for example, the whistle of a train when moving toward an observer appears higher then when it is moving away. When a light source is moving toward an observer it appears more blue than when moving away, then appears more red.

Dora case First of five extensive case histories reported by S. Freud. This one was written in 1901 and published as *Fragment of an Analysis of a Case of Hysteria* in 1905. Freud used the Dora case as a base to further his dream analysis and to account for the repressed part of mental life.

dorsal At or on the back.

dorso-ventral (anatomical) Extending from the dorsal to the ventral axes of the body, from the front to the back.

DOT Dictionary of Occupational Titles.

dotting test See *test, dotting*.

double alternation problem See *problem, double alternation*.

double aspect theory A metaphysical theory, based on Spinoza's philosophy, stating that mental and physical processes represent two aspects of the same occurrences.

double bind hypothesis See *hypothesis, double bind*.

double blind method A research design in which neither the investigator nor the subject knows the nature of the experimental conditions. For example, in drug research neither the investigator nor the participating patients know who is getting the real drug and who is getting the placebo.

double-entry table 1. Any statistical table in which values are entered both in the rows and in the columns. 2. A scatter diagram.

double orientation See *orientation, double*.

double representation The perception of two hues or brightnesses of an object when that object is illuminated by a light of a different color.

double sampling See *sampling, double*.

double vibration See *vibration*.

double vision See *diplopia*.

doubles, illusion of See *illusion of doubles*.

Downey's Will-Temperament Test See *test, Downey's Will-Temperament*.

Down's syndrome See *mongolism*.

DR or ΔR Symbol for change in response.

drainage hypothesis (W. McDougall) A theory of neural inhibition and facilitation which suggests that when two neural groups, anatomically close, are aroused, the neural impulse is drawn from the usual pathway of the weaker neural group and increases the impulse of the more active group.

drama therapy See *psychodrama*.

dramamine An antihistamine drug used to control motion sickness.

Draw-A-Person Quality Scale See *scale, Draw-A-Person Quality*.

Draw-A-Person Test See *test, Draw-A-Person*.

dream-day; daydream A fantasy while awake. The individual lets his mind wander aimlessly through gratifying images. The daydream is said to be motivated by unconscious and unfulfilled wishes.

dream determinant (psychoanalysis) The principle factor in determining the content and characteristic quality of a dream.

dream ego (C. G. Jung) The part of the ego that is dreaming.

dream interpretation The process of understanding the unconscious meanings of a dream. There are several levels of meaning. Aside from the symbolism that is individual and characteristic only of the individual and interpretable through dream analysis, it is held that some dream symbols are universal, the meanings of which are shared by all human beings.

dream, manifest content (psychoanalysis) The dream as it is remembered; the images, events, people, etc.; "the story line" of the dream.

dream, perennial A dream that, after having been dreamt in childhood, appears again in later years.

dream, reconstruction (D. B. Levin) A dream in which the sequence of dream elements seems to naturally incorporate a stimulus that wakes the sleeper. For example, the bell of an alarm clock waking the dreamer is included into the dream.

dream, secondary elaboration of The differences between the descriptions of a dream and the actual content of the dream. This process continues in the waking state so that a later description of the dream differs from an earlier one.

dream work (psychoanalysis) Transformation of an unconscious demand by a substitute wish-fulfillment in dreams. The transformation of the hidden, latent dream content into what the dreamer experiences (manifest dream) is called dream work. The dream work protects the sleep and prevents waking up.

dreams 1. Sensations, images, thoughts and emotions experienced in sleep. 2. (S. Freud) Dreams are guardians of sleep and protect the sleeper from being disturbed by unconscious conflicts and annoying external stimuli. Dreams are a compromise between the inner and outer disturbance of sleep and the desire to sleep. The sleeping person "dreams away," as it were, the disturbing factors. The content of the dreams reflects repressed demands for instinctual gratification. The mental functions of the dreams are unconscious with irrational primary processes with "all the absurdities, delusions and illusions" of a psychosis. A dream is a compromise; the unconscious, forbidden impulses appear in the dream in a disguised manner. This disguising is called dream-work, the unconscious wish is called latent dream, the story of the dream is called the manifest dream content. 3. (A. Adler) Dreams serve a problem-solving function offering cryptic solutions to difficulties the dreamer faces. 4. (H.S. Sullivan) Dream satisfies in a symbolic way the needs which could not be discharged in wakeful states thus reducing tension. 5. (W. Dement and C. Fisher) Dreams are sort of "safety valves" reducing the danger of emo-

tional disturbance. Deprivation could produce psychosis. 6. (R. Hernandez-Peon) Dreams are related to disinhibition of cortical and limbic neurons associated with the motivational and muscular systems. The neurons associated with memory functions determine the manifest dream content, the limbic neurons determine the latent dream content. 7. (M. Jouvet and J. Jouvet) The causal-positive area in the thromboencephalic part of the brain is the dream-center.

dreams, physiology of The period of dreaming differs from non-dreaming sleep states and periods of wakefulness. These periods are characterized by a low-voltage EEG pattern concomitant with rapid eye movements. The physiological arousal consists of changes in respiration, pulse rate, basal skin resistance, blood pressure and muscular activity. This state recurs periodically from ninety to one hundred twenty minutes which may be due to an internal physiological mechanism involving primitive cerebral structures and perhaps neurohumoral transmitters. If dreaming is prevented, a rebound occurs during the following night in which the subject regains the deficit. Prolonged suppression of dreaming results in serious personality disturbance.

Dreikurs, Rudolf (1897-1972) Viennese-born, American psychiatrist and educator. Developed Alfred Adler's system of "Individual Psychology" into techniques for understanding purposes of disturbing behavior in children, and for stimulating cooperative behavior without punishment or reward. Key assumption: the child strives to find a place amongst others. When discouraged from socially useful striving he pursues one or more of the socially useless "Four Goals:" 1) attention, 2) power, 3) revenge, 4) display of inadequacy. Founded Alfred Adler Institutes of Chicago and Tel Aviv. Inspired international movement of Family Education Centers, parent study groups. Opposed "transference" theories by instituting multiple psychotherapy to stress educational task of therapist.

drh schedule See *reinforcement, schedule of: differential reinforcement of high rates.*

drive 1. An impelling force, push, or pressure. 2. An inner urge that stimulates or prevents action. 3. (W. B. Cannon) A special localized sensation determined by organ stimulation, e.g. the hunger drive is hunger-sensation, pangs caused by the contraction of the stomach. 4. (S. Freud) Drive (Trieb) is an innate force, synonymous to instinct, that facilitates or prevents the discharge of energy; see *instinct*. 5. (C. L. Hull) A general energizer whose reduction is reinforcing. If the reinforcement takes place without learning, the drive is primary; if the reinforcement takes place after prior learning, it is a secondary drive. Thus the primary drives are the unlearned sources of energy in the organism. 6. (N. E. Miller and J. Dollard) Drive is a stimulus that impels the organism to make responses to cues in the stimulus situation. These responses become conditioned if they have been rewarded; thus reward is drive reducing. Primary drives, such as hunger and thirst, are based on physiological processes. Secondary or acquired drives are based on the primary drives.

7. (C. T. Morgan) See *Central Motivating State.*
8. (B. F. Skinner) Skinner uses the term drive as "a verbal device," a convenient way of referring to the effects of deprivation and satiation. **9.** (W. Stern) Drive is an innate disposition towards the implementation of one's own goals. There are four types of drives, namely: (1) self-preservation, (2) self-development, such as self-adornment, (3) social drives, and (4) human drives such as intellectual and idealistic strivings. **10.** (P. Teitelbaum) Drive is activation of unlearned behavior, in contradistinction from motive, which implies activation of learned behavior. **11.** (C. J. Warden) A behavioral tendency activated by an arousal stemming from deprivation and/or incentive. **12.** (R. S. Woodworth) Woodworth introduced the term drive in 1918 as a factor motivating human behavior. **13.** (P. T. Young) The energy of behavior; the sum of energy released in behavior.

drive, achievement The tendency to work with determination toward a specific end that is considered important by the individual.

drive, acquired 1. A need or motive that has been learned through one's life experience as opposed to being an innate drive. **2.** A drive specific to a particular species that comes to be satisfied by learned techniques. See *motivation.*

drive, aim-inhibited (S. Freud) Instinctual drives that are modified or held in suspension, under the influence of the ego and superego, allowing gratification different from the original aim. For example, libidinal drives which are powerfully cathected in a love object may become aim-inhibited and result in satisfaction derived from relation to the object without actual sexual gratification.

drive arousal Any of a combination of stimulus conditions that activate a specified drive. The conditions can be either external or internal to the organism.

drive discrimination (E. C. Tolman) A form of learning dependent on the type of deprivation which an organism has undergone which activates specific drives in the organism.

drive displacement After one drive has been aroused but gratification of that drive is prevented, the behavior may change and be appropriate for some other unaroused but gratifiable drive.

drive for self-aggrandizement Drive to maintain feeling of personal adequacy expressed primarily in competitive situations.

drive, homonomy (A. Angyal) The trend of the individual to adjust himself to the environment, merging his individuality in a union with a social group, or the world order.

drive, maternal The tendency of the female organism to care for her young which has both hereditary and learned components.

drive, primary Any drive which is universal in a given species, for which there is a physiological basis, and which is independent of learning.

drive reduction The lessening of drive behavior (the activity called a drive) and related conditions with the organism usually accomplished through satisfaction of the needs associated with the drive by satiation or through removal of drive arsenal.

drive-reduction theory See *theory, drive-reduction.*

drive, sensory An intense desire or need for a specific sensory experience.

drive state (P. Teitelbaum) The internal state, such as hunger, which influences the excitability of the nervous system and controls its feeding reflexes.

drive stimulus; S$_D$ (C. L. Hull) An afferent nerve activity arising in those organs in a drive state which, when reduced by some behavior, results in the reinforcement of that behavior.

drl schedule See *reinforcement, schedule of: differential reinforcement of low rates.*

DRQ See *discomfort-relief quotient.*

drug addiction A state of periodic or chronic intoxication detrimental to the individual and to society, produced by the repeated consumption of a drug (natural or synthetic). Its characteristics include: an overpowering desire or need (compulsion) to continue taking the drug and to obtain it by any means, a tendency to increase the dose, a psychic (psychological) and sometimes a physical dependence upon the effect of the drug.

drumstick A small protrusion from the nucleus of a polymorphonuclear leucocyte, found in three to five per cent of these cells in females but not in males.

dual file system A system in industrial personnel work of summarizing all information in two files: (a) individual endowment profiles, and (b) job profiles.

dual instinct theory 1. (S. Freud) The postulation of two inborn instincts, Eros and Thanatos, as the two forces of life. **2.** See *death instinct.* **3.** See *life instinct.*

dual personality See *personality, dual.*

dualism 1. An hypothesis that there are two fundamentally different entities or substances in the world, mind and matter. **2.** (psychology) The proposition that there is a distinction of some kind between the processes of the mind and the processes of the body and there is no way of reducing one to the other.

duct glands See *glands, exocrine.*

ductless glands See *glands, endocrine.*

dull normal A category of intelligence usually delimited by the I.Q. score range from 80 to 90.

duodenal ulcer See *ulcer, peptic.*

duplicity theory See *theory, duplicity.*

dura mater The thick, tough external membrane which covers the brain and spinal cord.

durance (H. A. Murray) The temporal unit of life activity which includes all proceedings occurring simultaneously.

duraplasty Treatment of defects in the dura mater.

Durham rule A 1954 law stating that an accused person is not held responsible for an act which is the product of mental defect or disorder.

Düss Fables See *Despert Fables.*

DV Dependent variable.

dwarfism A condition of extreme underdevelopment of the body resulting in small stature.

dwarfism, panhypopituitary A dwarfism which is characterized by the metabolic defects resulting from hypopituitarism.

dwarfism, renal A dwarfism which results from various kinds of chronic renal disease in children, such as congenital kidney malformation, chronic nephritis, renal tubular acidosis.

dyad (R. R. Sears) Two organisms conceived as a single unit because of an interdependence between some aspects of their action or motivational systems; a pair, neither of whose members can achieve full reinforcement, or gratification, without collaboration of the other; e.g., mother and child when attached, a loving husband and wife, twins when reared together, habitual enemies or rivals; a pair whose unique cathexes to one another prevent the replacement of either by a new member without significant emotional disturbance to the remaining original one. See *environmental event.*

dyadic theory (R. R. Sears) A personality or motivational theory that makes explicit the motivational interdependence of the members of two-person (dyadic) units; the dyadic quality of the relationship may be treated either as 1) a phenomenon to be explained developmentally, or as 2) the basic unit whose actions constitute the subject matter of the theory.

dynaception The process, related to sensory perception, in which the organism perceives and responds to his own need state.

dynamic apraxia See *apraxia, dynamic.*

dynamic crossroads Choice-points in the adjustment of the organism, permitting sequences of alternative responses in goal-seeking behavior. These choice-points plus the paths leading to and from them, compose the Adjustment Process Analysis Chart.

dynamic-effect law (R. B. Cattell) The proposition which holds that the habitualization of specific attentions and new behaviors is proportionate to their facilitation of goal attainment.

dynamic equilibrium A characteristic of a system in which the pattern of distribution of energy remains stable despite changes in the total amount of energy. A change in the amount of energy at any one point in the system results in a restructuring of the energy distribution towards the end of maintaining the original distribution pattern.

dynamic lattice (R. B. Cattell) A diagrammatic representation of the relation between an individual's goals and the relatively fixed habits which serve his dynamic purposes (attitudes, interests) in achieving these goals.

dynamic psychology See *psychology, dynamic.*

dynamic-situations principle (V. W. Voecks) The proposition that the stimulus configuration is never set as there are constant alterations of stimuli due to environmental and organismic changes, both of which affect which stimulus elements are received and how they are received.

dynamic structure factors Source traits found among attitude-strength measures of very varied content and representing both ergs and engrams. Distinguished from motivation component factors.

dynamic subsidiation The sequence of subsidiary goals which leads to a final goal.

dynamic theory (W. Köhler) The proposition which holds that brain activity is determined by continual energy changes rather than by fixed relations among anatomic brain structures.

dynamism 1. A persistent mode of behaving in a way which brings drive satisfaction; mechanism. 2. (H.S. Sullivan) The smallest unit in the study of an individual's functional activity, that is the relatively enduring pattern of behavior which continuously characterizes the individual in his interpersonal relations. Dynamisms may be either patterns arising from recurring physiological tensions manifested as integrative, disjunctive, or isolative tendencies, patterns arising from particular zones of interaction, or both.

dynamogenesis; dynamogen 1. The fact that changes in response are correlated with changes in sensory activity. 2. The fact that motor responses are initiated as a result of sensory stimulation.

dynamogenesis, principle of The proposition that response changes are proportional to the changes in sensory activity.

dysacousia A condition characterized by extreme discomfort caused by ordinary noise.

dysarthria The impairment of speech articulation caused by central nervous system disease.

dysbulia A difficulty in thinking characterized by an inability to concentrate, attend or maintain a train of thought.

dyseneia Defective speech articulation resulting from any kind of deafness.

dysergasia (A. Meyer) A term designating those syndromes usually associated with disordered brain physiology and characterized by hallucination, disorientation, and fears.

dysesthesia An inappropriate, excessive or diminished sensitivity to pain.

dysgenesis 1. Faulty development and infertility. 2. The condition in hybrids characterized by infertility with others of the hybrid stock and fertility with the members of either parent's stock.

dysgenic 1. A term describing those influences which are detrimental to heredity. 2. Biologically deficient.

dysgraphia The inability to express thoughts through writing or written symbols, caused by a brain lesion.

dyskinesia; dyskinesis A distortion of or inability to control involuntary movement characterized by involuntary muscular activity such as tics, spasms, or myoclonus.

dyslalia Defective speech.

dyslexia A reading disorder characterized by the inability to understand what one reads either silently or aloud.

dyslogia 1. An impairment of the ability to express ideas through speech caused by mental deficiency. 2. An impairment of speech due to mental deficiency.

dysmenorrhea Painful menstruation without apparent organic cause. The psychogenic factor is usually ambivalence concerning the female role.

dysmnesia An impairment of memory.

dysmutual neurosis See *neurosis, dysmutual.*

dysmutualism (B. B. Wolman) A type of mental disorder based on a form of social interaction characterized by an inconsistency of feelings and beliefs and extreme cyclic mood changes, including hysteria (on neurotic level) and manic-depressive psychosis.

dyspareunia 1. A deficient capacity for the enjoyment of sexual pleasure. 2. Painful sexual intercourse.

dysphagia An inability to swallow due to hysterical spasms of the throat muscles.

dysphemia A defective articulation of speech due to functional causes.

dysphonia Impairment of voice.

dysphoria A generalized feeling of anxiety and restlessness accompanied by depression.

dysphrasia A difficulty in speaking or writing which results from mental impairment.

dysplasis or displasia 1. Abnormal growth or development. 2. In terms of somatotype, the quantitative amount of a specific component or somatotype whether endomorphic, mesomorphic or ectomorphic, in different regions of the body. Also known as d-component.

dysplastic type See *type, dysplastic.*

dyspnoea; dyspnea A difficulty in breathing.

dyspraxia An impairment in the coordination of movement; an inability to carry out skilled movements.

dysthmia Despondent mood or disposition.

dystrophia See *dystrophy, pseudohypertrophic muscular.*

dystrophy, pseudohypertrophic muscular A familial disease characterized by progressive atrophy of the muscles following early hypertrophy, weakness, inability to rise and move naturally. It occurs in childhood.

E

e **1.** Abbreviation for error. **2.** (mathematics) Mathematical constant which is the base of natural logarithms having the value of 2.718281.

E **1.** Abbreviation for experimenter, often italicized. **2.** Abbreviation for environment.

$_S E_R$ See *excitatory potential.*

$_S E_R$ (C. L. Hull) Generalized reaction potential. The reaction potential of any amount of learning, is $_S E_R = D \times V_1 \times K \times _S H_R$ where D stands for drive operating during the learning process, multiplied by V_1 which is the dynamism of the signaling stimulus trace, multiplied by K which is the incentive reinforcement and by $_S H_R$, the habit strength.

$_S \overline{E}_R$ See *momentary effective reaction potential.*

E scale See *scale, E.*

ear Auditory sensory organ consisting of the outer ear, the middle ear, and the inner ear or labyrinth.

ear drum The tympanic membrane which stretches across the inner part of the external auditory canal and conducts vibrations when sound waves reach it.

ear, inner See *labyrinth.*

ear pulling **1.** Considered to be masturbatory equivalent in psychoanalytic theory. **2.** Viewed as substitute for thumb sucking by Kanner.

Earle, Pliny (1809-1892) American psychiatrist who held one of the first professorships of psychological medicine; author of *Curability of Insanity* (1877).

early recollections (A. Adler) The earliest childhood recollections offer the clue toward the understanding of a patient, for they represent the patient's attitude toward himself and life. Analysis of the early memories is of utmost importance in individual psychology psychotherapy.

Ebbinghaus, Hermann (1850-1909) German psychologist noted for his work in the field of memory and learning. He used experimentally the nonsense syllable. He developed the completion test which has been used in personality and intelligence tests. Serving as his own subject, Ebbinghaus investigated the memory process and association processes through studying the acquisition and retention of lists of words. Ebbinghaus established numerical indices of memory performance. He invented a method of measuring retention called "savings" in which he compared the number of trials to learn a list of nonsense syllables initially to the number of trials required for relearning, and elaborated the curve of retention. Ebbinghaus wrote several books, including *On Memory* (1885).

Ebbinghaus' curve of retention A forgetting curve obtained by Ebbinghaus who measured the retention of nonsense material. The curve demonstrates a rapid drop in retention of material immediately after learning followed by a more gradual decline later on.

Ebbinghaus illusion See *illusion, Ebbinghaus.*

ebriecation (Paracelsus) Term for mental illness associated with alcoholism.

ebriecation celeste (Paracelsus) Deranged exhibition of religious excitement and enthusiasm.

E/C intervening variable The factor that indicates the empirical difference of results between the experimental and the control conditions.

eccentric Deviating noticeably from normality in a manner considered to be odd or unusual without being a distinct sign of mental disorder, though sometimes, it is an early sign of such a disorder.

eccentric paranoia **1.** Paranoia characterized by acute emotional excitement with frequent hallucinations, abnormal motor activity, and intense involvement with deranged social schemes. **2.** Condition formerly called "religious mania" when involving religious ideas.

eccentric projection **1.** Location of sensation at the point in space of the stimulating body rather than at the point of sensation in the stimulated organism. Visual and auditory senses are usually projected in this way, while olfactory sensations are generally localized, tactual sensations are located at the point of sensation in the stimulated body. 2. A perceptual theory based upon these phenomena.

Eccles, John Carew (1903-   ) Neurophysiologist, specially interested in (1) Synaptic transmission in the central nervous system (Nobel award, 1963), (2) The central mechanisms concerned in the control of movement with special reference to the cerebellum, (3) The brain-mind problem. Published books on these three interests are (1) *Physiology of Nerve Cells* (1947); *Physiology of Synapses* (1964); (2) *The Cerebellum as a Neuronal Machine* (1967); *Facing Reality: Philosophical Adventures by a Brain Scientist* (1970).

ecdemomania Unhealthy impulse to roam or travel.

écho des pensées Hallucinations of thoughts reproduced as verbal images; thoughts are heard repeated in speech, including the announcement of future actions.

echo-phenomena A general term indicating repetitive behavior including echopraxia and echolalia.

echo principle Supposition that one animal will imitate another animal if they have been involved simultaneously in the same behavior.

echo-sign Epileptic speech disorder characterized by the repetition of a single word in a phrase.

echo-speech See *echolalia.*

echokinesis See *echopraxia.*

echolalia 1. Reiteration by imitation of the words or phrases of another person, characteristic of the catatonic schizophrenia. 2. Infantile speech patterns based on repeating sounds and words.

echolocation Also called facial vision. It is the ability to assess the location of objects from their reflected echoes; it is an unconscious process analogous to radar which detects radio signals above the surface and sonar which discovers sounds under water. Human echolocation was first described by D. Diderot and J. de R. D'Alembert, French philosophers in the eighteenth century. Diderot maintained that blind men judge proximity of fire by the degree of heat and can distinguish an open street by motions of air. Modern researchers (K. M. Dallenbach, D. R. Griffin, W. N. Kellogg) rejected the notion of facial vision but related the perception of blind people to their ability to locate auditory and tactile cues. Some animals display a high degree of echolocation. Dolphins follow fish and catch them following reflected echoes; rats emit sounds and avoid obstacles by perceiving the echoes of their sounds; and bats do not collide with the wires stretched in their caves.

echomatism See *echopraxia.*

echomimia See *echopraxia.*

echopathy Repetition by imitation of the words or actions of another person, characteristic of catatonic schizophrenia.

echophrasia See *echolalia.*

echopraxia Repetition through imitation of the actions or movements of another, as in "mirror-imaging," symptomatic of the catatonic schizophrenic.

eclactisma Movements of the lower portion of the body in a grand mal seizure of epilepsy.

eclampsia 1. Epileptic convulsion. 2. Recurrent convulsion occurring during late pregnancy and associated with kidney disorder.

eclecticism Organization of compatible facts and positions from diverse sources and incompatible theories into a consistent system.

eclimia 1. Large appetite and increased eating due to insatiable hunger. 2. Bulimia.

eclipse, mental (P. Janet) A belief that one's ideas are stolen from him, characteristic of schizophrenics.

ecmnesia Anterograde amnesia; a rare kind of amnesia.

ecnoia An extreme and prolonged fear reaction.

ecogenic component in an age curve (R. B. Cattell) The part of an age curve of a trait which is freed of influence due to peculiar historical epoch trend (the epogenic component). Ecogenic and epogenic components are to be separated by comparison of curves based on cross-sectional sampling with those from cursive longitudinal sampling.

ecological validity See *validity, ecological.*

ecology The study of organisms in relation to their physical environment and geographical surroundings.

ecology, human The study of human organisms in relation to the physical and social environment which constitutes their life space.

ecology, psychological The interaction of environmental variables and personal susceptibility in the development of a disorder.

ecomania Pathological attitude and behavior syndrome toward members of one's family.

econetics (R. B. Cattell) The subdivision of psychology concerned with relating the psychological meaning of a stimulus situation to the physical, biological, sociological, economic, etc., parameters. Psychophysics is, thus, a limited branch of econetics.

economic Psychoanalytic term for the production, distribution and consumption of psychic energy with the greatest gain for the least effort.

economic efficiency index An index expressing the efficiency of a test installation for industrial purposes by dividing the standard general validity by the cost (in expenditure on the time of various professional and clerical psychometric workers).

economic type See *type, economic.*

economical Minimum possible expenditure of energy resources or materials.

economics 1. Study of the production, distribution and exchange of material resources. 2. Theory that a person uses the least possible energy to attain a goal.

Economo's disease (K. von Economo) Lethargic encephalitis.

economy 1. Principle of arranging any system with minimum possible waste. 2. Tendency of an organism to avoid unnecessary expenditure of energy.

economy, principle of Rule in scientific investigation that the simplest of possible explanations be preferred; principle of parsimony.

ecophobia Fear of one's own house.

ecosomatogenic disorders (B. B. Wolman) Mental disorders of organic origin acquired through interaction with the physical environment. Brain injuries, toxic and infectious mental disorders belong to this category.

écouteur Person who experiences excessive pleasure by listening to sexual accounts.

ecphoria Recurrence of a memory trace or engram.

ecphorize To revive a memory trace or engram.

ecphory Reoccurrence of a memory trace or engram.

ecphronia Old term for neurotic mania and melancholy.

ecplexis (C. Galen) Stupor.

ecstasy 1. Overwhelming rapture or joy. 2. Religious trance.

ecstatic trance 1. Religious trance. 2. Trance-like state of overwhelming rapture or joy.

ECT Electroshock therapy. See *electric convulsive therapy*.

ectoderm Outer embryonic layer which gives rise to the epidermis, nails, hair, and other specializations of the outer membrane.

ectodermal Pertaining to the ectoderm or outermost embryonic layer which gives rise to the epidermis and its derivatives.

ectodermogenic neurosyphilis Syphilitic infection of the nervous system involving the cerebrospinal axis.

ectomorphic type See *type, ectomorphic*.

ectopia pupillae Abnormality of position of the pupil.

ectoplasm 1. Outer layer of a cell or unicellular organism. 2. In occultism and psychic research, a semisolid substance said to emanate from the body of a medium.

ectype Physical or mental constitution that varies markedly from the average.

eczema An inflammation of the skin characterized by itching, scaling and exudation of serous substances due to physical or psychogenic origin. Psychological causes involve feelings of insecurity, fears of rejection, and an inconsistent overprotective relationship with the mother.

edema, angioneurotic See *angioneurotic edema*.

edge details 1. A response to a Rorschach inkblot based on the contour of the edge. 2. A scoring category for the Rorschach test based on responses determined by the contour of the inkblot.

edging A unique kind of Rorschach test behavior in which the subject "edges" the cards, that is looking at the card with the surface held in a straight line with the line of vision.

edipism Injury to the eyes by oneself.

Edipus complex See *complex, Oedipus*.

educability Potentiality for learning, usually in reference to formal or school learning with I.Q. 50 or M.A. 6 as minimal necessary potential.

education 1. Progressive changes of a person affecting knowledge, attitudes, and behavior as a result of formal instruction and study. 2. Development of a person resulting from experience rather than from maturation. 3. Method of analysis through which a general principle emerges. 4. (C. Spearman) Process of relational thinking whereby knowledge of relations and the discovery of correlates leads to discovery of third and fourth neogenetic principles. 5. (H. S. Sullivan) Central processes located between the receptor functions and the effector functions.

education stage (C. G. Jung) The third stage of analytical psychotherapy in which the patient adapts to social pressure, demands and needs.

educational acceleration Progressing through an educational system more rapidly than normal either by skipping a grade or through special curricula.

educational age Performance in academic subjects measured in terms of the average chronological age performing at that level through the use of standardized achievement tests.

educational guidance Assisting students to pursue a suitable program of studies in relation to their interests, abilities, future plans, and environmental factors.

educational measurement 1. Appraising the abilities of a student through the use of a variety of tests. 2. Test construction and validation for use in schools. 3. Evaluating educational methods.

educational psychology See *psychology, educational*.

educational quotient Ratio of educational age to chronological age multiplied by 100 which is interpreted as an index of educational achievement.

$$E.Q. = \frac{E.A.}{C.A.} \times 100$$

Edwards Personal Preference Schedule (A. L. Edwards) A personality inventory introduced in 1953 which assesses fifteen of the manifest needs defined by H. A. Murray. Attempt was made to reduce variance of scores from social desirability by pairing items deemed equal in social desirability and requiring the subject to make a forced choice preference between these items. The subject's response is believed to reflect his needs rather than his conception of the more desirable characteristic.

EEG See *electroencephalogram.*

E-F scale Thirty item sub-scale of the Minnesota Multiphasic Inventory of Personality designed to measure ethnocentric and authoritarian attitudes.

effect **1.** Event that invariably follows a specific other phenomenon as in a causal relationship; a result. **2.** Major law of Thorndike's theory of learning stating that annoyance weakens and satisfaction strengthens a stimulus-response connection.

effect, halo The tendency to be influenced by a particular trait or overall impression of a person when rating another trait of that person.

effect, law of See *law of effect.*

effect, spread of The principle that the effect of rewards and punishments of a response spreads to other aspects of the situation.

effectance motive General motive encompassing all specific motives.

effective-habit strength ($_S\bar{H}_R$) (C. L. Hull) Functional habit strength; sum of the reaction evocation potentialities set up by a reinforcement process, or by multiple reinforcement processes ($_{SS}H_R$).

effective-reaction potential ($_S\bar{E}_R$) (C. L. Hull) Reaction potential less inhibitory potential.

effective stimulus Stimulus which elicits a response.

effector Nerve ending in a muscle or a gland which responds to impulses.

effeminacy Physical or psychological feminine characteristics in a man.

effeminate Word describing a man who displays marked feminine traits in appearance or in personality.

effemination **1.** State of being or becoming feminine in physical and psychological characteristics. **2.** Homosexuality in which the sexual feelings and the psychological make-up of a man resemble those considered typically feminine.

efferent Nerve fibers which conduct impulses from the central nervous system to muscles and glands.

efferent apraxia See *apraxia, dynamic.*

efferent motor aphasia See *aphasia, efferent motor.*

efficiency **1.** Ratio of energy expended to work done in a mechanism. **2.** Minimum time or energy expended for maximum accomplishment. **3.** (Signal detection theory) The square of the ratio of the empirically obtained detectability index for the human observer divided by the index for the ideal observer, the theoretically maximum performance,

$$\eta = \frac{(d' \text{ observed})^2}{d' \text{ ideal}}$$

efficiency, predictive See *predictive efficiency.*

efficient cause Total of the antecedent conditions of a given event or effect.

effluvium **1.** Emanations from spiritual bodies in psychical research. **2.** Body odor.

effort **1.** Work done voluntarily or without extrinsic coercion. **2.** Increased activity in the face of obstacles. **3.** Subjective experience of fatigue or strain accompanying strenuous physical or mental activity.

effort experience Kinesthetic experience originating in the muscles involved in activity or effort.

effort syndrome **1.** Physical symptoms, including shortness of breath, heart palpitation and fatigue out of proportion to the amount of exertion expended; associated with anxiety neurosis. **2.** Neurocirculatory asthenia.

egersis Extreme wakefulness.

ego **1.** The self, or the "I" which the individual experiences as himself. **2.** (psychoanalysis) Part of a person's mental apparatus which develops gradually under the influence of environmental forces or the id to protect the organism against threats from within and without. The unconscious material of the id becomes transformed into the preconscious ego, in which the primary mental processes give ground to the emerging secondary processes. The main task of the ego is self-preservation of the organism. It performs this task in relation to the external world and to the internal world and in relation to the id by applying the so-called "reality-principle." The ego carries out the intentions of the id but only under conditions that promise a successful fulfillment. The ego brings together, unifies and organizes the mental processes, eliminates contradictions and develops into a coherent and well-functioning unit, practices "reality testing" that is, checks and controls the correctness of perceptions, and steers the entire mental system, avoiding unnecessary risks. The ego adjusts to the environment through control of overt behavior and the regulation of motor functions. When the organism is exposed to external danger, the ego reacts with fear. When the inner pressure stemming from the unconscious threatens the ego, the feeling of anxiety serves as a danger signal.

ego-alien (psychoanalysis) Not in harmony with the ego or total self in terms of drives, intellect, emotions, or overt behavior. In this term ego connotes what would currently be called the total self rather than the psychoanalytic concept of ego.

ego-alter theory **1.** (H. Witkin) Theory that social interaction and social organization results from and is controlled by the individual's perception of himself in relation to the other or others. **2.** Theory that the development of social institutions is based on self-interest and the instinct of self-preservation.

ego analysis (psychoanalysis) Analysis of the strengths and weaknesses of the ego in order to make constructive use of these forces.

ego anxiety (psychoanalysis) **1.** Anxiety arising

from threat to the ego caused by the conflicting demands of the id, the ego, and the superego. **2.** Precipitate of ego defenses.

ego automatisms (psychoanalysis) Ego functions which are pre-conscious rather than conscious, such as driving a car or speaking a second language. Pathological ego automatisms resemble normal ego automatisms but are not appropriate to the situation, as in echolalia.

ego, auxiliary See *auxiliary ego.*

ego block Anything which interferes with the functioning and growth of the ego.

ego, body Mentally experienced representations of the bodily self.

ego boundaries (P. Federn) Hypothetical boundaries existing between the person and the outer world of reality and between the person and his inner unconscious world. In a well functioning individual, the boundaries are cathected and flexible so that the ego is able to admit certain aspects of the unconscious selectively and to test reality demands adequately. In maladjustment, one or both of the boundaries are either too rigid or too weak to exercise their functions properly.

ego cathexis (psychoanalysis) Channeling instinctual demands and impulses in a rational, well-adjusted manner by using avenues of gratification in which the demands of the id, the ego, the superego, and of the external world are brought to a rational harmony. Impulses that jeopardize the inner harmony become either "successfully repressed" or sublimated, that is, channeled into new and more acceptable channels.

ego complex (C. Jung) Psychic energy in the human mind centered around the ego or self.

ego defense (psychoanalysis) Protection of the ego from unacceptable impulses of the id through the use of unconscious defense mechanisms.

ego-deficiency symptoms (B. B. Wolman) Psychotic symptoms including loss of contact with reality, paranoid delusions, hallucinations, depersonalization and motor and speech disturbances which occur as a result of the collapse of the ego.

ego development 1. (S. Freud) The gradual differentiation and evolution of part of the id into the ego. The neonate's mental apparatus, the id, resembles a body floating in water. Under the influence of environmental forces that act on the surface of the id, this surface changes and develops into a sort of protective shell, called the ego. Part of the unconscious material of the id becomes transformed into the preconscious ego, in which the primary mental processes give ground to the emerging secondary processes. This development of ego allows the individual to protect himself from internal and external threats and to differentiate himself from the external world. **2.** (H. Hartmann) Development through maturation and learning of the primary and the secondary autonomous apparati of the ego which constitute the foundation for the ego's relation to external reality. The primary autonomous apparati include the inborn capacities of perception, motility, and thought; the secondary autonomous apparati develops as a result of defense against instinctual drive and leads toward a more structured and independent pattern of behavior.

ego, duplication of Delusion that the individual is more than one person or has multiple identities.

ego-dystonia Mental state of experiencing ideas or impulses which are unacceptable to the ego or self.

ego-eroticism (S. Freud) **1.** The investment of libido in one's own person; the direction of libido to oneself as opposed to external objects. **2.** The egoistic drives or energies that are at the disposal of erotic force and that serve pleasure and enhance the vital functions of the individual.

ego failure (psychoanalysis) Failure of the ego to keep balance among impulses coming from the id, demands of the superego, and external reality.

ego function (psychoanalysis) Activities of the ego as opposed to the id or the superego.

ego-ideal (S. Freud)**1.** In earlier works, synonymous with what was later called the superego; representing the biologically and cultural-historically evolved conscience which sets behavioral norms for the individual. **2.** In later works, the ego-ideal represents that part of the superego which carries the child's admiration for idealized parental figures. Identification by introjection results in the individual striving toward perfection by attempting to live up to the expectations or standards of the idealized parental figures, the ego-ideal.

ego-ideal, narcissistic Perfect self-image the child constructs of himself without reference to an ego-ideal based on identification with the parental figures.

ego identity (psychoanalysis) A person's experience of himself as persisting essentially unchanged on as a continuous entity through time as a result of the function of the ego which synthesizes one's ideals, behavior and societal role.

ego instincts (psychoanalysis) Instincts directed toward self-preservation.

ego-integrative Organization of personality into a whole through harmonizing of impulses and desires.

ego-involvement Personal indentification with, or commitment to, a situation or a task.

ego-libido (S. Freud) Libido invested in one's own person; libido directed toward one's self and toward self-preservation, as opposed to external objects.

ego, loss of boundaries of 1. Inability of an individual to separate his own self from another, or from the surrounding world. **2.** Breakdown of subject/object distinction.

ego, mental Mentally experienced representation of self or ego.

ego morphism 1. (L. Ackerson) Perceiving and interpreting the behavior of others and things in general the way one wants them to be. 2. Using one's personal motivational system as a general standard of reference against which the motives and actions of others are judged.

ego-neurosis (psychoanalysis) Disorder occurring when the weak or poorly organized ego is unable to cope with inner and outer pressures; a quantitative disharmony between the id, ego, and superego, and between the total personality and the outer world.

ego nuclei (M. Klein) Original components of the ego.

ego-object polarity Maintenance of a clear distinction between oneself and all that is other or not self.

ego perception (P. Schilder) The ego as a censor.

ego protective symptoms (B. B. Wolman) Neurotic symptoms including defense mechanisms indicative of the struggle of the ego to retain the control over unconscious impulses.

ego resistance (psychoanalysis) The action or defense mechanism of the ego that prevents the unconscious from becoming conscious.

ego retrenchment (psychoanlaysis) The lessening or the disappearance of the need for a particular function of the ego to occur through the use of defense mechanisms.

ego strength A source trait showing itself in good emotional stability and capacity to cope with emotional difficulties.

ego structure Persisting pattern of personality characteristics that influence ego processes.

ego subject (psychoanalysis) The ego as the object of its own libido or instincts as in narcissism and autoerotic gratifications.

ego-suffering (psychoanalysis) The direction of aggressive forces stored in the superego against the ego creating guilt feelings such as depression when the superego disapproves of the ego.

ego syntonic (psychoanalysis) Ideas, behavior or impulses which are acceptable to the ego or self.

egocentric 1. Interested in oneself and one's personal needs and concerns. 2. Behavior directed by personal needs and self-interest.

egohood Selfhood; individuality.

egoism 1. Action or behavior directed by one's personal needs and interests, disregarding the needs of others. 2. Social philosophy or ethical system based on self-interest as the primary motivation of behavior.

egoist One who is motivated primarily by self-interest.

egoistic 1. Concerned with one's own interests to the neglect of others. 2. Motivated by self-interest.

egoity Selfhood; egohood.

egoize To take excessive interest in one's self.

egology (S. Rado) Study of the ego or the "I".

egomania Extreme preoccupation with self.

egopathy Hostile feelings or actions arising from excessive feelings of self-importance and the subsequent desire to put others down.

egotheism Deification of the self.

egotism See *egoism.*

egotist 1. See *egoist.* 2. Conceited person; one who overevaluates himself.

egotistical Conceited; thinking very highly of oneself.

egotize 1. To take excessive interest in oneself or to act conceited. 2. To display egotism.

egotropic (A. Meyer) Egocentric or egocentricity.

egotropy (A. Meyer) Narcissism or egocentricity.

egregorsis Extreme wakefulness.

egrimony Obsolete term for sorrow or sadness.

eidetic Mental images of things previously seen characterized by clean or vivid visualization.

eidetic imagery Especially clear and detailed visual image of things previously seen, sometimes even months after the actual viewing of them.

eidetic type (E. R. Jaensch) Constitutional type based on different kinds of eidetic imagery experienced by people and associated with personality variables arising from differences in perceptual and cognitive functioning.

Eigenwelt (Existentialist) Man's relationship with himself.

Einstellung (German) Attitude or mental set which predisposes one to behave or respond in a certain way to particular situations.

eisotrophobia Fear of mirrors.

ejaculatio deficiens Inadequate ejaculation.

ejaculatio praecox Premature ejaculation; emission of semen during preparation for sexual intercourse before or immediately upon insertion.

ejaculation Expulsion of semen at orgasm.

ejaculation retardata Delayed or retarded ejaculation during sexual intercourse.

EKG see *electrocardiogram.*

elaboration Combining and expanding of ideas and motives characteristic of higher mental processes.

elation 1. Extreme joyful excitement. 2. Abnormal or exaggerated gaiety. 3. (W. McDougall) Emotional component of self-display.

elavil Common name for amitriptylene, an antidepressant drug.

Elberfeld horses Group of horses trained in Elberfeld, Germany around 1900 who appeared to be solving complicated mathematical problems though they were actually trained to tap their feet each time the trainer nodded his head.

elbow jerk 1. Sharp reflex of the forearm occasioned by striking the tendon just above the elbow when the arm is partly flexed at the elbow. 2. Triceps reflex.

elective anorexia Absence of appetite and restriction of the amount of food eaten through having an extremely negative reaction to the consumption of food.

Electra complex See *complex, Electra.*

electric convulsive (electroshock) therapy Introduced in 1938 by Cerletti and Bini in Rome, Italy. It is a modification of the original convulsive therapy with pharmacological means (metrazol) by von Meduna. Convulsive therapy is primarily based on an old observation that the symptoms of mental patients may disappear after spontaneous convulsions. The same could be achieved with artificially induced convulsions. Since 1952 the early complications of convulsive treatment are eliminated by means of chemical relaxation of all muscles. This is accomplished by injection of succinyl choline given after induction of barbiturate anesthesia. The treatment itself is given with a short bilateral electrical stimulus. It is painless, and the patient has complete amnesia for the entire procedure. After several treatments some memory disturbance exists but always disappears after a while as thorough psychological testing has proven. Unilateral stimulation over the non-dominant hemisphere avoids memory impairment but is therapeutically less effective. Indications are schizophrenia, and particularly depressions.

electric organ Specialized muscular tissue in some primitive fish which can generate potential and store charges and which transmits electric shock through the nervous system upon excitation.

electrical brain stimulation (ESB) It has been found that electrical stimulation of the brain by means of implanted electrodes can have both reinforcing and punishing effects on behavior, i.e. the organism will work to be electrically stimulated or will work to avoid electrical stimulation. What effects stimulation will have is a function of the intensity of stimulation and the locus of stimulation.

electroaesthesiometer A type of aesthesiometer which measures two-point or spatial thresholds by using an electromagnet to bring the stimulus point into contact with the skin.

electrocardiogram (EKG) Graphic record of the electrical activity accompanying the heartbeat made by an electrocardiograph and used as a diagnostic tool.

electroconvulsive therapy See *electric convulsive therapy.*

electrode Two-poled device used to transmit electric current to tissue; the positive pole is the anode; the negative pole is the cathode.

electrodermal response (EDR) See *galvanic skin response.*

electrodiagnosis 1. Use of electrical instruments to diagnose conditions of the body. 2. The application of electric current to muscles and nerves for diagnostic purposes.

electromyogram (EMG) Graphic record of electrical activity or currents in a muscle. Also called *electromyograph.*

electronarcosis A shock treatment which produces a sleep-like coma after an initial convulsive phase.

electrophobia Extreme fear of electricity.

electroretinogram (ERG) Graphic record of electrical activity in the retina of the eye.

electroshock therapy See *electric convulsive therapy.*

electrotaxis Response of organisms or cells, either attraction or repulsion, to electrical stimulation.

electrotherapy Application of electricity in the treatment of physical or mental disorder.

electrotonus The changed electrical and physical condition of a nerve or muscle due to the application of electric current.

element 1. A part or constituent of the whole, especially one that cannot be reduced to a simpler unit. 2. (W. Wundt, B. Titchener) The simplest units of consciousness. 3. (G. A. Kelly) One of the events or units of information that are abstracted from a specific construct by a particular person. 4. (information theory) Points in a sample space or a single unit or events in a collection of units or elements.

elementarism 1. Belief that a complex whole is reducible to and understandable in terms of its constituent parts which are considered to be independent units. 2. Any approach to psychology which analyzes behavior and mental processes in terms of mental elements. 3. When used derogatorily: preoccupation with simple parts at the expense of the whole.

eleutheromania Fanatical interest in freedom.

Elgin check list List of behavior patterns more often associated with the psychotic population than with the normal population.

elimination The expelling of feces and urine from the body.

elision The omission of syllables or sounds in speech.

Elizur's test for organicity See *test, Elizur's, for organicity.*

ellipsis 1. Omission of whole words in speech or writing with the result that the listener or reader must complete the thought himself. 2. (psychoanalysis) Omission of highly significant words or ideas which might be recovered through free association.

ellis harmonical Specialized reed instrument similar to the harmonium used to experimentally study and demonstrate exact intervals and pitches.

Ellis, Henry Havelock (1859-1939) British psychologist noted for his study of the psychology of sex.

elucidation stage (C.. G. Jung) The second stage of analytical psychotherapy in which interpretations of unconscious contents, especially transference material, are made.

emancipation 1. Independence of thought, feeling and behavior due to freedom from control by others, particularly from the control of parents. 2. (psychoanalysis) Resolution of the Oedipal complex and subsequent liberation from parental figures and authority.

emasculation Castration, either physical or psychological.

embarassment dream Dream in which the individual sees himself in a painful or shameful situation from which he cannot escape and which is thought to be related to painful childhood experiences.

embedded figure 1. Outline of person or object merged with background in such a way that it is difficult to perceive. 2. Hidden figure.

embolalia Meaningless words or phrases interspersed in spoken language.

embolism Obstruction or stoppage of a blood vessel by a blood clot or an air bubble.

embolism, cerebral Occlusion of a cerebral blood vessel by an embolus, the result appearing like a cerebral hemorrhage.

embolophasia See embolophrasia.

embolophrasia Repeated repetition of an unnecessary phrase in spoken language.

embryo Organism in its early stage of prenatal development; in the human species it is the first six to eight weeks after conception.

embryology The study of prenatal development of organisms.

embryonic Related to the embryo or the early stage of an organism's development.

emeotamania Desire to vomit, often associated with hysteria.

emergency situations Critical situations where the organism automatically prepares for sudden, sustained action such as fight or flight through the occurrence of automatic facilitating physiological reactions which are under the control of the sympathetic nervous system.

emergency theory of the emotions 1. (W. B. Cannon) Theory that the emotions and accompanying physiological changes controlled by the sympathetic portion of the autonomic nervous system prepare the organism for emergencies; visceral changes such as increased heart rate, rise in blood pressure and dilation of the pupils which are associated with certain emotions also prepare the organism for flight or fight when necessary. 2. (H. Selye) Theory that an organism's adaptation to emergencies or stress is comprised of three phases governed by the autonomic nervous system: the alarm phase in which the organism mobilizes its defenses; the resistance phase in which the body exerts its resources in order to meet continued stress successfully; and the exhaustion stage when the organism has used its protective resources and is no longer able to resist stress.

emergent 1. Phenomenon which cannot be predicted from its parts or reduced to its antecedent events or properties. 2. (Gestalt) The whole as being qualitatively different from its constituent parts and, as such, influencing them.

emergent evolution Theory that new and unpredicatable phenomena result from the combination or interaction of pre-existing factors or elements.

emetophobia Extreme fear of vomiting often associated with hysteria.

EMG See electromyogram.

emission 1. Discharge of semen. 2. Elicitation of a response not associated with an identifiable stimulus.

emission, nocturnal Discharge of semen in sleep.

emit Occurrence of a response not associated with any particular or identifiable stimulus.

Emmert's law See law, Emmert's.

emmetropia, emmetropis Normal vision due to perfectly functioning refractory system of the eye, which focuses rays directly on the retina without the necessity of accommodation.

emote To exhibit emotion.

emotion 1. A complex reaction consisting of a physiological change from the homeostatic state, subjectively experienced as feeling and manifested in bodily changes which are preparatory to overt actions. 2. (psychoanalysis) A derivative of instinctual drive representing the tension experienced by the individual making it necessary for him to discharge and eliminate the need. 3. (James-Lange theory) The perception of the physiological reaction to a stimulus. 4. (B. F. Skinner) A hypothetical state that is the predisposition to act in a certain manner that is the function of circumstances in the individual's history. 5. (Cannon-Bard theory) The result of impulses sent to the cortex by the hypothalamus which is stimulated to do so by the receptors of outside stimulation. Impulses to the viscera are sent simultaneously by the hypothalmus, resulting in the energy state accompanying emotion. 6. (K. Pribram) A process of disequilibration (affects, passions) and re-equilibration (coping) that depends on internal control as opposed to that which deploys planned action on the environment (motivation).

emotional 1. Characterized by or associated with emotion or the physiological changes which accompany emotion. 2. Tending toward emotional behavior or responses rather than cognitive behavior or responses.

emotional bias Prejudice based on emotional causes.

emotional blockage Inability to remember or to think coherently due to strong emotions usually associated with fear.

emotional centre Obsolete term for the portion of

the brain thought to control emotional functioning. Thalamic region seems to be related to the function of emotions.

emotional control Attempt by an individual to direct his own emotions or the emotions of another.

emotional disorder Mental disorder or condition in which emotional reactions are chronically inappropriate or disproportionate given the reality situation.

emotional expression Behavioral, visceral, muscular and glandular changes that occur while emoting.

emotional immaturity 1. Tendency toward emotional behavior characteristic of children or younger persons. 2. Failure to exhibit emotional behavior considered appropriate to one's age level. 3. Vague term for poor adjustment of any sort.

emotional instability Tendency toward rapidly changing and unpredictable emotional behavior.

emotional maturity Condition characterized by emotional development, and by exhibition of emotional behavior appropriate to adults rather than to children.

emotional pattern 1. The behavioral, physiological and peripheral responses, and the set of relationships, such as intensity and timing, among them usually associated with a particular emotion and supposed to be characteristic of it. 2. The pattern of emotional behavior characteristic of a given individual under various conditions.

emotional release 1. Outpouring of emotions which had been suppressed or pent up. 2. Catharsis of emotion.

emotional stability Characteristic of having good emotional control and consistency or of not reacting excessively to emotional situations.

emotional state Physiological, behavioral, and conscious condition of an organism during emotional or affective experiences and characteristic of emotions.

emotional surrender The fusion of patients with another person in a therapeutic setting resulting in loss of their individuality.

emotionalism, respiratory See *nervous pseudoasthma*.

emotionality 1. Indicates the degree to which a person reacts emotionally. 2. Characteristic of persons who tend to react strongly or excessively to emotional situations.

emotionality, home setting of Family situation or home environment characterized by an atmosphere based on emotional influences and factors rather than a rational foundation.

emotions, abnormal instability of 1. General term for pathological manifestations of affect or emotions. 2. Thymopathy.

emotive Stimuli or situations which evoke an emotional or affective response.

empathema Obsolete term for uncontrollable passion.

empathema atonicum (M. Good) Melancholy.

empathema entonicum (M. Good) Obsolete term for what is currently called the manic phase of manic-depressive psychosis.

empathema inane (M. Good) Psychomotor aggression.

empathetic 1. Characterized by empathy. 2. Intellectual rather than emotional identification.

empathize To experience empathy.

empathy 1. Ability to perceive the mood and feelings of another person. 2. Understanding of the feelings, sufferings, or situation of another person without these feelings being communicated by words.

emphrensy Obsolete term for enfrenzy.

empirical 1. Based on facts and experience, systematic observation and experiment rather than theory on general philosophical principle. 2. Valuing facts and devaluing speculation or rational theory.

empirical construct Hypothetical construct based on observed facts.

empirical equation Equation based on a set of observations rather than on rational deduction according to the criteria of closeness to fit and parsimony, not theoretical meaning or value.

empirical law 1. Principle based on empirical data or experimental findings which states the ongoing relationship between two or more sets of variables. 2. Law based on the inductive rather than the deductive process.

empirical test Testing of a hypothesis through the use of facts or experimentation.

empirical validity Validity of a test according to how well it actually measures what it was designed to measure, which is determined by correlating the test with another, independent measure.

empiricism 1. Philosophical theory that all knowledge originates in experience. 2. Observation in psychology, and sciences in general, which is based on empirical observations and objective facts obtained through natural observation and experimentation as the only valid method and data for scientific investigation. Operational definitions and methods are central and theory-building and hypothetical constructs are generally avoided.

employment psychology 1. Area of psychology which deals with selecting the most suitable and most likely to succeed of the applicants for a given occupation through the use of various testing methods. 2. Personnel selection.

empresiomania Pathological desire to set things on fire, more commonly called pyromania.

emprosthotonos Bending of the body forward.

empty organism Term used by opponents of the stimulus-response approach to psychology to criticize the lack of consideration of organismic factors and of hypothetical constructs in such an orientation.

empty set See *null set.*

empyreumatic Category of odors characterized by a tarry or smoky aroma.

emulation Conscious attempt to equal the performance of another with the connotation of imitating that other.

enantiodromia (C.G. Jung) Interplay of opposites through which everything is changed into its opposite eventually.

enantiopathic Leading to the arousal of an opposing passion.

enantiopathy Opposing passion.

encatalepsis (Hippocrates) Obsolete term for catalepsy.

encephalasthenia Extreme mental fatigue.

encephalitis Acute inflammation of the brain or its covering which sometimes results in neurological and personality changes which persist after the inflammation.

encephalitis, coxsackie Mild form of encephalitis, with headaches, lethargy, vomiting, fever and pain of the back of the neck. It is fatal in 80 per cent of the cases in neonates.

encephalitis, ECHO Encephalitis caused by one of the types of ECHO virus, usually types 4, 6, and 9.

encephalitis, epidemic See *encephalitis, lethargic.*

encephalitis, equine Type of encephalitis characterized by headache, nausea, fever, increasing lethargy and vertigo with occasional loss of consciousness and seizures; residual symptoms include intellectual and emotional aberrations, seizures, mental retardation, and visual and language difficulties.

encephalitis, herpes simplex Type of encephalitis with upper respiratory infection, fever and convulsions, from which the person does not awaken. There is often extensive damage to the brain.

encephalitis, Japanese Form of encephalitis with rapid rise of temperature, headaches, confusion and, commonly, transient paralysis of the limbs. Although usually leaving no sequelae, persistent difficulties include paralysis, headaches and, especially in children, intellectual retardation and personality changes.

encephalitis, lethargic 1. Sleeping sickness. 2. Inflammation of the brain often resulting in severe personality changes.

encephalitis, mumps A type of encephalitis caused by mumps, although the patients, while suffering from encephalitis, may show no signs of mumps. Symptoms include lethargy, varying degrees of delirium, stupor and coma, and neurological difficulties during the latter half of the first week of the illness. Brainstem symptoms include facial paresis and deafness, with progressive medullary involvement leading to death. The patient may suffer severe peripheral and sphincter weakness and will manifest symptoms of both upper and lower motor neuron difficulty.

Residuals are rare but hearing loss, persistent facial weakness, and personality changes have been reported.

encephalitis periaxialis diffusa See *Schilder's disease.*

encephalitis, rabies Transmitted to humans by the bite of a rabid animal; its symptoms include pain, chills and fever, nausea and vomiting, malaise, headache, vertigo and often mental confusion, irritability and hydrophobia, and most often death.

encephalitis, rubeola A form of encephalitis associated with rubeola, an exanthematous disease characterized by rash and fever. The patient develops encephalitis four to seven days after the appearance of the rash although the severity of the rubeola has no bearing on the likelihood of development of encephalitis. The encephalitis is associated with a rise in temperature, headache, vomiting, ataxia, lethargy frequently progressing to a comatose state, and occasionally seizures. The most common residuals are ataxia and personality changes.

encephalitis, St. Louis A form of encephalitis which usually strikes abruptly with temperature elevation, headache and symptoms and signs of meningeal inflammation. Some difficulties with judgment, emotions and personality may remain for several months or, occasionally, permanently.

encephalitis, varicella A type of encephalitis which occasionally follow a varicella infection, characterized by lethargy, irritability, ataxia, seizures, fever, and paralysis. Residual difficulties include paresis, ataxia, blindness, retardation, speech difficulties, and personality changes.

encephalization 1. The brain takes on progressively more control of the functioning of the nervous system and of the activities of the body; ascending the phylogenetic scale, in the evolution of a species, and in the development of the individual. 2. Formation of brain through an evolutionary process.

encephalocele Congenital hernia of the brain which protrudes through an opening of the skull.

encephalomalacia Softening of the brain due to an inadequate supply of blood and resulting in partial or complete deterioration.

encephalomyelitis Inflammation of the central nervous system.

encephalon The brain.

encephalopathia literatorum Obsolete term for mental malfunction allegedly resulting from intense studies.

encephalopathia puerperalis See *puerperal psychosis.*

encephalopathy A general name for various brain diseases.

encephalopathy, congenital Brain disease contracted in utero. It may be caused by the mother's infectious diseases such as syphilis, rubella (also called German measles), influenza, parasitic organisms, etc., blood toxins (toxemia), and intoxications with lead, carbon monoxide, arsenic, etc. The various forms of congenital encephalopathy are associated with mental retardation.

encephalopsychosis Mental disorder due to cerebral lesions or a definitely localized disease of the brain.

encephalopyosis Brain abscess.

encephalosis General term for degeneration of the brain through disease.

encoding 1. Transformation of messages into signals which can be transmitted by a communications channel. 2. Transformation of information by an individual into behavior which can function as a signal in a communications system.

encopresis Involuntary defecation not caused by illness or any organic malfunction and associated with poor toilet training or emotional problems when it occurs in children.

enculturation The process of adjusting to and accepting a culture.

end 1. The outcome or result desired from purposive behavior. 2. A goal or purpose.

end brush The termination of an axon which is finely branched.

end button; end foot Thickening or enlargement of nerve fibers of the end brush which are in contact with the dendrites of other cells at the synapse and are thought to be involved in the firing of cells.

end plate Specialized ending of a motor nerve fiber which makes contact with the muscle cell and transmits nerve impulses from the axon to the muscle fiber.

end pleasure (psychoanalysis) Intense pleasure associated with release from tension, especially that which occurs with orgasm.

end spurt Increase in energy and performance just before completing or learning an activity or work.

endocathection 1. (H. A. Murray) The investment of psychic energy in inner thought or emotion for its own sake. 2. Preoccupation with one's own thoughts or inner activities and the withdrawal from external and practical pursuits.

endocrine gland Ductless gland of internal secretion, such as the thyroid, whose products go directly into the bloodstream by osmosis.

endocrine glands See *glands, endocrine.*

endocrine psychosyndrome (M. Bleuler) The majority of endocrine diseases do not provoke a psychosis but they are, however, accompanied by marked personality changes. These personality changes which are described by the term "endocrine psychosyndrome" include 1) increased impulsiveness and excitability in acute cases and decreased in chronic cases; 2) dysfunction of biological rhythms—patients are either inactive and apathetic or tense and hyperactive; 3) mood fluctuations, irritability, anxiety, aggressivity and euphoric states; and 4) disturbances

in biological drives—alternations in the urge to be protected against heat and cold, to rest and relax versus being active, to behave sexually or aggressively toward mother or nurse. These morbid alternations may be lasting but more often they occur suddenly and disappear in the same abrupt fashion. These personality changes are similar to those seen in patients with localized cerebral diseases, particularly those of the brain stem and frontal lobes.

endocrinology Study of endocrine glands and internal secretions.

endocrinopathic Related to or associated with endocrinopathy.

endocrinopathy General term for any disorder caused by disease of the endocrine glands.

endocrinotherapy The use of preparation made from the secretion from the endocrine glands, such as the pituitary or the thyroid, as therapeutic treatment.

endoderm Inner embryonic layer which gives rise to the visceral organs and the digestive tract.

endogamy Restriction of marriage to one's own social group, kinship, one's caste or any other specific group to which the individual belongs through custom or tradition.

endogenous 1. Arisen from within a given system or structure, as from within the mind of the body or a given biological group. 2. Forms of mental deficiency that are hereditary or determined by genes.

endolymph The fluid in the semicircular canal and the labyrinth-like membrane of the internal ear.

endomorphic type See *type, endomorphic.*

endoplasm Inner cytoplasm of a cell.

endopsychic 1. That which is inside the mind; intrapsychic. 2. Referring to unconscious processes.

endopsychic censor See *censor, endopsychic.*

endothelium 1. The epithelium which lines blood vessels, lymph vessels, and the heart. 2. Simple epithelium which lines closed cavities in the body and which develops from the mesoderm.

endowment Natural, innate physical and mental potential; most often used with the connotation of superior potential.

enelicomorphism Attributing adult characteristics, behaviors, or abilities to the child; describing a child's characteristics, behaviors or abilities in adult terms.

enemophobia Fear of wind.

energy (physics) The capacity for doing work.

energy, kinetic Energy of a body in motion which is due to the motion.

energy, psychic 1. Capacity to do mental or psychic work. 2. Energy invested in or expended through psychological activities or processes or mental pursuits.

enervate 1. To lessen energy; to weaken. 2. To surgically remove nerves.

enfrenzy To drive crazy, upset or madden.

engineering psychology 1. Study of the relationships between man and machines. 2. Adjusting the design of machines to the needs and capacities of man. 3. Study of the effect of machines on man's behavior.

engram Intervening variable hypothesized to account for retention and thought to be a permanent change in the state of living tissue as the result of excitation such as that which occurs with learning.

enomania See *oinomania*.

enosimania An individual's obsessive conviction that he has committed an unforgivable sin.

entatic Stimulating; provoking sexual desire or sexual intercourse.

entelechy 1. Realization of a potentiality. 2. The completion or perfection of an act. 3. Non-mechanical or immaterial agent considered responsible for material or life processes.

enteroceptor See *interoceptor*.

enterocolitis Intestinal inflammation associated with nervous disorder.

enteroperipheral (H. Spencer) Obsolete term for experience which originates inside the body.

enteroptosis Sagging or prolapse of the intestines associated with a particular body type in constitutional medicine.

entheomania Extreme fear of evil spirits or demons.

entity 1. Relatively autonomous being or object. 2. Discrete part of reality which exists with some degree of independence and maintains itself.

entoderm See *endoderm*.

entomology Study of insects.

entomophobia Morbid fear of insects.

entoptic 1. Within the eye. 2. Visual responses which are generated by chemical conditions or mechanical processes inside the eye itself rather than by external stimuli.

entropy 1. That part of the energy in a thermodynamic system which is not available for work. 2. (psychoanalysis) The extent to which psychic energy cathected or invested in an object cannot be transferred. 3. (information theory) Specification of the number of possible outcomes a given event might have, increasing as the number of possible outcomes increases while the amount of information contained in any one outcome decreases with an increase in total possible outcomes.

entropy, social Principle that energy is consumed in social change leaving less available for further progress and eventually resulting in a static society.

entry (statistics) Number, value or symbol which is recorded in a particular position of a statistical calculation.

enucleation Removal of a whole organ or tumor without cutting into it, as in the removal of an eyeball.

enumeration Counting or identifying each member of a group one by one, often for purposes of classification or induction.

enuresis 1. Involuntary passage of urine. 2. Bed-wetting.

environment Sum total of external conditions, including social and physical factors, which have the potential to influence an organism. See *environmental psychology*.

environment, internal The total internal processes occurring within the body, tending toward maintaining homeostasis and considered to act as an influence on any of the organism's activities.

environmental event The actions or action-products of one member of a dyad that are essential for allowing the other member to complete his search for gratification or reinforcement; e.g., a mother's responsive smile to her supplicative infant, a wife's retributive criticism of a guilty husband.

environmental factors All external conditions which may affect the individual.

environmental-mold trait (R.B. Cattell) Personality trait developed by the influence of persistent characteristics of the environment.

environmental psychology Environmental psychology is a relatively new field of scientific inquiry which is concerned with the interrelationships between man's physical environment—particularly the built environment—and human behavior and experience. It crystallized as a field in psychology with the publication of *Environmental Psychology: Man and his Physical Setting* by H. M. Proshansky, W. H. Ittelson, and L. G. Rivlin. What distinguishes this field from others concerned with man's environment in relation to human behavior and experience, is its focus on the natural, on-going physical settings that define and guide human interaction. It is problem oriented, interdisciplinary in its conceptual and theoretical orientations, and eclectic in its methodological approaches. The "urban setting" is a primary focus in the interest of many environmental psychologists, studying such issues as "crowding," "safety," "privacy," "territoriality," "place identity," "cognitive mapping," and others in the settings of the home, the school, the office, the neighborhood, the hospital, and the recreational area. What must be noted is that its interdisciplinary emphasis is rooted in its need to have a close working relationship not only with environmental sociologists and anthropologists, but with designers, architects, planners, and other practitioners responsible for designing man's built environment.

envy Emotion stimulated by the desire to possess what someone else has.

enzygotic twins See *twins, identical*.

enzyme Organic substance which functions as a catalyst in plants and animals accelerating chemical transformations.

enzyme blocks Substances or circumstances which prevent enzymes from performing their function.

eonism See *transvestitism.*

eosinophilic diathesis (constitutional medicine) Eosinophilic condition resulting from arthritic diathesis.

eosinophils A type of blood cell which is reduced during physiological stress.

eosophobia Fear of sunrise, daybreak.

epencephalon (physiology) The hindbrain or cerebellum rubrick, located below the cerebrum and above the pons and the medulla.

ependyma Membraneous lining of the central canal of the spinal cord and of the ventricles of the brain.

ephemeral mania See *mania transitoria.*

ephialtes Obsolete term for nightmare.

ephialtes vigilantium Nightmare-like experience while-awake.

epicritic Related to highly developed cutaneous sensitivity capable of delicate discrimination.

epicritic sensibility (H. Head) Cutaneous sensitivity to light pressure and mild degree of temperature with finely localized responsiveness and highly developed discrimination.

epidemic catalepsy See *catalepsy, epidemic.*

epidemic encephalitis See *encephalitis, lethargic.*

epidemic hysteria See *hysteria, epidemic.*

epidemiologist A person who studies the incidence, distribution, and control of disease in a population.

epidermis The outermost layer of the skin composed of epithelial tissue protective in function.

epigastric Related to or part of the epigastrium which is the surface of the upper and middle portions of the stomach region.

epigastric reflex Feeling of weakness or sinking in the stomach area frequently associated with anxiety or fear.

epigenesis 1. Hypothesis that new phenomena not present in the original fertilized egg emerge over the course of embryonic development through the interaction of pre-existing elements with pre-natal environmental influences. 2. Appearance of new phenomena not present at previous stages in an organism's development.

epiglottis Elastic-like membraneous structure which covers the glottis, protecting it during swallowing.

epilempsis (Hippocrates) Obsolete term for epilepsy.

epilentia Obsolete term for epilepsy.

epilepsia corticalis continua See *epilepsy, continuous.*

epilepsia cursiva Obsolete term for aimless running as a symptom of epilepsy.

epilepsia dromica Epileptic behavior resembling chorea.

epilepsia gravior Obsolete term for grand mal seizure.

epilepsia mitior Obsolete term for petit mal epileptic seizure.

epilepsia partialis continua Rarely occurring variety of continuous epilepsy specifically characterized by the limitation of jerking movements to one part of the body, usually a peripheral part, and by the resemblance of the movements to irregular muscle contractions.

epilepsia trochaica See *epilepsia cursiva.*

epilepsia vertiginosa 1. Obsolete term for petit mal epileptic seizure. 2. Disorientation or dizziness which sometimes precedes or takes the place of a grand mal epileptic seizure.

epilepsy A group of brain disorders associated with changes in the electrical activity of the brain due to brain injury or infectious childhood diseases or endocrine disorders, or one of several other causes. Epilepsy is often characterized by some form of convulsion, though behavioral symptoms vary greatly involving recurrent mental, motor or sensory dysfunction with or without convulsive seizures or loss of consciousness.

The seizures may be either focal or generalized; the main forms are classified as *grand mal* or major, *petit mal* and *psychomotor.* The "grand mal" seizure is often preceded by an "aura" of psychic, motor or sensory disturbances which serves as a warning followed by complete loss of consciousness and falling to the ground; a tonic phase follows in which the individual stiffens and respiration stops; a clonic phase characterized by jerking movements of the whole body follows the tonic phase, completing the seizure. The "petit mal" seizure refers to recurrent mild seizures of short duration usually consisting of loss of awareness and a sense of disorientation. The "psychomotor" category includes short attacks of extreme motor activity, sometimes violent, of which the individual has no recollection. Some psychomotor epileptics are capable of committing serious crimes of violence without being aware of their own behavior.

epilepsy, affective (H. Bratz) A form of epilepsy involving exaggerated emotionality usually followed by a seizure. Also called reactive epilepsies by K. Bonhoeffer and epileptic swindle by E. Kraepelin.

epilepsy, akinetic Form of petit mal epileptic seizure characterized by sudden loss of muscle control, nodding of the head and falling.

epilepsy, autonomic Form of epileptic seizure confined to the autonomic nervous system and characterized by sweating, changes of temperature, tearing of the eyes, and other symptoms resulting from either sympathetic or parasympathetic discharges.

epilepsy, continuous Form of epileptic seizure characterized by continuous myoclonic attacks of one part or side of the body without loss of consciousness.

epilepsy, coordinated Form of epileptic seizure characterized by movements which appear coordinated, voluntary and purposeful, although they may be repeated and without direction.

epilepsy, cryptogenic Epilepsy for which no cause has been identified.

epilepsy, essential See *ideopathic epilepsy.*

epilepsy, inhibitory Rare variety of petit mal epileptic seizure characterized by short-term loss of movement in part of the body without tonic and clonic phases and sometimes accompanied by loss of consciousness.

epilepsy, Jacksonian (J. H. Jackson) Form of grand mal seizure caused by disease of the cortex in which increasingly severe clonic movements spread from one point outward to include either one or both sides of the body, the more generalized seizures followed by unconsciousness.

epilepsy, myoclonic Severe variety of petit mal epileptic seizure characterized by symmetrical jerking of various muscles; the myoclonic EEG pattern is a typical petit mal pattern combined with occasional multiple spike-and-wave complexes.

epilepsy, nocturnal Epileptic seizures which occur while sleeping.

epilepsy, psychic Any form of epileptic equivalent state associated with or precipitated by a mental or emotional incident; behavioral manifestations include excitement, depression, dream-like states, etc.

epilepsy, psychopathology of See *personality, epileptic.*

epilepsy, reactive Epileptic seizure which appears to be a reaction to some particular pain or injury, or to a specific pathological focal point.

epilepsy, regional See *epilepsy, myoclonic.*

epilepsy, residual (E. Kraepelin) Rarely used term for recurrent epileptiform attacks without noticeable changes in personality or strange behavior.

epilepsy, sensory Variety of petit mal epilepsy in which the individual experiences sensation disturbances such as loss of sensation on part or all of one side of the body.

epilepsy, sleep Obsolete term for narcolepsy.

epilepsy, tetanoid (J. Prichard) Epileptic seizure consisting of tonic phase only, not clonic.

epilepsy, tonic Epileptic seizure in which only tonic spasms are exhibited, not clonic.

epileptic aura See *aura, epileptic.*

epileptic clouded states Psychotic behavior exhibited by epileptics before or after a convulsive attack; some epileptics experience hallucinations or fears or become confused, excited or ecstatic. See *aura.*

epileptic deterioration See *deterioration, epileptic.*

epileptic equivalent See *equivalent, epileptic.*

epileptic psychopathic constitution See *constitution, epileptic psychopathic.*

epilepticism Obsolete term for status epilepticus.

epileptiform seizure See *seizure, epileptiform.*

epileptoid personality; epileptoidism A person who exhibits the personality traits associated with the epileptic personality syndrome which includes selfishness, aggressiveness, stubborn uncooperativeness and religious fanatacism; this personality pattern is not found in the majority of epileptics nor exclusively in them.

epileptology The study of epilepsy.

epileptosis (E. E. Southard) General term for the different forms of psychosis manifested by epileptics.

epiloia Tuberous sclerosis.

epinephrine See *adrenalin.*

epinephrine poisoning See *poisoning, epinephrine.*

epinosic gain See *epinosis.*

epinosic resistance See *resistance, epinosis.*

epinosis (psychoanalysis) Also called secondary gain. An advantage or gain such as achieving social approval, and sympathy derived from neurosis; may lead to resistance in psychoanalysis aimed at perpetuating the epinosic gain.

epiphenomenalism The theory that neural processes produce mental activities and consciousness and that mental activities, therefore, can have no determining influence on mental or physical events.

epiphenomenon 1. An event which occurs simultaneously with another event but has no causal relationship with it. 2. (pathology) A symptom not related directly to the etiology of the disorder or disease.

epiphora Excessive tears due to oversecretion or to obstruction of their flow.

epiphysis (cerebri) The pineal gland.

episcotiser Instrument for studying short exposure intervals composed of a rotating disc with adjustable open and closed sections which are interposed between an observe and visual stimulus.

episodic amnesia See *amnesia, episodic.*

epistasis A genetic process in which one combination of non-allelic genes or one hereditary factor has dominance over other such combinations.

epistatic Referring to a combination of non-allelic genes or to hereditary factors exercising dominance over such combinations.

epistemology The philosophical investigation of knowledge including its origin, nature, method and limits.

epistemophilia Love of knowledge and for the investigation into things.

epithalamus Brain tissue lying above the thalamus composed of the habenula, the pineal body and the posterior commissure.

epithelium Layer of thin cellular tissue which forms the epidermis, and covers the inner surfaces of the bodily organs or viscera and the hollow linings of the digestive, respiratory and genitourinary systems.

epochal amnesia See *amnesia, epochal.*

epogenic component in a trait age curve (R. B. Cattell) The departure of an age trend from that most typical for humans, by reason of the special qualities of an epoch. Thus, the population intelligence plots from 1910-1970 are skewed from the ecogenic normal by an unusually rapid increase of education.

epsilon movement See *movement, epsilon.*

equal and unequal cases method (psychophysics) A variation of the constant stimulus method in which paired stimuli are judged as either equal or unequal.

equal appearing intervals 1. (psychophysics) Intervals determined by the equal sense differences method of measurement; a technique in which an individual finds the midpoint between two different sense stimuli and the two resulting distances are considered equal. 2. (L. Thurstone) Application of the equal sense differences method to any type of scaling judgments by dividing the total number of items of questions into categories composed of equal intervals.

equal interval scale Scale with arbitrarily determined zero point and equal intervals.

equal sense-differences method (psychophysics) A method of measurement in which an individual finds the midpoint between two different sense stimuli, and the two resulting distances are believed to be equal.

equality, law of (Gestalt) Principle that parts of a figure or a field are perceived as being a group or a whole to the extent to which the parts are similar or equal.

equalization of excitation (K. Goldstein) The tendency for excitation to spread out evenly over a functional system thus gradually decreasing the excitation at the stimulus point and increasing in other parts of the system.

equally noticeable 1. (psychophysics) Just noticeable difference. 2. (psychophysics) Differences between stimuli that are believed to be psychologically equivalent differences since they are perceived the same number of times.

equated scores Scores from two different tests of the same variable weighted in such a way as to have a common basis for comparison.

equation method (psychophysics) A procedure in which the subject is asked to adjust a stimulus object to a fixed standard or criterion object. The subject may be asked to equate the two or to relate the stimulus object in some other prescribed way to the criterion.

equation specification An equation for estimating a person's test score knowing his strength in one trait and the loading of that factor on the test. It is a form of the multiple regression equation.

equation, system A mathematical statement of the dynamic aspects of a system based upon the given input and output.

equation, tetrad difference (C. Spearman) An early method of factor analysis used to determine whether the one-factor theory common to all variables of a set is correct. This method originally referred to the nature of intelligence. The equation states that the correlations among various combinations of four factors are due to one factor if the tetrad diferrence is equal to zero. For example, given four factors, *A, B, C, D,* if one assumes that *G* is the only factor present in all of the tests, accounting for the variance common to more than one of them, than any tetrad difference should equal to zero such as

$$r_{AB}\, r_{CD} - r_{AC}\, r_{BD} = 0$$

or any other combination of variables. If another factor is found to contribute to the variance of one pair of variables but not to another, then the tetrad difference will no longer be zero, i.e.,

$$r_{AB}\, r_{CD} - r_{AC}\, r_{BD} \neq 0$$

equilibration 1. Adjusting a measuring instrument by equating it with a standard. 2. (J. Piaget) The operation together of the two processes of assimilation and accomodation in the cognitive growth of the child. The child assimilates new information resulting in a modification of (accommodation) existing cognitive structures.

equilibrium 1. A stable or balanced condition within a system as in homeostasis. 2. Maintenance of balance and upright posture in the human body.

equine encephalitis See *encephalitis, equine.*

equipotent method (R. B. Cattell) A statistical device for comparing source trait factor scores across different cultural, age, etc., groups by adjusting the factor estimation weights peculiar to each group to produce equal multiple correlations of variables with factor scores in the groups compared.

equipotentiality 1. Uniform potential and manifestation of equal potential or power of any sort. 2. The potential for any portion of the embryonic tissue to produce or to develop into any of the parts of the mature organism. 3. Hypothesis that one sensory cue may be substituted for another. 4. Cerebral equipotentiality.

equivalence Relationship between two variables, stimuli, terms or responses such that one may be substituted for another within a specified situation without altering the situation.

equivalence belief (E. C. Tolman) A hypothesized state of an organism based on the organism's behavioral response which indicates the organism is acting toward a subgoal as it would toward the goal as if the subgoal were the goal; equivalence belief parallels secondary reinforcement in other theories.

equivalence coefficient The correlation coefficient of two supposedly equivalent forms of the same test given to the same subjects at about the same time; this coefficient indicates the degree of agreement or reliability between the two forms, a high equivalence correlation indicating high reliability and a low coefficient indicating low reliability.

equivalence, response The occurrence of the same or similar responses to the same or similar stimuli.

equivalence, stimulus The evocation of the same or very similar responses by different stimuli.

equivalence test A test which determines which aspects of a stimulus can be varied without changing an organism's previously trained response to that stimulus. Those variations of the original stimulus which continue to elicit the same response are considered equivalent.

equivalent, anxiety See *anxiety, equivalent.*

equivalent, epileptic Epileptic attacks which are neither grand mal nor petit mal but which take their place, as for example, psychomotor attacks and fugue states.

equivalent form See *form, equivalent.*

equivalent groups See *groups, equivalent.*

equivalent of anxiety attack See *anxiety, equivalent.*

equivalent, onanistic (S. Fercenzi) Any act which serves as a substitute for manual masturbation.

equivalents method (psychophysics) A method of measurement in which the subject must adjust a stimulus until it seems equal to a criterion object.

erectio deficiens Inadequate erection or lack of genital erection.

erection The swelling and hardening of erectile tissue such as the penis, clitoris or nipples through the accumulation of blood.

eremiophobia Morbid fear of isolated places or of seclusion.

eremophilia Abnormal and unhealthy desire to be alone.

eremophobia Morbid fear of being by oneself.

erethism Abnormally great degree of excitability, sensitivity or irritability in any or all parts of the body.

erethismic Pertaining to an abnormally great degree of psychical or physical stimulation.

erethismus ebriosorum Rarely used term meaning delirium tremens.

erethistic See *eristhismic.*

erethitic Associated with exaggerated excitement or excitability.

erethizophrenia Extreme cortical excitability.

ereuthophobia See *erythrophobia.*

Erfassungstypus (H. Rorschach) A subject's mode of approach to the test which is interpretively studied in terms of the sequence of location choices which occurs within each card and to the entire test, together with the ratio of types of location choices through the entire test, such as proportion of Whole responses to usual Detail responses to unusual Detail responses, etc. These data are generally considered as indicative of the style used by the subject in solving his problems.

erg (R. B. Cattell) A drive that has been demonstrated by the factor analysis of dynamic variables to be a unitary entity. A factor found in dynamic measures, operationally defining a specific drive or instinct, as clinically and biologically recognized, for example, sex, self-assertion, fear, etc. To be distinguished from drive in general or Ergic Tension.

ERG See *electroretinogram.*

ergasia (A. Meyer) General term for all of the psychobiological functions or activities within the person taken as a whole.

ergasiatry (A. Meyer) Psychiatry.

ergasic Related to ergasia; ergastic.

ergasiology (A. Meyer) Psychology.

ergasiomania An intense need to work and keep busy. This term is infrequently used today. Such a condition is seen in the manic state of manic-depressive psychosis.

ergasiophobia General fear of acting or of moving generated by the belief that one's actions will either cause harm to another or to oneself and often associated with the fear of castration and the Oedipal complex.

ergasthenia A somewhat outdated term for a frequently encountered condition of fatigue or debility due to overwork or excessive mental and/or physical functioning, particularly noticeable in the manic phase of extreme cases of manic-depressive psychosis.

ergastic Related to ergasia; ergasic.

ergic-tension equation The equation: $E = S/C + H + (P - aG)] - bG$ expressing the derivation of the ergic-tension level from the influences involved.

ergodialeipsis Activity which stops before being completed which is thought to be a form of blocking usually associated with schizophrenia.

ergograph Instrument which records the amount of movement of a particular group of muscles of a single part of the body during continuous activity usually in connection with fatigue experimentation.

ergonomics The scientific study of the relationships between men and machines, particularly the psychological, biological and cultural with the purpose of adapting machines and jobs to meet the needs of men and of choosing suitable persons for particular jobs or machines.

ergot *Claviceps purpurea,* a fungus which contains alcaloids used for treatment of migraine headaches.

ergot poisoning See *poisoning, ergot.*

Erlebnistypus (H. Rorschach) A key concept in Rorschach testing representing the ratio of human movement to weighted color responses. Sometimes referred to as experience balance, or experience type; a precise translation from the German has been, at best, difficult in terms of capturing the full sense of Rorschach's meaning. The interpretive meaning goes beyond experience, to a description of "how" a person lives in terms of tendencies and experiences. Depending on the nature of the ratio, a person might be described as extratensive, introversive, ambitent, coarcted, or dilated, any of which relates to styles of living and experiencing.

erogenous or erotogenic zones Areas of the body which give rise to sexual, erotic or libidinal feelings when stimulated.

Eros (S. Freud) Originally Freud postulated two forces present at birth whose aim is individual and species survival, that is, self-preservation and sexual instincts. Later, Freud combined the drive for life under the name Eros which encompasses love directed toward oneself and/or others. The instinctual drive has a source, object and aim.

erotic 1. Sexual sensations, stimuli or feelings which arise from the erogenous zones. 2. Emotions or feelings associated with sexual sensations. 3. Love.

erotic fever See *fever, erotic.*

erotic organ See *organ, erotic.*

eroticism or erotism 1. Sexual excitement. 2. A greater than average interest in sexual matters; the tendency to experience sexual arousal more often or more intensely than the average individual; the preoccupation with sexual concerns in areas such as literature, art or history. 3. Sexual arousal through stimulation of non-genital parts of the body such as the mouth or anus.

eroticism, anal See *anal eroticism.*

eroticism, lip Erotic satisfaction derived from stimulation of the lips.

eroticism, oral 1. Experiencing of pleasure from oral stimulation and activities such as biting, sucking, chewing and stimulation of the lips and inner mouth. 2. (psychoanalysis) Characteristic of the oral stage of pregenital libidinal development.

erotodromomania Pathological desire to travel, to escape from some upsetting sexual experience.

erotogenesis 1. Originating from sex. 2. The origination of sexual, erotic, or libidinal impulses of behavior.

erotographomania Pathological desire to write love letters in which the love is usually expressed in a vague or sublimated manner, often through religious symbolism.

erotomania Unrestrained and morbid desire for genital relations with members of the opposite sex which is believed to stem from unconscious homosexual impulses.

error 1. A mistake; deviation from what is accurate or true. 2. A belief in something that is not true. 3. (statistics) Deviation from a true score. 4. (experimental) Any change in the dependent variable which is not attributable to the independent variable, whether chance or constant error. 5. (behaviorism) Any inappropriate response which delays the occurrence of the correct response, or any deviation from the experimental conditions or from the requirements of the experimenter.

error, absolute The obtained measurement value or observed score minus the true value. The mean of the measurements is usually considered to be the true value. The sign of this deviation score is disregarded.

error, alpha (statistics) The probability that an obtained result has occurred by chance. This is the risk of mistakenly rejecting the null hypothesis which is kept at a minimal level. The two conventionally accepted levels are .05 and .01.

error, anticipatory An error committed by making a response before the correct time in serial learning experiments.

error, beta (statistics) The probability or risk of accepting the null hypothesis.

error-choice technique See *forced choice technique.*

error, compensating An error, whether positive or negative which cancels out one or more errors so that the average of the errors tends toward zero.

error, constant An experimental deviation from the correct value of a measure which is consistent in one direction. For example, subjects may consistently underestimate the length of a line.

error, estimation One half of the distance or difference between an upper or a lower threshold.

error, experimental Incorrect value in measurement or measurements due to poor experimental procedure of any sort which includes inadequacy of method, sampling and design, uncontrolled practice effects, and failure to adequately control experimental conditions.

error, instrumental A constant error caused by a precision instrument's deviation from the standard and corrected for by a constant factor.

error of estimate 1. (statistics) The error which occurs from estimating the value of one variable from the value of another variable when using a regression equation. 2. (psychometrics) The anticipated margin of error of an individual's predicted test score on a criterion variable due to the imperfect validity of a test 3. (psychophysics) The point of subjective equality less the standard criterion in comparative judgments.

error of expectation (psychophysics) In the method of limits it is the tendency for the subject to change his responses before a stimulus change because he feels that a stimulus change should have occurred.

error of habituation (psychophysics) In the method of limits it is the tendency for the subject to give the same response within a given series even though the stimulus has changed.

error of measurement 1. (psychometrics) Departure of an individual test score from its true value due to variations in conditions from one test to another. 2. Departure of an individual test score from its true value which is due to the unreliability of the testing instrument and/or of the tester or experimenter combined.

error of refraction The inability to focus visual images upon the retina due either to abnormalities in the optical characteristics of the cornea, lens, aqueous humor or vitreous humor, or to irregular shaping of the eyeball.

error stimulus (E. B. Titchener) An error committed in introspective reports of responding to a stimulus as perceived in terms of previous experience rather than responding to stimulus qualities which characterized the object.

error, systematic An error resulting from the manner of gathering or interpreting data which indicates bias.

error variance That portion of the total variance which is due to uncontrollable factors such as sampling errors or errors of measurement.

errorless discrimination See *discrimination, errorless.*

errors, chance Mistakes in measurement that are the result of unknown causes and, therefore, cannot be either controlled or predicted. The mean of a series of measurements is taken to be the true value and an accidental error is the departure from this mean. Accidental errors are considered to be due to random or chance factors.

erythema endemicum Pellagra.

erythredema Also called acrodynia. Occurs in infants, rarely in older children. Main symptoms: anorexia, perspiration, hypertension and moods shifting from apathy to explosive irritability. Linked to mercury poisoning.

erythrism The growth of red hair in certain areas of the body, usually the beard or pubic hair, while not in others which is considered a characteristic of certain body types in some older constitutional theories.

erythroblastosis fetalis A hemolytic disease of the newborn caused by the development of antibodies in the blood against the Rh - positive factors in the fetal blood. The increased amounts of bilirubin cause jaundice and often kernicterus.

erythrogenic Stimulus or radiant energy from which the sensation of red originates.

erythrophobia Fear of the color red which is usually associated with a fear of blood.

erythropsia Retinal condition in which everything appears tinted with red usually due to overexposure to strong white light.

escape behavior Behavior which removes an organism from a pain-producing situation.

escape training (experimental) Learning situation in which an organism is exposed to a noxious stimulus from which he may escape by eliciting a particular response.

Eshmun complex See *complex, Eshmun.*

esophagus The tube which connects the pharynx or mouth to the stomach; the gullet.

esophoria An inward deviation of the eye from the correct position necessary for binocular vision resulting from a muscular imbalance.

esoteric 1. Understood by, or made for only a special few. 2. Meant for only a special few who have been educated in certain teachings or doctrines. 3. Private or protected from public view.

esotropia Optical condition in which one eye deviates inward while the other focuses directly on the object.

ESP See *extrasensory perception.*

esprit de corps Common feeling shared by member of a group with the connotation of enthusiasm and loyalty.

Esquirol, Jean Etienne Dominique (1772-1840) French psychiatrist.

essay examination See *examination, essay.*

essential hypertension See *hypertension, essential.*

establishment (H. Murray) A division of personality along functional lines. Modified versions of Freud's id, ego and superego are the establishments.

Estes Statistical Model of Learning (W. K. Estes) Mathematical interpretation of Guthrie's non-continuity S-R learning theory based on the assumption that association occurs through contiguity. Estes' statistical model predicts response probability from a strictly contiguous association viewpoint without utilizing the concepts of reinforcement or extinction.

esthesia Sensitivity; capacity for sensation or feeling.

esthesiogenesis Producing of a sensory zone reaction.

esthesiometer See *aesthesiometer.*

esthete See *aesthete.*

esthetics See *aesthetics.*

estimate, unbiased An estimate based on an adequate and representative sample.

estimates 1. Values arrived at by rough rather than exact calculation or by global rather than specific inspection of the data from which the value is obtained. 2. (statistics) To infer a population measure from a sample measure.

estimation error, or difference See *error, estimation.*

estimation, magnitude (psychophysics) Direct scaling procedure in which a stimulus on a sensory continuum is selected by the experimenter and a number designating its subjective magnitude is assigned to it. The subject is then presented in turn with comparison stimuli and is instructed to assign to each comparison stimulus a number which looks as proportional to its subjective magnitude as compared to the standard. The judgments are in terms of subjective magnitudes consequently the resultant scale is directly obtained.

estimation method (psychophysics) The subject estimates the stimuli that are presented.

estimation, ratio (psychophysics) Direct scaling procedure in which the subject indicates when the sensory magnitudes of two stimuli stand in a specified ratio to each other. One stimulus is the standard and remains fixed throughout the series; the other stimulus is variable and is adjusted by the subject. The subject's task is to adjust the variable stimulus so that the stimulus magnitude provides a subjective ratio of the variable to the standard that is equal to the ratio specified by the experimenter. For example, the variable stimulus may be adjusted to appear one third as bright as the standard.

estrogen Any of the female hormones that stimulates the female to estrus, regulates the estrus cycle and influences the development of secondary sex characteristics.

estromania See *nymphomania.*

estrus or estric cycle The periodical state of sexual receptivity in female animals accompanied by physiological changes in the reproductive organs.

Eta coefficient (X) See *correlation ratio.*

ethics The study of moral values and moral behavior.

ethinamate Trademark valmid; a depressant.

ethnic 1. Groups of biologically related people. 2. Any division or group of people who are related on the basis of common customs or traits.

ethnocentrism 1. The tendency to consider one's group, usually national or ethnic, superior to other groups using one's own group or groups as the frame of reference against which other groups are judged. 2. A personality syndrome characterized by perception of social reality as composed of in-groups with which one identifies and out-groups toward which one is hostile; stereotyping people positively or negatively depending on their in-group or out-group membership; authoritarian and power-oriented social relations.

ethnography See *ethnology.*

ethnology The study of ethnic groups: their origins, customs, culture and pursuits in relation to their geography and to other ethnic groups.

ethnopsychology The comparative psychology of peoples and races, particularly nonliterate groups.

ethology 1. The science of ethics including the comparative study of ethical systems and the investigation of ethical systems in light of scientific principles. 2. The empirical investigation of character. 3. (sociology) The study of customs, mores and folk ways. 4. (psychology and biology) The comparative study of behavior, particularly lower forms of animal life in relation to their natural habitat.

ethos 1. The characteristic outlook or predominant disposition of a racial group or culture. 2. The underlying feeling or spirit associated with a particular outlook on life.

ethyl alcohol poisoning See *poisoning, ethyl alcohol.*

ethylene dichloride poisoning See *poisoning, ethylene dichloride.*

ethylene glycol poisoning See *poisoning, ethylene glycol.*

etiology The study of the origins and causes of disease.

ETS Educational Testing Service.

euergasia (A. Meyer) Normal or healthy mental functions.

eugenics The application of scientific genetics to the problem of improving the biological and psychological qualities of mankind. Positive eugenics attacks this task by methods favoring the early and productive unions of persons with superior genetic characteristics. More practicable is the implementation of a voluntary, minimal eugenics, operating through genetic counselling at heredity clinics, aiming at the elimination or reduction of the risks of the procreation of children with severe genetic physical or mental handicaps. Although eugenic ideas are found in Plato and were practised in the Oneida community in Vermont (1841), scientifically informed eugenics only came into its own through the writings of Sir Francis Galton at the turn of the century.

eumorph, eumorphic Person whose body type and build is average or normal.

eunuch A castrated male.

eunuchoidism Condition characterized by lack of fully developed sexual organs and the development of female secondary sex characteristics similar to those of a eunuch but due to disease.

eupareunia Sexual intercourse during which orgasm is achieved.

euphoria Attitude or mood of complete well-being and optimism.

euphoric That which is characterized by euphoria.

eupraxia Normal performance of coordinated movements.

eurhythmia Smooth congruent relations between different systems of the body.

eurotophobia Fear of the female genital organs.

eurymorph (H. J. Eysenck) A person whose body-build index is one or more standard deviations below the mean.

euryplastic Body type characterized by thick necks, short limbs and rounded body contour.

eustachian tube Small valved passageway which connects the middle ear with the mouth and functions to maintain an equilibrium of atmospheric pressure between the middle and the outer ear.

eusthenic (E. Kretschmer) Subdivision of the asthenic body type which borders on the athletic type.

eutelegenesis Artificial insemination.

euthanasia Mercy killing; the act of putting to death as painlessly as possible a person suffering from an incurable or painful disease.

euthenics The science concerned with improving the environment and living conditions in order to improve man.

euthymia A happy and tranquil mood or disposition.

evaluation 1. Determination of the relative value or importance of a score or phenomenon by appraisal or comparison with a standard. 2. (education) Global appraisal or measurement of educational progress or achievement.

evaluation, operation of (J. P. Guilford) Inspection or comparison of items of information with respect to given specifications in accordance with logical criteria, such as identity or consistency.

event 1. Occurrence or phenomenon which has a definite beginning and end. 2. Occurrence or series of occurrences which are related to an individual's needs in some way and thus form a unity. 3. (H. A. Murray) That part of a projective test which is related to a press or need.

evil eye A superstitious belief that certain people have the power to cause evil or to harm others by looking at them.

evil, St. John's Obsolete term for epilepsy.

evivation 1. Emasculation. 2. Delusion of a male that he has become a woman accompanied by stereotypically feminine feelings and desires.

evolutility (biological) Capacity of an organism to change through growth and physical development through nutrition.

evolution 1. Process of change through growth and orderly development. 2. Theory that present organisms have developed from pre-existing ones through genetic adaptations to the environment.

evolution, Darwin's theory of See *darwinism*.

evolutionism, evolutism Characterized by or related to evolution.

exacerbation To irritate or exaggerate the violent or bitter symptoms of a disease, of a person's feelings, or of behavior.

exaltation 1. Mood of great elation or positive excitement. 2. Abnormal increase in the amount of functioning of an organ.

examination anxiety 1. Nervous tension experienced prior to a test due to uncertainty regarding one's performance or ability. 2. (psychoanalysis) Pretest anxiety is exaggerated due to associations, often unconscious, between the test situation and childhood experiences where the individual was punished for doing wrong.

examination, comprehensive An examination, which is designed to assess a person's integration and comprehension of a broad field or a range of areas which have been studied for a long period of time.

examination, essay Examination in which one must write about one particular topic at some length.

examination, mental Test which is administered to assess an individual's mental level or the extent of a person's pathology.

examination, neurological The patient is examined to assess the presence and degree of damage to the nervous system. The content of a neurological examination is not homogenous and consistent, probably varying considerably among neurologists. An examination generally includes assessments of the intactness of reflex arcs, the strength of muscles, the quality of voluntary and involuntary movements, visual-motor behavior, quality of language, presence or absence of hyperkinesis. The electroencephalogram, angiogram and air encephalogram are used. Great weight is placed upon the patient's life history, especially the pattern of symptoms.

examination, psychiatric Examination of a mental patient aiming at diagnostic evaluation and planning of treatment. It may include several interviews and administration of psychological tests. The main components of the psychiatric examination are history-taking and diagnostic interviewing. In some cases, a neurological and/or any other medical examination may be necessary.

examination, psychiatric social Psychodiagnostic evaluation which takes into consideration the influence of sociocultural variables, such as socioeconomic status and family relations.

examination, psychological General term for a test which either measures or evaluates abilities, general or specific, or personality traits.

examination, psychometric A series of various psychological tests which are administered to an individual in order to test one or several of the factors in his mental ability, such as intelligence, special abilities and disabilities, manual skill, vocational aptitudes, interests, and personality characteristics.

exanthropia Obsolete term for disliking society.

excema, infantile A psychosomatic disturbance of the skin which occurs in infants.

exceptional Differing greatly from others within a given group in one or more characteristics frequently in reference to individual ability differences in children.

excitability 1. (physiological) Of a living tissue having the capacity to reach stimulation. 2. Characterized by an easily aroused or excessive emotional reaction. 3. Highly reactive.

excitant A stimulus; an object which has the capacity to elicit a response or activity from an organ.

excitation 1. The process of causing physiological change in a receptor by stimulation. 2. (I. P. Pavlov) A hypothetical nervous process of the conduction of energy from one center to another in the cortex. 3. The process of causing activity in a nerve or muscle of nerve action. 4. The hypothetical nervous system correlated to the strength of response evoked by a stimulus.

excitation, deflection of (S. Freud) The redirection of a response to a stimulus, from the psychical to the somatic sphere.

excitation gradient See generalization gradient.

excitation, somatic sexual (S. Freud) Ongoing visceral excitation caused by pressure on the nerve endings of the seminal vesicles.

excitatory agent A stimulus.

excitatory drive mechanisms Hormonal or neural mechanisms which cause drive-related behavior.

excitatory field Region of the brain near the termination of a neuron at the time it is activated by a specific sensory process.

excitatory irradiation See irradiation, excitatory.

excitatory post synaptic potential (EPSP) A type of synaptic event which causes a rapid depolarization of the neuron. These events convey the neural impulse across a synapse.

excitatory potential $_SE_R$ (C. L. Hull) The potentiality of reaction evocation on the hypothesized strength of a response tendency which is arrived at through combining the effects of habit strength and drive: $_SE_R = D \times _SH_R$.

excitatory tendency The capacity of a stimulus to elicit a response, usually in terms of quantitative ability.

excitement An emotional state characterized by impulsive behavior, activity and a feeling of anticipation.

excrement, abnormal attraction to See coprophilia.

executive area Cortical area which controls other cortical areas through a function of higher integration.

exercise 1. Repetition of an act in order to learn it or increase skill. 2. Physical activity to maintain health, improve muscles or for recreational purposes.

exercise, law of See law of exercise.

exhaustion 1. State of depleted metabolism or reduced catabolic rate resulting in fatigue and lowered responsiveness to stimulation. 2. Extreme metabolic depletion which constitutes the final phase of the adaptation syndrome. 3. Hypothetical state of an

action after responding characterized by a higher response threshold and reduced rate and strength of response which is hypothesized to be the result of the loss of energy which occurs with responding and is frequently not replaced.

exhibition need See need, exhibition.

exhibitionism A sexual impulse to exhibit one's genitals which may be displaced to other areas of the body.

exhilirant That which causes elation.

existence, absence of the feeling of physical See acenesthesia.

existential analysis (existentialism) A type of psychotherapy designed to help the individual to react spontaneously to life situations and to develop a sense of freedom and responsibility for his own actions.

existential crisis A crisis concerning the problem of finding meaning in life.

existential psychology See psychology, existential.

existential psychotherapy See psychotherapy, existential.

existentialism 1. (philosophy) The name for a group of philosophical systems developed by Sören Kierkegaard, Martin Heidegger, Jean-Paul Sartre and others. There is considerable diversity in their views; Kierkegaard stressed the paradoxality of the concept of being and the idea of individual device. Heidegger bridged existentialism and phenomenology, pointed to the inadequacy of scientific analysis, and developed an existentialist system of being. Sartre maintained that existence is absurd and there is no adequate explanation why things are the way they are. The idea of absurdity and futility of human life was developed by Albert Camus. 2. (psychology) K. Jaspers originated a psychiatric system based on existentialist philosophy. Distinguished between the empirical and the "true" self. Only in situations of extreme despair, called boundary situations, an individual can become aware of his true self. 3. (L. Binswanger) Combined some psychoanalytic ideas with Heidegger's version of existentialism. Neurosis must be explained not in terms of its etiology but its meaning to the patients. 4. (P. Tillich) Combined psychoanalytic ideas with existentialism and protestant philosophy. He maintained that self-affirmation leads to the discovery of being itself. 5. (R. D. Laing) Utilized existentialist concepts in interpreting schizophrenia as "divided self" between what one really is and where one is an object of other people's influences and is unable to live his own life.

exocathection (H. A. Murray) Preoccupation with external rather than internal events and involvement in the world of public affairs rather than private pursuits.

exocrine glands See glands, exocrine.

exogamy The restriction of marriage to a person outside one's own group as, for example, the practice of not marrying blood relatives.

exogenous, exogenetic, exogenic That which originates outside.

exolinguistics (information theory) The study of the relationships between the sender of a message, the receiver and the message itself.

exophoria An outward deviation of the eye due to a muscular imbalance.

exophthalmic goiter See *goiter, exophthalmic.*

exopsychic Mental activity which has effects outside the individual on the physical or social environment.

exosomatic method or technique Method which utilizes the resistance of the skin to external electric current in the measurement of psychogalvanic response.

exoteric The public or external aspect of a situation or of an interpretation of an idea or thought.

expansive Open, unrestricted feeling and expression in physical or verbal behavior.

expansive delusion Delusions of grandeur often accompanied by euphoric states including feelings of power, wealth, self-importance and well-being.

expansiveness 1. Personality trait characterized by extroverted behavior including friendliness, loquacity and hyper-reactivity. 2. (K. Horney) Neuroticism characterized by egotism, narcissism and perfectionism resulting from the belief of the individual that he has achieved his ideal self.

expectancy 1. (statistics) The probability of a thing occurring based on mathematical calculation. 2. An attitude of waiting for or anticipating something accompanied by attention and muscular tension. 3. An intervening variable or learned set which is inferred from behavior whereby a response to a certain cue or stimulus is assumed to lead to another particular situation on the basis of past experience or expectancy.

expectancy theory (E. C. Tolman) Cognitive learning consists of the acquisition of expectancies and of the resultant tendency to react to certain objects as signs of certain other objects previously associated with them in the environment.

expectation 1. State of anticipation of something often associated with tension or emotion. 2. (statistics) The probability of the occurrence of an event based on mathematical calculation. 3. The true or universal mean.

experience 1. The living through and personal encountering of an event. 2. Skill or understanding which is the result of living through something, or of practice, or of participation in something. 3. (E. B. Titchener) The whole of mental phenomena or of consciousness at any particular moment.

experience, accidental (psychoanalysis) Refers to experiences that are of external origin rather than inherent in the individual. Two types of accidental experiences are distinguished according to when they occur in the life or mental growth of the individual.

An accidental experience is called dispositional if it happens in the early years of development when it greatly influences the molding of character traits. If an accidental experience occurs later in life, it is called definitive and will have little or no influence on mental development. However, a definitive accident may be important in its affect upon the course of one's career.

experience, actual A summary score devised in the Beck approach to the Rorschach which is derived by adding the number of human movement responses to the weighted total of color responses. It is hypothesized to represent the total emotional resources, which, when related to intellect, yields an index of the psychological growth potential. It is also interpreted as the organized emotion operating in the life style of the individaul.

experience, affective An event in the life of an individual that involves feelings or emotions.

experience balance See *Erlebnistypus.*

experience type See *Erlebnistypus.*

experiment Controlled arrangement and manipulation of conditions in order to systematically observe particular phenomena with the intention of defining the influences and relationships which affect these phenomena. The variables or conditions in an experiment are the experimental variable which is systematically varied or manipulated by the experimenter; the dependent variable which is the phenomenon to be observed and is assumed to be affected by the manipulation of the experimental variable; all extraneous conditions are held constant as far as possible in that they do not confound results.

experiment, blank A kind of experimental control which calls for the occasional introduction of irregular conditions designed to prevent the subject from becoming automatic in his responses or from guessing what is coming. The results of these conditions are not included in the data analysis.

experiment, complication See *prior entry law.*

experiment, control A repetition of an experiment performed because the initial one was inadequately controlled or not controlled.

experiment, crucial An experiment which is critical to the acceptance or rejection of an hypothesis or a theory.

experiment of nature The investigation of the reaction of the individual organism to real environmental situations.

experimental control See *control, experimental.*

experimental design See *design, experimental.*

experimental error See *error, experimental.*

experimental group See *group, experimental.*

experimental method Scientific method and technique of testing hypotheses and gaining information through controlled experimentation.

experimental neurosis See *neurosis, experimental.*

experimental psychology See *psychology, experimental.*

experimental series 1. Trials or observations which are part of the experiment proper, as opposed to pretest, post-test or practice trials. 2. Those trials or observations which were made by the experimental group and those procedures which were applied to them as opposed to the control groups.

experimental variable See *variable, experimental.*

experimenter 1. One who designs or conducts an experiment. 2. Abbreviation "E."

experimentum crucis See *experiment, crucial.*

explanation 1. Simplification and classification of a concept or an idea. 2. Accounting for an event or for the nature of an object by delineating those conditions which gave rise to it. 3. Finding the underlying causes.

explicit 1. That which is stated directly or is clearly present in the data. 2. Overt.

explicit behavior Overt, outward, observable behavior, such as bodily movement.

exploitation Taking advantage of another person or group for one's own personal needs without consideration of the needs of that person or group.

exploitative character See *character, exploitative.*

exploratory behavior Movement or locomotion engaged in most frequently by children, animals and lower organisms when initially orienting themselves to new situations. These movements bring various aspects or pieces of the environment into view of the exploring organism.

explosive diathesis See *diathesis, explosive.*

exponent (mathematics) A symbol written as a superscript to another symbol or expression which indicates the power to which that symbol or expression is to be raised.

exposition attitude (H. A. Murray) The tendency to explain things, to judge, to define relationships, or to demonstrate.

expression 1. Anything an organism does which is considered to be indicative of the nature of the organism itself. 2. Verbal, facial or physical responses which are indicative of the emotional state of the individual. 3. (mathematics) A numerical or algebraic statement or symbol.

expression method The measurement of emotion or feeling through the investigation of the accompanying physical changes.

expressive 1. Responding of an organism. 2. Verbal, physical or facial gestures which indicate an emotion. 3. A portion of an event or situation which particularly indicates the nature of the total event or situation.

expressive aphasia See *aphasia, expressive.*

expressive function Anything an organism does

which is considered to be indicative of the nature of that organism.

expressive movements Distinctive bodily movements such as particular facial expressions or postures which can be used to differentiate one person from another. These are sometimes helpful to personality assessment.

expressive therapy See *therapy, expressive.*

expressivity The extent to which the genetic complement for a trait or disease, having achieved penetrance, expresses itself. In schizophrenia variable degrees of expressivity are illustrated by the spectrum from seclusive personality, slowly deteriorating schizophrenia of late onset, to rapidly deteriorating schizophrenia of early onset.

ext schedule See *reinforcement, schedule of: extinction.*

extended F+% A ratio used in the Rapaport approach to the Rorschach which is expressed as the number of "good" pure form responses in proportion to the total number of pure form responses, as related to the number of "good" form-dominated responses in proportion to the total number of form-dominated responses. The ratio is generally interpreted in terms of ego functioning.

extension 1. (physics) The occupying of space by physical objects. 2. The supporting and straightening function of a limb. 3. (logic) The category of object or events to which a term applies.

extension thrust See *reflex, extension thrust.*

extensity The psychological parallel of physical extension which is the raw material or sense data upon which a perception is based as opposed to the extension in space of a physical object.

extensor Muscle which functions to straighten a limb by contracting.

exteraceptor Sense organ which is stimulated by external sources of energy.

exteriorization The relation of one's private life or personal affairs to the external world and objective reality.

external auditory meatus Canal which connects the middle ear to the external ear.

external inhibition See *inhibition, external.*

external rectus External eye muscle which functions to move the eyeball outward.

external senses Sensory receptor mechanisms which are stimulated completely or primarily by external stimulation.

external validation Validation of a measure by correlating it with an appropriate external criterion as, for example, validating an aptitude test by establishing high positive correlation with school grades.

externalization 1. The arousal of a drive by external stimulation rather than by internal stimulation through a learning process of secondary reinforcement. **2.** The process of differentiating the individual self from the external environment which occurs in childhood. **3.** The projection of one's own personal feelings or perceptions onto the external environment. **4.** The attribution of particular aspects of experience to an environment perceived as outside one's own experience.

extinction 1. The gradual diminution of the conditioned response resulting from the withholding of the unconditioned stimulus or the instrumental reward. **2.** (I.P. Pavlov) A type of internal inhibition in which the conditioned response is temporarily decreased following the presentation of the conditioned stimulus without the unconditioned stimulus.

extinction, differential Extinction of one response while reinforcing the other.

extinction, latent Extinction which occurs without responding as a result of non-reinforced exposure to the previously reinforcing situation.

extinction ratio The ratio of unreinforced responses to reinforced responses emitted by the organism during the process of periodic instrumental reconditioning. Unreinforced responses do not elicit reward under experimental conditions; the reinforced response is the previously learned and extinguished response.

extinction (ext) schedule See *reinforcement, schedule of: extinction.*

extinction, secondary The weakening or extinction of conditioned responses. As the result of a particular conditioned response being extinguished, responses similar to the one being extinguished are likely to become extinct.

extinctive inhibition See *extinction, (I.P. Pavlov).*

extirpation The surgical removal or destruction of an organ.

extraception (H. A. Murray) Orientation or attitude characterized by skepticism and impersonal objectivity.

extrajection 1. (psychoanalysis) Defense mechanism consisting of the projection of one's own feelings, characteristics or processes onto another person. **2.** The symbolic representation of a psychic process or feeling as, for example, writing a poem about anger.

extramural That which occurs outside the walls of an institution.

extraneous 1. That which originates externally or pertains to an external or irrelevant factor. **2.** Something which is not pertinent to what is being investigated or considered.

extrapolate To infer or estimate from the narration of a variable within the known range the value of that variable beyond the given data or to extend its curve beyond the plotted range.

extrapunitive 1. (S. Rosenzweig) Frustration reaction in which the individual directs hostility, anger, or aggression against the person or thing which he perceives as the source of frustration. **2.** Personality type characterized by extrapunitive frustration reactions.

extrasensory perception or ESP Awareness or perception of an external event which is not mediated by any of the known senses. ESP includes the phenomena of clairvoyance, precognition and psychokinesis.

extraspectral hue Hue or color not present in the spectrum as, for example, purple, which lies between red and violet or blue.

extratensive A Rorschach postulate, referring to those instances where the sum of weighted color responses is substantially greater than the sum of human movement responses. When the ratio (Erlebnistypus) manifests such a characteristic, the person is considered to be one who derives his more basic gratifications from interactions with his environment.

extratensiveness (Rorschach) Characterized by strong responsiveness to the environment and outward orientation which may be either passive or active. Passive extratensiveness is associated with conformity and dependance in interpersonal relations and acceptance of surrounding situations; active extratensiveness is associated with creativity in interpersonal relations and striving toward external goals.

extraversion 1. Outward-directed personality orientation characterized by sociability, activity and interest in the public environment rather than inner directed attitudes and interests. **2.** (C. G. Jung) Movement of the libido toward the outer world resulting in all attitudes, values, and interests being directed toward the physical and social environment and an object-directed reference point. **3.** (J. H. Eysenck) A personality type based on particular neural structures which cause a rapid development of reactive inhibition, strong inhibition and a slow dissipation of inhibition. The neurotic form is hysterical conversion.

extraversion, active (C. G. Jung) Outward direction of libido which is willed by the subject rather than pulled from an external source or object.

extraversion-introversion (C. G. Jung) Bipolar personality dimension which in combination with the four features of thinking, feeling, sensation, and intuition, form the basis of personality typology through which people are divided into the following eight types: extraverted thinking, extraverted feeling, extraverted sensation, extraverted intuition, introverted thinking, introverted feeling, introverted sensation, and introverted intuition. The dimension ranges from outer-directedness on the extraverted extreme and inward-directedness on the introverted extreme.

extraversion, passive (C. G. Jung) Outward direction of libido which is compelled by the external object rather than subjectively directed.

extravert One who has an extraverted personality.

extraverted feeling type (C. G. Jung) Personality type characterized by acting according to the demands and expectations of a situation, feeling for external objects and the ability to establish friendships.

extraverted intuition type (C. G. Jung) Personality type characterized by a perception of the possibilities for manipulation and control of available external objects.

extraverted sensation type (C. G. Jung) Personality type characterized by a realistic, materialistic outlook and an orientation toward the sensory, concrete features of objects.

extraverted thinking type (C. G. Jung) Personality type characterized by dependence on sensory impressions as a basis for logical analysis and reality-construction, acceptance of the sensory world and an interest in facts and their classification.

extravisual Outside the field of vision.

extrinsic behavior See *behavior, extrinsic.*

extrinsic constant (T. Burrow) Secondary principle governing man's relationship to his environment; refers to cortex mediated behavior.

extrinsic eye muscles Those eye muscles that rotate the eyeball in different directions.

extrinsic motivation See *motivation, extrinsic.*

extrinsic reward See *reward, extrinsic.*

extrinsic thalamus See *thalamus, extrinsic.*

extrophy Malformation of an organ.

extropia The turning outward of one eyeball because of muscular imbalance when the other focuses on an object; walleyedness.

extroversion See *extraversion.*

exudative diathesis See *diathesis, exudative.*

exvia-invia (R. B. Cattell) Factorially established broad dimension within the area of behavior popularly referred to as extraversion-introversion. The precise core concept within extraversion-introversion.

eye Visual sensory receptor consisting of three layers: the scleratic layer including the white of the eye surrounding the corneal lens which focuses light, the choroid coat which functions to absorb light, and the innermost retinal layer containing the rods and the cones with the fovea on the center of clear vision at its rear. The portion of the eyeball within the eye socket is also part of the eye.

eye, compound A type of eye found in insects which consists of a series of optical systems whose focus is slightly different which results in the perception of a mosaic rather than a single image.

eye dominance 1. Greater use of one eye than of the other in fixating on objects and greater dependence on the impressions of that eye even though the other eye is functional. 2. One eye leads.

eye ground That which is seen by the viewer when looking at the back of the eyeball through the pupil with an opthalmoscope.

eye-hand coordination The cooperative functioning of the eyes and the hands when picking up or moving objects.

eye, light-adapted 1. The eye in its normal condition for daylight vision. 2. An eye which has been exposed to light of a high degree of intensity and has thereby become relatively insensitive to light of lower intensities.

eye movements The rotary movement and positional changes of the eye as a result of the functioning of the extrinsic eye muscles.

eye span The amount seen and comprehended in a single fixation pause of the eyes which is measured in terms of the number of letters or words comprehended in reading.

eye-voice span The distance in terms of letters by which the eye leads the voice in oral reading; the distance between what is being said and what is being focused on.

eyedness See *eye dominance.*

eyelash sign The spontaneous reflex movement of the eyelid when the eyelash is stimulated.

Eysenck, Hans J. (1916-   ) British psychologist, German born. He developed and experimentally tested descriptive theory of major dimensions of personality; developed and tested causal theories for these dimensions; linked drug action with personality, and demonstrated the importance of genetic factors in personality development. Originated (with P. Broadhurst) large-scale genetic studies of emotionality, conditioning and arousal in rats. Worked out (with D. Furneaux) model of IQ dependent on speed, error-checking and continuance aspects. Proposed and tested two-factor model for structure of social attitudes, relating these to the political party preference. Promoted development of clinical psychology in England, and played part in origin and growth of behavior therapy; founded and edits *The Journal of Behavior Research and Therapy.*

F

F   (Rorschach) Form response.

F-   (Rorschach) Poor form response.

F+   (Rorschach) Good form response.

F+% A traditional Rorschach calculation used in most approaches to the test, except that of Klopfer (See *form level rating*), and expressed as the proportion of "good" form responses in relation to the total number of form responses. Good and poor form have been variously defined in terms of normative frequency and/or examiners, opinion concerning the appropriateness of the area of the blot used for the response given. Low F+% is generally interpreted as "poor" reality testing.

F factor   (R.B. Cattell) The factor defining the personality dimension of surgency-desurgency; surgency is social, cheerful versus desurgency being dull, depressed; there is also a difference in tests of speed of reaction time, alkalinity of saliva, etc.

F ratio   (statistics) An index used to determine whether the difference between two statistics is statistically significant. The F ratio is found by dividing the larger variance (σ_1^2) by the smaller (σ_2^2). The formula is:

$$F = \frac{\sigma_1^2}{\sigma_2^2}$$

This F is looked up in a table of significance.

F scale (fascism scale)   (T. W. Adorno et al.) Questionnaire designed to assess how readily the subject would accept antidemocratic ideologies.

F score   A score on the Minnesota Multiphasic Inventory of Personality that indicates whether or not a testee has complied understandingly to the directions.

F test (F)   A variance test between two samples to determine whether the difference between them could be ascribed to chance.

Fables test   A mental test which may be used as a projective or intelligence test in which the subject is required to explain the lesson taught by the fable.

fabrication   1. An inappropriate response to test items, often of a fantastic nature. 2. See *confabulation*.

fabulation   Fabrication.

fabulized response   (Rorschach) Included in the Rapaport approach to the Rorschach, as a type of deviant verbalization in which the subject's response includes elaborate and unnecessary descriptions of a generally idiographic nature so as to personalize the response. Occurring in significant quantity in a single record they are considered indicative of psychopathology.

face-to-face group   Two or more people who are in such close proximity that direct interaction is possible.

face-to-face interview   See *interview, face-to-face*.

face validity   The extent to which a test seems to measure the variable to be tested because of its similarity to the criterion measure.

facial angle   An angle, intended to measure cranial development, which is formed by a line drawn from the base of the nostrils to the opening of the ear and from the base of the nostrils to the forehead.

facial nerve   See *nerve, facial*.

facial nucleus   A mass of cells in the base of the brain which give rise to the facial nerve.

facial vision   See *echolocation*.

facile ament   (A.F. Tredgold) Mentally defective individual who is "characterless, facile," and particularly amenable to suggestion.

facilitation   Physiological term referring to the excitation of one neuron by another: in meaning, identical with stimulation, except that it is customary to distinguish between excitation originating outside the nervous system (stimulation) and excitation originating within it (facilitation).

factitious   Man-made, artificial; not natural or spontaneous.

factor An underlying influence responsible for part of the variability of a number of behavioral manifestations. Therefore, an influence in behavior which is relatively independent of other influences and of a unitary nature.

factor analysis 1. Statistical procedure aimed at the generation of hypothetical variates that are weighted sums of observed variates. The former, fewer in number than the latter, are usually expected to describe, summarize, or explain the latter. 2. (C. Spearman) A data-reduction procedure whereby a matrix of obtained measurements of N individuals on n experimental variables is replaced by a smaller matrix of factor coefficients or loadings relating every variable to each of r factors, each an underlying variable, assumed to represent an ability or other kind of trait, which is conceived as a vector in r-dimensional space. ($N > n > r$). 3. (L.L. Thurstone) The technique used to show the correlation of all tests of mental ability. Thurstone found that all the tests were positively correlated, indicating a common factor among them. The analysis indicated the following seven primary mental abilities: verbal, number, spatial, perceptual, memory, reasoning and word fluency.

factor analysis, inverted See *Q technique.*

factor analytic studies Studies which attempt to delineate the underlying relationships in a series of correlations.

factor axes A set of coordinates which represents the relationships between factors and the relationships of factors to correlations in the matrix. Axes are located by factor rotation and are the solution regarded as best for a particular study.

factor, bipolar A factor which consists of two mutually exclusive, opposite extremes.

factor coefficient See *factor loading.*

factor, common See *factor, group.*

factor configurations The positions and relations of vectors or lines which represent the various tests in the correlation matrix. The relationship between the angles of each vector represents the correlation. A right angle is a zero correlation; the more acute the angle, the higher the correlation.

factor group A factor present in two or more, but not all tests of a set of tests being factor analyzed which accounts for the high intercorrelations of tests within the set and the lower intercorrelations of tests outside the group.

factor loading The amount of correlation that a given factor contributes to the variability of a test.

factor matrix A table of factor loadings resulting from a factor analysis; the columns represent the factors extracted and the rows represent the tests.

factor, number (N) A factor found in many tests of ability which is revealed by facility in the manipulation of numbers and in working out simple numerical operations.

factor, O Variables which are present in an orga-

nism at any given moment; internal factors which affect an organism's response such as drive or individual differences. Also called O-variables.

factor, position The influence geographical location or spatial arrangement has upon an organism's response to a particular stimulus as, for example, the tendency to turn a certain way in a maze.

factor, primary 1. (factor analysis) Any factor which satisfies the requirements of simple structure. 2. Any factor in a group of factors which could be divided without remainder and without overlapping the covariance of a matrix.

factor reflection Changing the algebraic signs of related measures in a correlation matrix in order to maintain unidirectionality of the variables, or the consequence of rotation.

factor resolution Synonymous with factor structure.

factor rotation In factor analysis movement of the axes of a plot of factors by rotation of their origin to psychologically meaningful positions. The points are then accurately plotted in new dimensions.

factor, second order A factor common to other factors.

factor structure Statistical end point of factor analysis, when the interrelations and relative positions of the vectors have been established and a coordinate system imposed upon their spatial distribution.

factor theories of learning 1. Contention that there are two aspects of learning (a) a mechanical, motor process and (b) a mental comprehension of the relationship. 2. A theory in conditioning which maintains that attitudes influence the incidence of conditioning and that stimulus properties determine the magnitude of the response. 3. A theory that says that instrumental and classical or Pavlovian conditioning constitute distinct and separable processes. The characteristics of each remain in dispute, but often instrumental conditioning is said to require reinforcement and occur in the central nervous system, while classical conditioning does not require reinforcement and occurs in the autonomic nervous system. There is currently a feeling that the two processes may be inseparable and the distinction may be a matter of degree resulting from the experimental procedure rather than in the organism.

factor theory Explanation and description of personality and intelligence in terms of statistically derived hypothetical factors used on factor analysis of results of written and motor tests.

factor theory of intelligence Theories of structure and function of intelligence based upon factor analysis of performance on primarily paper and pencil tests. C. Spearman hypothesized a single factor of intelligence which he called "general ability" or "g" and interpreted as a purely intellectual element, pure mind. L.L. Thurstone expanded the number of factors to "seven primary abilities" : V, verbal; N, number; S, spatial; M, memory; R, reasoning; W, word-fluency; and P, perceptual speed. J.P. Guilford developed a factor theory of intelligence in which each factor is specified by three dimensions: content, operation, and product. The contents are divided into figural, symbolic, semantic, and behavioral contents. The operations are divided into cognition memory, divergent production, and evaluation. The products are divided into implications, transformations systems, relations, classes, and units. Thus there are, in this schema, 120 different factors of intelligence of which Guilford maintains 82 have been demonstrated or discovered.

factor, unique (factor analysis) A factor found in only one test or measure of a correlation matrix; its variance is not shared with the other tests being factorized.

factor weight Synonymous with *factor loading.*

factorial 1. Combination of elements or factors, in several or all possible ways. 2. (statistics) A number, *N!*, read *"N factorial"* representing the product of all numbers from 1 to that number, e.g., 5! = 5 x 4 x 3 x 2 x 1 = 120.

factorial design See *design, factorial.*

factorial theory of personality See *personality, factorial theory of.*

factorial validity See *validity, factorial.*

factoring Process of finding factors. The procedure of factor analysis.

factors, constitutional Factors referring to neurophysiological and chemical aspects of the body.

faculty 1. A natural or learned ability to perform a certain act. 2. An obsolete term referring to supposed mental "powers" such as reason, memory, will, perception, and imagination.

faculty psychology (W. Wolff) A theory that the mind is made up of separate and independent areas of power, each of which can be strengthened by exercise.

fad A passing enthusiasm zealously pursued by an individual or group which is not directly useful and meets no major needs.

faeces amicae in os proprium inicere (W. Stekel) A form of sexual perversion in which feces are orally incorporated.

failure 1. Someone who has not achieved a minimum economic or social status or who has failed to attain goals he has set for himself. 2. Not obtaining the desired or anticipated results in an experiment.

faintness 1. Weakness in intensity. 2. A passing state bordering on loss of consciousness with symptomatic dizziness, overall weakness, and sometimes nausea.

faith Unconditional and complete acceptance of a belief or system of beliefs without substantial evidence, usually accompanied by strong emotions.

faith healing A method or practice of treating mental or physical illness through the patient's belief in divine intervention.

fall chronometer An instrument used to measure time intervals by the fall of a weight.

fallacia An illusion or hallucination.

fallacia optica Optical illusion or hallucination.

fallacy 1. Deception. 2. A false idea; also the liability to make a mistake. 3. Reasoning that fails to satisfy the conditions of logical proof or violates the laws of valid argument.

fallectomy A sterilization operation in whieh the fallopian tubes are cut and tied off.

falling sickness A colloquialism for epilepsy; also called caduca passio.

Falret, Jean-Pierre (1794-1870) A French psychiatrist known for his studies in suicidal tendencies. Also suggested the term "mental alienation" instead of mental illness. First in field to consider mania and depression as stages of the same disorder.

false alarm (psychophysics) A response by a subject as if a stimulus had been presented when in fact no stimulus was presented.

false association (W. Stekel) A dreamer's simultaneous identification with several persons who represent the same love object. Such associations are considered only partly valid and evasive since they may lead the analyst to details concerning one of the people with whom the dreamer identifies as his love object, when in reality this association pertains to another person who is a partial substitute for the real love object.

false negative The number of cases incorrectly excluded from a particular group by the application of certain standards of criteria.

false positive The number of cases incorrectly included in a particular group by the application of certain standards or criteria.

falsehood, unconscious A false or untrue statement made by an individual without his having any conscious awareness of its false nature. The individual has simply come to believe things about himself, other people or situations which are untrue.

falsification of memory 1. Detailed and seemingly lucid fabrications of gaps in memory associated with Korsakoff's psychosis. 2. Confabulations.

falsification, retrospective Adding false details and meanings to the recall of past experiences. A common practice of paranoid schizophrenics who may recall experiences which occurred prior to the formation of their delusional system from a delusional point of view.

fames bovina Obsolete term for oxlike hunger.

fames canina Obsolete term for doglike hunger.

fames lupina Obsolete term for wolfish hunger.

familial Pertaining to the family, referring to either heredity or heritage.

familial dysautonomia A hereditary dysfunction of the autonomous nervous system, emotional lability and indifference to pain. Occurs in infancy.

familial tremor A hereditary disease which starts in childhood, associated with tremor and hyperactivity.

familianism A tendency to maintain strong intra-familial ties which are culturally transmitted, resulting in intense solidarity among family members.

famille névropathique (J. Charcot) A group of degenerative diseases for which heredity was seen as the unique originating cause.

family 1. A group of persons related by blood or marriage, the specific members of which differ from culture to culture. Always includes a mother and children, nearly always includes the father. **2.** Metaphorically, any group bound by close ties. **3.** Biologically, a group of related *genera*, a subdivision of an *order* in the classification of organisms. **4.** The *human family:* all men, including extinct species. **5.** Any collection of closely related items: a family of words, a family of colors.

family behavior problem (social work) Denotes anti-social conduct of an individual within the patient group. Such behavior is usually associated with offenses or delinquency such as assault, and stealing.

family constellation (A. Adler) The number and characteristics of the members of a family, the patterns of their mutual relationships, and the order of birth. Considered an important factor in the development of the "style of life."

family life handicap (social work) A physical or psychological disability which interferes with or limits an individual's capacities for marriage and home-making.

family romance (psychoanalysis) Childhood fantasies in which: **1.** the child rejects his own parents and fantasizes that he is the offspring of other, more noble parents thereby making his own developmental need to separate from his real parents more acceptable. **2.** the child imagines himself saving the life of some great person, who is really a representative of a parent, and thus resolves his debt to his parents for having given him life.

family, schismatic (T. Lidz) Family in which there is chronic parental disharmony and in which the children are forced to take one or the other side in the ongoing battle; the parents tend to devalue each other, making appropriate sex role identification difficult for the children.

family, skewed (T. Lidz) Family in which one parent is overwhelming and engulfing and the other is appeasing and submissive, resulting in a lopsided parental situation. Such a family is characterized by a desperate need of all members to avoid anxiety and by the experiencing of individuation as total separation and loss.

family therapy See *psychotherapy, family.*

fanaticism Excessive enthusiasm for a point of view or cause, evidenced by intense emotions and extreme, though often transient, efforts in its behalf.

fancy Fantasy; whimsical imagination.

fancy, tendency to A tendency to imagine in a whimsical, wishful way which, in extreme cases, can become morbid and detrimental.

fantasm; phantasm A vivid, seemingly real image of an absent person or thing, or of what is assumed by the perceiver to be a disembodied spirit.

fantastic melancholia (E. Kraepelin) A term indicating a morbid mental state characterized by bizarre delusions and hallucinations such as evil spirits, death, animals' heads, monsters, angels, and floating heads.

fantasy; phantasy Imagining a complex object or event which is pleasant and wish-fulfilling in concrete symbols or images, whether or not the object or event exists.

fantasy cathexis See *cathexis, fantasy.*

fantasy formation; phantasy formation The process of daydreaming.

fantasy, pregnancy (psychoanalysis) The concept that the wish for a child in women is closely related to their oedipal wish of a child with the father, their wish for a penis, their desire for the mother's breast and the wish to retain feces, all of which are the same symbols expressed at different levels of development.

fantasying, active (psychoanalysis) A psychotherapeutic technique in which the patient is asked to spontaneously relate his imagery, the analysis of which enables the psychoanalyst to uncover the patient's inner conflicts and subsequently bring them into his conscious awareness.

far point The most distant point at which the eye can see an object distinctly under relaxed conditions.

far sight A condition of vision characterized by an inability to see near objects clearly, often accompanied by clear vision for distant objects. The most common cause is hyperopia, in which the light rays come to a focal point behind the retina.

farad Measure of electrical capacity. It has a charge of one coulomb when the difference in potential between the field and its boundaries is one volt. Usually measured in microfarads 1/1,000,000 farads.

fasciculus A bundle or cluster of nerve, muscle, or tendon fibers separated by connective tissue.

fasciculus cuneatus An important tract of the dorsal part of the spinal cord which mediates jointly with the fasciculus gracilis the proprioception of touch.

fasciculus gracilis An important tract in the dorsal part of the spinal cord which mediates jointly with fasciculus cuneatus the proprioception of touch.

fascination The partial mastery of what is experienced as an uncontrollable factor in one's environment by identifying with it. For example, an infant may pay rapt attention to a rattle waved before him, but if it is beyond his reach or if he has not yet learned to grasp and hold, his attention becomes greatly intensified, and he loses himself in the sight and sound of the rattle and thus becomes one with it.

fascinum An ancient belief that certain individuals possess an "evil eye" with which they can fascinate and subsequently injure others by looking at them.

fashion Specifically, irrational and transient manners of dress, but may also refer to customs, beliefs, and the arts.

fastidium cibi Loathing of food.

fastidium potus Loathing of drink.

fatalism **1.** The philosophical and religious doctrine that an individual's acts are predestined by a deity and are, therefore, not subject to change by his own will, the act of another person, or changes in his environment. **2.** The doctrine that volition or will cannot influence human behavior.

father complex See *complex, Electra.*

father figure **1.** A person who replaces one's real father and becomes the object of habitual responses originally developed in relation to the real parent. **2.** A mature individual with whom a younger, immature person identifies and who comes to exercise such parental functions as advice and encouragement.

father hypnosis (S. Ferenczi) The concept that submission to hypnotic states can be traced to blind obedience to one's parents, in this case the transference of paternal fixation; also called "fear-hypnosis."

father-ideal (psychoanalysis) That part of the ego-ideal which is derived from introjection of idealized parent figures. The father's image usually encompasses the images of both parents. The resulting ego-ideal is greatly influenced by the child's perceptions of the father's moral standards, ideas, and attitudes. Identification by introjection results in the individual's striving towards perfection by attempting to line up to the expectations and standards of the idealized father figure, the father-ideal.

father imago See *imago.*

father surrogate See *father figure; surrogate.*

father's womb The displacement of affection for one's mother onto the father and, thus, the father becomes "maternalized" and invested with a womb.

fatigue, combat A traumatic neurosis precipitated by the stress and anxiety of combat and characterized by anxiety and somatic disorders.

fatigue, condition of See *ergasthenia.*

fatuity **1.** Stupidity; anything fatuous. **2.** Idiocy; dementia.

fatuous **1.** Foolish; inane; absurd. **2.** Without reality; illusory.

fault **1.** A failing, generally minor in nature; shortcoming; blemish, as an imperfection or weakness in character. **2.** A failure to do what is right. **3.** Responsibility for wrongdoing; guilt.

faunorum ludibria An obsolete term for nightmare and sometimes, epilepsy.

faxen psychosis See *buffoonery psychosis.*

fear A strong emotion involving perception of danger, unpleasant agitation and often a desire to hide or to escape. Fear is accompanied by physiological changes, mostly of the sympathetic nervous system.

fear, conditioned Fear learned in a conditioning procedure which undergoes extinction if not reinforced intermittently.

fear, morbid of
air: aerophobia
animals: zoöphobia
anything new: kaino(to)phobia; neophobia
bacilli: bacillophobia
bad men: pavor sceleris; scelerophobia
barren space: cenophobia; kenophobia
bearing a monster: teratophobia
bees: apiphobia; melissophobia
being alone: autophobia; eremiophobia; monophobia
being buried alive: taphephobia
being locked in: claustrophobia; clithrophobia
being looked at: scopophobia
being touched: (h)aphephobia; haptephobia
birds: ornithophobia
blood: hematophobia; hemophobia
blushing: ereuthophobia
brain disease: meningitophobia
bridges: gephyrophia
burglars: scelerophobia
carriages: amaxophobia
cats: ailurophobia; galeophobia; gatophobia
change: kainophobia; kainotophobia; neophobia
childbirth: maieusiophobia
choking: anginophobia; pnigophobia
cold: cheimaphobia
color(s): chromatophobia; chromophobia
comet: cometophobia
confinement: claustrophobia
contamination: molysmophobia; mysophobia
corpse: necrophobia
crossing streets: dromophobia
crowds: demophobia; ochlophobia
dampness: hygrophobia
darkness: achluophobia; nyctophobia; scotophobia
dawn: eosophobia
daylight: phengophobia
death: thanatophobia
definite disease: monopathophobia
deformity: dysmorphophobia
demons: demonia; demonomania; entheomania
depth: bathophobia
devil: demonophobia; satanophobia
dirt: mysophobia; rhypophobia; rupophobia
disease: nosophobia; pathophobia
dog: cynophobia
dolls: pediophobia
dust: amathophobia
eating: phagophobia
electricity: electrophobia

emptiness: kenophobia
everything: panphobia; panophobia; pantophobia
excrement: coprophobia
eyes: ommatophobia
failure: kakorrhapiophobia
fatigue: kopophobia
fearing: phobophobia
feathers: pteronophobia
female genitals: eurotophobia
fever: fibriphobia; pyrexeophobia
filth: mysophobia; rhypophobia; rupophobia
fire: pyrophobia
fish: ichthyophobia
flash: selaphobia
flogging: mastigophobia
floods: antlophobia
flute: autophobia
fog: homichlophobia
food: cibophobia
forest: hylophobia
frogs: batrachophobia
functioning: ergasiophobia
ghosts: phasmophobia
girls: parthenophobia
glass: crystallophobia; hyelophobia
God: theophobia
gravity: barophobia
hair: trichopathophobia; trichophobia
heat: thermophobia
heaven: uranophobia
height: acrophobia; hyposophobia
hell: hadephobia; stygiophobia
heredity: patroiophobia
high objects: batophobia
house: domatophobia; oikophobia
ideas: ideophobia
infinity: apeirophobia
injury: traumatophobia
innovation: neophobia
insanity: lyssophobia; maniaphobia
insects: acarophobia; entomophobia
jealousy: zelophobia
justice: dikephobia
knives: aichmophobia
large objects: megalophobia
left: levophobia
light: photophobia
lightning: astraphobia; astrapophobia;
  kerauophobia
machines: mechanophobia
man: androphobia
many things: polyphobia
marriage: gamophobia
materialism: hylephobia
medicine(s); pharmacophobia
metals: metallophobia
meteors: meteorophobia
mice: musophobia
mind: psychophobia
mirrors: eisoptrophobia; spectrophobia
missiles: balistophobia
moisture: hygrophobia
money: chrematophobia
motion: kinesophobia
myths: mythophobia
naked body: gymnophobia

names: onomatophobia
needles: belonephobia
Negroes: negrophobia
night: noctiphobia; nyctophobia
northern lights: auroraphobia
novelty: kainophobia; kainotophobia; neophobia
odor(s): olfactophobia; osmophobia;
  osphresiophobia
open space(s): agoraphobia
pain: algophobia; odynophobia
parasites: parasitophobia
people: anthrophobia
place: topophobia
pleasure: hedonophobia
points: aicmophobia
poison: iophobia; toxicophobia
poverty: peniaphobia
precipice(s): cremnophobia
punishment: poinephobia
rabies: cynophobia
railroads or trains: siderodromphobia
rain: ombrophobia
rectal excreta: coprophobia
rectum: protophobia
red: erythrophobia
responsibility: hypengyophobia
ridicule: catagelophobia
right: dextrophobia
river: potamophobia
robbers: harpaxophobia
rods: rhabdophobia
ruin: ateophobia
sacred things: hierophobia
scabies: scabiophobia
scratch: amychophobia
sea: thalassophobia
self: autophobia
semen: spermatophobia
sex: genophobia
sexual intercourse: coitophobia
shock: hormephobia
sin: hamartophobia
sinning: peccatiphobia
sitting: thaasophobia
sitting down: kathisophobia
skin disease: dermatosiophobia
skin lesion: dermatophobia
skin (of animals): doraphobia
sleep: hypnophobia
small objects: microphobia; microbiophobia
smothering: pnigerophobia
snakes: ophidiophobia
snow: chionophobia
solitude: eremiophobia
sounds: acousticophobia
sourness: aerophobia
speaking: laliophobia
speaking aloud: phonophobia
spiders: arachneophobia
stairs: climacophobia
standing up: stasiphobia
standing up and walking: stasibasiphobia
stars: siderophobia
stealing: kleptophobia
stillness: eremiophobia
stories: mythophobia

strangers: xenophobia
streets: agyiophobia
string: linonophobia
sunlight: heliophobia
symbolism: symbolophobia
syphilis: syphilophobia
talking: laliophobia
tapeworms: taeniophobia
taste: geumaphobia
teeth: odontophobia
thinking: phronemophobia
thunder: brontophobia
time: chronophobia
travel: hodophobia
trembling: tremophobia
trichinosis: trichinophobia
tuberculosis: phthisiophobia; tuberculophobia
vaccination: vaccinophobia
vehicles: amaxophobia
venereal disease: cypridophobia; cypriphobia
void: kenophobia
vomiting: emetophobia
walking: basiphobia
water: hydrophobia
weakness: asthenophobia
wind: anemophobia
women: gynophobia; horror feminae
work: ponophobia
writing: graphophobia

fear neurosis (M. Prince) A neurotic complex in which the physiological manifestations of emotion occur without any conscious awareness of such emotion.

fear, real A fear of something real in one's environment as opposed to impulse fear which is purely instinctual or psychological in nature.

feature profile test A type of performance test in which the testee puts pieces of wood together to form a profile or head without being informed of the nature of the object.

febrile Feverish.

febriphobia Fear of fever.

febris hysterica Hysterical fever.

feces, faeces Excretions from the intestines out through the anus of unabsorbed food, indigestible matter, and intestinal secretions.

Fechner, Gustav Theodor (1801-1887) Inventor of psychophysics, and considered by some the founder of experimental psychology. His 1860 publicaton proposed three methods for measuring the relationship between subjective and objective quantities, and contained a statement of his famous law: $S = k \log R$, or, the magnitude of a sensation *(S)* is proportional to the logarithm of the magnitude of the stimulus (*R*, for Reiz, the German word for stimulus).

Fechner's colors See *Charpentier's bands.*

Fechner's paradox A phenomenon first observed by Fechner that when one eye is closed, there is an increase in brightness of a figure which had previously been viewed binocularly.

Fechner's shadow experiment An experimental

demonstration of Weber's law in which an individual compares the intensity of brightness of two shadows cast by one pole on a screen by two independent, variable light sources, a comparison of their difference threshold.

Fechner-Weber law (psychophysics) When stimuli progress in geometrical progression, sensations increase in arithmetical progression.

feeblemindedness General term for individuals of subnormal intellectual development and deficient mental functioning who fall into the more specific categories of moronity, imbecility, and idiocy, which includes a range of I.Q. from 20–69. Individuals of borderline deficiency, or I.Q. of 70–80 are not considered feebleminded. In Britain, feeblemindedness includes only the moron category, I.Q. 50–69.

feeblemindedness, affective (S. Ferenczi) A condition characterized by the inhibition of thought due to the extreme intensity of the feelings. During the time when affect is strong the individual's thought processes become inhibited, but when the emotion passes the usual capacity for clear thinking returns.

feedback 1. In a machine or electronic system, an automatic means of regulating performance by linking input to output. 2. (neurology) The afferent impulses from proprioceptive receptors which indicate the speed and extent of motor movements. Believed to be important in aiming, grasping, and placing movements. 3. (social psychology) Any kind of direct information from an outside source about the effects and/or results of one's behavior.

feedback and brain mechanism Feedback regulation of physiological processes, innate behavior, and voluntary activities is dependent on the functioning of different areas of the brain. The preliminary stages of the innate act seems to require an integrated performance of different parts of the brain while the consummatory act appears to be focal. The cephalic brainstem in coordination with the limbic portions of the cerebral hemisphere are important in emotion. Lesions of the postcentral cortex results in defective kinesthetic feedback from motor acts.

feedback, kinesthetic Stimulation generated during the execution of a motor response, often used equivalently with proprioceptive feedback. Research conducted by J.M. Notterman and others has shown the importance of kinesthetic feedback to the broad topic in conditioning and learning known as "response differentiation."

feedback, negative Information concerning the relative absence of a requisite substance in a system which leads to the correction of this error.

feeding problem Persistent and extreme difficulty in getting a child to eat adequate amounts of nutritious food, which is not uncommon and generally indicates emotional distress.

feeling 1. Subjective descriptor for awarenesses of bodily (neural) states that cannot be reliably referred to environmental events. 2. Tactile sensation. 3. Awareness of something, i.e. feeling of being accepted. **4.** Emotion, e.g., feeling happy, sad, angry, etc.

feeling, ataxic See *ataxia, introphysic.*

feeling, discharge of See *discharge of affect.*

feeling-into **1.** Empathy. **2.** (C. G. Jung) A literal translation of the German word, *Einfühlung,* which refers to a kind of perceptual process by which one attributes, thought feeling, essential psychic content to an object and, as a result, the object is introjected.

feeling-intuition See *feeling-aperception.*

feeling, oceanic Feeling of unlimited omnipotence.

feeling sensation See *affective sensation.*

feeling, superiority See *superiority feelings.*

feeling type See *type, feeling.*

feigned amnesia A convenient defense often used in an attempt to escape the repercussions of criminal or otherwise offensive behavior.

fellatic Pertaining to fellatio.

fellatio Oral stimulation of the penis.

fellator One who practices fellatio, generally used in reference to a male.

fellator, self See *auto-fellatio.*

fellatrice A female who practices fellatio.

felony A grave crime.

Fels Scales of Parental Behavior See *scales, Fels, of Parental Behavior.*

felt need See *need, felt.*

female epispadias Congenital split clitoris and defective labia.

female penis, fantasies of (psychoanalysis) The attempt of some neurotic males to allay unconscious fears of castration by attributing a penis to both men and women. Such fantasies often lead to voyeuristic and exhibitionistic behavior, and at times, to a compulsive need to perform cunnilingus.

female psychology See *psychology, female.*

feminine psychology Psychology of women which stresses the cultural and social factors influencing the development of a woman rather than biological ones.

femininity **1.** The quality or state of being a woman; the collective characteristics of women. **2.** In contrast to *femaleness* which refers to the proper XX chromosome structure, *femininity* is used to characterize the possession of the usual secondary sexual characteristics of women.

femininity, complex (M. Klein) The unconscious attempt by a boy to deal with fears of being castrated by his mother by identifying himself with her and wishing for a vagina and breasts. At the same time, his dread of taking on the feminine role often appears as its opposite, in an excess of aggression.

feminism **1.** The theory or practice of those who advocate legal and social change which will lead to political, economic, and social equality of the sexes. **2.** Feminine character or characteristics.

feminization The process of becoming more female, whether one is biologically male or female.

fenestra **1.** The Latin word for window. **2.** (biology) See *fenestra ovalis* and *fenestra rotunda.*

feral child A child or adult who has been nurtured and reared by animals and completely isolated from human contact.

Féré method See *galvanic skin response.*

Féré phenomenon See *galvanic skin response.*

Ferri, Enrico (1856-1929) Italian psychiatrist who specialized in forensic psychiatry.

Ferrier's experiment An experiment in which the subject puts his finger on a trigger and concentrates on thinking he is pressing it, but does not press it, until he experiences the sensation of pressing it which is a kinesthetic sensation coming from other muscles. This experiment was designed to show that there is no direct experience of motor impulses.

Ferry-Porter law See *Porter's law.*

fertility **1.** The capacity for breeding or reproducing in abundance. **2.** One's ability to produce ideas; creativity.

fertilization The process of sexual reproduction, specifically the union of a male (*sperm*) and female (*egg* or *ovum*) germ cell which produces one new cell (*zygote*). The essential feature is the fusion of the nuclei which contain the chromosomes, or genetic material.

fertilize **1.** To make an egg fertile and thus produce a zygote; to impregnate. **2.** To make fertile or enrich; to make productive.

festination Involuntary tendency to hasten one's movements.

fetish **1.** An inanimate object believed to possess magical powers; any object to which one habitually devotes extravagant emotions. **2.** Objects or nonsexual parts of the body which arouse and gratify sexual impulses.

fetishism **1.** The worship of inanimate objects believed to possess magical powers. **2.** A pathological condition in which sexual impulses are habitually aroused and gratified by a nonsexual part of the body or a possession of the loved one.

fetishism, acoustic A pathological condition in which one's sexual impulses are habitually aroused and gratified by listening to stories with sexual content.

fetishism, adherent (M. Hirschfeld) Fetishism is a sexual perversion involving the fixation of erotic interest on an object or part of the body that is not normally associated with sexual behavior. The fetishist adores or worships such an object as a substitute for a beloved person or deity. Adherent fetishism is the form of fetishism characterized by the fetishist donning clothes.

fetishism, beast The habitual arousal and gratification of sexual impulses by touching furs or animal skins.

fetishism, coherent (M. Hirschfeld) A form of fetishism in which possessions of the loved one are brought into immediate contact by the fetishist with his own body, but are not worn as clothing.

fetishist 1. One who believes that certain inanimate objects possess magical powers and worships them accordingly. 2. One who habitually gratifies sexual impulses by handling the possessions or nonsexual parts of the body of the loved one.

fetishistic 1. Relating to or exhibiting the worships of certain inanimate objects which are believed to possess magical powers. 2. Relating to or exhibiting a pathological condition in which sexual impulses are habitually aroused and gratified by the possessions or nonsexual parts of the body of the loved one.

fetology The study of the fetus.

fetus, foetus The unborn offspring of an animal which is in its more advanced stage of development, the earlier stage being referred to as the *embryo*. In human beings, from the end of the third month of pregnancy to birth.

fever, autarchic The false and unconditional belief of children in their own omnipotence rather than recognition of their degree of dependence on the environment.

fever, Christmas A general term referring to the various syndromes of psychosomatic illness which tend to occur around holidays.

fever, erotic The "fever" accompanying erotomania, or unrestrained desire for genital relations with members of the opposite sex.

fever, psychogenetic Fever induced by hypnotic suggestion.

FI schedule See *reinforcement, schedule of: fixed interval.*

fiber 1. A filament or threadlike structure which comprises tissue. 2. A nerve fiber or single neuron. 3. An axon or a dendrite.

fibers, commissural Neural tract which connects corresponding areas in the two hemispheres of the brain.

fibril Filament-like portion of a neuron which extends through its cell body and out to the periphery.

fibrillation The component hair-like filaments which comprise a fiber.

fibromyositis See *myositis.*

fiction 1. A feigned or imagined state of affairs not considered to be real. 2. A paradoxical concept which is taken as *if* it is true for the sake of argument, such as $\sqrt{-1}$. 3. (A. Adler) A complex set of principles by which one understands and evaluates his experience and which thus determines his life style.

fiction, directive A fantasy or idea of superiority which is originally conceived of as unconscious compensation for feelings of inferiority and which is later reacted to as if it were an absolute truth.

fidgetiness A state of restlessness or increased motor activity often caused by anxiety.

fidgets A vague uneasiness usually accompanied by increased motor activity.

fiducial interval See *interval, fiducial.*

fiducial limits See *limits, fiducial.*

field 1. An area having boundaries which define both the physical place as well as the kind of activity permitted. 2. (physics) The entire space in which a set of forces operate, such as a magnetic field. 3. (psychology) The complex totality of interdependent social, personal, and physical factors within which a psychological event takes place.

field cognition mode (E.C. Tolman) A particular organism's disposition or readiness, resulting from the interaction of perception, memory, and thought, to apprehend some specific characteristic of the field in which he behaves. Thus, the contribution of the organism to the stimulus aspect of the stimulus-response sequence is emphasized.

field expectancies (E. C. Tolman) A type of learning in which as a result of repeated presentations of a particular environmental situation, an organism acquires a set to be prepared for further stimuli of a field upon apprehension of the first group of stimuli from this field and set for the interconnections between these groups of stimuli.

field force (K. Lewin) A manifestation of directed energy (referred to by other psychologists as libido, instinct, or drive) which has a certain magnitude analogous to that of physical force and which must be defined in terms of the whole field in which it takes place.

field, leaving the (K. Lewin) An attempted reduction of conflict or frustration consisting of the individual's removal of himself from the situation.

field of attention Those stimuli or ideas to which the organism is attending at any given moment.

field of awareness See *field of consciousness.*

field of consciousness The totality of that which the individual is aware of at any given time.

field of regard All of the external world that can be seen by the moving eye with the head stationary, as distinguished from *visual field.*

field structure 1. The patterning of relations among the various parts of the *life space,* or psychological field. 2. The reasonably precise and hierarchical arrangement of psychological facts within the life space which lend it stability.

field theory (K. Lewin) A systematic, mathematically described theory of psychology and social psychology which emphasizes the interrelatedness of a present concrete event and the totality of influences both within an individual's personality and his environment which determine behavior. To view a situation in its totality, one must view it as a field, i.e., a totality of interdependent facts. The *psychological field,* or *life space,* of an individual is comprised of the interaction between his personality and his environment. Thus, individual behavior at any given time is the function of one's personality and environment. According to this theory, every concrete situation, rather than just recurring events, is regarded as conforming to psychological laws, and a complete scientific and mathematical representation of such a situation would complete the task of psychology.

fields of psychology Since its emergence as a separate field of study, psychology has expanded into a great number of areas. The most basic field of psychology is that of experimental psychology. This field is concerned with precise research of basic psychological problems. The processes investigated may be grouped into several clusters. One such cluster is concerned with the manner in which an organism gathers and receives information about its environment. A second cluster of problems concerns the modification of behavior. Here the psychologist deals with development, learning, thinking, and problem solving; in other words, the way in which the organism learns to react to his environment. A third cluster concerns itself with the general problem of the motivation of behavior, including such topics as reinforcement, emotions, and motives. Some psychologists stress the environmental, sociological point of view, whereas others are more interested in physiology. Those who adopt this latter point of view are the physiological psychologists. Their interests are quite similar to those of physiologists, and they have made great strides in determining the functions of the various areas of the brain. Some of their most recent work deals with the relationship between such physiological processes as reward, punishment, and attention to brain function.

Another field is that of comparative psychology. The comparative psychologist's main interest is in the differences of behavior among the species. They often work with lower animals because of the relative ease in studying their behavior.

Social psychology studies the various factors which are associated with the adjustment of the individual to the specific cultural environment in which he lives. Some of the topics which are of concern to the social psychologist are the conducting of public opinion polls, the social conditions which affect the emergence of religious and political leaders, measurement of attitudes and the determination of those factors which lead to attitude change, the effects of group membership upon individual behavior patterns, group problem solving, conformity and prejudice.

Educational psychology is concerned with the factors which affect performance in the school situation. This field is closely related to that of general psychology which studies learning and motivation in general. The educational psychologist must apply what is known in these areas to the specialized area of the school. It has often been necessary for the educational psychologist to develop his own techniques in dealing with these problems. An example of this is the development of teaching machines which present material in a way which maximizes effective learning.

The application of psychology to the industrial setting has been an important and widespread development, incorporating many different areas of general psychology. The industrial psychologist concerns himself with such problems as recruiting and training programs for employees, studying consumer motivation, maximizing production by increasing employee morale and motivation, designing advertising campaigns and designing more effective and safer equipment based on psychological knowledge.

The widespread use of psychological tests in schools, business, and the military has led to the development of a field of psychology known as psychometrics. The psychometrist is an expert in test construction, administration, and interpretation. He must have a strong working knowledge of statistical methods in order to assure the reliability and validity of the test results. The psychometrist may also be trained in the administration and interpretation of personality tests, as an adjunct to therapy.

Developmental psychology concerns itself with the patterns of development in children as they grow to adulthood. The developmental (or child) psychologists have accumulated such information as the age norms for weight, height, vocabulary development, motor skills, etc. They have also developed methods of child training, so as to assist the child in his task of growing up.

Some of the most pressing present-day social problems involve the abnormalities in the development and functioning of the personality. Personal maladjustment and mental illness are probably our major medical and social problem. The field of personality and abnormal psychology deals with these problems. Clinical psychologists devote themselves to the diagnosis of personality maladjustments. By means of tests and interviews they attempt to arrive at a meaningful classification of psychopathology. Others are interested in the origins of mental disorders. They have attempted to find the causes of maladjustment in early family life, the stressful events of infancy, physiological causes, social conditions, and others. Another group of clinical psychologists has attempted to develop methods of curing mental disorder. Their methods may be based on individual or group treatment, directive or nondirective participation by the therapist, long- or short-term periods of treatment. In spite of the many different forms the treatment may take, the goal is still the same: the removal of the abnormal condition.

Theoretical psychology is really a combination of all the other fields of psychology. Theoretical psychologists formulate broad scientific systems.

figural aftereffect (Gestalt psychology) A perceptual phenomena used to illustrate the tendency to maintain stability in figure-ground relationships by showing that the characteristics of one perceptual field may effect the perception of another.

figural cohesion (Gestalt psychology) The tendency of all the parts of a figure to perceptually remain together as one figure. For example, once seen as forming a square, a set of four dots tend to continue to be seen as a square, even when they are combined with other elements.

figural information See *information, figural.*

figural openness (Gestalt) Situation in which a figure or figural outline does not surround or enclose the area of a configuration.

figure-ground The principle that all perception and even awareness is fundamentally patterned into two parts or aspects that mutually influence each other: a) the *figure,* which has good contour, unity, and is perceived as being separate from the ground, and b) the *ground,* which is relatively homogeneous and whose parts are not clearly shaped or patterned.

figure, helpful In the fantasy world of a child, a beneficient and understanding male or female fairy-like creature to whom the child feels he can turn to for help.

filial generations The successive generations from a single parent or pair of parents which are designated as first filial (F_1), second filial (F_2) and so on.

filicide 1. Killing of one's own child. 2. One who has killed his own child.

filiform script Cursive writing, generally small and rapid, in which words trail off into a single line of indistinguishable letters.

film color A texture-free, soft color which lacks localization, as contrasted with the color of the surface of an object, and seems to hover before the observer like a film or cloud.

filter 1. Device which transmits only a particular variety and homogenous wave lengths. 2. Capacitor or choke circuit or their combination which regulates and smooths out current flow.

final 1. Last in a series of terms or trials. 2. Purposive; pertaining to ends or goals.

finalism See *teleology.*

fine grain rate See *rate, fine grain.*

fine tremor Tremor of 10-12 vibrations per second.

finger agnosia Inability to recognize one's fingers.

finger aphasia Inability to name one's fingers.

finger painting Making pictures or designs by applying paints directly to a surface with the fingers and hands. In psychology, it is often used as a projective technique, or means of stimulating free association.

finger spelling A mode of communication used among or with the deaf, and the deaf and blind, in which words are spelled out by means of specific finger movements. For a deaf and blind person to receive a message in this way, he cups his hands around the sender's and feels each movement of the sender's fingers.

finger-thumb opposition A significant step in child's motor coordination which occurs at about the age of one year, and which is characterized by picking up objects between the thumb and fingers (partial prehension) and, later, the thumb and fore-finger (final prehension), rather than by scooping movements with the palm and fingers.

fingers, insane A low grade inflammation of the fingers to which the mentally ill, particularly general paralytics, are liable. It is less common today than in the past which is probably due to improved hygiene in mental institutions.

Fisher's test See *test, Fisher's.*

fission 1. Any splitting or cleaving. 2. (biology) Asexual reproduction, characteristic of unicellular animals, in which the mature cell splits into two parts, each of which becomes a separate organism.

fissure Any of the deep grooves on the surface of the brain. Any of the shallower ones are known as a *sulcus.*

fissure of Rolando See *central sulcus.*

fissure of Sylvius A deep fissure located in the temporal cortex, which divides the temporal lobe from the parietal and frontal lobes. Also called the lateral fissure.

fistula A tube or opening in some tissue resulting from incomplete closure of a wound, surgery, or abnormal growth.

fit 1. (medicine) A sudden attack, or a convulsion. 2. (statistics) The agreement of probable data with actual data. 3. The adjustment of obtained data to conform to a predetermined standard.

fittest From Darwin's concept of the "survival of the fittest," referring to those organisms best adapted to their environment and who thus tend, in the "struggle for existence" to survive and propagate their species.

fixated conflict The condition in a stable course of behavior, settled upon after conflict, in which some ergic satisfactions are gained at the cost of loss of others, as shown by simultaneous positive and negative loadings.

fixatio mononoea An obsolete term for severe depression.

fixation 1. A persistent mode of behavior which has outlived its usefulness or has become inappropriate. 2. The strengthening of a memory or a motor habit by repetition. 3. The directing and focusing of one or both eyes on an object or point, so that the image falls on the *fovea.* 4. (psychoanalysis) A strong and relatively enduring emotional attachment, generally psychosexual in nature, to an object of infancy or childhood which persists into later life and, thus, makes the formation of new attachments and new patterns of behavior rather difficult if not impossible.

fixation, anxiety (psychoanalysis) The persistence into later life of anxiety which was originally associated with a dangerous situation of an earlier phase of development.

fixation, cannibalistic The fixation of the libido at the late oral, or biting, phase, which may lead to cannibalistic fantasies such as biting, eating, swallowing, and, thus, incorporating a hated object.

fixation, father An excessively emotional and possessive attachment to one's father, stemming from the period of infantile sexuality but continued long beyond the point at which Oedipal conflicts should normally have been resolved.

fixation hysteria See *hysteria, fixation.*

fixation, libido The retention of libido at an early phase of psychic growth.

fixation, mother An excessively emotional and possessive attachment to one's mother, stemming from the period of infantile sexuality but continued long beyond the point at which Oedipal conflicts should normally have been resolved.

fixation of affect The establishment of a strong and relatively enduring emotional attachment, generally psychosexual in nature, to an object of infancy or childhood which persists into later life and, thus, makes the formation of new attachments and new patterns of behavior rather difficult if not impossible.

fixation pause One of the brief moments during which the eyeball is not moving which makes visual discrimination possible.

fixed alternative Pertaining to a test or questionnaire which requires that the subject choose one answer from several limited alternatives.

fixed idea A persistent, firmly held, but often irrational idea which tends to dominate a person's mental life.

fixed-interval reinforcement Partial reinforcement schedule in which the subject is rewarded or reinforced consistently on his first response after the lapse of a certain prescribed amount of time after the preceding reinforcement.

fixed interval (FI) schedule See *reinforcement, schedule of: fixed interval (FI).*

fixed ratio reinforcement Partial reinforcement schedule in which the subject is rewarded or reinforced consistently with *n*th trial.

fixed ratio (FR) schedule See *reinforcement, schedule of: fixed ratio (FR).*

fixedness; functional fixedness An inability to be flexible in problem solving which is characterized by maintaining a certain set behavior despite its inappropriateness.

fixity, social Pertaining to societies or any grouping of people in which each individual's role, status and possibility for social interaction is rigidly defined, as in feudal or caste societies.

flaccid Readily yielding to pressure; soft, flabby; without muscular tone.

flagellant 1. One who whips himself or submits to whipping by others for religious purposes or sexual excitement. 2. A religious sect in the thirteenth century in Europe which believed in self-punishment and self-torture as an expression of the Lord's commandment for self-imposed suffering.

flagellantism Self-punitive and self-torturing behavior.

flagellate To scourge or whip.

flagellation The act of whipping, especially as a means for arousing religious or sexual emotions.

flagellator One who whips himself or others for religious purposes or sexual excitement.

flagellomania Sexual pleasure or stimulation from whipping or being whipped.

Flajane's disease See *goiter, exophthalmic.*

flattening of affect See *affect, flattening of.*

flavor A sensory impression from objects, mainly food, in the mouth which results from the combined experience of taste, smell, pressure, and temperature.

Flesch index Formulas used to compute the reading difficulty of a passage of English prose.

fleshy type (C. B. Davenport) Constitutional body type characterized by short limbs, thick neck, and rounded or fat body contour.

flexibilitas cerea See *catalepsy.*

flexibility 1. Adaptability; plasticity. 2. The ability to readily change set, modify behavior, and, thus, respond to changing conditions.

flexibility, waxy See *catalepsy.*

flexion The act of bending at the joint of a limb or part of the body, which is made possible by certain muscles called *flexors.*

flexor A muscle which serves to bend or flex a limb or part of the body.

flicker A sensation of fluctuating vision induced by a corresponding change in the visual stimulus.

flicker, auditory The perception of a periodically interrupted auditory stimulus as discontinuous.

flicker, binocular Flicker evoked by alternating stimuli rapidly from one eye to the other.

flicker, chromatic Flicker due to rapid periodic changes in hue, saturation, or both.

flicker, photometry Measurement and comparison of brightnesses by determining their critical flicker frequencies when reflected individually against a surface with the same illumination.

flight into health See *transference cure.*

flight of colors Visual afterimage of a succession of colors or white which sometimes occurs as an aftersensation to a bright or intense light stimulus.

flight of ideas A rapid and continuous flow of thought or speech which, while not disjointed or bizarre in content, is characterized by jumping from one topic to another, each topic being only superficially related to the previous one or intervening stimuli in the environment.

floccillation See *carphology.*

flogger See *flagellator.*

fluctuation 1. Constant change; moving back and forth as a wave. 2. (biology) Relatively slight changes or variations due to chance factors which are normally distributed about the mean of a species, as distinguished from mutations. 3. (perception) See *attention fluctuations.* 4. (statistics) Changes in the value of a statistical constant when calculated from successive but otherwise similar random samples.

fluctuations of attention See *attention fluctuations.*

fluency 1. The ability to verbally communicate with ease. 2. (factor analysis) A factor that characterizes the ability to rapidly think of and verbalize words and associations. It loads on items which require the subject to produce as many words as possible in a given period of time, verbalize associations to inkblots, complete stories, etc.

fluid 1. (psychology) Pertaining to an unstable, changing situation with few constraints in which an individual may act freely. 2. (field theory) Characterizing a *field* in which there is an easy flow of communication between the various forces or tensions of the field.

fluid general ability (R. B. Cattell) That form of general intelligence which is largely innate and which adapts itself to all kinds of material, regardless of previous experience with it.

fluttering hearts A perceptual illusion in which colored figures moved forward and back on a differently colored background appear to be moving from side to side.

focal Pertaining to a *focus.*

focal epilepsy See *Jacksonian epilepsy.*

focal length The specified distance from a given lens which is necessary to bring parallel rays of light to a focus.

focal symbiosis See *symbiosis, focal.*

focus 1. The point at which parallel rays of light are made to converge after passing through a given lens. 2. To adjust an optical system so as to bring parallel rays of light to a convergence point. 3. To center one's attention on a stimulus.

focus of attention That part of a complex experience which at a given moment is the clearest and most outstanding.

foliate papilla Minute, nipple-like protrusions, shaped like a leaf, which are found along the sides and back of the tongue.

folie The French word for *insanity* which, historically, has been used in combination with other qualifying French words to name various mental disorders.

folie à deux Simultaneous occurrence of the same mental disorder in two people who are closely associated with each other where one appears to have influenced the other.

folie à double forme An obsolete term for manic-depressive psychosis.

folie à quatre The simultaneous appearance of psychoses with similar delusional content in four members of the same family.

folie à trois The simultaneous appearance of psychoses with similar delusional content in three members of the same family.

folie ambitieuse A generic term referring to various forms of insanity in which grandiose ideas are present.

folie du doute (J. P. Falret) Form of anxiety neurosis or obsessive compulsive behavior characterized by excessive doubting to the point of madness as, for example, checking repeatedly to see that a door is locked.

folie morale, acquired (E. Kraepelin) Patients classified as psychopathic personalities may eventually develop a clearly defined psychotic condition. Kraepelin called this psychotic state an acquired form of folie morale or moral insanity. See *psychopathic personality; psychosis.*

folium A fold or convolution in the grey matter of the *cerebellum.*

folk psychology 1. The social psychology of non-literate, primitive societies. 2. A detailed study of the legends, beliefs, and customs of a particular race or people, especially primitive.

folklore Legends, beliefs, customs, folk-remedies, songs, and other fragments of culture which have survived from earlier, more primitive stages of a given society.

folkways Traditional patterns of behavior, including habits and customs, which characterize a given culture or social group and which exercise a strong though unconscious influence on the behavior of each member.

fontanel The "soft spot" in the cranium of an infant which is not ossified.

foot lambert (ftl) Unit of measure of luminance.

foot rule correlation See *correlation, Spearman foot rule.*

foramen magnum Opening in the occipital bone which the spinal cord passes through into the brain where it becomes the medulla.

force (field theory) A tendency to act in a certain direction; a cause of any activity.

forced choice technique (psychometrics) Method of assessing the attitudes of an individual or the social desirability of alternatives by directing the individual to choose between two equally unlikely, and undesirable alternatives as, for example, whether he prefers ugliness or laziness; the pattern of forced responses is then assessed.

forced color response A concept in Klopfer's approach to the Rorschach to denote instances in which the response includes the use of color, but not the color of the perceived object in its natural state. Instead, the subject has "forced" the use of color as it exists on the blot, as for example, "pink mountain lions."

forebrain The anterior brain portion of the embryo which develops into the diencephalon and the telencephalon from which arise the olfactory lobes, the cerebral hemispheres, the striate body and the thalamus.

forecasting efficiency index of (E) The measure of the extent to which one can predict one variable by knowing another variable and the relationship between them. The formula is:

$$E = 100\left[1 - \sqrt{\frac{N-1}{N-2}}\,(1-r^2)\right]$$

where N is the number of scores in the sample, and r is the correlation coefficient.

fore-exercise Period preceding an experiment or test, the purpose of which is to allow the subject to adapt to the situation or to estimate the approximate strength of the response which is to be measured.

forensic psychiatry See *psychiatry, forensic.*

foreperiod The initial time interval between the ready signal and the introduction of the stimulus in an experiment, especially reaction time experiments.

forepleasure (psychoanalysis) **1.** The pleasure, physical and emotional, occurring with increase in tension especially in sexual areas. **2.** The erotic pleasure which comes from stimulation of an erogenous zone prior to intercourse.

Forer Structured Sentence Completion Test See *test, Forer Structured Sentence Completion.*

foreshortening 1. The shorter appearance of the length of a line when it is viewed lengthwise; the shortening appears proportionately greater as the closer the line parallels the direction in which one is looking. **2.** The perceptual shortening in a painting or drawing according to the principles of perspective.

form 1. The outline, shape or pattern of arrangement of elements of an object or figure. **2.** (Gestalt) The nature of a whole in terms of its organized arrangement of parts or its unity.

form, alternate (psychometrics) Tests measuring the same thing but with unequal raw scores that have been standardized through the use of an equivalence table yielding scores that are comparable.

form-color response (FC response) (Rorschach) Response to a Rorschach inkblot test which is co-determined by form and color with form being the primary contributor. The form determinant appears to reflect the subject's reasoning powers and contact with the demands of reality. The color determinant appears to reflect affectivity and impulsiveness.

form, comparable (psychometrics) General term for different sets of test items which are considered to be different forms of the same test due to similarity of content structure, and the possibility of converting the raw scores from the tests to the same derived score scale.

form determinant The use of contour, shape or form as the basis for a Rorschach response which is thought to reflect the formal reasoning power and contact with reality demands of the respondent.

form, equivalent Tests measuring the same thing which have raw scores with the same statistical meaning on each form.

form level rating A method developed by Klopfer to evaluate the appropriateness of form used in the Rorschach more extensively than afforded by other systems. Each response is weighed on a scale ranging from +5.0 to −2.0 depending on the accuracy, specification, and organization of the percept.

form, number See *number form.*

form quality 1. (Gestalt) Properties of a whole or entity which does not reside in its constituent parts. **2.** Properties which a part possesses when a constituent of a particular unit or entity but not when in isolation or when it belongs to another unit. **3.** Gestalt qualitäten.

form response The most common type of Rorschach answer wherein the response is determined by the shape or form of the blot or the portion of the blot used. No other determinant such as color, movement, or shading is involved in the formulation of the percept. Form may also play a determining role in responses involving other features of the blot and when this occurs, scoring is modified accordingly, such as FC for a form-dominated color response, CF for a color dominated color response which also includes form.

formal discipline 1. Formal training or education. **2.** Doctrine that certain subjects should be studied for the constructive exercise of the mind or the positive effect such study will have on intellectual ability in general rather than for its own sake.

formalism The systemization of a field of knowledge through strict adherence to consistent orderly organization within a relatively rigid framework which directs and limits theorizing.

formant Elements which constitute the timbre or quality which makes one vowel sound different from another.

formative cell An embryonic cell.

formboard test See *test, formboard.*

fornication Generally, sexual intercourse involving persons who are not married to each other.

fornix A nerve fiber which connects the thalamus with the hippocampus.

foster placement The process of arranging for persons not related to a child to care for and support that child by taking the child into their home and family.

Four Picture Test See *test, Four Picture.*

fourfold table A statistical table composed of two sets of columns and two of rows.

Fourier's law (physics) Principle that any complex sound or light wave may be represented in the form of simple sine waves or as comprised of several simple vibratory movements.

Fournier's Test (A. F. Fournier) Test in which the individual is asked to stand up quickly, turn sharply and to start and stop walking on command in order to determine whether there is a disorder of muscular coordination or equilibrium in relation to walking.

fovea centralis Center of clearest vision which is a small depression in the retina.

foveal vision Seeing with the foveal region of the retina.

FPT See *test, Four Picture.*

FR schedule See *reinforcement schedule of: fixed ratio.*

fractional antedating goal response See *response, fractional antedating goal.*

fractionation Physiologically, the dropping-out of neurons from a neural system with repeated activity, the result of changed time properties of the system. The opposite of recruitment, when the changed time properties make it possible to "recruit" neurons not originally part of the system.

Fragesucht (German) A compulsion to ask questions without being interested in having them answered.

frame of reference 1. A system of attitudes and values which provide a standard against which actions, ideas, and results are judged and which to some extent controls or directs action and expression. **2.** The background against which a thing is perceived.

Franck Drawing Completion Test See *test, Franck Drawing Completion.*

fraternal twins See *twins, fraternal.*

free association 1. An unrestricted, random flow of words or ideas. **2.** (psychoanalysis) Method employed in which the patient says whatever comes into his mind and speaks freely in order to widen the therapist's access to the patient's unconscious mind and to allow the repressed memory of traumatic experiences to come to the surface in order that the trauma may be resolved.

free association period The main procedure in Rorschach testing in which the subject is handed the cards, one at a time, and asked to report what he is reminded of by the blot. The specific instructions to the subject are somewhat different than the free association procedure as employed in psychoanalysis, yet some overlap does exist. In Rorschach testing the subject is asked to report what he sees but is also free to elaborate as extensively or as minimally as he prefers.

free association test See *test, free association.*

free nerve endings The delicately branched endings of afferent neurons in the skin without specific nerve organs which are thought to be associated with sensitivity to temperature and to pain.

free recall test See *test, free recall.*

free will The philosophical and religious doctrine that attributes the cause of behavior to volition and independent decisions of the person rather than to external determinants.

freedom, degrees of See *degrees of freedom.*

Fregoli's phenomenon See *illusion of negative doubles.*

frequency 1. The number of cycles per second in a periodic vibration. **2.** The number of times a specific phenomenon occurs in a given class interval.

frequency curve or distribution A curve showing graphically the frequency of various values in each interval of the distribution.

frequency diagram The spatial or graphic representation of a frequency distribution.

frequency graph A graphic representation of a frequency distribution. The three most common are the histogram, frequency polygon, and the frequency curve.

frequency histogram A graphic representation of a frequency distribution consisting of a series of contiguous rectangles, of width proportional to the size of the class interval, and in height proportional to the frequencies in the various intervals.

frequency, law of See *law of frequency.*

frequency, marginal 1. (statistics) The sum of the frequencies of a column or a row in a double-entry table which are written in the lower right-hand margin of the table. **2.** (testing) The frequency of responses falling outside the modal response.

frequency polygon The graphic outline of the frequency distribution made by connecting the plot of the midpoints of the class intervals.

frequency table The systematical ordering in tabular form of the values of a frequency distribution.

frequency theory of hearing See *hearing, theory of: frequency theory.*

Freud, Anna (1895-   ) Youngest daughter of Sigmund Freud, born in Austria, active member of the International Psychoanalytical Association since 1922. Emigrated to England in 1938; Director of the Hampstead Child-Therapy Course and Clinic from 1947 onward. Many contributions to the developmental theory of psychoanalysis and its application to educational, diagnostic, therapeutic and preventive work.

Freud, Sigmund (1856-1939) Viennese psychiatrist, founder of psychoanalysis. Initially conducted research in neurology, then under the influence of Charcot, Liebeaut, and Breuer, treated mental disorders with hypnosis. Developed (jointly with Breuer) the cathartic method of treatment, then psychoanalytic technique. These joint studies were reported in Breuer and Freud's *Studies of Hysteria* (1894). Through the observation of his patients and the analysis of his own dreams, Freud discovered the phenomena of the unconscious and developed the technique of dream analysis (described in *The Interpretation of Dreams*, 1901). In 1905 Freud wrote *Three Essays on Sexuality* in which he applied the biogenetic principle to the study of the phylo and ontogenetic psychosexual development. In 1914, Freud discovered the phenomenon of narcissism and thus interpreted human behavior by means of a single innate drive, the force of love, that is support of life. This force, called Eros, had at its disposal the emotional energy of libido which could be sexual or desexualized, directed toward others (cathected) as object-love or toward oneself as narcissistic self-love. In 1920 Freud again revised his theory of instinctual drives by introducing the concept of the death instinct, called Thanatos, and destructive energy. In 1923 Freud elaborated the so-called structural theory, introducing the concept of a three-partite mental apparatus comprised of the id, ego and superego. In 1927 Freud published the *Future of an Illusion,* a psychoanalytic critique of religion; in 1930 he dissected contemporary civilization and in the last year of life wrote a critical essay on *Moses and Monotheism.*

Freud wrote and worked with patients almost until his last days, despite the fact that he suffered from cancer of the mouth and in the years 1923-1939 he underwent 33 surgical operations.

Freudian slip (psychoanalysis) A mistake or substitution of words in speaking or in writing. The mistake is contrary to the conscious wish of the individual. The individual expresses his unconscious and repressed wishes through the erroneous action.

Freudian theory See *psychoanalysis.*

Freudianism, Freudism See *psychoanalysis.*

frigidity 1. Coldness; absence of sexual feeling. 2. Blocking of the normal expression of sexual desire in females.

Froelich syndrome An endocrine disturbance affecting the pituitary gland and resulting in a condition with poor skeletal development, metabolic disturbances, obesity and arrested physical and behavioral development.

Fromm, Erich (1900-   ) Born in Germany, emigrated to United States in 1934. Has developed a revision of Freud's theory, emphasizing (1) the specific conditions of human existence, (2) the influence of social factors on character ("social character"), (3) the use of psychoanalysis for the understanding of social and historical processes and political leaders, (4) the relevance of values. Proposed a synthesis of Marx's and Freud's concepts. See *psychoanalysis; social character; ethics.*

frontal cortex See *cortex, frontal.*

frontal leucotomy Frontal lobotomy.

frontal lobe See *lobe, frontal.*

frontal lobe, structure and function of See *lobe, frontal, structure and function of.*

frontal lobes brain lesion See *brain lesion, of frontal lobes.*

frontal lobotomy See *lobotomy, frontal.*

Frosch, John (1909-   ) American psychiatrist and psychoanalyst. Editor of *Journal of American Psychoanalytic Association;* Editor of *Annual Survey of Psychoanalysis;* Professor of psychiatry, New York University College of Medicine. Has been a practicing psychoanalyst for 35 years. Has founded and been Editor-in-Chief of the *Journal of the American Psychoanalytic Association,* the official publication of the American Psychoanalytic Association for the past 25 years. Author of some 35 articles. His recent contributions have been in the area of the borderline problems both in the psychopathology, as well as in the treatment modalities. He has emphasized the concept of the psychotic character and described borderline patients who function most of the time as nonpsychotic, although they may have psychotic breaks from time to time. He has also made contributions to the understanding and the treatment of the disorders of impulse control with special emphasis on the impulse ridden character and introduced the concept of reality constancy as the counterpart to object constancy. This is an ego function which permits an individual to attain an appropriate relationship to reality but is severely disturbed in borderline and psychotic patients.

Frostig Sensory-Motor and Movement Skills Checklist See *checklist, Frostig Sensory-Motor and Movement Skills.*

frottage Sexual perversion in which orgasm occurs as a result of rubbing against a clothed person of the opposite sex in a crowd.

fructose intolerance A deficiency of fructose-1-phosphate alocase which leads to an inhibition of hepatic release of glucose, resulting in hypoglycemia when fructose containing foods are ingested.

fruity A type of smell typified by the smell of fruits.

frustration Interference with an ongoing action.

frustration aggression hypothesis (J. Dollard and N. E. Miller) Theoretical assumption based on psychoanalytic concepts, that frustration leads to aggression, whether implicit or explicit, and that aggression is always a sign of some sort of frustration.

fugue states 1. A long-term amnesia state characterized by the individual leaving his home and changing life-style and conduct. The individual has almost total loss of memory though skills are not affected. When the fugue ends, there is complete restoration of pre-fugue memory and a forgetting of the whole fugue period. 2. Period of absence associated with epilepsy.

Fullerton-Cattell law See *law, Fullerton-Cattell.*

function 1. (statistics) A quantity that varies with the variation of another quantity. The variation is not necessarily proportional. 2. The activity of an organism rather than non-activity; an ongoing process. 3. The purpose or end product of an organ or organism. **4.** That which is dependent on something else, stated non-quantitatively. **5.** A heading or categorical classification for activities. **6.** An activity or structure that is useful. **7.** (C. Jung) Any transitory manifestation of the psyche or libido.

function fluctuation The real variation on a source trait from time to time with internal and external conditions (not in the focal stimulus), differentiating the stability coefficient from the consistency coefficient.

function, power See *power function.*

functional autonomy See *autonomy, functional.*

functional autonomy principle (G. W. Allport) The principle that modes of behavior, though acquired, become independent of the original instigating drive.

functional disorder See *disorder, functional.*

functional fixedness See *fixedness.*

functional inferiority See *inferiority, functional.*

functional psychology See *functionalism.*

functional relation A dependency between variables such that a change in one will bring about a change in one or more of the others.

functional system (P. K. Anokhin) A unit of integrative activity of the brain and organism formulated in 1935 by P. Anokhin. Due to the development of the "systems approach" and "general systems theory," the functional system theory is obtaining a particular significance for research in biology, physiology, neurophysiology, psychology and other sciences where systems analysis is essential. The principal features of the functional system are as follows: (1) system organizing factor, which determines the formation of co-operative relationships between the system components toward obtaining a functional-useful result. Such co-operation of the system components can be possible when the system permanently sorts out "degrees of freedom" of every system component (such as, for example, the

synaptic formation on a neuron). Through return afferentation ("feed-back") the result produces a reorganizing effect upon the co-operative relationships between the system components. (2) Some specific key mechanisms (internal architectonics) enable the investigator to construct a continuous passage ("conceptual bridge") from the level of integration to the level of the finest mechanisms of the brain systemic activity, the molecular level included. These key mechanisms of the functional system provide it with uninterrupted self-organization and plastical adaptation toward changing external conditions. The functional system key mechanisms are the following: a) afferent synthesis, b) decision making, c) acceptor of action results, d) program of action, e) result of action, f) return afferentation which contains all parameters of the result, and g) collation of the real results with those that have been predicted before in the Acceptor of Action Results. By its constructive meaning the functional system theory permits study and evaluation of such compound processes of the whole organism which cannot be either investigated or understood without it.

functional unity **1.** The cooperative functioning of various parts or processes to produce an integrated whole or perform one action. **2.** Considering different behavioral patterns as stemming from one trait or organ. Such relationships are investigated systematically through factor analysis.

functionalism School of psychology founded at the end of the 19th century by James and Dewey. The major proponents include James R. Angell, Harvey A. Carr, and Edward Robinson. Functionalism began as a protest against structuralism, elementarism and a disjointed molecular approach to the subject matter of psychology. Functionalism treated psychological processes as functions within the context of Darwinian theory. The process of adjustment of the organism to the environment is central as is a purpositivistic interpretation of the process in which stimuli and responses are a chain of deeds and not separate entities. Functionalism dealt with the

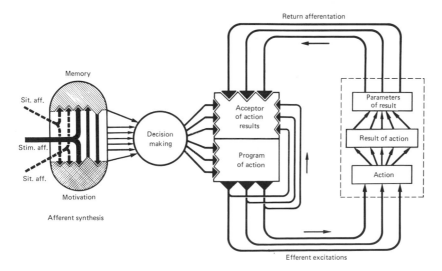

"how" and "why" of psychology rather than the "what." A molecular approach was emphasized in order to understand the totality of the organism and the functions of the mind as mediator between organism and environment. The process of the modification of behavior and of associationism was given importance, resulting in interest in habit formation, learning theory, and the concerns of educational and comparative psychology. Functional psychology also prepared the ground for behaviorism and conditioning as well as for the purposive-hormic theory of McDougall.

functions maintenance The physiological activities in an organism which preserve a state of relative inner equilibrium.

fundamental response processes Physiological processes assumed to underlie the fundamental colors.

fundamental tone The basic or lowest component of a compound tone which identifies the pitch.

furor, epileptic State of confusion followed by maniacal attack of violence or rage associated with epileptic equivalent attacks.

G

G factor See *general factor.*

G force The force required to go against the force of gravity.

g score A key scoring in the Hertz approach to the Rorschach which represents the manner in which a response is organized. See also *organizational activity; z score.*

gain An increment or increase in a variable.

gain, epinosic Secondary advantages obtained from illness such as the gratification of dependency needs.

gain, method See *gain, epinosic.*

gait, hemiplegic Gait characterized by stiffly held legs seen in hemiplegic patients.

gait-stuttering A halting and hesitant gait analogous to the stammer in speech.

galactosemia A congenital metabolic disturbance causing increased galactose in the blood often associated with mental retardation. Gastrointestinal disturbance of varying intensity is characteristic. If severe, death may occur. Cataracts appear between 4 to 8 weeks. Treatment consists of removal of galactose containing substances including milk.

galeanthropy The delusion of being a cat.

galeophobia Morbid fear of cats.

gallows humor See *humor, gallows.*

Galton bar (psychophysics) An apparatus for determining the threshold for visual linear distances by the method of just noticeable differences or the method of reproduction. It consists of a meter rod with four sides, one of which facing the experimenter has a millimeter scale. The other sides are painted in grey or black. The rod has riders on it, one at the center and two on opposite sides. One of the markers is placed at a standard distance from the center. The subject is asked to place the second marker at a distance equal to the standard marked off length.

Galton, Francis (1822-1911) Versatile British psychologist who, ten years after the publication of *The Origin of Species,* applied Darwinian evolutionary theory to individual differences in human mental capacity in his work, *Hereditary Genius.* Pioneer in mental testing, the eugenics movement, the use of the questionnaire method, and the development of the coefficient of correlation.

Galton's whistle (F. Galton) A high-pitched whistle used in the determination of the upper threshold of tonal hearing.

galvanic Referring to a steady, direct current such as one from a battery.

galvanic nystagmus See *nystagmus, galvanic.*

galvanic skin response The changes in the electrical resistance of the skin measured by a galvanometer. It is used as an indicator of emotional arousal and tension.

galvanometer A device used to measure the strength of an electric current in amperes and milliamperes.

galvanotropism or galvanotaxis An orienting response toward electrical stimulation.

gambler's fallacy The failure to recognize the independence of some events that occur in a sequence. A gambler who has lost 10 straight times and feels he has a better chance of winning because of his misfortune is an example of this fallacy.

game Play which is organized according to specific rules, usually competitive and with a definite goal.

game, hallucinatory Make-believe games created by the child in which he actively invents fantasy objects to amuse himself. These hallucinations differ from real hallucinations which are passively experienced as foreign in that the child realizes the unreality of his fantasy play and can easily revert back to reality when necessary.

game theory A mathematical theory which attempts to analyze conflict situations in terms of a

155

game in which each person seeks maximal gain and minimal loss.

gamete A mature germ cell (male or female) with haploid chromosome number.

gametogenesis The developmental process of the male and female gametes.

gamma (γ) (psychophysics) The distance of a stimulus from the threshold.

gamma movement See *movement, gamma.*

gammacism Speech impairment characteristic of young children in which velars g, k are replaced with dentals such as d and t.

gamogenesis Reproduction through fusion of two gametes.

gamonomania Excessive desire to marry.

gamophobia Fear of marriage.

gang A group of persons united together by common interests. It usually refers to children and often has antisocial connotations.

ganglia Groups of nerve cells whose cell bodies are located outside of the central nervous system.

gangliated Referring to a neuron which passes a ganglion on its course.

ganglion A group of nerve cells or cell bodies which are found outside the brain or spinal cord.

ganglioplexus A group of cell bodies found in a network of nerve fibers.

gangliosides Fat substances of the brain which contain a special fatty acid, neuraminic acid. Often associated with organic disorders caused by abnormal metabolic conditions, such as Tay-Sachs disease.

Ganser's syndrome See *syndrome, Ganser's.*

Ganzfeld A homogeneous visual field which is uniformly illustrated and which lacks any area or point of unique stimulation.

gargalesthesia A tickle sensation.

gargoylism See *Hurler's syndrome.*

gases, psychosis due to Mental disturbances resulting from the inhalation of poisonous gases such as carbon monoxide which produce a loss of consciousness and prolonged delirium, followed by difficulties in concentration, fatigue, and in some cases by impairment of intellectual functions.

gastric neurosis See *neurosis, gastric.*

gastro-intestinal tract The region of the stomach and intestines related to digestion.

gastropaths, false Individuals who are able to digest allegedly indigestible food but who develop food phobias for other foods due to psychological problems.

gastro-psychiatry A psychiatric term referring to a subject's preoccupation with his digestive system.

gastrula A stage in the development of an embryo following the blastula stage.

gastrulation The development of the didermic gastrula in the embryonic developmental process.

Gates-MacGinitie Reading Tests See *tests, Gates-MacGinitie Reading.*

gating The blocking of one set of sensations by another occurring usually during attention, when there is selective focusing on one set of sensations while others are held in the background.

gatophobia Fear of cats.

Gaucher's disease (P. C. E. Gaucher) A rare familial lipidosis occurring in both an acute infantile form and a more chronic adult form. Characterized by enlargement of the spleen, bronzing of the skin, anemia and, in infants, neurological involvement usually leading to death by age two.

Gaussian or Gauss's curve See *curve, normal distribution.*

gaze, fascinating The intensification of the eyes of the hypnotist on the subject in hypnosis.

gazing, crystal A technique used in hypnoanalysis in which a hypnotized subject is instructed to observe a glass ball or a mirror and to produce associations.

gelasmus Spasmodic laughter seen in hysterics.

Gelinean's syndrome (J. B. Gelinean) See *narcolepsy.*

gemmation A type of non-sexual reproduction in which the new organism develops as a bud from the parent.

gemmule A small copy of a cell found inside each cell.

Gemüt or Gemütsbewegung 1. A general term in German referring to the effective sphere of experience. **2.** Mood.

gender Denotes sex. It is solely determined by the difference in the physical structure and appearance of the subject, and is used to differentiate male and female.

gene The basic unit of heredity. Genes are arranged in a linear fashion along the chromosomes, each gene having a precise position or locus. From the chemical standpoint a gene is a portion of a DNA molecule coded for the synthesis of certain poly-peptide chain.

gene, dominant A member of an allele pair which if present determines the phenotype whether either member of the pair is the same or different.

gene, major A gene which has a noticeable phenotypic effect.

gene pair See *alleles.*

gene, recessive The subordinate member of a heterozygous allele pair which does not have an effect on the phenotype and can only exhibit its effect phenotypically in a homozygous state.

genealogical See *genealogy*.

genealogy The study of the descent of a person or family from a progenitor.

general ability 1. A term describing the ability to deal with a wide range of problems. 2. An ability necessary in all intellectual tasks and measured to a degree by cognitive tests. 3. (C. Spearman) See *general factor*.

general ability test A general intelligence test.

general adaptation See *general adaptation syndrome*.

general adaptation syndrome (H. Selye) Intense physiological changes in various organ systems of the body, especially the endocrine system as a result of stress. The sequence of bodily changes consists of the alarm reaction, resistance, and exhaustion.

general aptitude The potentiality to acquire proficiency in a diversity of skills with a given amount of formal or informal training.

general aptitude test battery A group of subtests developed by the United States Employment Service for use by their counselors. The subtests include a verbal aptitude, numerical aptitude, spatial aptitude, form perception, clerical perception, motor coordination and manual dexterity test.

general attitude type (C. Jung) A categorization of individuals determined by their habitual way of responding to stimuli, whether inward (introversion) or outward (extraversion).

general consciousness Experiences shared by all members of a group.

general factor 1. A factor common to all the tests being factor analyzed; also called G factor. 2. (C. Spearman) The G (general) factor is a common factor which represents a general ability.

general image An image representing anyone of a class of objects for a subject.

general inhibition (R. B. Cattell) A temperament factor in objective tests loading especially reduction of muscular movement under threat, larger G.S.R. response and avoidance of risk behavior. Indexed as U.I. 17 in the universal index series of factors and hypothesized as identical with Pavlov's temperament dimension in animals.

general intelligence A basic intellectual factor which functions in the solution of all intellectual problems.

general intelligence test See *test, intelligence*.

general juvenile paresis See *paresis, general juvenile*.

general norms Average, standard performance under specified conditions which is used as a base for comparison of other's performance under the same conditions.

general paralysis of the insane See *paresis, general*.

general paresis See *paresis, general*.

general psychology See *psychology, general*.

general semantics Science which deals with human reactions to symbols.

general systems theory (L. V. Bertalanffy) The "general systems theory" is a reaction of contemporary science to the overflow of fractional analytic and non-organized researches at the world's numerous laboratories. The "general systems theory" represented by the special annual edition of "General Systems Theory" and by the scientific "Society of General Systems Theory" seeks the most effective theoretical generalizations, which would permit finding a "key" toward the understanding of different classes of phenomena within the system. Failures of the wide application of the "general systems theory" are connected with some of its shortcomings such as: a) it still doesn't have a formulation of the system acceptable for a majority of the investigators; b) it hasn't revealed a system organizing factor, transferring the chaos of a great number of components into an organized multitude, into the system; c) the system is displayed as something homogeneous without operational architectonics which would permit the evaluation of the system functional effect.

generalization 1. A statement concerning the classification of a class of objects on the basis of one common denominator. 2. The subject's realization of a common principle in a class of objects or problems in concept formation and problem solving. 3. (I. P. Pavlov) Stimuli which were not used in the original conditioning procedure can evoke the conditioned response.

generalization gradient The decrease in the strength of the generalized conditioned response with decreasing similarity of the stimuli used in testing to the original stimulus.

generalized A judgment or principle which, having the qualities common to a class, applies to the members of this class.

generalized gangliosidosis A lipidosis, associated with the involvement of the central nervous system leading to mental retardation as well as liver and kidney failure. Progressive deterioration usually leads to death by age three.

generalized glycogenesis See *Pompe's disease*.

generalized inhibitory potential (C. L. Hull) Conditioned inhibition as a result of stimulus generalization.

generation 1. Act of producing offspring. 2. A group of individuals of the same genealogical rank. 3. A group of individuals living at the same time. 4. Statistical concept describing the average duration of life in a group.

generative Having the ability to reproduce.

generativity See *generative*.

generator potential Change in voltage in a receptor cell due to the depolarizing action of a stimulus.

generic 1. Pertaining to genus. 2. General, applying to all instances of a class.

generic image See *image, generic*.

genesis Origin; beginnings; inception.

genetic 1. Pertaining to origins, history or development; developmental, as, for example, genetic psychology. 2. The science of genetics, pertaining to genes. 3. Produced or determined by a gene or combination of genes. 4. When combined with nouns denotes "pertaining to generation" or "genesis" as in psychogenetic or psychogenic.

genetic marker A readily recognizable gene which can be used to determine whether another gene is on the same chromosome.

genetic method The understanding of behavior by tracing its hereditary origins and development.

genetic psychology See *psychology, genetic.*

genetic sequences The order in which structures or functions determined by genes appear in development.

genetic theory or viewpoint The point of view that stresses the importance of origins and developmental history in understanding phenomena.

geneticism The doctrine that behavior is inherited.

genetics The scientific study of heredity initiated by the hybridization studies of Gregor Mendel published in 1886.

genial Pertaining to the genetic quality of exhibition of genius.

geniculate bodies Slight enlargements on the lateral surface of the thalamus which function as relay stations for visual and auditory impulses to the appropriate centers in the cortex.

geniculate neuralgia Lesion of the facial nerve at the geniculate ganglion followed by facial paralysis.

genital Pertaining to the organs of reproduction.

genital character See *character, genital.*

genital eroticism Sexual excitement resulting from the stimulation of the genital organs.

genital love 1. Love of the genitals during the period of love of an object. 2. (psychoanalysis) Sexually mature love of another person.

genital primacy (psychoanalysis) State of psychosexual development in which the dominant sexual proclivity is coition.

genital primacy stage (psychoanalysis) The final stage of psychosexual development during which the emphasis is on coition and the pleasure is derived from the genital organs.

genital-psychical development Psychosexual development evaluated by the capacity to love on an adult level as opposed to physical prowess.

genital sensations Sexual sensations originating in the genital organs.

genital stage (psychoanalysis) The final stage of psychosexual development in which a person has an affectionate relationship with the sex partner.

genital zones The external genitals and adjacent areas from which genital sensations arise.

genitality Term referring to the genital aspects of sexuality; adult sexuality.

genitalize (psychoanalysis) Regarding objects as symbols of genitals.

genitals The organs of reproduction.

genius 1. High intellectual and creative ability 2. A person possessing such ability.

genome All the genes found in a haploid set of chromosomes.

genophobia Fear of sex.

genosomatogenic disorders (B. B. Wolman) Inherited organic mental disorders.

genotype The genetic characters inherent in the alleles present at a particular locus, or the sum total of these characters in the organism under consideration.

genotypical Pertaining to the genotype.

gens A division of an ethnic group whose line of descent runs through the males.

genus A biological classification which consists of closely related species.

geography, psychological The description of a community in terms of its location and psychological influences among members of the group and groups within the community.

geometric illusion A group of illusions determined by distorted lines which cause a misinterpretation of their relationships.

geometric mean The nth root of the product of n number of means. For example:

$$\bar{x}_g = \sqrt[n]{\bar{x}_1\bar{x}_2\bar{x}_3\ldots\bar{x}_n}$$

geometric-optic agnosia Lack of sense of direction.

geophagy The eating of dirt.

geotaxis A taxis in which the animal orients to the stimulation of gravity.

gephyrophobia Morbid fear of crossing a bridge or river.

geriatrics A branch of medicine concerned with old age and its ailments.

geriopsychosis A psychosis of old age characterized by the deterioration of the brain tissue and progressive mental deterioration.

germ 1. A mass of protoplasm capable of developing into a new organism. 2. A bud.

germ cell A reproductive cell.

germ plasm The tissue making up germ cells which is the main factor in the transmission of hereditary characteristics.

German, Gordon Allen (1935-   ) British

psychiatrist. Set up the first academic unit of psychiatry in East and Central Africa at Makerere University, Uganda, in 1966. Has demonstrated that the prevalence of mental disorder amongst Africans is at least as high as in developed countries; in particular that neurotic illness is a common development in unsophisticated Africans. Explored the nature of psychiatric disorder amongst African students; has put forward the hypothesis that the evil consequences of social change rather than social change *per se* are key factors in the etiology of mental illness.

germinal period The early period of embryonic life, approximately two weeks.

germinal vesicle The nucleus of the egg before the development of the polar bodies.

germinally affected Refers to an individual who carries a homozygous recessive gene pair for a morbid trait which is not manifested phenotypically.

gerontology The scientific study of old age.

gerontophilia Love of old people.

gerophilia See *gerontophilia.*

Gesell, Arnold (1880-1961) Child psychologist and pediatrician (Yale). Research on stages of motor development in infancy, popularizing concept of maturation as basis for development; devised method of co-twin control; author of widely read books on characteristics of children at successive age levels from birth to ten years.

Gesell Development Scales 1. Scales of development for infants and pre-school children based on normative data of children from the Yale Clinic of Child Development. **2.** See *infant schedule.* **3.** See *pre-school schedule.*

gestalt A configuration or figure whose integration differs from the totality obtained by summing the parts.

gestalt factor Any condition favorable to the perception of a whole or totality.

Gestalt psychology Gestalt psychology, a major revolution in psychology, was founded in Germany around 1910 by Max Wertheimer, Wolfgang Köhler, and Kurt Koffka. It started as a protest against the atomism and the narrowness of the prevailing psychology of the mind, but its criticisms were later applied also to the equally atomistic American behaviorism.

Scientific psychology at the turn of the century modeled itself after the physical sciences as it understood them, seeking to reduce the wealth of experience to elements of the mind. The exact nature and number of elements were under dispute, but sensory elements were generally agreed upon. It was assumed that there is a one-to-one correspondence between local sensory experience and local stimulation. This is the constancy hypothesis, the basis of traditional psychology.

Gestalt psychologists set out by rejecting the constancy hypothesis and other forms of elementarism

in psychology. Rather than starting with a preconception about the nature of scientific analysis, they undertook first of all to make their analysis relevant to its subject matter. This meant a starting point in phenomenology in the sense of a clear and unbiased view of phenomena. Re-examining scientific method, Gestalt psychologists asserted that it need not be atomistic. Field theory in physics provided them with a model entirely different from the interpretation of science by the traditional psychology. They found that in many situations, parts derive their nature and functions from the wholes in which they exist and cannot be understood apart from these wholes. Nor can such dynamic wholes be understood as a summation of independent local constituents. The processes in them are functions of interactions within the total relevant field.

From this point of view, many problems in perception were investigated; the approach was extended to thinking, memory and recall, to values and to problems of motivation, to social psychology and the psychology of art. Through the principle of isomorphism, the hypothesis that there is a structural similarity between the facts of organized experience and the corresponding cortical processes, certain problems of brain physiology were opened up to investigation by Gestalt psychologists. Isomorphism proved to be a powerful heuristic tool and led to the investigation of figural aftereffects, then to the demonstration of cortical currents corresponding to organized perceptions.

Gestalt therapy See *psychotherapy, Gestalt.*

Gestaltqualität The quality of the whole form or configuration as dependent on the combination and patterning of the elements.

gestation The carrying of the embryo in the uterus.

gestation period The period of development of an organism before birth.

gestational insanity A mental disorder which occurs during pregnancy.

Gestural Interverbal Test See *test, Gestural Interverbal.*

gestural-postural language See *language, gestural-postural.*

gesture A movement of a part of the body for the purpose of communication.

geumophobia Morbid fear of taste.

geusia The act of tasting.

Gheel colony A colony in Gheel, Belgium, in existence since the 13th century, which treats psychotic patients in private residences in the community.

ghost A disembodied being who retains some of the bodily characteristics such as visibility.

gibberish Incoherent, incomprehensible language.

Gibson, Eleanor J. (1910-   ) American psychologist, best known for research and theory on perceptual learning and development. Applied concepts of conditioning (generalization and differentiation) to verbal learning; made comparative studies of early experience and development of depth perception measured on the "visual cliff" (with Richard Walk); conducts basic research on reading skill and development of economical strategies of perceptual processing.

giddiness Dizziness; having the sensation of whirling about.

gifted 1. Possessing a high degree of intellectual ability. 2. Possessing a high degree of a special talent.

gigantism An abnormal increase in stature due to oversupply of the growth hormone by the anterior pituitary gland.

gigantosomia primordialis A rare form of gigantism characterized by well proportioned physique and a normal sex development.

gigolette Descriptive term for a young woman who engages in promiscuous love affairs.

gigolism 1. Term describing the action of a professional escort usually to members of the opposite sex. 2. Male prostitution.

gigolo 1. Man who serves as a paid escort for women. 2. Man who lives on the earnings of a professional prostitute.

girdle sensation The sensation created by a tightly worn belt appearing as a symptom in particular diseases such as tabis dorsalis.

given 1. Potentially specifiable but left undefined. 2. A set of data available at the inception of an investigation.

gland An organ which secretes substances used in the body or excreted. There are two types: endocrine or ductless glands which secrete their substances directly into the blood stream, and exocrine or duct glands whose secretions are discharged through a duct to the outside or other organs of the body.

gland, anterior pituitary A portion of the pituitary gland which responds to physical or emotional stress by secreting the adreno-corticotrophic hormone which stimulates the adrenal cortex to increase its production of hormones.

gland, parotid Large salivary gland located below the external ear under the jaw bone.

gland, pituitary An endocrine gland called the master gland which is located in the central part of the head. It is made of up two parts. The anterior pituitary controls growth and the activity of other endocrine glands. The posterior pituitary controls the water balance.

glands, adrenal A pair of endocrine glands lying over the kidneys. The adrenal medulla is the dark, central portion of the glands that produces epinephrine and norepinephrine (more commonly called adrenalin and noradrenalin). These hormones are important in the body's reaction to stress. The adrenal cortex, the yellowish outer layer of the adrenal glands, releases several hormones called steroids which are involved in the regulation of body metabolism and sexual functions.

glands, endocrine The ductless glands which secrete their substances directly into the bloodstream.

glands, exocrine The duct glands which secrete their substances through a duct to the outside or other organs of the body.

glands, sudoriferous Sweat glands.

glandular response The reaction of the gland when it is stimulated by a substance outside of the gland.

glans The bulblike end of the penis or clitoris.

glass sensation The visual quality produced by a transparent solid.

glaucoma A disease of the eye caused by increased internal pressure from the liquids leading to progressive visual impairment and finally blindness.

glia Specialized supporting tissue within the cerebrospinal axis; neuroglia.

glial diathesis A constitutional condition characterized by an abnormal growth of the primitive or more differentiated glial cells resulting in one of many degenerative scleroses of the corpora striata.

glioma A brain tumor.

gliosis Rapid increase in the production of neuroglia in the brain or spinal cord as a replacement process or due to inflammation.

global Taken as a whole, as an entirety without distinguishing the parts.

global aphasia See *aphasia, global.*

globus hystericus The sensation of having a lump in the throat or of a ball coming from the stomach to strangulate the person.

glossal Pertaining to the tongue.

glossiness A quality of the surface determined by the degree to which it reflects light.

glossodyma A burning sensation of pain in the tongue.

glossolalia Unintelligible speech such as occurs in hypnotic trances, religious ecstasies and sometimes in pathological mental disorders.

glossopharyngeal nerve The ninth cranial nerve which contains nerve fibers which mediate the sensation of taste.

glossospasm A spasm of the tongue consisting of an inward-outward movement, lasting several minutes.

glossosynthesis The formation of nonsense words.

glottis 1. The opening between the vocal cords. 2. The opening between the arytenoid of the larynx and the vocal cords found at the upper part of the trachea.

glove anesthesia A functional disorder in the

sensory field in which the person is insensitive to touch in an area corresponding approximately to the part covered by a glove.

Glover, Edward (1888-1972) M.D., L.L.D., Hon. Fel. Brit. Psycho. Soc. Originally specialist in diseases of chest. Since 1921, adopted psychoanalytic practice. Wrote extensively on clinical and theoretical aspects of psychoanalysis. Founded Criminological Institute and Clinic for Study and Treatment of Delinquency. Special interests include technique and theory of psychoanalysis, classification of mental disorders, also various social aspects. Author of textbooks of psychoanalytic theory and practice, also on problems of child development and war psychology.

glucose Blood sugar.

gluteal reflex A reflexive contraction of the glutea caused by the stroking of the buttocks.

gluttony Excessive eating.

glycogen Stored hydrocarbon which is used by the muscles and tissues in performing work.

glycogen storage diseases Group of diseases characterized by abnormal accumulations of glycogen in the body, each disease being characterized by a specific, genetically determined enzymatic deficiency resulting in a defect of carbohydrate metabolism. Disease types I, II, and III result in hypoglycemia and the associated central nervous system manifestations.

glycosuria The presence of sugar in the urine resulting from disease or a violent emotional reaction.

gnostic sensation Refers to epicritic sensations, the result of delicate sensory discrimination of the cutaneous receptors.

goal 1. The end result toward which a living organism is moving. 2. A place which contains a reward, an incentive. 3. A consummatory response.

goal-directed behavior Behavior which can be interpreted only in terms of the organism's intention to reach the goal.

goal gradient (C. L. Hull) The principle that in closer proximity to the goal, the experimental animal will speed up and make fewer errors in performance.

goal object The final result toward which the experimental subject is striving.

goal orientation 1. The positioning of the experimental animal or human subject toward the goal. 2. In maze learning, the tendency of the experimental animal to enter alleys in the direction of the goal.

goal response 1. A response directed toward the goal. 2. In instrumental conditioning, the response made toward the reward.

goal set An anticipation of the goal.

goal stimulus A proprioceptive stimulus which arises from goal-directed behavior.

Goetsch Test (E. Goetsch) A test for hyperthyroidism.

goiter, exophthalmic Disease caused by the overproduction of tyroxin by the thyroid gland. It is characterized by an enlargement of the thyroid gland, tachycardia, nervousness, loss of weight, muscular weakness, disturbances in carbohydrate metabolism and acute thyroid crises.

golden section The aesthetic division of a line or an area into two parts x and y, so that the ratio of x to y equals the ratio of y to the line or area.

Goldflam, Samuel (1852-1932) Polish neurologist who is known for his description of myasthenia gravis.

Goldstein, Kurt (1878-1956) German neurologist and Gestalt psychologist who emigrated to the United States in 1935. An organismic personality psychologist whose theory of motivation stressed self-actualization; he found (with Martin Scheerer) that brain injury makes behavior less abstract and more concrete.

Goldstein-Scheerer Tests See *tests, Goldstein-Scheerer.*

Golem Based on Jewish medieval tradition, a manmade huge monster created from clay by the supernatural power of Rabbi Livay.

Golgi apparatus Granule-like structures inside the neuron which are rich in ribonucleic acid and are believed to participate in the synthesis of substances used in maintaining the cell and of transmitter substances which excite or inhibit other cells.

Golgi-Mazzoni corpuscles Encapsulated end organs consisting of nerve endings surrounded by a capsule of tissue, similar to the Krause corpuscles, receptors for cold sensations.

Golgi tendon organ Kinesthetic end organs which are found in the tendons near the tendon-muscle junctures. By responding to changes in tendon tension, these nerve endings function to provide kinesthetic sensations.

gonad The sex gland.

gonadal, gonadial, gonadic Pertaining to the gonad.

gonadocentric Regarding the genitals as central points.

gonadotropic hormone A hormone secreted by the pituitary gland which stimulates the growth and development of the sperm and eggs in the gonads and causes the secretion of androgen and estrogen.

goneometer 1. An instrument for measuring angles. 2. An instrument which measures the amount of sway in psychological experiments.

good and evil test See *test, good and evil.*

good continuation (Gestalt psychology) The principle that a perceived element tends to continue in its direction.

good Gestalt A symmetrical, simple configuration.

good-me See *personified self.*

good object See *object, good.*

good shape (Gestalt psychology) The principle that figures, shapes or patterns are perceived in the most stable and uniform manner as possible.

Goodenough Draw-a-Man Test See *test, Goodenough Draw-a-Man.*

goodness of fit The degree to which any set of empirical observations conforms to a theoretical or standard value.

Gordon Holmes rebound phenomenon See *rebound phenomenon of Gordon Holmes.*

Gordon reflex (A. Gordon) A great toe reflex evoked in diseases of the pyramidal tract.

Gottschaldt figures Simple geometric figures hidden in more complex figures used to test form perception.

governess psychosis See *psychosis, governess.*

Grace Arthur Scale See *scale, Arthur Point of Performance Tests.*

gradation methods Psychophysical techniques measuring change in terms of small equal steps.

grade 1. A class consisting of things on the same position on a scale. 2. In United States schools, a class representing one academic year. 3. A rating on a test.

grade equivalent A score which reflects a person's achievement on a test or battery of tests according to grade norms.

grade scale See *scale, grade.*

grade score See *score, grade.*

graded rehearsal The rehearsal of behaviors which increase in difficulty.

gradient 1. Any regular change in a magnitude which slopes from high to low or vice versa. 2. A change in the motivation to respond which is dependent on a corresponding change in some dimension of stimulation such as time interval or distance.

gradient, anterior-posterior The more rapid growth of the head region in comparison with the tail region which results in the cephalocaudal sequence in development.

gradient, approach The degree of attractiveness of a positive goal increases as a function of nearness to it or as the goal is approached.

gradient, avoidance The attractiveness of a negative goal decreases as it is approached and the tendency to move away from the negative goal increases with closeness to it.

gradient of effect The principle that in a series of S-R sequences, those sequences which closely follow or precede a reinforced sequence have greater probability of occurrence than those which are remote.

gradient of reinforcement The generalization that the closer a response is to the reinforcement, the stronger it becomes.

gradient of response generalization The principle that upon learning to emit a particular response to a given stimulus, that stimulus will elicit similar responses from the animal. The greater the similarity in response, the more the stimulus will elicit it.

gradient of stimulus generalization The principle that when the animal learns to respond to a given stimulus, he will respond to similar stimuli. This response will not, however, be as strong.

Graduate Record Examination A combination of verbal and mathematical tests which are used as measures of aptitude to select candidates for graduate school. Also known as GRE.

grand mal A complete epileptic seizure consisting of a sudden loss of consciousness, tonic and clonic spasms, frothing at the mouth and often urine incontinence. Following the convulsions, the person is often confused and falls into a deep sleep. See *epilepsy.*

grandeur delusions See *delusions, grandeur.*

grandfather complex See *complex, grandfather.*

grandiose Referring to delusions of greatness and importance.

granular layers 1. The fourth layer of the central cortex consisting of many small multipolar cells with short peripheral processes. 2. The fifth and seventh layer of the retina.

graph The representation of the relationship between two variables by means of lines or geometric figures.

graph, correlation See *scatter diagram.*

graphic Representation by means of a graph.

graphic analysis See *analysis, graphic.*

graphic individuality See *individuality, graphic.*

graphic language See *language, graphic.*

graphic method See *method, graphic.*

graphic rating scale See *scale, graphic rating.*

graphic score See *score, graphic.*

graphodyne A mechanism for recording pressure in handwriting.

graphology The study of handwriting for the purpose of deducing the personality characteristics of the writer.

graphomania Intense impulse to write.

graphomaniac A person exhibiting an inordinate impulse to write.

graphomotor technique See *technique, graphomotor.*

graphophobia Fear of writing.

graphorrh(o)ea Disordered, often meaningless writing observed in pathological states.

graphospasm Writer's cramp.

grasping and groping reflex See *reflex, grasping and groping.*

gratification Satisfaction of a person's needs or desires.

gratification, self The satisfaction of one's own needs, particularly those having to do with enhancement of self through praise and prestige.

Graves' disease See *goiter, exophthalmic.*

gray matter The part of the brain and spinal cord chiefly made up of nerve cells.

Gray Oral Reading Test See *test, Gray Oral Reading.*

gray-out Partial loss of consciousness due to anemia of the brain or anoxemia.

GRE See *Graduate Record Examination.*

Great Mother See *Magna Mater.*

Greek love Homosexuality among males.

green A visual sensation resulting from the stimulation of the retina with radiation of approximately 510 millimicron wave lengths.

gregariousness 1. The proclivity to be in the company of others. 2. The tendency for animals to congregate in herds or flocks. 3. The tendency in humans to live in groups and to desire the company of others.

grey or gray The achromatic color ranging in shade between the extreme limits of black and white.

grief An emotional state resulting from the loss of an important object.

Grieg's disease Mental and physical retardation associated with a deformity of the frontal area of the cranium and characterized by a low forehead, wide bridge of the nose, increased distance between the eyes and divergent strabismus; hypertelorism.

Griffiths' Scale See *scale, Griffiths'.*

grimace A distorted facial expression due to organic or psychological causes.

Griselda complex See *complex, Griselda.*

gross score See *score, gross.*

ground The background in the relationship of figure and ground.

group Two or more individuals, assembled or dispersed, who are united by some common interest, characteristic or attachment and whose actions are interrelated.

group acceptance The reaction of group members to a new or prospective member which establishes the member's role in the group.

group analysis See *analysis, group; group psychoanalysis.*

group atmosphere The feelings and attitudes manifested in a group.

group behavior 1. The behavior of a group acting as a whole. 2. The actions of an individual member as influenced by being a member of the group. 3. Actions characteristic of individuals when in the group but not when outside the group.

group, blanket A group in which criteria for group membership do not exist.

group boundary The regulations which control group activities and group membership.

group, closed A psychotherapy group which does not admit new patients during the course of the treatment.

group consciousness 1. An awareness characteristic of the whole group which is more than the sum of the individual consciousness. This concept is synonymous with G. LeBon's group mind and group behavior. 2. An awareness of one individual in a group for another member or for the group as a whole.

group contagion The rapid spread of feelings through the group as a result of an empathic perception of the feelings in others.

group, control A group which is equivalent to the experimental group in every respect except for the independent variable which the experimental group is treated with and the control group is not.

group decision An opinion or judgment arrived at by the group either by consensus or by a majority vote of the members.

group differences Distinguishing disparities between two or more groups with respect to any specific variable.

group dimension A quantitative characteristic by means of which a group can be described.

group dynamics 1. The cause and effect relationships which exist in the group. 2. The study of the development of the cause and effect relationships within a group. 3. The techniques for changing the interpersonal relations and attitudes within a group.

group experiment An experiment performed on a large number of interrelated persons.

group, experimental The subjects in an experiment who are exposed to the independent or experimental variable and whose performance is thought to reflect the influence of that condition. This group is matched with the control group in every way except for their exposure to the experimental condition.

group feeling The desire to be with other members of a group.

group identification The process of internalizing the standards and ideals of the group.

group interval A class interval.

group interview The use of the interview technique with several individuals at once.

group marriage A marriage consisting of several men and women.

group, matched (experimental research) One of the groups used in an experiment which are made equivalent in every respect in order to ensure experimental control. Some groups undergo experimental manipulation while others do not. The resulting difference between the initially equal groups is a measure of experimental effect.

group mean *p* technique A longitudinal factor analysis carried out, not on an individual, but a group, all members experiencing the same sequence of stimuli.

group measures Measures which fall within intervals or classes of scores rather than a group of individual scores.

group, membership A group in which the person is an accepted member.

group mind (G. LeBon) A term used to explain the behavior of a group which cannot be accounted for by the sum of the traits of the individual members.

group morale The prevailing spirit in the group characterized by confidence and a willingness to strive for group goals.

group norm See *norm, group.*

group, open A psychotherapy group which admits new patients during the course of treatment.

group processes The methods used by a group to approach and solve problems and to meet objectives.

group psychoanalysis Psychoanalytic technique applied to the group treatment of mental disorders; a particular version of group psychotherapy based on psychoanalytic principles.

group psychotherapy See *psychotherapy, group.*

group psychotherapy, analytic See *psychotherapy, analytic group.*

group psychotherapy, didactic See *psychotherapy, didactic group.*

group psychotherapy, nondirective See *psychotherapy, nondirective group.*

group psychotherapy, psychoanalytic See *psychotherapy, psychoanalytic group.*

group rigidity Resistance to change in a group.

group, standardization The group of individuals used for establishing norms for a test which is believed to be representative of the population which will be tested in the future.

group structure The relationships of members in a group and the characteristics of the group which determine the interpersonal relations and its relationships with other groups.

group, structured (S. R. Slavson) A therapy group in which the selection of members is made according to the criterion of which individuals will effect a most therapeutic change on one another.

group superego The aspect of the superego based on identifications with peer groups as opposed to the portion of the superego derived from the introjection of parental values.

group test see *test, group.*

group therapy See *psychotherapy, directive group.*

group, therapy See *psychotherapy, group.*

group, transitional A psychotherapy group designed for children in the latency and puberty stage who cannot adjust to the demands of a social club but do not need intensive group psychotherapy.

grouped distribution A frequency distribution in which the values of a variable are expressed in ranges.

grouping 1. Putting together of objects, animals, humans, or concepts and ideas into one clan or category. 2. Combining scores into classes or categories. 3. (education) Assigning school pupils into classes or grades.

grouping error The error introduced when a set of observations is divided into class intervals due to the assumption that the data are uniformly distributed around the midpoint of each interval.

groups, equivalent (statistics) Two or more groups which exhibit approximately the same distribution on a particular variable. Mean, standard deviation and range are nearly the same, falling within previously set limits of each other.

growing pains 1. Physical pain experienced by the child or adolescent due to the overly rapid development of the bones. 2. Metaphorically, any stress due to development.

growth Refers to increments in size or amount.

growth curve A graphic representation of the growth rate of an organism over a period of time.

growth, differential Growth of one organ or structure proceeds at a different rate than another organ within the same organism.

growth, mental The increase with age of any psychological function, specifically of intelligence.

growth motivation See *motivation, growth.*

growth principle (C. R. Rogers) The principle that in an atmosphere free from coercion and distortion, the creative and actualizing tendencies within an individual will prevail leading to the development of a more adaptive, forward-moving and confident person, with feelings of positive self-regard and worth.

grumbling mania See *mania, grumbling.*

guessed mean *See mean, assumed.*

guidance A type of counseling in which an individual is assisted through the use of interviews and tests, in choosing educational and vocational careers which will offer him maximum satisfaction.

guidance, child A term which refers to the preventive measures oriented toward minimizing the possibility of mental disorders in adult life by offering didactic and therapeutic aid to the child and his family members, at a time when the intervention will have a critical prophylactic effect.

Guilford, Joy Paul (1897-   ) American multivariate experimental psychologist, known for his contributions to psychological measurement and the application of measurement methods and factor analysis to derivation of taxonomies of personality traits, including intellectual abilities. Probably his best contribution was his structure of intellect, a model representing systematically all currently conceivable varieties of intellectual functioning. The model has led to an operational-informational point of view in psychology, which regards the individual as a processor of information in specified codes, according to logical principles.

Guilford-Zimmerman Temperament Survey   A personality inventory published in 1949, which measures ten traits, products of factorial analyses: general activity, restraint, ascendance, sociability, emotional stability, objectivity, friendliness, thoughtfulness, personal relations, and masculinity. The survey is intended for use with individuals in grades 9 through 16 and with adults.

guilt   **1.** The realization that one has transgressed a moral, social or ethical principle, associated with a lowering of self-esteem and a need to make retribution for the transgression. **2.** (psychoanalysis) Feeling which is the result of a conflict between the superego and ego in which the superego, as the internal authority, punishes the ego in the form of feelings of low self-esteem and guilt for allowing the expression or existence of unacceptable impulses. The guilt feeling or moral anxiety in the most extreme form becomes a fear of annihilation, and panic that affection and narcissistic supplies will be withdrawn.

guilt proneness   A source trait distinct from superego strength but predisposing to guilt-prone, depressive, apprehensive behavior.

guilt, unconscious sense of   A term referring to the unconscious causes of guilt feelings. A more correct term would be an unconscious need for punishment.

gumma, intracranial   A form of cerebral syphilis in which a necrotic mass with a tendency to encapsulation and tibrosis may produce intracranial pressure. The associated mental symptoms include an acute organic reaction with delirium, memory loss of recent events and emotional variability. Upon increased intracranial pressure, stupor and a loss of sphincter control occur.

gust   A unit of taste which equals the subjective strength of a one per cent solution of sucrose.

gustation   The sense of taste with receptors on the tongue and soft palate.

gustatism   A syncratic sensation of taste with another sensory modality.

gustatory center   The center of taste.

gustatory-lacrimal reflex   Crocodile-tears syndrome.

Guthrie, Edwin R. (1886-1959)   Behaviorist at the University of Washington. Developed a theory of learning based upon a single law, which he used systematically to account for a broad range of behaviors, including social phenomena, personality and education: whenever a response occurs, it is linked permanently with each stimulus element present at the time the response is made.

Guttman scale   See *scale, Guttman.*

guttural   Pertaining to the throat such as sounds originating in the throat.

gynander, gynandromorph   An organism exhibiting both male and female characteristics due to the development of both types of sex tissue.

gynandroid, gynandromorphic, gynandrous   Referring to the hermaphroditic combination in an organism in which feminine features predominate.

gynandry   Feminine pseudohermaphroditism.

gynecomania   Intense desire for women.

gynephobia   Fear of women.

gynomonoecism   The ability of a genetic female to produce spermatozoa in the ovaries.

gyrectomy   The surgical ablation of any gyrous of the brain. As a treatment for certain forms of mental illness, part of the cortex is excised bilaterally from the frontal lobes of the brain.

gyrus   A fold or convolution on the surface of the cerebral hemisphere.

gyrus cinguli or cingulate   Also called gyrus callosus. The central fold of each cerebral hemisphere; it lies above the corpus callosum.

gyrus fornicatus   See *lobe, limbic.*

gyrus of Broca   (P. Broca).Motor speech area.

gyrus, paracentral   A convolution on the middle surface of the cerebral hemispheres which surrounds the upper end of the dentral fissure.

H

H **1.** See *mean, harmonic.* **2.** (C. L. Hull) Habit strength. Also $_sH_r$. **3.** Rorschach scoring symbol for the perception of human forms.

H test See *test, H.*

Haab's pupil reflex (O. Haab) The contraction of both pupils when the gaze is directed toward a bright object in a darkened room.

habenula **1.** The fibers which form the stalk of the pineal body and attach it to the thalamus. **2.** A small strip of flesh.

habit **1.** An acquired act that is practiced regularly and with a minimum of voluntary control. **2.** The tendency for a given stimulus to evoke a specific response on occasions subsequent to the original reaction. **3.** (J. Dewey) a) Complex and flexible mechanisms of behavior that control the interaction between organism and its environment; b) The mechanisms that "assimilate objective energies, and eventuate in command of environment;" c) Dewey distinguishes between routine habits, those which offer adjustment to a more or less static environment and intelligent habits, which guide the individual to a better adjustment to a changing situation. **4.** (C. L. Hull) a) Persistent patterns of behavior that are "set up by virtue of the law of reinforcement;" b) Reinforced conditioned-response patterns. See *habit formation, law of* and *habit strength.*

habit, accident The tendency to have accidents as a result of unconscious conflictual needs which are partially satisfied by the consequent injuries.

habit, act A characteristic mode of responding resulting from environmental influence.

habit, complaint (L. Kanner) A recurrent tendency to hypochondriachal complaints in children as a reaction to emotional or other difficulties.

habit, deterioration The loss of socialized behaviors as a result of a regression to less integrated patterns of behavior in mental and organic illnesses.

habit, family hierarchy (C. L. Hull) The grouping of alternate routes to a goal in the order of most to least preferred.

habit formation The establishment of behavior patterns.

habit formation, law of (C. L. Hull) An equation in mathematical learning theory that expresses the relation between habit strength and number of reinforcements. If reinforcements follow each other at evenly distributed intervals, everything else constant, the resulting habit will increase in strength as a positive growth function of the number of trials according to the equation: $_sH_R = 1 - 10^{-aN}$ where a is a constant that specifies the learning rate, N is the total number of reinforcements from Z, and Z is the absolute zero of the reaction potential.

habit hierarchy **1.** (C. L. Hull) The arrangement of responses in terms of their strength which depends on their temporal contiguity with the reinforced response. **2.** The hierarchical organization of simpler habits into more complex habit patterns.

habit, hysterical A hysterical reaction which develops from a voluntary to an automatic response by means of repetition.

habit, interference The weakening of one or both responses which have been established to the same situation.

habit, motor A habit defined in terms of the response movements which are involved.

habit, residual hysterical Hysteria which continues to exist because of the patient's lack of desire to get well.

habit, sensory A learned behavior which consists of the ability to differentiate between stimuli rather than learning to make specific responses.

habit strength (C. L. Hull) The strength of the habitual response which is dependent on the number of reinforcements, the amount of reinforcement, the temporal interval between stimulus and the response, and between the response and the reinforcement. Also known as $_sH_R$.

habit training The didactic process directed toward the establishment of habitual patterns of behavior in organisms.

habitat 1. Natural surroundings and conditions of an animal or vegetable species. 2. (A. Adler) The situations to which a person has been exposed including the social factors that have influenced him.

habituation The elimination of a response as a result of a continuous exposure to the stimulus which evoked the response.

habitus 1. The general characteristic appearance of the body of an organism. 2. The constitutional predisposition to a disease believed to be associated with a particular body type.

habitus, affective The affective organization of a person.

habitus apoplecticus See *type, apoplectic.*

habitus phthisicus (Hippocrates) A slender constitution thought to be characteristic of tubercular patients.

habromania Morbid gaiety.

haematophobia, hematophobia See *hemophobia.*

haemorrhage The eruption of blood from the vessels.

hair cells Cells with hairlike protrusions which function as receptors in the inner ear.

hair follicle An epithelial structure in the corium and hypodermis which contains the root of the hair filament.

hair pulling A compulsive symptom of pulling the hair from the head which is the expression of unconscious conflicts.

halfway house A facility providing professional supervision in a group living arrangement for the patient without a home who is ready to work after having been discharged from a hospital.

Hall, Granville Stanley (1844-1924) Early pioneer in and promoter of American psychology, a student of Wundt who founded and served as the first president of the American Psychological Association in 1892, while president of Clark University. He started the *American Journal of Psychology,* edited several other journals, and wrote books on individual differences, developmental psychology and other areas.

hallucinate To perceive an external stimulus in any sensory modality which has no basis in reality.

hallucinatio hypochondriasis An obsolete term for hypochondriasis.

hallucination The perception of an external object in any sensory modality, which arises within the individual himself, without any basis in reality.

hallucination, auditory A hallucination associated with sensations of hearing.

hallucination, diminutive visual See *hallucination, Lilliputian.*

hallucination, elementary auditory The hallucination of amorphous noises such as murmurs, knocks and shooting.

hallucination, extracampine A hallucination which is localized outside of the normal range of perception for the organ.

hallucination, genital The hallucination of being the victim of obscenity.

hallucination, gustatory The hallucination of sensations of taste.

hallucination, haptic A hallucination associated with sensations of touch.

hallucination, hypnagogic A hallucination occurring between the stage of wakefulness and sleep, usually recognized as an unreal perception.

hallucination, induced A hallucination evoked in a person by another person.

hallucination, Lilliputian The visual hallucination of objects which appear greatly reduced in size.

hallucination, macroptic The visual hallucination of objects which appear greatly increased in size.

hallucination, memory A visual image of previously repressed material.

hallucination, microptic See *hallucination, Lilliputian.*

hallucination, motor See *hallucination, psychomotor.*

hallucination, negative The failure to see an object when looking at it.

hallucination, negative memory The denial of an event which one has experienced.

hallucination, olfactory The hallucination of sensations of smell.

hallucination, psychic The hallucination of mental events.

hallucination, psychomotor The hallucination that certain parts of a person's body are moving or being moved.

hallucination, psycho-sensorial Hallucinations involving both mental events and the sensory organs.

hallucination, reflex A hallucination in one sensory area resulting from the stimulation of another sensory organ.

hallucination, retroactive See *hallucination, memory.*

hallucination, slow motion The hallucination that one is moving very slowly while everything around is accelerated.

hallucination, space-motor The sensation that one is moving at an accelerated pace.

hallucination, teleologic A hallucination in which the person is directed as to what course he should take.

hallucination, unilateral A hallucination involving only one side of the sensory apparatus.

hallucination, vestibular False sensory perceptions

resulting from the impairment of the vestibular apparatus which are usually restricted to visual and haptic hallucinations.

hallucination, visual A hallucination involving vision.

hallucinatory game See *game, hallucinatory.*

hallucinatory image A mental image which is mistaken for reality.

hallucinatory neuralgia See *neuralgia, hallucinatory.*

hallucinosis The state of having recurrent hallucinations.

hallucinosis, acute The sudden manifestation of hallucinations as a result of alcohol or drug intoxication or a traumatic event, which ceases within a period of weeks.

hallucinosis, alcoholic Hallucinatory states caused by alcohol with the exclusion of delirium tremens, Korsakov's psychosis, and alcoholic deterioration. The hallucinations are usually auditory and threatening to the affected alcoholic.

hallucinosis, diabetic Hallucinations occurring in diabetic individuals.

hallucinosis, uremic Hallucinations occurring in individuals with kidney disease.

halo 1. A ring of light around an object. **2.** Honor and glory with which a famous or beloved person is endowed.

halo effect See *effect, halo.*

halving method See *method, halving.*

hamartophobia Fear of sin.

Hamilton, Gilbert Van Tassel (1877-1943) American psychiatrist and psychobiologist. Pioneered research on frustration with inter-species comparisons, and developed the first sophisticated theory of objective psychopathology (diagnosis and treatment) based on behavioral principles of learning and frustration rather than mentalistic ones of dissociation and the unconscious. His later research on marriage began the integration of psychoanalytic and learning theories of personality development.

hammer See *malleus.*

Hampstead Baby Profile An instrument introduced by W. E. Freud in 1967 to assess the development of infants up to about six months of age, based on reports and home observations of the development of infants from the Well-Baby Clinic, a department of the Hampstead Child Therapy Clinic in Hampstead, England.

Hampstead Index A system of classification of the data of analytic hours introduced in 1955 by workers from the Hampstead Child Therapy Clinic in Hampstead, England, to provide more readily accessible analytic material for research, teaching and reference purposes. The original categories were evolved from a pilot study of fifty cases which were in daily analysis at the clinic.

Hampton Court Maze See *maze, Hampton Court.*

hand test See *test, hand.*

hand-to-mouth reaction A reaction of bringing all objects within reach of the hand to the mouth, observed in infants until approximately twelve months of age.

handedness Preferential use of one hand over the other.

handicap A disadvantage which prevents the individual from achieving success of some desired goal.

handicap, collective life A term used in social work referring to a person's handicap which interferes with his interpersonal relations.

handicap, family life A term used in social work referring to a person's handicap which interferes with his role in marriage.

handicap, perceptual A term for neurological dysfunction involving the higher mental functions emphasizing that the perceptual processes are involved in brain damage whether it relates to specific perceptual areas or to the person's perceptual organization in the environment.

handicraft Art or craft used as a means of therapeutic treatment.

handwriting scale See *scale, handwriting.*

Hanfman-Kasanin Concept Formation Test See *test, Hanfman-Kasanin Concept Formation.*

haphalgesia The experience of the sensation of pain upon touching an object.

haphephobia Fear of being touched.

haploid The chromosome number of a normal gamete which contains only one member of each chromosome pair. In man, the haploid number is 23.

haploidy The condition of having half the number of chromosomes present in somatic cells.

haplology The omission of syllables in words because of rapidity of speech.

haptephobia See *haphephobia.*

haptic Referring to the cutaneous sensory system.

haptics The investigation of the cutaneous sensory system.

haptometer An instrument for measuring sensitivity of touch.

hard colors Reds and yellows, the colors which separate most easily from the gray field of equal saturation and luminosity.

hard-of-hearing Having defective auditory acuity which can be improved by the use of a hearing aid.

harelip A cleft of the upper lip caused by a failure in the complete development of the fetus in the first eight to ten weeks after conception.

Harlow, Harry F. (1905-) American psychologist,

creator of the learning set phenomenon and the cloth and wire surrogate mothers. Experimentally analyzed the various love or affectional systems giving proper and appropriate emphasis to the age-mate or peer system as contrasted to the other system, particularly the maternal. Published extensive studies on cortical localization of learning, curiosity and manipulation, the induction of depression by various experimental techniques and the experimental alleviation of induced psychopathology.

harmavoidance need See *need, harmavoidance.*

harmonic 1. An overtone whose frequency of wave vibration is a multiple of the fundamental tone. **2.** Referring to the combination of simultaneous tones into chords.

harmonic analysis The resolution of a complex wave into its sine and cosine components by the use of Fourier's law or a harmonic analyzer.

harmonic mean See *mean, harmonic.*

harmony 1. The combination of parts into a congruous whole. **2.** Good, friendly relations among people. **3.** The combination of tones into chords which are arranged to yield a congruous whole in music.

harp theory of hearing See *hearing, theory of: resonance theory.*

harpaxophobia Fear of robbers.

harria (R. B. Cattell) A factor trait referring to assertive, decisive, realistic behavior.

Harrower inkblots (M. R. Harrower-Erickson and M. E. Steiner) The Rorschach inkblot test adapted for assessing groups. The cards are projected on a screen in front of the subjects who write down what they see. They then locate their responses on diagrams of the blots and add any additional information about their responses which will help the examiner score them. Instructions are given before each step to ensure that all of the information is obtained.

harshness 1. A quality of sounds due to an irregular wave form. **2.** A personality characteristic manifested by the lack of sympathetic understanding of others, an unpleasant manner and abrupt speech.

Hartley, David (1705-1757) British physician and philosopher, influenced by Newton, founder of British Associationism; endeavored to integrate philosophy with anatomy, physiology, and physics; based his system of physiological psychology on association. Chief work: *Observations on Man* (1749).

Hartmann, Heinz (1894-1970) Was among the second generation of European psychoanalysts who sought to develop further some aspect of Freudian theory. His *Ego Psychology and the Problem of Adaptation* (1939), regarded as a landmark not only in development of psychoanalysis but in the relationships of the schools, was well received by Anna Freud, and exerted influence in Europe and America. Hartmann revised the concept of the ego, freeing it in part from its dependence on the id.

Further investigation of the problem of the ego appeared justified in view of the fluctuation of Freud's thought on the role of the ego and his own warning not to draw sharp dividing lines between ego, superego, and id, but rather to allow "what we have separated to merge again." Today ego psychology is a central issue in psychoanalytical theory.

Hartmann, von E. (1842-1906) A German philosopher known for his introduction of the unconscious as a critical mental factor, for his opposition of the mechanistic materialism of his time and for his justification of philosophical pessimism which formed a bridge to the more extreme views of pessimism and nihilism of the twentieth century.

Hartnup disease A very rare aminoaciduria associated with mental retardation.

hashish See *cannabis.*

hate 1. An enduring character trait consisting of anger, aversion and the desire to hurt the other person. **2.** See *Thanatos.*

haut mal Grand mal epileptic attack; seizure.

Hawthorne experiment A study conducted at the Hawthorne Works of the Western Electric Company which pointed out the existence of implicit, informal group norms which affect the behavior of members in a group as opposed to explicitly stated rules which may not be adhered to by the members.

Hawthorne studies A pioneering series of studies started in 1927 and continuing into the early 1930's done at the Western Electric Company by Elton May, F. J. Roethlisberger, W. J. Dickson, and their associates. The studies showed the importance of the human quality and demonstrated that work efficiency was not just the product of physical or economic conditions. They led to seeing the importance of employee attitudes, a change to the indirect from the direct method of interviewing, the introduction of personal counseling and the awareness of the intricacies of social organization.

headache, lead-cap The sensation that the head is splitting or that one has a heavy weight or constriction around the head.

headache, migraine A headache of organic or psychological etiology characterized by periodic attacks, prodromal disturbances and pain. The physiological mechanisms underlying pain seem to involve the vascular stretching of the cerebral and cranial arteries resulting from vasodilation. Ergot and its derivatives offers relief. Migraines often occur in people who are hostile and envious of intellectually superior people.

head-banging Uncontrolled physical movements characteristic of a young child in a temper tantrum.

head-knocking Hitting the head against the wall or other objects seen in some infants and children.

head-rolling Semicircular movements of the head manifested by some infants before going to sleep.

health-conscience (R. H. Jokl) The transformation

of an unconscious sense of guilt into a conscious repudiation of the illness or symptom and alliance with ego attitudes which are healthy.

Healy Picture Completion Test See *test, Healy Picture Completion.*

hearing The perception of sounds through the auditory sensory apparatus.

hearing, color The syncretic sensation of seeing colors when sounds are heard.

hearing loss The degree of loss of the capacity to hear tones at particular frequencies, expressed in relative terms of the percentage of normal hearing or in absolute terms of decibals of loudness.

hearing, monaural Hearing with one ear.

hearing theories 1. Theories which attempt to explain how physical sound vibrations give rise to the neural impulses of hearing. There are five major theories: resonance theories, frequency theories, volley theories, hydraulic theories, and sound-pattern theories. 2. See *hearing, theory of: resonance theory*. 3. See *hearing, theory of: frequency theory*. 4. See *hearing, theory of: volley theory*. 5. See *hearing, theory of: hydraulic theory*. 6. See *hearing, theory of: sound-pattern theory.*

hearing, theory of: frequency theory (E. Rutherford) The theory that the basilar membrane responds as a whole to aural stimuli, then transmits the stimuli to the brain for analysis.

hearing, theory of: hydraulic theory (H. Meyer) The theory that hearing is dependent on the amount of basilar membrane involved in the sensation of different tones.

hearing, theory of: resonance theory (H. von Helmholtz) The theory that pitch is determined by the place on the basilar membrane which is stimulated, the short fibers being sensitive to high pitched sounds, the long fibers to the low-pitched sounds and the fibers in the middle of the membrane being attuned to sounds of medium pitch. Also known as the piano theory, place theory and harp theory.

hearing, theory of: sound-pattern theory The theory that the sense of hearing is dependent on the pattern of vibration on the basilar membrane.

hearing, theory of: volley theory (E. G. Wener and C. W. Bray) The theory that nerve fibers of the basilar membrane respond in groups or volleys, not in unison resulting in more transmission of aural impulses.

heart neurosis See *neurosis, cardiovascular.*

heart rate Rate of ventricular contractions per minute.

heat 1. A sensation experienced when the receptors for warm and cold are stimulated simultaneously. 2. See *estrus.*

heavy metal poisoning See *poisoning, lead; poisoning, arsenic; poisoning, mercury; poisoning, thallium; poisoning, barium.*

Hebb, D.O. (1904-   ) Canadian psychologist and author of a neurological theory of thinking. Showed that the development of intelligence and personality in the infant, and normal mental function at maturity, depend on environmental stimulation; "sensory deprivation" results in gross disorders of behavior.

Hebb's theory of perceptual learning (D. O. Hebb) A theory of learning based on the postulation of groups of sensory and motor neurons which work together called cell assemblies. The theory states that perception leads to the formation of interconnections between neural pathways which subsequently act as a unit. Separate assemblies can become coordinated to form a phase sequence which on the perceptual level enables an individual to perceive elements of a whole as a totality. The cell assemblies can undergo changes through fractionation, the loss of synchronization of neurons with the assembly or recruitment, the joining of neurons to the assembly. Learning is believed to result from facilitation established in which one or a group of assemblies facilitates the oncoming of some other units. When something has been learned, one stimulus sets off established phase sequences. In higher organisms, missing elements in a perceived totality do not alter the whole because of the ability to generalize and abstract.

hebephrenia One of the main schizophrenic syndromes. See *schizophrenia, hebephrenic.*

hebephrenia, engraffed (E. Kraepelin) Hebephrenia which is superimposed on an already existing disorder.

hebephrenic, depressive A form of hebephrenia characterized by cycles of depression.

hebephrenic, manic A form of hebephrenia characterized by cycles of mania.

hebephrenic schizophrenia See *schizophrenia, hebephrenic.*

hebetic Referring to puberty, specifically to mental illness during adolescence.

hebetude 1. Emotional apathy. 2. Lack of affect or interest exhibited through apathy, dullness, listlessness and indifference to surroundings and usually associated with schizophrenia. 3. Apathy and dullness from any cause.

hebetudinous Characterized by hebetude.

hebetudo animi Imbecility.

hebetudo mentis Imbecility.

heboid praecox See *praecox, heboid.*

heboidophrenia (K. L. Kahlbaum) Obsolete term referring to simple form of schizophrenia.

Hecker, Ewald (1843-1909) German psychiatrist who coined the term hebephrenia.

hederiform terminations Free nerve endings in the skin which serve as sensory end organs for pain.

hedonia Pleasure, enjoyment.

hedonic 1. Referring to the feeling of pleasure. 2. Referring to the dimension pleasure-unpleasure.

hedonism 1. The psychological principle that the person acts to gain pleasure and avoid pain. **2.** The philosophical doctrine which states that pleasure or happiness is the goal of conduct.

hedonophobia Fear of pleasure.

heel-to-knee test See *test, heel-to-knee.*

Heidbreder, Edna (1890-) American psychologist. Author of *Seven Psychologies* and papers on schools and systems of psychology; co-author (with D. G. Paterson, R. M. Elliott, D. Anderson, H. Toops) of *The Minnesota Mechanical Ability Tests*; constructed scales for measuring introversion–extraversion and inferiority attitudes which were among the first instruments available for the quantitative treatment of traits of personality; identified 'participant' and 'spectator' behavior in an experiment on thinking; conducted a series of experiments on concept-attainment in which that phrase was first defined and used as a technical psychological term.

Heidegger, Martin (1889-) German philosopher significant for existential psychology and psychiatry. Influenced by Edmund Husserl and Sören Kierkegaard. Taught that only man, of all beings, is aware of his existence and that he realizes his existence is not his making or his choice. Discovering his life oriented toward inescapable death, man experiences dread and anguish. He tries to overcome this by conforming to conventional modes of thinking, acting, and speaking. Such camouflages produce a feeling of guilt. Heidegger insisted that only by accepting the inevitability of death and nothingness can man have authentic existence and be truly free. The Swiss psychiatrist, Ludwig Binswanger, elaborated and applied this concept to the field of psychotherapy. Author of *Being and Time* (1927), *What is Metaphysics?* (1929), and a *Postscript* (1947).

Heidelberg man The primitive man reconstructed from the jaw dated in the early Middle Pleistocene age which was found in 1907 near Heidelberg, Germany.

Heinis constant A measure of the rate of mental growth computed by translating mental age units into values on a scale having theoretically equal mental growth units and dividing the result by chronological age.

Heinis law of mental growth The principle that intelligence increases with age according to the following formula:

$$y = 429(1-e^{\frac{CA}{6.675}})$$

where y = attained intelligence, e = the base of the natural logarithm, and CA = chronological age.

Hejna test See *test, Hejna.*

helicord 1. Referring to a spiral shape. **2.** A warped surface produced by a straight line moving so as to cut or touch a fixed helix.

helicotrema The opening which connects the scala vestituli with the scala tympani in the spinal canal of the cochlea.

heliocentric theory The theory that the sun is the center of the universe.

heliophobia Fear of sunlight.

heliotropism An orienting movement toward the source of light.

helix The curved part of the outer ear.

Heller's disease See *dementia infantilis.*

Hellwag's vowel triangle A graphic description of the interrelationship of vowel sounds:

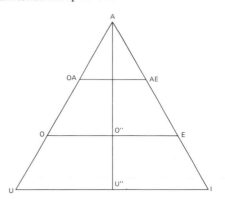

helmet, neurasthenic A feeling of pressure over the cranium characteristic of certain cases of neurasthenia.

Helmholtz, Hermann Ludwig Ferdinand von (1821-1894) German scholar, physicist, physiologist and psychologist who proposed the principle of conservation of energy, first measured the speed of the neural impulse, and did pioneer work in hearing, vision and perception. Formulated an influential place theory of pitch perception and three-cone theory of color vision. A scientific materialist, he held that perception is a matter of unconscious inference.

helper, magic (E. Fromm) A neurotic form of interpersonal relations in which one member endows the other member with omnipotent illusory power in the hope of obtaining security, support, and escape from frightening feelings of isolation.

helping, mania for A morbid need to participate in every action in order to gain an advantage for oneself.

helplessness, psychic (S. Freud) The experience of the young infant when he is in a dangerous situation in which he cannot gratify his needs which is the prototype for all later experiences of anxiety.

Helson, Harry (1898-) American psychologist, author of the theory of adaptation-level, has worked in psychophysics, sensory processes, perception, color vision, human factors in design of equipment, and other areas. Known also for Helson-Judd effect, reformulation of the Weber-Fechner law and theory of time-order effects (with Michels), and for studies of reversal of classical lightness contrast (von Bezold assimilation). His first major contribution, appearing in journal articles and later in book form, served to introduce Gestalt psychology to English readers. His most recent work, a study of the effects of spectral energy of light sources and chromaticity of backgrounds on pleasantness of object color is the most extensive study in the field of aesthetics of color. See *adaptation-level theory; color conversion; the U-hypothesis; assimiliation and contrast.*

hemathidrosis The elimination of blood pigments through the glands of the skin.

hemeralopia 1. Day blindness. 2. Night blindness.

hemeralopsia See *hemeralopia.*

hemeraphonia The loss of the voice during the day characteristic of hysteria.

hemianaesthesia A lack of sensitivity in one half of the body.

hemianalgesia A lack of pain in one half of the body.

hemianopia; hemiopia Unilateral or bilateral blindness in one side of the visual field.

hemianopsia, heteronymous Bitemporal loss of vision.

hemianopsia, homonymous Loss of vision in the left or right visual field of both eyes.

hemianthropia Insanity.

hemiballism Violent repeated movements, shaking and twisting of one side of the body resulting from a brain lesion on the opposite side of the body.

hemichorea Chorea in which the convulsive movements affect only one side of the body.

hemichorea, hysterical Hemichorea caused by hysteria.

hemichorea, paralytic Hemichorea occurring with hemiplegia.

hemichorea, post-hemiplegic Hemichorea which occurs following an attack of hemiplegia.

hemichorea, preparalytic Hemichorea which occurs before an attack of hemiplegia.

hemichorea, rheumatica Hemichorea occurring concomitant with rheumatism.

hemichorea, syphilitic Hemichorea caused by syphilis.

hemicrania 1. Migraine. 2. Pain occurring on one side of the head. 3. Partial anencephalia.

hemiopia See *hemianopia.*

hemiparesis Paresis of one side of the body.

hemiplegia Paralysis of one side of the body.

hemiplegia cruciata Paralysis of an upper extremity and a lower extremity of the opposite side.

hemiplegic gait See *gait, hemiplegic.*

hemispheres The two symmetrical halves into which the cerebrum is divided.

hemispherical dominance The tendency of one side of the body to control bodily movements resulting in laterality.

hemophilus influenzae meningitis See *meningitis, hemophilus influenzae.*

hemophobia Fear of blood.

hemoptysis, hysterical The spitting of blood caused by a psychic disorder.

hemorrhagic arsphenamine encephalitis See *encephalitis, hemorrhagic arsphenamine.*

hemothymia Morbid impulse for blood and murder.

Henle, Mary (1913-) American psychologist. Investigated substitution and other problems of topological psychology. (With MacKinnon) wrote an early laboratory manual in psychodynamics. Edited two volumes of papers on Gestalt psychology. Showed that deductive reasoning does not violate the rules of inference and conducted other studies of cognitive processes. Undertook studies in the history of psychology and systematic analyses of current theories.

hepatic Referring to the liver.

hepatolenticular degeneration See *Wilson's disease.*

Herbart, Johann Friedrich (1776-1841) German philosopher-psychologist, pioneer of quantitative psychology and, according to some, the first educational psychologist. Developed a mathematical theory of how ideas compete for a place in consciousness. His pedagogy was based on the concept of the *apperceptive mass*, the ideas presently in consciousness that determine its receptivity to new ideas.

Herbartian psychology (J. F. Herbart) A mechanistic version of the associationist psychology which emphasizes the competitiveness of ideas to reach consciousness. The central thesis of this system is the doctrine of apperception according to which new ideas must be related to a previously acquired mass of ideas, the apperceptive mass, before they can be understood.

herbivorous 1. Plant-eating. 2. (T. Bryant) A body type characterized by an athletic build.

Herculeus morbus Obsolete term for epilepsy.

herd instinct The tendency in certain animals to congregate in flocks or herds.

hereditarianism The point of view which emphasizes the importance of heredity in determining behavioral traits.

hereditary; hereditarial Referring to the mechanism of transmitting traits from generation to generation and to the characteristics to which one is predisposed resulting from the working of this mechanism.

hereditary predispostion An inborn tendency toward a particular disorder whose development depends on environmental influence.

heredito-constitutional Aspects of an organism's constitution which reflect the genotype.

heredity The process of transmitting characteristics from the progenitor to the offspring which is a function of genes found in chromosomes in the nucleus of each cell. These chromosomes are made of deoxyribonucleic acid (DNA) which contains a code determining particular characteristics of an organism. Hereditary transmission is restricted to the action of the sex cells, the sperm and ova, which fuse to form the new organism.

heredity, polygenic Heredity involving many different genes which are expressed in one phenotype.

hereism The existence of virtue, goodness and morality in the role of wife and mother named after Hera, the wife of Zeus.

Hering, Ewald (1834-1918) Physiologist at Prague who proposed an influential three-cone opponent-process theory of color vision. The cold colors (green, blue and black) result in anabolism, the warm (red, yellow and white) in catabolism of the photochemical substance in the retinal cones. Inventor of research apparatus and contributor to the psychology of memory.

Hering illusion See *illusion, Hering.*

Hering's after-image The positive afterimage perceived following a brief bright stimulus of the same hue and saturation as the original.

Hering's grays A set of fifty gray papers ordered from extreme white to extreme black in subjectively equal steps.

Hering's theory of color vision See *color vision, theory of: Hering theory.*

Hering's window An apparatus used to obtain colored contrast effects. This is a double window with a gray opening and another opening for a colored glass. Any intensities of the lights from the two halves of the window can be controlled by slides to eliminate brightness effects. Objects seen through this apparatus are of the same or complementary color depending on the color of the glass in the opening of the window.

heritable Inheritable.

heritable variation The variation existing in a species which is transmitted by the genes.

heritage 1. Characteristics transmitted biologically from generation to generation. 2. Social customs, traditions and mores transmitted from generation to generation.

hermaphrodite A bisexual (or ambisexual) individual. Such an individual has the external genital organs (penis or vagina) of one sex and the inner reproductive structure, and/or the gonads, and/or sex chromatin pattern of the other. In some cases the individual possesses genital organs of both sexes.

hero-birth, primordial image of (C. G. Jung) Source of the dream symbol of the individuality of a person on an unconscious level.

hero-worship (psychoanalysis) The tendency of people to seek another person to admire and to submit to as a prototype of the father whom they need and long for.

heroimania Morbid passion for heroin.

heroin A narcotic derivative of morphine which was formerly used as a sedative. Its manufacture or importation into the United States is presently prohibited due to the high danger of addiction and damage to mental and physical health.

herpes simplex encephalitis See *encephalitis, herpes simplex.*

Herpes zoster A skin eruption characteristic of inflammation of spinal or cranial ganglia of sensory nerves.

Herring revision A 1922 revision of the Simon-Binet intelligence test which was used as an alternate in place of the 1916 Stanford scale.

Hertwig-Magendie phenomenon (O. Hertwig and F. Magendie) A downward and inward deviation of the eyeball on one side and an upward and outward rotation of the eyeball on the opposite side sometimes charactertistic of a cerebellar lesion.

hertz (hz) Cycles per second; a specification of energy in waves, usually used for auditory stimuli.

hetaera; hetera Mistress, concubine.

hetaerism Referring to a common law marriage.

heterocentric Directed toward others, away from oneself.

heterochrony 1. A difference in the speed between two processes. 2. A difference in the time of development of an organ from the norm. 3. A difference in the chronaries of functionally related tissue parts.

heterodox 1. Referring to opinions and beliefs which differ from those which are generally accepted. 2. Characterizing a person who holds such beliefs.

heteroerotic Referring to sexual interest for persons other than oneself.

heteroerotism Sexual interest in persons other than oneself, especially of the opposite sex.

heterogamous Referring to the differences in the male and female gamete.

heterogeneity; heterogeny Referring to differences and dissimilarities of objects in organisms.

heterogeneous; heterogenous Characterized by heterogeneity.

hetero-hypnosis Hypnosis effected by one person on another.

heterolalia See *heterophemy.*

heteromorphosis The development of an organ or a part of an organ abnormal to the site after the removal of the original organ.

heteronomous super-ego See *super-ego, heteronomous.*

heteronomy 1. (A. Angyal) Referring to activities whose source is outside the self. 2. Referring to the direction of one person by another.

heteronymous hemianopsia See *hemianopsia, heteronymous*.

heterophasia See *heterophemy*.

heterophemy The unconscious unintended substitution of words for the desired ones.

heterophilic Characterized by interest in the opposite sex.

heterophonic An abnormal change of voice.

heterophoria Deviation of one eye from the correct position necessary for binocular vision resulting from a muscular imbalance.

heterorexia Morbid appetite.

heteroscendasticity Referring to a matrix in which the arrays have significantly different standard deviations.

heterosexual Referring to attraction for members of the opposite sex.

heterosexual nymphomania See *nymphomania, heterosexual*.

heterosexuality 1. Attraction for persons of the opposite sex. 2. A developmental level characterized by attraction for the opposite sex or the occurrence of sexual intercourse between members of the opposite sex. 3. The occurrence of sexual intercourse between members of the opposite sex.

heterosis An increase in growth and a healthier development manifested by first-generation hybrids.

heterosociality Social relationships with people of the opposite sex.

heterosomal Referring to the sex chromosome.

heterosome The chromosome which carries sex determinants.

hetero-suggestibility The influence of one person over another.

hetero-suggestion Suggestion which originates in another person.

heterotopia 1. The occurrence of an organ or part of an organ in an unnatural location. 2. The congenital development of gray matter of the spinal cord in the white matter area.

heterotropia See *strabismus*.

heterozygosis Having one or more heterozygous pairs of genes resulting from crossbreeding.

heterozygosity See *heterozygousness*.

heterozygote An individual who has two different alleles at a given locus on a pair of homologous chromosomes. Adjective: heterozygous.

heterozygotic, heterozygous Referring to heterozygote.

heterozygousness Refers to the condition of heterozygosis.

heuristic method Method which leads to the discovery of new thinking and investigation.

Heymans' law (C. Heymans) The law relating the threshold value of a stimulus to a simultaneously occurring inhibitory stimulus by the equation: $T_a = T_O + K_a$ where T_O is the threshold of a given stimulus, T_a is the threshold of the stimulus when it is raised by the occurrence of a second stimulus of intensity x and K_a is the coefficient of inhibition which is different in different modalities and with different individuals.

hibernation 1. The state of sleep during the winter characteristic of many animals. 2. A type of therapy using high dosages of chlorpromazine to produce prolonged sleep with a lowered body temperature.

hibernation of ament The loss of intellectual energy during the winter characteristic of imbecility.

hiccup, hysterical Hiccough due to mental causes.

hidden-clue test or situation A test requiring the subject to discover which aspect of the situation will lead to a reward.

hidden figure See *embedded figure*.

hidden self The dissociated aspect of the personality.

hierarchy correlation See *correlation, hierarchy*.

hierarchy of habits See *habit hierarchy*.

hieroglyphics A form of writing in which the symbols are pictures designating the word which is represented.

hieromania Mania for religion.

hieronosus (Linnaeus) Epilepsy.

hierophobia Fear of religious things.

high-grade defective See *defective, high-grade*.

higher centers; higher brain centers 1. Centers of the brain making up the cerebrum. 2. Centers of the brain concerned with complex functions such as learning, memory and intelligence.

higher level skills (R. H. Seashore) Work technique applicable to a variety of concrete tasks rather than a particular one.

higher mental processes See *mental processes, higher*.

higher mental processes, organization of See *mental processes, higher, organization of*.

higher-order conditioning See *conditioning, higher-order*.

higher response unit 1. A group of stimuli treated as a single stimulus. 2. A complex act formed by integrating simpler acts.

Hilgard, Ernest R(opiequet) (1904-) American psychologist and educator, known primarily for his earlier work on conditioned responses and theories of learning and his later work on experimental studies of hypnosis. His general position is a broadly heuristic one, often known in America as functional psychology. The position is represented in his general textbook of psychology and in his occasional writings on education, psychoanalysis, and social problems. See *conditioned responses; functionalism; learning theory; educational psychology;* and *hypnosis.*

hindbrain The part of the brain made up of the cerebellum, pons and medulla.

Hipp chronoscope (M. Hipp) A clock developed in 1842 and used in reaction-time experiments capable of recording time-intervals of 1/1000 of a second.

hippanthropy The belief that one is a horse.

hippocampus A large nuclear mass consisting of gray matter lying in the floor of the inferior horn of the lateral ventricle.

hippus Independent spasmotic pupillary motion.

hircine Pertaining to a cheese-like smell.

histidinemia A rare aminoaciduria associated with mental retardation.

histogram A graphic representation of a frequency distribution in the form of rectangular bars whose width is equal to the interval of the class and whose height reflects the number of cases in each class.

histology The branch of biology which deals with the study of the structure of tissues.

historical method (G. W. Allport) The study of individuals by tracing their life events.

histrionic personality disorder See *hysterical character.*

hit (psychophysics) A correct detection of a stimulus by the subject.

HIT See *Holtzman Inkblot Technique.*

Hitzig's girdle (E. Hitzig) Insensitivity to pain at the level of the breast which is a sign of tabes dorsalis.

hoarding orientation (E. Fromm) A non-productive life style consisting of the proclivity toward keeping one's feelings, thoughts and possessions to oneself as a means of security.

Hobbes, Thomas (1588-1679) English philosopher who countered Descartes' doctrine of innate ideas and foreshadowed the thesis of the mind as the tabula rasa in his theory that sense experience forms the content of the mind.

Hoch, Paul Kerry (1902-1964) Hungarian born American neuropsychiatrist, specialized in psychosomatic medicine, community psychiatry and hospital adminstration; was a New York State Commissioner of Mental Health.

hodological space (K. Lewin) A psychological space which differs from Euclidian space in that direction between regions is important and because the distance between regions is determined by the dynamic qualities of the regions, not by the absolute measure.

hodology (K. Lewin) The science of vectors, paths and the direction, distance and force which these locomotions represent reflecting motivations and tensions which guide behavior.

hodophobia Fear of traveling.

Hoffman (or Trommer's) sign (J. Hoffman) The snapping of the index or ring finger which produces the flexion of the thumb is a sign of hemisplegia of organic origin.

hog A slang term for a heroin addict who progressively increases his dose.

holergasia (A. Meyer) A psychosis which disrupts the entire personality.

holergasic, holergastic Referring to holergasia.

holism (K. Goldstein) The principle that an organism is not equal to the sum of its parts and must be studied as a whole. Biological phenomena such as a living organism cannot be evaluated quantitatively but must be described in terms of their qualitative organizations. Increasing knowledge of separate, individual parts does not augment our understanding of the totality except by understanding these parts as expressions of the functioning of the organism as a whole.

holistic psychology (A. Maslow) Human beings are fundamentally good and healthy. A full healthy and normal development consists of actualizing oneself and fulfilling one's potentialities. Human needs and motives must be presented in a hierarchical order starting with the most powerful physiological needs such as hunger and thirst, then safety, belongingness, love, esteem, and cognitive and esthetic needs.

holistic theory of intelligence The principle that intelligence is a function of the cerebrum as a whole.

holistic theory of personality See *holism.*

Holmes, Gordon, rebound phenomenon See *rebound phenomenon of Gordon Holmes.*

Holmgren test See *test, Holmgren.*

Holmgren wools The differently colored skeins of wool used in a test for colorblindness.

holograph A document in the handwriting of the author.

Holt, Robert R. (1917-   ) American psychologist. Developed methods of selecting psychiatric residents, and offered a resolution of the controversy over clinical vs. statistical prediction. Founded and directed (with G.S. Klein) a major center for experimental studies of psychoanalytic propositions (Research Center for Mental Health, NYU); developed a technique for objectively measuring adaptive and maladaptive regression (the primary process and its control) in Rorschach responses, dreams, and other verbal data, and applied it in studies of sensory deprivation, creativity, and LSD effects. Contributed to the clarification and critique of psychoanalytic and personality theories. Methodological and applied studies of personality assessment in clinical and social problems.

Holtzman Inkblot Technique (W. H. Holtzman) A projective test developed in 1961 consisting of forty-five inkblots plus two practice blots. The inkblots vary in color, symmetry, form and shading. The subject is asked to give one response to what he sees after which the examiner conducts a brief inquiry. There are two alternate forms allowing for the determination of test-retest rehability and the study of change within an individual. Factor analysis has shown that six variables are tapped: perceptual maturity and integrated ideational activity, perceptual sensitivity, psychopathology of thought, perceptual differentiation, inhibition or inability to perceive; and bodily preoccupation. The last three factors are not stable and differ according to the population tested.

homeopathic principle See *principle, isopathic.*

homeosis, homoeosis The development of an organ in an abnormal site.

homeostasis The maintenance of equilibrium among the bodily processes.

homeostatic systems 1. Mechanisms which maintain a homeostatic balance. 2. Physiological process which maintains internal stability in an organism whereby changes in the internal or external environment stimulate other processes to counteract these changes through a feedback mechanism. These mechanisms account for several aspects of innate behavior.

homichlophobia Fear of fog.

homicidomania A mania for killing.

homilophobia 1. Fear of sermons. 2. A fear that people in a group will criticize one's appearance.

homing The tendency and ability to return to the original home when removed to a distance characteristic of certain animal species.

homocystinuria Mental deficiency recessively inherited, associated with ocular changes including subluxated lenses. Homocystine is excreted in urine.

homoerotism, homoeroticism Erotic or libidinal feeling directed to a person of the same sex.

homogametic Producing one kind of germ cells. Females have XX chromosomes and are homogametic.

homogamous Evincing qualities of homogamy.

homogamy 1. Inbreeding in a genetically isolated group resulting in the development of similar traits among the members of the group. 2. A similiarity in trait or traits among husband and wife.

homogeneity; homogeny 1. The quality of likeness found in a group of people, data, or objects. 2. The measure of one single variable by items on a test.

homogeneity, test for See *test of independence.*

homogeneous reinforcement See *reinforcement, homogeneous.*

homogenitality Interest in the genitals of the same sex; homosexuality.

homology Correspondence of structure of organs but not necessarily of their function suggesting common ancestry.

homonomy drive See *drive, homonomy.*

homonymous hemianopsia See *hemianopsia, homonymous.*

homoscedasticity A double-entry table possessing the characteristic of its entries having equal variability.

homosexual impulses Sexual impulses directed toward a person of the same sex.

homosexuality 1. Sexual intercourse with a member of the same sex. 2. Sexual feelings for a member of the same sex.

homosociality Social relations with members of the same sex.

homozygote An individual possessing a pair of identical alleles at a given locus on a pair of homologous chromosomes.

Honi phenomenon The absence of the illusion effect of a distorted room in the Ames experiment when the subject is looking at a person whom he knows.

horizontal-vertical illusion See *illusion, horizontal-vertical.*

horme (W. McDougall) The urge to live which is the main purpose of all living organisms.

hormic psychology (W. McDougall) A theory of psychology introduced in 1908 and subsequently modified, based on the three main assumptions that behavior is purposive, that each individual is endowed with certain purposeful behavioral tendencies called instincts and that the entire behavior is determined by these instincts or their derivatives called sentiments or tastes. The basic construct is horme, the purpose to survive, to live, characteristic of all living organisms. To account for the continuity of evolution, a continuity is postulated between inorganic and organic matter suggesting that some trace of mental structure exists in inorganic matter whose activity is also purposive. Instincts, the inherited psychophysical propensities to action, consist of three kinds of functions; cognitive and conative which can be altered by experience, and affective functions which are inherited and cannot be modified by experience. Acquired behavior, however, can be transmitted to the next generation through genes. Seven primary instincts are postulated, each accompanied by an invariable primary emotion: escape associated with fear, combat, and anger, curiosity and wonder, repulsion and disgust, self assertion and elation, self-abasement and subjection and the parental instinct whose primary affect is tender emotion.

hormic theory (W. McDougall) See *hormic psychology.*

hormone A chemical substance produced in one organ and transported by the blood to other cells of the body where it has a physiological regularity effect.

hormone, adrenocorticotropic Secreted by the anterior pituitary gland. This hormone stimulates the adrenal cortex to secrete steroid hormones which in turn regulate the water balance and expenditure of energy.

hormone, corticotropic A hormone secreted by

the anterior pituitary gland which controls the functioning of the adrenal cortex.

hormones, adrenocortical Hormones secreted by the adrenal cortex which regulates the water balance and expenditure of energy.

hormones, sex Hormones of the male and female which cause the development of secondary sexual characteristics, influence the threshold of arousal, and the emotional manifestations of the sexual drive. Their secretion is affected by the emotional state of the individual.

Horn-Hellersberg Drawing Completion Test See *test, Horn-Hellersberg Drawing Completion.*

Horner's Law The principle that red-green color-blindness is transmitted from male-to male through the female.

Horner's syndrome See *syndrome, Horner's.*

Horney, Karen (1885-1953) Psychiatrist and psychoanalyst. Born in Berlin of Norwegian father and Dutch mother. Taught at Berlin Psychoanalytic Institute (1920-1932). Came to U.S. (1932). After 15 years of practice, part of that time in Germany, in Chicago, and in New York, she switched from Freudian orthodoxy, forming her own group, the American Institute of Psychoanalysis. Challenging the biological assumption of Freudian theory, she developed a neo-Freudian approach, stressing social factors in development and functioning of personality. Author of *The Neurotic Personality of Our Time* (1937); *New Ways in Psychoanalysis* (1939); *Our Inner Conflicts* (1945); and *Neurosis and Human Growth* (1950).

horopter (optics) The locus of points on which two eyes fixate which are reflected on corresponding points in the two retinas.

horoscope 1. A graphic representation of the positions of planets and signs of the zodiac used to predict future events. 2. The prediction of future events using such a diagram.

hospital, day A form of therapeutic facility introduced in the early 1930's which offers a full treatment program to patients who are well enough to remain at home for the night.

hospitalism (R. Spitz) A syndrome resulting from institutionalization in infancy with early separation from the mother characterized by a lag in mental and physical development, apathy, immobility, withdrawal reactions in the presence of strangers, frequent infections, cachexia, and sometimes death.

hostility The desire to harm another person.

House-Tree-Person test See *test, House-Tree-Person.*

Hovland, Carl Iver (1912-1961) Social psychologist (Yale). Collaborator with Hull in early studies of verbal learning. Research on communication and persuasion based on learning theory. Influential in organizational affairs in the social sciences nationally.

Hoyt formula (C. Hoyt) A formula for the computation of the reliability coefficient using analysis of

variance: $r = 1 - \dfrac{V_r}{V_e} = \dfrac{V_e - V_r}{V_e}$ where V_r is the variance for the remainder sum of squares and V_e is the variance for examinees.

H-T-P test See *test, House-Tree-Person.*

hue The perceived dimension of color which corresponds to the wave length of light which stimulates the retina.

Hull, Clark Leonard (1884-1952) American behavioristic psychologist. After early research on thinking, aptitude testing and hypnosis, he created a hypothetico-deductive theory of animal and human learning, in the form of a mathematically based "learning theory," which dominated research and theory in these fields for two decades from about 1930. Intellectual leader of the Yale Institute of Human Relations.

Hull's Mathematico-Deductive Theory of Learning (C.L. Hull) A theory of learning using mathematical equations, definitions and postulates to explain learning phenomena. The attempt is made to explain observable data in terms of neurophysiological events. Seventeen postulates and seventeen corollaries are presented. It is postulated that biological adaptation facilitates the survival of the organism and when this is not facilitated, the organism is in a state of need. When need is aroused, the organism acts to reduce the need. Behavior is thus goal directed toward the reduction of needs. Any behavior which reduces needs or drives (S_1) is a reinforcer. Conditioning or learning will not occur without need reduction, or reinforcement. Under conditions of reinforcement, specific stimuli evoke specific responses called habits. When the reinforcing need is removed, when habits no longer lead to biological adaptation, they become inhibited, weakened or extinguished. The number of reinforcements strengthens the stimulus-response connection or habit strength $(_SH_R)$. The resulting response or reaction potential $(_SE_R)$ is a function of the Drive (D) or (S_D) and of the reinforcement, or habit strength $(_SH_R)$. In the absence of drive or habit strength, performance will not occur. Two types of inhibitions are postulated, reactive (I_R) and conditioned $(_SI_R)$ inhibition. Reactive inhibition is the reaction of the organism to effort caused by fatigue, pain etc. The increase of this inhibition results in its conditioning producing $(_SI_R)$. In the absence of the goal stimulus or reinforcer, a component of the goal response can occur called the fractional anticipatory goal response (R_G). This serves to explain expectant behavior.

human engineering An applied area of psychology and engineering which concerns itself with the design of the physical conditions, machines and other equipment in relation to human capabilities, learning capacities, efficiency and comfort.

Hume, David (1711-1776) Influential Scottish philosopher who wrote a major history of England. He argued that the apparent necessary connection between cause and effect may be an illusion produced by repeated contiguity of "cause" and "effect" in time and space.

Humm-Wadsworth Temperament Scale See *scale, Humm-Wadsworth Temperament.*

humor 1. A positive, pleasant emotional attitude. 2. Any liquid secretion. 3. A comical attitude or expression.

humor, gallows Psychiatric term for humorous behavior under conditions of impending death.

hunger 1. Desire for food. 2. (experimental) Operational definition of a bodily state in terms of the number of hours of food deprivation. 3. Aching sensations in the stomach region due to muscle contractions. 4. A craving for something one is deprived of.

Hunt-Minnesota Test for Organic Brain Damage See *test, Hunt-Minnesota, for Organic Brain Damage.*

Hunter group A mucopolysaccharidosis inherited in a sex-linked recessive manner; similar to Hurler's syndrome but affected children are not as severely retarded in motor or intellectual development.

Huntington's chorea (G. Huntington) A chronic, progressive hereditary disease which is characterized by irregular movements, disturbance of speech and gradually increasing impairment of intellectual functioning.

Hurler's syndrome A mucopolysaccharidosis carried by single recessive genes, characterized by short stature, unusual skeletal deformities, grotesque facial features, deafness, congenital heart disease, mental retardation, and sometimes clouding of the corneas.

Hurst, Lewis Alfred (1911-   ) South African psychiatrist, whose main contributions have been in the areas of psychiatric genetics, electroencephalographic findings in schizophrenia, manic depressive psychosis, senility and the senile psychoses, and in transcultural psychiatry, notably psychopathology and attitudes to mental health in an urban Bantu group.

Husserl, Edmund Philosopher, born 1859, in Prossnitz, Mähren (now Prostejov, Moravia, Czechoslovakia) and died 1938 in Freiburg, Baden-Württemberg. Studied with Stumpf and Brentano and was for a short time an assistant to Weierstrass. Received Ph.D. in 1881. Taught as Privatdozent in Halle 1887-1901, as professor at Göttingen 1901-1916 and at Freiburg from 1916 until his forced retirement by the Nazis. His fundamental goal was a search for the "unshakable foundation of human knowledge." He distinguished sharply between psychology (an empirical science) and logic (an *a priori* science); between science (what is) and ethics (what ought to be); between philosophy viewed as an *a priori* discipline and viewed as historically relative. Paralleling the world of science is the *Lebenswelt*, the study of which is the first task of phenomenology. Husserl distinguished between an empirical and an *a priori* psychology. The former is concerned with the empirical ego and contents of thought of other persons; the latter is concerned with the transcendental ego, intentionality, and mental acts. For Husserl the primary goal is the description of pure intentionality. not objects-as-intended, Brentano's realistic position. Starting from a position near that of Stumpf and Brentano, he developed from a critical realism to a critical idealism. He strongly influenced Scheler, Heidegger, and Merleau-Ponty. Major works of interest to psychologists are: 1) *Die Idee der Phänomenologie: Vorlesungen* (1907) 2) *Cartesian Meditations* (1931) 3) *Die Krisis der Europäschen Wissenschaften und Die Transzendentale Phänomenologie* (1939—not completed at his death)

hybrid 1. The progeny of parents who belong to two different species. 2. The offspring of parents, one of whom has and one of whom lacks a particular unit character.

hydraulic theory of hearing See *hearing, theory of: hydraulic theory.*

hydrocephalus Enlargement of the cranium resulting from an excess of cerebrospinal fluid. Retardation is usually severe or profound.

hydrocephaly See *hydrocephalus.*

hydrochloric acid A strong acid present in gastric juices in a diluted form. Also called HCL.

hydrodipsomania Excessive thirst which occurs periodically.

hydro-encephalocele An aberration of brain development in which the brain cavity protruding from the skull connects with the cerebral ventricles.

hydromyelia A dilation of the central canal of the spinal cord associated with an increase of fluid in this canal due to tumors of cerebellum or injuries to the spinal chord or characterized by atrophy of the gray matter.

hydromyelocele The existence of an excess of fluid in the central canal of the spinal cord.

hydrophobia 1. Fear of water. 2. Rabies.

hydrotherapy Therapeutic treatment of disease using water administered internally or externally.

hydroxyprolinemia A rare aminoaciduria associated with mental retardation.

hyelophobia Fear of glass.

hygiene, mental The branch of hygiene dealing with the prevention of mental disorder and the preservation and maintenance of optimal modes of living and emotional health.

hygrophobia Morbid fear of moisture.

hylephobia Fear of forests.

hypacusia Partial impairment of hearing.

hypalgia, hysterical A decrease in the normal sensitivity of pain in various areas of the body of psychogenic origin. The insensitivity is a defense against repressed unconscious wishes which would cause anxiety if allowed to reach consciousness.

hyperactive Overactive.

hyperacusia, hyperacuses Supersensitivity of hearing.

hyperadrenocorticism A condition involving the overproduction of hormones of the adrenal cortex or the hyperfunctioning of the pituitary gland. It results in Cushing's syndrome.

hyperalgesia Excessive sensitivity to pain.

hyperalgia See *hyperalgesia.*

hyperammonemia A metabolic disorder associated with mental retardation and characterized by episodic vomiting, lethargy, stupor, decline of vision and microcephaly.

hyperbilirubinemia, neonatal A condition characterized by an excessive amount of bilirubin in the blood, often resulting in severe neurological involvement and severe psychological problems in the child.

hypercalcemia Excessive calcium in the blood causing suppression of CNS activity leading to coma.

hypercathexis The overcharge of psychic energy.

hypercathexis, self The overinvestment of psychic energy in oneself, seen in narcissistic individuals.

hyperenesthesia A feeling of extreme well-being.

hyperepidosis An excessive growth of a part of the body.

hyperergasia (A.Meyer) The manic, overactive state of manic-depressive psychosis.

hyperesophoria An upward and inward deviation of the eye due to a muscular imbalance.

hyperesthesia Excessive sensitivity especially to tactile stimuli.

hyperexophoria An upward and outward deviation of the eye due to a muscular imbalance.

hyperfunction Excessive functioning.

hypergenitalism Excessive development of the genital system.

hyperglycemia An excess of sugar in the blood commonly caused by diabetes mellitus. If untreated leads to diabetic acidosis and coma.

hypergnosis, hypergnosia The projection of inner conflicts onto the environment.

hyperhistidinemia A possibly hereditary metabolic disorder associated with mental retardation and characterized by speech defect.

hyperinstrumental neurosis See *neurosis, hyperinstrumental.*

hyperinsulinism An intermittent or continuous condition causing loss of consciousness caused by excessive production of insulin leading to hypoglycemia.

hyperkinesis Excessive movement or motor restlessness.

hyperkinesthesia Extreme sensitivity to sensations of the muscles, tendons and joints.

hyperlogia Excessive volubility of speech characteristic of excited psychotic states.

hyperlysinemia A rare aminoaciduria associated with mental retardation.

hypermania An extreme manic state characterized by excessive activity and excitement.

hypermetropia A condition of the eye in which incoming parallel light rays focus behind the retina due to an abnormal shortness of the eyeball or to subnormal refraction.

hypermnesia Unusual, exaggerated ability to remember.

hyperopia See *hypermetropia.*

hyperorexia Excessive desire for food.

hyperosmia Exaggerated sensitivity to odors.

hyperphagia Excessive eating. May be caused by diabetes mellitus or bilateral lesions in the ventromedial hypothalamus.

hyperphasia See *hyperlogia.*

hyperphoria An upward deviation of the eye due to a muscular imbalance.

hyperpituitary constitution See *constitution, hyperpituitary.*

hyperplasia Excessive multiplication of cells resulting in an increase in the size of tissues, organs, and bodily parts.

hyperpnoea Excessive rate of breathing.

hyperprolinemia A rare aminoaciduria associated with mental retardation.

hyperprosexia Exaggerated compulsive attention to a particular stimulus.

hypersarcosinemia A rare aminoaciduria associated with mental retardation.

hypersexuality An excessive need or existence of sexual activity.

hypersomnia Excessive sleepiness.

hypersthenic Referring to a condition marked by excessive lymphatic functioning and extreme tension and strength.

hypertelorism Excessive distance between two parts or organs.

hypertension, essential Chronic condition of high blood pressure without any discernible organic cause. The early phase of hypertension can be produced by emotional conflicts, physical work, and renal ischemia.

hyperthymia 1. Excessive sensitiveness. 2. Labile, excessive emotionality. 3. State of overactivity. 4. Extreme cruelty or recklessness.

hyperthyroidism A condition of excessive thyroid function characterized by an increased metabolic rate, restlessness and excitability and resulting in death if untreated.

hypertonicity, hypertonia Excessive state of tension in the muscles.

hypertrophy Excessive growth of an organ or tissue due to the multiplication of its cells.

hypervalinemia A rare aminoaciduria associated with mental retardation.

hypervectorial cathexis See *cathexis, hypervectorial.*

hypervectorial childhood neurosis See *neurosis, hypervectorial childhood.*

hypervectorial neurosis See *neurosis, hypervectorial.*

hypervectorial type See *type, hypervectorial.*

hypesthesia; hypaesthesia Impairment of sensitivity to tactile stimulation.

hyphedonia State in which diminution of pleasure sensations occurs in acts which normally give great pleasure.

hypnagogic Inducing sleep; pertaining to the beginning state of sleep.

hypnagogic imagery See *imagery, hypnagogic.*

hypnagogic intoxication See *intoxication, hypnagogic.*

hypnagogic phenomena See *phenomena, hypnagogic.*

hypnagogic reverie See *reverie, hypnagogic.*

hypnagogic visions See *imagery, hypnagogic.*

hypnalgia 1. Pain sensations occurring during sleep. 2. Pain occurring in dreams.

hypnenergia Obsolete term for somnambulism.

hypnic Pertaining to or causing sleep.

hypnoanalysis A form of psychotherapy combining psychoanalytic technique with hypnosis.

hypnobades Obsolete term referring to somnambulist.

hypnobadicus Obsolete term for, relating to, or affected by somnambulism.

hypnobains Obsolete term for somnambulism.

hypnobat Somnambulist; one who walks in his sleep.

hypnobatesis Obsolete term for somnambulism.

hypnobatia Obsolete term for somnambulism.

hypnocarcosis Deep state of sleep induced by hypnosis.

hypnocatharsis Free association while in a hypnotic state.

hypnodia Somnolence.

hypnodrama (J. L. Moreno and J. M. Enneis) A therapuetic technique used when the patient is under hypnosis of dramatizing the patient's conflict with the participation of the therapist or a professional actor in one of the roles.

hypnogenic Producing sleep or hypnosis.

hypnogenic spot See *spot, hypnogenic.*

hypnogenic zone See *spot, hypnogenic.*

hypnograph Instrument measuring physiological functions during sleep.

hypnoid Resembling hypnotic state or sleep.

hypnoidal Mild hypnotic state.

hypnolepsy Narcolepsy.

hypnology The science of hypnotism and sleep.

hypnonergia Obsolete term for somnambulism.

hypnopathy Narcolepsy.

hypnophobia Fear of falling asleep.

hypnophrenosis (C. H. Schutze) Pertaining to various types of sleep disturbance.

hypnopompic Pertaining to the state of awakening.

hypnosigenesis Hypnotic induction.

hypnosigenic Pertaining to hypnotic induction.

hypnosis An artificially induced sleep-like state characterized by increased suggestibility, decreased initiative and will to act on one's own, recollection of events not remembered in the normal state, and often amnesia for that which occurred while hypnotized. The hypnotic state may be superficial or deep depending on the subject's susceptibility. Anesthesia, paralysis and vaso-motor changes can be induced or removed under deep hypnosis. Hypnosis was first brought to psychologists' attention when A. Mesmer demonstrated his "animal magnetism" and "magnetic fluid." Though these concepts were rejected, suggestion and influencing others' minds were recognized as true phenomenon and named hypnotism by J. Braid, a British surgeon. Later, the French physician, A. Liebeault, published a book describing methods of treatment with the use of hypnosis. J. M. Charcot followed with proof that hysterical symptoms could be produced and removed by hypnotic suggestion. Hypnosis has been used in therapeutic treatment of neurotics since the time of S. Freud and J. Breuer.

hypnosis, catalyzing action of The use of hypnosis during various phases of psychotherapy for accelerating the recovery of unconscious material.

hypnosis, induction of The process by which a hypnotist hypnotizes a subject. One of several techniques such as verbal suggestion and/or mechanical or chemical aids may be used depending on the hypnotist's preference and skill, and on the subject's needs and susceptibility. Most techniques have in common the subject's fixation of attention to some small object and the reduction in usual sensory input and motor output through relaxation.

hypnosynthesis (J. H. Conn) A term for hypnotherapy which stresses its function in allowing the patient to view and evaluate his experience objectively and to understand his motives for his behavior.

hypnotherapy Psychotherapeutic treatment by means of hypnosis.

hypnotic 1. Pertaining to hypnosis. 2. A drug that induces sleep.

hypnotism The theory and practice of hypnosis.

hypnotizability Hypnotic susceptibility.

hypoacusia See *hypacusia.*

hypoadrenal constitution See *constitution, hypoadrenal.*

hypoaffective type See *type, hypoaffective.*

hypoalgesia Diminished sensibility to pain.

hypobulia Deficiency of will power.

hypocalcemia A disorder involving lowered calcium level in the blood. Associated with increased neuromuscular irritability leading to spasms. An idopathic form involves mental retardation.

hypocathexis The undercharge of psychic energy.

hypocathexis, self The underinvestment of psychic energy in oneself resulting from object hypercathexis.

hypochondria Hypochondriasis.

hypochondriasis An exaggerated and morbid concern with one's health often focused on a single organ and accompanied by the belief that one is plagued by serious bodily illnesses. It may occur as a specific neurosis or in association with other neurotic disorders.

hypochondrophthisis A rarely used term for body atrophy in hypochondriasis.

hypochoresis Defecation.

hypodermic 1. Referring to the area under the skin. 2. Placed under the skin. 3. An injection given beneath the skin. 4. The syringe used in a hypodermic injection.

hypoergasia Depressive stage in manic depressive psychosis.

hypoevolutism Inadequate morphological, physiological and psychological development. Term may pertain to either specific or general functions.

hypofunction Diminished function or activity.

hypogenitalism Various types of deficient genital development.

hypoglossal nerve See *nerve, hypoglossal.*

hypoglossal nucleus Mass of cell bodies in the lower medulla in which the hypoglossal nerve originates.

hypoglycemia Condition caused by low level of glucose in the blood due to excessive utilization of sugar or to interference with the formation of sugar in the blood. In newborns, symptoms may include tremors, cyanosis, seizures, respiratory problems and eye rolling. Later in life, symptoms associated with hypoglycemia are nervousness, profuse sweating and dizziness. There is an approximately 60 percent occurrence of mental retardation in children who develop hypoglycemia in the first year of life.

hypoglycemia, ketotic Symptoms of hypoglycemia occur after a short fast; can be precipitated by a high fat and low carbohydrate diet. Seen most frequently in children between 18 months and three years of age.

hypoglycemic therapy See *insulin shock therapy.*

hypognathous Condition of abnormally small lower jaw.

hypokinesis Abnormal reduction of muscle movement.

hypologia Abnormal poverty of speech usually of an organic nature.

hypomagnesemia A disorder of magnesium metabolism resulting in muscle spasm, tetany and seizures.

hypomania Generalized term for a mild form of mania.

hypomotility Hypokinesis.

hyponatremia A disorder involving low levels of blood sodium. Symptoms may include headache, lethargy, ataxia, hypertension. Seizures frequently occur in affected young children and infants. Death may occur in acute phase. Those surviving may suffer retardation, seizures and spasticity.

hyponoia Rare term for hypopsychosis.

hypopancreatic constitution See *constitution, hypopancreatic.*

hypoparathyroid constitution See *constitution, hypoparathyroid.*

hypophonia Incomplete use of voice due to uncoordination of the muscles used in sound production.

hypophoria A downward deviation of the eye due to a muscular imbalance.

hypophrasia Slowness or lack of speech such as is seen in depression. Bradyphasia.

hypophrenia Mental deficiency.

hypophrenosis (E. E. Southard) Feeblemindedness.

hypophysectomy Surgical removal of the pituitary body.

hypophysis; hypophysis cerebri See *gland, pituitary.*

hypopituitarianism Inadequate production of the pituitary hormones possibly resulting in impotence, sterility, amenorrhea, hypoglycemia, signs of adrenal cortical failure, hypometabolism and shrinkage of tissue and viscera.

hypopituitary constitution See *constitution, hypopituitary.*

hypoplasia 1. Underdevelopment of any tissue. 2. Refers to a manikin or a dwarf when relating to the whole organism.

hypoprosessis See *hypoprosexia.*

hypoprosexia Inadequate attentive ability.

hypopsychosis Diminution of mental activity.

hyposomia Condition resulting from inadequate amount of sleeping time.

hypostatic Referring to those combinations of non-allelic genes or hereditary factors which are mashed by other such combinations, the epistatic, in the genetic process of epistasis.

hypostenia Deficient strength; weakness.

hypotaxia, hypotaxis See *suggestion, affective.*

hypotension, orthostatic Low blood pressure when erect due to organic causes such as diabetes, multiple sclerosis, and adrenal malfunctions or seen as a side effect produced by antihypertensive or tranquilizing drugs.

hypothalamotomy Psychosurgical procedure causing partial ablation of the hypothalamic area.

hypothalamus Grouping of small nuclei forming part of the diencephalon and generally lying at the junction of the midbrain and thalamus. It is the most important central brain structure involved with autonomic nervous system functions, and together with its connections to the limbic system, is thought to play a major role in emotion and motivation.

hypothalamus, lateral The part of the hypothalamus responsible for the control of hunger arousal and food-related activity.

hypothesis **1.** An assumption; a guess. **2.** A tentative statement to be proven or disproven by evidence.

hypothesis, alternative **1.** (statistics) A statement contrary to the null hypothesis. It is known as H_A or H_1. **2.** (R. A. Fisher) A statement that the null hypothesis is false. If H_O = O, then $H_A \neq$ O where H_O is the null hypothesis, H_A is the alternative hypothesis, = means equal to, and ≠ means not equal to. **3.** (J. Neyman and E. S. Pearson) An exact alternate to the null hypothesis which makes the power analysis possible. If H_O=0, then H_A= specific number, where H_O is the null hypothesis, H_A is the alternative hypothesis, = means equal to.

hypothesis, double bind (G. Bates et al.) The theory that schizophrenia often develops in children who are involved in double bind situations. The child is faced with contradictory messages from his parents. However, the situation is not readily visible as such because the messages are sent on different levels or because of denial. The child cannot escape from the situation or comment on the contradiction, and feels damned regardless of whatever he does.

hypothesis (in animal learning) (D. Krech) A term applied to a type of response (whether correct or wrong) displayed by many species during the course of discrimination learning. As originally used by Krech, an hypothesis is a response pattern which can be demonstrated to be (1) systematic (occurring at a frequency beyond chance expectations), (2) purposive (persistence ultimately conditional upon goal attainment), (3) abstractive (guided by attributes common to a set of varying stimuli-configurations), (4) autonomous (reflecting the animal's predilections

and past experiences). See *continuity-non-continuity* (in learning theory).

hypothesis, mediumistic (H. G. Baynes) Hypothesis that the schizophrenic person is closer than others to the collective unconscious, is better able to foresee the unconscious trend of events and can therefore recognize early indications of his own disintegration.

hypothesis, Neyman-Pearson (statistics) A type of alternative hypothesis which states the exact size of the non-zero effect.

hypothesis, null (statistics) An hypothesis stating that an experimental effect does not exist, that the mean of a group is equal to zero, or that there is no difference between means. It is also known as H_O.

hypothetical construct See *construct, hypothetical.*

hypothetical process variable See *variable, hypothetical process.*

hypothetical state variable See *variable, hypothetical state.*

hypothetico-deductive method (C. L. Hull) A three-step research method applying rigorous deduction from a priori set principles. A system of clear and consistent definitions is introduced, followed by the proposal of a series of highly conceptualized postulates. From these, a series of detailed theorems is rigorously deduced.

hypothymia A condition of subnormal intensity of emotions; depression; despondency.

hypothyroid Inadequate thyroid secretion.

hypothyroidism A condition caused by a deficiency of thyroid hormones, expressed in advanced state as cretinism or myxedema and in mild form as a state having subnormal basal metabolic rates.

hypothyrosis Hypothyroidism.

hypotonia; hypotony Diminution of normal tension especially introcular pressure.

hypotonic **1.** Subnormal tension or strength. **2.** Pertaining to a solution whose osmotic pressure is less than any other solution taken as standard.

hypovigility Subnormal awareness or response to external stimuli, characteristically seen in all categories of schizophrenia.

hypoxemia A condition of deficient oxygen in the blood.

hypoxia A state in which there is an insufficient amount of oxygen available.

hypsophobia Fear of high places.

hysteria A mental disorder characterized primarily by dissociation, repression, emotional instability, suggestibility and a variety of psychogenic functional disorders. In the psychoanalytic system, it is classified as a psychoneurosis, two types being distinguished: the conversion type, comprised of mainly somatic symptoms often mimicking organic diseases; and the dissociative type, including alterations in conscious awareness such as amnesia, sleep-walking and split personalities.

Hippocrates coined the term from the Greek word hysteron, meaning uterus. Originally it was applied to a convulsive condition occurring in widows and spinsters presumably due to migration of the uterus. Freud followed by ascribing the cause of his patients functional disorders to frustrated sexual needs. The symptoms are still most commonly thought to arise from repressed conflicts, usually of a sexual nature.

hysteria, anxiety (S. Freud) A neurosis characterized by extensive use of the defense mechanism of displacement and often reaction formation and manifesting a variety of symptoms including hypochondriac fears, headaches, restlessness, anxiety states and general irritability.

hysteria, combat A functional disorder manifested during combat, the purpose being avoidance of further service in dangerous areas. Termed shell shock during World War I and battle fatigue during World War II.

hysteria, conversion A form of psychoneurosis characterized by the transformation of repressed intrapsychic conflicts into overt physical symptoms which have no physiological basis.

hysteria, epidemic Hysteria which appears to be attributable to interaction with an hysterical environment.

hysteria, fixation Form of hysterical conversion reaction in which a psychological problem manifests itself through a localized physical symptom.

hysteria, major A clinical syndrome characterized by several states: the aura, the stage of epileptoid convulsions, the stage of tonic followed by clonic spasms, the stage of dramatic emotional reactions, the stage of delirium. The stages do not necessarily follow the above order. The attack may last up to one half hour.

hysterical anesthesia See *anesthesia, hysterical.*

hysterical aphonia See *aphonia, hysterical.*

hysterical blindness See *blindness, hysterical.*

hysterical character See *character, hysterical.*

hysterical hypalgia See *hypalgia, hysterical.*

hysterical neurosis See *hysteria.*

hysterical paralysis See *paralysis, hysterical.*

hysterical personality See *character, hysterical.*

hysteriform Behavior disorders particularly of a motor nature such as convulsions, of hysteric orgin.

hysteroid Resembling hysteria.

hysterosyntonic Personality type representing a combination of hysterical and syntonic personalities.

I

I fraction Duration of inspiration divided by the total cycle of inspiration expiration.

I-persona (T. Burrow) The personality constellation which synthesizes man's socially symbolic functioning. It is purely partitive and the affective identity exhibited in interrelations.

$_sI_R$ See *inhibitory potential.*

iamatology The science of therapy.

iatrogenic neurosis; iatrogenic illness Behavior disorder induced by the physician's diagnosis or attitude.

iatrogeny The production of iatrogenic illness.

iatrotechnique Treatment method; iatrochemistry is synonymous with chemotherapy.

ICD See *International Classification System of Diseases.*

ichthyophobia Morbid fear of fish.

iconolatry Worship of images.

iconomania Morbid worshiping or collecting of images.

ictal emotions Suddenly occurring and vanishing emotions, especially depression and anxiety.

icterus gravis neonatorum See *kernicterus.*

ictus 1. Stress or accentuation of a tone or syllable. 2. Seizure or stroke.

ictus epilepticus Obsolete for sudden occurrence of an epileptic seizure.

id (S. Freud) The mass of unbound energies, both libidinal and aggressive, which constitute part of the unconscious and influence conscious action by seeking discharge and immediate gratification in accordance with its governing influence, the Pleasure Principle. It is comprised of whatever is innate, inherited or fixed in the constitution and is the link between somatic and mental processes. At birth all mental processes are part of the id. Through gradual contact with environmental demands, part of the unconscious id material becomes bound by pressures subserving these demands and undergoes development into preconscious material from which the ego emerges. The rest remains unconscious and unaltered.

More recent theorists suggest the ego and id are not entirely dichotomously differentiated structures, but rather operate along a continuum, both subserving motivation and discharge, and including ideational activity, with the id operating at the more primitive levels.

id—ego (psychoanalysis) The original psychic organization in the newborn out of which the id and ego develop.

id resistance See *resistance, id.*

id sadism See *sadism, id.*

idea 1. Cognitive process such as an image or thought which is not directly sensory in nature. 2. A plan of action or hypothesis.

ideal Thought of a personality, type of character, or line of action in emotionally colored terms as representing a goal to be sought after.

ideal, ego See *ego-ideal.*

ideal observer (signal detection theory) A function that relates an observation to the probability of that observation in a signal detection sensory experiment. The ideal observer is a mathematical expression of the maximum performance possible under the conditions of the experiment.

ideal type A perfect or near-perfect representation of all essential characteristics of a given species or category, though no single member embodies them all.

idealism A system of philosophical thought which attempts to explain the universe in terms of ideas, rather than in terms of matter or material things.

idealization Representation of an object in terms of one's ideals or desires.

idealized image (K. Horney) A false and exaggerated estimation of oneself, derived from what one would like to be rather than from what one actually is.

ideas, flight of See *flight of ideas.*

ideas, innate A philosophical doctrine which claims that all morally correct judgments and scientific principles consist of a priori knowledge of either universal principles governing reality or of objects transcending sensory experience. The knowledge is either present in the individual at birth, or stems from an inborn disposition of the mind to form conceptions under particular circumstances. Plato, ancient Stoics, Spinoza, and Descartes all employed the doctrine of innate ideas in the development of their philosophies.

ideas of reference A frequently occurring symptom of paranoid schizophrenia. The schizophrenic ascribes special importance to irrelevant events and believes that they are related to himself.

ideation Process of idea or image formation.

ideational Pertaining to idea or ideation.

ideational apraxia See *apraxia, ideational.*

ideational fluency The capacity to produce new ideas.

ideational learning See *learning, ideational.*

idée fixe See *fixed idea.*

idée, force (Fouillée) Postulate that ideas have dynamic influences and can serve as the source of actions.

identical Alike, the same; or similar in every respect.

identical components theory See *identical-elements theory.*

identical direction, law of The principle in binocular vision that objects are localized as if seen by a single, central eye.

identical-elements theory (E. L. Thorndike) Proposition that a new task will be learned more easily to the extent that it contains elements like those in already mastered tasks. Called identical components theory by R. S. Woodworth.

identical points Pair of points in the two retinae that receive stimuli from a single object at any distance and yield single vision, corresponding points.

identical series Type of recognition method used in the experimental study of learning.

identical twins See *twins, identical.*

identical visual direction law A pair of lines in objective space corresponding in direction in binocular vision, is seen in visual space as a single line. Objects on either line are seen as on a single line.

identification 1. The process of recognition. 2. (psychoanalysis) A defense mechanism consisting of the imitation of others in an effort to master too intense stimuli. Primary identification occurring in normal development during the oral stage is the beginning of the infant's perception of the external world and of his emotional attitudes towards others. It results from the wish to possess the object or the other and is exhibited by taking things into the mouth, thus incorporating whatever is loved and by introjecting others' traits. This is the basis of the superego. Secondary identification is pathological and may occur at later stages. It consists of assuming another's characteristics for purposes of either restoration or mastery. For example, a love-object lost through death, separation or rejection is re-established through identification with the object. Anxiety caused by a powerful enemy is subdued by the assumption of his powerful traits.

identification, crossparental The tendency to identify with the parent of the opposite sex associated with strong attachment to this parent.

identification test See *test, identification.*

identity 1. The condition of sameness in essential character. 2. The temporally persisting sense of being the same person whereby the individual orients himself to the external world. It is based primarily on coenaesthesia and the continuity of goals and memories. Psychologically, it is called personal identity.

identity, ego See *ego identity.*

identity crisis 1. Emotional disturbance seen particularly in young people. The individual has difficulty in experiencing or establishing a consistent personality irregardless of changes in time, circumstances, or roles. 2. (E. H. Erikson) Problems of adolescence or adulthood centering around a lack of a sense of personal identity.

identity hypothesis See *double aspect theory.*

ideogenetic Mental processes employing images of sense impressions rather than ideas that can be verbally expressed.

ideoglandular Glandular function evoked by mental impressions.

ideograph; ideogram 1. Pictograph; character or figure symbolizing an object or idea. 2. The graphic record obtained from apparatus recording the subject's unconscious movements.

ideokinetic See *ideomotor.*

ideokinetic apraxia Inability to carry out sequentially correct motor functions, though each single motor response may be intact.

ideology 1. A complex system of world, social and/or political philosophy. 2. Theory of the nature of ideas. 3. Psychology before that term was fixed.

ideometabolic Metabolic activity resulting from ideas.

ideomotor Referring to a motor action which is evoked by an idea.

ideomotor action Direct and automatic transfer of ideas into action, such as acts during states of absent-mindedness.

ideomotor apraxia Impairment or loss of the ability to carry out a complex act. The separate behaviors comprising the act may individually be performed properly but the sequence is not correct.

ideophobia Fear of ideas.

ideophrenia (J. Guislain) Delirium characterized by ideational disorders.

ideoreflex Transfer of an idea, suggested either from within or without, into action.

ideosynchysia Obsolete for delirium.

idioctonia Obsolete term for suicide.

idiocy The lowest class of mental deficiency composed of those whose IQ's are below 25. It is usually congenital and accompanied by physical defects.

idiocy, amaurotic family See *Tay-Sach's disease.*

idiocy, Kalmuk Mongolism; Down syndrome.

idiodynamics Point of view that only those environmental aspects that are relevant to a particular individual are attended to.

idioglossia Unintelligible speech.

idiographic Relating to the study of individual cases.

idiographic science (W. Windelband) A science that studies individual and unrepeatable phenomena, such as history. W. Dilthey, G. W. Allport and others maintained that psychology is an idiographic science.

idiokinesis Obsolete term for the origin of a new hereditary character through mutation.

idiolalia Private language invented by those of low mentality.

idiopathic 1. Primary disease of spontaneous origin, not resulting from an outside agent. 2. Diseases for which no cause is known.

idiopathic sterility Sterility related to lack of spermatozoa in the semen or faulty ovulation.

idiophenomena Phenomena which are idiographic, due to individual differences.

idiophonia Individual form of dysphonia.

idiophrenia Obsolete term for disorder resulting from organic brain disease.

idioplasm; idioplasma Obsolete for hypothetical structure of the germ plasm.

idioretinal Visual perceptions of light in the absence of external stimulation, caused by physiological changes occurring in the cortex or retina.

idiosome The central apparatus of an auxocyte.

idiosyncrasy A characteristic peculiar to an individual and that can be attributed to any general psychological factor.

idiosyncratic credit The sum of the positive dispositions of group members toward an individual. These credits represent status and allow deviation from group norms, innovation and assertion of influence. The freedom to behave in an idiosyncratic manner increases along with the amount of credit an individual accumulates. Idiosyncratic credit may be acquired as a result of perceived conformity and competence, although other factors such as seniority may enter in.

idiot An individual of the lowest level of mental deficiency, whose IQ is below 25. Idiots are not able to learn to speak, read, write, or avoid the common dangers of living.

idiot savant A mentally retarded person possessing extraordinary ability in one specific area.

idiotropic Introspective.

idiovariation Ongoing process of mutation in the genotypical structure of an organism.

idol 1. An effigy, natural object or image worshipped as a god. 2. (F. Bacon) A prejudice usually resulting from mass suggestion or tradition, that interferes with logical thinking.

idolomania Overly passionate worship of idols.

idolum Obsolete for illusion or hallucination.

I/E ratio Rate of inspiration divided by rate of expiration; it may be used as an index of emotionality. It is believed low I/E ratios are indicative of lying.

I/E scale See *scale, I/E.*

IES test See *test, IES.*

Illinois Test of Psycholinguistic Abilities (ITPA) See *test, Illinois, of Psycholinguistic Abilities.*

illness, advantage by See *epinosis.*

illness as self-punishment See *resistance, superego.*

illumination Amount of intensity of light energy that falls on a surface.

illusio sensus Hallucination.

illusion A subjective distortion, occurring in sense perception or memory, of what is objectively present.

illusion, Aristotle's The perception of one object as two, when the object is in contact with the tips of crossed middle fingers.

illusion, auditory A subjective distortion of an auditory stimulus.

illusion, Ebbinghaus The geometrical illusion that a circle surrounded by a ring of smaller circles is of a larger size than the same sized circle surrounded by a ring of circles larger than itself.

illusion, geometrical Class of optical illusions consisting of misperceived direction, size or distance.

illusion, Hering A geometrical optical illusion of straight parallel lines curving inwards when they intersect a series of lines which originate beyond the extremities of the straight lines and intersect above and below them.

illusion, horizontal-vertical The illusion that a vertical line drawn at right angles to a horizontal line of the same length is longer.

illusion, Jastrow An optical illusion consisting of the upper of two equal-sized ring sectors placed one above the other, appearing smaller.

illusion, Müller-Lyer The geometrical illusion that one line is longer than another of equal length when the former has obtuse angles at both ends while the latter has acute angles at both ends.

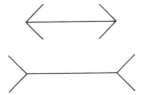

illusion, oculogyral The illusory perception of movement of a very dim light in a dark room which occurs following rotation of the body.

illusion of doubles Misidentification of known or unknown people in one's environment. It can occur as illusion of either positive or negative doubles. Also called Capgras' syndrome, or illusion of false recognition.

illusion of false recognition See *illusion of doubles.*

illusion of negative doubles Misidentification of known people in one's environment, as people whose appearances have been altered so they are no longer recognizable. Also called Fregoli's phenomenon.

illusion of orientation Misidentification of environmental stimuli due to impaired sensorium. It occurs in typhoid fever, malaria, pneumonia and scarlet fever.

illusion of positive doubles Misidentification of people in one's environment as friends or relatives.

illusion, optical An illusion of vision usually affecting spatial relations.

illusion, Ponzo The geometrical illusion that a horizontal line appearing within the smaller end of a pair of divergent vertical lines is longer than an equal-length line located at a point at which the vertical lines are farther apart.

illusion, staircase A reversible figure illusion whereby a staircase can be perceived both as from above or from below with both perspectives alternating.

illusion, Zoellner The geometrical illusion that two parallel lines are divergent occurring when one is crossed at sharp angles by many short slanting lines in one direction and the other is crossed by lines going in the opposite direction.

illusory movement See *movement, apparent.*

image A mental copy arising from memory of a sense experience in the absence of sensory stimulation.

image agglutinations (E. Kretschmer) Image groups occurring in dreams that are representative of the day's thoughts and are formed from the conglomeration of discrete images under the influence of affects.

image, body 1. Mental representation of one's body derived from internal sensations, emotions, fantasies, posture, experience of and with outside objects and people. 2. Internal, evaluative representation of one's body determined largely by how one thinks it looks to others. Also known as body concept.

image, generic A somewhat schematic image representing any one of a class of objects.

image, idealized See *idealized image.*

image, memory The revival in memory of a past experience, including the recognition that the original percept occurred in the past, in the absence of present sensory stimulation.

image, percept See *percept-image.*

image, primordial See *archetype.*

imageless thought A thought or train of thought lacking sensory content. Within the structuralists school, there was controversy as to whether such thought exists but recent experimental data indicates that it does.

imagery, composite A single image composed of parts of several sensory experiences of similar objects.

imagery, eidetic See *eidetic imagery.*

imagery, hypnagogic Vivid imagery, often of a hallucinatory nature, seen during the pre-sleep stage, and during the time of falling asleep.

imagery, hypnopompic Visions occurring during the state after sleep and prior to wakefulness.

imagination The constructive reorganization and employment of past perceptual experiences into ideational level images in a present experience. Imagination may be classified according to the function for which it is employed. For example, anticipatory imagination represents movement towards a future goal or the goal itself.

imagination, active (C. G. Jung) Technique of analytical psychotherapy used in dream interpretation in which the fantasy of the dream is elaborated through the observation of the fantasy material stimulated by the dream, leading to an understanding of the dream as a whole rather than an understanding of the components of the dream.

imagination, creative Self-initiated and self-organized imagination.

imagination, imitative Imagination which follows a pattern initiated and organized by another.

imago 1. (psychoanalysis) Unconscious, idealized representation of an important figure from childhood, usually a parent, often markedly influencing later life in the form of control of standard. 2. (C. G. Jung) Archetype.

imbalance, muscular Imbalance in muscles of the opposite function, especially used in reference to the extrinsic muscles of the eyeball causing difficulty in fixating an object with both eyes. Some varieties are heterophoria and strabismus.

imbecile A mentally deficient individual whose adult IQ is between 25 and 50 and whose mental age is between two and seven years.

imipramine Drug prescribed in the treatment of depression.

imitation The performance of an act in the same manner as another seen performing the act.

immanence, theory of life Closed circle hypothesis of life. Belief that the organism consists of parts or organs which function not only for themselves but also work to keep several other parts in optimal condition. Since each organ is involved in the functioning of others, the life process takes place within a closed circle.

immobility A state of temporary inability to move, as seen in the death-feigning response or sometimes in hypnosis.

immobility, social The societal condition in which individuals are not able to change their social class, role, status or occupation.

immobilization-paralysis See *paralysis, immobilization.*

immobilizing activity See *activity, immobilizing.*

immoral In violation of social or moral law.

impedance The property of an electrical circuit which limits the power of the current passing through it.

imperative Used in reference to actions an individual feels compelled to perform.

imperative, categorical (E. Kant) An unconditioned demand stemming from an inner law of ethics and morality which is universally binding. The imperative consists of the principle that one's actions are good only if they are valid for all rational beings in the same situation.

imperceptible A stimulus that is below the threshold of perception.

imperception Defective perception such as is seen in agnosia.

impersonal projection See *projection, impersonal.*

impersonation The deliberate assumption of another's identity, usually for purposes of obtaining an advantage or privilege.

impetus (psychoanalysis) The genetically determined force, strength, or energy of an instinctual drive.

implications, informational (J. P. Guilford) Extrapolations of information in the form of expectancies, predictions, or consequences.

implicit apprehension See *apprehension, implicit.*

implicit behavior See *response, implicit.*

implicit response See *response, implicit.*

impotence 1. The feeling that one is unable to control the course of events. 2. The inability of the male to perform sexual intercourse, related to the lack of erection or inadequate erection or too early ejaculation.

impotence, anal General constipation or the inability to defecate except under conditions of privacy, resulting from pathological concern with giving offense.

impotence, orgastic Inability in the male to achieve orgasm or complete sexual satisfaction despite normal erection and ejaculation.

impotentia generandi Inability of the male to copulate most often due to physiological pathology.

impression 1. The neural effect of sensory stimulation. 2. The psychic effect of stimulation in the form of an unanalyzed sensation.

impression, absolute A judgment of intensity, weight, brightness, etc. that is made without reference to or direct comparison with a standard.

impression method See *method, impression.*

imprinting (ethology) A learning process; the range of stimuli eliciting the following response in the young of several species becomes narrowed. This is limited to a sensitive period. This period ends in part because the bird flees from strange objects. It is often asserted but questionable that this process is irreversible or that this learning is accomplished without reinforcement.

improvement The progressive movement towards a given standard or skill in the experimental study of practice. It is exhibited by decrease in time taken to perform the task and increase in accuracy.

improvement over chance (statistics) A measure of the level of improvement in the dependent variable as compared with the average amount of improvement that would be expected from chance alone.

impuberty; impuberism The state of not having reached puberty, either chronologically or because of delayed physical or psychological development.

impulse 1. Incitement to action without reflection or deliberation. 2. The wave of active change continuing along a nerve fiber. 3. (psychoanalysis) The psychological presentation of an instinctual drive, in the form of a sudden inclination or desire arising immediately upon confrontation with a certain stimulus.

impulse, component Impulse arising from a component instinct.

impulse disorder See *disorder, impulse.*

impulse fear A fear that arises from an instinctual or psychological source, as opposed to real fear which is a fear of something real in one's environment.

impulsion Tendency to immediate action, originating from blind obedience to internal drives.

impulsive An act that is the immediate response without deliberation, to the presentation of a stimulus.

impunitive 1. (S. Rosenzweig) Frustration reaction in which the individual attempts to justify, rationalize or deny the frustration which has occurred rather than to blame either himself or others for it. 2. Personality type characterized by impunitive frustration reactions.

inaccessibility A state, characteristic of autism and schizophrenia, in which the individual is unresponsive to stimulation from others.

inadequacy Inability to deal competently with a situation due to lack of skill or mental ability.

inadequacy, constitutional Any hereditary physical or mental defect that is largely unmodifiable.

inadequacy, psychic (psychoanalysis) The feeling of inability to respond to sexual stimulation in a satisfactory manner.

inadequate personality See *personality, inadequate.*

inadequate stimulus See *stimulus, inadequate.*

inappetence Absence of desire or appetite.

inappropriate affect See *affect, inappropriate.*

inattention A state in which attention is not focused and wanders unselectively.

inattention, selective 1. (H. S. Sullivan) A process used by the self-system to limit and restrict awareness by causing anxiety provoking experiences, threatening to the individual's security and self-esteem, to be ignored, misunderstood, or forgotten. The necessity for restriction of awareness is the result of the limitations of experiences set forth in the socialization process which is transmitted first in one's early childhood at home and is continued through later educational processes. 2. See *defense, perceptual.*

inborn Innate; present in the organism at birth.

inbreeding Procreation among close relatives which automatically fixes the genes making them homozygous. It is sometimes arranged deliberately in certain species to maintain desirable, hereditary characteristics.

incendiary mania Pyromania.

incentive 1. Motive for behaving in a certain way. 2. External object which arouses or adds to already existing motivation to maintain a certain goal-directed behavior.

incest Sexual relations between opposite-sexed individuals, closely connected by blood kinship, the degree of the kinship being defined by law and social custom.

incest barrier (psychoanalysis) The limitation or prohibition placed upon the libido by social law concerning incest, resulting in guilt evoked by thoughts, fantasies or dreams of defying the barrier and in the loosening of libidinal attachment to the family in accordance with the barrier.

incest taboo See *taboo, incest.*

incidence The frequency with which a condition or event occurs within a given time and population.

incidental cue See *stimulus, incidental.*

incidental learning See *learning, incidental.*

incidental memory See *memory, incidental.*

incidental stimulus See *stimulus, incidental.*

incipient The beginning or initial phase of a process.

incipient movement See *movement, incipient.*

incoherence Lack of organization or systematic connection of parts, such as in unintelligible speech marked by disconnectedness.

incommensurable Magnitudes or variables requiring different unity scales or standards of measurement or estimation in order to be assessed accurately.

incompatible Statements, phenomena, or individuals which are inconsistent or not capable of existing together with the same system.

incomplete-pictures test See *test, incomplete pictures.*

incontinence Incapacity of self-control of body functions, particularly sexual impulses, urination, and defecation.

incoordination Lack of balance or harmony in movements resulting from the inadequate working together of muscles or muscle groups.

incorporation 1. Taking into the body and making part of oneself. 2. (psychoanalysis) A form of introjection in which attributes of another are taken into the mind of an individual following the model of oral ingestion and swallowing. It is the primary mechanism in identification.

increment The amount or rate of increase or decrease in the progressive change of a magnitude or variable.

incremental learning theory See *learning theory, incremental.*

incubation 1. A period of no apparent activity in a complex function during which development and change in the function may occur. 2. (G. Wallas) The second of the four stages of creative thought.

incubus Nightmare.

incus Anvil. The middle bone in the chain of small bones in the middle ear.

independence-dependence syndrome See *syndrome, dependence-independence.*

independence, test of See *test of independence.*

independent variable See *variable, independent.*

index A sign or number indicative of change in magnitude, or pointing to a state or fact.

index, cephalic Anthropometrical measurement,

given by dividing the maximum breadth of the head by the maximum length and multiplying by 100.

index consistency (i) An index measuring the extent to which members of a group give the same responses to identical stimuli within a certain time limit. The formula is:

$$i = \sqrt{\frac{1}{N}\Sigma\cos^\pi - \frac{(BC)^{1/2}}{(AD)^{1/2}(BC)^{1/2}}},$$

where A =the number of responses present both times; B and C = the number of responses present one time and not the other respectively, D= the number of responses denied or omitted both times, and N= the number of subjects.

index, cranial The cephalic index measured on the bare skull.

index of correlation See *correlation, index of.*

index of independence See *test of independence.*

index of refraction See *refraction, index of.*

index of reliability See *reliability, index of.*

index, predictive See *forecasting efficiency, index of.*

index, selection (H. J. Eysenck) A formula used in the determination of the discriminatory usefulness of a test: $D = \dfrac{P}{P+P_m+P_f}$ where P_m equals the proportion of persons who belong in a certain category and whose scores are appropriate to that category; P equals the proportion of individuals who belong in a category but whose scores do not place them there; and P_f equals the proportion of individuals not belonging in the category in which their scores place them.

indicator, mechanical A mechanical moving part of an instrument which gives information concerning the state of a phenomenon, usually by bringing a reference point into relation with a scale, such as pointers do on speedometers.

indifference of medium or indicator The principle that a personality dimension exists regardless of the form or existence of some particular scale or type of measurement. Thus, the same trait or factor can usually be measured by a number of distinct tests in either Questionnaire Rating, or Objective Test media of observation.

indifference point The transition zone between two opposing experiences, such as pleasure and pain, or variables.

indifferent stimulus See *stimulus, indifferent.*

indirect measurement See *measurement, indirect.*

indirect method of therapy See *psychotherapy, client centered.*

indirect scaling See *scaling, indirect.*

indirect vision See *vision, indirect.*

indissociation (J. Piaget) An early stage in the child's development of perception of the physical world in which phenomena are not sharply distinguished from each other or from the self.

individual differences See *differences, individual.*

individual psychology The name given by Alfred Adler to his personality theory. It is a holistic ego-psychology and a social psychology which assumes that life is movement and must endlessly strive for better adaptation to the environment. This was first called by Adler "The striving for superiority," while any lack of adaptation led to an "inferiority feeling." The age-old conflict as to the primacy of heredity or environment is resolved in this theory by seeing the child as utilizing heredity as well as environment in his endeavor to construct his personality. Within the limits of reality the child has great latitude for doing so. In the course of his striving for better adaptation the child will always set for himself a goal to strive for. Adler stated: "We cannot think, feel, will or act without the perception of a goal." The singlemindedness of this goal striving lead to a unified personality, and the mode of movement of the individual toward his goal was termed by Adler his "style of life." The social character of individual psychology was expressed by Adler as follows: "No psychologist is able to determine the meaning of any expression, if he fails to consider it in its social relation to society." Adler's psychological system was developed in a social science direction. Consciousness itself is considered a social product, and character traits are in Adler's system only the external aspects of the social relationship an individual has to the problems of the outside world. In its stress on ego-psychology and its fight against drive-psychology, the "Individual Psychology" states that instincts would be an inadequate guide for man through the intricacies of our complex world; only goal-directed man can find his way, since all human history is nothing but the activity of man, aiming at his own goals. Adler also contended that civilization, culture, art and science could never have been created by man, if his basic striving had been "back to the womb."

Individual psychology sees neuroses and psychoses as being safeguarding devices, designed (unconsciously) by the individual to defend his self-esteem and his idealized ego against a threatened collapse, when faced with a social problem for which he feels unprepared. His lack of "social interest" forces him from social reality into a world of pretense and illusion. Special innovations in the treatment techniques are the use of "early recollections" and "birth order position" and a relentless stress on the (not conscious) purposiveness of the symptoms.

The optimistic tenor of individual psychology led to the acceptance of its tenets by a great many educators, the child guidance movement and the general public. Societies, individual psychology clinics and Adlerian Institutes carry on the work of "Individual Psychology" in most western countries.

individual response See *response, individual.*

individual test See *test, individual.*

individualism 1. A strong personal attitude or action exhibiting an attitude of independence from group standards. **2.** The theory that the individual is of paramount importance and should take precedence over social or legal action.

individuality, graphic The unique characteristics of a person's handwriting which make possible the identification of the writer.

individualization The process by which an organism becomes different from all others.

individuation **1.** The process by which an organism moves or differentiates from the general class to an individual mode of existence, through the development of particular structures, parts, and functions. **2.** (C. G. Jung) The process by which the various systems within the personality, such as archetypes and complexes, develop to the fullest capacity and become distinct from the original, undifferentiated wholeness in which they originate. Realization of self, the ultimate result, cannot occur unless all systems are completely differentiated and permitted conscious expression. Underdeveloped systems attempt to attract energy from more fully developed ones, causing resistances to growth, irrational behavioral outlets for expression, and consequently neurosis. **3.** (M. S. Mahler) A phase of development, occurring usually between the eighteenth and 36th month, during which the infant manifests progressive independence of the mother through growing ability to satisfy his own desires by increased mobility, dexterity, and tolerance of the mother's absence. The individuation process marks the end of the symbiotic mother-child relationship, during which the infant is completely dependent on the mother.

indoctrination **1.** Instruction designed to gain complete and uncritical acceptance rather than critical consideration. **2.** Preliminary training, the purpose of which is to introduce new members to the policies, mores, and practices of a group.

induced color See *color, induced.*

induced movement See *movement, induced.*

induced tonus See *tonus, induced.*

induction **1.** The process of deriving the general from the particular. **2.** Arousal in one area resulting from the spread of activity from another part in physiology. **3.** See *induction, positive.* **4.** See *induction, negative.*

induction coil An electrical device consisting of two coils, used for physiological stimulation and for the administration of shock in psychological experiments.

induction, negative (I. P. Pavlov) The concentration of inhibition due to preceding excitation of neighboring areas.

induction, positive (I. P. Pavlov) The concentration of excitation in a stimulated area due to preceding inhibition of neighboring areas.

induction test See *test, induction.*

industrial psychology The branch of applied psychology concerned with the application of psychological techniques and findings to the solution of problems arising in the industrial or economic field. The first applications were in the use of intelligence and aptitude tests as aids in determining selection and replacement of employees. More recent developments include the involvement of industrial psychologists in training procedures, the counseling of employees, determining effective methods of communication between workers and employers, and in designing the most suitable and effective equipment and working conditions. Industrial psychology is now called industrial and organizational psychology. It is essentially the application of many areas of psychology not only to industry itself but to other organizations where people work. Over the years it has deepened and broadened its scope to include more complex aspects of human behavior in a greater variety of settings. There are three major aspects within the field of industrial and organizational psychology: personnel psychology, industrial-social psychology and human engineering. More recently the term organizational psychology has come to replace the label industrial-social psychology and human factors engineering is replacing human engineering.

inertia **1.** The tendency of matter to retain its state of rest or motion as long as it is not acted upon by an external force. **2.** The property in the nervous system of time lag between a stimulus and the onset of its physiological effect.

infancy The earliest period of postnatal life, prior to the learning of speech, in which the individual is totally dependent upon parental care.

Infant Schedule A Gesell Development Scale used to determine the level of linguistic, motor, and social behavior in infants.

infant test See *test, infant.*

infantile excema See *excema, infantile.*

infantile polymorphous perversion See *perversion, infantile polymorphous.*

infantile psychosis: treatment design (M.S. Mahler & M. Furer) Infantile psychosis can be treated only through restoration, as completely as possible, of the mother-child symbiotic dual unity and subsequent facilitation of a separation-individuation process. Mahler & Furer designed a mother-therapist-child tripartite treatment situation in which the first goal was to re-establish a symbiotic-like union with the mother via the therapist as a bridge. This situation facilitated a subsequent separation-individuation process which also enabled the therapist to reconstruct traumata in the psychotic child's past and to observe the emergence of many hitherto absent developmental phenomena. The conflict between the ego and the id produced neurotic-like symptoms which could be dealt with therapeutically.

This therapeutic action research design must be modified for a more general application because of the forbidding cost in manpower. Yet it reaffirms the theory of the symbiosis origin of human emotional development and may eventually facilitate rehabilitation of early and severely disturbed children. The emotional availability of a mothering person in the treatment of the erstwhile psychotic infant is an absolute necessity.

infantile sadism   See *sadism, infantile.*

infantile spastic diplegia   Bilateral congenital brain defects, or lesions acquired at birth causing the limbs (particularly the lower) to become weak and spastic, Other symptoms may include involuntary movements, ataxia and sometimes mental deficiency.

infantile symbiotic psychosis   See *psychosis, symbiotic.*

infantilism   Regression or arrested physical or mental development in an older child or adult, characterized by behavior resembling that of the infant.

infarction, myocardial   A coronary occlusion produced in the cardiac muscle and related to the existence of hypertension, obesity, diabetes, peptic ulcer, renal disease, and smoking.

infavoidance need   See *need, infavoidance.*

inference   A judgment or conclusion reached on the basis of former judgments.

inferiority complex   See *complex, inferiority.*

inferiority feelings   **1.** Feelings of weakness, helplessness and inadequacy. **2.** (A. Adler) Feelings of inferiority, arising from the sense of imperfection and incompletion in a particular sphere of life, which motivates the individual to strive for a higher level of development and as such, are the cause of all improvement in life situation. Each time a new level of achievement is reached, inferiority feelings reappear, continuing to mitigate upward movement. If inferiority feelings become exaggerated by adverse conditions in the home, pathological inferiority complex may develop.

inferiority, functional   (A. Adler) One of a subgroup of organ inferiority characterized by work that is quantitatively or qualitatively insufficient to satisfy a standard of required effectiveness.

inferiority, morphologic   (A. Adler) One of the subgroups of organ inferiority characterized by a defect in the shape, size, or strength of a particular organ.

inferiority, organ   (A. Adler) The belief that the actual or subjectively felt defect in an organ causes feelings of inferiority and attempts at compensation for these feelings.

infertility   The inability to produce offspring.

infinite   **1.** A quantity greater than any definite quantity. **2.** Not bounded or limited.

infinitesimal   **1.** A quantity less than any definite quantity. **2.** Minute.

informal test   See *test, informal.*

information   **1.** Knowledge of a particular fact or circumstance gained or given through communication, research or instruction. **2.** (behavior theory) That aspect of a stimulus used by the subject in his response. **3.** (information theory) The quantitative property of the set of all possible items that can be communicated under a defined set of circumstances, rather than that item which is actually communicated or its content. If all items of a source of possible items can be predicted, no information will be conveyed by the communication. If all items are as likely to be communicated, maximum information will be conveyed. The bit is the unit of information. **4.** (J. P. Guilford) That which an organism discriminates. Intellectually processed information has some degree of structure, with both substantive (content) and formal (product) aspects.

information, behavioral   (J. P. Guilford) Information involved in human interactions where the attitudes, needs, desires, moods, feelings, intentions, perceptions, thoughts, etc. of other people and of ourselves are involved. Conveyed by expressive behavior or "body language" as well as by word symbols.

information content   See *content, informational.*

information, figural   (J. P. Guilford) Information in concrete form, as perceived or as recalled in the form of images. The term "figural" implies at least minimal structure. Subclasses are along sensory-input lines—visual, auditory, kinesthetic, etc.

information, semantic   (J. P. Guilford) Information in the form of meanings to which words commonly, although not always, become attached, hence most notable in verbal thinking and verbal communication, but not identical with words as symbols. Meaningful pictures can also convey semantic information.

information, symbolic   (J. P. Guilford) Information in the form of denotative signs, having no significance in and of themselves, such as numbers, letters, and words (as letter structures).

information test   See *test, information.*

information theory   **1.** The branch of science dealing with the transmission of information as a formal mathematical concept, and originally stemming from probability theory and electrical communications. Modern information theory is based primarily on the work of R. V. L. Hartley who set forth the idea that information could be identified as a stochastic process, one that gives rise to a sequence of symbols to which probability laws apply, and could thus be measured in terms of what could have been communicated under a defined set of circumstances, rather than what actually is communicated.

C. E. Shannon and N. Wiener elaborated the scheme and are largely responsible for the promulgation of information theory in the social sciences, their formulations having been enthusiastically accepted by psychologists such as G. A. Miller and F. C. Frick. Shannon's and Wiener's elaborations consist essentially of the idea that communication is a statistical process which can only be described in probabilistic terms. Maximum information is conveyed when any one item of a source of possible items, is as probable as any other. No information is conveyed when all items of a source of possible items are completely predictable. Based on these premises, a measure of the amount of information associated with a given message was derived by defining a set of conditions the measure had to satisfy. The only measure for any item of a group of items, which satisfies all conditions set forth is the negative logarithm, to the base 2, of the probability of that item. The average information of the group of items, is the average weighted logarithmic measure.

Currently information theory is being applied as a means of psychological experimentation such as language, perception, reaction time, and statistical analyses. 2. (industrial psychology) The science of the transmission and measurement of information. The basic measure is the "bit." In information theory channel capacity refers to the limit of information that can be handled by any communications channel and, by analogy, human channel capacity refers to the maximum limit of the information that can be received by a human through all sensory modalities. The theory is applicable in human factors engineering, such as determining the perceptual load imposed upon an operator by a sensory-motor task.

informational classes See *classes, informational.*

informational content See *content, informational.*

informational implications See *implications, informational.*

informational product See *product, informational.*

informational relations See *relations, informational.*

informational systems See *systems, informational.*

informational transformations See *transformations, informational.*

informational units See *units, informational.*

infrahuman 1. Species, other than man. 2. Characteristics of a human that resemble those of a lower animal.

infundibulum The stalk by which the pituitary body is attached to the forebrain.

ingratiation A strategy used by a lower status individual to make himself more attractive to a person with higher status and to reduce the power differential between them.

in-group A closely knit group of individuals who feel they belong with each to the exclusion of others.

inherent Existing in, belonging to and permanently forming a part of an individual or object.

inheritance 1. Traits transmitted from parent to offspring. 2. The process by which traits are transmitted from parent to offspring.

inhibited mania See *mania, inhibited.*

inhibition 1. The stopping of a process in progress or the prevention of a process from starting when the eliciting stimulus is present. 2. A mental state which results in a hesitancy or blockage of action. 3. (psychoanalysis) The prevention of instinctual impulses from reaching consciousness due to the

action of the ego or the superego. 4. (I. P. Pavlov) A hypothetical cortical process of the diminution or cessation of activity in the cerebrum.

inhibition, aim See *drive, aim-inhibited.*

inhibition, associative 1. The weakening of an established bond due to a new association which is made to one of the members of the original association. 2. The difficulty of establishing a new associative bond because of previously existing associations.

inhibition, conditioned (I. P. Pavlov) The suppression of the conditioned response upon the pairing of the conditioned stimulus with another stimulus without presenting the unconditioned response.

inhibition, conditioned reactive (C. L. Hull) The hypothetical state caused by the conditioning of reactive inhibition to the stimulus that is present when a conditioned response is extinguished, thereby causing the stimulus to have an inhibitory power.

inhibition, differential A hypothesized force within an organism acquired through conditioning causing a decrease in the tendency to respond to one stimulus while a tendency to respond to another, similar, stimulus is left intact.

inhibition, external (I. P. Pavlov) The extinction or cessation of a conditioned response when an extraneous stimulus is presented simultaneously with the conditioned stimulus.

inhibition, extinctive See *extinction, (I. P. Pavlov).*

inhibition, internal (I. P. Pavlov) The principle that an inhibitory process arises in the nervous system to counteract the strength of the conditioned response when the reinforcement is given and causes the diminution of the response when the reward is withheld.

inhibition of delay (I. P. Pavlov) An inhibition which reduces the time interval between the conditioned stimulus and the conditioned response.

inhibition of inhibition See *disinhibition.*

inhibition of reinforcement (C. I. Hovland) The temporary reduction of a conditioned response occurring within reinforcement trials presented in short succession which is reversible following a rest period.

inhibition, proactive The hypothetical process which is used to account for the relatively poorer learning rate of elements later in a series as compared to the learning rate of elements coming earlier in a series.

inhibition, reactive (C. L. Hull) The tendency toward a lessened strength of response due to practice or activity. It is independent of reinforcement and dependent on the time interval since the last response and the number of preceding responses. It is also called I_R.

inhibition, retroactive The interference with or impairment of the usual effects of a learning activity when the activity is followed closely by some other activity, especially activity similar to the first.

inhibition, specific Inhibition of an ego function such as locomotion or eating, which if performed would cause severe anxiety.

inhibitory epilepsy See *epilepsy, inhibited.*

inhibitory post synaptic potential (IPSP) A type of synaptic event which has the same form as the excitatory past synaptic potential (EPSP), but which produces a brief hyperpolarization which manifests itself as an inhibition of the neuron when it would normally respond.

inhibitory potential (C. L. Hull) sI_R; a temporary state of the organism, hypothesized to exist as the result of a response and to reduce the potential of the response's recurrence.

inhibitory reflex See *reflex, inhibitory.*

initial cry See *cry, epileptic.*

initial spurt The relatively high level of performance at the beginning of a series of tasks such as appears frequently in a work curve.

initiative The individual's capacity for independent action in starting a series of events, or the action itself.

injury Impairment of a structure or function in an organism due to damage from other than natural biological processes.

ink-blot test See *test, Rorschach inkblots.*

innate Present in the individual at birth.

innate ideas See *ideas, innate.*

inner-directed (D. Riesman) An individual whose reactions to various environmental pressures are consistent and based on an early-instilled value system.

inner ear See *labyrinth.*

inner-personal region See *region, inner personal.*

innervation 1. The supply of efferent nerves to a muscle or gland. 2. The excitation of a muscle or gland by an efferent nerve.

innervation ratio The number of muscle fibers in a motor unit per neuron.

input 1. The energy or effort put into a system. 2. (computer technology) The properly coded information fed into the computer. 3. The current or voltage applied to an electronic device or circuit.

inquiry The second major procedure in Rorschach testing, following the completion of the free association period (except in the Rapaport system where the inquiry is conducted after the free association to each card). The basic format generally followed is for the examiner to present the cards to the subject a second time, asking non-directive questions so as to understand which portion of the blot was used in the response and which determining features of the blot stimulated the percept. See also *direct inquiry; analogy period; testing-of-limits.*

insanity The legal term for severe mental disorder involving irresponsibility and incompetence in the conduct of the individual's affairs.

insanity, adolescent 1. (E. Hecker) An obsolete term for hebephrenia. 2. Any psychotic disorder that occurs in adolescence.

insanity, affective Another expression for what is now called affective psychosis.

insanity, legal Any type or degree of mental disorder which entails legal consequences such as commitment to an institution, appointment of a guardian, or relief of responsibility for crime or contract. Legal insanity involves ignorance of right and wrong, the existence of delusions or the presence of an irresistible impulse.

insanity, moral 1. (J. Prichard) Rarely used term describing individuals who manifest uncontrollable violence and extreme lack of concern for the well-being of others without any intellectual impairment. 2. Extreme cases of psychopathic personality.

insanity, normal (C. G. Jung) Temporary supplanting of conscious autonomy by the unconscious giving rise to bizarre behavior characteristic of insanity, but occurring in normal individuals usually during periods of great stress.

insemination The act of fertilizing or impregnating.

insensibility Temporary or permanent absence of a particular quality or mode of sensation.

insight 1. Mental discernment or apprehension of the true nature of a problem, object, person, or situation. 2. The faculty involved in grasping the inner character or underlying truth. 3. (psychoanalysis) Awareness of the meaning and unconscious origin of one's behavior, symptoms, and the emotional processes which underlie them, this being a prerequisite to any therapeutic change. 4. (Gestalt) The main factor in learning characterized by grasping of those relationships leading to the solution of a problem, based on perceptual reorganization of previous experience. Once insight occurs it can promptly be repeated and applied to new situations.

insight therapy See *therapy, insight.*

insomnia Chronic inability to sleep.

inspection technique See *technique, inspection.*

inspiration 1. The drawing in of air to the lungs. 2. The sudden grasp of the nature of a problem or the occurrence of a creative idea that does not result from previous reasoning or trial and error.

inspiration-expiration ratio See *I–E ratio.*

instability 1. Excessive or rapidly changing emotions or moods. 2. Lack of steadiness of purpose and self-control.

instigation (quantitative) Total combined strength of all instigators to a given response affecting an organism at one time, whether facilitative or inhibitory.

instigator A specifiable antecedent to which a given

response is the consequence; *external* instigator is a perceived object or event that initiates or facilitates an action; *internal* instigator may be inferred from external indices of internal changes (e.g., thirst drive equals hours of water deprivation), past experiences (e.g., high achievement motives equals history of parental reward for successful achievement), verbal report (e.g., "I am hungry," or "I am angry.").

instinct 1. An innate activity pattern or tendency to action common to a given species. 2. (S. Freud) A constant psychic force with the organism stemming from a certain bodily deficiency or disequilibrium, the aim of which is to remove the excitation and restore equilibrium through its investment in or attachment to an object that will bring satisfaction to the organism. In his final revision of instinct theory, Freud postulated the existence of only two primary instincts, Eros, the aim of which is to bind together, and Thanatos, the aim of which is to destroy connections and reduce living things to an inorganic state. The two instincts may combine into aggressive and sexual instincts of various forms. For example, in sadism, the destructive force is stronger than the aim for intimate union. 3. (W. McDougall) An inherited psychophysical disposition which determines what particular objects the individual will perceive, what he will experience emotionally about them, and how he will react to them behaviorally. McDougall believed the emotional component of instinct is inherited and cannot be modified by experience, as can the sensory and motor components and therefore identification of the distinct primary emotions was the only method of discovering what and how many instincts there are. A list of the primary emotions and thus the primary instincts was compiled and continuously revised. Some of the core instincts include escape, combat, curiosity, repulsion, self-assertion, self-abasement, and parental. 4. (K. Lorenz) Energy which initiates and drives certain behavior patterns and is specific to them. The instinctive activity is characterized by being stereotyped, common to all members of at least one sex of a species, innate, always completed once it is set into motion, and is the goal and terminus of the instinct.

instinct, aggressive See *Thanatos.*

instinct, component (psychoanalysis) Any of the various pregenital impulses arising from stimulation and tension in specific zones and organs. Each component instinct is disconnected and independent of the others in seeking gratification until puberty when they become fused, and are subordinated to genital primacy, subsequently comprising the elements of forepleasure. Examples are sucking, biting, sadism and masochism, all of which can be pathological if used as the source of end-pleasure.

instinct, death See *Thanatos.*

instinct, destructive See *Thanatos.*

instinct, life See *Eros.*

instinct, self-preservation See *Eros.*

institution, mental See *mental hospital.*

institutionalization 1. The placing of an individual in an institution for corrective or therapeutic purposes. 2. The process by which an individual adapts to the behavior patterns characteristic of the institution in which he lives.

instruction The process of imparting knowledge systematically.

instrument Any device used in measuring or recording data.

instrument factor (R. B. Cattell) A false factor, i.e., not a real personality factor, which sometimes appears when many behaviors are measured by one kind of instrument and which is peculiar to the instrument.

instrumental Behavior performed in order to achieve a certain end, as in the subject's response in instrumental conditioning.

instrumental conditioning See *conditioning, operant.*

instrumental error See *error, instrumental.*

instrumental learning See *conditioning, operant.*

instrumentalism 1. (J. Dewey) A position attempting the application of scientific methods and critical intelligence to moral and social beliefs through the notion that theory and practice are not opposed and irreconcilable. Using the model of scientific inquiry which, Dewey believed, showed that theory and practice were in fact interdependent, Dewey formulated the view that general ideas are instruments for the reconstruction and reorganization of problem situations. The idea's truth lies in its capacity to reorganize the components of an experience in such a way as to resolve the problem in accordance with the rules of disciplined inquiry. Thus ideas prescribe behavior. 2. (B. B. Wolman) A sociopsychological attitude. Selfishness based on viewing others as instruments to be used for the satisfaction of one's own needs. Originates in the parasitic infant-mother relationship.

insufficiency, segmental (A. Adler) Inferiority of a body segment usually observable by a skin disorder of that segment.

insula See *Reil, island of.*

insulin A hormone secreted by the beta cells of the islets of Langerhans in the pancreas, the purpose of which is to reduce the blood-sugar level. Deficiency in its production results in diabetes for which it is used as a drug.

insulin coma See *coma, insulin.*

insulin shock therapy Treatment method, introduced by M. Sakel, consisting of the production of hypoglycemic comas and at times, convulsions induced by insulin administration.

insulin treatment, ambulatory (P. Polatin and H. Spotnitz) A modified insulin treatment used to relieve extreme anxiety and tension as well as the physical effects of these symptoms, such as appetite and weight loss. Small doses of insulin are administered intramuscularly, inducing hypoglycemia rather than coma. The patient is fully conscious during treatment. This is known also as sub-shock or sub-coma insulin treatment.

insulinoma The presence of a tumor in the pancreas which causes it to produce large quantities of insulin irrespective of the body's needs.

insurance, narcissistic (S. Rado) The mechanism which inhibits the critical judgment of the ego and thus allows for gratification of forbidden aggressive tendencies resulting in narcissistic satisfaction.

intake The initial contact between patient and therapist usually in the form of an evaluative interview upon admission to a clinic or hospital.

integral 1. An integer or whole number. 2. The result of mathematical process of integration.

integrated motivation component (R. B. Cattell) That component in motivation for a given course of action of which the person is fully aware and which is integrated with his conscious intentions and skills.

integration 1. The process or result of the unification of parts into a whole. 2. (psychology) The process by which different parts or characteristics of an individual are combined, organized and worked together at a higher level as a complex whole. 3. (neurology) The combination of discrete neural impulses in a center producing a unified and coordinated activity. 4. (mathematics) The summing of a differential series.

integration, primary (psychoanalysis) The conscious recognition of the child, usually before age 5, that his body and mind are distinct from the environment.

integration, secondary (psychoanalysis) The process by which psychic components, especially pre-genital sexual components, are unified and socialized into an adult or genital level.

integration, social 1. The process of unifying diverse elements of a group or society in such a way that all are guaranteed the same rights and liberties. 2. The process by which an individual adapts to group standards.

integrative learning (R. B. Cattell) A type of rewarded learning, important for personality development, in which the organism learns to make a choice or compromise between different goal satisfactions in the interests of a greater satisfaction (of all drives) for the organism as a whole. A learning to control by adjusting goals as distinct from Means—End Learning which is simply the learning of paths to a given goal.

intellect 1. The cognitive aspect of the mind including processes of reasoning, relating, judging and conceiving. 2. Mental ability.

intellect, structure of (J. P. Guilford) A comprehensive and systematic organization of intellectual abilities, known and hypothesized, in a three-dimensional facet- or matrix-type model, in which the abilities are parallel and are distinguished with respect to kinds of operations, kinds of informational content and kinds of products of information.

intellectual 1. Ideas and conceptions having to do with the intellect. 2. Thinking or reasoning of a high quality. 3. A person of high intellect whose interests are mainly in the area of learning and ideas.

intellectual operations See *operations, intellectual.*

intellectualism The doctrine that reduces all mental processes to only the cognitive aspect of the mind, attempting to explain emotion and volition in terms of the intellect.

intellectualization 1. The attempted analysis of a problem in purely intellectual terms. 2. A defense mechanism employing intellectual functions in the attempt to understand or explain a personal problem for the purpose of avoiding the acknowledgement of emotion evoked by the problem.

intelligence 1. In its Latin origin, it meant "information," a conception shared today in military circles. Biologically, with the naturalists, in contrast to "instinct" it meant an organism's ability to cope with its environment through learning. In contemporary psychology it is generally defined as a hypothetical construct from which stem an individual's abilities to deal with abstractions, learning, and novel situations. The level of intelligence is measured by standardized intelligence tests, its degree being proportional to the complexity of the test problems. 2. (A. Binet) The ability to judge, comprehend, and reason. Differences in intelligence are identified with differences in developmental levels as represented by the average capacities of individuals of various ages. The measure of an individual's intelligence is his mental age, or the developmental level he achieves, divided by his actual chronological age. 3. (E. L. Thorndike) A composite of a multitude of separate elements of ability broadly categorized within the ability to understand and deal with people (social intelligence), the ability to understand and deal with objects and the appliance of science (concrete intelligence), and the ability to understand and deal with verbal and mathematical symbols (abstract intelligence). Thorndike's is a multi-factor theory of intelligence stating that each mental act involves a number of minute elements operating together. Because many of these operate together and are common to several different mental acts, they can be also classified into separate groups such as verbal meaning, visual perception of relations or comprehension, all of which can then be measured yielding an index of intelligence. 4. (C. Spearman) A general factor (g) of mental energy possessed by all individuals in varying degrees which operates in all mental activities in amounts that differ according to the tasks' demands. In addition to g, each particular type of mental activity includes its own specific factor (s). Spearman's is thus a two-factor theory of intelligence, the g-factor being regarded as the essential measure of intelligence and therefore that which must be tapped in testing. An intelligence test conforming to this theory would include items saturated with g so that measurement would cause the testee's level of g to emerge and the effects of s to cancel out. 5. (L.L. Thurstone) A composite of a number of groups of mental operations, each having its own unifying primary factor that is relatively independent of the others. In addition, a second-order general factor is responsible for part of the common ground between some primary factors. Some of the primary factors which have been identified are: the number factor, the ability to do numerical calculations rapidly and accurately; the role memory factor, the ability to memorize quickly; and the verbal factor, involved in verbal comprehension. 6. (D. Wechsler) The individual's global capacity to act purposefully, to think rationally, and to deal effectively with his environment. Intelligence is not, however, the sum of these abilities, because such factors as drive, incentive and motivation influence intelligent behavior, as does the particular way in which the various abilities are combined. In addition, excess of anyone's ability does not necessarily add to behavior's effectiveness as a whole. Despite the fact that intelligence is not the sum of intellectual abilities, it can only be evaluated quantitatively by the measurement of the various aspects of these abilities. If general intelligence is not equated with intellectual ability, there is no contradiction. In Wechsler's system, intelligence is measured by the comparison of an individual's performance with the mean for his chronological age group. This procedure yields an Intelligence Quotient, without the use of the Mental Age concept which is considered erroneous because it presupposes a constancy of relationship between mental and chronological age which is known not to exist.

intelligence, abstract   The ability to understand and manage abstract concepts, relationships, and symbols.

intelligence, borderline   The level of intelligence which lies between the normal and subnormal levels. The individual is usually considered legally competent but slightly subnormal in intelligence.

intelligence, coefficient of   An index of relative intelligence obtained by dividing the testee's score by the norm for his chronological age.

intelligence, concrete   The ability to deal with situations and problems in a practical and effective way.

intelligence, marginal   The level of intelligence which is between mental deficiency and normalcy.

intelligence, mechanical   The inborn capacity to understand mechanical objects and mechanisms.

intelligence, multimodal theory of   The theory that intelligence is made of a group of abilities or factors rather than one single factor.

intelligence, nonverbal   Intelligence which is measured by nonverbal or performance tests such as visual-motor coordination.

intelligence quotient   (W. Stern) An index of rate of development in certain aspects of intelligence during childhood, found by determining what percent a child's mental age is of his chronological age. Among late adolescents and adults, it is an index of relative standing in similar aspects of intelligence, on a standard scale whose mean in the general population is 100 and whose standard deviation is approximately 16. A "verbal IQ" emphasizes abilities important for

general academic aptitude. A "nonverbal IQ" stresses abilities important for mechanical aptitude.

intelligence scale   A standardized intelligence test.

intelligence test   See *test, intelligence.*

intelligibility   Capable of being readily understood.

intend   In psychological contexts "intend" has different meanings. William James has been quoted using the term in the following clause, "What intelligent consciousness 'means' or intends . . ." This usage is common in introspective psychology in which the meaning of a term is the object to which it refers. The word "hammer" refers semantically (intends) to the thing hammer. The word "hammer" may, however, have other pragmatic meanings. The term "intent" is distinguished from "intend" in that the former is used as a present resolve to perform some future action, whereas the latter is used in the perceptual sense of present consciousness which has a relation to an object or a content.

intensity   1. (physics) The magnitude of energy or force per given unit. 2. The unanalyzable quantitative attribute of experience which is roughly correlated with the intensity of the physical energy of the stimulus. 3. The strength of any behavior, emotion, or motivation.

intent analysis   See *analysis, intent.*

intentional accident   See *accident, intentional.*

intentionality   Source of the notion of intentionality is the classical conception in which an individual interacts with an object in such a way that perception of an object is the result of a fusion of *eidola* from the object and a ray emanating from the subject. According to Plato, perception is an interaction of the object with the individual such that wine tastes sour to a sick individual. On the level of thinking, the nature of intentionality is that judgments are "of something" (Plato, *Theaetetus,* 189A).

The term was used by scholastic scholars to distinguish types of mental acts. *First intention* referred to the formation of classes by comparing objects. *Second intention* is what we would call today a second abstractive process from the comparison of classes. As a result of second intentions the primitive terms of logic, such as identity and difference, were constructed.

In the context of mental phenomena, intentionality refers to a relation between an object and a mental act. Within Aristotle's naive realism and substance theory of mind, objects impress their form on the mind, which has the capacity of becoming any form. The form of the object was held to exist in the mind intentionally. This is known as the doctrine of intentional inexistence.

For Brentano intentionality characterized relations between humans and other objects but was not to be found in the physical world. Thus, the distinction between the mental and the physical was the property of intentionality.

Recently G. Bergmann has defined intentionality as "means" in the sentence, "The proposition this is green means this is green." "Means" refers to an intentional relation that is analytic, specific to a world in which there are minds, and which subsists as a logical form.

inter response time Time between two successive responses; the response-response interval. IRT's may selectively be reinforced yielding the drl and drh schedules; the former being differential reinforcement of low rates of responding, or large IRT's, the latter being differential reinforcement of high rates of responding, or small IRT's.

inter schedule See *reinforcement, schedule of: interpolated.*

interaction, afferent (C. L. Hull) The hypothesized mutual influence of the peripheral neural processes involved in perception.

interaction principle (C. L. Hull) The principle that all active afferent neural impulses interact at any given moment and partially change as a result of each varying combination.

interaction process analysis (F. Bales) A method consisting of four major categories and twelve sub-categories by which reactions of members of a group are analyzed for emotional and problem solving responses.

interactional psychoanalysis See *psychoanalysis, interactional.*

interactional psychotherapy See *psychotherapy, interactional.*

interactionism A theory postulating reciprocal causation or interaction between mind and body as the solution to the psycho-physical problem.

interactionist approach The Hertz approach to Rorschach interpretation which seeks to integrate Rorschach configurations with socio-educational-situational-life style variables so as to create a broader and potentially objective configurational pattern.

interactive measurement See *measurement, interactive.*

interactive scale units Units on a psychological scale which are derived from actual physical and social effects of behavior and are thus in units compatible with those of physics. (Opposed to solipsistic measurement, within the individual.)

interbehavior (J. R. Kantor) Adjustive interaction between an organism and its environment.

interbehavioral psychology See *psychology, interbehavioral.*

interbrain Diencephalon.

intercalation The automatic, illogical and irrelevant insertion of a sound or word between other words or phrases.

intercept The distance from a point of origin to the point at which a line crosses a reference axis.

intercorrelation The correlation of each variable with each of the other variables in a group, usually arranged in tabular form.

intercourse 1. Interaction in any modality of two or more individuals or groups. 2. Coitus.

intercourse, buccal The application of the mouth to the genitals.

intercranial stimulation (ICS) See *electrical brain stimulation.*

interego (W. Stekel) Proposed substitute for Freud's term superego to imply the function of the intermediary between crude libidinal impulses and their final conscious aims according to moral principles.

interest 1. An enduring attitude consisting of the feeling that a certain object or activity is significant and accompanied by selective attention to that object or activity. 2. A state of motivation which directs activity toward certain goals. 3. The element, either acquired or congenital in an individual's make-up, from which an individual would be unable to learn. 4. (K. Pribram) The resultants of emotional (affective) and motivational (appetitive) processes.

interest, doctrine of The belief that learning cannot occur without the student's feeling of interest in the subject or activity and that education should begin with an appeal to the present interests with the aim of continuing to induce broadened and more varied ones.

interest inventory See *inventory, interest.*

interference 1. Conflict caused by incompatible or competing motives, ideas, precepts, or acts. 2. The inhibition of a piece of learning or an association by a conflicting memory or thought. 3. A diminution in the amplitude of sound or light waves taking place when two waves which are out of phase, occur simultaneously.

interference tube A complex conducting tube arranged such that sound waves of different lengths periodically cancel those tones to which they are tuned, producing tones of any required degree of purity.

interindividual cathexis See *cathexis, interindividual.*

interjection theory The theory which attributes the origin of spoken language to automatic or forced exclamatory sounds.

interlock schedule See *reinforcement, schedule of: interlocking.*

interlocking reinforcement See *reinforcement, interlocking.*

interlocking (interlock) schedule See *reinforcement, schedule of: interlocking.*

intermediate gene See *gene, intermediate.*

intermittence tone See *tone, interruption.*

intermittent reinforcement See *reinforcement, intermittent.*

intermittent schedule See *reinforcement, intermittent schedule of.*

intern An individual who has completed a given course of formal instruction and subsequently practices the profession for which he was trained, under the supervision of experienced professionals.

internal capsule A relatively large tract of nerve fibers passing through the corpus striatum.

internal consistency, coefficient of An index of the degree to which a consistent score can be obtained from different parts of a test, as exhibited by the degree to which testees score comparably. The degree of internal consistency is usually computed by correlating split-halves of the test items, or by the Hoyt or Kuder-Richardson formulas.

internal ear See *labyrinth.*

internal environment See *environment, internal.*

internal inhibition See *inhibition, internal.*

internal reinforcement See *reinforcement, internal.*

internal secretion See *secretion, internal.*

internal validation See *validation, internal.*

internalization (psychoanalysis) The process by which interactions between the individual and the external world are replaced by inner representations of them and their results. The process contributes to super-ego formation and the substitution of outer for inner controls.

International Classification System of Diseases The classification system of diseases, developed by the World Health Organization for uniform use throughout the world. The classifications of mental disorders and diseases of the nervous system and sense organs follow:

MENTAL DISORDERS (290-315)

Psychoses (290-299)
290 Senile and presenile dementia
291 Alcoholic psychosis
292 Psychosis associated with intracranial infection
293 Psychosis associated with other cerebral condition
294 Psychosis associated with other physical conditions
295 Schizophrenia
296 Affective psychoses
297 Paranoid states
298 Other psychoses
299 Unspecified psychosis
Neuroses, personality disorders, and other nonpsychotic mental disorders (300-309)
300 Neuroses
301 Personality disorders
302 Sexual deviation
303 Alcoholism
304 Drug dependence
305 Physical disorders of presumably psychogenic origin
306 Special symptoms not elsewhere classified
307 Transient situational disturbances
308 Behavior disorders of childhood
309 Mental disorders not specified as psychotic associated with physical conditions

Mental retardation (310-315)
310 Borderline mental retardation
311 Mild mental retardation
312 Moderate mental retardation
313 Severe mental retardation
314 Profound mental retardation
315 Unspecified mental retardation
DISEASES OF THE NERVOUS SYSTEM AND SENSE ORGANS (320-389)
Inflammatory diseases of central nervous system (320-324)
320 Meningitis
321 Phlebitis and thrombophlebitis of intracranial venous sinuses
322 Intracranial and intraspinal abscess
323 Encephalitis, myelitis, and encephalomyelitis
324 Late effects of intracranial abscess or pyogenic infection
Hereditary and familial diseases of nervous system (330-333)
330 Hereditary neuromuscular disorders
331 Hereditary diseases of the striatopallidal system
332 Hereditary ataxia
333 Other hereditary and familial diseases of nervous system
Other diseases of central nervous system (340-349)
340 Multiple sclerosis
341 Other demyelinating diseases of central nervous system
342 Paralysis agitans
343 Cerebral spastic infantile paralysis
344 Other cerebral paralysis
345 Epilepsy
346 Migraine
347 Other diseases of brain
348 Motor neuron disease
349 Other diseases of spinal cord
Diseases of nerves and peripheral ganglia (350-358)
350 Facial paralysis
351 Trigeminal neuralgia
352 Brachial neuritis
353 Sciatica
354 Polyneuritis and polyradiculitis
355 Other and unspecified forms of neuralgia and neuritis
356 Other dieases of cranial nerves
357 Other diseases of peripheral nerves except autonomic
358 Diseases of peripheral autonomic nervous system
Inflammatory diseases of the eye (360-369)
360 Conjunctivitis and opthalmia
361 Blepharitis
362 Hordeolum
363 Keratitis
364 Iritis
365 Choroiditis
366 Other inflammation of uveal tract
367 Inflammation of optic nerve and retina
368 Inflammation of lacrimal glands and ducts
369 Other inflammatory diseases of eye
Other disease and conditions of eye (370-379)
370 Refractive errors
371 Corneal opacity

372 Pterygrium
373 Strabismus
374 Cataract
375 Glaucoma
376 Detachment of retina
377 Other disease of retina and optic nerve
378 Other diseases of eye
379 Blindness
Diseases of the ear and mastoid process (380-389)
380 Otitis externa
381 Otitis media without mention of mastoiditis
382 Otitis media with mastoiditis
383 Mastoiditis without mention of otitis media
384 Other inflammatory disease of ear
385 Meniere's disease
386 Otosclerosis
387 Other disease of ear and mastoid process
388 Deaf mutism
389 Other deafness

internship, in clinical psychology One year of supervised training in a clinical facility including diagnosis, therapy, research, seminars, and conferences required to obtain a Ph.D. degree.

internuncial neurons See *neurons, internuncial.*

interoceptive system The system of receptors located within the body as distinguished from the exteroceptive system, situated near the surface of the body, and the proprioceptive system, situated within the body tissue.

interoceptor A sense organ or receptor located inside the body in contrast to one located at the surface or within the body tissue. It receives stimuli related to visceral processes.

interocular distance The distance between the central points of the pupils of the two eyes when they are in the normal position for fixation.

interosystem (R. Monroe) Any system which functions wholly within the organism and is controlled by the autonomic nervous system, such as the cardiac and respiratory systems.

interpersonal psychotherapy See *psychotherapy, interpersonal.*

interpersonal theory See *theory, interpersonal.*

interpolated reinforcement See *reinforcement, interpolated.*

interpolated (inter) schedule See *reinforcement, schedule of: interpolated.*

interpolation The calculation, either graphically or by mathematical formula, of a value between two values in a series of measurements.

interposition The partial obscuring of one object by another, used as a monocular cue in the perception of distance and depth.

interpretation **1.** The description, formulation, or reformulation of data, an event, or thought in a more familiar or significant way. **2.** (psychoanalysis) The therapist's formulation or description of the patient's productions, particularly translation of resistances, defenses, and symbols into terms which are understandable by the patient.

interpretation, allegoric The view that assumes a symbolic expression is intentional on the part of the speaker.

interpretation, anagogic (C. G. Jung) Interpretation of dreams based on the premise that they not only reflect conflict stemming from infantile wishes, but also the idealistic strivings of the unconscious.

interpretation of dreams See *dream interpretation.*

interpretive therapy See *therapy, interpretive.*

interquartile range (statistics) The distance between the first and third quartiles, encompassing the central fifty percent of the values in the distribution.

interruption tone See *tone, interruption.*

intersensory perception See *perception, intersensory.*

intersexuality The possession of sexual traits of both sexes, especially secondary sex characteristics.

interstimulation Behavior which is modified by the presence or perceived presence of others, whether there is intentional communication or not.

interstitial neurosyphilis See *syphilis, cerebral.*

intertone A tone of intermediate pitch between two tones of nearly equal pitch produced when the two tones are sounded together.

intertrial interval See *interval, intertrial.*

interval, class (i) (statistics) The number of score units between the upper and lower limits, or the range of values of a class in a frequency distribution.

interval estimation (statistics) The estimate of the population parameter in terms of a range of values within which the parameter lies with a certain degree of probability. The length of the confidence interval depends on the variance of the derived sampling distribution.

interval, fiducial The distance between certain points or limits beyond which a statistic is not expected to occur except by chance in more than a stated percentage of the samplings.

interval, intertrial The interval of time between successive presentations of the stimuli.

interval, median The class interval containing the median.

interval, mode The class interval which includes the mode.

interval of uncertainty (IU) The range between the upper and lower thresholds in judgments of difference.

interval reinforcement See *reinforcement, interval.*

interval scale See *scale, interval.*

interval schedule See *schedule, interval.*

intervention **1.** Behavior by an organism designed

to alter the environment or its relation to the environment. **2.** The therapist's direction of or influence on a client's actions.

interview A conversation between a therapist, counselor, or other professional, and a patient, client, or perspective employee, designed to elicit information for the purpose of assessing diagnosis, treatment, qualifications, or aid in research or guidance. According to the purpose of the interview it may be conducted using a directive or non-directive approach. For therapeutic purposes, the non-directive approach is usually preferred.

interview, amytal Interview conducted with the patient having been injected with small doses of amytal, inducing a completely relaxed and serene state which facilitates the communication of thoughts and the expression of previously repressed memories, affects and conflicts.

interview counseling An interview of an individual with a professional counselor who offers advice and guidance in the appropriate problematical area.

interview, diagnostic An interview whose purpose is to establish a diagnosis, treatment and prognosis of a disorder of the one interviewed.

interview, face-to-face A type of interview during which the therapist and patient sit opposite each other, characteristic of supportive interviewing and some forms of insight interviewing, such as Sullivanian therapy.

interview, stress An interview during which the interviewee is under intentionally induced emotional tension.

interview, structured An interview which has a definite predetermined cause.

interviewer bias The effect of the interviewer's opinions, values, expectations, and prejudices upon the process and interpretation of an interview.

intimacy, principle of (Gestalt psychology) The principle that Gestalts are wholes composed of interdependent parts, none of which may be changed without changing the whole.

intoxication A condition of exhilaration, depression, or alternating states between the two, caused by poisoning due to the ingestion of alcohol, drugs, or poison.

intoxication, hypnagogic Obsolete term for a hypnopompic state in which process of awakening generates dream images which persist into and may induce action in the awakened state.

intraception (H. A. Murray) Orientation or attitude characterized by humanism, feeling and imagination.

intracranial Within the cranium or brain.

intracranial tumor See *tumor, intracranial.*

intraindividual cathexis See *cathexis, intraindividual.*

intraocular modification Any change that takes place in the visual stimulus during its passage from the cornea to the ocular nerve, as a result of the general or individual structure of the eye.

intrapsychic Arising from or occurring within the psyche, mind, or personality, such as intrapsychic conflicts, the expressions of the existence of two opposing impulses or motivations within the individual.

intrapunitive See *intropunitive.*

intrinsic behavior See *behavior, intrinsic.*

intrinsic constant See *central constant.*

intrinsic eye muscles Muscles of the iris and of the ciliary body of the eye.

intrinsic motivation See *motivation, intrinsic.*

intrinsic reward See *reward, intrinsic.*

intrinsic thalamus See *thalamus, intrinsic.*

introception Internalization of a social group's standards or motives.

introjection The desire to swallow the love object and to identify with it is called introjection. Introjection expresses the primitive and ambivalent attitude that combines love and destruction in a cannibalistic incorporation of the love object, and in identification with the object incorporated. When certain adults are unable to develop more mature object relationships, their weak egos regress to the oral defense mechanism of introjection. Neurotic identification with the love object becomes the only possible object relationship.

introjection, projection and introjection process The process of learning and experiencing consisting of introjection, projection, and introjection. The person projects internal states into the environment, then introjects or is receptive to those aspects which will affect him. The introjections circularly determine the following projections. As a result of this process, the world is a meaningful part of the person and exists only as an aspect of that person. It also provides the individual with a system of values which affects his actions, and experiences.

intropunitive **1.** (S. Rosenzweig) Frustration reaction in which the frustrated individual blames himself for what happened and feels guilty, ashamed, or humiliated because of it. **2.** Personality type characterized by intropunitive frustration reactions.

introspection Observation and contemplation of one's own mental processes, and experiences; systematic self-observation.

introspectionism (W. Wundt) The method of psychology which holds that introspection is the basic method of psychological investigation.

introspective psychology See *introspectionism.*

introversion **1.** Inner-directed personality orientation characterized by interest in personal thoughts and feelings rather than in social concerns or external matters. **2.** (C. G. Jung) Dominance of subjective perception and cognition resulting in self-centered orientation and involvement with one's own inner world. 3. (H. J. Eysenck) A personality type based on particular neural structures which cause a slow development of reactive inhibition, weak inhibition and fast dissipation of inhibition. The neurotic form is characterized by anxiety and depression symptoms.

introversion, active (C. G. Jung) Inward direction of libido which is willed by the subject or a voluntary preoccupation with internal subjective reality.

introversion-extraversion 1. (H. J. Eysenck) A factor analyzed bipolar variable basic to the personality. 2. See *introversion*. 3. See *extraversion*.

introversion, passive (C. G. Jung) Inward direction of libido due to an inability to direct it toward external objects or an inability to relate to external reality.

introversive A Rorschach postulate, referring to those instances where the sum of human movement responses is substantially greater than the weighted sum of color responses. When the ratio (Erlebnistypus) manifests such a characteristic, the person is considered prone to derive his more basic gratifications from within himself rather than from interaction with his environment.

introversiveness (Rorschach) Characterized by inwardness and a tendency to interpret the world according to personal needs and values usually accompanied by a strong imagination and well-developed cerebral and autonomic processes.

introvert One who has an introverted personality or orientation.

introverted feeling type (C. G. Jung) Personality type characterized by a dominant subjective orientation such that the individual lives within his own internal world of emotions as a daydreamer or quiet, peaceful person.

introverted intuition type (C. G. Jung) Personality type characterized by attention to imagery which influences activity and a tendency to live within himself.

introverted sensation type (C. G. Jung) Personality type characterized by attendance to the external world through perceptions dominated by the individual's subjective internal state.

introverted thinking type (C. G. Jung) Personality type characterized by thorough organization of ideational patterns until they suit the individual, and some success in social contacts.

introverted type See *type, introverted*.

intuition Direct and immediate perception, judgment or knowledge, arrived at without prior conscious cogitation or reflective thinking.

intuitionism The philosophical theory stressing intuitive knowledge of fundamental truths in ethics, concerning right and wrong, and aesthetics, concerning beauty.

intuitive type See *type, intuitive*.

invalid 1. A conclusion, argument, or method which is not logically correct because of violation of the established rules of logic. 2. A test which does not measure that which it was designed to measure.

invariance 1. The property of remaining constant despite changes in other conditions. 2. The tendency of an image to retain its original size regardless of changes in the distance of the surface upon which it is projected.

inventive-response test An "open-ended" test in which the subject is restricted in response only by the instructions, as opposed to a selective-response test in which given response alternatives restrict the possible responses.

inventory A catalog or list used for assessing the presence or absence of certain behaviors, interests, attitudes or other items regarded as relevant for a given purpose.

inventory, adjustment A technique used to obtain evidence concerning an individual's adjustment from the individual himself. Also called surveys, schedules or questionnaires. An adjustment inventory contains statements or questions believed to be indicative of good or bad adjustment. The subject is requested to show what is generally or typically true of himself by choosing either "yes-no," "agree-disagree," or "like-dislike," depending on the particular inventory being used. The answers are scored and then compared to norms based on large samples of individuals.

In some cases, such as the SRA (Science Research Associates) Youth Inventory, the subject marks the appropriate answer space only if the statement applies to him. The following are some statements from a few of the areas covered by the SRA Youth Inventory:

Area	Illustrative Item
My School	1. I have difficulty keeping my mind on my studies.
Looking Ahead	35. What shall I do after high school?
About Myself	81. I feel "low" much of the time.

Inventory, Bell Adjustment A personality questionnaire used with subjects fourteen and up, yielding scores on home, health, social and emotional adjustment.

inventory, interest A questionnaire used in personality diagnosis, vocational guidance and personnel selection, consisting of items designed to reveal objects and activities preferred by or interesting to the individual.

Inventory, Minnesota Counseling (R. F. Berdie and W. L. Layton) An inventory developed from 1953 to 1957 designed for use with secondary school and college applicants in counseling.

inventory, personality A questionnaire or checklist which is usually answered by an individual about himself. It generally consists of numerous statements about personal characteristics to which the individual must respond, indicating whether they apply to him or not with "yes," "no" or "doubtful." Norms based on large representative samples are used in interpreting and comparing results.

inventory test See *test, inventory.*

inverse correlation See *correlation, inverse.*

inverse relationship Any relationship in which high values of one variable are associated with low values of the other.

inverse square law See *law, inverse square.*

inversion A choromosomal aberration in which a segment of a chromosome is reversed.

inversion, amphigenous Condition in which the homosexual individual engages in sex relations with those of the opposite sex, in contrast with absolute inversion.

inversion of affect See *affect, inversion of.*

invert An individual who prefers sexual partners of the same sex.

inverted factor analysis See *Q technique.*

investment 1. (psychoanalysis) The psychic energy expended upon an object. 2. The potential amount of affect or psychic energy with which an object is charged. Also called cathexis.

inviolacy motive (H. A. Murray) The need to defend onself and prevent self-depreciation.

involuntary An action which occurs without intention or volition.

involution Retrograde change in development accompanied by physiological and psychological deterioration as in senility and sometimes menopause.

involutional depression See *psychotic reaction, involutional.*

involutional melancholia See *psychotic reaction, involutional.*

involutional psychotic reactions See *psychotic reactions, involutional.*

Iowa Tests of Basic Skills See *tests, Iowa, of Basic Skills.*

I-P-I process See *introjection, projection, and introjection process.*

iproniazid A compound $C_3H_{13}N_3O$ which was used as a monoaminooxidase inhibitor antidepressant drug with mental patients until 1961 when it was withdrawn from the market because of the danger of causing an irreversible jaundice.

ipsation Autoerotism.

ipsative method A method of measuring traits using the individual's own behavior as the standard for comparison.

ipsative scale See *scale, ipsative.*

ipsative scoring (R. B. Cattell) Standardization of

scores obtained for a given individual. The ipsative scoring accounts for the mean and standard deviation of similar responses given by a certain individual to a variety of stimuli and/or on numerous occasions.

ipsilateral On the same side.

IQ See *intelligence quotient.*

iris The pigmented muscular disc of the eye, located in front of the lens and surrounding the pupil, the contractions of which regulate the amount of light entering the eye.

irradiation 1. The spreading of rays of light. 2. An ostensible increase in the size of a small bright stimulus seen on a dark background. 3. The spread of an afferent impulse to adjacent fibers as it approaches and travels through the central nervous system. 4. A spread of excitation in muscle fibers upon increase in the intensity of stimulation. 5. (I. P. Pavlov) The spread of excitation and inhibition through the cerebral cortex. 6. (I. P. Pavlov) The elicitation of the conditioned response by stimuli similar to the conditioned stimulus. 7. The exposure of tissues to radiation.

irradiation, excitatory (I. P. Pavlov) The spreading out of stimulation in the cerebrum.

irradiation theory See *theory, irradiation.*

irrational type See *type, irrational.*

irreality level (K. Lewin) The region of the individual's life space in which actions and thoughts are determined more by needs and desires than by objective recognition of situations. Prejudices and fantasies are of the irreality level.

irreality-reality dimension (K. Lewin) The continuum on which behaviors can be ordered according to the degree they are regulated by either needs and desires, or by the reality demands of the environment.

irritability 1. The characteristic property of living matter of being capable of responses to stimulation or excitation. 2. Over-sensitivity to stimulation.

IRT See *inter response time.*

ischnophonia; ischophonia Stammering or stuttering.

Ishihari test See *test, Ishihari.*

Island of hearing See *tonal islands.*

Island of Reil See *Reil, island of.*

Islands of Langerhans See *Langerhans, islands of.*

isochronism 1. Correspondence in time or frequency of occurrence between two processes. 2. Having the same chronaxy.

isocortex The most common type cortex of the cerebral hemispheres, composed of six layers of cells originating in the gray matter. Also called neocortex.

isogenic Having identical genotypes as in identical

twins, triplets, etc. A homograft is accepted in these cases.

isolate 1. To separate, set apart, or abstract from a class. 2. (psychoanalysis) To separate ideas or memories from their affect. 3. (J. L. Moreno) The individual who scored lowest in a group on the sociogram.

isolation (S. Freud) A defense mechanism of the ego. It consists of interposing of a refractory period in which the individual refrains from thinking and acting. It is usually an aftermath of a traumatic or severely unpleasant experience.

isolation defense See *defense, isolation.*

isolation effect The isolation of an item by use of distinctive type or color in the center of a group in serial learning, resulting in the facilitation of learning.

isolation, psychic (C. G. Jung) Withdrawal from social contacts for fear that some unconscious material might be divulged.

isometric twitch See *twitch, isometric.*

isomorphism 1. (logic) A one-to-one relation between the elements of two distinct sets. 2. (Gestalt) The proposition that there exists a one-to-one correspondence between a stimulus and the excitatory fields in the brain; that is, if there is a perceived difference of size there will be a corresponding difference in the size of the excitatory fields.

isopathic principle See *principle, isopathic.*

isophilia (H. S. Sullivan) Affectionate behavior with the absence of expressed or sublimated genital lust, towards individuals of one's own sex.

isophonic contour A graphic representation of the interdependent relationships between the physical properties of a sound and the corresponding auditory experiences.

isopodic method (R. B. Cattell) A method of comparing source trait factor scores across cultural or age groups by producing comparability of a) the scaling of the variables themselves, and b) the factor estimation weights.

isosensitivity function See *receiver operating characteristic.*

isotropic Items or attributes placed in an ordered series on any nonquantitative basis, as for example, army ranks.

isovaleric acidema A rare aminoaciduria associated with mild mental retardation.

isthmus 1. The neck or the connecting part of an organ. 2. The part of the brain which connects the spinal cord with the forebrain and the cerebellum.

item analysis See *analysis, item.*

item difficulty The level of difficulty of a test item. The frequency with which it is passed or failed in a given testee population.

item scaling A statistical procedure used for assigning a test item to its place, determined by its level of difficulty.

item selection The process by which an item is selected for use on a test on the basis of its validity, reliability, scorability, scalability, and unique contribution.

item validity See *validity, item.*

item weighting The process by which a test item is assigned the proportion of the total score it will determine.

items, stop Starred items in personality inventories which are used to screen individuals who may need psychological help.

ITPA See *test, Illinois, of Psycholinguistic Abilities.*

IU See *interval of uncertainty.*

Ivanov-Smolensky technique See *technique, Ivanov-Smolensky.*

J

J (C. L. Hull) Delay in reinforcement.

j The number of standard deviations from the mean.

j coefficient See *coefficient, j.*

J curve See *curve, J.*

Jackson, John Hughlings (1834-1911) A British neurologist who described the seizures due to focal lesions of the cerebral cortex, since called Jacksonian epilepsy. He is also credited with the classic study of aphasia, and with J. A. L. Clarke, the first full description of syringomyelia. His description of paralysis of one-half of the palate, pharynx, and larynx, and flaccid paralysis of the homolateral sternocleidomastoid and part of the trapezius resulted in its being known as Jackson's syndrome.

Jackson's law The principle that in deterioration in mental functioning resulting from disease, the order of degeneration is the reverse of the order of development or acquisition.

jactation or jactitation Excessive restlessness characterized by irregular and convulsive movements of the body.

James-Lange theory Two separate, distinct theories about emotions which are often commonly and incorrectly viewed as one. **1.** C. Lange (1834-1900), a Danish physiologist, studied the circulatory system and concluded that emotions were identical with experiences of vascular change. **2.** W. James (1842-1910) incorporated Lange's idea into his own theory which stated that bodily changes, particularly visceral and muscular changes, immediately followed the perception of an emotion-provoking situation and that one's experience of these physiological changes is the emotion. This theory challenged the popular view that emotions preceded and caused bodily changes.

James, William (1842-1910) American psychologist and philosopher, developed pragmatic philosophy and functionalistic psychology. His main work, *Principles of Psychology* (1878), introduced an evolutionary-biological approach to mental life viewed as an important tool in adjustment to life. His theory of emotions assumes that bodily changes follow directly the perception of existing fact, and that our feeling of the same dangers as they occur is the emotions. Thus we feel sorry because we cry, not vice versa. James introduced the concept of "stream of consciousness." Consciousness itself is a product of evolution and has been evolved as all other functions. James stressed pleasure and usefulness as the main motives of behavior.

Janet, Pierre (1859-1947) French student of Charcot who had competed with Freud. Studied dissociation and hysteria, and pioneered interest in the unconscious. Fully at home in both medicine and general psychology, he tried to bring the two closer together.

Jansky-Bielschowsky disease See *Tay-Sachs disease.*

Japanese encephalitis See *encephalitis, Japanese.*

jargon aphasia See *aphasia, jargon.*

Jaspers, Karl (1883-1969) A Swiss-German existentialist philosopher. Prior to his philosophical work, Jaspers was a practicing psychiatrist. His emphasis, as such, was on the need for detailed descriptions of patient's subjective experiences and on the necessity of empathy with patients' feelings in order for therapy to be successful. *Die Psychologie der Weltanschauungen* ("Psychology of Personal Views on Life") marked his move towards philosophy. As a philosopher, Jaspers' aim was to provide a theory encompassing all problems related to man's existence. Thus he distinguished three modes of being: "being-there," the objective world known through observation and experiment; "being-oneself," man's personal existence dependent upon awareness of self, liberty, and assertion of self by decision and choice; and "being-in-itself," the representative of the world in its transcendence. According to Jaspers, man can participate in all modes at once but can never fully grasp the entire meaning of existence. Communication is central to Jaspers' theory. Man exists only to the extent that he is in communication with others, or to the extent that another existence reflects him. Though he is alone in dealing with inescapable situations such as death, anguish, and struggle, he is not isolated. Freedom, in essence, is man's search for communication with the existence of others.

Jastrow cylinders A series of hollow, weighted rubber cylinders used for the determination of thresholds for pressure and kinaesthesis in lifting.

Jastrow illusion See *illusion, Jastrow.*

Java man Pithecanthropus erectus.

jealousy, projected Jealousy derived from an individual's own actual infidelity or from repressed desires for it.

Jendrassik reinforcement See *reinforcement, Jendrassik.*

jnd See *just noticeable difference.*

job analysis A thorough examination and breakdown of the ability and experience requirements, work conditions and opportunities for advancement on a particular job or occupation.

job placement The assignment of a person to a job usually on the basis of his aptitude, interest, experience, and personality.

Jocasta complex See *complex, Jocasta.*

joints, disturbances of 1. Disturbances of joints and the muscular system due to organic or psychogenic causes. 2. See *arthritis, rheumatoid.* 3. See *back disorders, psychogenic.*

Jones, Ernest (1879-1958) British psychiatrist and psychoanalyst. One of the earliest disciples of S. Freud; the first British psychoanalyst. Wrote extensively on psychoanalytic technique, dream interpretation, nightmares, etc. Author of the most detailed biography of S. Freud.

Jordan curve See *curve, Jordan.*

Joseph's syndrome A rare aminoaciduria associated with seizures.

Jost's law See *law, Jost's.*

judgment 1. The process of discovering an objective or intrinsic relationship between two or more objects, facts, experiences or concepts. 2. That faculty which enables an individual to make judgments. 3. A

critical evaluation of a person, object or situation. 4. (psychophysics) A subject's verbal responses to stimuli, concerning its presence or absence and magnitude used for the determination of threshold.

judgment, absolute In a series of comparisons, the evaluation of the first of a pair of items prior to the presentation of the second member of the pair.

judgment, comparative A report which declares the subject's perception of how two or more stimuli compare on a particular dimension.

judgment, moral (J. Piaget) Judgment concerning whether an act is right or wrong. The moral judgment is a function of development.

Juke family (R.L. Dugdale) The history of this family was studied in the early part of the century in an attempt to show a family with low intelligence also has generally low social competence.

Jung, Carl Gustav (1875-1961) Swiss psychiatrist, founder of "analytical psychology." Discovered "feeling-toned complexes" (1904-09); proposed psychogenic theory of schizophrenia (1907); cooperated with Freud (1907-1913); introduced principle of analysis of analysts (1912); separated from Freud on account of his divergent concepts of libido and of incest. Described psychological typology ("extra- and introversion," 1921). Defined psyche as self-regulating system, aiming at individuation, manifested in compensatory function of dreams, with the symbol as "transformer of energy." Distinguished three layers of psyche: consciousness, the personal unconscious, and the collective unconscious, the latter containing the "archetypes." Explored psychological significance of myth, religion, and alchemy; formulated concept of "synchronicity" as a principle of "acausal connection."

Jung association test See *test, Jung association.*

Jungian typology See *extraversion-introversion.*

just noticeable difference The least difference, usually in a quantitative aspect, between two stimuli, one of which is barely above the threshold. Statistically, the difference is not detected as often as it is.

just noticeable differences method See *method, just noticeable differences.*

juvenile delinquency See *delinquency, juvenile.*

juvenile general paresis See *paresis, general juvenile.*

K

k **1.** (mathematics) The most commonly used symbol for representing a constant. **2.** (statistics) The coefficient of alienation, given by the formula

$$\sqrt{1 - r^2}$$

where r is the correlation coefficient. **3.** (Rorschach) The symbol used to represent a response in which shading was a determinant.

K (C. L. Hull) Incentive motivation considered as a part of reaction potential.

K' (C. L. Hull) The physical reward or incentive in motivation.

K complex See *complex, K.*

K scale See *scale, K.*

Kahlbaum, Karl Ludwig (1828-1899) A German psychiatrist who described in 1863 mental deterioration in adolescence and called it *paraphrenia hebetica.* In 1874 he described catatonic stupor and called it *Spannungs Irrsinn* (insanity of tension); he believed that the stupor was caused by a brain disease.

Kahn Test of Symbol Arrangement See *test, Kahn, of Social Arrangement.*

Kalinowsky, Lothar B. (1899-   ) Born in Berlin, Germany; psychiatrist and neurologist. Interested in somatic treatments in psychiatry since working with malaria treatment in the Viennese Clinic of Wagner-von Jauregg. After work in German neuropsychiatric centers he worked with the Italian psychiatrists Cerletti and Bini at the time of their discovery of electric convulsive treatment. Since 1940 in the United States, continues his work in the field of somatic treatments. Wrote various books, the latest (with H. Hippius) in 1969, *Psychopharmacological Convulsive and other Somatic Treatments in Psychiatry.*

Kallikak family (H. H. Goddard) A ficticious name given by H. H. Goddard to a family he studied intensively, one branch (496 individuals) of which was noted for its good citizenship and in several cases, distinguished service to the community, while the other branch (480 individuals) showed almost without exception, a record of criminality, degeneracy, insanity, and severe mental retardation.

Kallmann, Franz J. (1897-1965) Psychiatrist and geneticist, born and trained in Germany, lived and worked in United States from 1936. Developed genetic theory of schizophrenia based on extensive study of families and twins, showing that the risk of schizophrenia in relatives varies directly with the degree of genetic closeness; formulated hypothesis that predisposition is inherited and manifestation depends on constitutional and environmental factors; provided evidence by studies of twins for the role of genetic factors in manic-depressive psychosis, involutional psychosis, homosexuality, and the aging process; demonstrated increasing marriage and fertility rates among hospitalized schizophrenic patients; concerned from an early date with problems of genetic counseling in a psychiatric setting; studied family and mental health problems of persons with early total deafness and established in New York the first psychiatric service for the deaf.

Kanzer, Mark (1908-   ) American psychoanalyst. Main studies have been in the application of psychoanalysis to the understanding of human behavior and the promotion of its potentialities 1) through investigations of the history of psychoanalysis; 2) the evaluation of its methods both in the clinical and behavioral fields; 3) in analytic education, research and administrative organizations; 4) in definition of its terms and concepts.

Kappa effect (J. Cohen) See *Tau effect.*

Kardiner, Abram (1891-   ) Past Director of Psychoanalytic Clinic and Clinical Professor of Psychiatry at Columbia University. Efforts directed chiefly to a study of human adaptation as seen through traumatic neuroses and cross cultural studies of human development. Books written include: *The Individual and his Society* (1939), *The Traumatic Neuroses of War* (1941), *The Psychological Frontiers of Society* (1945), *The Mark of Oppression* (with L. Ovesey) (1951), *Sex and Morality* (1954), *War Stress and Neurotic Illness* (1947), *They Studied Man* (1958).

karyotype The chromosomal set of an individual; often applied to their photo-micrographs arranged according to a standard classification.

kathisophobia Fear of sitting down.

Keeler polygraph Lie detector.

Kelley's constant process (psychophysics) A technique for the treatment of data from the constant stimulus method, consisting of fitting the data to the normal ogive by using the standard deviation instead of h.

Kelly, George Alexander (1905-1967) American clinical psychologist; pioneer in clinical psychology; the first to found a psychological clinic for service and training; proposed a personality theory based on the thesis that the important determinant of a person's behavior is his own conception of the world in which he lives and the people he meets; his chief two-volume work, *The Psychology of Personal Constructs* (1955), and his clinical methods had much influence and stimulated research here and abroad; he taught at Ohio State University for 20 years; lectured in Europe, South America, and the Caribbean area.

keltolagnia Sexual excitement associated with stealing.

Kelvin scale See *scale, Kelvin.*

kenophobia; cenophobia Fear of large, empty spaces.

Kent-Rosanoff test See *test, Kent-Rosanoff.*

Kent Series of Emergency Scales See *scales, Kent Series of Emergency.*

keraunophobia Fear of lightning.

kernicterus A disease occurring in infancy manifested by jaundice two or three days after birth, which if untreated, produces convulsions, rigidity, coma and death in 75% of the cases. Mental deficiency, epilepsy, chorea or athetosis often result in those who survive. Also called icterus gravis neonatorum. It is caused by blood incompatibility of blood groups Rh, A, B and O of the fetus with the mother's blood.

kerosene poisoning See *poisoning, kerosene.*

ketotic hypoglycemia See *hypoglycemia, ketotic.*

key 1. A central concept upon which others depend or which facilitates understanding of other concepts. 2. A list of symbols or correct answers used in coding or decoding information, or in scoring a test. 3. (operant conditioning) Any object movement which opens or closes an electric circuity thus meeting the criterion of a reinforcement eligible response.

Kierkegaard, Sören (1813-1855) Danish philosopher and writer on theology. Objected to Hegelian rationalism and based his philosophy on the absolute dualism of faith and knowledge, and of thought and reality. Considered himself a "religious author," but was not renowned so much for his theological ideas as for his penetrating analysis of man's inner experiences, man's existential problems. Was probably the first to use the term "existence" in the sense existentialists now use it. His main theme is man and his conflicts; man striving for eternity with an infinite God, but frustrated by his own temporality and finitude. Emphasized that religion was a matter for the individual soul. Author of *Either-Or* (1843), *The Concept of Dread* (1844), and *The Sickness Unto Death* (1849). Discovered in the 20th century. Major influence on existential philosophers such as Martin Heidegger.

kinephantom A movement illusion seen in shadow movement, in which the shadows of moving objects, such as the spokes of a wheel, are seen as moving in the opposite direction from that of the object.

kinesthesis The sense of body movement and movements of particular body parts, such as muscles, tendons and joints. In conjunction with the static sense derived from the semicircular canals of the ear, it yields information concerning the position of the body and limbs in space. Kinesthesis is divided into: muscle sense, sensors within the muscles which are stimulated by muscle contraction; tendon sense, sensors within the tendons; and joint sense, sensors on joint surfaces which are stimulated by joint flexion.

kinesthetic aphasia See *aphasia, afferent motor.*

kinesthetic apraxia See *apraxia, afferent.*

kinesthetic feedback See *feedback, kinesthetic.*

kinesthetic memory See *memory, kinesthetic.*

kinesthetic method See *method, kinesthetic.*

kinesthetic response See *response, kinesthetic.*

kinetic aphasia See *aphasia, efferent.*

kinetic apraxia See *apraxia, efferent.*

kinky hair disease A genetic, sex-linked transmitted metabolic disorder which results in a slight aminoaciduria in the urine and an excess of glutamic acid in the blood. The main clinical features are mental and physical retardation, lack of pigmentation in the hair, epilepsy and microcephaly.

kinship system See *system, kinship.*

Kirchhoff, Theodor (1853-1922) A German psychiatrist and noted historian of psychiatry.

Kjersted-Robinson law The principle that the amount of information learned during a segment of the total learning time is relatively independent of and constant for different lengths of material.

Klein, Melanie (1882-1960) Born in Vienna and died in London. Analyzed by Ferenczi and Abraham, she became an original thinker in the field of psychoanalysis and her technical and theoretical work deeply influenced modern psychoanalytic theory. Pioneered the psychoanalysis of children and evolved the play technique which became the basis of most techniques in child psychotherapy. Her theoretical contributions include the description of the early roots of the Oedipus complex and of the superego, and a conceptualization of the early infantile development in terms of the depressive and the paranoid-schizoid positions. The light she threw on the dynamics of early infantile stages is of particular importance for the understanding and psychoanalytical treatment of psychotic states. In 1926, she came to London and exerted a marked influence on the British Psychoanalytic Society.

Klein's, Melanie, contribution to psychoanalysis Melanie Klein, the originator of the technique of psychoanalysis of children, evolved a play technique which gave her a means for direct investigation of the mind of a small child, and enabled her to extend and deepen psychoanalytic knowledge. Her early discoveries established the existence of pregenital forms of the Oedipus complex and the superego, and the importance of unconscious fantasy in all aspects of mental functioning. In the latter part of her scientific work she formulated her findings in terms of development of positions. The *paranoid-schizoid* position gets organized in the first months of life. It is characterized by the infant's relation to part objects, primarily the breast. The leading mechanisms of defense are splitting, projective identification and introjection. Both the object and the ego are split into good and bad. The prevalent anxiety is persecutory. Envy is an important pathogenic factor. The *depressive* position is organized when the infant perceives the mother as a whole person. It is characterized by integration, awareness of separateness from the object, and ambivalence. The prevalent anxiety is a loss of the loved object, and guilt. The depressive anxiety and guilt are defended against by manic defenses, but they also give rise to more positive developments linked with reparation. The roots of the Oedipus complex are in the oral phase in the depressive position following the recognition of the mother's separate existence as a person. Jealousy gradually replaces envy. The points of fixation of psychotic illnesses lie in the paranoid-schizoid position and early stages of the depressive position.

kleptomania An obsessive impulse to steal often in the absence of economic motive or desire for the particular objects stolen.

Klineberg, Otto (1899-   ) American social psychologist, born in Quebec, Canada. Research and publications concerning problems of ethnic relations and race differences, international affairs, culture and personality, social and cultural aspects of mental health. Actively engaged in the international development of psychology. Taught for over 30 years at Columbia University, New York; visiting professor, University of Sao Paulo, Brazil; University of Hawaii; University of Paris and Ecole des Hautes Etudes, Paris, 1962-   . Member of Secretariat, Unesco, 1948-49, 1953-55. Former Secretary general and President, International Union of Psychological Science; President and Honorary President, World Federation for Mental Health; Honorary President, European League for Mental Hygiene. One of the first psychologists to question, on the basis of empirical research, the theory of innate psychological differences between racial and ethnic groups. See *race*.

Klinefelter's syndrome See *syndrome, Klinefelter's.*

klinotaxis A taxis which does not require a receptor itself capable of discriminating the direction of the stimulus source. If the receptor is not equally accessible to stimulation in all directions, the animal can compare intensities by moving the receptors first one way, then another. In these successive comparisons the organism turns until the two sides are equally stimulated.

Klopfer system An approach to the Rorschach test developed by Bruno Klopfer, essentially based on a phenomenological approach to understanding behavior and thinking. It has become the most widely used approach to the Rorschach in the United States.

Klüver-Bucy syndrome See *syndrome, Klüver-Bucy.*

knee A deviation from a smooth curve which is often seen in the early acceleration of interval or ratio segments and which consists of a period of compensatory low response rate following a brief period of rapid responding.

knee jerk reflex See *reflex, patellar.*

knox cube test See *test, Knox cube.*

Koenig cylinders A series of tuned, metal cylinders which emit tones of very high frequency, used in the determination of the upper threshold of pitch.

Koffka, Kurt (1886-1941) European-born American psychologist. With Max Wertheimer and Wolfgang Köhler, founder of Gestalt psychology. He was the first to introduce Gestalt psychology to America (1922). Extended this approach to developmental psychology (*Growth of the Mind*); later undertook a systematic overview of the whole field of psychology from the Gestalt point of view (*Principles of Gestalt Psychology*, 1935). Made many experimental and theoretical contributions to perception, including studies of the perception of motion, the constancies, visual organization, and a clarification of the problem of the nature of the stimulus.

Köhler-Restorff phenomenon The occurrence of greater frequency of recall in right associates experiments, when the pair is presented in isolation in comparison to presentation as one pair in a series.

Köhler, Wolfgang (1887-1967) European-born American psychologist. With Max Wertheimer and Kurt Koffka, founder of Gestalt psychology. Critic of prevailing atomistic theories in psychology, he examined the relations between field theory in physics and the theories and findings of Gestalt psychology, showing similarities between the behavior of physical and of perceptual organizations. This line of thinking later led him to investigation (with Wallach and others) of figural aftereffects and finally to the demonstration (with Held and others) of cortical currents corresponding to organized perceptions. Made many theoretical and empirical contributions to perception. Investigated problem solving in chimpanzees and clarifed concept of insight. (With von Restorff) discovered the isolation effect in memory; contributed to theory of memory and recall; developed nonassociationistic theory of the nature of associations. Analyzed values in terms of requiredness, rejecting purely subjective and relativistic interpretations. His analysis of evolutionary theory showed that the nativism-empiricism dichotomy is insufficient, since it neglects all those factors, either inherited or acquired that organisms share with the rest of nature.

Kohs Block Design Test See *test, Kohs Block Design.*

Kolb, Lawrence C. (1911-   ) American psychiatrist, educator, author. Contributed to understanding of the body image separating clinically the healthy from the psychopathological responses following trauma, mutilation and disease, and described the features which discriminate body concept and percept as well as delineating preventive and therapeutic approaches to the variant expressions. Also wrote on related pain expressive behavior and its management; superego defects productive of homosexual acting out. Earlier work on the traumatic neuroses induced by environmental stress and physiology of micturition. In recent years has chaired the Columbia University Department of Psychiatry, and directed the New York State Psychiatric Institute. Author of *Urban Challenges to Psychiatry; Mental Deficiency* and 150 other articles.

Korsakoff psychosis See *psychosis, Korsakoff.*

Korsakov's syndrome or psychosis Excessive neural irritation generally caused by alcoholism and severe deficiencies in food intake, characterized by disturbances of memory and loss of orientation.

Korte's laws Laws stating the conditions for optimal apparent movements when two stationary visual stimuli are given in succession. They are: 1) when intensity is held constant, the time interval for optimal phi directly varies with the distance between stimuli; 2) when time is held constant, the distance for optimal phi varies directly with intensity; 3) when distance between stimuli is held constant, intensity for optimal phi varies inversely with the time interval.

KPR See *Kuder Preference Record.*

K-R formulas See *coefficient of equivalence, Kuder-Richardson.*

Kraepelin, Emil (1856-1926) German psychiatrist, a student of Wundt, who, in applying Wundtian methods to the study of abnormal states, was a pioneer in experimental psychopathology. Late in the nineteenth century he formulated a system for classifying the psychoses that has been highly influential ever since. He classified mental disease into two major groups: dementia praecox and manic depressive psychoses. Maintained strict somatic view; helped to initiate abnormal psychology. Author of *Lehrbuch der Psychiatrie* (1933).

Krafft-Ebing, Richard (1840-1903) A German psychiatrist primarily noted for his work in sexology. He was the first to definitely establish the relationship between general paralysis and syphilis before the Wassermann reaction was discovered and in his work *Psychopathia Sexualis* in 1886, he described aberrations of the sexual drive.

Krause's corpuscle See *corpuscle, Krause's.*

Krech, David (né Krechevsky, I.) (1909-   ) American experimental psychologist, brain researcher, social psychologist and textbook author. His behavioral research culminated in his "hypothesis" and "non-continuity" theories for animal cognitive learning; after early ablation experiments on animal brains, he initiated the Berkeley research program on brain chemistry and behavior and made the initial observation of chemical and anatomical brain residuals consequent upon psychologically enriched experiences; founded, in 1936, the Society for the Psychological Study of Social Issues; with collaborators wrote three texts: *Theory and Problems of Social Psychology, Individual in Society, Elements of Psychology.*

Kretschmer, Ernst (1889-1964) German neuropsychiatrist and psychotherapist. Designed the first psychiatric characterology, described the sensitive psychogenesis of delusions and postulated multidimensional diagnosis and therapy. Psychophysiological theory of hysteria (conscious will and hypobulic mechanisms). Understanding of neurosis caused by ambivalence of impulses and insufficiency of maturation; connection between adolescence and psychic disorders. Wrote first *Medical Psychology.* Found correlation between schizophrenia and leptosome, athletic, dysplastic body built; between manic-depressive psychoses and pyknic habitus. Constitutional correspondence: leptosome-schizothyme, athletic-barykinetic, pyknic-cyclothyme temperaments. Investigated relationship between character, genius and society.

Kubie, Lawrence S. (1896-   ) American psychiatrist and psychoanalyst; taught, practiced and conducted research in psychiatry, clinical neurology, experimental neuropathology, psychoanalysis, and psychosomatic medicine. Kubie examined critically the fundamental concepts of psychoanalytic theory and practice, as well as the biological basis of psychiatry, and tried to reconcile the constitutional factors with psychoanalysis.

Kuder Preference Record A self-report inventory designed to reveal relative interest in ten broadly defined vocational areas, such as scientific, musical, etc. by the administration of items dealing with the interests as well as five sections dealing with personality data, such as family relations, and conflict avoidance.

Kuder-Richardson coefficients of equivalence See *coefficients of equivalence, Kuder-Richardson.*

Kuf's Disease (H. Kufs) A type of amaurotic familial idiocy which occurs in the teens. Also see *Tay-Sachs disease.*

Kuhlmann-Anderson Test See *test, Kuhlmann-Anderson.*

Kuhlmann-Binet Test See *test, Kuhlmann-Binet.*

Külpe, Oswald Philosopher, psychologist. Born August 3, 1862 in Kandava, Latvia; died December 30, 1915 in Munich of influenza. In 1881 he studied history at Leipzig, then followed several years of academic *Wanderjahren* studying at Berlin, Göttingen, and Dorpat. He received his Ph.D. at Leipzig under Wundt in 1887. He was professor at Würzburg in 1894; in 1909 he went to Bonn and in 1912 to Munich.

Külpe is best known in psychology as the founder of the Würzburg School of *Denkpsychologie.* His intellectual development went from early adherence to Wundt's psychology of contents towards Brentano's psychology of acts. His is a middle position between these two extremes in that he recognized the existence of conscious contents (Gedanken), relations between them, and psychic functions like abstracting (Denken). Impalpable acts were a species of *Denken* and included the attribution of meaning, thinking and judging, which were conceived to be other than relations between contents.

Compared with Brentano, who was a distinguished Aristotelian scholar, Külpe was an outstanding Kantian scholar. His general philosophical position was that of Critical Realism.

His students included K. Bühler, O. Selz, and E. Bloch. Wertheimer received his degree at Würzburg at the time of Külpe's leadership, but could not be considered one of the followers of the school.

Külpe published quantitatively little by the scale of academicians of his time, but qualitatively his work was well reasoned and therefore influential. Among his works are: 1893, *Grundiss der Psychologie,* English translation by Titchener; 1895-1929, *Einleitung in die Philosophie,* (many editions); 1907-1912, *I. Kant* (two editions).

Kundt's rule The principles that: 1) distances which have been divided by regular gradation lines appear greater than those which are unmarked and 2) that in the attempt to bisect a horizontal line using only one eye, there is a liklihood that the dividing point will be placed too near the nasal side of the eye used.

kurtosis (Ku) The relative degree of flatness or peakedness in a frequency curve in the region of the mode.

kuru A neurological disorder, occurring mainly in Australia and the South Pacific, the etiology of which is unknown. It results in progressive motor incoordination, mental disturbances especially in affect, and often death within six to nine months after onset.

Kwashiorkor A tropical and subtropical children's disease caused by an inappropriate protein diet. Main symptoms include impaired growth, edema, severe apathy and often mental retardation.

Kwint psychomotor test See *test, Kwint psychomotor.*

kymograph An instrument essentially consisting of a rotating drum covered with paper, used for making graphic records of temporal variations in physiological and psychological processes.

kymography A technique used for the measurement of motions in an organ.

kyphoscoliosis A lateral curvature of the spine with an anteroposterior hump on the spinal column.

kyphosis An angular curvature of the spine which resembles a mild humpbacked condition.

L

L Lumen.

sL_R (C. L. Hull) The stimulus strength which will just barely evoke a response; reaction threshold.

L-data Life-record data, obtained by rating the individual as he reacts in life situations. Quantifiable data not arising from standard key-score tests; hence, subject to disagreement among observers as to the score value to be assigned a given performance. L-Data constitute one of the three Media of Observation, the other two being Q-Data and T-Data.

L method (statistics) A short cut method for selecting a small number of items which will predict a criterion as well as or better than one that was computed from the entire pool or population from which the smaller sample was drawn.

laboratory training A general term for group approaches in which the goals are some degree of self-understanding, the understanding of the conditions which facilitate or inhibit group functioning, the understanding of interpersonal operations in groups and developing skills for diagnosing individual, group and organizational behavior. The primary use of these groups is in industry where problems arise due to interpersonal or group conflicts. The first organization to offer such assistance to industry was the National Training Laboratories or NTL.

labyrinth Part of the auditory apparatus composed of a system of intercommunicating canals and cavities within the cochlea.

lacuna A gap in evidence or data occurring in memory or consciousness.

Ladd-Franklin, Christine (1847-1930) American psychologist. A versatile scientist who was trained at Johns Hopkins, Göttingen, and Berlin. Probably best known for her theory of color vision, an elaboration of Hering's evolutionary color vision theory. An associate editor of Baldwin's *Dictionary of Philosophy and Psychology* (1901-02) and a frequent contributor to mathematical, philosophical, and psychological publications. She lectured in logic and psychology at Johns Hopkins (1904-1909). In 1910 moved to Columbia where she remained until her death.

Ladd-Franklin theory See *color vision, theory of: Ladd-Franklin theory.*

lagophthalmos, lagophthalmus A disturbance of the seventh cranial nerve consisting of the failure of the upper eyelid to move downward when the individual attempts to close his eyes.

Laing, Ronald D. (1927-   ) Scottish psychiatrist and psychoanalyst. Experiences as practicing psychiatrist led to questioning psychiatric assumptions as to what mental illness is. Research in mental hospital, clinic, and home settings, brought to light many observations in social *impasses,* and the behavior that ensues. Work with psychedelics in social situations led to need to envisage chemistry *in vivo,* as part of the social process, conditioned thereby, and conditioning. Subsequently involved in developing theory in the area between social controls, behavior, and experience. Presently associated with experiments with reciprocal influences of disturbed and disturbing environment and disturbed and disturbing modes of experience.

laissez-faire group (K. Lewin) Group in social psychology with a passive leader who avoids taking the initiative.

lallation 1. Infantile or unintelligible speech. 2. The substitution of the *l* sound for more difficult consonants such as *r.*

Lamarckian evolution (J.B.P.A. de Monet de Lamarck) The theory that characteristics acquired during the life of an organism through use, disuse, or adaptation of organs to changes in the environment can be transmitted to the offspring.

lambda (λ) Wave length.

lambda ratio A primary Rorschach index as formulated in the Beck approach to the test and represented by the proportion of pure form responses to all non-pure responses in the record. It is related to,

215

but computed differently than, the F% used in other approaches to the test. Either lambda or the F% are interpreted as representing affect-free functioning.

lambert A unit of luminance equal to the brightness of a perfectly diffusing surface reflecting light at a rate of one lumen per square centimeter, or to $1/\pi$ candles per square centimeter. The millilambert, one thousandth of a lambert, is more commonly used.

Lambert's law A law of the relation between physical intensity of light and the angle of incidence with the reflecting surface, stating that the incidence, emission and reflection of light, vary directly as the cosine of the angle of the rays perpendicular to the surface.

La Mettrie, Julien Offray de (1709-1751) French physician-philosopher who also worked in Holland and Germany. Holding that thought is only the outcome of the mechanical action of the brain and nervous system, he was an extreme scientific materialist and hedonist. Among his influential writings was *Man, a Machine,* published in 1848.

Landolt circles Incomplete circles having gaps of varying sizes used in the determination of visual acuity.

Lange, Carl George (1834-1900) A Danish physiologist who almost simultaneously with William James, proposed a theory of emotions stating that emotion is the organism's feeling of the physiological changes which directly follow perception of an object, situation or thought. This has since been known as the James-Lange theory of emotion.

Langerhans, islands of Small masses of cells in the pancreas which secrete insulin.

language centers Areas in the cerebral cortex which function in different aspects of spoken and written language and in music.

language, gestural-postural A form of non-verbal communication by means of gestures and postures.

language, graphic Communication by means of recorded symbols.

language, irrelevant (L. Kanner) Words, utterances, or phrases within the context of intelligible speech or alone, which are understood and have meaning for only the speaker. Irrelevant language is seen most commonly in schizophrenia and early infantile autism.

Laplacian curve The normal frequency curve.

lapsus calami A slip of the pen.

lapsus linguae A slip of the tongue.

lapsus memoriae A slip of the memory.

larval sadism See *sadism, larval.*

larvated epilepsy See *epileptic equivalent.*

laryngeal reflex See *reflex, laryngeal.*

laryngograph An arrangement for obtaining a graphic record on a kymograph of movements of the larynx during speech.

laryngoscope An instrument composed essentially of a system of mirrors, used in examining the larynx.

Lasegue sign A symptom indicative of disease of the sciatic.

Lashley jumping stand Apparatus used to train and test animal visual discrimination. The subject, most often a rat, stands on a platform and is faced with two doors, one of which is locked. Each door has a different stimulus pattern. The response is the rat jumping through the unlocked door to the food reinforcement on the other side.

Lashley, Karl Spencer (1890-1958) American physiological psychologist who discovered in pioneer ablation experiments on the rat, that memory for learned habits is not precisely localized in the brain; performance decrement is proportional to the *amount* of brain tissue removed, not to its *location.* Formulated the principles of mass action and equipotentiality in brain function.

latency stage (S. Freud) The fourth stage of psychosexual development occurring from the age of six to eleven during which the Oedipal incestuous and aggressive wishes have been repressed and the child identifies with the parent of the same sex. During this stage, the child gives up interest in persons of the opposite sex which are prototypes of the parent, and tends to associate with members of his own sex.

latent dream content See *content, dream, latent.*

latent extinction See *extinction, latent.*

latent learning See *learning, latent.*

latent structure analysis See *analysis, latent structure.*

lateral dominance See *dominance, lateral.*

lateral fissure See *fissure of Sylvius.*

lateral geniculate body A sensory relay nucleus which is part of the visual system. It is part of the thalamus where the optic tract synapse joins with visual fibers which project to the visual region of the cerebral cortex.

lateral hypothalamus See *hypothalamus, lateral.*

Latin square An experimental pattern or design which provides as many different trials as there are experimental conditions, every subject being exposed to all conditions in varying serial orders from other subjects.

law, Bell-Magendie A statement of the principle that the ventral roots of the spinal nerves are motor in function while the dorsal roots are sensory in function.

law, Donder's Principle that the position of the eyes in looking at an object is independent of the movement of the eyes to that position; regardless of previous fixation points, every point on the line corresponds to a definite, invariable angle of the eyes.

law, Emmert's Generalization that a projected image, either eidetic image or after-image, tends to increase in size in proportion to the distance to which it is projected onto a ground.

law, Fullerton-Cattell   A generalization proposed as a substitute for Weber's law which states that the errors of observation and of just noticeable differences are proportional to the square root of the magnitude of the stimuli, though subject to variations which must be accounted for in each case.

law, inverse square   A law of physics which states that the intensity of energy emanating from a stimulus, decreases proportionately to the square of the distance from the source to the sense receptor. Sound, light, heat, and odor follow this principle.

law, Jost's   The principle that given two associations of equal strength and unequal age, repetition increases the strength of the older more than the younger, and the older loses strength less rapidly with the passage of time.

law of advantage   Also called principle of advantage; the principle that when two or more incompatible and inconsistent responses occur to the same situation one has an advantage over the others, being more reliable and occurring more frequently.

law of assimilation   (E. L. Thorndike) Also called law of analogy; it is a replica of association by similarity. It says that learners tend to reply in a similar way as they replied before to a similar situation.

law of Bichat   Proposed by Marie Francois Bichat (1771-1802), a French anatomist. There are two main body systems which are in inverse relationship, called the vegetative and the animal, with the former providing for assimilation and augmentation of mass and the latter providing for the transformation of energy.

law of categorical judgment   (W. S. Torgenson) A theory derivative of the law of comparative judgment which should provide an equal interval category scale. It assumes: 1) the psychological continuum of an individual can be divided into categories 2) a category boundary is not a stable entity but projects a normal distribution on the continuum 3) the subject's responses are predicated on the position of the category boundary; thus, the boundaries between adjacent categories behave like stimuli. The law of categorical judgment may be written:

$$C_A - R_1 = Z_{A1} \sqrt{\sigma_A{}^2 - \sigma 1^2 - 2r_{A1}\sigma_A\sigma_1}$$ which is

directly comparable to the law of comparative judgment of Thurstone.

law of closure   See closure.

law of coercion to cultural-genetic mean   (R. B. Cattell) The tendency of social pressure to force behavior to the existing central norm.

law of comparative judgment   (L.L. Thurstone) A mathematical model which explicates a theoretical assumption about the effects of the stimulation by two stimuli, S_1 and S_2

$$R_2 - R_1 = Z_{21} \sqrt{\sigma_2^2 + \sigma_1^2 - 2r_{21}\sigma_1\sigma_2}$$

in which R_2 is the mean of the responses to stimulus two; R_1 is the mean of the responses to stimulus one; Z_{21}, the standard score of the distribution of differences between the two distribution responses to the two different stimuli, $\sigma_2{}^2$, the standard deviation of the distribution of the responses to stimuli two; $\sigma_1{}^2$, the standard deviation of responses to stimuli one.

law of content   1. The principle that the meaning of verbal material or mental processes is influenced by the situation surrounding them. 2. The hypothesis that the degree of retention depends on the similarity between the learning situation and the retention condition.

law of effect   (E. L. Thorndike) Learning theory law stating that annoyance weakens and satisfaction strengthens a stimulus-response connection.

law of exercise   (E.L. Thorndike) Principle that repetition of an act promotes learning and makes subsequent performance of that act easier, other things being equal.

law of frequency   The principle that the more an act or an association is repeated the more rapid is the acquisition or learning of that act or association, other things being equal.

law of prepotency of elements   (E. L. Thorndike) The learner tends to select relevant elements in his response to a complex situation.

law of readiness   (E. L. Thorndike) The proposition which holds that when a conduction unit is ready to conduct, conduction by it is satisfying, as long as nothing is done which alters its action.

law of recapitulation   See biogenetic law.

law of recency   1. The principle or generalization that a specific item will tend to remind the individual of a more recent association than one farther in time. 2. The generalization which holds that the more recent the item, event or experience, the better it is remembered.

law of use   The generalization that an association or a function is facilitated by use or practice.

law, power   See Steven's power law.

law, Talbot-Plateau   Principle that with a surface illuminated by a light flickering so quickly no interruption is apparent, the brightness is less than the brightness of steady illumination to a degree equal to the ratio between the time during which the light actually reaches the surface and the whole period.

laws, Mendelian   See Mendelian laws.

lead poisoning   See poisoning, lead.

leadership   1. The exercise of authority in initiating, directing, or controlling the behavior or attitudes of others, with their consent. 2. Those qualities of personality and training which make the guidance and control of others successful.

learning, approach   Learning specific behaviors in order to attain particular rewards.

learning, avoidance A type of training in which the organism is allowed to avoid a noxious stimulus if he makes the required response.

learning, conceptual The learning of new concepts or the alteration of old ones.

learning contingencies Variables present in the learning situation.

learning, continuity theory of The principle that in discrimination learning, there is an increment of learning for every reinforced response to the stimulus.

learning curve A graphic representation of the changes at successive units of practice over the course of learning. Units of practice, recorded on the abscissa, are usually in terms of time spent or number of trials required; the progress in performance, recorded on the ordinate, is usually in terms of amount recalled, time required for successful completion of the task, or number of errors. The form of the curve differs according to the measure used for the ordinate.

learning, ideational Learning involving the use of ideational material, either as in learning through the connection of ideas or memorization, in contrast to rote and motor learning.

learning, incidental The occurrence of learning in the absence of formal instruction, intent to learn and ascertainable motive. If indeed there is no motive operating, incidental learning suggests contiguity alone is a sufficient condition for learning.

learning, instrumental See *conditioning, operant.*

learning, latent Learning which is not manifested in performance but which reveals itself in later performances that follow an intervening activity which does not involve the behavior in question nor any reward for behavior. The change in performance is attributed to the addition of a motive in later performances.

learning, linear-operator model of (B. B. Bush and F. Mosteller) Mathematical model of learning which assumes that an organism perceives and responds to some fraction of the total stimulus complex. This fraction of stimulus elements attended to is measured as a kind of sum of the weighted element. This theory incorporates two parameters a) the positive influence of reinforcement and b) the negative punishing influence of the work required in responding. The linear-operator is: $Qp = p\ a(1-p)-bp$ where Qp is the operator Q operating on p, the probability that a response will occur during a specified time, a is the parameter associated with reward, b is the parameter associated with work or punishment, p is the probability of the response.

learning, motor Any form of learning which is described in terms of the activities of muscles and glands which it involves.

learning, perceptual Learning of a new perceptual response or learning which consists of modifying an already existing perceptual response.

learning, programmed A learning method consisting of materials which are presented in a predetermined order with provisions enabling the student to check his answers and to proceed at his own pace. The most common method of programmed learning involves the use of teaching machines, although some programs have been prepared in workbook form.

learning, response Learning to make a specific set of responses to reach a goal rather than learning the route or topography of the environment.

learning, reversal Experimental technique in which the correct response, usually one of two possible responses, after some specified amount of training, is changed to the other response.

learning, serial or serial-order Learning of responses in a specific order which is often used in rate learning.

learning set 1. A generalized approach to problem situations which includes the assumption by the subject that a specific method can be discovered to solve the problem. The approach itself is a result of learning. 2. An orienting factor which determines which kinds of responses will be made and which kinds omitted in a particular kind of problem situation. The manner of approach to solving the situation has been previously learned, not the particular solution.

learning, social Learning of social standards, values and customs.

learning, subliminal The acquisition of a habit which cannot be remembered because the learning of it was not on a conscious level or because it has not progressed far enough.

learning theory A large body of concepts exploring the process of learning, starting with associationism, through the various theories of conditioning and cognition. At the present time, several theoretical systems and subsystems started by Pavlov, Bekhterev, Hull, and Skinner as well as specialized approaches of the mathematical learning theories, gestalt inspired learning theories and others vie for the so far unattainable position of a generally accepted theory of learning.

learning theory, incremental The average measure of learning as presented in the typical learning curve shows a gradual change over trials. This is so common that it has provided a basis for the inference that learning is a gradual process. It is contended that a stimulus is complex and gradually more and more stimulus elements come to be associated to the reinforced response.

learning types Individual kinds of learners distinguished by the types of imagery they tend to rely on and the methods of learning they employ.

learning, verbal The learning to respond verbally to a verbal stimulus, ranging from learning to associate two nonsense syllables to learning to solve complex problems stated in verbal terms.

learning, whole method of Learning characterized by the successive repetition of the complete material, from the beginning to the end.

least action, law of (Gestalt) The principle that an organism will tend to follow the course of action which requires the least effort or expended energy under prevailing conditions. Course of action and energy expended can be influenced by the particular individual's personality characteristics so that an objectively easy course may be difficult for an individual because of the amount of emotional investment required. Also called principle of least energy expenditure, and least effort principle.

least group size The principle that the optimal size of a class or learning group is the smallest number of individuals which represent all the abilities required for the learning tasks to be undertaken.

least noticeable difference See *just noticeable difference.*

least squares method See *method of least squares.*

leaving the field See *field, leaving the.*

left-right agnosia See *apractagnosia.*

legal insanity See *insanity, legal.*

legal responsibility See *responsibility, legal.*

Leibniz, Gottfried Wilhelm von (1646-1716) German philosopher and mathematician. He developed an elaborate systematic position, published as the *Monadology* in 1714, which contained a strict parallelist analysis of the mind-body problem: mental and bodily events are like synchronous clocks that do not affect each other.

Leigh's encephalomyelopathy A genetic metabolic disorder transmitted by an autosomal recessive resulting in high level pyruvates in the blood. The main clinical features are failure to thrive, lack of movement, hypotonia, spasticity, absent reflexes, optic atrophy, nystagmus, and convulsions.

Leiter International Performance Test See *test, Leiter International Performance.*

lencotomy, frontal Frontal lobotomy.

Lennox syndrome A type of myoclonic epilepsy in older children.

Lennox, William Gordon (1884-1960) An American neurologist noted for his work in epilepsy.

lens A transparent structure in the eye capable of changing its convexity, the function of which is to form an image on the retina of the object being looked at. Also called crystalline lens.

lens, corneal A plastic lens worn on the tears of the cornea which is used to correct impaired vision. Also known as contact lens.

leptokurtosis The relative degree of peakedness about the mode of a frequency curve.

leptomorph (H. J. Eysenck) A person whose body-build index is one or more standard deviations above the mean.

leptosome An individual of slender or asthenic body build.

LES See *local excitatory state or potential.*

lesbianism Homosexuality in women.

lesion A change in tissue due to injury, disease or surgical procedures.

Lesse, Stanley (1922-   ) American psychiatrist and neurologist. Demonstrated the direct relationship between the quantitative degree of anxiety and the development and amelioration of other symptoms and signs, and the predictable relationship between the various components of anxiety to each other. Introduced futurologic research with projections as to how the health sciences will be at the end of the century. Introduced future oriented psychotherapy as a therapeutic technique. Described the multivariant masks of depression, performed the original research studies and presented the initial publications on the use of psychotherapy in combination with tranquilizing drugs and antidepressant drugs. Presented the original descriptions of the psychopathology and psychodynamics of pain of psychogenic origin, particularly a typical facial pain. Described psychotherapy as a placebo phenomenon and interrelated unintended psychotherapeutic effects with placebo effects. Research into the relationship of socioeconomic and sociopolitical phenomena and its relationship to psychotherapeutic techniques.

lethal disease Fatal disease, a disease that ends in death.

lethal equivalent A gene carried in the heterozygous state which if homozygous, would be lethal. Thalassemia minor and major, approximate this situation.

lethargic encephalitis See *encephalitis, lethargic.*

leucotomy Lobotomy.

leucotomy, pre-frontal Pre-frontal lobotomy.

leukodystrophy See *sulfatide lipidosis.*

level 1. An area, region, position or degree in which all things are equal in quality. **2.** (psychophysics) The condition of reactivity of a receptor compared with its established average threshold. **3.** The position or rank obtained on a test. **4.** The plane or standard of intellectual, sensory and motor efficiency.

level, maintenance 1. A state of development at maturity when the organism's growth, weight, and size stabilize and remain at this maximal level. **2.** The unvarying ability to perform an act due to overlearning or repeated practice.

leveling effect An effect due to practice or repetition under certain conditions of measurement, which results in a second set of observations to cluster more closely around the mean, the standard deviation and range being less than in the first set of observations.

levitation Rising in the air without material support, usually in reference to dream experience.

Levy inkblots A special series of inkblots which are designed to facilitate movement (*M*) responses.

Lewin, Kurt (1890-1947) German child psychologist; emigrated to America in 1933. Created a field theory of action and emotion modeled on modern physical theory and topology. Known especially for studies of conflict, level of aspiration, substitution, regression, and for development of research and theory on small group dynamics. Applied latter to problems of food utilization and housing congestion in World War II. See *field theory; topological psychology.*

LGB See *lateral geniculate body.*

libertarianism See *free will.*

libertine Sexually unrestrained and promiscuous individual.

libertinism Unrestrained sexual activity especially with reference to the male.

libidinal types (S. Freud) Freud distinguished three libidinal types, the erotic, obsessional and narcissistic. See *type.*

libido (S. Freud) A quantitatively variable force related to sexual excitation. The totality of mental energy at the disposal of Eros, the instinct of love.

libido object See *object, libido.*

lie detector Apparatus which measures physiological changes in pulse, respiration, blood pressure and psychogalvanic skin response of a person to whom questions are posed which he must answer. The assumption is that the emotional disturbance associated with telling a lie will exhibit itself in the above physiological changes though such physiological changes accompany emotionality of any sort.

Liebeault, Ambroise-August (1823-1904) A French physician who was one of the first to employ hypnosis in the treatment of his patients and is one of those responsible for its growth as a method of treatment.

life-goal (A. Adler) The goal of attaining superiority to compensate for an individual's real or imagined inferiority. It is present implicitly in all strivings though is seldom consciously acknowledged.

life history A detailed description of the environmental and internal events in the development of an individual or group from birth to the present or death.

life instinct See *Eros.*

life lie (A. Adler) An individual's belief that he will fail in his life plan because of circumstances beyond his control.

life plan (A. Adler) The complete pattern of defensive behaviors used by an individual to prevent his assumed superiority from being disproved by reality.

life space (K. Lewin) The entire set of phenomena in the environment and in the organism itself which influence present behavior or the possibility of behavior. Emphasis is placed on the interaction between the organism and its environment in an organized, unified field.

life span 1. The length of life from birth to death of an individual. 2. The characteristic length of life of a species.

life style (A. Adler) The characteristic mode of living of a person, of the way in which he pursues his goals.

light-adapted eye See *eye, light-adapted.*

likelihood criterion ratio (signal detection theory) The decision rule the subject uses to determine his responses in a psychophysical experiment. It can be estimated in the experiment by the likelihood ratio.

likelihood ratio 1. (J. Neyman and E. S. Pearson) A procedure for finding the best statistic test for testing any hypothesis which will give the most powerful test for the hypothesis. It consists of the probability of obtaining the sample result under the null hypothesis relative to the probability of obtaining the sample result under the alternate hypothesis. 2. (signal detection theory) An expression of the likelihood that the observed responses obtained arose from signal plus noise relative to the likelihood that the responses arose from noise alone.

Likert scale See *scale, Likert.*

limbic lobe See *lobe, limbic.*

limbic system A group of functionally related structures including the transitional cortex and subcortical nuclei, about which much controversy exists as to function and definition, but generally thought to be related to the integration of emotional patterns and primary drives.

limen See *threshold.*

limen, absolute (RL) See *threshold, absolute.*

limen gauge (Von Frey) An instrument consisting of two levers, one which is activated by a spring that is controlled by the other lever, used for the application of pressure to the skin at regular intervals.

limen, sense See *threshold, absolute.*

liminal sensitivity See *sensitivity, liminal.*

liminal stimulus See *stimulus, liminal.*

limit, physiological See *physiological limit.*

limited aims psychotherapy See *psychotherapy, limited aims.*

limited hold (operant conditioning) On interval schedules, FI, VI, etc., the organism is eligible for reinforcement after a time from the previous reinforcement. When the organism is eligible, a response is reinforced (reinforcement occurs only after a response). Limited hold is the period during which a response will be reinforced. At the end of the limited hold, a response is not reinforced until the next limited hold occurs.

limited-term psychotherapy See *psychotherapy, limited-term.*

limits and differences method (E. Kraepelin) A modification of the limits method, consisting of the statistical treatment of judgments obtained by the normal limits method.

limits, fiducial The points or limits to the right or left of some measure of central tendency beyond which a statistic is not expected to occur except by chance alone in more than a stated percentage of the samplings.

limits method See *method, just noticeable difference.*

limophoitas Psychotic episode caused by starvation.

limophtisis Physical and mental emaciation caused by starvation.

Lincoln-Oseretsky Motor Development Scale See *scale, Lincoln-Oseretsky Motor Development.*

line of direction The line of sight from an object to the nodal points of the eyes.

line of regard See *regard, line of.*

linear correlation See *correlation, linear.*

linear function A relationship between two variables which is represented by a straight line whose equation is $y = mx + b$ where m is the slope of the line and b is the point at which the line crosses the y axis.

linear graph The representation of the relationship between two variables by means of lines.

linear-operator model of learning See *learning, linear-operator model of.*

linear perspective See *perspective, linear.*

linear regression A regression whose equation develops a line that best fits the mean of the rows or columns in a correlation table, and is approximately straight.

linear system A system in which the units of input are summated in a simple straight line method; or in which the response to a complex input is the summation of the individual responses of the input.

linguistics The scientific study of the origin, structure, and evolution of language.

link analysis The design of systems in which connections between parts are as efficient as possible, the number of links being minimal and their value maximal. For example, the design of an efficient typewriter keyboard.

link-defect hypothesis An explanation for the abnormalities of perception, attention, cognition, etc. in mentally defective children. Mental functions are seen as complex processes which are formed in the course of a child's development. If the process of formation is disturbed, if a step or link is missed due to illness, trauma, inborn defect, etc., the disturbance may affect further mental development and lead to a number of secondary symptoms and consequences.

Link Instrument Trainer An apparatus used in training airplane pilots, which without leaving the ground, simulates operating conditions for a plane.

linkage 1. The tendency for characteristics to be linked together in hereditary transmission, the offspring showing either both traits or neither. **2.** The connection between stimulus and response.

linophobia Fear of ropes.

lip eroticism See *eroticism, lip.*

lip key An instrument used in reaction time experiments for measuring the start of lip movements in speech.

lip-reading A method used by the deaf for understanding spoken speech, consisting of observation of the speaker's lip movements.

lipid histiocytosis, kerasin type See *Gaucher disease.*

lipid histiocytosis, phosphatide type See *Niemann-Pick disease.*

lipidoses, cerebral A group of rare diseases characterized by the accumulation of particular complex lipids in the central nervous system and associated with a mental defect which is familial, an enlarged liver and spleen.

lipidosis Disorder of lipid metabolism.

lipids A group of non-water soluble fats; a major chemical component of the brain.

Lissajou's figures Closed figures produced by the reflection of a beam of light from small mirrors attached to the surfaces of two tuning forks which vibrate in perpendicular planes to one another.

Lissauer's dementia paralytica See *dementia paralytica, Lissauer's.*

Listing's law A law of eye movement stating that when the eye moves from the primary position to another position, the axis around which the eye in the new position moves, is the same as if the eye had turned around a fixed axis at right angles to the initial and final lines of regard.

literacy test See *test, literacy.*

lithic diathesis A hereditary metabolic dysfunction characterized by renal disorders and a tendency to form urinary calculi.

Little Hans (S. Freud) A case of a phobia of a horse in a five year old boy analyzed by S. Freud and Hans' father. A classical illustration of the dynamics of the phobia, in that there is a clear sexual component, for Hans was in a state of intensified sexual excitement with nightly masturbation, with repression (of Hans' death wishes for the father), projection (Hans feared that someone would do to him what he wished to do), and displacement (from the father onto the horse), with concern about the missing penis of the woman, the anatomical difference being seen as a possible consequence of masturbation.

Little's disease See *infantile spastic diplegia.*

Lloyd Morgan's canon The principle that in the interpretation of behavior, attribution of the behavior in terms of lower rather than higher level of functioning is preferred.

load **1.** The number of patients or clients a therapist, social worker, or counselor conducts treatment with. **2.** (statistics) The multiplication of a set of values by a constant for the purpose of rendering the set comparable to another set. **3.** (statistics) A weight or factor loading.

loading A value varying between +1 and -1 which is obtained from factor analysis and shows the extent to which increases in the strength of a factor bring about increases in the dependent behavior score.

lobe **1.** A rounded projection of an organ. **2.** One of the main sections of the cerebrum; the frontal, parietal, temporal, occipital, or central lobes.

lobe, central See *Reil, island of.*

lobe, frontal The part of each central hemisphere in front of the central fissure.

lobe, frontal, structure and function of The frontal lobe is characterized by the predominance of associative layers and fiber tract connections to other cortical areas through which it receives processed information from subcortical layers. As a result of these interconnections, these areas influence both afferent and efferent stimulation. It has been found that the frontal lobes are important in regulating complex behavior, the organization and planning of purposeful activities, and the coordination of intention with the action. Lesions of these areas result in the impairment of planned, purposeful behavior.

lobe, limbic A convolution on the medial surface of the brain, consisting of the gyrus cinguli, isthmus hippocampi, and the gyrus hippocampi. Also called gyrus fornicatus.

lobe, occipital The dorsal portion of the cerebral hemispheres of the brain which contains the centers for vision.

lobe, parietal The part of the cerebral cortex between the frontal and occipital lobes and behind the central fissure.

lobe, temporal The section of the cerebral hemisphere lying below the lateral fissure and in front of the occipital lobe, that is the cortical area for the reception of auditory stimuli.

lobectomy Surgical removal of a lobe or an organ or gland. Commonly refers to the removal of the prefrontal region of the frontal lobes.

lobectomy, pre-frontal Surgical removal of the prefrontal region of the frontal lobes of the brain.

lobotomy The surgical severing of the nerve fibers of the frontal lobes of the brain which connect with the thalamus and the hypothalamus. This is a form of psychosurgery which is sometimes used in the treatment of mental disorder.

lobotomy, frontal See *lobotomy.*

lobotomy, transorbital A surgical procedure consisting of partial ablation of the prefrontal area, preferred to the classical prefrontal lobotomy because undesirable side effects such as incontinence and apathy are less likely to occur.

local excitatory state or potential The reaction of nervous tissue to stimuli consisting of a localized increase in negativity on the surface of the membrane and in a spike potential if the stimulation is above threshold.

local rate See *rate, local.*

local sign See *sign, local.*

localization **1.** The mental reference of a sensory or perceptual process to its source in space. **2.** The reference of mental and nervous functions to their particular sources in the various parts of the nervous system.

location chart (Rorschach) Reproductions of the inkblots on a single side of the record blank used by the examiner for the purpose of locating and recording the positions of the subject's responses.

location score One of the major components in Rorschach scoring or coding which denotes the general area of the blot used in a response, such as the whole blot, a common detail area, or an unusual detail area.

Locke, John (1632-1704) Philosopher and politician and early British empiricist. Held that the *idea* is the fundamental unit of mind; all ideas come from sensation or reflection. Formulated the principle of association, and distinguished between *primary* qualities of perception (number, weight, etc.) which correspond to characteristics of the real object and *secondary* qualities (color, sound, etc.), which are "aroused in us" by the powers of the real object.

locomotion **1.** The movement of an organism from one area to another. **2.** (K. Lewin) A change in the valence or value of regions within the individual's life space resulting in a change in the relationship of the individual to his life space.

locomotor The organs upon which movement from place to place depends.

locomotor ataxia See *tabes dorsalis.*

locus **1.** A place or spot on the surface of the body or an organ. **2.** (mathematics) The sum of all possible positions of a moving element.

Loeb, Jacques (1859-1924) German zoologist and physiologist who moved to America in 1891. Developed the tropistic theory of animal behavior. He also proposed that associative memory is the criterion of consciousness.

logagnosia; logamnesia Sensory aphasia.

logarithmic curve See *curve, logarithmic.*

logarithmic mean See *mean, logarithmic.*

logic, affective A sequence of judgments which on the surface appear to be logical chains connected by reasoning but in actuality are linked by emotional factors.

logical construct See *construct, hypothetical.*

logical positivism Also called physicalism; a philosophical school associated with a group of Viennese philosophers (Wiener Kreis, that is, the Vienna Circle) who saw the main task of philosophy in stating scientific data in the language of physical science and development of a system of symbolic logic to be used as the vehicle for scientific research and communication. The logical positivists maintained that a great many philosophical issues must be dismissed as pseudo-problems. C.L. Hull, K. Lewin, B.F. Skinner, S.S. Stevens, and other psychologists have been influenced by the logical positivists.

logistic curve See *curve, logarithmic.*

logospasm Explosive speech.

loloneurosis Stammering.

lolopathy Speech disorder.

lolophegia Inability to speak caused by paralysis of facial muscles.

lolophobia Morbid fear of speaking.

Lombroso, Cesare (1836-1909) Italian anthropologist and criminologist who wrote on the connection between genius and insanity. He advocated the view of the innate disposition to criminal behavior associated with degeneration of hereditary cells. He found most criminals have physical signs (stigmata of degeneration) bearing witness to the innate, constitutional disposition to crime.

long-circuiting The renunciation of immediate satisfaction in the interests of attaining relatively remote goals. A recently discovered, objective test factor, indexed as U.I. 35, is believed to embody the most important features of this concept.

long term memory (LTM) See *memory, long term.*

longitudinal studies Studies which focus on the change in a person or group of people over an extended period of time.

Lopez Ibor, Juan Jose (1907-   ) Spanish psychiatrist, head of Department of Psychiatry and Psychological Medicine at the Madrid University. Former President of the World Psychiatric Association, Honorary Member of the Royal Psychiatric College, London, Member of the Academia Leopoldina Gesellschaft, German Fed. Republic, Honorary Member of the American Psychiatric Association. Developed a new theory of schizophrenic characteristics and new concepts of depressions, partly extended in the concept of depressive equivalents (Maudsley Lecture, 1970). Described anxiety equivalents which include ailments considered to be neurological, such as paresthesic meuralgia, etc. Studied psychological aspects of anxiety; 1st publication "Vital Anxiety" (*Angustia Vital,* 1950), 2nd edition in 1960. Introduced new ideas concerning the dynamic of neuroses, published as "Neuroses as illness of the mind" (*Neurosis como enfermedades del animo,* 1966), and modified the therapeutic technique. Apart from these clinical and psychological publications, conducted physiopathological studies of anxiety and the use of neuroleptics. Several publications on social psychiatry, psychiatric assistance and its organization, especially in European countries. Also critical studies on the results obtained in the so-called "Therapeutic Communities." Wrote on depressions in young people and their relation to severe cases of drug addiction. Presently studies the subconscious elements of psychotherapeutic directions from Mesmer toward post-Freudian techniques.

Lorenz, Konrad (1903-   ) Austrian physician, founder of ethology, director of Max Planck Institute for Behavior Physiology. Discovered several aspects of animal behavior, among them the innate behavior coordinaters (Erbkoordinationen), fixed action patterns (F.A.P.) stimulus selection, signal movements in introspecific communication. He found "inner releasing schemata," imprinting, and other phylogenetically determined behavior mechanisms. Lorenz developed new observational and experimental techniques in the study of animal behavior.

Lowe's syndrome A genetic metabolic disorder which appears to be sex-linked resulting in aminoaciduria in the urine and acidosis in the blood. The main clinical features are mental retardation, glaucoma, cataracts, rickets and hypotonia.

LS See *sensitivity, luminal.*

LSD See *lysergic acid diethylamide.*

lumbar puncture The withdrawal of a sample of cerebrospinal fluid for diagnostic purposes, by the insertion of a hypodermic needle between the lumbar vertebrae.

lumen The strength of light energy or the unit of luminous flux, determined by the amount of light within a solid angle of unit size coming from a uniform point source of one candle-power.

luminal Common name for phenobarbital.

luminance Light energy transmitted, reflected or emitted from a source; the actual strength of light in the whole of the space involved.

luminosity The physical correlate of brightness of light, dependent on and modified by the prevailing physical conditions such as distance, reflectance, and conditions of illumination, and not on the physical intensity of the light itself.

luminosity, absolute The relative brightness of a light expressed in absolute terms such as lumens per watt.

luminosity coefficients The numbers which any color mixture data must be multiplied by in order that the sum of the three products equals the luminances of the particular desired color sample.

luminosity curve The brightness value of the various spectral stimuli through the visible range, plotted as curves with wave length on the abscissa and luminosity on the ordinate.

luminous flux The rate of passage of light determined by the experience of the brightness it produces on a surface at right angles to its direction.

lupus erythematosis A chronic lupus disease of the skin of unknown origin sometimes affected by emotional factors which is characterized by red, scaly patches of different sizes.

Luria, A.R. (1902-   ) Soviet psychologist and neuropsychologist. His basic works were concerned with the analysis of brain mechanisms of psychological processes, psychological methods of diagnostics of local brain lesion, as well as the basic problems of the development of behavioral process and the role of speech in organization of human behavior. Main publications: *The Nature of Human Conflicts; Higher Cortical Function in Man; Human Brain and Psychological Processes; Restoration of Functions after Brain Trauma; Traumatic Aphasia; The Mind of a Mnemonist; The Man with a Shattered World; The Working Brain.*

Luria technique (A. R. Luria) A method for measuring emotional tensions in which the subject simultaneously responds to words in a free association test and presses the fingers of one hand on a sensitive tremor recorder while holding the other hand as still as possible.

lust for life **1.** (I. P. Pavlov) The main reflex whose goal is self-preservation. It is composed of positive movement reflexes toward conditions favorable for life and negative movement reflexes guarding the organism against injury. **2.** (B. B. Wolman) All living organisms carry a certain amount of mental energy, a derivative from the universal biochemical energy. This energy is activated by threats to one's life. The built-in release apparatus, the force that opens the valves or ignites the motor and facilitates the discharge of energy is called a drive or instinctual drive. Since this force activates the energies for survival, it was named "Lust for Life." At a certain level of evolution, a part of this force has been directed into procreative activities, and the Lust for Life can be channelled into a drive for war, called Ares, and the drive for love, called Eros.

Lustprinzip (S. Freud) The urge for immediate discharge of energy which brings satisfaction to libidinal or destructive drives. Usually translated as the pleasure principle.

lux A unit of illumination, equal to the density of luminance flux on a surface area of one square meter which is at right angles to the rays and at a distance of one meter or foot from a point source of one candle-power.

lycanthopy The belief by an individual that he can change himself into a wolf.

lygophilia A morbid desire to stay in dark and gloomy places.

lymph A body fluid, chiefly derived from the blood but which also may contain food products, that slowly travels through the lymphatic system of ducts and vessels to the large veins near the heart where it is transferred into the blood stream.

lymphoma A group of malignant diseases of lymphoid tissue.

Lyon hypothesis This hypothesis seeks to explain the puzzle that females homozygous for an X-limited mutant gene are no more markedly affected than homozygous males. Some mechanism of dosage compensation is indicated. Dr. Mary Lyon (1962) stated a detailed hypothesis containing the following three points 1) the condensed sex chromosome is genetically inactivated, 2) the inactivated X could be either the paternal or maternal X in the cells of the same individual and, 3) the inactivation occurs early in embryonic life.

lypothymia **1.** Depression. **2.** Involutional psychosis.

lysergic acid diethylamide (LSD) One of a group of psychomimetic drugs which produces symptoms similar to those of psychosis such as disturbance in thought processes, severe anxiety, general confusion and delusions.

lyssophobia Fear of going insane.

M

m 1. In general formulas, symbol for a number. 2. Meter. 3. (Rorschach) Inanimate movement.

M 1. Symbol for arithmetic mean. 2. Symbol for illumination. 3. (C. Hull) Symbol for the maximum learning. 4. (Rorschach) Movement response. 5. Associative memory factor symbol.

MA See *mental age.*

Mach, Ernst (1838-1916) Austrian philosopher, and a physicist, a thinker and an experimentalist. Made many contributions, theoretical and experimental, to the study of vision, hearing, and to time and space perception; tried to make psychology less philosophical, more quantitative and objective; his ideas influenced logical positivism (the "Vienna Circle"), American operationism, and Einstein's earlier work; William James called him "pure intellectual genius."

Machover Draw-A-Person Test See *test, Draw-a-Person.*

MacQuarrie Test for Mechanical Ability See *test, MacQuarrie for Mechanical Ability.*

macrocephaly Increase in size of brain leading to mental retardation, impaired vision and sometimes convulsions.

macrocosm The universe or society as a totality.

macrogenitosomia A syndrome characterized by premature physical development concomitant with the occurrence of secondary sex characteristics. It is caused by tumors of the pineal gland.

macropsia An impairment of vision in which objects appear larger than they really are due to retinal pathology.

macroscopic 1. Large enough to be seen without the aid of special lenses. 2. Perceived as a whole disregarding the details.

macrosplanchnic Referring to a body build in which the trunk is disproportionately large in relation to the extremities.

macula acoustica A thickening of the utricle and saccule wall in the inner ear made up of cells of unknown functions.

macula lutea A yellowish area about 2 millimeters in diameter in the center of the human retina containing the fovea.

Maddox rod test See *test, Maddox rod.*

magazine (operant conditioning) Device which makes food, water, etc. available to the organism usually during reinforcement.

Magendie, François (1783-1855) French physiologist, pioneer of experimental physiology, author of several medical books. He made important contributions to medicine; demonstrated in 1822 that the dorsal roots of the spinal nerves were sensory in function and the ventral roots motor; the claim of famous British anatomist, Charles Bell, to priority in this discovery (1809) began one of the greatest controversies, never conclusively settled.

magic 1. The act of producing desired effects and control of natural phenomena through various techniques such as prayer or incantation. 2. The production of illusions by means of sleight of hand.

magical thinking See *thinking, magical.*

magilalia Hesitancy in speaking.

Magna Mater 1. The symbol of universal motherhood. 2. (C. G. Jung) The archetypal primordial image of the mother, based on the cult of Cybele, a goddess known to the Romans as the Great Mother of the Gods.

magnetism, animal (F. A. Mesmer) The hypothetical force which induces hypnosis by being transferred from the hypnotist to the subject.

magnitude estimation See *estimation, magnitude.*

magnitude scales See *scales, magnitude.*

Mahler, Margaret Schoenberger (1897-) American psychoanalyst and child psychiatrist. M.D. (Jena, Germany), Sc.D. (Med.) Honoris Causa. Faculties New York and Philadelphia Psychoanalytic Institutes. Psychoanalyst-Teacher. Director of Research Masters Children's Center, New York City. Recipient of: Brill Memorial Plaque, 1962, of the New York Psychoanalytic Society; Agnes Purcell McGavin Award of the A.P.A., 1969; The Scroll of the N.Y. Psychoanalytic Institute, 1970 Freud Anniversary Lectureship; The Frieda Fromm-Reichman Award of 1970 of the American Academy of Psychoanalysis; A Festschrift: Separation-Individuation with contributions of 27 psychoanalysts. Author of more than eighty scientific articles, chapters and books, some of them translated into Italian, German, French and Spanish. Pioneering contributions to psychoanalytic developmental psychology, to the natural history of infantile psychosis and to tics and motor neurosis in child- and adulthood as well as the application of the concepts of separation-individuation to reconstruction in the psychoanalytic situation of borderline cases (adult and adolescent).

maieusiophobia Morbid fear of childbirth.

main score (H. Rorschach) The number of responses to inkblots which the subject gives during the test precluding the additional responses which are added as afterthoughts.

maintenance functions See *functions, maintenance.*

maintenance level See *level, maintenance.*

maintenance schedule See *schedule, maintenance.*

major gene See *gene, major.*

major solution See *solution, major.*

Make-A-Picture-Story Test See *test, Make-A-Picture-Story.*

make-believe The pretense that fantasy is a real characteristic of children's play and associated with varying degrees of recognizing the unreality of the situation.

maladaptation The failure of an organism to develop biological characteristics necessary to insure success in interaction with the environment.

maladjustment The failure of an individual to develop behavioral patterns necessary for personal and social success.

malaise A slight feeling of being ill or unwell.

malformation An abnormal development of an organ or part of the body.

malfunction Failure of an organismic process, organ or system to work properly.

malignant Referring to a disease or tumor with a poor prognosis, usually threatening life.

malingering The pretense of illness or disability in order to obtain certain benefits.

malleation A repeated spasmodic motion of the hands involving striking at an object.

malleus Bony transmitter of aural vibrations from the outer ear through the middle ear to the inner ear.

Malleus Maleficarum A book depicting the ideology of the witch-hunting movement written by J. Sprenger and H. Kraemer in 1487 with the approval of the Church, the University of Cologne and the monarch, Maximilian I, king of Rome. The textbook describes the destruction of heretics and the mentally ill, branded as witches, with detailed instructions on the process of identifying and convicting these individuals.

malpractice Behavior of a professional person contrary to the established ethical code due to negligence, ignorance or intent which may result in legal action.

Malthus' theory; Malthusianism (T. R. Malthus) The doctrine concerning population growth which states that the population of a species increases geometrically while the food supply increases arithmetically suggesting the necessity of some form of population control including war, famine, and natural disasters.

malum minus The petit mal type of epilepsy.

mammalia The highest class of vertebrates which includes organisms which bear their young within a uterus, nourish them by milk from the mammary glands after birth and have hair.

mammalingus (E. Jones) The concept of fellatio towards a woman which stresses the woman's act of suckling the man.

mammillary bodies Two small rounded bodies in the posterior hypothalamus.

man-to-man rating See *rating, man-to-man.*

management, psychology of The manipulation and direction of people and their work environment in order to obtain more effective and favorable results.

mand (B. F. Skinner) A speech sequence whose function is to make a demand on the recipient who subsequently grants the request thus rewarding the speaker.

mandala 1. An oriental geometric circular symbol representing unity. 2. (C. G. Jung) The symbol expressing the archetype of man's striving for unity. It is representative of the integration of the conflicting elements of conscious and unconscious through the emergence of the self.

mania 1. Impulsive, uncontrollable behavior characterized by violent and excessive motor activity and excitement. 2. The overactive phase of manic-depressive psychosis. 3. Uncontrollable urge to do a certain thing.

mania a potu Alcoholically induced state characterized by extreme excitement and sometimes other-directed violence.

mania, absorbed A condition in which the patient has focused his attention upon his own thoughts to the exclusion of reality. This situation has been distinguished from a condition which it resembles called a stupor because in the latter situation this is a lack of attention and mental activity.

mania, acute Manic state which has sudden onset

and terminates rather than persisting over a long period of time.

mania, akinetic A disorder characterized by the symptoms of mania as well as lack of movement.

mania, ambitious Obsolete term for delusions of grandeur or any mental disorder characterized by grandiose ideas.

mania, anxious Variation of manic-depressive psychosis characterized by anxiety and excitement rather than depression.

mania, Bell's (L. V. Bell) Acute mania.

mania, chronic Mania or manic state which persists over a long period of time or permanently.

mania, collecting Uncontrollable urge to collect things, often useless items, and thought to be associated with anal erotic impulses.

mania concionabunda Obsolete term for strong uncontrollable urge to give speeches to the public.

mania, ephemeral See *mania transitoria.*

mania errabunda Obsolete term for uncontrollable desire to wander aimlessly away from home which is often associated with senility.

mania, grumbling The state of exaltation and restlessness concomitant with feelings of dissatisfaction, capriciousness and complaining.

mania, incendiary Pyromania.

mania, inhibited (E. Kraepelin) Variation of the manic state characterized by cheerfulness, inhibited psychomotor activity and flight of ideas.

mania, metaphysical Obsolete term for folie du doute.

mania, mitis Mild form of mania currently called hypomania.

mania, muscular Obsolete term for mania characterized by normally voluntary muscular movements occurring automatically.

mania, recurrent General term for mania which occurs periodically.

mania, puerperal Obsolete term for mania occurring after childbirth and previously thought to be attributable in a casual way to the puerperium, though today the puerperium is considered just one of several contributing factors.

mania, recurrent General term for mania which occurs periodically.

mania, religious Acute state of excitement characterized by religious hallucinations and hyperactivity.

mania senilis Mania associated with old-age and senility.

mania sine delirio Mild form of mania currently called hypomania, a more appropriate term.

mania, stuporous Manic phase of mania in which an individual is aloof and often does not talk.

mania transitoria Obsolete term for rare variety of spontaneous mad exaltation which is characterized by incoherence, insomnia and total or partial lack of awareness of surroundings.

mania, wandering Form of mania in which the individual has uncontrollable urge to leave home and wander about.

maniac One who exhibits mania or maniacal behavior.

maniacal chorea Chorea accompanied by extreme mental disturbance.

maniaphobia Morbid fear of going insane.

manic behavior Elated, hyperactive behavior.

manic-depressive psychosis See *psychosis, manic-depressive.*

manic-depressive psychosis, circular type See *psychosis, manic-depressive, circular type.*

manic depressive psychosis, depressed type See *psychosis, manic depressive, depressed type.*

manic-depressive psychosis, manic type See *psychosis, manic-depressive, manic type.*

manifest anxiety scale See *scale, manifest anxiety.*

manifest dream content See *content, dream, manifest.*

manifest schizophrenia See *schizophrenia, manifest.*

manifold 1. A group of objects which have something in common. 2. A classification which contains two or more subdivisions.

Manikin Test See *test, Manikin.*

manipulanda (E. C. Tolman) The aspects of an object or situation which allow the animal to manipulate it motorically.

manipulandum (operant conditioning) That part of the experimental chamber upon which the organism responds. This term, no longer the preferred term is being replaced by the word operandum.

manometric block Obstruction of the free flow of cerebrospinal fluid.

manoptoscope An apparatus consisting of a hollow cone through which the subject looks, which measures eye dominance.

mantle The part of brain which includes corpus callosum, fornix and the convolutions.

mantle layer The middle embryonic layer of the neural plate which develops into the gray matter of the central nervous system.

manual method See *method, manual.*

maple syrup urine disease A rare aminoaciduria associated with mental retardation. A hereditary metabolic disorder. In infantile form it is associated with hypertonicity, vomiting, seizures and often death.

MAPS See *test, Make-A-Picture Story.*

marasmus 1. A wasting or withering of the tissues, usually from improper nutrition. **2.** (R. Spitz) A condition in infants in which there is a gradual wasting of the body. The last stage of the grief reaction, in infants older than six months who are separated for a long period from their primary caretaker.

Marbe's law More common responses in word association tests have a shorter latency than the less common responses.

marginal intelligence See *intelligence, marginal.*

marginal layer The outer layer of the walls of the embryonic neural plane which gives rise to the nerve fibers.

marginal man (social psychology) A person who is not assimilated into a group or culture and is uncertain about his group membership.

marihuana; marijuana A drug derived from the hemp plant, cannabis indica, which produces feelings of mental exaltation, loss of inhibitions, intoxication and a distorted sense of time.

mark 1. A distinguishing characteristic. **2.** A score indicating the value or level of the performance of a subject.

marker variable or marker A variable, usually a test score, previously known to load (correlate with) a factor highly and consistently through different studies. Therefore, (a) a marker which loads highly on a factor helps to identify that factor, and (b) scores on marker tests can be used to estimate scores on the factor (Factor Score).

market research See *research, market.*

marketing orientation (E. Fromm) A non-productive life-style characterized by the perception of oneself as a commodity and of one's self-worth as dependent on one's market value.

Markov process (statistics) A model which represents joint probabilities sequentially and conditional probabilities in order to determine statistically the future values of a random variable.

masculine protest 1. (A. Adler) The desire to dominate and be superior. **2.** (A. Adler) The desire of the female to be a male.

Mashburn Complex Coordinator An apparatus to measure eye-hand and eye-foot coordination. The subject is asked to line up rows of red and green lights with a stick and rudder bar; the score is the number of matchings in a limited amount of time.

masked epilepsy See *epileptic equivalent.*

masking 1. The partial or complete obscuring of sensory stimulus by another. **2.** The partial or complete interference of one tone by another.

Maslow's theory of personality (A. H. Maslow) The theory that two basic types of motivation are important: deficiency motivation as oxygen, food and water, and growth motivation, strivings for knowledge and self-actualization. There is a postulated hierarchy of motivation according to which physiological needs must be satisfied first followed by safety needs, love, esteem needs and finally the need for self-actualization.

masochism 1. Sexual perversion in which the individual derives sexual pleasure from the infliction of pain upon himself. **2.** The deriving of pleasure from being maltreated or from suffering. **3.** (psychoanalysis) Aggression turned toward the self because of the anxiety inherent in expressing it outward.

mass action, principle of (K. S. Lashley) The theory that learning depends on the areas of the cortex as a whole based on animal experiments which have shown that the effect of brain tissue removal on learning depends on the quantity of ablated tissue rather than its location.

mass communication See *communication, mass.*

mass contagion See *contagion, mass.*

mass media of communication See *communication, mass media of.*

mass method See *method, mass.*

mass movement See *movement, mass.*

mass observation See *observation, mass.*

mass polarization See *polarization, mass.*

mass psychology See *psychology, mass.*

mass reflex See *reflex, mass.*

Masserman, Jules H. (1905-   ) American neurologist, psychiatrist and psychoanalyst. After early work on cerebrospinal fluid and neurophysiology, conducted research demonstrating the following biodynamic principles applicable to animals and man: 1) that behavior is actuated by varying physiologic needs, 2) that it is contingent on the organism's genetic and experiential *concepts* of its milieu, 3) that versatility of adaptation to stress is similarly determined and 4) that when these adaptive ranges are exceeded in circumstances of conflict or uncertainty, somatic dysfunctions and drug addictions stereotyped, regressive or "dereistic" patterns develop analogous to clinical neuroses or psychoses. As President of the International Association of Social Psychiatry (1970-   ), Masserman proposed that all effective therapy must satisfy three ultimate (Ur-) needs of man: 1) physical well-being and creativity, 2) social security and 3) philosophic serenity.

Author of 8 books, editor of 34 others, and contributor of over 250 articles on history, music, biography and philosophy as well as neurology, pharmacology and psychiatry.

Masson disc A white disc upon which black squares are arranged along one radius so that when the disc is rotated, a series of concentric rings of diminishing grayness is seen. The first ring from within which becomes indistinguishable from the background reflects the difference threshold of brightness vision.

mastery motive See *motive, mastery.*

masturbation The deriving of sexual satisfaction by manual or mechanical stimulation of the genitals.

MAT See *test, Miller Analogies.*

matched group See *group, matched.*

matched sample See *sample, matched.*

matching test See *test, matching.*

mate 1. To copulate. 2. To enter into a long-term relationship with a member of the opposite sex.

materialism 1. A philosophical point of view that matter is the only reality. 2. A value system which stresses the pursuit and acquisition of material goods and comforts at the expense of intellectual and cultural activities.

maternal behavior See *behavior, maternal.*

maternal drive See *drive, maternal.*

maternal overprotection See *overprotection, maternal.*

mathematical axis 1. A straight line around which a plane figure can be rotated to form a solid figure. 2. A pair of intersecting coordinates which are used to determine the position of a point or a series of points forming a surface or curve.

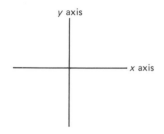

mathematical model See *model, mathematical.*

mathematico-deductive method See *method, mathmatico-deductive.*

matriarchy 1. A society in which lineage and inheritance are determined through the female line. 2. A society ruled by a woman.

matrix 1. The context. 2. (mathematics) A table of numbers arranged in rows and columns which undergoes certain mathematic operations.

matrix correlation See *correlation, matrix.*

matrix, product (factor analysis) The result obtained when factor loadings of variables are multiplied together.

maturation The process of changing from an immature (small, undifferentiated) to a mature or adult state.

maturation-degeneration hypothesis The principle that an organism's functions and abilities develop to a certain optimal stage then decline.

maturation hypothesis or theory The theory that some modes of behavior are solely determined by heredity but cannot be manifested until the appropriate organs and neural connections have matured.

maturity, emotional See *emotional maturity.*

maturity rating See *rating, maturity.*

MAVA See *multiple abstract variance analysis.*

maximal sensation See *sensation, maximal.*

maximum likelihood estimators (statistics-R.A. Fisher) Statistics chosen as estimators of population parameters which will maximize the likelihood of the sample results that are observed to occur.

Maxwell discs Slotted color discs which overlap when fitted on a rotating spindle. When rotated at a speed above the critical flicker frequency, a color mixture occurs whose hue and brightness is proportional to the amount of color exposed by the overlapping.

Maxwell triangle See *color triangle.*

Maxwell's demons (C. Maxwell) A metaphorical way of discussing physical forces and concepts as if they were humanlike with human attributes.

maze An apparatus of varying complexity used to study learning and motivation behavior which consists of a series of pathways, some of which are blind alleys, which eventually lead to the end or goal point.

maze, Hampton Court A 6 by 8 foot instrument designed to test learning in rats introduced by W. S. Smell, and based on the pattern of Hampton Court, England.

maze, multiple T A series of T maze runways with the starting box at the base of the first T and the goal at one end of the last cross bar.

maze, stylus A maze which a person traces with a stylus.

maze, T A pathway in the shape of a T with the starting box at the base and goal boxes at either ends of the cross piece. For each trial, reinforcement may be available in either or both goal boxes. Often used in animal learning and discrimination studies with the discrimination stimuli at the choice point.

McArdle's syndrome See *syndrome, McArdle's.*

McDougall, William (1871-1938) British-born psychologist and physician. Professor of psychology, Harvard University (1920-1927), Duke University (1927-1938). Chief exponent of hormic psychology whose basic proposition is that all behavior is purposive or goal-seeking. Opposed concept of psychology as science of consciousness; was first to propose definition of psychology as the study of behavior. Wrote *Physiological Psychology* (1905), *Introduction to Social Psychology* (1908), *The Group Mind* (1920), *Outline of Psychology* (1923), *Outline of Abnormal Psychology* (1926), and *The Energies of Men* (1932).

MCI See *inventory, Minnesota Counseling.*

MCI See *mother-child interaction.*

McNaghten rule See *M' Naghten rules.*

mdn See *median.*

Mead, Margaret (1901-   ) American anthropologist. Developed method of studying childhood in primitive cultures; the study of cultural character; extended its application to the study of modern cultures and the study of cultures at a distance; developed the theory of cultural transformation through across the board cultural change and the application of anthropological methods to culture building.

mean $(\bar{x})$ A measure of central tendency which is the arithmetic average of the scores. Obtained by the formula: $\bar{x} = \frac{\Sigma x}{N}$, x refers to the individual scores, N is the number of scores, and Σ is to take the sum of the values represented by the expression.

mean, assumed An arbitrary value near the middle of a group distribution which is chosen in a short-cut method of determining the mean. The algebraic sum of the deviations from the assumed mean divided by the number of deviations is subsequently added or subtracted from the assumed mean to arrive at the actual mean of the series.

mean deviation See *deviation, average.*

mean-error procedure See *adjustment method.*

mean geometric See *mean, logarithmic.*

mean gradation method See *equal sense differences method.*

mean, harmonic The reciprocal of the arithmetic mean of the reciprocals of a series of values. The formula for H or M_H is

$$\frac{1}{H} = (\frac{1}{N})\Sigma(\frac{1}{X})$$

where N = number of cases and X = any score.

mean, logarithmic The nth root of the product of n number of values or means, used in averaging ratios, rates of change, and means which are distinctly different but which have comparable standard deviations. Also called geometric mean. The formula is:

$$M_2 = \sqrt{a \cdot b \cdot c}$$

mean rate See *rate, mean.*

mean square The square root of the average of the squares of all the values in a set.

mean-square contingency coefficient (statistics) A statistic which determines whether the entries in a two-way contingency table could have been produced by chance factors. The symbol is Φ^2.

mean-square error See *variance.*

mean variation See *deviation, average.*

meaning 1. That which is intended. 2. That which a symbol or symbolic act signifies. 3. The emotional or cognitive import of something for an individual.

meaning, context theory of (E. Titchener) The hypothesis that the meaning of an experience consists of the mental images which are associated with this experience. The meaning develops from actual sensory experience which is gradually replaced by mental images which symbolize the experience.

means-end capacity (E. C. Tolman) The hypothesized ability of an organism to respond to relationships between means objects and goal objects, specifically to respond to cues which lead to the goal such as distances, directions, and sequence.

means-end expectancy (E. C. Tolman) A state of expectation for the goal resulting from the immediate perception of means-end stimuli.

means-end learning A type of rewarded learning in which skills are acquired for the purpose of achieving a single, relatively restricted goal, usually tangible and external; for example, a rat satisfying hunger by running a maze.

means-end readiness (E. C. Tolman) A state of innate or acquired readiness to form particular expectancies.

means-end relations (E. C. Tolman) The intervening objects and signs between a means and an end goal which are meaningful to an organism due to his previous experience.

measure 1. A quantitative result of measurement. 2. A standard used in measurement. 3. A statistic.

measurement, absolute 1. A measurement that disregards the plus or minus sign of the value. 2. A measurement that is obtained by units derived from that which is being measured and is, therefore, independent of comparison with other variables.

measurement, direct Measurements taken directly without transformation to another scale of measurement.

measurement, indirect Measurement in which the obtained values must be transformed to another scale or used in an intermediary process to obtain the desired quantification such as in the calculation of rectangular area from values of length and width.

measurement, interactive (R. B. Cattell) Measurement reflecting the exchange between an individual and his environment.

measurement, mental 1. The use of quantitative methods to measure psychological processes. 2. Psycho-physical methods of measurement.

measurement methods See *methods, measurement.*

meatus The external and internal canals of the temporal bone of the skull. The external passage leading from the outside to the middle ear cavity transmits soundwaves from the outside to the ear. The internal canal which leads from the cavity of the inner ear to the interior of the skull transports the auditory and facial nerves with blood-vessels.

mechanical aptitude See *aptitude, mechanical.*

mechanical indicator See *indicator, mechanical.*

mechanical intelligence See *intelligence, mechanical.*

mechanical stimulation See *stimulation, mechanical.*

mechanism 1. A system which operates like a machine. 2. The manner in which an end is produced. 3. A habitual manner of behaving which accomplishes a desired end. 4. (psychoanalysis) Unconscious determinants of behavior resulting from repressed wishes and impulses.

mechanistic theory The doctrine that all aspects of the universe including organisms and their psychological processes can be explained in terms of mechanical laws. Free will, motivation and purpose are denied as important variables in attaining ends.

mechanoreceptor Nerve structures (receptors) which are stimulated by movement of or change of pressure within the organ in which they are located.

mecholyl A drug which causes a rapid drop of blood pressure.

Medea complex See *complex, Medea.*

median (md) A measure of central tendency which is the point that divides the distribution into two parts such that an equal number of scores fall above and below the point.

median deviation See *deviation, median.*

median grey A brightness of gray forming the midpoint of a scale of brightness ranging from pure white to pure black.

median interval See *interval, median.*

mediate 1. Interposed between two items. 2. To act as an arbitrator between disputants. 3. To be a link between two processes, specifically thought processes. 4. Dependent upon an intervening process.

mediate association See *association, mediate.*

mediated generalization Similar responses and associated proprioceptive stimuli that becomes attached to different stimuli, consequently retarding the formation of a discrimination. This concept has been used to extend the stimulus-response formulations to symbols using human subjects.

mediation theory The doctrine that stimuli do not directly initiate behavior but stimulate intervening processes which activate the instrumental behavior.

mediator (communication theory) Functions of receiving and sending message are united. A system between the source and destination of a message.

medicine 1. Any substance, material or method used in the treatment of disease. 2. The science of treating diseases. The branches of medicine include: 1) Anatomic medicine, dealing with anatomic changes in diseased organs and their association to symptoms manifested during life; 2) Clinical medicine, the study of disease by direct observation and treatment of the patient; 3) Experimental medicine, based upon experiments on animals and the observation of pathologic changes induced in diseases and the effect of drugs dispensed; 4) Physical medicine, a consultative, diagnostic, and therapeutic aid coordinating and integrating the use of physical and occupational therapy, and physical rejuvenation on the professional direction of the ailing and injured; 5) Preventive medicine, dealing with any activity which seeks to prevent disease, prolong life, and support physical and mental health and effectualness, especially the science of etiology and epidemiology of disease processes. They deal with those predisposing factors increasing an individual's suseptibility to disease, the initiating and precipitating factors of disease, and those factors which in noninfective or degenerative disease, result in their advance; 6) Psychosomatic medicine, dealing with the interrelationship between the psychic and physical components of illness; 7) Social medicine, an approach to the preservation and promotion of health, and to the prevention, amelioration, and cure of disease, having its foundation in a dynamic sociology and biology, comprised of the study of man and his environment. It is an attempt at the integration of the fields of clinical and social pathology, their workers, and their methods. The data so obtained is consistently guided by the concepts of the normal variability of human beings, and their capacity for adaptability.

medicine, constitutional The branch of medicine which concerns itself with the patient's constitution and his vulnerability to disease.

medium 1. The instrumentality through which something is accomplished. 2. Anything which fills the space through which a substance such as waves passes. 3. (parapsychology) A person who is believed to be controlled by disembodied spirits during a trance and to be able to receive and to impart messages from deceased people.

medulla 1. The inner part of an organ. 2. Abbreviation for medulla oblongata, the bulb at the top of the spinal cord which is the lowest part of the brain and the seat of nerve centers controlling autonomic functions such as respiration, heart rate, and gastrointestinal functions, and contains all of the ascending and descending fiber tracts interconnecting the brain and the spinal cord with many important nerve cell nuclei.

Meduna, Ladislas J. von (1896-1964) Hungarian-born American psychiatrist who suggested the use of convulsive agents in the treatment of schizophrenics.

megalocephalia See *macrocephaly.*

megalomania An exaggerated overestimation of one's own value, importance and abilities.

Meier Art Judgment Test See *test, Meier Art Judgment.*

meiosis The special type of cell division occurring in the gonads by which the gametes, containing the haploid chromosome number, are produced from diploid cells. This mechanism ensures that the chromosome number does not double with each new generation.

mel A unit of a ratio scale for pitch developed by

establishing a tone of 1,000 cycles per second equal to 1000 mels. The steps of the scale are constructed by the method of fractionation whereby the subject adjusts a stimulus tone equal to one-half the standard tone of 1000 mels, then adjusts the next tone and continues in this manner to produce a scale of subjectively equal intervals.

melancholia, abdominal   (T. S. Clouston) Describes patients suffering from profound depression with intensely believed in delusions concerning the stomach and bowels.

melancholia, agitated   The expression, melancholia agitata, was employed in the latter half of the nineteenth century to refer to the excited phase of catatonia. The Anglicized term, agitated melancholia, then became associated with manic-depressive psychosis and involutional melancholia. Neither term is much in use today. The condition described by the term agitated melancholia involves a state of severe anxiety, most commonly occurring late in life.

melancholia; melancholy   1. An obsolete term for intense depression, loss of interest in external stimuli, and feelings of guilt. 2. (psychoanalysis) The pathological reaction to a loss of an object characterized by intense depression, disinterest in the outside world and guilt feelings resulting from previously repressed intense hostility directed at the internalized object.

melancholic type   See *type, melancholic.*

membership character   See *character, membership.*

membership group   See *group, membership.*

memory   1. The characteristic of living organisms involving the reliving of past experience and consisting of four phases: learning, retention, recall, and recognition. 2. The totality of experiences which can be remembered. 3. A specific past experience which is recalled.

memory afterimage   See *afterimage, memory.*

memory, associative   The recalling of a past experience by remembering a fact or incident associated with it which evokes the experience.

memory color   The effect of a color perceived previously on a present experience of the same color.

memory, curve   See *curve, retention.*

memory drum   An apparatus for the presentation of material to be learned by the subject at a constant rate of speed. It is used to test verbal recall of serially presented words and of paired associate words.

Memory-for-Designs Test   See *test, Memory-for-Designs.*

memory image   See *image, memory.*

memory, incidental   The occurrence of a memory without intent to remember.

memory, kinesthetic   Memory that is in terms of ideal representation of movement sensations.

memory, long term (LTM)   The ability to respond to a stimulus, recite a list, remember an association, and so on, after a long period of time since the material was presented. Its slow rate of decay and great amount of remembered material distinguish it from short term memory.

memory, operation of   (J. P. Guilford) The commission of information to memory storage, to be distinguished both from the memory store itself and from the process of retrieval of information from storage.

memory, organic   A change in living tissue which persists and modifies subsequent activity of that tissue and which results from the activity or functioning of the tissue itself.

memory, physiological   (M. Prince) The storing of somatic experiences without the organism's awareness of it.

memory, racial   The part of person's mental apparatus which is believed to be inherited from ancestors, and transmitted from generation to generation.

memory, screen   (psychoanalysis) Fragmentary childhood memories which are similar in structure to manifest dream content in that they have been subjected to the operations of condensation and displacement, and usually serve as a cover for other repressed memories. Also called cover memory.

memory, short term (STM)   The correct recall or appropriate performance immediately or shortly after the presentation of the material. Its rapid decay and limited amount of material distinguishes it from long term memory.

memory span   Greatest number of items an individual can correctly reproduce immediately after one presentation. Series of items of a single type.

memory-span method   Test of memory span by the presentation of several series of items varying in length from what is expected the subject will recall to what is known to be beyond his ability to recall. The number correctly reproduced in fifty percent of the trials is taken as the measure of memory span.

memory system   An artificially developed device for remembering material usually consisting of the formation of associative connections between the material to be learned and previous knowledge.

memory trace   The hypothetical neurological change which occurs when material is learned; it is postulated to account for the retention of learned material.

memory, unconscious   (psychoanalysis) Repressed ideas and affects which influence behavior through their derivatives which enter consciousness.

menarche   The first menstruation in the human female.

mendacity   Pathological lying.

Mendel, Gregor Johann (1822-1884)   Czech priest and biologist, abbot of the Augustinian monastery in Brno, Czechoslavakia; laid foundation for modern genetics; experimented on crosses between varieties of plants, mostly peas; discovered two laws of inheritance (Mendel's laws); his published report of 1866 was ignored for over 30 years; died without recognition for his scientific work.

Mendelian Law of Independent Assortment The principle that alleles or homologous chromosomes segregate independently of other alleles in other chromosome pairs.

Mendelian Law of Segregation The principle that genes maintain their integrity as they divide and recombine from generation to generation.

Mendelian laws Laws of hereditary transmission of characteristics which state that traits are inherited according to the Mendelian ratio which refers to the frequency of dominant to recessive phenotypes in the particular generation. The crossing of pure dominant with pure recessive parents produces a first generation consisting of three dominant phenotypes to one recessive.

Mendelian ratio The frequency of the dominant and recessive phenotype in the offspring from a specific type of mating.

Mendelism The doctrine of inheritance based on the principles that elements called genes exist which are responsible for the transmission of unit characters, and that the genetic elements are segregated independently of each other in the reproduction process.

meninges The three membranes, the dura matter, the arachnoid layer and the pia matter which cover the brain and spinal cord.

meningitis Inflammation of the meninges.

meningitis, cryptococcus A form of meningitis, frequently associated with leukemia and lymphoma in children, in which signs and symptoms include a positive Kernig's sign, nuchal rigidity, increased intracranial pressure, irritability, somnolence, anorexia, vomiting and fever.

meningitis, hemophilus influencae Type of meningitis with symptoms of anorexia, fever and seizures. Sequelae include upper motor neuron disease with resultant spasticity, hemiparesis, deafness, intellectual and motor retardation, seizures, and rarely, brain abcesses.

meningitis, neonatal Occurring in .01 percent of full-term infants, its symptoms include vomiting, anorexia, lethargy, twitchings, tremors, increase in startle response, jaundice, bulging fontanelle, and seizures.

meningitis, pneumococcal A type of meningitis with symptoms including lethargy, fever and seizures.

meningitis, staphylococcal A relatively rare form of bacterial meningitis which usually results from an infection of the skin, ears, or paranasal sinuses. There are multiple intracerebral and meningeal abscesses along with lethargy, fever and seizures leading to death if not properly treated. Sequelae include

spasticity, deafness, seizures, and motor and mental retardation.

meningitis, streptococcal A form of bacterial meningitis most commonly found in the first few months of life in which a focus of infection in the skin, ears, and nasopharynx is frequently present. It results in a deposition of a purulent exudate over the convexity of the brain along with lethargy, fever, and seizures. Sequelae include spasticity, deafness, seizures, and motor and mental retardation.

meningovascular syphilis See *syphilis, meningovascular.*

menopause Also called climacterium; the normal cessation of menstruation which takes place usually in the late forties.

menotaxis A taxis in which the animal orients at a constant angle rather than directly toward or away from the stimulus source.

menstruation The monthly discharge of blood and uterine material which occurs in the sexually mature female.

mensuration The measurement process.

mental abilities, primary 1. The hypothetical fundamental and basic units which constitute all distinguishable mental abilities. 2. (L. L. and L. G. Thurstone) Seven unit traits, derived through factor analysis, which are held to account for most variance in ability: verbal comprehension (V); word fluency (W); number (N); space (S); associative memory (M); perceptual speed (P); and reasoning (R) or induction (I).

mental age (A. Binet) The degree of intelligence of an individual determined by comparing his ability with the ability of other individuals of the same age. This concept is based on the principle that intellectual ability can be measured and that it increases progressively with age.

mental apparatus See *apparatus, mental.*

mental chemistry The doctrine that mental elements are fused by association into complex processes which no longer resemble the original elements.

mental deficiency See *deficiency, mental.*

mental development See *development, mental.*

mental disease See *disease, mental.*

mental disorder 1. Behavior disorder. 2. Severe maladjustment. 3. Includes mental diseases and all forms of psychopathological behavior.

mental disorders, classification of See *classification of mental disorders.*

mental disorders of old age See *senility.*

mental examination See *examination, mental.*

mental faculty See *faculty psychology.*

mental function 1. A mental process. 2. A particular type of ability such as intelligence.

mental growth See *growth, mental.*

mental growth curve See *curve, mental growth.*

mental healing The curing of disorders by suggestion or faith.

mental health A state of relatively good adjustment, feelings of well-being and actualization of one's potentialities and capacities.

Mental Health Study Act An act passed by the Congress of the United States of America in 1955 pointing out the human and economic problems of mental illness and stating its support of research aiming at the prevention of mental disorders.

mental hospital An institution, either privately or state owned, in which in and out rehabilitative care is administered to mentally disturbed persons through various forms of therapy, such as psychotherapy, occupational therapy, and chemotherapy.

mental hygiene See *hygiene, mental.*

mental illness A disorder of behavior of organic or non-organic origin which is severe enough to require professional help. This term is used exchangeably with mental and behavior disorder.

mental institution See *mental hospital.*

mental maturity 1. The attainment of an adult level of mental development. 2. An average adult level of intelligence.

mental measurement See *measurement, mental.*

mental process See *process, mental.*

mental processes, higher Complex functions such as thinking, intelligence, memory, in contrast to sensory or motor functions.

mental processes, higher, organization of Higher mental processes are described in terms of two principles: the reflex structure of mental activity and the systemic organization of higher mental processes in man which are of social origin. The reflex processes underlying mental activity are complex and dynamically organized involving different cerebral structures. The mental functions are dynamic systems in which different groups of cortical areas participate. These higher mental processes are developed from intercommunication among individuals and are mediated by a second signaling system. At different stages of development, the same mental function involves different cortical areas and dynamic systems.

mental retardation 1. Subnormal intellectual development due to social and environmental factors with no organic component, carrying with it the implication of reversibility. 2. See *deficiency, mental.*

mental scale See *scale, mental.*

mental set See *set, mental.*

mental structure See *structure, mental.*

mental test See *test, mental.*

mentalism The doctrine that mental phenomena or mental processes cannot be reduced to physical phenomena.

menticide The systematic attempt to break down a person's beliefs, standards, and values and to inculcate other views.

meprobamate A minor tranquilizer, usually prescribed for anxiety, phobic states, insomnia, irritability and hyperactivity.

mercury poisoning See *poisoning, mercury.*

merergasia (A. Meyer) A syndrome consisting of a partial disorganization of personality.

merit ranking Ordering of data, persons, objects, etc. with respect to the magnitude of a particular trait.

merit rating The evaluation of an individual's performance on a specific job or task.

merit scale Ranking of data or subjects according to the average of merits which were assigned by the raters.

Merkel corpuscle A sense receptor, believed to be associated with pressure and touch which is located in the mouth and tongue.

Merkel's laws (Merkel) A principle which holds that equal above threshold sense differences correlate with equal stimulus differences.

Merleau-Ponty, Maurice (1907-1961) French existential philosopher. Attempted to integrate phenomenology and psychology. Made perception the foundation of his philosophy because he regarded it as man's primordial contact with the world. Wrote *The Structure of Behavior* (1942) and *Phenomenology of Perception* (1945).

Merrill-Palmer scale (Merrill, Palmer) A test designed to measure intellectual ability, including verbal and performance materials within a 93 item-series that has been standardized for children ages 24-63 months.

mescaline A narcotic drug which produces auditory and visual hallucinations. It is derived from the cactus plant. Mescaline, when ingested, is known to alter one's state of consciousness and has been used in therapy to make a patient behave as if he were back in his childhood. The drug can produce an effect which simulates a psychotic state. The intake of mescaline produces hallucination (a feeling that part of the body is missing), the tasting and smelling of peculiar odors, the development of paranoid ideas, the hearing of colors, the seeing of sounds, depressive or euphoric states. Some physiological effects are dilation of the pupils, body tremors, poor coordination, and difficulty in spatial discrimination.

mesencephalon The midbrain consisting of the corpora quadrigemina, lamina, the cerebral peduncles, the tegmentum and the nerve tracts known as the crura cerebri. It developed from the middle portion of the primitive embryonic brain.

Mesmer, Franz Anton (1734-1815) Austrian physician; believed in animal magnetism, an invisible power, which some men could utilize to cure diseases; expelled from Vienna for practicing what came to be called mesmerism, moved to Paris, where his method of treatment gained wide popularity; commission of scientists and physicians under presidency of Benjamin Franklin verified mesmeric phenomena but attributed them to causes other than animal magnetism; unable to prove his theory, branded as an impostor, had to leave Paris; died in Switzerland.

mesmerism (F. A. Mesmer) Obsolete term for hypnotism.

mesmerization Hypnosis.

mesmerize To hypnotize.

mesoblast See *mesoderm.*

mesocephalic The moderate relationship of the head between its length and width. In somatometry, having a cephalic index of 76.0 to 80.9.

mesoderm The middle layer in an embryo which develops into bone and muscle. Also called mesoblast.

mesodermogenic neurosyphilis See *neurosyphilis, mesodermogenic.*

mesognathous A condition in which the upper jaw has a mild degree of anterior projection when compared to the profile of the facial skeleton. In craniometry, having a gnathic index of 98.0 to 102.9.

mesokurtosis A frequency curve whose distribution, particularly its peak, is similar to the peak found in a normal curve.

mesomorphic type See *type, mesomorphic.*

mesomorphy (W. Sheldon) One of the three basic bodily builds which relates to the 3 primary temperments. According to this classification, the physique is marked by a prominence of muscle, bone and connective tissue.

mesosomatic (E. J. Eysenck) A subject who falls within one standard deviation of the mean after standard scores for height and chest measurements have been multiplied.

message 1. Symbolic communication between individuals. 2. (communications theory) The part of the output of one unit which is fed into the receiver of another unit as input.

messenger RNA A type of ribonucleic acid which transfers genetic information from the cell nucleus to the cytoplasm.

metabolism The physical and chemical reactions of the organism by which protoplasm is produced and destroyed and which manufacture energy necessary for the organism to perform its vital activities.

metacholine chloride A compound used as a measure of gross autonomic activity and to predict differential response to electroshock therapy.

metachromatic leukodystrophy See *sulfatide lipidosis.*

metaerg (R. B. Cattell) A trait, motivational in nature, which is affected by environmental factors, as opposed to constitutional influences.

metagnomy A belief that knowledge can be obtained by superhuman methods from spiritual beings; superhuman knowledge.

metalanguage 1. The aspect of language concerned with rules for the correct use of language such as grammar and syntax. 2. Terminology which expresses from dissimilar disciplines in a common manner.

metallophonia A metallic quality of the voice.

metals, psychosis due to Psychotic symptoms may appear in persons who have had prolonged exposure to metallic poisoning, such as lead or mercury. Because of the effects of these toxins on the neurological structures, patients may not recover, although recovery is not ruled out.

metamers Colors with different spectral qualities but which are perceived as identical under specific conditions.

metamorphopsia The distortion of visually perceived objects when the retina has been displaced.

metamorphoses, delirium of See *lycanthropy.*

metamorphosis 1. Radical, striking change. 2. The abrupt, observable change in the post-embryonic development of an organism, such as a tadpole into a frog.

metamorphosis sexualis paranoica A rare delusion, seen in paranoid patients who believe that they have been changed into the opposite sex.

metamphetamine A drug of the amphetamine group used in the treatment of depression and, in children, in the treatment of hyperactive behavior. However, it is infrequently prescribed because of cardiovascular effects when given in high dosages.

metaphase A stage in mitosis when the split chromosomes group together in the equatorial plane of the spindle. The metaphase occurs after the prophase and before the anophase.

metaphoric language 1. The use of metaphors. 2. In psychoanalytical theory, a form of thinking which resembles the primary process. The metaphor is a device which expresses a vital emotion and experience which originally occurred in the pregenital stage and of repressed Oedipal wishes. Metaphoric thinking may take place in dreams and in regressed states of neurotics.

metaphorical combinations A connection between different spheres of experience made by symbols or images.

metaphrenia A condition which is characterized by a compulsion with time and money.

metaphysical mania See *mania, metaphysical.*

metaphysics The branch of philosophy which concerns itself with the ultimate nature of existence. It includes ontology, the science of being, cosmology, the science of the nature of the universe and more widely epistemology, the theory of knowledge.

metapsychics See *parapsychology*.

metapsychology (psychoanalysis) The study of mental processes in terms of dynamic, economic, structural, genetic, adaptive and topographic approaches. *Dynamic:* deals with two innate motivational forces (instinctual drives), namely the libidinal Eros and the aggressive Thanatos. *Economic:* dwells upon the use of mental energies. *Structural:* divides the personality structure into id, ego and superego. *Genetic:* analyzes the origin of the mental phenomena and their development. *Adaptive:* deals with the interaction with the environment and the ensuing intrapsychic harmony. *Topographic:* divides the mind into conscious, preconscious and unconscious.

metatheory See *metapsychology*.

metathetic (S. S. Stevens) A sensory continuum in which just noticeable differences are thought to be subjectively equal. The physiological processes underlying the discrimination for metathetic continua are suggested to be the substitution of one locus of neural activity for another locus of activity. Pitch is one such continuum.

metempirical Beyond the empirical method; speculative or intuitive; evading empirical evidence.

metempsychosis A belief in the transmigration of the human soul into another corporal being.

metencephalon The part of the embryonic brain from which the medulla oblongata develops.

methadone A synthetic narcotic drug which is used in the relief of pain and the treatment of heroin addiction.

methamphetamine hydrochloride A central stimulant and vasoconstrictor compound soluble in water which is a methyl derivative of amphetamine or a desoxyn derivation of ephedrine.

methionine A rare aminoaciduria associated with mental retardation.

method A systematic procedure; a chosen path of dealing with facts or hypotheses.

method, absolute-judgment A psychophysical method that involves the evaluation of each of a series of stimuli without direct comparison to a standard; the utilization of absolute impressions.

method, association The study of association responses to given stimuli in an attempt to determine personality or behavioral traits.

method, biographical The systematic utilization and analysis of background information of a person in the investigation of cause-and-effect relationships between events in the person's life and development.

method, constant See *method, constant stimulus*.

method, constant stimulus (G. T. Fechner) A psychophysiological technique used for determining absolute and difference thresholds by requiring the subject to compare various stimuli with a standard or by stating when he notices a given stimulus. The thresholds are then determined as the value which is perceived in exactly fifty per cent of the cases.

method, contingency (statistics) A method of determining the degree to which two variables are dependent on each other. It is obtained by taking a function of the differences between the actual frequencies of the cells of a two-way table and the frequencies that would be estimated if the two variables were independent.

method, cross-sectional A method of studying large groups of people by assessing their standing on a particular variable at a given time rather than looking at how they change on this variable over a longer period of time. This method is used to establish standards.

method, graphic 1. The use of graphs to present or to analyze data. 2. A technique of recording responses in the form of a graph.

method, halving A psychophysical technique of constructing ratio scales of sensory magnitude in which the subject is asked to compare pairs of stimuli so that the intervals between them are perceived as equal.

method, impression A method used in the experimental study of feeling, that is dependent on the subject's introspective report of the affective experience produced by various stimuli.

method, just noticeable difference (psychophysics) A procedure for determining the smallest difference in a stimulus that can be discriminated by a subject. The technique consists of increasing the difference between two nondiscriminable stimuli, decreasing the difference between two discriminable stimuli, and taking the average of the point at which difference between the former is discerned and the point at which difference between the latter is imperceptible.

method, kinesthetic A technique for treating speech and reading defects and disabilities by focusing attention onto the various movement sensations associated with correct and faulty speech and reading.

method, limits See *method, just noticeable difference*.

method, manual The method of communication among deaf people consisting of sign language and gestures.

method, mass A technique for measuring large numbers of persons simultaneously.

method, mathematico-deductive (C. L. Hull) The use of mathematical equations to delineate postulates and definitions from which detailed theorems are deduced.

method, metric 1. The use of quantitative measurement, especially measurement using the metric system. 2. (psychophysics) Psychophysical methods of measurement.

method, minimal change (psychophysics) A technique for determining the differential threshold. The experimenter presents the subject with a series of stimuli which vary slightly in ascending or descending order which the subject is asked to compare with a standard.

method, moving average (statistics) A method of evening-out a series of items by substituting for frequencies of a number of groups, the average of the groups.

method, moving total (statistics) A method of evening-out a series of items by replacing each item with the sum of the item and a number of neighboring items.

method, Müller-Urban (psychophysics) A technique used to analyze data obtained by the method of constant stimuli based on the assumption that the best measure of the absolute or difference threshold value is the median of the best fitting ogive curve for the observed distribution.

method, multigroup (R. B. Cattell) A factor analytic procedure of simultaneously extracting the factors from the correlation matrix instead of successively.

method, multiple-choice A test or experiment in which the subject or animal is given several choices, only one of which is correct or which leads to a reward. In a discrimination experiment, the correct choice is usually marked by a specific cue which the animal must learn.

method, obstruction A technique for measuring the relative strength of various drives or motivations by juxtaposing one against the other in order to see which will determine an animal's behavior. The animal is forced to endure a negative stimulus in order to reach a positive goal; the technique measures to what extent a negative stimulus will be endured in particular conditions.

method of adjustment (psychophysics) The subject manipulates a continuously variable comparison stimulus until it appears equal to the standard stimulus. Several measures are usually taken. It is often used to determine the differential threshold or the point of subjective equality (PSE).

method of least squares (mathematics) A method for obtaining the best fitting curve for a series of quantitative data by making minimum the sum of the squares of the differences between the points to be fitted and the corresponding points on the fitted line.

method of limits (psychophysics) Most commonly used method for determining absolute thresholds. The experimenter presents a series of stimuli, each differing by a small discrete amount from the preceding stimulus. For each stimulus in the series the experimenter records the response of the subject. In this method usually two types of stimulus series are employed: a) an ascending series in which the initial stimulus of the series is presented below the threshold and each succeeding stimulus is increased by a constant small step until the subject reports detection; b) A descending series in which the initial stimulus is above the threshold and each succeeding stimulus is decreased by a constant small step.

method of residues See residues, method of.

method of successive-intervals See successive-intervals, method of.

method of successive-practice See successive-practice, method of.

method, prompting The method of measuring retention by the number of prompts needed to reproduce a previously presented series of items until the entire series can be reproduced without prompting.

method, rank order A method of ranking items or events according to the order of their rank.

method, right and wrong cases See method, constant stimulus.

method, scientific The techniques and procedures of naturalistic observation and experimentation used by scientists to deal with facts, data and their interpretation according to certain principles and precepts.

method, scopic A method of recording quantitative data by means of visual observation as opposed to graphic methods in which they are recorded by instruments.

method, sense ratio See estimation, ratio.

method, serial-anticipation See method, prompting.

method, subtraction 1. A method used to obtain a value of interest by subtracting the value of one observation from another. 2. (psychophysiology) In reaction time experiments, a method for measuring the amount of time necessary to make a choice, by subtracting from the time of the compound reaction, the amount of time used in the simple reaction.

method, successive-approximation See conditioning, approximation.

method, successive reproduction A method for measuring retention by asking the subject to reproduce learned material at relatively long intervals.

methodology A branch of logic and/or philosophy of science which analyzes research procedures.

methods, measurement Quantitative methods in psychological experiments. The measurement of psychological constructs by tests, and scales which are treated statistically.

methyl alcohol poisoning See poisoning, methyl alcohol.

methylphenidate A central nervous system stimulant frequently prescribed for the treatment of depression.

metonymy Disturbance in the logical use of language; the use of inappropriate, non-idiomatic, autistic forms of speech.

metrazol A trade name for pentylenetetrazol which in doses of 0.1 gr (1 ½ gr) is used as a circulatory and respiratory stimulant and in doses of 0.4-0.5 gr (6–7½ gr) is given intravenously and used in shock treatment of mental disorders.

metric method See method, metric.

metronome An apparatus which marks off short periods of time. It is used in timing various activities and was formerly used in obtaining graphical records of time intervals in psychological experiments.

metronoscope An apparatus which exposes short pieces of reading material for variable intervals to test or practice reading speed.

Metropolitan Achievement Tests See *tests, Metropolitan Achievement.*

Meyer, Adolf (1866-1950) American psychiatrist who stressed a holistic and integrative view including counseling, advice, and social service. The patient was viewed as a psychobiological whole. He interpreted behavior in terms of overt reactions and did not concern himself with a postulated set of unconscious mechanisms. The approach was keeping an open mind with the patient in order to understand the patient's cues. He introduced the term "mental hygiene" which developed into a movement for the prevention and cure of mental illness.

Meynert, Theodore (1833-1892) Viennese physician who emphasized the neurological and physiological aspect of mental disorder. He theorized that psychosis is due to a variety of changes in the circulatory nervous system and developed a classification of mental illness on a purely anatomical basis involving the working of the central nervous system.

M-F test 1. Test for measuring an individual's psychosocial gender role (masculinity or femininity). **2.** A test for such measurement in adults devised by L. M. Terman and Catherine C. Miles.

Michigan Picture Test See *Test, Michigan Picture.*

Michotte, Albert van den Berk (1881-1965) Belgian phenomenological experimental psychologist at the University of Louvain. During World War II, he and his students undertook extensive experiments on the perception of motion and of causation, demonstrating (contrary to David Hume's philosophical analysis) that impressions of causality depend not upon past experience but upon time, space, and speed relationships in the stimulus pattern.

microcephaly A condition characterized by the smallness of the head with associated subnormal mental development, produced by an incomplete development of the brain due to a premature closing of the skull.

micron The unit of length equal to one millionth of a meter.

microphobia Morbid fear of small objects.

microphonia Weak, hardly audible voice.

micropsia Disorder of visual perception in which objects are perceived much smaller than they really are.

microsplanchnic (A. Viola) A body type characterized by a small trunk and relatively long limbs.

microtome An instrument used for cutting thin sections of tissue for microscopic preparations.

micturition Discharge of urine; urination.

midbrain See *mesencephalon.*

midparent The average measure for both parents of any characteristic such as height.

midpoint The halfway point in a given interval or range.

midrange values The mean of the highest and lowest scores in a distribution which is a crude measure of central tendency.

midscore The median.

Mignon delusion The delusional fantasy of a child that his parents are not his real parents and that his true parents are distinguished people.

migraine headache See *headache, migraine.*

milestone sequence (J. Loevinger) A trait which develops in stages independent of age.

milieu therapy A therapeutic process which stresses changes in the patient's physical and social environment, with emphasis on the social.

military psychology See *psychology, military.*

Mill, James (1773-1836) British philosopher-empiricist whose doctrine represented the culmination of the philosophy of associationism. A strict elementist, he held that the mind consists of sensations and ideas; there is only one principle needed to explain mind: association. Any mental whole equals the sum total of its constituent elements.

Mill, John Stuart (1806-1873) British empiricist whose influential "mental chemistry" differed sharply from the arch-associationism of his father, James Mill. Compounds of ideas can, he held, have properties not deducible from the properties of the elemental ideas composing them. Also influential was his epistemological position that matter is the permanent possibilities of sensation.

Mill's canons (J. S. Mill) Five principles of inductive reasoning: the law of agreement states that given a large number of instances of a phenomenon which have a common factor, that factor causes the phenomenon most probably; the law of difference which holds that differences occurring among otherwise similar phenomena are due to events preceding them; the law of agreement and difference which states that the factor which is present when the phenomenon is present and absent if the event is absent must be a cause of the occurrence; the law of residues which states that the unexplained residue of an event is due to an unexplained remainder in the preceding condition; and the law of concomitant variation which states that the factors which vary together have a common cause.

Miller Analogies Test See *test, Miller Analogies.*

Miller, Neal E. (1909-   ) American psychologist. Developed and experimentally tested theory of conflict and displacement, developed (with John Dollard) learning theory of psychotherapy, showed that fear can motivate, and reduction in it reinforce, learning; credited (with Delgado and Roberts) with first demonstration of instrumental learning motivated by direct electrical stimulation of the brain, one of the early investigators to use a variety of behavioral techniques to study the effects of direct electrical and chemical stimulation of the brain, proved that such stimulation of specific sites in hypothalamus can have a variety of motivational effects similar to those of normal hunger and thirst; proved that a variety of autonomically mediated visceral responses are subject to instrumental learning.

millilambert A measuring unit of luminance equal to one thousandth of a second.

millimicron A unit of measurement for light waves equal to one thousandth of a micron or one millionth of a millimeter.

mimesis 1. Imitation. 2. Meaningful response to species-specific behavior without previous learning.

mind 1. The organized totality of mental or psychical processes of an organism. 2. The totality of structures which are postulated to account for the occurrence of behaviors and processes. 3. (structuralism) The sum total of conscious experience. 4. The self or psyche. 5. The intellect. 6. A characteristic manner of thinking, feeling, and behaving such as the American mind.

mind-body problem The philosophical and psychological issue concerning the relation of the mind or mental processes to the body, the physical or physiological processes. Several views have been suggested: the theory that the mind and body are separate and should be studied as such is called dualism. The view that the mind and body influence each other is known as interactionism. According to the theory of psychophysical parallelism, the mind and body have parallel effects and change in parallel manner but do not interact. The isomorphic view is that a point-by-point correspondence exists between conscious experience and brain areas. The double language theory states that mental and bodily processes describe the same phenomenon in two different terminologies. Epiphenomenalism holds that mental processes are products of bodily processes and unimportant in themselves. The materialistic view also states that only the body is real while the idealistic viewpoint is that the mind is real and that bodily activity is simply a phenomenon of the mind.

mind, collective 1. A consensus. 2. The mental processes or behaviors which characterize the group rather than the individuals.

miniature system See *system, miniature.*

minimal brain dysfunction syndrome A concept which attempts to explain the etiology of learning disturbances for which there are no severe neurological signs. Developmental dyscrasias, learning disabilities and visual—motor perceptual irregularities are taken as signs of brain dysfunction, reflecting disorganized central nervous system functioning. The concept is applied to children with average, below average and above average intelligence with mild to severe learning and/or behavioral disabilities, manifested by impairment in perception, conceptualization, language, memory, and control of attention, impulse or motor function.

minimal change method See *method, minimal change.*

minimum audible field (MAF) Auditory threshold measuring technique in which the subject faces the source of sound in a free field room. The sound intensity is measured at the position in which the observer's head was located.

minimum audible pressure Auditory threshold measuring technique in which the sound intensity is measured against the eardrum.

Minnesota Clerical Aptitude Test See *test, Minnesota Clerical Aptitude.*

Minnesota Counseling Inventory See *inventory, Minnesota Counseling.*

Minnesota Multiphasic Personality Inventory A paper-and-pencil personality questionnaire with 550 items consisting of items borrowed from older inventories and rephrased diagnostic cues used by clinical workers. The subject answers true, false or cannot say to such items as: "I believe I am being plotted against"; "I drink an unusually large amount of water everyday"; "I wish I could be as happy as others seem to be." The content of the items are diverse, reporting observable behavior, feelings, symptoms of abnormal behavior, and general social attitudes. Scoring yields a profile on the subject with separate scores for scales of: hypochondriasis; depression; hysteria; psychopathic deviation; masculinity-femininity; paranoia; psychasthenia; schizophrenia; hypomania. Also scored are control scales (?,L,F,K) which identify or make allowance for exceptional response styles. ? identifies the frequency of the cannot say response. The L score, or Lie score, indicates the trustworthiness of the subjects answers. The F, or False, score consists of responses given extremely rarely; a high F indicates carelessness, misunderstanding and otherwise invalid answers. The K scale assesses the subject's defensiveness and is used as a weight in correcting the regular scale.

Minnesota Paper-Form Board A test of mechanical ability introduced in 1948 which consists of problems requiring the subject to identify the correct geometric figures from five choices when only two or more parts of the figure are shown. The test is believed to measure the ability to visualize and manipulate geometric forms which is related to mechanical ability.

Minnesota Rate of Manipulation Test See *test, Minnesota Rate of Manipulation.*

Minnesota Spatial Relations Test See *test, Minnesota Spatial Relations.*

Minnesota Test for Aphasia See *test, Minnesota, for Aphasia.*

miolecithal Referring to eggs which have little or no yolk.

miosis See *myosis.*

mirror drawing Drawing performed while viewing the design and one's hand in the mirror, used in psychological experiments or test of eye-hand coordination.

mirror reading See *reading, mirror.*

mirror reversal **1.** The reversal of right and left positions of objects when they are perceived in the mirror. **2.** A change in the right and left positions of an object.

mirror writing Reverse writing that looks as usual writing when put against a mirror.

misanthropy Aversion, dislike of mankind.

miscegenation Mixing of different races in marriage.

misogynist A person who hates women.

misogyny Hatred of women.

misologia Fear and aversion of speaking.

misoneism Avoidance of change and dislike of new subjects, events and people.

misopedia Hatred of children.

miss (signal detection theory) One of four possible outcomes in a single trial of a signal detection experiment. Both a signal and noise are presented together and the subject incorrectly responds that no signal was presented, only the noise. The other three possible outcomes are a hit, false alarm, and a correct rejection.

mitis mania See *mania, mitis.*

mitochondria Bodies in the cell which oxidize sugars and fats to produce adenosine triphosphate, an energy-rich substance utilized by the cells.

mitosis Cell division which results in the formation of two daughter cells, each having one-half of the chromosomal material from the original cell. This process begins with the division of the fertilized ovum and continues in the somatic cells of the body.

mix schedule See *reinforcement, schedule of: mixed.*

mixed (mix) schedule See *reinforcement, schedule of: mixed.*

mixed schizophrenic See *schizophrenic, mixed.*

mixoscopia An unusual form of voyeurism where orgasm is reached while looking at sexual relations between one's love object and another person.

mixovariation (genetics) Combination of several hereditary factors over several generations.

MMPI See *Minnesota Multiphasic Personality Inventory.*

M'Naghten Rules A legal test of insanity. Often used in the U.S.A. A person accused of a crime must be declared legally insane and thus not guilty by reason of insanity if the court decides that "he was laboring under such a defect of reason, from disease of the mind, as not to know the nature and quality of the act he was doing or . . .did not know he was doing what was wrong."

mneme (R. Semon) The basic principle which is believed to account for memory. The memory trace.

mnemonics Artificial devices used to facilitate recall and memory.

mnemotaxis A taxis in which the animal orients on the basis of a whole configuration of stimulus cues and not to the selective stimulation of special parts of the receptor.

mnemotechnics The art of facilitating memory.

mobility, social Pertaining to societies or any grouping of people in which the role and status of each individual is flexible and changing, thus allowing for free interaction among its members.

mobilization vs. regression (u.i. 23) in the Universal Index (R. B. Cattell) A source trait visible as a pattern in objective tests and characterized at one pole by ability to mobilize one's skills quickly and at the other by general regression of interest and control.

modality In personality, the division into ability, temperament, and dynamic traits.

modality, sense See *sense.*

mode (M_O) **1.** (statistics) A measure of central tendency which is the most frequently occurring value in a series. **2.** The peak (or peaks) in a frequency curve. **3.** A characteristic action pattern which satisfies needs.

mode, crude (statistics) The midpoint of the interval containing the greatest number of cases.

mode interval See *interval, mode.*

mode, parataxic (H. S. Sullivan) The second stage in perceiving. The child in parataxic mode perceives the world in a prelogical order viewing himself as the center of the universe.

mode, prototaxic (H. S. Sullivan) The earliest stage in perceiving. The infant's prototaxic mode is a state of unconscious and diffused experiences.

mode, refined (statistics) An estimation of the mode of a population from which a given sample was drawn.

mode, syntaxic (H. S. Sullivan) The third stage in perceiving. The school-age child learns to validate his perceptions against the perceptions of others and arrives through this consensual validation at a correct perception of reality.

model **1.** A copy of the authentic thing. **2.** A criterion or something ideal used for comparison purposes. **3.** An actual representation of how a system functions with all of its interrelated parts. **4.** A system of principles or hypotheses which is postulated to explain relationships in the data and is usually presented in mathematical terms.

model, conceptual A graphic or schematic representation of a concept.

model, mathematical The use of mathematical formulas or equations to systematize and order psychological data showing the relationship of some aspects of the data to others.

model, mathematical learning Use of mathematics to describe, summarize, and express relationships, predict and suggest further investigation in the field of learning. Feedback models, cybernetics, information-theory, and game theory have been the sources of the most influencial mathematical models of learning.

model, schematic A model which manifests the significant relationships between concepts.

model, stochastic See *stochastic models of behavior.*

modeling A behavior therapy technique designed to modify behavior through perceptual learning and by allowing the individual to imitate.

modification 1. Any change in structure, function or behavior. 2. (genetics) Any change in the phenotype due to environmental influences without a corresponding change in the genotypic configuration.

modifiers (modifying genes) Genes, usually polygenes, which influence the penetrance and expressivity of specific genetic mechanisms. In the view of Franz J. Kallmann these genes relate to constitution or somatotype which influences the manifestation of both schizophrenic and manic-depressive psychosis.

modulation theory (R. B. Cattell) The theory that a stimulus situation can be divided into two parts—a *focal stimulus* and an *ambient stimulus*—the second of which is capable of momentarily changing the individual's level on states and certain traits. The behavioral equation thus acquires modulator (s) terms, in addition to behavioral indices (b) terms, the former changing the state level, the latter expressing the effect of the state upon behavior.

modulator, visual (R. Granit) A hypothesized receptor in the retina which yields the sensation of a specific hue.

Moebius, Paul Julius (1853-1907) A German psychiatrist and sexologist. He studied famous men and originated the branch of psychiatry called pathography which deals with psychopathology in superior men.

mogigraphia Writer's cramp.

molar behavior See *behavior, molar.*

molecular behavior See *behavior, molecular.*

molimen Physiological and psychological distress which causes difficulties in performing even simple tasks.

molimen, menstrual Premenstrual tensions which may include psychological and physiological symptoms.

molimen, virile Obsolete term for fatigue characteristic of the climacterium in the male.

moment 1. A very small interval of time. 2. The measure of a force determined by its effect in causing circular movements in a body. 3. (statistics) The average of the deviations from the mean, after each deviation has been raised to a certain power. The general formula is $\Sigma\ (x^n)/N$ where x is any deviation, n is the power to which X is raised, N is the number of cases in the series, and Σ is the summation sign.

momentary effective reaction potential ($_S\bar{E}_R$) (C. L. Hull) Reaction potential modified by the oscillation factor.

moments of a distribution (statistics) The expectations of different powers of the random variable. The first moment about the origin of a random variable x is $E(x)$= mean. The second moment is $E(x^2)$, the third is $E(x^3)$, etc. When the mean is subtracted from x before it is raised to a power, the moment is about the mean. $E(x - E(x))^2$ is the second moment about the mean; $E(x - E(x))^3$ is the third moment about the mean, etc. The higher moments reflect features of the distribution such as the degree of skewness or kurtosis which are important for statisticians in developing theoretical distribution which will fit the observed data.

monadic theory A psychological theory which treats each organism as an independent unit; e.g., most cognitive and developmental stage theories (Freud, Werner, Piaget).

monaural hearing See *hearing, monaural.*

mongolism; mongoloidism A common subgroup of mental deficiency. Retardation is usually moderate. Characterized by broad face, flat nose, slanted eyes, coarse and deeply fissured tongue, and broad and clumsy hands and feet. Also called Down syndrome. Typically, mongoloids have 47 chromosomes, having trisomic chromosome 21.

monism A philosophical theory of unity of nature. A belief that mind and matter are one and the same thing.

monitor To watch or supervise an individual or machine in order to insure continued normal functioning.

monoamine oxidase; MAO An enzyme which can oxidase or inhibit various amino substances.

monochorionic twins See *twins, identical.*

monocular vision See *vision, monocular.*

monogamy Marriage of one woman to one man.

monohybridity; monohybridism A state of being heterozygous for one single pair of genes.

monomania 1. Obsolete: a mild form of insanity in which the patient's mind concentrates on one topic only. 2. Exaggerated concern with one idea or topic.

mononoea See *monomania.*

monoplegia Paralysis of one limb or any other one part of the body.

monosomy A condition in which one chromosome of a pair is missing, resulting in a single member of that pair instead of the normal diploid number. Thus in Turner's syndrome there is a single X chromosome instead of the normal female double X complement.

monovular twins See *twins, identical.*

monozygote That which develops from one egg or zygote as, for example, identical twins.

monozygotic A term used to describe twins derived from a single fertilized ovum. Synonyms – identical or uniovular twins. Also see *twins, identical.*

monozygotic twins See *twins, identical.*

Monroe Diagnostic Reading Test See *test, Monroe Diagnostic Reading.*

mood complex See *complex, mood.*

mood system See *complex, mood.*

Mooney Problem Checklist An inventory developed in 1950 for use with persons in high school and college which consists of a record of different types of problems. The individual is asked to consider this list and to choose those problems which are relevant to him. The checklist is used as a screening device for finding people with problems, and as a means to facilitate counseling or psychological interviews.

moral anxiety See *anxiety, superego.*

moral idiot (E. Bleuler) An individual in whom the ability to sympathize with others is absent while his ability to experience other kinds of emotions is essentially unimpaired.

moral imbecile (E. Bleuler) An individual whose ability to sympathize with others is inadequately developed while his ability to experience other kinds of emotions is essentially unimpaired.

moral insanity See *insanity, moral.*

moral judgment See *judgment, moral.*

moral oligophrenic (E. Bleuler) Individual whose ability to sympathize with others is either stunted (moral imbecile) or entirely absent (moral idiot), while his ability to experience other kinds of emotions is essentially unimpaired.

moral realism (J. Piaget) The attitude characteristic of small children that morality is inherent in an act as an objective fact and that it is observable to all.

moral treatment in psychiatry The forerunner of the modern therapeutic community which emphasized the humane treatment of mentally ill people. The movement dates back to the thirteenth century when psychotic patients were taken care of in the homes of citizens of Gheel in Belgium and was propelled by the liberation of patients from chains by P. Pinel in 1793. B. Rush supported this movement in the United States emphasizing the release of patients from mechanical restraint, the improvement in patient care, kindness, attention to the patient's psychological needs, and a stress on supporting the patient's self-respect.

morale An attitude in individuals or in a group characterized by confidence, control, and motivation.

morality, sphincter (S. Ferenczi) The rudiments of the superego which originate from the rewards and punishments centering around toilet training.

Morel, Benedict Augustin (1809-1873) French psychiatrist who viewed most mental diseases as a result of "hereditary weakness." He believed that mental disease is a product of a hereditary malformation called degeneration, and they are accompanied by a series of symptomatic physical signs called "stigmate of degeneration." He divided all mental diseases into five groups, namely hereditary, toxic, sympathies (brain disease), emotional (hysteria,) and sociopathic psychoses. He coined the term dementia praecox, later called schizophrenia.

Moreno, J.L. (1890-   ) American psychiatrist of Austrian education. Credited with the development of sociometry and psychodrama. Coined the terms encounter and encounter group, group therapy and group psychotherapy; developed a psychodramatic theory of personality and its application to 1) the treatment of mental disorders, 2) analysis of social and cultural phenomena, and 3) a new theory of society (sociatry).

mores Social customs without legal sanction which are believed to be conducive to social welfare and which put a pressure on the members to conform under the threat of societal condemnation.

Morgan, Conway Lloyd (1852-1936) Early comparative psychologist who in 1894 formulated a psychological version of the principle of parsimony, later known as Lloyd Morgan's canon: one must not interpret an animal's activity as the outcome of the exercise of a higher psychical faculty, if it can be interpreted as the outcome of the exercise of one which stands lower in the psychical scale.

Morgan's canon (L. Morgan) The principle that a behavior should not be interpreted as the result of the functioning of a higher mental process if it can be explained in terms of a lower psychical process.

moria An obsessive desire to joke.

Moro response The infant's response to stimuli such as a strong blow to the surface on which he is lying, characterized at first by general clutching movements of the extremities and gradually evolving into a discrete rapid body jerk. Also known as the startle response.

moron A level of feeblemindedness which is defined as the range of IQ from fifty to seventy. This category includes people who are believed to be capable of supporting themselves by performing simple tasks under supervision.

morpheme The smallest linguistic unit which is still meaningful.

morphine A colorless, narcotic drug derived from opium which is chiefly used to reduce pain and to induce sleep.

morphinomania Morbid desire or craving for morphine.

morphogenesis The structural development of parts of an organism.

morphologic inferiority See *inferiority, morphologic.*

morphology The branch of biology dealing with the study of form and structure of organisms.

Morquio's syndrome A type of mucopolysaccharidosis which is transmitted in an autosomal recessive fashion and characterized by normal intelligence, cloudy corneas, and severe bony changes leading to marked curvature of the spine.

mortido S. Freud called the mental energy at the disposal of Eros, the life instinct, libido, but did not coin any term for the destructive energy activated by the instinct of death, Thanatos. E. Federn called the destructive energy mortido; B. B. Wolman called it destrudo.

morula A stage in the embryological development of an organism before the fertilized egg reaches the thirty-two cell stage and the formation of the blastula.

mosaic An individual or tissue with at least two cell lines differing in genotype or karyotype, derived from a single zygote.

Mosaic Test See *test, Mosaic.*

mother-child interaction (MCI) (generic) Standardized assessment situations in which mother-child interactions are observed and recorded for either monadic or dyadic analysis.

mother complex See *Oedipus complex.*

mother figure 1. A person who replaces one's real mother and becomes the object of habitual responses originally developed in relation to the real parent. 2. A mature individual with whom a younger, immature person identifies and who comes to exercise such parental functions as advice and encouragement.

mother hypnosis (S. Ferenczi) The concept that submission to hypnotic states can be traced to blind obedience to one's parents, in this case transference of maternal fixation; also called "coaxing-hypnosis."

mother imago See *imago.*

mother, schizophrenogenic (A. Kanner) A woman whose behavior causes her child to become a schizophrenic.

mother substitute See *surrogate.*

mother surrogate See *mother figure; surrogate.*

motion study The study of the movements made in the performance of a task in order to determine the most efficient method of carrying out this task.

motivation 1. A process (appetitive as opposed to affective) that effects changes in the environment (acts) consonant with internal representations (plans, programs). 2. (V. G. Dethier) A specific state of endogenous activity in the brain which, under certain internal conditions and sensory input, leads to behavior which results in changes in the interior milieu and reduction of the initial activity.

motivation component factors (R. B. Cattell) Components, found in measurement *devices,* which may enter into any dynamic structure factor—principally, factors *a* (conscious id), β (realized ego), γ (ideal self), and δ (unconscious, physiological).

motivation, conjunctive (H. S. Sullivan) The desire for a lasting satisfaction.

motivation, deficiency (A. H. Maslow) Needs for food, oxygen and water which motivate behavior. These needs must be satisfied before other needs, higher in the hierarchy are considered.

motivation, extrinsic Motivation which stems from positive or negative reinforcements which are external to the behavior itself rather than inherent in it: studying to get good grades not because the studying is enjoyable.

motivation, growth (A. H. Maslow) Strivings toward self-actualization and knowledge which motivate behavior when lower physiological needs are satisfied.

motivation, intrinsic Motivation as an incentive which originates within the behavior itself rather than externally as in playing a musical instrument for enjoyment.

motivational hierarchy (A. Maslow) A hierarchy of human motives which determine behavior. The physiological needs are postulated to be the most basic. Needs for security and safety are at the next level. Love, affection, and belongingness form the next category followed by needs for esteem, mastery, competence and prestige. The highest level need is the need for self-actualization which does not appear until the lower level needs are satisfied.

motive 1. A state within an organism which energizes and directs him toward a particular goal. 2. The reason an individual offers to explain his behavior. 3. An unconscious cause of behavior.

motive, affiliative Need or tendency to depend upon or seek out others, for the purpose of forming friendships and other kinds of attachments.

motive, mastery The drive to achieve, to be successful.

motone (H. A. Murray) A motor-muscular action pattern.

motoneuron A neuron which is directly connected to a muscle or gland thus stimulating or inhibiting it.

motor abreaction See *abreaction, motor.*

motor aphasia See *aphasia, motor.*

motor apraxia See *apraxia, motor.*

motor area The area of the cortex consisting of the ascending precentral Rolandic convolutions and neighboring areas which when electrically stimulated elicits contraction of certain muscles and the associated bodily movement.

motor end plate   See *motor point.*

motor equivalence   The principle that a goal can be reached by many different actions requiring different muscular movements.

motor function   Any activity resulting from the excitation of muscles and glands by efferent neural fibers.

motor habit   See *habit, motor.*

motor learning   See *learning, motor.*

motor nerve   See *nerve, motor.*

motor neuron   See *neuron, motor.*

motor point   The point of contact between a motor neuron and a muscle.

motor primacy theory   The theory that the mechanisms underlying motor functions develop before those responsible for sensory functions.

motor reaction type   See *reaction type, motor.*

motor root   A ventral root of the spinal cord involved in motor functions.

motor sensation   See *sensation, motor.*

motor set   See *set, motor.*

motor theory of consciousness   (J. B. Watson) The principle that the subjective perception of consciousness depends on the motor and glandular reactions the subject makes.

motor unit   The motor neuron, its axon and the muscular and glandular areas which it supplies.

motoric region   (K. Lewin) The expressive part of personality, reflected by the external appearance and responses of the person.

motorium   The brain areas which directly control the activity of the voluntary or skeletal muscles.

mouches volantes   French word meaning flying flies which is used to refer to minute particles in the vitreous or aqueous humor of the eye which sometimes appear to be in motion in the field of vision. They are usually unnoticeable.

movement, alpha   A form of apparent movement where there appears to be change of size in parts of a figure exposed in succession.

movement, apparent   Subjective visual perception of movement in the absence of real physical movement. The most common examples are the phi phenomenon, the autokinetic effect, and the aftereffect of seen movement.

movement, beta   A form of apparent movement occurring when different sized or positioned objects exposed in succession give the appearance of movement. The time interval between exposures is crucial. Also called optimal movement.

movement, delta   A form of apparent movement obtained under certain conditions of stimulus size, intensity of illumination and distance and time between stimuli. When these requirements are met and the second stimulus is brighter than the first, movement of the brighter stimulus to the darker stimulus is reported.

movement determinant   See *movement response.*

movement, epsilon   The visual perception of movement when a white line against a black background is changed into a black line against a white background, one of various types of apparent movement.

movement, gamma   A form of apparent movement characterized by perceived expansion and contraction of a figure which is suddenly shown or withdrawn, or is exposed to sudden change in illuminations.

movement, illusion   See *movement, apparent.*

movement, incipient   The imperceptible or barely perceptible beginning of a movement that is not overtly carried out such as occurs in the speech organs during internal speech.

movement, induced   The illusory movement of the inner object of a pair of stimulus elements arranged such that one is the surround for the other, regardless of which object is set in motion. The perceived direction of movement is rigidly determined by the direction of the objectively moving surround.

movement, mass   (sociology) A unified attempt by a large number of individuals to effect a social change by working as a group.

movement, optimal   See *movement, beta.*

movement response   A Rorschach response in which the subject perceives in the "static" blots some form of action, expression, posture, or life. Rorschach restricted this classification to those responses in which the movement was human or human–like and used the symbol *M* for the scoring. Rorschach's basic position is also followed in the Beck and Rapaport approaches to the test; however, other approaches such as Klopfer, Hertz, and Piotrowski have defined two other classes of movement responses. One involves animal movement which is scored *FM* and the second involves movement perceived in inanimate objects, scoring using the symbol *m*. Human movement responses are generally conceded to be related to the inner life of the subject, especially his organized fantasy world while animal and inanimate movement responses are interpreted as being less sophisticated or controlled energies.

movement, stroboscopic   The illusion of movement occurring when fixed, separate stimuli are presented in succession. The most common example is the motion picture where if succession is rapid enough, there is no perceived separation of images but rather perceived smooth motion.

Movigenic Movement Scale   See *scale, Movigenic Movement.*

moving average method See *method, moving average.*

moving total method See *method, moving total.*

Mowrer, O. Hobart (1907-   ) American psychologist whose work includes three stages: 1) research on visual and vestibular functions with special reference to spatial orientation and reflex habituation; 2) work with laboratory animals involving issues in systematic learning theory, analogues of certain clinical dynamisms, competitive and cooperative problem solving, and signaling behaviors from which human language evolved; and 3) interest in disordered interpersonal relationships and their rectification in small groups and the role of psychopharmacology in this connection.

mucopolysaccharidosis Disorder of mucopolysaccharide metabolism.

mucous colitis See *colitis, mucous.*

Müller, Georg Elias (1850-1934) Early German experimental psychologist at the University of Göttingen. Did seminal research in psychophysics, vision, physiological psychology, and memory. He discovered the associative and retroactive inhibitions, the paired associates type of learning, and developed better and more reliable apparatus. He also furthered the studies in color vision, space perception, and attention. He was the head of the Göttingen laboratory, a rival of Wilhelm Wundt's Leipzig laboratory, which under his direction became an influential experimental center, turning out many distinguished students and much important research.

Müller, Johannes (1801-1858) German physiologist and comparative anatomist, professor at Berlin University; experimented on sensation; published monumental *Handbook of Human Physiology* which contained new physiological material; formulated theory of specific nerve energies which profoundly influenced research on sensation; coined the phrase "nemo psychologus nisi physiologus" (no one can be a psychologist unless he is a physiologist).

Müller–Lyer illusion See *illusion, Müller-Lyer.*

Müller–Schumann Law The principle that the association of two items causes difficulties in associating either one with a third item.

Müller–Urban method See *method, Müller–Urban.*

Müller–Urban weights (psychophysics) A technique used for determining the best value of h, the measure of precision of the fit of the data under the normal curve. When p=.50, the weight equals the maximal value of 1.00. At the extremes of the distribution, p.=.01 and p=.99, the weights are at a minimum.

mult schedule See *reinforcement, schedule of: multiple.*

multicellular Many-celled.

multidimensional analysis of deviant behavior The analysis of a person in terms of a number of variables chosen for their importance in the establishment and maintenance of social response patterns.

multigroup method See *method, multigroup.*

multimodal theory of intelligence See *intelligence, multimodal theory of.*

multiple abstract variance analysis (MAVA) design A research design for discovering relative proportions of environmental vs. hereditary determination for personality traits (Nature-Nurture Ratio).

multiple choice method See *method, multiple-choice.*

multiple choice test See *test, multiple choice.*

multiple correlation See *correlation, multiple.*

multiple determination coefficient See *coefficient, multiple determination.*

multiple discrimination technique (statistics) A technique in which a subject is assigned a number which places him in more than one category. It is a form of the Fisher's discriminant function technique.

multiple-factor Pertaining to a theory or process which is believed to have more than one factor underlying it.

multiple-factor inheritance The transmission of a trait determined by more than one pair of genes.

multiple personality See *personality, multiple.*

multiple regression equation See *regression equation, multiple.*

multiple response, principle of A complex and varied reaction to a new stimulus.

multiple response test See *test, multiple response.*

multiple (mult) schedule See *reinforcement, schedule of: multiple.*

multiple sclerosis Hardening of the nerve tissues causing emotional disorder, speech defects, tremor, etc.

multipolar nerve cell A cell which has more than one pole.

multivariate analysis (statistics) Any technique designed to assess the existence and size of effect of many variables acting simultaneously.

multivariate experiment An experimental design in which several stimulus conditions are simultaneously varied and/or several responses simultaneously measured, the relations being determined factor analytically or by path coefficients, partial correlations, etc.

mumps encephalitis See *encephalitis, mumps.*

Murphy, Gardner (1895-   ) American psychologist. Wrote extensively on history of psychology and social psychology. Conducted research in social and developmental psychology jointly with his wife Lois

B. Murphy. Created the biosocial theory of personality based on the analysis of biological and social factors, conditioning and perception. Developed a field-theoretical approach to social problems and studied, on behalf of UNESCO, social tensions in India.

As Director of Research at the Menninger Foundation directed a major program in personality, stressing developmental factors and perceptual learning, and developed (with E.E. Green) the concept of biofeedback as applied to self-deception. Also contributed to research in parapsychology.

Murphy, Lois Barclay (1902-   ) American specialist in child development. Introduced American study of childhood sympathy; coping styles and devices; vulnerability and resilience. With Ruth Horowitz (Hartley) and L.K. Frank introduced the concept of "projective techniques"; integrated projective methods and naturalistic observations in studies of individual children. Directed a multi-disciplinary longitudinal series studying mid-west children. Contributed to integration of child development and psychoanalytic theory. Collaborated with Gardner Murphy on a volume on experimental social psychology, and with others in psychodynamic studies of learning at the college level.

Murray, H. A. (1893-   ) American psychologist who developed a system of needs believed to be characteristic of man and presented them in his book *Explorations in Personality*. He was instrumental in beginning an assessment of men in the United States Army during the Second World War. He is best known for his projective technique, the Thematic Apperception Test which is designed to elicit interpersonal conflicts related to the above needs.

muscle spindle See *spindle, muscle.*

muscle, striate or striped A skeletal muscle which is under voluntary control and has a striped appearance.

muscular mania See *mania, muscular.*

music preference test A test of personality through measuring factors of appreciative response to music.

mutagen Any substance or force which increases the mutation rate, e.g. ionizing radiation.

mutation A permanent heritable change in the genetic material. It is usually defined as a change in a single gene and is then often named a point mutation, in contrast to the less common usage to indicate a change in the number or arrangement of chromosomes. Schizophrenia and manic-depressive disorder if caused by single recessive and single dominant mode of inheritance respectively must have originated as point mutations. According to Frazer Roberts, genetic diseases which originate in this way through mutation often run an evolutionary course from dominance to recessiveness.

mutism 1. The lack of speech, resulting from congenital deafness, lack of proper development of the speech apparatus. **2.** The voluntary or involuntary lack of speech due to emotional conflicts.

muton In molecular genetics, the unit of mutation, possible as small as one nucleotide pair.

mutualism (B. B. Wolman) A sociopsychological give and take attitude based on the desire to satisfy the needs of others and have one's own needs satisfied by them. Mature sexual relationship is the prototype of mutualism.

mydriasis Dilation of pupils.

mydriatics Cocaine, atropine, epinephrine and any other substance that causes dilation of the pupils.

myelination; myelinization The formation of myelin or its accumulation in the process of development or regeneration of a nerve.

myelitis Inflammation of the spinal cord or of the bone marrow.

myeloblastoma A malignant tumor caused by overgrowth of myeloid cells.

Myers-Briggs Type Indicator (I. B. Myers) A test designed in 1962 on the assumption that individuals differ in their preferences in perception and judgment. It measures the four sets of traits postulated by C. G. Jung: extraversion—introversion, sensing—intuiting, thinking—feeling, and judgment—perception. Each item calls for a choice between two contrasting alternatives, which are both from the same category. The subject's score is based on the number of times he chooses a category. His type is designated by the letters of his predominant mode in each of the categories.

myocardial infarction See *infarction, myocardial.*

myoclonic epilepsy See *epilepsy, myoclonic.*

myoclonus Alternating contraction and relaxation of a muscle which usually does not cause movement.

myokinetic psychodiagnosis (E. Mira) A technique based on the symbolic interpretation of movements developed in 1940. The subject is blindfolded and asked to draw ten lines with each hand, to the left, or right toward and away from the subject, with the drawing board in a vertical position, upward or downward; the lines are measured in terms of slope and direction of drift of center of gravity. Based on work with abnormal subjects, the movements are interpreted as distinct personality signs. Drifts away from the body are believed to indicate aggressive attitudes toward others. An inward drift is thought to refer to self-aggression or suicidal trends. An upward drift indicates elation; a downward drift, depression.

myopathy Any disease of the muscle.

myopia Nearsightedness.

myopsychopathy Muscular disease frequently associated with mental disorder or mental deficiency.

myosis Extreme contraction of the pupil of the eye due to drugs or disease.

myositis Inflammation of the muscle tissue due to muscle tension of physical or psychogenic origin.

The psychogenic cause is a chronically suppressed emotional state.

mysoline Common name for the anticonvulsant drug, primodine.

mysophobia Fear of contamination.

mysticism 1. The belief in supernatural, religious and/or spiritual sources of knowledge. **2.** The belief in direct contact with God or other spiritual forces.

mythological image See *archetype.*

mythological theme See *theme, mythological.*

mythomania A morbid interest in and liking of myths often accompanied by distortions and fabrications.

myxedema; myxodema A disorder due to a decrease or absence of the thyroid hormone characterized by a sallow, thick skin, low metabolism, and physical and mental retardation. It is a constitutional disorder occurring in adults and older children.

N

N **1.** (statistics) The number of observations in the data. **2.** (C. L. Hull) The number of rewards which are given. **3.** Symbol for need in the Thematic Apperception Test.

naïve misperception That demonstrated factor in misperception which arises from interpreting others' behavior in terms of one's own, as a result of low intelligence or limited experience.

Nancy School A school founded by H. Bernheim in 1882 which promulgated the belief that hypnotism is a natural phenomenon induced by suggestion.

nanism Dwarfism.

nanometer (ηm) N M = 10^{-9} meter, formerly called a millimicron; the preferred term is now nanometer.

narcissism **1.** Love of the self; egoism. **2.** (psychoanalysis) Erotic gratification derived from love of one's own body, qualities and attributes. **3.** (K. Horney) The loving of the unrealistic attributes of the idealized image of oneself.

narcissism, primary (psychoanalysis) The earliest stage of life in which all the energies at the disposal of the love instincts are invested in oneself.

narcissism, secondary Narcissism occurring in later life when object love is thwarted and libido is turned back to one's own person.

narcissistic disorders **1.** Behavior disorders characterized by excessive narcissism. **2.** (S. Freud) Schizophrenia is a narcissistic disorder because schizophrenics are unable to develop object relations. Schizophrenia represents a regression to narcissism, that is loss of objects, loss of contact with reality and breakdown of the ego. As a result, schizophrenics are unable to develop transference. **3.** (B. B. Wolman) The hyperinstrumental-narcissistic type of disorders characterized by intense self-cathexis of libido and object cathexis of destrudo. More severe cases of this disorder are the sociopathic, i.e., psychopathic personality and psychopathic psychosis.

narcissistic insurance See *insurance, narcissistic.*

narcoanalysis Treatment of mental disorders with the use of chemically induced sleep. Widely used in the second World War with intravenous injections of sodium amythal or sodium pentothal. Also used for extracting confessions from criminals under the name truth serum. Various forms are called narcosynthesis, narcosuggestion, and narcotherapy.

narcolepsy Recurrent and sudden uncontrollable tendency to fall into deep sleep of short duration associated with epilepsy, some tremors and encephalitis.

narcomania A morbid desire for relief from physical pain by using narcotics.

narcosynthesis The use of the material obtained from a patient under narcotics for a postnarcotic psychotherapy.

narcotherapy The use of narcotics in the treatment of mental disorder.

narcotic Sleep-inducing drug.

nardil A common name for phenelzine.

nares The nasal passages.

National Intelligence Scale See *scale, National Intelligence.*

nativism A theory that maintains that practically all functions of the organism, including the mental ones are inherited.

natural sciences Sciences which study nature; e.g. physics, chemistry, biology, geology, etc. W. Windelband counterposed the natural sciences to cultural sciences (humanities). Some philosophers of science maintain that all sciences are natural sciences, for psychology, sociology, history, archeology, etc., study certain fractions of the universe.

natural selection (C. Darwin) The survival of the fittest in the struggle for survival. As a result of this struggle, the poorly equipped individuals, unable to adjust to changing conditions, perish, while the superior individuals survive.

naturalistic observation Observation conducted in natural surroundings, such as practiced by J. Piaget in developmental psychology and K. Lorenz in ethological studies of animals.

nature-nurture problem One of several highly controversial issues in psychiatry and psychology related to the relative importance of heredity (called nature) versus environment (called nurture) in the development of normal and abnormal behavior. The nativists stress the role of heredity, while the empiricists emphasize the effect of sociocultural and socioeconomic factors, family dynamics and rearing practices, etc.

nature-nurture ratio A statistic giving the extent to which endowment of a personality trait tends to be fixed genetically rather than determined by environmental experience.

Neanderthal man An extinct, prehistorical human race. Its remnants were found in the valley of Neanderthal.

near-point-of convergence The limit of seeing a close point as single. If the object is brought closer to the eyes, it looks double.

Necker cube An ambiguous figure that is a line drawing of a cube drawn as if it were transparent, with all twelve angles showing. When regarded steadily, there is continuous shift in the angle of interpretation, for example it can be regarded as viewed from above or below.

necromimesis Belief that one is dead.

necrophilia Desire for sexual relations with a corpse.

necrophobia Morbid fear of dead bodies.

need 1. The condition of lacking, wanting or requiring something which if present would benefit the organism by facilitating behavior or satisfying a tension. 2. (H.A. Murray) A construct representing a force in the brain which directs and organizes the individual's perception, thinking, and action, so as to change an existing, unsatisfying situation. A need may be evoked by internal processes or environmental forces and is accompanied by particular emotions and modes of behavior designed to change the initiating circumstance and satisfy the organism. From intensive study of a number of subjects, Murray compiled a list of common essential needs. The original list includes needs for: *abasement,* to admit inferiority, blame, error, to accept punishment or criticism and to passively submit to external forces; *achievement,* to independently master objects, others, and ideas, and to increase self-esteem by successful exercise of talent; *affiliation,* to draw near, cooperate and remain loyal to another who is seen as similar to oneself and a friend; *aggression,* to oppose, fight, injure or punish another; *autonomy,* to be independent, unattached, and unrestricted; *counteraction,* to overcome failure and weakness through resumed action and repression of fear; *dependence,* to defend oneself against assault, criticism, and blame and to justify or conceal a failure, error, or humiliation; *deference,* to support, praise,

honor, or admire a superior and to conform to custom; *dominance,* to influence or control others' behavior; *exhibition,* to impress others; *harmavoidance,* to avoid pain, injury, illness, and death; *infavoidance,* to avoid humiliation; *nurturance,* to support, protect, comfort, heal and gratify the needs of the helpless; *order,* to organize, balance, and arrange objects in the environment; *play,* to seek enjoyment and relaxation without further purpose; *rejection,* to separate oneself from a negatively cathected object; *sentience,* to seek and enjoy sensuous impressions; *sex,* to form and pursue an erotic relationship; *succorance,* to be gratified by an allied object and always have support and protection; *understanding,* to question, answer, speculate, formulate, analyze, and generalize.

need, cognizance (H.A. Murray) The need to investigate, explore, observe, be curious, and ask questions.

need, construction (H.A.Murray) The need to organize and build things.

need, felt A need of which one is consciously aware.

need, gratification Reduction of a need through consummatory behavior.

negative acceleration A gradual decline of speed; a consecutively smaller increment, e.g. mental growth slows down with age.

negative attention seeking See *attention seeking, negative.*

negative doubles, illusion of See *illusion of negative doubles.*

negative feedback See *feedback, negative.*

negative induction See *induction, negative.*

negative movement reflex See *reflex, negative movement.*

negative Oedipus complex Oedipal involvement with the parent of the same sex.

negative reinforcement See *reinforcement, negative.*

negative response See *response, negative.*

negative taxis See *taxis.*

negative therapeutic reaction See *resistance, superego.*

negative transference See *transference, negative.*

negative tropism See *tropism.*

negativism, sexual (M. Hirschfeld) Lack of sexual interests believed to be caused by a deficiency of the sexual glands.

nembutal Common name for pentobarbital.

neocortex See *isocortex.*

neololia A tendency of forming new words, neologisms.

neomnesis Selective memory with a particular ability for recollection of recent events.

neonatal hyperbilirubinemia See *hyperbilirubine-mia, neonatal.*

neonatal meningitis See *meningitis, neonatal.*

neonate Newborn.

neopallium A large part of the cerebral hemisphere with the exclusion of the rhinencephalon.

neophobia Morbid fear of anything new.

neophrenia (K.L. Kahlbaum) An obsolete term for childhood psychosis.

neoplasm A new growth, tumor.

neopsychoanalysis A school of psychoanalysis which repudiates the importance of biology, the instincts, and the role of insight in promoting thera-peutic change.

neostriatum Parts of the corpus striatum which in-cludes the putamen and caudate nucleus.

nerve A bundle of neuron fibers.

nerve, abducens; abducent The sixth cranial nerve. It innervates the external rectus muscle of the eye, carrying to this muscle a motor component and carrying from it a sensory component mediating proprioception.

nerve, auditory or acoustic The portion of the eighth cranial nerve concerned with hearing.

nerve block Disruption of the passage of nerve exci-tation.

nerve ending The termination of a nerve either in a center or periphery but not at a synapse.

nerve, facial The seventh cranial nerve which carries efferent impulses to the facial muscles and afferent impulses from the taste buds in the front portion of the tongue.

nerve, hypoglossal The twelfth pair of cranial nerves. A motor nerve innervating the muscles of the tongue.

nerve, motor An efferent nerve which transmits impulses to muscles and glands.

nerve, oculomotor The third cranial nerve con-taining components which innervate all the extrinisic eye muscles except the superior oblique and the lateral rectus and containing afferent proprioceptive fibers.

nerve, optic The second cranial nerve which func-tions as a connection between the visual centers and the retina.

nerve, pathetic See *nerve, trochlear.*

nerve, pneumogastric See *nerve, vagus.*

nerve, sensory Afferent nerve from a sense receptor to the central nervous system.

nerve, trochlear The fourth cranial nerve which car-ries different impulses to the superior oblique eye muscles.

nerve, vagus The tenth cranial nerve which distrib-utes motor and sensory nerve fibers to many parts of the body, including the lungs, stomach area, external ear, larynx, pharynx and heart.

nerves, cranial Twelve pairs of nerves originating or terminating within the cranium.

nervous pseudo-asthma Physiological changes in res-piration due to emotion as, for example, shortness of breath, constriction of the throat, or panting. Also known as respiratory emotionalism.

nervous system The entire apparatus comprised of nerve tissues, including: 1. the cerebrospinal nervous system, which is comprised of the brain, the brain stem, the spinal cord, all cranial and peripheral nerves and ganglions and 2. the autonomic nervous system, comprised of the parasympathetic or cranio-sacral division, the sympathetic or peripheral and orthosympathetic or thoracicolumbar divisions.

nervous system, autonomic A system of ganglia, nerves, and plexuses which innervate the viscera, heart, blood vessels, smooth muscles, and glands. It was once thought to be completely self-regulating, but is now known to be only partially independent. Includes the sympathetic and parasympathetic ner-vous system.

nervous system, conceptual A model which attempts to present the neurological or physiological correlates of behavioral acts. It is a hypothetical model and chiefly of heuristic value.

nervous system, parasympathetic A subdivision of the autonomic nervous system which selectively stimulates various visceral organs, stimulation result-ing in an effect opposite from the sympathetic ner-vous system.

nervous system, sympathetic A component of the autonomic nervous system which centers about two chains of ganglia running along the sides of the spinal cord and connects with many sympathetic ganglia, facilitating widespread discharge. Stimulation by this system usually results in an effect opposite from the parasympathetic nervous system.

nervous tissue Accumulation of nerve cells, i.e. the neurons.

neural circuit The path of transmission of an im-pulse from a receptor via connecting neurons to an effector.

neural conduction See *conduction, neural.*

neural crest See *cephalogenesis.*

neural current The electrical change which occurs along nerve fibers and across the synapse during the transmission of an impulse.

neural excitation The activity in a neural fiber in-duced by stimulation of the neuron.

neural fold See *cephalogenesis.*

neural groove See *encephalogenesis.*

neural induction The effect which one neuron or group of neurons has on another. Positive induction means that neural activity is facilitated. Negative induction refers to the inhibition of neural activity.

neural noise Spontaneous neural activity occurring in the nervous system which may give rise to sensations when in fact no stimulus was presented. During threshold determinations neural noise may be responsible for many responses during latch trials. Since neurons are spontaneously active, stimulation does not so much initiate neural activity but modifies existing activity.

neural plate See *cephalogenesis.*

neural reinforcement See *reinforcement, neural.*

neural reverberation (D.O. Hebb) The maintenance and continuation of neural activity after the stimulus which initiated it ceases.

neural satiation A state of relative insensitivity to stimulation in the nerve fibers directly following a period of stimulation by a group of closely related stimuli.

neural set See *set, neural.*

neural tube See *cephalogenesis.*

neuralgia Sharp, stabbing, paroxysmal pain of a nerve without structural changes in the nerve.

neuralgia, hallucinatory The sensation of local pain with no actual peripheral nerve pain.

neuraminic acid An acid obtained from the ganglioside part of brain lipids. Also found in mammary glands of some animals.

neurasthenia See *asthenic reaction.*

neurasthenia, abdominal A type of neurasthenia in which the dominant symptoms are those which relate to the gastrointestinal tract.

neurasthenia, aviator's A neurosis believed to occur among aviators and characterized by anxiety, restlessness, and various physical symptoms.

neuraxis The brain and the spinal cord.

neurin 1. The protein substance of nerve tissue. 2. (W. McDougall) The energy believed to account for nerve excitation.

neurinomatosis; neurofibromatosis A tumorous disease. A growing number of neurofibromas appear in the skin and along peripheral nerves. Often associated with mental retardation. Transmitted by dominant genes.

neurite Axon.

neuritis Inflammation of peripheral nerves.

neuroarthritism A disease of gout and neurological rheumatoid disease.

neurobiotaxis The tendency of nerve cells to draw to the source of their nutrition.

neuroblast A newly formed nerve cell.

neurocirculatory asthenia 1. Anxiety neurosis characterized by shortness of breath, heart palpitations, and a vague feeling of effort and fatigue out of proportion with amount of energy expended. 2. Effort-syndrome.

neurocyte Nerve cell; neuron.

neurodermatitis A skin disease characterized by localized, circumscribed, symmetrical patches of pruritic dermatitis which is exacerbated by emotional problems.

neurofibril A fibril of a nerve cell.

neurofibroma A tumor characterized by proliferation of neurofibrils.

neuroglia 1. Supporting tissues in nerve cells derived mainly from the ectoderm. 2. Certain cells of the nervous system such as astrocytes and oligodendroglia.

neurohumor The chemical substance in the nerve cell which facilitates the conduction of nerve impulses at the synapse.

neurological examination See *examination, neurological.*

neurology A branch of medicine devoted to the study and treatment of anatomy and physiology of normal and abnormal structure and functions of the nervous system.

neuromuscular junction The point where a motor nerve meets the muscle it activates.

neuron The complete nerve cell, the basic structural and functional unit of the nervous system. It consists of the axon, dendrites, cell body, and myelin sheath.

neuron, bipolar A neuron which is characterized by the extension in opposite directions of the two long processes of the cell—the axon and dendrite. This cell is contrasted with the regular sensory neuron which is characterized by the cell body's being off to one side while the axon seems to be continuous with the dendrite.

neuron, motor An efferent neuron which transmits impulses to muscles and glands.

neurons, internuncial Neurons which connect sensory and motor neurons within the central nervous system.

neuropathic diathesis See *diathesis, neuropathic.*

neuropathy Any disease of the nervous system.

neurophysiology The branch of physiology which deals with the functions of the nervous system especially the study of the transmission of the nerve impulse.

neuropil A network of neurofibrils which are nonmyelinated at the synaptic function between two neurons.

neuropsychiatry In the nineteenth century, the name of the profession and discipline concerned with the diseases of the nervous system, organic and non-organic. Today, the term is used for a branch of psychiatry distinctly concerned with neurological causes, symptoms and cures of mental disorders.

neuropsychology A branch of psychology which studies the nervous system and its impact on behavior. A great many psychologists in the U.S.S.R. are neuropsychologists.

Neurosis (300) Also called psychoneurosis, a loosely used term applied to a variety of comparatively mild disorders. The following description is taken with abbreviations from the Diagnostic and Statistical Manual of Mental Disorders (DSM II) published by the American Psychiatric Association in 1968. Anxiety is the chief characteristic of the neuroses. It may be felt and expressed directly, or it may be controlled unconsciously and automatically by conversion, displacement and various other psychological mechanisms. Generally, these mechanisms produce symptoms experienced as subjective distress from which the patient desires relief.

The neurosis, as contrasted to the psychoses, manifests neither gross distortion or misinterpretation of external reality, nor gross personality disorganization. A possible exception to this is hysterical neurosis which some believe may occasionally be accompanied by hallucinations and other symptoms encountered in psychosis. Traditionally, neurotic patients, however severely handicapped by their symptoms, are not classified as psychotic because they are aware that their mental functioning is disturbed.

300.0 Anxiety neurosis
This neurosis is characterized by anxious over-concern extending to panic and frequently associated with somatic symptoms. Unlike phobic neurosis, anxiety may occur under any circumstances and is not restricted to specific situations or objects. This disorder must be distinguished from normal apprehension or fear, which occurs in realistically dangerous situations.

300.1 Hysterical neurosis
This neurosis is characterized by an involuntary psychogenic loss or disorder of function. Symptoms characteristically begin and end suddenly in emotionally charged situations and are symbolic of the underlying conflicts. Often they can be modified by suggestion alone.

300.13 Hysterical neurosis, conversion type
In the conversion type, the special senses or voluntary nervous system are affected, causing such symptoms as blindness, deafness, anosmia, anaesthesias, paraesthesias, paralyses, ataxias, akinesias, and dyskinesias. Often the patient shows an inappropriate lack of concern or belle indifference about these symptoms, which may actually provide secondary gains by winning him sympathy or relieving him of unpleasant responsibilities. This type of hysterical neurosis may be distinguished from psychophysiologic disorders, which are mediated by the autonomic nervous system; from malingering, which is done consciously; and from neurological lesions, which cause anatomically circumscribed symptoms.

300.14 Hysterical neurosis, dissociative type

In the dissociative type, alterations may occur in the patient's state of consciousness or in his identity, to produce such symptoms as amnesia, somnambulism, fugue, and multiple personality.

300.2 Phobic neurosis
This condition is characterized by intense fear of an object or situation which the patient consciously recognized as not real danger to him. His apprehension may be experienced as faintness, fatigue, palpitations, perspiration, nausea, tremor, and even panic. Phobias are generally attributed to fears displaced to the phobic object or situation from some other object of which the patient is unaware. A wide range of phobias has been described.

300.3 Obsessive compulsive neurosis
This disorder is characterized by the persistent intrusion of unwanted thoughts, urges, or actions that the patient is unable to stop. The thoughts may consist of single words or ideas, ruminations, or trains of thought often perceived by the patient as nonsensical. The actions vary from simple movements to complex rituals such as repeated handwashing. Anxiety and distress are often present either if the patient is prevented from completing his compulsive ritual or if he is concerned about being unable to control it himself.

300.4 Depressive neurosis
This disorder is manifested by an excessive reaction of depression due to an internal conflict or to an identifiable event such as the loss of a love object or cherished possession.

300.5 Neurasthenic neurosis (Neurasthenia)
This condition is characterized by complaints of chronic weakness, easy fatigability, and sometimes exhaustion. Unlike hysterial neurosis the patient's complaints are genuinely distressing to him and there is no evidence of secondary gain.

300.6 Depersonalization neurosis (Depersonalization syndrome)
This syndrome is dominated by a feeling of unreality and of estrangement from the self, body, or surroundings. This diagnosis should not be used if the condition is part of some other mental disorder, such as acute situational reaction. A brief experience of depersonalization is not necessarily a symptom of illness.

300.7 Hypochondriacal neurosis
This condition is dominated by preoccupation with the body and with fear of presumed diseases of various organs. Though the fears are not of delusional quality as in psychotic depressions, they persist despite reassurance. This condition differs from hysterical neurosis in that there are no actual losses or distortions of function.

300.8 Other neuroses
This classification includes specific psychoneurotic disorders not classified elsewhere such as "writer's cramp" and other occupational neuroses.

neurosis, actual (psychoanalysis) A neurosis involving a physiological as opposed to psychological basis for symptoms. Originally this concept was associated with Freud's first or toxicologic theory of anxiety. The existence of actual neuroses as clinical entities separate from the psychoneuroses has been questioned by other investigators. See *psychoneurosis; neurosis.*

neurosis, anxiety A controversial term. The Diagnostic and Statistical Manual of Mental Disorders (II) describes it as follows: Characterized by anxious over-concern extending to panic and frequently associated with somatic symptoms.

neurosis, cardiovascular A neurosis with manifestations of cardiovascular disorder which have no physiological basis.

neurosis, character See *character neurosis.*

neurosis, combat See *fatigue combat.*

neurosis, dysmutual (B.B. Wolman) A neurosis characterized by inconsistency in interpersonal relations and manifested in dissociative and conversion reactions.

neurosis, experimental 1. State of stereotyped, compulsive or inhibited behavior, hyper-emotionality, chaotic and random responding, or inability to respond induced in experimental animals by impossible tasks or difficult discrimination problems particularly when failure to make the correct response results in severe punishment. 2. (I.P. Pavlov) An induced acute neurotic state in animals produced by requiring very fine discriminations which the animal is unable to perform. Differences in the preneurotic behavior of the animals are related to the type of neurosis which develops.

neurosis, gastric A disturbance of digestion due to a psychological conflict involving dependent infantile fixations.

neurosis, hyperinstrumental (B.B.Wolman) A neurosis manifesting anxiety and depressive reactions and characterized by intense selfish, narcissistic interest in oneself.

neurosis, hypervectorial (B.B.Wolman) A neurosis manifesting obsessive, phobic, or neurasthenic reactions and characterized by excessive object hypercathexis.

neurosis, transference (psychoanalysis) An artificial neurosis occurring during psychoanalytic treatment in which the patient re-enacts all of his Oedipal conflicts with the analyst, who represents the important figures in the patient's life.

neurosis, traumatic A neurotic disorder precipitated by a trauma such as an incident or emotional upheaval.

neurosis, vegetative Neurosis characterized by disturbances of the autonomic nervous system functioning where the outward-directed action is suppressed and the withheld emotional tension induces chronic internal vegetative changes.

neurosyphilis Syphilis which affects the nervous system resulting in locomotor ataxia if the spinal cord is affected or general paresis in infections of the brain.

neurosyphilis, interstitial See *syphilis, cerebral.*

neurosyphilis, mesodermogenic Neurosyphilis involving the meninges, blood vessels and neural membranes which develop from mesodermal embryonic layers.

neurotic One who exhibits neurotic behavior.

neurotic character See *character neurosis.*

neurotic depressive reaction See *depression, reactive.*

neurotic process factor (R. B. Cattell) A characterological trait factor whose scores are of crucial importance in influencing the severity and expression of neurosis. Among Neurotic Contributory factors, that subclass which most significantly and meaningfully discriminates between neurotics and normals, hence is believed to be central in the etiology of neurosis.

neurotic resignation See *resignation, neurotic.*

neurotic symptoms Some symptoms, such as anxiety, apprehension, depressive moods, excessive fatigue, etc. are common to most if not to all neuroses. Some other symptoms, such as compulsions are typical only for a certain type neurosis.

neurotic trend See *trend, neurotic.*

neuroticism 1. The condition of being neurotic. 2. (R. B. Cattell) Neurosis which is characteristic in varying degrees of all people.

neurovegetative system The parasympathetic branch of the autonomic nervous system which is the aspect of the nervous system controlling the vegetative processes.

neurovisceral gangliosidosis See *generalized gangliosidosis.*

neutral stimulus See *stimulus, neutral.*

neutralization (H. Hartmann) The transformation of aggressive and sexual energy into energy which is free from the pressure of instinctual needs and is available for use in the development of ego functions.

neutralizer (S. Slavson) A term in group psychotherapy for a member who controls and nullifies the aggressive and impulsive behaviors of other members.

nevus; naevus Birthmark.

new look (D. Krech) A phrase from women's fashions (circa 1948 when longer, fuller skirts replaced short, spare war-time dresses) applied by Krech to the then new approach to perceptual research which emphasized the dependence of perception upon the psychological attributes of the perceiver. This research concern threatened for a time to become a "movement." The incipient "movement" however quietly reverted to what has become a continuing research and theoretical orientation.

Newcomb, Theodore M. (1903-) American social psychologist. Demonstrated close relationship in small college community between attitude change and position in status structure; 25 years later, these changes persisted on the part of individuals whose social environments were supportive of changed attitudes. Showed, in different setting, that interpersonal attraction among initial strangers changed over period of months in ways predictable from similarity of relatively unchanging values and attitudes. Extended this formulation, derived from Heider's balance theory, by showing that positive and negative attraction have different effects on interpersonal balance.

nexus 1. The connection between two variables. **2.** The causal connection between two items or variables which makes them interdependent.

Neyman-Pearson hypothesis See *hypothesis, Neyman-Pearson.*

nialamide An antidepressant drug of the monoamine oxidase inhibitor group used in the treatment of depression.

niamid Common name for nialamide.

Niemann-Pick disease A lipidosis similar to Tay-Sachs disease but not confined to the first year of life.

Nietzsche, Friedrich (1844-1900) German philosopher, advocate of extreme individualism. Invented the term "id", representative of unconscious blind forces. Criticized the overvaluation of consciousness, maintaining that it is merely the surface, while "the great basic activity is the unconscious."

nightmare 1. A dream depicting fearful events and marked by acute anxiety. According to psychoanalytic theory: 1) a nightmare represents the failure of the dream's function of protecting sleep; 2) in a nightmare a wish one is afraid of comes true. **2.** (E. Jones) Nightmares originate in incestuous impulses symbolized by witches, devils, and vampires.

nirvana 1. A state of satisfaction and bliss. **2.** (Buddhism) The state of life which is the prime goal when all desires are eliminated and the self is merged with the cosmos.

nirvana-principle (S. Freud) The inherent tendency of drives to eliminate all energy and to bring the life processes to an end, to reduce them to the inorganic state, thus attaining perfect equilibrium.

Nissl granules Granular bodies found in the cell body and dendrites of a neuron; chromophil granules.

no-threshold aminoacidurias See *aminoacidurias, no-threshold.*

nocireceptor A receptor for pain stimuli.

noctambulism Sleepwalking or somnambulism.

nocturnal enuresis Bedwetting at night, in sleep.

nocturnal epilepsy See *epilepsy, nocturnal.*

noise, neural See *neural noise.*

noise, sensory See *neural noise.*

nomenclature of mental disorders The American Psychiatric Association published in 1968 the Diagnostic and Statistical Manual of Mental Disorders (DSM II). See *Classification of mental disorders.*

nominal aphasia See *aphasia, nominal.*

nominal scale A scale in which numbers are assigned to events or event classes for identification and with no reference to any property of the event or class. Thus the number does not represent any dimension of the event or class, e.g. numbers on the members of a football team.

nominalism (philosophy) A theory that maintains that only objects and bodies exist, while concepts, abstractions, and generalizations are merely names of classes or groups of objects or bodies.

nominating technique A rating technique in which the rater chooses the person who conforms best or worst to the criterion. J.L. Moreno's sociogram and B.B. Wolman's statogram apply this technique.

nomograph; nomogram 1. (mathematics) A graphic presentation of a mathematical function or of any other relationship. **2.** (statistics) A graphic presentation consisting of three parallel lines representing three interrelated variables; the values of two are known and the value of the third is inferred by dividing a straight edge.

nomology 1. The science of law. **2.** (A. Kaplan) Referring to cases or experiments whose focus is the testing of hypotheses for the purpose of deriving general laws.

nomothetic Referring to methods and procedures used to formulate general laws or statements.

nomothetic science (W. Windelband) A science which aims at the discovery of general laws.

non-additive A group of elements which cannot be added to one another.

non-continuity (in learning theory) See *continuity-non-continuity (in learning theory).*

nondetermination coefficient See *coefficient, non-determination.*

nondirective group psychotherapy See *psychotherapy, nondirective group.*

nondirective psychotherapy See *psychotherapy, client centered.*

nondiscriminated avoidance See *avoidance, free operant.*

non-disjunction The failure of two members of a chromosome pair to disjoin during the anaphase of cell division, so that both pass to the same daughter cell. This is the underlying reason of trisomy 21 accounting for one variant of Down's syndrome or mongolism.

non-linear regression See *regression, nonlinear.*

non-permissiveness (developmental psychology) In child rearing, preventing the occurrence of undesired behaviors by non-punitive means, such as 1) distraction, 2) negative evaluation in advance, 3) expression of counter-values with expectancy that child will adopt them. See *permissiveness.*

nonsense figure A figure which has no meaning in terms of resembling real objects or geometric figures.

nonsense syllables (H. Ebbinghaus) A group of letters which can be pronounced but which are meaningless as words. They are used in the rote-learning experiments.

nonverbal intelligence See *intelligence, nonverbal.*

nonverbal tests See *tests, nonverbal.*

noology The study of the human mind.

noradrenaline Norepinephrine.

norepinephrine A substance secreted by the adrenal medulla and formed at sympathetic nerve endings which functions as a neural transmitter and produces bodily reactions characteristic of emotional excitement.

norm, composite A norm arrived at by combining two or more scores.

norm, group 1. Representation of the performance of a given group. 2. Social norm.

norm-of-reaction concept The principle that each genotype has a range of possible phenotypes that can be developed depending on the influence of the environment.

norm, percentile (statistics) A norm which is defined in terms of the percentage standing of scores or individuals in the population in question as opposed to the means or averages.

normal; normality; normalcy 1. Being and acting according to some accepted standards. 2. Being healthy, wholesome, and free of conflict.

normal distribution curve or frequency See *curve, normal distribution.*

normal insanity See *insanity, normal.*

normative science A science that sets norms and determines what ought to be done, e.g. education is such a science, for it determines the ends and means of upbringing children, teaching and guiding.

normative scoring Standardization of scores obtained by a sample or a population. Normative scoring standardization uses the mean and the sigma of scores of a sample or a population.

nortriptyline An anti-depressant drug of the tricyclic compound group used in the treatment of depressions.

nosogenesis; nosogeny The beginning and development of a disease.

nosology The study and classification of diseases; this term applies also to the study of behavior disorders.

nosophobia Morbid fear of diseases.

nostalgia Homesickness.

not-me See *personified self.*

("not-R") The residual responding which makes up the behavior stream apart from the experimentally measured response, R.

Nothnagel, C. W. H. (1841-1905) Austrian neurologist who is known for his early work on the localization of brain function.

notogenesis The stage of embryonic development in which the notochord and the mesoderm develop.

notomania Excessive homesickness.

Notterman, Joseph M. (1923-   ) American experimental psychologist. Main studies in field of feedback paradigms of behavior. Principle research in kinesthetic feedback of motor responses, particularly in context of operant conditioning. Has demonstrated that systematic variations in response force, duration, and time integral of force ("effort") occur as a function of reinforcement contingencies, and response-induced feedback. Has also written extensively on perception of changing stimuli as related to feedback control of behavior, and on heart rate conditioning.

noumenal Pertaining to perception or knowledge based on pure thought with no reference to time or space.

nous (Greek) Reason.

noxious Harmful, damaging, hurting.

nuclear cluster A correlation cluster which consists of the variables overlapping from several phenomenal clusters.

nuclear sexing procedures Screening techniques helpful in the search for anomalies of the sex chromosomes.

nucleus 1. The central part of a living cell containing specialized substances, which is distinctly separated from the rest of the cell material or cytoplasm. 2. The central or focal part about which material gathers. 3. A group of cells within the cerebrum of the brain. 4. A cluster.

null hypothesis See *hypothesis, null.*

null set ($\emptyset$) A set containing no objects or elements.

nulliplex inheritance Inheritance which is determined by two recessive genes, each contributed by one parent.

Number Completion Test See *test, Number Completion.*

number factor See *factor, number.*

number form An imaginary form which represents a number series; each number has a definite position in space.

numerical value   A number which is expressed as an absolute number, regardless of the sign.

nursing, psychiatric   See *psychiatric nursing.*

nurturance need   See *need, nurturance.*

nurture   The environmental aspects which influence an organism from the time of conception. This term is used in the nature-nurture controversy which attempts to assess whether heredity or environment is the determining influence in development.

nutrient   A substance which can be absorbed into the body and transformed into food for the tissues.

nyctalopia   Inability to see in darkness.

nyctophobia   Morbid fear of darkness.

nymphomania   An excessive heterosexual drive in females.

nymphomania, heterosexual   Excessive desire of woman for men.

nystagmus   A fluctuating movement of the eyeballs which may be congenital or due to intracranial disease.

nystagmus, galvanic   Nystagmus produced by passing an electric current through the labyrinthine area.

O

O **1.** Abbreviation for observer; plural: Os. **2.** Abbreviation for organism. **3.** (Rorschach) Abbreviation for original response. **4.** Abbreviation for oscillation. **5.** (structuralism) The trained introspectionist who observes.

$_sO_R$ (C. L. Hull) Behavioral oscillation or the oscillatory weakening potential which is associated with $_sE_R$, effective reaction potential.

O factor See *factor, O.*

O-technique (R. B. Cattell) A factor analysis technique which correlates the relationships among functions by yielding a correlation of classes of occasions and, by inference, their similarity. This technique is used to compare the same person on different occasions, as, for example, on two different tests.

O variable See *variable, O.*

oasthouse urine disease A rare aminoaciduria associated with mental retardation; malabsorption of methionine.

object **1.** Anything which is concrete, stable, and visible. **2.** Any aspect of the environment of which an individual is aware or towards which an attitude is directed or to which a response is made which may be material, abstract or social. **3.** An aim, purpose or goal of an individual or group. **4.** A stimulus or that which elicits an instinctive response or reaction. **5.** Anything which exists independent of a perceiver or subject.

object-assembly test See *test, object-assembly.*

object cathexis See *cathexis, object.*

object, good (M. Klein) The introjected object which helps and supports the ego in binding its death instinct by libido.

object hypercathexis The overinvestment of psychic energy in objects outside of oneself.

object libido (psychoanalysis) Sexual energy or drive which is directed outward toward external objects or persons rather than toward the erogenous zones or the self.

object loss **1.** (psychoanalysis) The real loss of a loved one due to death, illness, or some other cause. **2.** (psychoanalysis) The experiencing of loss of love by an individual even though such a loss of love or threat of loss has not really happened.

object love (psychoanalysis) The direction of sexual energy or libido outward to an external object or person and the investment of libido in an external object.

object relations (psychoanalysis) The relationships of an individual including those in which there is either libidinal and/or aggressive instinctual gratifications and those where instinctual gratification is sublimated. These include primitive types of relationships such as symbiotic and transitional object relations and mature forms of object relations.

object relations technique A projective technique used with children, consisting of two sets of four pictures of one-person, two-person, three-person, and group relationships. Color is used to intensify the threat element and to encourage emotional involvement.

objective-analytic (O-A) battery A group of tests for measuring each of the eighteen main personality dimensions found in Objective Tests. A general purpose test for objective test measurement of personality factors.

objective anxiety See *anxiety, objective.*

objective examination An examination which has a scoring standard so prescribed and unequivocal as to leave no element of subjectivity or chance to the scorer. The most common types of such tests are completion tests, multiple choice and true-false.

objective test A test in which the subject's behavior is measured, for inferring personality, without his being aware in what ways his behavior is likely to affect the interpretation.

oblique muscles A pair of eye muscles, the inferior and the superior which rotate the eyeball. The inferior oblique rotates the eyeball downward and outward and the superior oblique rotates the eyeball upward and outward.

oblique solution (factor analysis) A set of factors which are correlated since they are not at right angles to each other.

obliviscence 1. Forgetfulness. 2. The gradual disappearance of ideas over time.

obnubilation Obscuring of consciousness; stupor.

obscenity Violation of established norms of what is believed to be proper, modest or in good taste; lewd or pornographic actions or communication. This includes pictures, gestures, writings, and speech often dealing with the subjects of sex or excretory functions. The interpretation of and criteria for what constitutes obscenity varies culturally and is often determined legislatively or in the courts.

observation 1. An intentional or explicit examination of a situation or thing in order to ascertain facts or particulars about it. 2. A score or value which represents an observed fact. 3. The communication, usually casual, of what has been observed.

observation, mass The technique of ascertaining public opinion through the sampling of opinions of representative people of a group.

observer 1. An individual who examines a situation or an object closely in order to report on it or understand it clearly. 2. One who participates in introspective observations. 3. Abbreviation: "O."

observer, participant One who observes a social event or happening while participating in it himself simultaneously.

observer reliability The degree to which two observers agree on some measure of behavior observation when they observe the same series of events independently; Pearson r is a common expression of agreement when the measure is of frequency of occurrence in a set of 30 or more observations; "percent agreement" is often used when each observation involves 2 or more parameters (e.g., agent, object, intensity, category of action), the formula being 2 × total number of agreements on recorded observations by A and B divided by the total number of recorded observations by A plus same by B.

obsession An idea or impulse which persistently preoccupies an individual even though the individual prefers to be rid of it. Obsessions are usually associated with anxiety or fear and may be of relatively long or short duration and may constitute a minimal or a major disturbance of or interference with normal functioning and thinking.

obsessional neurosis See *neurosis, obsessive-compulsive.*

obsessive-compulsive behavior Behavior characterized by repetitive, irrational thoughts called obsessions and actions called compulsions.

obsessive-compulsive neurosis See *neurosis, obsessive-compulsive.*

obstacle sense The ability to avoid objects in one's way without seeing them usually developed by blind persons and sometimes by others; this depends largely upon echo-location which is hearing sounds bounce off objects.

obstipation Severe constipation usually of functional origin.

obstruction The sudden ceasing, blocking or disappearance of thought which is a symptom of mental disturbance.

obstruction method See *method, obstruction.*

obtained score A raw score which is a score obtained directly from a test and one which has not been converted to standard units or submitted to any statistical treatment.

Occam's razor The principle of scientific thinking which states that the most simple adequate explanation of a thing is to be preferred to any more complex explanations.

occasionalism (philosophy) A post-Cartesian school which proposes that God intervenes in bodily and psychic processes which may be transformed into each other without any other intervention.

occipital lobe See *lobe, occipital.*

occipital lobe brain lesion See *brain lesion, of occipital lobe.*

occipitoparietal brain lesion See *brain lesion, occipitoparietal.*

occlusion 1. The obstruction of a passageway. 2. The exhibition of fewer than the usual number of motor unit responses due to an overlap of neuronal fields.

occultism The belief that nature can be controlled through magical procedures. Also the attempt to control nature through such means.

occupational ability The measurement of an individual's aptitude for a certain vocation or work by means of a standard test; several different occupational ability tests are usually administered at one time and the results are reported as a profile or pattern.

occupational analysis See *job analysis.*

occupational norm The average or usual score or pattern of scores for a particular occupational category or profession.

occupational test See *test, occupational.*

occupational therapy See *therapy, occupational.*

oceanic feeling (psychoanalysis) Sensation of unlimited omnipotence, of boundlessness, and of being at one with the universe.

ochlophobia Fear of crowds.

ocular dominance See *dominance, ocular.*

ocular pursuit See *pursuit, ocular.*

oculocardiac reflex See *reflex, oculocardiac.*

oculogyral illusion or movement See *illusion, oculogyral.*

oculomotor nerve See *nerve, oculomotor.*

odd-even technique A method of estimating test reliability by determining the correlation between the odd and the even test items and applying the Spearman-Brown formula to compensate for attenuation caused by splitting the test.

odor prism (H. Henning) A diagrammatic illustration of the relations between the six basic classes of odors and the mixed colors.

odorimetry Olfactometry or the measurement of odors.

oedipal conflict (S. Freud) Conflict experienced by the boy during the phallic stage concerning his incestuous wishes for his mother and fear that the father will castrate him.

Oedipus complex See *complex, Oedipus.*

ogive 1. A curve which has a double bend. 2. (statistics) A mathematical curve which is shaped like the letter S.

Ohm's law 1. (acoustics) The ear hears a complex tone as a combination of simpler tones; often the ear can break down a complex tone into its simpler components by a physical separation of the complex acoustic wave.2. (electricity) The amount of electrical current in a circuit is directly proportional to the electro-motive force and inversely proportional to the circuit resistance.

oikiomania Pathological attitude and behavior syndrome toward members of one's own family.

oikiophobia See *oikophobia.*

oikofugic Relating to the urge to travel or wander about.

oikophobia Fear of one's own home or house.

oikotropic Homesick.

oinomania Excessive desire for liquor caused by excessive drinking; dipsomania.

old age, mental disorders of See *senility.*

olfaction The sense of smell, the receptors of which are located in the nose and are made up of hair cells in the olfactory epithelium.

olfactometer An instrument used in threshold experiments to regulate the intensity and the amount of a smell stimulus.

olfactory area The part of the cerebral cortex where the centers for smell are located.

olfactory brain The rhinencephalon.

olfactory bulb, or lobe One of two oval masses of grey matter located on the bottom of the cranium above the nasal cavity extending outward toward the eyes. These bulbs or lobes mediate smell and are an extension of the cerebrum.

olfactory cells Spindle-shaped cells in the nasal cavities, membranes which function as sense receptors for smell stimuli.

olfactory nerve The first cranial nerve which connects the olfactory region in the cerebrum with the olfactory cells.

oligoencephaly (C. E. Benda) The primary oligophrenia, an idiopathic mental deficiency characterized by asymmetries in the physical development. There are usually noticeable differences between the right and left sides of the body, irregularities in the nervous system, and low resistance to disease.

oligomenorrhea Scanty, infrequent menstruation sometimes due to psychological regression to the oral state of development because of fear of the sexual role.

oligophrenia Mental deficiency.

oligophrenic response A peculiar type of Rorschach response in which discrete parts of figures, particularly human, are reported while the majority of subjects see the entire figure. These types of responses, generally rare, are most commonly associated with severe intellectual retardation or those severe disturbances in which intellectual ties to reality are extensively impaired.

omission training A type of training in which a particular undesired response is not rewarded.

omnibus test See *test, omnibus.*

omnipotent infantile sadism See *sadism, omnipotent infantile.*

onanism 1. Coitus interruptus or withdrawal of the penis before ejaculation. 2. Masturbation.

onanistic equivalent See *equivalent, onanistic.*

one-tailed test See *test, one-tailed.*

one-trial learning 1. The total mastery of a skill or of an association on the first trial; the mastery of an increment of learning or association on one trial. 2. (E. R. Guthrie) The acquisition of the complete associative strength of a stimulus pattern on the first pairing of it with a response. 3. (B. F. Skinner) Maximum probability that a particular response will follow a particular stimulus as the outcome of one rewarded pairing.

one-way screen A screen or mirror which can be seen through from only one direction. This allows an individual to observe a person or group without the observed knowing they are being watched.

oneirism Experiencing of a dreamlike state while awake.

onomatomania Obsession by words or names.

onomatophobia Fear of hearing a particular name.

onomatopoiesis Creating a word which imitates the sound of the action or thing which the word represents. The creation of such words is characteristic of certain forms of schizophrenia.

ontogenesis; ontogeny The origin and development of the individual organism.

ontogenetic; ontogenic Relating to ontogenesis.

ontology The branch of philosophy concerned with the study of the nature of being.

onychophagia (A. Kanner) Nailbiting which is thought to be a form of neurotic behavior and a means of releasing inner tension.

oocyte The female egg cell before the maturation process is complete.

oogonia The first phase in the development of mature female reproductive cells.

open-cue situation Learning situation in which the means or materials necessary for solution of the problem or attainment of the goal are available to the subject. The task is to use the means appropriately in order to reach the goal.

open-ended question Any question which allows the person answering flexibility of form and substance in his response.

open group 1. A group which admits new members. 2. A psychotherapeutic group in which every member follows his own therapeutic course; when some members are discharged (or leave), new members are admitted.

operandum (operant conditioning) Any object movement which is classified as a response and as such is reinforced. The word operandum is preferred and is replacing the earlier word, "manipulandum."

operant (B. F. Skinner) A unit of behavior defined by its effect on the environment. It is a class of responses all members of which are equally effective in achieving reinforcement under a set of given conditions.

operant avoidance See *avoidance, free operant.*

operant behavior Behavior which is identified in terms of its effect on the environment.

operant, concurrent (operant conditioning) Two or more topologically different responses, at least with respect to locus, capable of being performed at the same time or in rapid succession with little mutual interference. Stimuli and reinforcements are independently programmed for each response.

operant conditioning See *conditioning, operant.*

operant level (operant conditioning) The rate of occurrence of the operant before conditioning, before it occasions reinforcement.

operant reserve See *reflex, reserve.*

operating characteristic 1. The probability of accepting the null hypothesis in every possible situation of a test of significance. 2. Quantitative statement of the expected effects of a particular procedure or thing.

operation of cognition See *cognition, operation of.*

operation of convergent production See *convergent production, operation of.*

operation of divergent production See *divergent production, operation of.*

operation of evaluation See *evaluation, operation of.*

operation of memory See *memory, operation of.*

operational analysis (communication theory) The quantitative analysis of output and input in a transmission system; such a system may be composed of organisms or other measurable units.

operational definition A definition of a fact or a concept in terms of "operations" such as controlled observation or experimentation performed by the researcher. Intelligence, e.g., is what intelligence tests measure.

operational-informational psychology See *psychology, operational-informational.*

operational term A term which has been defined by the procedures used to arrive at it.

operationalism See *operationism.*

operationism (P. W. Bridgman) A radical version of empiricism. According to Bridgman, any scientific concept must be presented in terms of the operations performed by the scientist. Accordingly, the true meaning of a term is to be found by observing what a man does with and not by what he says about it. Although at a later stage (1936), Bridgman assumed that in final analysis "science is only my private science," a great many psychologists embraced operationism as the proper guidepost in psychological research. According to S. S. Stevens "the propositions of science have empirical significance only where their truth can be demonstrated by a set of concrete operation," and "only those propositions which are public and repeatable are admitted to the body of science."

operations, intellectual (J. P. Guilford) Major kinds of intellectual activities or processes; things that an organism does in the construction of information and its use. One of the parameters of the structure of intellect, including the categories of cognition, memory, divergent production, convergent production, and evaluation.

operator (mathematics) A symbol which indicates an operation is to be performed on another symbol or number.

operon Unit or gene action postulated by Jacob and Monod, consisting of an operator gene and a closely linked structural gene(s) whose action it controls.

ophidiophilia Morbid attraction for snakes.

ophidiophobia Morbid fear of snakes.

ophthalmia Inflammation of the outer tissues of the eye, especially of the conjunctiva.

ophthalmology Branch of medicine which deals with the structure, the functions, and the diseases of the eye.

ophthalmometer Instrument which measures the curvature of the front surface of the eye.

opiate 1. Drug which contains opium or a derivative of opium. 2. Anything which relaxes, soothes, or quiets a person.

opinion poll A survey of opinions which is gathered by questioning a sample of people on a specific issue or issues.

opinionaire Questionnaire used in a study of public opinion.

opiomania Addiction to opium or an opium derivative.

opium A narcotic drug which comes from a species of poppy and which depresses the higher nervous centers and induces a euphoric condition. Codeine and morphine are the most common derivatives.

opposites test See *test, opposites.*

optic atrophy See *atrophy, optic.*

optic chiasma See *chiasma.*

optic disc Retinal area where the optic nerve fibers gather before leaving the retina. This area is extremely insensitive to light and is called the blind spot.

optic lobes The upper part of the corpora quadrigemina.

optic nerve See *nerve, optic.*

optic thalamus See *thalamus.*

optical axis The line passing through the curvature center of both the lens and the cornea which is the center of vision.

optical illusion See *illusion, optical.*

optimal movement See *movement, beta.*

optical projection See *projection, optical.*

optimal stimulation principle (C. Leuba) Generalization that an organism learns those responses and behaviors which lead to an optimal level of excitation and stimulation.

optimal tension level The amount of tension thought to be necessary for mental health.

optimism An attitude or personality trait characterized by cheerfulness; a tendency to have faith in the future and the tendency to perceive most situations and things as good.

optimum adjustment See *adjustment, optimum.*

optional-content drawings A projective technique used with children in which the child is asked to draw whatever he wishes or to complete elaborate already provided stimulus patterns, sometimes being asked to relate a story concerning the drawing. Drawings and stories are both interpretable.

optogram A light-reflecting image of an object on the retina.

optokinetic reaction Eye movements which are caused by visual stimulation and the apparent movement which sometimes results in the visual field.

optometry 1. The measurement of the eye and its

functions. 2. The applied art of improving vision by fitting glasses or suggesting visual exercises and training but not through the use of surgery or the prescription of drugs.

oral-aggressive type See *type, oral-aggressive.*

oral character See *character, oral.*

oral characteristics Traits of a person which reveal a fixation at the oral stage characterized by dependence, and passivity.

oral dependence (psychoanalysis) The desire to return to the security of the infantile oral stage of development which consisted of the protection of the mother in combination with the intense gratification provided by the mother's breasts and milk.

oral eroticism or erotism See *eroticism, oral.*

oral incorporation (psychoanalysis) The desire to incorporate the mother or any other love object.

oral-passive type See *type, oral–passive.*

oral personality See *character, oral.*

oral sadism See *sadism, oral.*

oral stage (S. Freud) The first psychosexual stage occurring in the first year of life during which the infant's sexual pleasure is derived from the stimulation of the mouth. The infant's first sexual excitations are related to sucking in the feeding process, which becomes the prototype of later sexual satisfaction and the mother, the object involved in the feeding process becomes the prototype of all later love object relations.

oral test See *test, oral.*

orality See *eroticism, oral.*

order need See *need, order.*

order of a matrix (statistics) Matrix size stated in terms of the number of its rows and its columns which is written in this form: "in the order of *m* by *n* (rows by columns)."

order of magnitude Arrangement of values, objects or data in a sequence which goes from the lowest or smallest in magnitude to the highest or largest.

order of merit Arrangement of people, data or objects in a sequence determined by their magnitude or importance with respect to a particular characteristic or quality.

ordinal Pertaining to or indicating order or succession as in ordinal numbers.

ordinal position A specific position in a succession, usually indicated by the ordinal numbers.

ordinal scale See *scale, ordinal.*

ordinate 1. The vertical axis of a two-dimensional graph. 2. The shortest distance from a point to the horizontal axis of a two dimensional chart measured along a line parallel to the vertical axis.

Orestes complex See *complex, Orestes.*

orexis The conative and affective components of an act or behavior as opposed to the cognitive aspect.

organ A structure of an organism which is specialized for a particular function or functions.

organ, erotism The investment of erotic energy in an organ or part of one's body.

organ inferiority See *inferiority, organ.*

organ of Corti Numerous hair cells in a bony cavity of the inner ear which move when stimulated by sound or air waves and set off neural impulses which produce auditory sensations.

organ, sense **1.** An end organ usually including the endings of afferent neurons and associated cells which are specialized to receive specific types of stimulation. **2.** A receptor.

organic variable or O variable See *variable, organic or O.*

organic view of psychopathology The belief that mental disturbances are caused by hereditary factors or acquired through physical damage or disease.

organicism **1.** Philosophical view that life is the end-product of organization. **2.** Principle that all disorders are organic in origin, whether mental or physical. **3.** (H. Spencer) Belief that social groups are analogous to individual persons.

organism Any living being which has the potential to maintain itself and exist independently as a self-contained system with functions such as respiration, digestion, etc. This includes all plants and animals.

organismic **1.** Of an organism or pertaining to one. **2.** Any psychological viewpoint which rejects a dualistic approach to the organism and utilizes a holistic or functionalist orientation in psychological investigation and experimentation as, for example, organismic psychology and behaviorism. **3.** Characteristics of an integrated organism which are the product of integration and interactivity. **4.** (J. R. Kantor) Interbehavioral psychology.

organismic psychology **1.** Psychological orientation which stresses investigation of the total biological organism as the proper subject matter of psychology. A molar of holistic approach is characteristic as is the rejection of dualism and mind-body distinctions. **2.** (J. R. Kantor) School of psychology which states that psychological organisms are simultaneously physical and biological objects which always function as a whole within a definite environment. The subject matter of psychology is the interbehavior of organism with objects, events, and other organisms. The field of interbehavior between organism and environment is the subject matter of psychology.

organization **1.** The arrangement of elements or parts in an integrated or cooperative way. **2.** The amount of integration or cooperation in a complex whole. **3.** (Gestalt) The process through which psychophysical excitations form themselves into an integrated stable field or gestalt.

organizational activity The composite perceptual-association process which appears in some but not all Rorschach responses. It is most clearly identified where two or more elements of a blot are organized into a relationship with a meaning described to the organized elements. Rorschach implied that all percepts using the entire blot manifest organizational activity. Beck and Hertz (see *z score* and *g score*) have developed a quantitative method for differentiating the organizational activity when it occurs to the whole blot or as it occurs by combining adjacent or distant details of the blots. The organizational activity is interpreted as directly related to intellectual functioning but also involving non-intellectual features.

organon **1.** Body of principles and tenets which indicate how knowledge should be acquired, investigated and increased. **2.** A scientific method.

organotherapy Treatment of a body with natural organic substances such as, for example, hormones, with the intention of restoring health to the body by replacing or supplementing a vital substance that was lacking.

orgasm, alimentary (S. Rado) Experience of well-being and release of tension by an infant at the height of breast-feeding.

orgastic impotence See *impotence, orgastic.*

orgiastic **1.** Like an orgy in nature. **2.** Characterized by excitement, frenzy, or emotional intensity.

orgone theory (W. Reich) A dissident psychoanalytic theory that there is a vital, primal raw-material energy called orgone which permeates the space and accounts for the functions of life.

orientation **1.** Awareness of one's position or direction in space and time whether in relation to other persons, situations, physical reality or a goal. **2.** The tendency to move toward a source of stimulation or a particular direction, as in tropisms. **3.** A pre-disposition or frame of reference which influences reactions to certain stimuli, situations or behaviors. **4.** (personnel) The process of initiating an individual to a work situation and of instructing him about rules, regulations and responsibilities as an introduction to a new situation, particularly a new job. **5.** The position a thing or organism is in or the position taken by it. **6.** General viewpoint which influences choice of scientific method, selection of methodology, etc.

orientation, double (E. Bleuler) Ability to maintain contact with reality and acceptable daily functioning on same level while exhibiting delusions in certain areas.

orientation, illusion of See *illusion of orientation.*

orienting response A reaction of attention to a given stimulus.

origin, arbitrary (statistics) Any arbitrary chosen zero point against which other values are defined by being measured as deviations.

original response A special Rorschach scoring category, using the symbol O, to denote responses which occur no more than once in 100 records.

original score See *score, raw.*

ornithophobia Fear of birds.

orthodox analysis See *psychoanalysis.*

orthogenesis (biology) The theory that maintains that nature has an intrinsic tendency to develop in a definite direction determined by the germ plasm.

orthogenic Corrective, improving, making things straight.

orthognatic or orthognathous skull A skull with a profile of 85° to 93°. The forehead and the jaws form an almost vertical line.

orthogonal solution (factor analysis) A solution in which the axes symbolizing factors are at right angles with one another which indicates they are uncorrelated or independent.

orthopsychiatry A cross disciplinary science combining child psychiatry, developmental psychology, pediatrics, and family care, devoted to the discovery, prevention and treatment of mental disorders in childhood and adolescence.

orthoptics System of training techniques which are designed to facilitate cooperative functioning of the two eyes especially in cases of muscular imbalance.

orthorater Brand name of an instrument which tests visual acuity, color vision, steropsis, and phoria.

orthostatic hypotension See *hypotension, orthostatic.*

orthriogenesis (P. Federn) Regaining of its full development by the ego which is said to occur spontaneously at the moment of awakening when the ego has its cathexis restored which had disappeared in sleep.

oscillation 1. Swinging back and forth or fairly steady direction reversal. 2. (C. L. Hull) The continual quantitative and qualitative variability of response to the same environmental stimulation which is thought to be a function of the normal probability law. 3. (factor analysis) The amount of general response variability which characterizes a person's responses to the same situation or test on different occasions.

oscillation behavioral $_S O_R$ (C. L. Hull) The incessant variability or oscillatory weakening potential of the effective reaction potential $_S \bar{E}_R$; the reaction potential's standard deviation.

oscillograph An instrument which produces a graphic record of the wave form of an electric current.

oscillometer An instrument which records mechanical oscillations or vibratory motion.

Oseretsky scale See *scale, Oseretsky.*

osmosis A penetration of a porous substance, membrane, etc. by fluids.

osphresiolagnia Morbid concern with bodily odors.

osphresiophobia Morbid fear of odors.

Ostwald colors A large series of achromatic and chromatic color samples classified according to an arbitrary letter-number notation system. Each color sample represents a particular pigment mixture of full color content, white content, and black content.

OT See *occupational therapy.*

Otis Quick-Scoring Mental Ability Test See *test, Otis Quick-Scoring Mental Ability.*

Otis Self-Administering Test of Intelligence See *test, Otis Self-Administering, of Intelligence.*

otitis media Inflammation of the middle ear.

otogenic tone See *tone, otogenic.*

otohemineurasthenia Deafness in one ear caused by non-organic factors.

otoliths Small calcium deposits in the endolymph of the inner ear which help maintain equilibrium by activating neuronal endings when the head moves.

otology The science of the ear.

outer-directed (D. Riesman) Individual who is motivated by public opinion rather than by his own convictions and who tends to conform to the desires of other persons, seeking social approval as a primary goal.

outgroup 1.(social psychology) Any group to which a designated person does not belong. 2.Any persons who are not members of a particular group being considered. 3. Any individuals, whether members of a group or not, who do not belong to one's own group.

outpatient treatment Ambulatory, non-hospital treatment in private practice or a clinic.

ovariotomy Removal of the ovaries by surgery.

ovary The female reproductive organ which produces the ovum or egg cell and the female sex hormones, the estrogens. It is one of a pair of glandular organs which are connected to the uterus by the fallopian tubes.

over-all rate See *rate, over-all.*

overachievement Performance which exceeds expectations made on the basis of mental aptitude.

overcompensation Using more effort than is necessary to make up for weakness or deficiency.

overdetermination (S. Freud) The assumption that mental processes are caused by more than one factor, that is, they are overdetermined.

overflow aminoacidurias See *aminoacidurias, overflow.*

overinclusion (N. Cameron) Inability to eliminate inappropriate or inefficient responses associated with a particular stimulus from the behavioral repertoire.

over-learning Learning in which practice continues after the desired criterion of learning is reached.

overprotection, maternal Excessive protection and indulgence of the child by the mother which usually results in later passivity, dependence, and inability to tolerate frustration in the overprotected child.

overreaction   A greater reaction than would be expected to a situation, usually of an emotional nature.

overt behavior   See *behavior, overt.*

ovoplasm   The cytoplasm of an unfinished ovum.

ovum   A female germ cell.

oxycephaly   Having an elongated or can-shaped head.

oxyesthesia   Hypersensitivity; hyperesthesia.

oxygeusia   Unusually acute sense of taste.

oxyopia   Excellent vision; unusually sharp vision.

oxyphonia   Unusually shrill voice.

ozostomia   Bad breath; halitosis.

P

P 1. Person. 2. Perceptual speed. 3. Probability ratio. 4. (H. J. Eysenck) Symbolizes the degree of personality organization. 5. (Rorschach) Popular response scoring code. 6. (physiology) Symbolizes drive state.

p factor A factor of behavioral inertia; the tendency to maintain an activity once it has started.

P-technique (R. B. Cattell) A factor analytic design which measures a single person on the same set of variables over a number of different occasions. Correlations between the variables are computed over these occasions as entries, then factor analyzed. P-technique and Incremental Factor Analysis are the two main methods for determining dimensions of personality change-over-time (or states).

padded cell See *cell, padded.*

pain 1. The opposite of pleasure; that which is not pleasant. 2. The sensation which results from too much stimulation of the free nerve endings pain receptors in the skin and where tissue is damaged.

pain, referred Pain which is perceived or felt as coming from some other location than that which was stimulated.

pain sense See *sense, pain.*

pain spot A small area of the skin especially sensitive to pain.

paired associates Pairs of words or nonsense syllables used in experiments of learning.

paired associates method The method of measuring retention in which items to be learned are presented in pairs. In testing retention the first member of each pair is given and the subject asked to respond with the second.

paired-choice tests See *tests, paired-choice.*

paired-comparison method A technique used in psychophysics and social psychology in which the subject is asked to compare each stimulus with every other.

Paired Hands Test of Friendliness See *test, Paired Hands, of Friendliness.*

paleologic thinking (Van Domarus) Paralogic thinking which is characteristic of schizophrenic thinking disorders.

paleomnesis Memory of the distant past of one's life.

paligraphia Obsessive repetition of letters, words, or phrasing in writing.

palilalia Speech disorder consisting of the increasingly rapid repetition of words and phrases.

palilexia Abnormal rereading of words and phrases.

pallesthesia Sensitivity to vibrations experienced when a vibrating tuning fork is placed over bony surfaces.

pallium Old word for the cerebral cortex; neo-pallium refers to newer areas and archi-pallium to older areas of the cortex.

palmar reflex or response See *reflex, palmar.*

palmesthesis See *pallesthesia.*

palmistry Interpreting the personality characteristics, past or future of an individual by reading the lines and other characteristics of the hand.

palsy, cerebral See *cerebral palsy.*

panel design See *design, panel.*

panhypopituitary dwarfism See *dwarfism, panhypopituitary.*

panic, primodial Combination of fright and anger reaction with disorganized motor responses characteristic of many schizophrenic children.

panmixia Equal, unrestricted mating of different races or different ethnic groups.

panphobia; panophobia; pantophobia Fear of everything.

panpsychism Belief that only psychological or mentalistic reality exists.

pansexualism The view that human behavior and motivation can be fully explained in terms of the sex drive or motive.

Panum's area Areas of the two retinas within which one identical stimulus is perceived when two separate stimuli are presented, one in each eye, in which case they fall within the limits of Panum's area and binocular fusion occurs.

paper and pencil test See *test, paper and pencil.*

papilledema Usually bilateral edema, or accumulation of fluids in the optic nerve often caused by brain tumor.

parabiosis Temporary loss of nerve conductivity.

parabulia Inability to make decisions.

paracentral vision See *vision, paracentral.*

parachromatopsia Partial color-blindness.

paracousia; paracusia; paracusis 1. Deafness to deep tones which is selective or relative. 2. The supposed ability of partially deaf people to hear better when there is background noise. 3. Any hearing disorder except deafness.

paracusis imaginaria Hallucination of audition.

paradigm A pattern or model which illustrates all the possible functions or forms.

paradoxia sexualis Manifestation of sexual impulses or behavior not characteristic of the chronological age of the individual.

paradoxical cold The sensation of coldness when a relatively warm object stimulates a cold receptor or spot on the skin.

paradoxical warmth The sensation of warmth when a relatively cold object stimulates a warm receptor or spot on the skin.

paragenital Intercourse in which conception is prevented.

parageusia 1. A distorted or perverted sense of taste. 2. Taste hallucination.

paragrammatism Speech disorder in which there is faulty syntactical or grammatical relationships.

paragraphia The omission and incorrect inclusion of words in speech or writing due to cerebral injury or nervous disorder.

parahypnosis The kind of sleep occasioned by hypnotism and sleep walking.

parakinesia Movement carried out in a grotesque, awkward manner.

parakinesis The lifting up of material things by supernatural powers in psychical research.

paralalia Speech disorder characterized by the inability to make certain sounds or the emission of incorrect sounds.

paralalia literalis The inability to form certain sounds correctly often accompanied by stammering.

paraleresis A mild form of delirium.

paralexia The incorrect reading of words including the transposition of word order and the inclusion of additional words.

paralipophobia Fear of neglecting responsibilities.

parallax The apparent movement of objects when the viewpoint is shifted laterally in the field of vision. Things beyond the fixated point move with the shift; things closer to the observer than the fixated point appear to move against the direction of the shift.

parallax, binocular Difference in optic angle or viewpoint of the eyes due to their separation laterally.

parallax threshold (binocular vision)

$$p = \left(\frac{a}{y-x} - \frac{a}{y}\right) = \frac{ax}{y(y-x)}$$

where x is the distance of two points, y is the further point, distant from the nodal point of both eyes, a is the stereo base (interocular distance) and p is the parallax threshold measured in radians.

parallel law (T. Fechner) Psychophysical generalization that when two different intensity stimuli are presented to a sense modality, sensory adaptation and fatigue result in a decrease of the absolute intensity, but the ratio of the difference between the two stimuli remains the same.

parallel proportional profiles (R. B. Cattell) Procedure method of factor analysis which utilizes several matrices at once and applies the parsimony principle to the complete set instead of applying it to analysis of each matrix separately.

parallelism, psychological Doctrine that assumes the relationship between mental and physical processes to be parallel and concomitant without assuming any causal connection between them.

paralog Nonsense word of two syllables.

paralogia The suppression of a logically connected idea in speech and the substituting of another one related to it.

paralogia, metaphoric Speech disorder characterized by the suppression of a general idea by a more narrow idea which replaces it.

paralogia, thematic Abnormal speech characterized by the incessant preoccupation with one subject.

paralogical thinking Irrational, fallacious thinking without the person being aware of the logical errors.

paralogism Fallacy which is not intentioned or goes unnoticed.

paralysis Partial or complete impairment of function in the voluntary musculature.

paralysis agitans See *Parkinsonism.*

paralysis, familial periodic A paralysis due to an

autosomal mode of inheritance characterized by spontaneous attacks or attacks induced by the injection of salt-retaining adrenocortical steroids which may last from a few hours to several days.

paralysis, general   See *paresis, general.*

paralysis, hysterical   Paralysis which is psychogenic in origin rather than organic.

paralysis, immobilization   The often hysterical persistence of immobilization of a limb or body part after healing, in patients who have been immobilized for some time by casts or splints.

paralytic abasia   See *abasia.*

paralytic dementia   See *paresis.*

parameter   Any device employed in psychoanalytic technique which is not interpretation is called a parameter. Examples are advice, reassurance, suggestion, etc. A parameter should not be used until and unless the analyst is convinced that without it the analysis will not progress. The classic example is that of advising a phobic patient to confront his feared situation, after exhaustive analysis has failed to impel him to go of his own will. In employing a parameter, the analyst must be convinced that nothing else will suffice to move the patient, that it can be given up as quickly as possible, and that the patient attains full insight into the reasons for using it.

paramimia   Apraxic disorder in which gestures are distorted and do not express feelings.

paramnesia   1. Déjà vu or false recognition. 2. Memory distortion or false memory.

paramutualism   See *dysmutualism.*

paranoid; paranoea   Psychotic disorder characterized by extensive systemized delusions with little deterioration or general dementia. Most usual are delusions of persecution, of grandeur, or of both.

paranoid character   See *character, paranoid.*

paranoid defenses   Feelings that others are hostile to oneself.

paranoid personality   See *character, paranoid.*

paranoid reactions   Ascribing one's own feelings, mostly hostile ones, to other people.

paranoid schizophrenia   See *schizophrenia, paranoid.*

paranosic gain   See *paranosis.*

paranosis   Also called primary gain. The alleviation of anxiety resulting from the reduction of instinctual pressure through their partial discharge in the formation and maintenance of neurotic symptoms.

paraphasia   Habitual inclusion of extremely inappropriate words or phrases in one's speech.

paraphasia, verbal   Verbal response characterized by the introduction of inappropriate words or phrases and associated with lesions of the auditory speech areas of the cortex.

paraphia   1. Distorted or perverted sense of touch. 2. Malfunction of tactile sensibilities.

paraphilia   Sexual perversion or distortion of sexuality.

paraphonia   Pathological change in voice quality or any other abnormal voice condition.

paraphrasia   Misuse or improper construction of words and phrases.

paraphrenia   An obsolete term for schizophrenia and paranoia.

paraphrenia hebetica   (K. L. Kahlbaum) An obsolete term for mental deterioration in adolescence.

paraplegia   Paralysis of the lower limbs which is sometimes affected by emotional problems.

parapraxis   A generic term for minor errors in behavior such as slips of the tongue, small accidents, forgetting things and mistakes in writing.

parapsychology   The study of forms of interaction between individual and environment which cannot at present be explained in terms of known physical energies. Attempts to achieve the full description and systematic understanding of alleged telepathy (communication between one organism and another through means other than the known senses); clairvoyance (perception of objective stimuli or events by extra-sensory means); precognition (telepathy or clairvoyance relating to *future* occurrences); and psychokinesis (the control of the movements of physical objects without the use of known physical energies). It attempts to gather, classify, and explain all such events, and to develop experimental control, full replication, and a systematic scientific-philosophical interpretation.

parasexuality   Perverted or abnormal sexual behavior.

parasitophobia   Fear of parasites.

parasomnia   Sleep disturbances or perversions usually associated with nervous system lesions.

parasympathetic nervous system   See *nervous system, parasympathetic.*

parataxic   1. Characterized by emotional maladjustment. 2. Referring to a lack of congruity among various aspects of the personality.

parataxic distortion   See *distortion, parataxic.*

parataxic mode   (H. S. Sullivan) A prelogical second mode of experiencing the world characterized by an autistic interpretation of events and people and a subjective, personal system of communication. It is associated with young children and sometimes seen in adults.

parateresiomania   1. Extreme impulse to observe or to peep. 2. Scoptophilia.

parathion poisoning   See *poisoning, parathion.*

parathymia   Display of an inappropriate reaction or of the opposite mood from what would be expected from the situation. This is an affect disturbance characteristic of schizophrenia.

parathyroidism Over-functioning of the parathyroid glands.

paratype Environmental influences.

parceled factor analysis (R. B. Cattell) A method of economically factoring large matrices by packaging the variables and undoing later.

parenchyma; parencyme The actual specific tissue of a gland or an organ as opposed to the connective or supporting tissue.

parental attitudes Attitudes which parents exhibit towards their children have a great effect upon the shaping of the child's development from infancy and subsequent personality characteristics and behavior as, for example, attitudes of rejection or lack of a meaningful relationship with the mother appear to be factors connected with psychopathic personality patterns.

paresis Partial motor paralysis characteristic of psychosis which results from a syphilitic infection of the brain.

paresis, afferent (O. Foerster) A disturbance of movement due to very severe lesions of the postcentral area in which the patient cannot carry out movements because impulses are transmitted simultaneously to agonist and antagonist muscles, although he retains strength in his muscles. In less severe cases, the person may be unable to place his hand in a desired position or to manipulate objects.

paresis, general A psychosis due to syphilis of the central nervous system. It is characterized by a variety of mental and neurological symptoms resulting from progressive brain pathology.

paresis, general juvenile A psychosis due to inherited syphilis which does not differ appreciably from the adult form, usually observed in children aged 12-14.

paresthetic acathisia See *acathisia, paresthetic.*

parietal brain lesion See *brain lesion, parietal.*

parietal cortex, structure and function of See *cortex, parietal, structure and function of.*

parietal lobe See *lobe, parietal.*

Parkinson, James (1755-1824) British physician best known for his treatise on a neurological condition currently called parkinsonism or Parkinson's disease which is characterized by the symptoms of rigidity, tremor, akinesia, and loss of movement.

Parkinsonism; Parkinson's disease A syndrome which in the idiopathic case is characterized by tremor, rigidity, a masking of the face, and a loss of spontaneous and automatic movement. It predominantly occurs in males over the age of fifty. The onset is usually slow, insidious, and local and gradually spreads to other parts of the body producing an abnormal posture and gait, and distortions in the musculature of the body. The symptoms are exacerbated by emotional stress and abate during sleep.

parnate Common name for tranylcypromine, a powerful antidepressant.

parole Release from imprisonment or from restraint upon the condition of good behavior, usually used in reference to the discharge of prisoners from penal institutions or correctional facilities with the condition that they report to a parole officer.

parosmia Disturbance of the olfactory sense.

parotid gland See *gland, parotid.*

paroxysm Spasm; convulsion.

paroxysmal choreoathetosis Tonic or choreotype movements of limbs, trunk and face. Probably inherited.

paroxysmal trepidant abasia See *abasia.*

Parry's disease See *goiter, exophthalmic.*

parsimony law Scientific principle which states the simplest of alternative explanations of a situation or phenomenon is to be preferred.

Parson Language Sample A diagnostic language test derived from Skinnerian learning theory with an emphasis on the delineation of observable vocal and nonvocal responses, thus allowing the definition of the conditions controlling the responses. The seven subtests reflect Skinner's major classes of language behavior: naming response; verbal repetition response; response showing comprehension; gestural exchange; and demand response. The first three subtests assess vocal responses; the next three assess nonvocal responses; and the seventh assesses both vocal and nonvocal responses.

part method of learning See *learning, part method of.*

parthenogenesis Development of an organism from an unfertilized egg which occurs primarily in some insects, crustacea, and worms.

parthenophobia Morbid fear of girls.

partial correlation See *correlation, partial.*

partial regression equation See *regression equation, multiple.*

partial reinforcement See *reinforcement, partial.*

participant observer (H. S. Sullivan) The role of the therapist consisting at once of skill and expertise in both observation of the patient's interactions and participation in the interpersonal process of therapy.

participation, law of 1. Taking part in an activity or occurrence. 2. (L. Levy-Bruhl) Tendency to perceive similar things as not just similar but the same which is characteristic of primitive thinking and also functions in magic. 3. (J. Piaget) Tendency of children to confuse their wishes with outer events.

participation, mystical (L. Levy-Bruhl) Condition in which an individual experiences himself as one with the object of his perception or thought and is unable to distinguish between himself and such an object.

partile (statistics) Generic name for one of a set of points which divide a serially ordered distribution into any number of groups or classes, each of which includes an equal number of scores or values. The most common partile division is into 100 equal points each of which is a percentile.

partition measure (statistics) Any division which separates one part of a frequency distribution from another as, for example, a partile measure.

partition scales See *scales, partition.*

parturition The act of childbirth.

passive-aggressive personality See *personality, passive-aggressive.*

passive vocabulary The amount of words a child understands without being able to use them actively in speaking.

passivism Total sexual submission of males.

pastoral psychiatry See *psychiatry, pastoral.*

PAT See *test, Picture Arrangement.*

patellar reflex See *reflex, patellar.*

paternalism 1. The principle or practice of dealing with individuals in the way a father relates to his children which implies protection and control. 2. Denial of the right to control their own affairs to adults who occupy a subordinate position.

path 1. Conduction line along a nerve network. 2. An alley in a maze. 3. (K. Lewin) That part of the psychological environment along which locomotion occurs. The direction and regions along which locomotion occurs is determined by the strength and fluidity of region boundaries and by dynamic factors.

path-transformation coefficient (R. B. Cattell) A statistic which relates experiences on life-adjustment paths to learning and other forms of personality change. It states what such path experience does to the individual, after the path or choice has been made; that is, it states, in the broadest sense, what he learns from it.

pathergasia (A. Meyer) Any physical defect or malfunction which interferes with the personal psychological adjustment of the individual.

pathermia (R. B. Cattell) One pole of a personality dimension, characterized by emotional immaturity and affectivity, in the sense of reacting to problems with cognitively unfocused feelings rather than with realism and objectivity.

pathetic nerve See *nerve, trochlear.*

pathetism Hypnotism; mesmerism.

pathobiology The study of diseases or disorders which are biological in origin.

pathocure Disappearance of a neurotic condition at the same time an organic disease occurs.

pathogen Any organism, generally a microorganism, that can infect a host with a disease, i.e. that gives rise to pathology or suffering.

pathogenesis 1. The process by which suffering and disease is generated. 2. The history and origins of suffering and disease.

pathogenic Having the potential to give rise to suffering or disease.

pathognomy 1. Diagnosis of or recognition of the characteristics of a disease. 2. Recognition of the characteristics of feelings and emotions.

pathological Abnormal; caused by disease.

pathology 1. A condition of the organism that gives rise to suffering. Usually implies an abnormal or disordered condition of the body or its parts. 2. The medical discipline which studies such conditions.

pathomimesis; pathomimicry Mimicking or feigning of a disease.

pathomorphism Abnormal body build.

pathopsychology See *psychopathology.*

pathos 1. Great suffering, mental anguish or unhappiness, psychological in origin rather than physiological. 2. That which arouses sympathy or sorrow. 3. The private emotional components of an art work rather than its universal elements. 4. (sociology) The feeling that a revered tradition or idea should not be criticized or discussed.

patient A person who receives treatment.

Paton, Stewart American psychiatrist and neurologist who wrote the first American psychiatric textbook (1905) and established the first American University mental health clinic at Princeton University (1910).

patrilineal Kinship or relationship on the father's side.

pattern analysis See *analysis, pattern.*

pattern discrimination Responding to a whole pattern rather than to the individual components which comprise it.

pattern, sensory Perceptual or sense data which exhibit overall unity or interrelationship such that the total design on the relationships is emphasized rather than the sensory properties taken separately.

pattern similarity coefficient (R. B. Cattell) A statistic (r_p), ranging from +1.00 to -1.00, which expresses the degree of similarity or dissimilarity between two Profiles of Factor Scores. (Profiles can be for single individuals or for groups of individuals). This statistic takes into account shape, level, and emphasis of the profiles, and, for profile comparison purposes, therefore, it is superior to the usual correlation coefficient, which considers only shape. Also known as Profile Similarity Coefficient.

pattern, variable (T. Parsons and E. Shils) Five bipolar dimensions along which any action may be categorized and its meaning defined: 1) specific or diffuse, 2) affective or non-affective, 3) performance quality or quantity, 4) particular or universal, 5) self-oriented or collectively oriented.

patterning 1. Imposing a pattern or system of organization upon a group of data. **2.** Learning to respond to a whole set of data or stimuli pattern rather than to parts.

Pavlov, Ivan Petrovich (1849-1936) Russian physiologist, created an epoch in some fields of physiology, such as digestion and the higher nervous activity. In 1874 he graduated from Petersburg University and in 1879 from the Petersburg Medico-Surgical Academy. After graduation from the Academy he went abroad where he worked at the laboratories of Ludwig and Heidenhain. In 1874-1885 he worked at the Clinic of the Russian clinician-therapeutist S. P. Botkin, as the head of Botkin's experimental physiological laboratory. In 1890 Pavlov was appointed Professor of Pharmacology at the Medico-Surgical Academy and in 1896 Head of the Physiology Department of the Academy. In 1904 Pavlov was awarded the Nobel prize for his work on the physiology of digestion where the surgical method of application of chronical fistula was first employed systematically. In 1905 Pavlov was elected as a member of the Russian Academy of Sciences. I. P. Pavlov discovered a new regularity of the brain activity, the conditioned reflex. This "Doctrine on the higher nervous activity" became a new chapter in the physiology of the brain. During 35 years of research in this field Pavlov and his numerous disciples covered a wide range of fundamental problems in the study of the brain related also to such sciences as medicine, pedagogy, art, etc. Pavlov discovered a new form of inhibition specific for the higher nervous activity which he called "internal inhibition" or "conditional inhibition", different from all other types of specific and unconditioned inhibitions. The conditioned-reflectory regularities have become a general model of the entire behavior, and the study of neurophysiological mechanisms and the theory of the higher nervous activity can be rightfully considered milestones in the history of the science of the brain.

Pavlovian conditioning See *conditioning, Pavlovian.*

pavor nocturnus (Latin) Night panic. Waking up in the middle of the night panic stricken, agitated, and sometimes hallucinated, then falling back asleep with complete amnesia.

Payne Sentence Completion Blank A projective technique for children in the upper grades and high school which requires the child to complete a sentence stem.

Pcs (S. Freud) The preconscious. The middle layer in Freud's topographic theory of personality, between the conscious and unconscious layers. The preconscious contains memory traces. It is, as it were, in one's mind but not on his mind at a particular moment.

PE See *probable error.*

Peabody Picture Vocabulary Test See *test, Peabody Picture Vocabulary.*

peak top diagram A diagram constructed by plotting each frequency above the midpoint of its class interval and connecting the points by a line.

Pearson, Karl (1857-1936) British biomathematician and statistician who, in addition to undertaking extensive statistical investigations of psychological questions, invented the product-moment coefficient of correlation, r, which has been named after him. He devised the system of generalized frequency curves; invented "chi-square" test of good fit and worked out its distribution; derived "Pearson's product moment" formula and two equivalent formulas; elaborated correlation theory on three variables and on other aspects of correlation and of regression.

Pearsonian correlation See *correlation, product movement.*

peccotiphobia Morbid fear of committing a sin.

pecking order 1. Hierarchy of privilege and dominance observed by some animal groups, and particularly studied in chickens. **2.** Accepted hierarchy of privilege and dominance established in some small groups by intimidation and aggressiveness.

pedagogical psychology See *psychology, educational.*

pederasty Anal intercourse with a boy or young man.

pederosis (A. Forel) A sexual desire for children commonly found among certain types of psychopathic personalities and also some psychoneurotic patients.

pediatrics A branch of medicine devoted to the study, treatment and prevention of childhood diseases.

pedication Pederasty.

pedigree Genealogy.

pedigree method The study of the distribution of traits in families in order to determine hereditary mechanisms. This method is of historical interest.

pedologia Soviet name for the study of child development. Child psychologists in the U.S.S.R. in the years 1918-1935 were called pedologists.

pedomorphism Attributing childish characteristics, behaviors, or abilities to adults; describing adult characteristics, behavior or abilities in childish terms.

peduncle A stalklike bundle of nerve fibers connecting various parts of the brain.

peduncle, cerebellar One of three bonds of fibers connecting the cerebellum to the brain stem.

peduncle, cerebral One of two large bands of white matter containing descending axons of upper motor neurons connecting the cerebral hemispheres with the pons and forming the main connection with the spinal cord.

Peking man (anthropology) A primitive form of man similar to the Neanderthal man the remains of which were found near Peking.

pellagra A nutritional deficiency of nicotinic acid characterized by diarrhea and dermatitis of sun-exposed surfaces and in severe cases, disturbances of the central nervous system, such as delirium, acute mania and depression.

pellet **1.** Small piece of food usually standardized by size, weight, and content which is used in animal experimentation. **2.** Small round object which is used in infant development studies for the infant to manipulate.

penetrance The percentage of cases in which genetic complement for a trait or disease is manifested in the developed organism or phenotype. The penetrance of the single genetic mechanism in schizophrenia is calculated as being of the order of 60 to 70% in the twin-family studies of Franz J. Kallmann.

peniaphobia Morbid fear of becoming poor.

penilingus Fellatio.

penis envy (S. Freud) A reaction of little girls at the phallic stage to the discovery of sexual differences. The girls feel they have been deprived of the penis (castrated) and wish to have it back. The resolution of the feminine castration complex and Oedipal wish is associated with the substitution of desiring having a child instead of having a penis.

penology The scientific study of the treatment of criminals which may be punitive or preventive in orientation.

pentobarbital A drug of the barbiturate family used to alleviate acute anxiety and fear.

pentothal Trademark for thiopental, a narcotic.

peotillomania Pulling of one's own penis as a nervous tic and not masturbation.

peptic ulcer See *ulcer, peptic.*

percentile **1.** (statistics) One of the 99 points which divide a group of scores or ranked distribution into 100 equal parts, each containing 1/100th of the scores or people. Percentiles are ranked from the bottom up from 1 to 99. Thus, the 62nd percentile indicates that 62% of the total group are below that point and 38% fall above it. **2.** (statistics) Centile rank or division.

percentile curve See *curve, percentile.*

percentile norm See *norm, percentile.*

percentile rank See *rank, percentile.*

percentile scale See *scale, percentile.*

percentile score See *score, percentile.*

percept **1.** The object of perception. **2.** A single instance of perception. This refers to the perceptual experience but not to the physical objects of perception which are stimuli.

percept-image A concrete fantasy or memory image of hallucinatory clarity, commonly seen in schizophrenic patients.

perception **1.** The process of obtaining information about the world through the senses. **2.** (nativism) The view that perception of the world as it exists is inborn. The adherents of this group were R. Descartes and I. Kant. **3.** (empiricism) The view that perception is based on previous experience, on the association of elements. This view is characteristic of British

associationists. **4.** (E.B. Titchener and W. Wundt) Perception is the result of learning added to raw sensations. The perceptions must be analyzed in order to yield the more basic psychological elements of sensation. **5.** (J.J. Gibson) Perception is the result of physical stimuli impinging on sense receptors. The emphasis is on the biological context which is believed to explain true perception. **6.** (Gestalt) Perception results from an innate organizing process. The basic unit is a configuration which is a whole that is greater than the sum of its parts and which determines the parts. An isomorphism between the organizing processes in perceived configurations and the chemical-electrical events taking place in the brain is postulated. **7.** (A. Ames) The transactional approach states that perception is based on assumptions about the construction of reality. Each individual is believed to develop a restricted set of perceptions through his own unique transactions with the environment to handle the infinite variety of possible retinal images which he receives. Perception becomes a learned act of constructing reality to fit one's assumptions about it.

perception, allocentric (E. G. Schachtel) Perception which is independent of the individual's immediate needs, of the stereotyped interpretation or the symbolic representation of an object.

perception, automorphic The tendency to view or think of others as similar to oneself, strengthened by ignoring differences and accentuating similarities.

perception, binocular Perception of only one visual field through the cooperative acting of both eyes. Binocular vision is the primary way of perceiving three-dimensionality and of seeing things in space in reference to the person seeing.

perception, extra-sensory See *extra-sensory perception.*

perception, intersensory Perception with more than one sense modality.

perception of time (P. Fraisse) The attention to, or apprehension of, change through the integration of a series of stimuli and characterized by the ability to conceive of duration, simultaneity, and succession. The perception of time is generally broken down into various categories: conditioning to time, which includes the temporal orientation of organisms, the periodicity of their behavior in terms of the circadian, or day-night, 24-hour cycle; the perception of the passage of time, duration, the ability to estimate various segments of time (ten seconds, ten minutes, etc.); control over time which is characterized by an active orientation of the self in time, in the present, the past and the future; and the experience of time, which includes the differences between "psychological" time and "clock" time and how the individual views and experiences time—its passage, its role in his life, and what it is.

perception, sense The awareness of the world as based on the stimulation of the sense organs.

perception, social **1.** Perception of social phenomena which includes persons and groups. **2.** Perception of the behaviors of another which reveal his feelings, intentions, and attitudes.

perception, subliminal The perception of stimuli below the threshold which are not perceived consciously but can influence behavior.

perceptual anchoring A frame of reference against which a perceptual response or judgment is made. This frame of reference in combination with the properties of the object itself influences the response.

perceptual defense See *defense, perceptual.*

perceptual distortion See *distortion, perceptual.*

perceptual field All those elements of the external environment which an organism perceives or experiences as he experiences them. This may include illusory or distorted elements.

perceptual handicap See *handicap, perceptual.*

perceptual learning See *learning, perceptual.*

perceptual restructuring The process of changing an already existing perception which entails changing the pattern of a percept.

perceptual schema The cognitive patterns which serve as a frame of reference against which an organism reacts to the environment and external stimuli.

perceptual segregation Separation of part of a perceptual field from the total field.

perceptual set See *set, perceptual.*

perceptual speed One of several hypothetical units which constitute the primary mental abilities. This ability consists of quick, efficient handling of perceptual forms.

perceptualization 1. Organization of sensory elements into a meaningful whole. 2. Awareness of a new or different meaning for a percept.

percipient 1. The perceiver. 2. (parapsychology) The person who receives the messages in telepathic communication.

performance 1. Activity. 2. Behavior in which an organism engages in response to a task or activity which leads to results, especially to a result which modifies the environment in some way.

performance curve See *curve, performance.*

performance test See *test, performance.*

periblepsis Strange staring expressing bewilderment, typical for a delirious state.

perimacular vision See *vision, perimacular.*

perimeter (vision) Instrument which maps the visual areas of the retina defining the sensitivity of the retinal field by determining what can be seen when different parts of the field are stimulated. It is used to measure the extent of achromatic and chromatic vision and to isolate areas of visual defect. The device consists of a circular band which rotates upon which stimuli are moved outward and inward. The subject fixates his eye at the center of rotation.

period 1. (physics) The time interval of a complete cycle of an event which happens regularly as, for example, the time it takes for a sound to occur. 2. (physiology) The length of time the menstrual flow lasts, or the menstrual period.

period, absolute refractory Short period of time following the discharge of a neuron, during which the neuron cannot be fired again.

periodic mania See *mania, periodic.*

periodic reinforcement Reinforcement which occurs intermittently rather than continuously according to a consistent predetermined time schedule.

peripheral region (K. Lewin) In differentiated personality structure, the peripheral region represents the acquired and not-fundamental personality traits.

peripheral vision Vision which takes place in the outer regions of the retina; the area of rods and color vision.

peripheralism A position which maintains that behavior should be viewed as a function of events taking place in the periphery of the organism.

peristalsis Progressive wavelike contraction which occurs in the alimentary tract forcing the contents of the tract downward.

peritoneum Membrane lining of the inside of the abdominal cavity which surrounds the enclosed viscera.

permeable 1. That which can be penetrated, permeated or passed through without being ruptured as with membranes which allow certain liquid to pass through. 2. A boundary which can be penetrated from the outside. 3. (topology) The degree to which activities or regions can be affected by forces from outside the region of the life space. 4. (G. A. Kelly) A construct which has the capacity to accept new elements into its field of applications.

permissive relation The relation of one factor to another such that a certain level must be reached on the former before the latter can function on the criterion at all.

permissiveness (developmental psychology) Allowing a child to express his feelings and ideas in ways that are cognitively and emotionally appropriate to his age and experience; often used in reference to parental non-punitive treatment of sexual, aggressive, or other behavior which by tradition is subject to socialization pressures.

permutations A statistical rule concerning the number of ways that N objects may be arranged in order according to the formula:
$$N! = (1)(2)(3)...(N-1)\ (N) \text{ where } 0! = 1$$

perphenazine A drug used as a tranquilizer and in the treatment of nausea.

perseveration 1. A tendency for organismic activity to occur without exteroceptive or specifiable stimuli. 2. A tendency to finish whatever was begun or difficulty experienced in changing methods while doing a task. 3. Pathological repeating of a word or phrase.

perseverative trace   See *trace, perseverative.*

persona   (C. G. Jung) An autonomous partial system or complex representing an individual's conscious attitude toward the outer world in accordance with his own inner archetypal needs. The ego is the core of the persona.

personal data sheet   A questionnaire which asks for specific biographical information about the individual usually inquiring about name, age, sex, occupation, interests, etc. It may include some psychological questions but based on habits and factual data rather than personality questions which would necessitate inferences.

personal document analysis   (G. W. Allport) In accordance with his idiographic view of psychology, Allport stressed the importance of analysis of personal diaries, letters, inventories, etc. as case study research techniques.

personal equation   1. Difference in performance which is due to individual differences. 2. Difference in simple reaction time between two persons. 3. Personal idiosyncrasies which must be considered in analyzing situations if the actual dynamics of situations are to be determined.

personal identity   See *identity.*

personal unconscious   See *unconscious, personal.*

personalistic psychology   See *psychology, personalistic.*

personality   The pattern of traits characterizing an individual person, trait here meaning any psychological characteristic of a person, including dispositions to perceive different situations similarly and to react consistently despite changing stimulus conditions, values, abilities, motives, defenses, and aspects of temperament, identity, and personal style. Though the pattern of such characteristics is necessarily unique, personality comprises all of a person's traits, not merely the ones that differentiate him from others. A descriptive, not a causally efficacious concept, personality (and traits) may be interpreted in terms either of observable consistencies in behavior or of inferred dispositions to behave (behavior being construed in the widest sense, to include implicit, only self-observable thoughts, feelings and emotions, impulses, dreams, and percepts, as well as actions and words observable by others). The full pattern or organization of traits becomes manifest only over the entire life span, so that personality is, in Murray's phrase, the study of lives; but the term is commonly used to refer to the observable and inferrable pattern at any one time. Personality is not synonymous with person, a more inclusive term denoting an individual human organism, which consists not only of a personality but that of a physique, an anatomy, a physiology, a social role and status, a being who expresses and transmits a culture—the focus of all the human (e.g., behavioral and medical) sciences.

personality (a psychometric conception)   An individual's unique pattern of characteristics, including his positions on a large number of trait variables.

personality, anal   See *character, anal.*

personality, basic   (A. Kardiner and R. Linton) A theory which maintains that common child raising methods practiced in a given society determine certain basic personality traits such as, e.g. assertion, aggressiveness, cooperation, etc. These traits, called "basic personality" determine the ethnic or national characteristics common to all members of a given social group notwithstanding the differences between the various individuals.

personality, compulsive   A personality type characterized by an excessive rigid involvement with standards, morality and conformity and a tendency to be orderly, inhibited and pedantic.

personality disorder, iatrogenic   Personality disorder caused by diagnostic or treatment exacerbation.

personality disorders   See *character disorders.*

personality, dual   1. Dissociation. 2. A form of personality disorder in which the personality is divided, as it were, into two separate, distinct parts, each of which functions with its own fairly independent organization and mental life though there is some degree of unity between them.

personality dynamics   The motivations, emotions, and other internal forces which underlie behavior.

personality, epileptic   Complex of negative traits and related behavioral manifestations including aggressiveness, selfishness, religious fanaticism, morbid egotism, temper tantrums and stubborn uncooperativeness found in some epileptics. This personality syndrome is not exhibited by the majority of epileptics nor exclusively by epileptics; the relationship between epilepsy and this pattern is unclear.

personality, factorial theory of   (R. B. Cattell) Concluding that clinical observation alone is not sufficiently reliable to develop and test theories of personality structure, Cattell began in 1940 what became a thirty-year factor analytic investigation of correlations, over people and over time, in life (L), questionnaire (Q) and behavioral test (T) data. The resulting concepts in traits and states, e.g., surgency, ego strength, regression, superego, anxiety and arousal, cover some *thirty primaries, twelve secondaries,* etc., in a hierarchy. A specific response behavior a_j is estimated according to the model:

$$a_j = b_{j1}\,T_1 + \ldots b_{jp}T_p + b_{j1s}S_1 + \ldots b_{jsq}S_q +$$

specific terms, where the T's are p broad common traits and the S's are q broad common states. The model, when the T's are known ability, temperament and dynamic traits, has yielded excellent criterion predictions. The b terms (behavioral indices or loadings) describe the environment, thus brought to interaction with the individual personality vector of T's. The *dynamic calculus* is the more specialized development of this theory in the dynamic realm.

personality, inadequate   Class of personality disturbances in which the individuals are characterized by inadaptability, social incompatibility and inadequate responses to intellectual, emotional, social, and physical demands without being grossly physically or mentally deficient on examination.

personality inventory See *inventory, personality.*

personality measurement A general term for a variety of psychological techniques which measure various aspects of personality. Personality measurement techniques include paper-pencil tests, projective techniques, interest inventories, attitudes scales, rating and performance techniques, etc.

personality, multiple An extreme form of dissociative reaction to stress in which two or more separate personalities exist. The person may shift from one personality to another which is often very different from the other. Each personality has no memory of the other's thoughts and actions. One of the personalities may function unconsciously and be aware of the conscious personality but it manifests itself early indirectly as in automatic writing.

personality, oral See *character, oral.*

personality, passive-aggressive Behavior syndrome characterized by passivity and aggressiveness with the aggressiveness often expressed passively by obstructionism, stubbornness, pouting, etc. This pattern usually reflects hostility and resentment at the individual's inability to establish a satisfactory relationship with a person or institution upon which he is overdependent.

personality, prepsychotic An individual whose behavior is indicative of an approaching psychosis.

personality, sociopathic Personality disorder characterized by poor social relationships and inability to conform to cultural, ethical, and social norms. This broad category may include antisocial, asocial, or dyssocial attitudes and behavior and often sexual anomalies.

personality sphere (R. B. Cattell) Essentially, the range of measurable human personality.

personality tests See *tests, personality.*

personality, theories of: biological 1. Theories of personality which emphasize the biological nature of personality. 2. See *constitutional theory of personality: W. H. Sheldon.* 3. See *holistic theory of personality.* 3. See *Maslow's theory of personality.*

personality trait Any respect in which one person differs from others. It can often be represented by a linear dimension. Otherwise, it is a matter of presence or absence, or membership in categories.

personality types Classification of human beings according to certain distinct personality features and typical behavioral patterns. There are several personality typologies (Eysenck, Freud, Fromm, Hippocrates, Jung, Kretschmer, Sheldon, Wolman, etc.), which describe particular personality types. See *type.*

personification 1. Attribution of personal characteristics to inanimate objects, an abstraction, or various phenomena of nature. 2. (H.S. Sullivan) An abstract of what an individual perceives as the pattern of another's interaction with him or his interaction with another, based on feelings, attitudes and conceptions which grow from recurrent interpersonal experiences with need satisfaction and anxiety. Personifications are not accurate representations of the person to whom they refer but images formed to better deal with others. The individual's first personifications are of the good mother, who satisfies needs, and the bad mother, who causes anxiety, neither of which is a true picture of the 'real' mother.

personified self (H.S. Sullivan) The personification referring to one's self, based on the rudimentary personifications of: good-me, the organization of interpersonal experiences in which satisfaction and tenderness have been forthcoming from the mother because she was pleased with the infant's behavior; bad-me, the organization of interpersonal experiences in which anxiety has been evoked by the mother; and not-me, the organization of interpersonal experiences in which horror, dread, and intense-anxiety has been evoked. The personified self is part of the self-system and as such works to protect the individual from anxiety threatening to his security by interfering with objective self-evaluation.

personnel management Supervision of the employees of a firm or institution which entails interviewing job applicants, selection, training and placement of personnel, and dealing with problems which affect employees.

personnel psychology Personnel psychology is perhaps the earliest aspect of industrial and organizational psychology. It revolves around the study of individual differences and the comparative analysis of candidates for a position. Its roots stem from psychometrics, educational psychology, learning theory and applied personality theory. Organizational psychology studies people within organizations to implement effective coordination and control. It is closely related to social psychology and sociology. In human factors engineering, the working environment is manipulated to bring about compatibility with the individual. Human factors engineering is related to the general field of applied psychology, to industrial engineering and to psychophysiology.

personnel research See *research, personnel.*

personology 1. The study of personality. 2. The principle that behavior should be studied in terms of its relevance to the personality. 3. (H. A. Murray; R. W. White) Scientific biography; the study of lives.

perspective, aerial A cue to depth perception in which as distance increases color quality becomes less saturated and increasingly blurred while outlines within the image become less sharp.

perspective, alternating Changes in the perception of a stimulus pattern that lead to multiple interpretations as a result of the sense of a third dimension, created by the part of a figure or drawing that appears, alternately, closer and farther away as the figure is fixated. See *ambiguous figures; reversible figures.*

perspective, angular Represents the relationship between lines in the visual field and those formed by the images of the lines projected on the retina.

perspective, linear The apparent change in size of objects at different distances from the eye and the principles according to which distance determines the varying sizes of the visual image.

perturbation (information theory) A disturbance or excess presented with or superimposed upon the necessary information of a message. Such disturbance tends to obscure the message and thus lessens the probability that the receiver will respond appropriately to the message.

perversion A socially disapproved or prohibited form of conduct, particularly in sexual life. Interpretation varies and the term itself is becoming outmoded.

perversion, infantile polymorphous (S. Freud) The theory that a child's sexual instinct has no specific direction which results in the child's inclinations which might be considered perverted if performed by an adult.

pesticide poisoning See *poisoning, DDT; poisoning, parathion.*

petrification The process of being petrified or turned to stone which is sometimes interpreted as being a punishment for unacceptable voyeuristic or scopophilic impulses.

peyote An hallucinogenic drug derived from a cactus which causes psychedelic effects such as radical mood changes, delusions and hallucinations.

PF Study See *Picture-Frustration Study.*

Pfaffmann, Carl (1913-   ) U.S. physiological psychologist, pioneered electrophysiological studies of sense of taste. First to show limited specificity of single afferent taste fibers and introduced the neural pattern concept of taste discrimination. Showed that increased taste preferences not due to increased sensitivity of receptor. With Carr also found no receptor change from gonadal hormones again indicating stability of peripheral receptors. With Pfaff and Scott did find differential processing of olfactory information in preoptic brain area related to mating behavior and olfactory sensory responses in hypothalamus. His correlated studies of physiology and behavior clarified mechanisms underlying the sensory basis of reinforcement and the "Pleasures of Sensation."

Phaedra complex See *complex, Phaedra.*

phagocyte White blood cell; defends the organism against foreign bodies.

phagomania Morbid urge for overeating.

phagophobia Morbid fear of food and of gaining weight.

phallic character (psychoanalysis) An individual with permanent and consistent patterns of functioning which reflect reaction formation to castration fear experienced during the oedipal stage. Self-assuredness and boastfulness, combined with narcissism, vanity and sensitiveness are the main characteristics. Exhibitionistic and overtly aggressive behavior is a reaction formation to castration fear. In women, penis envy may be elaborated either by the assumption of a masculine role or by vindictive behavior toward males.

phallic sadism See *sadism, phallic.*

phallic stage (S. Freud) The third stage of psychosexual development occurring from the age of three to seven during which the child derives pleasurable sensations from stimulation of the genital organs. During this stage, each child has the desire to displace the parent of the same sex and to possess the parent of the opposite sex. These wishes are repressed because of castration anxiety for the boy and fear of loss of the mother's love for the girl.

phallic symbol (S. Freud) In dreams, knives, sticks, swords, etc. are phallic symbols as they represent the phallus.

phallus Penis in a state of erection.

phaneromania A morbid, compulsive urge to touch one's own body, e.g. such as one's nose, breasts, lips, etc.

phantasm See *fantasm.*

phantasmagoria Raising or recalling spirits of the dead.

phantasmoscopia Hallucinations of ghosts and spirits.

phantasy See *fantasy.*

phantasy formation See *fantasy formation.*

phantom limb The illusion of sensations in an amputated limb or stump. The prosthesis can even be experienced as a natural limb.

pharmacogenetics The sphere of biochemical genetics dealing with drug responses and their genetically controlled variations. Genetically controlled variation in response to certain anti-depressant agents is an example.

pharmacologic therapy Chemotherapy; treatment of mental patients with chemical substances, especially stimulants for depressive states and tranquilizers for excited states.

pharynx A part of the throat which leads to the larynx and esophagus.

phase difference (audition) Differences in the phase sequences of two sound waves as when crest does not correspond with crest and trough does not correspond with trough. Phase difference aids in the localization of sounds.

phase sequence (D.O. Hebb) A series of cell-assembly actions, theoretically constituting the stream of thought.

phasmophobia Morbid fear of ghosts.

phenelzine An antidepressant drug of the monoamine oxidase inhibitor group used in the treatment of depression and psychosis.

phengophobia Morbid fear of daylight.

phenobarbital A drug of the barbiturate family

used in the alleviation of acute anxiety and fear and also to control seizures.

phenocopy A phenotypic trait resulting from a specific genotype is mimicked by the interplay of an environmental effect, e.g., temperature or sunlight which duplicates hereditary traits of the skin.

phenomena, hypnagogic Processes occurring during the hypnagogic state.

phenomenal field See *field of consciousness.*

phenomenal regression See *regression, phenomenal.*

phenomenal report A verbal report of what one has experienced in a given experimental situation from a phenomenological viewpoint.

phenomenal self See *self, phenomenal.*

phenomenon, autokinetic The perception by various individuals of different amounts of apparent movement when exposed to a stationary light for some time.

phenomenology 1. The science of the subjective processes by which phenomena are presented. It deals with mental processes and concentrates on the ideal, essential elements of experiences. 2. The investigation of occurrences or phenomena as they happen directly in experience without interpretation.

phenomotive (W. Stern) A motive which can be discovered and observed introspectively.

phenothiazine poisoning See *poisoning, chlorpromazine.*

phenylketonuria (PKU) A genetic metabolic disorder transmitted as an autosomal recessive causing a lack in the enzyme necessary for the oxidation of phenylalanine resulting in an accumulation of phenylpyruvic acid. The clinical picture is of a severely retarded child with blond hair, blue eyes, fair skin, eczema and microcephaly.

phenylpyruvic oligophrenia See *phenylketonuria.*

phenylthiocarbamide A substance whose taste in people is determined by a single gene pair. The ability to taste is dominant.

phi coefficient (r_ϕ) The measure of association appropriate when two variables are divided into two qualitatively separate classes of observations, working from a four-fold contingency table. The formula is:

$$r\phi = \frac{bc - ad}{\sqrt{(a+c)\ (b+d)\ (a+b)\ (c+d)}}$$

where the letters refer to the cell and marginal frequencies.

phi-gamma function ($\phi(\tau)$) The integration of a normal distribution of psychophysical judgments obtained by the method of constant-stimulus difference stated in terms of h; an index of precisely how closely the data are centered about the mean. The formula is:

$$P = \int_{-\infty}^{\tau} \frac{11}{\sqrt{\pi}}\ e^{-\tau}\, d\gamma,$$

where the $\int_{-\infty}^{\tau}$ is the derivative from negative infinity to gamma, e is the common log base

(2.718281) raised to the negative gamma power ($-\tau$) and $d\tau$ is the change observed in the gamma value.

phi-gamma hypothesis The assertion or assumption that the data obtained by the method of constant stimulus difference will fit the phi-gamma function.

phi phenomenon (M. Wertheimer) The production of apparent movement by the successive appearance of two stationary stimuli, like the flashing of two lights. It is perceived as the movement of a single stimulus from one point in space to another.

philomimesia A compulsion to imitate and/or mimic.

philosophy of psychology Philosophical problems in psychology, such as theory formation, conceptualization, causation, reductionism, etc. Most of these problems belong to philosophy of science applied to psychology.

phlegmatic type See *type, phlegmatic.*

phobia Morbid fear based on displacement of an original fear, e.g., a patient afraid of his aggressive, genocidal impulses may develop agoraphobia, (fear of open places), thus preventing himself from acting out his aggressive impulses.

phobia, animal 1. Severe and unreasonable fear of animals, which may come from learning by experience or by being told of danger from imagination concerning the feared animal or identification with someone who fears the animal in question. 2. (psychoanalysis) Extreme fear of an animal involving the repression and projection of unacceptable impulses onto the animal.

phobia, school Fear of attending school, most commonly seen in elementary school children usually as a result of anxiety about separation from the mother.

phobic reactions Irrational fearful responses.

phobophobia A morbid fear of ever experiencing fear.

phocomelia A deformity of limbs in which the hands are attached directly to the shoulders with arms missing.

phonantograph An instrument which records sound waves graphically.

phonation Production of the sounds of speech.

phone Element of speech; a single symbol in the system of phonetics.

phoneidoscope A device which facilitates the visual observation of sound waves by reflecting light off a film which is made to vibrate.

phonelescope An instrument which makes possible the observation, measurement, and photographic recording of sound waves through the use of a recorder which is attached to a vibrating diaphragm.

phoneme 1. Similar speech sounds which are considered to be the same sound and may be spelled with the same or with equivalent letters. 2. An hallucination in which speaking or distinct sounds are heard as in hearing "voices".

phonetics Study of the production of vocal sounds with emphasis on their relation to language, though including psychological, physiological, and physical relationships and data.

phonism A form of synasthesia in which a sensation of sound is produced by a sensation in another sense modality or a thought.

phonogram 1. A symbolic illustration of a vocal sound. 2. A diagram which illustrates the vocal organs in the process of producing vocal sounds.

phonomania Homicidal impulses.

phonophobia Morbid fear of sounds including one's own voice.

phonoscope or phonoprojectoscope General term for any instrument which makes sound waves visible.

phoria The way the eyes turn or orient themselves to sight an object.

phorometry Measurement of the amount of balance or imbalance which exists in the external muscles which turn the eyeballs.

phosphene A phosphorescent form of light seen in the dark which is produced by the eyeball being distorted due to the normal process of accommodation and convergence or to pressure externally or to mechanical distortion.

phot A unit of illumination the same as that light produced at a surface which is one centimeter distant from a uniform point source of light of one candlepower strength.

photerythrosity Increased sensitivity to the red end of the spectrum exhibited by some people.

photic driving Stimulation of the brain rhythmically through the application to the eyes of a stroboscopic light to heighten brain waves. Alpha rhythm may be made to correspond with the light.

photism 1. Hallucination of light. 2. A form of synesthesia, in which a visual sensation of color or light is produced by a sensation in another sense modality or thought.

photochromatic interval Stimulus intensity range over which colored or chromatic stimulus can be perceived as light but cannot yet be seen as color or hue.

photoma Visual hallucination; seeing a flash of light without external stimulation.

photomania A morbid craving for light.

photometric measure Measure of light energy given in photometric terms as opposed to physical terms or sensation terms.

photometry The science of the measurement of light.

photophobia An extreme dislike of light.

photopic adaptation See *adaptation, brightness.*

photopic vision See *vision, photopic.*

photoreceptor Receptors which are stimulated by light and function in vision such as the retinal rods and cones.

phototropism An automatic movement (tropism) toward light (positive) or away from light (negative) caused by chemical or physical factors.

phrenitis (Hippocrates) An ancient term for the inflammation of the brain.

phrenology An obsolete theory which linked mental faculties to particular parts of the skull and maintained that the shape of the skull is indicative of the predominance of a particular faculty.

phronemophobia A morbid fear of reasoning.

phthisic type See *type, phthisic.*

phyloanalysis (T. Burrow) Method of treating behavior disorders which is based on the assumption that the disorders of individuals and of society are the result of impaired tensional balance which affects the individual's internal and external relationships.

phylobiology (T. Burrow) Behavioral science which investigates the phyletic motivation of organisms' reactions as they mediate the individual's rapport with the environment. It assumes biological unity to be a central principle directing motivation.

phylogenesis; phylogeny The origin and evolutionary development of a species.

phylogenetic; phylogenic Pertaining to the origin and development of a species.

phylogenetic principle See *principle, phylogenetic.*

phylogeny The evolutionary development of a species.

phylum Classification of biological species.

physical therapy See *physiotherapy.*

physicalism See *logical positivism.*

physiogenesis The origin of a normal or abnormal function of the organism.

physiognomy 1. Using the external appearance of the face and other external bodily features as a means of mental characteristics or attitudes. 2. Facial expression.

physiological age The level of physiological development attained at a certain chronological age.

physiological limit The point beyond which there can be no further gain in efficiency due to practice. The limit is not necessarily set by the physiological structure of the organism.

physiological memory See *memory, physiological.*

physiological psychology See *psychology, physiological.*

physiological therapy See *therapy, physiological.*

physiology Branch of biological science which investigates the functions of living organisms or of their parts and structures.

physiopathology Study of physiological disorders including both organic and functional disturbances.

physiotherapy Branch of medicine which deals with physical forms of treatment such as hydrotherapy, massage, and the use of light, heat, cold, etc.

physique Overall body structures and organization; general physical appearance.

physostigmine poisoning See *poisoning, physostigmine*.

pia mater Vascular membrane consisting of a network of blood vessels enclosed in thin tissue covering the surface of the brain and the spinal cord.

Piaget, Jean (1896-1980) Swiss psychologist, who started his scientific career as a zoologist and later, as a philosopher. His diverse interests led him to do postdoctoral work with the psychiatrist, Bleuler, in Zurich and with Dr. Simon in Paris. It was during an attempt to standardize Burt's reasoning tests upon Parisian children that the zoologist and philosopher was transformed into the child psychologist and epistemologist. After his work in Paris, Piaget was successively Director of Research at the Rousseau Institute in Geneva, Privat Docent at the Faculty of Science of the University of Geneva, Professor of Psychology and of the Philosophy of Science at the University of Neuchatel, Professor of General Psychology at the University of Lausanne, Professor of Sociology and of Experimental Psychology at the University of Geneva. He was named Titular Professor of Genetic Psychology at the Sorbonne in 1952. Piaget is currently co-director of the Institute of Educational Science in Geneva, as well as Professor of Experimental Psychology at the Faculty of Science at the University of Geneva. Piaget devoted his research and theoretical talents to the systematic understanding of the mental evolution of the child, as well as to problems of epistemology. His current bibliography totals to more than 18,000 printed pages. Many of his works have been translated into numerous languages and some of them are now regarded as classics in the field. Piaget has received honorary degrees from universities around the world, including, most recently, the University of Pennsylvania. He is the founder of the Center for the Study of Genetic Epistemology in Geneva, which each year brings together scholars from all over the world to deal with problems of epistemology. Under Piaget's editorship, the Center has published more than twenty volumes of original research on epistemological problems.

piano theory of hearing See *hearing, theory of: resonance theory*.

pica **1.** The eating of non-nutritional substances such as paint, cornstarch or hair. **2.** The craving for unusual foods which occurs frequently during pregnancy.

Pickford Projective Pictures Test See *test, Pickford Projective Pictures*.

Pick's disease (A. Pick) A presenile endogeneous disorder of insidious origin characterized by a progressive state of dementia resulting from circumscribed cerebral atrophy. A disturbance of abstract thinking and aphasia may occur. The onset occurs usually in the range of forty-five to fifty years with a preponderance of women being afflicted.

pictograph; pictogram See *ideogram*.

Picture Arrangement Test See *test, Picture Arrangement*.

picture completion test See *test, picture completion*.

Picture-Frustration Study (S. Rosenzweig) A controlled projective technique introduced in 1945 which measures a person's reaction to frustration. It consists of twenty-four cartoon-like drawings, each depicting a situation in which one person is frustrated by another. The comments of the frustrator are written and the subject is asked to provide the response of the frustrated person which is interpreted in terms of direction of the response and type of response. An overall conformity rating can be determined. There is a form for adults, for children and for the study of attitude toward minority groups developed by J. F. P. Brown.

picture impressions test See *test, picture impressions*.

picture interpretation test See *test, picture interpretation*.

Picture World Test See *test, Picture World*.

Piderit drawings Large series of very simple outlines of the human face which illustrate various emotional expressions. These are cut up into interchangeable pieces which are used to study how changing the expression on one part of the face affects overall expression and also to see how many potential varieties of emotional facial expression there are.

Piéron, Henri (1881-1964) One of the first major experimental psychologists in France, long-time professor at the Collège de France in Paris. Author of books on experimental psychology in 1928 and on mental development and intelligence in 1930, he also edited the major French psychological journal, *L'Année Psychologique*.

pigmentary retinal lipoid neuronal heredo-degeneration See *Spielmeyer-Vogt's disease*.

Pillars of Corti See *rods of Corti*.

pilomotor response See *response, pilomotor*.

pilot study A short-range exploratory study which is carried out as preparation for a larger, more involved study in order to test the feasibility of proposed methods or projects and to ascertain to some degree what problems may be encountered and what the outcome may be.

pineal body or gland; epiphysis cerebri **1.** A small glandular outgrowth of the thalamic region at the top of the third ventricle. **2.** According to Descartes, the place where soul and body interact.

Pinel, Philippe (1745-1826) French psychiatrist who during the French Revolution removed the chains from the inmates of the Salpetriere hospital and introduced a liberal approach to the inmates whom he perceived as victims of diseases, deserving humane treatment.

Pinel's system (P. Pinel) Eighteenth century classification system of mental disorder which divided psychiatric disorders into four categories: melancholias, manias with delirium, manias without delirium, and dementia or mental deterioration. The Pinel system included a systematic description of mental disturbances and of symptoms.

pinocytosis Absorption of fluid by cells which is a means of metabolic transport in the central nervous system.

Pintner-Paterson Scale of Performance Tests See *tests, Pintner-Paterson Scale of Performance.*

Piotrowski system An approach to the Rorschach test developed by Zygmunt Piotrowski. It represented an empirically based approach which differs significantly from methods developed by H. Rorschach and other Rorschach systematizers.

Piper's law The threshold for luminance in a consistently stimulated area of the retina is inversely proportional to the square root of the stimulated area.

pitch, absolute 1. The pitch of a sound as a function of its vibration rate. **2.** Ability to recognize and reproduce notes accurately without comparing any particular note or tone with another.

Pithecanthropus erectus An extinct ape considered to be closely related to modern man and classified as the lowest human in the evolutionary scale yet discovered. The species is identified and represented by a skull found in Java.

pithecoid Like an ape or monkey.

pithiatism 1. The use of persuasion or forced suggestion to treat hysteria and other nervous disorders. **2.** Rarely used term for hysteria.

Pitre's rule The general course of recovery from aphasia for a multilingual person begins first and is most complete with the most familiar, fluent language and proceeds gradually to less well-known languages.

pituitarism Pituitary gland overactivity.

pituitary-adrenal axis A system in the body of an organism which responds to situations of stress by secreting a hormone from the pituitary gland which activates the adrenal gland to secrete its substances that are necessary for the organism to fight harm or infection.

pituitary gland, hypophysis cerebri See *gland, pituitary.*

PKU See *phenylketonuria.*

place theory of hearing See *hearing, theory of: resonance theory.*

placebo 1. A substance with no medicinal properties which causes a patient to improve because of his belief in its efficacy. **2.** (experimental) A substance administered to a control group in an experiment in which the experimental group receives a drug in order to eliminate the effect of the act of administering the drug.

placebo therapy See *therapy, placebo.*

placement (personnel) Assignment of people to jobs according to abilities, experience, and interests in order that the person be well-suited and satisfied in the job.

placement test See *test, placement.*

placenta Vascular structure in mammals which attaches the fetus to the uterus and transmits nourishment and respiration from the mother to the fetus.

placing reaction When a few weeks old infant is supported under his arms and the dorsal part of the feet touches a table, he lifts his legs and places the feet on the table.

plan A neural program for effective action.

planchette Instrument used in automatic writing experiments. It consists of a pencil just above or on a smooth surface which records involuntary movements of the hand.

plantar reflex See *reflex, plantar.*

plantigrade Type of standing or locomotion in which the whole foot touches the ground as in bears and man.

plasm 1. Plasma or liquid portion of blood and lymph. **2.** Cellular substance.

plasma The liquid portion of blood and lymph consisting of a solution containing proteins and similar to interstitial body fluid.

plasmon (biology) Hereditary elements in the egg cytoplasm as opposed to the genome characteristics.

plasticity 1. Potential for flexible response. **2.** Adaptability. **3.** Teachability or possessing the capacity for learning.

plateau A flat period in a learning curve which indicates an apparent stop of learning which occurs temporarily during the process of learning a complicated task or skill.

Plato (427-347 B.C.) Greek philosopher, born in Athens, wrote Phaedo, Republic, Symposium and several other works. Plato believed in immortality of the soul. The soul has three parts, the highest one being the reason; the middle emotion and will; the lowest part is comprised of sensuous desires and appetites. The reason is located in the brain, the emotions in the heart, and the appetites in the liver. The rational part of the soul existed before birth; when the soul enters the human body, it acquires the two irrational parts.

platycephaly Flattening of the crown of the skull.

platykurtosis The relative degree of flatness of a frequency curve.

play need See *need, play*.

play therapy With children, the use of dolls and other play material as a measure of securing free expression of feelings and ideas; attributes of the play, including thematic content and organization, are treated as expressions in the therapeutic sense, with the usual interventions: reflection, interpretation, confrontation, etc.

pleasure-pain principle See *principle, pleasure-pain*.

pleasure principle (S. Freud) The principle which dominates id activity, calling for immediate reduction of tension through the satisfaction and gratification of all instinctual demands and impulses.

"pleasures of sensation" The hedonic or affective responses to certain classes of stimuli. Thus moderately sweet solutions are pleasant. Other stimuli may elicit displeasure, e.g. bitter solutions or pain prick. Weak lights and sounds may be pleasant, intense sounds and lights, unpleasant. Such affective aspects of sensation relate to the value or reinforcement value of stimuli as contrasted with the cognitive purely informational properties of sensory experience.

pleiotropy If a single gene or gene pair produces multiple effects, it is said to exhibit pleiotropy. Certain neurological syndromes exemplify this.

pleniloquence Compulsive, excessive talking.

pleocytosis Excessive cells in the cerebrospinal fluid associated with meningeal irritation.

pleonexia Morbid greediness.

plethysmograph An instrument used to record changes in the volume of a part of a body resulting from fluctuations in blood supply.

plexus A network of nerves, blood vessels, veins or lymphatics.

plot 1. (statistics) To record scores or make entries on a scatter diagram or frequency table. 2. Scatter diagram.

pluralism 1. The condition or situation of being plural. 2. Philosophical doctrine that reality consists of several irreducible, ultimate elements rather than only one.

plutomania Extreme greediness or desire for riches.

PMD See *dystrophy, pseudohypertrophic muscular*.

pneumococcal meningitis See *meningitis, pneumococcal*.

pneumogastric nerve See *nerve, vagus*.

pnigerophobia Morbid fear of being smothered.

pnigophobia Morbid fear of choking.

Poetzl phenomenon To dream about parts of a tachistoscopically viewed picture which were not consciously noticed or reported at the time of viewing.

Poggendorf illusion A geometrical illusion that the seen sections of a straight diagonal line, the center part of which is concealed behind a pair of vertical or horizontal parallel lines, are not parts of the same line.

poinephobia Morbid fear of being punished.

point-biserial correlation See *correlation, point-biserial*.

point, critical See *critical point*.

point estimation (statistics) The use of sample values or statistics to predict population parameters. It is so called because a single value or point in the space of all values is taken as an estimate.

point for point correspondence The relationship between two variables so that for every point on one variable, there is a corresponding point on the other variable.

point hour ratio Grade-point average which is an index of grades with each course letter grade weighted according to the number of credit hours the course is assigned and given a numerical value according to a sliding scale as follows: $A = 4, B = 3, C = 2$, and $D = 1$. The over-all average is calculated by multiplying the numerical value by the number of credit hours of the course and dividing the sum of these scores by the total number of credit hours.

point of regard See *regard, point of*.

point of subjective equality (PSE) (psychophysics) The value of the comparison stimulus energy which is equally likely to be judged as higher or lower than the test stimulus. It is the value of the comparison stimulus that is subjectively equal to the standard stimulus for the given stimulus conditions.

point-sampling A succession of behavior observations made for only an instant at regular intervals; measure is the frequency of occasions on which the act was occurring at the instant of recording.

point scale See *scale, point*.

point, score See *score, raw*.

"poison-pen" psychotherapy See *psychotherapy, "poison-pen"*.

poisoning, arsenic Early signs of acute toxicity are limited; mainly to gastrointestinal symptoms of vomiting and watery, bloody diarrhea. In the terminal stages, seizures and coma are present. Chronic toxicity is characterized by burning sensations, optic neuritis and chronic gastrointestinal upset.

poisoning, atropine Symptoms include blurred vision, fever, lethargy, delirium, excitability, confusion, comas, seizures resulting from the disruption of parasympathetic nervous system functioning by the inhibition of the acetylcholine effect. In cases of acute toxicity, permanent central nervous system effects are not common.

poisoning, barium Acute toxicity results in muscle spasms, vomiting, weakness, cardiac irregularities and, if untreated, death. Chronic toxicity is rare.

Severe and prolonged seizures may result in chronic cerebral changes.

poisoning, bromate Predominant symptoms of poisoning are those of renal and central nervous systems. In acute toxicity the patient vomits violently and experiences colic and diarrhea, with lethargy, coma and seizures following. Difficulties with anuria are very common and may lead to permanent renal failure and death.

poisoning, carbon monoxide Inhalation of carbon monoxide results in tissue anoxia, with symptoms ranging from headache to light-headedness to coma and death. Permanent intellectual impairment is a common consequence when the person has been comatose.

poisoning, carbon tetrachloride May occur through ingestion or inhalation with primary symptoms of liver, kidney, and central nervous system damage. If chronic may lead to confusion, blurred vision, personality alteration and memory loss.

poisoning, chlorpromazine Acute toxicity with this tranquilizing drug of the phenothiazine group. It causes lethargy, usually some degree of hypotension, nausea, occasionally visual difficulties, tremors and disturbance in voluntary motor movement. Residuals are rare, but include hepatic and hematologic difficulties.

poisoning, DDT Acute toxicity with the common insecticide results in irritability, excitability, muscular tremors, weakness and eventually major motor seizures. Chronic exposure can result in paresthesias, tremors, and personality changes. There are often permanent residuals if the patient has reached the seizure stage.

poisoning, epinephrine Causes stimulation of the sympathetic nervous system and acute toxicity. Leads to central nervous system excitement, irritability, fever, rapid heart activity, dilation of the pupils and frequently, seizures and ensuing coma. Chronic toxicity may lead to personality disorders.

poisoning, ergot Causes contraction of the smooth muscles of the gut, uterus and arterioles and results in light-headedness, seizures and coma.

poisoning, ethyl alcohol Toxicity leads to central nervous system symptoms including incoordination, slowing of reaction time, blurred vision progressing to gross incoordination, impairment of judgment, stupor, and coma.

poisoning, ethylene dichloride Primary involvement is of the central nervous system with lesser involvement of the liver, kidney and heart. Symptoms of poisoning, include stupor, progressing to coma along with vomiting and hypertension.

poisoning, ethylene glycol Results in kidney and liver damage and symptoms include stupor, coma and possibly seizures.

poisoning, heavy metal See *poisoning, lead; poisoning, arsenic; poisoning, mercury; poisoning, thallium; poisoning, barium.*

poisoning, kerosene The patient suffers from pulmonary edema, with central nervous system depression leading possibly to coma and seizures. Chronic exposure may lead to peripheral neuritis and personality changes.

poisoning, lead Acute toxicity leads to nausea, vomiting, weakness, and pain in the extremities and abdomen. Chronic lead poisoning leads to peripheral neuritis and involvement of the central nervous system with resultant changes in level of consciousness, convulsions, changes in pulse rate, spasticity and, commonly, mental retardation.

poisoning, mercury Acute toxicity leads to gastrointestinal disturbances of vomiting, abdominal colic, and bloody diarrhea and sometimes to prominent central nervous system symptoms. Chronic toxicity leads to fatigue, irritability, muscular weakness, psychotic personality changes and, occasional seizures.

poisoning, parathion A type of organo phosphate insecticide with symptoms including nausea, epigastric pain, excessive perspiration, vomiting, diarrhea, respiratory failure and central nervous system involvement manifested in anxiety, confusion, withdrawal, depression and later, coma. Permanent central nervous system residuals including changes in personality, judgment and intellect have been reported.

poisoning, phenothiazine See *poisoning, chlorpromazine.*

poisoning, physostigmine Acute toxicity with this autonomic group drug leads to abdominal colic, perspiration, tremors, bronchospasm, seizures, coma and death.

poisoning, salicylate Usually caused by acetysalicylic acid (aspirin) overdose, early symptoms of toxicity are hyperventilation and vomiting, followed by lethargy, disorientation and coma. Chronic toxicity symptoms include muscle tenderness and spasm, decreased auditory acuity, paresthesias, excitability, delirium, and hallucinations.

poisoning, thallium Toxicity results in neurological symptoms including myoclonic jerking and rigidity. Chronic ingestion often results in residual cerebral difficulties including intellectual, motor and personality changes.

poisoning, toluene Toluene is a common constituent of airplane glue and is thought to be the offending agent in patients who suffer from toxicity secondary to glue sniffing. Symptoms include light-headedness, euphoria, headache, visual blurring, tremors and, in later stages, coma and seizures. Chronic symptoms include personality changes, irritability and headache.

poisoning, trichloroethylene Acute toxicity results in central nervous system depression initially, leading to light-headed sensations, headache and hyperactivity followed by coma. Chronic toxicity often leads to lethargy and personality change. Liver damage is occasionally a limiting factor in the patient's recovery.

poisoning, triorthocresyl phosphate The usual sequelae of ingestion are demyelinization of peripheral nerves and, to some extent, degenerative changes within the spinal cord. Lower motor neuron paralysis, particularly of the distal muscles of the extremities, is common. Acute toxicity leads to weakness of the distal muscles with footdrop, wrist drop, loss of deep tendon reflexes and, in more severe cases, weakness of the ocular, laryngeal, and respiratory muscles.

Poisson distribution See *distribution, Poisson.*

Poisson series A frequency distribution in which the frequencies are listed by:

$$e^{-m} \ \left(1, m, \frac{m^2}{2!}, \frac{m^3}{3!}, \frac{m^4}{4!} \ldots \right)$$

where m is the mean value of the distribution, and e^{-m} is the common log base (2.718281) raised to the negative mean value of the distribution.

polar continuum A continuum or series which ranges from one opposite to another. The opposite are the end points as in the personality scale for submission-dominance.

polar variable See *variable, polar.*

polarization, mass The focusing of attention of a large number of people upon the same information or communication.

poliodystrophy See *Alper's disease.*

poliomyelitis A disease, often paralytic, which includes symptoms of malaise, muscle pains, stiffness and motor weariness. Difficulties with this autonomic nervous system lead to symptoms of hypertension, perspiration and, occasionally, vomiting. Death is more common in adults than in children.

polyandry Marriage of one woman with more than one man.

polychloric correlation See *correlation, polychloric.*

polychromatic Multi-colored.

polydactylism Possessing more than five fingers or toes.

polydipsia Excessive craving for fluids.

polygamy Marriage of one man with more than one woman, or one woman with more than one man.

polygenic Polygenic inheritance is inheritance by many genes at different loci, with small additive effects. Synonyms: multifactorial or quantitative. This type of mechanism is the major one involved in the genetic transmission of intelligence.

polygenic heredity See *heredity, polygenic.*

polygraph An apparatus for the simultaneous recording of a number of physiological reactions or activities.

polygyny Marriage of one man with more than one woman.

polyhybridity; polyhybridism (genetics) Difference in more than three hereditary characteristics in a hybrid or a hybrid possessing several hereditary differences.

polymorphism 1. The derivation of several varieties of animal or individual from the same parent. **2.** Organism which passes through several stages or forms or possesses several varieties.

polyneuritic psychosis See *Korsakov's syndrome.*

polyneuritis Condition of inflammation of several peripheral nerves simultaneously which is due to an infection or to poisoning and causes great pain, atrophy of muscles, and paralysis.

polyopia Abnormality of the refractive visual mechanism which causes several images of an object to form on the retina.

polyparesis See *paresis, general.*

polypeptidorrhachia Meningitis caused by polypeptides in the cerebrospinal fluid.

polyphagia Excessive craving for food.

polyploid Any multiple of the basic haploid chromosome number, other than the diploid number.

polypnoea Respiration which is heavy, forced or rapid and may be due to physical or psychical causes.

Pompe's disease A genetic metabolic disorder transmitted by autosomal recessive gene resulting in an excess of glycogen in the blood leucocytes and body tissues. The main clinical features are: failure to thrive, cardiomegaly and later cardiac failure, hypotonia, and enlarged tongue.

ponophobia Morbid fear of being overworked.

pons Varolii Part of the hind brain whose nerve fibers arch across the medulla connecting the cerebrum and the cerebellum.

Ponzo illusion See *illusion, Ponzo.*

pooling procedures Combining scores from different tests or values obtained through using various measures and treating them as one variable which often entails weighting some of the values in order to compensate for differences in scoring or methods of measures from one procedure to the other.

popular response A Rorschach scoring category, using the symbol P, to denote responses which occur very frequently. Authorities differ on the statistical criterion necessary for a response to be classified as popular. Rorschach suggested any response occurring once in three records while others have varied the criterion upward to as much as once in six records. Lists of popular responses vary from system to system with the largest number, 15, provided in the Beck approach.

population 1. All of the organisms living in a particular geographical area as opposed to a limited number of the total which is a sample. **2.** The total group of cases or people upon which a statement is based rather than the smaller sample which is observed or experimentally tested as representative of the total group.

porencephaly Presence of cavities in the substance of the brain due to a developmental abnormality.

poriomania Extreme desire to wander aimlessly which is sometimes associated with criminal behavior and/or amnesia during the travelling period.

pornographomania Extreme desire to write obscene letters.

porphyria Inherited metabolic disorder characterized by pathological amounts of porphyrins in the blood, urine, and other tissues.

Porter's law Generalization that increase in the critical flicker-fusion frequency is a function of the log brightness of the stimulus independent of the wavelength.

Porteus Maze Test See *test, Porteus Maze.*

position 1. The location of a thing in space in relation to other objects or to some reference point. 2. (social psychology) The rank or location of a person within a social structure or hierarchy of influence or power. 3. Taking a stand in relation to a theoretical issue or preference for a particular attitude. 4. (topology) Life space region in which a thing occurs, an event happens, or a fact lies.

position factor See *factor, position.*

position, primary The position of the eyes when the head is erect and the eyes are fixated on an object that is distant and straight in front in the median and horizontal planes.

position, secondary Any position of the eyes other than the primary position, especially rotation from the primary position around either the vertical or horizontal axis.

positive abnormalities Personal traits which have a positive and helpful effect on an individual's personal and social functioning.

positive after-image See *after-image, positive.*

positive attention seeking See *attention seeking, positive.*

positive correlation See *correlation, positive.*

positive doubles, illusion of See *illusion of positive doubles.*

positive induction See *induction, positive.*

positive movement reflex See *reflex, positive movement.*

positive-positive conflict See *conflict, approach-approach.*

positive reward See *reinforcement, positive.*

positive taxis See *taxis.*

positive transference. See *transference.*

positive tropism See *tropism.*

positivism Philosophical and scientific viewpoint that knowledge concerns observable phenomena, experience and facts and which regards metaphysical concepts and questions about ultimate reality as unnecessary and unscientific. This approach in psychology underlies behaviorism and involves a reductionistic and empirical orientation.

post-infectious psychosis See *psychosis, post-infectious.*

postpartum psychosis See *psychosis, postpartum.*

postpuberal stage See *stage, postpuberal.*

postremity principle (V.W. Vocks) Organisms tend to repeat a certain pattern of behavior performed in a given situation when a similar situation occurs.

postulate An underlying principle which is thought or assumed to be true. Scientists set postulates in the belief that these postulates have heuristic value and will be of help in further research.

postural reflexes See *reflexes, postural.*

potamophobia Morbid fear of rivers.

potassium metabolism disturbance Characterized by weakness, paralysis of the flaccid variety and, frequently, electrocardiogram changes.

potence; potency 1. Power or authority. 2. Latent power. 3. The ability of the male to perform the sex act. 4. (topology) The relative amount of influence any particular part of the life space has upon behavior.

potential 1. Having potency. 2. Latent ability to do something especially in relation to intellectual capability or talent. 3. Amount of electrical charge.

potlatch (anthropology) Ritual of some Northwest American Indians in which the giving away or destroying of possessions results in a gaining of prestige.

power 1. (mathematics) The product of a number multiplied times itself one or more times. The number of times it is to be multiplied is signified by the superscript. 2. Muscular strength. 3. The degree of magnification of a lens. 4. The control which a person has over other people; social power. 5. The degree to which a person possesses a trait. 6. (B.B. Wolman) A behavioral dimension defined as ability to satisfy needs. The amount of power an individual possesses indicates how well he can protect life and satisfy the needs of his own and of others. Omnipotence is the summit of power, death is the zero point. Power can be used for satisfaction of needs or for the prevention of satisfaction. The direction power is used is called acceptance.

power factor 1. A general intellectual factor which indirectly affects all aspects of intelligence and energizes them, reflecting the efficiency level of overall brain functioning. 2. (B.B. Wolman) The ability to satisfy needs of oneself and of others, or both, or to prevent their satisfaction. In interindividual relations power can be used for the protection or the destruction of life and can be presented in a linear scale ranging from a zero point which indicates no power to higher plus numbers indicating more and more power.

power function (statistics) An index of whether or not a given hypothesis should be rejected at a given level of risk when other related hypotheses are assumed as true.

power law See *Steven's power law.*

power politics type See *type, power politics.*

power spectrum (audition) Graphic illustration of the mean square amplitude of a sound wave which is used to analyze the intensity of a mixed noise or sound.

power test See *test, power.*

practice curve A curve which represents progress in learning. The number of trials is marked along the horizontal axis, the successes and/or failures are marked along the vertical axis.

practice effect The amount or degree of improvement which results from practice.

practice limit The law of diminishing returns applies to most cases of practice. Where there are no returns (no improvement) the practice has reached its limit.

practice material Material given to a testee before a test which enables some degree of familiarization with the test, and puts the testee at ease.

practice theory of play (K. Groos) The belief that children's play prepares them for future tasks in life. This theory was based mainly on observation of animal life.

pragmatism (C. Peirce and W. James) A philosophical-epistemological theory. According to Peirce, pragmatism is a method of classification of the meaning of linguistic signs thus permitting unambiguous communication of knowledge. According to James, the meaning and truth of ideas depends on their testability in real life. The main task of thought is the achievement of "satisfactory relations with our surroundings."

Prägnanz, law of (Gestalt) The general principle of learning in Gestalt psychology; Prägnanz means the goal directed tendency to restore the balance of the organism. Whenever there is a disequilibrium of forces in a psychological field, a learning process takes place and restores the equilibrium. Since learning is an improvement in Gestalt, the tendency to attain the most complete figure is called Prägnanz.

praxiology 1. Psychology viewed as the study of actions, and overt behavior. 2. (B.B. Wolman) Any normative science, such as, e.g. education, social philosophy, ethics, etc., that sets norms and goals for human actions.

precipitating factor The onset of mental i.e. behavior disorders is usually caused by several factors, mainly the predisposing ones acting upon an organism for a long time and the precipitating factors that turn a latent condition into a manifest disease or disorder.

precision index; *h* Indicates how close the measures come to the mean.

$$h = \frac{1}{\delta \sqrt{2}}$$

precision law (Gestalt) Shaping up of perception; assuming precise contours. Precision law is another version of Prägnanz.

precocity A too early, somewhat premature development.

precognition (parapsychology) Knowledge of a future event which could not have been rationally inferred.

preconditioning Presentation of two stimuli consecutively without reinforcement. The conditioning of the experimental subject to the second stimulus is called preconditioning.

preconditioning, sensory (W. J. Brogden) Procedure in which two conditioned stimuli are paired during preconditioning sessions. One conditioned stimulus is then paired with the unconditioned stimulus during the conditioning stage of the experiment after which the other conditioned stimulus, the one not paired with the unconditioned stimulus, is tested for conditioning.

preconscious (S. Freud) The middle stratum or "mental province" in Freud's topographic theory lying between the conscious and the unconscious. It includes what the individual is unaware of at a certain moment but may become conscious of at any time.

predelay reinforcement See *reinforcement, predelay.*

predementia praecox The personality configuration of the pre-schizophrenic characterized by evasion into day-dreams and flight from reality demands.

predication 1. Attributing certain characteristics to the subject of a proposition as in associating a predicate with a subject. 2. The psychological processes involved with making an association between concepts or ideas.

predictability See *predictive efficiency.*

prediction A statement concerning future outcome of an event. In a testing situation, the predictive value is related to the validity coefficient.

predictive efficiency A measure of the proportion of correct predictions of a test.

predictive index See *forecasting efficiency, index of.*

predictive validity The degree to which a test measures what it is supposed to measure; it is ascertained by comparing it to an independent interim.

predisposing factors in mental disorders Factors which increase the probability of the development of a mental disorder.

preference method A research technique. The experimental subject is presented with two mutually exclusive stimuli and he has to choose one of them.

"Preformationist" Concept of Development An approach to understanding the development of the child which assumes that the basic developmental pattern exists at birth. According to this concept, the human personality emerges to its full maturity according to a preformed pattern.

preformism The belief that any evolutionary process and individual development is an evolvement of preexisting conditions in respectively, the origins of nature and/or embryonic state.

prefrontal area The anterior part of the frontal lobe of the brain.

prefrontal leucotomy See *lobotomy.*

prefrontal lobectomy See *lobectomy, prefrontal.*

preganglionic neuron A neuron of the autonomic nervous system; its cell body is located in the spinal cord or brain and its axon terminates in an autonomic ganglion.

pregenital phases of sexuality (S. Freud) The oral, anal, and urethral phases of psychosexual development.

pregnancy fantasy See *fantasy, pregnancy.*

prejudice An attitude which predisposes an individual to make either negative or positive judgments about persons, objects, concepts, or groups, prior to objective evaluation. The term is usually applied when negative attitudes are held.

premenstrual tension Premenstrual disturbances of mood.

premonition 1. An anxiety ridden anticipation of an adverse event. 2. (parapsychology) A supernatural revelation of future adversities.

premorbid history The history of an individual before his illness or disorder.

premotor cortex, brain lesions of See *brain lesions, of premotor cortex.*

premsia (R. B. Cattell) One pole of a personality dimension, characterized by protected emotional sensitivity, dependence, lack of aggressiveness, and tender-mindedness.

prenatal development See *development, prenatal.*

preparatory interval The time between a ready or warning signal and the presentation of a stimulus.

preparatory response Any response which does not directly bring satisfaction or is not immediately goal-directed but which is related to goal activity.

prepotence (A. A. Ukhtomski) The modification of an action caused by the force of sheer neural strength with no regard for reality, adaptiveness, and with no benefit of cognition and little involvement of affect.

prepotent response The response which is made when stimuli appropriate to two separate responses are present.

prepsychotic personality See *personality, prepsychotic.*

prepubertal stage The transitional period, usually one or two years, between childhood and adolescence which directly precedes puberty.

prerecognition hypothesis An inferred or unverbalized expectation of what is about to occur which is thought to be generated by previous experiences in similar situations.

Pre-School Schedule A Gesell Development Scale used to determine the level of linguistic, motor, and social behavior in pre-school children.

presenile psychosis See *Alzheimer Disease; Pick's Disease.*

presentation 1. The exposing of a subject in an experiment to the stimulus object. 2. The materials used as stimuli in an experiment. 3. The qualities and aspects of a thing as known. 4. The object known through the act of perceiving. 5. (J. F. Herbart) The second of the five formal steps in teaching which involves any form of placing subject matter in question before the person so that he might understand. 6. (psychoanalysis) The means through which an instinctual drive is expressed, including the instinct and some vehicle of expression.

press (H. A. Murray) The property of power an environmental object or person holds, having a facilitating or impeding effect on the individual's efforts to achieve a certain goal. Some press, significant in childhood are press-birth of sibling, press-family discord, and press-sex exposure.

press, alpha (H. A. Murray) The properties of environmental objects and people as they exist in reality.

press, beta (H. A. Murray) The properties of environmental objects and people as they are interpreted or perceived by the individual.

pressure balance 1. A mechanism used to control the amount and rate of application of pressure to the skin. 2. An instrument employed for testing judgments of lifted weights.

pressure gradient (psychophysiology) The gradual diminution in all directions from the center of pressure when point pressure is applied to the skin.

pressure, social See *social pressure.*

presthesia An abnormal exceptional cutaneous sensation such as tingling, itching, and burning occurring in spinal cord lesions, in peripheral neuritis and as a conversion symptom of psychogenic origin.

prestige motive The desire or push to gain position in the eyes of one's peers or in general.

preverbal construct See *construct, preverbal.*

Pribram, Karl H. (1919-) American brain scientist and experimental psychologist. Known for pioneering experiments relating cerebral function to behavior. Discovered the effects of limbic forebrain stimulation on visceral-autonomic functions and of limbic resection on the four F's (feeding, fighting, fleeing and sex); the relationship of frontal to limbic cortex and both to context-dependent cognitive processes; the separate roles in visual, auditory, gustatory and somesthesic memory of portions of the primate posterior association cortex; the primarily sensory nature of the functions of motor cortex in controlling behavioral acts (via receptor regulation). Developed and extensively tested an influential cognitive theory of motivation based on computer technology (with George Miller and Eugene Galanter); and a theory of perception based on optical information processing (holography).

primacy, law of The proposition that that which is learned first in a series will be remembered better than the others.

primacy zone (psychoanalysis) In the psychosexual development of the individual, the erotic zone which is in ascendancy at the moment, i.e. in the phallic stage, the phallic zone is primary.

primal-horde stage A hypothetical stage in the development of human society, occurring before the primitive clan stage in which human groups probably consisted of a dominant male, his females, and subordinate males.

primal sadism See *sadism, primal.*

primal scene (psychoanalysis) A recollection, which may be actual observation, fantasy, or some mixture of the two, from childhood which relates to an early sexual experience, especially concerning sexual intercourse between the parents.

primary color See *color, primary.*

primary correlation See *correlation, primary.*

primary data The data as originally obtained and collected, before sorting, classification, and analysis.

primary drive See *drive, primary.*

primary factor See *factor, primary.*

primary gain See *paranosis.*

primary group An intimate face-to-face group, such as the family or a small club, which exerts an enduring influence on the individual.

primary hue A color primary.

primary integration See *integration, primary.*

primary mental abilities See *mental abilities, primary.*

primary narcissism See *narcissism, primary.*

primary position See *position, primary.*

primary process See *process, primary.*

primary process thinking See *thinking, primary process.*

primary quality A fundamental or basic aspect of an object which is necessary for the object's perceptual existence. Thus the orange color of an orange is not primary while its spatial dimensions are.

primary reinforcement See *reinforcement, primary.*

primary repression See *repression, primary.*

primary stimulus generalization See *stimulus generalization, primary.*

primate The highest order of mammals including the lemuridae, a sub-order of monkey-like animals, and the anthropoidae, a suborder which includes monkeys, apes, and man.

prime number A number which can be divided only by itself or by the number one.

primidone An anticonvulsant drug closely related to the barbiturates, used in the treatment of epilepsy.

primipara A female who has only once borne offspring.

primordial dwarfism See *dwarfism, primordial.*

primordial image See *archetype.*

primordial panic See *panic, primordial.*

Prince, Morton (1854-1929) American psychiatrist, who described cases of multiple personality.

principle 1. A working hypothesis or a maxim used in guiding conduct. 2. A guideline or canon of scientific investigation. 3. A fundamental law or statement of a unity in nature. 4. The essential ingredient of a substance which produces its characteristic reaction.

principle, constancy (S. Freud) The proposition that the mental apparatus attempts to maintain excitation at the lowest or at a constant level. The mind strives towards rest or repose and, when excited, acts so as to remove the excitation and thus return to a quiescent state. Freud's constancy principle corresponds to homeostasis.

principle, homeopathic See *principle. isopathic.*

principle, interaction See *interaction principle.*

principle, isopathic (E. Jones) A term to describe the process in which the cause of something can cure its effect, i.e. guilt caused by hate is relieved with the expression of that hate.

principle of color conversion (H. Helson) In any viewing situation there is established a level of adaptation such that objects with reflectances (luminances) above adaptation level are tinged with the hue of the illuminant, objects below adaptation level are tinged with the after-image complementary to the hue of the illuminant, while objects near, or at, adaptation level are either achromatic or are of weak or uncertain chromaticity.

principle of dynamogenesis See *dynamogenesis, principle of.*

principle of inertia (F. Alexander) The same principle as that of repetition-compulsion, but with stress laid upon the fact that the tendency to automatic action is greater than activity which involves constantly changing and active mental efforts.

principle of interdependence The basic format for the Piotrowski interpretation of Rorschach data predicated on the application of logical relationships between Rorschach components. It is similar, but not identical, to the configuration principle following more closely along lines such as would be found in the programming of a computer.

principle of intimacy See *intimacy, principle of.*

principle of least energy expenditure See *least action, law of.*

principle of reduced cue See *reduced cue, principle of.*

principle, phylogenetic The doctrine which holds that the individual tends in the course of his own development to exhibit behaviors that repeat the history of his species; ontogeny (individual development) recapitulates phylogeny (species development).

principle, pleasure See *pleasure principle.*

principle, pleasure-pain (psychoanalysis) Bipolar principle that people attempt to seek pleasure and avoid pain. The stimulation of the organism by inner or external forces causes disbalance of energy or tension. Tension is experienced as unpleasure or pain, and the instinctual forces press for an immediate discharge of energy so as to re-establish the equilibrium that existed previously. The discharge of energy brings relief and is experienced by the individual as pleasure or gratification of the instinctual demands. The perfect pleasure is the perfectly balanced state of the organism.

prior entry, law of The principle that of two perceived stimuli, one attended to and the other not, the stimulus that is attended to will be perceived as having been introduced significantly sooner than the other.

prism A wedge-shaped lens possessing the property to refract or bend light waves passing through it so that the light waves are broken down into their component wave lengths, resulting in the spectrum, or band, of colors.

prism diopter (optics) The strength of a prism measured by 100 times the tangent of the angle through which the light waves are refracted.

prison neurosis See *chronophobia.*

prison psychosis See *psychosis, prison.*

privation A condition of an involuntary lack of the means necessary for the satisfaction of a need.

privileged communication A legal, medical, or psychotherapeutic document or recorded statement which is not accessible to public inspection. The communication between psychiatrists and psychologists and their patients or clients is privileged communication.

proactive inhibition See *inhibition, proactive.*

probabilism The position that it is possible to make predictions of future events through the use of logical operations in a rational and empirical study of past experience. A one-to-one correspondence between cause and effect is not assumed; rather, it is assumed that predictions with validity can be made within the limits of mathematical probability.

probabilistic functionalism A theoretical approach holding that behavior is best understood in terms of its probable success in attaining goals.

probabilities, complementary The sum of the probabilities that an event occurs and does not occur, given by the formula: $p + q = 100$ where p is the probability that an event accurs and q that it does not occur.

probability 1. (mathematics) The degree to which it is likely that an event will occur as opposed to alternate events which might occur. The formula most often used is

$$P(A) = \frac{\#(A)}{\#(S)}$$

where $(P)A$ refers to the probability of event A. $\#(A)$ is the number of outcomes in event A and $\#(S)$ is the total number of outcomes in the entire population of the experiment. 2. The quality of being probable, or likely of occurring. 3. See *probability theory.*

probability, conditional The relative frequency with which one event occurs as dependent upon the occurrence of another event.

probability curve A normal frequency curve unless otherwise qualified.

probability function The relation that is graphed in a normal frequency curve.

probability integral 1. The integral of the probability function. 2. The area falling below the normal frequency curve between two given abscissa points.

probability learning In choice behavior the probability of a response tends to approach the probability of the reinforcement.

probability matching In a choice situation in which the only discriminative stimulus is the reinforcement or lack of reinforcement of the previous trial the probability of a subject's responses come to match the probability of the reinforcement.

probability of response The actual frequency of occurrence of a response in relation to the theoretical maximum frequency of that response under a specified set of stimulus conditions.

probability ratio The ratio obtained by dividing the number of circumstances under which an event could occur by the total number of events that could occur in a certain defined set. It is written: P/Q.

probability sampling See *sampling, random.*

probability table A table which gives the frequency with which a given variable will probably occur given certain specified conditions.

probability theory The treatment of probability, the science of measuring or predicting chance, in mathematics based upon the postulates regarding the uniformity of nature, laws of change, equality of opportunity of occurrence of events, and the cancellation of complementary errors with sufficient observations.

probable error (PE) The index of a measure is variability derived in terms of the extent to which the obtained values of the measure deviate from the mean of the measure. The probable error is equal to

0.6745 of the standard error, half of the deviations from the mean falling within ± 1 probable error.

proband In genetic family trait studies, the original cases which must be representative of the trait in question that are the starting points of the family study.

probation A period of time in which a person is allowed to prove his ability to meet set requirements whether of achievement or of conformity to social regulations.

probe technique Common method to measure short term retention. A series of items are presented to the subject, who is tested on only one of them. At the time of the presentation the subject does not know which item will be tested.

problem behavior 1. Behavior perplexing to the observer or to the actor. 2. Behavior which creates a problem for the actor or others due to the antisocial or abnormal nature of the behavior.

problem box A box which must be opened in order to receive a reward. The opening of the box requires the successful manipulation of the fastenings.

problem checklist A self-report form consisting of various situations that often give rise to concern (sex, academic, vocational achievement), the subject being asked to check those items he feels are particularly pressing for him.

problem child See *child, problem.*

problem, double alternation An experimental situation in which the strategy for maximum success requires the subject to respond twice in one way and then to respond twice in another way. No extroceptive stimulus or cue is used to signal the response alternation.

problem solving The process involved in the determination of the correct sequence of alternatives leading to a desired goal.

proceeding (H. A. Murray) The physiologist's basic data or unit of observation consisting of interaction of sufficient duration to include the important elements of a particular behavioral sequence.

process, analytic In psychoanalysis as a psychotherapeutic method, includes establishing the analytic situation, the growth and interpreting of the transference neurosis and the working through of the end phase. The regression in the treatment resulting in the emergence of unresolved childhood conflicts and in their eventual resolution allows for greater maturity, mastery and insight on the part of the patient.

process, interpersonal The quality of psychotherapy characterized by the attitudes, affects, etc. of the patient and psychotherapist towards each other which are not products of the transference or countertransference.

process, mental 1. Action of an organism which involves the mind. 2. The phenomena of mental life.

process, primary The mental process in the id by which there is immediate and direct satisfaction of libidinal or instinctual wishes. Primary processes are unconscious and include such irrational elements as condensation, distortion, displacement, etc.

process schizophrenia See *schizophrenia, process.*

process, secondary (psychoanalysis) The activity of the conscious part of the psyche which determines and governs the ego activity that will be used in order to satisfy instinctual impulses.

process, unconscious The mental processes which exist at the unconscious level.

process variable, hypothetical See *variable hypothetical process.*

processing error An error which is introduced into the data in the process of producing, collecting, or analyzing.

processomania A term for mania for litigation introduced by Bianchi.

prochlorperazine Compasine, a tranquilizer.

procreation The biological processes of reproduction of the species.

prodigy A person manifesting any outstanding trait, ability, or quality, especially at an early age.

prodrome Early warning sign or symptom of an oncoming disease.

product, informational (J. P. Guilford) A parameter of the structure of intellect, it is the formal aspect of information, by which it is classified in six categories—units, classes, relations, systems, transformations, and implications.

product matrix See *matrix, product.*

product moment In correlation technique, the deviations from the means of the variables, or from some other measure as origin, raised to a power, multiplied and summated.

product moment correlation (r) See *correlation, product moment.*

product, scalar See *scalar product.*

product scale An original scale consisting of a series of products or performances that are assigned numbers representing merit against which the performance or product of a subject is judged, his performance being given the number of the standard performance it most closely resembles.

production methods (psychophysics) The subject directly manipulates the stimuli so they reflect a specified subjective relation.

productive character orientation (E. Fromm) A life style characterized by an interest in people and things and by giving rather than taking.

profession An occupation which requires general and specialized education at a high level and which generally has some code of ethics defining the role the profession should play in society.

professional code A set of ethical principles

adopted by a professional group to serve as a guideline for the performance of the respective members.

proficiency An ability of a certain degree, usually of a high degree, that is necessary for the performance of a task or the involvement in a vocation.

profile analysis A procedure used in assessing an individual's uniqueness and trait organization which consists of establishing patterns of traits in the profile of the individual.

profile chart A curve which unites points depicting the individual's scores on various measures, the various scores having been made comparable by a statistical treatment.

profile test See *test, profile.*

progeria A kind of dwarfism combined with infantile traits and premature senility.

progesterone A hormone secreted by the ovaries which prepares the uterus lining for pregnancy.

prognathous A term describing a skull which is characterized by the protrusion of the upper jaw beyond the plane of the forehead.

prognosis A prediction of the outcome of an activity or process, especially of a disease or mental disorder, including an indication of the duration, severity, and course.

prognostic test See *test, prognostic.*

program A list of coded instructions for the computer which are necessary to solve a problem.

programmed learning See *learning, programmed.*

programming A method of preparing a computer to perform certain operations on data fed into the machine by instructing the computer in "language" which it can read and understand.

progression, law of (J. Delboeuf) The proposition that successive increments of sensation increase in an arithmetic progression while the corresponding stimulus increments increase in a geometric progression.

progressive matrices test See *test, progressive matrices.*

progressive relaxation See *relaxation, progressive.*

project A planned undertaking or procedure, with a well worked-out field but not necessarily a fully defined goal.

projection 1. (anatomy) A protruding part. 2. The transmission of nerve impulses to specific areas of the cerebral cortex from lower centers. 3. The attribution of one's faults to others. 4. (testing) The perception of one's needs and goals in unstructured stimuli. 5. (psychoanalysis) Projection is a defense mechanism diametrically opposed to introjection. It is an externalization of wishes that leads to paranoid distortion of reality. The primitive, archaic ego draws a line between "something to be swallowed," which is pleasurable, and "something to be spit out," which is unpleasurable. What was "inside" was believed to be a part of the ego, and what was spit out becomes an alien body. When the weak ego harbors desires and feelings that invite the superego's harsh disapproval, the ego may ascribe them to the outer world. Forbidden homosexual impulses are a case in point, for most homosexuals "project" their homosexual urges and believe that other people of the same sex desire them. Neurotic and psychotic individuals, who cannot admit their own hostility will frequently ascribe it to others in delusions of persecution.

projection fibers Neurons which lead into and away from sensory areas.

projection, impersonal Attributing one's unobjectionable, impersonal or neutral actions or qualities to another.

projection, optical 1. The formation of an image of an object using an optical instrument such as a slide projector. 2. The objective referent of sensation in the environment. 3. The localization of objects in space which correspond to the image on the retina as determined by the refractive mechanism of the eye.

projective doll play See *doll play, projective.*

projective play Play in which the child using play materials such as dolls and a doll house, expresses unconscious ideas, attitudes, and feelings that the child would otherwise be unable to express and that are useful in coming to an understanding of the dynamics of the child.

projective techniques Methods used to discover an individual's attitudes, motivations, defensive maneuvers and characteristic ways of responding through analysis of their responses to unstructured, ambiguous stimuli.

prolactin A pituitary hormone associated with the secretion of milk.

prolegomena A lengthy and detailed introduction to a scholarly work or course of study.

proliferation A multiplication of cells in a living body, especially through cell division.

prolonged sleep treatment See *sleep treatment, prolonged.*

promiscuity Non-selectivity in social or sexual intercourse.

prompting method See *method, prompting.*

pronation Movement into a prone position, especially a movement of the hand orienting the hand downward.

proof Facts, evidence or valid generalizations which convincingly support a proposition. Proof may be inductive, reasoning from the particular to the general, or deductive, reasoning from the general to the specific.

propaganda Actions or expressed opinions of individuals or groups which are actively organized in an attempt to influence the actions or opinions of other individuals or groups.

propaganda analysis See *analysis, propaganda.*

propensity 1. An hypothesized strong and persistent characteristic of a person, from hereditary sources or from habit, which leads or inclines the person to certain goal-seeking behavior. 2. (W. McDougall) A substitution for instinct to avoid difficulties with the latter term. 3. (R. B. Cattell) A disposition permitting the individual to acquire certain behaviors more readily than others. The dispositions may be innate or acquired. See *erg; metanerg.*

proper subset See *subset, proper.*

prophecy formula (statistics) A formula used in the estimation of scores expected on some future measurement.

prophylaxis The prevention of disease or disorder through the use of systematic measures.

proposition 1. A formulation of a plan or procedure to be acted upon. 2. (logic) A verbal or symbolic statement which is offered to be tested for truth.

propositional speech Speech which is characterized by the meaning yielded from relationships among the words as opposed to the meaning yielded from the addition of the distinct words.

proprioception The sense of body position and movements.

proprioceptive cues Cues which are sensitive to body position or movement.

proprioceptive sensation See *sensation, proprioceptive.*

proprioceptor A receptor which is sensitive to the position and movement of the body and its limbs which include: (1) receptors sensitive to the body's orientation in space, and to body rotation which are located in the vestibule of the inner ear and in the semicircular canals; and (2) receptors which are sensitive to the position and movement of body members, giving rise to kinesthetic sensations, located in the muscles, tendons, and joints.

proprium (G. W. Allport) Aspects of the personality which seem peculiarly individual and collectively constitute the individual's uniqueness and sense of individuality.

prosencephalon The forebrain.

Proshansky, Harold M. (1920-   ) American psychologist. Began his research in social perception working with Gardner Murphy and Otto Klineberg. Carried out the first systematic attempt to use an especially designed projective technique to measure a social attitude. Subsequently continued to do research on perception, attitude changes, and ethnic prejudice. Most significant contribution came as a result of his collaboration with W. H. Ittelson and L. Rivlin in their pioneering research in the definition of the field of environmental psychology. Since 1958 has developed with Ittelson and Rivlin a behavioral mapping technique for the study of how individuals use physical space, and continues to carry out research with respect to such physical settings as hospitals, family settings, and others. See *environmental psychology.*

prosthesis An artificial device substituting for a missing part of the body such as, e.g., an amputated leg.

protanopia Partial color blindness; inability to distinguish between blue-green and red.

protein A complex nitrogeneous substance of high molecular weight which is found in different forms in animals and plants and is a characteristic of living matter.

protensity The attribute of a mental process characterized by its temporality or movement forward in time.

protest, masculine (A. Adler) Submission to inferiority is feminine, rebellion against it is masculine. The rebellion against inferiority, whether experienced by men or women, was called by Adler "masculine protest." The masculine protest is a universal and normal compensatory mechanism.

prothetic (S. S. Stevens) A sensory continuum in which just noticeable differences are thought not to be subjectively equal. It is suggested that the physiological processes underlying sensory discrimination for prothetic continua involve the addition of neural excitation to ongoing neural activity. Two prothetic continua are brightness and loudness; apparently it is the Stevens' power law that relates stimulus energy to subjective sensation.

protocol sentences (L. J. J. Wittgenstein) A fundamental concept in logical positivism, first introduced by Wittgenstein in 1921. The protocol sentences, also called basic statements, represent simple names of simple objects arranged in a most simple order. R. Carnap assumed that these sentences describe what is given in immediate sensory experience; thus they need no further explanation. They can be expressed in any form of language. O. Neurath maintained that these protocol sentences must be conveyed in an intersubjective language.

protoneuron A most primitive nerve unit which hypothetically exists in lower organisms which have no nervous system. Protoneurons transmit impulses indiscriminately, in all possible directions.

protoplasm The essential substance of living cells.

prototaxic; prototaxic mode (H. S. Sullivan) The first and earliest mode of experience characteristic of an infant which is undifferentiated, global, unorganized. It consists of changing momentary states which are unformulated and incommunicable.

prototype 1. (biology) The earliest, aboriginal type. 2. The original pattern from which other patterns evolved.

protozoa (biology) Most primitive organisms; some of them are unicellar, some multi-nucleic organisms or colonies.

proverb test See *test, proverb.*

proximal variable See *stimulus, proximal.*

proximity principle (Gestalt) Wertheimer distinguished several determinants in the organization of perception, among them proximity, similarity and closure. Proximity of dots to one another determines their perception as a figure.

proximo-distal trunk The development of the body proceeds from the center toward its distant parts; e.g. the shoulders develop before the arms, the arms grow before the hands.

pruritus, psychogenic An irritating itching of psychogenic origin in which an inhibited sexual excitement is a dynamic factor.

PSE See *point of subjective equality.*

psellism Speech defect; stammering.

pseudo conditioning See *conditioning, pseudo.*

pseudoamentive syndrome in childhood schizophrenia (B. B. Wolman) The most severe level of childhood schizophrenia, corresponding roughly to the dementive level of schizophrenia in adults. In the most severe cases, development is stopped before it had a chance to start; motor coordination, metabolism, sleep and waking states, food intake, speech and mental development are affected.

pseudogeusia False perception of taste.

pseudohypertrophic muscular dystrophy See *dystrophy, pseudohypertrophic muscular.*

pseudohypoparathyroidism Failure of venal tubes to respond to parathyroid hormone. Symptoms include hypocalcemia, mental retardation and skeletal deformities.

pseudologia fantastica Morbid extensive fabrication aimed at self-aggrandizement, easily renounced when confronted with facts.

pseudomental deficiencies Conditions simulating mental deficiency in which there is a deficit in intellectual development and inadequate behavior which are not the result of poor innate intellectual endowment. A combination of factors such as auditory or visual handicaps and emotional disturbances may interfere with intellectual development to the point that the child appears mentally defective.

pseudonomania The impulse to falsify.

pseudoscope An optical instrument which transposes the visual images so that what is normally seen by the left eye is seen by the right and vice versa and which inverts distance relations so that hollow objects appear solid and solid objects appear hollow.

psi process (parapsychology) The intra-individual mental processes, unable to be described in terms of presently accepted natural laws, which are involved in the ability to send or receive telepathic messages.

psoriasis A skin disease characterized by chronic inflammation, red patches with white scales which is of organic or psychogenic origin. The psychogenic causes relate to wishes for exhibitionism which are punished.

psychalgia Experiencing pain without an organic cause.

psychasthenia (P. Janet) Janet divided all neuroses into hysterias and psychasthenias; psychasthenia included anxiety stages, phobias and obsessions.

psyche Mind, self, soul; the spiritual as distinct from the bodily nature of persons.

psychedelic drugs Drugs which produce a mental state characterized by an 'expanded' sense of consciousness, extreme feelings of despair or euphoria and sometimes concomitant perceptual distortions and hallucinations.

psychergograph An apparatus designed for the measurement of fatigue and discrimination, used for submission of a series of new stimuli for the discrimination as soon as a correct response was made to a former stimulus. Also called serial discrimeter.

psychiatric criminology A branch of psychiatry devoted to the study, diagnosis, treatment, and prevention of mentally abnormal criminals. Psychiatric criminology is also related to the study of the legal aspects of crime and the judicial and penitentiary systems.

psychiatric interview Usually, the initial interview with a patient to be admitted for treatment in a public or private ambulatory or confined setting. The aim of the psychiatric interview is to establish a tentative diagnosis of the disorder.

psychiatric nosology A classification of mental disorders.

psychiatric nursing A specialty in nursing. A psychiatric nurse is a registered nurse who has received advanced training in clinical psychiatry and holds, usually, an M.A. degree. Most frequently a psychiatric field nurse plays the role of a ward administrator and mother-surrogate to hospitalized patients, and assists the psychiatrists in all aspects of psychiatric treatment.

psychiatric social examination See *examination, psychiatric social.*

psychiatric social work A social work specialty devoted to mental disorders emphasizing the role of community and family life on the origin of mental disorders and their prevention.

psychiatric social worker A social worker who specializes in dealing with mentally disturbed people. Psychiatric social workers work in mental hospitals and clinics, conduct field studies, visit the families of the patients, place patients in institutions and homes and administer intake interviews related to the social background and etiology of mental disorders. A great many psychiatric social workers take an active part in the psychotherapeutic process either jointly with psychiatrists and clinical psychologists or independently.

psychiatrist A physician who specializes in the diagnosis and treatment of mental disorders using physical, chemical or psychological methods. Psychiatrists work in mental hospitals, clinics, and private practice, as well as in public mental health and research.

psychiatry Psychiatry started as a medical specialty related to the study, diagnosis, treatment and prevention of organic and non-organic mental disorders. Psychiatry today includes a variety of scientific disciplines such as endocrinology, biochemistry, genetics, neuropathology, psychoanalysis, psychopharmacology, psychopathology, sociology, and various theories of normal and abnormal behavior, and it deals with problems related to public mental health, social and community problems and a host of research problems in several aspects of medicine, psychology, and the social sciences.

psychiatry, child A branch of psychiatry devoted to the study, diagnosis, treatment and prevention of mental disorders in children and adolescents.

psychiatry, community A branch of social psychiatry applied to cooperation with communities and prevention of mental disorders. Community psychiatry deals with the establishment of mental health centers, clinics and after-care institutions.

psychiatry, forensic The field of applied psychology or psychiatry which concerns itself with legal, judicial, or correctional procedures. The focus of clinical expertise is typically on such matters as the determination of responsibility or sanity of a defendant in a criminal trial, suitability for guardianship or custody of a child in divorce proceedings, commitment of an incompetent to a state mental hospital, recommendation for parole of an offender, etc.

psychiatry, hospital A branch of psychiatry related to establishing, directing and reforming institutionalized treatment of mental disorders. The main areas of research of hospital psychiatry are the conversion of custodial type hospitals in therapeutic centers and the development of new methods of treatment and staff-patient relationships in mental hospitals.

psychiatry, pastoral 1. A branch of psychiatry related to religion. 2. Psychiatric type counseling with mental patients, conducted by clergymen.

psychiatry, political A study of psychopathological phenomena in public life.

psychiatry, psychoanalytic A branch of psychiatry which applies psychoanalytic principles and techniques to the study, diagnosis, treatment and prevention of mental disorders.

psychiatry, social The study of social and cultural factors of mental disorders. Social psychiatric research encompasses ethnology, cultural anthropology, sociology, social psychology, mental hygiene, community psychiatry, hospital psychiatry, language and communication and several other ancillary disciplines. Social psychiatry studies the roles of sex, socioeconomic class, ethnic group, ecology and their impact on the etiology and choice of symptoms in various types of behavior disorders, as well as the epidemiology of mental disorders.

psychic 1. Related to psyche, mind. 2. (parapsychology) An individual or an object believed to be involved with supernatural, spiritual powers.

psychic apparatus See *apparatus, mental.*

psychic determinism A belief that the entire overt and covert behavior can be presented as a chain of causes and effects.

psychic impotence 1. Pathological temporary inability to perform actions and mental activity ordinarily performed. 2. Impotence resulting from psychological factors.

psychic inadequacy See *inadequacy, psychic.*

psychic isolation See *isolation, psychic.*

psychic research (parapsychology) Study of supranatural phenomena such as occultism, extrasensory perception and telepathy.

psychical satiation See *satiation, psychical.*

psychoacoustics A discipline that links physics and psychology which deals with the physical phenomena of sound as related to audition, as well as with the physiology and psychology of sound receptor processes.

psychoactive agent 1. Psychotropic drug. 2. A chemical substance that affects the mind. A mood altering drug; a drug that alters states of consciousness.

psychoanalysis A scientific approach to the study of human functioning, normal and abnormal, originated by Sigmund Freud and expanded in method, form, content, theory, and application by him and his followers.

Psychoanalysis is (1) a particular method of investigating the mind; (2) a systematic body of knowledge arrived at by use of a specific method, accompanied by a gradually evolving body of theory which has expanded, particularly with the development of ego psychology, from an early preoccupation with psychopathology into a general psychology; (3) a specific method of treatment of psychological disorders.

1. The psychoanalytic method of investigation is designed to bring about accessibility to the unconscious process in the patient in a setting which enables him to master, through insight, the forces hitherto totally unknown to him which have seriously impaired his ability to feel and to function satisfactorily in his life situation. By the use of free association, the reclining position, the benevolent but neutral attitude of the analyst, the frustration of infantile wishes in relation to the analyst, and the requirement that the patient will verbalize what he might otherwise carry out in action, regression is brought about in relation to the analyst. This, encouraged by the analyst's interventions to remove resistances (consisting mostly of ego defenses), facilitates the appearance of the transference neurosis, together with the therapeutic alliance. The latter may be described as the effect of a split in the patient's ego, whose healthy part enables him to ally himself with the analyst in an attempt to elicit the unconscious, regressive memories and experiences which come to consciousness in the transference neurosis. Dreams, fantasies, behavior, thought processes, cognitive and affective processes are made comprehensible through interpretation, the basic tool of psychoanalysis.

The process of working-through, a repetition and

elaboration of the relationship between the present and the past, results in the final resolution of the terminal phase of analysis.

2. The psychoanalytic body of knowledge has been refined and reformulated into a general theory called *metapsychology*. The facets of metapsychology are (1) the dynamic, referring to the constantly active interplay of forces within the individual; (2) the economic, referring to the shifts of psychic energy; (3) the genetic, which means the instinctual and ego developmental sequences culminating in the formation of the individual personality; (4) the structural, referring to the characteristics and interactions within and between the id, ego, and superego, and the adaptive. Certain analysts might add the topographical aspect, the unconscious, preconscious, and conscious characteristics of psychic functioning, but others would maintain that these terms can apply to each one of the metapsychological concepts, and therefore cannot be put into a separate category.

3. Psychoanalysis as a therapy has been most effective in its purest form in the treatment of psychoneurotic individuals who are capable of the therapeutic split of the ego and the alliance with the analyst described above, who are sufficiently intelligent to grasp the interpretations presented to them, and whose life situation is not so irreversibly traumatic as to be impervious to change. It is also necessary for individuals in analysis to have a sufficiently intact ego to be able to synthesize their insights so as to formulate and independently carry out their own individual way of life.

The consistent handling of the transference and the analysis of resistances are the main elements of the psychoanalytic technique. The increasing knowledge of ego psychology, especially concerning early developmental phases, has provided new means of strengthening the ego, neutralizing aggression and preparing otherwise inaccessible patients for a closer approach to psychoanalytic treatment proper. Improved methods and extra-analytic devices (parameters) have been applied especially in psychoanalytically-oriented psychotherapy. The aim of all types of psychoanalytic treatment is to enable the patient to develop the capacity to love, to work effectively, and to function in society with a well-defined and satisfying sense of identity.

psychoanalysis, didactic Psychoanalysis of an individual in fulfillment of requirements to become a psychoanalyst.

psychoanalysis, direct (J. Rosen) A method of psychotherapy, used primarily with schizophrenics, characterized by an attempt to convey to the patient the therapist's ability to fully understand what is going on in the patient's mind. This is accomplished through direct interpretation of the patient's behavior, letting him know in definitive terms how the therapist sees his behavior.

psychoanalysis, interactional (B. B. Wolman) A modification of psychoanalytic theory and technique. This theory introduced the concept of interindividual cathexis and the driving force called Lust for Life, divided in two instinctual drives, Eros (love) and Ares (destructiveness). The interactional

psychotherapeutic technique is based on explicit manipulation of transference viewed as interindividual cathexis and on search for identity.

psychoanalysis, transactional (E. Berne) A theoretical and treatment approach which emphasizes the levels of interactions and communications within a person and among individuals. The levels in interactions in a person are denoted "adult," "parent," and "child"; therapy consists in analyzing the origin and development of these levels and in determining ways to integrate them within the personality.

psychoanalyst A psychiatrist or clinical psychologist who is fully trained in the theory and practice of psychoanalysis and who employs these principles in treatment.

psychoanalytic group psychotherapy See *psychotherapy, psychoanalytic group.*

psychoanalytic psychiatry See *psychiatry, psychoanalytic.*

psychoanalytic psychology See *psychology, psychoanalytic.*

psychoanalytic psychotherapy See *psychotherapy, psychoanalytic.*

psychobiogram (E. Kretschmer) A means of investigating the personality, the first two parts consisting of data relating to the individual's history and heredity and the other parts consisting of data relating to the individual's temperament, social attitudes, physical findings, intelligence, etc.

psychobiology (A. Meyer) An organismic approach to the study and treatment of normal and abnormal behavior which emphasizes the holistic functioning of the individual in his environment.

psychodiagnosis, automated The diagnosis of mental disorders using machinery which elicits and records the diagnostic information.

psychodiagnostics The use of the individual's behavior and results on psychological tests for the study of the individual's personality.

psychodometer A mechanical device utilizing a tuning fork, which is used in the measurement of response time.

psychodrama (J. L. Moreno) A projective technique and form of group psychotherapy in which a person is asked to act out meaningful situations in the presence of people who act as auxiliary egos confronting the person on various issues, the therapist, and the audience. Each member of this drama has specific functions designed to help the subject understand himself and to act spontaneously which facilitates self-understanding.

psychodynamics, adaptational (S. Rado) A system of psychoanalytic psychotherapy which emphasizes the need to counter the regressive trend in psychoanalytic treatment with a force toward progression. That is, in psychoanalytic treatment, the patient, following a regressive trend, tends to parentify the therapist. In this system, the therapist counters this trend by not allowing himself to be pushed into the role of parent, thus bolstering the patient's self-confidence. There is an emphasis on understanding the patient in terms of motivation and control, the cultural context, and background and life-history.

psychoepistemology (J. P. Guilford) Basic kinds of information as distinguished in the structure of intellect in terms of interactions of kinds of content and kinds of products.

psychogalvanic response; psychogalvanic reflex See *galvanic skin response.*

psychogalvanometer Lie detector.

psychogenesis. 1. Having psychological origins; developing from a thought or idea; generated by the mind, as for example, a psychogenic disorder. **2.** Having psychological determinants.

psychogenic disorder A functional disorder having no observable organic basis which is probably due to emotional conflict or stress.

psychogeusia Perception of taste.

psychognosis Diagnosis of mental state.

psychokinesis; psychokinesia; PK (parapsychology) The hypothetical ability of an individual to directly influence the movement or condition of an inanimate object or of a physical system without any known physical or sensory mediation.

psycholagny Fantasy that causes sexual arousal.

psycholepsis; psycholepsy A sudden and intense decrease in one's normal level of mental tension, resulting in depression, which is generally associated with individuals who are emotionally unstable.

psycholinguistics The investigation and study of the relationships between the language spoken by an individual or group and the characteristics of the individual or group.

psychological examination See *examination, psychological.*

psychological field See *life space.*

psychological scale See *scale, psychological.*

psychological space See *life space.*

psychological test See *examination, psychological.*

psychological warfare A general concept which refers to the total attempt to lower the ability of the enemy to wage war by weakening his morale, and to raise one's own ability to wage war.

psychologist A psychologist, whatever his specific field, has two roles of a professional man and scientist. As a professional psychologist he holds a job and earns a living, and as a scientist he is interested in expanding the knowledge of behavior and in developing theories which will provide interpretation of this knowledge. The number of vocational settings in which the professional psychologist may find himself is quite large. He may find himself at a school,

prison, hospital, clinic, in business, the military, or government.

Traditionally, psychology is an academic subject. Most psychologists teach in a college or university, devoting themselves to teaching and research. Depending on particular circumstances, the proportion of time devoted to both areas varies greatly. Typically, the psychologist teaches three to four courses, and spends the rest of his time carrying on research, either on his own, or with the cooperation and assistance of his colleagues and students. He may also spend some of his time in the administrative problems involved in departmental education. Other psychologists have their primary appointment as members of a hospital or clinic. The duties of the clinical psychologist often are more varied than those of the academic psychologist. Again, depending on individual circumstances, the clinical psychologist may do either research, or therapy, or a combination of both. Very often the clinical psychologist also holds a position as a member of the staff at a college; either one associated with the hospital or clinic at which he works, or at a nearby university. In some cases his primary appointment is in the university, and his secondary post is in a guidance clinic or hospital operated by the school.

An increasing number of psychologists work directly for industry or as a part of the military. In such a position they may involve themselves with the various problems of training, selection, morale, social relations, or the adaptation of equipment to the capacities of the human operator, or any of the other problems involving human factors that industry or the military may encounter. Like his colleagues, the industrial or military psychologist may hold a secondary appointment with a nearby college or university.

psychologist, consultant A psychologist who professionally helps organizations with their psychological problems.

psychologist, consulting A psychologist who professionally helps individuals with problems of vocational, educational, and maladjustment nature.

psychologist, school A psychologist specializing in problems associated with elementary and secondary educational systems, who utilizes psychological concepts and methods in programs or actions which attempt to improve learning conditions for students. Such actions include counseling teachers and students, diagnostic testing in areas of personality and scholastic ability, designing more efficient and psychologically sound classroom situations, and acting as a catalyst for teacher involvement in reforms and innovations.

psychology Psychology is the science of human and animal behavior. Behavior is part of the totality of life processes. Life processes include metabolism, growth, decline, digestion, elimination, circulation. These physiological processes and especially those related to the nervous and glandular systems, form the foundation of behavior. Behavior means the action of the organism as a whole. When an organism runs for life, his various organs, such as the heart, lungs, muscles, are involved. The study of the structure and function of the various organs belong to physiology, but the escape from danger is an action of the organism as a whole; it is its behavior. Behavior is thus the subject matter of psychology. Behavior includes several types of action. In the first category belong the overt and observable actions of the organism, such as its reactions to external stimuli and spontaneous acts stemming from within. All organisms respond to the sight or smell of food; all organisms seek food spontaneously; all organisms fight for survival and most engage in sexual and parental activities.

Psychologists try to assess correctly what organisms do. They use observation, experimentation, measurement, and other research methods. Psychologists study first what organisms do and how they do it, but the scientific inquiry does not stop at the what and the how level. Sciences reach beyond the observable data looking for actions that are unobservable in a direct manner but which can be inferred. When a scientist sees smoke, he seeks the causes of the smoke. Astronomers discovered remote planets before they could be seen; the impact of these remote planets led scientists to assume their existence which was later proved with the help of powerful telescopes.

A similar development took place in psychology. When an experimenter applies a mild electric shock to a subject's finger, the subject withdraws the finger immediately. The observable facts are stimulus and response, but a response is not merely the result of a stimulus. Not all human beings respond in the same way to a given stimulus; some people react vehemently, while others may inhibit their response. Some severely disturbed individuals, schizophrenics, may not react at all to a stimulus which would cause pain and tears in others.

But what is pain? Physiologists study nerve centers' reaction to pain but can psychologists confine their study to facial expressions, tears, and screams? All these symptoms are the smoke that implies the existence of fire. Pain may lead to facial grimaces, tears, and screams. External observers can see the observable reactions, but only the person who experiences the pain, as it were, knows the cause of his grimaces and tears. This observation of one's own feelings and thoughts, called introspection, is associated with the name of William Wundt.

The introspective data are less objective and less reliable than data obtained by rigorous observation and experimentation. Yet it is an undeniable fact that one may be in pain even when the wound is not visible and one may experience auditory hallucinations and hear voices when no one is around. Psychologists have thus developed sophisticated research methods for objective study of those introspective, covert parts of human behavior. There is, however, also a third category of behavior, in addition to the observable and introspectionistic data. One may be unaware of one's true feelings and desires and be surprised when these hidden, unknown-to-oneself wishes lead to overt and unpredictable actions. People may be surprised by their own irrational reactions; some people forget or deny their sexual and aggressive impulses that come true in their dreams, slips of the tongue, and occasionally in uncontrollable overt actions.

The entire province of behavior which cannot be observed from without or by introspection is called unconscious or unconsciousness, and is associated with the name of Sigmund Freud.

psychology, abnormal Psychopathology; a branch of psychology devoted to the study of abnormal behavior; a study of behavior and personality disorders, including neuroses, psychoses, psychosomatic and organic mental disorders, and mental deficiencies.

psychology, analytical The system created by Carl Gustav Jung. It distinguishes three layers of the psyche: *conscious mind, personal unconscious* "comprising all acquisitions of personal life," and *collective unconscious,* not individually acquired but inherent in the specifically human psychic structure and as such the impersonal substratum of the psyche. The collective unconscious contains the *archetypes* as "determinants" or "regulators" of all psychic processes. Archetypes as such are irrepresentable patterns of behavior. Jung has used the analogy of the axial system of crystals, performing the crystalline structure in the mother liquid without material existence of its own. Archetypes manifest themselves in consciousness as *archetypal images* or ideas which are constellated by the encounter with reality, e.g. man and woman *project* on each other the contrasexual images of *anima* resp. *animus;* mother is experienced as the Great Mother, nourishing and devouring, etc.

Jung's *typology* describes two attitude types: *extra-* and *introversion,* and four function types: intellect, intuition, feeling, sensation. Attitude types as well as function types stand in a complementary relationship, e.g. where intellect is the superior (differentiated) function, feeling is inferior. This polarity creates a dynamic tension, aiming at the *union of opposites.*

The psyche is a *self-regulating system* in which conscious and unconscious stand in a compensatory relationship, the latter functioning as the regulator of the former. The unconscious has thus a potentially constructive function; the causal point of view has to be complemented by a *final point of view* which interprets psychological facts as symbolic expressions of psychic development. The *constructive/ prospective* aspect of the unconscious expresses itself mainly in *dreams* (for which reason dream analysis plays a predominant role in psychotherapy). They are "the self-portrayal, in symbolical form, of the actual situation in the unconscious." *Symbols* express contents which transcend consciousness; they are the "best possible expression for a complex fact not yet clearly apprehended by consciousness" (this in contradistinction to a semeiotic use of symbols designating a known thing, as in psychoanalysis). Thus they are *transformers of energy.* The psyche aims at constantly progressing assimilation of unconscious contents, leading to the integrated personality (*process of individuation*). The center of the total personality is the *self,* in contradistinction to the *ego* as center of consciousness.

psychology and other sciences A considerable part of human behavior depends upon the biochemical changes in nerve cells, metabolic processes, and glandular secretion. Modern study of heredity revealed that what one inherits from his parents is largely the result of chemical processes.

Other sciences closely related to psychology are neuroanatomy and neurophysiology. Neurological studies of the structure and functions of the nervous system form an indispensable prerequisite for the understanding of human behavior. The central and autonomic parts of the nervous system control human behavior and a considerable part of abnormal behavior is caused by deficiences and diseases in the nervous system.

Also history, the science of human past, and the study of contemporary and past cultures and social systems can be of great help in understanding human nature. A psychologist versed in history, anthropology, and sociology is able to develop a broader outlook on human behavior.

The relationship between psychology and the sciences that study the organism and society is a close one. Psychology deals with the interaction between organism and environment. There is a particular area where medical science and psychology are closely interrelated. A special science of psychosomatics studies the impact of psychological factors on the organism. Peptic ulcers, for instance, are a physical disease caused by emotional disturbances.

The knowledge of psychology may prove indispensable for the understanding of social institutions and cultural issues in the past and the present. Psychology holds a key position in behavioral sciences, and is often used as a basic explanation for a variety of social phenomena. Psychology helps to explain the origin and the development of government, law, economic life, education, and mental health and at the present time psychological research is applied to all these areas.

psychology, applied 1. The utilization of theories and principles developed through psychology for practical ends. 2. General term for various subdivisions of psychology each of which deals with a specific practical end. These include educational psychology, vocational guidance and counseling, psychology of learning, industrial psychology, human engineering and personnel psychology. Applied psychology also includes psychotechnology which is the body of principles utilized in applied psychology and psychotechnics which deal with the specific procedures and skills of applied psychology.

psychology, atomistic Any system of psychology which suggests that psychological phenomena should be broken down into their component elements for investigation which exist independent of the whole and that psychology should be approached by dealing with small, simple bits of behavior or of mental content. Early behaviorism, associationism, and sensationism were atomistic psychologies.

psychology, clinical A branch of psychology devoted to the study, diagnosis and treatment of behavior disorders.

psychology, comparative A branch of psychology which deals with the comparison of behaviors of organisms of different species.

psychology, content F. Brentano distinguished between psychology concerned with the act of perceiving (the act psychology) and the one concerned with what is perceived (the content psychology). According to this distinction, the psychological systems of Wundt, Ebbinghaus, Titchener, et al. were content psychologies.

psychology, correctional The application of techniques of clinical and counseling psychology to the rehabilitation of offenders during incarceration. More broadly, the participation of psychologists in the personnel aspects of prison administration and supervision of inmate behavior and welfare.

psychology, counseling A branch of psychology related to clinical psychology but different in that the problems it deals with are generally of a less serious nature. Personal, as well as vocational and academic guidance is provided.

psychology, criminal The study of the personalities, motives, etiology and pathology of criminals as well as psychological intervention in correctional procedures and rehabilitation.

psychology, depth Any psychological theory which studies unconscious phenomena, e.g. psychoanalysis, individual psychology, analytical psychology.

psychology, differential Branch of psychology which studies individual and group psychological differences, their kind, cause, amount and consequences.

psychology, dynamic 1. Any psychological system which is primarily concerned with cause and effect relationships or which stresses drives and motives. 2. (R. S. Woodworth) An outgrowth of the functionalism of Dewey and James, this psychological theory is primarily concerned with the causation of behavior which is defined in terms of a dynamic factor. The living organism is interjected between the stimulus and the response. The stimulus-response relation is the mechanism of behavior but the driving power behind it is the drive that activates the mechanism. The S-R chain was modified into an S-O-R chain, O standing for the structures and functions of the organism. The concept of general motivation was introduced; the motivating drives can be organic, such as hunger or fatigue, or inorganic, such as self-assertion or curiosity. To the observable stimulus and response factors were added the drives that act as motivating forces within the organism and together with the stimuli represent the totality of factors that cause action.

psychology, educational A branch of psychology concerned especially with increasing the efficiency of learning by applying psychological knowledge about learning and motivation to practices and procedures in school.

psychology, existential A movement in psychology based on the philosophical principles of existentialism which emphasizes that each individual must exert his freedom of choice in a chaotic world. This orientation opposes the abstractions of both academic psychology and traditional psychoanalysis while emphasizing the importance of individual existence.

psychology, experimental 1. The use of systematic, controlled scientific methodology in the investigation of psychological phenomena. 2. The systematic presentation of the methodology and results of an experiment, usually within the context of a laboratory experiment.

psychology, female The psychological study of women with special reference to their particular needs, problems and experiences. There are a wide range of approaches to the field of study, ranging from orthodox psychoanalytic concepts, to K. Horney's and C. M. Thompson's, and to more recent and radical ideas which have discarded such concepts as penis envy in an attempt to develop new and nonstereotypical means of studying women.

psychology, general A set of psychological data and theories which apply to people in general.

psychology, genetic The branch of psychology which studies phenomena in terms of their hereditary origin and development.

psychology, Gestalt See *Gestalt psychology.*

psychology, holistic-dynamic (A. Maslow) Maslow's theory is based on the innate goodness of human nature. The fundamental human needs are good or neutral rather than evil. A normal development consists primarily of self-actualizing and fulfillment of the inner potentialities. Men are made bad by adverse environmental factors.

psychology, humanistic An offshoot of existentialism and phenomenology, the humanistic school was started by A. Maslow and A. Sutich. Humanistic psychology stresses the holistic approach, creativity and self-actualization, intentionalism, free choice and spontaneity.

psychology, interbehavioral (J. R. Kantor) The definition of psychology as the study of evolved interaction between the organism and the environment. The unit of study is the event consisting of the interbehavior of the organism with other organisms and objects which are existentially and structurally separate. Configurations constituting events are determined by previous interbehaviors.

psychology, introspective See *introspectionism.*

psychology, mass The study of the behavior of groups or crowds.

psychology, military The branch of psychology which concerns itself with psychological problems in the Armed Forces, such as selection, assignment, training, morale, and motivation of personnel, and the design of military equipment.

psychology, operational-informational (J. P. Guilford) An act-content system of psychology based upon the structure of intellect, in which the taxonomy of acts includes five basic kinds of operation, and the taxonomy of content is a psychoepistemology.

psychology, organismic 1. Several psychological theories stress the role of the organism in its totality and its adjustive functions. 2. (K. Goldstein) Goldstein's organismic theory is best known under the name of holism or holistic theory. 3. (J. R. Kantor) Under the influence of Adolf Meyer's psychobiology, Kantor views all actions of the organism in their totality; physical and mental functions are but two aspects of interbehavior, that is adjustive interaction between the organism and its environment. Kantor rejects the idea that psychological phenomena must be reduced to physiology. 4. (A. Angyal) Angyal introduced the concept of "biosphere" which represents a holistic unity of the organism and its environment, thus coming close to both K. Goldstein and K. Lewin. The biosphere can be divided into organism (subject) and environment (object). The biosphere has three dimensions, namely the vertical, progressive, and transverse. The vertical dimension reflects overt behavior motivated by the deeper layers of personality; the progressive dimension includes goal-directed behavior; and the transverse dimension serves the overall coordination of personality.

psychology, pedagogical See *psychology, educational.*

psychology, personalistic A psychological school that was started under the influence of Dilthey's "understanding" psychology, Windelband's concept of idiographic sciences, and Brentano's intentionality. Edward Spranger's personalistic theory combined the above mentioned three elements stressing the need to understand the unique and goal-directed patterns of every human being. These particular patterns are "personality types" and Spranger's theory evolves around the understanding of human personality. Wilhelm Stern developed a full-fledged personalistic theory, describing personality as "unitas multiplex", unity in complexity. Stern maintained that personality is comprised of traits which are organized in a particular manner, making each person unique. Gordon W. Allport represented the American school of personalism; he viewed personality traits as determinants of human behavior. A personality trait is a neuropsychic system which controls the perception of stimulus and responses to them. Personality structure is a dynamic organization of these psychological systems which determines the individual's adjustment to his environment.

psychology, physiological Branch of psychology which experimentally investigates the physiological bases of behavior including the anatomical structures and physiological processes which are related to psychological events, psychological process, and mental functions. The nervous system, the endocrine system, and neurological processes are central areas of concern.

psychology, psychoanalytic A system of psychology which applies the principles of psychoanalysis to the study of personality and behavior.

psychology, schools of See *schools of psychology.*

psychology, social The branch of psychology concerned with the study of individuals in groups. It deals with the psychological processes and interpersonal interactions in groups and between groups. The emphasis is on individual behavior rather than on the group as a unity.

psychology, stimulus-response A branch of psychology which focuses on determining the relationship between stimuli and responses. While central processes which may be involved in this connection may be postulated, the emphasis is usually on the objective features of the overt stimulus and response.

psychology, structural A school of psychology that started under the influence of W. Wundt. The subject matter of psychology is experience; the method of psychology is a specific type of observation, introspection, which is the self-observation of the experiencing individual. The mind is viewed as a sum of mental states and processes. The basic units of consciousness are sensations, images and affections. Sensations are the elements of perception, images are the elements of ideas, and affections are the elements of emotions. Each of these units can be further classified according to the attributes of quality, intensity, duration, and clearness except for affections for which clearness has no meaning. Questions concerning these mental processes can be posed by asking "what," "how," and "why." "What" and "how" seek to describe mental phenomena, "what" deals with facts, and "how" with combinations of facts and their interrelationships. In order to answer "why" physiological parallels of psychological phenomena must be investigated. The primary aim of psychology, however, is to analyze the structure of the mind, the morphological aspects rather than to investigate the function of mental processes. This school of thought was dominant in Germany and the United States until the 1920's when Functionalism and Behaviorism were introduced.

psychology, topological (K. Lewin) A descriptive psychological system using the terms of the formal relationships of the geometrical system known as topology. Using the theoretical relationships among the various terms, empirically testable hypotheses are generated.

psychology, understanding (W. Dilthey) The main object of the natural sciences is to explain (*erklären*), but the task of psychology is to understand (*verstehen*). Psychological research must deal with the human mind as a whole, and understand the totality of life in human inner experience. Psychology is a humanistic science (*Geisteswissenschaf*) in contradistinction to the empirical, natural sciences. According to Dilthey, psychology should be the foundation of all humanistic sciences such as the study of religion, law, economics and political science, for "all cultural systems . . . can be understood only in terms of the mind."

psychomathematics The use of certain mathematical formulas to work out variations of human personality and abilities.

psychometric constant delta Δ A constant in the method of constant stimuli, the product of h times I, h being equal to $\dfrac{1}{\sigma\sqrt{2}}$ and I being equal to a constant of the individual observer.

psychometric examination See *examination, psychometric.*

psychometric function A mathematical formula which expresses the relation between the quantitative variation in a stimulus and the judgments of a subject who is reporting about the stimulus.

psychometry 1. The measurement of individual differences in behavior. 2. (parapsychology) The alleged process of obtaining information concerning a human event by touching an object related to the event.

psychomotor attack Form of epileptic seizure characterized by short attacks of extreme motor activity, sometimes violent, of which the individual has no subsequent recollection, and which usually originates in the temporal lobe. Lesions of the posterior inferior surface, the lateral part, or the insula of the frontal lobe can also initiate the seizure.

psychomotor center The area of the cerebrum which is involved in the control of movement that is psychically rather than extra-psychically or organically determined.

psychomotor retardation The slowing down of psychomotor reactions.

psychomotor tests See *tests, psychomotor.*

psychoneural parallelism The proposition which holds that there is a corresponding neural activity for every conscious or mental event.

psychoneurosis See *neurosis.*

psychoneurotic schizophrenia See *schizophrenia, psychoneurotic.*

psychonomics 1. A term for psychic laws. 2. (rare) The study of environmental factors in relation to psychological development.

psychonosology The classification of mental disorders.

psychopath, constitutional An old term for antisocial personality.

psychopathology The study of mental, that is, behavior disorders.

psychopathology of epilepsy See *personality, epileptic.*

psychopedics The branch of psychology dealing with the guidance and psychological treatment of children.

psychopharmacology 1. The study of chemical substances that affect the mind. 2. The study of the effects of chemical substances upon mental states.

psychophysical dualism See *dualism.*

psychophysical function See *psychometric function*.

psychophysical method The standard methods used in investigating psychophysical problems such as the method of average error, method of equal-appearing intervals, constant methods and method of limits.

psychophysics 1. The branch of psychology which investigates the relationships between stimulus magnitudes, the differences between stimuli and the corresponding sensory experiences. **2.** (G. Fechner) The science of the relations between mind and body. **3.** (logical positivism) The utilization of a human as an instrument of observation of a variable, the variable being one that can be arranged along a physical continuum, governed by a set of specified conditions.

psychophysiological disorders Physical disorders, presumably of psychogenic origin, which are characterized by physiological changes accompanying certain emotional states.

psychophysiology See *psychology, physiological*.

psychoprocess Term referring to central controls which determine which stimuli will affect the organism.

psychoses, alcoholic Psychoses caused by poisoning with alcohol.

psychosexual immaturity The inability to respond sexually at an age-appropriate level.

psychosexual stages (S. Freud) Five biologically determined stages of development: the oral, anal, phallic, latency, and genital stages.

psychosis Mental disorder that interferes seriously with the usual functions of life. The following overall description is taken from the Diagnostic and Statistical Manual (DSM) of the American Psychiatric Association published in 1968. A detailed description of the various psychoses is given elsewhere in the Dictionary in alphabetic order.

Psychoses are described in two places in the Manual, here with the organic brain syndromes and later with the functional psychoses. The general discussion of psychosis appears here because organic brain syndromes are listed first in DSM-II.

Patients are described as psychotic when their mental functioning is sufficiently impaired to interfere grossly with their capacity to meet the ordinary demands of life. The impairment may result from a serious distortion in their capacity to recognize reality. Hallucinations and delusions, for example, may distort their perceptions. Alterations of mood may be so profound that the patient's capacity to respond appropriately is grossly impaired. Deficits in perception, language and memory may be so severe that the patient's capacity for mental grasp of his situation is effectively lost.

Some confusion results from the different meanings which have become attached to the word "psychosis". Some non-organic disorders, in the well-developed form in which they were first recognized, typically rendered patients psychotic. For historical reasons these disorders are still classified as psychoses, even though it now generally is recognized that many patients for whom these diagnoses are clinically justified are not in fact psychotic. This is true particularly in the incipient or convalescent stages of the illness.

II-A. PSYCHOSES ASSOCIATED WITH ORGANIC BRAIN SYNDROMES (290-294)

290 Senile and pre-senile dementia
.0 Senile dementia
.1 Pre-senile dementia
291 Alcoholic psychosis
.0 Delirium tremens
.1 Korsakov's psychosis (alcoholic)
.2 Other alcoholic hallucinosis
.3 Alcohol paranoid state ((Alcoholic paranoia))
.4 Acute alcoholic intoxication
.5 Alcoholic deterioration
.6 Pathological intoxication
.9 Other (and unspecified) alcoholic psychosis

292 Psychosis associated with intracranial infection
.0 Psychosis with general paralysis
.1 Psychosis with other syphilis of central nervous system
.2 Psychosis with epidemic encephalitis
.3 Psychosis with other and unspecified encephalitis
.9 Psychosis with other (and unspecified) intracranial infection

293 Psychosis associated with other cerebral condition
.0 Psychosis with cerebral arteriosclerosis
.1 Psychosis with other cerebrovascular disturbance
.2 Psychosis with epilepsy
.3 Psychosis with intracranial neoplasm
.4 Psychosis with degenerative disease of the central nervous system
.5 Psychosis with brain trauma
.9 Psychosis with other (and unspecified) cerebral condition

294 Psychosis associated with other physical condition
.0 Psychosis with endocrine disorder
.1 Psychosis with metabolic or nutritional disorder
.2 Psychosis with systemic infection
.3 Psychosis with drug or poison intoxication (other than alcohol)
.4 Psychosis with childbirth
.8 Psychosis with other and undiagnosed physical condition
(.9 Psychosis with unspecified physical condition)

II-B. NON-PSYCHOTIC ORGANIC BRAIN SYNDROMES (309)

309 Non-psychotic organic brain syndromes ((Mental disorders not specified as psychotic associated with physical conditions))
.0 Non-psychotic OBS with intracranial infection

(.1 Non-psychotic OBS with drug, poison, or systemic intoxication)
    .13 Non-psychotic OBS with alcohol (simple drunkenness)
    .14 Non-psychotic OBS with other drug, poison, or systemic intoxication
.2 Non-psychotic OBS with brain trauma
.3 Non-psychotic OBS with circulatory disturbance
.4 Non-psychotic OBS with epilepsy
.5 Non-psychotic OBS with disturbance of metabolism, growth or nutrition
.6 Non-psychotic OBS with senile or pre-senile brain disease
.7 Non-psychotic OBS with intracranial neoplasm
.8 Non-psychotic OBS with degenerative disease of central nervous system
.9 Non-psychotic OBS with other (and unspecified) physical condition
    (.91 Acute brain syndrome, not otherwise specified)
    (.92 Chronic brain syndrome, not otherwise specified)

III. PSYCHOSES NOT ATTRIBUTED TO PHYSICAL CONDITIONS LISTED PREVIOUSLY (295-298)

295 Schizophrenia
.0 Schizophrenia, simple type
.1 Schizophrenia, hebephrenic type
.2 Schizophrenia, catatonic type
    .23 Schizophrenia, catatonic type, excited
    .24 Schizophrenia, catatonic type, withdrawn
.3 Schizophrenia, paranoid type
.4 Acute schizophrenic episode
.5 Schizophrenia, latent type
.6 Schizophrenia, residual type
.7 Schizophrenia, schizo-affective type
    .73 Schizophrenia, schizo-affective type, excited
    .74 Schizophrenia, schizo-affective type, depressed
.8 Schizophrenia, childhood type
.90 Schizophrenia, chronic undifferentiated type
.99 Schizophrenia, other (and unspecified) types

296 Major affective disorders (affective psychoses)
.0 Involutional melancholia
.1 Manic-depressive illness, manic type ((Manic-depressive psychosis, manic type))
.2 Manic-depressive illness, depressed type ((Manic-depressive psychosis, depressed type))
.3 Manic-depressive illness, circular type ((Manic-depressive psychosis, circular type))
    .33 Manic-depressive illness, circular type, manic
    .34 Manic-depressive illness, circular type, depressed
.8 Other major affective disorder ((Affective psychoses, other))
(.9 Unspecified major affective disorder
    (Affective disorder not otherwise specified)

(Manic-depressive illness not otherwise specified)

297 Paranoid states
.0 Paranoia
.1 Involutional paranoid state ((Involutional paraphrenia))
.9 Other paranoid state

298 Other psychoses
.0 Psychotic depressive reaction ((Reactive depressive psychosis))
(.1 Reactive excitation)
(.2 Reactive confusion)
    (Acute or subacute confusional state)
(.3 Acute paranoid reaction)
(.9 Reactive psychosis, unspecified)

299 Unspecified psychosis)
    (Dementia, insanity or psychosis not otherwise specified)

psychosis, acute shock A sudden but short term psychological disturbance common during active warfare. This condition is marked by complete unconsciousness, insensitivity to pain, fluttering eyelids, closed eyes, and flaccid limbs.

psychosis, affective The name given to what used to be called an affective disorder. An affective psychosis is characterized by derangements of mood involving the domination of mental activity by either extreme depression or elation.

psychosis, akinetic (C. Wernicke) The extreme catatonia that is marked by stupor and almost no movement is referred to as akinetic motor psychosis.

psychosis, alcoholic Psychotic state caused by alcohol poisoning. There are five types of alcoholic psychoses, namely alcoholic deterioration, alcoholic hallucinosis, alcoholic paranoia or paranoid state, delirium tremens, and Korsakov's psychosis.

psychosis, alcoholic, paranoid type Also called alcoholic paranoia. A paranoid state accompanied by jealousy and delusions of infidelity by the alcoholic spouse or lover.

psychosis, alternating A term descriptive of manic-depressive psychosis which involves alternating symptoms of elation and depression.

psychosis, arteriosclerotic A severe psychic disturbance associated with arteriosclerosis with symptoms ranging from mild emotional deviations to extreme psychotic responses and disorders of intellect, thought, and orientation.

psychosis, circular See *psychosis, manic-depressive.*

psychosis, climacteric See *psychosis, involutional.*

psychosis, governess Schizophrenia in a very severe form.

psychosis, iatrogenic A severe behavior disorder induced by the physician's diagnosis, attitudes and/or behavior and not the result of the specific treatment for the complaint.

psychosis, Korsakoff A disorder, generally caused by alcohol, metallic poisons, infections or the encephalopatimes, which is characterized by polyneuritis as the outstanding physical condition and loss of memory for current events as the outstanding mental condition.

psychosis, manic-depressive A psychosis characterized by extreme mood swings, remission and recurrence. It is usually observed in patients with no history of affective psychosis and in the absence of an apparent precipitating event.

psychosis, manic-depressive, circular type A psychosis characterized by at least one occurrence of both a depressive episode and a manic one.

psychosis, manic depressive, circular type, depressed The depressed episode of the manic-depressive psychosis, circular type.

psychosis, manic-depressive, depressed type A psychosis consisting of depressed episodes and characterized by a depressed mood, mental and motor retardation, apprehension, and agitation. Hallucinations and delusions which occur are due to the mood disorder.

psychosis, manic-depressive, manic type A psychosis consisting of manic episodes which are characterized by extreme elation, flight of ideas, loquacity, accelerated speech and accelerated motor activity.

psychosis, organic Severe mental disorder which is due to an empirically identifiable structural change or impairment of the nerve tissues, such as alcoholic psychosis.

psychosis, post-infectious A mental disorder which follows an acute disease such as influenza, pneumonia, typhoid fever, and acute rheumatic fever. Its characteristics include mild confusion and suspicion, irritability and depressive reactions.

psychosis, postpartum A psychotic episode precipitated by giving birth.

psychosis, prison A kind of mental disorder which is precipitated by imprisonment, the form of the disorder depending upon the individual involved.

psychosis, schizoaffective A disorder which is manifested by disturbances of thinking, mood, and behavior, especially with pronounced elation or depression. DSM II lists this disorder as one of the types of schizophrenia.

psychosis, symbiotic (M. S. Mahler) A form of mental illness occurring in children aged one to four whose origin lies in the symbiotic phase. This syndrome develops when the young child finds it impossible to separate from his mother and fails to progress to the next stage of separation and individuation because of panic inherent in this separation. Psychosis develops when the symbiotic union of mother and child is threatened. The belief is that a constitutional predisposition toward the development of this state must be present in a child who then responds to the mother in ways to elicit from her similar symbiotic needs.

psychosis, toxic-infectious A mental disorder which accompanies or follows an infective illness or poisoning by some external poison. It is characterized by delirium, dazed and stuporous condition, epileptiform attacks, hallucination, and incoherence and confusion.

psychosis, Windigo A psychosis found in certain Indian tribes, the Ojibwa, Chippewa, Eastern Cree, which is characterized by a morbid craving for human flesh and by the delusion of a transformation into Windigo, a mythological giant feared by the tribes.

psychosocial That which is both social and psychological.

psychosocial stages of development (G. M. Gilbert) According to biosocial theory, an epigenetic series of psychosocial stages from infancy to mature social adulthood best depicts the development of the integrated human personality. The stages suggested are: 1) (birth to 3rd year) ego emergence and dependency; 2) (3rd to 7-8th year) primary group interaction; 3) (7-8th year to puberty) secondary socialization; 4) (puberty through adolescence) adult role anticipation; 5) (early adulthood) social role assumption.

psychosomatic Involving both the mind and the body, psyche and soma.

psychosomatic disorder Generally a disorder of the body having psychogenic determinants.

psychosomatic medicine A specialty in medicine dealing with the diagnosis and treatment of psychosomatic disorders.

psychostimulants Drugs which stimulate the nervous system. See *amphetamines; methylphenidate; tranylcypromine; phenelzine; nialamide.*

psychosurgery Introduced by the Portuguese neuropsychiatrist Moniz in 1935; had been preceded by some operations on mental patients performed by the Swiss psychiatrist Burckhardt in 1890. After Moniz, Freeman and Watts in the United States standardized the operation performing cuts in the connections between frontal lobe cortex and thalamus (lobotomy). Today smaller, so-called stereotaxic operations are aimed at circumscribed structures in the brain. Electrocoagulation or radium-like substances are used.

psychosynthesis (S. Potter) A movement counter to psychoanalysis which attempts to restore useful inhibitions and to return the id to its rightful place. There is the attempt to keep the id and ego separate with the reality oriented ego in a dominant position.

psychotechnics The use of psychological principles, laws and knowledge in the attempt to control or alter behavior.

psychotechnology The body of psychological facts, principles, methods and concepts which are used in the application of psychology to practical problems.

psychotherapist A person who is trained in and practices psychotherapy.

psychotherapy Psychotherapy is a loose term encompassing a variety of treatment techniques of organic and non-organic mental (i.e., behavior) disorders. In a narrower and most commonly used sense psychotherapy means psychological treatment of mental disorders in contradistinction to the physical and chemical treatment methods. Psychotherapy is practiced primarily by psychiatrists and clinical psychologists, but several other professionals, notably the psychiatric social workers, psychiatric nurses, pastoral counselors, general physicians and others practice psychotherapy to some extent.

With the advent of Freud's discoveries, psychotherapy has been viewed as a form of psychological treatment in which a trained person (psychotherapist) establishes a professional relationship with a person (patient, client) suffering from emotional problems for the purpose of alleviating or modifying troublesome symptoms or patterns of behavior. The resulting changes are seen as promoting personality growth and mental health.

Freud attempted to draw a sharp distinction between psychoanalysis (as a method of treatment) and other forms of psychotherapy, which he regarded as closer to suggestion and hypnosis. In contrast, psychoanalysis was characterized as a radical treatment designed to overcome infantile conflicts. Extending over months and years, psychoanalysis focuses on a thorough analysis of (a) the transference and (b) resistances. The therapist's technical maneuvers are restricted to clarifications and interpretations of the patient's free associations, with a minimum of suggestion, advice, and directiveness. These maneuvers are considered to strengthen the patient's ego by undoing repressions and other defenses. "Orthodox psychoanalysis" has given way to numerous modifications, such as "psychoanalytically oriented psychotherapy" or "psychotherapy based on dynamic principles," which make use of Freudian teachings but adapt them in various ways to the needs of the patients and other circumstances. Differences between therapeutic approaches tend to be in degree rather than kind.

All forms of psychotherapy are based on common psychological principles operating in any helping relationship, including comfort, support, guidance, reassurance, guilt-reduction through confession, and hope. The therapist fosters an atmosphere of trust through interest, respect, understanding, and empathy, and he encourages open and direct communication by refraining from criticism and censure. These so-called nonspecific factors generally result in a diminution of fears and anxieties and mobilize the patient's abilities to cope with his problems. Intertwined with the nonspecific factors are more specific techniques designed to produce changes in symptoms (e.g., phobias, obsessive-compulsive acts), and maladaptive patterns of behavior. These techniques. include not only interpretations of unconscious fantasies and beliefs but also suggestions, modeling of fearless behavior, setting an example of reasonableness and rationality, promoting the acquisition of self-understanding through insight, and the management of reward and punishment. Through his interaction with the therapist and experimentation outside the therapeutic situation, the patient acquires more adaptive skills in interpersonal relations. Consequently, psychotherapy is not a form of medical treatment for a disease (formerly called "neurosis"), but it represents a more or less systematic attempt to help a patient achieve maturity, autonomy, responsibility, and skill in adult living.

Psychotherapy takes many forms (e.g., group psychotherapy, psychodrama, play therapy), is based on diverse theoretical principles and assumptions, and is being extended to widely divergent patient groups. Psychotherapy is now frequently distinguished from behavior modification, an approach based on learning theories, with focus on the direct modification of symptoms.

psychotherapy, active analytical (W. Stekel) A method of dream interpretation, also called active analysis, in which the analyst intervenes directly in a patient's free associations by making revelations and giving advice suggested by the manifest dream content.

psychotherapy, Adlerian (A. Adler) The rationale of this psychotherapy is derived from A. Adler's individual psychology. There are no rigid rules in this treatment method, and the individual-psychological treatment is conceived as a relationship in which two people have to cooperate in a common task. Transference phenomena are viewed as the patient's distortions, and the therapist must interpret them as such. The task of the physician or psychologist is to give the patient the experience of contact with a fellow-man, and then to enable him to transfer this awakened social feeling to others.

psychotherapy, ambulatory The treatment of persons with psychological and behavior disorders on an out-patient basis.

psychotherapy, analytic group (S. R. Slavson) A method of treatment of behavior disorders in which interpretations are offered to patients, activity and verbalization are encouraged and interpreted in the hope of achieving insight. A particular version of group psychoanalysis.

psychotherapy, analytical (C. G. Jung) Psychoanalytic treatment similar to Freud's technique in that free association and dream interpretation are used but deviating from it in that libido is viewed as the general energy of life manifesting itself in creativity as well as sexual drive, and the mind is viewed as bipolar in nature, with one side in ascendency. Dream analysis is employed not only as a means of understanding the causative role of past experiences in present problems but also as a means of understanding the current concerns and future hopes of the patient. Four stages of the analysis are distinguished but not seen as consecutive or mutually exclusive and in each there is a different technical approach: the first stage is confession (cathartic method); the second stage is elucidation or interpretation (especially of the transference); the third stage is education (adapting to social demands and pressures); the fourth stage is transformation or individuation where the unique pattern of the patient is discovered and developed. The goal of the analysis is seen as the development of the unique pattern of personality with a re-balancing of the compensatory relationship between the conscious and the unconscious, accomplished by a progressive integration or constructive synthesis of unconscious contents into the conscious. Towards this goal, the analysis is seen as a dialectical process between two people, the analyst being part of the process and approaching each patient individually. The chair, as well as the couch, is used to facilitate the dialectic interpretations of the transference and dreams are often prospective or constructive rather than reductive in that the transference and dreams are seen as communications of unconscious parts of the personality to be integrated into the conscious as well as expressions of regressive and repressed infantile sexual impulses. "Active imagination" is often used in understanding the dream because free associations to the dream reveal meanings of specific contents and not the meaning of the dream itself.

psychotherapy, assignment (J. L. Moreno) Psychotherapeutic help given to a patient in a small work or play group after the group has been assessed sociometrically.

psychotherapy, client-centered (C. Rogers) Client-centered therapy is a continually developing approach to human growth and change, developed originally by Carl Rogers in the 1940's. Its central hypothesis is that the growth potential of any individual will tend to be released in a relationship in which the helping person is *experiencing* and *communicating* attitudes of realness, caring, and a deeply sensitive non-judgmental understanding. These concepts have been carefully defined theoretically as congruence, unconditional positive regard, and empathy. This kind of a relationship has been shown by empirical research to have constructive effects with troubled persons, normal people (in encounter groups), hospitalized schizophrenics, and students in classrooms.

Client-centered therapy is process oriented, not diagnostically or theoretically oriented. It draws its hypotheses from the raw data of the process of therapy as preserved in recorded and filmed interviews. It has been determined to test all its hypotheses through appropriate research and has probably sponsored more investigations than any other approach.

It is a mode of dealing with persons which has application in every field of human endeavor where healthy psychological growth and improvement in interpersonal relationships constitute goals. It has found use not only in psychotherapy, but in education, in conflict situations (racial and industrial), religious work, social work, encounter groups, and international student groups.

psychotherapy, dance Dance techniques to express one's unconscious conflicts used for psychotherapeutic purpose.

psychotherapy, didactic group A method of treatment of individuals in a group in which the group experience serves to educate the individual about the processes of psychotherapy, and to help him to clarify his own problems. The pedagogical methods may include the patient's bringing up problems for general discussion, the therapist lecturing on particular topics, and/or the use of a textbook to suggest topics of discussion which the patients may comment on or associate to.

psychotherapy, direct (K. Platonov) A therapeutic method which uses explanation and persuasion to arouse the patient's cortex, and to remove pathological bonds in the cortex by means of conscious and critical analysis of the pathogenic situation by the therapist.

psychotherapy, directive A form of psychotherapy in which the therapist plays an active role giving reassurance and advice, asking questions and offering information.

psychotherapy, directive group (S. R. Slavson) A type of therapeutic treatment for a group designed to help the group members adjust to their environment which includes activities such as didactic and educational group work, group counseling and guidance, and therapeutic recreation.

psychotherapy, existential Therapy based on phenomenological and existential principles. This therapeutic technique emphasizes the direct approach to life and a thorough investigation of the individual's experiences and consciousness in order to reconstruct and unify the individual's existence. The various existential techniques stress the understanding of the individual and giving meaning to his life.

psychotherapy, family Psychotherapy in which the processes of the family as a unit as well as the individual family members are treated. The family meets as a group with the psychotherapist and interpretations are made of the interactions among the family members and of individual psychodynamics involved in those interactions.

psychotherapy, filial (B. G. Guerney) Play psychotherapy in which parents are trained and used as psychotherapists with their own children.

psychotherapy, Gestalt (F. Perls, P. Goodman, R. Hefferline) A form of psychotherapy based on the theory that psychopathology results from the disturbance of figure-ground development. The therapy consists of analyzing the internal experience in order to achieve a "good gestalt" within the person. Dissociated areas of the personality are thus accepted.

psychotherapy, group A form of treatment of behavior disorders in which two or more patients and the psychotherapist participate to resolve difficulties and effect therapeutic changes.

psychotherapy, implosive A therapy developed by Stampfl based on the technique of extinguishing fear reactions by having the patient imagine the feared stimuli. The therapy is called implosive because the patient is not actually harmed while imagining. A frightening stimulus is apt to produce an inner explosion—an implosion—of panic.

psychotherapy, interactional (B. B. Wolman) A psychotherapeutic technique. The rationale is derived from Wolman's modification of psychoanalysis and the assumption that psychotherapy is an interactional process. The main features of this technique are the manipulation of transference phenomena and adjustment of the technique to the type of sociogenic disorder, namely the hyperinstrumental, dysmutual, and hypervectorial, and the five levels of regression, namely neurotic, character neurotic, latent, manifest, and dementive psychotic.

psychotherapy, interpersonal (H. S. Sullivan) A treatment technique which emphasizes the interpersonal nature of the events occurring in the treatment as well as in the patient's life in an attempt to help the patient become conscious of those parts of himself he has a stake in keeping out of awareness.

psychotherapy, limited aims Psychological treatment with goals which are somewhat more restricted than usual, due often to forces or conditions in the patient's life not allowing for longer, more comprehensive treatment. A goal of this treatment is often the solution of some pressing life problems rather than the in-depth analysis and restructuring of the patient's personality.

psychotherapy, limited term Psychotherapy in which the termination date is established at the inception of treatment.

psychotherapy, nondirective See *psychotherapy, client-centered.*

psychotherapy, nondirective group A form of group psychotherapy utilizing concepts derived from the Rogerian school of client-centered therapy. The basic assumption is that man has inherent potential for goodness, and self-healing. The focus of the group is the problem of most concern to the group or individual. The belief is that in an accepting, secure atmosphere the individual recognizes his needs and learns ways to obtain satisfaction. The role of the leader is that of a catalyst who clarifies and guides but never interprets.

psychotherapy, "poison-pen" (J. G. Watkins) The use of the writing of angry letters for cathartic purposes which are discussed with the therapist rather than mailed.

psychotherapy, psychoanalytic A simplified and shorter method of treatment based on modified principles of psychoanalysis.

psychotherapy, psychoanalytic group 1. A form of group psychotherapy utilizing the concepts of psychoanalysis. 2. (A. Wolf) The application of psychoanalytic concepts as transference, free association, dreams, and historical development in groups. The group re-creates the original family facilitating the resolution of problems. The members serve as co-therapists and representative of standards for each other, especially through the use of the technique of "going around," in which each member free associates about another member. The group meets once a week with the therapist and once a week without him. 3. (S. H. Foulkes) A meeting of six to eight people with a group analyst once a week where no directions are given. Any communication is considered free association and a reflection of the group

interaction. The role of the therapist is that of a conductor who interprets and analyzes and offers minimal private information. 4. (W. R. Bion) The treatment of individuals in a group where the focus is on group behavior. The group is seen as a series of emotional states or basic assumption cultures. Its behavior is analyzed in terms of its movements to or away from the central problem. 5. (H. Thalen) Treatment of individuals in a group where the focus is on group interaction which is seen as a functional process. Emphasis is placed on the emotional and cognitive factors in the group and the relationship of the individuals to the group culture. 6. (B. B. Wolman) A psychotherapy group must be balanced vertically and horizontally, according to Wolman's classificatory system of mental disorders. The vertical balance requires participation of hyperinstrumental, hypervectorial and dysmutual patients, with none of these three clinical types dominating the group. The horizontal balance is based on avoidance of too extreme differences in the level of regression; e.g. a group comprised largely of character neurotics may have neurotic and latent psychotic members, but must not accept manifest or dementive psychotics.

psychotherapy, rational (A. Ellis) Rational psychotherapy or rational-emotive therapy (RET) is a form of cognitive-behavior therapy which emphasizes a philosophic rather than a psychodynamic approach to the prevention and treatment of emotional disturbances. It utilizes emotive-evocative techniques (such as direct confrontation) and behavior therapy methods (such as activity homework assignments). It especially teaches the individual that his emotional Consequences (C) do not stem mainly from the Activating Events (A) of his past or present life but from his Belief System (B); and it shows him how to clearly distinguish his rational Beliefs (rB's) from his irrational Beliefs (iB's) about himself and the world and how to use the logico-empirico or scientific method of vigorously Disputing (D) his irrational Beliefs until he significantly changes them. RET thereby helps the individual minimize his current self-defeating behavior and his future disturbability by becoming more realistic (that is, desiring rather than demanding) in his general outlook.

psychotherapy, reconstructive A form of psychotherapy which focuses on the reconstruction of childhood and adult experiences which are instrumental in the patient's problems.

psychotherapy, relationship Psychotherapy in which the relationship between the psychotherapist and patient serves as the means and end of the psychotherapy. The relationship becomes the significant growth experience, with the focus on the patient's experiencing himself within the context of the relationship. Reliance is placed on the dynamic effect of various maneuvers in the relationship or on the supportive value that a positive, friendly contact with another human being can have to another troubled, confused, or unhappy person.

psychotherapy, role-divided Individual or group psychotherapy in which more than one therapist participates.

psychotherapy, short contact Psychotherapy of short duration often used in child-guidance clinics.

psychotherapy, will (O. Rank) A form of psychotherapy, based on the theory of the birth trauma. Rank encouraged the patient to assert his will, as in the separation from the womb, to achieve independence.

psychotic An individual afflicted with psychosis.

psychotic depressive reaction A form of psychosis which is characterized by a depressive mood attributable to some event or experience, with no history of repeated depressions or mood swings.

psychotic, involutional See *psychotic reactions, involutional.*

psychotic reactions, involutional Psychotic reactions usually seen in menopausal women but also in aging men. It is characterized by intense depression and feelings of worthlessness.

psychotomimetic Appearing to mimic a psychosis. As for example, the effects of lysergic acid diethylamide.

psychotomimetic drugs Drugs which produce a state similar to that of psychosis.

ptosis 1. Falling. 2. Paralytic drooping of the eyelid.

pubertas praecox See *macrogenitosomia.*

puberty The developmental state or period in which the reproductive organs reach maturity and the individual begins to exhibit secondary sex characteristics. Although there is much variability among individuals, the end of the stage for males is generally given as fourteen and thirteen for females.

puberty rites Initiation through precept and ritual into the adult life of a community consisting of indoctrination into tribal lore, ceremonies, etc.

pubesence; pubescency The period or process of reaching puberty.

public opinion The general state of feeling, opinion, or attitude of a large and major segment of the population on an issue or group of issues.

pudendum; pudenda The external genital organ.

puerilism The condition of acting like a boy or child; an adult participating in immature behavior.

puerperal mania See *mania, puerperal.*

pulfric phenomenon or effect When an object is moving in a pendular movement in one plane it will appear to be moving in an ellipse whose plane is perpendicular to the frontal plane when viewed through a filter of medium density.

punched card technique The use of cards with holes punched in them at appropriate places to record and process data, usually in a computer system.

punishment training A type of training in which a particular response elicits a negative reinforcer.

pupil The aperture on the iris of the eye which changes dimension in response to the brightness of light and to control the amount of the light passing through it on the way to the retina.

pupillary reflex See *reflex, pupillary.*

Purdue pegboard A test measuring gross arm, wrist and finger movements which requires the subject to combine pegs, washers, and collars into various assemblages.

Purdue perceptual-motor survey A test for the qualitative assessment of perceptual-motor abilities in the early grades. The survey consists of twenty-two scorable items divided into eleven subtests: walking board, jumping, identification of body parts, imitation of movement, obstacle course, muscular strength tests, angels in the snow, chalkboard, rhythmic writing, ocular control, and visual achievement forms.

pure C response The Rorschach response determined only by color, with no form involvement whatsoever. Such responses, sometimes described as crude color responses, are generally interpreted as representing a substantial loss of control with emotion being in near complete command of behavior. It is typically found in records of very seriously disturbed subjects.

pure line See *line, pure.*

pure number (statistics) A number which is not dependent on the units of measurement of the quantities used in its determination.

pure stimulus act See *act, pure stimulus.*

puritis 1. Itching resulting from sensory nerve irritation. 2. Functional or psychological itching.

Purkinje afterimage The second positive visual aftersensation, appearing most plainly in the hue complementary to that of the primary sensation.

Purkinje cell See *cell, Purkinje.*

Purkinje figures The shadowy network on the retina which results from the thin network of blood vessels lying between the sensitive cells and the incoming light and which may be seen under certain conditions.

Purkinje phenomenon With decreasing illumination, the red or long-wave end of the spectrum decreases in brilliance more rapidly than the blue, or short-wave end.

Purkinje-Sanson images The three images of an object an eye is fixated on which can be seen by an observer of the eye. The images are reflected from the surface of the cornea, from the front of the cornea, and from the back of the cornea.

purposive psychology The belief that behavior, rather than being simply a complex set of reflexes or mechanistic physiological processes, is characterized by purpose.

purposivism An approach to psychology holding

that purposes interact with certain stimulus conditions in yielding behavior.

pursuit, ocular The continuous perception of a moving object by successive fixations of the eyes.

pursuit reaction Movements meant to maintain the perception of a moving stimulus.

pursuitmeter An instrument which measures the subject's ability to manipulate his behavior in accord with changes in a constantly moving stimulus.

Putnam, James Jackson (1846-1918) An American psychiatrist who founded the American Psychoanalytic Society in 1910.

puzzle-box An enclosure which prevents the experimental animal from attaining the goal box until he has successfully manipulated a mechanism which opens the enclosure.

pygmalionism The condition characterized by the falling in love with one's own creation.

pygmeism A constitutional anomaly which is characterized by a dwarfed but well-proportioned body when viewed in comparison with others in the specific racial group.

pyknic type See *type, pyknic.*

pylorus The opening which leads from the stomach into the duodenum.

pyramidal tract The nerve fibers which pass through the medullary pyramids and form an efferent path originating in the precentral gyrus of the cerebral cortex, and leading to the motor centers of the brain stem and cord.

pyrexiophobia Fear of fever.

pyrolagnia Experiencing of sexual arousal and excitement at the sight of fire.

pyromania Pathological desire to set things on fire, or empresiomania.

pyromania, erotic See *pyrolagnia.*

pyromaniac Person who exhibits pyromania.

pyrophobia Fear of fire.

pyrosis Heartburn.

Q

Q 1. See *quartile deviation*. 2. See *questionnaire*.

Q 1. A symbol for luminous energy. 2. (Rorschach) A general symbol sometimes used by the examiner to indicate qualification, restriction, or a self-doubting expression on the part of the subject.

Q-correlation See *P-technique*.

Q data (or factors) Responses and response factors based on questionnaire behavior taken only as behavior.

Q-sort (W. Stephenson) A personality inventory introduced in 1953 in which the subject or a judge is asked to sort a series of statements into a pile showing which best applies to the subject.

Q-technique 1. A factor analysis from correlating persons instead of tests. The transpose of R-technique. 2. (R. B. Cattell) A factor analysis technique which investigates the relationships among people by correlating the performance of different persons in relation to a population of tasks under constant conditions.

Q' technique Finding types as clusters, not factors, from an r (shape method) or r_p matrix of relations among person profiles, preferably scored on factors as elements.

quadriplegia A kind of paralysis which affects both the arms and legs.

quale Any bit of experience which is investigated as it is without referring to the context, relations, or meaning involved with it.

qualification grid A "ready reckoner" device for calculating job adjustment or success scores from personality factor profiles, with an implicit formula.

quantum hypothesis See *quantum theory*.

quantum theory (G. von Bekesy) The hypothesis that changes in sensation occur in discrete steps and not on a continuum. This implies that sensory discrimination is fundamentally a discontinuous process characterized by finite quantal steps. This is predicated on the all-or-nothing principle in neural activity.

quartile 1. One of the three points which divide a serial ranked distribution into four segments, each segment containing one-fourth of the scores. 2. One of the four segments of the subdivided segment.

quartile deviation A rough measure of variability which is equal to one-half of the distance separating quartiles one and three.

quasi measurement The attachment of a numerical value to a datum even though the rules of measurement proposed by a theorist are not followed.

quasi need (K. Lewin) A state of tension which initiates activity directed at a specific goal with its origin not in a biological deficit but in an intention or purpose.

quaternity 1. A unit which is composed by the union of four factors. 2. (C. G. Jung) Describes the four dimensional structural concept of personality, the four dimensions being: thinking, feeling, intuiting, and sensing.

questionnaire; questionary A set of questions, often elaborate, which is designed so as to investigate a given subject.

Quincke's tubes 1. A set of glass tubes which produce sound when blown across the open end and which are used to obtain high pitches in studies of hearing. 2. A kind of interference tube.

quota control A technique used in population sampling where the number chosen of a certain element is proportionate to the number of elements in the population as a whole.

quota sampling See *sampling, stratified*.

quotient The number which is yielded when one number (the dividend) is divided by another number (the divisor).

quotient, intelligence See *intelligence quotient*.

R

r   See *correlation, product moment.*

r   (statistics) The symbol for the product-moment correlation coefficient.

R   **1.** A symbol for response; see *response.* **2.** A symbol which denotes a general reasoning factor in reference to primary mental ability. **3.** (Rorschach) A symbol which stands for the total number of responses given by a subject to the Rorschach test.

R   **1.** (statistics) A symbol of the multiple correlation coefficient. **2.** (Statistics) A symbol for foot-rule correlation, a rarely used statistic.

R$_G$ (C. L. Hull) The symbol representing a goal-attaining, or consummatory, response.

r$_t$ (statistics) The symbol for the tetrachoric correlation coefficient.

R-correlation   (R. B. Cattell) A factor analysis technique which investigates how closely two functions or tasks are related by correlating them for a large number of subjects.

R-technique   A design which measures a group of persons on the same set of variables at one occasion then factor analyzes the correlations between these variables to determine personality dimensions descriptive of inter-individual differences at any one time (or traits).

rabies   See *encephalitis, rabies.*

rabies encephalitis   See *encephalitis, rabies.*

race   (physical anthropology) A large subdivision of mankind characterized by a common ancestry and having a number of common characteristics, particularly physical or visible.

racial memory   See *memory, racial.*

racial prejudice   The irrational belief in the association of good or bad qualities to any one racial group.

racial unconscious   See *collective unconscious.*

racism   A belief which utilizes common ancestry or somatic racial characteristics as the basis for discrimination in the granting of political, social, or economic rights.

radiance   The measure of radiant energy in terms of the emission rate and the area of the source. It is the analog of luminance, the measure of radiant energy in terms of the light produced.

radical   **1.** A term descriptive of persons, plans, etc. which seek rapid, fundamental and substantive change. **2.** (mathematics) The sign for square root, m, indicating that the quantity within is to be factored into its roots.

radix   A term used for nerve fibers located at the point of entry or departure from the central nervous system.

ramifying linkage method   (R. B. Cattell) A system method for isolating all types or clusters in an r or r_p matrix.

ramus; ramus communicans   **1.** A branch from a nerve or vein. **2.** One of the nerve tracts which connects the sympathetic ganglia (the sympathetic nervous system) to the spinal cord (central nervous system) and to visceral and peripheral organs.

random   Occurring by chance, without voluntary control.

random activity   Movement that is carried out without foresight or plan or purpose, that is not the result of instinct or habit, that is not directed toward any goal and that is not elicited by any specific cueing stimulus.

random error   **1.** That part of variability which can be attributed to chance. **2.** The average deviation of a sample from the mean of a large number of observed values or scores.

random observation   Any observation which is not part of a systemized series of observations and which has not been planned in advance.

random sample   A number of cases of any sort drawn from a population in such a way that every item in the population has an equal chance of being chosen as every other.

random sampling See *sampling, random.*

range 1. (statistics) A measure of variability that is computed by subtracting the lowest score in a distribution from the highest score. 2. (sociology) Any geographical area occupied by a species, group or individual.

range effect In a pursuit or tracking reaction, the making of too small a movement when the target motion is large and too large a movement when the target motion is small.

range of audibility or hearing The range which stretches between the upper and lower limits of hearable tones, measured in cycles per second. The average range is 20 to 20,000 cycles per second.

rank 1. (noun) The position of an item or datum in relation to others which have been arranged according to some specific criterion. 2. (verb) To put items in an order, from lowest to highest (or highest to lowest) according to some criterion.

rank correlation See *rank-difference correlation.*

rank-difference correlation (*p*) A technique for ference between two sets of values or magnitudes which have been ranked,

$$p = 1 - \frac{\sigma \Sigma d^2}{N(N^2-1)}$$

where d is the difference between ranks, N is the number of cases ranked, and Σ means the sum of all the values represented by d^2.

rank order The arrangement of a series of values, scores, or individuals in the order of their magnitude (decreasing or increasing). The intervals between the values are not necessarily equal.

rank-order method See *method, rank-order.*

rank, percentile (statistics) The position or magnitude of a value or score in a sequentially-ordered series defined in terms of the percentage of values or scores which fall at or below that position.

ranked distribution See *distribution, ranked.*

rapport 1. A comfortable and warm atmosphere between two individuals, especially between a tester and the testee. 2. A special relationship which exists between the hypnotist and his subject, rendering the latter extremely sensitive to stimuli from the former. 3. (parapsychology) The relationship between a medium and the spirit control.

rare detail; dr (Rorschach) A response on Rorschach utilizing a small and generally unused portion of the blot.

rat-man (S. Freud) A patient of Freud's who had suffered from severe obsessions and fears. Freud used his knowledge of the case, gained through an eleven month analysis, to illustrate the dynamics of the obsessive-compulsive neurosis.

rate, compensatory (operant conditioning) A higher than average response rate following a lower than normal rate, tending to restore the over-all rate to its earlier value. Also possibly a lower than normal rate following a higher rate with the same effect on over-all rate.

rate, fine grain (operant conditioning) The response rate, number of responses by time, over the shortest unit of time.

rate, local (operant conditioning) Response rate over a short time; it is given by the tangent of the cumulative curve at any point ignoring the fine curve.

rate, mean (operant conditioning) Responses per unit of time calculated for an interval during which local rates have changed.

rate, over-all (operant conditioning) Mean response rate for a long period of time, from minutes to hours. Frequently applied to response rates between reinforcements.

rate, response (operant conditioning) Responses per unit of time usually responses per second.

rate, running (operant conditioning) The sustained constant rate, often the only important rate other than zero which is often observed in some schedules.

rate score The number of test items which are completed in a specified amount of time.

rate, terminal (operant conditioning) The response rate reached at the moment of reinforcement.

rate test See *test, rate.*

rating 1. The analysis of qualitative data by scaling. The essential operation consists of making a judgment about an aspect of the data in terms of more, equal, or less. 2. The rank or score given to data.

rating behavior See *behavior, rating.*

rating, man-to-man The comparison of an individual with other individuals who exemplify different degrees of a trait to determine the subject's endowment of this trait.

rating, maturity The determination of the degree of an individual's development along a certain dimension in comparison with the norm of the group to which he belongs.

rating scale An instrument which allows a rater to record the estimated magnitude of a trait or quality for the case in question.

rating, sociability An index of the degree to which a person is sociable and interacts with others.

ratio 1. A relationship between two things, whether in number, degree, or quantity. 2. Specifically, a quotient, as in intelligence quotient, which is equal to the product of the mental age divided by the chronological age.

ratio, affective A calculation, used in the Beck approach to the Rorschach, representing the ratio of number of responses given to the last three cards of the test versus the number given to the first seven cards. Since the last three cards are the only ones in the test which are entirely chromatic, the ratio is believed to afford some index of the manner in which the subject responds to the external world. Other approaches to the Rorschach, such as Klopfer, Hertz, and Piotrowski, include emphasis on the number of responses to the last three cards but compute the ratio differently, as a percentage (8-9-10%) by comparing these responses to all of the responses in the protocol.

ratio correlation See *correlation, ratio.*

ratio estimation See *estimation, ratio.*

ratio, Mendelian See *Mendelian ratio.*

ratio scale See *scale, ratio.*

ratiocination The act or process of thinking, reasoning or of drawing a deductive conclusion.

rational equation A mathematical equation which embodies an hypothesis derived from data and based on assumptions regarding the nature of a specific psychological process. They are generated in an attempt to predict psychological phenomena, the general nature of the parameters being dictated by theory and the exact values determined by the available data.

rational learning Meaningful learning which includes an understanding of the material and an understanding of the relationships among the component facts.

rational number Any number which can be expressed as the quotient of two whole numbers or integers.

rational psychotherapy See *psychotherapy, rational.*

rational type See *type, rational.*

rationale The basic or underlying reason for an opinion, hypothesis or action.

rationalization An effort to distort reality in order to protect one's self-esteem. In its attempt to mediate between the id and reality, the weak ego ascribes rationality to the irrational demands of the id. A strong ego can cope with failures and frustrations, but a weak ego would rather distort the truth than admit defeat. Rationalization is used as a cover-up for mistakes, misjudgments, and failures. It tries to justify behavior by reasons that are made to sound rational.

A common type of rationalization is known as "sour grapes," taking its name from the fable about the fox who, upon failing to get the grapes he desired, consoled himself by calling them "sour." People rationalize in the same way; it takes a mature personality with a strong ego to admit that not all desirable grapes are also attainable. A neurotic tends to make himself believe that sweet grapes are sour rather than admit that he failed.

rauwolfia compounds Compounds derived from the rauwolfia plant and used in the treatment of the psychoses. See *reserpine.*

Ravens Controlled Projection Test See *test, Ravens Controlled Projection.*

raw score See *score, raw.*

Ray, Isaac (1807-1881) American psychiatrist. One of the pioneers of the mental hygiene movement and one of the founding fathers of the American Psychiatric Association.

Rayleigh equation A quantitative statement describing the proportion of red and green stimuli necessary for the normal human eye to perceive yellow. The normal mixture is a spectrum red of 670 mμ and a spectrum green of 535 mμ to yield a yellow of 589 mμ, while, for color-blind or -weak person, more red or green may be required, depending on the predominant weakness.

reaction A response of an organism to a stimulus.

reaction, complex In a reaction time experiment, the requirement that the subject choose or make a discrimination between two or more stimuli.

reaction, compound In a reaction time experiment, the requirement that the subject discriminate between two stimuli or recognize a stimulus before reacting.

reaction, confirming The hypothetical reaction which occurs in the nervous system of the organism when the goal is achieved.

reaction formation (psychoanalysis) A defense mechanism which consists of counteracting the unconscious drive derivative with the opposite conscious attitude such as feeling conscious aversion toward a person toward whom the individual feels unconscious attraction. A strong ego is in control of the entire system; it satisfies some of the id cravings, while it postpones or modifies others and flatly rejects and suppresses those demands which it deems unacceptable. A weak ego resorts to the use of defense mechanisms against impulses. One of these defenses is the development of an attitude diametrically opposed to the id desires. For instance, an individual with strong homosexual impulses may crusade against homosexuality. An individual who hates his father and is very unhappy about it may develop a ritual of affection directed toward his father; an individual torn by an impulse to be dirty may develop compulsive cleanliness.

reaction key A switch interrupting a circuit, much like a telegraph key, which is used in measuring reaction time.

reaction threshold See *threshold, response.*

reaction time 1. The minimal amount of time between the onset of the stimulus and the beginning of the subject's response. 2. See *reaction time: sensory preparation.* 3. See *reaction time: motor preparation.*

reaction time, choice When a subject has learned various responses to various stimuli, the time measured from the presentation of a certain stimulus to the beginning of the response of the subject that is correct for that stimulus.

reaction time, cognitive The time measured from the presentation of a stimulus to the beginning of the response of the subject when he has recognized the stimulus.

reaction time, discrimination The time measured from the presentation of two stimuli to the beginning of the subject's response to the correct stimulus.

reaction time, motor preparation The readiness of the subject to make a particular movement as a response in a reaction time experiment.

reaction time, sensory preparation The readiness of the subject to receive a particular stimulus in a reaction time experiment.

reaction type In reaction time experiments, those people whose responses are governed or dominated by a particular set, either sensory or motor.

reaction type, motor In reaction time experiments, those individuals whose behavior is characterized by a set to respond as quickly as possible with attention to the movement.

reaction type, sensory In reaction time experiments, those individuals whose behavior is characterized by a set to apprehend the incoming stimuli.

reactive epilepsy See *epilepsy, reactive.*

reactive inhibition, conditioned See *inhibition, reactive conditioned.*

reactive schizophrenia See *schizophrenia, reactive.*

readiness law See *law of readiness.*

reading disability Problem or disturbance in the reading ability or progress of a child. It can be due to or associated with a number of factors, including lower scores on the Verbal, Performance and Full Scales of the Wechsler Intelligence Scale for Children (WISC); higher Performance Scale scores than Verbal Scale scores on the WISC; slow development of vocabulary; difficulty with auditory-visual integration and with the perception of auditory stimuli; visual-perceptual difficulties; difficulty in copying a visually presented standard pattern; neurological dysfunction; and inadequate resolution of internal and external conflicts.

reading, mirror Reading from right to left.

reading quotient An index, obtained by dividing the child's reading age, as obtained from a standardized test, by his chronological age, reflecting the child's reading ability in comparison with other children his age.

reading readiness Denotes the stage at which the child, due to developmental, experimental and situational factors, is able to profit by certain conditions of reading instruction.

reading, remedial Specific techniques designed to correct particular faulty reading habits.

reading span The number of words which can be perceived and comprehended by the subject in a single fixation period, that is, the period of time when the eye is not moving in the reading process.

reagin An antibody which may precipitate intense allergic responses.

real 1. Whatever exists. 2. (J. F. Herbart) The world is comprised of small units or things which he called the "reals." All reals react to external pressure by self-preservation. The human soul is one of those reals and ideas or presentations are the self-preservation reactions of the soul. The totality of these ideas form the consciousness.

real anxiety See *anxiety, real.*

real base factor analysis (R. B. Cattell) A system whereby factors are not artificially reduced to equal unit variance, but retain their real differences of "size" from experiment to experiment. This permits an integration of psychometric and manipulative experimental approaches not previously possible. With this design there goes also the possibility of referring scores to a true zero.

realism Philosophical school which accepts the existence of the universe independently of human cognition. Naive realism assumes that the world is as perceived by the sensory apparatus; critical realism views human perception as imperfect and demands validation of perceptions by improved cognitive tools, measurement and critical analysis.

realism, moral (J. Piaget) Children's belief that the right and wrong ideas are objective, rigid and self-evident.

reality The aspect of the universe which is not fantasied.

reality principle (S. Freud) The guiding principle of the ego in contradistinction to the id's pleasure principle; it is the ability to postpone or renounce immediate gratification in order to avoid unpleasant consequences and/or secure a greater reward in the future.

reality testing (S. Freud) An ego function; an appraisal and evaluation of inner and external stimuli of the possibilities of successful satisfaction of instinctual impulses, of the inner resources and of the totality of circumstances followed by an adjustment to the external requirements.

reality therapy See *therapy, reality.*

reasoning Rational, logical thinking.

rebound phenomenon of Gordon Holmes A test for ataxia illustrating the lack of cerebellar control of coordinated movement.

recall The repetition of reinstitution in memory of previously learned materials.

recall method Method of measuring retention by reproduction of items which were presented to an adopted criterion of learning.

recall test See *recall method.*

recapitulation theory The premise that the individual organism in the process of growth and development passes through a series of stages representing stages in the evolutionary development of the species. Also called the biogenetic law.

receiver (communication theory) The structure or process which translates a signal into a message; in an animal it is the sense organs and their connections to the brain.

receiver operating characteristic curve (signal detection theory) Usually referred to as the ROC curve. It is a description of a subject's performance in a signal detection psychophysical experiment. The ROC is the probability of a correct detection by the subject, of a signal when the signal is given, a hit, plotted as a function of the probability of the subject's reporting that a signal was presented when actually there was no signal presented; a false alarm. The ROC is a graphic description of the sensory capacities of the individual subject.

receiving hospital An institution which is designed specifically to receive people suspected of mental disorder for diagnosis and early or short treatment. Commitment is not required although if short treatment is not deemed desirable, the patient is normally referred to other institutions for treatment.

recency, law of See *law of recency.*

recenter To substitute a better figure-ground relation for an inadequate one; to transfer the anchor of a perceptual field to a different part.

recept 1. (neurology) The process or change which occurs in the afferent side of a neural transit. **2.** A mental image formed from that which is common in a series of percepts.

receptive character See *character, receptive.*

receptor A specialized part of the body connected to sensory neurons sensitive to different kinds of stimuli. There are four general classes of receptors: photic receptors which respond to light; mechanical receptors which respond to mechanical stimuli; chemical receptors; and thermal receptors sensitive to warm and cold.

recessive A gene is recessive when it is expressed only when homozygous.

recessive gene See *gene, recessive.*

recessive trait See *trait, recessive.*

recidives in schizophrenia See *schizophrenia, recidives in.*

recidivism The repetition or occurrence of criminal or delinquent behavior or of mental disorder, especially when recurrence leads to a second conviction or commitment.

reciprocal inhibition (C. S. Sherrington) A term which indicates that elicitation of a particular spinal reflex is accompanied by the inhibition of another, and vice versa. Its use was expanded by Wolpe to subsume all cases in which the elicitation of one response seems to bring about a decrement in the strength of a simultaneous response. When a learned response is reciprocally inhibited, its habit strength is

diminished. This fact has been the basis of numerous methods of weakening unadaptive habits, especially anxiety response habits, and has been a central focus of behavior therapy.

reciprocal innervation 1. A system whereby contraction of one of a pair of antagonistic muscles results in the relaxation of the other. **2.** In the autonomic nervous system, an arrangement in which stimulation of the same organ by the sympathetic nervous system results in an opposite effect from the parasympathetic.

reclining position of the patient The requirement of psychoanalytic treatment that the patient lie on a couch which facilitates the development of transference.

recognition method Means of measuring information retention by administering tests on which items that have been presented earlier appear along with new related items, and requesting the subject to choose those which have been previously presented.

recognition test See *recognition method.*

reconditioning The strengthening or re-establishment after extinction of a conditioned response through the reintroduction of the unconditioned stimulus.

reconstruction (psychoanalysis) One of the tasks in psychoanalytic treatment. Recollection of the past in transference permits the resolution of repressed infantile conflicts. S. Freud compared reconstruction to archeological excavation.

reconstruction method Method of measuring retention or learning in which the subject is asked to reconstruct items in the order they were originally presented. The degree to which the reconstruction coincides with the original order is taken as the measure of retention. The number of trials or time required to reproduce the arrangement correctly is taken as the measure of learning.

reconstructive psychotherapy See *psychotherapy, reconstructive.*

record, cumulative (operant conditioning) A graph produced by the cumulative recorder of response rate. On the vertical axis the cumulative number of responses is recorded; on the horizontal axis cumulative time is recorded. Usually events such as reinforcements, stimulus changes, etc. are indicated.

recorder, cumulative (operant conditioning) Most common device used to record responses in operant conditioning. It produces a graph of the total number of responses as a function of time. In other words it provides a graph of the response rate. When in operation a motor drives paper at a constant speed. Each response moves a recording pen a constant amount. The result is a graph with time on the abscissa and responses on the ordinate.

recovery Regaining health; restoration of a normal physical or mental state.

recovery, spontaneous 1. The reappearance of an

extinguished conditioned response following rest. The response is weaker and will be extinguished if not reinforced. 2. The disappearance of symptoms and general improvement of mental patients without treatment.

recovery time   The period of time which follows a response in which the response cannot be repeated or elicited.

recreational therapy   See *therapy, recreational.*

recruitment   See *fractionation.*

rectilinear distribution   See *distribution, rectilinear.*

rectilinear regression   See *regression, linear.*

recurrent mania   See *mania, recurrent.*

red nucleus   A group of neurons located in the front part of the tegmentum in the midbrain, giving rise to the rubrospinal fluid.

redintegration   1. The re-establishment or re-forming of a whole. 2. The principle which is characterized by the recall of other elements in the whole or the whole itself when a few of the elements are present in consciousness. 3. (H. Hollingworth) The principle which holds the psychological consequence of an event as a whole tends to be elicited by the presence of a single element of that event. 4. The principle which holds that a stimulus which is contiguous with a response elicited by another stimulus will in the future tend to elicit that response, i.e., the principle operative in classical conditioning.

reduced cue, principle of   A learning principle which holds that with repetition of a stimulus-response unit a progressively smaller part of the stimulus is required to elicit the response.

reduced eye   A simplified and schematic representation or model of the average, unaccommodated human eye.

reduced score   A score which has been lessened by some constant in order to facilitate computation.

reduction division   (biology) The formation of gametes or sex cells through a process in which half of the normal number of chromosomes go to the daughter cells; meiosis.

reductionism   The belief that a certain science can be presented in terms of another science, either in the methods of research (methodological reductionism) or in its data and theory (theoretical reductionism)

reductionism, methodological   The application of research techniques borrowed from one scientific discipline to research problems of another discipline, e.g. Pavlov borrowed his psychological research techniques from biology; Margaret Mead, in anthropology, borrowed from psychology.

reductionism, theoretical   The belief that the entire subject matter of one science can be presented in terms of another science, e.g. psychology can be presented in neurophysiological terms. In psychology one can distinguish six distinct approaches to this problem: 1) Radical reductionism (Bekhterev, Hebb, Watson, et al.) which assumes identity in the subject matter described in both sciences. 2) Hoped-for-reductionism (Pavlov, Freud, Hull, et al.) which assumes that some day psychological data will be presented in physico-chemical terms. 3) Logical reductionism (Feigl, Nagel, et al.) assumes that the logical constructs can be presented in the same way in both sciences. 4) Transitionism (B. B. Wolman) assumes an evolutionary mind-body continuum. 5) Rejection of reductionism (K. Lewin, Skinner). 6) Dualism (practically all psychologists prior to the twentieth century) which believes in two separate substances, mind and body.

reductive interpretation   (C. G. Jung) An interpretation in which behavioral products are not seen as symbols but rather as a sign or symptom of the unconscious processes.

redundancy   See *T function.*

reference axes   (factor analysis) The axes of two orthogonal, or independent factors in relation to the location of other factor axes.

reference group   (sociology) A group with which an individual identifies himself. When an individual's behavior at a particular time is determined by the norms of one of the groups he belongs to (e.g. his economic, religious, or occupational group).

reference, ideas of   Morbid viewing of one's own emotions, thoughts, and attitudes projected on others as originating in them.

reference, objective   A quality of pointing to the objective world which is inherent in certain perceptual processes.

reference vector   (factor analysis) The set of coordinates or axes that test vectors are located in reference to, giving grounding lines or planes which allow the geometrical and trigonometrical expression of the mathematical relations found in the correlation matrix. These axes must retain the same origin as the test vectors in rotation but may be rotated around the origin.

referent   The object, abstraction, event, or experience to which the meaning of a word or other symbol points.

referral   Referring a client or patient to another therapist, agency, or institution.

referred pain   See *pain, referred.*

referred sensation   See *sensation, referred.*

refined mode   See *mode, refined.*

reflected color   Color which is perceived as reflected from an object.

reflection   1. See *introspection.* 2. Going over the meaning, value, or significance of experiences, facts, or events. 3. (physics) The reversal or turning back of particles or waves which strike a surface. 4. The image of an object in a mirror. 5. (factor analysis) The alteration of the algebraic signs in some of the columns and the corresponding rows in order to make consistent the interpretation of the factor loadings as related to certain tests.

reflection angle (optics) The angle formed by the path of a beam of light and the line perpendicular to the surface at the point from which the beam is reflected.

reflection of feelings (C. Rogers) A counseling or psychotherapeutic technique in which the therapist restates or reiterates what the patient has said in an attempt to accentuate the emotional tone rather than the intellectual meaning.

reflection response (Rorschach) A response in which one-half of the inkblot is reported as a reflection of the other half.

reflex 1. A simple stimulus response connection believed to be unlearned and characteristic of a species. 2. (H. Spencer) The simplest reactions which are unflexible and gross adjustments to the environment. 3. (I. P. Pavlov) Inborn permanent and unchangeable reactions of organisms to stimulation from the external world which take place through the activity of the nervous system. 4. (B. F. Skinner) Any observed correlation of stimulus and response which constitutes the simple unit of behavior. 5. A mechanical act requiring no thought.

reflex, abdominal Contraction of the muscles in the abdominal wall in response to the stroking of the skin of the belly.

reflex, acute affective (E. Kretschmer) An involuntary emotional reaction to definite and strong stresses that fades away after a period of rest. Originally identified in soldiers during wartime. Two examples are compulsive crying and fine muscular tremblings.

reflex, alternating response Two responses or reflexes that follow one another in their occurrence, usually in a series. For example, the alternating flexion and extension in walking movements.

reflex-arc (J. Dewey) The neurological unit which in theory consists of the receptor, an intermediate neuron and an effector.

reflex, attention A reflexive change in pupil size when attention is fixed upon something suddenly.

reflex, audito-oculogyric Movement of the eyes in the direction of a sudden sound.

reflex, axon A peripheral reflex which is thought to be mediated by collateral branches of the afferent neurons activating an effector, a muscle or a gland.

reflex, Bekhterev-Mendel (V. M. Bekhterev and K. Mendel) A dorsal flexion of the foot with a flexion of the knee and hip on the same side upon release of a foot passively bent in a plantar direction. This reflex is seen in pyramidal tract disease.

reflex, blinking The closing of the eyelids caused by the exposure to bright light, by an attention shift or by tearing.

reflex circle The tendency for muscle contractions

to stimulate proprioceptive reflex loops, strengthening in turn the muscular contraction.

reflex circuit See *reflex-arc.*

reflex, conditioned (I. P. Pavlov) A new and temporary connection between stimulus and response which is the main function of the higher parts of the central nervous system. It is formed when an indifferent stimulus is simultaneously presented with a stimulus which elicits an unconditioned reflex. Following repeated presentations, the indifferent stimulus alone will evoke the same reflex.

reflex, consensual eye The contraction of the pupil in the shaded eye when the other pupil is stimulated by a bright light.

reflex, cranial A reflex controlled by one of the cranial nerves.

reflex, direct Reflex in which both the receptor and effector are on the same side of the body.

reflex, grasping and groping The reflexive clutching by the fingers or toes of any object that stimulates the palm or sole.

reflex, inhibitory The reflexive relaxation of one of a pair of antagonistic muscles following the excitation of the other muscle of the pair.

reflex, knee jerk See *reflex, patellar.*

reflex, laryngeal Coughing caused by irritation of the larynx.

reflex, mass Indiscriminate response of a large group of effectors to a given stimulus.

reflex, negative movement (I. P. Pavlov) A form of the general instinct of life consisting of movements which guard the organism against injury.

reflex, oculocardiac A decrease of heart rate as a result of pressure upon the eyeballs.

reflex or response, palmar Reflexive hand-grasp action of the newborn.

reflex, patellar Spontaneous forward extension of the lower leg elicited by a sudden sharp tap against the patellar tendon which is just below the knee cap.

reflex, plantar Spontaneous flexing of the toes which is produced by stroking the sole of the foot.

reflex, positive movement (I. P. Pavlov) One form of the general instinct of life consisting of movements toward conditions favorable for life.

reflex, pupillary The change in the size of the pupil as the muscle of the iris contracts or relaxes, responding to altered light intensity or to a changed fixation point.

reflex reserve (B. F. Skinner) Total number of responses made when the response no longer occasions reinforcement, i.e. during extinction. It was a measure of resistance to extinction. The term is no longer used.

reflex, Schaeffer (M. Schaeffer) A pathological reflex manifested by dorsal reflexion of the big toe when the Achilles tendon is pinched.

reflex sensitization principle The proposition which holds that a response may sometimes be elicited by a previously less effective or neutral stimulus following repeated elicitation of a response by a stimulus.

reflex, spinal A reflex which is mediated by the spinal cord and does not require the brain for the connection of afferent and efferent fibers.

reflex time; reflex latency The time which is measured from the application of a stimulus and the beginning of a reflex response.

reflex, unconditioned (I. P. Pavlov) An innate reflex derived from the reflex of life whose purpose is the preservation of life, which is connected with a definite sensory mechanism or analyzer and a center in the nervous system.

reflexes, allied Two or more simultaneous or closely associated reflexes that combine to form a response unit.

reflexes, postural The group of reflexes which help to maintain posture and keep the body in relatively stationary position.

reflexology 1. A system of laws in the field of learning experiments, in which a simple reflex connection, such as might be due to a neurological reflex arc, is supposed to exist between the stimulus and the response. 2. (V. M. Bekhterev) A theory that explains all behavior in terms of conditioned and unconditioned reflexes or combinations of them.

refraction A change or bending in the direction of flow of a wave, especially of a light wave.

refraction, index of A number giving the degree to which a light wave is bent in the passage from one transparent medium to another and dependent upon the nature of the two media and the curvature of the bounding surface.

refractory period 1. A brief period of time which follows the stimulation of a nerve during which it cannot be restimulated by another stimulus. 2. A brief period of time which follows the initial movement of a movement system or set of similar movements in which a second movement cannot be initiated even if it is not antagonistic to the first.

refractory period, relative A period of time following stimulation of a nerve in which the nerve can be restimulated only by the application of a significantly more powerful stimulus.

regard, field of Total space visible by rotation of the eye with the head stationary.

regard, line of An imaginary straight line from the fixation point to the center of the rotation of the eye.

regard, point of Fixation point.

regeneration (biology) Restoration of a lost part of the body by growth.

region, inner personal (K. Lewin) That part of the personality, topographically represented as a concentric circle within the larger circle representing the perceptual-motor region. The inner personal region is composed primarily of needs (physiological conditions, desires, intentions), some of which are peripherally located and therefore more accessible to the environment than others which are more centrally located.

regional epilepsy See *epilepsy, myoclonic.*

register, vocal See *vocal register.*

regnancy (H. A. Murray) The unit composed of the total physiological processes occurring at a single moment, which constitute dominant configurations in the brain. A single process comprising part of the regnancy is referred to as a regnant process.

regnant construct See *construct, regnant.*

regression 1. A movement backward. 2. A return to earlier or less mature behaviors or earlier or less mature levels of organization of behavior. 3. (psychoanalysis) One of the defense mechanisms in which the individual, faced with an anxiety arousing instinctual wish or impulse, returns to a stage which has previously been cathected by libido and is thus less anxiety and guilt provoking. There are two forms of regression: that in which there is a return to the original object and that in which there is a return to the level of infantile sexual organization. The return to an earlier level of organization always carries with it characteristics of the later level, possibly allowing the reworking of earlier conflicts by a more mature ego organization. 4. During the generalized weakening of retention, the tendency for memories to be lost in the inverse order of their acquisition. 5. (genetics) In individuals of the species, the tendency to return to the typical form. 6. (conditioning) The reappearance of a previously extinguished conditioned response after punishment. 7. (conditioning) During the extinction of a conditioned response to a stimulus, the reappearance of a previously extinguished conditioned response to that same stimulus. 8. (statistics) The relationship between two paired variables in which the predicted score of the dependent variable is nearer to the sample mean than is the value of the independent variable.

regression analysis (statistics) Adapted from the least square multiple regression equation, this procedure is used in predicting the value of a continuous, quantitative variable from a non-quantitative category or rating score.

regression coefficient (b) 1. (statistics) the multiplier of the independent term in the linear regression equation. It is represented by the formula:

$$b = r \, \frac{\sigma_y}{\sigma_x}$$

where r is the correlation coefficient, and x is the variance of a particular set of scores. 2. The constant in a linear regression equation which measures the slope of a regression line.

regression curve A smooth curve fitted to the means of a group of variables in a correlation table.

regression curvilinear See *regression line, curvilinear.*

regression equation An equation taking the form $Y = bX + a$ and employed for computing the deviation from average of one variable from the given value of another by the formula:

$$Y^1 = by.x\ (X-M_x) + M_y, \text{ where}$$
$$Y^1 = \text{the predicted score}$$
$$by.x = \text{regression coefficient}$$
$$M_x = \text{mean of } x$$
$$M_y = \text{mean of } y$$
$$X = \text{given x value.}$$

regression equation, multiple (statistics) Equation for computing a criterion variable score for an individual from his scores on several other variables. The criterion valuable score is derived from the correlation of each of these variables with the criterion and from their intercorrelations.

regression equation, partial See *regression equation, multiple.*

regression, filial The tendency of parents who possess characteristics that widely depart from the mean of the species to produce offspring who depart less widely.

regression in the service of the ego (E. Kris) A temporary return to an earlier level of functioning to serve reality needs. This regression aids ego functions being controlled, circumscribed and reversible and promotes imaginative creative thinking because the primary processes become available to secondary process functions.

regression line 1. A line that shows the relationship between two variables. 2. A line that is the best fit for a relationship according to some theorem. It may be a curve or a straight line.

regression line, curvilinear The line that best fits the means in a correlation table. A regular curve, not a straight line.

regression, linear The regression that occurs when the line that best fits the means in a correlation table forms a line that is approximately straight.

regression, non-linear A regression line that is not a straight line. It includes curvilinear regression lines.

regression, phenomenal The size of an object one perceives that lies between what would be expected from the actual physical stimulus size of the object and what would be expected from object constancy. This entails a shift toward true physical size and away from perfect perceptual constancy.

regression, teleologic (S. Arieti) Regression for the purpose of avoiding anxiety and re-establishing a psychic equilibrium, a typical occurrence in schizophrenia.

regressive behavior Behavior more appropriate to an earlier level of development.

regressive electroshock therapy See *therapy, regressive electroshock.*

regulator gene According to the operon theory of gene action of Jacob and Monod, a regulator gene synthesizes a repressor substance which inhibits the action of a specific operator gene, thus preventing the synthesis of messenger RNA by that operon.

rehabilitation The process of restoring a person to the best possible level of functioning following a physical, mental or emotional disorder. This process involves training him to find employment and helping him to adjust to his status in the interpersonal sphere.

reification Dealing with ideas and concepts as if they were concrete objects.

Reil, island of A section of the cortex located at the bottom of the Sylvian fissure and covered by cortical folds present only in primates. Also called insula.

Reilly bodies Unusual cytoplasmic granules in white blood cells.

reinforcement 1. (I. P. Pavlov) Reinforcement takes place when the conditioned stimulus is presented simultaneously or at an effective interval before the unconditioned stimulus. 2. (E. L. Thorndike) Pleasure producing, rewarding stimuli, called "satisfiers," stamp in, that is strengthen the responses. Thorndike's "stamping in" corresponds to reinforcement. 3. (C. L. Hull) Primary reinforcement takes place whenever an effector activity (R) is closely associated with a stimulus afferent impulse or trace (s) and the conjunction is closely associated with the rapid diminution in the motivational stimulus (S_D or S_G), there will result an increment (Δ) to a tendency for that stimulus to evoke the response 4. (B. F. Skinner) Presenting a reinforcing stimulus when a response occurs, or arranging such presentation is operant reinforcement. Presenting a conditioned and an unconditioned stimulus at approximately the same time is respondent reinforcement.

reinforcement, accidental The unplanned coincidence of a response and a reinforcing event. For example, in certain programs designed to establish a discrimination, the appearance of the discriminative stimulus may coincide with a response in its absence. Also called incidental or spurious reinforcement.

reinforcement, alternative Reinforcement that occurs according to either a fixed-ratio or fixed-interval schedule, depending on which condition is satisfied first. For example, the alternative conditions might be 50 responses or two minutes. In such a situation, if the 50 responses occurred before the two minutes passed, a reinforcement would be given; if not, reinforcement would take place after the two minute time period had elapsed.

reinforcement, aperiodic Reinforcement schedule in which reinforcement occurs irregularly and intermittently, not continuously.

reinforcement, conditioned A rewarding event or

state of affairs which obtains its effectiveness from a prior learning or conditioning experience.

reinforcement, differential Selective reinforcement of a response to one stimulus with a greater amount of reinforcement than a response to another stimulus. This operation results in discrimination.

reinforcement, homogeneous The simultaneous presentation of two stimuli each of which elicits the same or similar response.

reinforcement, interlocking A kind of intermittent reinforcement consisting of decreasing ratio of required responses per reinforcement.

reinforcement, intermittent See *reinforcement, schedule of.*

reinforcement, intermittent schedule of See *reinforcement, schedule of.*

reinforcement, internal A bodily process which increases the probability of the occurrence of a certain response.

reinforcement, interpolated The insertion of one block of one schedule of reinforcements into another for a brief period of time.

reinforcement, Jendrassik A method of increasing a reflex response, usually the patellar reflex, by having the subject interlock his hands and pull and presenting the usual stimulus the moment the subject begins to pull.

reinforcement mechanisms Areas of the brain which are positively or negatively reinforcing. The posterior hypothalamus and midbrain have positive rewarding qualities more effective as rewards than food. Stimulation of the dorsal diencephalic zone is a negative reinforcement which an organism tries to avoid.

reinforcement, negative The use of coercive stimuli for reduction or prevention of probability of reinforcement.

reinforcement, neural The rewarding effect that one response has on a simultaneously occurring response resulting in a stronger response.

reinforcement of affect (S. Freud) The process in which the suppressed ideas and the mechanism of suppression combine their forces producing mutual cooperation.

reinforcement, partial **1.** Intermittent reinforcement or reinforcement which does not occur on every trial but only sporadically, resulting in slower learning rate and slower extinction rate than continuous reinforcement. **2.** Presentation of only part of a reward or of reinforcing conditions.

reinforcement, positive A reinforcer which when presented as a consequence of a particular response or behavior increases the occurrence of that response.

reinforcement, predelay A modification of the delayed response technique. The experimental arrival is rewarded at a certain place, then prevented for a while from returning to that place. The return of the animal to the same place after a period of delay.

reinforcement, primary **1.** A stimulus increasing the probability of a response without necessitating the learning of the value of the reinforcer. **2.** The reduction of a primary-drive state through drive-stimulus reduction.

reinforcement, schedule of (operant conditioning) In the operant situation usually not every response is reinforced. In the laboratory and in life, similar behaviors seldom have the same effect upon the environment in two instances; therefore, the effect called reinforcement is seldom the consequence of every response. Most reinforcements are intermittent. A schedule of reinforcement is the prescription or rule for presenting and terminating reinforcing stimuli that are contingent upon behavior.

The schedule specifies in what way the presentation of the reinforcing stimulus is dependent upon the occurrence of the response. A schedule, therefore, may be defined without reference to its effect upon behavior.

Schedules have regular, orderly and profound effects on the organism's behavior. Each schedule produces a characteristic behavior which may be steady, constant, or cyclic with predictable changes. Just by looking at a record of responses it is often possible to tell what schedule was operative without knowing what type of organism was responding.

reinforcement, schedule of: adjusting (ADJ) Intermittent schedule in which the value of the interval or ratio is changed in some systematic way after reinforcement as a function of the immediately preceding performance. The change in performance requirement occurs from reinforcement to reinforcement in the adjusting schedule while in the interlocking schedule the change in requirement occurs within the reinforcement.

reinforcement, schedule of: alternate (ALT) Intermittent reinforcement schedule in which a response is reinforced either by a fixed ratio or fixed interval schedule whichever is satisfied first. Thus, e.g. in ALT FI 5 FR 300, the first response is reinforced either after a period of 5 minutes if 300 responses have not been made, or upon the completion of 300 responses before 5 minutes have past.

reinforcement, schedule of: chained (CHAIN) Intermittent schedule similar to a tandem schedule; however, a stimulus change is correlated to the completion of the first part of the schedule. The second stimulus controls behavior appropriate to the second part of the schedule.

reinforcement, schedule of: concurrent (CONC) (B. F. Skinner) Two or more schedules independently arranged, but operative at the same time. Each independent schedule is programmed on a separate operandum. For example, in a CONC FI 5 FR 300 reinforcements are programmed to be delivered on one operandum after the first response, five minutes after the previous reinforcement has been delivered on that operandum; at the same time reinforcements are programmed to be delivered after 300 responses on the other operandum. The organism has free access to both operandi; however, since it is impossible to respond on both operandi simultaneously, the organism chooses the operandum, thus choosing the schedule. Concurrent schedules are one way of studying choice behavior and establishing preferences with an operant paradigm.

reinforcement, schedule of: conjugate (B. F. Skinner) Schedule in which responses initiate or terminate a constant, subthreshold change in stimulation. Thus, for example, if the subject does not respond, the intensity of illumination constantly but gradually decreases until darkness is reached. If the subject responds, the stimulus change can be terminated or reversed; the more he responds, the brighter it gets. The point is, in conjugate schedules, that stimulus intensities are scheduled to change on a continuum and responses either terminate or reverse the direction of this.

reinforcement, schedule of: conjunctive (CONJ) (B. F. Skinner) Intermittent reinforcement schedule in which both a ratio and interval must be satisfied for a response to occasion a reinforcement. Thus, for example, in ALT FI 5 FR 300 a response is reinforced 5 minutes after the previous reinforcement and after at least 300 responses have been made.

reinforcement, schedule of: continuous (CRF) (B. F. Skinner) A nonintermittent reinforcement schedule in which every emitted response is reinforced.

reinforcement, schedule of: differential reinforcement of high rates (DRH) (B. F. Skinner) Reinforcement occurs when the response rate is above some specified value.

reinforcement, schedule of: differential reinforcement of low rates (DRL) (B. F. Skinner) Reinforcement schedule in which a response is reinforced only when a specific time has elapsed since the immediately preceding response. Thus reinforcement is contingent upon a low rate of responding.

reinforcement, schedule of: extinction (EXT) (B. F. Skinner) A nonintermittent schedule in which every emitted response has the same effect on the environment, i.e. no response is reinforced.

reinforcement, schedule of: fixed interval (FI) (operant conditioning) Intermittent reinforcement schedule in which the presentation of the reinforcing stimulus to the organism is contingent upon the first response the organism makes after a fixed period of time since the previous reinforcement. All other responses made before or after the reinforcement have no effect upon the presentation of the reinforcement. This schedule is designated usually in minutes; thus FI 5 means that the first response made five minutes after the previous reinforcement is reinforced.

reinforcement, schedule of: fixed ratio (FR) An intermittent reinforcement schedule in which a response is reinforced upon completion of a fixed number of responses counted from the preceding reinforcement. The ratio refers to the ratio of responses to reinforcement. This schedule is indicated by the addition of the ratio after FR; thus in FR 100 the one-hundredth response after the previous reinforcement is reinforced.

reinforcement, schedule of: interlocking (INTER) Intermittent reinforcement schedule in which a response is reinforced upon completion of a number of responses; but this number changes during the interval that follows the previous reinforcement. For example, immediately after reinforcement, 300 responses may be required for another reinforcement; but this may be reduced as a linear function of time, so that after 10 minutes one response will occasion reinforcement. Therefore, if the organism responded rapidly it would have to have emitted nearly the 300 responses. If responding was slower, it would have been reinforced after a smaller number of responses. Of course, many different cases are possible. In an increasing interlocking schedule ratio, requirements increase as some function of time.

reinforcement, schedule of: intermittent (B. F. Skinner) One or two classes of reinforcement schedules in which only certain selected occurrences of a response are reinforced. The schedule is the rule followed by the environment; in an experiment, by the apparatus in determining which among the many occurrences of a response will be reinforced. The intermittent schedules include: fixed ratio (FR), fixed interval (FI), variable ratio (VR), variable interval (VI), alternative (ALT), conjunctive (CONJ), interlocking (INTER), tandem (TAND), chained (CHAIN), adjusting (ADJ), multiple (MULT), mixed (MIX), interpolated (INTER), concurrent (CONC). The second class of reinforcement schedules is the non-intermittent schedules.

reinforcement, schedule of: interpolated (INTER) (B. F. Skinner) An intermittent schedule in which a small block of reinforcements, contingent on one schedule, may be introduced into a background of another schedule. For example, a block of 10 reinforcements on a FR 50 is inserted into a six hour period of reinforcement on FI 10.

reinforcement, schedule of: mixed (MIX) Intermittent schedule similar to a multiple schedule except stimuli are not correlated with the schedules. For example, MIX FI 5 FR 50 indicates a schedule in which reinforcement occurs after either a 5 minute interval or 50 responses. These possibilities occur either randomly or in a determined proportion in a given program.

reinforcement, schedule of: multiple (MULT) Intermittent schedule consisting of two or more independent schedules alternating at random and presented successively to the organism. Each schedule correlates with a different discriminative stimulus which is presented as long as the schedule is operative. For example, in MULT FI 5 FR 100 the response key is sometimes red, and sometimes green, the former when reinforcement is occasioned after 100 responses.

reinforcement, schedule of: non-intermittent (B. F. Skinner) One of two classes of reinforcement schedules in which every response has the same environmental effect, i.e. each response is equally effective in producing reinforcement. The non-intermittent schedules are continuous reinforcement (CRF) and extinction (EXT). The second class of reinforcement schedules is the intermittent schedules.

reinforcement, schedule of: second order The behavior specified by a complete schedule is treated as a unitary response which is itself reinforced according to some schedule of primary reinforcement; thus a way of specifying schedules of schedules. For example, FR 3 (FI 2) indicates a second order schedule in which primary reinforcement is contingent upon completion of three successive FI 2 schedules. This schedule FR 3 (FI 2) in which there are no extroceptive stimulus changes upon completion of the FI schedules is, in the terminology of Ferster and Skinner, a tandem schedule, TAND FI 2 FI 2 FI 2.

reinforcement; schedule of: tandem (TAND) Intermittent schedule in which reinforcement is contingent upon the completion of two schedules, the second beginning when the first has been completed. However, there is no change in stimulus correlated with the change in schedule. For example, in TAND FI 10 FR 5, reinforcement occurs after 5 responses, counted only after a response that occurred 10 minutes after the previous reinforcement. In TAND FR 300 FI 5, 300 responses must be made, followed by a 5 minute period whereupon a response occasions the reinforcement.

reinforcement, schedule of: variable interval (VI) Intermittent reinforcement schedule in which responses are reinforced after a time interval from the previous reinforcement. This time interval is variable between reinforcements and is usually a random series of intervals having a given mean and lying within an arbitrary range. The average interval of reinforcements, usually in minutes, is indicated by addition of a number to the letters VI, thus VI 5 indicates a variable interval schedule with a mean interval of 5 minutes.

reinforcement, schedule of: variable ratio (VR) Intermittent reinforcement schedule in which a response is reinforced upon completion of a number of responses counted from the preceding reinforcement. The specific ratios are from a random series of ratios having a given mean and lying within an arbitrary range. The mean ratio may be noted by a number; for example, VR 100 indicates that on the average, the one-hundredth response is reinforced.

reinforcement, secondary A stimulus which derives its reinforcing qualities from previous conditioning experience in which it has been associated with a primary reward.

reinforcement, serial Reinforcement of any particular response in serial learning.

reinforcement, successive differential See *conditioning, approximation.*

reinforcement withdrawal A therapeutic method of withholding reinforcement for responses to reduce the probability of the recurrence of these responses.

reinforcer, conditioned A stimulus which has reinforcing properties by virtue of previous learning or conditioning experience.

reinforcing stimulus The unconditioned or rewarding stimulus which is presented or naturally experienced following the subject's having performed the correct response.

reintegration See *redintegration.*

Reix limen (RL) (psychophysics) German phrase for absolute threshold.

rejection 1. The act of determining something or somebody as worthless, or tossing something aside as unimportant, or of refusing to place or locate something in a certain class or category. **2.** (psychoanalysis) A mechanism involving the denial of gratification to an instinctual demand while tolerating the existence of the demand in the conscious mind.

rejection need See *need, rejection.*

relapse A recurrence of symptoms after cure or a period of improvement.

relation measure (statistics) A mathematical formulation which describes the change in one variable paralleling the change in another variable.

relations, informational (J. P. Guilford) Definitive connections between items of information based on variables or points of contact that apply to them.

relationship psychotherapy See *psychotherapy, relationship.*

relative refractory period See *refractory period, relative.*

relativism, cultural The belief that the concepts of behavior disorders depend on a particular cultural setting, and individuals believed to be mentally disturbed in one culture may appear normal in another.

relaxation, progressive (E. Jacobson) A relaxation training technique in which the person, starting with the most easy muscles to control, learns to relax muscle groups, leading eventually to being able to relax his whole body.

relaxation therapy See *therapy, relaxation.*

relearning and saving method See *saving method.*

release phenomenon 1. (neurology) The activity in a lower center of the brain when a higher controlling center is not functioning. **2.** The inhibited motor discharge occurring when a higher brain center is damaged.

release therapy See *therapy, release.*

releaser (ethology) A stimulus which is highly specific and which elicits species-specific behavior.

reliability The degree to which results are consistent on repetition of the experiment.

reliability coefficient See *coefficient, reliability.*

reliability, index of An estimate of the correlation between the obtained scores on a test and the theoretically true scores on the test.

reliability sampling A measure of the reliability of two or more samples derived from the same population.

reliability, split-half method of A measure of reliability in which items from one part of a test are correlated with items from another part of the test.

religious mania See *mania, religious.*

religious therapy See *therapy, religious.*

religious type See *type, religious.*

remedial instruction Didactic techniques used with children with learning difficulties

remedial reading See *reading, remedial.*

remission Disappearance of symptoms.

remote association In verbal learning, the connection between one item in a list and one removed from it by at least two steps.

remote association test See *test, remote association.*

remote conditioning See *track conditioned response.*

renal aminoacidurias See *aminoacidurias, renal.*

renal dwarfism See *dwarfism, renal.*

renifleur An individual for whom sexual excitement is associated with certain odors.

repetition compulsion 1. (S. Freud) The conservative tendency of instincts to recreate and repeat an earlier state. The repetition of the experience is an active attempt to master the anxiety experienced previously. It functions to bind energy and reduce tension and manifests a tendency of the instincts to return to the inorganic state. 2. An irrational need to repeat a particular behavior.

repetition, law of The proposition which holds that a function is facilitated by being used or exercised and is weakened by disuse.

replication The breaking down of an experiment into various components, each containing the essential parts to allow for a comparison between the several replicas, enabling the discrimination between the effect of the experimental conditions and those of irregular or variable conditions.

report method Method of measuring retention in which the subject is asked to report his observations after witnessing an event or examining a picture or number of objects for a given length of time. The number of correctly reported items is taken as the measure of retention.

representation An obsolete term (*Darstellung*) used loosely as an idea, concept, perception, etc.

representative design 1. (E. Brunswik) An experimental procedure utilizing the covariation of a group of variables in the study of stimulus-response relationships. 2. A type of experiment in which a representative or stratified sample of subjects is included.

representative factors 1. Those activities which are hypothesized to allow the organism to continue or to renew a response despite the withdrawal of the original stimulus. 2. The verbal symbols and imagery serving as mediators of ideational activity.

representative measure or score A number—the mean or median, for example—which can stand for all the scores collectively.

representative sampling See *sampling, representative.*

repression (psychoanalysis) The main defense mechanism. Repression is an unconscious exclusion from the consciousness of objectionable impulses, memories and ideas. The ego, as it were, pushes the objectionable material down into the unconscious and acts as if the objectionable material were nonexistent.

repression, primary (psychoanalysis) That process which originally expels the instinctual derivative from the conscious mind.

repression resistance See *resistance, repression.*

repression, secondary (psychoanalysis) That process which prevents the return to the conscious mind of the expelled instinctual derivative.

reproduction 1. The making or creation of a near copy of something. 2. (biology) The creation of a new organism by a parent organism or by parent organisms. 3. (learning) The doing of a task in the manner in which it was first learned.

reproduction method 1. See *adjustment procedure.* 2. A means of assessing retention through the reproduction as completely as possible of learned material.

reproductive facilitation (learning) An increase in the level of reproduction of some learned material as a result of some activity which occurs between the learning trials and the reproduction trials.

reproductive function 1. The sum of the activities, operations or processes involved in the making or creation of a new organism. 2. A specific act, such as sexual intercourse, involved in the creation of a new organism.

reproductive interference (learning) A decrease in the reproduction of some learned material as a result of some activity which occurs between the learning trials and the reproduction trials.

reproductive strength An expression of the summation of all factors which tend to increase the probability that a specific response will be made.

research 1. A detailed and systematic attempt, often prolonged, to discover or confirm through objective investigation the facts pertaining to a specified problem or problems and the laws and principles controlling it. 2. Library, record, document, or other investigation which attempts to uncover or develop new facts concerning some subject, especially towards the end of developing an historical understanding or perspective of the subject.

research for action Research aiming at social change.

research, market 1. The systematic investigation of buying and selling behavior. 2. The systematic investigation of the expected volume of sales under specific circumstances.

research, personnel Investigation of the individual and of groups with reference to work situations and work conditions both physical and social as a means of dealing with personnel needs and problems and of meeting management needs and goals.

reserpine A purified alkaloid extract of Rauwolfia which produces a generally depressant effect. It has been used in the treatment of the psychoses, hyper-aggressivity and hyperactivity. The complications—initial considerable sleepiness, increase in heart rate and, in high doses, Parkinsonian symptoms—have led generally to the use of the phenothiazines in the treatment of these conditions.

residential treatment See *treatment, residential.*

residual 1. That which remains after certain events or processes, especially accidents, illnesses or operations. Residual vision is the vision which remains after being partially blinded. 2. The difference between a computed and observed value. 3. (factor analysis) The variance remaining once the variance of all factors has been extracted.

residual epilepsy See *epilepsy, residual.*

residual matrix The matrix which remains following the extraction of the variance due to a factor.

residues, method of (J. S. Mill) One of the working principles of induction which holds that the unexplained remainder of an antecedent condition or event results in the unexplained remainder of an effect.

resignation, neurotic (K. Horney) A solution for inner conflicts, involving the avoidance of and withdrawal from the situations, events and experiences which would tend to bring the conflict into awareness.

resistance (psychoanalysis) Resistance is a continuation of repression which interferes, often actively, with the progress of the analysis. The patient resists in various ways, working for or reaching the goal for which he entered analysis. It is an expression of the wish to maintain the repression of the unconscious desires. The analysis of the resistances, along with the analysis of the transference, forms the basic task of psychoanalysis.

resistance, epinosic Resistance aimed at the perpetuation of secondary gain. The patient may wish to stay neurotic and gain all the sympathy and consideration that can be wrung from the sick role. It comes from the ego, as if the ego feared to give up its neurotic mechanisms and face a head-on collision with instinctual forces. This form of resistance occurs most frequently at the beginning of treatment, and in the final stage, when the patient is expected to abandon infantile modes of emotional life.

resistance, id (psychoanalysis) Resistance dominated by the repetition compulsion. The resistance takes the form of repeating the same process rather than recollecting it. Id resistances cannot be easily lifted because they hinge on the basic rules of unconscious behavior—the constancy and pleasure principles. A prolonged process of working through is required.

resistance, repression (psychoanalysis) Resistance in which the patient attempts to maintain the repression of unacceptable instinctual derivatives by forgetting most recent events; by being unable to free associate; by preventing a continuous flow of free associations in that they go in every possible direction; and by accepting the analyst's interpretation and applying it to everyone but himself.

resistance, superego Resistance to psychoanalytic treatment stemming from the superego. It originates from a sense of guilt requiring punishment for alleviation and, therefore, opposes any success in treatment. Also called negative therapeutic reaction.

resistance, transference Resistance in which the patient attempts to avoid the treatment of the neurosis by acting-out his transference-love or -hate for the analyst. The task of the analyst is to transform the acting-out of these past feelings into a recollection of them.

resolving power 1. The ability or capacity of the eye to perceive two distinct objects when the two objects are viewed simultaneously. 2. The ability of the eye to perceive two distinct objects when the two objects are casting images in close proximity on the retina.

resonance 1. The vibration of an object resulting from force applied with periodic frequency, especially the vibrations in an object in response to external sound. 2. A deep, rich and vibrant vocal quality.

resonance theory of hearing See *hearing, theory of: resonance theory.*

resonator An instrument or device which makes use of the principle of resonance in the intensification of a tone.

respiratory disorders See *disorders, respiratory.*

respondent behavior Behavior which is elicited by a particular stimulus.

response; R 1. An answer, especially a formal answer, such as to a question on a test or questionnaire. 2. Any process in the body, muscular, glandular, etc., which results from stimulation. 3. A psychic process which results from previous psychic processes, sensory or imaginal. 4. Any overt or covert behavior; the class or the organisms executing processes.

response amplitude 1. A quantitative measure of a response, assessed in terms of some predetermined dimension. 2. See *response magnitude.*

response, antedating A response which occurs earlier than usual in a sequence of events.

response, anticipatory See *error, anticipatory.*

response circuit The neuronal chain or loop from the receptors to the effectors.

response class; R class A category of behaviors or parts of behaviors of an organism all of which tend to produce the same, or similar, effects on the organism's environment or changes in his relation to the environment.

response, consummatory A concluding response in a series of responses which brings the organism to a state of adjustment in a situation which has been partly or totally determined by the preparatory responses.

response, content (Rorschach) A scoring category for responses of what the subject sees such as a bat or an ice-cream sundae.

response, differential Response to only one of several stimuli; as a consequence of training, responses to the other stimuli do not occur.

response differentiation See *conditioning, approximation.*

response equivalence See *equivalence, response.*

response, fractional antedating goal 1. A component of the goal response which occurs in the absence of its goal reinforcer. It occurs earlier in the series of conditioned component responses than it originally occurred. 2. Symbol: r_G.

response generalization principle The principle which holds that when an organism is conditioned to a particular stimulus, that stimulus becomes effective in eliciting other responses.

response hierarchy A class of behaviors, parts of behaviors, or behavior patterns which are arranged in the order of the probability of their elicitation in a certain stimulus situation.

response, implicit Muscular and glandular responses not directly observable without the appropriate instruments.

responses incompatible Responses which cannot occur at the same time and place though either may be elicited by the same stimulus.

response, individual A response to a word on an association test that is uncommon and does not appear on standard lists, such as the Kent-Rosanoff, of response frequencies.

response inhibition (O. H. Mowrer) The inhibition of a response by internal cues in the presence of the eliciting stimulus.

response, kinesthetic (Rorschach) A response which projects movement, action, or life onto the inkblots.

response latency 1. Time between stimulus onset and the response in experimental procedures with discrete trials or inter-response times in operant conditioning procedures. 2. A measure of response strength.

response learning See *learning, response.*

response magnitude See *response strength.*

response, negative A response which tends to move the organism away from something, which tends to remove the organism from exposure to a stimulus, either by leaving the situation or by behavior designed to remove or cancel the stimulus in question.

response-oriented theories or systems All approaches to or systems of psychology whose primary datum or dependent variable is the response. Such systems include functional psychology, behaviorism, stimulus-response psychology, act psychology and reaction psychology.

response pattern A qualitative and quantitative grouping of responses into a distinct unit of activity.

response, pilomotor Spontaneous reaction of the hair moving or stiffening as occurs in times of fear and shivering or with goose-pimples.

response probability 1. Relative frequency of a response over a number of opportunities. 2. A possible measure of response strength.

response-produced conflict A conflict caused by the elicitation of a response which has been previously punished.

response-reinforcement contingency The relationship between a response and the rewarding stimulus.

response, selective A response which has been differentiated and chosen from a number of possible alternative responses.

response, serial A response occurring in an ordered sequence of responses.

response set 1. In reaction time experiments or similar situation, the concentration on the muscular, or response, phase of the experiment rather than on the sensory, or perceptual phase in which the subject is ready to perceive the stimuli. 2. The readiness to respond in a certain pattern, to perform one type of response over another.

response-shock interval (B. F. Skinner) The time which elapses between the last response and the occurrence of a shock as an aversive stimulus in avoidance conditioning.

response, species specific See *behavior, species specific.*

response, stereotyped 1. A behavior or response that is consistently occasioned by some problem situation, varies little in its topography, and is little altered by its consequences. 2. Successive occurrences of a response which does not vary in its topography.

response strength A measure of the magnitude or intensity of a response. It is important to realize that a response is an arbitrarily defined bit of behavior and among the measures of response strength are frequency, latency rate, amplitude, duration. There is no simple relationship among these measures and each can be independently effected by the reinforcement contingencies. Thus it is not justified to say that response strength changed unless the aspect of the response being measured is specified.

response threshold   See *threshold, response.*

response time   See *reaction time.*

response topography   See *topography, response.*

response variable   See *variable, response.*

responses, chained (operant conditioning)   A sequence of responses in which one response produces the necessary stimulus conditions for the next response. The topography of the chained responses may or may not be the same.

responsibility, legal   The accountability for actions and their consequences in those who are assumed to be able to conform to laws, customs, and standards of the society.

rest-cure   A method of treatment not widely used or recognized, which stresses the importance of rest, environmental change, fattening diet, massage and mild exercise.

restructure   1. (E. C. Tolman) To alter the relative position of part-regions without changing their total number. 2. (K. Lewin) The basic change in the relationships of the psychological field, usually through changes internal to the person rather than changes in the environment or external conditions.

retained members method   A type of recall method of measuring retention using a series of items to be learned that exceeds the memory span and giving an insufficient number of presentations for complete learning.

retardate, familial   Diagnostic term referring to a mildly retarded individual with a genealogical history of retardation who exhibits no physiological causes for the retardation.

retardation   1. The slowing down of a process. 2. The slowing down of an individual's mental development. 3. (I. P. Pavlov) A type of internal inhibition in which the conditioned response is delayed due to the presentation of the unconditioned stimulus several minutes after the beginning of the conditioned stimulus.

retention   1. (physiology) The inability or refusal to empty the bladder or rectum. 2. (learning) The fact that a learned behavior will persist after a period of time has passed in which the behavior has not been performed.

retention curve   See *curve, retention.*

reticular activating system   A structure consisting of a network of nerve fibers found at the upper part of the spinal cord whose function is to regulate attention and arousal by activating the cerebral cortex and to screen out sensory stimuli.

reticuloendothelial system   Hypothesized by F. J. Kallman to be Macrophage system (RES), man's defense mechanism against schizophrenia.

reticulum   (biology) A finely interwoven network in a cell or in some delicate tissue system.

retifism   A pathological condition in which one's sexual needs are satisfied by the foot or shoe of the loved one which is responded to as if it were the genitals.

retinal disparity   See *disparity, retinal.*

retinal field   The specific pattern of rods and cones activated by the particular image falling on the retina.

retinal image   The image of external objects formed on the retina by the structures of the eye.

retinal light   An idioretinal sensation of light, occurring in the absence of any type of stimulation and presumably due to the intrinsic neuronal activity of the cortex and retina.

retinal oscillations   The excitation effect of a single momentary stimulus characterized by variations in the state of excitation of the visual neural apparatus and experienced as a succession of dark and bright phases.

retinal rivalry   An irregular alternation of images when the two eyes are focused on different sensory fields that cannot be somehow fused or are not subject to a unitary interpretation.

retinal zones   See *color zones.*

retinene   A retinal pigment which is related to carotene and from which, in the presence of vitamin A and certain proteins, visual purple is formed.

retinitis   Inflammation of the retina.

retinoscope   A mirror with a small aperture at its center through which light passes and through which the observer is able to examine the interior of the eye.

retroactive association   A connection which is made between an item in a list to be learned and any item which precedes it in the list.

retroactive inhibition   See *inhibition, retroactive.*

retrobulbar   1. Situated behind the eyeball. 2. Behind the medulla oblongata.

retrogenesis   The hypothesis which holds that new growth process develops out of undifferentiated tissue rather than out of a fully developed structure.

retrospection   The systematic review and observation of an experience after it has already happened, especially as soon after its occurrence as possible.

return afferentation   (P.K. Anokhin) A pattern of afferent parameters characterizing the useful result received by the functional system. Return afferentation is composed of quite various sensory modalities, which on the whole give an adequate reflection of the result received (visual, tactile, auditory, etc.). It must be distinguished from the proprioceptive afferentation which, though being a "return" from muscles, has a correcting effect upon the action itself. The result of this correction is a pattern of afferent excitations which corresponds to the result received in accordance with the decision made and with the acceptor of action results already formed, where collation of both complexes of afferent features takes place. The difference between the parameters of the return afferentation and of those predicted on the basis of afferent synthesis elicits disintegration that serves as a stimulus to the immediate formation of a new, more adequate program. The idea and formulation of the return afferentation were elaborated on the basis of study of an organism's compensatory adaptation under disturbed functions by P. K. Anokhin. Being a pattern of afferent parameters of the result received, the return afferentation is anticipation of the "feed-back" as the basic regularity of cybernetics.

return sweep The movement of the eyes in reading from the end of one line back to the beginning of the next.

reverberatory circuit A neuronal system in the brain or autonomic nervous system which is able to maintain activity after the demise of the initiating impulse. It is known to exist in the autonomic nervous system and hypothesized to exist in the central nervous system.

reverie A dream-like state in which the subject experiences visions or ideational mental processes.

reverie, hypnagogic Reverie occurring in a hypnagogic state.

reversal (psychoanalysis) The transformation of one instinctual derivative into its opposite.

reversal learning See *learning, reversal.*

reversible figure A specific form of ambiguous figure in which there is a ready and rapid reversal of the perspective.

reversible perspective See *alternating perspective.*

reversion 1. The inheritance and manifestation of a recessive trait that was not manifested in the parent(s). 2. A regression or return to an earlier developmental level. 3. Atavism, or the reappearance of a hereditary characteristic after absence in immediately preceding generations.

revival The recall or reproduction of an experience.

reward A stimulus, stimulus-object, situation or verbal statement which is presented upon completion of a successful performance of a task and which tends to increase the probability of the behavior involved.

reward expectancy (E. C. Tolman) A hypothesized process which is aroused when an organism encounters the circumstances which have been associated with a reward. It is a set or readiness which moves the animal to search for a goal, is built up over a number of trials and is associated with a certain place or pathway.

reward, extrinsic A reward which is external to the behavior being rewarded or which is perceived by the subject as not being logically or intrinsically connected to the thing being rewarded.

reward, intrinsic A reward which is closely connected to or part of the behavior or task being rewarded and cannot be separated from it.

reward learning (or operant conditioning) Learning new paths or responses towards a goal, under the influence of the 'law of effect', i.e. the tendency of rewarded behaviors to be remembered. See *operant conditioning.*

reward, positive See *reinforcement, positive.*

reward, primary A stimulus object or situation which is satisfying for the organism without the animal's having to learn to like it—food, drink, sex objects.

reward, secondary See *reinforcement, secondary.*

reward training A type of learning in which a correct response is rewarded.

Rh blood factor An agglutinating factor present in the blood named after the rhesus monkey in whom it was first found. When introduced into an organism who lacks it, it causes the production of antibodies. Rh positive in children of Rh negative mothers causes jaundice, paralysis and convulsions at birth and mental deficiency.

rheobase The strength of direct electrical current which is just sufficient to excite a nerve or muscle.

rheotropism; rheotaxis A tropistic response to water in which the tropism is a turning in line with the direction of the flow of water.

rheumatoid arthritis See *arthritis, rheumatoid.*

rhinencephalon The area of the brain which includes the olfactory bulb and a portion of the forebrain in the lateral fissure which includes the hippocampus pyriform lobes and fornix. It is chiefly concerned with the reception and integration of olfactory impulses and with the regulation of appropriate motor activities in response to such impulses.

RHO: ρ The coefficient of correlation for squared rank differences:

$$\rho = 1 - \frac{6 \Sigma D^2}{N(N^2 - 1)}$$

with D equal to the deviation in ranks and N the number of ranked cases.

rhodopsin Visual purple, the pigmented substance which stimulates the rods of the retina. It bleaches in bright white light and recovers in darkness and is thought to be the material involved in the reception of faint visual stimuli.

ribosomal RNA A type of ribonucleic acid which lines up amino acids in the ribosomes to form proteins according to a particular sequence.

ribosomes Small bodies in the cytoplasm of a cell which synthesize proteins.

Ribot, Théodule Armand (1839-1916) French psychologist who, while not undertaking many experiments himself, wrote many books on psychology. He familiarized himself with the new developments in British and German psychology, publishing books on these in French in 1870 and 1879.

right and wrong cases method See *method, constant stimulus.*

right and wrong test   See *M'Naghten rules*.

right associates method   A common procedure in the investigation of learning and retention. Items which are generally verbal are presented in pairs; the first of each pair, generally not in the same order as the first series, is presented briefly and the subject attempts to reproduce the second, yielding the number of retained members or successes.

righting reflex   A reflex or reflexive act which serves to return the organism to an upright position when thrown off balance or when placed on its back.

rigidity   1. (physiology) A state of strong muscular contraction. **2.** The inability to alter one's opinions, attitudes or actions when they are inappropriate.

risk level   The percentage of samples which can be expected to fall outside the particular statistical limits, such as the five or ten per cent level. Therefore, at the five percent level, the chances are one out of twenty, that the obtained statistic, with repeated samplings, will be significantly less or greater than one would expect from chance fluctuation.

ritalin   Common name for methylphenidate.

RNA (ribonucleic acid)   A nucleic acid formed upon a DNA template and taking part in the synthesis of polypeptides. There are three varieties: 1) Messenger RNA—the template upon which polypeptides are synthesized. 2) Transfer RNA (soluble RNA), which collaboratively with ribosomes brings activated amino acids into position along the messenger RNA template. 3) Ribosomal RNA, a component of the ribosomes, which serves as a non-specific site of polypeptide synthesis.

RNA, effects of behavior on   Experiments have shown that rotation in rabbits cause the production of RNA in the nerve associated with equilibrium. The process of learning has been found to produce a change in RNA bases.

RNA, virus   A type of messenger RNA which codes genetic information for virus protein *in vitro* and codes for more than one distinct protein.

R-O-C   See *Receiver Operating Characteristic Curve*.

rod vision   Vision in which only the rods function, the cones not being involved.

rods of Corti   Tiny columnar cells which line the organ of corti in the inner ear, forming arches.

rods; retinal rods   Structures in the retina which are rod shaped and which are thought to be the specific structures for the reception for grey or achromatic visual qualities at the lower intensities.

Roe, Anne (1904-   )   American psychologist. Except for several years as a Training Unit Chief in the Veterans Administration, has been chiefly engaged in research. Made earliest clinical studies of living artists and scientists. Developed new classification of occupations based on psychological aspects, and has contributed largely to theoretical development of field of occupational psychology. Other research topics have included intellectual functions in normal, asphasic, and mentally disordered adults; behavior of newborn infants; development of foster children from different backgrounds; behavior and evolution; psychology of creativity; relations between early experiences and career patterns; aspects of use of woman-power.

Rogers, Carl R. (1902-   )   American psychologist and educator. Developed the client-centered approach to psychotherapy and the principles and theory which were deduced from his experience in working with individuals in the therapeutic process. Led and sponsored research in the process of psychotherapy, its outcomes, the attitudinal conditions which foster therapeutic growth and personal growth, and the application of these principles in groups as diverse as college students and confirmed schizophrenics. His theory is based on the hypothesis that given the proper psychological climate of attitudinal conditions, the individual has within himself the capacity and the strength to gain insight into and to cope with his problems. He and others have put this hypothesis to work in ways which have helped to revolutionize the concept of the helping relationship in therapy, in educational guidance, in education itself, in encounter groups, in the ministry and in other professions.

Rolando's fissure   Central sulcus.

Rolando's sulcus   Central sulcus.

role   A pattern of behavior that is characteristic or expected of an individual occupying a particular position within a social system.

role action pattern   The pattern of special responses that actually distinguishes a person in a particular role.

role construct repertory test   See *test, role construct repertory*.

role-directed   psychotherapy   See *psychotherapy, role-directed*.

role playing   1. The taking on or performing of a role. **2.** Behaving according to a role which is not ones own. **3.** A means of studying a role in all its manifestations and concrete details by enacting the role in a contrived situation, allowing for a better and more objective understanding. **4.** (psychotherapy) The adoption of the role of an important other in the person's life so as to come to a better understanding of the other or the adoption of social roles so as to better understand how he conceives of and functions in them.

role therapy   See *therapy, role*.

Romberg sign   The swaying which is evident in a person with locomotor ataxia when he tries to stand quietly with eyes closed and feet together.

root conflict   A central conflict having its roots in infancy and playing a part in the entire development of the personality, especially in the formation of later conflicts and complexes.

root-mean-square (RMS)   The square root of the

sum of several values squared, divided by the number of values in the sample. The formula is:

$$RMS = \sqrt{\frac{\Sigma X^2}{N}}$$

root, sensory Any dorsal root of the spinal cord involved in sensory functions.

root, spinal The end part of the spinal nerves which connects with the spinal cord, including the ventral motor roots and dorsal sensory roots.

rooting reflex The head-turning and mouth-opening movements in the infant when his cheek is stroked which is involved in the reflex to turn toward the breast when being nursed.

Rorschach, Hermann (1884-1922) Swiss psychiatrist who in 1911 at the age of 27 began his experiments with inkblots to study reflex hallucinations. Studying as many as 40 inkblots, Rorschach ultimately settled on the 10 which comprise his now famous test. Rorschach's monograph, *Psycho-diagnostik,* had been intended as a preliminary report; however, a few months following its publication in 1921, he developed peritonitis after an attack of appendicitis and died in April, 1922, at the age of 37. His work, though incomplete, became a milestone from which much of modern clinical psychology developed. See *test, Rorschach inkblots.*

Rorschach test See *test, Rorschach inkblots.*

Rosenzweig Picture-Frustration Test See *test, Rosenzweig, Picture-Frustration.*

Rossolimo reflex (G. I. Rossolimo) A plantar flexion of the toes which is elicited by tapping the balls of the toes. It is a pathological reflex exhibited when the lower motor neuron is removed from the usual suppressor effect of higher centers, such as in lesions of the pyramidal tract.

rotary pursuit A pursuit reaction test requiring the subject to follow the path of an irregularly moving object with an indicator.

rotation A technical term for the shifting of factor axes and their hyperplanes from the positions initially obtained after Factor Extraction.

rotation, orthogonal (factor analysis) A rotation of the factor axes to the point where they meet at right angles. The correlation of two factors in this configuration is zero.

rotation perception The sensation which occurs when there is an alteration in the rate or direction of the rotation of a person's body, resulting from movement of the fluids in the semicircular canals which excites the receptors. When the rate of rotation is reduced the sensation is that of rotating in the opposite direction.

rotation system A method sometimes used in group therapy in which the therapist works with the individual patient in a sequence in front of the group.

rote learning Memorization in which the task is to commit the various components of the material to memory with little or no understanding, requiring only the ability to later reproduce what has been learned in the exact form in which it was presented.

Rotter Incomplete Sentence Blank A projective technique for college age individuals developed in 1950 by J. B. Rotter and J. E. Rafferty. It is designed to estimate the person's degree and areas of maladjustment for diagnostic purposes.

rounding off Process of eliminating or discarding one or more digits to the right of a particular digit. The last digit is increased by one if the dropped digit directly following it is greater than five. If this digit is less than five, the preceding digit is left unchanged. When this digit is exactly five, the preceding digit if it is odd is increased, while if it is even it is left unchanged.

RR interval See *inter response time.*

R/S See *response-shock interval.*

RS interval See *avoidance, free operant.*

rubeola encephalitis See *encephalitis, rubeola.*

Rubin, Edgar J. (1886-1951) Danish phenomenologist, a student of G. E. Müller at Göttingen, whose 1915 doctoral dissertation, in which he studied the difference between figure and ground in visual perception, greatly influenced later Gestalt psychology. Occupied the chair in psychology at Copenhagen for many years.

Rubin's figure An ambiguous figure which can be perceived either as a goblet or as two profiles facing each other.

Ruffini corpuscle or cylinder A specialized, branched-nerve end organ found in the subcutaneous tissues which is thought to mediate warmth sensations.

Ruffini papillary ending Nerve endings thought to mediate pressure sensation which are located in the papillary layer of the skin.

run 1. A single exposure to a task or stimuli or a single performance of a task, i.e., a trial. **2.** An execution of an operation which may then be repeated. **3.** To repeatedly expose an animal to an experimental situation such as a maze.

running rate See *rate, running.*

runway A straight pathway, usually without interruption, leading from the starting box to the goal box in which some form of reinforcement, usually positive, is available. The runway is usually either covered or elevated.

Rush, Benjamin (1745-1813) Often called the father of American psychiatry. In 1812 he wrote *Diseases of the Mind,* the first textbook on mental diseases by an American. He was a prime force in the push to get American medicine and the public at large to accept the idea that insanity was the result of internal disturbances rather than of mysterious outside forces. Rush believed in the relief a patient might experience upon talking to a doctor but also advocated treating patients more actively, and somewhat inhumanely—using tricks, terrifying the patient, and tranquilizing and gyrating chairs. Althought he used seemingly merciless devices, Rush was sincere in his concern for his fellow human beings and managed to help change the American medical profession's approach to the treatment of mental disorder.

S

S 1. A symbol for stimulus. 2. A symbol for sensory intensity, when the response is the stimulus. 3. A symbol for the space factor of the factors comprising primary mental abilities. 4. (psychophysics) A symbol for the standard stimulus.

(S) 1. A symbol for a subject in an experiment. 2. (Rorschach) A symbol for a response to white space on the card.

σ^2 The symbol used to refer to variance.

σ_M The symbol used to refer to the standard error of the mean.

Σ The symbol for summation. It is placed before a variable all of whose values are algebraically summed. It is read "sum of."

S^- (respondent conditioning) In Pavlovian conditioning discrimination studies, the test stimulus that is presented to the subject but which has never been paired with the US. Thus if the subject discriminates, the S^- should not elicit the conditioned response.

S^t (respondent conditioning) In Pavlovian conditioning discrimination studies, the CS that is consistently paired with the US.

S^A (operant conditioning) In discrimination studies the stimulus in the presence of which a response is never reinforced.

S^D (operant conditioning) The discriminative stimulus in discrimination studies. The stimulus in the presence of which responses are reinforced and responses in the absence are not reinforced.

S_D See *drive stimuli.*

S_G (C. L. Hull) A symbol for fractional goal stimulus, which is a proprioceptive stimulus resulting from a fractional antedating goal response (r_G).

$S \leftrightarrow R$ (J. R. Kantor) A symbol denoting stimulus-response interaction or interbehavior.

S curve See *curve, S.*

S factor A special or specific factor derived in a factor-analysis of tests of ability which is unique for the test in question, representing the kind of ability necessary to do well on the test.

S population See *stimulus, population.*

S variable See *stimulus variable.*

saccadic movement A rapid jump of the eye from one fixation point to another, especially in reading.

sacral division An anatomic division of the autonomic nervous system comprising that part in the region of the sacrum.

sadism A sexual perversion in which sexual excitement and orgasm are dependent upon the infliction of pain and humiliation of others.

sadism, anal (psychoanalysis) The manifestation of destructive and aggressive tendencies in the anal stage of development.

sadism, id The most primitive instinctual destructive urges seen in the early years of infancy, related to the desire for omnipotent gratification.

sadism, infantile Sadism occurring in early childhood.

sadism, larval (M. Hirschfeld) Concealed sadism.

sadism, omnipotent infantile See *sadism, id.*

sadism, oral Aggressive, primordial urges toward omnipotent mastery and gratification expressed in fantasy through the oral apparatus.

sadism, phallic Aggressive urges in the phallic stage of development during which the child interprets the sexual act as a violent, aggressive activity.

sadism, primal The part of the death instinct which remains within the person, partially bound with the libido and partially directed at the self.

sadism, superego The aggressive, cruel aspects of the conscience part of the superego whose energy is derived from the aggressive, destructive forces of the id. The intensity of this sadism depends on the intensity and strength of the child's own infantile violent and sadistic fantasies which are controlled by the superego.

sadism, unconscious Primordial destructive wishes which one is born with which in the infant are directed toward omnipotent power in fantasy and partially exist in the unconscious fantasies of adults.

sadomasochism The tendency toward both sadism and masochism. There is the simultaneous existence of submissive and aggressive attitudes in social and sexual relations with others, usually with the presence of a considerable degree of destructiveness.

safety motive 1. (K. Horney) A measure by which the neurotic attempts, in indirect ways, to protect himself from the hostility in his environment and, more broadly, to protect himself from any kind of threat. 2. The tendency to seek security.

sagittal 1. A term describing the arrow-shaped suture located between the two parietal bones of the skull. 2. A plane which divides the body into halves, passing through the sagittal suture along the long axis of the body.

sagittal axis (optics) The line or plane passing outward from the center of the retina, through the center of the lens and pupil, and projecting to the center of the object in view in the field of vision.

sagittal fissure The large longitudinal fissure dividing the two cerebral hemispheres.

Saint Dymphna Patron of the mentally disturbed, who was murdered in Gheel, Belgium by her psychotic father.

Saint John's evil Obsolete name for epilepsy.

Saint Vitus' dance See *chorea, Sydenham's acute.*

Sakel, Manfred (1900-1957) A German psychiatrist who developed the idea of using insulin to treat psychotics, especially the inducement of insulin shock in schizophrenics.

salaam spasm Movements of the head and upper part of the body which are rhythmic and periodic; usually seen in children.

salicylate poisoning See *poisoning, salicylate.*

salient variable similarity index for factors (s) A formula based on a count of salients, common salients, and common variables in the studies, whereby the P value of a given factor match between studies can be assessed.

salivary reflex The reflex characterized by the production and flow of saliva upon perceiving food.

salpingectomy A sterilization operation in which the fallopian tubes are cut and tied off.

saltatory spasm A clonic spasm causing the patient to leap or jump.

Saltpetriére school A school of psychopathology founded by J. Charcot and based on hypnotic phenomena.

sample A subgroup of a population which is used as a representative of an entire population and from which conclusions are drawn which are said to be characteristic of the entire population.

sample bias Any factor in a sample or in the method of drawing a sample that lessens the representative quality of that sample.

sample, matched A sample which is equivalent in all necessary respects to another sample under consideration.

sample, stratified A sample which has been divided into separate, non-overlapping categories. The sample is obtained by random selection and the number of cases in each category is proportional to the number in the population.

sampling The process by which a subset of persons or observations from a larger set is drawn and studied in order to make inferences about the characteristics of the larger population.

sampling, area Survey procedure which takes all of a particular class of respondents within a specified area such as one ten-block square or from within several specifically selected areas which are chosen to be representative of a larger area.

sampling block 1. The categorization of respondents or elements to be sampled into groups which are representative of the total population and the selection of a certain number of cases from each category. 2. The selection of respondents from each of certain geographic areas.

sampling, controlled Sampling methods in which the influenced factors are regulated and not left to chance.

sampling, double Using two different techniques for generating samples at different stages of the investigation. A form of mixed sampling.

sampling errors Errors resulting from the fact that the sample is not completely representative of the population. The standard error is obtained by subtracting the mean of the sample from the population mean.

sampling population The population from which the sample is going to be drawn.

sampling, random (experimental) The procedure of choosing a representative sample from a population whereby everyone in the parent population has an equal chance of being chosen. This procedure is used when the population values of the variables of interest are unknown.

sampling, representative The drawing of a sample which adequately reflects the characteristics of the population from which the sample is drawn.

sampling servo An instrument used in the measurement at regular intervals of errors in a process, applying corrections proportional to the error.

sampling stability A state which is achieved when successive samplings from a population yield consistent results and are regarded as reliable.

sampling, stratified (experimental) The procedure of choosing a representative sample from a population by choosing specific individuals who are similar to the people in the population. This procedure is used when the population values of the variables of interest are known.

sampling theory The theory which is involved with drawing samples which are representative of a population.

sampling validity A measure to determine how well a certain test item measures what the test as a whole is measuring.

sampling variability A measure of the extent to which a sample differs from a truly random sample which is estimated from the standard deviation.

San Filippo syndrome A mucopolysaccharidosis not involving skeletal abnormalities. Initially, mild retardation followed by rapid deterioration between the second and fourth years.

sanguine type See *type, sanguine.*

Sansom image See *Purkinje-Sansom image.*

saphism Female homosexuality; lesbianism; the name saphism is derived from Sapho, an ancient Greek poetess.

Sargent Insight Test See *test, Sargent Insight.*

SAT See *test, scholastic aptitude.*

satiation, psychical (K. Lewin) The experience that upon repetition of an act, the act gains a negative valence for a person causing him to try to leave the situation. The process of satiation is identified by the criteria of variation, dissolution of perceptual and action unities, inattention and forgetting. The speed of satiation depends on the structure of the task, upon the state of tension of the whole person, upon whether the task is a peripheral or central one, and upon the personality of the person. Satiation shows that repetition of a task does not always result in an improvement in performance.

satisfaction 1. The state of pleasure in an organism when it has achieved the goal of the dominant motivating tendencies. 2. The feeling state in a person who has gratified an appetite or motive.

satisfier (E.L. Thorndike) A reward or any external situation or circumstance leading to satisfaction.

saturated test (factor analysis) A test having a high factor loading—a high correlation with a certain factor.

saturation 1. With colors, purity and fullness of hue of the color. 2. (factor analysis) The degree to which a test is correlated or loaded with a certain factor. 3. (chemistry) The degree to which a chemical substance has been dissolved or absorbed by a liquid.

satyriasis Excessive sexual drive in males.

savant, idiot See *idiot savant.*

saving method (H. Ebbinghaus) The method of measuring retention which can be used when a subject has forgotten what he has learned. The difference between the time required for the first and subsequent learnings or the time saved is taken as the measure of retention present at the time of relearning. Also called relearning and saving method.

scala A perilymphatic space of the cochlea.

scala media The smallest tube of the cochlea which contains the organ of Corti.

scala tympani A spiral tube in the cochlea filled with endolymph, extending from the round window to the apex connecting to the scala vestibuli.

scala vestibuli A spiral tube in the cochlea, filled with a fluid which receives sound vibrations from the stapes, communicating them to the organ of Corti.

scalability 1. The ability to be arranged in a normal progression or to be fitted into a progression. 2. The characteristic of a test or test item that makes it possible to estimate a subject's response to any single item, knowing his test score.

scalar analysis The process of determining where an item is situated on a scale.

scalar product (statistics) The length of vector A multiplied by the length of vector B, multiplied by the cosine of the angular separation between the two vectors. The scalar product is the cosine of the angle if the two vectors are of unit length.

scale 1. Any series of items which is progressively arranged according to value or magnitude into which an item can be placed according to its quantification. 2. A physical device which is representative of a scale (yardstick). 3. A series of test items which have been arranged according to their value or magnitude of difficulty. 4. The rules which are applied when assigning an item to a class. 5. (L. Guttman) An attitude-measuring device which meets the standards for being scaled.

scale, A Questionnaire designed to measure degree of intolerance for ambiguity, vagueness and indefiniteness.

scale, absolute A scale that begins at an absolute zero point and has equal intervals between all subsequent points on the scale.

scale, additive A scale whose units can be summated because the units are equal at all points on the scale.

scale, age Also called age-equivalent scale. A scale in which the units of measurements are the differences between successive age equivalents, each difference assumed to be equal to any other.

scale, age-equivalent Also called age scale. A scale whose units of measurement are the differences between successive age equivalents, each difference assumed to be equal to any other. For example, a child with a mental age of ten is said to be one year older mentally than a child whose development is that of nine-year-olds. See *age equivalent.*

scale, allergic potential Scale developed for the evaluation of a patient's predisposition to allergic reaction, using family history of allergy, eosinophilic count, skin-test reactions and how easily a certain clinical symptom can be diagnosed as related to certain allergens.

scale, analytical A test or scale designed and used for a diagnostic purpose.

scale, Arthur Point of Performance Tests (G. Arthur) An intelligence test for school children developed in 1933 which consists of eight performance subtests. Six of these subtests are restandardized versions of the Pintner-Paterson Scale, the Knox Cube Test, the Seguin Form Board, the Two-Figure Form Board, the Casuist Form Board, the Manikin, the Feature Profile, the Mare and Foal, and the Healy Picture Completion I. The two additional tests are the Porteus Maze and the Kohs Block Design Test. The scale yields an IQ score which is determined by the number of successes, or the time required on each test, or the degree of accuracy or a combination of these. An alternate form of the scale is available for retesting and for use with pre-school children. This version consists of four of the subtests from Form I plus the Arthur Stencil Design.

scale, attitude A measuring device consisting of a set of items, of predetermined scale value, which are to be marked as favorable or unfavorable.

scale, attitude toward disabled persons (H. E. Yuker, J. R. Block, and W. J. Campbell) A scale introduced in 1960 to ascertain attitudes toward disability.

scale, Bayley, of Infant Development (N. Bayley) Test to assess an infant's developmental progress which reflects the notion that development is an interaction of mental, physical and social factors. Includes a motor scale, mental scale and a behavioral index, although the index is not as carefully standardized.

scale, Bogardus Social Distance A rating scheme requiring the subject to indicate the degree of intimacy to which he would be willing to accept a certain person or a representative of a certain social group.

scale, bril A scale of visual brightness based upon the fractionation method for scaling subjective magnitude.

scale, California Infant, for Motor Development Test battery divided into subtests, seventy-six items used in assessing motor development from birth to three years. Representative items are: sits with support expected at 3.5 months; walks alone two or three steps without support at 13.0 months; walks alone upstairs at 24.3 months; walks upstairs, alternating forward foot at 35.5 months; and, the last item in the test, walks downstairs, alternating forward foot at 50.0 months.

scale, chromatic Musical scale with half-tone intervals between the notes.

scale, Columbia Mental Maturity (B. Burgomeister,

L. H. Blum, I. Lorge) A scale of general ability developed in 1953 for children aged three to twelve. It consists of sets of drawings printed on a card. The child is asked to point to the one which does not belong with the others.

scale, continuous A scale in which the function or trait is measured on a continuum.

scale, developmental A check list or inventory of behaviors. The behaviors of an individual are checked on the inventory, compared with the norms of the scale and an estimate of the individual's developmental stage is reached.

scale, diatonic A stepwise organization of tones which forms the basis of most western music. A diatonic scale can be formed with any tone as a starting point by producing two successively higher tones each separated from each other by whole steps. Between the third and the fourth tone is a half step. Whole steps separate the fourth from the fifth, the fifth from the sixth, and the sixth from the seventh. Between the seventh and the eighth is a half step. Thus, the successive eight tones, the octave, are separated from each other by whole steps except between the third and fourth tones and between the seventh and eighth tones which are separated by half steps. This is the major scale. In the minor scale, of equal importance, the half steps between the sixth, seventh, and eighth tones are varied depending on the specific form desired; but invariably the half step is between the second and third tones.

scale, difficulty A test in which the items are arranged in order of difficulty.

scale, Draw-A-Person Quality (M. E. Wagner and H. J. P. Schubert) A scale based on the Draw-A-Person Test in which the person's drawing is scored according to an artistic scale of 0 to 8.

scale, E Attitude scale which measures tendency toward ethnocentrism.

scale, grade A scale, standardized to measure a person's development in terms of grade norms.

scale, graphic rating A type of rating scale for describing the strength of a particular characteristic representative of a person. The scale is usually in the form of a line with gradations marking the range of the trait from minimum to maximum.

scale, Griffiths' (R. Griffiths) A scale introduced in 1954 to assess the abilities of infants. It determines the level of development of five areas: locomotor, personal-social, hearing and speech, hand and eye development, and performance. The scale yields a general quotient derived by dividing the mental age by the chronological age.

scale, Guttman (L. Guttman) A unidimensional attitude scale in which the items are arranged in such a way that a person who agrees with a particular item automatically agrees with the items lower in rank and disagrees with those higher in rank.

scale, Humm-Wadsworth Temperament (D. G. Humm and G. W. Wadsworth) A personality inventory introduced in 1935 designed to assess if a person has paranoid, hysteric, manic, depressive, or schizoid tendencies.

scale, I/E Introversion/extroversion scale; a scoring key for the Minnesota Multiphasic Personality Inventory, yielding points on the introversion and extroversion dimension.

scale, interval A type of scale which does not have an absolute zero point but possesses equal intervals and magnitude.

scale, ipsative A scale which employs the characteristic behavior of an individual as the standard of comparison, so that a response is rated in terms of how it compares to the individual's common response.

scale, K A scoring scale of the Minnesota Multiphase Personality Inventory used for the detection of malingering.

scale, Kelvin A temperature scale using absolute zero or the complete lack of heat, -273° C, as its starting point. Also called absolute scale.

scale, Likert A type of attitude scale which requests the subject to indicate the degree of agreement or disagreement, on a three- or five-step scale, with stated attitudes.

scale, Lincoln-Oseretsky Motor Development A sensorimotor diagnostic test battery with thirty-six items of high reliability and good discrimination for children between six and fourteen years of age. The test is useful in the assessment of general motor ability rather than in the differential evaluation of psychomotor abilities.

scale, mental A scale involving the application of different numerical scores to different levels of mental performance.

scale, national intelligence A group test developed for the National Research Council of America consisting of a battery of tests designed to assess intelligence. There are two forms, Form A and Form B.

scale, nominal The simplest type of scale which labels objects by letters or numbers for identification or classification. It does not possess equal intervals, magnitude relationships or an absolute zero point.

scale, ordinal A type of scale which arranges objects with reference to their magnitude and assigns numbers accordingly—first, second, third, etc. It does not possess equal intervals or an absolute zero point.

scale, percentile A scale which indicates the percentile rank of each score or value of the population.

scale, point Test items or set of problems each of which is assigned a numerical score. Performance is rated according to total number of points earned.

scale, psychological A device used in the measurement and assessment of psychological functioning, such as attitudes, mental ability, degree of psychopathology, etc.

scale, ratio A type of scale with magnitude, an absolute zero point, and equal intervals which can be added or divided. All statements of ratio must be based on this scale.

scale, sixteen D (N. Bayley) A score defining the level of intelligence derived from a multiple of the standard deviation from the mean score obtained at age sixteen on several standardized tests. This score allows for the comparison of growth levels at different ages determined by tests having disparate age ranges and scoring systems.

scale, stuttering Iowa A scale which is composed of thirty-three nine-second samples of phonographically recorded stuttered speech, ranked using the equal-appearing intervals method on the basis of the degree of stuttering which is thought to be manifested in the samples. A stutterer in speech is compared with the samples and then assigned the scale value of the sample which it most closely resembles.

scale, T A scale which is based on the standard scores of the distribution obtained from unselected twelve-year-olds for any given test. The distribution is given a mean of fifty. Any score which equals five times the value of the standard deviation either above or below the mean is given the value of zero or one hundred. The scores between zero and one hundred progress in steps equal to .1 standard deviation.

scale, Taylor Manifest Anxiety (J. A. Taylor) A verbal measure of anxiety developed in 1956 which consists of a questionnaire made up of items believed to indicate anxiety to which the subject must answer true or false according to whether the statement describes him. This scale has a statistically significant but not very high validity when compared with physiological and other verbal measures of anxiety.

scale, Thorndike's Handwriting (E. L. Thorndike) A scale composed of handwriting samples rated in terms of the probability they exhibit against which another sample may be compared and then graded.

scale, Thurstone Attitude A scale constructed using the method of equally appearing intervals and consisting of a series of statements assigned a scale value of favorability in respect to a specified attitude object, on the basis of the proved judgments of a hundred or more raters. The score is the mean of the total of the values of those with which the subject indicates he agrees.

scale, value 1. The number that is assigned to an item according to a certain scale. 2. The number or name that is assigned to a division or a point on a scale; the reference points.

scale, Vineland Social Maturity (E. A. Doll) A survey of a person's maturity and social development introduced in 1936 and designed for use with individuals from infancy to the age of thirty years. The scale determines the levels of development in six categories: self-help, self-direction, locomotion, occupation, communication and socialization, from interviews with someone who knows the person or the subject himself. Items are grouped according to age and scored yielding a social age which is divided by the chronological age to produce a social quotient.

scale, Wechsler Adult Intelligence (D. Wechsler) An intelligence test developed and standardized in 1955 on white subjects, ages 16-64. It is a modified version of the Wechsler-Bellevue scale consisting of eleven subtests. The six verbal subtests include Information, Comprehension, Arithmetic, Similarities, Digit Span and Vocabulary. The performance tests are Digit Symbol, Picture Completion, Block Design, Picture Arrangement and Object Assembly. These subtests measure verbal, numerical, social and visual-motor capabilities. The test yields a Verbal, Performance and Full Scale Intelligence Quotient with a mean of 100 and a standard deviation of 15. Also known as the WAIS.

scale, Wechsler-Bellevue (D. Wechsler) An intelligence test for adults developed in 1939 and standardized on an American population aged 7-69. It consists of eleven subtests. The six verbal subtests are Information, Comprehension, Digit Span, Arithmetic, Similarities and Vocabulary. The five performance tests include Picture Arrangement, Picture Completion, Block Design, Object Assembly and Digit Symbol. These subjects measure verbal, numerical, social and perceptual-motor abilities. For a more recent version, see *Wechsler Adult Intelligence Scale.*

scale, Wechsler Intelligence, for Children (D. Wechsler) An intelligence test for children ages 5 years 0 months to 15 years 11 months developed and standardized in 1949 on a group of white children. The scale consists of twelve subtests, one of which is an alternate performance test. The verbal tests are Information, Comprehension, Arithmetic, Similarities, Vocabulary and Digit Span. The performance tests include Picture Completion, Picture Arrangement, Block Design, Object Assembly, Coding and the alternate test, Mazes. These tests measure verbal, numerical, social and visual-motor adaptability. The test yields a Verbal, Performance and Full Scale Intelligence Quotient with a mean of 100 and a standard deviation of 15. Also known as the WISC.

scale, Wechsler Preschool and Primary, of Intelligence (D. Wechsler) An intelligence scale for children ages 4-6½ developed and standardized in 1963. It includes eleven subtests of which one verbal subtest is an alternate. The six verbal subtests are Information, Vocabulary, Arithmetic, Similarities, Comprehension and the alternate test, Sentences. The performance tests include Animal House, Picture Completion, Mazes, Geometric Design and Block Design. These tests assess verbal, numerical, social and visual-motor capabilities. The test yields a Verbal, Performance and Full Scale Intelligence Quotient score with a mean of 100 and a standard deviation of 15. Also known as the WPPSI.

scales, confusion Scales produced by indirect scaling procedures are sometimes called confusion scales.

scales, Fels, of Parental Behavior (H. Champney) Scales designed to assess the child's home environment as a function of parental behavior and introduced in 1941. Thirty scales comprise this battery appraising dimensions such as child-centeredness, protectiveness, readiness of criticism, restrictiveness of regulations, severity of penalties, discord at home. The ratings are based on information obtained during several home visits including clinical impressions which are analyzed in terms of intra-rater and inter-rater reliability.

scales, handwriting (T. S. Lewinson and J. Zubin) A series of twenty-two scales developed in 1942 to evaluate the dynamic aspects of handwriting and describe an individual's movement impulses which are expressed in the handwriting. Each scale, representing one element of handwriting is divided into seven categories: the middle, called the balance, subdivides the scale into the contraction categories which indicate increasing degrees of control and the release categories which indicate increasing degrees of undercontrol. Twenty subjects were tested, both normal and abnormal, to produce the frame of reference for these scales. The findings suggest that the most striking difference between the normal and abnormal performance is in the consistency of handwriting, normals being consistent and abnormals manifesting variability.

scales, Kent Series of Emergency A brief general intelligence test consisting of ten orally given questions used in situations requiring a quick estimate of intellectual ability. Also called the Kent EGY test.

scales, magnitude Direct ratio scales based on the direct judgment of the ratios.

scales, partition Of direct equal interval scales based on the direct judgment of the intervals.

scaling The methods of determining which properties of a number scale apply to the dimension of objects, and which transformations of the scale values leave these scale dimensions invariate. Three characteristics of a scale are order, distance, and origin. Depending on whether none, one, two, or three of these are present in a scale, the scale is designated as nominal, ordinal, interval, or ratio. The type of valid mathematical functions possible on a scale is determined by the type of scale and its characteristics.

scaling, age-grade Standardizing a test on a population of school children who are at the normal or average age for their grade in school.

scaling, direct (S. S. Stevens) Methods of obtaining units of measurement on a scale in which direct quantitative judgments of a particular stimulus dimension are made by the subject. The subject not only judges stimuli A B on a given continuum as he does in an indirect scaling procedure, but he specifies the particular relationship among the subjective experiences, e.g. the subject may adjust stimulus B so that it appears one half the size of stimulus A.

scaling, indirect Methods for obtaining scales of sensation in which the subject differentiates stimuli on the basis of order, e.g. which tone is louder, stimulus A or B? If A is judged as louder 50% of the time, it is concluded that stimulus A is louder than stimulus B. If stimulus B is just noticeably higher than stimulus A and stimulus C is just noticeably higher than stimulus B, then the distance on the psychological continuum that separates B and A is assumed to be equal to the distance that separates C and A: one "just noticeable difference", one jnd. Thus jnd's are assumed to be equal, and a scale constructed on this assumption is an indirect scale.

scaling, test The procedure of assigning test items to specific positions on a scale after having administered the scale to a trial sample of people.

scallop (operant conditioning) A positively accelerated part of a cumulative response record indicating an increase in the response rate. The scallop is the typical steady state performance of a FI.

scalogram A cumulative scale, also called Guttman scale.

scapegoating **1.** Process by which a person, group or object becomes the focus of displaced aggression. **2.** (family therapy) Process in which one member of the family is identified as the "bad" or "crazy" member and is regularly put into a position in which other members of the family unconsciously support, as well as outwardly condemn, his unacceptable activities; the problems of the family are blamed upon this member.

scatology Morbid interest in excrement.

scatter **1.** The degree to which a distribution of measurements or scores are closely grouped around the mean or dispersed over a wide range, most commonly measured by the standard deviation. **2.** The extent to which items passed or failed by an individual on a test are of widely varying levels of difficulty.

scatter analysis See *analysis, scatter.*

scatter diagram A correlation diagram or chart that shows the relationship of two variables. The scores for the X variable are plotted along the horizontal axis and the scores for the Y variable are entered along the vertical axis. A point is made at each intersection.

scatterplot See *scatter diagram.*

Schaeffer reflex (M. Schaeffer) See *reflex, Schaeffer.*

schedule **1.** A detailed plan for a series of operations. **2.** A form used to guide experimental proceedure and gathering of data. **3.** A questionnaire.

schedule, Edwards Personal Preference An instrument used with college students and adults which is designed, through a forced-choice method, to show the relative importance within the subject of fifteen key needs or motives, including achievement, dominance, debasement, change, nurturance, autonomy.

schedule, maintenance The provision of food, water and exercise to maintain an organism at a stable level of growth.

schedule of reinforcement See *reinforcement schedule.*

schedule of reinforcement: adjusting (ADJ) See *reinforcement, schedule of: adjusting.*

schedule of reinforcement: alternate ALT See *reinforcement, schedule of: alternate.*

schedule of reinforcement: chained (CHAIN) See *reinforcement, schedule of: chained.*

schedule of reinforcement: concurrent (CONC) See *reinforcement, schedule of: concurrent.*

schedule of reinforcement: conjugate See *reinforcement, schedule of: conjugate.*

schedule of reinforcement: conjunctive (CONJ) See *reinforcement, schedule of: conjunctive.*

schedule of reinforcement: continuous (CRF) See *reinforcement, schedule of: continuous.*

schedule of reinforcement: differential interresponse time reinforcement See either *reinforcement, schedule of: differential reinforcement of low rates of responding (DRL)* or *reinforcement, schedule of: differential reinforcement of high rates of responding (DRH).*

schedule of reinforcement: extinction (EXT) See *reinforcement, schedule of: extinction.*

schedule of reinforcement: fixed interval (FI) See *reinforcement, schedule of: fixed interval.*

schedule of reinforcement: fixed ratio (FR) See *reinforcement, schedule of: fixed ratio.*

schedule of reinforcement: interlocking (INTER) See *reinforcement, schedule of: interlocking.*

schedule of reinforcement: intermittent See *reinforcement, schedule of: intermittent.*

schedule of reinforcement: interpolated (INTER) See *reinforcement, schedule of: interpolated.*

schedule of reinforcement: mixed (MIX) See *reinforcement, schedule of: mixed.*

schedule of reinforcement: multiple (MULT) See *reinforcement, schedule of: multiple.*

schedule of reinforcement: nonintermittent See *reinforcement, schedule of: nonintermittent.*

schedule of reinforcement: second order See *reinforcement, schedule of: second order.*

schedule of reinforcement: tandem (TAND) See *reinforcement schedule of: tandem.*

schedule of reinforcement: variable interval (VI) See *reinforcement, schedule of: variable interval.*

schedule of reinforcement: variable ratio (VR) See *reinforcement, schedule of: variable ratio.*

schedule, self-demand A schedule for feeding infants in which the infant is fed when he gives indications of being hungry rather than by a predetermined schedule of feeding time.

schedule, Sidman Avoidance See *avoidance, free operant.*

Scheie's syndrome A disorder of mucopolysaccharide metabolism which is transmitted as an autosomac recessive trait and is characterized by a coarse appearance, cloudy corneas, limitation of motion at the joints, normal intellect, and cardiac vascular changes.

schematic model See *model, schematic.*

Schilder's disease One of the group of progressive diffuse sclerosis diseases commonly occurring early in life and characterized by symptoms such as visual failure, mental deterioration and spastic paralysis. Also called encephalitis periaxialis diffusa.

schismatic family See *family, schismatic.*

schizoaffective psychosis See *psychosis, schizoaffective.*

schizogenic family A family unit believed to have caused schizophrenia in one or more of its children.

schizogenic mothers See *schizophrenogenic mothers.*

schizoid 1. Pertaining to schizophrenia. 2. Schizoid character. 3. Schizophrenic-like behavior.

schizoid character An individual with a character disorder characterized by social withdrawal. Such individuals are shy, oversensitive, seclusive and often appear detached and eccentric, and sometimes withdraw into autistic fantasies and daydreams though some reality contact is maintained.

schizoid personality see *schizoid character.*

schizophrenia A group of psychotic reactions characterized by fundamental disturbances in reality relations and concept formations, and behavioral, affective and intellectual disturbances in varying degrees. There is often progressive deteriorating and regressive behavior. Several varieties classified according to symptomatology are distinguished. Formerly called dementia praecox.

schizophrenia, ambulatory 1. Schizophrenic disorder which does not require hospitalization. 2. Relates to schizophrenic patients who are treated on an out-patient basis.

schizophrenia, aretic (B.B. Wolman) An aggressive, pugnatious syndrome of childhood schizophrenia.

schizophrenia, autistic The autistic phase in childhood schizophrenia.

schizophrenia, catatonic A type of schizophrenia characterized by conspicuous motor behavior, exhibiting either marked generalized inhibition, such as stupor, mutism, negativism, waxy flexibility and inaccessibility to external stimuli, or excessive motor activity and excitement.

schizophrenia, childhood Diagnostic category for those children exhibiting a schizophrenic state, including such symptoms as withdrawal from people and reality, escape into a fantasy world, disturbance in the ability to make affective contact with the world, autistic thought processes, mutism, excessive inhibition or uninhibition of impulse expression, identification with animals or objects, stereotyped gestures, impassivity or extreme outbursts of rage and anxiety, bizarre posturing, and vasovegetative functioning.

Childhood schizophrenia is seen as a mental catastrophy that took place even before the ego had the opportunity to grow and exert control over the id; there is an arrest in the development of the personality structure. This is in contradistinction to adulthood schizophrenia which is seen as the failure of an impoverished ego; the personality structure is regressed.

schizophrenia, childhood, sociopsychosomatic theory of (B. B. Wolman) The classification of childhood schizophrenia based on etiology and personality characteristics which corresponds to particular stages in which the disorder was proposed. The pseudo amentive schizophrenia, formed during the pre-verbal stage, is the most severe form of this illness and corresponds to dementive schizophrenia in adults. The other three types of schizophrenia are the autistic, corresponding to adult hebephrenia; the symbiotic, parallel to adult catatonia; and the aretic, which corresponds to the adult paranoid syndrome.

schizophrenia, deteriorating stage of The stage at which the patient is in a regressed affectless stage.

schizophrenia, hebephrenic A type of schizophrenia characterized by marked silliness, inappropriate affect, giggling, delusions, hallucinations and regressive behavior.

schizophrenia, latent A form of schizophrenia in which the person has not yet broken with reality but may develop a psychosis if exposed to unfavorable circumstances of life. It is characterized by a considerable unevenness in mental functioning with mental functioning breaking down in emotionally loaded areas and threatening situations, strict control of id impulses, coldness, shallowness, non-attachment, and difficulty in accepting friendship and love.

schizophrenia, manifest A schizophrenic reaction which is observable. A fully developed schizophrenic disorder.

schizophrenia, mixed A form of schizophrenia characterized by symptoms usually manifested in two or more of the four categories of schizophrenia: hebephrenic, simple, catatonic and paranoid, so that a classification in one of the above categories cannot be made.

schizophrenia, paranoid A type of schizophrenia characterized by autistic thinking, delusions of persecution and/or grandeur, ideas of reference and often hallucinations.

schizophrenia, postemotive Schizophrenia, the onset of which is precipitated by a severe physical, social or sexual trauma.

schizophrenia, process Several authors distinguish process schizophrenia from reactive schizophrenia.

The process schizophrenia is characterized by a gradual decline of activity, dullness, autism, ideas of reference, thought disturbances, prolonged history of maladjustment, poor physical health, difficulties at home and in school, abnormal family relationships and somatic delusions.

schizophrenia, psychoneurotic (P. Hoch and P. Polatin) A syndrome characterized by a pervading anxiety which affects all areas of life and the presence of all symptoms of neurotic illnesses at the same time. The patient may have short psychotic episodes or may become schizophrenic in the future.

schizophrenia, reactive Schizophrenia characterized by a radical onset, oscillations between excitement and stuporous depression and by periods of almost normal functioning alternating with states of confusion.

schizophrenia, recidives in Recurring and intermittent schizophrenic episodes which occur after a long remissions period, the recurring episodes often duplicating past episodes although there are often new features.

schizophrenia, simple A type of schizophrenia characterized chiefly by reduction in external attachments and interests and impoverishment of human relationships, often accompanied by apathy and indifference.

schizophrenia, sociopsychosomatic theory of See *sociopsychosomatic theory of schizophrenia.*

schizophrenia, thanatotic (K. R. Eissler) Schizophrenic syndrome associated with the wish to die.

schizophrenic paradox (B. B. Wolman) Schizophrenic's renunciation of his own life in order to protect those who are supposed to protect him.

schizophrenic reaction See *schizophrenia.*

schizophrenogenic mothers (A. Kanner) Mothers whose personality and behavior are believed to have caused schizophrenia in their offspring.

schizothyme 1. Person who has schizothymic tendencies. **2.** (E. Kretschmer) Person characterized by a schizothymic temperament, one of two basic temperaments.

schizothymia Schizoid-like behavior or characteristics within the limits of normality.

schizothymic 1. Schizoid behavior or characteristics within the limits of normality. **2.** (E. Kretschmer) Basic temperament characterized by introversion, sensitivity, moodiness and seriousness, associated with the asthenic and the athletic body types and to a lesser degree with the dysplastic type.

schizothymic type See *type, schizothymic.*

Schoenfeld, William N. (1915-) American psychologist and university educator. Principal research areas: behavior theory, conditioning, social psychology, psychophysics and perception. Co-author (with F.S. Keller) of first textbook based on reinforcement theory; and, formulator of first systematic organization of reinforcement schedules (as presented in *Stimulus Schedules: the t-t Systems,* with B. K. Cole, et al., co-authors).

scholastic achievement test See *test, scholastic achievement.*

scholastic aptitude test See *test, scholastic aptitude.*

school and college ability test See *test, school and college ability.*

school phobia See *phobia, school.*

school psychologist See *psychologist, school.*

schools of psychology There are several independent theoretical systems in psychology not related to one another. Historically speaking, the earliest two systems were proposed by Plato and Aristotle, and later by Plotinus, St. Augustine and others influenced by Plato, and St. Thomas Aquinas and others inspired by Aristotle. In modern times the faculty psychology competed with associationism.

The nineteenth century witnessed the birth of scientific research in psychology; Wundt and Titchener developed the structural psychology (structuralism) and James Dewey, Angell and others started the functional psychology (functionalism).

The main currents in twentieth century psychological theory can be roughly divided into three major groups or schools, namely the conditioning-behavioristic school which includes the teachings of Pavlov, Watson, Hull, Skinner and others; the psychoanalytic school which encompasses the works of Freud, Adler, Jung, Sullivan and others; the third current which includes several distinct schools, such as personalistic psychology, phenomenology, Gestalt, field theory and others.

Schopenhauer, Arthur (1788-1860) German philosopher. Developed a solipsistic theory of cognition viewing the world as man's will and idea. Believed that insanity (madness-Irrsinn) originates in the unconscious.

Schreber case (S. Freud) Interpretation of an autobiographical description of a paranoid schizophrenic by the judge David Paul Schreber.

science 1. An organized and systematic body of knowledge. **2.** The study of phenomena in order to produce precise and valid information hitherto unknown with proof to support its validity.

scientific method See *method, scientific.*

scintillating scotoma See *scotoma, scintillating.*

sciosophy Non-scientific system of thought such as astrology.

scleroderma A disease characterized by patches of hardened skin tissue, atrophy of the epidermis and pigmentation. Psychogenic causes may lead to susceptibility to the disorder in patients who are threatened by a loss of security.

sclerosis, tuberous See *epiloia.*

scopic method See *method, scopic.*

scopophilia; scoptophilia Sexual pleasure derived from looking; also called voyerism.

score 1. A quantitative value assigned to a datum, usually a test response, attitude, etc. 2. The sum or total of a number of credits or scores obtained by an individual.

score, accuracy The proportion or number of test items that the subject answered correctly.

score, age Also called age equivalent score. A test score that expresses the individual's performance as the age at which most individuals reach that particular level of performance. See *age equivalent*.

score, composite The average of a person's scores when they are expressed in common units. The scores may be weighted.

score criterion The dependent variable in an experimental situation.

score, crude 1. The raw score which has not been analyzed. 2. The approximate score.

score, derived 1. A score derived by the mathematical manipulation of another score or measure. 2. A score that has been converted from one scale into the units of another scale.

score, deviation (statistics) An individual score obtained by subtracting from any raw scores. Another value may be substituted for the mean, but it will be indicated.

score, grade A score which describes a person's achievement in terms of grade level for which his performance is average.

score, graphic A score which is represented by a line or other figural diagram.

score, gross The score expressed in the original units of measurement.

score, original See *score, raw*.

score, percentile A score which indicates the percentage of cases or persons falling below a particular score in a given sample.

score, point See *score, raw*.

score, raw A score which is presented in the original test units; a value that has not been treated statistically.

score, sigma See *score, standard*.

score, standard 1. Any score using as its unit the standard deviation of a population which it is using as its criterion. 2. The difference between the obtained score (x) and the mean (M_x) divided by the standard deviation (σ). It is known as the z score. The formula is:

$$z = \frac{x - M_x}{\sigma_x}$$

score, time The amount of time required to perform a particular task.

score, transmuted A score which has been translated into the units of another scale.

score, z See *score, standard*.

scores, additional Used in the Klopfer approach to the Rorschach to identify responses which have more than one determining feature, i.e. form, color, movement, or shading. Klopfer's system requires that only one determinant be selected as the "main" feature responsible for the response. Where multiple determinants occur, one is selected as "main" and the others are scored as "additional." Klopfer's method of interpretation generally weighs additional scorings differently from main scores.

scores, ungrouped Scores which have not been tabulated into classes or groups.

scoring, configural A method of determining a subject's criterion score used in pattern analysis. Each individual in a particular answer pattern is assigned the same score for that pattern. This set of scores is the best prediction of the subject's criterion score according to the least squares requirement.

scoring, differential Procedure of scoring responses on a battery of tests in different ways so as to get measures of more than one variable.

scotoma A blind or partially blind spot in the visual field surrounded by normal or near normal vision.

scotoma, central A blind or partially blind spot limited to the area of the retina normally associated with clearest vision (the macular luteu).

scotoma, mental Lack of insight; mental blind spot.

scotoma, scintillating The usually temporary appearance of bright flashes before the eyes.

scotopic adaption Adaption to darkness.

scotopic vision Twilight vision.

screen memory Recollection of an insignificant item used unconsciously as resistance against recalling an emotionally significant event.

screening The selection of individuals or items for inclusion or exclusion in a test group, procedure or other situation.

scrying Crystal gazing.

SD (σ) See *standard deviation*.

seance A group meeting or sitting, usually in darkness, for the purpose of obtaining and investigating psychic phenomena.

Sears, Robert R. (1908-   ) Child psychologist whose behavioral research explored the influence of parental child-rearing practices on aggression, dependency, sex-typing, identification and other motivational systems. Devised standardized methods of behavior observation for fantasy expression (doll play) and mother-child interactions. Emphasized dyadic approach to theoretical analysis of personality development. See dyad.

Sechenov, Ivan Mikhailovich (1829-1905) Russian physiologist considered to be the "Father of Russian Physiology"; created the school of Russian physiologists. Between 1850 and 1855, Sechenov was a student of the Faculty of Medicine of the Moscow University, where he had a chance to listen to K. F. Rulye, F. I. Inozcmtzev, et al. Sechenov was influenced by the revolutionary ideas of a leader of Russian Enlightenment, N. G. Chernishevskiu. Sechenov worked at European laboratories under C. Ludwig, J. Müller, Du Bois-Reymond, Claude Bernard, et al. He was interested in the physiology of the nervous system where he made a remarkable discovery, namely the process of central inhibition. In the book, *Reflexes of the Brain* (1863) Sechenov demonstrated the possibility of scientific materialistic interpretation of man's psychic activity. He also investigated gas exchange and gas contents in blood; he introduced the method of "Toricelli vacuum" for extraction of gases from blood.

second order factor A factor which describes the correlations among first-order factors after they have been rotated to simple structure. A dimension of co-variation in the correlations between factors. Second order factors describe more massive, broader organizations of personality.

second order schedules See *reinforcement, schedule of: second order.*

second signal system (I. P. Pavlov) The ability to signal to oneself, in contrast to the external signal of the conditioned stimulus.

secondary correlation See *correlation, secondary.*

secondary elaboration (S. Freud) The putting together of non-related elements or thoughts and considering them to be a whole, as in dreams.

secondary extinction See *extinction, secondary.*

secondary gain See *epinosis.*

secondary inhibitor A neutral stimulus which becomes an inhibitor as a result of its association with an inhibitor.

secondary integration See *integration, secondary.*

secondary narcissism See *narcissism, secondary.*

secondary position See *position, secondary.*

secondary process See *process, secondary.*

secondary reinforcement See *reinforcement, secondary.*

secondary repression See *repression, secondary.*

secondary reward See *reinforcement, secondary.*

secondary sex characteristics See *sex, secondary characteristics.*

secretion Production of substance by a bodily organ, e.g. tears; the secretion of the tear glands is exogenous and the thyroxin hormone, secretion of the thyroid gland, is endogenous.

secretion, internal The secretion of the endocrine glands.

security operations (H. S. Sullivan) Activities employed by the self-system to reduce or relieve tension and maintain self-esteem and a feeling of safety.

sedative Any drug which quiets functioning or activity. The barbiturate, a cellular depressant, is commonly used.

segmental behavior Behavior controlled by a segment of the spinal cord.

segmental insufficiency See *insufficiency, segmental.*

segregation 1. (genetics) Breaking up of a pair of gametes permitting new combinations of genes in sexual reproduction 2. (Gestalt) Breaking up of elements in perception and forming a new figure-ground combination. 3. (social psychology) Isolating of individuals or groups from the rest of the population; forming ghettos and/or forming separate dwelling units, schools, and means of locomotion for the segregation of groups in order to isolate them from the non-segregated population.

seizure, audiogenic Convulsion caused by prolonged exposure to intense high frequency sound.

seizure, conversion A seizure due to psychological causes with no organic or physical basis.

seizure, epileptiform 1. A convulsion or attack which resembles an epileptic attack but which is caused by some other disease or injury to the brain. 2. Hysterical behavior which leads to epileptic-like symptoms such as convulsions.

seizure, gustatory A form of epilepsy in which the seizure pattern includes the sensation of a peculiar taste.

selection 1. (statistics) The choice of an item, individual, or experimental stimulus for inclusion in a group, test, category or experiment. 2. (genetics) The process by which particular genes or gene combinations change from generation to generation as a result of biological advantages favoring change. 3. (industrial psychology) The process of selection attempts to optimize the number of successful employees hired by an organization. It represents the earliest function performed by psychologists employed in industry beginning with the work of Münsterberg, published in 1913.

selection, artificial The process by which animals or plants that possess desirable characteristics are chosen for hybridizing or homogeneous breeding.

selection index See *index, selection.*

selection method See *method, recognition.*

selection, natural (C. Darwin) Biological law synonymous to the survival of the fittest. In the process of natural selection, individuals who carry characteristics which do not foster successful adjustment to the environment cannot survive, thus they do not transmit maladjustive traits, and only the traits which help survival are genetically transmitted.

selection ratio A statistical technique that gives the functional value of any selection instrument. The selection ratio is defined as the ratio of the number of available jobs to the number of applicants for the jobs.

selective answer test   See *test, selective answer.*

selective inattention   See *inattention, selective.*

selective response   See *response, selective.*

selective silence   A brief period occurring in conversation, association tests, or therapy, in which a subject withholds a response, indicating an anxiety-provoking topic has been touched upon.

self   1. The ego. **2.** The traits and characteristics making up the individual. **3.** (W. James) That which a person considers part of or representing himself. There are many selves representing an individual, such as the material self, the social self, and the spiritual self. **4.** (C. G. Jung) An archetype which develops during middle age and represents the reconciliation of opposites and the fusion of the conscious and the unconscious. It is the center of the personality providing stability and equilibrium and is thus the goal of life. It does not develop until the other aspects of the personality are developed and individuated. **5.** (C. Rogers) The portion of the personality which consists of perceptions of "I" or "me" and develops out of the organism's interaction with the environment. It strives for consistency, introjects the values of others which may be perceived in a distorted way, and changes as a result of maturation and learning. **6.** (H. S. Sullivan) See *self-system.* **7.** (A. Adler) A subjective system which makes experiences meaningful for the individual and seeks experiences which will fulfill the person's life style. It gives meaning to life creating the goal as well as helping to fulfill it.

self-acceptance   A healthy attitude toward one's worth and limitations consisting of an objective recognition of each quality and an acceptance of each as being part of the self.

self-actualization   1. (K. Goldstein) Striving toward completeness; fulfillment of one's potentialities. **2.** (A. Maslow) Developing and fulfilling one's innate, positive potentialities.

self-administering test   See *test, self-administering.*

self-analysis   See *analysis, self.*

self-cathexis   See *cathexis, self.*

self-concept   The individual's appraisal or evaluation of himself.

self-consistency   1. Individuals, items, or theories which do not contradict themselves in any aspect, action or phase. **2.** (B. Lecky) A theory of personality growth which postulates that growth consists of the development of a self-image and progressive harmonizing of subsequent behavior consistent with that image.

self-correlation   See *correlation, self.*

self-demand schedule   See *schedule, self-demand.*

self-distribution   See *distribution, self.*

self-dynamism   (H. S. Sullivan) See *self-system.*

self-effacement   (K. Horney) One of the major neurotic solutions to conflict consisting of identification with the hated self and consequent idealization of compliancy, dependency, and love.

self-extinction   (K. Horney) Neurotic behavior in which the individual has no experience of himself as an entity, attempts to live through others' experiences, and sees himself only as a reflection of others.

self-feeling   (W. McDougall) Various simple feelings which form the nucleus of an individual's self-regard. They may be of either a positive nature, derived from praise or achievement, or of negative nature, resulting from criticism or under-achievement.

self-gratification   See *gratification, self.*

self-gratification mores   (G. Murphy) The mores which set forth the means for obtaining non-utilitarian satisfactions. Also called self-maintenance mores.

self-hypercathexis   See *hypercathexis, self.*

self-hypocathexis   See *hypocathexis, self.*

self-image   (K. Horney) The perfect and ideal self which the individual imagines himself to be after identification with an idealized conception of what he should be.

self-inventory   A self-making questionnaire on which the subject marks the traits he believes are his own.

self-maintainence mores   See *self-gratification mores.*

self-marking test   See *test, self-marking.*

self, phenomenal   1. The self as it is experienced directly as the focus in the interaction of person and environment. **2.** The self as it is personally perceived and directly known as in the self-image or self-concept.

self-preservation instinct   See *Eros.*

self-report inventory   See *self-inventory.*

self-sentiment   (R. B. Cattell) A control of impulse, temperamental capacity to integrate, and strong investment of appropriate behavior integrated about the self-concept (or, roughly, self-respect). Aspects of this concept are involved in questionnaire factor Q_3 (usually called Self-Sentiment Control), objective test factor UI 36 (usually called Strength of Self-Sentiment Development), and a purely dynamic factor measured by the Motivational Analysis Test. Since these three factors are not identical empirically, they are best thought of as representing somewhat different aspects of the self-sentiment concept, with some common core of similarity.

self-system   (H. S. Sullivan) A secondary dynamism, dissociated from the rest of the personality, the organization of which controls awareness. It includes the personified self as well as the processes by which anxiety-provoking experiences and perceptions are kept from awareness. The self-system is purely the product of interpersonal experiences arising from anxiety encountered in the pursuit of need satisfaction and has no particular zones of interaction or physiological apparatus behind it but rather uses all zones and apparatus.

semantic aphasia See *aphasia, semantic.*

semantic conditioning Conditioning of a word to an object which the word represents.

semantic differential test See *test, semantic differential.*

semantic information See *information, semantic.*

semantic therapy An ancillary method in psychotherapy; the explanation of meaning of words is used to help emotional conflicts.

semantics The study of meaning of symbols; interpretation of symbols.

semiotics The study of relationships between verbal and other symbols, and what they represent.

senile dementia See *dementia, senile.*

senility 1. A general term including a variety of mental disorders occurring in old age which consist of two broad categories, organic and functional disorders. Organic disorders are characterized by intellectual impairment, poor memory, and labile emotions, due to infection, intoxication, circulatory disturbances or brain disease. The functional disorders include physical reactions of vertigo, fatigue, and headaches and psychological reactions of insomnia, doubt, hypochondriasis, delusions and feelings of physical decline. 2. See *dementia, senile.* 3. See *geriopsychosis.* 4. See *psychotic reactions, involutional.*

sensation Immediate elementary experiences requiring no verbal, symbolic or conceptual elaboration, and related primarily to sense organ activity such as occurring in the eye or ear and in the associated nervous system leading to a particular sensory area in the brain. In so far as the only verifiable statements about sensations become statements about behavior, sensation denotes a construct whose meaning is derivative of responses of the organism to specified stimuli.

Sensation is typically though somewhat vaguely and arbitrarily distinguished from perception in that the latter tends to be more complex and more dependent upon learning, motivational, social and personality factors than the former.

sensation, affective Also called feeling-sensation. An inseparable blending of feeling or affective elements with sensation elements.

sensation increment (psychophysics) An increase in the intensity of the subjective sensory experience.

sensation level The degree of intensity of a sensation such as in audition; the intensity in decibels of a sound.

sensation, maximal The intensity level of the sensation which is not augmented upon increase of the physical stimulus.

sensation, motor Sensation which arises from the receptors in the muscles, joints, and tendons.

sensation, proprioceptive Sensation from inside the body.

sensation, referred The experience of sensation at a point other than that which was stimulated.

sensation, subjective Sensations which do not result from external stimulation but are related to phenomena within the organ such as ringing in the ears.

sensation threshold See *threshold, absolute.*

sensation type See *type, sensation.*

sensation unit 1. A small discriminible experience which can occur in any sensory modality. 2. The just-noticeable-difference. 3. (audition) A unit of physical intensity of a stimulus equal to the decibel. It is measured in logarithms and is abbreviated as SU.

sense 1. At least five criteria differentiate among primary sense modalities. They have 1) different receptive organs that 2) respond to characteristic stimuli. Each set of receptive organs has 3) its own nerve that goes to 4) a different part of the brain and 5) the resultant sensations are different on the basis of these criteria. Nine and perhaps eleven different senses have been identified: vision, audition, kinesthesis, vestibular, tactile, temperature, pain, taste, and smell. 2. The activity of a sense organ and correlated neural activity. 3. Apparently intuitive judgment in which the relevant stimuli are unidentified or obstructed.

sense, cutaneous The sense of pressure, pain, cold, warmth and touch whose receptors lie beneath the skin or in the mucous membranes.

sense datum That fundamental unit which is experienced upon stimulation of a sense receptor.

sense distance The interval on a scale of sensation which separates two sensations.

sense experience The awareness of the sensation resulting from the stimulation of the sensory receptor.

sense-feeling The dimension of pleasantness and unpleasantness of a sensory experience.

sense limen See *threshold, absolute.*

sense modality See *modality, sense.*

sense organ See *organ, sense.*

sense, pain Sensory modality of free nerve endings receptive to pain which is distributed over the periphery of the body and many internal surfaces.

sense perception See *perception, sense.*

sense quality 1. The character of a sensation which distinguishes it from other senses. 2. A sense datum characteristic of a particular modality.

sense-ratios method See *method, sense-ratios.*

sense, systemic The sense whose receptors lie in the internal organs. Also known as interoceptive sense.

sensed difference A noticeable difference between two sensations which are presented simultaneously or successively.

sensibility The capacity to sense or to be stimulated by sense stimuli.

sensibility, differential Ability to discriminate between two stimuli as measured by a differential threshold.

sensibility, subcutaneous Sensitivity to stimulation of the receptors lying beneath the skin.

sensitive zone A part of the body highly responsive to a particular kind of stimulus, e.g. skin is a tactile sensitive zone.

sensitivity 1. The reciprocal of threshold; one over threshold. 2. The responsiveness of an organism to stimulus energy or energy changes.

sensitivity, absolute The ability to respond to stimuli of minimal intensity.

sensitivity, liminal An individual's sensory acuity as measured by the average stimulus that just barely evokes a response.

sensitivity training Training in human relations which is an outgrowth of the thinking of K. Lewin and C. Rogers and began with the meeting of a group in Bethel, Maine in 1947. The focus of the group is personal and interpersonal interactions. The members are taught to observe their interactions with others and the nature of the group process. There are many forms and emphases in the groups. The groups may be composed of strangers or they may be acquainted with each other. They may be workers in an organization, couples, male, female, etc. Some groups meet once a week, some more often, even during an entire weekend. There is at least one leader whose function is to facilitate the understanding of interpersonal relations. Presently, this term usually refers to groups in which personal and interpersonal issues are the primary forces rather than the observation of group processes or organizational behavior.

sensitization The process of a receptor becoming more susceptible to a given stimulus.

sensor A receptor that responds to energy or energy changes.

sensori-motor activity Responses resulting from the reception of sensory stimulation.

sensorium 1. Obsolete term for the sensory areas of the brain. 2. The total sensory mechanism.

sensory Referring to the total apparatus and experience of sensation including the sense organs, stimuli impinging on the sense receptors, afferent neurons, brain centers' receiving the impulses and the processes involved in the experience of sensation.

sensory adaptation 1. The decrease in sensitivity to stimuli due to prolonged stimulation, also called negative adaptation. 2. The continuation of effective sensory responsiveness to changing stimulation.

sensory aphasia See *aphasia, sensory*.

sensory apraxia See *apraxia, sensory*.

sensory areas Areas in the cerebral cortex which receive neural impulses from sense organs.

sensory basis of reinforcement Property of many sensory stimuli that reinforce behavior in their own right as a result of their stimulus properties and innate central nervous system connections. Head turning to one side or the other may be rapidly conditioned in the neonate by presentation of a sweet nipple. Patterns of visual or auditory stimuli may reinforce motor responses that turn on such stimuli. Adversive reinforcement is also observed in which organisms avoid and learn instrumental responses to turn off or reduce noxious stimulation.

sensory circle Area of the skin in which two points stimulating the skin are perceived as a single point. This was explained as the skin area in which the terminals of a single sensory neuron are distributed.

sensory clearness See *attensity*.

sensory code The information content of a pattern of neural discharge frequencies about the nature of the stimulus impinging on a sense receptor.

sensory cortex See *cortex, sensory*.

sensory deprivation See *deprivation, sensory*.

sensory development, stages of (E. Schactel) Modes of perceiving, by which the individual objectifies his environment and shapes his experiences, which define an ontogenic hierarchy ranging from the dominance of autocentric modes (olfactory, gustatory, tactile) to the dominance of allocentric modes (auditory and visual).

sensory discrimination See *discrimination, sensory*.

sensory drive See *drive, sensory*.

sensory epilepsy See *epilepsy, sensory*.

sensory field The totality of stimuli which impinge on a receptor or organism as a whole at a specific time.

sensory habit See *habit, sensory*.

sensory integration (H. Birch and M. Bitterman) The postulate that the contiguous stimulation of two afferent areas results in a relationship between them whereby the activation of one will cause the other to be aroused.

sensory interaction The reciprocal interdependence of sensory processes occurring simultaneously.

sensory-motor arc Path of a neural impulse from the receptor through its afferent fibers to the central nervous system where it synapses with motor, efferent fibers which eventually terminate with response effectors.

sensory nerve See *nerve, sensory*.

sensory noise See *neural noise*.

sensory organization 1. The process by which

sensory processes become meaningfully coordinated. 2. (Gestalt) The patterning of stimuli in the sensory field which produces a meaningful percept.

sensory pattern See *pattern, sensory.*

sensory preconditioning See *preconditioning, sensory.*

sensory process 1. The process underlying sensation which originates in the receptor. 2. The process of becoming aware of sensations.

sensory projection area See *sensory areas.*

sensory reaction type See *reaction type, sensory.*

sensory receptors See *receptor.*

sensory root See *root, sensory.*

sensory stimulus See *stimulus, sensory.*

sensory system The sensory unit consisting of the sensory organs, afferent neurons and the sensory projection areas in the cerebral cortex.

sensual Referring to satisfaction obtained from indulging in activities involving the senses, such as food and sex.

sensum See *sense-datum.*

sensuous Referring to the sense aspect of experience or the ability for the senses to be aroused.

sentence completion test See *test, sentence completion.*

sentence repetition test See *test, sentence repetition.*

sentience 1. The capacity of the organism to receive stimuli. 2. Sensation without concomitant associations which is hypothesized as the most primitive form of cognition.

sentience need See *need, sentience.*

sentiment 1. An attitude. 2. An emotional disposition. 3. A soft, gentle feeling. 4. An expression of a subdued emotion, or of an emotionally colored attitude.

separation anxiety (psychoanalysis) Anxiety caused in a child by actual separation from his mother or by a threat thereof.

separation-individuation, normal (M. S. Mahler) From the fifth month on, the infant begins to differentiate gradually his own self, especially his bodyself boundaries, from the symbiotic dual unit; he starts to disengage himself and to separate his mental representation from that of his mother. Toward the end of the second quarter of the first year, there are unmistakable signs that symbiosis is overlapped by what Mahler calls the "separation-individuation" process. During the process of the child's separation-individuation, the mother's role shifts from that of complement and buffer (as it had been in the autistic and symbiotic phases) to that of support and encouragement for the toddler's strivings toward and gradual attainment of ego, i.e. self-autonomy.

separation-individuation: subphases of the normal process Four steps or subphases of the separation-individuation process were described by Mahler and her co-workers: 1) Differentiation (also called "hatching" from the symbiotic dual unity's common membrane); 2) The Practicing Period; 3) The Rapprochement Subphase (Mahler); 4) The Subphase "On the Way to Emotional Object Constancy."

sequels The pathological aftereffect of an illness.

sequence 1. (mathematics) A series of consecutive quantities in which each is obtained by performing a specific operation on the preceding quantity. 2. (H. Rorschach) The order of the different types of responses which the subject makes, such as whole and detail response.

sequence alternation One element of basic Rorschach interpretation in which the sequence of response determinants, such as movement, form, color, or shading, are studied in their consecutive relation to each other. This method of response analysis often reveals those responses which are most idiographic to the individual.

sequence analysis In Rorschach interpretation, the examination of each response in its chronological order in the protocol for basic structure, relevance to the blot area relation to preceding and subsequent responses, and its basic content. It is generally considered the second of three interpretive steps in working with Rorschach data, the first being interpretation from quantitative structural data and the third being a broad qualitative analysis of verbalizations and content.

sequential analysis Discussion of results obtained in research which aims at acceptance, rejection or modification of conclusions arrived at in that research.

sequential test See *test, sequential.*

serial-anticipation method See *method, prompting.*

serial discrimeter See *psychergograph.*

serial or serial-order learning See *learning, serial or serial-order.*

serial position effect The effect of a position of a certain item within a series on the speed of learning process.

serial reinforcement See *reinforcement, serial.*

seriation 1. Forming of series. 2. Organizing of data into statistical series.

series, Poisson See *Poisson series.*

serotonin A substance found in the brain, the intestines, and the platelets which induces vasoconstriction and muscular contraction. It has been suggested that this substance is involved in the development of mental disorders. This hypothesis is based on studies which show that certain indoles which antagonize serotonin produce aberrant behavior and that the displacement of serotonin from the brain by certain psychotropic drugs produces abnormal behavior in animal and human subjects. It may be that abnormal levels of serotonin underlie mental disorders.

serpasil Common name for reserpine, a purified alkaloid extract of rauwolfia.

servomechanism A system or mechanism which controls the rate of operation of another system according to a specified plan such as a thermostat.

set 1. (mathematics) A well defined collection of elements. 2. A temporary but often recurring tendency of a person or an organism to respond toward certain environmental stimuli in a predetermined way. 3. The establishment of a fixed behavior pattern; stereotyping.

set learning See *learning, set.*

set, mental Readiness for a particular kind of action usually due to instructions given previously.

set, motor The readiness of an organism to react motorically in a particular way to an expected stimulus which involves the adjustment of the muscles in anticipation of the action.

set, neural A readiness of an organism to respond in a specific way which is explained in terms of a state of neural excitation of a response circuit.

set, perceptual A predisposition to perceive the environment in a particular way, usually influenced by some sort of pattern.

set, postural Tonic muscle contractions which ready the organism to begin a specific action.

set, stimulus A readiness to attend to the stimulus rather than on making a response in reaction time experiments.

sex 1. Male or female gender. 2. Biological division of animal and human organism on the basis of their reproductive role. The male organism produces spermatozoa and possesses a necessary fertilization organ; the female organism produces ova capable of becoming fertilized by the spermatozoa and possesses the necessary organs for prenatal and postnatal care of the offspring.

sex chromosomes Chromosomes responsible for sex determination. In man, XX is female and XY is male.

sex determination Genetic mechanism which determines the difference between the two sexes, specifically the sex chromosomes X and Y. Under usual conditions a fertilized egg with two XX chromosomes becomes a female; a fertilized egg with one X and one Y chromosome becomes a male.

sex differences Innate or acquired, organic and/or behavioral differences between the two sexes.

sex hormones See *hormones, sex.*

sex-influenced A trait which is not sex-linked but is expressed to a different degree or with a different frequency in male and female is termed sex-influenced. Involutional psychosis is a good example.

sex-limited A trait expressed in one sex only is termed sex-limited.

sex-linkage Inheritance by genes on the sex chromosomes. Several neurological syndromes exhibit sex-linked transmission.

sex need See *need, sex.*

sex reversal 1. Changing of the anatomical sex. 2. Change in fundamental sexual characteristic. In some cases, when the female ovaries or male gonads are destroyed, or when there is an innate pathological discrepancy between the chromosomal and anatomical change, the apparent sexual characteristics and behavior can be changed into opposites.

sex role Behavioral patterns expected from an individual by his social group believed to be typical of his sex. Some sex determinant behavioral patterns are biologically determined, such as, e.g. menstruation and pregnancy in females. Certain behavior patterns are culturally influenced, such as, e.g. ascendance-submissiveness, or occupational choices. Sex role is often called psychosexual role.

sex, secondary characteristics Characteristics which distinguish between the sexes and are not directly related to sexual and reproductive functions, e.g. pubic hair, voice, stature, etc.

sex-typed skills Skills which are designated as either masculine or feminine.

sex-typed trait A trait identified as either masculine or feminine.

sex-typing The designation in a culture of certain behaviors as feminine or masculine and the training of children to adhere to these roles.

sexism A belief that utilizes sex differences as the basis for discrimination in the granting of political, social or economic rights.

sexoesthetic inversion The assumption of manners, habits, and garments of the opposite sex.

sexology Scientific study of sexual life.

Sexton, Virginia Staudt (1916-) American psychologist. Principal research interests: history of psychology; international developments in psychology; and psychology of women. Published (with H. Misiak) *Catholics in Psychology* (1954); *History of Psychology: an Overview* (1966); and *Historical Perspective in Psychology: Readings* (1971).

sexual behavior The totality of normal and abnormal, conscious and unconscious, overt and covert sensations, thoughts, feelings and actions related to sexual organs and other erotogenic zones, including masturbation, heterosexual and homosexual relations, sexual deviations, goals and techniques.

sexual deviation 1. Sexual behavior which does not conform with social norms of a certain culture. 2. The Diagnostic and Statistical Manual of the American Psychiatric Association (DSM II, 1968) describes sexual deviation as follows:

.0   Homosexuality
.1   Fetishism
.2   Pedophilia
.3   Transvestitism
.4   Exhibitionism
.5   Voyeurism
.6   Sadism
.7   Masochism
.8   Other sexual deviation

sexual exhibitionism See *exhibitionism.*

sexual frigidity Sexual inadequacy in females; covers a variety of symptoms, such as lack of sexual desires, total inability of reaching orgasm, inability of reaching vaginal orgasm or orgasm in coitus, complete or partial anesthesia of sexual organs, vaginism, etc.

sexual negativism See *negativism, sexual.*

sexual perversion See *sexual deviation.*

sexual reflex 1. Erection. 2. Orgasm.

sexual reproduction The process of creating a new organism through the union of male and female sex cells.

sexual selection Selection of sexual mates which leads to natural selection. The prevalence of certain sex characteristics sought after fosters, through heredity, a prevalence of these characteristics in the forthcoming generations.

sexual symbolism The use of substitute objects to represent sexual organs or actions, such as receptacles for female organs and sharp objects for male organs.

Sh R (Z. Piotrowski) Shading response is a Rorschach inkblot test indicating self-control and inhibition of overt emotional reactions.

shading response A type of Rorschach response in which the chiaroscuro features (light-dark distribution) contribute to the development of a response in a manner other than creating a textural quality or a sense of depth. Shading responses are generally considered indicative of painful affects, mainly anxiety.

shading shock An unusual or startle response of Rorschach subjects to the achromatic or chiaroscuro features of the blots. It may be manifest in delayed reaction time, alteration in approach, reduction of response quality and/or frequency. It is generally interpreted as a response to threat and associated with insecurity, extensive anxiety, or over-emphasis on introspection.

shadow (C. G. Jung) The archetype consisting of man's animal instincts inherited in his evolution from lower life forms. It contains sexual and aggressive impulses which cannot be approved by the conscious ego. When these impulses pierce the consciousness they may be repressed into the personal unconscious and form a part of a complex.

Shannon's tenth theorem See *Ashby's Law of Requisite Variety.*

shape constancy Perceiving an object as having the same shape irrespective of the perceiver's vantage point.

shaping See *conditioning, approximation.*

Sheldon, William H. (1899-) American psychologist. Developed and experimentally investigated a constitutional theory of personality. Investigated the composition of the human body, the components of temperament, and the relation between physiology and personality; developed 7-point measuring scales for assessing body-type and temperament; applied theoretical findings to the area of delinquency; investigated the relation between physical structure and organic disease. See *constitutional theory of personality.*

shell shock See *battle fatigue.*

Sherrington, Charles S. (1857-1952) Distinguished British neurophysiologist. His 1906 *Integrative Action of the Nervous System* presented the results of many experiments on reflexes, the synapse, and the control of reflex arcs by higher nervous centers, and developed many concepts and principles (such as neural summation, reciprocal inhibition, and facilitation) that served as the foundation of physiological psychology for many decades.

shifting, law of (E.L. Thorndike) The law of associative shifting means that it is easy to have associated the responses which the learner is capable of with situations to which he is sensitive.

shock therapy The treatment of mentally ill persons by passing an electric current through the brain or by the administration of drugs which produces convulsions.

short term memory (STM) See *memory, short term.*

Siamese twins See *twins, Siamese.*

sickle-cell anemia See *anemia, sickle-cell.*

Sidman avoidance schedule See *avoidance, free operant.*

sigma (σ) 1. One thousandth of a second. 2. The symbol of standard deviation.

sigma score See *standard score.*

sign-gestalt (E.C. Tolman) The process of cognitive learning is based on expectations of attainment of certain goals or objects called sign-gestalts.

sign learning (O.H. Mowrer) Learning by contiguity with the participation of autonomic nervous system.

sign, local (H. Lotze) An inherent qualitative factor by means of which one visual or tactual sensation can be distinguished from others in respect to position in space.

sign-significance relation The expectancy of a given phenomenon.

sign stimulus See *stimulus, sign.*

sign stimulus, super-normal See *stimulus, super-normal sign.*

signal detection theory (psychophysics) A method of dealing with sensory discrimination without using the threshold concept, since classical psychophysics assumes that there is a real sensory threshold. Signal detection theory provides a method of separating the sensitivity of the subject from his criterion of response. The basic signal detection experiment involves the detection of signals (stimuli) that are weak relative to a background noise against which they are presented. This detection becomes a function of the signal intensity and background noise intensity. On some trials the noise is presented without a signal and on other trials both are presented together. The subject attempts to determine if the signal was present or not. There are four possible results on any trial; the signal may or may not be presented and in each case the response may or may not be correct.

A response is a function of the stimulus input, the sensations, and the decision rule used by the subject. The specific decision rule in the specific situation depends on the value or relative loss of the types of errors and the relative worth of the types of correct responses; this defines the optimum strategy. The subject's sensitivity is depicted as a graph of the probability of a yes response to the signal and noise together—a correct determination; as a function of the probability of a yes response to the noise alone—a false alarm. Any deviation from this obtained function, called d', on the receiver operating characteristic (ROC) curve is indicative of a change in the subject's sensitivity. Thus the ROC curve serves as a baseline or characteristic performance level with which to compare other individuals or changes in the sensitivity of the same individual as a function of some independent variable.

significance (statistics) A statement that the probability of obtaining the observed effect by chance only is small and designated by the alpha error.

significant difference A difference between two statistics, computed from two separate samples. This difference is of a magnitude such that the probability that the samples were drawn from the same universe is less than some predetermined level.

similarity paradox See *Skaggs-Robinson hypothesis.*

simple interview An interview with an individual who forms part of a sample of a population.

simple schizophrenia See *schizophrenia, simple.*

simple structure A criterion for rotation of factors, which is attained when the number of zero or near-zero loadings (Hyperplane Count) is maximized for each factor.

single variable, rule of The rule of experimentation which states that only one factor at any given time should be treated as an independent variable. When two equivalent groups differ, the difference can be attributed to only one factor.

sitomania Morbid craving for food; bulimia.

sitophobia Fear of food.

situation, analytic Setting of the psychoanalytic process, characterized by a one-to-one relationship between analyst and patient, the patient being required to recline so he cannot see the analyst and to relate without censoring all thoughts and feelings as they occur.

situation test See *test, situation.*

situationism (K. Lewin) Dealing with psychological phenomena in a given situation at a given time. Viewing behavior in a context of interaction between the organism and its environment as it occurs at a certain moment, as a momentary situation.

sixteen D scale See *scale, sixteen D.*

size constancy See *constancy, size.*

size-weight illusion See *illusion, size-weight.*

SK See *skewness.*

Skaggs-Robinson hypothesis (E. B. Skaggs and E.S. Robinson) The learning of identical materials, the learning of one enchancing the retention of the other; as the materials become more dissimilar, one interferes with the retention of the other, and when the material is completely dissimilar, retention increases again, although it never attains the level obtained at the point of maximal similarity of material.

skew-deviation See *Hertwig-Magendie phenomenon.*

skewed family See *family, skewed.*

skewed regression See *regression, non-linear.*

skewness (SK) The extent to which a frequency curve is twisted, so that it extends farther to one side of the central tendency than to the other. It is positively skewed if it leans to the right and negatively skewed if it leans to the left.

skiascope An instrument used for measuring the refractive condition of the eye.

skill An acquired aptitude.

Skinner, B.F. (1904-) American psychologist, working in the experimental analysis of operant behavior. Developed laboratory methods and extended principles to verbal behavior, psychotherapy, education, and the design of cultures. See *operant behavior.*

Skinner box A typical research apparatus is a device known as the Skinner box, named for its inventor B. F. Skinner. The dimensions of the box are about 12 inches cubed. There is a small lever projecting out of one wall of the apparatus. When the experimental animal (usually a rat) depresses the lever, a piece of food is released into the compartment for the animal to consume. The animal is rewarded for pressing the lever, and thus continues to press it as long as it is hungry. The pattern of the animal's behavior can be varied by varying the procedure. For example, if the animal receives food once for every ten pressings, he will press the bar very rapidly. On the other hand, if it receives food only on the first response after a one minute period has lapsed, his behavior will be quite different. As a rule, the animal does very little for the first part of the minute, but toward the end of the time limit it presses the bar rapidly.

Skinner's operant conditioning See *conditioning, operant.*

Slater, Eliot T. O. (1904-) British psychiatrist. Principally engaged in work on the genetics of mental disorders. Studied parents and children of manic-depressives, proposing hypothesis of major dominant gene. Conducted the first British major study of twins of psychotic patients. Twin studies, and later follow-up studies, of "hysteria" led to the conclusion that this was a pseudo-syndrome without genetical basis. Studies of schizophrenia-like psychoses in epileptics (with A.W. Beard and E. Glithero) suggested a discrete syndrome of organic but not genetic causation. Twin studies (with J. Shields) in the neuroses suggested an important genetical contribution to anxiety states, but a negligible one to the reactive depressions.

sleep 1. A state of bodily rest combined with inhibition of voluntary activities, decrease in metabolism, and complete or partial suspension of consciousness. 2. (I. P. Pavlov) Sleep is the most general internal inhibition which creates a balance between the processes of destruction and restoration. 3. (S. Freud) A temporary regression into a position resembling intrauterine life. 4. (H. Pieron) During the waking state a fatigue product, called hypnotism, is accumulated in the blood and cerebrospinal fluid. The abundance of hypnotism produces sleep; sleep metabolizes the hypnotism and restores the balance in the organism. 5. (E. N. Harvey, G. A. Hobart and A. L. Loomis) There are five identifiable electro-encephalic stages in sleep, called stages 0, 1, 2, 3, 4, respectively. Stage 1 EEG is accompanied by rapid eye movements and dreaming. 6. (N. Kleitman) Sleep is the phylogenetically fundamental passive state. On the lower levels of evolution, in decorticated animals and newborn infants, the environmental or inner stimuli may interrupt the state of sleep and elicit temporary states of "wakefulness necessity." One must also distinguish between primitive sleep and wakefulness controlled by subcortical centers, and the cortical sleep and wakefulness controlled by the cortex. 7. (W. R. Hess) Sleep is an active inhibitory state controlled by the parasympathetic nervous system; sleep provides for rest and relaxation. 8. (W. H. Magoun) The synchronized EEG in sleep is caused by the thalamus-cortical system, driven by the pontine mechanisms which produces a reduction in the visceral process. The sleep mechanism is inhibitory in Pavlovian sense and operates opposite the reticular activating system. 9. (R. Hernandez-Peon) There is no one sleep center. The sleep system is influenced by the neocortex, medulla and the limbic system.

sleep deprivation, effects of See *deprivation, sleep.*

sleep epilepsy See *epilepsy, sleep.*

sleep treatment, prolonged A treatment technique of mental disorders in which extended sleep is induced by chemicals.

slip, Freudian See *Freudian slip.*

slip of the tongue, or lapsus linguae The inclusion of an incorrect word or phrase in speech which changes the meaning of the sentence. This was interpreted first in psychoanalysis and now quite generally interpreted as expressing a repressed wish or unconscious desire of the individual.

slope (mathematics) The inclination of a line as compared to any base line. The slope of a line can be computed by dividing the vertical distance between two points by the horizontal distance. The formula, given two points (X_1, Y_1) (X_2, Y_2) is:

$$SLOPE = \frac{Y_2 - Y_1}{X_2 - X_1}$$

slope of a curve (mathematics) The inclination of a line tangent to a curve at any point. The value is constantly changing.

slow learner A child who cannot learn at the same rate as his peers because of mental retardation or slower development, but who can profit from academic training at a slower rate.

small-sample method A mathematical technique which permits drawing conclusions from a small number of cases.

Smith, Mahlon Brewster (1919-) American social psychologist. Developed (with J. S. Bruner and R.W. White) an early comprehensive account of how social and political attitudes are embedded in the functioning of personality; contributed to the reconceptualization of "mental health" as personal effectiveness and competence; sponsored the application of social psychology to such topical social problems as prejudice, student protest, and population; promoted a view of human agency intended to bridge the gap between polarized humanistic and scientific psychologies.

smooth curve A curve with little if any deviations from its direction.

Snellen chart or test (H. Snellen) A test of visual acuity consisting of a chart of printed letters ranging from very large to very small which the subject is asked to read at a predetermined distance.

Snezhnevsky, Andrei V. (1904-) Soviet psychiatrist. Main studies in the field of clinical psychiatry. Studied and elaborated a classification of schizophrenia based on the principle of development. Has distinguished three main typical groups of schizophrenia proceeding continuously, without remissions (sluggish, paranoid and malignant forms of schizophrenia), leading to a gradual and gross deterioration; mixed or shift-like forms including a development with attacks and residual psychotic changes between the attacks (and in the form of pseudoneurotic, pseudopsychopathic, hypochondriacal, paranoidal, etc.) and distinct personality changes; recurrent schizophrenia developing in acute affective and affective delusional attacks and with minimal personality changes. Also many works in psychopharmacology.

sociability Desire to be with other people; enjoying human company.

sociability rating See *rating, sociability.*

sociable or social type See *type, sociable or social.*

social adaptation The changes necessary to meet the demands made by society and interpersonal situations. See *adaptation.*

social atom See *atom, social.*

social attitude See *attitude, social.*

social behavior 1. Behavior of an individual dependent on the presence of other people. 2. Behavior of a group, social unit or social organization.

social character (E. Fromm) By social character it is understood to mean the character matrix shared by members of a social group such as a tribe, nation, or class. It develops in the process of active adaptation to the economic, social and cultural conditions common to the group. The effect of the social character is to make people *desire* doing what they *have* to do in their socially determined role. The social character has a two-fold function: it furnishes society with the specific psychical energies it needs for its proper functioning, and it gives the individual a sufficient degree of satisfaction from behaving according to his character traits, while making him conform with society. The social character is transmitted to the child through the character structure of the parents and through methods of child rearing and education which in themselves are mainly socially determined. The family is the "psychological agency" of society which mediates the social influence in early childhood.

Because social change occurs more rapidly than change in educational methods and ideologies, there is often a "lag" between a traditional form of social character and new social conditions to which it is not properly adapted. This lag often leads to serious maladjustments in the social process.

The concept of social character was first employed by E. Fromm in 1932, using the term "social libidinous structure," and from 1941 onwards the term "social character".

social character typology (D. Riesman) The postulation of three character types: tradition-directed, inner-directed, and other-directed whose formation is influenced by society.

social class A group of people united because of their fulfillment of certain criteria, e.g., wealth, education, family background, religion, etc.

social climate The totality of social factors affecting the behavior of a group and its members.

social climbing Vertical social mobility; moving from a lower social class toward a higher one.

social continuity See *continuity, social.*

social control See *control, social.*

social conventions See *conventions, social.*

social distance scale See *scale, Bogardus Social Distance.*

social dynamics The causes and motives of social behavior.

social exchange A profit-centered view in which social interactions are designed to maximize gain for both parties through exchange of rewards; i.e. one rewards the other with something (some statement or behavior) which is more valuable to the receiver than to himself, and in exchange receives a reward which is more valuable to him than to the other individual.

social facilitation The energizing effect of a group on the motivation and effort of any given member.

social factors Influences stemming from interindividual relations, social organizations, social institutions, norms, or beliefs.

social influence The ability of an individual or a group to affect or control some aspect of some other individual or group.

social instinct (A. Adler) An innate ability for co-operation, for "seeing with the eyes of another person." The child's innate impulses of affection are directed toward others and, in normal development, the striving for superiority is blended with the social interest.

social integration See *integration, social.*

social learning See *learning, social.*

social maturity An index of the level of social development including the acquisition of social behavior and standards expected at a particular age.

social medicine See *medicine, social.*

social mobility Flexibility and fluidity of a social organization which permits groups and individuals to change their social affiliation and status.

social norm Rule of conduct established by a social organization.

social perception See *perception, social.*

social pressure Any type of coercion or force applied by an institution or group of individuals.

social process 1. A social interaction between individuals. 2. Social change.

social psychology See *psychology, social.*

social status The position of an individual within his group in relationship to other group members.

social stratification The division of a society into strict social classes.

social structure The organization of a group in terms of the stratification of persons, interpersonal relationships and any other factors which differentiate the group from other groups.

social work The profession which concerns itself with the amelioration of social conditions in a community.

socialization 1. The process in and by which the individual learns the ways, ideas, beliefs, values, patterns and norms of his particular culture and adapts them as a part of his own personality. 2. The process of bringing the industry and services of a country under governmental control for the benefit of all people in the country.

socialized anxiety See *anxiety, socialized.*

sociatry (J. L. Moreno) A special approach to the problems of social psychiatry which applies Moreno's rationale of social acceptance and rejection, spontaneity, etc. as the main determinants in psychopathology.

society 1. A large number of mutually interdependent individuals. 2. Social organization; a group formed for a fulfillment of a certain task.

sociocenter (J. L. Moreno) The person who is most often chosen in a sociometric test.

sociocentrism An assumption that a particular society is or should be the determinant of the behavior of its members.

sociocultural determinants The social organization, the legal and political system, social norms, religion, economics and other aspects of the ways and manners of a particular society viewed as determinants of individuals' normal or abnormal behavior.

sociodiagnostic technique (B. B. Wolman) A technique of diagnosing behavior disorders using overt interindividual behavior as the main clue. This sociopsychological technique is derived from experimental studies with statogram and uses the power and acceptance dimensions for the assessment of the clinical type of particular sociopsychogenic mental disorder. The sociodiagnostic technique uses Sociopsychological Inventory of Observation and Sociopsychological Diagnostic Interview.

sociodrama (J. L. Moreno) The use of role playing and dramatization to teach socially acceptable behaviors.

sociogenesis The process by which other persons affect the self, either the body or the mind.

sociogenic mental disorders (B. B. Wolman) Mental disorders are either inherited, acquired, or caused by a combination of both. If they are inherited, they are transmitted through the genes. Those mental disorders which are not inherited are acquired through interaction with either the physical or the social environment. Thus mental disorders can be divided into three large categories related to their origins. Those that originate in the organism through heredity or through interaction with the physical environment (injuries, poisons, and so on) are somatogenic (soma means body). The inherited disorders are genosomatogenic, for they are caused by genes; the physically acquired mental disorders are ecosomatogenic, for they are caused by interaction with the environment, the ecos. All other disorders stem from faulty interindividual relations, i.e. they are psychosocial, but since the interaction with the social environment is the cause of morbid conditioning and cathexis, we shall call these disorders sociogenic or sociopsychogenic.

In sociogenic or psychosociogenic disorders the social interaction is the cause, and the psychological or behavioral symptoms are the result.

sociogram (J. L. Moreno) A diagram in which group interactions are analyzed on the basis of mutual attractions or antipathies between group members.

WOLMAN'S CLASSIFICATION OF SOCIOGENIC MENTAL DISORDERS

	Hyperinstrumental Type (I)	*Dysmutual Type (M)*	*Hypervectorial Type (V)*
Neurotic Level	HYPERINSTRUMENTAL NEUROSIS (Certain anxiety and depressive neuroses)	DYSMUTUAL NEUROSIS (Dissociative and conversion neuroses)	HYPERVECTORIAL NEUROSIS (Obsessional, phobic, and neurasthenic neuroses)
Character Neurotic Level	HYPERINSTRUMENTAL CHARACTER NEUROSIS (Sociopathic or psychopathic character)	DYSMUTUAL CHARACTER NEUROSIS (Cyclothymic and hysteric character)	HYPERVECTORIAL CHARACTER NEUROSIS (Schizoid and compulsive character)
Latent Psychotic Level	LATENT HYPERINSTRUMENTAL PSYCHOSIS (Psychopathic reactions bordering on psychosis)	LATENT DYSMUTUAL PSYCHOSIS (Borderline manic-depressive psychosis)	LATENT VECTORIASIS PRAECOX (Borderline and latent schizophrenia)
Manifest Psychotic Level	HYPERINSTRUMENTAL PSYCHOSIS (Psychotic psychopathy and moral insanity)	DYSMUTUAL PSYCHOSIS (Manifest manic-depressive psychosis)	VECTORIASIS PRAECOX (Manifest schizophrenia)
Dementive Level	COLLAPSE OF PERSONALITY STRUCTURE		

sociology The science of human societies, groups, organizations and institutions.

sociometry (J. L. Moreno) A technique for the measurement of attraction and repulsion among people which uses the method of the sociogram.

socionomics The study of nonsocial factors, such as geographical factors, rivers, climate, etc. on social life and social organizations.

sociopath See *personality, sociopathic.*

sociopathic personality See *personality, sociopathic.*

sociopharmacology The study of the effects of drugs upon social systems and upon persons other than the drug taker.

sociopsychogenic disorders See *sociogenic mental disorders.*

socio-psychological-diagnostic interview (B. B. Wolman) Reflects the subject's perception of himself and his environment in terms of power and acceptance. The interviewer conducts an open-end, focused-type interview. The subject is requested to tell his life history, dwell on his childhood memories, describe his past experiences, etc. The interviewer avoids asking any direct questions, but encourages a free flow of communication and whenever necessary tries to bring out a point by asking a question, such as "And what happened next? What did you do? How did you feel about it? And what was the reaction of others?" etc.

socio-psychological-diagnostic inventory of observation (B. B. Wolman) Roughly corresponds to the technique of statogram. In the Inventory of Observations the observer or observers carefully record the overt patterns of behavior of the subject and categorize them in terms of power and acceptance. The observers register empirical data, record them carefully, and tabulate. To increase the objectivity of observations one can employ several observers and correlate their ratings. This observation includes actions (eating, sleeping, working, entertainment) and other interaction and communication with other individuals.

sociopsychosomatic theory of schizophrenia (B. B. Wolman) Morbid environmental factors—especially the disturbed intrafamilial setting (social)—cause disbalance in interindividual cathexis of libido and destrudo, which in time affects the intra-individual balance of cathexis and disorganizes the personality structure (psychological). The disorganized personality affects adversely the functions of the glandular and nervous system causing morbid changes in the organism (somatic). Hence the causal sociopsychosomatic chain.

sociotype Stereotype applied to a certain social group or clan.

sodium amytal See *amytal.*

sodium pentothal See *thiopental.*

sodomy 1. Sexual intercourse through the anus. 2. Sexual intercourse between a human being and an animal.

solipsism An epistemological theory promoted by A. Schopenhauer and others which implies that whatever exists is a product of will and ideas of the perceiving individual.

solution, comprehensive (K. Horney) The identification of the self with the idealized self in order to protect oneself from intrapsychic conflict.

solution learning (O. H. Mowrer) Acquisition of a tendency to action which is the solution to some problem. Solution learning is problem solving, drive reducing and gives pleasure.

solution, major (K. Horney) The neurotic tendency to deny or repress two of the three interpersonel orientations and to recognize only one as a means of reducing basic anxiety.

soma The body; the tissues of the body.

somatic Pertaining to the tissues of the body.

somatic disorders 1. Disorders of the organism. 2. Behavior disorders of organic origin; somatogenic disorders.

somatogenesis Having origins in the tissues of the body.

somatogenic disorders (B. B. Wolman) All mental or behavior disorders can be divided into somatogenic, which are caused by physiochemical factors and socio- or psychosociogenic ones caused by interaction with the social environment. The somatogenic disorders can be divided into genosomatogenic, i.e. inherited and ecosomatogenic, i.e. acquired in interaction with physiochemical world, such as poisons, infections, etc.

somatophysic Refers to a psychological disorder which has a somatic basis.

somatoplasm (biology) The protoplasm of the cells of a living organism.

somatopsychic Transformation of or transition from an organic to a non-organic process. The influence of alcohol or drugs on behavior is a somatopsychic process.

somatotonia (W. H. Sheldon) Temperament component characterized by physical and personal assertiveness, striving for power, desire for risk, and need for adventure and competition, associated with the mesomorphic body-type.

somatotype Body type.

somatotypology The classification of persons according to body type or physical characteristics, usually with the implication that certain physiological characteristics and body types are correlated differentially with personality characteristics and personality variables.

somesthesia The overall bodily sense, including kinesthesis, tactile and other sensations.

somnambulism 1. Execution of complex acts, such

as walking or talking, during sleep that normally take place in the waking state. **2.** Refers to hypnotic phase in which subject may appear awake and in control of actions, though his behavior is directed by the hypnotist.

somnambulism, cataleptic Cataleptic state taking place during somnambulism.

somnambulism, complete (P. Janet) Temporary, hypnotically induced state which is forgotten by the subject sometime after hypnosis is over.

somnambulism, ecstatic State of ecstasy occurring during somnambulism.

somnambulism, monoideic (P. Janet) Ideational processes centering around a single idea occurring during a somnambulistic state.

somnambulism, polyideic (P. Janet) Ideational content containing many ideas occurring during a somnambulistic state.

somnambulist One who performs complex acts, such as walking and talking, during sleep.

somniferous Sleep-producing.

somniloquy Talking in sleep.

somnolence **1.** Drowsiness, sleepiness. **2.** Unnatural prolonged drowsiness.

sonant A vocal speech sound.

sone A unit of the ratio scale of loudness which is equal to a loudness at a frequency level of 1000 cycle tone forty decibels above the mean threshold.

sonometer An instrument consisting of one or more strings stretched over a resonating box used in auditory experiments and demonstrations.

sophism A subtly fallacious argument.

soporific A substance which induces sleep.

sorting test See *test, sorting.*

soul **1.** (Aristotle) The vital aspect of life. **2.** (theology) An entity which is believed to exist permanently even after death. **3.** An obsolete term for the mind. **4.** Emotional factors as opposed to the intellectual aspect of personality.

sound-pattern theory of hearing See *hearing, theory of: sound-pattern theory.*

sound pressure level (SPL) Usual reference level used in specifying decibels or sound intensity. SPL is .0002 dyne per square centimeter. When using decibels the reference pressure level is always indicated, for example, 20 db (SPL).

sound spectrograph A device which produces a quantitative representation of a sound. It is a group of sound filters each of which passes energy of only a narrow frequency band. The output voltage of each filter adjusts the brightness of a light which produces a trace on a moving formant belt, thus producing a graphic representation of the components of a sound.

source (communication theory) A system that emits a message.

source trait (R. B. Cattell) A factor-dimension, stressing the proposition that variations in value along it are determined by a single, unitary influence or source.

South African Picture Analysis Test See *test, South African Picture Analysis.*

space error A bias in the judgment of the position of stimuli because of its spatial relationship to the observer.

space perception Three dimensional perception.

space response A type of Rorschach response which includes the use of the white areas of the card rather than the properties of the blot itself. Scored S, it is generally considered a perceptual reversal of figure-ground and interpreted as a form of negativism and/or non-conformity.

spacial summation The addition of two or more volleys which results in one motor response. These volleys of nervous impulse can be summated, provided they reach a synapse at approximately the same time.

span of attention The number of objects, digits or letters perceived on a brief exposure, usually measured on a tachistoscopic exposure.

spasm Involuntary, localized, usually slow, sometimes prolonged muscular contractions which may occur anywhere in the body.

spasm, nodding (A. Kanner) Vertical or rotary head movement of infants.

spastic acathusia See *acathusia, spastica.*

spastic colitis See *colitis, spastic.*

spasticity Muscular tension often associated with clonic movements.

spatial threshold The smallest distance between two points on the skin surface at which two simultaneous tactile stimuli are perceived as two and not as one.

spaying Removing the ovaries of a female animal; sterilization.

Spearman-Brown formula A procedure used in the estimation of the reliability of a test which has been changed by the addition or subtraction of similar items:

$$R_n = \frac{nr_m}{1+(n-1)r_m}$$

being the estimated reliability coefficient of a test with n items, r_m being the obtained reliability coefficient of the original test with m items.

Spearman, Charles E. (1863-1945) British quantitative psychologist. Invented the rank-difference coefficient of correlation, ρ (Greek letter rho), which has been named after him. Formulated the two-factor theory of human capacity (performance of a task is a function of G, general intelligence, and of S, the ability specific to the performance of the task), and was a forerunner of later developments in factor analysis.

Spearman footrule See *correlation, Spearman footrule.*

special education Education of children with physical, sensory, intellectual and emotional handicaps, deficiencies or disorders.

special purpose test See *test, special purpose.*

species 1. Clan; category. 2. (biology) Biological clan of animals or plants; subdivision of a genus.

species specific behavior See *behavior, species specific.*

specific energy of nerves A belief that each nerve is capable of reacting in a certain way only, irrespective of the nature of the stimuli.

specific inhibition See *inhibition, specific.*

specification equation An equation which predicts performance on a specific behavior or task for an individual, from knowledge of 1) the association of that behavior with a set of factors, and 2) the individual's endowment on each of the factors.

specificity 1. Typical or characteristic of a certain class or category of objects or events. 2. Typical of a certain biological species, bodily organ or part of an organism.

spectrometer An apparatus which measures the lengths of the waves of colors on a spectrum.

spectroscope An apparatus which gives a spectrum.

spectrum 1. The colors obtained by refraction of a wave of light in a prism. 2. The energy of light obtained by refraction.

speculation Non-empirical reasoning; reasoning without factual evidence.

speech agnosia See *agnosia, speech.*

speed practice Learning process with time intervals between the successive trials.

speedometer (operant conditioning) A stimulus, some dimension of which changes as a function of the rate of responding over some period of time.

spells, breath-holding A condition simulating epilepsy, observed during crying, set off by an event that made the child angry or afraid. The child seems as if in a rage, begins to hold his breath and becomes cyanotic around the lips; there may also be loss of consciousness and/or convulsive movements.

Spence, Kenneth W. (1907-1966) American psychologist and learning theorist. A follower of C. L. Hull, Spence deemphasized the physiological aspects of Hull's theory and rejected the need-reduction concept as the prerequisite for reinforcement. Introduced the response-competition concept based on non-reinforcement and maintained that reinforcement is necessary for the classical aversive conditioning, but not for the instrumental aversive learning. Wrote *Behavior Theory and Conditioning, Behavior Theory and Learning,* and several other studies.

Spencer, Herbert (1820-1903) British evolutionary associationist who wrote major works about the sciences of the mid-nineteenth century. He championed double-aspect monism as a solution to the mind-body problem, and was one of the first to suggest that behavior is a continual adjustment to life circumstances, thus anticipating the later functionalist school.

Spens syndrome (T. Spens) See *Stokes-Adams syndrome.*

sperm; spermatozoan Mature male germ cell.

spherical aberration Failure of rays of light to be refracted by a lens, caused by a curvature of the lens.

sphincter morality (S. Ferenczi) A psychoanalytic term for superego forerunners related to parental prohibitions in toilet training at the anal stage.

sphingolipids A type of lipid; the abnormal metabolism and storage of sphingolipids is associated with metabolic disorders such as Gaucher's Disease and Tay-Sach's Disease.

sphygmomanometer An apparatus which measures the arterial tensions and blood pressure.

Spielmeyer-Vogt disease Juvenile form of amaurotic family idiocy which occurs between the ages of six and twelve and is characterized by mental dysfunction, blindness and death within two years.

spina bifia (myelomeningocele) A birth defect which involves a developmental failure of the bilateral dorsal laminae of the vertebrae to fuse in the midline and develop a single dorsal spinal process. The developmental failure may not be accompanied by spinal-cord or nerve-root abnormality and may be covered by normal skin. When associated with defective formation of the spinal cord, the defective cord and the meninges are visible on the back. This condition is generally accompanied by muscle weakness, skin sensitivity below the defective part of the spinal cord, poor innervation of the bowel and bladder, and various degrees of hydrocephalus, neuromuscular problems, such as difficulties in walking and muscle imbalance leading to curvature in posture.

spinal cord A part of the central nervous system extending from the medulla oblongata to the filum terminale at the level of the first (sometimes second) lumbar vertebra.

spinal nerve See *nerve, spinal.*

spinal reflex See *reflex, spinal.*

spinal root See *root, spinal.*

spinal tonus The tonus retained by the spinal cord following severence of the nerve fibers leading to the brain.

spindle, muscle A receptor found in the equatorial region of muscles which consists of muscle fibers activated by sensory nerve endings, all of which are enclosed in a tissue fluid and a capsule of connective tissue. The spindle has nerve endings of two kinds, depending on their appearance which function as receptors: the annulospiral endings and flower-spray endings.

spindle tendon See *Golgi tendon organ.*

spiritism 1. Belief in spirits, ghosts, etc. 2. Belief in the possibility of communication with deceased people.

spiritualism A monistic philosophical theory which assumes that the world is comprised of one non-material element.

spirograph An instrument which measures and records the rate and amount of breathing.

spirometer A mechanism used for measuring the amount of air exhaled in one breath independent of the air remaining in the lungs.

split-half correlation See *correlation, split-half.*

split-half method of reliability See *reliability, split-half, method of.*

split personality An obsolete term indicating dissociation and amnesia; also called multiple personality.

spontaneity test See *test, spontaneity.*

spontaneity therapy See *therapy, spontaneity.*

spontaneity training See *training, spontaneity.*

spontaneous behavior See *behavior, spontaneous.*

spontaneous recovery See *recovery, spontaneous.*

spontaneous recovery rate The rate of the disappearance of symptoms without treatment.

spot, hypnogenic Point on the body which when touched will induce a hypnotic state.

Spranger, E. (1882-1963) German philosopher who developed what is termed the "psychology of structure" emphasizing the whole mental life as a unique structure not to be reduced to more elementary levels. He studied the individual as a whole in relation to his historical environment and identified six ideal cultural types of man based on six human values or goals. These types include the theoretical or knowledge-seeking, the esthetic, the economic or practical, the religious, the social or sympathetic and the practical.

spread of effect See *effect, spread of.*

spurious correlation See *correlation, spurious.*

SR A symbol for stimulus response, or the stimulus response relationship. The symbol is also written *S-R* and *S→R*, stimulus leading to response.

SRA mechanical aptitude test See *test, SRA mechanical aptitude.*

SS interval See *avoidance, free operant.*

stabilimeter A device for measuring the amount of bodily sway a person evinces when he is blindfolded in an erect position attempting not to move.

stability coefficient See *coefficient, stability.*

stage A naturally occurring level in the developmental process which is separate from other levels.

stage, postpubertal Period just after puberty during which much of the growth of the skeleton is completed.

stages of sensory development See *sensory development, stages of.*

staircase illusion See *illusion, staircase.*

stammering See *stuttering.*

standard 1. A model or criterion of performance. 2. A fixed unit of measurement used for comparison and in the development of scales.

standard deviation (statistics) The index of variability of a distribution. It is derived by the following formula:

$$SD \text{ or } \sigma = \sqrt{\frac{\Sigma(X\text{-}M)^2}{N}}$$

where *SD* or σ is the symbol for standard deviation, *X* is any number, *M* is the mean of the distribution, *N* refers to the size of the sample, Σ is the summation sign and $\sqrt{}$ is the square root sign.

standard error of difference The difference between two means divided by the standard error of that difference. The formula is:

$$\sigma \text{ diff.} = \sqrt{\sigma_{M_1}^2 + \sigma_{M_2}^2} = \sqrt{\frac{\sigma_1^2}{N_1} + \frac{\sigma_2^2}{N_2}}$$

where M = mean and σ = the standard error of the mean. It is also known as the critical ratio.

standard error of estimate (σ_{est} or σ_{xy}) The standard deviation of the difference between the actual values of the dependent variable and those values which are estimated from a regression equation. The formula is:

$$\sigma_{est} = \sigma_0 \sqrt{1\text{-}r^2}$$

where σ_0 is the standard deviation of the dependent variable and *r* is the correlation coefficient.

standard error of mean (σ_{DM} or σ_M) An estimate of the amount that an obtained mean varies by chance form the true mean. The formula is:

$$\sigma_M = \sqrt{\sigma^2 M} = \frac{\sigma}{\sqrt{N}}$$

where σ_M is the standard error of estimate, and *N* is the size of the sample on which the means are based.

standard measure See *standard score.*

standard observer A hypothetical individual who has normal sensory receptors.

standard ratio See *standard difference.*

standard score See *score, standard.*

standard stimulus One of a group or pair that is used as a basis of comparison with the others in an experiment.

standardization The procedure of establishing standards or norms, uniform procedures and acceptable deviations from the norm for a test by administering it to a large group of representative individuals.

standardization group See *group, standardization.*

standardized test See *test, standardized.*

Stanford Achievement Test See *test, Stanford Achievement.*

Stanford Binet An English language revision and reconstruction of the Binet-Simon intelligence test by L.M. Terman of Stanford University. First revision in 1916; second (with Maud A. Merrill) in 1937; third in 1959.

stanine (statistics) A unit of measure developed by the United States Air Force during World War II which is equal to one-ninth of the range of standard scores of a normal distribution. It has a mean of five and a standard deviation of absolute two.

stapes One of the three auditory ossicles in the middle ear resting against the membrane of the vestibular window of the cochlea. Also known as the stirrup.

staphylococcal meningitis See *meningitis, staphylococcal.*

startle reflex See *Moro response.*

state (R. B. Cattell) Dimension describing change-over-time within a single individual or in groups of individuals. Essentially, a factor-dimension in *intra*-individual change as contrasted with a Trait which describes *inter*-individual differences at any one time. State dimensions are discovered by P-Technique or by Incremental Factor Analysis.

state, hypothetical variable See *variable, hypothetical state.*

static convulsion See *convulsion, static.*

static reflex A postular reflex which maintains the balanced posture of the body (stance reflex) or restores it (righting reflex).

static sense The sense of equilibrium of posture. The receptors of the static sense organ are located in the semicircular canals in the inner ear.

stasis State of rest; static state.

statistic Any value that expresses the end result of mathematical operations which represents a population or a sample.

statistical constant A value or number that represents or describes the population from which the sample was drawn. The means and standard deviations are examples.

statistical table The arrangement of statistical data in horizontal or vertical rows to exhibit any relationships that might occur.

statistical universe 1. The basis underlying statistical inferences. 2. The population of cases from which samples can be drawn.

statistics 1.The branch of mathematics that gathers and evaluates numerical data, and treats them such

that the relation between these facts is clearly shown. 2. A set of values that expresses the end result of mathematical operation which represents a population or sample.

statistics, descriptive A branch of statistics which includes the organizing, summarizing and describing of quantitative information or data.

statistics, nonparametric The branch of statistics which deals with distributions that are not normal and makes no assumptions with regard to the distribution of the population being sampled.

statogram (B. B. Wolman) A research technique in social psychology used for evaluating the status of individuals in small groups. The members of a group rate one another in terms of power and acceptance on quasi-Cartesian coordinates.

statokinetic reflexes Postural reflexes which adjust the balance posture while the body is in motion.

statue of Condillac The French philosopher-sensualist Condillac maintained that mental life started with simple sensations. He imagined a statue to be endowed first with the olfactory sense, then the other senses until it developed a full scale mental life.

status Position; state.

status epilepticus Series of grand mal epileptic seizures without interruption which is the most frequent cause of death in epileptics.

staves (R. B. Cattell) Units in a scale for converting questionnaire raw scores to units which are standard relative to the population. Exactly like stens, except that staves are only a five-point scale, extending from two and one-half standard deviations below the population average (stave 1) to two and one-half standard deviations above (stave 5). Stave 3 represents the population average.

Stekel, Wilhelm (1868-1940) Viennese psychiatrist and sexologist, one of Freud's earliest associates. Developed a modified psychoanalytic technique in which the analyst directly intervenes in the patient's life.

stens (R. B. Cattell) Units in a standard ten scale, in which ten score points are used to cover the population range in fixed and equal standard deviation intervals, extending from two and one-half standard deviations below the mean (sten 1) to two and one-half standard deviations above the mean (sten 10). The mean is fixed at 5.5 stens. First proposed by Cattell in 1949, questionnaire raw scores are usually converted to stens, when intending to use them normatively (to compare obtained values with population values).

step interval See *class interval.*

stereoscope (C. Wheatstone) Device invented in 1833 for simultaneous presenting to each eye of one individual separate two-dimensional pictures of the same event. The resultant two separate retinal images are identical to those that would be produced by the three-dimensional real event and the impression of depth is produced from the binocular view of the two pictures.

stereoscopic vision Binocular depth vision resulting from the slightly different retinal projections of the same stimulus. This inevitably occurs since the two eyes are not positioned identically in space.

stereotaxic atlas (psychophysiology) A map of the brain which is requisite in experiments or studies of brain stimulation.

stereotaxis An orienting response to a solid object simulus with a direct and immediate reaction to the stimulus.

stereotype A rigid or biased perception in which individuals are ascribed certain (usually negative) traits regardless of whether they possess these traits, merely because of their membership in a specific national or social group.

stereotyped behavior See *response, stereotyped.*

stereotyped response See *response, stereotyped.*

sterility The inability to produce offspring due to organic or psychological causes.

Stern, William (1871-1938) A German experimental and differential psychologist at Hamburg, who also contributed to child psychology and to applications of psychology to industry and law. He invented the concept of the intelligence quotient, the I.Q., defined as the ratio of mental age to chronological age (times 100).

steroid disorder An undesignated metabolic disorder, transmitted by an autosomal recessive gene, which results in a general slight aminoaciduria and an excess of glutamic acid in the blood. Clinical signs include mental and physical retardation, lack of pigmentation in the hair and microencephaly.

Stevens' power law (S. S. Stevens) A formulation relating the objective stimulus energy to the subjective sensory experience. It contends that for certain sensory systems equal physical ratios are psychologically equal. In normal tests of the power law the stimulus values are transformed to logarithms so as to mark off equal stimulus ratios and plotted on the x axis of a graph. Since the psychological ratios are also thought to be equal, the response values, plotted on the y axis, are also transformed to logarithms. If the resultant plot of the log of the response as a function of the log of the stimulus is a straight line, the prediction of the power law is fulfilled. This law has been proposed as an alternative to the psychophysical function proposed by Fechner, but neither function is truly satisfactory and both functions cannot be correct at the same time. Consequently the power function has been the center of controversy in psychophysics for the past thirty years.

stilling test See *test, stilling.*

stimulation 1. The activation of a sense receptor by a form of energy or energy change. 2. The excitation of an organism by a change of energy whether internal or external.

stimulation, mechanical Stimulation of a reception by means of pressure.

stimuli, accidental Those chance happenings that occur in the environment of a sleeping individual which seem to become part of or to precipitate dreams. For example, a muscle cramp may start a dream of being hurt in that particular area of the body.

stimulus 1. An object or an action that elicits action. 2. (physiology) Any inner or outer factor that causes the organism to act. 3. (psychology) Any action or situation that elicits response.

stimulus, adequate A stimulus which excites the receptor appropriate to the particular stimulus.

stimulus attitude 1. The subject's readiness to respond to a particular stimulus. 2. The subject's set to attend to specific qualities of the stimulus.

stimulus, aversive A stimulus that, when applied after a response, decreases the tendency for that response to be activated in similar situations.

stimulus-bound 1. Referring to perception which is almost wholly determined by the stimulus aspects. 2. Pertaining to an individual whose reactions are inflexible and almost totally determined by the stimulus situation. 3. Referring to the perception of striking or outstanding aspects of a situation to the exclusion of less central aspects.

stimulus, comparison See *comparison stimulus.*

stimulus, conditioned (CS) A stimulus which, through classical conditioning, has become an effective stimulus for a response which was originally elicited by another stimulus, the unconditioned stimulus (UCS).

stimulus, consummatory A stimulus which triggers off a consummatory response.

stimulus continuum A continuous series of stimuli such that between any two, there is always a third.

stimulus control (operant conditioning) The extent to which the value of an antecedent stimulus determines the probability of the occurrence of a conditioned response. It is measured as a change in response probability as a function of change in stimulus value. The greater the change in response probability, the greater the amount of stimulus control with respect to the stimulus continuum that is varied. In operant conditioning this term has come to be the favored term over the terms stimulus generalization and discrimination primarily because these latter terms come from attempts to describe processes rather than empirical functions.

stimulus-controlled P-technique A P-technique which enters the score values for the intensity of manipulated stimuli as well as for levels of response.

stimulus differentiation 1. (Gestalt) The process whereby parts of a homogeneous whole become distinguished in the visual field. 2. The process whereby an organism learns to distinguish two or more stimuli which previously elicited the same response.

stimulus, discriminative In operant conditioning the stimulus which elicits the correct response.

stimulus, distal A stimulus in the environment that acts upon a sense receptor indirectly, through the action of a proximal stimulus, e.g. the chair in the environment is the distal stimulus. The retinal image caused by the chair is the proximal stimulus.

stimulus equivalence See *equivalence, response.*

stimulus error See *error, stimulus.*

stimulus generalization, primary The elicitation of a response learned to a certain stimulus by stimuli that are like or similar to the original stimulus.

stimulus, inadequate A stimulus which excites the receptor for which it is not the appropriate stimulus, resulting in subjective sensation that is inappropriate to the stimulus but in accordance with the receptor. For example, a wool object applied to a receptor for warmth is sensed as warm.

stimulus, incidental A stimulus occurring in a situation for which it is neither essential nor intentional but which nevertheless influences the subject's response.

stimulus, indifferent A stimulus to which a subject has not yet responded in a particular way, as often occurs at the beginning of conditioning experiments to what is to become the conditioned stimulus.

stimulus, liminal A physical stimulus which is just at the threshold or just barely evokes a sensory response on one half of the trials.

stimulus, neutral (I. P. Pavlov) A stimulus which does not elicit conditioning if applied without the unconditioned stimulus.

stimulus pattern A configuration which consists of a conglomeration of stimuli harmoniously grouped together.

stimulus population A finite number of independent environmental events, only one sample of them being effective at any one time.

stimulus-produced conflict A conflict produced by a stimulus which has been associated with both reward and punishment.

stimulus, proprioceptive Stimulus produced by the act of responding. A response produces sensations which themselves have stimulus qualities.

stimulus, proximal A stimulus that effects a sense receptor directly, e.g. the feel of a pencil, or heat, or an image on the retina.

stimulus schedule The rule whereby an experimentally specified stimulus is intruded into an organism's behavior stream; "reinforcement schedule" is the special case where the intruded stimulus is of the sort historically called a "reinforcement."

stimulus, sensory Any stimulus which affects a sense organ.

stimulus set See *set, stimulus.*

stimulus, sign A part or change in a part of the environment that is correlated with some species specific behavior which is not a reflex response.

stimulus, standard See *standard stimulus.*

stimulus, structured A complex stimulus consisting of distinct interrelated parts.

stimulus, subliminal A stimulus whose magnitude is below the threshold of a receptor.

stimulus, super-normal sign A sign stimulus with one or more of its dimensions amenable to quantification along a continuum. The stimulus occurring in the field is at a point on the continuum; while stimuli below this value occasion responses of less magnitude, stimuli above this value occasion responses of greater magnitude.

stimulus threshold See *threshold, stimulus.*

stimulus, unconditioned A stimulus which evokes an unconditioned response and may serve as a reinforcing agent. Such a stimulus evokes a response without prior learning or conditioning.

stimulus value The qualitative description of the stimulus, usually referring to the intensity of the stimulus.

stimulus variable See *variable, stimulus.*

St. Louis encephalitis See *encephalitis, St. Louis.*

stochastic Relating to events whose probability of occurrence constantly changes.

stochastic models of behavior Theories of learning which view behavior as a stochastic chain.

stochastic processes A branch of probability theory dealing with sequences of events whose probabilities are constantly changing.

Stokes-Adams syndrome (W. Stokes and R. Adams) Heart block due to functional or organic causes.

stop items See *items, stop.*

story recall test See *test, story recall.*

Stout, George Frederick (1860-1944) British systematic psychologist, a forerunner of William McDougall. He emphasized conation (or striving) in his psychology, developing a functional or act psychology that contrasted sharply with the dominant German structuralism. His 1899 *Manual of Psychology* was for decades the most widely accepted systematic psychological statement in Great Britain.

strabismus Failure of eye coordination causing lack of proper fixation in the form of either divergent or convergent squint.

straight-jacket A canvas jacket used to restrain a violent, usually mentally ill patient.

stratification A horizontal layering of a group or society.

stratified sample See *sample, stratified.*

stratified sampling See *sampling, stratified.*

Stratton's experiment (G. M. Stratton) An experiment designed to investigate the relationship between vision and tactual-motor coordination. The experiment consists of wearing prisms which turn the visual field through an angle of 180 degrees and studying the effects of this reversed visual experience or tactual-motor experience.

stream of consciousness (W. James) The belief that consciousness is a stream of thought, a changing continuum, a unity in diversity rather than a series of discrete separate elements.

streptococcal meningitis See *meningitis, streptococcal.*

stress **1.** A condition of physical or mental strain which produces changes in the autonomic nervous system. **2.** Emphasis on particular words in speaking.

stress interview See *interview, stress.*

stretch reflex Contraction of a muscle as a result of a rapid stretching of the muscle.

striate or striped muscle See *muscle, striate or striped.*

striate body, or striatum A part of the base of each cerebral hemisphere composed of nerve fibers making up the caudate nucleus, lenticular nucleus and internal capsule.

strip key A scoring key which is designed to allow comparison of the key with the subject's responses by aligning the two.

striped muscle See *muscle, striate or striped.*

stroboscopic movement See *movement, stroboscopic.*

stroke A sudden and severe seizure which may be due to a lesion in the brain or spinal cord leading to paralysis.

Strong vocational interest blank An inventory designed to assess the extent to which an individual's interests and preferences match those of successful persons in specific occupations in order to predict which career choice would be desirable for the subject. It consists of four hundred items which cover various areas of occupation, amusement, academic subjects and personality traits. The inventory may also be scored for non-occupational interests which can be used in guidance and counseling.

Stroop Test See *test, Stroop.*

structural psychology See *psychology, structural.*

structure-function principle (A. Gesell) In experimental studies with infants, Gesell has proven that development depends both on maturation and learning. When an infant tries to learn a certain behavioral pattern ("function") before he is mature enough (his "structure" is not ready) he will not make much progress in learning. Hence, the structure-function principle which means when the structure is ready, the function may start—that is, maturation must come ahead of learning.

structure, mental **1.** A hypothetical construct which is believed to account for similarities or recurrence of behavior. **2.** A personality viewed as a stable complex organization of interrelated traits.

structured interview See *interview, structured.*

structured learning theory (R. B. Cattell) That portion of learning theory, complementary to *reflexology*, which explains the emergence of personality and dynamic *structures*, rather than atomic *conditioned reflexes*. It involves description of learning change by the tri-vector analysis: 1) A vector of trait change, 2) of behavioral index (loading) change, and 3) of modulation index change. Under (1) it develops the theory regarding the learning of motivational *sets*. It operates with multivariate, matrix-expressed calculations.

structured stimulus See *stimulus, structured.*

study of values See *Allport-Vernon-Lindzey Study of Values.*

Stumpf, Karl (1848-1936) German psychologist and philosopher. As a law student at Würzburg Stumpf came under the influence of Brentano and, following his advice, went to Göttingen to study with Lotze, under whom in 1868 he received his Ph.D. with a thesis on Plato. From 1870-1873 he was a Privatdozent at Göttingen and then went to Würzburg. In 1879 he was called to Prague where he became an associate of Mach, Hering, and Marty. He was in Halle in 1884 and went to Munich in 1889. Finally, in 1894 he was appointed professor at Berlin, where he remained until his retirement in 1921.

Along with the work of other scientifically-minded philosophers of his time, Stumpf's work is an attempt to supplant Kantian *a priori* schemes with empirical ones. In his first book, which was on the psychological sources of space perception, he defended a nativisitic interpretation which, along with the contributions of Hering, became one of the supports of Gestalt theory.

As a psychological systematist he distinguished four closely related disciplines: Phenomenology, Logology, Psychology, and Eidology. Phenomenology is concerned with the contents of consciousness in the manner of Wundt. Logology is concerned with the relations in these contents that are presumably directly presented, a view shared with Wm. James. Psychology is concerned with mental acts in the Brentano tradition. Eidology is an effort to account for presentations of memory in the absence of external stimulation in sentences like, "I like red." To Gestalters these distinctions seemed too much in the act psychology tradition and thus too imbued with the "old psychology."

Stumpf strongly influenced Wm. James and in turn wrote a book about him (1927). In 1900 he founded the *Verein für Kinderpsychologie* . He studied the language of his son. These interests led him to sponsor Köhler's study of anthropoids in Tenerife. He had as students, Köhler, Koffka, and Lewin, but they later abandoned his work under the influence of Wertheimer.

stupor, catatonic See *catatonic stupor.*

stupor, epileptic State which frequently follows a

grand mal epileptic seizure in which the individual is almost unconscious.

stuporous mania See *mania, stuporous.*

stuttering A speech nonfluency in which the even and regular flow of words is disrupted by rapid repetition of speech elements, spasms of the breathing and vocalization muscles, and hesitations. There are various forms of this nonfluency, including neurogenic, in which fluency is affected by the periodic and uncontrolled release of electrical potential in areas of the brain which subserve speech formulation or which innervate articulatory musculature; sensorimotor, in which fluency is affected by a physiological delay in the return of various sensory dimensions of the speech signal back to the speaker; evaluational forms, in which fluency is affected by the overmonitoring and criticizing by significant others of the child's developmentally expected nonfluencies, resulting in the disruption of the automaticity of speech due to the child's own criticism of the nonfluencies; and psychogenic, in which fluency is affected by an internal conflict over the content of the speech.

stuttering Iowa scale See *scale, stuttering Iowa.*

style of life See *life style.*

stylus maze See *maze, stylus.*

subception The perception of a stimulus on a preverbal level as evinced by an emotional reaction which is detected by a psychogalvanometer or a longer verbal reaction time to the stimulus.

sub-coma insulin treatment See *insulin treatment, ambulatory.*

subconscious An ambiguous term referring to partial unconscious.

subconscious personality (M. Prince) A condition where complexes of subconscious processes have been constellated into a personal system manifesting a secondary system of self-consciousness endowed with volition, intelligence, etc. This personality is capable of communication and occasionally may become the only personality capable of remembering its own personal subconscious life and can give information about subconscious processes.

subconscious process (M. Prince) A process of which the personality is unaware and thus it is outside personal consciousness but which is a factor in determination of conscious and bodily phenomena, or produces effects analogous to those which might be directly or indirectly induced by consciousness.

subcortical 1. Referring to neural structures lying below the cortex which mediate functions that are not controlled by the cortex. 2. Relating to functions which are not controlled by the cortex.

subculture A subgroup of a culture which has its separate mores and customs but which shares some of the basic customs with the general culture.

subcutaneous sensibility See *sensibility, subcutaneous.*

subject 1. An individual who participates in an experimental situation. 2. Topic; theme; matter.

subject complex See *complex, subject.*

subjective 1. Referring to the subject or person. 2. Referring to experience available only to the subject of the experience. 3. Characterizing systems of psychology which focus on the subject and his personal experiences. 4. Not available to consensual validation. 5. Referring to judgments made without the use of devices or instruments. 6. Referring to sensations originating in internal states. 7. Hallucinatory, illusory. 8. Dependent on the person's own standard prejudices and experiences.

subjective equality, point of 1. The subject's choice of a point in a continuous series of stimuli at which two stimuli appear to be equal. 2. (psychophysics) A point in a continuum which is judged to be equal to a standard by one of the following methods: the value which is chosen most frequently as equal to the criterion; the point of intersection between values which are judged greater than the standard and those which are chosen as smaller than the standard' or the point midway between the upper and lower thresholds. 3. (comparative psychology) A point when the experimenter does not perceive any noticeable differences in the organism's responses to two stimuli.

subjective sensation See *sensation, subjective.*

subjective test See *test, subjective.*

subjectivism 1. The tendency to evaluate experiences in terms of one's own personal frame of reference. 2. The theoretical viewpoint which stresses personal experience as the sole basis of reality.

sublimation A successful and normal defense against instinctual wishes is called sublimation. Sublimation is a cathexis of instinctual energy into a substitute aim or object or both; it is a channeling of the instinctual demands into a new desire or idea and a desexualized cathexis of libido or destrudo.

sublimation theory of cultural evolution (S. Freud) The theory that aim-inhibited creative activities advance development of cultural civilization.

subliminal 1. Below the absolute threshold of perception. 2. Pertaining to stimuli which are not perceived consciously but which are perceived on a preverbal level and influence behavior.

subliminal learning See *learning, subliminal.*

subliminal perception See *perception, subliminal.*

subliminal stimulus See *stimulus, subliminal.*

subnormal Below the normal level, inferior.

suboccipital puncture (Ayer) A procedure developed for the determination of spinal subarachnoid block and other therapeutic purposes.

subset ($\subseteq$) B is a subset of A if every element of B is also in A. $B \subseteq A$.

subset, proper ($\subset$) B is a proper subset of A if every element of *B* is also in *A,* and there is at least one element of *A* that is not in *B. B⊂A.*

subshock therapy See *therapy, subshock.*

subsidiation A term referring to the fact that achievement of most or all goals requires prior achievement of a series of sub-goals. For example, before achieving the goal "having one's own home," one may first have to achieve sub-goals as "getting a better-paying job," "gaining the confidence of a banker," etc., the latter two being subsidiated to the former.

substance Essence; the essential part; the main part of an issue, problem or communication.

substantia nigra A layer of pigmented gray matter which separates the dorsal from the ventral part of the cerebral peduncle.

substantive sets (W. James) A part of the stream of consciousness consisting of definite and distinct objects or persons as opposed to transition states which are denoted by prepositional words.

substitution test See *test, code.*

subtest A part of a test or test battery.

subtraction method See *method, subtraction.*

subvocal speech Movements of the mouth, larynx and tongue without making audible sounds.

successive-approximation method See *conditioning, approximation.*

successive contrast See *contrast, color.*

successive differential reinforcement See *conditioning, approximation.*

successive-intervals, method of A modified version of the method of equal-appearing intervals in which the intervals are differentiated verbally or by the use of samples.

successive-practice, method of A method designed to assess the effect of transfer of training by measuring the amount of time saved in learning B as a function of having learned A. A control group is given B to learn without having learned A and the two groups are compared.

successive reproduction method See *method, successive reproduction.*

succorance need See *need, succorance.*

sudoriferous glands See *glands, sudoriferous.*

sufficient reason, law of (G. V. Leibniz) The principle which states that the occurrence of an event can always be understood given sufficient information.

suggestibility The readiness to accept suggestions.

suggestion, affective (E. Jones) The emotional rapport that exists between the subject and the hypnotist in a hypnotic setting. Called hypotaxia by Durand.

suicide Killing oneself.

sulcus Shallow grooves on the surface of the brain.

sulfatide lipidosis A rare lipidosis unusual in that symptoms do not appear until the child is one to one and a half years of age. Weakness progresses to spasticity and severe mental and motor retardation.

sulfatide variants Conditions which may represent a bridge between the lipidoses and mucopoly-saccharidoses.

Sullivan, H. S. (1892-1949) American psychiatrist and neo-psychoanalyst who developed his own system of psychology deviating from S. Freud farther than any other psychoanalyst. He abandoned the Freudian concepts and terminology, borrowing only some principles in human dynamics such as unconscious motivation, defense mechanisms, and dream interpretation. Sullivan was influenced by A. Meyer's biological method and G. Mead's and K. Lewin's theories of social status, role and interpersonal relation. He distinguished between physical and cultural phenomena. He dealt with bodily needs in a consistently reductionist manner. Sullivan introduced the theory that the release of energy is always controlled by social relations. He specified that the development of personality is the result of interpersonal relations. He theorized that there exists two basic needs, the need for security and the need for satisfaction. A conflict between the two is believed to cause emotional problems. Sullivan introduced a new terminology into his system such as the self-dynamism and re-defined already existing terms such as anxiety. His greatest contribution was in stating that men become themselves in relation to others, that growth, motivation, adjustment and disturbances can be understood only in their social inter-relationships.

summation 1. The total of a series, or aggregate. The symbol for summation is Σ (sigma). 2. In sensation, the increased intensity effect of the rapid presentation of two stimuli (sensory summation effect). When the stimulation impulses are presented in rapid succession it is known as temporal summation. When the impulses are presented to adjacent areas it is known as spatial summation. 3. A single effect produced by two or more factors. 4. The occurrence of a different kind of response when mild stimuli are applied in succession.

summation curve The graphic representation of a cumulative frequency distribution.

summation tone A combination tone, heard when two tones, separated by 50 cps or more, are sounded simultaneously. The resultant summation tone is the sum of the two frequencies.

superego (S. Freud) The intrapsychic, mostly unconscious structure of personality which represents societal and cultural standards. The critical self-attitude of a part of the ego exercising the power of censorship in dreams and serving as the main force in repressing instinctual wishes, and the ideal aspirations of the person which the person may not always rise to. The superego develops as a result of an introjection and identification of the child with the parents. The origin is seen in pregenital stages when the child internalizes the prohibitions and restraints of the parents because of the fear of punishment and the need for their love. The full development of the superego does not occur before the end of the phallic stage, when at the height of the Oedipal phase, fear of castration for the boy, and fear of the loss of love for the girl, forces each to give up their erotic love for the parents of the opposite sex and to regress from object relationship to identification by introjection. The introjected parental figures become the superego with the parental standards and punitive attitudes, and the ego-ideal, the child's admiration for the parents. The hostility of the child for the parents becomes the energy at the disposal of the superego, which once directed at the parents, now becomes aimed at the self. The relation between ego and superego parallels that of the child to the parents. The superego rewards the ego with feelings of self-esteem when it is good and punishes it when the ego is bad with feelings of guilt and low self-esteem. As the person develops, the mature superego becomes more impersonal, incorporating societal and objective standards by which the person lives which are no longer bound to parental demands.

superego anxiety See *anxiety, superego.*

superego, double The presence of two usually antagonistic consciences in a person representing disparate standard of conduct.

superego, group (S. R. Slavson) Term referring to the modification of the superego due to experiences with groups of people exclusive of the parents.

superego, heteronomous A type of superego which demands that the ego behave according to the demands of the moment rather than to a set of internalized standards.

superego, parasite of the   Standards and values which take over the functions of the superego for varying lengths of time causing feelings of high and low self-esteem.

superego, primitive A superego which exists earlier and apart from the parental superego. It is believed to be hereditary and to function in organizing the differentiation of the cells in the fetus, according to the principles of development of the particular species.

superego resistance See *resistance, superego.*

superego sadism See *sadism, superego.*

superego strength A source trait governing conscientious, persevering, unselfish behaviors and impelling the individual to duty as conceived by his culture.

superior adult test See *test for superior adults.*

superiority feelings 1. An attitude that one is better in some or all ways than most other people which, although it may be true in some cases, is generally disproportionately displayed and thus, is viewed as a defense against intense feelings of inferiority. 2. (M. Klein) The displacement onto an intellectual level of

a boy's feelings of inferiority which he over-compensates for by viewing himself as superior to girls in the area of sex simply because he possesses a penis.

super-normal sign stimulus See *stimulus, super-normal sign.*

superstition 1. Explanation of events by a belief usually surviving in a distorted form from an earlier religious system now not accepted in a current religious system nor in the body of established facts. 2. (B. F. Skinner) In an operant conditioning experimental situation, when given periodic reinforcements, hungry animals develop repetitive behavior the precise form of which varies from one experimental subject to another but is constant for a single subject.

supportive therapy See *therapy, supportive.*

suppression 1. (physiology) Inhibition of an activity. 2. (psychoanalysis) Conscious repression of a desire or an idea.

suppression area Any area of the cortex which inhibits other cortical activity when stimulated.

suppression, conditioned The presentation of the neutral stimulus with or without the unconditioned aversive stimulus, eventually occasions a decrease of whatever behavior the organism is engaged in at that particular time.

suppression of insight (G. M. Gilbert) A defense mechanism in which the individual resists integrating the cognitive elements of a particular kind of experience that would lead to ego-threatening insights. This mechanism is particularly applicable to attempts to resolve social value and role conflicts of guilt, e.g. hypocritical inconsistency between professed principles and actions in role behavior. The mechanism has some elements in common with cognitive dissonance and denial, but differs from repression in being semi-conscious and merely suppressing the accompanying anxiety.

suppressor variable A variable in a prediction battery which has a zero correlation with the criterion but correlates highly with some other predictor in the battery. Its effect is that it subtracts the variance from the predictor variables not correlated with the criterion, increasing the predictive value of the battery.

suprapatellar reflex A swift reflex in the leg elicited when the index finger, placed above the patella with the leg extended, is struck. The result is a kickback of the patella.

suprarenal glands See *adrenal glands.*

surface color See *color, surface.*

surgency (R. B. Cattell) The high-score (positive) pole of a personality dimension found in questionnaire data, characterized by cheerfulness and alertness.

surgery, emotional reactions to Experiments have shown that the presence of moderate pre-operative fear results in an absence of emotional disturbance during the stressful period following the operation, while the pre-operative presence of extreme fearfulness or the absence of fear, results in post-operative anxiety, anger, and resentment.

surrogate 1. A person who functions in an individual's life as a conscious or unconscious substitute for someone else, generally a parent. 2. (psychoanalysis) A person unconsciously substituted for one of the parents. Because the surrogate figure is frequently not consciously recognized as such, unacceptable id-originated feelings toward the person being substituted for, are often expressed in dreams toward the surrogate.

sursumvergence A movement of one eye upwards in relation to the other.

survey research The assessment of public opinion using questionnaire and sampling methods.

survey tests See *tests, survey*.

survival value The value of a quality or trait in prolonging the life of an organism or species.

suture of nerve Artificial connection of the cut ends of a nerve trunk in order to allow the end which is attached to the cell body to develop along the nerve while the other end degenerates.

Sydenham's chorea See *chorea, Sydenham's*.

syllogism A kind of reasoning consisting of three statements, two premises and a conclusion. Acceptance of the premises leads to the acceptance of the conclusion which may not always be true.

Sylvian fissure The lateral fissure separating the temporal and parietal lobes.

symbiosis 1. A relationship consisting of two species which cannot survive without each other. 2. A normal developmental level following birth when the infant is physiologically and psychologically dependent on the mother and when he is not yet separated from the mother as a distinctly separate individual. 3. (E. Fromm) A neurotic dependence of one individual on another. 4. (M. S. Mahler) A pathological involvement between mother and child typical for the symbiotic syndrome in childhood schizophrenia.

symbiosis, focal Extremely strong bond between a young child with personality disturbance and one of his parents, revolving around a particular and exclusive set of ego functions, such as intellectual functioning or motor skills.

symbiosis, normal (M. S. Mahler) Normal symbiosis is ushered in by cracking of the autistic shell and the lifting of the innate strong stimulus barrier protecting the young infant up to the third or fourth week of life, with the result of inside and outside stimuli impinging from now on upon him. As the instinct for self-preservation has atrophied in the human young, the ego has to take over the role of managing the human being's adaptation to reality, a role that the id is unable to fulfill. The mental apparatus of the young infant is unable to organize his inner and outer stimuli in such a way as to insure his survival, and the psycho-biological rapport between the nursing mother and the baby complements the infant's undifferentiated ego. Empathy on the part of a mother is, usually, the human substitute for those instincts on which the altricial animal relies for its survival. Normal symbiosis develops concomitantly with the above mentioned lowering of the innate stimulus barrier (J. Benjamin), through the repetitious experience of an outside mothering agency which alleviates the need hunger tension and functions as an auxiliary ego (R. Spitz).

Symbiosis refers to a stage of sociobiological interdependence between the one to five month old infant and his mother, to a stage of preobject or need satisfying relationship, in which the self and the maternal intrapsychic representations have not yet been differentiated: from the second month on the infant behaves and functions as though he and his mother were an omnipotent dual unity within one common boundary (the symbiotic membrane).

The mother's availability and the infant's innate capacity to engage in the symbiotic relationship marks the inception of ego-organization by the establishment of intrapsychic connections on the infant's part between memory traces of gratification and the Gestalt of the human face, and signals a shift of cathexis from inside the body (viscera of the autistic phase) to the periphery, the sensory perceptive organs, from coenesthetic (R. Spitz) to diacritic organization.

symbiotic child psychosis (M. S. Mahler) The crucial disturbance in child psychosis consists of the lack or loss of the ability to utilize the mother during the early phases of life as a complement to and organizer of maturation. This causes an absence of a human beacon of orientation, both in the world of reality and in his own inner world, and a gross impairment of the integrating, synthesizing and organizing functions of the ego.

In symbiotic psychosis (Mahler) disturbances in maturation and/or development seriously interfere with the progress of the subsequent separation-individuation process, and results in fixation at or regression to a distorted symbiotic phase, uneven growth, and a striking vulnerability of the ego to minor frustrations.

The symbiotic infantile psychosis is often precipitated by acute panic evoked by such routine separation experiences as enrollment in nursery school, the birth of a sibling, and so on. Basically, however, the symbiotic child psychosis is a reaction of the child to the inherent maturational pressures toward intrapsychic separation from the mother. The paradigm of inherent maturational pressure is behaviorally manifested by the onset of the autonomous locomotor capacities that enable and prompt the toddler to physically separate from the mothering person.

The clinical picture is most often dominated by agitated biphasic fusion and violent isolation attempts, by agitated catatonic-like temper tantrums and panic stricken behavior, followed by bizarrely distorted efforts at restitution.

In many cases of the primarily symbiotic syndrome, the child is compelled to take recourse to a secondary retreat into a quasi-stabilizing (secondary) autism, disrupted by occasional aggressive destructive behavior.

symbiotic phase (M. S. Mahler) A stage of development occurring approximately from the age of three months to about two years when the infant relies on his mother for the satisfaction of his physical and emotional needs. During this stage, the infant, having no separate image of himself as an individual, remains emotionally fused with the mother.

symbiotic psychosis See *psychosis, symbiotic.*

symbiotic relatedness A parasitic style of relating to others in terms of the gratification of one's own neurotic needs.

symbiotic syndrome in childhood schizophrenia 1. See *psychosis, symbiotic.* 2. (B. B. Wolman) The second most severe level of childhood schizophrenia, corresponding to catatonia in adulthood. It is characterized by the child's inability to separate from his mother.

symbol arrangement test See *test, symbol arrangement.*

symbol elaboration test See *test, symbol elaboration.*

symbol of a construct (G. A. Kelley) A factor representing the construct which conceptualizes it as well as itself.

symbol substitution test See *test, code.*

symbolic information See *information, symbolic.*

symbolic interpretation Interpretation of the person's thoughts, dreams, and behavior as derivatives of unconscious conflicts.

symbolism 1. The use of symbols. 2. (psychoanalysis) The use of symbols to represent repressed material.

symbolism, abstract Symbols that signify abstract concepts, for example, the cross and the swastika. Abstract symbolism has had an important role in religious mythology. Although the origin of the symbols may have been forgotten, the ideas which were behind them have remained.

symbolism, anagogic An indirect representation of objects of ideas that have an ideal, spiritual or moral significance.

symbolism, cryptogenic (E. Silberer) The representation of mental functions in the form of imagery.

symbolism, dream See *dream work.*

symbolism, functional (E. Jones) A form of symbolism which arises due to the hindering influence of an affective complex.

symbolism, threshold (E. Silberer) Symbolism occurring in the transition stage from one state of consciousness to another.

symbolism, true Symbolism which represents unconscious material and is unvariable in meaning independent of individual differences. It is believed to evolve from previous generations and have parallels in other races, myths and cultures.

symbolization (psychoanalysis) The unconscious process of utilizing symbols so that unconscious material can be allowed into consciousness.

Symond's Picture-Study Test See *test, Symond's Picture-Study.*

sympathectomy The surgical excision of the sympathetic division of the autonomic nervous system.

sympathetic ganglion Any of the nerve clusters of the sympathetic division of the autonomic nervous system which are found on both sides of the spinal cord.

sympathetic nervous system See *nervous system, sympathetic.*

sympathin A neurohormonal substance. The form E is believed to be produced by a combination of chemical substances discharged in excited effector cells and the endings of sympathetic nerves. The form I is believed to be produced by a combination of chemical substances discharged in inhibited effector cells and the endings of sympathetic nerves.

symptom 1. An event indicative of something. 2. Any event or sign indicative of disease or disorder.

symptom, accessory (E. Bleuler) A secondary symptom not basic to schizophrenia such as hallucinations, delusions, speech and writing disturbances.

symptom, fundamental (E. Bleuler) A symptom which is pathognomonic of schizophrenia, such as disturbances of affect, of thought, autism and schizophrenic dementia.

symptom, primary defense (S. Freud) The first defensive measures such as shame taken in the development of obsessional neurosis against memories of pleasurable sexual activities.

symptom remission The temporary disappearance of the symptoms of a disorder.

symptom, secondary defense (S. Freud) Defensive measure taken in obsessional neurosis when the primary defenses have failed. These include obsessive thought, compulsive activities, doubting, and precautionary and penitential actions.

symptom-substitution theory An expression of the contention that simple removal of a symptom through behavior modification, hypnosis or suggestion will result in the appearance of another symptom. The theory rests on the assumption that the personality is a closed-energy system, with the offending behavior or symptom serving as a mechanism for the expression of an internal conflict of drives.

symptomatology The study of symptoms.

symptoms, ego deficiency (B. B. Wolman) Psychotic symptoms indicative of failure of the ego, e.g. delusions, hallucinations, depersonalization, incontinence, etc.

symptoms, ego protective (B. B. Wolman) Neurotic

symptoms indicative of ego's struggle for retaining a behavioral control, e.g. repression, isolation, compulsive acts, phobias, etc.

Synanon A residential treatment facility for drug addicts organized by a former alcoholic, C. E. Dederich in 1958. It is a secular treatment center staffed by non-professional former drug addicts. Membership is voluntary and the focus is on personal and social responsibility which is discussed in group therapy sessions.

synapse The junction between two nerve cells, neurons. The neural impulse is transmitted across synapses by chemical action of a neurotransmitter.

synaptic conduction The transmission of a nerve impulse across the synapse.

synaptic knob or bouton The bulblike area in the unmyelinated portion at the ending of the axon which releases substances to transmit the nerve impulse from one neuron to another.

synaptic resistance The facilitation or inhibition of the transmission of the nerve impulse occurring at the synapse.

synchronism 1. The occurrence of several developmental disturbances at one time. 2. (C. G. Jung) An acausal principle which refers to events which occur together in time but which do not cause one another. This principle is evinced in phenomena such as clairvoyance, telepathy and archetypes.

syncope Temporary loss of consciousness due to cerebral anemia. Fainting.

syncope, vasodepressor A temporary disturbance of the cardiovascular homeostasis causing fainting due to the sudden drop in blood pressure. It may be of physical or psychogenic origin.

syncretism 1. The combination of many elements into one system disregarding the inherent contradictions. 2. (J. Piaget) A level of thinking found in young children characterized by accidental connections made among elements with the absence of any causal or logical types of associations.

syndromal analysis See *analysis, syndromal.*

syndrome A cluster of symptoms indicative of a clinical entity.

syndrome, abstinence Constellation of symptoms seen when medication is withdrawn from a patient physiologically dependent on an addictive.

syndrome, adaptation (H. Selye) A cycle of extensive physiological changes in the endocrine and other organ systems due to prolonged and intense stress. The first response to stress, called the alarm reaction, is the release of metabolites in the affected tissues. If this phase is not too severe, the metabolites will stimulate the anterior lobe of the pituitary to release a hormone that influences secretion in the cortex of the adrenal gland which aids the body in its resistance (the countershock phase). Should this intense stimulation continue, however, the adrenal cortex will persist in releasing its hormones. Such prolonged exposure would eventually wear down the adaptive

mechanisms and the individual would enter a stage of exhaustion until the adrenal cortex is unable to secrete any more hormones and the organism dies.

syndrome, Bassen-Kornzweig Mental deficiency associated with a genetic metabolic disorder; abetalipoproteinemia.

syndrome, Brown-Sequard (C. E. Brown-Sequard) A syndrome following the hemisection of the spinal cord resulting in paralysis of movement on one side and of sensation on the opposite side.

syndrome, Capgras A condition described by Jean Marie Joseph Capgras (1873-1950), a French psychiatrist. The patient, upon meeting a familiar person, concludes that this person is an impostor who has assumed the real person's physical identity.

syndrome, carotid sinus A syndrome caused by pressure applied over the carotid sinus which results in weakness, slowing of the heart, a decrease in blood pressure and often fainting.

syndrome, *cri du chat* See *cri du chat syndrome.*

syndrome, dependence-independence Inconsistent interpersonal behavior most commonly seen in latent schizophrenics, comprised of marked shifts in mood from dependent feelings manifested through expectations of strength, unconditional love, and protection from relations, to independent feelings; when dependence needs are frustrated, manifested through aggressive, rebellious, and domineering behavior.

syndrome, deprivation In young children, a constellation of symptoms and behaviors, usually associated with maternal loss or absence, characterized by withdrawal, lack of responsiveness to the environment and often depression.

syndrome, disparagement A pattern of self-denigration in certain areas of accomplishment as well as a generalized tendency to disparage the abilities of others.

syndrome, Ganser's (S. J. M. Ganser) A syndrome consisting of the giving of irrelevant, often absurd answers to questions.

syndrome, general adaptation See *general adaptation syndrome.*

syndrome, Horner's (J. H. Horner) Ptosis of the eyelid resulting from paralysis of the nerve fibers or from lesions of the cervical sympathetic nerve fibers, usually associated with enopthalmus and absence of sweating on the affected side of the head and the face.

syndrome, Hunt Ramsay (J. Ramsay Hunt) Dyssynergia cerebellaris. A geniculate neuralgia associated with severe pain in the middle ear, hyperacusis, facial paralysis and decline in taste and salivation, often associated with herpes zoster infection.

syndrome, hyperventilation Respiratory alkalosis resulting from over-breathing and characterized by dizziness, sometimes loss of consciousness, numbness and tonic or clonic motor reactions. The syndrome may be due to anxiety, fear, drugs, or organic brain disease.

syndrome, Klinefelter's (H. F. Klinefelter) A disorder of a defective hormonal balance and underdeveloped testes in males, related to an extra X chromosome. Mental retardation is often present.

syndrome, Klüver-Bucy (H. Klüver and P. C. Bucy) A syndrome, the symptoms of which are loss of the ability to recognize others, loss of fear, and rage reactions, increased sexual activity, memory defects, bulimia, and hypermetamorphosis. It was originally described by Klüver and Bucy in monkeys whose temporal lobes had been removed.

syndrome, mast Presenile dementia inherited through the recessive gene with an onset in the early teens causing intellectual deterioration, spasticity, and dysarthria and by the age of thirty to forty, resulting in complete incapacitation.

syndrome, McArdle's (B. McArdle) A defect of the mitochondrial enzymes which is inherited as a recessive gene. It is characterized by weakness, pain, and stiffness following exercise due to the excessive deposit of glycogen in the muscles resulting from the deficiency of the enzyme, mycophosphorylase.

syndrome, Münchausen (R. Asher) A syndrome characterized by the presentation of false symptoms and false medical and social histories.

syndrome, Pötzl (O. Pötzl) Symbol agnosia for written material with disturbances of color vision found in the presence of lesions in the medullary layer of the lingual gyrus of the dominant hemisphere, including damage of the corpus callosum.

syndrome, Rubinstein-Taybi (J. H. Rubinstein and H. Taybi) A form of mental retardation characterized by congenital malformation including broad thumbs and toes.

syndrome, Sjögren-Larsson (S. Sjögren and T. Larsson) Hereditary syndrome characterized by mental retardation, spastic paralysis and ichthyosis, and occurring through the autosomal recessive type of transmission.

syndrome, striatal Disease of the striatum characterized by rigidity, tremor, hypokinesis, impairment of associated movements and an absence of sensory disturbances or true paralysis.

synergism The principle that responses or ideas result from the combination of coordinated factors working together.

synergism, sexual Sexual excitation resulting from the combined effect of many stimuli occuring simultaneously.

synergy (R. B. Cattell) The energy, representable by an ergic vector by which a group operates, summing the attitude vectors representing the interest strengths of members in the group life.

synonym-antonym test See *test, synonym-antonym.*

syntactic aphasia See *aphasia, syntactic.*

syntality (R. B. Cattell) That which determines a group's performance when its situation is given. Analogous to personality in the individual.

syntaxic See *syntaxic mode.*

syntaxic mode (H. S. Sullivan) The third, logical mode of experiencing the world characterized by consensually validated experiences, judgments and observations and an interpersonal system of communication.

synthesis The combination of elements into a whole.

syntone One who is in affective harmony with the environment.

syntonia A personality trait characterized by a high degree of emotional responsiveness to the environment.

syntonic Possessing the qualities of a syntone.

syntonic ego See *ego-syntonic.*

syntropic Pertaining to syntropy.

syntropy (A. Meyer) Harmonious association with others.

syphilis A prenatal or acquired venereal disease due to systemic infection with *treponema pallidum* and almost always acquired in sexual intercourse. Lesions may be produced in any tissue or organ of the body with symptoms characteristic of the site of involvement.

syphilis, cerebral See *syphilis, meningovascular.*

syphilis, meningovascular Syphilis of the central nervous system involving the leptomeninges and the cerebral arteries. Symptoms do not differ from those caused by other cerebral lesions.

syphilitic insanity Obsolete term for psychosis caused by syphilis.

syphilophobia Fear of syphilis.

system 1. A set of elements which are orderly interrelated to make a functional whole. 2. A set of concepts which provide the framework for arranging the facts and data of a science.

system, action (A. Kardiner) A bodily system which allows an organism to fulfill a need or desire.

system, anabolic The system in constitutional medicine which corresponds to the megalosplanchnic habitus.

system analysis Analysis of the functioning of a system which includes an identification and measurement of errors, and a modification of the system in order to correct the mistakes.

system, dynamic A system which involves a stable exchange of energy among the parts depending on their interrelationships.

system equation See *equation, system.*

system, kinship (anthropology) The types and degrees of kinship, the terms by which they are defined, and the behavior patterns associated with them in any given culture or society.

system, miniature A set of principles and theoretical laws which are organized to explain a psychological process or group of related psychological facts.

system, perceptual-conscious (S. Freud) The surface aspect of the ego which is directed onto the external world, mediates perceptions of it and produces the phenomena of consciousness through its functioning. This system is the receptor of stimulation from without and from the inside of the mind.

system research Research involving the investigation of new system designs and the examination of the relationship of man to machine with a view to developing and improving existing systems.

system, sign (P. Schilder) The utilization of language as the chief instrument in psychotherapy.

systematic desensitization (J. Wolpe) A behavior therapy technique in which deep muscle relaxation is used to inhibit the effects of graded anxiety-evoking stimuli. The patient is trained to relax muscles beyond the point of normal tonus, and anxiety-evoking situations, e.g. those characterizing a phobia are ranked according to their anxiety potency for him. In systematic desensitization, the weakest situation is presented to the imagination of the fully relaxed patient, repeatedly, until it no longer evokes anxiety, and then in progressively stronger situations. There are many variants of this technique, using real stimuli instead of imaginery ones, and various anxiety-inhibiting responses other than relaxation.

systematic error See *error, systematic.*

systemic 1. Referring to a system. 2. Referring to the body systems.

systemic-localization concept The principle that higher mental functions called systems are localized in specific areas of the brain.

systemic sense See *sense, systemic.*

systemogenesis (P. K. Anokhin) An evolutionary trend based on the original theory of the functional system. This trend reveals new regularities of the brain development in ontogenesis and phylogenesis of animals and man. The main features of systemogenesis are the accelerated and selective development of those structures in ontogenesis which form vitally significant functional systems of a new-born immediately after birth, such as respiration, blood circulation, sucking, feeding, etc. Maturation of structures necessary for these functional systems is rather selective and does not depend upon degree of maturation of the entire organ. For example, the nerve cells of the facial nerve nucleus innervating orbicularis oris, completely mature at a definite time, and their axons innervate the muscle fibers through developed neuromuscular synapses, while other motor neurons of the facial nerve nucleus have not matured yet. Such a type of maturation of the functional system but not of the organ is basic in the evolution of organisms and that is why it was called systemogenesis and not organogenesis.

systems, informational (J. P. Guilford) Organized items of information; complexes of interrelated or interacting parts.

systems theory An approach to knowledge in which a unit is seen as being a subsystem of a larger and more comprehensive system and also seen as being comprised of various and smaller subsystems. The interactions of the various systems, subsystems, and components of subsystems are focused upon, resting on the assumption that a unit cannot be studied with no understanding of how that unit fits into other larger and smaller systems.

systole The period of active contraction of the heart muscle.

Szondi test See *test, Szondi.*

T

t 1. Any particular case in a series. 2. The amount of time passed since a stipulated event. 3. (statistics) The ratio of a statistic to its standard error. It is also written with subscripts indicating the value which is observed, (t_{obs}), or a critical value (t_{crit}).

T Transmittance of radiant power.

T 1. (Rorschach) The total time required to respond to all the inkblots. 2. Temperature given in degrees absolute. 3. Point of transition. 4. A total, sometimes written with subscripts indicating which scores are summed.

T.A. Toxin-antitoxin.

$_st_R$ (C. Hull) The median reaction time or latency.

$_sT_R$ (C. Hull) The reaction time or latency.

T data (R. B. Cattell) Data obtained through the use of tests.

T distribution See *test, t.*

T function A measure of the reduction of the amount of information needed to locate an element in one category or classification if it has already been located in other categories. The amount of relatedness in the classification of elements.

T group A sensitivity training group in which the focus is the learning of human relation skills and personal and interpersonal issues.

T maze See *maze, T.*

T maze, multiple See *maze, multiple T.*

T scale See *scale, T.*

T technique (R. B. Cattell) Factor analysis of a correlation matrix from correlating, on a sample of people, the various occasions on which the same test is repeated.

T-TAT See *test, Thompson, Thematic Apperception.*

t test See *test, t.*

TAB (statistics) The estimated frequency of the cell as the intersection of the Ath row and the Bth column.

tabes dorsalis Degeneration of posterior column of spinal cord leading to loss of proprioceptive feedback from muscles and consequent incoordination of walking movements (locomotor ataxia).

table, correlation See *correlation table.*

table, double-entry A statistical table arranged in rows and columns. Two entering arguments or values are needed to specify a value in the table.

taboo, incest The prohibition of sexual intercourse between close relatives.

taboo; tabu A social prohibition of objects, persons, dress, words, or actions usually stemming from early cultural conceptions of the object as magical or sacred and thus associated with power, danger, and by extension, the unclean.

tabula rasa (J. Locke) The mind of a newborn child is like a clean slate (tabula rasa), and whatever is in the human mind, is derived from the sensory perceptions.

tachistoscope An apparatus used in experimental studies of perception, learning, etc., for exposure of small pictures, digits and letters for brief intervals.

tachycardia Rapid heart rate which may be due to functional or organic causes.

tachylogia Abnormally rapid speech.

tact (B. F. Skinner) Verbal response secondarily reinforced.

tactile agnosia See *agnosia, tactile.*

tactile circle An area of skin whose two tactile stimuli are perceived as one.

tail (statistics) The end area of a frequency curve beyond a specified ordinate which is usually less than a third of the distribution. A distribution curves into a tail-like formation toward the base-line at the extremes.

Talbot-Plateau law See *law, Talbot-Plateau.*

talent High level innate ability in a particular area such as music.

tally The recording of a single mark for each occurrence of a certain event or characteristic in order to maintain a cumulative tabulation.

tand schedule See *reinforcement, schedule of: tandem.*

tandem (tand) schedule See *reinforcement, schedule of: tandem.*

taphaophilia Attraction for a cemetery.

taphophobia Fear of being buried alive.

tapping test See *test, dotting.*

tarantism Compulsion to dance.

taraxein A chemically unstable protein fraction which is reportedly present in the blood of schizophrenic patients and is believed to be a chemical manifestation of an inborn error of metabolism. Taraxein is said to inhibit the interaction of a brain enzyme and a chemical, diamine, which is produced under situations of psychological stress. This inhibitory action underlies the development of mental disorder. Several experiments have shown that the injection of a protein fraction from the plasma of schizophrenic patients produces psychotic-like behavior in normal subjects.

Tarchanoff phenomenon Electrodermal response; production of a mild electric current on the surface of the skin.

Tartini's tone Difference in tones.

taste bud Nerve ending of the gustatory sense located in the mouth.

TAT See *test, thematic apperception.*

Tau effect (H. Helson) The interaction of time and space such that if three spots are successively stimulated on the skin, or three lights are flashed successively, if the time between the second and third is less (greater) than that between the first and second, the distance between them is perceived to be smaller (greater) than that between the first two. The converse of this effect, named the Kappa effect, is found when observers are asked to judge the time when the distance between spots is varied; then the shorter (longer) distance is perceived to be stimulated more rapidly (less rapidly) than the longer (shorter) distance between the stimuli.

tautaphone (D. Shakow and S. Rosenzweig) A projective device introduced in 1940 consisting of a record of random vocal sounds which the subject is asked to interpret.

taxis The involuntary movement of a motile organism or organic bodies involving a change of place toward (positive taxis) or away (negative taxis) from a source of stimulation. Several types of taxes have

been distinguished: klinotaxis, tropotaxis, telotaxis, menotaxis, anemotaxis, and geotaxis.

taxonomic system A system of classification of data according to their natural relationships.

Tay-Sachs disease A type of lipidosis characterized by hypertonicity, listlessness, blindness, spasitic paralysis, convulsions and retardation. Progressive deterioration usually leads to death by age three. About 80 percent of those affected are of Jewish descent.

Taylor Manifest Anxiety Scale See *scale, Taylor Manifest Anxiety.*

taylorism (industrial psychology) A theory of increased efficiency and productivity in business, management and industry.

teaching machine A system of programmed instruction in which the child works independently and at his own pace on academic material presented to him through a console on a mechanical apparatus. The material is presented in either a linear manner or a branching manner.

technique, critical incident A method of studying organisms by observing selected samples of their behavior and making inferences about the total organism.

technique, graphomotor A projective technique in which the subject is asked to move the pencil freely on a piece of paper. The clinician subsequently interprets the drawing.

technique, inspection (R. Monroe) Abbreviated technique for evaluating the Rorschach using only those response patterns which are significant for a given purpose rather than attempting an over-all personality description.

technique R See *correlation, R.*

tele 1. Purpose. 2. (J. L. Moreno) A unit of attraction or repulsion measured by sociogram.

telecephalon The anterior part of the forebrain which includes the olfactory lobes, cerebral cortex and corpora striata.

teledendrite Terminal arborization of an axon.

telegnosis (parapsychology) Clairvoyance.

telekinesis (parapsychology) Movement of objects believed to take place without application of physical force.

telemetry A technique for measuring autonomic body changes from the distance using devices such as a miniature radio transmitter which is sensitive to perspiration, changes in heart rate, blood pressure and respiration rate, muscle tension and electrical conductance of the skin.

teleologic regression See *regression, teleologic.*

teleology 1. The study of behavior as it is related to purposes or as being purposive. 2. The belief that behavior is defined and set off from other phenomena in that it is purposive. **3.** (philosophy) The doctrine that goals have a causal influence on present events, that the future as well as the past affect the present. **4.** (theology) The belief that a universal purpose or design exists which pervades reality, and that all events tend toward its ultimate fulfillment.

telepathy Extrasensory perception of thought without the use of any known means of communication.

telodendron Teledendrite.

telotaxis A taxis in which, as in tropotaxis, the animal makes simultaneous comparisons of stimulus intensity. However telotaxis does not depend on a balance between sources of stimulation; if there are two stimulus sources operating through the same modality the animal orients toward one or the other and not intermediately suggesting that one stimulus source is inhibited.

temperament **1.** The predisposition of a person to emotional reactions. **2.** (Hippocrates) A personality type characterized in terms of a humoral theory. There are four types: choleric, melancholic, sanguine and phlegmatic. **3.** (I. P. Pavlov) A personality type which has its basis in the excitation and inhibition processes of the nervous system. There are four types, the excitatory or choleric, the inhibitory or melancholic and the central or equilibrated type which consists of a quiet or phlegmatic and lively or sanguine type.

temperature spot Skin surface that is exceptionally sensitive to temperature.

Temple-Darley Test See *test, Temple-Darley.*

temporal lobe See *lobe, temporal.*

temporary reflex See *reflex, conditioned.*

tender feeling (W. McDougall) An innate inclination for taking care of children and helpless individuals.

tenderness (K. Abraham) The wish to preserve and to take care of. It starts at the anal-retentive phase of psychosexual development.

tendon Fibrous tissue connecting a muscle to a bone.

tendon reflex A contraction of a muscle.

tension **1.** (physiology) Strain which results from muscular contraction and through which muscles, tendons, etc. are stretched and maintained in that position. **2.** Physical sensations which result from muscular strain, tension, and contraction. **3.** Condition of anxiety, tension, and uneasiness which occurs from readiness to alter behavior or readiness to act, especially in situations of threat. **4.** Emotional strain. **5.** (K. Lewin) A state of disequilibrium between an organism and its environment.

tension system (K. Lewin) A state of disequilibrium between the individual and his environment. This objective state of disequilibrium is perceived by the individual as a need. Tension and need are two sides of the tension system which entails the psychological field of the individual as well as the objective state of disequilibrium.

teratology The study of malformations of the body.

Terman, Lewis Madison (1877-1956) American educational psychologist, widely known for test construction. Designed and standardized an American revision of the Binet-Simon intelligence test (Stanford Binet), bringing the IQ concept into widespread usage, and directed construction of the Stanford Achievement Test. Conducted a lifetime longitudinal research on the development of gifted children, and also made naturalistic, test-based studies of masculinity-femininity and marital happiness. See *IQ; Stanford Binet; M-F Test.*

Terman-McNemmar Test of Mental Ability See *test, Terman-McNemmar, of Mental Ability.*

terminal bulb See *synoptic knob.*

terminal stimulus The highest intensity of a stimulus to which the organism is capable of responding.

terminology A system of terms, symbols and names used in a particular discipline, profession or occupation.

test **1.** A standardized set of questions which are administered to a group or to individuals in order to assess the presence or absence of a particular skill or knowledge. **2.** A measurement which produces quantitative data. **3.** (statistics) A set of operations designed to assess the significance of a stated hypothesis. **4.** (logic) An operation designed to determine the truth or validity of a hypothesis.

test, ability Standardized test of maximum performance designed to reveal the level of present ability, either in general or in a specific direction.

test, absurdities A task in which the individual must detect and point out the absurdity in a picture, story or writing. An absurdity is an incongruity, something that is obviously the opposite of that which is accepted as fact or truth. The Stanford-Binet tests of intelligence include both picture and verbal absurdities tasks. An example of a verbal absurdity is as follows: "They found a young man locked in his room with his hands tied behind him and his feet bound together. They think he locked himself in." After the presentation of a statement of this type, the subject is asked, "What is foolish about that?"

test, accuracy A test that considers only correctness as the criterion and the time taken to perform the tasks is not important.

test, ACE The American Council on Education test of intelligence, primarily designed for upper high school students and college freshmen. A language score, a quantitative score and a total score can be obtained for this test.

test, achievement A test designed to measure the level of proficiency by testing the individual's performance in a particular area.

test, adult-child interaction (J. F. Alexander) Eight card TAT-like test designed to facilitate the categorization of scores in terms of: 1) what kinds of stimuli were employed (symbolization); 2) positive and negative affects and activities (emotional perception); and 3) frequency and degree of organization of a series of defined elements in the story (behavioral continuum).

test age The score which is obtained from an age-equivalent scale.

test, aiming A task involving quick precise eye-hand coordinations. Aiming is measured by a stylus-and-hole apparatus. The subject's task is to thrust the stylus into progressively smaller holes or into holes momentarily uncovered by a rotating shutter. without touching the sides of the holes. There is also an aiming test that is of paper and pencil design which requires the subject to place dots in small circles as rapidly as he can. This version of the test involves motor speed as well as precision of movement.

test, alternate-response A test composed of a number of questions, each having only two possible answers. The subject is required to choose one of the alternatives such as Yes-No or True-False.

test, altitude A test specifically designed to obtain a measure of the maximum level of difficulty that an individual can achieve in problem solving.

test, analogies Test which requires supplying a fourth term to correctly complete a relationship of four terms in which the relationship between the first and second terms is the same as that between the third and fourth terms, i.e. M is to N as O is to ———.

test, aptitude A compilation of tasks which are chosen and standardized so as to yield scores which enable a prediction of a subject's future performance on tasks which are somewhat similar to the tasks on the test.

test, Army Alpha Verbal intelligence tests used by the army during World War I, 1917-1918, in combination with the Army Beta test. Also called the Army Alpha Intelligence Test.

test, Army Alpha Intelligence See *test, Army Alpha.*

test, Army Beta Non-verbal intelligence test used by the army during World War I, 1917-1918, in combination with the Army Alpha test. Also called the army Beta Intelligence Test.

test, Army General Classification Also called AGCT. World War I brought with it the necessity of developing a method of measuring the intelligence of the normal adult. The Army Alpha and Army Beta Tests, which were developed at that time, laid an important foundation for the future of mental testing. It was shown that the mental test was much more than a device to help identify the feeble-minded, and that there are degrees of mental ability among those considered normal. The army testing program also brought out the fact that mental testing does not have to be the costly individual proce-

dure previously held to be the only method. Also convincingly shown was the value of the tests for the practical classification of men. The psychologists in World War I had their greatest achievement in the development of the group intelligence test. Following World War I the tests were released for civilian use and group testing continued to be expanded.

There were many tests modeled after the army plan and the psychologists of World War II were faced with the task of sifting the available testing devices in order to find the ones which were or could be made suitable to their needs. In contrast to World War I, military organization had become more complex and individual roles were more highly specialized and therefore, needs were also more specific and varied.

The problem of group intelligence testing had been further clarified during the years between the two wars, and a new Army General Classification Test was prepared and used in World War II. This group intelligence test was used by the army to classify inductees according to their abilities to learn military duties. The technical kind of learning involved in military service forced the emphasis to be on verbal comprehension, quantitative reasoning, and spatial perception. The three subtests designed to measure these processes were a vocabulary test, an arithmetic test, and a block-counting test. Scores were changed to standard units with a mean of 100 and a standard deviation of 20. These final scores were similar to IQ scores but with a greater spread around the mean. Therefore, the very high or very low scores would be of slightly less significance than if computed by the usual method for IQs. The scores obtained from the AGCT are not in part a function of chronological age. See *Army Alpha Test; Army Beta Test.*

test, association A technique designed to assess a person's reaction to specific stimuli such as words or colors. The subject may be given a general instruction of saying whatever comes to his mind or may be told to respond in a specified manner.

test, auditory apperception (D. R. A. Stone) An auditory projective test introduced in 1953 consisting of five 45-rpm records which have a variety of sounds. There are ten sets of three types of sounds. After hearing a set, the subject is asked to tell a story about the sounds, including what led up to them, what is happening and how it will end. The test is recommended for use with blind subjects or groups.

test, ball and field A Stanford-Binet test item which requires the child's demonstrating through drawing how he could search for an object lost in a field.

test, Bárány (R. Bárány) The rotation of a subject positioned so that his head lies in each of the three planes bringing the three semicircular canals vertical to the direction of rotation.

test, Behn-Rorschach (H. Behn and H. Rorschach) Companion test to the original Rorschach, used for research or with subjects overly familiar with the standard Rorschach.

test, Bender Visual-Motor Gestalt (L. Bender) Test

of visual-motor and perceptual functioning requiring the subject to reproduce nine geometric designs characterized by their patterning or configuration, each design presented on a different card. Distortions in the copied designs can be the result of neural injury, variations in level of intellectual performance, or emotional disorder.

test, Bennett Differential Aptitude (G. K. Bennett) Aptitude tests used for grades eight to twelve which measure numerical, verbal, mechanical, and abstract reasoning, spatial relations, language usage, and clerical speed and accuracy.

test, Bennett, of Mechanical Comprehension (G. K. Bennett) A test of mechanical ability with several levels of difficulty for high school students and adults which uses mechanical problems in printed form.

test, best answer, or **test, best reason** A test in which a number of different answers or solutions to a problem are presented along with a problem; the testee chooses the answer or solution he thinks is the best one.

test, Binet-Simon (A. Binet and T. Simon) A series of tests developed in 1905 and 1908 for use in the assessment of school children in France and since adapted for use in many other countries. The test underwent several revisions in France and elsewhere.

test, Blacky pictures (G. S. Blum) Cartoons of a dog family with questions derived from a psychoanalytic framework, focusing on castration fears, sexual activity, sibling rivalry and so on.

test, block design A kind of performance test which requires the subject to reproduce standard designs with various colored blocks.

test, Bolgar-Fischer World (H. Bolgar and L. Fischer) A projective technique developed in 1947 which consists of miniature objects such as houses, animals, vehicles. The subject is asked to do whatever he wants with them. The examiner discusses the subject's work inquiring in order to obtain qualitative data. The test can be used with adults or children.

test, bone-conduction A procedure designed to assess how well the subject can hear sounds transmitted to the internal ear via the skull bones. If the subject can hear well, hearing loss can be determined to be due to defective conduction in the middle ear.

test, Bryngelson-Glaspey (B. Bryngelson and E. Glaspey) A test which determines proficiency in articulation of speech sounds. The test, introduced in 1941, consists of stimuli pictures designed to elicit verbal responses which assess individual sound in initial, medial and final position and in sound clusters.

test, cause and effect A test which requires the testee to state or choose from available options the cause of a specified effect or the effect of a specified cause.

test, CAVD (E. L. Thorndike) A battery of four intelligence tests: completion, arithmetic problems, vocabulary, and following directions.

test chart A chart which is employed in the assessment of visual acuity.

test, children's apperception (L. Bellak and S. S. Bellak) A projective test modeled after the Thematic Apperception Test and intended for children from three to ten years of age. The test has two forms, one in which the characters are animals and the other in which they are children.

test, code A test which requires substitution of one set of symbols by another, e.g. digit-symbol test.

test, color sorting See *test, Holmgren.*

test, completion A test in which the subject is asked to fill in the missing word, letter or phrase.

test, comprehension 1. A form of aptitude test in which the subject is asked to evaluate what he would do in a specific practical situation. 2. A test which assesses a person's comprehension of a written passage by means of questions, following the selection, which the person is asked to answer.

test, d reaction In reaction-time experiments, the test in which the subject must withhold his response until he has made an identification of which of the two stimuli has been presented.

test, developmental, of visual-motor integration (K. E. Beery and N. A. Buktenica) Form-copying test for the assessment of the degree of integration of visual and motor skills; used with children fourteen years of age.

test, dexterity Test to measure the speed and accuracy in performance of manual tasks.

test, diagnostic A test for the purpose of identification of the nature and source of the individual's difficulties. For example, a reading test can identify the source of an individual's poor scholastic performance.

test, diagnostic word A test which presents auditory verbal stimuli to determine the intensity threshold at which speech can be understood.

test, differential aptitude (DAT) A battery of eight aptitude tests including tests of verbal, numerical, abstract, and mechanical reasoning, and spacial relations, clerical speed and accuracy, and two language tests. It is designed for use by high school students.

test, directions An intelligence test in which the testee is directed to perform tasks on the assumption that the ability to follow directions is indicative of intelligence.

test, disarranged sentence Test item in which the task is to rearrange the given series or words into a meaningful sentence.

test, dotting A paper and pencil test of motor ability in which the subject makes as many dots as possible in a unit of time. Also called the tapping test. In a variant of this, the aiming test, the subject is required to aim his dots one in each of a series of randomly placed circles.

test, Downey's Will-Temperament (J. Downey) A personality scale introduced in 1924 based on the assumption that various performance tasks, such as writing, express personality characteristics. It consists of twelve such tasks.

test, draw-a-person (K. Machover) A projective test developed in 1948 and based on F. Goodenough's test of intellectual ability determined from children's drawings. The subject is asked to draw a person, then a person of the opposite sex. He is then asked specific questions about his drawings. There is one list of questions for children and one for adults which inquire about age, schooling, ambition, marital status of the drawn people. This test is believed to yield information concerning the subject's self-image and body image.

test, Elizur's, for organicity Test for brain damage involving figure copying, clock-design constructs, and a digit test. Scores in the organic range on two of the three scales indicate organic damage.

test for homogeneity See *test of independence*.

test for superior adults Test developed for the assessment of superior adults such as the three grades of tests in the Terman-Merrill tests which are used for adults up to a mental age of over twenty-two.

test, Forer Structured Sentence Completion (B. R. Forer) An inventory introduced in 1950 designed to evaluate problematical areas such as interpersonal relations, aggression, and anxieties to plan a course of therapy. It consists of one hundred items. There are separate forms for males and females.

test, formboard Any of a group of performance tests which requires fitting geometric forms or blocks into depressions on a board.

test, four pictures (D. J. Van Lennep) A projective test introduced in 1948 consisting of four ambiguous pictures showing figures which are alone and in groups. The subject must make up one story integrating the four pictures. Analysis of the results involves the content and formal dimensions such as time and space.

test, Franck Drawing Completion (K. Franck) A projective instrument used with children ages six and over in which the child is presented with various stimulus patterns and asked to complete them or make a drawing out of them. The instrument is particularly geared for the assessment of masculinity-femininity.

test, free association A test or examination in which the subject is asked to make an association as quickly as possible to each stimulus presented. Any modality of stimulus or of response may be employed but verbal stimuli and responses are the most frequently used. The nature of the response and the time interval between the stimuli and the response are evaluated in terms of the subjects' attitudes, personality or other variables.

test, free recall A test in which the subject responds with associations to the test stimuli.

test, Frostig, of Visual Motor Development (M. Frostig) A test which is designed to assess the development of perceptual disturbances in which the child is required to perform various perceptual tasks.

test, gestural interverbal A subtest of the Parson Language Sample designed to assess skills of the gestural exchange class of language behavior.

test, good and evil The precursor of the right and wrong test which is used to determine a person's responsibility in a criminal action. Based on the M'Naghten rule of 1843, English law stipulates that to plead insanity as a defense in a criminal case, it must be shown that the accused was not cognizant of what he was doing or that he did not know that this action was wrong.

test, Goodenough Draw-A-Man (F. Goodenough) A test of intelligence for children up to eleven years old in which the child is asked to draw a man. The drawing is scored according to the amount of detail present. It was introduced and standardized in 1926.

test, Gray Oral Reading (W. S. Gray) An individually administered test designed for use with children in grades one to twelve in the assessment of speed, accuracy, and comprehension in oral reading which consists of a series of standardized reading paragraphs.

test, group A test designed to be given to more than one person at a time.

test, H A test of the significance of the differences between two sets of ranked data.

test, hand A projective technique in which children six years of age and over are shown a series of nine drawings of hands in various ambiguous poses and are asked what the hand is doing. The last card is blank and requires the child to imagine a hand and describe what it is doing. The scoring, similar to that of the Rorschach and TAT, provides measures of affection, dependence, tension and aggression.

test, Hanfmann-Kasanin Concept Formation (E. Hanfmann and J. S. Kasanin) A test originally concerned with the performance of schizophrenics, designed to determine a person's ability to classify twenty-two blocks each being in one of five colors, six shapes, two heights and two widths, into four categories: tall-wide, flat-wide, tall-narrow, and flat-narrow. Performance is analyzed with respect to the person's interpretation of the task, nature of the attempts at solution, and discovery of the correct solution, each of which is classified according to three levels: the primitive, the intermediate and the conceptual which are scored 1, 2, and 3 respectively. These scores are arbitrary values which have not been determined experimentally. This test yields an over-all evaluation of a person's performance and is used to determine deterioration in conceptual thinking.

test, Healy Picture Completion (W. Healy) 1. A performance test in which the subject is asked to complete the missing parts of a picture by choosing pieces from a larger number of possibilities. The time limit is ten minutes. This test is a subtest of the Pintner-Paterson Scale of Performance Tests. 2. See *tests, Pintner-Paterson Scale of Performance.*

test, heel-to-knee A test for ataxia in which the patient, who is in a reclining position, is asked to raise his foot high, touch the knee with the opposite heel and move the heel along the shin with his eyes open or closed.

test, Hejna (R. F. Hejna) A test to assess speech articulation developed in 1959 which consists of pictures designed to elicit verbal responses which will include specific sounds.

test, Holmgren (A. F. Holmgren) A test for color blindness in which the subject must classify skeins of wool according to three sample colors.

test, Horn-Hellersberg Drawing Completion (C. C. Horn and E. F. Hellersberg) A projective technique used with children in which the child is given a series of stimulus patterns and asked to make a complete drawing out of each. There is a published list of popular responses for grade-school children.

test, house-tree-person (J. N. Buck) A projective test introduced in 1948 in which the subject is asked to draw a house, a tree, and a person, each of which is believed to be a self-portrait. The drawings are evaluated in terms of sequence, style and area. The tester conducts an extensive interview following the test. This test is believed to reflect personality characteristics and assess intelligence.

test, Hunt-Minnesota, for Organic Brain Damage (H. F. Hunt) A test designed for the detection of organic brain damage, introduced in 1943. It consists of three parts: the vocabulary subtest of the 1937 Stanford-Binet Test, six memory and recall tests, and nine tests which are used to predict validity. In the vocabulary test the number of words the subject defines correctly reflects his basic verbal ability before the deterioration occurred. The validation tests consist of items of information, of counting forward and backward and of following specific instructions; subjects who cannot perform these tests are considered too disturbed, uncooperative or too deteriorated to be tested. The subject receives a score of each of the validation tests to determine whether he scores below the critical score ascertained as necessary for taking the test. This test was developed for use with individuals sixteen years of age and older. It was standardized on a small group of thirty-three patients, aged sixteen to seventy, who had been diagnosed as suffering from organic brain damage.

test, identification A test requiring the subject to name an object or part of a picture pointed to by the examiner.

test, IES An instrument, based on a psychoanalytic framework, developed and designed to measure impulses, ego and superego in children ten years of age and over.

test, Illinois, of Psycholinguistic Abilities (ITPA) A test based on communications theory designed to assess differential language abilities that are considered important in communications and learning disorders. It consists of twelve subtests which attempt to assess the child's communication skills in: 1) three processes of communication (reception, expression and organized process); 2) two levels of language organization (representational and automatic); 3) two channels of language input (auditory and visual); and 4) two channels of language output (verbal and manual expression). The test assesses the degree of the child's ability to, understand spoken words, comprehend visual stimuli, manipulate linguistic symbols meaningfully, express ideas with spoken words, express ideas using movement, produce the correct patterns of standard American language, remember auditory stimuli, remember and reproduce nonmeaningful visual figures, identify a common object from an incomplete visual presentation, fill in the deleted parts from an auditory perception, and synthesize separate parts of a word presented orally to produce an integrated whole word.

test, incomplete pictures A test of visual organization in which the subject is required to identify a common object presented in a series of successively completed drawings of that object as early in the sequence as possible. Also used as an indicator of the degree of psychotic impairment.

test, individual A test designed to be administered usually by a specially trained individual to only one person at a time.

test, induction A test often used as a measure of general intelligence, requiring the subject to derive a principle from several particular instances.

test, infant A test measuring infant behavioral development consisting of the performance of various tasks that are expected to be performed at the individual infant's chronological age.

test, informal A nonstandardized test designed to give an approximate index of an individual's level of ability.

test, information 1. A mental test designed to sample the subject's knowledge of a variety of general facts which theoretically are available to everyone. 2. One of the verbal sub-tests appearing on the Wechsler Intelligence Scales.

test, intelligence 1. A standardized test which measures a wide range of abilities, including verbal, numerical and social competence. 2. See *Stanford-Binet.* 3. See *Wechsler-Bellevue Scale.* 4. See *Wechsler Adult Intelligence Scale.* 5. See *Wechsler Intelligence Scale for Children.* 6. See *Wechsler Preschool and Primary Scale of Intelligence.*

test, inventory A test covering major areas of pupil achievement for the purpose of yielding a profile of individuals' strengths and weaknesses.

test, Ishihari A test used in the detection of color blindness consisting of a number of plates in which figures printed in different hues appear against backgrounds of random dots of varying saturation and brightness. The difference in hue between the figure and ground is not apparent to the color-blind person.

test item A question, an item or a problem which elicits a response which can be measured as a single unit and related to the skill the test is measuring as a whole.

test, Jung association (C. G. Jung) A word association test used in conjunction with physiological measures of emotion yielding strong evidence of emotional reactions to specific words. It is used for the purpose of uncovering complexes and aiding diagnosis.

test, Kahn, of Symbol Arrangement (E. Kahn) A structured play test used in diagnostic evaluation of children and sometimes adults. For use with those six years of age or older, the test involves the arrangement of sixteen small plastic objects, such as dogs, hearts, stars and butterflies.

test, Kent-Rosanoff (G. H. Kent and J. Rosanoff) A free association test consisting of one-hundred words, the associations to which have been standardized so that the frequency of different associations is known and used in determining relative normalcy or eccentricity of thought.

test, Knox Cube (H. A. Knox) A performance in which the subject taps a series of four cubes in various sequences prescribed by the examiner.

test, Kohs Block Design (S. C. Kohs) A performance test of intelligence in which multicolored cubical blocks are arranged by the subject to form designs, the patterns of which are the same as those appearing on presented cards. It is part of the Arthur Performance Scale.

test, Kuhlmann-Anderson (F. Kuhlmann and R. G. Anderson) A series of test batteries designed to measure general intelligence from kindergarten to adulthood.

test, Kuhlmann-Binet (F. Kuhlmann and A. Binet) Binet intelligence tests which have been revised for the purpose of administration for the U.S.A. population.

test, Kwint Psychomotor An inventory of psychomotor activities based on age, and designed for use with brain-damaged children.

test, Leiter International Performance (R. G. Leiter) A series of nonverbal intelligence tests consisting of picture completion tasks, number series, concealed figures and various wooden blocks which are to be matched by the subject according to colors, pictures and forms. The test is designed to be culture-free.

test, literacy A test measuring the ability to read or write.

test, MacQuarrie, for Mechanical Ability (T. W. MacQuarrie) A paper-and-pencil test, which includes such tasks as the tracing of a line through a series of broken lines, an assessment of tapping, block analysis, and counting and pursuit. It is heavily weighted for skills in eye-hand coordination and spatial relations.

test, Maddox Rod (E. E. Maddox) A test of muscular imbalance of the eyes. It uses one or more parallel glass rods fitted in an opaque disk. The rod or rods are held in front of one eye at a time through which the eye perceives a candle flame which is converted by the rod into a line of light. The differential images perceived by the two eyes reflect the degree of heterophogia.

test, make-a-picture-story (E. S. Schneidman) A projective technique designed in 1947 which consists of twenty-two background pictures and sixty-seven separate figures of people of different ages and occupations. The subject is required to choose people for each scene and to make up a story about it. The choice of people, their location, and the story are interpreted to provide information about conflicts, interpersonal relations and self-image.

test, manikin (R. Pintner and D. Paterson) One of the subtests in the Pintner-Paterson Scale of Performance Tests introduced in 1917. It consists of pieces of a man, wooden legs, arms, head and body, which the subject must put together to make a man. The score depends on the quality of the performance.

test, matching A test which requires the subject to choose items from one list and match them with items from a second list according to prescribed criteria.

test, Meier Art Judgment (N. C. Meier) A test of aesthetic judgment introduced in 1940 for use with children in grades seven to twelve. It consists of one hundred pairs of uncolored pictures, one of which is a reproduction of a masterpiece and the other of which is altered in a way to make it inferior. The subject is asked to indicate his preference. His aesthetic judgment is considered to be an index of his artistic capability and talent and to indicate his future success in the field of art.

test, memory-for-designs An instrument designed for use in the assessment of the organic consequences of brain injury. Fifteen geometric figures are presented, each for five seconds, and then removed, the patient then drawing each from memory. Scores from zero to four are assigned on the basis of configuration, Gestalt, reversal and rotation.

test, mental 1. The measurement of the presence, absence or degree of particular mental abilities. 2. An intelligence test.

test, Michigan Picture A projective test focusing on school difficulties.

test, Miller Analogies (W. S. Miller) A test designed in 1926 to predict scholastic ability at the graduate school level. It consists of one hundred mostly verbal analogies covering a wide variety of fields of specialization. The subject is asked to determine analogy relationships among words. The time limit is fifty minutes.

test, Minnesota Clerical Aptitude A test of clerical ability introduced in 1946 which consists of two subtests, numbers and names, each of which is made up of identical and nonidentical pairs which the subject has to detect. The tests are designed to measure perception of detail and perceptual speed.

test, Minnesota, for Aphasia (H. Schuell and J. J. Jenkins) A test for aphasia developed in 1961. It consists of a variety of linguistic tasks which require the subject to respond orally and in writing.

test, Minnesota Rate of Manipulation A test of the rapidity of movement in working at simple tasks with the hands and fingers. It consists of two parts. Part one requires the subject to place sixty blocks into sixty holes in a board. Part two requires the subject to pick up each block, turn it over, and replace it with the opposite hand. The score is the total time required to perform these tasks.

test, Minnesota Spatial Relations A test of mechanical aptitude introduced in 1930 which consists of a series of four boards, each of which has fifty-eight cutouts of different shapes. The subject is required to replace them in their correct places. The test is believed to measure speed and accuracy in the perception of details in mechanical and spatial relations.

test, Monroe Diagnostic Reading (M. Monroe) A test developed in 1930 to diagnose the factors which interfere with an individual's ability to read, exclusive of intelligence. The test consists of nine parts, some visual and some auditory, which deal with the sensory aspects and the mechanics of reading and writing and attempt to delineate the auditory and visual deficiencies. It is designed for children in grades one to five.

test, mosaic A projective instrument used with children two and over in the assessment of global personality traits. The test requires the choice of various ambiguous forms (circles, triangles, etc.) of five colors (red, yellow, blue, green, black and white), and organization of those forms into something the child wishes to make, using as many pieces as he likes. The child's method of procedure and finished product are analyzed in terms of choices of pieces and colors and the finished design.

test, multiple choice A type of test which requires the subject to choose the answer he thinks is the best answer or solution to a question or problem.

test, multiple response A test in which the testee is required to choose more than one of the given optional answers as correct.

test, number completion A test which requires the subject to complete a series of numbers according to an inherent rule, such as 4, 16, 64, _____.

test, object assembly 1. A test in which the subject must put together pieces or objects which have been disassembled. 2. Test which uses a jigsaw puzzle.

test, occupational A test designed to measure ability for a given occupation.

test of independence A test of the degree of agreement between actual and expected frequencies in a plot of two or more variables. Also called test for homogeneity.

test, omnibus A type of test in which different kinds of tasks or items are distributed throughout the test rather than being grouped together by kind as in battery tests. There is only one timing and one score for such a test.

test, one-tailed (statistics) A test of the null hypothesis which distributes the risk of rejecting the null hypothesis falsely in one tail of the sampling distribution obtained under the null hypothesis. The power is greater than the two-tailed test if the results obtained are in the direction anticipated by the experimenter. If not, the power is decreased.

test, opposites Test in which the subject is instructed to respond with the opposite of a stimulus word.

test, oral A test in which the testee is required to give his response orally.

test, Otis Quick Scoring Mental Ability (A. S. Otis) Three forms of group intelligence tests for different school levels: the Alpha test for grades 1-4, the Beta test for grades 4-9, and the Gamma test for grades 9-16. The tests contain a spiral mixture of verbal, spatial and numerical items and yield a single raw score which can be converted into age norms.

test, Otis Self-Administering, of Intelligence (A. S. Otis) Verbal intelligence test consisting of two forms: intermediate examination for grades 4-9 and higher examination for grades 9-16. The test may be used as a group or an individual test, has self-contained items, and is easy to administer and to score.

test, paired hands, of friendliness A projective instrument used in the assessment of children's social relatedness. Slides of two hands, one white and one black, are projected in various positions and the child chooses answers from a multiple-choice answer sheet.

test, paper and pencil Test in which answers must be written.

test, Peabody Picture Vocabulary A decoding or receptive vocabulary test in which the child is required to understand the words spoken by the examiner and to select which of the four pictures is most related to the word. The test is untimed and takes about ten minutes to administer. Norms are available for ages two to eighteen.

test, performance A test which requires nonverbal responses rather than verbal. Such tests minimize the role of language and often involve concrete materials, such as blocks, form boards, etc.

test, Pickford Projective Pictures (R. W. Pickford) A projective instrument used for children ages five to fifteen consisting of 120 ambiguous line drawings of people in a variety of situations. It is designed to serve as a cathartic experience for the child as well as a means of understanding the child's dynamics. The recurrent themes in the large number of stories reflect the child's worries and preoccupations.

test, picture arrangement (S. S. Tomkins) A projective test introduced in 1957 which consists of a set of twenty-five plates, each having three drawings depicting the activities of a person. The subject is required to arrange the drawings in sequence and to tell a story about what is happening. The sequences and the stories are interpreted in terms of quantitative and qualitative criteria respectively. There are norms for the sequences of normal and abnormal subjects.

test, picture completion Performance type intelligence test in which the subject is required to find the missing part or parts in a drawing or group of drawings of animals or objects.

test, picture impressions A projective instrument used with adolescents and adults, specifically designed to study the patient's expectations regarding the therapist. The four pictures have drawings of a person in a short white laboratory coat.

test, picture interpretation Intelligence test in which the subject must interpret what a picture is about. The subject's response is then assessed. Enumeration is considered a lower response than description which is less advanced than an interpretive response.

test, picture world A projective instrument, used with children six and over, consisting of unambiguous and reality-oriented scenes about which the child writes his own story, adding additional objects and figures from a list of thirty-six if he wishes so. The child is instructed to make up a world that is as he sees it or as he would like it to be.

test, placement Test designed to determine the most appropriate class or course of studies for individual students based on their abilities, achievements and interests.

test, Porteus Maze (G. Arthur) A performance test in the Arthur Point Scale of Performance Tests introduced in 1933 and revised in 1943. It consists of a set of mazes of increasing difficulty, each found on a separate sheet. The subject is asked to trace each maze from beginning to end. The test is given to children five to fourteen years old for the assessment of intelligence.

test, power A test which is used to measure the level of achievement an individual can reach.

test, power of See *power function.*

test, profile An instrument which yields several separate measures of different variables resulting in a picture, or profile of the individual's characteristics across several areas.

test, prognostic An instrument which is designed so as to enable the prediction of the possible degree of achievement of a certain skill under specified conditions.

test, progressive matrices (J. C. Raven) A nonverbal scale of mental ability used in evaluating the individual's ability to apprehend relationships between geometric figures and designs, to perceive the structure of the matrix and of the figure (part) necessary to complete each system of relations (the matrix) presented. The test evaluates the individual's ability to discern and utilize a logical relationship, requiring analytical and integrating operations. There are several sets of the scales: one is for children six and over and adults, and one is for use with the highest quarter of intelligence.

test, proverb An instrument which requires the subject to explain the meaning of proverbs.

test, psychological See *examination, psychological.*

test, rate A test of many items of comparable difficulty which is taken within a certain proscribed time limit, the testee being required to finish as many items as possible with no expectation that all the items will be completed. The score is the total of all the correct responses.

test, Raven's Controlled Projection (J. C. Raven) A projective technique used in the assessment of social attitudes, habits and personal relationships in children ages six to twelve. The child is asked to draw whatever occurs to him and simultaneously relate a story about an imaginary child. The examiner provides the framework of the story and the child provides the details in response to eleven questions about preferences, fears, fantasies, feelings and parents.

test, remote association A test of creativity developed by S. A. Mednick in 1962 which requires the person to provide a word which links three ostensibly unrelated words. Correct responses are determined according to the criteria of remoteness and usefulness.

test-retest coefficient The correlation coefficient between the two administrations of the same test or of comparable forms of the same test.

test, role construct repertory (G. Kelly) A test developed in 1955, which determines the dimensions along which people classify other people.

test, Rorschach Inkblots (H. Rorschach) A projective test consisting of ten cards on which either black and white, black and white with color, or colored asymmetrical inkblots appear. The subject is presented the cards in a prescribed sequence and requested to tell the examiner what the inkblots could be. Responses are scored according to the various determinants used in a particular response and are indicative of the particular cognitive style and defensive patterns characterizing the individual's personality structure as a whole.

test, Rosenzweig Picture-Frustration (S. Rosenzweig) A projective instrument used with children and adults that is useful for sampling reactions to frustration and for determining whether aggression is directed inwardly or externally. The pictures are highly structured scenes of interpersonal frustration events such as the destruction of a treasured object. The scoring system is relatively objective.

test, Sargent Insight (H. D. Sargent) A projective instrument which combines sentence completion technique with thematic technique. A series of cartoon-like pictures are presented and a story is begun for the child. The themes covered deal with problem solving in relation to parents, other adults, children, school failure, loss of a loved one, illness, and concepts of time and distance. Scoring focuses on expressions of affect, defenses against affect, and thought processes which are indicative of maladjustment.

test, scaled A test in which the questions are arranged in order of increasing difficulty.

test scaling See *scaling, test.*

test, scholastic achievement Test which measures the testee's knowledge and ability within a certain area of study, such as literature, mathematics, french, chemistry, etc.

test, scholastic aptitude A combination of verbal and mathematical tests used to select candidates for college admission.

test, school and college ability A group of test batteries consisting of a sentence completion, vocabulary, calculation, and quantitative reasoning subtest, each of which is designed to assess the person's capacity to master educational requirements at the next level.

test, seashore musical ability A series of tests consisting of recorded tasks of pitch and loudness discrimination, tonal memory, rhythm, time and timbre, used for the identification of an individual's relative musical ability.

test, selective answer A test in which questions are presented along with several alternative answers from which the testee must choose the one that is correct, e.g. a multiple choice test.

test, self-administering A test in which the instructions for completion are given directly and clearly in order that the subject can easily follow them without further assistance.

test, self-marking A test which is designed in such a way that the subject's answers are recorded as right or wrong automatically.

test, semantic differential A paper-and-pencil test which provides the subject with a series of pairs of opposite adjectives, such as "rough-smooth," "active-passive," and requires him to locate himself (or any other person) on the continuum between each of the adjective pairs. The resulting semantic spaces can be defined statistically; adjectives that are associatively similar are identified and their psychological distance from other adjectives is determined.

test of sensorimotor functions Instruments and techniques designed to assess the child's developmental status and progress in perceptual and motor behaviors. See *scale, Lincoln-Oseretsky Motor Development; scale, California infant, for Motor Development; Purdue Perceptual-Motor Survey; scale, Movigenic Movement.*

test, sentence repetition A test in which the subject is asked to repeat verbatim after the examiner a series of increasingly difficult sentences.

test, sequential (statistics) A test used to determine the point at which the addition of further data would not increase the obtained level of significance.

test, similarities A test in which the subject is required to state the similarity between two items or to arrange items according to their likeness.

test, situation A test which requires the subject to solve an artificial real life problem in order to assess his capability of doing so in a real life situation.

test sophistication The gain or change in a test score due to past familiarity with that test or type of test.

test, sorting 1. A test used to determine conceptualization by presenting a subject with a series of objects which he must categorize. 2. See *Q-sort.*

test, South African Picture Analysis A projective TAT-type instrument designed to measure the subject's relationship to God as well as to man. The stories given to pictures with both human and humanlike animals, are interpreted in an existential framework.

test, special-purpose A relatively brief test designed to measure either some single factor-dimension or some special combination of factors in a single score.

test, spontaneity (J. L. Moreno) A test in which an individual is placed in a life-like situation with people with whom he is emotionally involved or others who symbolize these people so that he can act out his feelings and practice new behaviors toward them.

test, SRA mechanical aptitude A test of mechanical aptitude which involves three subjects designed to assess mechanical information used in the names and uses of tools, form perception and spatial visualization, and the solution of problems using shop arithmetic.

test, standardized A test which is compiled empirically, has definite directions for administration and use, has adequate norms, and has data on reliability and validity.

test, Stanford Achievement A test designed for use in measuring a pupil's progress in paragraph meaning, word meaning and grammatical usage.

test, stilling A test which is composed of a chart of many dots of various hues, saturations, and intensities. The charts are used in the detection of color weakness as the dots are arranged to form numbers which are visible to the naked eye but not to the eye with color weakness.

test, story recall A test involving the subject's ability to recall and reproduce details of a story which has been presented to him.

test, Stroop (J. R. Stroop) A test developed in 1935 designed to measure an individual's degree of cognitive control. It consists of a series of colored cards on which names of colors other than the color of the cards are printed. The individual is asked to name the color of the card rather than to read the name written. The degree to which individuals are subject to the interference of the printed words is the measure of cognitive control.

test, subjective Any test which cannot and does not employ any objective criteria for scoring purposes.

test, survey Tests to investigate and study the level and status of a whole group and class.

test, symbol arrangement (T. C. Kahn) A projective test developed in 1955 which consists of sixteen plastic geometric shapes, such as hearts, dogs, anchors, crosses. The subject is asked to group the objects into rectangles designated as "love," "hate," "bad," "good," "living," "dead," "small," and "large" on a piece of felt which is divided into fifteen numbered parts. He is asked to free associate to the meaning of each object. A scoring system is available which purports to yield information about the subject's unconscious process of symbolization.

test, symbol digit See *test, code.*

test, symbol elaboration A projective technique used with children ages six and over in which the child is provided with eleven stimulus patterns and asked to elaborate them by drawing.

test, symbol substitution See *test, code.*

test, Symonds Picture-Study (P. M. Symonds) A projective technique, designed for use with adolescents, which closely parallels the TAT although the figures in the pictures are more youthful and the pictures more depressive in tone. The subject tells a story to each of the pictures which include a large number of situations and interpersonal relationships. The stories are then analyzed in terms of such themes as family relationships, aggression, economic concern, punishment and separation.

test, synonym-antonym A test requiring the subject to indicate whether pairs of words which are presented are the same or opposite in meaning.

test, Szondi (L. Szondi) A projective test developed in 1947 in Hungary and introduced in the United States in 1949. It consists of forty-eight cards, which are divided into six sets. The cards have portraits of faces of mental patients on them representing the categories of homosexuality, sadism, epilepsy, hysteria, catatonic schizophrenia, paranoid schizophrenia, depression and mania. Each set of cards has one card representing a category. The subject is asked to choose two cards which he likes best and two which he least likes in each set. The distribution of chosen cards is interpreted in terms of which categories the subject identifies with and which traits he rejects.

test, t (statistics) The ratio of a statistic or its standard error used especially when the number of cases in the sample is small. The statistical significance of *t* is dependent on its size and the number of degrees of freedom, or the number of observations minus the number of independent restrictions placed on the sample. A common use of this test is the determination of the significance of the differences between two means.

test tapping See *test dotting.*

test, Temple-Darley (M. C. Temple and F. L. Darley) A test of articulation developed in 1960 which has standardized stimulus pictures, words and administrative procedures.

test, Terman-McNemar, of Mental Ability (L. M. Terman and Q. McNemar) A group administered verbal scale of mental ability which is designed for use with grades seven through twelve, with norms provided for ages ten through nineteen years eleven months. There are seven subjects, including information, synonyms, logical selection, classification, analogies, opposites and best answer.

test, thematic Any test in which a person is asked to tell a story.

test, thematic apperception (C. D. Morgan and H. A. Murray) A projective test introduced in 1935 consisting of thirty pictures plus one blank card which are used in combinations depending on the sex and age of the subject. The subject is told that the test is one of imagination without right and wrong answers. He is asked to make up a story for each picture which has a beginning describing what has led up to the depicted scene, a middle giving an account of what is occurring in the picture and the feelings of the characters involved, and an end telling what the outcome will be. There is no time limit in this test. The stories should be recorded verbatim. Following the testing procedure, the tester may conduct an interview to obtain more specific information about the given stories for diagnostic purposes.

test, Thompson Thematic Apperception (C. E. Thompson) A projective test developed in 1949 based on the Thematic Apperception Test. The test consists of pictures of Negro figures in various combinations and situations. The subject is asked to tell a story about each picture which is interpreted in terms of formal structure and content.

test, true-false A form of test in which the subject is presented with certain statements and is required to check whether each statement is true or false. The test may consist of statements concerning a certain area of study or general statements that concern the individual.

test, Twitchell-Allen Three-Dimensional Personality (A. Twitchell-Allen) A projective technique used with children consisting of a set of twenty-eight ceramic figures, relatively culture-free and free-form and of neutral color, laid out in a predetermined order in front of the child. The child tells three stories and names each piece, two stories being told to pieces he selects and arranges and one being told to three standard pieces selected and arranged by the examiner. The examiner records verbal associations, stories and expressive motor behavior such as gestures, facial expressions and movements. The several recommended scoring procedures include the naming test in which the child's responses are categorized as to content, determinants, form quality and originality, as in Rorschach scoring; a psychodynamic approach in which stories are analyzed in terms of themes such as sexual, relationship to authority, and struggle between independence and dependence; and an analysis of verbal form and content, taking into account the number of words, parts of speech, and number of different persons in the story. The test is one of the few standardized projective techniques that can be used with visually handicapped children.

test, two-tailed (statistics) A nondirectional test of the null hypothesis in which the risk of rejecting the null hypothesis falsely is distributed equally in the two tails of the sampling distribution obtained under the null hypothesis. This test has the greatest power unless it is known that the data implies directionality.

test, U (statistics) A nonparametric test used to determine the significance of the differences between means for unmatched groups.

test value A temporary value determined by a few observations which is used to limit the variability of an experimental variable.

test, vector (statistics) The representation of a test by a vector or straight line.

test, verbal 1. Any test which is constructed so as to require verbal ability to perform the tasks. 2. Any test which measures general verbal ability.

test, Vigotsky (L. S. Vigotsky) A test of concept formation in which the subject is required to sort blocks of different sizes, shapes and colors.

test, visual apperception A projective technique designed for use with subjects twelve years of age and over. The subject is presented with twelve plates consisting of lines randomly drawn under controlled conditions and is asked to color in whatever object or pattern he sees in the doodles and title the finished drawing.

test, visual-motor Gestalt See *test, Bender Visual-Motor Gestalt*

test, vocabulary A test which is designed so as to assess the skill a person has in using and understanding words.

test, Weigl-Goldstein-Scheerer (E. Weigl, K. Goldstein and M. Scheerer) A test of concept formation introduced in 1941 which requires the subject to sort a variety of geometric figures according to color and form and to shift from one category to another. The subject must also verbalize his act to allow for discrimination of concrete from abstract behavior.

test, Wepman, of Auditory Discrimination (G. P. Wepman) An individually administered examination that requires five to ten minutes to administer and, attempts to determine whether or not auditory discrimination deficits are present. The subject is required to determine whether two words pronounced by the examiner are alike or different.

test, whisper A crude form of hearing test in which the subject, standing with one ear plugged twenty feet from the examiner who pronounces test words in a distinct whisper, tries to hear the words without looking at the examiner's lips.

test, wiggly block A test of manual dexterity requiring the subject to reassemble nine blocks cut by wavy lines from a rectangular block.

test-wise A term used to describe a person who, having taken a number of tests, will tend to be relatively less naive and have more of an advantage over a person who has not taken a lot of tests.

test, word association 1. A projective technique consisting of a list of words which is presented to the subject one at a time. The subject is asked to respond with the first word which comes to his mind. The verbal responses, and non-verbal reactions are recorded. This test is used to assess general adjustment and neuroticism. 2. (C. G. Jung) A test designed for the detection of "complexes" which was developed in 1906. It consists of one hundred words which represent the common emotional "complexes." The verbal content and non-verbal responses are interpreted. 3. (G. H. Kent and A. J. Rosanoff) A test consisting of one hundred words designed in 1910 for the purpose of differentiating between normal and mentally ill people. Standardized norms are available for common and uncommon responses which are believed to differentiate normal from abnormal individuals. This is not always true. 4. (D. Rapaport, et al.) A test developed in 1946 consisting of a list of words designed to provide clinical information concerning the degree of maladjustment and impairment of thought organization. Many of the stimulus words elicit responses involving psychosexual matters.

test, word-building A test requiring the subject to construct as many words as possible out of a given number of letters.

test, work-limit A kind of test in which each subject performs the same task, the differences between them dependent upon the time required.

test, X-O (S. Pressley) A test which pioneered in the area of attitudes and interests. The subject either crosses out or circles certain preferences.

testability Characterizing propositions or statements which can be tested for truth.

testing The administration of a test or tests.

testing-of-limits A special type of structured Rorschach inquiry suggested by B. Klopfer, and usually involving suggestions to a subject concerning certain percepts or characteristics of percepts not mentioned by the subject but ordinarily seen by most subjects. If, after direct suggestion, the subject still maintains no awareness of the percepts in question, the examiner may use a more direct form of suggestion so as to ascertain the extent to which the subject is able to see popular or conventional concepts. Testing-of-limits ordinarily occurs only after the formal inquiry has been completed.

testis One of the ball-shaped organs located in the scrotum, and constituting the vertebrate male sex glands.

testosterone One of the male sex hormones.

tests, battery of 1. A group or series of related tests that are administered at one time. 2. A group or series of tests which, when combined, yield a single score.

tests, Benton Visual Retention (A. L. Benton) Ten geometric designs are exposed to a child, each for ten seconds, then removed while the child draws the design. The test measures visual perception, immediate memory and psychomotor reproduction. Used with children eight years of age and over; useful in the detection of severe brain damage in older children.

tests, California Achievement (L. P. Thorpe and W. W. Clark) Four batteries of tests, including primary, elementary, intermediate and advanced (running from grade 1 to grade 13), covering the same general areas of reading vocabulary, arithmetic reasoning, reading comprehension, arithmetic fundamentals, spelling, and mechanics of English and grammar, although content and difficulty change with increasing levels. Except for spelling, each test is divided into subtests that are seen as parts of the larger area of school learning; widely different subtest scores are seen as significant for diagnostic purposes.

tests, California, of Mental Maturity (L. P. Thorpe and W. W. Clark) Scales arranged on five levels all testing the same factors, such as memory and logical reasoning with the content of each scale adapted to the appropriate level of form and difficulty. At the earliest levels there is an emphasis on nonverbal materials, with increasing use of word knowledge, number concepts and complex nonverbal material at higher levels.

tests, California, of Personality (L. P. Thorpe, W. W. Clark and E. W. Tiegs) A set of five scales introduced in 1953, the primary, elementary, intermediate, secondary and adult, which assess the principal sources of an individual's problems. The questions of the test determine the presence of traits in two categories: personal adjustment and social adjustment. Personal adjustment consists of feelings of self-reliance, personal worth, personal freedom, and belonging, withdrawing tendencies and nervous symptoms. Social adjustment refers to social standards, social skills, anti-social tendencies, family relations, school relations, occupation relations and community relations.

tests, clerical Usually a battery of tests, which includes tasks such as filing, checking, simple bookkeeping, routine mathematical operations, and sometimes stenography and machine calculation.

tests, concept formation 1. Methods of studying how people form concepts and levels of concept formation. 2. See *test, Weigl-Goldstein-Scheerer.* 3. See *test, Vigotsky.*

tests, cumulative Tests which measure traits and abilities which increase with age. Scoring is established on a minimally inferential level, usually establishing a criterion and determining a person's score deviation from the criterion.

tests, Gates-MacGinitie Reading A series of reading tests designed to assess vocabulary, comprehension, speed and accuracy in reading at the primary levels.

tests, Goldstein-Scheerer (K. Goldstein and M. Scheerer) Five tests designed in 1941 to assess abstracting ability and the capacity to form concepts in abnormal subjects. There is no standardization data or norms available. The tests are used as qualitative measures of the presence of organic disorders. The five tests consist of the following: 1) Goldstein-Scheerer cube test—seeks to determine the subject's ability to copy designs which are constructed with superimposed lines to help the subject who has previously failed to analyze the design. 2) Gelb-Goldstein color sorting test—assesses the subject's ability to sort woolen skeins according to color. 3) and 4) Gelb-Goldstein—Weigl—Scheerer object sorting test and the Weigl-Goldstein-Scheerer color-form sorting test—determine the subject's ability to sort objects according to color, form, and material and to shift from one category to another. 5) Goldstein-Scheerer stick test—requires the subject to reproduce a series of figure designs from memory by means of sticks.

tests, Iowa, of Basic Skills A battery of educational achievement tests which provides scores on reading, vocabulary, language, arithmetic and work-study skills. There are norms for each grade at the beginning, middle and end of the year. The measured skills are all assessed in sections that become increasingly more difficult with some overlap between grades.

tests, Metropolitan Achievement An instrument used in the assessment of achievement levels for grades 1-2, 3-4, 5-6, 7-8. At the elementary level the test provides in three hours of testing, nine scores assessing vocabulary, reading and arithmetic skills and language usage. Tests of social studies, science and study skills are included at the higher levels.

tests, nonverbal Tests which do not utilize verbal material for presentation or solution of the problem. They are also known as performance tests.

tests, paired-choice Personality tests which consist of paired items and require the subject to choose which of the statements most applies to him or to a situation.

tests, personality Any test or technique used to evaluate personality or to rate personality characteristics or personal traits.

tests, Pintner-Paterson scale of performance (R. Pintner and D. Paterson) A group of fifteen performance tests designed for the evaluation of mental ability in persons having serious hearing and speech defects and for non-English speaking individuals, introduced in 1917. The age range of this scale is four to fifteen years although this does not apply to all of the subtests. Three different scoring methods may be used: median mental age, point score, and percentile rank. This scale does not measure the same abilities as verbal tests and should be used to supplement the latter.

tests, psychomotor Tests of motor skill in which

the score is dependent upon a certain degree of precise coordination of a sensory process and a motor activity.

tests, sentence completion 1. Projective tests which consist of a series of sentence stems of one or more words which the subject is asked to furnish. They are believed to reflect attitudes, motives and conflicts. The first was developed by A.D.A. Teadler in 1930 which was modified by A. R. Rohde in 1946. 2. See *Rotter Incomplete Sentence Blank.* 3. See *test, Forer Structured Sentence Completion.*

tests, timed A test which has time limits.

tests, vocational aptitude A test which is constructed to measure and evaluate potential achievement in a specific profession through the assessment of ability, personality traits and interests.

tetanoid epilepsy See *epilepsy, tetanoid.*

tetanus 1. A state of continuous muscle contraction. 2. An infectious disease characterized by tetanus.

tetany A pathological condition or disease which is characterized by the presence of intermittent tetanus, particularly of the extremities.

tetartanopia Partial blindness which affects one fourth of the field of vision.

tetrachoric correlation See *correlation, tetrachoric.*

tetrachromatism The theory that there are receptors in the eye for four colors.

tetrad difference equation See *equation, tetrad difference.*

texture gradient Characterizes the perceived increase in density and loss of the separateness of the perceptual field elements with increasing distance from the eye.

texture response A type of Rorschach response in which the chiaroscuro (light-dark) features of the blot convey the impression of tactuality to the subject, whose response becomes determined, at least in part, by this impression. Texture responses are generally interpreted as representing deprivation of the more infantile erotic needs.

thalamic theory of the emotions (W. B. Cannon and P. Bard) A theory stressing the role of the hypothalamus in the emotions. The theory holds that emotion provoking stimuli give rise to impulses stimulating the hypothalamus in turn activating the cortex and the visceral processes, the cortical activity arousing the emotional experience and the visceral activity preparing the individual for activity.

thalamotomy A rarely used procedure in the treatment of depressive states in which there is a bilateral destruction of the medial thalamic nuclei.

thalamus Mass of gray matter consisting of numerous nuclei in the diencephalon which relays impulses from various sensory organs to the cortex.

thalamus, extrinsic Dorsal thalamic nuclei which function to relay incoming impulses from other mechanisms.

thalamus, intrinsic Dorsal thalamic nuclei which relay incoming impulses which originate within other thalamic nuclei.

thalassophobia A morbid fear of the sea.

thalidomide A drug used as a tranquilizer, sedative or hypnotic. When used during pregnancy it causes limb and brain damage to the fetus.

thanatophobia Fear of death.

Thanatos (S. Freud) A drive toward death. It is present in all organisms arising from the time when organic material developed from inorganic material. With the start of life the death instinct, Thanatos, was born, which aimed at the destruction of life and the re-establishment of inanimate nature. The life force, Eros, and the death force Thanatos, are inseparable. Eros seeks to bring organic material together into larger units whereas the death instinct seeks to disperse organic materials and return life to its original inorganic state. All masochism, sadism, hostility, destruction, violence, etc., are thought to be an expression of the death instinct.

thanatotic (K. Eissler) A term describing a person who manifests the death instinct.

thema (H. A. Murray) A molar behavioral unit consisting of the interaction between press, the instigating situation, and the operating need.

thematic apperception test See *test, thematic apperception.*

thematic test See *test, thematic.*

theme, mythological (C. G. Jung) The themes revealed in a people's myths are seen as derived from themes that are present in the collective unconscious.

theomania The delusion that one is God.

theophobia The pathological fear of God.

theorem A scientific proposition, statement or premise, expressed in scientific terms, symbols or mathematical equation.

theorem of intellectual unity and hierarchy of specific intelligences (C. Spearman) A certain proportion of the variance in any intellectual task can be accounted for by a factor of "general intelligence" (g). However, there are elements to each intellectual task which are common to the specific task and not common to all the tasks.

theoretical type See *type, theoretical.*

theory Any scientific system is comprised of empirical data derived from observation and/or experimentation, and of their interpretation. The set of statements of propositions explaining factual data is called theory. Some scientists start with empirical data while others pose several theoretical statements and deduce from them the empirical laws. Whichever way scientists proceed, a theory is a system of hypothetical statements concerning a certain area of scientific inquiry.

theory, crisis (G. Caplan, et al.) The idea that particular stages of development are crisis periods during which the individual is susceptible to change. During these times the person may progress or regress. Intervention at these times consists of aiding the individual to progress.

theory, drive-reduction 1. The proposition that all motivated behavior rises out of drives or needs and the responses which satisfy those drives or needs tend to be strengthened or reinforced. 2. The proposition that all motivation is based on the reduction of a drive, need for drive stimulus and the responses which tend to reduce the drive.

theory, duplicity The proposition, now established as fact, that there are separate receptors for color vision (cones) and brightness vision (rods). Cones are primarily sensitive to differences in wave length and rods are primarily sensitive to intensity of light waves.

theory, interpersonal (H. S. Sullivan) The belief that personality development is solely the result of interpersonal experiences and situations and can only be observed and studied as it is manifested in such situations. Sullivan postulated that satisfaction and security are the two basic goals of human activity, satisfaction resulting from the fulfillment of bodily needs and security from the feeling of well-being derived from acceptance and love by significant others in the environment. Both needs are present at birth and patterns of comfort and frustration are first established through the infant's and mother's interrelations. The individual's unique patterns of interrelations are called dynamisms, the most important of which is the self-dynamism or self-system, which is formed early by the experience of anxiety. Gradually the infant learns which behaviors, thoughts and actions serve to avoid destruction of the euphoric feeling of satisfaction and security and evoke love and approval from the mother, and which do not. The resulting pattern of protective behaviors and controls form the self-system, which continues to be modified in later life by various threats to one's security. Associated with behavior resulting in satisfaction and security is the individual's perception of himself as "good-me". Associated with forthcoming anxiety is the self perception of "bad-me". When the child's interactions result in intense anxiety his perception of himself as perpetrator is dissociated and becomes "not-me". Sullivan terms these perceptions personifications and states that they also exist in reference to others, for example, the caring, loving mother is "good mother", while the mother in situations associated with the child's anxiety is "bad mother". Sullivan was also concerned with the relation of cognitive processes to personality. He distinguished three modes of cognitive experience: the prototaxic, consisting of sensations, images and feelings found in its purest form in infancy, the parataxic, the next to develop, consisting of the ability to see causal relationships between events occurring close in time but not being logically related, and the syntaxic, the highest and most uncommonly experienced mode of thinking, consisting of consensually validated symbol activity particularly of a verbal nature which produces logical order among experiences. Any of these may be the mode of experience in a given situation depending on the particular interpersonal relationship involved.

theory, irradiation 1. The theory, based on the application of irradiation phenomena to learning, that learning consists of the selective reinforcement of one of many occurring responses. 2. (I. P. Pavlov) The spread of excitation or inhibition in nerve centers.

theory of knowledge See *epistemology.*

theory of the ideal observer See *ideal observer.*

theory, quantum See *quantum theory.*

theory, sampling See *sampling theory.*

theory, signal detection See *signal detection theory.*

therapeutic community (M. Jones) A plan for the transformation of the traditional custodian type mental hospitals into centers of incessant therapeutic activity. According to Jones' idea, the entire time a patient spends in a mental hospital must be utilized for therapeutic purposes. Even the architecture of the hospital, its furniture, daily routines, diet, entertainment, etc. must form a part of an overall therapeutic program.

therapeutic milieu A therapeutic setting for mental patients in which all personnel are trained in interpersonal and therapeutic techniques and in which the patients take responsibility to help each other. Frequent patient-staff group meetings are held in order to facilitate interpersonal communication.

therapist One who is trained in and skilled at the use of techniques for the treatment of various disorders.

therapy 1. Activities undertaken to cure diseases and to ameliorate suffering, e.g. psychotherapy, chemotherapy. 2. The curative effects of such activities.

therapy, active See *psychotherapy, activity group.*

therapy, activity group See *psychotherapy, activity group.*

therapy, adjuvant or adjunctive Supplementary or contributory techniques used in psychotherapy such as occupational therapy. Often used synonymously with adjunctive psychotherapy.

therapy, analytic See *psychotherapy, psychoanalytic.*

therapy, art Participation in the arts such as dance, music, painting and sculpture used as a therapeutic method to offer the patient opportunities for sublimation, outlets to distance himself from his problems and occasions to increase his self-esteem through achievement.

therapy, aversion A behavior therapy technique in which an undesired response such as pleasurable emotion to a fetishistic object is inhibited by the evocation of an incompatible response to which the person reacts with avoidance. Stimuli to such responses are either physical, e.g. electrical shock or noxious odors, or conditioned, e.g. the evocation of nausea by suggested images (covert sensitization). See *reciprocal inhibition.*

therapy, crisis Therapy provided on a "drop-in" emergency basis.

therapy, directive group See *psychotherapy, directive group.*

therapy, expressive Therapy which encourages the individual to express feelings without inhibitions and to talk openly about personal problems.

therapy, insight Form of psychotherapy which focuses on the uncovering of the deep causes of the patient's conflicts, and the adjustment or removal of the defenses against this insight. This type of therapy aims at helping the patient toward greater self-understanding and utilization of his resources.

therapy, interpersonal See *psychotherapy, interpersonal.*

therapy, interpretive Psychotherapy focused on the patient's verbal expression of conflicts and their symbolic meaning with the belief that the process will teach the patient to eventually solve his problems alone.

therapy, occupational The treatment of mental or physical disorders by giving the patient useful or interesting work to do. The intention is usually to exercise particular muscles and to improve the individual's mental outlook.

therapy, physical See *physiotherapy.*

therapy, physiological Therapeutic techniques including electroconvulsive shock treatment and drug therapy.

therapy, placebo Any treatment or therapy which has an affect on the patient's symptoms, disease or psychological state because it reinforces the patient's expectations though it does not really act on the individual's condition.

therapy, play See *psychotherapy, play.*

therapy, reality (W. Glasser) A method of treatment in which the therapist plays an active role and the patient is held responsible for his behavior. It is theorized that a person will act the right way if he has fulfilled two basic needs, the need for feelings of self-worth and respect and love for others. Fulfillment of these needs is a sign of responsibility. The therapist focuses on helping the patient do better and be more responsible. It is the patient's responsibility however to change his behavior.

therapy, recreational A kind of therapy in which the patient is encouraged to participate in some form of play or recreation in order to enjoy it for its own sake.

therapy, regressive electroshock Electroshock treatment in which the patient is given a shock resulting in a short convulsive period and then, through the use of mild electrical current, is maintained in a sleep-like state.

therapy, relaxation A kind of therapy in which there is an emphasis on teaching the patient how to relax in the belief that muscular relaxation and lack of tension will promote the decrease of psychological distress and tension.

therapy, release (D. Levy) A short-term child therapy concerned with specific symptoms resulting from a traumatic event. It consists of the expression of the traumatic situation which caused the symptoms through play, allowing the child to master his repressed emotions. This type of therapy is believed to be a good prophylactic technique to avert the consolidation of neurotic responses to traumatic situations.

therapy, religious Psychotherapeutic help obtained in various aspects of the church such as the confessional which offers a verbal catharsis, pastoral counseling, and participation in church sponsored activities.

therapy, role (G. A. Kelly) A form of therapy in which the focus is on helping the client reformulate his constructs or form new ones as a prelude to initiating new modes of action. The relationship of the therapist with the client is a cognitive one. The emphasis is on the present.

therapy, spontaneity (J. L. Moreno) Psychodrama and sociodrama techniques designed to allow the person to act out his conflicts and to practice new behaviors which are more adaptable.

therapy, subshock Shock therapy in a mild degree.

therapy, supportive A type of therapy in which the therapist actively offers reassurance, suggestion, advice, and persuasion to help the person resolve his problems. The therapist attempts to foster a positive relationship and to utilize it to promote improvement. Adjunctive methods may be used, such as physical and/or occupational group, drug or hypnotherapy.

therapy, three-cornered See *psychotherapy, role-divided.*

thermal 1. Pertaining to heat. 2. Warm; hot.

thermal sensitivity The ability to discriminate temperature.

thermalgia Sensation of burning pain.

thermanaesthesia Loss of ability to discriminate heat or cold by touch.

thermestosiometer An instrument which measures the sensitivity to heat of different areas of the skin.

thermocouple A thermoelectric device used to measure differences in temperature.

thermohyperaesthesia Abnormal sensitivity to temperature stimuli.

thermohypesthesia Abnormal insensitivity or indifference to heat or contact with heated objects.

thermoneurosis An elevation of body temperature due to neurosis.

thermophobia Morbid fear of heat.

thermoreceptor Nerve structures (receptors) which are stimulated by temperature fluctuations.

thermotaxis 1. The regulation of body temperature. 2. The involuntary movement of an organism toward or away from heat.

thermotropism The involuntary movement of an organism or cells involving change or movement or growth toward or away from heat.

thesis 1. A proposition which is formally offered for proof or disproof. 2. A systematic treatise, generally dealing with one specific problem. 3. In American universities a treatise written in partial fulfillment for an advanced degree.

thinking 1. Cognitive behavior which uses symbols. 2. Representational or symbolic mental process. 3. Manipulation of concepts and precepts. 4. The train of ideas. 5. (J. Dewey) Problem solving activity involving primarily ideational activity. 6. (J. B. Watson) Subvocal or covert speech.

thinking, abstract Thinking which is characterized by the use of abstractions and generalizations.

thinking, associative A form of thinking based on the use of associative connections.

thinking, autistic (E. Bleuler) Thought processes which have meaning to the thinking individual himself; turning away from reality and seeing life in fantastic pictures.

thinking, conceptual, and brain processes Thinking on an abstract level which is dependent on the integrative processes of the cortex. Localization of this function in a specific area of the brain does not exist.

thinking, concrete (K. Goldstein) A form of thinking found especially in brain-injured individuals when the frontal lobes are impaired. Its characteristics include an inability to detach the ego from the inner or outer sphere of experience; an inability to assume or to shift a specific mental set; a confusion about spatial relationship; an inability to concentrate on two tasks simultaneously, to integrate parts into a whole or to analyze a totality; and an inability to judge, reflect about or plan for the future.

thinking, magical A form of developmentally primitive thinking seen in young children, psychotics and normal individuals under conditions of stress and fatigue characterized by primary process, animism, prelogical, and superstitious thought processes.

thinking, primary process Form of thought which is characterized by rules of primary process rather than secondary process. Such thinking reflects a tendency towards condensation and displacement. Fantasy or day-dreaming is a form of primary process thinking.

thinking type See *type, thinking.*

thiopental A barbiturate which is used intravenously as an anaesthetic in surgery and has been used to stimulate the release of repressed feelings.

thioridazine Mellaril; a tranquilizer used in the treatment of psychoses.

thombencephalon The hind brain.

Thompson, Clara (1893-1953) American psychiatrist and neo-psychoanalyst, follower of H. S. Sullivan School; historian of psychoanalysis.

Thompson Thematic Apperception Test See *test, Thompson Thematic Apperception.*

thorazine Common name for chlorpromazine.

Thorndike, Edward L. (1874-1949) Educational psychologist (Columbia Teachers' College), known for his 1) original work on trial-and-error learning in cats, 2) statement of the law of effect, 3) development of educational psychology and experimental education through authoritative textbooks based on the three problems of motivation, capacity, and learning, 4) construction of achievement and higher level intelligence tests, and 5) research on verbal learning.

Thorndike-Lorge list A 30,000 word list showing frequencies of English words based on written material such as books and magazines. Words which occur more than 100 times per million are designated AA and those which occur between 50 and 100 times per million as A. The book also includes lists of words occurring four times per 18,000,000 words. These lists are used in verbal and association learning in order to evaluate the results.

Thorndike's Handwriting Scale See *scale, Thorndike's Handwriting.*

Thorndike's trial and error learning (E. L. Thorndike) The theory that learning proceeds through neural connections between stimulus and response, a stimulus and response being connected when a response to a stimulus leads to a state of satisfaction or pleasure.

threctia (R. B. Cattell) The low-score pole of the Parmia-Threctia personality dimension, characterized by timidity, withdrawal, and susceptibility to threat.

three-component theory 1. See *trireceptor theory.* 2. See *trichromatic theory.*

threptic A conveniently brief term (borrowed by Cattell from Aristotle) for defining "the portion of a trait or a trait variance which is environmentally determined." Thus, *genetic* and *threptic* are complementary terms to be used in behavior genetics in reference to experimentally determinable quantities.

threshold, or limen (psychophysics) The minimum stimulus energy or energy change necessary for the experimental subject to indicate an awareness of the stimulus change. Stimulus energy values are usually determined several times for the same subject; the threshold is arrived at by one of several possible statistical treatments of the determined values. Thus the threshold value is statistical, and as such affected by several types of experimental errors as well as the changes within the physiology and nervous system of the subject himself. Thus, a threshold determination does not truly represent one absolute value, but rather a best guess from a range of possible values.

threshold, absolute (RL) The minimum intensity or frequency at which a stimulus will be perceived. See *differential threshold.*

threshold, arousal The minimum amount of stimulation necessary to produce arousal.

threshold, brightness The minimal intensity of a visual stimulus required to differentiate it as brighter than the surrounding or adjacent visual field.

threshold, difference The minimum difference between two stimuli that can be responded to as different under the given experimental conditions. Also referred to as the just noticeable difference and JND.

threshold, response Minimal value of a state variable that will evoke a response; the state variable is a conceptualization of all internal and external determinants of the response.

threshold, sensation See *threshold, absolute.*

threshold, stimulus The class of stimuli that occasion at a stated probability a defined response class, e.g. the threshold traditionally is the stimulus that has a 50% probability of occasioning the response.

thromboangitis obliterans A disease of the peripheral nerves, arteries, and veins with associated venous and arterial thrombosis, often leading to gangrene. It usually occurs in young and middle-aged males who are heavy smokers. Also called Buerger's disease.

thumb-sucking An early manipulation of the body, believed to serve as substitute erotic gratification and calming purposes generally seen only from birth to early childhood.

Thurstone Attitude Scale See *scale, Thurstone Attitude.*

Thurstone, Louis L. (1887-1955) Quantitative psychologist at Chicago who contributed substantially to the development of the theory of factor analysis, and undertook major factor analyses of human intelligence in a search for primary mental abilities. After he identified seven, he constructed tests to measure them in a more refined manner.

Thurstone's theory of primary mental abilities (L. L. Thurstone) The theory is based upon relationships which were found among tests of ability using multiple factor analysis. All of a number of tests correlated, indicating the presence of common factors of which he identified seven: verbal ability (V), the use and understanding of verbal concepts; spatial (S), the dealing with objects in space and the utilization of spatial relationships; reasoning (R), the apprehension and employment of abstract relationships in the solution of problems; word fluency (WF), thinking of words rapidly; number (N), the rapid and correct performance of fundamental mathematical opera-

tions; memory (M), learning and retaining information; perceptual (P), rapid and accurate object identification. Thurstone is in opposition to those which hold that there is a unitary ability involved in intelligence and holds that intelligence can be truly measured only by a measurement and percentile ranking of the seven primary abilities of the theory.

thwart Prevention of a consummatory response; one of three is usually used: 1. Withholding the stimulus for the response when the stimulus usually appears as the consequence of previous responses. 2. Mechanically preventing the response, e.g. by making rigid the response key in the Skinner box. 3. By placing the animal in a conflict situation.

thymergasia (A. Meyer) Pathological affective and emotional processes.

thymopathy General term for abnormal instability of the emotions.

thymus An organ located in the anterior superior mediastinum. It develops until the second year of life and atrophies after the age of fourteen.

thyroid dwarfism See *cretinism.*

thyroid gland One of two endocrine glands at the base of the neck which secretes thyroxin, a hormone which influences growth and development.

thyrotropic hormone Also TSH. A hormone secreted by the pituitary gland which stimulates the activity of the thyroid gland.

tic 1. An uncontrolled nervous twitch which is of neurogenic or psychological origin. The psychogenic component is a hysterical conversion symptom, whose origin is defensive or reflexive movements. 2. Any compulsive habit.

tic douloureux Facial neuralgia characterized by excruciating sharp pain.

time agnosia Loss of knowledge about or loss of ability to use time.

time and motion study The observation and analysis of movements in a task with an emphasis on the amount of time required to perform the task.

time-corrected P technique P technique in which lead-and-lag (staggered) correlations are carried out to maximize the correlations among variables.

time, d reaction A form of a choice reaction time experiment; the subject withholds the response until he has identified the stimulus.

time error A tendency to incorrectly judge objects dependent on their position in time; e.g. of two identical tones sounded in succession, the first will generally be judged louder.

time limit method A procedure in which the test score is arrived at by the totaling of all items done correctly within a certain time limit, the time limit being established so as to preclude all the tasks being completed.

time out (TO) (operant conditioning) Time, usually in minutes, during which behavior characteristically does not occur. With pigeons, TO is usually arranged by turning off all lights in the apparatus. With the rat, TO is usually arranged by previously established discriminative stimulus. TO's are used as markers in a series of events, as probes, as a method to eliminate proprioceptive stimulus effects of earlier behaviors, and recently as a form of aversive stimulation.

time perception   See *perception, time*.

time-sampling   Continuous behavior observations recorded by pre-established categories, made in successive time intervals, each of which is treated as an independent observation unit; interval may be of any appropriate duration; behavior measure is given in terms of number or proportion of intervals containing a given category. See *point-sampling*.

time score   See *score, time*.

timed tests   See *tests, timed*.

tinnitus   A condition characterized by ringing in the ears and other noises in the head caused by disturbances in the receptor mechanisms.

tissue   Any organismic structure which is composed of similar elements or cells having a common function.

Titchener, Edward Bradford (1867-1927)   British-born psychologist and systematist whose principal contributions were made in the United States. Studied at Oxford, and at Leipzig with Wundt; became professor of experimental psychology at Cornell (1892) where he remained for his entire academic life. Representing the Wundtian tradition with faithful dedication to the pursuit of the pure scientific psychology of the generalized normal adult mind, he became the leading protagonist of structural psychology in opposition to functionalism. Never became part of American psychology. Author of numerous books and articles including *Experimental Psychology: A Manual of Laboratory Practice* (1901-1905); *A Textbook of Psychology* (1909-1910), and *Systematic Psychology: Prolegomena*, a posthumous work (1929).

TO   See *time out*.

toilet training   Teaching children the socialized manner, time and place of urination and defecation.

tolerance of incongruity   The ability to consider incompatible ideas without anxiety and the use of defenses.

Tolman's purposive behaviorism   (E. C. Tolman) A system of psychology, rooted in behaviorism, which is a stimulus-response theory interpolated by the interpretation of non-observable factors. Observable factors are the initiating causes of behavior and the behavior itself. The former consists of five independent variables: 1) the environmental stimuli (S); 2) physiological drive (P); 3) heredity (H); 4) previous training (T); and 5) maturity or age (A). Behavior is a function of (f) the five, B=f(S,P,H,T,A). Environmental stimuli and physiological drive are releasing variables; heredity, previous training and age are guiding variables.

The theory holds that the organism actively looks for significant stimuli to plan his "map" and is not the passive receptor of physically present stimuli; behavior is purposive and cognitive. Behavior is not a sequence of causes and effects but a chain of goals and actions leading to the goal object. Behavior is determined by the goal-directed perceptions of the totality of the situation, or the sign-gestalt expectations, a combination of motivating and perceptual elements.

tonal bell   (C. E. Ruckmick) A bell-shaped model illustrating the interrelations among the tonal attributes—tonal brightness, volume and tonality.

tonal gap   A range of pitches to which an individual is insensitive or partially insensitive although he is sensitive to tones on either side.

tonal islands   A region of an individual's normal acuity for pitch or frequency that is surrounded by areas of insensitivity to tones.

tonal pencil   A diagrammatic scheme representing the relation of pitch to volume.

tonal scale   The range of frequencies audible to the normal human ear—20 to 20,000 cycles per second.

tonal volume   A tone's extensity or space-filling attribute.

tonality   1. (experimental psychology) The attribute of a pitch by which a tone sounds more closely related to its octave than to the tone adjacent to it in the scale. 2. (music) The relationships among a scale's tones and chords to the keynote or tonic.

tone   1. A sound whose physical stimulus or source is a periodic vibration or sound wave in an elastic medium. 2. A unit of measure of the musical interval. 3. An instrument's characteristic timbre. 4. See *tonus*. 5. A quality of the general level of background emotion or feeling.

tone, interruption   A tone produced by regular and rapid successive interruptions of a continuous and uniform tone, the pitch of which corresponds to the frequency of the interruptions.

tone, otogenic   A perceived tone which is stimulated by activity within the auditory mechanism rather than by external sound waves.

tone variator   A device used in the production of pure tones of variable pitch.

tongue apraxia   Lack of purposeful tongue movements.

tonic   1. Pertaining to tonus. 2. Characterized by a continuous state of muscular tension or contraction.

tonic contraction   The contraction of the groups of muscle maintaining muscular tonus.

tonic convulsion   See *convulsion, tonic*.

tonic epilepsy   See *epilepsy, tonic*.

tonic fits   See *cerebellar fits*.

tonic immobility   1. Total immobility occurring in some animals as a reaction to certain stimuli; death feigning. 2. Slight contraction of large muscle groups sufficient to cause tautness but not movement.

tonic reflex A continuous or immediately renewed tonus which is maintained by some specified stimulus condition.

tonicity Normal state of tension of any organ or muscle.

tonitrophobia Morbid fear of thunder.

tonoscope A mechanism used in converting sound waves to light and, through the stroboscopic effect, measuring changes in pitch.

tonus Slight degree of contraction normally occurring in muscles not in active movement. In skeletal muscles due to low frequency efferent impulses; an inherent property of smooth muscles.

tonus, induced Muscle tone caused by movement in another part of the body.

topalgia Pain localized in a certain spot.

topectomy A modification of the lobotomy in which small incisions are made in the frontal lobe and thalamus in an attempt to alleviate psychotic symptoms.

topographical theory (S. Freud) Division of the human mind in three layers or strata—conscious, preconscious, and subconscious.

topography, response (experimental) Full quantitative specification of all relevant, physically measurable dimensions of a response.

topological psychology See *psychology, topological.*

topology (mathematics) A part of geometry which investigates properties of a figure which remain unchanged under continuous transformation. These properties are non-quantitative, non-metrical, thus neither magnitudes nor distances count.

topophobia Morbid fear of places, especially open spaces such as streets.

torpor Total inactivity.

torticollis Spasmodic contraction of the muscles of the neck. Also called wryneck.

total correlation See *correlation, total.*

totem (anthropology) An animal, plant, or inanimate object which is venerated as the group's symbol, the symbol of the group's protective deity or the symbol of the spirit kin of the group.

totemism The use of symbolic objects to assure a degree of psychological safety.

touch spot An area of skin surface exceedingly sensitive to tactile stimuli.

touching (sensitivity training) The use of physical contact among the members of a sensitivity group toward the end of breaking down defenses and barriers to interpersonal communication.

toxemia Blood poisoning.

toxic-infectious psychosis See *psychosis, toxic-infectious.*

toxicity, corticosteroid Large doses of corticosteroids may produce symptoms ranging from mild personality change to psychosis and coma, and in some cases, even death.

toxicomania Addiction; craving to be poisoned.

toxicophobia Morbid fear of being poisoned.

toxin Poisonous product of vegetable or animal cells; organic poison.

toxoplasmosis, congenital A disease caused by infection by a parasitic protozoa, called toxoplasma. When contracted by a pregnant woman, it may cause encephalomyelitis and severe mental deficiency.

t-r systems Systematic organizations of stimulus schedules; the temporal parameters of these two systems subsume all stimulus schedules within a single descriptive framework, the traditional "contingent schedules of reinforcement" appearing as special or limiting cases of the system's parameters.

trace conditioned response A response resulting from the presentation of a conditioned stimulus followed by a blank interval and then by reinforcement.

trace, perseverative (C. L. Hull) A neural impulse which continues with diminishing strength for a short period following the cessation of the firing of a neuron.

tradition directed (D. Riesman) A term describing a person whose behavior is dictated by rules, rituals and relationships derived from past generations and modified only slightly by later generations.

train (experimental) To subject an animal to a series of procedures such that the animal behaves in a desired fashion.

training, spontaneity (J. L. Moreno) Training in acting more naturally and spontaneously in real-life situations by practicing these behaviors in a supporting environment.

trait 1. An inherited or acquired characteristic which is consistent, persistent and stable. 2. (G. W. Allport) A combination of motives and habits; it is a neuropsychic system that determines to a great extent which stimuli will be perceived (selective perception) and what kind of response will be given (selective action). Each individual's traits determine his behavior in a unique way.

trait dissection theory of environmental and genetic influence The model which does not divide a factorial source trait into genetic and threptic variance components but supposes that heredity and environment yield discernibly different factor trait patterns. These may appear as "eidolons," i.e. cooperative factor patterns not far from being mutual images.

trait organization The dynamic and cause and effect interrelationships among the various traits which compose the individual's personality.

trait profile A chart or diagram which depicts the relative standings of a number of traits as measured by tests or other instruments.

trait, recessive A genetically controlled trait which remains latent or subordinate to a dominant trait except in those cases in which both members of the gene pair are recessive.

trait, unique 1. A personality trait possessed by an individual, and not found exactly the same in other people. 2. (statistics) A trait which shows a zero correlation when compared to other traits being measured.

trait variability The spread, divergence or scatter exhibited by the individual on various trait measures.

trait view theory (R. B. Cattell) The theory that the distortion in the estimation of a trait level, either in another (rating) or in oneself (questionnaire response) is a piece of behavior to be predicted like any other from the individual's trait endowment and a behavioral equation specific to the rating or test-taking situation. This model enables one to estimate the true trait levels from the given rating or test levels.

trance 1. A sleeplike state which is characterized by a reduced sensitivity to stimuli and a loss or alteration of knowledge of what is happening. 2. The hypnotic state.

tranquilizer Any drug which has a sedative effect without inducing sleep.

tranquilizing treatments A therapeutic treatment consisting of the administration of drugs to calm or soothe patients.

transaction A psychological event or behavior in which all parts of the unit are understood through their interaction with the physical and social environment.

transactional analysis See *analysis, transactional.*

transactional theory of perception (A. Ames) A complex theory holding that our fundamental perceptions are learned reactions based on our interactions and transactions with the environment. On the basis of past experience, the individual builds up expectancies of what will be perceived and the individual brings them to new experiences and will make perceptions of those experiences conform to the expectancies.

transcendent function (C. G. Jung) A unifying mechanism within a person which aims to unite all of the opposing, divergent trends within the personality to form a perfect whole, if not at a conscious level, then at an unconscious one.

transection Section or cutting across the long axis of, e.g. a fiber, an axon, or the spinal cord.

transfer 1. The effect of either increasing or decreasing the strength of a response complex as a consequence of performing some other response. 2. The effect of a set of responses to one set of stimuli when the same set of responses are made to a different set of stimuli.

transfer of training (educational psychology) A theory which maintains that a proficiency acquired in a branch of knowledge or a skill helps in the acquisition of knowledge or skill in another field.

transfer RNA Ten to twenty percent of the ribonucleic acid which combined with certain amino acids complements the messenger ribonucleic acid during protein synthesis.

transferability coefficient (R. B. Cattell) A correlation showing how much a test measures with one kind of subject the same thing that it measures with other kinds of subjects.

transference (psychoanalysis) The patient transfers his past emotional attachments to the psychoanalyst in accordance with the repetition compulsion principle. The analyst is a substitute for the parental figure. Transference may be either negative or positive. In positive transference the patient loves the analyst and wishes to obtain love and emotional satisfaction from him. In negative transference the patient views the analyst as an unfair, unloving, rejecting parental figure and accuses him of all his parents' past injustices. Interpretations of transference make the patient aware of the fact that his infatuation with the analyst is not related to the analyst as a person but is simply a reflection of previous emotional entanglements. Interpretation is necessary for modification of behavior. In the psychoanalytic situation, regression to childhood is necessary for the resolution of conflicts rooted in the past.

transference, negative Reliving of hostile feelings toward parents or parental substitute in psychotherapeutic setting and experiencing hostility toward the psychologist or psychoanalyst.

transference neurosis Reenacting of the infantile roots of the neurotic conflict in psychoanalytic treatment with the psychoanalyst representing the parental figure.

transference, positive See *transference.*

transference resistance See *resistance, transference.*

transformation 1. (logic) Substitution of a symbol or a proposition by another performed in accordance with the rules of formal logic. 2. (mathematics) A change in mathematical formula without changing the content or the value, performed through operations accepted in a particular branch of mathematics, e.g. $a + b$ can be transformed into $b + a$.

transformation stage (C. G. Jung) The fourth stage of analytical psychotherapy in which the patient comes to discover and develop his unique and individual personality pattern.

transformations, informational (J. P. Guilford) Changes of various kinds—redefinitions, shifts, revisions, or other modifications—in existing items of information or in their roles.

transformism 1. A theory of transformation. 2. (biology) Theory of evolution.

transitionism (B. B. Wolman) The proposition that mental phenomena should be explained as a derivative and a continuation of somatic processes.

translocation The transfer of a piece of one chromosome to a non-homologous chromosome, as occurs, for example, in a variant of Down's syndrome of mongolism, where a translocation occurs between a chromosome 21 and one of the D group, such as chromosome number 15. If two non-homologous chromosomes exchange places, the translocation is reciprocal.

transmission 1. Transferring or sending over of objects, symbols and words in communication. 2. (genetics) Carrying of genetic traits from one generation to another. 3. (neurology) Firing of one neuron by another. 4. (medicine) Communicating a disease; contagion. 5. (communication theory) Sending a message. 6. (anthropology and sociology) Carrying over of cultural norms and values.

transmission unit A logarithmic unit of sound intensity, such as decibel.

transmittance Percentage of light energy transmitted through a medium.

transmitter 1. (communication theory) The means by which a message is encoded and begun on its way through a channel. 2. Any device for relaying a message in the form of a signal to a receiver.

transmutation of measures The alteration of a set of measures into an equivalent system.

transmuted score See *score, transmuted.*

transorbital lobotomy See *lobotomy, transorbital.*

transposition 1. A change or interchange in position of two or more elements in a system. 2. (music) The change of a musical composition from one key to another. 3. The reaction to the relationships among stimuli rather than to the absolutes of the stimuli, e.g. the organism's learning that to be rewarded he must go to the smaller of two circles and transferring the learning to a situation in which the originally smaller circle is now the larger and reward requires going to the now smaller circle.

transtype variables Variables which can be measured upon members of many different types and species, and thus lead to dimensions on which all types can be placed.

transvaluation of psychic values A significant shift in the value system and the adoption of a new, if not opposite, one.

transverse 1. Lying or going across. 2. Lying at right angles to the body's longitudinal axis of the body.

transvestism See *transvestitism.*

transvestite 1. One who dresses in clothes of the opposite sex or has strong desire to do so. 2. One who experiences sexual sensation when wearing clothes of the opposite sex.

transvestitism Strong desire to dress in the clothes customarily associated with the opposite sex. 2. Sensation of sexual excitement when wearing clothes of the opposite sex.

tranylcypromine An antidepressant drug of the monoamine oxidase inhibitor group prescribed in the treatment of depressive psychosis.

trapezoid body A strand of fibers located in the pons arising from the cells of the cochlear nucleus.

trauma 1. A physical injury or wound or an experience which inflicts injury on the organism. 2. Psychological damage or an experience inflicting psychological damage.

traumatic neurosis See *neurosis, traumatic.*

traumatophilia Desire to be hurt; accident proneness.

traumatophilic diathesis See *diathesis, traumatophilic.*

traumatophobia Morbid fear of being hurt.

treatment, ambulatory Treatment of noninstitutionalized patients; outpatient treatment.

treatment, residential Psychotherapeutic treatment offered in an institutional setting which involves a total program for supporting the child's ego strengths, reinforcing his ego weaknesses, and providing him with adults and peers who will help him to develop more effective modes of interaction.

treatment, variable An experimental or independent variable.

trembling abasia See *abasia.*

tremograph A device used in the measurement of the amount of involuntary fine movement made by a member of the body or by the whole body.

tremophobia Morbid fear of trembling.

tremor Repeated spastic motions; trembling.

trend analysis (statistics) The analysis of a series of measurements of a variable, taken at different points of time, to discover if there is a direction of change.

trend, neurotic (K. Horney) The group of tendencies in an individual developed during childhood which strive to attain maximum security, thus reducing basic anxiety. Horney distinguished three trends: toward people, away from people, and against people.

trephine 1. A small drill, generally hollow inside, used to cut a hole or plug in the skull. 2. To cut a hole, or plug, in the skull.

treppe The tendency for a muscle tissue contraction to become progressively stronger in response to a stimulus of constant intensity.

trial A single opportunity in which a specific response is elicited or can occur.

trial and error learning See *learning, trial and error.*

trial and error, vicarious (experimental) Movement of the head of an animal looking at alternative pathways in a maze or at other possible avenues.

tribade A woman with an exceedingly large clitoris who plays the male role in lesbian relations.

trichlorethylene poisoning See *poisoning, trichlorethylene.*

trichotillomania A compulsion to pull one's own hair.

trichromatic theory A theory on color vision which is based upon the facts of color mixture.

tricyclic compounds Antidepressant drugs used which appear to act by altering cellular permeability, thereby decreasing the storage or degradation of norepinephrine.

tridimensional theory of feeling (W. Wundt) The position that affect or feeling has three dimensions: pleasantness-unpleasantness; excitement-quiescence; tension-relaxation.

trigeminal nerve See *nerve, trigeminal.*

trigeminal nucleus A bunch of nerve cells located in the pons and medulla giving rise to the trigeminal nerve.

triorthocresyl phosphate poisoning See *poisoning, triorthocresyl phosphate.*

triple-X syndrome An anomaly of the sex-chromosome in which the patient is anatomically female but has the sex-chromosome complement XXX. The syndrome is often associated with mental retardation.

trireceptor theory A theory which holds that there are three types of receptors in the eye, corresponding to the three color primaries of trichromatic theory.

triskaidekaphobia A morbid fear of the number 13.

trisomy The state of having one extra chromosome per cell, so that there are three representatives per cell of that chromosome instead of the usual diploid number. In Down's syndrome or mongolism there is a trisomy of the twenty-first chromosome. Severe mental retardation, deformities of mouth and eyes, etc. are caused by 13 chromosome trisomy. Physical and mental defects are caused by trisomy of the 18 chromosome.

tristimulus value The hue of a sample color stated in the amounts of the three primaries needed to create it.

tritanopia A rare type of partial color blindness characterized by the confusion of reddish blue and greenish yellow stimuli.

troland A measure of retinal illuminance which corrects for the energy lost in the eye.

tropism The involuntary movement of an organism involving change in orientation or growth either toward (positive tropism) or away (negative tropism) from a source of stimulation. See *taxis.*

tropotaxis A taxis in which the sense receptors are bilaterally symmetrical enabling simultaneous comparisons of stimulation intensity. Thus the animal can orient to a stimulus source without lateral swings or wavy movements necessary in klinotaxis.

truancy Absence from school or home without permission usually due to psychological problems involved in each situation.

true-false test See *test, true-false.*

truism A statement of the obvious.

truncated distribution See *distribution, truncated.*

truth serum The use of narcotics such as sodium amythal or sodium pentothal injected intravenously for extracting confessions from subjects.

TSH See *thyrotropic hormone.*

TU See *transmission unit.*

tube feeding Forcefeeding patients who refuse to eat by means of a nasal catheter that terminates in the stomach.

tubectomy Excision of the uterine tube.

tube feeding Forcefeeding patients who refuse to eat by means of a nasal catheter that terminates in the stomach.

tuberculomania A form of hypochondriasis; the morbid belief that one has tuberculosis.

tuberous sclerosis See *epiloia.*

tumescence Swelling of tissue, especially central tissue.

tumor, intracranial A localized intracranial lesion of neoplastic or chronic inflammatory origin, which causes a rise in intracranial pressure. Symptoms may include headache, vomiting, papilledema, aphasia, convulsions, coma, and progressive confusion and disorientation.

tune 1. The adjustment of the frequency of mechanical device's sounding body so that it emits a tone of some required pitch. 2. A series of musical notes making a melody.

tuning fork A two-toned device made of highly tempered metal which when struck emits a perceptually pure tone of some pitch.

tunnel vision Restriction of vision to the central area of the retina with no peripheral vision.

Turner's syndrome (H. H. Turner) The affected individuals are anatomically females, but have a deficiency in ovarian tissue and concomitant sexual infantilism. Chromosome complement is XO. Mental retardation is often present.

twilight vision The type of vision occurring under conditions of minimal illumination.

twin One of two offspring gestated simultaneously and born at the same birth.

twinned To be born as a twin.

twinning Refers to giving birth to or being a twin.

twins, enzygotic See *twins, identical.*

twins, fraternal Twins which develop from two separate ova fertilized at the same time; can be of the same or of a different sex since they have different genetic structures.

twins, identical Twins which develop from a single fertilized ovum in the same chorionic sac and consequently, of the same sex and the same genetic structure.

twins, monochorionic See *twins, identical.*

twins, monovular See *twins, identical.*

twins, monozygotic See *twins, identical.*

twins, Siamese Monozygotic twins joined together at birth over some portion of their bodies due to incomplete splitting of the egg during pre-natal development.

twitch A sudden localized convulsive muscle contraction.

twitch, isometric A slight muscular contraction occurring as a response to a new stimulus without significant shortening of the muscle.

Twitchell-Allen Three-Dimensional Personality Test See *test, Twitchell-Allen Three-Dimensional Personality.*

two-aspect theory A theory of the mind-body problem in which mind is body seen from one viewpoint and body is mind seen from another.

two-factor theory (O. H. Mowrer) First introduced about 1950 to distinguish between conditioning (Pavlov) and habit formation (Thorndike, Hull). Later (circa 1960) it proved possible to derive the latter from the former; and the two factors which have since been emphasized are positive (rewarding) reinforcement and negative (punishing reinforcement).

two factor theory of avoidance conditioning A theory which explains the avoidance of an aversive stimulus. When the organism avoids the stimulus, it is reinforced by the non-occurrence of an event. According to the theory, the situation in which the aversive stimulus initially occurred is classically conditioned to the aversive stimulus. The situation becomes, through classical conditioning, a conditioned aversive stimulus. The escape from this conditioned stimulus is reinforcing. The escape is acquired by instrumental conditioning. Thus avoidance conditioning becomes a special case of escape conditioning and incorporates both classical and instrumental conditioning.

two point threshold The minimum distance separating two pointed objects at which, when applied to the skin, they can be perceived as two separate objects.

two-tailed test See *test, two-tailed.*

two-way table See *scatter diagram.*

Tyler, Leona E. (1906-) American psychologist. Author of books on individual differences, tests and measurements, counseling, developmental, and clinical psychology. President of American Psychological Association, 1972-73. Research and theoretical contributions on development of interests and organized choices.

tympanic membrane The eardrum.

type 1. A category or class of people or things distinguished by the possession of some common characteristic and grouped together on that basis. 2. A person who serves as an ideal example of a group due to possessing fully the characteristics which define that group and distinguish it from others. 3. Pattern of characteristics according to which people are categorized. 4. The end portions of a continuous variable as in an aggressive type or tall type.

type, aesthetic (E. Spranger) Personality type characterized by individualism and interest in universal harmony, beauty and gracefulness.

type, affective reaction A term used to describe any behavior disorder in which the main symptoms are of an affective or emotional nature. See *affective disorders.*

type, apoplectic (Hippocrates) Body type characterized by a thickset, rounded physique.

type, asthenic (E. Kretschmer) Body type associated with schizothymic temperament.

type, athletic (E. Kretschmer) Body type characterized by well-proportioned body, well-developed muscular-skeletal structure, and physical strength and prowess associated with the schizothymic temperament.

type, body Any classificatory scheme of individuals which uses macroscopic anatomical characteristics as guidelines, usually with the assumption that certain psychological characteristics are associated with certain body types.

type, cerebral (L. Rostan and C. Sigaud) Constitutional type distinguished by a predominance of brain and nervous system over body.

type, cerebrotonic (W. H. Sheldon) Basic temperament component characterized by a rigidity in posture and in movement, inhibition in social situations, self-worry and hypersensitivity, associated with the ectomorphic body type.

type, choleric (Hippocrates) Constitutional type characterized by an abundance of yellow bile in the body which was thought to result in an irritable personality type.

type, cyclothymic (E. Kretschmer) One of two basic personality types which is primarily associated with the pyknic body-type in Kretschmer's constitutional system. Should a cyclothymic ever become psychotic, his psychosis will be manic-depressive.

type, dysplastic (E. Kretschmer) Body type characterized by deviant features, uneven combination of elements, and structure too irregular to be classified in any of the three basic categories of asthenic, athletic or pyknic; most often associated with schizothymic temperament.

type, economic (E. Spranger) The economic personality type is characterized by concern about practical matters, self-preservation and economic security. Material values and success are primary goals.

type, ectomorphic 1. Somatotype characterized by fragile physique, predominance of linearity, and relatively great surface area as compared to body mass. 2. (W. H. Sheldon) Body type correlated with the cerebrotonic temperament.

type, endomorphic 1. Somatotype characterized by a predominance of structures developed from the internal organs on the endodermal embryonic layer and by soft and round body features. 2. (W. H. Sheldon) Body type correlated with the viscerotonic temperament.

type, erotic (S. Freud) The main interest of the erotic type is loving and even more, being loved. Should such a normal type deteriorate, he will become a hysteric.

type, esthetic See *type, aesthetic.*

type, extraverted (C. G. Jung) Personality type characterized by movement of the libido outwards toward the world resulting in all attitudes, values, and interests being directed toward the physical and social environment or an object-directed reference point.

type, fallacy The false assumption that the extremes along a continuum are distinct groups discontinuous from the intermediate range of the continuum rather than an extension of it.

type, feeling (C. G. Jung) Personality type characterized by the dominance in the conscious of the feeling function.

type, hyperinstrumental (B. B. Wolman) A narcissistic type of mental disorder characterized by tendencies to use others, which at the neurosis level is seen as anxiety and depression reactions, and at the psychosis level manifests itself as psychotic psychopathy and so-called "moral insanity."

type, hypervectorial (B. B. Wolman) A type of mental disorder developed in an over-demanding home environment which manifests itself on the neurotic level as obsessive, phobic, or neurasthenic reactions and at the psychotic level becomes schizophrenia called by Wolman *vectoriasis praecox.*

type, hypoaffective (N. Pende) The constitutional type characterized by deficient emotional reactivity.

type, introverted (C. G. Jung) Personality type characterized by a dominance of subjective perception and cognition resulting in a self-centered orientation and involvement with one's own inner world.

type, intuitive (C. G. Jung) Personality type characterized by the dominance in the conscious of the feeling function, which is an irrational process based on the immediate perception of relationships.

type, irrational (C. G. Jung) Personality type characterized by a dominance of either the sensation or intuition functions which are associated with the

intensity of perceptions rather than rational judgments.

type, learning See *learning type.*

type, melancholic (Hippocrates) A constitutional body type characterized by an abundance of black bile in the body which was thought to result in a personality type characterized by sadness.

type, mesomorphic 1. Somatotype characterized by a predominance of structures developed from the bone, muscle and connective tissue, the mesodermal embryonic layer. 2. (W. H. Sheldon) Body type correlated with the temperament component of somatotonia. 3. (H. J. Eysenck) A person whose body-build index falls within one standard deviation of the mean.

type, narcissistic (S. Freud) The main interest is self-preservation with little if any concern for other people, and very weak if any superego.

type, obsessional (S. Freud) The main characteristic of the obsessional type is his very strong dictatorial superego, conscience and conservatism. This type may develop the neurotic pattern of obsessive-compulsive neurosis.

type, oral-aggressive (psychoanalysis) Personality type characterized by hostile, critical, negativistic, and overdemanding attitude.

type, oral passive (psychoanalysis) Personality type characterized by passivity, overdependence, inability to accept frustrations and disappointments, day dreaming about personal desires and the feeling that the world owes him protection and concern.

type, personality See *personality types.*

type, phlegmatic (Hippocrates) Constitutional type characterized by an abundance of "phlegm" in the body which was thought to result in an apathetic personality type.

type, phtisic (Hippocrates) Slender, flat-chested body build believed to prove a tendency to develop tuberculosis. Analogous to Kretschmer's asthenic type.

type, power politics (E. Spranger) Personality type characterized by the desire to control people and perception of the world in terms of power, of overcoming obstacles and of domination, and an interest in politics and methods of influencing and ruling.

type, pyknic (E. Kretschmer) Body type characterized by short limbs, thick neck, and rounded or fat body contour, associated with the cyclothymic temperament.

type R conditioning See *conditioning, instrumental.*

type, rational (C. G. Jung) Personality type characterized by a dominance in the conscious of either the thinking or feeling functions which are associated with reasoning and judgments.

type reaction See *reaction, type.*

type, religious (E. Spranger) Personality type characterized by a mystical outlook and the pursuit of unity between man and universe. Contemplation and a search for eternal unity are primary goals.

type S conditioning See *conditioning, Pavlovian.*

type, sanguine (Hippocrates) A personality type characterized by warmth, ardor, and/or optimism and thought to be the result of the influence of blood.

type, schizothymic (E. Kretschmer) One of two basic personality temperament's in Kretschmer's constitutional system. This temperamental type is associated primarily with the asthenic and athletic body-type. Should a schizothymic ever be psychotic, he will be a schizophrenic.

type, sensation (C. G. Jung) Personality type characterized by the dominance in the conscious of the sensation function, which is an irrational process associated with intensity of perceptions and a concern for the reaction of the individual to the outer world.

type, sociable, or social (E. Spranger) Personality type characterized by friendliness, congeniality, and consideration and compassion for others. The desire to help people is a primary goal.

type T (E. Jaensch) A personality type prone to eidetic imagery.

type, theoretical (E. Spranger) The theoretical personality type is characterized by an inquisitive intellectual approach to life which is systematic and rational and which attempts to see the world as a systematic logically ordered unity.

type, thinking (C. G. Jung) Personality type characterized by the dominance in the conscious of the thinking function which is a rational process of reasoning, judgment and interpretation of the perceived objects and relationships.

type, visual Person who thinks in visual terms and uses visual imagery predominantly.

typology 1. The study of types. 2. A particular system used in the classification of individuals into types.

tyrosinosis An overflow aminoaciduria disease with a probable deficiency of p-hydroxyphenylpurivic acid oxidase. In the acute variety the patient experiences in the first few months of life vomiting, diarrhea, enlarging abdomen, and failure to thrive, with death usually occurring within a period of a few months. The chronic type is similar with the onset later in life, with death usually occurring in the first decade of life. The main clinical features are progressive hepatic and renal failure, failure to thrive, and mild mental retardation.

U

U fibers Short fibers in the cerebral cortex which interconnect adjacent cortical gyri.

U-hypothesis (H. Helson) In most organic responses there is a region of optimal functioning wherein errors are minimal and beyond (above and below) which errors rapidly increase. Even classical curves of visual and auditory sensitivity can be regarded as inverted U-functions since they exhibit maximal regions of sensitivity and brightness as a function of wave length, loudness as a function of frequency, etc.

U test See *test, U.*

ucs (psychoanalysis) Abbreviation for unconscious.

ulcer, duodenal See *ulcer, peptic.*

ulcer, peptic Ulcer due to an inordinate secretion of gastric juices affecting the gastric or duodenal mucosa or the mucosa of the stomach and jejunum of physical or psychological origin. Psychogenic causes involve frustrated wishes for dependency which are transformed regressively into wishes to be fed.

ulcerative colitis See *colitis, ulcerative.*

ulnar nerve An afferent sensory nerve found in the hand.

umbilical cord Cord which connects the navel of a fetus to the placenta of the mother.

unbiased estimate See *estimate, unbiased.*

uncertainty interval See *interval of uncertainty.*

unconditioned reflex See *reflex, unconditioned.*

unconditioned response See *response, unconditioned.*

unconditioned stimulus See *stimulus, unconditioned.*

unconscious 1. (philosophy) Several philosophers and scientists, among them Galen, Plotinus, St. Augustine, St. Thomas Aquinas, Montaigne, and Descartes, were aware of unconscious processes.

Paracelsus (1493-1541) implies the influence of ideas people are unaware of. Several authors described their dreams, analyzed the irrational elements in their behavior, and described the surprising motives they were driven by without being aware of them. The idea of unconscious has become a topic of general interest when F. A. Mesmer (1733-1815) claimed to be able to cure people by "magnetic" processes; the hypnotic states, induced by Mesmer, were obviously unconscious. In 1890 G. H. Schubert published a book on "Dream Symbolism." A. Schopenhauer (1788-1860) explained the origins of mental illness by repression of ideas which hurt one's interests and conscious wishes. J. F. Herbart (1716-1841) presented mental life as a struggle of ideas for a place in human consciousness; the repressed ideas continue struggling to attain the conscious surface.

The term unconscious was probably used in print for the first time in 1860 by the French writer H. I. Amiel who wrote about *La Vie Inconsciente* (the unconscious life). This term appeared in 1878 in the dictionary of the French Academy and in 1868 E. von Hartmann published a comprehensive work *The Philosophy of Unconscious.* 2. (psychoanalysis) In years 1872-1880 there appeared several works dealing with the various aspects of unconscious and the works of Charcot, Bernheim, Liebeault and Janet introduced the concepts of unconscious motivation to psychiatry and psychology. S. Freud developed the concept of unconscious as a part of an overall "topographic" description of "mental layers" or "provinces." The human mind is divided into what one is aware of, i.e. his conscious or consciousness and what he is unaware of, or his unconscious. The unconscious is divided into preconscious and unconscious proper. The preconscious includes all that one has in his mind but not on his mind at a particular moment.

The mind of a newborn child is totally unconscious and only a part of it ever becomes preconscious and conscious. The unconscious processes are "primary processes;" and they are totally irrational, inaccessible to the conscious mind. Their existence can be inferred from dreams, amnesias, slips of the tongue, and symptom formation. Some unconscious wishes are thrown back into the unconscious even before the individual becomes clearly aware of them; such a rejection of the unconscious wishes and impulses is called repression.

unconscious, collective (C. Jung) The part of the unconscious composed of acquired traits and cultural patterns transmitted by heredity that is the foundation of the whole personality structure. It is universal, all men being essentially the same, is almost totally divorced from anything personal or individual, and is continuously accumulating memory traces as a result of man's repeated experiences over generations. Archetypes are its structural components.

unconscious memory See *memory, unconscious.*

unconscious, personal (C. G. Jung) The surface layer of the unconscious, consisting of subliminal perceptions, repressed, suppressed, forgotten and/or ignored experiences, and fantasies and dreams of a personal nature, all of which can be accessible to consciousness.

unconscious process See *processes, unconscious.*

unconscious sadism See *sadism, unconscious.*

underachiever A person who does not perform as well as would be expected from known characteristics or abilities, particularly from measures of intellectual aptitude.

understanding need See *need, understanding.*

undifferentiated areas (K. Lewin) The life space of an individual which has not been structured and differentiated through learning and perception into inner and outer regions of personality. The life space of a neonate is an undifferentiated field or area.

undoing (psychoanalysis) The mechanism of undoing represents a far-reaching loss of contact with reality. Undoing is a fallacious belief that one can undo or nullify previous actions that make one feel guilty. A strong ego admits past blunders and a mature individual assumes responsibility for his behavior. A weak ego fears the superego's reproaches and acts in accordance with a belief that wishing to nullify past deeds can effect such nullification. The mechanism of undoing is a patent distortion of truth; it is a kind of magic. Freud pictured the ego as trying to "blow away" not only the consequences of an event, but the fact that the event itself ever took place.

unequivocal Not ambiguous; clear; open to only one interpretation.

unfinished task See *Zeigarnik effect.*

Ungestalt (Gestalt) Not a Gestalt; that which is not united or an integrated whole.

ungrouped scores See *scores, ungrouped.*

unidextrality The use of one hand or side of the body rather than the other.

unidimensional Possessing only one direction.

unimodal A frequency distribution curve having only one mode or peak.

unintegrated motivation component (R. B. Cattell) That component in a person's motivation for a given course of action which has poor reality contact and manifests itself mainly through "I wish" expressions.

uniocular One-eyed; pertaining to only one eye.

unipolar 1. Having only one pole. 2. Referring to variables, tests, or scales which are meaningful at one extreme but not at the other.

unique factor See *factor, unique.*

unique trait A set of characteristics patterned idiosyncratically in an individual, so that other individuals cannot meaningfully be given scores on this trait. Differences between individuals on unique traits tend to be qualitative.

unitas multiplex (W. Stern) A unity composed of elements which contains more than mere empirical unity. The personality is a unitas multiplex because it is a product of the converging influences of hereditary and environmental factors.

units, informational (J. P. Guilford) Relatively segregated or circumscribed items of information having "thing" character. May be close to Gestalt psychology's "figure on a ground."

universal set (S) A set which includes all objects to be considered in any particular discussion.

universe, statistical See *statistical universe.*

unreality feeling See *depersonalization.*

uraniscolalia Speech defect caused by cleft palate.

Urban's tables The tables of the Müller-Urban weights.

urethra The organ which conducts urine from the bladder.

urethral character See *character, urethral.*

urethral phase (S. Freud) The developmental stage between anal and phallic stages. Urethral eroticism is basically autoerotic; it may, however, turn toward others with fantasies about urinating on them or being urinated on. The training in bladder control leads to conflicts with parents, and bedwetting children tend to become over-ambitious, as if trying to re-establish their self-esteem.

urolagnia An unusual preoccupation with urine because pleasure is derived from this source.

US Unconditioned stimulus.

use, law of See *law of use.*

utilitarianism An ethical philosophical, social and economic theory which sets practical achievements and well-being of people as the supreme value. The greatest possible happiness of the greatest number of people is believed to be the supreme moral value.

utility index (R. B. Cattell) A validity coefficient calculated for a prediction made one year from the time of testing and with known intervening events.

utricle An expansion in the vestibule of the inner ear associated with the balance receptors in the semicircular canals.

uvula Lump of tissue hanging from the soft palate.

V **1.** A verbal comprehension factor. **2.** (Rorschach) Referring directly to the vista response. **3.** Referring to volume. **4.** (C. L. Hull) The magnitude of the intensity of a potential reaction.

V factor A verbal comprehension factor.

V test (statistics) A modification of the t test used when the samples are large and the variance is unequal.

vaccinophobia A morbid fear of receiving vaccinations.

vacuum activity (etiology) The occurrence of a fixed action pattern in the apparent absence of its usual releaser. It is hypothesized that this occurs because of a high drive state.

vaginal plexus Vaginal nerve network.

vaginism; vaginismus A symptom of frigidity; a painful contraction of vaginal muscles which prevents sexual intercourse.

vagotomy The cutting of the vagus nerve.

vagotonia A condition due to the overactivity of the vagus nerve.

vagus nerve See *nerve, vagus*.

valence **1.** (E. C. Tolman) Objects that attract an organism have a positive valence, those that repel have a negative valence. Thus valence is a determinant of actions leading toward or away from an object-goal. **2.** (K. Lewin) The concept of valence corresponds to a field force which has the structure of a positive central field; that is all forces in this field are directed toward the attracting-positive valence or away from negative-repulsive valence.

validation **1.** The process in which the degree of validity of a measuring instrument is determined. **2.** The process of establishing the objective proof of a proposition, measuring instrument, etc.

validation, consensual (H. S. Sullivan) A technique developed in the syntaxic stage of checking one's perceptions against the perceptions of others which correspond to reality. It is similar to S. Freud's reality testing.

validation, internal A means of improving the validity of a measuring device by consisting of checking for high correlations between the scores on various subitems of the test and the total score.

validity A test's ability to predict performances other than performance on itself, that is, a test's correlation with a factor, life-situation performance, clinical category placement, etc. There are several varieties of validity.

validity, concurrent The measure of the extent to which a test measures what it is supposed to measure by correlating the results of the tests with the results of the person's performance or a task which the test presumably assesses. The two correlated measures must be taken at the same time with no time lapse.

validity, content A measure of how well items of a test correspond to the behavior which the test attempts to assess or predict.

validity criterion An independent external measure of what a test is devised to measure.

validity, ecological (E. Brunswik) An established relationship within a set of environmental circumstances between a proximal stimulus and a distal stimulus, such that the presence or occurrence of the proximal stimulus increases the probability that the distal stimulus is also operative and vice versa.

validity, factorial (psychometrics) Validity of a test measured by correlation of the test with a factor derived by factor analysis.

validity, item The extent to which a test item measures what it is intended to measure.

validity, predictive See *predictive validity*.

validity, sampling See *sampling, validity*.

valium Common name for diazepam, a tranquilizing drug.

value **1.** The degree of worth or excellence assigned to or derived from an object. **2.** A quantitative score or measure. **3.** (mathematics) The magnitude of something, or the number or symbol representing the magnitude. 4. An abstract concept which determines for a person or some social group the relative worth of various goals or ends. 5. The location of some visual datum on the scale of white to black. 6. (economics) The determination of what an object will bring in exchange on the market.

value, absolute The mathematical value of a number without regard to its positive or negative sign.

value, difficulty Measure of the discriminating power of a test item in terms of the percent of a specified group who answer the item correctly.

value judgment A reaction to persons, objects, places, events, etc. on the part of an individual in terms implying or employing an assessment of their worth in relation to others rather than in terms of their objective characteristics.

value system A set of values adopted by an individual or society, governing the behavior of the individual or the members of the society, often without the conscious awareness of the individual or the members of the society.

van Bogaert-Nyssen disease (L. van Bogaert and R. Nyssen) Sclerosis and a degenerative disease of the nervous system. Appears late in life.

variability 1. The degree to which scores in a set differ from each other or from their central tendency. The most common measures are: the range, which is the distance from the highest to the lowest score in a distribution; the average deviation (*AD*), or the average of the differences from the mean of each value in a series,

$$AD = \frac{\Sigma \ |X - \bar{X}\ |}{N}$$

and finally the standard deviation (*S²*) which is an index of the variability of a whole distribution:

$$S^2 = \frac{\Sigma (X - \bar{X})^2}{N-1}$$

2. The ability or capacity of an individual or a species to change.

variability coefficient See *coefficient, variation.*

variability, sampling See *sampling variability.*

variable 1. A factor the quantity of which can be increased or decreased either in discrete steps or along some continuum without any other concomitant change in that factor. 2. Anything that can change or take on different characteristics appropriate to specified conditions.

variable, autochthonous Factors within a system that change relatively independently of forces outside the system. In psychology, common examples are metabolic changes, appetites such as hunger, thirst, and sex, and neural noise from spontaneous neural discharge.

variable, continuous A variable, the possible values of which are on a continuum. When between any two values of a variable it is possible to find an intermediate value, the variable is called continuous.

variable, controlled See *variable, independent.*

variable, criterion A variable the value of which serves as a standard to compare results of other variables.

variable, dependent A parameter, usually in an experimental setting, whose values are hypothesized to change as a consequence of changes in the independent variable, i.e. the parameter directly manipulated by the experimenter.

variable, discontinuous See *variable, discrete.*

variable, discrete A variable, the possible values of which do not form a continuum but a certain scale in which there are no intermediate values between two given values. Thus, there are definite, discrete, and abrupt changes in quantity on this scale.

variable, distal (E. Brunswik) A variable which does not directly effect a receptor but is mediated by the action of a proximal variable.

variable error See *error, chance.*

variable, experimental The independent variable in an experiment which is systematically manipulated in order to observe and investigate its influence on other dependent variables.

variable, hypothetical process A class of hypothetical constructs. It is a process hypothesized to occur on the basis of observed effects. The process is also hypothesized to have properties or effects other than those that lead to its postulation.

variable, hypothetical state (K. W. Spence) Hypothetical relatively permanent condition or state of an organism which is assumed to result from past interactions with the environment. The state variables are usually specific to fairly circumscribed sets of stimuli and seldom to the total state of the organism.

variable, independent 1. A variable that can be observed and assessed as a determinant of behavior. 2. The variable that is altered independently of any other variable, usually by the experimenter. 3. (E. C. Tolman) The initial causes of behavior of which there are six: a) the environmental stimulus, b) physiological drive, c) heredity, d) previous training, e) maturity or age, f) some organismic factors. Experimental independent variables include a) preceding experimental presentations of the stimuli, b) previous occurrences of the behavior, c) the instances of reinforcement of the behavior, d) the drive level or deprivation level of the organism, e) the appropriateness of the goal object, f) the types of stimuli, g) the types of responses required, h) the experimental apparatus. 4. (B. F. Skinner) The external conditions of which behavior is a function.

variable interval reinforcement Partial reinforcement schedule in which reinforcement occurs on the first trial after varying time lapses, but on the average after a certain amount of time.

variable interval (VI) schedule See *reinforcement, schedule of: variable interval (VI).*

variable, intervening 1. The unobserved, inferred factors that connect the observed independent variable, the stimuli, with the observed dependent variables, the responses. Thus intervening variables are hypothetical statements about entities, events or processes occurring within the behaving organism. The status of intervening variables in scientific thinking has not been settled. Distinctions have been made between hypothetical constructs, and intervening variables. The former, also called existential constructs, postulate the existence of entities that "fill out" the space between the observables, for example, the theory of genes "fills out" Mendelian genetics. The intervening variable is often defined only in terms of the independent and dependent variables, thus it has a specific and limited operational meaning. **2.** (E. C. Tolman) The intervening variable is a part determinant of behavior, being divided into immanent purposive and cognitive determinants, capacities, and behavior adjustments. These cannot be observed, only inferred. A subsequent revision of this theory postulated (a) need-systems, the drive situation or physiological deprivation at a given time; (b) belief-value, relative value of goal objects to the organism; (c) behavior-spaces, the space, or environment in which the organism operates.

variable, O Factors which are present in an organism at any given moment; internal variables which affect an organism's response to a stimulus. These include drive and individual differences such as age. Also called O factors.

variable, organic or O An internal state or process of the organism or person which, together with the immediate stimulus, co-determines the response, as for example, an illness or a general attitude.

variable, polar (J. Loevinger) A variable which increases as a function of age.

variable, proximal See *stimulus, proximal.*

variable ratio reinforcement Partial reinforcement schedule in which reinforcement occurs in an irregular pattern every nth trial, on the average.

variable ratio (VR) schedule See *reinforcement, schedule of: variable ratio (VR).*

variable, response Dependent variable in psychological research that changes with concomitant changes in the stimulus variable.

variable, stimulus **1.** The independent variable in psychological research. It is a measurable dimension of a stimulus complex. Changes in the stimulus variable occasion concomitant changes in the response variable. **2.** (psychophysics) Any of the set of stimuli that are compared to standard stimulus.

variance The measure of the extent to which individual scores in a set differ from each other. It is the square of the standard deviation computed by the formula:

$$S^2 = {}_i\Sigma(X_i - M)^2 \over N$$

where S and X are the symbols for sample and population variance respectively, M is the mean of the set, N is the size of the set and Σ is the summation sign.

variance analysis See *analysis of variance.*

variance, common factor See *communality.*

variation **1.** Change. **2.** Difference. **3.** (biology) The change in an organism or species resulting from hereditary or environmental influences. **4.** (statistics) The extent of deviation of scores from the mean of the distribution.

variation coefficient See *coefficient, variation.*

varicella encephalitis See *encephalitis, varicella.*

vasodepressor syncope See *syncope, vasodepressor.*

vasopressin Pituitary hormone mainly used for antidiaretic effect.

vectorialism (B. B. Wolman) A sociopsychological attitude based on the desire for helping others without expecting anything in return; it is an unselfish, giving attitude. Originates in the parent-child core.

vectoriasis praecocissima (B. B. Wolman) Childhood schizophrenia. See *vectoriasis praecox.*

vectoriasis praecox (B. B. Wolman) Schizophrenia. A term introduced in 1957, based on the division of non-organic mental disorders into hypervectorial (schizotype), hyperinstrumental (narcissistic), and dysmutual (cyclic). Vectoriasis praecox indicates a too early and extreme object hypercathexis, called hypervectorialism.

vegetative nervous system The autonomic nervous system.

vegetative neurosis See *neurosis, vegetative.*

vehicle (R. B. Cattell) A mode of expression of interest or motivation which expresses partly the strength of a capacity, e.g. memory, which needs to be discounted in assessing the interest strength itself.

ventromedial nucleus of the hypothalamus The portion of the hypothalamus which controls the cessation of eating.

verbal aphasia See *aphasia, motor.*

verbal behavior See *behavior, verbal.*

verbal catharsis See *catharsis, verbal.*

verbal conditioning in behavior therapy See *behavior therapy, verbal conditioning.*

verbal learning See *learning, verbal.*

verbal paraphasia See *paraphasia, verbal.*

verbal test See *test, verbal.*

verbomania Morbid need for excessive talking; logozzhea.

verbone (H. A. Murray) A verbal reaction pattern.

vergence A turning movement of the eyes.

veridical A term describing that which corresponds to objective reality.

verification **1.** The use of empirical data to prove or disprove an hypothesis or the process of proving or disproving an hypothesis using empirical data. **2.** (esthetics) A stage of artistic thought or creation in which the observer or artist reviews an artistic object to ascertain whether the intended effect was achieved.

vermis The median lobe of the cerebellum.

vernier A closely calibrated scale, ancillary to a larger scale which allows the reading off of fractions from a larger scale.

Verstehende Psychologie See *psychology, understanding.*

vertex 1. The uppermost point of a geometric figure. 2. Referring to the top of the head. 3. The point where two angular lines meet.

vertical axis See *Y axis.*

vertical group structure (B. B. Wolman) The distribution of severity of disorder in a psychotherapeutic group.

vertical mobility (sociology) Moving upward of a social class system; climbing up the social ladder.

vertigo A state of dizziness.

vesania (B. de Sauvage) An obsolete term for all mental disorders introduced in 1763.

vesicle A sac-like structure which contains liquid.

vestibule A bony cavity in the inner ear's labyrinth composed of two sacs—the utricle and saccule—and containing fluid. The hair cells in the utricle and saccule are sensitive to acceleration and deceleration of the body, being the receptor apparatus for that sense.

VI schedule See *reinforcement, schedule of: variable interval.*

vicarious arousal An emotional response aroused by an empathetic understanding of what another person is experiencing.

vicarious conditioning Learning through observation without practice.

vicarious functioning Behavioral pattern in which one psychological process is substituted for another.

vicarious learning Learning through indirect experience.

vicarious trial and error See *trial and error, vicarious.*

Viennese Circle See *logical positivism.*

Vierordt's Law (K. von Vierordt) The two-point threshold of a mobile part of the body is lower than for a less mobile part of the body.

Vigotsky Test See *test, Vigotsky.* Also spelled Vygotsky.

Vincent learning curve (L. E. Vincent) A method used in comparing the learning curves of individuals who take different numbers of trials or different lengths of time to achieve the specified criterion of learning. Each subject's data are broken down into equal intervals—either of time or number of trials—allowing the construction of a curve with all subject's having the same beginning and end points but with different amounts of learning exhibited in any one interval.

Vineland Social Maturity Scale See *scale, Vineland Social Maturity.*

viraginity A woman being or acting in man-like fashion.

virilism The development in a woman of the male secondary sex characteristics.

virus RNA See *RNA, virus.*

viscera The organs enclosed in the large cavities of the body, especially the abdominal and thoracic cavities.

visceral drive A drive which is based upon a physiological need.

visceral reflex The response, regulated by the sympathetic and parasympathetic nervous system, of the viscera to conditions of stress.

visceral sense A collective term for all those sensations emanating from the viscera.

visceroceptor; visceroreceptor A receptor organ in one of the viscera.

viscerogenic A term describing that which originates in the viscera.

viscerotonia (W. H. Sheldon) Temperament component characterized by love of food, enjoyment of physical relaxation and comfort, sociability and affection, associated with the endomorphic body-type.

visibility coefficient A number designating the visibility of a specified sample of radiant energy, usually of a single spectral wave length.

visibility curve A graphic representation of the relation of visual intensity, called brilliance, to the wave length.

vision 1. The seeing sense with the eye as the receptor whose normal stimulus is light or radiant energy ranging from about 400 to 760 millimicrons. 2. That which is seen. 3. The act of seeing.

vision, distance 1. Seeing objects that are more than twenty feet away. 2. Ability to discriminate among stimuli twenty feet or more away.

vision, indirect Vision of objects stimulating the marginal area of the retina.

vision, monocular Vision with one eye.

vision, paracentral Seeing through use of the area immediately surrounding the fovea centralis.

vision, perimacular Vision which utilizes the part of the retina which surrounds the macula.

vision, photopic Vision under conditions of fairly strong illumination such that full discrimination of colors is possible since the cones are functional; color or daylight vision.

vision theory See *color vision theory; duplicity theory.*

visions, hypnagogic See *imagery, hypnagogic.*

vista response A type of Rorschach response in which the chiaroscuro (light-dark) features of the blot convey the impression of depth or dimensionality. Vista responses are generally interpreted as a form of self-examination and/or attempts to distantiate from the environment.

visual acuity The ability of the visual mechanism to discriminate two points in the visual field; the closer together the two points, the greater the acuity.

visual adaptation The ability of the eyes to adjust to conditions of continued stimulation or lack of stimulation. See *adaptation, brightness; adaptation, color.*

visual agnosia See *agnosia, visual.*

visual agraphia See *agraphia, visual.*

visual alexia See *alexia, visual.*

visual aphasia See *aphasia, visual.*

visual apperception test See *test, visual apperception.*

visual aurae See *aurae, visual.*

visual axis The straight line running from the external fixation point through the nodal point of the eye to the point of clearest vision on the retina.

visual displacement The angles describing the eyes' deviations from the primary position when viewing objects.

visual field 1. All of the external world that is visible to the unmoving eye of any particular observer at a given moment. 2. The perceived three-dimensional space that forms a frame of reference for perceived objects, forms, distances and movements.

visual fixation The movement of the eyes so that the images fall on the central part of the retina.

visual induction The effect on the perceptual reaction to one area of the visual field caused by the stimulation from another area of the visual field.

visual-motor Gestalt test See *test, Bender Visual-Motor Gestalt.*

visual organization The complex relationships existing among the various elements of the visual field, reflecting the fact that the phenomenal visual field always appears patterned and meaningful.

visual process 1. Activity of the organism contributing to seeing; operations of the eye, nerve tracts and brain centers involved in seeing. 2. The operation of sight in general.

visual projection The process involving the attribution of objective location to a visually perceived object.

visual purple A substance found in the rods of the retina which bleaches in white light and which is believed to be involved in the reception of faint visual stimuli.

visual-righting reflex An alteration in the position of the head when there is a change from one fixation point to another.

visual space The visual field or the three-dimensional subjective field in which objects are perceived and located.

visual type See *type, visual.*

visual yellow A yellow substance which is sometimes found in the retina when visual purple has been bleached by exposure to light.

vital statistics Data concerning birth and death rates concerning human beings.

vitalism 1. A philosophical theory of life which maintains that living organisms contain elements not existing in the inanimate nature and these elements account for irreducibility of life to inanimate processes. 2. (Hans Driesch) Presented as a theory of autonomy of the life processes. The life of an organism is entelechy, i.e. realization of a potentiality, sort of a purposeful evolvement. According to Driesch, entelechy is like an artist who uses a material medium within its limitations (easel, paint, etc.) but only he creates the work of art. McDougall, Kantor and other psychologists have been influenced by vitalism.

vitality 1. The property or quality of being alive, or being able to maintain life. 2. Vigor, energy or endurance.

vocabulary test See *test, vocabulary.*

vocal cords The ligaments of the larynx involved in the production of vocal sounds.

vocal immaturity Voice disorder due to the inhibition of laryngeal growth, usually caused by dysfunctioning of the sex glands, and characterized by a voice of higher than normal frequency.

vocal register The pitch range of an individual voice.

vocational aptitude Particular abilities a person possesses which allow the making of a prediction concerning the person's future success in a given field.

vocational aptitude tests See *tests, vocational aptitude.*

vocational counseling See *counseling, vocational.*

vocational guidance Aiding a person in the choice of an occupation.

vocational interest blank See *strong vocational interest blank.*

Vogt-Spielmeyer Disease (O. Vogt and W. Spielmeyer) A variant of Tay-Sachs Disease. See *Tay-Sachs Disease.*

voice dysmaturity Voice disorder resulting from various conditions, such as defects of the larynx, which directly interfere with the development and function of the laryngeal structures.

volition 1. The process of deciding upon a course of

action without external pressure. **2.** Voluntary activity. **3.** (content psychology) A complex experience consisting primarily of kinesthetic sensations and images of a goal.

volley theory of hearing See *hearing, theory of: volley theory.*

voluntarism A philosophical doctrine which assumes the superiority of the will over reason.

voluntary movement 1. Movement resulting from conscious intention to move. **2.** Movement of striated muscles under the control of the central nervous system.

von Bezold assimilation In the field of color vision von Bezold showed that certain patterns of white lines on chromatic surfaces lightened and black lines darkened the surfaces thus reversing the usual classical lightness contrast effects. Found by H. Helson and colleagues to hold usually for narrow lines on gray as well as chromatic backgrounds.

voyeurism Sexual gratification obtained from peeping, especially from watching people engage in sexual intercourse.

VR schedule See *reinforcement, schedule of: variable ratio.*

vulnerability index of a scale to motivational distortion (R. B. Cattell) An index, obtainable factor analytically, which expresses the distortion in a given questionnaire scale in a given test situation as a function of strength of need to distort. The administration of two scales for the same trait, but of differing vulnerability indices, permits estimation of the true, undistorted score.

Vvedensky, Nikolay Yevgenyevich (1852-1922) Russian physiologist, a disciple of I. M. Sechenov. In 1874 he was arrested, being accused of political propaganda and spent three years in prison. After graduation from the University he worked at Sechenov's laboratory. In 1889 he was appointed as Professor of the Petersburg University.

In 1900 he was elected as an Honorable President of Congress of Medicine in Paris. Vvedensky continued Sechenov's trend in the field of physiology of the nervous system. Investigating the problem of the nervous inhibition and of relation of the inhibitory processes to the excitation of the nervous system, he discovered excitation in nerves is a rhythmic one. He elaborated the theory of parabiosis as a state of a "stable unfluctuated excitation" (*Excitation, Inhibition, and Narcosis,* 1901). Vvedensky showed that the inhibitory process can be formed inside the nervous substrate under increase of frequency and power of the coming nervous impulses (Pressimum). Later on, this phenomenon was called the "Vvedensky inhibition."

Vygotski, Lev Semionovich (1896-1934) Soviet psychologist, one of the founders of modern scientific psychology in the U.S.S.R. His basic contribution to psychology is the introduction of sociohistoric approach to the psychological sciences and the concept of higher psychological processes which are social by origin, intermediated by tool or sign, and conscious and voluntary. According to his observations, higher psychological processes (as voluntary action, active attention, higher form of memorizing) were started as processes divided between two persons (adult and child) and mainly are inter-psychological processes; only then with the development of child's own speech (first overt, then abbreviated and last, internal) these processes become interiorized and an inter-psychological system of processes is formed. Vygotski studied the development of child's own speech; he proved that not only the contents but the structure of the word meanings undergo development, and the system of psychological processes underlying higher psychological functions basically changes during the child's development. His book *Thought and Language* was published in Russian posthumously (1934) and was translated into several languages and had a profound impact upon the development of psychology in the U.S.S.R.

W

w (Rorschach) A response to a card which utilizes most of the inkblot, although not including some small part of the blot.

w 1. (statistics) A weight; also written *W*. 2. A will factor.

W 1. (physics) Work measured in joules. 2. (statistics) Referring to a weight; also written w. 3. (statistics) The coefficient of concordance. 4. (psychophysics) The Weber fraction. 5. The word fluency factor. 6. (Rorschach) Referring to the whole response.

W% (Rorschach) The percentage of the total number of responses to the cards which are responses to the whole card.

W response (Rorschach) A response to a card which utilizes the whole inkblot.

Wagner von Jauregg, Julius (1857-1940) An Austrian psychiatrist and neurologist known for the development of a fever treatment for general paresis.

WAIS See *Wechsler Adult Intelligence Scale.*

Wallerian degeneration (A. V. Waller) (neurology) The breakdown of the myelin sheath of portions of the axon; secondary degeneration.

wandering mania See *mania, wandering.*

wanderlust See *wandering mania.*

war neurosis See *combat neurosis.*

warm spot A tiny spot on the surface of the skin particularly sensitive to heat.

warm-up Increase in the magnitude of some aspect of the response occasioned by the first few trials independent of any reinforcement contingency.

Wartegg drawing completion form A projective technique used with children five and over which consists of a form with eight two-inch boxes, each containing a small stimulus: a line or dots or geometric detail. The child is asked to finish the drawings, title them and tell which he likes best and least.

Formal aspects as well as content of the drawings are considered in the assessment and scoring.

Washburn, Margaret Floy (1871-1939) American psychologist and pioneer in struggle for equal educational opportunities for women. Studied with Cattell at Columbia and obtained her doctorate under Titchener at Cornell. Taught philosophy and psychology at Vassar College (1903-37). Widely known for her theory of motor consciousness, for her editorial services on several psychological journals, and for her election (1921) as president of the American Psychological Association, the second woman so honored.

Wassermann Test A test or a sample of the blood or cerebrospinal fluid for the presence of syphilitic infection.

Watson, John Broadus (1878-1958) American psychologist, founder of behaviorism, whose textbooks on comparative (1914) and general psychology (1918), and popular writings on child rearing (1920's), were highly influential in turning American psychological study away from mental content and toward behavior.

Watson's behaviorism (J. B. Watson) A system of psychology holding strictly to the principle that the only valid material for study is that which can be observed from without—the overt and observable behavior of the organism, its muscles, glands and tissues—eliminating states of consciousness as objects of investigation. The goal of his system was to interpret all behavior in physical-chemical terms. The system proposes that all behavior is learned, the instincts being rejected as causative influences. Behavior is viewed as the result of a stimulus-response connection, the connections in existence being those which have been practiced the most recently and frequently. The theory applied the concept of conditioning to the most complex forms of learning and to the emotions. Behavior, even the most complex, was reduced to a sensory-central-motor chain of stimuli and responses. Thus all behavior was divided into explicit and implicit, the

405

explicit behavior including observable activities such as talking, walking, etc., and the implicit one including visceral activities, glandular secretion, etc.

wave amplitude The height of a wave measured from the crest to the trough.

wave frequency The number of times per second a complete wave pattern passes a specific stationary point.

wave length The distance, at a specified point in time, between two adjacent crests of a wave. The wave length is in an inverse relation with frequency.

wave of excitation 1. An electrochemical change which is propogated in wave form through a living tissue. 2. A neural impulse when seen as an electrochemical change.

waxy flexibility See *catalepsy.*

WAY technique A projective technique in which the subject is asked to write three short answers to the question "who are you?"

Weber, Ernst Heinrich (1795-1878) Pioneer German sensory psychophysiologist, the first to study touch and kinesthesis in elaborate experiments. Discovered a major psychophysical principle which G. T. Fechner later called Weber's law: $\Delta I / I = k$; that is the just noticeable increment (ΔI) in stimulus intensity is a constant fraction (k) of the intensity (I) already present.

Wechsler Adult Intelligence Scale See *scale, Wechsler Adult Intelligence.*

Wechsler-Bellevue Scale See *scale, Wechsler-Bellevue.*

Wechsler, David (1896-   ) American psychologist, author of widely used individual intelligence scales which bear his name: the Wechsler-Bellevue, the Wechsler Adult Intelligence, the Wechsler Intelligence Scale for Children, and the Wechsler Preschool and Primary Scale of Intelligence. First to combine verbal and non-verbal tests into a composite scale, and to introduce the concept of the non-intellective factors of intelligence. Proponent of the view that most intellectual abilities begin to decline at relatively early age (25 or sooner). Principal fields of research: intelligence, diagnostic use of mental test and range of human capacities.

Wechsler Intelligence Scale for Children See *scale, Wechsler Intelligence, for Children.*

Wechsler Preschool and Primary Scale of Intelligence See *scale, Wechsler Preschool and Primary, of Intelligence.*

weight coefficient (statistics) A constant number which is multiplied with a variable so as to alter or modify its relative contribution to a total score or to the variance of the total score.

weighting The determination of the relative influence any one element should have in the total by the assignment of a constant by which that element is multiplied.

Weigl-Goldstein-Scheerer Test See *test, Weigl-Goldstein-Scheerer.*

Weigl-Goldstein-Scheerer Color Form Sorting Test, See *test, Weigl-Goldstein-Scheerer Color Form Sorting.*

Weissmannism A theory of genetics which negates the principle that acquired characterictics are inherited and postulates a continuity of germ plasm through generations.

Weltanschauung A German word meaning view of the universe, used to describe one's total outlook on life, society and its institutions.

Wepman Test of Auditory Discrimination See *test, Wepman, of Auditory Discrimination.*

Werner, Heinz (1890-1964) A psychologist who was trained in Germany but later moved to the United States. He is known for his development of the sensory-tonic field theory of perception and an organismic theory of development.

Werner-Strauss theory (H. Werner and A. Strauss) An attempt at explaining the difficulties brain-injured children have in learning situations. Brain-injured children tend to be seriously handicapped in the visual, tactual and auditory fields by background interference, leading to a chaotic and disturbing impression of the world around them. Special teaching and training approaches are thought to be needed, aimed at overcoming the excessive distractibility of the brain-injured child by diminishing irrelevant stimuli and at teaching him how to tackle perceptual difficulties by taking him through a carefully designed program of exercises.

Wernicke, Carl (1848-1905) A German neurologist known for his work in aphasia. One of the brain areas is named after him.

Wernicke's agnosia See *agnosia, Wernicke's.*

Wernicke's area An area of the cerebrum in the temporal region that was once thought to be the center for understanding spoken language. The area is involved in language but the relationship is more complex than once thought.

Wertheimer, Max (1880-1943) European-born American psychologist. With Wolfgang Köhler and Kurt Koffka, founder of Gestalt psychology. His experiments on apparent movement (phi phenomenon), published in 1912, launched this new psychology. Showed in many contexts that organized wholes cannot be treated as sums of elements "from below," but must be approached "from above," in terms of whole properties and the dynamics of the whole. Demonstrated factors of organization in perception. Undertook major studies and analyses of productive thinking, attempting to describe the processes that occur in it and to show that neither association theory nor the application of traditional logic can account for thinking at its best. Applied Gestalt approach to an understanding of certain problems in ethics, the nature of truth, democracy and freedom.

Wetzel fibers (N. E. Wetzel) An instrument used in plotting interrelations of height, weight, and age over a period of years with norms of development being derived from the interrelations.

Wever-Bray phenomenon (E. G. Wever and C. W. Bray) Cochleal electrical activity in response to external stimulation combined with the action potential of the auditory nerve.

Wherry-Doolittle technique (statistics) A short-cut method used in selecting a small number of tests from a larger number, so the smaller number will yield a correlation with a criterion with only slightly less validity than the multiple correlation of all the tests with the criterion.

whisper test See *test, whisper.*

white matter The areas of the brain which are light gray in color from the myelin covering of the nerve fibers.

white-space response (Rorschach) A response utilizing a portion of the card which is not covered by the inkblot.

White, William A. (1870-1937) An American psychiatrist who was instrumental in bridging the gap in America between academic psychiatry and psychoanalysis.

whole method of learning See *learning, whole method of.*

whole response A Rorschach response which involves the use of the entire blot. Scored *W*, these responses are generally indicative of one's organizational talents.

wholism See *holism.*

Whorf's hypothesis (B. L. Whorf) Differences in language and linguistic habits lead to differences in behavior in general.

Wiersma, Enno Dirk (1858-1940) A Dutch psychiatrist and neurologist who studied genetic origins of mental disorders.

Wiggly Block Test See *test, Wiggly Block.*

Wiktiko psychosis See *psychosis, Wiktiko.*

wild boy of Aveyron (J. Itard) A boy found living in the woods, thought to be a feral child, and brought under the care of Dr. Itard. The boy was unsocialized and spoke no language. The attempt to train him made some inroads but was, for the most part, unsuccessful.

will 1. The capacity which is involved in the ability to participate in conscious activity. **2.** The total impulses, conscious and unconscious, of the person.

will therapy See *psychotherapy, will.*

will to power (A. Adler) The guiding force in development which consists of a striving for superiority and dominance.

Wilson's disease (S. A. K. Wilson) Hepatolenticular degeneration due to a genetic mechanism consisting of several alleles which results in changes in the level of ceruloplasmin.

windigo See *psychosis, Wiktiko.*

windmill illusion The illusion that, without real change in direction, the direction of spin of a spoked wheel changes intermittently.

WISC See *Wechsler Intelligence Scale for Children.*

Wisconsin General Test Apparatus (WGTA) Apparatus used to test discrimination in primates in which the subject chooses between two food cups. The cup that contains the reinforcement is randomly changed from trial to trial.

wit-work (S. Freud) The psychological processes, mostly unconscious, which produce wit. They are similar to the processes involved in dream-work.

witchcraft The belief and practice of magic and sorcery.

withdrawal symptoms Symptoms exhibited by drug addicts when they are removed from the addicting drug, including anxiety, cramps and profuse perspiration.

Wittkower, Eric David (1899-   ) Psychoanalyst. Pioneer in psychosomatic medicine. Has published several books (largely on psychosomatic subjects) and over 125 scientific articles. Recent interests include the cultural aspects of and variations in mental disorder.

wolf child See *feral child.*

Wolpe, Joseph (1915-   ) American, previously South African, psychiatrist, central figure in the development of behavior therapy. Demonstrated that experimental neuroses, whether produced by conflict or noxious stimulation, are learned behavior. Derived from these experiments general theory of neuroses as persistent unadaptive habits acquired by learning in anxiety-generating situations. Evolved reciprocal inhibition theory of psychotherapy on observation that experimental neuroses are progressively diminished through evocation of competing responses, such as feeding in the presence of the stimuli to weak neurotic responses. On this paradigm developed systematic desensitization and other techniques for eliminating human neurotic habits. Major publications: *Psychotherapy by Reciprocal Inhibition,* and *Practice of Behavior Therapy.*

Woodworth personal data sheet (R. S. Woodworth) A personality inventory developed in 1920 which consists of one-hundred sixteen items requiring a "yes" or "no" answer. The inventory is a screening device for neurosis where a "yes" answer is a neurotic one. The subject's score of "yes" answers plus his responses on critical items determine his position in the neurotic category.

Woodworth, Robert Sessions (1869-1962) American psychologist who served psychology for more than 70 years as experimentalist, teacher, textbook writer and editor. Studied with James at Harvard and Cattell at Columbia. Joined teaching staff at Columbia in 1903 and maintained his association with this university until his death. Revised Ladd's *Physiological Psychology* (1911). During World War I designed *The Personal Data Sheet*, a personality inventory to detect emotional instability for military purposes. (Became prototype for subsequent personality questionnaires). An advocate of dynamic psychology—published *Dynamic Psychology* (1917) —and analysis of dynamic interaction of motivation with perception, learning, and thinking. Wrote an introductory text, *Psychology* (1921) in five editions; *Contemporary Schools of Psychology* (1931, rev. 1948, and a final revision, prepared with Mary Rose Sheehan, published posthumously, 1964); and *Dynamics of Behavior* (1958).

word association test See *test, word association.*

word-building test See *test, word-building.*

word count An assessment and study of the frequency with which certain words or classes of words are used in a representative sample of speech or writing.

work decrement (experimental) Decrease in the magnitude of some aspect of the response system as a function of frequency of the response.

work-limit test See *test, work-limit.*

work sample Selected operations or tasks which are taken as representative of some job, often used in the selection of new employees or in the validation of other tests.

working mean See *mean, assumed.*

working through (psychoanalysis) The process in which the patient re-experiences and encounters over and over again the troubling conflicts until he is able to master them and face them independently and successfully in everyday life.

world test See *test, Bolgar-Fischer World.*

WPPSI See *Wechsler Preschool and Primary Scale of Intelligence.*

writer's cramp A painful spasm of the muscles of the forearm, hand and fingers of psychogenic origin.

Wundt, Wilhelm (1832-1920) German physiologist and psychologist; professor at Leipzig (1875-1917) where he founded the first laboratory for experimental psychology. Developed his scientific psychology of consciousness based directly on experience, from physiology and psychophysics. Trained many early pioneers of psychology from various countries. Author of numerous books and articles on physiology, psychology and philosophy. Probably his most important volume is *Principles of Physiological Psychology* (1873-1874), which presented his system and launched psychology as an independent science.

Würzburg school A school of psychology in Germany, important for its contributions concerning the effect that the preparation of a subject has on an experiment, the fact that responses are not mere products of the stimuli but also depend upon some factors within the mind of the subject, and the influence of what were called determining tendencies (hypnotic or experimental suggestions).

X

x 1. The deviation of a class from the mean value of the x variable. 2. Refers to a standardized score which is more commonly referred to as z. 3. The midpoint of an interval. 4. An uncommon response in the Rorschach test in which the subject reports seeing part of an animal in an inkblot to which the most common response is that of seeing a whole or entire animal.

X 1. The most commonly used symbol employed to denote the range of possible scores. 2. Any raw score of the X distribution.

$\overline{X}$ The overlined capital stands for the arithmetic mean of a group of scores.

X′ The capital letter prime stands for a score in the original scale units predicted from another group of scores, Y.

X_O Any variable whose changes are dependent upon the changes in another variable.

$X_1 X_2$ The predicted raw score.

X axis The horizontal axis or abcissa which at a right angle to the Y axis, forms a reference by which any point in space can be located.

x chromosome One of the sex determining chromosomes. Females have xx chromosomes; males have xy chromosomes.

X coordinate See *X axis.*

X-O test See *test, X-O.*

X value The distance from any point to the X axis measured on a line parallel to the Y axis.

xanthocyanopia; xanthocyanopsia Partial color blindness; red and green are not perceived.

xenophobia An extreme fear of strangers.

xi (psychophysics) The point of subjective equality or the point at which the probability of a judgment "greater" is equal to the probability of a judgment "lesser".

Y

y (statistics) The deviation of a value from the class mean ordinate value. **2.** (mathematics) The height or value of an ordinate, the qualitative value representing the distance from the X axis along any line parallel to the Y axis.

Y **1.** That which is being predicted by other variables. The dependent variable. **2.** Any raw score of the Y distribution. **3.** (Rorschach) An inkblot response which is determined by a flat gray surface.

Y axis The vertical axis or ordinate which at a right angle to the X axis, forms a reference by which any point in space can be located.

y chromosome One of the sex determining chromosomes. See *x chromosome.*

Y coordinate See *Y axis.*

y intercept (mathematics) The distance from the origin to the point where a line crosses the Y axis.

Y value The distance from any point to the X axis measured on a line parallel to the Y axis.

year scaling See *age-equivalent scale.*

yellow-sighted A heightened color sensitivity for yellow or the tendency to see all objects tinged with yellow.

yellow spot See *macula lutea.*

Yerkes-Bridges point scale An early adaptation of the Binet scale for American conditions which utilized points rather than months of mental age.

Yerkes, Robert Mearns (1876-1956) Yale psychologist and primatologist. Known for 1) invention of numerous laboratory devices for comparative studies of animal behavior, 2) early research on aggressive instincts in cats, 3) formulation of Yerkes-Dodson law, 4) supervision (with L. M. Terman) of army intelligence testing in World War I, and 5) extensive research studies of chimpanzees and gorillas in his Yale Laboratories of Primate Biology (1925-1946).

yoga A method of contemplation used in Indian religious training. Yoga means, literally, yoking or harnessing, controlling one's faculties. The aim of yoga is to separate the eternal element in man from the psychophysical organism by striving for a conscious state in which mental activities, such as perception and imagination, can be suspended. There are physical as well as mental exercises and techniques aimed at attaining this state.

yoked boxes (operant conditioning) Experimental control procedure which separates reinforcement frequency from other variables. In one isolated experimental chamber the organism is reinforced according to the schedule, usually an FR. In another completely isolated experimental chamber, another subject becomes eligible for reinforcement whenever the organism in the first chamber is reinforced. Only when a response in the first experimental chamber is reinforced is a response in the second chamber reinforced. When an FR schedule is operative in the first chamber, usually a VI schedule is operative in the second chamber.

yoked control Experimental control technique in which the experimental subject's reinforcement is dependent upon his responses while for another control subject, the reinforcements are delivered as they were for the experimental subject regardless of the responses of the control subject.

Young-Helmholtz theory See *color vision, theory of: Young-Helmholtz theory.*

Young, Paul Thomas (1892-) American psychologist, pioneer in the experimental study of motivation and the affective processes. Known for 1) experimental studies of food preferences, palatability, appetite, dietary habits, 2) the role of hedonic processes in behavior and development, 3) experimental studies of sound localization with a right-left reversing pseudophone.

Z

z (statistics) A standardized score which shows the relative status of that score in a normal distribution. Any raw score may be converted into this score by means of the formula:

$$z = \frac{x\text{-}M}{S}$$

where x is the score, M is the mean of scores and S is the standard deviation of the sample of scores.

Z (statistics–R.A. Fisher) A one-to-one function of r_{xy} known as the Fisher r to Z transformation. It is used to test hypotheses about $_{xx}$ as well as confidence intervals on large samples from bivariate normal populations. For each r there is only one Z value. The Z value is used because for almost any value of $_{xy}$, the sampling distribution of Z value is approximately normal. Transformation values are found in appendices of statistical textbooks.

z score A major scoring used in the Beck approach to the Rorschach to evaluate the organizational activity which occurs as certain responses are formulated. Scores are given on a weighted basis depending on the difficulty and complexity of the organization.

Zeigarnik effect (B. Zeigarnik and K. Lewin) An experimental study of uncompleted tests. Settings of a task or a goal creates tension, and the individual tends to act in order to remove the tension by locomotion in the direction of the goal. As long as the task is not completed, a force corresponding to the valence of the goal region motivates the individual, thus the uncompleted tasks are better remembered than the completed ones.

Zeitgeist The spirit of the times; the prevailing cultural climate at a certain epoch.

Zen Buddhism A form of Mahayana Buddhism found chiefly in Japan but recently having an influence in the West, especially the United States. Zen, meaning literally meditation, stresses spiritual discipline through meditation leading to sudden illumination or satori, a stage on the road to full enlightenment. There is a belief in rebirth, the necessity of attaining release, and the possibility of attaining Buddhahood, as well as an emphasis on the spontaneity of illumination and the rapport existing between the individual and nature. Illumination is gained when the unity which transcends the differences between immediate experience and cerebration is recognized and known.

Zen psychology A treatment approach originating in the Orient which concerns itself with existential questions of meaning and strives to attain a state of oneness with the universe which is called "satori". Specific techniques are available to reach this goal, such as training in particular physical posture and meditation, the aim of which is the suppression of worldly desires and conflicts.

Zeno's arrow A logical argument forwarded by the sophistic philosophers in ancient Greece which attempted to prove that motion is impossible.

zero, absolute 1. The temperature at which there is no longer any molecular motion, equivalent to -273 degrees C. or –459 degrees F. 2. The point on a measuring scale where that which is being measured no longer exists, where nothing of the variable remains.

zero correlation See *correlation, zero.*

zero-order (statistics) Pertaining to a correlation coefficient which has no variables held constant when computed. It is written r_{12}, referring to the correlation of variables 1 and 2.

Zoellner illusion See *illusion, Zoellner.*

zone, hypnogenic See *spot, hypnogenic.*

zooerasty Sexual intercourse of a human with an animal.

zoology The science of animal life.

zoomorphism An interpretation of human behavior in terms of animal behavior; uncritical application of data obtained from comparative psychology to human behavior.

zoophilia An excessive attraction to animals.

zoophobia A morbid fear of animals.

Zubin, Joseph (1900-) American psychologist and psychopathologist concerned with introducing objective approaches to evaluation of treatment of mental disorders, improvement of classification and diagnosis by use of systematic structured interviews, development of suitable statistical techniques and experimental laboratory and field investigation methods for detection and diagnosis of mental disorders.

Zürich school Carl G. Jung and his followers.

zygote The fertilized ovum.

APPENDIX A

CLASSIFICATION
OF
MENTAL DISORDERS

by

AMERICAN PSYCHIATRIC ASSOCIATION

THE USE OF THIS MANUAL: SPECIAL INSTRUCTIONS

Abbreviations and Special Symbols

The following abbreviations and special symbols are used throughout this Manual:

WHO — The World Health Organization

ICD-8 — The **International Classification of Diseases, Eighth Revision,** World Health Organization, 1968. For use in the United States see: **Eighth Revision International Classification of Diseases Adapted for Use in the United States,** Public Health Service Publication No. 1693, U. S. Government Printing Office, Washington, D. C. 20402.

DSM-I — **Diagnostic and Statistical Manual, Mental Disorders,** American Psychiatric Association, Washington, D. C., 1952 (out of print).

DSM-II — This Manual: **Diagnostic and Statistical Manual of Mental Disorders,** Second Edition, American Psychiatric Association, Washington, D. C., 1968.

[ ] — The brackets indicate ICD-8 categories to be avoided in the United States or used by record librarians only.

* — Asterisk indicates categories added to ICD-8 for use in the United States only.

(( )) — Double parentheses indicate ICD-8 terms equivalent to U. S. terms.

OBS — Organic Brain Syndrome(s), i.e. mental disorders caused by or associated with impairment of brain tissue function.

The Organization of the Diagnostic Nomenclature

While this Manual generally uses the same diagnostic code numbers as ICD-8, two groups of disorders are out of sequence: *Mental retardation* and the *Non-psychotic organic brain syndromes. Mental retardation* is placed first to emphasize that it is to be diagnosed whenever present, even if due to some other disorder. The *Non-psychotic or-*

ganic brain syndromes are grouped with the other organic brain syndromes in keeping with psychiatric thinking in this country, which views the organic brain syndromes, whether psychotic or not, as one group. Furthermore, the diagnostic nomenclature is divided into ten major subdivisions, indicated with Roman numerals, to emphasize the way mental disorders are often grouped in the United States.

The Recording of Diagnoses

Every attempt has been made to express the diagnoses in the clearest and simplest terms possible within the framework of modern usage. Clinicians will significantly improve communication and research by recording their diagnoses in the same terms.

Multiple Psychiatric Diagnoses

Individuals may have more than one mental disorder. For example, a patient with anxiety neurosis may also develop morphine addiction. In DSM-I, drug addiction was classified as a secondary diagnosis, but addiction to alcohol, for example, could not be diagnosed in the presence of a recognizable underlying disorder. This manual, by contrast, encourages the recording of the diagnosis of alcoholism separately even when it begins as a symptomatic expression of another disorder. Likewise mental retardation is a separate diagnosis. For example, there are children whose disorders could be diagnosed as "Schizophrenia, childhood type" and "Mental retardation following major psychiatric disorder."

The diagnostician, however, should not lose sight of the rule of parsimony and diagnose more conditions than are necessary to account for the clinical picture. The opportunity to make multiple diagnoses does not lessen the physician's responsibility to make a careful differential diagnosis.

Which of several diagnoses the physician places first is a matter of his own judgment, but two principles may be helpful in making his decision:

1. The condition which most urgently requires treatment should be listed first. For example, if a patient with simple schizophrenia was presented to the diagnostician because of pathological alcohol intoxication, then the order of diagnoses would be first, *Pathological intoxication,* and second, *Schizophrenia, simple type*.

2. When there is no issue of disposition or treatment priority, the more serious condition should be listed first.

It is recommended that, in addition to recording multiple disorders in conformity with these principles, the diagnostician *underscore* the disorder on the patient's record that he considers the underlying one. Because these principles will not always be applied or used consistently, statistical systems should account for all significant diagnoses recorded in every case.

Qualifying Phrases and Adjectives

The ICD is based on a classification scheme which allots three digits for the designation of major disease categories and a fourth digit for the specification of additional detail within each category. DSM-II has introduced a fifth digit for coding certain qualifying phrases that may be used to specify additional characteristics of mental disorders. This digit does not disturb the content of either the three- or four-digit categories in the ICD section on mental disorders.

These terms are as follows:

(1.) In the brain syndromes a differentiation of acute and chronic conditions may be provided by .x1 *acute* and .x2 *chronic*. This will help maintain continuity with DSM-I. These qualifying adjectives are recommended only for mental disorders specified as associated with physical conditions and are, of course, unnecessary in disorders seen only in an acute or chronic form.

Those who wish to continue the distinction made in DSM-I between "acute" and "chronic" organic brain syndromes must now add these as qualifying terms. Note also that a recorded diagnosis which merely indicates an organic brain syndrome and does not specify whether or not it is psychotic will now be classified under *Non-psychotic organic brain syndromes*.

(2.) The qualifying phrase, .x5 *in remission,* may also be used to indicate a period of remission in any disorder. This is not synonymous with *No mental disorder.*

(3.) With a few exceptions, all disorders listed in parts IV through IX may be classified as .x6 *mild,* .x7 *moderate,* and .x8 *severe.* But exceptions must be made in coding *Passive-aggressive personality, Inadequate personality,* and the two sub-types of *Hysterical neurosis* because their basic code numbers have five digits. *Antisocial personality* should always be specified as mild, moderate, or severe.

(4.) As explained on page **439**, the qualifying phrase *not psychotic* (.x6) may be used for the psychoses listed in pages **430-468** when the patient's degree of disturbance is not psychotic at the time of examination.

Associated Physical Conditions

Many mental disorders, and particularly mental retardation and the various organic brain syndromes, are reflections of underlying physical conditions. Whenever these physical conditions are known they should be indicated with a separate diagnosis in addition to the one that specifies the mental disorder found.

THE DIAGNOSTIC NOMENCLATURE:
List of Mental Disorders and Their Code Numbers

I. MENTAL RETARDATION

Mental retardation (310-315)

310 Borderline mental retardation

311 Mild mental retardation

312 Moderate mental retardation

313 Severe mental retardation

314 Profound mental retardation

315 Unspecified mental retardation

The fourth-digit sub-divisions cited below should be used with each of the above categories. The associated physical condition should be specified as an additional diagnosis when known.

.0 Following infection or intoxication

.1 Following trauma or physical agent

.2 With disorders of metabolism, growth or nutrition

.3 Associated with gross brain disease (postnatal)

.4 Associated with diseases and conditions due to (unknown) prenatal influence

.5 With chromosomal abnormality

.6 Associated with prematurity

.7 Following major psychiatric disorder

.8 With psycho-social (environmental) deprivation

.9 With other [and unspecified] condition

II. ORGANIC BRAIN SYNDROMES

(Disorders Caused by or Associated With Impairment of Brain Tissue Function) In the categories under IIA and IIB the associated physical condition should be specified when known.

II-A. PSYCHOSES ASSOCIATED WITH ORGANIC BRAIN SYNDROMES (290-294)

290 Senile and pre-senile dementia
   .0 Senile dementia
   .1 Pre-senile dementia

291 Alcoholic psychosis
   .0 Delirium tremens
   .1 Korsakov's psychosis (alcoholic)
   .2 Other alcoholic hallucinosis
   .3 Alcohol paranoid state ((Alcoholic paranoia))
   .4* Acute alcohol intoxication*
   .5* Alcoholic deterioration*
   .6* Pathological intoxication*
   .9 Other [and unspecified] alcoholic psychosis

292 Psychosis associated with intracranial infection
   .0 Psychosis with general paralysis
   .1 Psychosis with other syphilis of central nervous system
   .2 Psychosis with epidemic encephalitis
   .3 Psychosis with other and unspecified encephalitis
   .9 Psychosis with other [and unspecified] intracranial infection

293 Psychosis associated with other cerebral condition
   .0 Psychosis with cerebral arteriosclerosis
   .1 Psychosis with other cerebrovascular disturbance
   .2 Psychosis with epilepsy
   .3 Psychosis with intracranial neoplasm
   .4 Psychosis with degenerative disease of the central nervous system
   .5 Psychosis with brain trauma
   .9 Psychosis with other [and unspecified] cerebral condition

294 Psychosis associated with other physical condition
   .0 Psychosis with endocrine disorder
   .1 Psychosis with metabolic or nutritional disorder
   .2 Psychosis with systemic infection

.3 Psychosis with drug or poison intoxication (other than alcohol)

.4 Psychosis with childbirth

.8 Psychosis with other and undiagnosed physical condition

[.9 Psychosis with unspecified physical condition]

II-B NON-PSYCHOTIC ORGANIC BRAIN SYNDROMES (309)

309 Non-psychotic organic brain syndromes ((Mental disorders not specified as psychotic associated with physical conditions))

.0 Non-psychotic OBS with intracranial infection

[.1 Non-psychotic OBS with drug, poison, or systemic intoxication]

.13* Non-psychotic OBS with alcohol* (simple drunkenness)

.14* Non-psychotic OBS with other drug, poison, or systemic intoxication*

.2 Non-psychotic OBS with brain trauma

.3 Non-psychotic OBS with circulatory disturbance

.4 Non-psychotic OBS with epilepsy

.5 Non-psychotic OBS with disturbance of metabolism, growth or nutrition

.6 Non-psychotic OBS with senile or pre-senile brain disease

.7 Non-psychotic OBS with intracranial neoplasm

.8 Non-psychotic OBS with degenerative disease of central nervous system

.9 Non-psychotic OBS with other [and unspecified] physical condition

[.91* Acute brain syndrome, not otherwise specified*]
[.92* Chronic brain syndrome, not otherwise specified*]

III. PSYCHOSES NOT ATTRIBUTED TO PHYSICAL CONDITIONS LISTED PREVIOUSLY (295-298)

295 Schizophrenia

.0 Schizophrenia, simple type

.1 Schizophrenia, hebephrenic type

.2 Schizophrenia, catatonic type

.23* Schizophrenia, catatonic type, excited*
.24* Schizophrenia, catatonic type, withdrawn*

.3 Schizophrenia, paranoid type

.4 Acute schizophrenic episode

.5 Schizophrenia, latent type

.6 Schizophrenia, residual type

.7 Schizophrenia, schizo-affective type

    .73* Schizophrenia, schizo-affective type, excited*

    .74* Schizophrenia, schizo-affective type, depressed*

.8*   Schizophrenia, childhood type*

.90* Schizophrenia, chronic undifferentiated type*

.99* Schizophrenia, other [and unspecified] types*

296 Major affective disorders ((Affective psychoses))

.0 Involutional melancholia

.1 Manic-depressive illness, manic type ((Manic-depressive psychosis, manic type))

.2 Manic-depressive illness, depressed type ((Manic-depressive psychosis, depressed type))

.3 Manic-depressive illness, circular type ((Manic-depressive psychosis, circular type))

    .33* Manic-depressive illness, circular type, manic*

    .34* Manic-depressive illness, circular type, depressed*

.8 Other major affective disorder ((Affective psychoses, other))

[.9 Unspecified major affective disorder]
    [Affective disorder not otherwise specified]
    [Manic-depressive illness not otherwise specified]

297 Paranoid states

.0 Paranoia

.1 Involutional paranoid state ((Involutional paraphrenia))

.9 Other paranoid state

298 Other psychoses

.0 Psychotic depressive reaction ((Reactive depressive psychosis))

[.1 Reactive excitation]

[.2 Reactive confusion]
        [Acute or subacute confusional state]
[.3 Acute paranoid reaction]
[.9 Reactive psychosis, unspecified]

[299 Unspecified psychosis]
        [Dementia, insanity or psychosis not otherwise specified]

IV. NEUROSES (300)

300 Neuroses
  .0 Anxiety neurosis
  .1 Hysterical neurosis
      .13* Hysterical neurosis, conversion type*
      .14* Hysterical neurosis, dissociative type*
  .2 Phobic neurosis
  .3 Obsessive compulsive neurosis
  .4 Depressive neurosis
  .5 Neurasthenic neurosis ((Neurasthenia))
  .6 Depersonalization neurosis ((Depersonalization syndrome))
  .7 Hypochondriacal neurosis
  .8 Other neurosis
  [.9 Unspecified neurosis]

V. PERSONALITY DISORDERS AND CERTAIN OTHER NON-PSYCHOTIC MENTAL DISORDERS (301—304)

301 Personality disorders
  .0 Paranoid personality
  .1 Cyclothymic personality ((Affective personality))
  .2 Schizoid personality
  .3 Explosive personality
  .4 Obsessive compulsive personality ((Anankastic personality))
  .5 Hysterical personality
  .6 Asthenic personality
  .7 Antisocial personality
  .81* Passive-aggressive personality*
  .82* Inadequate personality*

.89* Other personality disorders of specified types*

[.9 Unspecified personality disorder]

302 Sexual deviations

.0 Homosexuality

.1 Fetishism

.2 Pedophilia

.3 Transvestitism

.4 Exhibitionism

.5* Voyeurism*

.6* Sadism*

.7* Masochism*

.8 Other sexual deviation

[.9 Unspecified sexual deviation]

303 Alcoholism

.0 Episodic excessive drinking

.1 Habitual excessive drinking

.2 Alcohol addiction

.9 Other [and unspecified] alcoholism

304 Drug dependence

.0 Drug dependence, opium, opium alkaloids and their derivatives

.1 Drug dependence, synthetic analgesics with morphine-like effects

.2 Drug dependence, barbiturates

.3 Drug dependence, other hypnotics and sedatives or "tranquilizers"

.4 Drug dependence, cocaine

.5 Drug dependence, Cannabis sativa (hashish, marihuana)

.6 Drug dependence, other psycho-stimulants

.7 Drug dependence, hallucinogens

.8 Other drug dependence

[.9 Unspecified drug dependence]

VI. PSYCHOPHYSIOLOGIC DISORDERS (305)

305 Psychophysiologic disorders ((Physical disorders of presumably psychogenic origin))

.0 Psychophysiologic skin disorder

.1 Psychophysiologic musculoskeletal disorder

.2 Psychophysiologic respiratory disorder

.3 Psychophysiologic cardiovascular disorder

.4 Psychophysiologic hemic and lymphatic disorder

.5 Psychophysiologic gastro-intestinal disorder

.6 Psychophysiologic genito-urinary disorder

.7 Psychophysiologic endocrine disorder

.8 Psychophysiologic disorder of organ of special sense

.9 Psychophysiologic disorder of other type

VII. SPECIAL SYMPTOMS (306)

306 Special symptoms not elsewhere classified

.0 Speech disturbance

.1 Specific learning disturbance

.2 Tic

.3 Other psychomotor disorder

.4 Disorders of sleep

.5 Feeding disturbance

.6 Enuresis

.7 Encopresis

.8 Cephalalgia

.9 Other special symptom

VIII. TRANSIENT SITUATIONAL DISTURBANCES (307)

307* Transient situational disturbances[1]

---

[1] The terms included under DSM-II Category 307*, "Transient situational disturbances," differ from those in Category 307 of the ICD. DSM-II Category 307*, "Transient situational disturbances," contains adjustment reactions of infancy (307.0*), childhood (307.1*), adolescence (307.2*), adult life (307.3*), and late life (307.4*). ICD Category 307, "Transient situational disturbances," includes only the adjustment reactions of adolescence, adult life and late life. ICD 308, "Behavioral disorders of children," contains the reactions of infancy and childhood. These differences must be taken into account in preparing statistical tabulations to conform to ICD categories.

.0* Adjustment reaction of infancy*

.1* Adjustment reaction of childhood*

.2* Adjustment reaction of adolescence*

.3* Adjustment reaction of adult life*

.4* Adjustment reaction of late life*

IX. BEHAVIOR DISORDERS OF CHILDHOOD AND ADOLESCENCE (308)

308 Behavior disorders of childhood and adolescence[2] ((Behavior disorders of childhood))

.0* Hyperkinetic reaction of childhood (or adolescence)*

.1* Withdrawing reaction of childhood (or adolescence)*

.2* Overanxious reaction of childhood (or adolescence)*

.3* Runaway reaction of childhood (or adolescence)*

.4* Unsocialized aggressive reaction of childhood (or adolescence)*

.5* Group delinquent reaction of childhood (or adolescence)*

.9* Other reaction of childhood (or adolescence)*

X. CONDITIONS WITHOUT MANIFEST PSYCHIATRIC DISORDER AND NON-SPECIFIC CONDITIONS (316*—318*)[†]

316*[††] Social maladjustments without manifest psychiatric disorder

.0* Marital maladjustment*

.1* Social maladjustment*

.2* Occupational maladjustment*

.3* Dyssocial behavior*

.9* Other social maladjustment*

---

[2] The terms included under DSM-II Category 308*, "Behavioral disorders of childhood and adolescence," differ from those in Category 308 of the ICD. DSM-II Category 308* includes "Behavioral disorders of childhood and adolescence," whereas ICD Category 308 includes only "Behavioral disorders of childhood." DSM-II Category 308* *does not* include "Adjustment reactions of infancy and childhood", whereas ICD Category 308 does. In the DSM-II classification, "Adjustment reactions of infancy and childhood" are allocated to 307* (Transitional situational disturbances). These differences should be taken into account in preparing statistical tabulations to conform to the ICD categories.

317* Non-specific conditions*

318* No mental disorder*

XI. NON-DIAGNOSTIC TERMS FOR ADMINISTRATIVE USE (319*)†

319* Non-diagnostic terms for administrative use*

  .0* Diagnosis deferred*

  .1* Boarder*

  .2* Experiment only*

  .9* Other*

---

† The terms included in this category would normally be listed in that section of ICD-8 that deals with "Special conditions and examinations without sickness." They are included here to permit coding of some additional conditions that are encountered in psychiatric clinical settings in the U. S. This has been done by using several unassigned code numbers at the end of Section 5 of the ICD.

†† This diagnosis corresponds to the category *Y13, **Social maladjustment without manifest psychiatric disorder** in ICDA.

THE DEFINITIONS OF TERMS

I: MENTAL RETARDATION[1] (310—315)

Mental retardation refers to subnormal general intellectual functioning which originates during the developmental period and is associated with impairment of either learning and social adjustment or maturation, or both. (These disorders were classified under "Chronic brain syndrome with mental deficiency" and "Mental deficiency" in DSM-I.) The diagnostic classification of mental retardation relates to IQ as follows[2]:

310 Borderline mental retardation—IQ 68—83

311 Mild mental retardation—IQ 52—67

312 Moderate mental retardation—IQ 36—51

313 Severe mental retardation—IQ 20—35

314 Profound mental retardation—IQ under 20

Classifications 310-314 are based on the statistical distribution of levels of intellectual functioning for the population as a whole. The range of intelligence subsumed under each classification corresponds to one standard deviation, making the heuristic assumption that intelligence is normally distributed. It is recognized that the intelligence quotient should not be the only criterion used in making a diagnosis of mental retardation or in evaluating its severity. It should serve only to help in making a clinical judgment of the patient's adaptive behavioral capacity. This judgment should also be based on an evaluation of the patient's developmental history and present functioning, including academic and vocational achievement, motor skills, and social and emotional maturity.

315 Unspecified mental retardation

This classification is reserved for patients whose intellectual functioning

---

[1] For a fuller definition of terms see the "Manual on Terminology and Classification in Mental Retardation," (Supplement to *American Journal of Mental Deficiency,* Second Edition, 1961) from which most of this section has been adapted.

[2] The IQs specified are for the Revised Stanford-Binet Tests of Intelligence, Forms L and M. Equivalent values for other tests are listed in the manual cited in the footnote above.

has not or cannot be evaluated precisely but which is recognized as clearly subnormal.

Clinical Subcategories of Mental Retardation

These will be coded as fourth digit subdivisions following each of the categories 310-315. When the associated condition is known more specifically, particularly when it affects the entire organism or an organ system other than the central nervous system, it should be coded additionally in the specific field affected.

.0 Following infection and intoxication

This group is to classify cases in which mental retardation is the result of residual cerebral damage from intracranial infections, serums, drugs, or toxic agents. Examples are:

Cytomegalic inclusion body disease, congenital. A maternal viral disease, usually mild or subclinical, which may infect the fetus and is recognized by the presence of inclusion bodies in the cellular elements in the urine, cerebrospinal fluid, and tissues.

Rubella, congenital. Affecting the fetus in the first trimester and usually accompanied by a variety of congenital anomalies of the ear, eye and heart.

Syphilis, congenital. Two types are described, an early meningo-vascular disease and a diffuse encephalitis leading to juvenile paresis.

Toxoplasmosis, congenital. Due to infection by a protozoan-like organism, Toxoplasma, contracted in utero. May be detected by serological tests in both mother and infant.

Encephalopathy associated with other prenatal infections. Occasionally fetal damage from maternal epidemic cerebrospinal meningitis, equine encephalomyelitis, influenza, etc. has been reported. The relationships have not as yet been definitely established.

Encephalopathy due to postnatal cerebral infection. Both focal and generalized types of cerebral infection are included and are to be given further anatomic and etiologic specification.

Encephalopathy, congenital, associated with maternal toxemia of pregnancy. Severe and prolonged toxemia of pregnancy, particularly eclampsia, may be associated with mental retardation.

Encephalopathy, congenital, associated with other maternal intoxications. Examples are carbon monoxide, lead, arsenic, quinine, ergot, etc.

Bilirubin encephalopathy (Kernicterus). Frequently due to Rh, A, B, O blood group incompatibility between fetus and mother but may also follow prematurity, severe neonatal sepsis or any condition producing high levels of serum bilirubin. Choreoathetosis is frequently associated with this form of mental retardation.

Post-immunization encephalopathy. This may follow inoculation with serum, particularly anti-tetanus serum, or vaccines such as smallpox, rabies, and typhoid.

Encephalopathy, other, due to intoxication. May result from such toxic agents as lead, carbon monoxide, tetanus and botulism exotoxin.

.1 Following trauma or physical agent

Further specification within this category follows:

Encephalopathy due to prenatal injury. This includes prenatal irradiation and asphyxia, the latter following maternal anoxia, anemia, and hypotension.

Encephalopathy due to mechanical injury at birth. These are attributed to difficulties of labor due to malposition, malpresentation, disproportion, or other complications leading to dystocia which may increase the probability of damage to the infant's brain at birth, resulting in tears of the meninges, blood vessels, and brain substance. Other reasons include venous-sinus thrombosis, arterial embolism and thrombosis. These may result in sequelae which are indistinguishable from those of other injuries, damage or organic impairment of the brain.

Encephalopathy due to asphyxia at birth. Attributable to the anoxemia following interference with placental circulation due to premature separation, placenta praevia, cord difficulties, and other interferences with oxygenation of the placental circulation.

Encephalopathy due to postnatal injury. The diagnosis calls for evidence of severe trauma such as a fractured skull, prolonged unconsciousness, etc., followed by a marked change in development. Postnatal asphyxia, infarction, thrombosis, laceration, and contusion of the brain would be included and the nature of the injury specified.

.2 With disorders of metabolism, growth or nutrition

All conditions associated with mental retardation directly due to metabolic, nutritional, or growth dysfunction should be classified here, including disorders of lipid, carbohydrate and protein metabolism, and deficiencies of nutrition.

Cerebral lipoidosis, infantile (Tay-Sach's disease). This is caused by a single recessive autosomal gene and has infantile and juvenile forms. In the former there is gradual deterioration, blindness after the pathognomonic "cherry-red spot," with death occurring usually before age three.

Cerebral lipoidosis, late infantile (Bielschowsky's disease). This differs from the preceding by presenting retinal optic atrophy instead of the "cherry-red spot."

Cerebral lipoidosis, juvenile (Spielmeyer-Vogt disease). This usually appears between the ages of five and ten with involvement of the motor systems, frequent seizures, and pigmentary degeneration of the retina. Death follows in five to ten years.

Cerebral lipoidosis, late juvenile (Kuf's disease). This is categorized under mental retardation only when it occurs at an early age.

Lipid histiocytosis of kerasin type (Gaucher's disease). As a rule this condition causes retardation only when it affects infants. It is characterized by Gaucher's cells in lymph nodes, spleen or marrow.

Lipid histiocystosis of phosphatide type (Niemann-Pick's disease). Distinguished from Tay-Sach's disease by enlargement of liver and spleen. Biopsy of spleen, lymph or marrow show characteristic "foam cells."

Phenylketonuria. A metabolic disorder, genetically transmitted as a simple autosomal recessive gene, preventing the conversion of phenylalanine into tyrosine with an accumulation of phenylalanine, which in turn is converted to phenylpyruvic acid detectable in the urine.

Hepatolenticular degeneration (Wilson's disease). Genetically transmitted as a simple autosomal recessive. It is due to inability of ceruloplasmin to bind copper, which in turn damages the brain. Rare in children.

Porphyria. Genetically transmitted as a dominant and characterized by excretion of porphyrins in the urine. It is rare in children, in whom it may cause irreversible deterioration.

Galactosemia. A condition in which galactose is not metabolized, causing its accumulation in the blood. If milk is not removed from the diet, generalized organ deficiencies, mental deterioration and death may result.

Glucogenosis (Von Gierke's disease). Due to a deficiency in glycogen-metabolizing enzymes with deposition of glycogen in various organs, including the brain.

Hypoglycemosis. Caused by various conditions producing hypoglycemia which, in the infant, may result in epilepsy and mental defect. Diagnosis may be confirmed by glucose tolerance tests.

.3 Associated with gross brain disease (postnatal)

This group includes all diseases and conditions associated with neoplasms, but not growths that are secondary to trauma or infection. The category also includes a number of postnatal diseases and conditions in which the structural reaction is evident but the etiology is unknown or uncertain, though frequently presumed to be of hereditary or familial nature. Structural reactions may be degenerative, infiltrative, inflammatory, proliferative, sclerotic, or reparative.

Neurofibromatosis (Neurofibroblastomatosis, von Recklinghausen's disease). A disease transmitted by a dominant autosomal gene but with reduced penetrance and variable expressivity. It is characterized by cutaneous pigmentation ("café au lait" patches) and neurofibromas of nerve, skin and central nervous system with intellectual capacity varying from normal to severely retarded.

Trigeminal cerebral angiomatosis (Sturge-Weber-Dimitri's disease). A condition characterized by a "port wine stain" or cutaneous angioma, usually in the distribution of the trigeminal nerve, accompanied by vascular malformation over the meninges of the parietal and occipital lobes with underlying cerebral maldevelopment.

Tuberous sclerosis (Epiloia, Bourneville's disease). Transmitted by a dominant autosomal gene, characterized by multiple gliotic nodules in the central nervous system, and associated with adenoma sebaceum of the face and tumors in other organs. Retarded development and seizures may appear early and increase in severity along with tumor growth.

Intracranial neoplasm, other. Other relatively rare neoplastic diseases leading to mental retardation should be included in this category and specified when possible.

Encephalopathy associated with diffuse sclerosis of the brain. This category includes a number of similar conditions differing to some extent in their pathological and clinical features but characterized by diffuse demyelination of the white matter with resulting diffuse glial sclerosis and accompanied by intellectual deterioration. These diseases are often familial in character and when possible should be specified under the following:

Acute infantile diffuse sclerosis (Krabbe's disease).

Diffuse chronic infantile sclerosis (Merzbacher-Pelizaeus disease, Aplasia axialis extracorticalis congenita).

Infantile metachromatic leukodystrophy (Greenfield's disease).

Juvenile metachromatic leukodystrophy (Scholz' disease).

Progressive subcortical encephalopathy (Encephalitis periaxialis diffusa, Schilder's disease).

Spinal sclerosis (Friedreich's ataxia). Characterized by cerebellar degeneration, early onset followed by dementia.

Encephalopathy, other, due to unknown or uncertain cause with the structural reactions manifest. This category includes cases of mental retardation associated with progressive neuronal degeneration or other structural defects which cannot be classified in a more specific, diagnostic category.

.4 Associated with diseases and conditions due to unknown prenatal influence

This category is for classifying conditions known to have existed at the time of or prior to birth but for which no definite etiology can be established. These include the primary cranial anomalies and congenital defects of undetermined origin as follows:

Anencephaly (including hemianencephaly).

Malformations of the gyri. This includes agyria, macrogyria (pachygyria) and microgyria.

Porencephaly, congenital. Characterized by large funnel-shaped cavities occurring anywhere in the cerebral hemispheres. Specify, if possible, whether the porencephaly is a result of asphyxia at birth or postnatal trauma.

Multiple-congenital anomalies of the brain.

Other cerebral defects, congenital.

Craniostenosis. The most common conditions included in this category are acrocephaly (oxycephaly) and scaphocephaly. These may or may not be associated with mental retardation.

Hydrocephalus, congenital. Under this heading is included only that type of hydrocephalus present at birth or occurring soon after delivery. All other types of hydrocephalus, secondary to other conditions, should be classified under the specific etiology when known.

Hypertelorism (Greig's disease). Characterized by abnormal development of the sphenoid bone increasing the distance between the eyes.

Macrocephaly (Megalencephaly). Characterized by an increased size and weight of the brain due partially to proliferation of glia.

Microcephaly, primary. True microcephaly is probably transmitted as a single autosomal recessive. When it is caused by other conditions it should be classified according to the primary condition, with secondary microcephaly as a supplementary term.

Laurence-Moon-Biedl syndrome. Characterized by mental retardation associated with retinitis pigmentosa, adiposo-genital dystrophy, and polydactyly.

.5 With chromosomal abnormality

This group includes cases of mental retardation associated with chromosomal abnormalities. These may be divided into two sub-groups, those associated with an abnormal number of chromosomes and those with abnormal chromosomal morphology.

Autosomal trisomy of group G. (Trisomy 21, Langdon-Down disease, Mongolism). This is the only common form of mental retardation due to chromosomal abnormality. (The others are relatively rare.) It ranges in degree from moderate to severe with infrequent cases of mild retardation. Other congenital defects are frequently present, and the intellectual development decelerates with time.

Autosomal trisomy of group E.

Autosomal trisomy of group D.

Sex chromosome anomalies. The only condition under the category which has any significant frequency is Klinefelter's syndrome.

Abnormal number of chromosomes, other. In this category would be included monosomy G, and possibly others as well as other forms of mosaicism.

Short arm deletion of chromosome 5—group B (Cri du chat). A quite rare condition characterized by congenital abnormalities and a cat-like cry during infancy which disappears with time.

Short arm deletion of chromosome 18—group E.

Abnormal morphology of chromosomes, other. This category includes a variety of translocations, ring chromosomes, fragments, and iso-chromosomes associated with mental retardation.

.6 Associated with prematurity

This category includes retarded patients who had a birth weight of less than 2500 grams (5.5 pounds) and/or a gestational age of less than 38 weeks at birth, and who do not fall into any of the preceding categories. This diagnosis should be used only if the patient's mental retardation cannot be classified more precisely under categories **.0** to **.5** above.

.7 Following major psychiatric disorder

This category is for mental retardation following psychosis or other major psychiatric disorder in early childhood when there is no evidence of cerebral pathology. To make this diagnosis there must be good evidence that the psychiatric disturbance was extremely severe. For example, retarded young adults with residual schizophrenia should not be classified here.

.8 With psycho-social (environmental) deprivation

This category is for the many cases of mental retardation with no clinical or historical evidence of organic disease or pathology but for which there is some history of psycho-social deprivation. Cases in this group are classified in terms of psycho-social factors which appear to bear some etiological relationship to the condition as follows:

Cultural-familial mental retardation. Classification here requires that evidence of retardation be found in at least one of the parents and in one or more siblings, presumably, because some degree of cultural deprivation results from familial retardation. The degree of retardation is usually mild.

Associated with environmental deprivation. An individual deprived of normal environmental stimulation in infancy and early childhood may prove unable to acquire the knowledge and skills required to function normally. This kind of deprivation tends to be more severe than that associated with familial mental retardation (q.v.). This type of deprivation may result from severe sensory impairment, even in an environment otherwise rich in stimulation. More rarely it may result from severe environmental limitations or atypical cultural milieus. The degree of retardation is always borderline or mild.

.9 With other [and unspecified] condition.

II. ORGANIC BRAIN SYNDROMES

(Disorders caused by or associated with impairment of brain tissue function)

These disorders are manifested by the following symptoms:

- (a) Impairment of orientation
- (b) Impairment of memory
- (c) Impairment of all intellectual functions such as comprehension, calculation, knowledge, learning, etc.
- (d) Impairment of judgment
- (e) Lability and shallowness of affect

The organic brain syndrome is a basic mental condition characteristically resulting from diffuse impairment of brain tissue function from whatever cause. Most of the basic symptoms are generally present to some degree regardless of whether the syndrome is mild, moderate or severe.

The syndrome may be the only disturbance present. It may also be associated with psychotic symptoms and behavioral disturbances. The severity of the associated symptoms is affected by and related to not only the precipitating organic disorder but also the patient's inherent personality patterns, present emotional conflicts, his environmental situation, and interpersonal relations.

These brain syndromes are grouped into psychotic and non-psychotic disorders according to the severity of functional impairment. The psychotic level of impairment is described on page 439 and the non-psychotic on pages 447-448.

It is important to distinguish "acute" from "chronic" brain disorders because of marked differences in the course of illness, prognosis and treatment. The terms indicate primarily whether the brain pathology and its accompanying organic brain syndrome is reversible. Since the same etiology may produce either temporary or permanent brain damage, a brain disorder which appears reversible (acute) at the beginning may prove later to have left permanent damage and a persistent organic brain syndrome which will then be diagnosed "chronic". Some brain syndromes occur in either form. Some occur only in acute forms (e.g. *Delirium tremens*). Some occur only in chronic form (e.g. *Alcoholic deterioration*). The acute and chronic forms may be indicated for those disorders coded in four digits by the addition of a fifth qualifying digit: .x1 *acute* and .x2 *chronic*.

THE PSYCHOSES

Psychoses are described in two places in this Manual, here with the organic brain syndromes and later with the functional psychoses. The general discussion of psychosis appears here because organic brain syndromes are listed first in DSM-II.

Patients are described as psychotic when their mental functioning is sufficiently impaired to interfere grossly with their capacity to meet the ordinary demands of life. The impairment may result from a serious distortion in their capacity to recognize reality. Hallucinations and delusions, for example, may distort their perceptions. Alterations of mood may be so profound that the patient's capacity to respond appropriately is grossly impaired. Deficits in perception, language and memory may be so severe that the patient's capacity for mental grasp of his situation is effectively lost.

Some confusion results from the different meanings which have become attached to the word "psychosis." Some non-organic disorders, (295-298), in the well-developed form in which they were first recognized, typically rendered patients psychotic. For historical reasons these disorders are still classified as psychoses, even though it now generally is recognized that many patients for whom these diagnoses are clinically justified are not in fact psychotic. This is true particularly in the incipient or convalescent stages of the illness. To reduce confusion, when one of these disorders listed as a "psychosis" is diagnosed in a patient who is not psychotic, the qualifying phrase *not psychotic* or *not presently psychotic* should be noted and coded .x6 with a fifth digit.

Example: 295.06 *Schizophrenia, simple type, not psychotic.*

It should be noted that this Manual permits an organic condition to be classified as a psychosis only if the patient is psychotic during the episode being diagnosed.

If the specific physical condition underlying one of these disorders is known, indicate it with a separate, additional diagnosis.

II. A. PSYCHOSES ASSOCIATED WITH ORGANIC BRAIN SYNDROMES (290—294)

290 Senile and Pre-senile dementia

290.0 Senile dementia

This syndrome occurs with senile brain disease, whose causes are largely unknown. The category does not include the pre-senile psychoses nor other degenerative diseases of the central nervous system. While senile brain disease derives its name from the age group in which it is most commonly seen, its diagnosis should be based on the brain disorder present and not on the patient's age at times of onset. Even mild cases will manifest some evidence of organic brain syndrome: self-centeredness, difficulty in assimilating new experiences, and childish emotionality. Deterioration may be minimal or progress to vegetative existence. (This condition was called "Chronic Brain Syndrome associated with senile brain disease" in DSM-I.)

290.1 Pre-senile dementia

This category includes a group of cortical brain diseases presenting clinical pictures similar to those of senile dementia but appearing characteristically in younger age groups. Alzheimer's and Pick's diseases are the two best known forms, each of which has a specific brain pathology. (In DSM-I Alzheimer's disease was classified as "Chronic Brain Syndrome with other disturbance of metabolism." Pick's disease was "Chronic Brain Syndrome associated with disease of unknown cause.") When the impairment is not of psychotic proportion the patient should be classified under *Non-psychotic OBS with senile or pre-senile brain disease.*

291 Alcoholic psychoses

Alcoholic psychoses are psychoses caused by poisoning with alcohol (see page **439**). When a pre-existing psychotic, psychoneurotic or other disorder is aggravated by modest alcohol intake, the underlying condition, not the alcoholic psychosis, is diagnosed.

Simple drunkenness, when not specified as psychotic, is classified under *Non-psychotic OBS with alcohol.*

In accordance with ICD-8, this Manual subdivides the alcoholic psychoses into *Delirium tremens, Korsakov's psychosis, Other alcoholic hallucinosis* and *Alcoholic paranoia.* DSM-II also adds three further subdivisions: *Acute alcohol intoxication, Alcoholic deterioration* and *Pathological intoxication.* (In DSM-I "Acute Brain Syndrome, alcohol intoxication" included what is now *Delirium tremens, Other alcoholic hallucinosis, Acute alcohol intoxication* and *Pathological intoxication.*)

291.0 Delirium tremens

This is a variety of acute brain syndrome characterized by delirium, coarse tremors, and frightening visual hallucinations usually becoming more intense in the dark. Because it was first identified in alcoholics and until recently was thought always to be due to alcohol ingestion, the term is restricted to the syndrome associated with alcohol. It is distinguished from *Other alcoholic hallucinosis* by the tremors and the disordered sensorium. When this clinical picture is due to a nutritional deficiency rather than to alcohol poisoning, it is classified under *Psychosis associated with metabolic or nutritional disorder.*

291.1 Korsakov's psychosis (alcoholic) Also "Korsakoff"

This is a variety of chronic brain syndrome associated with long-standing alcohol use and characterized by memory impairment, disorientation, peripheral neuropathy and particularly by confabulation. Like delirium tremens, Korsakov's psychosis is identified with alcohol because of an initial error in identifying its cause, and therefore the term is confined to the syndrome associated with alcohol. The similar syndrome due to nutritional deficiency unassociated with alcohol is classified *Psychosis associated with metabolic or nutritional disorder.*

291.2 Other alcoholic hallucinosis

Hallucinoses caused by alcohol which cannot be diagnosed as delirium tremens, Korsakov's psychosis, or alcoholic deterioration fall in this category. A common variety manifests accusatory or threatening auditory hallucinations in a state of relatively clear consciousness. This condition must be distinguished from schizophrenia in combination with alcohol intoxication, which would require two diagnoses.

291.3 Alcohol paranoid state ((Alcoholic paranoia))

This term describes a paranoid state which develops in chronic alcoholics, generally male, and is characterized by excessive jealousy and delusions of infidelity by the spouse. Patients diagnosed under primary paranoid states or schizophrenia should not be included here even if they drink to excess.

291.4* Acute alcohol intoxication*

All varieties of acute brain syndromes of psychotic proportion caused by alcohol are included here if they do not manifest features of delirium tremens, alcoholic hallucinosis, or pathological intoxication. This diagnosis is used alone when there is no other psychiatric disorder or as an additional diagnosis with other psychiatric conditions including alcoholism. The condition should not be confused with *simple drunkenness*, which does not involve psychosis. (All patients with this disorder would have been diagnosed "Acute Brain Syndrome, alcohol intoxication" in DSM-I.)

291.5* Alcoholic deterioration*

All varieties of chronic brain syndromes of psychotic proportion caused by alcohol and not having the characteristic features of Korsakov's psychosis are included here. (This condition and Korsakov's psychosis were both included under "Chronic Brain Syndrome, alcohol intoxication with psychotic reaction" in DSM-I.)

291.6* Pathological intoxication*

This is an acute brain syndrome manifested by psychosis after minimal alcohol intake. (In DSM-I this diagnosis fell under "Acute Brain Syndrome, alcohol intoxication.")

291.9 Other [and unspecified] alcoholic psychosis

This term refers to all varieties of alcoholic psychosis not classified above.

292 Psychosis associated with intracranial infection

292.0 General paralysis

This condition is characterized by physical signs and symptoms of parenchymatous syphilis of the nervous system, and usually by positive serology, including the paretic gold curve in the spinal fluid. The condition may simulate any of the other psychoses and brain syndromes. If the impairment is not of psychotic proportion it is classified *Non-psychotic OBS with intracranial infection*. If the specific underlying physical condition is known, indicate it with a separate, additional diagnosis. (This category was included under "Chronic Brain Syndrome associated with central nervous system syphilis (meningoencephalitic)" in DSM-I.)

292.1 Psychosis with other syphilis of central nervous system

This includes all other varieties of psychosis attributed to intracranial infection by **Spirochaeta pallida.** The syndrome sometimes has features of organic brain syndrome. The acute infection is usually produced by meningovascular inflammation and responds to systemic antisyphilitic treatment. The chronic condition is generally due to gummata. If not of psychotic proportion, the disorder is classified *Non-psychotic OBS with intracranial infection.* (In DSM-I "Chronic Brain Syndrome associated with other central nervous system syphilis" and "Acute Brain Syndrome associated with intracranial infection" covered this category.)

292.2 Psychosis with epidemic encephalitis (von Economo's encephalitis)

This term is confined to the disorder attributed to the viral epidemic encephalitis that followed World War I. Virtually no cases have been reported since 1926. The condition, however, is differentiated from other encephalitis. It may present itself as acute delirium and sometimes its outstanding feature is apparent indifference to persons and events ordinarily of emotional significance, such as the death of a family member. It may appear as a chronic brain syndrome and is sometimes dominated by involuntary, compulsive behavior. If not of psychotic proportions, the disorder is classified under *Non-psychotic OBS with intracranial infection.* (This category was classified under "Chronic Brain Syndrome associated with intracranial infection other than syphilis" in DSM-I.)

292.3 Psychosis with other and unspecified encephalitis

This category includes disorders attributed to encephalitic infections other than epidemic encephalitis and also to encephalitis not otherwise specified.[1] When possible the type of infection should be indicated. If not of psychotic proportion, the disorder is classified under *Non-psychotic OBS with intracranial infection.*

292.9 Psychosis with other [and unspecified] intracranial infection

This category includes all acute and chronic conditions due to nonsyphilitic and non-encephalitic infections, such as meningitis and

---

[1] A list of important encephalitides may be found in "A Guide to the Control of Mental Disorders," American Public Health Association Inc., New York 1962, pp. 40 ff.

brain abscess. Many of these disorders will have been diagnosed as the acute form early in the course of the illness. If not of psychotic proportion, the disorder should be classified under *Non-psychotic OBS with intracranial infection*. (In DSM-I the acute variety was classified as "Acute Brain Syndrome associated with intracranial infection" and the chronic variety as "Chronic Brain Syndrome associated with intracranial infection other than syphilis.")

293 Psychosis associated with other cerebral condition

This major category, as its name indicates, is for all psychoses associated with cerebral conditions *other* than those previously defined. For example, the degenerative diseases following do *not* include the previous senile dementia. If the specific underlying physical condition is known, indicate it with a separate, additional diagnosis.

293.0 Psychosis with cerebral arteriosclerosis

This is a chronic disorder attributed to cerebral arteriosclerosis. It may be impossible to differentiate it from senile dementia and presenile dementia, which may coexist with it. Careful consideration of the patient's age, history, and symptoms may help determine the predominant pathology. Commonly, the organic brain syndrome is the only mental disturbance present, but other reactions, such as depression or anxiety, may be superimposed. If not of psychotic proportion, the condition is classified under *Non-psychotic OBS with circulatory disturbance*. (In DSM-I this was called "Chronic Brain Syndrome associated with cerebral arteriosclerosis.")

293.1 Psychosis with other cerebrovascular disturbance

This category includes such circulatory disturbances as cerebral thrombosis, cerebral embolism, arterial hypertension, cardio-renal disease and cardiac disease, particularly in decompensation. It excludes conditions attributed to arteriosclerosis. The diagnosis is determined by the underlying organ pathology, which should be specified with an additional diagnosis. (In DSM-I this category was divided between "Acute Brain Syndrome associated with circulatory disturbance" and "Chronic Brain Syndrome associated with circulatory disturbance other than cerebral arteriosclerosis.")

293.2 Psychosis with epilepsy

This category is to be used only for the condition associated with "idiopathic" epilepsy. Most of the etiological agents underlying chronic brain syndromes can and do cause convulsions, particularly syphilis, intoxication, trauma, cerebral arteriosclerosis, and intra-cranial neoplasms. When the convulsions are symptomatic of such diseases, the brain syndrome is classified under those disturbances rather than here. The disturbance most commonly encountered here is the clouding of consciousness before or after a convulsive attack. Instead of a convulsion, the patient may show only a dazed reaction with deep confusion, bewilderment and anxiety. The epileptic attack may also take the form of an episode of excitement with hallucina-tions, fears, and violent outbreaks. (In DSM-I this was included in "Acute Brain Syndrome associated with convulsive disorder" and "Chronic Brain Syndrome associated with convulsive disorder.")

293.3 Psychosis with intracranial neoplasm

Both primary and metastatic neoplasms are classified here. Reactions to neoplasms other than in the cranium should not receive this diagnosis. (In DSM-I this category included "Acute Brain Syndrome associated with intracranial neoplasm" and "Chronic Brain Syndrome associated with intracranial neoplasm.")

293.4 Psychosis with degenerative disease of the central nerv-ous system

This category includes degenerative brain diseases not listed previous-ly. (In DSM-I this was part of "Acute Brain Syndrome with disease of unknown or uncertain cause" and "Chronic Brain Syndrome associated with diseases of unknown or uncertain cause.")

293.5 Psychosis with brain trauma

This category includes those disorders which develop immediately after severe head injury or brain surgery and the post-traumatic chronic brain disorders. It does not include permanent brain dam-age which produces only focal neurological changes without sig-nificant changes in sensorium and affect. Generally, trauma pro-ducing a chronic brain syndrome is diffuse and causes permanent brain damage. If not of psychotic proportions, a post-traumatic per-sonality disorder associated with an organic brain syndrome is clas-sified as a *Non-psychotic OBS with brain trauma.* If the brain injury occurs in early life and produces a developmental defect of intelligence, the condition is also diagnosed *Mental retardation.* A head injury may precipitate or accelerate the course of a chronic brain disease, especially cerebral arteriosclerosis. The differential diagnosis may be extremely difficult. If, before the injury, the patient had symptoms of circulatory disturbance, particularly arteriosclerosis, and now shows signs of psychosis, he should be classified *Psychosis with cerebral artiosclerosis*. (In DSM-I this category was divided between "Acute Brain Syndrome associated with trauma" and "Chronic Brain Syndrome associated with brain trauma.")

293.9 Psychosis with other [and unspecified] cerebral condition

This category is for cerebral conditions other than those listed above, and conditions for which it is impossible to make a more precise diagnosis. [Medical record librarians will include here *Psychoses with cerebral condition, not otherwise specified*.]

294 Psychosis associated with other physical condition

The following psychoses are caused by general systemic disorders and are distinguished from the *cerebral* conditions previously described. If the specific underlying physical condition is known, indicate it with a separate, additional diagnosis.

294.0 Psychosis with endocrine disorder

This category includes disorders caused by the complications of diabetes other than cerebral arteriosclerosis and disorders of the thyroid, pituitary, adrenals, and other endocrine glands. (In DSM-I "Chronic Brain Syndrome associated with other disturbances of metabolism, growth or nutrition" included the chronic variety of these disorders. DSM-I defined these conditions as "disorders of metabolism" but they here are considered endocrine disorders.)

294.1 Psychosis with metabolic or nutritional disorder

This category includes disorders caused by pellagra, avitaminosis and metabolic disorders. (In DSM-I this was part of "Acute Brain Syndrome associated with metabolic disturbance" and "Chronic Brain Syndrome associated with other disturbance of metabolism, growth or nutrition.")

294.2 Psychosis with systemic infection

This category includes disorders caused by severe general systemic infections, such as pneumonia, typhoid fever, malaria and acute rheumatic fever. Care must be taken to distinguish these reactions from other disorders, particularly manic depressive illness and schizophrenia, which may be precipitated by even a mild attack of infectious disease. (In DSM-I this was confined to "Acute Brain Syndrome associated with systemic infection.")

294.3 Psychosis with drug or poison intoxication (other than alcohol)

This category includes disorders caused by some drugs (including psychedelic drugs), hormones, heavy metals, gasses, and other intoxicants except alcohol. (In DSM-I these conditions were divided between "Acute Brain Syndrome, drug or poison intoxication" and "Chronic Brain Syndrome, associated with intoxication." The former excluded alcoholic acute brain syndromes, while the latter included alcoholic chronic brain syndromes.)

294.4 Psychosis with childbirth

Almost any type of psychosis may occur during pregnancy and the post-partum period and should be specifically diagnosed. This category is not a substitute for a differential diagnosis and excludes other psychoses arising during the puerperium. Therefore, this diagnosis should not be used unless all other possible diagnoses have been excluded.

294.8 Psychosis with other and undiagnosed physical condition

This is a residual category for psychoses caused by physical conditions other than those listed earlier. It also includes brain syndromes caused by physical conditions which have not been diagnosed. (In DSM-I this condition was divided between "Acute Brain Syndrome of unknown cause" and "Chronic Brain Syndrome of unknown cause." However, these categories also included the category now called *Psychosis with other [and unspecified] cerebral condition*.)

[294.9 Psychosis with unspecified physical condition]

This is not a diagnosis but is included for use by medical record librarians only.

II. B. NON-PSYCHOTIC ORGANIC BRAIN SYNDROMES (309)

309 Non-psychotic organic brain syndromes ((Mental disorders not specified as psychotic associated with physical conditions))

This category is for patients who have an organic brain syndrome but are not psychotic. If psychoses are present they should be diagnosed as previously indicated. Refer to pages 438-439 for description of organic brain syndromes in adults.

In children mild brain damage often manifests itself by hyperactivity, short attention span, easy distractability, and impulsiveness. Sometimes the child is withdrawn, listless, perseverative, and unresponsive. In exceptional cases there may be great difficulty in initiating action. These characteristics often contribute to a negative interaction between parent and child. If the organic handicap is the major etiological factor and the child is not psychotic, the case should be classified here. If the interactional factors are of major secondary importance, supply a second diagnosis under *Behavior disorders of childhood and adolescence;* if these interactional factors predominate give only a diagnosis from this latter category.

309.0 Non-psychotic OBS with intracranial infection

309.1 Non-psychotic OBS with drug, poison, or systemic intoxication

> **309.13* Non-psychotic OBS with alcohol* (simple drunkenness)**
>
> **309.14* Non-psychotic OBS with other drug, poison, or systemic intoxication***

309.2 Non-psychotic OBS with brain trauma

309.3 Non-psychotic OBS with circulatory disturbance

309.4 Non-psychotic OBS with epilepsy

309.5 Non-psychotic OBS with disturbance of metabolism, growth or nutrition

309.6 Non-psychotic OBS with senile or pre-senile brain disease

309.7 Non-psychotic OBS with intracranial neoplasm

309.8 Non-psychotic OBS with degenerative disease of central nervous system

309.9 Non-psychotic OBS with other [and unspecified] physical condition

> **[.91* Acute brain syndrome, not otherwise specified*]**
>
> **[.92* Chronic brain syndrome, not otherwise specified*]**

III. PSYCHOSES NOT ATTRIBUTED TO PHYSICAL CONDITIONS LISTED PREVIOUSLY (295—298)

This major category is for patients whose psychosis is not caused by physical conditions listed previously. Nevertheless, some of these patients may show additional signs of an organic condition. If these organic signs are prominent the patient should receive the appropriate additional diagnosis.

295 Schizophrenia

This large category includes a group of disorders manifested by characteristic disturbances of thinking, mood and behavior. Disturbances in thinking are marked by alterations of concept formation which may lead to misinterpretation of reality and sometimes to delusions and hallucinations, which frequently appear psychologically self-protective. Corollary mood changes include ambivalent, constricted and inappropriate emotional responsiveness and loss of empathy with others. Behavior may be withdrawn, regressive and bizarre. The schizophrenias, in which the mental status is attributable primarily to a *thought* disorder, are to be distinguished from the *Major affective illnesses* (q.v.) which are dominated by a *mood* disorder. The *Paranoid states* (q.v.) are distinguished from schizophrenia by the narrowness of their distortions of reality and by the absence of other psychotic symptoms.

295.0 Schizophrenia, simple type

This psychosis is characterized chiefly by a slow and insidious reduction of external attachments and interests and by apathy and indifference leading to impoverishment of interpersonal relations, mental deterioration, and adjustment on a lower level of functioning. In general, the condition is less dramatically psychotic than are the hebephrenic, catatonic, and paranoid types of schizophrenia. Also, it contrasts with schizoid personality, in which there is little or no progression of the disorder.

295.1 Schizophrenia, hebephrenic type

This psychosis is characterized by disorganized thinking, shallow and inappropriate affect, unpredictable giggling, silly and regressive behavior and mannerisms, and frequent hypochondriacal complaints. Delusions and hallucinations, if present, are transient and not well organized.

295.2 Schizophrenia, catatonic type
295.23* Schizophrenia, catatonic type, excited*
295.24* Schizophrenia, catatonic type, withdrawn*

It is frequently possible and useful to distinguish two subtypes of catatonic schizophrenia. One is marked by excessive and sometimes violent motor activity and excitement and the other by generalized

inhibition manifested by stupor, mutism, negativism, or waxy flexibility. In time, some cases deteriorate to a vegetative state.

295.3 Schizophrenia, paranoid type

This type of schizophrenia is characterized primarily by the presence of persecutory or grandiose delusions, often associated with hallucinations. Excessive religiosity is sometimes seen. The patient's attitude is frequently hostile and aggressive, and his behavior tends
to be consistent with his delusions. In general the disorder does
not manifest the gross personality disorganization of the hebephrenic
and catatonic types, perhaps because the patient uses the mechanism of projection, which ascribes to others characteristics he cannot accept in himself. Three subtypes of the disorder may sometimes
be differentiated, depending on the predominant symptoms: hostile,
grandiose, and hallucinatory.

295.4 Acute schizophrenic episode

This diagnosis does not apply to acute episodes of schizophrenic
disorders described elsewhere. This condition is distinguished by
the acute onset of schizophrenic symptoms, often associated with
confusion, perplexity, ideas of reference, emotional turmoil, dream-
like dissociation, and excitement, depression, or fear. The acute
onset distinguishes this condition from simple schizophrenia. In time
these patients may take on the characteristics of catatonic, hebephrenic or paranoid schizophrenia, in which case their diagnosis
should be changed accordingly. In many cases the patient recovers
within weeks, but sometimes his disorganization becomes progressive. More frequently remission is followed by recurrence. (In DSM-I
this condition was listed as "Schizophrenia, acute undifferentiated
type.")

295.5 Schizophrenia, latent type

This category is for patients having clear symptoms of schizophrenia
but no history of a psychotic schizophrenic episode. Disorders sometimes designated as incipient, pre-psychotic, pseudoneurotic, pseudopsychopathic, or borderline schizophrenia are categorized here. (This
category includes some patients who were diagnosed in DSM-I under
"Schizophrenic reaction, chronic undifferentiated type." Others formerly included in that DSM-I category are now classified under
Schizophrenia, other [and unspecified] types (q.v.).)

295.6 Schizophrenia, residual type

This category is for patients showing signs of schizophrenia but who, following a psychotic schizophrenic episode, are no longer psychotic.

295.7 Schizophrenia, schizo-affective type

This category is for patients showing a mixture of schizophrenic symptoms and pronounced elation or depression. Within this category it may be useful to distinguish excited from depressed types as follows:

295.73* Schizophrenia, schizo-affective type, excited*

295.74* Schizophrenia, schizo-affective type, depressed*

295.8* Schizophrenia, childhood type*

This category is for cases in which schizophrenic symptoms appear before puberty. The condition may be manifested by autistic, atypical, and withdrawn behavior; failure to develop identity separate from the mother's; and general unevenness, gross immaturity and inadequacy in development. These developmental defects may result in mental retardation, which should also be diagnosed. (This category is for use in the United States and does not appear in ICD-8. It is equivalent to "Schizophrenic reaction, childhood type" in DSM-I.)

295.90* Schizophrenia, chronic undifferentiated type*

This category is for patients who show mixed schizophrenic symptoms and who present definite schizophrenic thought, affect and behavior not classifiable under the other types of schizophrenia. It is distinguished from *Schizoid personality* (q.v.). (This category is equivalent to "Schizophrenic reaction, chronic undifferentiated type" in DSM-I except that it does not include cases now diagnosed as *Schizophrenia, latent type* and *Schizophrenia, other [and unspecified] types.)*

295.99* Schizophrenia, other [and unspecified] types*

This category is for any type of schizophrenia not previously described. (In DSM-I "Schizophrenic reaction, chronic undifferentiated type" included this category and also what is now called *Schizophrenia, latent type* and *Schizophrenia, chronic undifferentiated type.*)

296 Major affective disorders ((Affective psychoses))

This group of psychoses is characterized by a single disorder of mood, either extreme depression or elation, that dominates the mental life of the patient and is responsible for whatever loss of contact he has with his environment. The onset of the mood does not seem to be related directly to a precipitating life experience and therefore is distinguishable from *Psychotic depressive reaction* and *Depressive neurosis*. (This category is not equivalent to the DSM-I heading "Affective reactions," which included "Psychotic depressive reaction.")

296.0 Involutional melancholia

This is a disorder occurring in the involutional period and characterized by worry, anxiety, agitation, and severe insomnia. Feelings of guilt and somatic preoccupations are frequently present and may be of delusional proportions. This disorder is distinguishable from *Manic-depressive illness* (q.v.) by the absence of previous episodes; it is distinguished from *Schizophrenia* (q.v.) in that impaired reality testing is due to a disorder of mood; and it is distinguished from *Psychotic depressive reaction* (q.v.) in that the depression is not due to some life experience. Opinion is divided as to whether this psychosis can be distinguished from the other affective disorders. It is, therefore, recommended that involutional patients not be given this diagnosis unless all other affective disorders have been ruled out. (In DSM-I this disorder was considered one of two subtypes of "Involutional Psychotic Reaction."

Manic-depressive illnesses (Manic-depressive psychoses)

These disorders are marked by severe mood swings and a tendency to remission and recurrence. Patients may be given this diagnosis in the absence of a previous history of affective psychosis if there is no obvious precipitating event. This disorder is divided into three major subtypes: manic type, depressed type, and circular type.

296.1 Manic-depressive illness, manic type ((Manic-depressive psychosis, manic type))

This disorder consists exclusively of manic episodes. These episodes are characterized by excessive elation, irritability, talkativeness, flight of ideas, and accelerated speech and motor activity. Brief periods of depression sometimes occur, but they are never true depressive episodes.

296.2 Manic-depressive illness, depressed type ((Manic-depressive psychosis, depressed type))

This disorder consists exclusively of depressive episodes. These episodes are characterized by severely depressed mood and by mental and motor retardation progressing occasionally to stupor. Uneasiness, apprehension, perplexity and agitation may also be present.

When illusions, hallucinations, and delusions (usually of guilt or of hypochondriacal or paranoid ideas) occur, they are attributable to the dominant mood disorder. Because it is a primary mood disorder, this psychosis differs from the *Psychotic depressive reaction,* which is more easily attributable to precipitating stress. Cases incompletely labelled as "psychotic depression" should be classified here rather than under *Psychotic depressive reaction.*

296.3 Manic-depressive illness, circular type ((Manic-depressive psychosis, circular type))

This disorder is distinguished by at least one attack of both a depressive episode *and* a manic episode. This phenomenon makes clear why manic and depressed types are combined into a single category. (In DSM-I these cases were diagnosed under "Manic depressive reaction, other.") The current episode should be specified and coded as one of the following:

296.33* Manic-depressive illness, circular type, manic*

296.34* Manic-depressive illness, circular type, depressed*

296.8 Other major affective disorder ((Affective psychosis, other))

Major affective disorders for which a more specific diagnosis has not been made are included here. It is also for "mixed" manic-depressive illness, in which manic and depressive symptoms appear almost simultaneously. It does not include *Psychotic depressive reaction* (q.v.) or *Depressive neurosis* (q.v.). (In DSM-I this category was included under "Manic depressive reaction, other.")

[296.9 Unspecified major affective disorder]
[Affective disorder not otherwise specified]
[Manic-depressive illness not otherwise specified]

297 Paranoid states

These are psychotic disorders in which a delusion, generally persecutory or grandiose, is the essential abnormality. Disturbances in mood, behavior and thinking (including hallucinations) are derived from this delusion. This distinguishes paranoid states from the affective psychoses and schizophrenias, in which mood and thought disorders, respectively, are the central abnormalities. Most authorities, however, question whether disorders in this group are distinct clinical entities and not merely variants of schizophrenia or paranoid personality.

297.0 Paranoia

This extremely rare condition is characterized by gradual development of an intricate, complex, and elaborate paranoid system based on and often proceeding logically from misinterpretation of an actual event. Frequently the patient considers himself endowed with unique and superior ability. In spite of a chronic course the condition does not seem to interfere with the rest of the patient's thinking and personality.

297.1 Involutional paranoid state ((Involutional paraphrenia))

This paranoid psychosis is characterized by delusion formation with onset in the involutional period. Formerly it was classified as a paranoid variety of involutional psychotic reaction. The absence of conspicuous thought disorders typical of schizophrenia distinguishes it from that group.

297.9 Other paranoid state

This is a residual category for paranoid psychotic reactions not classified earlier.

298 Other psychoses

298.0 Psychotic depressive reaction ((Reactive depressive psychosis))

This psychosis is distinguished by a depressive mood attributable to some experience. Ordinarily the individual has no history of repeated depressions or cyclothymic mood swings. The differentiation between this condition and *Depressive neurosis* (q.v.) depends on whether the reaction impairs reality testing or functional adequacy enough to be considered a psychosis. (In DSM-I this condition was included with the affective psychoses.)

[298.1 Reactive excitation]

[298.2 Reactive confusion]
[Acute or subacute confusional state]

[298.3 Acute paranoid reaction]

[298.9 Reactive psychosis, unspecified]

[299 Unspecified psychosis]
[Dementia, insanity or psychosis not otherwise specified]

This is not a diagnosis but is listed here for librarians and statisticians to use in coding incomplete diagnoses. Clinicians are expected to complete a differential diagnosis for patients who manifest features of several psychoses.

IV. NEUROSES (300)

300 Neuroses

Anxiety is the chief characteristic of the neuroses. It may be felt and expressed directly, or it may be controlled unconsciously and automatically by conversion, displacement and various other psychological mechanisms. Generally, these mechanisms produce symptoms experienced as subjective distress from which the patient desires relief.

The neuroses, as contrasted to the psychoses, manifest neither gross distortion or misinterpretation of external reality, nor gross personality disorganization. A possible exception to this is hysterical neurosis, which some believe may occasionally be accompanied by hallucinations and other symptoms encountered in psychoses.

Traditionally, neurotic patients, however severely handicapped by their symptoms, are not classified as psychotic because they are aware that their mental functioning is disturbed.

300.0 Anxiety neurosis

This neurosis is characterized by anxious over-concern extending to panic and frequently associated with somatic symptoms. Unlike *Phobic neurosis* (q.v.), anxiety may occur under any circumstances and is not restricted to specific situations or objects. This disorder must be distinguished from normal apprehension or fear, which occurs in realistically dangerous situations.

300.1 Hysterical neurosis

This neurosis is characterized by an involuntary psychogenic loss or disorder of function. Symptoms characteristically begin and end suddenly in emotionally charged situations and are symbolic of the underlying conflicts. Often they can be modified by suggestion alone. This is a new diagnosis that encompasses the former diagnoses "Conversion reaction" and "Dissociative reaction" in DSM-I. This distinction between conversion and dissociative reactions should be preserved by using one of the following diagnoses whenever possible.

300.13* Hysterical neurosis, conversion type*

In the conversion type, the special senses or voluntary nervous system are affected, causing such symptoms as blindness, deafness, anosmia, anaesthesias, paraesthesias, paralyses, ataxias, akinesias, and dyskinesias. Often the patient shows an inappropriate lack of concern or *belle indifférence* about these symptoms, which may actually provide secondary gains by winning him sympathy or relieving him of unpleasant responsibilities. This type of hysterical neurosis must be distinguished from psychophysiologic disorders, which are mediated by the autonomic nervous system; from malingering, which is done consciously; and from neurological lesions, which cause anatomically circumscribed symptoms.

300.14* Hysterical neurosis, dissociative type*
In the dissociative type, alterations may occur in the patient's state of consciousness or in his identity, to produce such symptoms as amnesia, somnambulism, fugue, and multiple personality.

300.2 Phobic neurosis
This condition is characterized by intense fear of an object or situation which the patient consciously recognizes as no real danger to him. His apprehension may be experienced as faintness, fatigue, palpitations, perspiration, nausea, tremor, and even panic. Phobias are generally attributed to fears displaced to the phobic object or situation from some other object of which the patient is unaware. A wide range of phobias has been described.

300.3 Obsessive compulsive neurosis
This disorder is characterized by the persistent intrusion of unwanted thoughts, urges, or actions that the patient is unable to stop. The thoughts may consist of single words or ideas, ruminations, or trains of thought often perceived by the patient as nonsensical. The actions vary from simple movements to complex rituals such as repeated handwashing. Anxiety and distress are often present either if the patient is prevented from completing his compulsive ritual or if he is concerned about being unable to control it himself.

300.4 Depressive neurosis
This disorder is manifested by an excessive reaction of depression due to an internal conflict or to an identifiable event such as the loss of a love object or cherished possession. It is to be distinguished from *Involutional melancholia* (q.v.) and *Manic-depressive illness* (q.v.). *Reactive depressions* or *Depressive reactions* are to be classified here.

300.5 Neurasthenic neurosis ((Neurasthenia))
This condition is characterized by complaints of chronic weakness,

easy fatigability, and sometimes exhaustion. Unlike hysterical neurosis the patient's complaints are genuinely distressing to him and there is no evidence of secondary gain. It differs from *Anxiety neurosis* (q.v.) and from the *Psychophysiologic disorders* (q.v.) in the nature of the predominant complaint. It differs from *Depressive neurosis* (q.v.) in the moderateness of the depression and in the chronicity of its course. (In DSM-I this condition was called "Psychophysiologic nervous system reaction.")

300.6 Depersonalization neurosis ((Depersonalization syndrome))

This syndrome is dominated by a feeling of unreality and of estrangement from the self, body, or surroundings. This diagnosis should not be used if the condition is part of some other mental disorder, such as an acute situational reaction. A brief experience of depersonalization is not necessarily a symptom of illness.

300.7 Hypochondriacal neurosis

This condition is dominated by preoccupation with the body and with fear of presumed diseases of various organs. Though the fears are not of delusional quality as in psychotic depressions, they persist despite reassurance. The condition differs from hysterical neurosis in that there are no actual losses or distortions of function.

300.8 Other neurosis

This classification includes specific psychoneurotic disorders not classified elsewhere such as "writer's cramp" and other occupational neuroses. Clinicians should not use this category for patients with "mixed" neuroses, which should be diagnosed according to the predominant symptom.

[300.9 Unspecified neurosis]

This category is not a diagnosis. It is for the use of record librarians and statisticians to code incomplete diagnoses.

V. PERSONALITY DISORDERS AND CERTAIN OTHER NON-PSYCHOTIC MENTAL DISORDERS (301—304)

301 Personality disorders

This group of disorders is characterized by deeply ingrained maladaptive patterns of behavior that are perceptibly different in quality from psychotic and neurotic symptoms. Generally, these are life-long patterns, often recognizable by the time of adolescence or earlier. Sometimes the pattern is determined primarily by malfunctioning of the brain, but such cases should be classified under one of the non-psychotic organic brain syndromes rather than here. (In DSM-I "Personality Disorders" also included disorders now classified under *Sexual deviation, Alcoholism,* and *Drug dependence.*)

301.0 Paranoid personality

This behavioral pattern is characterized by hypersensitivity, rigidity, unwarranted suspicion, jealousy, envy, excessive self-importance, and a tendency to blame others and ascribe evil motives to them. These characteristics often interfere with the patient's ability to maintain satisfactory interpersonal relations. Of course, the presence of suspicion of itself does not justify this diagnosis, since the suspicion may be warranted in some instances.

301.1 Cyclothymic personality ((Affective personality))

This behavior pattern is manifested by recurring and alternating periods of depression and elation. Periods of elation may be marked by ambition, warmth, enthusiasm, optimism, and high energy. Periods of depression may be marked by worry, pessimism, low energy, and a sense of futility. These mood variations are not readily attributable to external circumstances. If possible, the diagnosis should specify whether the mood is characteristically depressed, hypomanic, or alternating.

301.2 Schizoid personality

This behavior pattern manifests shyness, over-sensitivity, seclusiveness, avoidance of close or competitive relationships, and often eccentricity. Autistic thinking without loss of capacity to recognize reality is common, as are daydreaming and the inability to express hostility and ordinary aggressive feelings. These patients react to disturbing experiences and conflicts with apparent detachment.

301.3 Explosive personality (Epileptoid personality disorder)

This behavior pattern is characterized by gross outbursts of rage or of verbal or physical aggressiveness. These outbursts are strikingly different from the patient's usual behavior, and he may be regretful and repentant for them. These patients are generally considered excitable, aggressive and over-responsive to environmental pressures. It is the intensity of the outbursts and the individual's inability to control them which distinguishes this group. Cases diagnosed as "aggressive personality" are classified here. If the patient is amnesic for the outbursts, the diagnosis of *Hysterical neurosis, Non-psychotic OBS with epilepsy* or *Psychosis with epilepsy* should be considered.

301.4 Obsessive compulsive personality ((Anankastic personality))

This behavior pattern is characterized by excessive concern with conformity and adherence to standards of conscience. Consequently, individuals in this group may be rigid, over-inhibited, over-conscientious, over-dutiful, and unable to relax easily. This disorder may lead to an *Obsessive compulsive neurosis* (q.v.), from which it must be distinguished.

301.5 Hysterical personality (Histrionic personality disorder)

These behavior patterns are characterized by excitability, emotional instability, over-reactivity, and self-dramatization. This self-dramatization is always attention-seeking and often seductive, whether or not the patient is aware of its purpose. These personalities are also immature, self-centered, often vain, and usually dependent on others. This disorder must be differentiated from *Hysterical neurosis* (q.v.).

301.6 Asthenic personality

This behavior pattern is characterized by easy fatigability, low energy level, lack of enthusiasm, marked incapacity for enjoyment, and oversensitivity to physical and emotional stress. This disorder must be differentiated from *Neurasthenic neurosis* (q.v.).

301.7 Antisocial personality

This term is reserved for individuals who are basically unsocialized and whose behavior pattern brings them repeatedly into conflict with society. They are incapable of significant loyalty to individuals, groups, or social values. They are grossly selfish, callous, irresponsible, impulsive, and unable to feel guilt or to learn from experience and punishment. Frustration tolerance is low. They tend to blame others or offer plausible rationalizations for their behavior. A mere history of repeated legal or social offenses is not sufficient to justify this diagnosis. *Group delinquent reaction of childhood (or adolescence)* (q.v.), and *Social maladjustment without manifest psychiatric disorder* (q.v.) should be ruled out before making this diagnosis.

301.81* Passive-aggressive personality*

This behavior pattern is characterized by both passivity and aggressiveness. The aggressiveness may be expressed passively, for example by obstructionism, pouting, procrastination, intentional inefficiency, or stubbornness. This behavior commonly reflects hostility which the individual feels he dare not express openly. Often the behavior is one expression of the patient's resentment at failing to find gratification in a relationship with an individual or institution upon which he is over-dependent.

301.82* Inadequate personality*

This behavior pattern is characterized by ineffectual responses to emotional, social, intellectual and physical demands. While the patient seems neither physically nor mentally deficient, he does manifest inadaptability, ineptness, poor judgment, social instability, and lack of physical and emotional stamina.

301.89* Other personality disorders of specified types (Immature personality, Passive-dependent personality, etc.)*

301.9 [Unspecified personality disorder]

302 Sexual deviations

This category is for individuals whose sexual interests are directed primarily toward objects other than people of the opposite sex, toward sexual acts not usually associated with coitus, or toward coitus performed under bizarre circumstances as in necrophilia, pedophilia, sexual sadism, and fetishism. Even though many find their practices distasteful, they remain unable to substitute normal sexual behavior for them. This diagnosis is not appropriate for individuals who perform deviant sexual acts because normal sexual objects are not available to them.

302.0 Homosexuality

302.1 Fetishism

302.2 Pedophilia

302.3 Transvestitism

302.4 Exhibitionism

302.5* Voyeurism*

302.6* Sadism*

302.7* Masochism*

302.8 Other sexual deviation

[302.9 Unspecified sexual deviation]

303 Alcoholism

This category is for patients whose alcohol intake is great enough to damage their physical health, or their personal or social functioning, or when it has become a prerequisite to normal functioning. If the alcoholism is due to another mental disorder, both diagnoses should be made. The following types of alcoholism are recognized:

303.0 Episodic excessive drinking

If alcoholism is present and the individual becomes intoxicated as frequently as four times a year, the condition should be classified here. Intoxication is defined as a state in which the individual's coordination or speech is definitely impaired or his behavior is clearly altered.

303.1 Habitual excessive drinking

This diagnosis is given to persons who are alcoholic and who either become intoxicated more than 12 times a year or are recognizably under the influence of alcohol more than once a week, even though not intoxicated.

303.2 Alcohol addiction

This condition should be diagnosed when there is direct or strong presumptive evidence that the patient is dependent on alcohol. If available, the best direct evidence of such dependence is the appearance of withdrawal symptoms. The inability of the patient to go one day without drinking is presumptive evidence. When heavy drinking continues for three months or more it is reasonable to presume addiction to alcohol has been established.

303.9 Other [and unspecified] alcoholism

304 Drug dependence

This category is for patients who are addicted to or dependent on drugs other than alcohol, tobacco, and ordinary caffeine-containing beverages. Dependence on medically prescribed drugs is also excluded so long as the drug is medically indicated and the intake is proportionate to the medical need. The diagnosis requires evidence of habitual use or a clear sense of need for the drug. Withdrawal symptoms are not the only evidence of dependence; while always present when opium derivatives are withdrawn, they may be entirely absent when cocaine or marihuana are withdrawn. The diagnosis may stand alone or be coupled with any other diagnosis.

304.0 Drug dependence, opium, opium alkaloids and their derivatives

304.1 Drug dependence, synthetic analgesics with morphine-like effects

304.2 Drug dependence, barbiturates

304.3 Drug dependence, other hypnotics and sedatives or "tranquilizers"

304.4 Drug dependence, cocaine

304.5 Drug dependence, Cannabis sativa (hashish, marihuana)

304.6 Drug dependence, other psycho-stimulants (amphetamines, etc.)

304.7 Drug dependence, hallucinogens

304.8 Other drug dependence

[304.9 Unspecified drug dependence]

VI. PSYCHOPHYSIOLOGIC DISORDERS (305)

305 Psychophysiologic disorders ((Physical disorders of presumably psychogenic origin))

This group of disorders is characterized by physical symptoms that are caused by emotional factors and involve a single organ system, usually under autonomic nervous system innervation. The physiological changes involved are those that normally accompany certain emotional states, but in these disorders the changes are more intense and sustained. The individual may not be consciously aware of his emotional state. If there is an additional psychiatric disorder, it should be diagnosed separately, whether or not it is presumed to contribute to the physical disorder. The specific physical disorder should be named and classified in one of the following categories.

305.0 Psychophysiologic skin disorder
This diagnosis applies to skin reactions such as neurodermatosis, pruritis, atopic dematitis, and hyperhydrosis in which emotional factors play a causative role.

305.1 Psychophysiologic musculoskeletal disorder
This diagnosis applies to musculoskeletal disorders such as backache,

muscle cramps, and myalgias, and tension headaches in which emotional factors play a causative role. Differentiation from hysterical neurosis is of prime importance and at times extremely difficult.

305.2 Psychophysiologic respiratory disorder
This diagnosis applies to respiratory disorders such as bronchial asthma, hyperventilation syndromes, sighing, and hiccoughs in which emotional factors play a causative role.'

305.3 Psychophysiologic cardiovascular disorder
This diagnosis applies to cardiovascular disorders such as paroxysmal tachycardia, hypertension, vascular spasms, and migraine in which emotional factors play a causative role.

305.4 Psychophysiologic hemic and lymphatic disorder
Here may be included any disturbances in the hemic and lymphatic system in which emotional factors are found to play a causative role. ICD-8 has included this category so that all organ systems will be covered.

305.5 Psychophysiologic gastrointestinal disorder
This diagnosis applies to specific types of gastrointestinal disorders such as peptic ulcer, chronic gastritis, ulcerative or mucous colitis, constipation, hyperacidity, pylorospasm, "heartburn," and "irritable colon" in which emotional factors play a causative role.

305.6 Psychophysiologic genito-urinary disorder
This diagnosis applies to genito-urinary disorders such as disturbances in menstruation and micturition, dyspareunia, and impotence in which emotional factors play a causative role.

305.7 Psychophysiologic endocrine disorder
This diagnosis applies to endocrine disorders in which emotional factors play a causative role. The disturbance should be specified.

305.8 Psychophysiologic disorder of organ of special sense
This diagnosis applies to any disturbance in the organs of special sense in which emotional factors play a causative role. Conversion reactions are excluded.

305.9 Psychophysiologic disorder of other type

VII. SPECIAL SYMPTOMS (306)
306 Special symptoms not elsewhere classified
This category is for the occasional patient whose psychopathology is

manifested by discrete, specific symptoms. An example might be anorexia nervosa under *Feeding disturbance* as listed below. It does not apply, however, if the symptom is the result of an organic illness or defect or other mental disorder. For example, anorexia nervosa due to schizophrenia would not be included here.

306.0 Speech disturbance

306.1 Specific learning disturbance

306.2 Tic

306.3 Other psychomotor disorder

306.4 Disorder of sleep

306.5 Feeding disturbance

306.6 Enuresis

306.7 Encopresis

306.8 Cephalalgia

306.9 Other special symptom

VIII. TRANSIENT SITUATIONAL DISTURBANCES (307)

307* Transient situational disturbances[1]

This major category is reserved for more or less transient disorders of any severity (including those of psychotic proportions) that occur in individuals without any apparent underlying mental disorders and that represent an acute reaction to overwhelming environmental stress. A diagnosis in this category should specify the cause and manifestations of the disturbance so far as possible. If the patient has good adaptive capacity his symptoms usually recede as the stress diminishes. If, however, the symptoms persist after the stress is removed, the diagnosis of another mental disorder is indicated. Disorders in this category are classified according to the patient's developmental stage as follows:

---

[1] The terms included under DSM-II Category 307*, "Transient situational disturbances," differ from those in Category 307 of the ICD. DSM-II Category 307*, "Transient situational disturbances," contains adjustment reactions of infancy (307.0*), childhood (307.1*), adolescence (307.2*), adult life (307.3*), and late life (307.4*). ICD Category 307, "Transient situational disturbances," includes only the adjustment reactions of adolescence, adult life and late life. ICD 308, "Behavioral disorders of children," contains the reactions of infancy and childhood. These differences must be taken into account in preparing statistical tabulations to conform to ICD categories.

307.0* Adjustment reaction of infancy*

Example: A grief reaction associated with separation from patient's mother, manifested by crying spells, loss of appetite and severe social withdrawal.

307.1* Adjustment reaction of childhood*

Example: Jealousy associated with birth of patient's younger brother and manifested by nocturnal enuresis, attention-getting behavior, and fear of being abandoned.

307.2* Adjustment reaction of adolescence*

Example: Irritability and depression associated with school failure and manifested by temper outbursts, brooding and discouragement.

307.3* Adjustment reaction of adult life*

Example: Resentment with depressive tone associated with an unwanted pregnancy and manifested by hostile complaints and suicidal gestures.

Example: Fear associated with military combat and manifested by trembling, running and hiding.

Example: A Ganser syndrome associated with death sentence and manifested by incorrect but approximate answers to questions.

307.4* Adjustment reaction of late life*

Example: Feelings of rejection associated with forced retirement and manifested by social withdrawal.

IX. BEHAVIOR DISORDERS OF CHILDHOOD AND ADOLESCENCE (308)

308* Behavior disorders of childhood and adolescence ((Behavior disorders of childhood))[2]

This major category is reserved for disorders occurring in childhood and adolescence that are more stable, internalized, and resistant to

---

[2] The terms included under DSM-II Category 308*, "Behavioral disorders of childhood and adolescence," differ from those in Category 308 of the ICD. DSM-II Category 308* includes "Behavioral disorders of childhood and adolescence," whereas ICD Category 308 includes only "Behavioral disorders of childhood." DSM-II Category 308* *does not* include "Adjustment reactions of infancy and childhood," whereas ICD Category 308 does. In the DSM-II classification, "Adjustment reactions of infancy and childhood" are allocated to 307* (Transitional situational disturbances). These differences should be taken into account in preparing statistical tabulations to conform to the ICD categories.

treatment than *Transient situational disturbances* (q.v.) but less so than *Psychoses, Neuroses,* and *Personality disorders* (q.v.). This intermediate stability is attributed to the greater fluidity of all behavior at this age. Characteristic manifestations include such symptoms as overactivity, inattentiveness, shyness, feeling of rejection, over-aggressiveness, timidity, and delinquency.

308.0* Hyperkinetic reaction of childhood (or adolescence)*

This disorder is characterized by overactivity, restlessness, distractibility, and short attention span, especially in young children; the behavior usually diminishes in adolescence.

If this behavior is caused by organic brain damage, it should be diagnosed under the appropriate non-psychotic *organic brain syndrome* (q.v.).

308.1* Withdrawing reaction of childhood (or adolescence)*

This disorder is characterized by seclusiveness, detachment, sensitivity, shyness, timidity, and general inability to form close interpersonal relationships. This diagnosis should be reserved for those who cannot be classified as having *Schizophrenia* (q.v.) and whose tendencies toward withdrawal have not yet stabilized enough to justify the diagnosis of *Schizoid personality* (q.v.).

308.2* Overanxious reaction of childhood (or adolescence)*

This disorder is characterized by chronic anxiety, excessive and unrealistic fears, sleeplessness, nightmares, and exaggerated autonomic responses. The patient tends to be immature, self-conscious, grossly lacking in self-confidence, conforming, inhibited, dutiful, approval-seeking, and apprehensive in new situations and unfamiliar surroundings. It is to be distinguished from *Neuroses* (q.v.).

308.3* Runaway reaction of childhood (or adolescence)*

Individuals with this disorder characteristically escape from threatening situations by running away from home for a day or more without permission. Typically they are immature and timid, and feel rejected at home, inadequate, and friendless. They often steal furtively.

308.4* Unsocialized aggressive reaction of childhood (or adolescence)*

This disorder is characterized by overt or covert hostile disobedience, quarrelsomeness, physical and verbal aggressiveness, vengefulness, and destructiveness. Temper tantrums, solitary stealing, lying, and hostile teasing of other children are common. These patients usually have no consistent parental acceptance and discipline. This diagnosis should be distinguished from *Antisocial personality* (q.v.), *Runaway reaction of childhood (or adolescence)* (q.v.), and *Group delinquent reaction of childhood (or adolscence)* (q.v.).

308.5* Group delinquent reaction of childhood (or adolescence)*

Individuals with this disorder have acquired the values, behavior, and skills of a delinquent peer group or gang to whom they are loyal and with whom they characteristically steal, skip school, and stay out late at night. The condition is more common in boys than girls. When group delinquency occurs with girls it usually involves sexual delinquency, although shoplifting is also common.

308.9* Other reaction of childhood (or adolescence)*

Here are to be classified children and adolescents having disorders not described in this group but which are nevertheless more serious than transient situational disturbances and less serious than psychoses, neuroses, and personality disorders. The particular disorder should be specified.

X. CONDITIONS WITHOUT MANIFEST PSYCHIATRIC DIS- ORDER AND NON-SPECIFIC CONDITIONS (316*—318*)

316* Social maladjustments without manifest psychiatric dis- order

This category is for recording the conditions of individuals who are psychiatrically normal but who nevertheless have severe enough problems to warrant examination by a psychiatrist. These conditions may either become or precipitate a diagnosable mental disorder.

316.0* Marital maladjustment*

This category is for individuals who are psychiatrically normal but who have significant conflicts or maladjustments in marriage.

316.1* Social maladjustment*

This category is for individuals thrown into an unfamiliar culture (culture shock) or into a conflict arising from divided loyalties to two cultures.

316.2* Occupational maladjustment*

This category is for psychiatrically normal individuals who are grossly maladjusted in their work.

316.3* Dyssocial behavior*

This category is for individuals who are not classifiable as anti-social personalities, but who are predatory and follow more or less criminal pursuits, such as racketeers, dishonest gamblers, prostitutes, and dope peddlers. (DSM-I classified this condition as "Sociopathic personality disorder, dyssocial type.")

316.9* Other social maladjustment*

317* Non-specific conditions*

This category is for conditions that cannot be classified under any of the previous categories, even after all facts bearing on the case have been investigated. This category is not for "Diagnosis deferred" (q.v.).

318* No mental disorder*

This term is used when, following psychiatric examination, none of the previous disorders is found. It is not to be used for patients whose disorders are in remission.

XI. NON-DIAGNOSTIC TERMS FOR ADMINISTRATIVE USE (319*)

319* Non-diagnostic terms for administrative use*

319.0* Diagnosis deferred*

319.1* Boarder*

319.2* Experiment only*

319.9* Other*

APPENDIX B

ETHICAL STANDARDS
OF PSYCHOLOGISTS

by
AMERICAN PSYCHOLOGICAL ASSOCIATION

ETHICAL STANDARDS OF PSYCHOLOGISTS [1]

The psychologist believes in the dignity and worth of the individual human being. He is committed to increasing man's understanding of himself and others. While pursuing this endeavor, he protects the welfare of any person who may seek his service or of any subject, human or animal, that may be the object of his study. He does not use his professional position or relationships, nor does he knowingly permit his own services to be used by others, for purposes inconsistent with these values. While demanding for himself freedom of inquiry and communication, he accepts the responsibility this freedom confers: for competence where he claims it, for objectivity in the report of his findings, and for consideration of the best interests of his colleagues and of society.

Specific Principles

Principle 1. Responsibility. The psychologist, [2] committed to increasing man's understanding of man, places high value on objectivity and integrity, and maintains the highest standards in the services he offers.

a. As a scientist, the psychologist believes that society will be best served when he investigates where his judgment indicates investigation is needed; he plans his research in such a way as to minimize the possibility that his findings will be misleading; and he publishes full reports of his work, never discarding without explanation data which may modify the interpretation of results.

b. As a teacher, the psychologist recognizes his primary obligation to help others acquire knowledge and skill, and to maintain high standards of scholarship.

c. As a practitioner, the psychologist knows that he bears a heavy social responsibility because his work may touch intimately the lives of others.

Principle 2. Competence. The maintenance of high standards of professional competence is a responsibility shared by all psychologists, in the interest of the public and of the profession as a whole.

a. Psychologists discourage the practice of psychology by unqualified persons and assist the public in identifying psychologists competent to give dependable professional service. When a psychologist or a person identifying himself as a psychologist violates ethical standards, psychologists who know firsthand of such activities attempt to rectify the situation. When such a situation cannot be dealt with informally, it is called to the attention of the appropriate local, state, or national committee on professional ethics, standards, and practices.

b. Psychologists regarded as qualified for independent practice are those who (a) have been awarded a Diploma by the American Board of Examiners in Professional Psychology, or (b) have been licensed or certified by state examining boards, or (c) have been certified by voluntary boards established by state psychological associations. Psychologists who do not yet

---

[1] Copyrighted by the American Psychological Association, Inc., January 1963. Reprinted (and edited) from the *American Psychologist,* January 1963, and as amended by the APA Council of Representatives in September 1965 and December 1972.

[2] A student of psychology who assumes the role of psychologist shall be considered a psychologist for the purpose of this code of ethics.

meet the qualifications recognized for independent practice should gain experience under qualified supervision.

c.   The psychologist recognizes the boundaries of his competence and the limitations of his techniques and does not offer services or use techniques that fail to meet professional standards established in particular fields. The psychologist who engages in practice assists his client in obtaining professional help for all important aspects of his problem that fall outside the boundaries of his own competence. This principle requires, for example, that provision be made for the diagnosis and treatment of relevant medical problems and for referral to or consultation with other specialists.

d.   The psychologist in clinical work recognizes that his effectiveness depends in good part upon his ability to maintain sound interpersonal relations, that temporary or more enduring aberrations in his own personality may interfere with this ability or distort his appraisals of others. There he refrains from undertaking any activity in which his personal problems are likely to result in inferior professional services or harm to a client; or, if he is already engaged in such an activity when he becomes aware of his personal problems, he seeks competent professional assistance to determine whether he should continue or terminate his services to his client.

Principle 3. Moral and Legal Standards. The psychologist in the practice of his profession shows sensible regard for the social codes and moral expectations of the community in which he works, recognizing that violations of accepted moral and legal standards on his part may involve his clients, students, or colleagues in damaging personal conflicts, and impugn his own name and the reputation of his profession.

Principle 4. Misrepresentation. The psychologist avoids misrepresentation of his own professional qualifications, affiliations, and purposes, and those of the institutions and organizations with which he is associated.

a.   A psychologist does not claim either directly or by implication professional qualifications that differ from his actual qualifications, nor does he misrepresent his affiliation with any institution, organization, or individual, nor lead others to assume he has affiliations that he does not have. The psychologist is responsible for correcting others who misrepresent his professional qualifications or affiliations.

b.   The psychologist does not misrepresent an institution or organization with which he is affiliated by ascribing to it characteristics that it does not have.

c.   A psychologist does not use his affiliation with the American Psychological Association or its Divisions for purposes that are not consonant with the stated purposes of the Association.

d.   A psychologist does not associate himself with or permit his name to be used in connection with any services or products in such a way as to misrepresent them, the degree of his responsibility for them, or the nature of his affiliation.

Principle 5. Public Statements. Modesty, scientific caution, and due regard for the limits of present knowledge characterize all statements of psychologists who supply information to the public, either directly or indirectly.

a.   Psychologists who interpret the science of psychology or the services of psychologists to clients or to the general public have an obligation to report fairly and accurately. Exaggeration, sensationalism, superficiality, and other kinds of misrepresentation are avoided.

b.   When information about psychological procedures and techniques is given, care is taken to indicate that they should be used only by persons adequately trained in their use.

c.   A psychologist who engages in radio or television activities does not participate in commercial announcements recommending purchase or use of a product.

Principle 6. Confidentiality. Safeguarding information about an individual that has been obtained by the psychologist in the course of his teaching, practice, or investigation is a primary obligation of the

psychologist. Such information is not communicated to others unless certain important conditions are met.

a.   Information received in confidence is revealed only after most careful deliberation and when there is clear and imminent danger to an individual or to society, and then only to appropriate professional workers or public authorities.

b.   Information obtained in clinical or consulting relationships, or evaluative data concerning children, students, employees, and others are discussed only for professional purposes and only with persons clearly concerned with the case. Written and oral reports should present only data germane to the purposes of the evaluation, every effort should be made to avoid undue invasion of privacy.

c.   Clinical and other materials are used in classroom teaching and writing only when the identity of the persons involved is adequately disguised.

d.   The confidentiality of professional communications about individuals is maintained. Only when the originator and other persons involved give their express permission is a confidential professional communication shown to the individual concerned. The psychologist is responsible for informing the client of the limits of the confidentiality.

e.   Only after explicit permission has been granted is the identity of research subjects published. When data have been published without permission for identification, the psychologist assumes responsibility for adequately disguising their sources.

f.   The psychologist makes provisions for the maintenance of confidentiality in the preservation and ultimate disposition of confidential records.

Principle 7. Client Welfare. The psychologist respects the integrity and protects the welfare of the person or group with whom he is working.

a.   The psychologist in industry, education, and other situations in which conflicts of interest may arise among various parties, as between management and labor, or between the client and employer of the psychologist, defines for himself the nature and direction of his loyalties and responsibilities and keeps all parties concerned informed of these commitments.

b.   When there is a conflict among professional workers, the psychologist is concerned primarily with the welfare of any client involved and only secondarily with the interest of his own professional group.

c.   The psychologist attempts to terminate a clinical or consulting relationship when it is reasonably clear to the psychologist that the client is not benefiting from it.

d.   The psychologist who asks that an individual reveal personal information in the course of interviewing, testing, or evaluation, or who allows such information to be divulged to him, does so only after making certain that the responsible person is fully aware of the purposes of the interview, testing, or evaluation and of the ways in which the information may be used.

e.   In cases involving referral, the responsibility of the psychologist for the welfare of the client continues until this responsibility is assumed by the professional person to whom the client is referred or until the relationship with the psychologist making the referral has been terminated by mutual agreement. In situations where referral, consultation, or other changes in the conditions of the treatment are indicated and the client refuses referral, the psychologist carefully weighs the possible harm to the client, to himself, and to his profession that might ensue from continuing the relationship.

f.   The psychologist who requires the taking of psychological tests for didactic, classification, or research purposes protects the examinees by insuring that the tests and test results are used in a professional manner.

g.   When potentially disturbing subject matter is presented to students, it is discussed objectively, and efforts are made to handle constructively any difficulties that arise.

h.   Care must be taken to insure an appropriate setting for clinical work to protect both client and psychologist from actual or imputed harm and the profession from censure.

i.   In the use of accepted drugs for therapeutic purposes special care needs to be exercised by the psychologist to assure himself that the collaborating physician provides suitable safeguards for the client.

Principle 8. Client Relationship. The psychologist informs his prospective client of the important aspects of the potential relationship that might affect the client's decision to enter the relationship.

a. Aspects of the relationship likely to affect the client's decision include the recording of an interview, the use of interview material for training purposes, and observation of an interview by other persons.

b. When the client is not competent to evaluate the situation (as in the case of a child), the person responsible for the client is informed of the circumstances which may influence the relationship.

c. The psychologist does not normally enter into a professional relationship with members of his own family, intimate friends, close associates, or others whose welfare might be jeopardized by such a dual relationship.

Principle 9. Impersonal Services. Psychological services for the purpose of diagnosis, treatment, or personalized advice are provided only in the context of a professional relationship, and are not given by means of public lectures or demonstrations, newspaper or magazine articles, radio or television programs, mail, or similar media.

a. The preparation of personnel reports and recommendations based on test data secured solely by mail is unethical unless such appraisals are an integral part of a continuing client relationship with a company, as a result of which the consulting psychologist has intimate knowledge of the client's personnel situation and can be assured thereby that his written appraisals will be adequate to the purpose and will be properly interpreted by the client. These reports must not be embellished with such detailed analyses of the subject's personality traits as would be appropriate only after intensive interviews with the subject. The reports must not make specific recommendations as to employment or placement of the subject which go beyond the psychologist's knowledge of the job requirements of the company. The reports must not purport to eliminate the company's need to carry on such other regular employment or personnel practices as appraisal of the work history, checking of references, past performance in the company.

Principle 10. Announcement of Services. A psychologist adheres to professional rather than commercial standards in making known his availability for professional services.

a. A psychologist does not directly solicit clients for individual diagnosis or therapy.

b. Individual listings in telephone directories are limited to name, highest relevant degree, certification status, address, and telephone number. They may also include identification in a few words of the psychologist's major areas of practice; for example, child therapy, personnel selection, industrial psychology. Agency listings are equally modest.

c. Announcements of individual private practice are limited to a simple statement of the name, highest relevant degree, certification or diplomate status, address, telephone number, office hours, and a brief explanation of the types of services rendered. Announcements of agencies may list names of staff members with their qualifications. They conform in other particulars with the same standards as individual announcements, making certain that the true nature of the organization is apparent.

d. A psychologist or agency announcing nonclinical professional services may use brochures that are descriptive of services rendered but not evaluative. They may be sent to professional persons, schools, business firms, government agencies, and other similar organizations.

e. The use in a brochure of "testimonials from satisfied users" is unacceptable. The offer of a free trial of services is unacceptable if it operates to misrepresent in any way the nature or the efficacy of the services rendered by the psychologist. Claims that a psychologist has unique skills or unique devices not available to others in the profession are made only if the special efficacy of these unique skills or devices has been demonstrated by scientifically acceptable evidence.

f. The psychologist must not encourage (nor, within his power, even allow) a client to have exaggerated ideas as to the efficacy of services rendered. Claims made to clients about the efficacy of his services must no go beyond those which the psychologist would be willing to subject to professional scrutiny through publishing his results and his claims in a professional journal.

Principle 11. Interprofessional Relations. A psychologists acts with integrity in regard to colleagues in psychology and in other professions.

a.   Each member of the Association cooperates with the duly constituted Committee on Scientific and Professional Ethics and Conduct in the performance of its duties by responding to inquiries with reasonable promptness and completeness. A member taking longer than 30 days to respond to such inquiries shall have the burden of demonstrating that he acted with "reasonable promptness."

b.   A psychologist does not normally offer professional services to a person receiving psychological assistance from another professional worker except by agreement with the other worker or after the termination of the client's relationship with the other professional worker.

c.   The welfare of clients and colleagues requires that psychologists in joint practice or corporate activities make an orderly and explicit arrangement regarding the conditions of their association and its possible termination. Psychologists who serve as employers of other psychologists have an obligation to make similar appropriate arrangements.

Principle 12. Remuneration. Financial arrangements in professional practice are in accord with professional standards that safeguard the best interest of the client and the profession.

a.   In establishing rates for professional services, the psychologist considers carefully both the ability of the client to meet the financial burden and the charges made by other professional persons engaged in comparable work. He is willing to contribute a portion of his services to work for which he receives little or no financial return.

b.   No commission or rebate or any other form of remuneration is given or received for referral of clients for professional services.

c.   The psychologist in clinical or counseling practice does not use his relationships with clients to promote, for personal gain or the profit of an agency, commercial enterprises of any kind.

d.   A psychologist does not accept a private fee or any other form of remuneration for professional work with a person who is entitled to his services through an institution or agency. The policies of a particular agency may make explicit provision for private work with its clients by members of its staff, and in such instances the client must be fully apprised of all policies affecting him.

Principle 13. Test Security. Psychological tests and other assessment devices, the value of which depends in part on the naivete of the subject, are not reproduced or described in popular publications in ways that might invalidate the techniques. Access to such devices is limited to persons with professional interests who will safeguard their use.

a.   Sample items made up to resemble those of tests being discussed may be reproduced in popular articles and elsewhere, but scorable tests and actual test items are not reproduced except in professional publications.

b.   The psychologist is responsible for the control of psychological tests and other devices and procedures used for instruction when their value might be damaged by revealing to the general public their specific contents or underlying principles.

Principle 14. Test Interpretation. Test scores, like test materials, are released only to persons who are qualified to interpret and use them properly.

a.   Materials for reporting test scores to parents, or which are designed for self-appraisal purposes in schools, social agencies, or industry are closely supervised by qualified psychologists or counselors with provisions for referring and counseling individuals when needed.

b.   Test results or other assessment data used for evaluation or classification are communicated to employers, relatives, or other appropriate persons in such a manner as to guard against misinterpretation or misuse. In the usual case, an interpretation of the test result rather than the score is communicated.

c.   When test results are communicated directly to parents and students, they are accompanied by adequate interpretive aids or advice.

Principle 15. Test Publication. Psychological tests are offered for commercial publication only to publishers who present their tests in a professional way and distribute them only to qualified users.

a.   A test manual, technical handbook, or other suitable report on the test is provided which describes the method of constructing and standardizing the test, and summarizes the validation research.

b.   The populations for which the test has ben developed and the purposes for which it is recommended are stated in the manual. Limitations upon the test's dependability, and aspects of its validity on which research is lacking or incomplete, are clearly stated. In particular, the manual contains a warning regarding interpretations likely to be made which have not yet been substantiated by research.

c.   The catalog and manual indicate the training or professional qualifications required for sound interpretation of the test.

d.   The test manual and supporting documents take into account the principles enunciated in the *Standards for Educational and Psychological Tests and Manuals.*

e.   Test advertisements are factual and descriptive rather than emotional and persuasive.

Principle 16. Research Precautions. The psychologist assumes obligations for the welfare of his research subjects, both animal and human.

The decision to undertake research should rest upon a considered judgment by the individual psychologist about how best to contribute to psychological science and to human welfare. The responsible psychologist weighs alternative directions in which personal energies and resources might be invested. Having made the decision to conduct research, psychologists must carry out their investigations with respect for the people who participate and with concern for their dignity and welfare. The Principles that follow make explicit the investigator's ethical responsibilities toward participants over the course of research, from the initial decision to pursue a study to the steps necessary to protect the confidentiality of research data. These Principles should be interpreted in terms of the contexts provided in the complete document [3] offered as a supplement to these Principles.

a.   In planning a study the investigator has the personal responsibility to make a careful evaluation of its ethical acceptability, taking into account these Principles for research with human beings. To the extent that this appraisal, weighing scientific and humane values, suggests a deviation from any Principle, the investigator incurs an increasingly serious obligation to seek ethical advice and to observe more stringent safeguards to protect the rights of the human research participants.

b.   Responsibility for the establishment and maintenance of acceptable ethical practice in research always remains with the individual investigator. The investigator is also responsible for the ethical treatment of research participants by collaborators, assistants, students, and employees, all of whom, however, incur parallel obligations.

c.   Ethical practice requires the investigator to inform the participant of all features of the research that reasonably might be expected to influence willingness to participate, and to explain all other aspects of the research about which the participant inquires. Failure to make full disclosure gives added emphasis to the investigator's abiding responsibility to protect the welfare and dignity of the research participant.

----

[3] *Ethical Principles in the Conduct of Research with Human Participants,* available upon request from the American Psychological Association.

d.   Openness and honesty are essential characteristics of the relationship between investigator and research participant. When the methodological requirements of a study necessitate concealment or deception, the investigator is required to ensure the participant's understanding of the reasons for this action and to restore the quality of the relationship with the investigator.

e.   Ethical research practice requires the investigator to respect the individual's freedom to decline to participate in research or to discontinue participation at any time. The obligation to protect this freedom requires special vigilance when the investigator is in a position of power over the participant. The decision to limit this freedom gives added emphasis to the investigator's abiding responsibility to protect the participant's dignity and welfare.

f.   Ethically acceptable research begins with the establishment of a clear and fair agreement between the investigator and the research participant that clarifies the responsibilities of each. The investigator has the obligation to honor all promises and commitments included in that agreement.

g.   The ethical investigator protects participants from physical and mental discomfort, harm and danger. If the risk of such consequences exists, the investigator is required to inform the participant of that fact, secure consent before proceeding, and take all possible measures to minimize distress. A research procedure may not be used if it is likely to cause serious and lasting harm to participants.

h.   After the data are collected, ethical practice requires the investigator to provide the participant with a full clarification of the nature of the study and to remove any misconceptions that may have arisen. Where scientific or humane values justify delaying or withholding information, the investigator acquires a special responsibility to assure that there are no damaging consequences for the participant.

i.   Where research procedures may result in undesirable consequences for the participant, the investigator has the responsibility to detect and remove or correct these consequences, including, where relevant, long-term aftereffects.

j.   Information obtained about the research participants during the course of an investigation is confidential. When the possibility exists that others may obtain access to such information, ethical research practice requires that this possibility, together with the plans for protecting confidentiality, be explained to the participants as a part of the procedure for obtaining informed consent.

k.   A psychologist using animals in research adheres to the provisions of the Rules Regarding Animals, drawn up by the Committee on Precautions and Standards in Animal Experimentation and adopted by the American Psychological Association.

l.   Investigations of human subjects using experimental drugs (for example: hallucinogenic, psychotomimetic, psychedelic, or similar substances) should be conducted only in such settings as clinics, hospitals, or research facilities maintaining appropriate safeguards for the subjects.

Principle 17. Publication Credit. Credit is assigned to those who have contributed to a publication, in proportion to their contribution, and only to these.

a.   Major contributions of a professional character, made by several persons to a common project, are recognized by joint authorship. The experimenter or author who has made the principal contribution to a publication is identified as the first listed.

b.   Minor contributions of a professional character, extensive clerical or similar nonprofessional assistance, and other minor contributions are acknowledged in footnotes or in an introductory statement.

c.   Acknowledgment through specific citations is made for unpublished as well as published material that has directly influenced the research or writing.

d.   A psychologist who compiles and edits for publication the contributions of others publishes the symposium or report under the title of the committee or symposium, with his own name appearing as chairman or editor among those of the other contributors or committee members.

Principle 18. Responsibility toward Organization. A psychologist respects the rights and reputation of the institute or organization with which he is associated.

a.   Materials prepared by a psychologist as a part of his regular work under specific direction of his organization are the property of that organization. Such materials are released for use or publication by a psychologist in accordance with policies of authorization, assignment of credit, and related matters which have been established by his organization.

b.   Other material resulting incidentally from activity supported by any agency, and for which the psychologist rightly assumes individual responsibility, is published with disclaimer for any responsibility on the part of the supporting agency.

Principle 19. Promotional Activities. The psychologist associated with the development or promotion of psychological devices, books, or other products offered for commercial sale is responsible for ensuring that such devices, books, or products are presented in a professional and factual way.

a.   Claims regarding performance, benefits, or results are supported by scientifically acceptable evidence.

b.   The psychologist does not use professional journals for the commercial exploitation of psychological products, and the psychologist-editor guards against such misuse.

c.   The psychologist with a financial interest in the sale or use of a psychological product is sensitive to possible conflict of interest in his promotion of such products and avoids compromise of his professional responsibilities and objectives.